PETERSON'S

1999

PROFESSIONAL DEGREE PROGRAMS IN THE *Visual* & *Performing* **Arts**

5th edition

ENDORSED BY THE NATIONAL ASSOCIATION
FOR COLLEGE ADMISSION COUNSELING

PETERSON'S
Princeton, New Jersey

About Peterson's

Peterson's is the country's largest educational information/communications company, providing the academic, consumer, and professional communities with books, software, and online services in support of lifelong education access and career choice. Well-known references include Peterson's annual guides to private schools, summer programs, colleges and universities, graduate and professional programs, financial aid, international study, adult learning, and career guidance. Peterson's Web site at petersons.com is the only comprehensive—and most heavily traveled—education resource on the Internet. The site carries all of Peterson's fully searchable major databases and includes financial aid sources, test-prep help, job postings, direct inquiry and application features, and specially created Virtual Campuses for every accredited academic institution and summer program in the U.S. and Canada that offers in-depth narratives, announcements, and multimedia features.

Visit Peterson's Education Center on the Internet (World Wide Web) at
http://www.petersons.com

ISSN 1073-2020
ISBN 0-7689-0112-X

Printed in the United States of America

10 9 8 7 6 5 4 3 2 1

CONTENTS

▲

Are you developing a portfolio? Need more time performing as a musician or an actor? Want to try your hand at filmmaking? The Gallery of Summer Programs describes summer courses that can help you expand your artistic experiences and explore professional careers in the arts.

INTRODUCTION

▲

This book, designed especially to help arts students identify the right college program to get them on their way toward achieving their professional goals, will help you answer questions like:

- What kind of school should you attend? A music conservatory? A large state university?
- Should you pursue the Bachelor of Fine Arts degree or enroll in a Bachelor of Arts program?
- What are your chances of getting into an arts program?
- How realistic are your worries that there are already enough "starving artists" in the world (whose ranks you certainly *don't* want to join)? Are your parents concerned too?

Peterson's Professional Degree Programs in the Visual and Performing Arts offers guidance from staff members at top music, art, theater, and dance programs as well as detailed information on professional degree programs in each field offered at U.S. and Canadian institutions. The guide should be used as a *first step* when identifying potential programs; students are encouraged to consult with their school counselors and arts teachers for additional guidance.

The Professional Degree Versus the Liberal Arts Degree

Perhaps one of the largest difficulties you face as an arts student is deciding which kind of degree to pursue and at what type of school—the options may seem a little overwhelming.

Although the details vary from program to program and among art, dance, music, and theater, "professional" degrees—such as the Bachelor of Fine Arts or the Bachelor of Music—generally differ greatly from "liberal arts" degrees—the Bachelor of Arts and Bachelor of Science, for example. Professional degree programs are more likely to require that a much higher percentage of course work be in the chosen arts field—say, 75 percent. The remaining academic course work to be taken will most likely also incorporate the arts into its curriculum.

A student in a professional degree program will generally have a particular focus—an individual musical instrument or style, for example. A liberal arts degree student's studies will be more general, covering a wider range of subject areas, with less emphasis on performance or studio work. This is not to say that a liberal arts degree cannot prepare you for a career in your chosen field—these degrees may be especially appropriate for you if you are unsure of what specialty you want to pursue or if you want a more generalized educational program.

You may be unsure whether you want to pursue a degree at an institute that focuses solely on the arts or at a liberal arts college or university that provides a greater diversity in course offerings. Again, one choice is not necessarily better than the other—it depends on your goals. Many professional programs will be more competitive in the particular field you want to enter—your audition or portfolio review is then all-important. A liberal arts college or university may be more difficult academically; there your SAT scores, for example, will play a bigger role in the admissions decision. Perhaps you want to be around other artists all day, every day, surrounded by music practice rooms and other musicians or in the company of future

---

PERFORMING ARTS COLLEGE FAIRS

The National Association for College Admission Counseling sponsors Performing Arts College Fairs each fall. These events are for college and college-bound students interested in pursuing undergraduate and graduate programs of study in the areas of music, dance, and theater. Attendees learn about educational and career opportunities, admission and financial aid, audition and entrance requirements, and other information by meeting with representatives from colleges, universities, conservatories, festivals, and other educational institutions. The fairs are scheduled in cities across the country.

For information about the 1999 Performing Arts College Fair schedule, call the Information Line at 703-836-2222.

sculptors and painters. Then a professional program may be appropriate for you. Perhaps you would like to focus on one of the arts but also have the opportunity to study history; then a liberal arts program may be more suitable than a professional degree program.

Remember, there is no "best" school, only the best school *for you.* Start examining your goals, your interests, your personality, and your talents. Read the articles of guidance that open each of the Program Descriptions sections in this book. And by all means, talk to your teachers and guidance counselors. Ask them for their assessment of your strengths and weaknesses, and for their views on which educational setting may be most helpful to you.

How Is This Book Organized?

This book is divided into four main parts:

- Quick-Reference Chart of Programs
- Program Descriptions (divided into Art, Dance, Music, and Theater sections)
- Majors Index
- School Index

ARTS RECOGNITION AND TALENT SEARCH

ARTS is a national program designed to identify, recognize, and encourage young people who demonstrate excellence in dance, music, music/jazz, theater, visual arts, photography, and writing. ARTS is a program of the National Foundation for Advancement in the Arts (NFAA), an independent, nongovernmental institution dedicated to the support of young artists.

NFAA earmarks up to $300,000 in cash awards for ARTS applicants whose work has been judged as outstanding by a national panel of experts. In addition, through the Scholarship List Service, NFAA provides the names of all ARTS applicants who are seniors in high school to colleges, universities, and professional institutions who are actively recruiting students in the creative and performing arts. NFAA is also the exclusive agent for nominating selected ARTS awardees to the White House Commission on Presidential Scholars, which names Presidential Scholars in the arts.

For an application form and more information, contact the NFAA at 1-800-970-ARTS.

NATIONAL PORTFOLIO DAYS

Each year members of the National Portfolio Day Association sponsor National Portfolio Days in thirty-five cities across the nation and in Canada. These events provide an opportunity for students interested in pursuing undergraduate or graduate study in the visual arts to meet with representatives from some of the most outstanding colleges, universities, and independent schools that teach art and design. Attendees have their portfolio of artwork reviewed and gain guidance about their future artistic development. Participating institutions also provide information about programs of study, careers in art, admission requirements, financial aid, and scholarships.

Posters announcing dates and locations are mailed in September to high school art departments, or call 612-874-3760 for more information.

Quick-Reference Chart of Programs

If you want to find out quickly which professional degrees are offered by a specific school, turn to the **Quick-Reference Chart** on pages 12–37. Organized geographically, this chart provides the most basic information about each school in the guide:

- Institution name and location.
- Professional degrees offered in music, art, theater, and dance. Acronyms appear in this column; the full names of the degrees are spelled out within the appropriate profile.
- Total undergraduate enrollment (and graduate if applicable). Specific program enrollments can be found within each profile.
- Tuition and fees for the 1997–98 or 1998–99 academic year. For public institutions where tuition differs according to residence, the state tuition is shown. More detailed expense information can be found within each profile.

Program Descriptions

This guide profiles professional degree programs only. The **Program Descriptions** are divided into four sections: Art (beginning on page 38), Dance (beginning on page 217), Music (beginning on page 255), and Theater (beginning on page 480).

At the beginning of each the four sections, you'll find invaluable information about the different types of programs available, what the admissions process entails (including auditions and portfolios), how to evaluate your own educational goals and needs, and what to look for in a program.

Program Descriptions appear following these articles. They are listed in alphabetical order by institution name.

Peterson's obtained program information through a questionnaire completed by music, art, theater, and dance program directors in the spring and summer of 1998. While the editors believe that the information in this book is accurate and up to date, Peterson's does not assume responsibility for the quality of the programs or the practices of the institutions. Students are encouraged to obtain as much information as possible from the schools themselves.

Majors Index

This index presents 313 undergraduate professional degree major fields of study that schools' responses to Peterson's annual survey indicate are currently offered most widely. The Majors Index, which begins on page 551, is divided into four sections: Art, Dance, Music, and Theater. The majors in each section appear in alphabetical order, each followed by an alphabetical list of the schools that offer a professional degree program in that field.

The terms used for the majors are the most widely used. However, many institutions use different terms for the same or similar areas. Readers should go to http://www.petersons.com to contact a school and ask for its catalog or see its program description in this book for the school's exact terminology. In addition, while the term "major" is used in this guide, some schools may use other terms, such as concentration, program of study, or field.

School Index

The index, which begins on page 594, lists every professional degree–granting institution in the guide and gives the page number(s) on which its Program Description(s) can be found.

The Gallery of Summer Programs

If you want to get a jump on developing your portfolio or experiencing visual or performing arts courses before entering college, this section, on pages 548–549, displays some summer programs that are available to high school students at certain colleges.

PROFILE EXPLANATION

▲

Criteria for Inclusion

Peterson's Professional Degree Programs in the Visual and Performing Arts 1999 covers accredited baccalaureate-degree-granting institutions in the United States, U.S. territories, and Canada. Institutions have full accreditation or candidate-for-accreditation (preaccreditation) status granted by an institutional or specialized accrediting body recognized by the U.S. Department of Education or Council for Higher Education Accreditation. Recognized institutional accrediting bodies, which consider each institution as a whole, are the following: the six regional associations of schools and colleges (Middle States, New England, North Central, Northwest, Southern, and Western), each of which is responsible for a specified portion of the United States and its territories; the Accrediting Association of Bible Colleges (AABC); the Accrediting Council for Independent Colleges and Schools (ACICS); the Accrediting Commission of Career Schools/Colleges of Technology (ACCSCT); the Distance Education and Training Council (DETC); the American Academy for Liberal Education; the Council on Occupational Education; and the Transnational Association of Christian Schools (TRACS). Program registration by the New York State Board of Regents is considered to be the equivalent of institutional accreditation, since the Board requires that all programs offered by an institution meet its standards before recognition is granted. A Canadian institution must be chartered and authorized to grant degrees by the provincial government, affiliated with a chartered institution, or accredited by a recognized U.S. accrediting body. There are recognized specialized accrediting bodies in over forty different fields, each of which is authorized to accredit specific programs in its particular field. This can serve as the equivalent of institutional accreditation for specialized institutions that offer programs in one field only (schools of art, music, optometry, theology, etc.). For a full explanation of the accrediting process and complete information on recognized accrediting bodies, the reader should refer to *Peterson's Directory of College and University Administrators*.

In addition to the above, a profiled institution must grant one or more of the following undergraduate professional degrees in art, dance, music, or theater:

- Bachelor of Apparel Design
- Bachelor of Architecture
- Bachelor of Art Education
- Bachelor of Arts
- Bachelor of Arts/Bachelor of Fine Arts
- Bachelor of Arts/Bachelor of Music
- Bachelor of Arts in Music
- Bachelor of Church Music
- Bachelor of Dance Arts
- Bachelor of Design
- Bachelor of Fashion Design and Merchandising
- Bachelor of Fine Arts
- Bachelor of Fine Arts/Master of Arts
- Bachelor of Fine Arts/Master of Art Teaching
- Bachelor of Graphic Design and Advertising
- Bachelor of Industrial Design
- Bachelor of Interior Architecture
- Bachelor of Interior Design
- Bachelor of Music
- Bachelor of Music/Bachelor of Music Education
- Bachelor of Music/Bachelor of Science
- Bachelor of Musical Arts
- Bachelor of Music Education
- Bachelor of Music Education/Music Therapy
- Bachelor of Music Therapy
- Bachelor of Sacred Music
- Bachelor of Science
- Bachelor of Science/Bachelor of Fine Arts
- Bachelor of Science in Design
- Bachelor of Science/Master of Science

Many of these institutions also offer advanced degrees at the master's or doctoral level:

- Master of Architecture
- Master of Art Education
- Master of Arts
- Master of Arts/Master of Fine Arts
- Master of Arts/Master of Science
- Master of Arts Management
- Master of Arts in Teaching
- Master of Church Music
- Master of Design
- Master of Education
- Master of Fine Arts
- Master of Industrial Design
- Master of Interior Architecture
- Master of Landscape Architecture
- Master of Liturgical Music
- Master of Music

- Master of Musical Arts
- Master of Music Education
- Master of Music Therapy
- Master of Professional Studies
- Master of Sacred Music
- Master of Science
- Master of Science in Teaching
- Doctor of Arts
- Doctor of Music
- Doctor of Musical Arts
- Doctor of Music Education
- Doctor of Philosophy

1 The **institutional control** of the institution: Private institutions are designated as *independent* (nonprofit), *independent/religious* (sponsored by or affiliated with a religious group or having a nondenominational or interdenominational religious orientation), or *proprietary* (profit-making). Public institutions are designated by their primary source of support, such as *federal, state, commonwealth* (Puerto Rico), *territory* (U.S. territories), *county, district* (an administrative unit of public education, often having boundaries different from units of local government*)*, *city, state and local* ("local" refers to county, district, or city), or *state-related* (funded primarily by the state but administered autonomously). The **student body type** categories are *men* (100 percent of student body), *primarily men, women* (100 percent of student body), *primarily women*, and *coed*. **Campus setting** is either *urban, suburban, small town,* or *rural*. The year in which the program was established may be listed. **Total enrollment** cites the number of matriculated undergraduate and (if applicable) graduate students at the institution, both full-time and part-time, as of fall 1997.

2 List of **degrees** and areas of study available in the program. The degrees listed (both undergraduate and graduate) are purely professional in scope and definition. Institutions may also offer B.A., B.S., M.A., and M.S. degrees that are considered "professional" based upon the prescribed curriculum and course load within the discipline. In a professional degree program, the majority of the curriculum is made up of course work within the particular arts field, while the rest of the program involves traditional liberal arts course work. A professional degree program allows students to focus most of their studies in art, dance, music, or theater and emphasizes professional training and acquiring professional skills in such areas as performance, exhibition, and education. **Majors and concentrations** listed are for the undergraduate degree program. Fields mentioned here may represent the general field in which a major or concentration is contained. Programs may also have more detailed majors and concentrations not listed here that are extremely unique in scope, as well as areas of specialization within a particular major or area of study (see Majors Index on page 551). If students enrolled at the institution may take courses at another college or university, this information is presented under the listing of **cross-registration**. The final part of this paragraph may include information about whether the professional program is accredited (or a candidate for accreditation) by a national accreditation body. A description of the acronym(s) listed is provided on page 7.

3 The **enrollment** numbers here are for fall 1997 and include the number of students enrolled in the specific degree program at the following levels (if applicable): *undergraduate, graduate, nonprofessional degree (undergraduate and graduate)*.

4 **Art student profile** contains whole-figure percentages for the total program enrollment and includes the following categories: *minorities, female, male, international*.

5 **Faculty** numbers for undergraduate and graduate (if applicable) faculty members teaching full-time and part-time in the respective area of study. A percentage of full-time faculty members who have appropriate terminal degrees in their field is listed, as is the ratio of undergraduate students to faculty members teaching undergraduate courses. Finally, a mention if graduate students teach undergraduate courses in the program.

6 Student life lists **program-related organizations** and campus activities in which visual and performing arts students may participate. The availability of **housing** opportunities designated solely for visual and performing arts students is mentioned here as well.

7 If provided by the institution, the one-time application fee is listed. **Expenses** are given for the 1998–99 academic year (actual or estimated) or for the 1997–98 academic year if more recent figures were not yet available at the time of data collection. Annual expenses may be expressed as a *comprehensive fee* (this includes full-time tuition, mandatory fees, and college room and board) or as separate figures for full-

▼ CENTER FOR CREATIVE STUDIES— COLLEGE OF ART AND DESIGN

Detroit, Michigan

1 Independent, coed. Urban campus. Total enrollment: 975. Art program established 1926.

2 **Degrees** Bachelor of Fine Arts in the areas of fine arts, crafts, photography, graphic communication, industrial design, interior design, animation/digital media. Majors and concentrations: animation, art direction, art/fine arts, ceramic art and design, commercial art, computer art, furniture design, glass, illustration, interior design, jewelry and metalsmithing, painting/drawing, photography, printmaking, product design, sculpture, studio art, textile arts, transportation design. Cross-registration with Association of Independent Colleges of Art and Design. Program accredited by NASAD.

3 **Enrollment** Fall 1997: 975 total; all undergraduate.

4 **Art Student Profile** 41% females, 59% males, 21% minorities, 4% international.

5 **Art Faculty** 196 total (full-time and part-time). 45% of full-time faculty have terminal degrees. Graduate students do not teach undergraduate courses. Undergraduate student–faculty ratio: 11:1.

6 **Student Life** Student groups/activities include Student Council, Black Artists Researching Trends, Industrial Design Society of America. Special housing available for art students.

7 **Expenses for 1998–99** Application fee: $35. Tuition: $14,280 full-time. Mandatory fees: $216 full-time. College room only: $3100. Room charges vary according to housing facility. Special program-related fees: $150–$300 for lab/material fees.

8 **Financial Aid** Program-specific awards for 1997: 1 Award of Excellence for high school seniors ($14,280), Entering Scholarships for entering students ($1500–$4000), 12 Walter B. Ford Scholarships for entering students ($8000).

9 **Application Procedures** Students admitted directly into the professional program freshman year. Deadline for freshmen and transfers: continuous. Notification date for freshmen and transfers: August 15. Required: high school transcript, college transcript(s) for transfer students, interview, portfolio, SAT I or ACT test scores (minimum combined ACT score of 20), minimum 2.5 high school GPA. Recommended: essay, 2 letters of recommendation. Portfolio reviews held throughout the year on campus; the submission of slides may be substituted for portfolios for large works of art or when distance is prohibitive.

10 **Web Site** http://www.ccscad.edu.

11 **Undergraduate Contact** Director of Admissions, Center for Creative Studies—College of Art and Design, 201 East Kirby Street, Detroit, Michigan 48202; 800-952-ARTS, fax: 313-872-2739.

time *tuition, mandatory fees, college room and board,* or *college room only*. For public institutions where tuition differs according to residence, separate figures are given for area and/or state residents and for out-of-state residents. If the institution charges **special program-related fees** for students in the visual and performing arts, these are listed as well.

8 Provides information regarding any college-administered **financial aid** opportunities dedicated exclusively for undergraduate students in the program. Keep in mind that while these awards are only for students in the program, program students may qualify for other financial aid opportunities at the institution as well.

9 This section indicates if students are admitted directly into the professional program when they enroll for the freshman year or if they must apply for admission into the professional program at some point in their undergraduate career. Admission **application deadlines** and dates for notification of acceptance or rejection into the program are given either as specific dates or as *continuous* for freshmen and transfers. Continuous means that applications are processed as they are received, and qualified students are accepted as long as there are openings. Continuous notification means that applicants are notified of acceptance or rejection as applications are processed up until the date indicated or until the actual beginning of classes. Application requirements are grouped into either *required* or *recommended*. In addition to these requirements, an institution may indicate if *auditions* or *portfolio reviews* are held and where they are held (on or off campus).

10 **Web site** provides the Internet address of the program or institution.

11 The name, title, mailing address, phone number, and fax number of the person to contact for further information are given at the end of the profile. Where applicable, a graduate contact is listed as well.

Research Procedures

The data contained in the college chart, profiles, and index were collected between spring and summer 1998 through Peterson's Annual Survey of Professional Degree Programs in the Visual and Performing Arts. Questionnaires were sent to the more than 1,100 programs that meet the criteria for inclusion outlined above. All data included in this edition have been submitted by officials (usually program directors, department heads, or admissions personnel) at the institutions themselves.

ACCREDITING ASSOCIATIONS

AAMT	American Association for Music Therapy
ASLA	American Society of Landscape Architects
CUMS	Canadian University Music Society
CUPTP	Consortium of Undergraduate Professional Training Programs
FIDER	Foundation for Interior Design Education Research
IDSA	Industrial Designer's Society of America
NAAB	National Architecture Accrediting Board
NAMT	National Association for Music Therapy
NASAD	National Association of Schools of Art and Design
NASD	National Association of Schools of Dance
NASM	National Association of Schools of Music
NAST	National Association of Schools of Theatre
NCATE	National Council for Accreditation of Teacher Education

---

In addition, the great majority of institutions that submitted data were contacted directly by Peterson's editorial staff to verify unusual figures, resolve discrepancies, and obtain additional data. All usable information received in time for publication has been included. The omission of any particular item from an index or profile listing signifies either that the item is not applicable to that institution or that data were not available. Because of the comprehensive editorial review that takes place in our offices and because all material comes directly from college officials, we have every reason to believe that the information presented in this guide is accurate. However, students should check with a specific college or university at the time of application to verify such figures as tuition and fees, which may have changed since the publication of this volume.

COVERING YOUR COLLEGE COSTS

▲

A college education is expensive: more than $100,000 for four years at some of the high-priced colleges and universities and more than $50,000 even at many lower-cost, state-supported colleges. Figuring out how you and your family will come up with the necessary funds to pay for your education requires planning, perseverance, and learning as much as you can about the options available.

For most families, paying the total cost of a student's college education out of savings is not possible. Obviously, the more your family has saved, the better off you will be and the less you will need to earn and borrow. But paying for college should not be looked at merely as a four-year financial commitment. While some of the money you need will likely come from funds that you and your parents have managed to save, some will come from a portion of your or your parents' current income. The rest will come from future earnings, through loans you or your parents will pay off later.

So if your family has not saved the total amount or does not earn enough, you can still attend college. That's where financial aid comes in. The amount you and your family will have to contribute toward your college expenses will be based upon how much you and your family already have and how much you earn. But if this is not enough, the rest of the expenses will be met through financial aid programs.

Financial Aid Basics: How Financial Aid Is Awarded

When you apply for aid, your family's financial situation is analyzed using a government-approved formula called the Federal Methodology. The result of this is the amount you and your family are expected to contribute toward your college expenses, called your Expected Family Contribution or EFC. If this is equal to or more than the cost at a particular college, then, of course, you have no need for additional funds. However, even if you don't have financial need, you may still qualify for aid since there are many grants, scholarships, and loans that do not consider financial need.

If the cost of education is greater than your EFC, then you will likely qualify for assistance, possibly enough to meet the full cost.

Total Cost of Attendance
– Expected Family Contribution
= Financial Need

The total aid you are awarded by any one college will likely differ from the amount offered by other colleges you may be applying to because, among other things, the costs of attendance are different. But, in theory, your EFC should remain about the same regardless of which college you attend.

Sources of Financial Aid

The largest single source of aid is the federal government, which awards some $47 billion to more than 8 million students each year. But the federal government is not the only source of financial aid. The next-largest sources of financial aid are the colleges and universities themselves. Institutions award an estimated $10 billion to students each year. Some of this aid is awarded to students who have a demonstrated need based on either the Federal Methodology or another formula, the Institutional Methodology, which is used by some colleges to award their own funds in conjunction with federal aid. Some aid is not based on need and is called merit aid. Merit-based aid is usually awarded based on a student's academic performance or specific talents or abilities or to students the institutions most want to attract. A college may also use merit-based aid to help meet its enrollment goals.

Another large source of financial aid is state government. All fifty states offer grant aid, most of which is need based, but some of which is merit based. Most state programs award aid only to students attending college in that state.

Other sources of financial aid include private agencies, foundations, corporations, clubs, fraternal and service organizations, civic associations, unions, and religious groups that award grants, scholarships, and low-interest loans. Some employers provide tuition reimbursement benefits for employees.

More information about these different sources of aid is available from high school guidance offices, public libraries, and college financial aid offices and directly from the sponsoring organizations. In addition, Peterson's offers a personalized computer search that includes its entire private aid database—over 2,000 sources—as well as college-administered financial aid and government aid that might be available to you. For more information about this service or about purchasing your own scholarship search software program, call a Peterson's Software Representative at 1-800-338-3282.

Applying for Financial Aid

Every student must complete the Free Application for Federal Student Aid (FAFSA) to be considered for federal aid. The FAFSA is available in your high school guidance office and many public libraries or directly from the U.S. Department of Education. Students can apply for aid over the Internet by using the interactive FAFSA on the Web. FAFSA on the Web can be accessed at http://www.fafsa.ed.gov/. You can get either the paper application or a computer diskette by calling the U.S. Department of Education at 1-800-433-3243.

To award their own funds, many schools require a second application, the Financial Aid PROFILE. The PROFILE asks additional questions that some colleges and awarding agencies feel provide a more accurate assessment of the family's ability to pay for college. It is up to the college to decide whether it will use only the FAFSA or both the FAFSA and the Financial Aid PROFILE.

So, the first thing you will have to do is determine whether you will need to fill out only the FAFSA or whether you will also have to complete the PROFILE. The listings later in this book will tell you what forms are required. But you should also read the schools' brochures, or speak to someone in the financial aid office, just to make sure.

If Every College You're Applying to in 1999 Requires Just the FAFSA

. . . then it's pretty simple: Complete the FAFSA sometime after January 1, 1999, being certain to send it in before any college-imposed deadlines. (You are not permitted to send in the 1999–2000 FAFSA before January 1, 1999, which should not pose a problem because most college application deadlines are in February or March.) It is best if you wait until you have all your financial records for the previous year available, but if that is not possible, you can use estimated numbers.

After you send in your FAFSA, either on paper or electronically, you'll receive a Student Aid Report (SAR) in the mail that reviews the information you reported and contains your EFC. If you used estimated numbers to complete the FAFSA, you may have to resubmit the SAR with any corrections to the data. The college(s) you have designated on the FAFSA will receive the information you reported and will use that data to make their decision. In many instances, the colleges you've applied to will ask you to send copies of your and your parents' income tax returns for 1998 plus any other documents needed to verify the information you reported.

If the College Requires the PROFILE

Step 1: Register for the Financial Aid PROFILE in the fall of your senior year in high school.

Registering for the Financial Aid PROFILE begins the financial aid process. You register by calling the College Scholarship Service at 1-800-778-6888 and providing basic demographic information, a list of colleges to which you are applying, and your credit card number to pay for the service. You can also register by using the College Board's ExPAN admission application service or by accessing College Board Online on the Internet (http://www.collegeboard. org).

Registration packets with a list of the schools requiring the PROFILE are available in most high school guidance offices and on the College Board Online Web site.

There is a fee for using the Financial Aid PROFILE application ($19.50 for the first college and $14.50 for each additional college). You may pay for the service by credit card when you register. If you do not have a credit card, you will be billed. The electronic registrations on the World Wide Web and ExPAN have systems built in to ensure that your credit card number cannot be stolen.

Step 2: Fill Out Your Customized Financial Aid PROFILE

A few weeks after you register, you'll receive in the mail a customized financial aid application that you can use to apply for institutional aid at the colleges you've designated, as well as from some private scholarship programs like National Merit. The PROFILE contains all the questions necessary to estimate your EFC plus the questions that the colleges and organizations you've designated require you to answer. Your individualized packet will also contain a cover letter instructing you what to do and informing you about deadlines and requirements for the colleges and programs you designated when you registered for the PROFILE, codes that indicate which colleges wanted which additional questions, and supplemental forms if any of the colleges to which you are applying require them (e.g., the Business/Farm Supplement when parents own their own business or the Divorced/Separated Parents Statement).

Make sure you submit your PROFILE by the earliest deadline listed. Two to four weeks after you do so, you will receive an acknowledgment of receipt and a report estimating your EFC (only the FAFSA can be used to get an official EFC) and another calculated family contribution using the second formula, the Institutional Methodology, which uses the additional data elements you provided in your PROFILE.

Financial Aid Awards

After you've submitted your financial aid application and usually after you've been accepted for admission, each college will send you a letter containing your financial aid award. Most award letters show the college's budget, how much you and your family are expected to contribute, and the amount and types of aid awarded. Most students who are eligible for aid are awarded aid from a combination of sources and programs; hence your award is often called a "package." For first-year students, award letters are often sent with, or soon after, the letter of admission.

Financial Aid Programs

There are three types of financial aid: scholarships (also known as grants or gift aid), loans, and student employment. Scholarships and grants are outright gifts and do not have to be repaid. Loans must be repaid, usually after graduation; the amount you have to pay back is the total you've borrowed plus an interest charge. Student employment is a job arranged for you during the academic year. Loans and student employment programs are generally referred to as self-help aid.

The federal government has two large grant programs—the Federal Pell Grant and the Federal Supplemental Educational Opportunity Grant; a student employment program called the Federal Work-Study Program; and several loan programs, including one for parents of undergraduate students.

The Subsidized Direct Stafford Student Loan, the Subsidized FFEL Stafford Student Loan, and the Federal Perkins Loan are all need-based, government-subsidized loans. Students who borrow under these programs do not have to pay interest on the loan until after they graduate or leave school. The Unsubsidized Direct Stafford Loan, the Unsubsidized FFEL Stafford Student Loan, and the parent loan (PLUS) program are not based on need, and borrowers are responsible for interest even while the student is in school.

If You Don't Qualify for Need-Based Aid

If you are not eligible for need-based aid, you and your college should try to put together a combination of nonfamily resources that will lessen the burden on your parents.

There are three sources to look into. First is the search for merit scholarships, which you can start at the initial stages of the aid application process. Merit-based awards are becoming an increasingly important part of college financing plans, and many colleges award these grants to students they especially want to attract. As a result, applying to a school at which your qualifications put you at the top of the entering class may be a good idea since you may receive a merit award. It is also a good idea to look for private scholarships and grants, especially from local service and community groups.

The second source of aid for those not qualifying for need-based assistance is employment, during both the summer and the academic year. The student employment office at your college should be able to help you locate a school-year job. Many colleges and local businesses have vacancies remaining even after they have hired students who are receiving work-study financial aid.

The third source is borrowing through the Unsubsidized FFEL Stafford Student Loan or the Unsubsidized Direct Stafford Student Loan, both of which are open to all students. The terms and conditions are similar to the subsidized loans. The biggest difference is that the borrower is responsible for the interest while still in college, although most lenders permit students to delay paying the interest right away and add the accrued interest to the total amount owed.

After you've contributed what you can through scholarships, working, and borrowing, your parents will have to figure out how they will meet their share of the college bill, that is, the Expected Family Contribution. Most colleges offer monthly payment plans that spread the cost over the academic year. For many parents, the monthly payments still turn out to be more than they can afford, so they can borrow through the Federal Parent Loan for Undergraduate Students (PLUS), through one of the many private education loan programs available, or through home equity loans and lines of credit. Families seeking assistance in financing college expenses might also seek the advice of professional financial advisers and tax consultants.

Students and parents who are interested in more information about financing a college education and in learning more about the financial aid application process for 1999–2000 should read the 1999 edition of *Peterson's College Money Handbook.*

QUICK-REFERENCE CHART
OF PROGRAMS

▲

	Art	Dance	Music	Theater	Enroll-ment	Tuition and Fees	Page
Alabama							
Alabama State University			BMEd, MMEd		5,273	$2030*	M258
Auburn University	BFA, MFA		BMEd, PhD	BFA	21,505	$2610*	A55, M264, T486
Birmingham-Southern College			BM, BMEd		1,531	$13,960*	M271
Jacksonville State University	BFA		BMEd, MMEd		7,619	$2060*	A97, M329
Samford University			BM, BMEd, MM		4,485	$9432*	M387
Troy State University			BMEd, MS		6,468	$2250*	M409
The University of Alabama	BFA, MFA		BM, MM, DMA		18,324	$2594*	A170, M411
The University of Alabama at Birmingham	BFA				14,933	$2850*	A170
University of Montevallo	BFA		BM, BMEd, MM	BFA	3,125	$3180*	A188, M435, T533
University of North Alabama	BFA		BM, BMEd		5,575	$2184*	A190, M439
University of South Alabama	BFA		BM, BMEd, MEd	BFA		$2838*	A195, M447, T536
Alaska							
University of Alaska Anchorage	BFA		BM, BMEd		14,765	$2466**	A171, M412
University of Alaska Fairbanks			BM		7,686	$2410*	M412
Arizona							
Al Collins Graphic Design School	BA					NR	A44
Arizona State University	BFA, MFA	BFA, MFA	BM, MM, DMA	BA, BFA, MFA, PhD	44,255	$2059*	A49, D221, M262, T485
Northern Arizona University			BM, BMEd, MM		19,618	$2080*	M366
The University of Arizona	BFA, MA, MFA	BFA, MA/MFA	BM, MM, DMA	BFA, MFA	33,737	$2058*	A171, D240, M413, T524
Arkansas							
Arkansas State University	BFA		BM, BMEd, MM, MMEd	BFA	10,012	$2280*	A50, M263, T485
Harding University	BFA, BS		BMEd		3,754	$7712*	A91, M318

* Expenses for 1997–98.   ** Expenses for 1998–99.   *** Estimated expenses for 1998–99.   NR = Not reported.

	Art	Dance	Music	Theater	Enroll-ment	Tuition and Fees	Page
Arkansas—*continued*							
Henderson State University			BM		3,773	$2166*	M320
Ouachita Baptist University			BM, BMEd	BA	1,619	$8090*	M376, T514
Southern Arkansas University–Magnolia			BMEd		2,676	$1896*	M396
University of Arkansas	BFA, MFA		BM, MM		14,322	$2661*	A172, M413
University of Arkansas at Monticello			BMEd			$2040*	M414
University of Central Arkansas	BFA		BM, MM		8,938	$2692*	A174, M416
Williams Baptist College	BFA				708	$5260*	A213
California							
Academy of Art College	BFA, MFA				4,976	$14,910*	A41
American Academy of Dramatic Arts/West				AA, Cert	200	$9600*	T485
American InterContinental University	BFA				500	$11,250*	A46
Art Center College of Design	BFA, BS, MA, MFA				1,433	$17,180*	A51
Art Institute of Southern California	BFA				196	$10,900*	A53
Biola University			BM		3,257	$14,286*	M270
California College of Arts and Crafts	BARC, BFA, MFA				1,073	$15,950*	A62
California Institute of the Arts	BFA, MFA	BFA, MFA	BFA, MFA	BFA, MFA	1,140	$18,185**	A64, D224, M277, T491
California State University, Chico	BFA				14,247	$2075*	A65
California State University, Fullerton	BFA, MFA		BM, MM		24,906	$1947*	A65, M278
California State University, Long Beach	BFA, MFA	BFA, MFA	BM, BMEd, MM, MMEd		27,809	$1846*	A65, D225, M278
California State University, Los Angeles			BA, BM, MA, MM		19,160	$1757*	M279
California State University, Northridge			BM, MM		27,653	$1980*	M279
California State University, Sacramento			BM, MM		23,481	$1982*	M279
Chapman University		BFA	BM, BMEd	BFA	3,806	$18,750*	D225, M286, T493
College of Notre Dame			BM, MM		1,782	$14,976*	M291
Design Institute of San Diego	BFA				253	$9200*	A82
Dominican College of San Rafael	BFA				1,465	$15,424*	A82
Holy Names College			BM, MM		861	$13,870*	M320
La Sierra University	BFA				1,466	$14,025*	A103
Mount St. Mary's College			BM		1,984	$15,216*	M358
Musicians Institute			BM			$12,000*	M359
Otis College of Art and Design	BFA, MFA				726	$16,300***	A132

* Expenses for 1997–98.   ** Expenses for 1998–99.   *** Estimated expenses for 1998–99.   NR = Not reported.

QUICK-REFERENCE CHART OF PROGRAMS

	Art	Dance	Music	Theater	Enroll-ment	Tuition and Fees	Page
California—*continued*							
Pacific Union College			BM		1,570	$14,055**	M377
San Diego State University			BM, MA, MM		29,898	$1854*	M388
San Francisco Art Institute	BFA, MFA				680	$17,400*	A149
San Francisco Conservatory of Music			BM, MM		261	$16,550*	M388
San Francisco State University			BM, MA, MM		27,420	$1982*	M390
San Jose State University	BFA, BS, MA, MFA		BM		26,897	$2017*	A150, M390
Sonoma State University	BFA				7,050	$2130*	A158
University of California, Irvine		BFA, MFA	BA, BM, MFA			NR	D241, M415
University of California, Santa Barbara		BFA	BM, MM, DMA	BFA	18,940	$4098*	D241, M416, T525
University of Redlands			BM, MM		1,490	$18,545*	M445
University of Southern California	BFA, MFA		BM, MA, MM, MMEd, DMA	BFA, MFA	28,342	$20,480*	A196, M448, T536
University of the Pacific	BFA		BA, BM, MA, MM		5,585	$19,365**	A201, M455
Colorado							
Colorado Christian University			BCM, BM, BMEd		1,910	$10,010*	M293
Colorado State University	BA, BFA, MFA		BM, MM		22,344	$3083*	A74, M293
Metropolitan State College of Denver	BFA				17,343	$1976*	A115
Rocky Mountain College of Art & Design	BFA				388	$9727*	A147
University of Colorado at Boulder	BFA, MFA	BFA, MFA	BM, BMEd, MM, MMEd, PhD, DMA	BFA, PhD	25,109	$2939*	A174, D242, M420, T526
University of Colorado at Denver	BA, BFA				13,092	$2204*	A175
University of Denver	BFA, MA, MFA		BM, MA, MM		8,667	$17,886*	A176, M422
University of Northern Colorado			BM, BMEd, MM, MMEd, DA, DMEd		11,860	$2578*	M441
Connecticut							
Albertus Magnus College	BFA			BFA	1,549	$17,262*	A43, T483
Central Connecticut State University				BFA	11,625	$3614*	T492
Lyme Academy of Fine Arts	BFA				80	$8690*	A107
Paier College of Art, Inc.	BFA				261	$10,595*	A135
University of Bridgeport	BA, BFA, BS		BM		2,427	$13,644*	A172, M414
University of Connecticut	BFA, MFA		BA, BM, BS, MA, MM, PhD, DMA	BFA, MA, MFA	18,205	$5242*	A175, M420, T527

	Art	Dance	Music	Theater	Enroll-ment	Tuition and Fees	Page
Connecticut—*continued*							
University of Hartford	BFA, MFA	BFA	BA, BM, MM, MMEd, PhD, DMA	BFA	7,089	$18,224**	A178, D242, M423, T528
Western Connecticut State University			BM, BS, MS			$2062*	M469
Delaware							
University of Delaware	BFA, MFA		BM, BMEd, MM		18,230	$4574*	A176, M421
District of Columbia							
American University	BFA, MFA				10,710	$18,555*	A48
The Catholic University of America			BM, MA, MLM, MM, DMA		5,616	$17,110*	M283
The Corcoran School of Art	BFA				380	$12,800*	A77
The George Washington University			BM		19,356	$21,360*	M315
Howard University	BFA, MFA		BM, BMEd, MM, MMEd	BFA	10,438	$8985*	A92, M322, T500
Florida							
Barry University	BA, BFA, MA, MFA, MS		BM	BA	6,899	$13,550*	A57, M267, T486
Florida Atlantic University	BFA, MFA		BM	BFA, MFA	18,823	$2022*	A87, M311, T499
Florida Baptist Theological College			BM		486	$2934*	M311
Florida International University	BFA, MFA		BM, MM	BFA	30,012	$2035*	A88, M311, T499
Florida Southern College			BM, BMEd, BSM		1,775	$10,604*	M312
Florida State University	BFA, MFA	BFA, MFA	BM, BMEd, EdD, MA, MM, MMEd, PhD, DM	BFA, MFA	30,401	$1988*	A88, D227, M312, T499
The Harid Conservatory			BM		61	$0*	M319
International Academy of Merchandising & Design, Inc.	BFA				500	$10,785**	A96
Jacksonville University	BAE, BFA	BFA	BFA, BM, BMEd	BFA	2,157	$13,900*	A98, D228, M329, T502
New World School of the Arts	BFA	BFA	BM	BFA	359	$1478***	A125, D231, M361, T508
Palm Beach Atlantic College			BM		1,932	$9900*	M377
Ringling School of Art and Design	BFA				850	$13,250*	A143
Stetson University			BM, BMEd		2,857	$15,765*	M402
University of Central Florida	BFA		BM, BMEd, MMEd	BFA	28,685	$2025*	A174, M417, T526

* Expenses for 1997–98.   ** Expenses for 1998–99.   *** Estimated expenses for 1998–99.   NR = Not reported.

	Art	Dance	Music	Theater	Enroll-ment	Tuition and Fees	Page
Florida—*continued*							
University of Florida	BA, BFA, MFA	BFA	BM, MM	BFA, MFA	41,713	$1930*	A177, D242, M422, T528
University of Miami	BFA, MFA		BM, MM, MS, DMA	BFA	13,651	$19,512*	A184, M430, T531
University of North Florida	BFA		BM		11,389	$2006*	A192, M442
University of South Florida			BA, BM, BS, MA, MM, PhD		34,036	$2086*	M450
The University of Tampa			BM		2,896	$14,652*	M450
University of West Florida	BFA				8,038	$1985*	A202
## Georgia							
American InterContinental University	BFA				1,016	$10,300*	A47
Armstrong Atlantic State University			BMEd		5,696	$1962*	M263
Atlanta College of Art	BFA				420	$12,250*	A54
Augusta State University	BFA		BM, BMEd		5,479	$1926*	A56, M265
Berry College			BM		2,070	$10,210*	M270
Brenau University	BFA	BFA	BM	BA, BFA	2,366	$10,740*	A61, D222, M274, T489
Brewton-Parker College			BM		1,652	$5760*	M275
Clayton College & State University			BM		4,713	$2168*	M288
Columbus State University			BM, MM		5,405	$2463*	M294
Covenant College			BM		945	$12,900*	M297
Georgia College and State University			BA, BM, BMEd		5,512	$2064*	M315
Georgia Southern University	BFA, MFA		BM, MM		13,963	$2256*	A89, M315
Georgia Southwestern State University	BFA, BS				2,414	$2145*	A89
Georgia State University	BFA, MFA		BM, MM		24,276	$2673*	A90, M316
Kennesaw State University			BM, BMEd		13,108	$2013*	M332
Mercer University			BM, BMEd		6,801	$14,656*	M350
Savannah College of Art and Design	BARC, BFA, MA, MARC, MFA				3,464	$13,500**	A150
Shorter College	BFA		BCM, BFA, BM, BMEd		1,639	$8260*	A156, M392
State University of West Georgia	BFA, MEd		BM, MM		8,422	$2088*	A162, M402
University of Georgia	BFA, MFA		BM, BMEd, MM, MMEd, DMA		29,693	$2838*	A178, M423
Valdosta State University	BFA, MAE		BM, MMEd	BFA	9,779	$1974*	A206, M462, T541

	Art	Dance	Music	Theater	Enroll-ment	Tuition and Fees	Page
Hawaii							
University of Hawaii at Manoa	BFA, MFA	BFA, MFA	BM, MM, PhD		17,356	$2950*	A179, D243, M424
Idaho							
Boise State University			BM, BMEd, MM, MMEd		15,433	$2294*	M271
Idaho State University			BM, BMEd	BFA, MA	11,886	$1984*	M323, T500
University of Idaho			BM, BMEd, MA, MM		11,027	$1942*	M425
Illinois							
American Academy of Art	BFA				420	$13,480**	A45
American Conservatory of Music			BM, MM, DMA		73	$9600*	M260
Barat College		BFA			749	$12,570*	D221
Bradley University	BA, BFA, BS, MA, MFA		BM	BA, BS	5,861	$12,690*	A60, M274, T489
DePaul University			BM, MM	BFA, MFA	17,804	$13,490*	M301, T496
Eastern Illinois University			BM, MM		11,777	$3112**	M303
Elmhurst College			BM		2,842	$11,900*	M308
Harrington Institute of Interior Design	BFA				384	$10,466*	A91
The Illinois Institute of Art	BA, BFA				600	$9984*	A92
Illinois State University	BFA, MA, MA/MS, MFA		BM, BMEd, MM, MMEd		20,331	$4123**	A93, M323
Illinois Wesleyan University	BFA		BFA, BM, BMEd	BA/BFA, BFA	2,021	$18,376**	A93, M324, T501
International Academy of Merchandising & Design, Ltd.	BFA				815	$9900*	A96
Millikin University	BFA		BFA, BM, BMEd	BFA	1,997	$14,138*	A117, M353, T507
Moody Bible Institute			BM		1,404	$830*	M356
Northern Illinois University	BFA, MFA		BM, MM	BFA, MFA	22,082	$3837*	A127, M366, T511
North Park University			BM, BMEd		2,004	$14,690*	M368
Northwestern University			BA/BM, BM, BM/BS, MM, PhD, DM		15,487	$22,458**	M369
Quincy University	BFA				1,149	$12,410*	A141
Roosevelt University			BM, MM	BFA, MFA	6,605	$11,030*	M383, T518
Saint Xavier University			BM		3,719	$12,560*	M386
School of the Art Institute of Chicago	BFA, BIA, MA, MFA, MS				2,228	$17,160*	A151

* Expenses for 1997–98.   ** Expenses for 1998–99.   *** Estimated expenses for 1998–99.   NR = Not reported.

	Art	Dance	Music	Theater	Enroll-ment	Tuition and Fees	Page
Illinois—*continued*							
Southern Illinois University at Carbondale	BFA, MFA		BM, MM		21,908	$3420*	A158, M396
Southern Illinois University at Edwardsville	BFA, MA, MFA		BM, MM		11,207	$2665**	A158, M397
University of Illinois at Chicago	BFA, MA, MFA				24,578	$3898*	A179
University of Illinois at Urbana–Champaign	BFA, MFA, DA	BFA, MFA	BM, BMEd, MM, MMEd, DMA	BFA, MFA, PhD	36,019	$4120*	A180, D243, M425, T529
VanderCook College of Music			BMEd, MMEd		173	$10,350*	M463
Western Illinois University	BFA				12,200	$3,037*	A211
Wheaton College			BM, BMEd		2,725	$13,780*	M473
Indiana							
Ball State University	BFA, MA		BM, BS, MM, DA		19,419	$3414*	A56, M266
Butler University		BFA	BM, BMEd, MM, MMEd		3,911	$15,690*	D223, M277
DePauw University			BM, BMA, BMEd		2,334	$17,050*	M301
Grace College			BM		800	$9820*	M317
Huntington College			BM		814	$12,800**	M323
Indiana State University	BFA, MFA		BM, BMEd, MM, MMEd		10,784	$3196*	A93, M325
Indiana University Bloomington	BFA, MA, MAT, MFA, PhD		BM, BMEd, BOM, MA, MM, MOM, MS, DM		34,937	$3929*	A94, M325
Indiana University–Purdue University Fort Wayne	BFA		BM, BMEd, BMT		10,749	$3321*	A95, M326
Indiana University–Purdue University Indianapolis	BA, BAE, BFA, MAE				27,036	$3441*	A95
Indiana University South Bend	BFA		BM, BMEd, BS, MM, MS		7,169	$2985*	A95, M326
Oakland City University			BA, BMEd		NR		M370
Saint Mary's College	BA/BFA		BM		1,347	$15,652*	A148, M385
Taylor University			BM, BMEd		1,884	$13,484*	M405
University of Evansville	BFA		BM	BA/BFA	3,023	$13,880*	A177, M422, T527
University of Notre Dame	BFA, MA, MFA				10,275	$19,947*	A193
Valparaiso University			BM, BMEd, MM		3,603	$15,060*	M462

	Art	Dance	Music	Theater	Enroll-ment	Tuition and Fees	Page
Iowa							
Clarke College	BFA				1,160	$12,439*	A70
Coe College			BM		1,318	$16,320*	M290
Cornell College			BM, BMEd		1,079	$17,840*	M296
Drake University	BAE, BFA		BM, BMEd, MM, MMEd	BA/BFA, BFA	5,184	$15,200*	A82, M302, T497
Iowa State University of Science and Technology	BFA, MA, MFA		BM, BMEd		25,384	$2766*	A96, M327
Iowa Wesleyan College			BMEd		804	$12,220**	M327
Maharishi University of Management	BFA, MA, MFA				1,422	$14,670***	A108
Morningside College			BA, BM, BMEd		1,166	$12,306**	M357
Simpson College			BM		1,958	$13,095*	M393
The University of Iowa	BFA, MA, MFA, PhD	BFA, MFA	BM, MA, MFA, PhD, DMA		28,409	$2760*	A180, D244, M426
University of Northern Iowa	BFA, MA		BM, MM		13,503	$2752*	A192, M442
Wartburg College			BM, BMEd, BMEd/MT		1,528	$13,610*	M466
Kansas							
Baker University			BM, BMEd		796	$10,900*	M265
Emporia State University	BFA		BM, BMEd, MM, MMEd	BFA	5,320	$1982***	A85, M308, T498
Fort Hays State University	BFA, MFA		BM		5,616	$1992*	A88, M313
Friends University		BFA	BM, BMEd		2,729	$9975*	D228, M313
Kansas State University	BFA, MFA		BM, BMEd, MM		20,306	$2467*	A99, M332
Pittsburg State University	BFA, BSEd, MA		BM, BMEd, MM		6,355	$2016*	A138, M379
Southwestern College			BM		826	$9260*	M398
University of Kansas	BFA, MFA		BFA, BM, BMEd, MM, MMEd, PhD, DMA	BFA, MFA	27,567	$2385*	A181, M426, T529
Washburn University of Topeka	BFA		BM, BMEd		6,281	$3150*	A208, M466
Wichita State University	BA, BAE, BFA, MA, MFA	BFA	BM, BMEd, MM, MMEd	BFA	14,061	$1986*	A213, D252, M474, T545
Kentucky							
Campbellsville University			BM, MM		1,521	$7302*	M281
Cumberland College			BM		1,698	$8430*	M299
Eastern Kentucky University			BM, BMEd, MM	BFA	15,424	$2060*	M304, T497

* Expenses for 1997–98.   ** Expenses for 1998–99.   *** Estimated expenses for 1998–99.   NR = Not reported.

	Art	Dance	Music	Theater	Enroll-ment	Tuition and Fees	Page
Kentucky—*continued*							
Georgetown College			BM, BMEd		1,626	$10,190*	M314
Kentucky State University			BM, BMEd		2,288	$2050*	M333
Kentucky Wesleyan College			BM, BMEd		777	$9730**	M334
Morehead State University			BM, BMEd, MM		8,200	$2150*	M357
Murray State University	BFA		BM, BMEd, MMEd		8,811	$2300**	A124, M359
Northern Kentucky University	BFA		BM	BFA	11,763	$2120*	A127, M367, T512
Union College			BM, BMEd		1,016	$9340*	M410
University of Kentucky			BM, MA, MM, PhD, DMA	BFA	23,540	$2736*	M427, T530
University of Louisville	BA, BFA, BS		BM, MAT, MM, MMEd		20,283	$2630*	A181, M427
Western Kentucky University	BA, BFA	BFA	BM	BFA	14,543	$2140*	A211, D251, M469, T544
Louisiana							
Centenary College of Louisiana			BM, BMEd		986	$11,400*	M284
Louisiana College			BM		925	$6763*	M340
Louisiana State University and Agricultural and Mechanical College	BFA, MFA		BM, BMEd, MM, DMA		28,066	$2711*	A107, M340
Louisiana Tech University	BFA, BIRD, MFA		BA, BFA		9,500	$2567*	A107, M341
Loyola University New Orleans			BM, BMEd, BMT, MM, MMEd, MMT		5,079	$13,354*	M341
McNeese State University			BM, BMEd, MMEd		8,117	$2012*	M349
Nicholls State University			BMEd		7,173	$2507*	M363
Northeast Louisiana University			BM, BMEd, MM		10,942	$1952*	M366
Northwestern State University of Louisiana			BM, BMEd, MM		8,873	$2177*	M369
Southeastern Louisiana University			BM, BMEd, MM		15,241	$2155***	M394
Southern University and Agricultural and Mechanical College			BM		9,815	$2068*	M398
Tulane University				BFA, MFA	10,921	$22,720**	T524
University of Southwestern Louisiana		BFA	BM, BMEd, MM	BFA	17,020	$1947*	D248, M450, T537
Xavier University of Louisiana			BM		3,506	$8215*	M477

	Art	Dance	Music	Theater	Enroll-ment	Tuition and Fees	Page
Maine							
Maine College of Art	BFA, MFA				313	$15,005*	A108
University of Maine			BM, BMEd, MM, MMEd		8,917	$4344*	M428
University of Southern Maine	BFA		BM		10,236	$3938*	A196, M449
Maryland							
Frostburg State University	BFA				5,199	$3544*	A89
Johns Hopkins University			BM, MM, DMA		5,022	$21,700*	M331
Maryland Institute, College of Art	BFA, BFA/MA, BFA/MAT, MA, MFA				1,143	$16,760*	A110
Salisbury State University	BFA, BS				6,022	$3842*	A148
Towson University		BFA	BM, BS, MM, MS		15,524	$4120*	D240, M408
University of Maryland, College Park			BA, BM, BS, MM, PhD, DMA		32,711	$4460*	M428
Massachusetts							
Anna Maria College	BA, BFA		BM		1,668	$12,240*	A49, M261
Art Institute of Boston	BFA				447	$11,770*	A52
Atlantic Union College			BM		722	$12,000*	M264
Berklee College of Music			BM		2,933	$15,100**	M268
Boston Architectural Center	BARC, BIRD, MARC, MIntD				854	$5691*	A59
Boston Conservatory		BFA, MFA	BM, BMEd, MM	BFA, MM	501	$15,925*	D221, M272, T487
Boston University	BFA, MFA		BM, MM, DMA	BFA, MFA	29,387	$23,148**	A60, M273, T488
Emerson College				BFA, MA	3,885	$17,826*	T498
Emmanuel College	BFA				1,552	$14,550*	A85
Gordon College			BM		1,375	$15,760**	M316
Massachusetts College of Art	BFA, MFA				2,289	$3964*	A114
Montserrat College of Art	BFA				333	$11,680*	A120
New England Conservatory of Music			BM, MM, MMEd, DMA		800	$18,000*	M360
Salem State College				BFA		NR	T518
School of the Museum of Fine Arts	BA/BFA, MFA				1,133	$15,890*	A153
Suffolk University	BFA				6,290	$12,920*	A163
University of Massachusetts Amherst	BFA, MA, MFA, MS	BFA	BM, MM, PhD		24,884	$5572*	A182, D244, M429

* Expenses for 1997–98.   ** Expenses for 1998–99.   *** Estimated expenses for 1998–99.   NR = Not reported.

	Art	Dance	Music	Theater	Enroll-ment	Tuition and Fees	Page
Massachusetts—continued							
University of Massachusetts Dartmouth	BFA, MAE, MFA				6,366	$4254**	A182
University of Massachusetts Lowell	BFA				12,322	$4422*	A184
Michigan							
Adrian College	BFA				1,000	$12,830*	A42
Albion College	BFA				1,500	$16,806*	A44
Alma College			BM		1,407	$14,238*	M259
Andrews University	BFA		BM, MM		3,152	$11,577*	A48, M260
Aquinas College	BFA		BM		2,458	$12,950*	A49, M262
Calvin College			BMEd		4,071	$12,250*	M280
Center for Creative Studies—College of Art and Design	BFA				975	$14,496**	A68
Central Michigan University	BFA, MFA		BM, BMEd, MM		24,747	$3546*	A69, M285
Cornerstone College			BM, BMEd		1,160	$10,026**	M296
Eastern Michigan University			BM, BMEd, BMT, MA		22,730	$3529*	M304
Grand Valley State University	BFA		BA, BM, BMEd		15,676	$3408*	A90, M317
Hope College			BM, BMEd		2,911	$14,878*	M321
Kendall College of Art and Design	BFA				560	$10,700*	A100
Lawrence Technological University	BFA, BS				3,645	$9340*	A104
Marygrove College			BM		3,603	$9410*	M347
Michigan State University	BFA, MFA		BM, MM, PhD, DMA		42,603	$4789*	A116, M351
Northern Michigan University			BMEd		7,787	$2986*	M367
Oakland University			BM, MM		14,379	$3734*	M371
Siena Heights University	BFA				1,287	$10,700*	A157
University of Michigan	BFA, MFA	BDA, BFA, MFA	BFA, BM, BMA, MM, DMA	BFA, MFA, PhD	36,995	$5878*	A185, D244, M431, T531
University of Michigan–Flint	BFA, BS		BMEd	BFA	6,488	$3559*	A186, M432, T532
Wayne State University	BFA, MA, MFA		BM, MM	BFA, MFA, DA	30,729	$3486*	A209, M467, T542
Western Michigan University	BFA, MFA	BFA	BM, MM	BFA	26,132	$3655*	A212, D252, M469, T544

	Art	Dance	Music	Theater	Enroll-ment	Tuition and Fees	Page
Minnesota							
Augsburg College			BA, BM, BMEd, BS		2,817	$14,616***	M264
Bethel College			BM, BMEd		2,612	$13,840**	M270
College of Visual Arts	BFA				225	$10,020**	A73
Concordia College			BM		2,931	$12,655**	M295
Crown College			BCM, BMEd, MA		713	$9335*	M298
Mankato State University	BFA, MA		BM, BS, MM		12,507	$2983*	A110, M343
Minneapolis College of Art and Design	BFA, MFA				598	$15,810*	A118
Moorhead State University	BFA		BM, BS, MA, MS		6,466	$2908**	A123, M356
St. Cloud State University	BFA		BA, BM, BS, MM		13,946	$3082*	A147, M385
St. Olaf College			BM		2,975	$16,500*	M386
University of Minnesota, Duluth	BFA, MFA		BM, MMEd	BFA	9,653	$4316*	A186, M433, T532
University of Minnesota, Twin Cities Campus	BFA, MFA	BFA	BM, MM, DMA		45,410	$4450*	A187, D245, M433
Mississippi							
Alcorn State University			BM, BMEd		2,847	$2429*	M259
Delta State University	BFA		BMEd, MMEd		4,012	$2354*	A81, M301
Jackson State University			BM, BMEd, MMEd		6,333	$2380*	M329
Mississippi College			BM, BMEd, MM		3,532	$8364**	M353
Mississippi State University	BFA, MFA		BMEd		15,628	$2731*	A119, M354
Mississippi University for Women	BFA		BM		3,309	$2284*	A120, M354
Mississippi Valley State University			BMEd		2,234	$2353*	M354
University of Mississippi	BFA, MA, MFA		BM, MM, DA		11,179	$2731*	A187, M433
University of Southern Mississippi	BFA, MAE, MFA	BFA	BM, BMEd, MM, MMEd, DMA	BFA, MFA	14,599	$2590*	A197, D247, M449, T537
William Carey College			BM	BFA		$6624*	M475, T545
Missouri							
Avila College				BA, BFA	1,246	$10,860*	T486
Calvary Bible College and Theological Seminary			BMEd		613	$4570*	M280
Central Methodist College			BM, BMEd		1,292	$10,710**	M284

* Expenses for 1997–98.   ** Expenses for 1998–99.   *** Estimated expenses for 1998–99.   NR = Not reported.

	Art	Dance	Music	Theater	Enroll-ment	Tuition and Fees	Page
Missouri—*continued*							
Central Missouri State University	BFA		BM, BMEd, MA	BFA	10,320	$2640*	A69, M285, T492
Columbia College	BFA				7,435	$9244*	A75
Culver-Stockton College	BFA		BMEd	BFA	994	$9200*	A80, M299, T495
Evangel College	BFA		BM		1,616	$8850**	A86, M309
Kansas City Art Institute	BFA				607	$16,930**	A99
Lincoln University			BMEd		3,041	$2076*	M339
Lindenwood University	BA, BFA, MA, MFA				4,788	$10,150*	A104
Maryville University of Saint Louis	BA, BFA				3,055	$10,910*	A112
Southeast Missouri State University			BM, BMEd, MMEd		8,231	$3000*	M395
Southwest Baptist University			BM		3,593	$8347*	M398
Southwest Missouri State University	BFA	BFA	BM, BS, MM	BFA	16,468	$3214**	A160, D238, M399, T520
Stephens College	BFA	BFA		BFA	819	$14,830*	A162, D239, T521
Truman State University	BFA, MAE		BM, MA		6,421	$3274*	A168, M410
University of Missouri–Columbia	BFA, MFA		BM, BS, MA, MEd, MM, PhD		22,552	$4280*	A187, M434
University of Missouri–Kansas City		BFA	BM, BMEd, MM, MMEd, DMA		10,445	$4278*	D245, M434
University of Missouri–St. Louis	BFA		BM, MMEd		15,576	$4396*	A188, M435
Washington University in St. Louis	BFA, MFA				11,606	$22,422**	A209
Webster University	BA, BFA, MA	BA, BFA	BM, BMEd, MM	BFA	11,756	$10,910*	A210, D251, M468, T543
Montana							
Montana State University–Bozeman			BMEd		11,603	$2677*	M355
The University of Montana–Missoula	BFA, MA, MFA	BFA	BM, BMEd, MM, MMEd	BFA, MFA	12,124	$2630*	A188, D246, M435, T533
Nebraska							
Bellevue University	BFA				2,928	$3650*	A59
Concordia College	BFA				1,191	$11,310**	A76
Hastings College			BM		1,059	$11,368*	M319
Nebraska Wesleyan University			BM	BFA	1,709	$11,220*	M360, T508
University of Nebraska at Kearney			BFA, MMEd		7,133	$2269*	M436
University of Nebraska at Omaha			BM, MM		13,710	$2356*	M436
University of Nebraska–Lincoln	BFA, MFA	BFA	BM, BMEd, MM, DMA	BFA, MFA	22,827	$2829*	A189, D246, M437, T533

	Art	Dance	Music	Theater	Enroll-ment	Tuition and Fees	Page
Nevada							
University of Nevada, Las Vegas	BFA, MFA		BM, MM		19,249	$1642*	A189, M437
University of Nevada, Reno			BM, MA, MM	BFA	12,442	$2109*	M437, T534
New Hampshire							
Keene State College			BM		4,409	$4340*	M332
Rivier College	BA, BFA				2,886	$13,190**	A145
University of New Hampshire	BFA		BM, MS		13,960	$5889*	A189, M438
New Jersey							
Caldwell College	BFA				1,827	$10,800*	A62
Centenary College	BFA				959	$13,260*	A67
The College of New Jersey	BA, BFA		BM, MMEd		6,780	$4843*	A71, M291
Kean University	BFA, MA				11,537	$3669*	A100
Montclair State University	BFA	BFA	BA, BM, MA	BFA	12,808	$3694*	A120, D231, M355, T507
New Jersey City University	BFA, MFA				8,503	$3828*	A124
Rowan University			BM		9,367	$4241*	M384
Rutgers, The State University of New Jersey, Mason Gross School of the Arts	BFA, MFA	BFA	BM, MM, DMA	BFA, MFA	48,341	$5366*	A113, D231, M349, T506
Seton Hall University	BA, BS, MA		BM, BMEd		10,114	$13,600*	A155, M390
Westminster Choir College of Rider University			BM, MM		437	$15,430*	M470
William Paterson University of New Jersey			BA, BM		8,941	$3786*	M475
New Mexico							
College of Santa Fe	BA, BFA		BFA	BFA	1,417	$13,240*	A72, M292, T493
Eastern New Mexico University	BFA		BM, BMEd, MM	BFA	3,495	$1716*	A84, M305, T498
New Mexico Highlands University	BFA				2,544	$1662*	A124
New Mexico State University	BFA, MFA		BM, BMEd, MM		15,067	$2196*	A125, M361
University of New Mexico	BFA, MFA, PhD		BM, BMEd, MM, MMEd		23,956	$2165*	A190, M438
New York							
Adelphi University				BFA	5,594	$14,720*	T483
Alfred University	BFA, MFA				2,329	$19,000*	A44
American Academy of Dramatic Arts				AOS, Cert	159	$10,100**	T483
Brooklyn College of the City University of New York	BFA, MFA		BM, MM	BFA, MFA	15,007	$3413*	A62, M276, T490

* Expenses for 1997–98.   ** Expenses for 1998–99.   *** Estimated expenses for 1998–99.   NR = Not reported.

	Art	Dance	Music	Theater	Enroll-ment	Tuition and Fees	Page
New York—*continued*							
Cazenovia College	BFA				897	$11,990***	A67
City College of the City University of New York			BFA, MA		12,061	$3309*	M288
College of New Rochelle	BFA				7,065	$11,100*	A72
The College of Saint Rose	BFA, MS				3,973	$11,719*	A72
Concordia College			BM		599	$11,990*	M295
Cooper Union for the Advancement of Science and Art	BFA				883	NR	A77
Cornell University	BFA, MFA				18,428	$21,914*	A78
Daemen College	BFA, BS				1,914	$10,980*	A80
Fashion Institute of Technology	BFA, MA				11,696	$2710*	A86
Five Towns College			BM, BMEd, MMEd, MOM		584	$9220**	M310
Hofstra University				BFA	12,439	$13,544*	T500
Houghton College			BM		1,411	$12,765*	M321
Hunter College of the City University of New York	BFA, MA, MFA		BM, MA		19,689	$3329*	A92, M322
Ithaca College	BFA, BFA		BOM, MM	BFA	5,897	$16,900*	A97, M327, T501
The Juilliard School		BFA	BM, MM, DMA	BFA	782	$15,000*	D229, M331, T503
Lehman College of the City University of New York	BFA, MFA				9,386	$3320*	A104
Long Island University, C.W. Post Campus	BFA, BS, MA, MFA, MS	BFA	BFA, MA	BFA, MA	8,171	$14,530*	A105, D230, M339, T504
Long Island University, Southampton College	BFA				1,563	$14,600*	A106
Manhattan School of Music			BM, MM, DMA		835	$17,900*	M342
Manhattanville College	BFA		BA, BM, MAT		1,925	$17,300*	A109, M343
Mannes College of Music, New School for Social Research			BM, MM		7,179	$15,670*	M344
Marymount Manhattan College		BFA		BFA	2,140	$12,290*	D231, T506
Nazareth College of Rochester			BM		2,782	$12,985*	M359
New School Jazz and Contemporary Music			BA/BFA, BFA			NR	M345
New York Institute of Technology	BFA				8,982	$10,630*	A125
New York School of Interior Design	BFA, MFA				625	$12,670**	A126
New York University	BFA	BFA, MFA	BM, BS, MA, MM, PhD, DA	BFA, BFA, MFA, MFA	36,684	$21,730*	A126, D232, M361, T509
Niagara University				BFA	3,079	$12,890*	T510
Nyack College			BM, BSM		1,433	$11,100*	M370

	Art	Dance	Music	Theater	Enrollment	Tuition and Fees	Page
New York—*continued*							
Pace University				BFA	13,317	$13,820*	T514
Parsons School of Design, New School for Social Research	BFA, MFA				7,179	$18,540*	A135
Pratt Institute	BARC, BFA, BID, MARC, MFA, MID, MPS, MS				3,640	$17,151*	A138
Purchase College, State University of New York	BFA, MFA	BFA	BFA, MFA	BFA, MFA	3,297	$3879*	A140, D235, M380, T517
Queens College of the City University of New York			BM, MA, MS		16,381	$3393*	M382
Rochester Institute of Technology	BFA, MFA, MST				12,352	$16,359*	A146
St. John's University	BFA				18,523	$12,230*	A148
School of Visual Arts	BFA, MFA				5,195	$13,890*	A154
State University of New York at Binghamton			BM, MM		12,156	$4110*	M400
State University of New York at Buffalo	BFA, MFA		BM, MM		23,429	$4340*	A160, M401
State University of New York at New Paltz	BFA, MA, MFA, MS			BFA	7,641	$3885***	A161, T520
State University of New York College at Brockport		BFA, MFA			8,492	$3915*	D238
State University of New York College at Fredonia	BFA		BFA, BM, BS, MM	BFA	4,593	$4075*	A161, M401, T521
State University of New York College at Potsdam			BM, MM		4,038	$3899*	M298
Syracuse University	BFA, BID, MFA, MID		BA, BM, MM	BFA, BS, MFA	14,557	$18,056*	A164, M403, T522
University of Rochester			BM, MA, MM, MM/PhD, PhD, DMA		8,451	$21,020*	M305
North Carolina							
Appalachian State University	BFA		BM, MM		12,108	$1840*	A49, M261
Barton College	BA, BFA, BS				1,303	$10,150**	A57
East Carolina University	BFA, MFA	BFA	BM, MM	BFA	18,271	$1848*	A83, D227, M303, T497
Guilford College	BFA				1,402	$14,750*	A90
Lenoir-Rhyne College			BMEd		1,616	$12,386**	M338
Mars Hill College			BFA, BM	BFA	1,244	$8900*	M347, T505
Meredith College			BM, MM		2,552	$8490*	M350
Methodist College			BM		1,720	$11,900***	M350
North Carolina Agricultural and Technical State University			BA	BFA	7,468	$1622*	M363, T510

* Expenses for 1997–98.   ** Expenses for 1998–99.   *** Estimated expenses for 1998–99.   NR = Not reported.

	Art	Dance	Music	Theater	Enroll-ment	Tuition and Fees	Page
North Carolina—*continued*							
North Carolina Central University			BA, BM		5,664	$1944*	M364
North Carolina School of the Arts		BFA	BM, MM	BFA, MFA	773	$2522*	D232, M364, T511
Queens College			BM		1,652	$9410**	M381
Salem College			BM		1,002	$12,415*	M387
University of North Carolina at Asheville	BFA				3,179	$1834*	A190
The University of North Carolina at Chapel Hill			BM, MAT		24,231	$2224*	M439
University of North Carolina at Charlotte	BFA		BM		16,511	$1777*	A191, M440
University of North Carolina at Greensboro	BFA, MFA	BFA, BS, MA, MFA	BM, MM, DMA	BFA, MFA	12,308	$2031*	A191, D246, M440, T534
University of North Carolina at Pembroke			BM		3,034	$1536*	M440
Western Carolina University	BFA			BFA		NR	A211, T543
Wingate University			BMEd		1,230	$11,690*	M476
North Dakota							
North Dakota State University				BFA, MA	9,408	$2566*	T511
University of North Dakota	BFA, MFA		BM, MM	BFA	10,363	$3118*	A192, M441, T534
Ohio							
Art Academy of Cincinnati	BFA, MA				185	$10,925*	A50
Ashland University			BM		5,737	$13,601*	M263
Baldwin-Wallace College			BM, BMEd		4,539	$13,275*	M265
Bowling Green State University	BFA, BS, MFA		BM, MM		17,328	$4422*	A60, M273
Capital University	BFA		BA, BM		3,988	$14,760*	A66, M281
Cedarville College			BMEd		2,559	$9312*	M284
Central State University			BM		1,051	$3318*	M286
Cincinnati Bible College and Seminary			BM		915	$6190**	M287
Cleveland Institute of Art	BFA				481	$13,170*	A70
Cleveland Institute of Music			BM, MM, DMA		360	$17,029*	M289
Cleveland State University			BM, MM		15,655	$3528*	M290
The College of Wooster			BM, BMEd		1,714	$19,230*	M292
Columbus College of Art and Design	BFA				1,547	$11,880*	A75
Denison University	BFA			BFA	2,025	$20,250*	A82, T496
Heidelberg College			BM		1,480	$16,260***	M319
Kent State University	BA, BFA, MA, MFA	BFA	BM, MM, PhD	BFA, MFA	20,743	$4460*	A101, D230, M333, T504

	Art	Dance	Music	Theater	Enroll-ment	Tuition and Fees	Page
Ohio—*continued*							
Lake Erie College	BA, BFA	BA, BFA	BA, BFA	BA, BFA	701	$13,750*	A103, D230, M334, T504
Miami University	BFA, BS, MA, MFA		BM, MM	BFA, MA	16,328	$5512*	A115, M351, T506
Mount Union College			BM, BMEd		1,935	$14,290*	M358
Oberlin College			BM, MM, MMEd		2,904	$22,438*	M371
Ohio Northern University	BFA		BM	BFA	2,927	$19,815**	A128, M372, T512
The Ohio State University	BFA, MFA	BFA, MFA	BM, BMEd, MA, MM, PhD, DMA		48,278	$3660*	A128, D233, M372
Ohio University	BFA, MFA	BFA	BM, MM	BFA, MFA	19,564	$4275*	A129, D233, M373, T513
Ohio Wesleyan University	BFA		BM		1,893	$20,040**	A129, M373
Otterbein College			BFA, BMEd	BFA	2,697	$14,997*	M376, T513
The University of Akron	BFA	BFA	BM, MM		23,538	$3660*	A170, D240, M411
University of Cincinnati	BFA, MFA	BFA	BM, MM, DMA, DMEd	BFA, MFA	28,161	$4359*	A174, D241, M417, T526
University of Dayton	BFA		BM, BMEd		10,208	$14,670**	A175, M421
University of Toledo			BM, BMEd, MM, MMEd	BFA	20,307	$3952*	M455, T539
Wittenberg University			BM, BMEd		2,088	$19,140*	M476
Wright State University	BFA	BFA	BM, MMEd	BFA	15,343	$3708*	A214, D253, M477, T545
Xavier University	BA, BFA				6,504	$14,520**	A214
Youngstown State University	BFA		BM, MM		12,324	$3558*	A215, M478
Oklahoma							
Cameron University			BM		5,147	$2180*	M280
East Central University			BS		4,087	$1812*	M303
Northwestern Oklahoma State University			BM, BMEd		1,871	$1802*	M368
Oklahoma Baptist University	BFA		BM, BMEd		2,211	$8336**	A129, M374
Oklahoma Christian University of Science and Arts			BMEd		1,904	$8278*	M374
Oklahoma City University			BM, BMEd, MM		4,323	$8512*	M374
Oklahoma State University	BFA		BM		19,350	$2357*	A130, M375
Oral Roberts University			BM, BMEd		3,966	$10,460**	M376
Phillips University			BMEd, BMT		584	$7300**	M379
Southeastern Oklahoma State University			BM, BMEd		3,946	$1879*	M395

* Expenses for 1997–98.   ** Expenses for 1998–99.   *** Estimated expenses for 1998–99.   NR = Not reported.

	Art	Dance	Music	Theater	Enroll-ment	Tuition and Fees	Page
Oklahoma—*continued*							
Southwestern Oklahoma State University			BM, BMEd, MMEd		4,478	$1798*	M399
University of Central Oklahoma			BM, BMEd, MM		13,928	$1806*	M417
University of Oklahoma	BFA, MFA	BFA, MFA	BFA, BM, BMA, BMEd, MM, MMEd, PhD, DMA	BFA, MA, MFA	25,975	$2311*	A193, D247, M443, T535
University of Tulsa			BM, BMEd		4,171	$12,930*	M455
Oregon							
The Art Institutes International at Portland	BAD, BIRD				148	$8900*	A54
Marylhurst University	BFA		BM			$9960*	A112, M348
Oregon College of Art and Craft	BFA				87	$10,425*	A131
Oregon State University	BFA				14,490	$3540**	A132
Pacific Northwest College of Art	BFA				243	$11,268**	A134
Portland State University			BM, MM		16,997	$3357*	M379
Southern Oregon University	BFA			BFA	5,426	$3204*	A159, T519
University of Oregon	BFA, MFA		BM, MA, MM, PhD, DMA		17,530	$3408*	A194, M443
University of Portland			BMEd, MA		2,606	$15,520*	M444
Willamette University			BM		2,502	$20,290*	M474
Pennsylvania							
Beaver College	BA, BFA				2,705	$15,840*	A58
Bucknell University			BM		3,543	$21,210*	M276
Carnegie Mellon University	BFA, MFA		BFA, MM	BFA, MFA	7,912	$20,375*	A67, M282, T492
Clarion University of Pennsylvania	BFA		BM, BS	BFA	5,948	$4419*	A69, M288, T493
The Curtis Institute of Music			BM, MM		162	$695*	M299
Duquesne University			BM, BS, MM, MMEd		9,500	$14,066*	M302
Edinboro University of Pennsylvania	BFA, BS, MFA				7,083	$4193*	A85
Grove City College			BM		2,292	$6576*	M318
Immaculata College			BM, MA		2,312	$12,115*	M324
Indiana University of Pennsylvania	BFA, MFA		BFA		13,736	$4204*	A94, M325
Kutztown University of Pennsylvania	BFA, MAE				7,920	$4219*	A102
Lebanon Valley College			BM, BS		1,856	$15,980*	M337
Lock Haven University of Pennsylvania			BA, BFA		3,538	$4062*	M339

	Art	Dance	Music	Theater	Enroll-ment	Tuition and Fees	Page
Pennsylvania—*continued*							
Mansfield University of Pennsylvania			BM, MM		2,907	$4404*	M346
Marywood University	BA, BFA, MA, MFA		BM, MA		2,948	$14,003*	A113, M348
Moore College of Art and Design	BFA				385	$15,500**	A122
Moravian College			BM		1,830	$17,276*	M356
Pennsylvania Academy of the Fine Arts	BFA, MFA					NR	A136
Pennsylvania State University University Park Campus	BFA, BS, MFA		BM, BMA, BS, MA, MEd, MM, PhD	BFA, MFA	40,538	$5832*	A137, M378, T515
Philadelphia College of Bible			BM		1,280	$9520**	M378
Point Park College		BA, BA/BFA		BA/BFA	2,270	$11,406*	D233, T515
Rosemont College	BFA				947	$13,340*	A147
Seton Hill College	BFA, MA		BM		1,078	$12,640*	A156, M391
Slippery Rock University of Pennsylvania	BFA		BM, BS		7,038	$4302*	A157, M394
Susquehanna University			BM		1,725	$18,350*	M403
Temple University	BFA, MEd, MFA	BFA, MEd, MFA, PhD	BM, BS, MM, MMT, PhD, DMA		27,670	$6150*	A168, D239, M308
University of the Arts	BFA, BS, MA, MAT, MFA, MID	BFA	BM, MAT, MM	BFA	1,624	$15,070*	A200, D249, M454, T538
West Chester University of Pennsylvania	BFA		BM, BS, MM		11,430	$4162*	A210, M468
Westminster College			BM		1,571	$15,430**	M471
Rhode Island							
Rhode Island College	BA, BFA, BS, MAT		BM, BS, MMEd		8,622	$3076*	A141, M382
Rhode Island School of Design	BFA, MARC, MFA, MIARC, MID, MLARC				2,001	$19,670*	A142
University of Rhode Island			BA, BM, MM	BFA	13,437	$4592*	M446, T535
South Carolina							
Anderson College			BMEd		1,012	$9475*	M260
Coker College			BMEd		970	$13,400*	M291
Columbia College		BFA	BM		1,368	$12,150*	D225, M294
Converse College	BA, BFA		BM, MM		1,474	$14,445*	A76, M296
Furman University			BM		2,840	$16,419*	M313
Lander University			BMEd			$3600*	M335
Newberry College			BM, BMEd		716	$12,326*	M360

* Expenses for 1997–98.   ** Expenses for 1998–99.   *** Estimated expenses for 1998–99.   NR = Not reported.

	Art	Dance	Music	Theater	Enroll-ment	Tuition and Fees	Page
South Carolina—continued							
University of South Carolina	BFA, MFA		BM, MM, MMEd, PhD, DMA		25,447	$3534*	A195, M447
Winthrop University	BA, BFA, MA, MFA		BM, BMEd, MM, MMEd		5,574	$3938*	A214, M476
South Dakota							
Northern State University			BMEd		2,646	$2535*	M367
South Dakota State University			BMEd, BS		8,867	$2912*	M394
University of South Dakota	BFA, MFA		BM, MM	BFA, MFA	7,392	$3012*	A196, M448, T536
Tennessee							
Austin Peay State University	BFA				7,803	$2280*	A56
Belmont University	BFA		BM, MM, MMEd		2,986	$10,300*	A59, M268
Carson-Newman College			BM		2,308	$10,610**	M282
East Tennessee State University	BFA, MA, MFA		BM, MMEd		11,596	$2100*	A84, M307
Fisk University			BA, BM, BS		765	$7750*	M309
Lambuth University			BM		1,012	$6194*	M335
Lee University			BMEd, MCM		2,870	$5638*	M337
Maryville College			BM		955	$14,425*	M348
Memphis College of Art	BFA, MFA				260	$11,500**	A114
Middle Tennessee State University	BFA		BM		18,366	$2196*	A116, M352
O'More College of Design	BFDM, BGDA, BIRD				149	$7955*	A130
Southern Adventist University			BMEd		1,695	$9736*	M396
Tennessee Technological University			BM		8,263	$2116*	M405
Tennessee Wesleyan College			BMEd		756	$7050***	M405
Union University			BM		1,953	$8180*	M410
The University of Memphis	BA, BFA, MA, MFA		BM, MM, DMA	BFA, MFA	19,851	$2412*	A184, M429, T530
University of Tennessee at Chattanooga	BFA, BS		BM, MM		8,528	$2200*	A197, M451
The University of Tennessee at Martin	BFA	BFA	BM	BFA	5,997	$2240*	A197, D248, M451, T538
University of Tennessee, Knoxville	BFA, MFA		BM, BMEd, MM		25,397	$2576*	A198, M451
Vanderbilt University			BM, BM/MEd		10,210	$21,478*	M462
Texas							
Abilene Christian University	BFA		BA, BM		4,507	$9180*	A41, M258

	Art	Dance	Music	Theater	Enroll-ment	Tuition and Fees	Page
Texas—*continued*							
Angelo State University			BM		6,234	$2242***	M261
Baylor University	BFA		BM, BMEd, MM	BFA, MFA	12,472	$10,266**	A57, M267, T487
Dallas Baptist University			BM		3,493	$7800*	M300
East Texas Baptist University			BM		1,292	$6750*	M307
Hardin-Simmons University			BM, MM		2,312	$8130*	M318
Howard Payne University			BM		1,489	$7620*	M321
Lamar University			BM, MM, MMEd		9,677	$1868*	M335
Midwestern State University	BFA		BM	BFA	5,770	$2091*	A117, M353, T507
Prairie View A&M University			BM		6,004	$2364*	M380
Rice University	BFA, MA		BM, MM, DMA		4,209	$14,306*	A143, M383
Sam Houston State University	BFA, MFA	BFA, MFA	BM, BMEd, MM, MMEd		12,712	$1586*	A149, D237, M387
Southern Methodist University	BFA, MFA	BFA, MFA	BM, MM, MMT	BFA, MFA	9,708	$16,790*	A159, D238, M397, T519
Southwestern University			BM	BFA	1,215	$14,000*	M399, T520
Southwest Texas State University	BFA		BM, MM		20,652	$2214*	A160, M400
Stephen F. Austin State University	BFA, MFA		BM, MA, MM	BFA, MA	12,041	$2188*	A162, M402, T521
Sul Ross State University	BFA, MEd					$1680*	A164
Tarleton State University			BA, BM	BFA		$2464*	M404, T523
Texas A&M University–Commerce	BFA, MFA		BM, MM, MS		7,693	$2286*	A165, M406
Texas A&M University–Corpus Christi	BFA		BM		6,024	$1954*	A166, M406
Texas A&M University–Kingsville	BFA, MS		BM, MM		6,050	$2180*	A166, M406
Texas Christian University	BFA, MA, MFA	BFA, MFA	BM, BMEd, MM, MMEd	BA, BFA	7,273	$11,090*	A166, D239, M407, T523
Texas Southern University	BA		BA, MA, MEd	BA	7,282	$2064*	A167, M407, T524
Texas Tech University	BFA, MFA, DA		BM, MM, MMEd, PhD		25,022	$2607*	A167, M408
Texas Wesleyan University			BA, BMEd		3,136	$7950*	M408
Texas Woman's University	BFA, MFA				9,378	$1980**	A167
Trinity University			BM		2,560	$14,724***	M409
University of Houston	BA, BFA, MFA		BM, MM, DMA	BA, MA, MFA	31,602	$1993***	A179, M424, T529
University of Mary Hardin-Baylor	BFA				2,313	$6944*	A182

* Expenses for 1997–98.   ** Expenses for 1998–99.   *** Estimated expenses for 1998–99.   NR = Not reported.

	Art	Dance	Music	Theater	Enroll-ment	Tuition and Fees	Page
Texas—*continued*							
University of North Texas	BFA, MFA		BM, MM, DMA		25,013	$2187*	A193, M442
The University of Texas at Arlington	BFA		BM		19,286	$2088*	A198, M452
The University of Texas at Austin	BFA, MFA	BFA	BM, MM, DMA	BFA, MFA, PhD	48,857	$2866*	A198, D248, M452, T538
The University of Texas at El Paso	BFA, MA		BM, MM, MMEd		15,176	$2266*	A199, M453
The University of Texas at San Antonio	BFA, MFA		BM, MM		17,494	$2744**	A199, M453
The University of Texas at Tyler	BFA		BM		3,393	$2084*	A199, M454
The University of Texas–Pan American	BFA, MFA					$1973*	A200
University of the Incarnate Word			BM, BMEd, BMT		3,312	$10,840*	M454
Wayland Baptist University			BM		4,190	$6470*	M467
West Texas A&M University	BFA, MA, MFA	BFA, MA	BM, MA, MM		6,489	$1744*	A212, D252, M472
Utah							
Brigham Young University	BA, BFA, MFA		BM, MM	BFA, MFA	32,161	$2630*	A61, M275, T489
University of Utah	BFA, MFA	BFA, BFA, MA, MFA, MFA	BM, BMEd, MM, MMEd	BFA, MFA	25,883	$2601*	A202, D249, M456, T539
Utah State University	BFA, MFA		BM, BS	BFA, MFA	21,234	$2175*	A205, M461, T541
Weber State University	BFA				14,613	$1935*	A210
Vermont							
Johnson State College	BA, BFA, MFA			BFA	1,622	$4641*	A99, T503
University of Vermont			BA, BM, BS		10,368	$7550*	M456
Virginia							
Christopher Newport University			BM		4,878	$3466*	M287
George Mason University		BFA, MFA	BM, MA		23,826	$4296*	D228, M314
James Madison University	BFA, MFA		BM, MM		14,115	$4148*	A98, M330
Liberty University			BM		6,646	$8500**	M338
Longwood College	BFA		BM	BFA	3,352	$4416*	A106, M340, T505
Norfolk State University			BM, MM		7,659	$3000*	M363
Old Dominion University	BFA, MA, MFA		BA, BM, BMEd		18,557	$3976*	A130, M375
Radford University	BFA, MFA, MS	BFA	BM, MS		8,534	$3180*	A141, D236, M382

	Art	Dance	Music	Theater	Enroll-ment	Tuition and Fees	Page
Virginia—*continued*							
Shenandoah University		BFA, MFA	BM, BMT, BS, MM, MMEd, MS, DMA	BA, BFA	1,927	$14,400*	D237, M391, T518
University of Richmond			BM		4,425	$18,595**	M447
Virginia Commonwealth University	BFA, MFA, PhD	BFA	BM, MM	BFA, MFA	22,702	$4111*	A206, D250, M464, T542
Virginia Intermont College	BFA	BFA	BFA	BFA	848	$10,650*	A207, D251, M464, T542
Virginia State University	BFA		BM, BMEd		4,200	$3307*	A208, M464
Washington							
Central Washington University			BM, MM		8,438	$2826*	M286
Cornish College of the Arts	BFA, BFA	BFA	BM	BFA, BFA	621	$11,658*	A80, D226, M297, T495
Eastern Washington University			BAE, BM, MA		7,537	$2622**	M305
Pacific Lutheran University	BFA		BM, BMA, BMEd		3,555	$15,680**	A133, M377
University of Puget Sound			BM		3,011	$18,940*	M445
University of Washington	BFA, MFA		BM, MM, DMA		35,367	$3366*	A202, M457
Walla Walla College			BM		1,653	$12,693*	M465
Washington State University	BFA, MFA		BM, BMEd, MA		20,243	$3394*	A208, M466
Western Washington University			BM, MM		11,476	$2772*	M470
West Virginia							
Marshall University	BA, BFA, MA		BFA, MA	BFA	13,388	$2184*	A110, M346, T505
Shepherd College	BFA				4,025	$2228*	A156
West Virginia University	BFA, MA, MFA		BM, MM, DMA	BFA, MFA	22,238	$2336*	A213, M472, T544
West Virginia Wesleyan College			BM, BMEd		1,686	$16,750***	M473
Wisconsin							
Alverno College			BM		2,072	$9722*	M259
Cardinal Stritch University	BFA				5,316	$10,130*	A66
Lawrence University			BA/BM, BM		1,179	$19,620*	M336
Milwaukee Institute of Art & Design	BFA				503	$14,800*	A117
St. Norbert College			BM		2,000	$14,434*	M386
Silver Lake College			BM, MM		1,050	$9986**	M392
University of Wisconsin–Eau Claire	BFA		BM, BMEd, BMT		10,484	$2872*	A203, M457

* Expenses for 1997–98. ** Expenses for 1998–99. *** Estimated expenses for 1998–99. NR = Not reported.

	Art	Dance	Music	Theater	Enroll-ment	Tuition and Fees	Page
Wisconsin—*continued*							
University of Wisconsin–Green Bay			BM		5,419	$2738*	M458
University of Wisconsin–Madison	BFA, BS, MFA		BM, MMA, MMEd, DMA		40,196	$3242***	A203, M458
University of Wisconsin–Milwaukee	BFA, MFA	BFA, MFA	BFA, MM	BFA, MFA	21,525	$3327*	A203, D250, M459, T539
University of Wisconsin–Oshkosh	BFA		BM, BMEd		10,960	$2609*	A204, M459
University of Wisconsin–River Falls			BMEd		5,441	$2750***	M459
University of Wisconsin–Stevens Point	BFA		BM, MMEd	BFA	8,446	$2790*	A204, M460, T540
University of Wisconsin–Stout	BFA, BS				7,418	$2806*	A204
University of Wisconsin–Superior	BFA, BS, MA		BM, BMEd	BFA	2,574	$2652*	A205, M460, T540
University of Wisconsin–Whitewater	BFA		BM, MMEd		10,563	$2772*	A205, M460
Viterbo College			BM, BMEd		2,622	$11,690**	M465
Wyoming							
University of Wyoming		BFA	BM, BMEd, MM, MMEd	BFA	11,094	$2330*	D250, M461, T540
Canada							
Acadia University			BAIM, BM		3,964	$5202*	M258
Alberta College of Art and Design	BFA				785	$2022*	A43
Brock University			BM		11,135	$3458*	M275
Carleton University			BM		17,541	$3528*	M282
Concordia University	BFA, MFA, PhD	BFA	BFA	BFA	29,271	$2286**	A76, D226, M295, T494
Dalhousie University			BA, BM		12,387	$3850*	M300
Lakehead University	BA, BFA		BM		6,787	$3563*	A103, M334
Mount Allison University	BFA		BM		2,474	$4017*	A123, M358
Nova Scotia College of Art and Design	BD, BFA, MFA				657	$3596*	A127
Queen's University at Kingston	BFA				15,973	$3778*	A140
St. Francis Xavier University			BM		4,048	$3898*	M385
Simon Fraser University	BFA, MFA	BFA, MFA	BFA, MFA	BFA, MFA	18,759	$2517*	A157, D237, M392, T519
University of Alberta			BM, BM/BEd, MA, MM, PhD, DM		28,613	$3446*	M412
University of British Columbia	BA, BFA, MA, MFA, PhD		BM, MA, MM, PhD, DMA	BA, BFA, MFA	32,110	$2551*	A173, M414, T525
The University of Calgary	BFA, MFA		BM, MM, PhD		23,737	$3366*	A173, M415

	Art	Dance	Music	Theater	Enroll-ment	Tuition and Fees	Page
Canada—*continued*							
University of Manitoba	BFA				21,083	$4180*	A181
University of Prince Edward Island			BM		2,934	$3507*	M444
University of Regina	BFA, MFA		BM, BMEd, MA, MM			$3042*	A195, M446
Wilfrid Laurier University			BM, BMT		7,857	$3488*	M474
York University	BFA, MFA	BFA	BFA	BFA, MFA	37,900	$3750*	A215, D253, M478, T547

* Expenses for 1997–98.   ** Expenses for 1998–99.   *** Estimated expenses for 1998–99.   NR = Not reported.

ART PROGRAMS

Professional or Bachelor of Fine Arts (B.F.A.) degrees allow students to focus most of their studies in art—up to 70 percent of all course work. These degrees aren't for every student interested in art. If you prefer a broader liberal arts background or you're not ready for the keener competition of a B.F.A. program, a liberal arts degree with an art major may be best. For information on B.A. programs, consult *Peterson's Guide to Four-Year Colleges*. But if a professional degree is what you're looking for, *Peterson's Professional Degree Programs in the Visual and Performing Arts* will help you choose a program that can launch you on a successful art career.

Your first step? To decide the type of school that will best suit your needs and goals. Professional degrees are offered by independent art schools as well as colleges and universities offering the full range of majors. Art schools and more comprehensive colleges each have a distinctive campus culture.

Independent Art Colleges

At an independent art college, all the resources of an institution—faculty, facilities, student services, and educational programs—focus on the needs of the developing professional artist. Because art colleges are usually small, students and faculty members interact closely. There's a strong sense of community. The focus is on preparing students for a career in art, so these schools usually offer extensive course work in art and design and many opportunities for specialization.

While the liberal arts programs at professional art colleges do not offer the broad choices found at universities, they are usually designed to integrate the study of studio art and liberal arts. For example, a physics course might focus on light and color—the content might then be integrated with concepts that are addressed in a studio course. Students majoring in graphic design might be encouraged to take psychology because this field involves marketing and management. Frequently, the liberal arts programs at art colleges emphasize courses related to creative expression—visual, verbal, and written—as well as art history, criticism, and other areas of the humanities.

University Art Programs

Students who wish to merge their ability in art with other interests and want to interact with students engaged in the study of many different disciplines might choose a university. Although not developed to support the specific needs of artists, the university can offer resources such as sports facilities, a comprehensive library, or a computer center. There are social clubs (such as fraternities and sororities), theater groups, and student government organizations, all of which provide opportunities for students to participate in the larger life of the university and meet students with other interests and talents.

Usually offered outside the department or school of art, liberal arts programs offer a wide range of electives from many disciplines, including business, languages, literature, and sciences. Art students interested in developing in-depth study in a liberal arts subject can often do so through the options of minors or dual majors. The university B.F.A. program in the visual arts will be rigorous and professional, typically offering a broad range of courses and electives. Universities will vary, though, as to whether or not areas for specialization are available.

The Admission Process and Criteria

The best way to enhance your chances of being accepted into a B.F.A. program is to seek early counseling and review of your work. Visit several schools or send a slide portfolio for advice. You might also want to attend one of the two dozen National Portfolio Days sponsored each year across the country

HOW DO YOU KNOW A PROGRAM IS RIGHT FOR YOU?

What makes a program right for someone makes it very wrong for someone else. You'll have to consider your own needs, talents, and interests if you want to make the best choice. Here are some questions to ask to help target your search:

- Are you happiest in a big school or small? Big city or small town? What is the overall environment of the school?
- How many people are majoring in the program you are interested in? What is the student-faculty ratio in your area of study?
- Where do the students in the program come from? Is this a regional school of commuting students, or does it attract students from all over the region—or country? What is the age group?
- Tour the facilities and ask which ones are available to you. Is there independent studio space for painting majors? Is there a foundry for sculptors? What kind of computer equipment does the school have?
- How many courses are offered in your area of interest?
- What opportunities will you have for professional exposure? Are there exhibition opportunities on or off campus? Are there student memberships in professional organizations? Are there opportunities for reality-based course work, such as designing a poster for a community group?
- Does the program feature visiting artists or critics so you can meet practicing professionals and learn the latest theories and techniques? Who are they? How many come each semester? Do they lecture in an auditorium, or do they come into the studios and talk and work with students?
- Does the program arrange job internships? Internships are one of the best tickets to a job following graduation. You'll want to know examples of recently awarded internships and with whom the students worked, as well as whether credit was given.
- Check the faculty biographies in the college catalog to see what degrees faculty members have and from which institutions. Look for a high percentage of M.F.A.'s or equivalent degrees as well as at their professional experience in terms of awards and exhibitions. Check the liberal arts faculty as well, because liberal arts are part of the B.F.A.
- A good B.F.A. program should have a career development center that helps students in both placement and assessment. Are the opportunities local and/or national? Does the center help students assess their abilities, skills, and interests early on and assist them in putting together their programs of study?
- Are recent graduates of the program working in their chosen field? What kind of entry-level jobs did they get? What internships helped them? What aspects of their college curriculum helped them?

by the National Portfolio Day Association of major art colleges and universities. Your portfolio will be reviewed by representatives from a number of colleges, and they can give advice on how to build on existing strengths. Call 612-874-3760 for more information.

In addition, consider attending summer programs in art (see *Peterson's Summer Opportunities for Kids and Teenagers* for several leading art programs held in the U.S. and abroad). Admission committees see enrollment in one of these programs as a demonstration of a high level of commitment to art. Summer art programs can also be invaluable when developing your portfolio.

Most universities have application deadlines. Art colleges are more inclined to have rolling admissions, partly because the portfolio plays such an important part in their evaluation and they want to give students the time and opportunity to build the best portfolio. Some art colleges send faculty or admission staff members to high schools to do presentations and evaluate portfolios. More often, students send their portfolio—usually on slides or videotape—with the rest of their admission materials. Many art colleges and universities encourage students to visit for a personal interview and portfolio review, though few require it.

The portfolio will weigh heaviest in the admission decision for art colleges, followed by the academic record. Traditionally, most art colleges have placed more weight on humanities courses than on math and the sciences in their evaluation of transcripts, except in the case of architecture candidates. However, in recent years this has been changing, and many art schools are now looking more closely at academics and placing equal importance on all courses taken. When reviewing course work, art colleges look at what kind of high school students attend. Is it a vocational school or a private prep school? Are the courses Advanced Placement or standard? Test scores are generally used more for placement than for admission.

The admission process can be different at universities, since art students are applying for admission to the university itself. Universities generally evaluate test scores and grades first, then portfolios—or at least place equal weight on art and academics.

Portfolio Evaluation

When evaluating portfolios, universities usually use faculty members from the department or school of art. Art colleges use trained admission staff members who are usually artists themselves, as well as faculty members. Portfolio evaluators at the more selective art colleges and universities are looking for more than raw talent. They are looking for a particular level of competency and technical skill as well as conceptual ability. The emphasis placed on concept versus skill will vary from college to college because each has a different philosophy of education and programmatic thrust and will look for students who are a good match for that institution. Every college, however, is looking for students who demonstrate through their artwork that they are creative, intellectually curious, and seriously invested and committed—even compelled—to make art. For more advice on the preparation of art portfolios, see the column titled "Words of Wisdom" in this article.

WORDS OF WISDOM

Sure-fire Tips to Breathe Life into Your Portfolio

- Perfect craftsmanship isn't everything. Adjudicators will look for how students handle problems or come up with unusual solutions to problems.
- Develop your own forms and styles; go beyond the usual.
- Do as much drawing and painting from real life as possible—draw subject matter from still lifes and landscapes. Observational drawing is key. You may even want to consider enrolling in a life drawing class.
- You'll need to show that you know how to look at a three-dimensional object and transfer it to a two-dimensional surface.
- You won't win points in the long run by using photos as drawing or painting aides. Since the contrast of shadows and light and composition are already in place, you won't actually compose the subject by yourself.
- Remember—your portfolio should represent your interests, not the latest trends.

▼ ABILENE CHRISTIAN UNIVERSITY

Abilene, Texas

Independent, coed. Urban campus. Total enrollment: 4,507. Art program established 1901.

Degrees Bachelor of Fine Arts in the areas of graphic design, art marketing, art, art education, graphic design-advertising. Majors and concentrations: ceramic art and design, graphic design, jewelry and metalsmithing, painting/drawing, sculpture. Cross-registration with Hardin-Simmons University, McMurry University.

Enrollment Fall 1997: 78 total; all undergraduate.

Art Student Profile 65% females, 35% males, 5% minorities, 2% international.

Art Faculty 9 total (full-time and part-time). 100% of full-time faculty have terminal degrees. Graduate students do not teach undergraduate courses. Undergraduate student–faculty ratio: 12:1.

Expenses for 1997–98 Application fee: $25, $45 for international students. Comprehensive fee: $12,990 includes full-time tuition ($8730), mandatory fees ($450), and college room and board ($3810). College room only: $1610. Room and board charges vary according to board plan and housing facility. Special program-related fees: $25–$125 per course for supplies.

Financial Aid Program-specific awards for 1997: Juanita Tittle Pollard Scholarship for program majors ($125–$1000), Whitefield Scholarships for program majors.

Application Procedures Students admitted directly into the professional program freshman year. Deadline for freshmen and transfers: continuous. Required: high school transcript, college transcript(s) for transfer students, letter of recommendation, SAT I or ACT test scores. Recommended: interview.

Undergraduate Contact DeAnn Boring, Administrative Coordinator, Department of Art, Abilene Christian University, ACU Station, PO Box 27987, Abilene, Texas 76999; 915-674-2085, fax: 915-674-2051.

▼ ACADEMY OF ART COLLEGE

San Francisco, California

Proprietary, coed. Urban campus. Art program established 1929.

Degrees Bachelor of Fine Arts in the areas of advertising design, computer arts, fashion, fine arts, graphic design, illustration, interior architecture and design photography, product and industrial design, motion pictures/video. Majors and concentrations: computer art, computer graphics, fashion design and technology, film and video production, industrial design, painting/drawing, printmaking, sculpture. Graduate degrees offered: Master of Fine Arts in the areas of advertising design, computer arts, fashion, fine arts, graphic design, illustration, interior architecture and design, photography, product and industrial design, motion pictures/video. Program accredited by NASAD, FIDER.

Enrollment Fall 1997: 5,000 total; 3,886 undergraduate, 645 graduate, 469 non-professional degree.

Art Student Profile 50% females, 50% males, 30% minorities, 35% international.

Art Faculty 465 total undergraduate and graduate (full-time and part-time). 10% of full-time faculty have terminal degrees. Graduate students do not teach undergraduate courses. Undergraduate student–faculty ratio: 20:1.

Student Life Student groups/activities include American Society of Interior Designers, Western Art Directors Club.

Expenses for 1997–98 Application fee: $100. Tuition: $14,850 full-time. Mandatory fees: $60 full-time. College room only: $6500. Special program-related fees: $45–$150 per semester for studio lab fee.

Application Procedures Students apply for admission into the professional program by sophomore year. Deadline for freshmen and transfers: continuous. Required: college transcript(s) for transfer students, minimum 2.0 high school GPA, high school transcript or GED. Recommended: minimum 3.0 high school GPA.

Web Site http://www.academyart.edu.

Undergraduate Contact Mr. Ron Bonn, Director of Admissions, Academy of Art College, 79 New Montgomery Street, San Francisco, California 94105; 415-263-4127, fax: 415-263-4130.

Graduate Contact Mr. Jim Short, Graduate Admissions Manager, Academy of Art College, 79 New Montgomery Street, San Francisco, California 94105; 415-274-2285, fax: 415-263-4124.

More About the Academy

Program Facilities The Academy is comprised of fifteen buildings in downtown San Francisco, including four art galleries and five dormitories. The newest building is an open studio and loft space for photography students to shoot large commercial product layouts. It also contains individual work spaces for M.F.A. students who create on large canvases. The eight-story Multimedia Center has more than 500

Academy of Art College *(continued)*

computers, including 84 Silicon Graphics work stations (the Academy is the only authorized Silicon Studio in Northern California). A new concentration in the Illustration Department, character animation, combines drawing techniques with 3-D computer rendering to help students submit portfolios to companies like Walt Disney, DreamWorks, and Warner Brothers, which recruit at the school. The Motion Picture/Video Department has nine AVID digital and 28 electronic editing suites as well as a full array of 16mm, 35mm, Beta SP, Sony DVCam, and Panasonic SVHS video cameras. The Fine Arts Sculpture building is 100,000 square feet of space that includes a 25-foot high ceiling equipped with cranes for large metal sculptures. The library has expanded to include scanners directly linked to the Computer Education Center and access to the World Wide Web.

Faculty, Resident Artists, and Alumni Nearly all of the Academy's instructors are professional artists and designers. Internationally known artists lecture and show their works in Academy galleries throughout the year.

Student Exhibit Opportunities More than eighty student shows are exhibited each year in the four main galleries. Each May the Spring Show takes over five of the eight floors of the Multimedia Center for three weeks. The annual AAC Fashion Show highlights senior and M.F.A. collections in a runway show to which international designers are invited.

Special Programs The Academy's outstanding ESL program—Engligh for Art—features a state-of-the-art Tannberg multimedia language lab and allows international students to learn English while taking foundation art/design courses. The product/industrial design department has added a new concentration in transportation design, with underwriting from Volkswagen. Additional classes have been added to the curriculum in the Liberal Arts area of compelling communications that train students to act in film and video productions. A Western Art Director's Club and a student chapter of ASID (American Society of Interior Designers) are located on campus.

▼

The Academy of Art College, San Francisco, is experiencing unprecedented growth in several departments. An analysis of this phenomenon shows that the largest group of potential students comes not so much because of direct advertising as "friends" of students or alumni or word-of-mouth recommendation. Certainly the Academy's state-of-the-art computers, equipment, labs, and studios are a contributing factor. Very popular at the Academy are the Career Days organized by the newly expanded Career Services Department. At least once each semester representatives from such companies as Walt Disney, Pixar, Industrial Light & Magic, Warner Brothers, Sony Digital, Columbia Tri-Star, Digital Domain, DreamWorks, McCann-Erickson, Hallmark, and other companies visit the campus. They assess student portfolios as well as explain exactly what qualities they look for in recruiting talent. One of the reasons they add the Academy to their recruiting rounds is because of the extensive drawing foundations classes all students must take. As one represantitive put it: "We look for artists primarily, who happen to use the computer as a tool." These meetings are so well attended that they are video-taped to allow students to view them several times.

Perhaps the most important reason students and graduates recommend the Academy is the professional-level instruction they receive. Most instructors are full-time art and design professionals who teach part-time, but a solid full-time core of department directors and assistant directors helps to maintain the focus and philosophy. Graduates of the Academy who recommend the school to friends often cite the professional level of instruction. One example is Craig Nelson, the Fine Arts Department Director, whose twenty-six years of credits include motion pictures (*Dirty Harry, Slapshot, Moscow on the Hudson*), advertising (the National Football League, Disneyland, Toyota) and album covers (Neil Diamond, Natalie Cole, Rickie Nelson). Foundations Department Director William Maughan is renowned for his Civil War-era prints and French landscapes. He has been commissioned by Signet, Avon, and Pinnacle Books, CBS-TV, *Cosmopolitan, Good Housekeeping*, and Universal Studios.

Photography Director James Wood was voted one of the top fifty advertising photographers in the world by Canon. He and David Pfeill, Director of Graduate Motion Pictures, spend half their time in Los Angeles working in the "real world." Patrick Kriwanek, Director of Motion Pictures/Video, has worked with Fox TV Network, LucasFilm, and Saul Zaentz and has produced TV commercials and more than fifty music videos.

Graphic Design Director Howard York has worked for more than thirty years with design clients including Sanyo, Exxon/Esso, Holiday Inns, Taco Bell, Embassy Suites, and Polaroid; one project took him five years to complete, the Riyadh, Saudi Arabia, airport for which he created more than 30,000 trilingual signs. Fashion Department Director Gladys Perint Palmer has taught at St. Martins in London and Parsons in New York, as well as covered fashion worldwide for several publications; her freelance clients include Oscar de la Renta, Emporio Armani, Missoni, Saks, and Fendi. Jeff Teague is a concept car designer who has styled automobiles for twenty years for Volkswagen, Mitsubishi, and Ford.

The new Director of the Advertising Design Department, Brian McCarthy, has worked thirty years as a creative director in top agencies in New York and San Francisco, including McCann-Erickson. The new Director of the Computer Arts Department, Rob Gibson, has been teaching Silicon Studio animation classes since 1992 and worked as a Senior Animator for Forensic Technologies, International, of San Francisco.

▼ ADRIAN COLLEGE
Adrian, Michigan

Independent, coed. Small town campus. Total enrollment: 1,000. Art program established 1962.

Degrees Bachelor of Fine Arts in the areas of art, interior design. Majors and concentrations: art education, art/fine arts, arts management, interior design, pre-art therapy. Cross-registration with Siena Heights University, Fashion Institute of Technology, Center for Creative Studies-College of Art and Design, The American College (London, Los Angeles, Atlanta).

Enrollment Fall 1997: 75 total; all undergraduate.

Art Student Profile 66% females, 34% males, 10% minorities, 4% international.

Art Faculty 10 total undergraduate (full-time and part-time). 100% of full-time faculty have terminal degrees. Graduate students do not teach undergraduate courses. Undergraduate student–faculty ratio: 10:1.

Student Life Student groups/activities include American Society of Interior Designers, Fashion Club, Art Club.

Expenses for 1997–98 Application fee: $20. Comprehensive fee: $16,950 includes full-time tuition ($12,730), mandatory fees ($100), and college room and board ($4120). College room only: $1880.

Financial Aid Program-specific awards for 1997: Studio Art Scholarships for program majors and minors ($3000–$6000).

Application Procedures Students admitted directly into the professional program freshman year. Deadline for freshmen and transfers: August 15. Required: high school transcript, college transcript(s) for transfer students, minimum 2.0 high school GPA, SAT I or ACT test scores (minimum combined ACT score of 16), portfolio for scholarship consideration. Recommended: essay, minimum 3.0 high school GPA, 2 letters of recommendation. Portfolio reviews held numerous times on campus and off campus in Fort Wayne, IN; the submission of slides may be substituted for portfolios when distance is prohibitive or scheduling is difficult.

Undergraduate Contact Ms. Janel Sutkus, Director of Admissions, Adrian College, 110 South Madison Street, Adrian, Michigan 49221; 800-877-2246, fax: 517-264-3331, E-mail address: admissions@adrian.edu.

▼ ALBERTA COLLEGE OF ART AND DESIGN

Calgary, AB, Canada

Province-supported, coed. Urban campus. Total enrollment: 785. Art program established 1926.

Degrees Bachelor of Fine Arts in the areas of ceramics, drawing, glass, jewelry and metals, painting, printmaking, sculpture, textiles, photographic arts, visual communications, interdisciplinary studies. Majors and concentrations: art/fine arts, ceramic art and design, commercial art, computer graphics, glass, graphic arts, illustration, interdisciplinary studies, jewelry and metalsmithing, painting/drawing, photography, printmaking, sculpture, studio art, textile arts. Cross-registration with University of Calgary.

Enrollment Fall 1997: 730 total; 708 undergraduate, 22 non-professional degree.

Art Student Profile 55% females, 45% males, 3% international.

Art Faculty 92 total (full-time and part-time). 25% of full-time faculty have terminal degrees. Graduate students teach a few undergraduate courses. Undergraduate student–faculty ratio: 18:1.

Student Life Student groups/activities include gallery exhibitions.

Expenses for 1997–98 Application fee: $25 Canadian dollars. Tuition and fee charges are reported in Canadian dollars. Canadian resident tuition: $2022 full-time. Full-time tuition varies according to student level. International student tuition: $8872 full-time. Special program-related fees: $2–$6 per credit for supplemental materials.

Financial Aid Program-specific awards for 1997: 100–120 General Scholarships for program students ($700), International Entrance Scholarships for international program students ($2000).

Application Procedures Students apply for admission into the professional program by sophomore year. Deadline for freshmen: April 15; transfers: March 1. Notification date for freshmen: June 15; transfers: April 15. Required: essay, high school transcript, college transcript(s) for transfer students, portfolio, 60% average GPA on 4 grade-12 subjects. Recommended: minimum 2.0 high school GPA. Portfolio

reviews held twice on campus; the submission of slides may be substituted for portfolios for large works of art, three-dimensional pieces, or when distance is prohibitive.

Web Site http://www.acad.ab.ca.

Undergraduate Contact Mr. Kevin Bird, Admissions Officer, Registrar's Office, Alberta College of Art and Design, 1407-14 Avenue NW, Calgary, AB T2N 4R3, Canada; 800-251-8290, fax: 403-289-6682, E-mail address: kevin.bird@acad.ab.ca.

More About the College

Program Facilities The Alberta College of Art & Design (ACAD) is a public college that offers four-year diploma programs and a Bachelor of Fine Arts degree in visual arts and design, including ceramics, drawing, glass, jewelry and metals, painting, printmaking, sculpture, textiles, interdisciplinary studies, photographic arts, and visual communications. The College is located in Calgary, Alberta, Canada, in a 245,000-square-foot building designed specifically as an art college. ACAD studios are spacious and well-equipped. The College is the home of two contemporary art galleries, a well-stocked art supply/bookstore, a tool bank, a wood shop, an audiovisual resource center, several computer labs, a library, and a cafeteria.

Faculty, Resident Artists, and Alumni All ACAD instructors are professional artists whose own work is exhibited locally, nationally, and internationally. Practicing professional artists from across the country and around the world come to ACAD to give workshops and lectures. Recent visiting artists have included New York performance artist Karen Finley and environmental artist Alan Sonfist.

Student Performance/Exhibit Opportunities Ongoing student exhibitions take place in the student gallery and throughout the building. There are a number of exhibiting galleries and artist-run centers in the city that support and encourage emerging artists.

Special Programs ACAD has an active student exchange program, which allows students to spend their third year studying at other art colleges and institutes across North America and in Great Britain, France, Germany, Norway, Sweden, and Australia.

▼ ALBERTUS MAGNUS COLLEGE

New Haven, Connecticut

Independent-Roman Catholic, coed. Suburban campus. Total enrollment: 1,549. Art program established 1925.

Degrees Bachelor of Fine Arts in the area of art. Majors and concentrations: graphic design, photography, studio art. Cross-registration with University of New Haven, Quinnipiac College.

Enrollment Fall 1997: 6 undergraduate.

Art Faculty 5 total (full-time and part-time). 100% of full-time faculty have terminal degrees. Graduate students do not teach undergraduate courses.

Expenses for 1997–98 Application fee: $35. Comprehensive fee: $24,898 includes full-time tuition ($16,864), mandatory fees ($398), and college room and board ($7636). Special program-related fees: $40–$50 per course for consumable art supplies.

Application Procedures Students apply for admission into the professional program by freshman year. Deadline for freshmen and transfers: continuous. Required: high school transcript, college transcript(s) for transfer students, mini-

Albertus Magnus College (continued)

mum 2.0 high school GPA, 2 letters of recommendation, SAT I or ACT test scores. Recommended: interview.

Undergraduate Contact Mr. Richard Lolatte, Dean of Admissions, Albertus Magnus College, 700 Prospect Street, New Haven, Connecticut 06511; 203-773-8501, fax: 203-773-9539.

▼ ALBION COLLEGE

Albion, Michigan

Independent-Methodist, coed. Small town campus. Total enrollment: 1,500. Art program established 1977.

Degrees Bachelor of Fine Arts in the area of visual arts. Majors and concentrations: art/fine arts.

Enrollment Fall 1997: 32 total; 4 undergraduate, 28 non-professional degree.

Art Student Profile 75% females, 25% males, 5% minorities, 5% international.

Art Faculty 6 total (full-time and part-time). 100% of full-time faculty have terminal degrees. Graduate students do not teach undergraduate courses.

Student Life Student groups/activities include Art Club, Senior Exhibition.

Expenses for 1997–98 Application fee: $20. One-time mandatory fee: $100. Comprehensive fee: $21,786 includes full-time tuition ($16,640), mandatory fees ($166), and college room and board ($4980). College room only: $2450. Special program-related fees: $25–$50 per course for lab fees.

Financial Aid Program-specific awards for 1997: 8 Fine Arts Scholarships for freshmen ($1000), 4 Janson Scholarship for program majors ($500), 1 Taup Scholarship for program majors ($1000).

Application Procedures Students admitted directly into the professional program freshman year. Deadline for freshmen and transfers: continuous. Required: high school transcript, college transcript(s) for transfer students, letter of recommendation, portfolio, SAT I or ACT test scores. Recommended: essay, minimum 2.0 high school GPA, interview. Portfolio reviews held throughout the year on campus and off campus in Interlochen, MI; the submission of slides may be substituted for portfolios whenever needed.

Undergraduate Contact Director of Admissions, Albion College, 616 East Michigan, Albion, Michigan 49224; 517-629-0321, fax: 517-629-0509.

▼ AL COLLINS GRAPHIC DESIGN SCHOOL

Tempe, Arizona

Proprietary, coed. Art program established 1978.

Degrees Bachelor of Arts in the area of visual communication. Program accredited by ACCSCT.

Enrollment Fall 1997: 120 undergraduate.

Art Faculty 7 total (full-time and part-time). 100% of full-time faculty have terminal degrees. Graduate students do not teach undergraduate courses. Undergraduate student–faculty ratio: 20:1.

Financial Aid Program-specific awards available.

Application Procedures Students admitted directly into the professional program freshman year. Deadline for freshmen and transfers: continuous. Required: essay, high school

transcript, interview. Recommended: portfolio. Portfolio reviews held continuously by appointment on campus.

Web Site http://www.alcollins.com.

Undergraduate Contact Steve Fireng, Associate Director Outside Marketing, Al Collins Graphic Design School, 1140 South Priest Drive, Tempe, Arizona 85281; 602-966-3000, fax: 602-902-0663.

▼ ALFRED UNIVERSITY

Alfred, New York

Independent, coed. Rural campus. Total enrollment: 2,329. Art program established 1900.

Degrees Bachelor of Fine Arts in the areas of ceramics, graphic design, two-dimensional studies and electronic art, three-dimensional studies. Majors and concentrations: art education, art history, ceramics, electronic arts, glass, graphic design, painting/drawing, photography, printmaking, sculpture, video art, wood. Graduate degrees offered: Master of Fine Arts in the areas of ceramics, glass, sculpture. Cross-registration with State University of New York College of Technology at Alfred. Program accredited by NASAD.

Enrollment Fall 1997: 453 total; 426 undergraduate, 26 graduate, 1 non-professional degree.

Art Student Profile 60% females, 40% males, 7% minorities, 2% international.

Art Faculty 37 total undergraduate and graduate (full-time and part-time). 99% of full-time faculty have terminal degrees. Graduate students do not teach undergraduate courses. Undergraduate student–faculty ratio: 13:1.

Student Life Student groups/activities include The Robert Turner Student Gallery exhibitions, Alternative Cinema, Annual Outdoor Light Exhibition. Special housing available for art students.

Expenses for 1997–98 Application fee: $40. Comprehensive fee: $25,406 includes full-time tuition ($18,498), mandatory fees ($502), and college room and board ($6406). College room only: $3334. Full-time tuition and fees vary according to program and student level. Room and board charges vary according to board plan and housing facility. Special program-related fees: $5–$60 per credit hour for material fees.

Financial Aid Program-specific awards for 1997: portfolio scholarships for students with an exceptional portfolio ($3500–$5500), 300 Art and Design Grants for program majors demonstrating need ($500–$4200), 1–2 Scholastic Art Awards for students with an exceptional portfolio ($500–$1000).

Application Procedures Students admitted directly into the professional program freshman year. Deadline for freshmen: February 1; transfers: April 1. Notification date for freshmen: March 15; transfers: April 15. Required: essay, high school transcript, college transcript(s) for transfer students, letter of recommendation, SAT I or ACT test scores, slides of portfolio, application by freshman deadlines for transfer applicants having completed fewer than 24 studio art credits. Recommended: minimum 3.0 high school GPA, interview. Portfolio reviews held numerous times depending on the number of applicants (all portfolios are reviewed on campus by a committee of Art and Design Faculty) on campus.

Web Site http://www.alfred.edu.

Contact Ms. Katherine McCarthy, Director, Admissions Office, Alfred University, Saxon Drive, Alfred, New York 14802; 800-541-9229, fax: 607-871-2198, E-mail address: adm.www@ bigvax.alfred.edu.

More About the University

Program Facilities Extensive facility includes state-of-the-art printmaking studio, expansive painting studios, new photography and video labs, ceramics studios equipped with thirty-eight indoor and outdoor kilns, hot and cold glass shop and neon fabrication studio, sculpture studios (foundry and fabrication shop), excellent wood shop, comprehensive computer facility for graphic design, and other specialized areas. Facilities provide an optimum working environment. The Fosdick-Nelson Gallery presents exhibitions of national and international scope. Scholes Library of Ceramics houses an extensive collection of books on the arts and art history, including a rich collection of all facets of glass and ceramic art. Museum of Ceramic Art provides students with the opportunity for hands-on study of ceramic art objects.

Faculty, Resident Artists, and Alumni Faculty members are practicing artists who exhibit extensively both nationally and internationally. Students are well exposed to contemporary art through faculty members and the active visiting artists program. The visiting artists program sponsors yearly thematic art events. This year's program, "The Relevant, the Significant and the Beautiful," featured Janet Wolff, Professor of Art History, Visual and Cultural Studies; Chad Latz, printmaker and maker of artist books; David Dunlap, collaborative works; and Pan Chun Fang and Xu Chen Quan, Yixing teapot masters. Other visiting artists include John Wood, photographer and printmaker; Roscoe Mitchell, New Music/solo saxophone; and Steff Geissbuhler, designer.

Recent exhibitions include *Furniture and Sculpture* by Phillip Tennant, *Pervasive Sentiments: The Coney Island Series* by Pike Powers, *The Photography National* curated by Charles Stainback, and *Companeras: Women, Art and Social Change in Latin America* curated by Betty LaDuke.

Renowned alumni include Joel Phillip Myers, glass; Ken Price, ceramics; and Michael Lax, industrial design.

Special Programs Freshman Foundation is a unique team-taught interdisciplinary course. The four-year program culminates in the all-school celebration of the Senior Show. Students may enroll in a core of psychology classes designed to prepare them for graduate study in art therapy or obtain K–12 certification in art education, both of which offer strong career options. A junior-year study-abroad program offers exchange opportunities in England and Italy.

▼ ALLEN R. HITE ART INSTITUTE

See University of Louisville

▼ AMERICAN ACADEMY OF ART

Chicago, Illinois

Proprietary, coed. Urban campus.
Degrees Bachelor of Fine Arts. Program accredited by ACCSCT.
Enrollment Fall 1997: 438 total; 408 undergraduate, 30 non-professional degree.
Art Student Profile 35% females, 65% males, 37% minorities, 1% international.

Art Faculty 37 total (full-time and part-time). 65% of full-time faculty have terminal degrees. Graduate students do not teach undergraduate courses. Undergraduate student–faculty ratio: 22:1.
Student Life Student groups/activities include Student Juried Competitions, Gallery 37, Ravinia Poster.
Expenses for 1998–99 Application fee: $25. Tuition: $13,480 full-time. Special program-related fees: $400 per course for computer lab access fee.
Financial Aid Program-specific awards for 1997: 3 High School Scholarship Competitions for high school seniors ($6740).
Application Procedures Students admitted directly into the professional program freshman year. Deadline for freshmen and transfers: continuous. Required: high school transcript, college transcript(s) for transfer students, interview. Recommended: essay, minimum 2.0 high school GPA, portfolio. Portfolio reviews held continuously on campus; the submission of slides may be substituted for portfolios when distance is prohibitive or for large works of art.
Web Site http://www.aaart.edu.
Undergraduate Contact Ione Fitzgerald, Admissions Director, American Academy of Art, 332 South Michigan Avenue, Suite 300, Chicago, Illinois 60604; 312-461-0600, fax: 312-294-9570, E-mail address: aaart@interaccess.com.

More About the School

Program Facilities The location and facilities are superb for students' studying the visual arts. The Academy of Art is

American Academy of Art (continued)

located at 332 South Michigan Avenue within walking distance of the Art Institute of Chicago, the Terra Museum of American Art, and the Museum of Contemporary Art. The facilities are designed to give students space to work comfortably in the studios, electronic design labs, and general education classrooms.

Faculty, Alumni, and Visiting Artists The Academy's faculty are professional artists with vast experience in the worlds of commercial and fine art. The faculty of approximately 40 instructors teach in the departments of Fundamentals of Art (Chair, Robert Krajecki), Life Drawing (Chair, Mary Phelan), Commercial Arts (Chair, Richard Kryczka), Electronic Design (Chair, Kathleen Kirka), and Fine Arts (Chair, Ted Smuskiewicz).

Distinguished Academy alumni include: Haddon Sundblom, Illustrator/Creator of the Coca-Cola Santa Claus; Gil Elvgren and Joyce Ballantyne, Illustrators/Pin-up era; Irving Shapiro, Watercolor Artist and former Director of the Academy; Roger Brown, Artist, Harry Who group; Howard Terpning, Western Painter; Thomas Blackshear, Illustrator; John Tobias, Artist/Animator/Co-Creator of Mortal Kombat Game; Alex Ross, Artist, Marvel and DC Comics.

Selected visiting artists to the Academy in the 1997–98 academic year include Mark Joyal, Art Director at Foote, Cone & Belding Advertising and Doug Klauba, Advertising & Editoral Illustrator, represented by Monroe, Goodman Talent.

Student Exhibitions Annual student exhibitions include the Student Juried Show, the Senior Show, and the B.F.A. group shows, all held in the Bill L. Parks Gallery at the Academy.

Special Programs The school offers a study abroad program in Florence, Italy, in classical drawing and painting available to students in the B.F.A. degree program.

▼

The American Academy of Art has built an extraordinary reputation for more than 75 years for educating competent, successful artists. The mission of the academy is to prepare students to become professionals in the visual arts. A professional artist nurtures a sense of artistic adventure while developing a sense of artistic discipline.

The philosophy of the academy is classical in its view that, to be successful, an artist must first master the media available and learn to depict the world in a realistic manner. The artist trained in the fundamentals of art and both traditional and contemporary mediums is well equipped to become tomorrow's visionary.

The American Academy of Art was founded in 1923, by Frank Young Sr., an internationally recognized authority in advertising design. He believed the academy should provide the best instruction, attract the best students, and neglect nothing that will help them to build successful careers. We aspire to these same goals today. In 1992, Richard Otto became the fourth owner and president of the school and with him, the academy continues its tradition of excellence that has been the cornerstone of the school since its beginning.

The American Academy of Art offers a Bachelor of Fine Arts degree (with a concentration in Commercial Art or Fine Art) and Associate of Applied Science degrees in either Commercial Art or Fine Art. Students develop essential drawing, painting and design skills in studio art classes, and critical thinking abilities in general education curriculum.

All students complete one year of foundation studies, which include Fundamentals of Art I/II and Life Drawing I/II. In the second year students can choose specializations in the following areas of commercial arts: advertising design, electronic design, graphic design, or illustration; or fine arts: life drawing, oil painting, painting, or watercolor painting. The degree curriculum is based on 75 percent studio and 25 percent general education course work. The student body is approximately 400 students. Incoming students include high school graduates and transfer students from a variety of post-secondary schools.

The prime location on Chicago's Michigan Avenue and proximity to not only the major art museums but also to the myriad of galleries and gallery districts support the visual experiences that the students can draw upon. The Harold Washington Library Center and the Chicago Public Library's Culture Center are invaluable resources for their extensive collections; both are walking distance from the academy.

Career services is a referal program offered to degree seeking students, graduates, and alumni of the American Academy of Art. The career services coordinator assists in identifying potential employers and locating jobs. Listings are updated continuously and obtained directly from employers, professional journals, and other relevant job sources. Internships are available to students in the final year of study at the academy. Intern positions are available at advertising agencies; design, animation, and fine art studios; and galleries in the Chicago area.

The academy's student activity advisor develops and facilitates activities for the student body, including student government, art-related field trips and movies, visiting artists/speakers, and our annual faculty vs. student softball game.

▼ AMERICAN INTERCONTINENTAL UNIVERSITY

Los Angeles, California

Proprietary, coed. Urban campus. Total enrollment: 500.

Degrees Bachelor of Fine Arts in the areas of interior design, fashion design, visual communication, video production, fashion marketing. Majors and concentrations: fashion design and technology, graphic arts, interior design. Program accredited by FIDER.

Enrollment Fall 1997: 450 undergraduate.

Art Student Profile 64% females, 12% minorities, 63% international.

Art Faculty 54 total (full-time and part-time). 100% of full-time faculty have terminal degrees. Graduate students do not teach undergraduate courses. Undergraduate student–faculty ratio: 10:1.

Student Life Student groups/activities include American Society of Interior Designers, Comma Club, Dressers Club.

Expenses for 1997–98 Tuition: $11,250 full-time. College room only: $4185.

Financial Aid Program-specific awards for 1997: 1 Travilla Scholarship for fashion design majors ($10,000), 1 High School Scholarship Competition for incoming freshmen ($10,000), 1 Emilio Pucci Scholarship for incoming freshmen ($1800), 1 Founders Scholarship for juniors ($10,000).

Application Procedures Students admitted directly into the professional program freshman year. Deadline for freshmen and transfers: continuous. Required: essay, high school transcript, college transcript(s) for transfer students, 2 letters of recommendation. Recommended: interview, portfolio. Portfolio reviews held 5 times on campus; the submission of slides may be substituted for portfolios for large works of art, three-dimensional pieces, or when distance is prohibitive.

Undergraduate Contact Mr. Alan Gueco, Director of Admissions, American InterContinental University, 1651 Westwood Boulevard, Los Angeles, California 90024; 310-470-2000, fax: 310-477-8640, E-mail address: amla@ix.netcom.com.

▼ AMERICAN INTERCONTINENTAL UNIVERSITY

Atlanta, Georgia

Proprietary, coed. Urban campus. Total enrollment: 1,016.

Degrees Bachelor of Fine Arts in the areas of interior design, fashion design, visual communication/commercial art, video production. Majors and concentrations: fashion design and technology, graphic arts, illustration, interior design, photography, video production, visual communication.

Enrollment Fall 1997: 700 total; all undergraduate.

Art Student Profile 76% females, 24% males, 21% minorities, 22% international.

Art Faculty 40 total (full-time and part-time). 100% of full-time faculty have terminal degrees. Graduate students do not teach undergraduate courses. Undergraduate student–faculty ratio: 12:1.

Student Life Student groups/activities include American Society of Interior Designers, Portfolio Club, Dressers Club.

Expenses for 1997–98 Application fee: $35. Tuition: $9578 full-time. Mandatory fees: $722 full-time. College room only: $4050.

Financial Aid Program-specific awards for 1997: 1 Travilla Scholarship for fashion design majors ($9360), 1 High School Scholarship Competition for incoming freshmen ($9360), 1 Emilio Pucci Scholarship for incoming freshmen ($1800).

Application Procedures Students admitted directly into the professional program freshman year. Deadline for freshmen and transfers: continuous. Required: essay, high school transcript, college transcript(s) for transfer students, 2 letters of recommendation, SAT I or ACT test scores.

Web Site http://www.aiuniv.edu.

Undergraduate Contact Ms. Suzanne McBride, Vice President for Admissions, American InterContinental University, 3330 Peachtree Road, Atlanta, Georgia 30326; 404-231-9000, fax: 404-231-1062.

More About the School

Facilities Each campus of AIU provides a professional environment for students. Leading edge technologies are integrated throughout the design and media arts departments to ensure that curricula are industry-relevant. Some of the special features include: state-of-the-art computer graphics labs with power Macintosh stations, scanners, and color printers; design labs with PC stations for interior design and fashion design, CAD software, and industry relevant equipment; photographic labs with black/white and color darkroom and photo studio; video production facilities with control room, programmable lighting system, AVID digital non-linear editing stations, audio facilities with a MIDI/Electronic Music suite and an audio suite with 32-channel stereo mixer, cassette, CD, DAT, and both analog and digital multi-track recorders and digital effects, and a full compli-

ment of field production equipment; interior design resource library; and a media center with Internet, CD-ROM, 25,000 volume library, periodicals, and audiovisuals.

Special Programs AIU offers a special orientation program for international students as well as an Intensive English Program. A study abroad program is available to students from American colleges and universities who wish to study in London or Dubai (students from over 300 institutions have participated) and a study in America program is available to students from international colleges and universities who wish to study in Atlanta or Los Angeles. AIU also has an accelerated degree program option for students who qualify. In addition, AIU's First Year Experience ensures that students are prepared for a successful academic experience at the university level.

AIU is accredited by the Commission on Colleges of the Southern Association of Colleges and Schools (SACS). Its BFA program in interior design in Atlanta and Los Angeles holds professional-level accreditation from the Foundation for Interior Design Education Research (FIDER). AIU has applied for specialized accreditation with the National Association of Schools of Art and Design (NASAD).

▼

For more than 27 years, American InterContinental University (AIU) has been a leader in design and media arts education. AIU's School of Design and Media Arts offers bachelor's degree programs in graphic design, illustration, photography, video production, interior design, and fashion and costume design. The programs are professionally oriented to integrate practical experiences with traditional design theory. The curriculum is aligned with today's digital and other technologies to ensure students are provided knowledge, skills, and techniques necessary to become successful professionals. Best of all, students may begin classes in their major from the very first quarter.

Design and media arts at AIU begin with a strong foundation in the basics. With an ideal student/faculty ratio (15:1), AIU's personal approach to education fosters creative

American InterContinental University (continued)

growth. A variety of studio classes, one-on-one teaching, collaborative/team-based learning, independent study, and lectures ensure that students refine their talent and develop their technical skills.

One measure of a university's quality is its faculty. AIU's faculty members are committed, practicing art, design, and media professionals who bring real-world experiences into the classroom and offer students the opportunity to work on current and conceptual projects with real clients. Classroom experiences are enhanced through field trips, study tours, student/faculty/professional exhibitions, and visiting industry guests. On-campus professional organizations and clubs such as the American Society of Interior Designers, International Society of Interior Designers, Fashion Association, Dressers Club, and Portfolio Club further involve students with professionals in the community. An extensive internship program enables students to gain invaluable practical training through work and study with major corporations and important design firms throughout the world such as Sony, CBS, Donna Karan, Burberry, Elizabeth Emanuel, Liberty of London, Saks Fifth Avenue, Design Continuum, Fox Television, MTV, and International Marketing Partners.

AIU offers a friendly, nurturing environment. Campuses in Atlanta, Los Angeles, London, and Dubai are centrally located to provide students with vital career and cultural resources as well as social and intellectual activities. Many students "go global" and transfer among the AIU campuses. These campuses, coupled with students from more than 100 countries, provide a truly international environment. The cultural diversity of students, faculty, and staff on each campus enables the student to gain a global perspective and forge friendships that will last a lifetime.

Graduates of AIU are sought by leading corporations and firms involved in design and media arts. Career placement services and opportunities are an important aspect of the AIU experience. Each year AIU brings employers and alumni who are recruiting for their own employment needs to the campuses to interview graduating students. Students at AIU begin career planning and developing their portfolio in their first year. As they progress through the program their portfolio is enhanced so that by the time they reach their senior year, they have developed a comprehensive professional portfolio. In other words, AIU transforms creative students into talented, working professionals.

▼ AMERICAN UNIVERSITY
Washington, District of Columbia

Independent-Methodist, coed. Suburban campus. Total enrollment: 10,710. Art program established 1942.
Degrees Bachelor of Fine Arts in the area of studio art. Majors and concentrations: art/fine arts, arts administration, graphic arts, painting/drawing, printmaking, sculpture, studio art. Graduate degrees offered: Master of Fine Arts in the areas of painting, printmaking, sculpture. Cross-registration with consortium of Washington universities.
Enrollment Fall 1997: 325 total; 200 undergraduate, 25 graduate, 100 non-professional degree.
Art Student Profile 50% females, 50% males, 8% minorities, 20% international.

Art Faculty 23 total undergraduate and graduate (full-time and part-time). 100% of full-time faculty have terminal degrees. Graduate students do not teach undergraduate courses. Undergraduate student–faculty ratio: 12:1.
Student Life Student groups/activities include Thursday Night Artist on Art Lecture Series, Visiting Artists Programs, semester in Italy.
Expenses for 1997–98 Application fee: $45. Comprehensive fee: $25,805 includes full-time tuition ($18,300), mandatory fees ($255), and college room and board ($7250). College room only: $4640. Room and board charges vary according to board plan. Special program-related fees: $400 for studio program in Italy.
Application Procedures Students apply for admission into the professional program by sophomore year. Deadline for freshmen: February 1; transfers: July 1. Notification date for freshmen: April 1; transfers: August 1. Required: high school transcript, college transcript(s) for transfer students, 2 letters of recommendation, SAT I test score only. Recommended: minimum 3.0 high school GPA, interview, portfolio. Portfolio reviews held continuously on campus; the submission of slides may be substituted for portfolios (slides preferred).
Web Site http://www.american.edu/academic.depts/cas/art.
Contact Ms. Glenna Haynie, Administrator, Department of Art, American University, 4400 Massachusetts Avenue, NW, Washington, District of Columbia 20016; 202-885-1670, fax: 202-885-1132.

▼ ANDREWS UNIVERSITY
Berrien Springs, Michigan

Independent-Seventh-day Adventist, coed. Small town campus. Total enrollment: 3,152. Art program established 1951.
Degrees Bachelor of Fine Arts in the areas of graphic design, fine arts, digital art and design, photography,ceramics, painting and printmaking.
Enrollment Fall 1997: 30 undergraduate.
Art Student Profile 50% females, 50% males, 23% minorities, 17% international.
Art Faculty 5 total (full-time and part-time). 100% of full-time faculty have terminal degrees. Graduate students do not teach undergraduate courses. Undergraduate student–faculty ratio: 15:1.
Student Life Special housing available for art students.
Expenses for 1997–98 Application fee: $30. Comprehensive fee: $15,087 includes full-time tuition ($11,340), mandatory fees ($237), and college room and board ($3510). College room only: $2070. Special program-related fees: $25–$100 per course for material fees.
Financial Aid Program-specific awards for 1997: 1 Maria and Constantine Constantine Scholarship for painting majors ($300), 1 Benjamin and Greta Gordon Scholarship for painting majors ($300).
Application Procedures Students apply for admission into the professional program by sophomore year. Deadline for freshmen and transfers: continuous. Required: high school transcript, 2 letters of recommendation, SAT I or ACT test scores, minimum 2.5 high school GPA. Recommended: college transcript(s) for transfer students, portfolio for transfer students. Portfolio reviews held by appointment at student's convenience on campus.
Web Site http://www.andrews.edu/ART/.
Undergraduate Contact Mr. Steve Hanson, Chair, Department of Art, Art History, and Design, Andrews University, Berrien

Springs, Michigan 49104-0190; 616-471-3281, fax: 616-471-6900, E-mail address: slhanson@andrews.edu.

▼ ANNA MARIA COLLEGE

Paxton, Massachusetts

Independent-Roman Catholic, coed. Rural campus. Total enrollment: 1,668.

Degrees Bachelor of Fine Arts in the area of studio art; Bachelor of Arts in the areas of art education, art therapy, art and business, art. Cross-registration with Worcester Consortium.

Enrollment Fall 1997: 27 total.

Art Student Profile 78% females, 22% males, 1% minorities, 4% international.

Art Faculty 8 total (full-time and part-time). Graduate students do not teach undergraduate courses. Undergraduate student–faculty ratio: 3:1.

Student Life Student groups/activities include senior art exhibit, student/teacher exhibit, gallery sitting. Special housing available for art students.

Expenses for 1997–98 Application fee: $30. Comprehensive fee: $17,496 includes full-time tuition ($11,600), mandatory fees ($640), and college room and board ($5256). Special program-related fees: $25 per course for model fees, $40 per course for studio fee, $130 per course for art practicum internship.

Application Procedures Students admitted directly into the professional program freshman year. Deadline for freshmen and transfers: continuous. Required: essay, high school transcript, college transcript(s) for transfer students, minimum 2.0 high school GPA, 3 letters of recommendation, portfolio, SAT I or ACT test scores. Recommended: interview. Portfolio reviews held by appointment on campus; the submission of slides may be substituted for portfolios when distance is prohibitive.

Web Site http://www.anna-maria.edu.

Undergraduate Contact Ms. Chris Soverow, Director of Admissions, Anna Maria College, Box 78, Paxton, Massachusetts 01612-1198; 508-849-3360, fax: 508-849-3362, E-mail address: csoverow@anna-maria.edu.

▼ APPALACHIAN STATE UNIVERSITY

Boone, North Carolina

State-supported, coed. Small town campus. Total enrollment: 12,108.

Degrees Bachelor of Fine Arts in the areas of art, graphic design, studio art. Majors and concentrations: art education, art/fine arts, arts administration, ceramic art and design, fibers, graphic design, jewelry and metalsmithing, painting/drawing, printmaking, sculpture, studio art. Program accredited by NASAD.

Enrollment Fall 1997: 360 total; 300 undergraduate, 60 non-professional degree.

Art Student Profile 50% females, 50% males, 2% minorities, 2% international.

Art Faculty 25 total (full-time and part-time). 100% of full-time faculty have terminal degrees. Graduate students do not teach undergraduate courses. Undergraduate student–faculty ratio: 16:1.

Student Life Student groups/activities include Student Art League, National Art Education Association Student Chapter, American Institute of Graphic Arts Student Chapter.

Expenses for 1997–98 Application fee: $25. State resident tuition: $900 full-time. Nonresident tuition: $8028 full-time. Mandatory fees: $940 full-time. College room and board: $3008. College room only: $1740. Room and board charges vary according to board plan and housing facility.

Financial Aid Program-specific awards for 1997: 8 Fine Arts Scholarships for freshmen, juniors, and seniors ($1000), 8 Talent Awards for program majors ($1800), 8 Work Study Awards for program majors ($1200–$1600), 1 Apartment Scholarship for talented program juniors or seniors ($6000).

Application Procedures Students admitted directly into the professional program freshman year. Deadline for freshmen: April 1. Required: high school transcript, slides of portfolio. Recommended: minimum 3.0 high school GPA. Portfolio reviews held 3 times on campus.

Undergraduate Contact Ms. Judy Humphrey, Director of Portfolio Reviews, Art Department, Appalachian State University, 233 Wey Hall, Boone, North Carolina 28608; 704-262-2220, fax: 704-262-6312.

▼ AQUINAS COLLEGE

Grand Rapids, Michigan

Independent-Roman Catholic, coed. Suburban campus. Total enrollment: 2,458. Art program established 1965.

Degrees Bachelor of Fine Arts in the areas of drawing, painting, printmaking, photography, sculpture, ceramics. Majors and concentrations: art/fine arts.

Enrollment Fall 1997: 50 total; 20 undergraduate, 30 non-professional degree.

Art Student Profile 75% females, 25% males, 5% minorities.

Art Faculty 6 total (full-time and part-time). 100% of full-time faculty have terminal degrees. Graduate students do not teach undergraduate courses. Undergraduate student–faculty ratio: 12:1.

Student Life Student groups/activities include Student Art Club.

Expenses for 1997–98 Application fee: $25. Comprehensive fee: $17,274 includes full-time tuition ($12,910), mandatory fees ($40), and college room and board ($4324). Full-time tuition and fees vary according to course load.

Financial Aid Program-specific awards for 1997: 1–2 Hoffius Art Scholarships for sophomores or juniors ($1000).

Application Procedures Students apply for admission into the professional program by sophomore year. Deadline for freshmen and transfers: continuous. Required: high school transcript, portfolio, ACT test score only (minimum combined ACT score of 18), minimum 2.5 high school GPA. Recommended: letter of recommendation, interview. Portfolio reviews held twice on campus.

Web Site http://www.aquinas.edu.

Undergraduate Contact Ms. Paula Meehan, Dean of Admissions, Aquinas College, 1607 Robinson Road, SE, Grand Rapids, Michigan 49506-1799; 616-459-8281 ext. 5205, fax: 616-732-4435, E-mail address: meehapau@aquinas.edu.

▼ ARIZONA STATE UNIVERSITY

Tempe, Arizona

State-supported, coed. Suburban campus. Total enrollment: 44,255.

Arizona State University (continued)

Degrees Bachelor of Fine Arts in the area of art. Majors and concentrations: art education, ceramics, drawing, fibers, intermedia, jewelry and metalsmithing, painting, photography, printmaking, sculpture. Graduate degrees offered: Master of Fine Arts in the area of art.

Enrollment Fall 1997: 1,050 total; 800 undergraduate, 150 graduate, 100 non-professional degree.

Art Student Profile 50% females, 50% males, 15% minorities, 10% international.

Art Faculty 58 total undergraduate and graduate (full-time and part-time). 98% of full-time faculty have terminal degrees. Graduate students teach a few undergraduate courses. Undergraduate student–faculty ratio: 16:1.

Student Life Student groups/activities include undergraduate exhibition, Step Gallery exhibitions, Northlight Gallery exhibitions.

Expenses for 1997–98 Application fee: $40 for nonresidents. State resident tuition: $1988 full-time. Nonresident tuition: $8640 full-time. Mandatory fees: $71 full-time. College room and board: $4500. College room only: $2700. Room and board charges vary according to board plan and housing facility. Special program-related fees: $15–$45 per class for expendable materials.

Financial Aid Program-specific awards for 1997: 25 Regents Tuition Scholarships for academically qualified applicants ($1500), 1 Nelson Undergraduate Scholarship ($3000).

Application Procedures Students admitted directly into the professional program freshman year. Deadline for freshmen and transfers: continuous. Required: high school transcript, minimum 2.0 high school GPA, SAT I or ACT test scores, portfolio for computer animation applicants, minimum 2.5 college GPA for nonresident transfer students. Portfolio reviews held in fall and spring on campus; the submission of slides may be substituted for portfolios (slides preferred).

Web Site http://www.asu.edu/cfa/art/.

Undergraduate Contact Mr. Glenn Hanson, Undergraduate Advisor, School of Art, Arizona State University, Tempe, Arizona 85287-1505; 602-965-6296, fax: 602-965-8338.

Graduate Contact Ms. Rita Rosenthal, Graduate Student Advisor, School of Art, Arizona State University, Box 871505, Tempe, Arizona 85287-1505; 602-965-6303, fax: 602-965-8338.

▼ ARKANSAS STATE UNIVERSITY

State University, Arkansas

State-supported, coed. Small town campus. Total enrollment: 10,012. Art program established 1936.

Degrees Bachelor of Fine Arts in the areas of studio art, art education, graphic design. Majors and concentrations: art education, ceramics, graphic design, painting/drawing, photography, printmaking, sculpture, studio art. Program accredited by NASAD.

Enrollment Fall 1997: 143 total; 133 undergraduate, 10 non-professional degree.

Art Student Profile 48% females, 52% males, 8% minorities.

Art Faculty 13 total (full-time and part-time). 100% of full-time faculty have terminal degrees. Graduate students do not teach undergraduate courses. Undergraduate student–faculty ratio: 10:1.

Expenses for 1997–98 Application fee: $15. State resident tuition: $2000 full-time. Nonresident tuition: $5090 full-time.

Mandatory fees: $280 full-time. College room and board: $2840. Room and board charges vary according to board plan and housing facility.

Financial Aid Program-specific awards for 1997: 5 art scholarships for art majors ($1900–$2000).

Application Procedures Students apply for admission into the professional program by sophomore year. Deadline for freshmen and transfers: continuous. Required: high school transcript, portfolio, SAT I or ACT test scores, minimum 2.0 college GPA for transfer students. Portfolio reviews held on campus; the submission of slides may be substituted for portfolios for three-dimensional work.

Web Site http://www.astate.edu/docs/acad/cfa/art.

Undergraduate Contact Mr. Curtis Steele, Chair, Art Department, Arkansas State University, PO Box 1920, State University, Arkansas 72467; 870-972-3050, fax: 870-972-3932, E-mail address: csteele@aztec.astate.edu.

▼ ART ACADEMY OF CINCINNATI

Cincinnati, Ohio

Independent, coed. Urban campus. Art program established 1869.

Degrees Bachelor of Fine Arts in the areas of fine art, communication design, studio with an emphasis in art history/museum studies. Majors and concentrations: computer graphics, graphic design, illustration, painting/drawing, photography, printmaking, sculpture. Graduate degrees offered: Master of Arts in the area of art education. Cross-registration with members of the Greater Cincinnati Consortium of Colleges and Universities. Program accredited by NASAD.

Enrollment Fall 1997: 198 total; 176 undergraduate, 22 graduate.

Art Student Profile 48% females, 52% males, 7% minorities, 4% international.

Art Faculty 50 total undergraduate and graduate (full-time and part-time). 98% of full-time faculty have terminal degrees. Graduate students do not teach undergraduate courses.

Expenses for 1997–98 Application fee: $25. Tuition: $10,800 full-time. Mandatory fees: $125 full-time.

Financial Aid Program-specific awards for 1997: 20–25 Entrance Scholarships for incoming students ($1500–$6000).

Application Procedures Students admitted directly into the professional program freshman year. Deadline for freshmen and transfers: continuous. Notification date for freshmen and transfers: August 1. Required: essay, high school transcript, college transcript(s) for transfer students, minimum 2.0 high school GPA, letter of recommendation, interview, portfolio, SAT I or ACT test scores. Recommended: minimum 3.0 high school GPA. Portfolio reviews held continuously on campus and off campus in 18 cities on National Portfolio Days; the submission of slides may be substituted for portfolios when distance is prohibitive.

Web Site http://artacademy.edu.

Contact Ms. Sarah Colby, Director of Enrollment Services, Art Academy of Cincinnati, 1125 Saint Gregory Street, Cincinnati, Ohio 45202; 800-323-5692, fax: 513-562-8778.

▼ Art Center College of Design

Pasadena, California

Independent, coed. Suburban campus. Total enrollment: 1,433. Art program established 1930.

Degrees Bachelor of Fine Arts in the areas of advertising, illustration, graphic design, photography, fine arts, film; Bachelor of Science in the areas of environmental design, product and transportation design. Majors and concentrations: advertising design and communication, art/fine arts, environmental design, film studies, graphic arts, illustration, industrial design, painting/drawing, photography, product design, transportation design. Graduate degrees offered: Master of Fine Arts in the areas of communication and new media design, fine arts, film; Master of Arts in the area of art theory and criticism. Cross-registration with Occidental College, California Institute of Technology. Program accredited by NASAD.

Enrollment Fall 1997: 1,433 total; 1,334 undergraduate, 99 graduate.

Art Student Profile 39% females, 61% males, 36% minorities, 26% international.

Art Faculty 385 total undergraduate and graduate (full-time and part-time). 2% of full-time faculty have terminal degrees. Graduate students do not teach undergraduate courses. Undergraduate student–faculty ratio: 12:1.

Student Life Student groups/activities include Contraste (Hispanic student group), Black Student Union, Industrial Design Society of America Student Chapter.

Expenses for 1997–98 Application fee: $45. Tuition: $17,180 full-time.

Financial Aid Program-specific awards for 1997: 300 Art Center Scholarships for program majors ($500–$4295), 30 Entering Grants for program majors ($2500), 9 Art Center Outreach Grants for Hispanic, African-American, Native American students ($4295), 6 Ford Minority Scholarships for Hispanic, African-American, or female transportation designers ($4295).

Application Procedures Students admitted directly into the professional program freshman year. Deadline for freshmen and transfers: continuous. Notification date for freshmen and transfers: continuous. Required: essay, high school transcript, college transcript(s) for transfer students, portfolio, SAT I or ACT test scores, minimum TOEFL score of 550 for international students. Recommended: minimum 3.0 high school GPA, interview. Portfolio reviews held continuously on campus.

Web Site http://www.artcenter.edu.

Contact Ms. Kit Baron, Vice President, Student Services, Art Center College of Design, 1700 Lida Street, Pasadena, California 91103; 626-396-2373, fax: 626-795-0578, E-mail address: admissions@artcenter.edu.

More About the College

Facilities Art Center is an acknowledged leader in providing new technologies and state-of-the-art facilities to its students. Features include a distinctive contemporary campus in the hills overlooking Pasadena's Rose Bowl; 215,000-square-foot glass and steel building designed by Craig Ellwood; 11,000-square-foot computer graphics lab with 115 Macintosh stations, sixty Silicon Graphic platforms, and one of the world's largest computer-aided industrial design (CAID) networks as well as a vast array of software to introduce students to the newest digital technologies; photography areas with black-and-white labs with seventy-five enlargers, color lab with 20-inch fully automated E-6 processor, 20-inch

Art Center College of Design

fully automated cibachrome processor, and 20-inch RA4 fully automated processor; two 4,600-square-foot shooting stages providing twenty-six shooting states equipped with seamless background colors, including one 15 × 30 flying flat; and digital imaging facilities including Kodak XL 7700 thermal printer, RFS 2035 film scanners, H-P Paint Jet printer, 840 AV workstation, and a Microtech 4 × 5 film scanner and Agfa flatbed transparency scanner.

Special Programs The College encourages a global and international approach to design education. Art Center encourages a wide variety of internship opportunities with major corporations and firms such as Ford, General Motors, Walt Disney Pictures, Reebok, Microsoft, Frogdesign, and Weiden and Kennedy. Students may also accept paid mentorship positions or enroll in a mentorship class to assist local Pasadena high school students.

▼

Art Center was founded in 1930 in downtown Los Angeles with a single purpose—to educate students for careers of achievement in the visual arts professions. The founder, Tink Adams, vowed to work closely with the leaders of industry to prepare professionals for meaningful careers. This tradition of close industry relationships continues today at the Pasadena campus.

Recognized by *U.S. News & World Report* as one of the leading visual arts colleges in the country in "The Best Specialty Schools" category, Art Center attracts attention from firms throughout the world. Companies such as Ford, Nike, Honda, Sony, Hallmark, and Kodak have decided to sponsor special student research projects at the College. Students have the opportunity to work with real clients on futuristic and conceptual projects.

In addition to visiting industry guests, the College features a faculty of practicing professionals who reinforce this tradition of real-world influence. Most are part-time faculty members who maintain their own distinctive client lists.

Fine arts students have an opportunity to work with some of the most provocative artists and painters working today, such as Mike Kelley, Steve Prina, and Jeremy Gilbert-Rolfe.

Art Center acknowledges and encourages the dissolution of boundaries between disciplines, and, although students apply to and study within specific majors, there are opportunities for new kinds of art-making based on digital and other technologies. A common link among students in all majors has become the computer. The College's mission is

Art Center College of Design *(continued)*

to lead the way for the industry in exploring new roles for design, photography, and film.

The average freshman at Art Center is 23 years old; all students must declare a major before entering the College. This has resulted in a mature and focused student body. Campus life, too, is influenced by the maturity of the students. There is no on-campus housing. Students choose from an abundance of housing within the Pasadena and Los Angeles area.

Art Center's graduates have made significant marks in the world of art and design, and alumni return to the campus to recruit for their own employment needs. The high demand for Art Center graduates is attributable to the degree of specialization and professionalism required of the students. In excess of 200 firms visit the College to interview graduating students each year, and job listings are printed regularly for the use of students and alumni. Some of the firms that have recruited on campus are Harcourt Brace & Co.; Warner Brothers Records; The Walt Disney Company; Ford Motor Company; General Motors Corporation; Mattel Toys; Ogilvy and Mather; Goodby, Berlin, and Silverstein; Virgin Records; Landor Associates; Honda; Texas Instruments; L.A. Gear; Young and Rubicam; Nike; Hal Riney and Partners; Mercedes-Benz; MCA-Universal Studios; Motorola; Hallmark Cards; Neiman Marcus Direct; and CALTY Design Research.

Located on an idyllic campus in suburban Pasadena, Art Center offers a contemplative environment juxtaposed with the internationalism of Los Angeles and the Pacific Rim. Art Center encourages a diverse population of students and faculty. The goal in bringing together a community of students from throughout the United States and the world is to develop new solutions to design issues and to promote the importance of design within the world communities. It is within this context that students receive highly individualized and rigorous programs of study. Critical thinking as well as development of technical skills is emphasized.

▼ ART INSTITUTE OF BOSTON

Boston, Massachusetts

Independent, coed. Urban campus. Art program established 1912.

Degrees Bachelor of Fine Arts in the areas of fine arts, illustration, design, fine arts/illustration, illustration/design, photography. Majors and concentrations: animation, art/fine arts, documentary photography, editorial illustration, graphic design, illustration, painting, painting/drawing, photography, printmaking, sculpture. Cross-registration with Boston Architectural Center, Pine Manor College, The Association of Independent Colleges of Art and Design, Berklee College of Music. Program accredited by NASAD.

Enrollment Fall 1997: 473 total; all undergraduate.

Art Student Profile 55% females, 45% males, 6% minorities, 14% international.

Art Faculty 73 total (full-time and part-time). 99% of full-time faculty have terminal degrees. Graduate students do not teach undergraduate courses. Undergraduate student–faculty ratio: 13:1.

Student Life Student groups/activities include Peer Advisors, student exhibitions in galleries and sites around Boston, Graphic Artists Guild student membership. Special housing available for art students.

Expenses for 1997–98 Application fee: $30. Comprehensive fee: $18,870 includes full-time tuition ($11,100), mandatory fees ($670), and college room and board ($7100). Full-time tuition and fees vary according to program. Special program-related fees: $770 per year for photography department fees, $770 per year for design department fees, $670 per year for other department fees.

Financial Aid Program-specific awards for 1997: 14 Merit Scholarships for incoming students ($1000–$6000), 1 Presidential Scholarship for incoming students ($11,200), 139 Art Institute of Boston Grants for those demonstrating need ($500–$2500), 15 Portfolio Scholarships for enrolled students ($500–$5550).

Application Procedures Students admitted directly into the professional program freshman year. Deadline for freshmen and transfers: continuous. Required: essay, high school transcript, college transcript(s) for transfer students, interview, portfolio, SAT I or ACT test scores. Recommended: minimum 2.0 high school GPA, 2 letters of recommendation. Portfolio reviews held as needed on campus and off campus; the submission of slides may be substituted for portfolios if a campus visit is impossible.

Web Site http://www.aiboston.edu.

Undergraduate Contact Ms. Diana Arcadipone, Dean of Admissions, Art Institute of Boston, 700 Beacon Street, Boston, Massachusetts 02215; 617-262-1223, fax: 617-437-1226, E-mail address: admissions@aiboston.edu.

Visiting artist Richard Yarde comments on a student's work in the AIB fine arts studios.

More About the School

Program Facilities The Art Institute of Boston's (AIB) facilities include a 1,500-square foot Exhibition Gallery; painting/drawing studios; individual fine art senior studio spaces; installation spaces and exhibition spaces throughout the college; two Macintosh computer laboratories; an animation laboratory that includes an Oxberry Master Series animation stand; a production room; gang photography labs with color and black-and-white systems, a nonsilver facility, several studios, and a yearlong photo gallery exhibiting student work; a wood shop; metals studio with welding equipment; a printmaking lab with etching press and lithography press; and clay lab with kilns. The library collection contains more than 9,000 books, 70 serial titles, 30,000 slides, over 250 videos, a video viewing room, and a picture reference file of 10,000 photographs and illustrations. The library is the Boston conservator of the National Gallery of Art's American

Art Collection on videodisc, a visual reference of more than 26,000 images that span three centuries, and has the complete Institute of Contemporary Art video collection. The AIB library is a member of the Boston Regional Library System, and students and faculty members have full privileges at the library at Suffolk University, Boston.

Special Programs The duPont Lecture Series brings the work of accomplished minority photographers to the college; frequent visits to the college by known artists; a collaboration with Maine Photographic Workshop; study-abroad programs in France and at The Art Institute of Florence, Lorenzo de Medici; internships at art galleries, design and animation studios, and advertising agencies; freelance and placement listings through artists' resources, counseling, guidance, and tutoring services. Pre-college classes give high school students an opportunity to earn college credit and develop portfolios.

▼

The Art Institute of Boston (AIB) is an independent college of art that was founded in 1912. Its programs are studio intensive, integrating liberal arts courses specifically designed to broaden students' intellectual and artistic perceptions. The Art Institute of Boston provides a supportive environment to enable students to succeed in their careers—the atmosphere is both challenging and nurturing, helping to maximize personal growth, intellectual growth, and artistic potential.

AIB is small and intimate, and most students and faculty members know each other by the end of the first semester. The Art Institute of Boston has an exceptional faculty, many of whom are well-known practicing artists, designers, illustrators, and photographers. Some of AIB's faculty members include Professor and Chair of the Foundation Department, Nathan Goldstein, a recognized authority on art education, lecturer and artist; Christopher James, Professor and Chair of the Photography Department, an internationally renowned photographer who has won numerous awards and fellowships and whose work is in museum collections around the world; Jane Tuckerman, Associate Professor of Photography, a widely-exhibited photographer and recipient of an NEA fellowship and other prestigious grants and fellowships; and Anthony Apesos, Associate Professor and Chair of the Fine Arts Department, who is an accomplished painter, lecturer, and art critic.

The faculty members at The Art Institute of Boston serve as mentors to their students and are very accessible to them. Students at AIB benefit from lectures, exhibitions, and the visiting artists who contribute to the positive energy of studio critiques and workshops. Activities and opportunities for growth and learning at AIB include student exhibitions on and off-campus, lectures, workshops, field trips to galleries in New York and New England, and a visiting artist program. Acclaimed artists such as Chuck Close, Duane Michals, Edward Sorel, Milton Glaser, Roy DeCarava, Luis Gonzalez Palma, and Andres Serrano have recently been guest lecturers at the college.

Education at AIB is not confined to the studios and galleries of the college. Students benefit from the talent and experience of the faculty and the extensive connections to the Boston art and business communities that the college has nurtured. Boston is a thriving cultural and commercial center, home to countless museums and galleries, symphonies, and theaters and renowned for its medical centers, financial institutions, and universities. These communities provide venues for a wealth of internships and full-time employment. In addition to yearlong exhibitions of student work throughout the College, students exhibit at numerous galleries around Boston. Students are encouraged to show their work long before graduation, gaining valuable life experiences outside the classroom.

The practical aspect of developing a career in art is part of the formal curriculum at AIB. By the time students graduate, they are well prepared for their professions through courses exclusively devoted to career-related skills such as presentation and portfolio building, and learning to make contacts in their fields. AIB graduates cite the practical skills and the encouragement they received as key factors in building the confidence needed to succeed in their careers.

▼ ART INSTITUTE OF SOUTHERN CALIFORNIA

Laguna Beach, California

Independent, coed. Small town campus. Total enrollment: 196. Art program established 1962.

Degrees Bachelor of Fine Arts in the areas of drawing/painting, graphic design, illustration. Majors and concentrations: art/fine arts, graphic arts, graphic design, illustration. Cross-registration with Concordia University (CA). Program accredited by NASAD.

Enrollment Fall 1997: 184 total; all undergraduate.

Art Student Profile 39% females, 61% males, 24% minorities, 14% international.

Art Faculty 37 total (full-time and part-time). 80% of full-time faculty have terminal degrees. Graduate students do not teach undergraduate courses. Undergraduate student–faculty ratio: 9:1.

Student Life Student groups/activities include Student Government, student exhibitions, American Institute of Graphic Arts.

Expenses for 1997–98 Application fee: $35. Tuition: $10,900 full-time.

Financial Aid Program-specific awards for 1997: 64 Competitive Scholarships for enrolled students ($700–$1200).

Application Procedures Students apply for admission into the professional program by sophomore year. Deadline for freshmen and transfers: continuous. Required: essay, high school transcript, college transcript(s) for transfer students, minimum 2.0 high school GPA, 2 letters of recommendation, interview, portfolio. Recommended: minimum 3.0 high school GPA, SAT I or ACT test scores. Portfolio reviews held 8-10 times on campus and off campus in various locations; the submission of slides may be substituted for portfolios when distance is prohibitive.

Undergraduate Contact Ms. Susan DeRosa, Admissions Advisor, Art Institute of Southern California, 2222 Laguna Canyon Road, Laguna Beach, California 92651-1136; 714-497-3309, fax: 714-494-4399.

More About the Institute

The Art Institute of Southern California (AISC), located in Orange County's Laguna Beach, is a small, fully accredited, specialized school for students interested in becoming artists or designers. The college combines personal attention with the best in faculty members and facilities to attain this goal. AISC's sole purpose is to help train students to become professional artists or designers. AISC is accredited by WASC and NASAD.

Art Institute of Southern California *(continued)*

Program Facilities At the Art Institute, students pursue four-year Bachelor of Fine Arts degrees in drawing and painting, graphic design, or illustration, where the work in the studio is complemented by a diverse liberal arts course of study. All classes needed for the degree are taught on AISC's 11-acre campus.

AISC offers students excellent facilities; the recently redesigned Barbara Auerbach Computer Facility exclusively features Macintosh Power PCs for student use, as well as two scanners and color and laser printers. Drawing, painting, three-dimensional, and photographic studios are designed to fit the needs of students in the visual arts. All studios are accessible to students for their use when classes are not in session.

Faculty AISC's faculty members have been selected for their professional experience and teaching abilities. All studio instructors are practicing artists or designers, and most hold terminal degrees in their field of study.

Special Programs Students enjoy small class sizes and individual attention. In addition, AISC's administration realizes the high cost of college education and has worked to keep tuition costs at less than 75 percent of all other accredited colleges offering similar programs.

▼ THE ART INSTITUTES INTERNATIONAL AT PORTLAND

Portland, Oregon

Proprietary, coed. Urban campus. Total enrollment: 148. Art program established 1963.

Degrees Bachelor of Interior Design; Bachelor of Apparel Design. Majors and concentrations: apparel design, interior design, retail management.

Enrollment Fall 1997: 148 total; all undergraduate.

Art Student Profile 86% females, 14% males, 16% minorities, 2% international.

Art Faculty 30 total (full-time and part-time). 20% of full-time faculty have terminal degrees. Graduate students do not teach undergraduate courses. Undergraduate student–faculty ratio: 7:1.

Student Life Student groups/activities include American Society of Interior Designers Student Chapter, Fashion Group Student Chapter.

Expenses for 1997–98 Application fee: $35. Tuition: $8900 full-time. Special program-related fees: $85–$120 for laboratory fees.

Financial Aid Program-specific awards for 1997: 1 Fashion Group Scholarship for artistically talented ($1000), 1 Make it Yourself With Wool Scholarship for artistically talented ($500).

Application Procedures Students admitted directly into the professional program freshman year. Deadline for freshmen and transfers: continuous. Required: essay, high school transcript, college transcript(s) for transfer students, minimum 2.0 high school GPA, measles immunization. Recommended: minimum 3.0 high school GPA, interview, portfolio, SAT I or ACT test scores. Portfolio reviews held continuously on campus.

Undergraduate Contact Ms. Kelly Alston, Director of Admissions and Enrollment Management, The Art Institutes Interna-

tional at Portland, 2000 Southwest Fifth Avenue, Portland, Oregon 97201; 503-228-6528, fax: 503-228-4227.

More About the College

Special Programs The Art Institutes International at Portland offers a baccalaureate degree as well as an Associate of Art degree and an Associate of Science degree in six fields of study.

Apparel Design: Design houses, pattern publishers, and manufacturers are after experienced employees. Apparel designers and developers combine imagination with technical experience to produce within a highly competitive field. Our instructors teach everything from concept and pattern design to the creation itself.

Computer Animation: Enter the computer-driven world of 3-D. Drawing, color, design, and computer science provide a foundation for 3-D modeling and desktop video production.

Graphic Design: Develop a portfolio that shows an agency, TV station, or graphic design studio what you know about design, illustration, composition, computer graphics, and concept.

Interior Design: Develop the skills needed to create all spaces, components, and elements designed for human needs and human spirits. Learn to transform space with color, texture, fabric, and light. Add drafting, sketching, and business skills to a sense of aesthetics.

Merchandising Management: Learn to buy, market, sell, and manage an operation as well as develop the skills and artistry that will attract the eye of the shopper.

Multimedia: As a student of this program, you'll learn how to integrate sound, text, graphic arts, animation, video, and film to create powerful new methods of communication.

▼ ATLANTA COLLEGE OF ART

Atlanta, Georgia

Independent, coed. Urban campus. Total enrollment: 420. Art program established 1928.

Degrees Bachelor of Fine Arts. Majors and concentrations: advertising design, art/fine arts, communication design, computer animation, computer art, computer graphics, digital art, digital imaging, digital multi-media, electronic arts, graphic design, illustration, individualized major, interior design, painting/drawing, photography, printmaking, sculpture, video art. Cross-registration with Atlanta Regional Center for Higher Education (ARCH). Program accredited by NASAD.

Enrollment Fall 1997: 420 total; all undergraduate.

Art Student Profile 48% females, 52% males, 29% minorities, 5% international.

Art Faculty 73 total (full-time and part-time). 98% of full-time faculty have terminal degrees. Graduate students do not teach undergraduate courses. Undergraduate student–faculty ratio: 12:1.

Student Life Student groups/activities include Performance Art Club, Cipher of Peace, Graphic Designers Club. Special housing available for art students.

Expenses for 1997–98 Application fee: $25. Tuition: $11,900 full-time. Mandatory fees: $350 full-time. Full-time tuition and fees vary according to course load. College room only: $3750. Special program-related fees: $10–$85 per per course for various course-specific materials.

Financial Aid Program-specific awards for 1997: President's Scholarships for incoming students, Dean's Scholarships for incoming students, School of Excellence Awards for incoming students, awards for students with minimum 3.5 GPA.

Application Procedures Students admitted directly into the professional program freshman year. Deadline for freshmen and transfers: continuous. Required: essay, high school transcript, college transcript(s) for transfer students, minimum 2.0 high school GPA, portfolio, SAT I or ACT test scores. Recommended: minimum 3.0 high school GPA, 3 letters of recommendation, interview. Portfolio reviews held continuously on campus and off campus in various high schools in U.S. and abroad; the submission of slides may be substituted for portfolios.

Web Site http://aca.edu.

Undergraduate Contact Ms. Carol Lee Conchar, Director of Enrollment Management, Atlanta College of Art, 1280 Peachtree Street, NE, Atlanta, Georgia 30309; 800-832-2104, fax: 404-733-5107, E-mail address: acainfo@woodruff.arts.org.

More About the College

Program Facilities Studios: Black-and-white color, nonsilver and cibachrome photography darkrooms, drawing and painting, video shooting and editing, computer graphics and animation, woodworking, metal, foundry, ceramics, blacksmithing, lithography, intaglio, screen print, paper and book-making, individual student workspace in design, senior painting, and sculpture. Gallery: Student exhibition space, ACA Gallery of Contemporary Art and Design. Library; 29,000 volumes primarily dedicated to contemporary art, 70,000 slides, 200 journals, and 1,000 artists' books.

▼

The Atlanta College of Art is a thriving artistic community that offers the student an opportunity to engage creative people unified through the search for artistic excellence. Students from all over the globe form ACA's creative community. ACA offers majors in drawing, electronic arts (computer animation, digital art, digital multimedia, or video), painting, photography, printmaking, sculpture, interior design, or communication design (advertising design, graphic design, or illustration). One of the great strengths of the ACA curriculum is that students may build an individualized major from several studio disciplines.

The first-year curriculum, considered to be somewhat unique among art colleges, combines a comprehensive training in visual art skills and media with the conceptual rigor needed to be a successful artist and designer today. The student encounters the role of the artist in the diverse cultures of our world. The Global Perspectives on Art course, which is the foundation of the general education requirement, prepares the student for the intensive study of the relationship between art and culture.

The faculty at ACA is committed to the education of the artist and designer. The faculty comprises award-winning artists, designers, and scholars. In addition, well-known visiting artists and designers regularly invigorate the life of the College through lectures and workshops. An international artist and designer residency program was established in 1993 to bring global issues in art and design directly into the ACA community.

Professional skills are reinforced through courses such as "The Artist as Professional" and through student internships at regional art and design institutions such as the High Museum of Art, Sandler Hudson Gallery, Art Papers, and notable companies such as IBM, CNN, and Coca-Cola. Many of these internships result in full-time employment after graduation.

Extensive renovations to the Woodruff Arts Center were completed in time for the 1996 Olympic Games. This $15-million makeover includes new professional and student galleries, a greatly expanded two-story library, additional studio space, and renovations to Lombardy Hall, the college residence hall. The Electronic Media Center is well known in the region for its computer, sound, and video technology. Advanced painting, sculpture, and design students have their own studio spaces, and most work areas are available 24 hours a day. The library houses a fine regional collection of contemporary art references, including an outstanding collection of artist-made books. The ACA gallery is well known in Atlanta for its collection of nationally and internationally known contemporary art.

The ACA campus is part of the Woodruff Arts Center, which includes the High Museum of Art, The Alliance and Studio Theaters, and the Atlanta Symphony Orchestra. The Atlanta College of Art is also a member of the Atlanta Regional Center for Higher Education (ARCH). Through ARCH, students at ACA have access to libraries, lectures, and exhibitions at all of the thirteen member institutions. Cross-registration with institutions such as Georgia Institute of Technology, Emory University, Spelman College, and Agnes Scott College make it easy for students to expand their education experience beyond the ACA campus.

▼ AUBURN UNIVERSITY

Auburn University, Alabama

State-supported, coed. Small town campus. Total enrollment: 21,505. Art program established 1927.

Degrees Bachelor of Fine Arts in the areas of art/fine arts, graphic arts. Majors and concentrations: ceramics, graphic design, illustration, painting/drawing, printmaking, sculpture, studio art. Graduate degrees offered: Master of Fine Arts in the area of art/fine arts. Program accredited by NASAD.

Enrollment Fall 1997: 1,056 total; 250 undergraduate, 6 graduate, 800 non-professional degree.

Art Student Profile 53% females, 47% males, 2% minorities, 1% international.

Art Faculty 23 total undergraduate and graduate (full-time and part-time). 100% of full-time faculty have terminal degrees. Graduate students teach a few undergraduate courses. Undergraduate student–faculty ratio: 10:1.

Auburn University *(continued)*

Student Life Student groups/activities include Auburn Students in Graphic Design, Association of Visual Artists.

Expenses for 1997–98 Application fee: $25, $50 for international students. State resident tuition: $2610 full-time. Nonresident tuition: $7830 full-time. Full-time tuition varies according to program. College room only: $1905. Room charges vary according to housing facility. Part-time mandatory fees per term: $145 for state residents, $435 for nonresidents. Special program-related fees: $20–$65 per course for material fees.

Financial Aid Program-specific awards for 1997: 7 scholarship program for art majors ($250).

Application Procedures Students admitted directly into the professional program freshman year. Deadline for freshmen and transfers: September 1. Notification date for freshmen and transfers: continuous. Required: high school transcript, college transcript(s) for transfer students, portfolio, SAT I or ACT test scores. Portfolio reviews held 4 times on campus; the submission of slides may be substituted for portfolios when distance is prohibitive.

Undergraduate Contact Jeff Lewis, Academic Advisor, Department of Art, Auburn University, 101 Biggin Hall, Auburn University, Alabama 36849-5125; 334-844-4373, fax: 334-844-4024, E-mail address: lewisjs@mail.auburn.edu.

Graduate Contact Mark Price, Graduate Program Officer, Department of Art, Auburn University, 101 Biggin Hall, Auburn University, Alabama 36849-5125; 334-844-4373, fax: 334-844-4024.

▼ AUGUSTA STATE UNIVERSITY

Augusta, Georgia

State-supported, coed. Urban campus. Total enrollment: 5,479. Art program established 1958.

Degrees Bachelor of Fine Arts in the area of art. Majors and concentrations: studio art.

Enrollment Fall 1997: 80 undergraduate.

Art Student Profile 48% females, 52% males, 13% minorities.

Art Faculty 13 total undergraduate (full-time and part-time). 100% of full-time faculty have terminal degrees. Graduate students do not teach undergraduate courses. Undergraduate student–faculty ratio: 10:1.

Expenses for 1997–98 Application fee: $10. State resident tuition: $1680 full-time. Nonresident tuition: $6141 full-time. Mandatory fees: $246 full-time. Special program-related fees: $45 per course for studio lab fee.

Financial Aid Program-specific awards for 1997: 1 department scholarship for program majors ($500), 1 Mary Byrd Scholarship for graduates of local Georgia high schools ($1000), 1 Nathan Bindler Award for artistically talented program majors ($500), 2–4 Pamplin Scholarships for program majors ($500).

Application Procedures Students admitted directly into the professional program freshman year. Deadline for freshmen and transfers: August 15. Required: high school transcript, minimum 2.0 high school GPA, 2 letters of recommendation. Recommended: portfolio, SAT I or ACT test scores. Portfolio reviews held once on campus; the submission of slides may be substituted for portfolios when distance is prohibitive.

Undergraduate Contact Dr. Clayton Shotwell, Chairman, Fine Arts Department, Augusta State University, 2500 Walton Way, Augusta, Georgia 30904-2200; 706-737-1453, fax: 706-737-1773, E-mail address: cshotwel@aug.edu.

▼ AUSTIN PEAY STATE UNIVERSITY

Clarksville, Tennessee

State-supported, coed. Suburban campus. Total enrollment: 7,803.

Degrees Bachelor of Fine Arts in the areas of studio arts, graphic design, art education. Majors and concentrations: art education, ceramics, drawing, graphic design, illustration, painting, photography, pottery, printmaking, sculpture. Program accredited by NASAD.

Enrollment Fall 1997: 170 undergraduate.

Art Faculty 20 total (full-time and part-time). 90% of full-time faculty have terminal degrees. Graduate students do not teach undergraduate courses.

Student Life Student groups/activities include Student Art League.

Expenses for 1997–98 Application fee: $15. State resident tuition: $1816 full-time. Nonresident tuition: $6412 full-time. Mandatory fees: $464 full-time. College room and board: $3260. College room only: $1770. Special program-related fees: $15 per course for ceramics, sculpture, photography, printmaking material fees.

Financial Aid Program-specific awards for 1997: 10–14 Center for the Creative Arts Scholarships for program majors ($500–$1000), 5 endowed scholarships for program majors ($1000).

Application Procedures Students apply for admission into the professional program by sophomore year. Deadline for freshmen and transfers: July 27. Required: high school transcript, college transcript(s) for transfer students, ACT test score only (minimum combined ACT score of 19), portfolio and minimum 3.0 high school GPA for scholarship consideration, minimum 2.75 high school GPA. Portfolio reviews held on campus; the submission of slides may be substituted for portfolios for three-dimensional work.

Undergraduate Contact Ms. Cynthia Marsh, Chair, Department of Art, Austin Peay State University, PO Box 4677, Clarksville, Tennessee 37044; 931-648-7333, fax: 931-648-5997.

▼ BALL STATE UNIVERSITY

Muncie, Indiana

State-supported, coed. Suburban campus. Total enrollment: 19,419.

Degrees Bachelor of Fine Arts in the area of art. Majors and concentrations: ceramic art and design, drawing, graphic design, jewelry and metalsmithing, painting, photography, printmaking, sculpture. Graduate degrees offered: Master of Arts in the area of art. Program accredited by NASAD.

Enrollment Fall 1997: 365 total; 275 undergraduate, 15 graduate, 75 non-professional degree.

Art Student Profile 52% females, 48% males, 5% minorities, 2% international.

Art Faculty 29 total undergraduate and graduate (full-time and part-time). 90% of full-time faculty have terminal degrees. Graduate students do not teach undergraduate courses. Undergraduate student–faculty ratio: 13:1.

Student Life Student groups/activities include National Art Education Association Student Chapter, Fine Arts League, Crafts Guild.

Expenses for 1997–98 Application fee: $25. State resident tuition: $3316 full-time. Nonresident tuition: $8872 full-time. Mandatory fees: $98 full-time. College room and board: $4120.

Financial Aid Program-specific awards for 1997: 3–4 Freshmen Scholarship Awards for outstanding freshmen program applicants ($1000), 7 Fine Art Scholarships for outstanding freshmen program applicants ($1000), 5 Ruth Swain Scholarship for outstanding sophomores, juniors, or seniors ($1000).

Application Procedures Students admitted directly into the professional program freshman year. Deadline for freshmen: April 1; transfers: continuous. Notification date for freshmen: May 1. Required: high school transcript, college transcript(s) for transfer students, portfolio, SAT I or ACT test scores (minimum combined SAT I score of 1000, minimum combined ACT score of 21), slides of portfolio for scholarship consideration. Recommended: minimum 2.0 high school GPA. Portfolio reviews held once on campus; the submission of slides may be substituted for portfolios if a campus visit is impossible.

Web Site http://www.bsu.edu/cfa/art/index.html.

Undergraduate Contact Ms. Barbara Giorgio-Booher, Primary Department Advisor, Department of Art, Ball State University, Muncie, Indiana 47306-0405; 765-285-5841, fax: 765-285-5275, E-mail address: bgiorgio@wp.bsu.edu.

Graduate Contact Dr. Thomas M. Spoerner, Chairperson, Department of Art, Ball State University, Muncle, Indiana 47306-0405; 765-285-5838, fax: 765-285-5275, E-mail address: tspoerne@wp.bsu.edu.

▼ BARRY UNIVERSITY

Miami Shores, Florida

Independent-Roman Catholic, coed. Suburban campus. Total enrollment: 6,899. Art program established 1951.

Degrees Bachelor of Fine Arts in the areas of art, photography; Bachelor of Arts in the area of biomedical and forensic photography. Majors and concentrations: ceramics, painting, photography. Graduate degrees offered: Master of Fine Arts in the area of photography; Master of Science in the area of art therapy/clinical psychology; Master of Arts in the area of photography.

Enrollment Fall 1997: 50 total; 40 undergraduate, 10 graduate.

Art Student Profile 64% females, 36% males, 52% minorities, 71% international.

Art Faculty 7 total undergraduate and graduate (full-time and part-time). 100% of full-time faculty have terminal degrees. Graduate students do not teach undergraduate courses. Undergraduate student–faculty ratio: 14:1.

Student Life Student groups/activities include art and photography clubs and associations.

Expenses for 1997–98 Application fee: $30. Comprehensive fee: $19,400 includes full-time tuition ($13,290), mandatory fees ($260), and college room and board ($5850). Full-time tuition and fees vary according to location. Room and board charges vary according to board plan. Special program-related fees: $36 per course for supplies.

Application Procedures Students admitted directly into the professional program freshman year. Deadline for freshmen and transfers: continuous. Required: essay, high school

transcript, college transcript(s) for transfer students, 3 letters of recommendation, interview, portfolio, SAT I or ACT test scores (minimum combined SAT I score of 1000), minimum 2.5 high school GPA. Portfolio reviews held twice on campus; the submission of slides may be substituted for portfolios if placed in notebook form.

Contact Ms. Derna M. Ford, Chair, Department of Fine Arts, Barry University, 11300 Northeast Second Avenue, Miami Shores, Florida 33161; 305-899-3422, fax: 305-899-2972, E-mail address: dford@buaxp1.barry.edu.

▼ BARTON COLLEGE

Wilson, North Carolina

Independent, coed. Small town campus. Total enrollment: 1,303.

Degrees Bachelor of Fine Arts in the areas of graphic design, ceramics, painting, photography; Bachelor of Science in the area of art education K-12; Bachelor of Arts in the area of studio art.

Enrollment Fall 1997: 76 total; 70 undergraduate, 6 non-professional degree.

Art Student Profile 60% females, 40% males, 15% minorities, 1% international.

Art Faculty 5 total (full-time and part-time). 100% of full-time faculty have terminal degrees. Graduate students do not teach undergraduate courses. Undergraduate student–faculty ratio: 16:1.

Expenses for 1998–99 Application fee: $20. Comprehensive fee: $13,928 includes full-time tuition ($9462), mandatory fees ($688), and college room and board ($3778). College room only: $1732. Full-time tuition and fees vary according to course load. Room and board charges vary according to board plan and housing facility.

Financial Aid Program-specific awards for 1997: 1 Bessie Massengill Award for sophomores and juniors ($1000), 1 TEAM Award for sophomores and juniors ($1000), 1 National Scholastic Award for freshmen ($1000).

Application Procedures Students admitted directly into the professional program freshman year. Deadline for freshmen and transfers: continuous. Required: high school transcript, college transcript(s) for transfer students, letter of recommendation, SAT I or ACT test scores. Recommended: minimum 2.0 high school GPA, interview.

Undergraduate Contact Mr. J. Chris Wilson, Chair, Art Department, Barton College, College Station, Wilson, North Carolina 27893; 919-399-6476, fax: 919-237-4957.

▼ BAYLOR UNIVERSITY

Waco, Texas

Independent-Baptist, coed. Urban campus. Total enrollment: 12,472.

Degrees Bachelor of Fine Arts in the areas of painting, printmaking, graphic design, ceramics, sculpture, art education. Majors and concentrations: art education, ceramic art and design, commercial art, painting/drawing, printmaking, sculpture.

Enrollment Fall 1997: 800 undergraduate.

Art Student Profile 75% females, 25% males, 3% minorities, 7% international.

Baylor University (*continued*)

Art Faculty 13 total (full-time). 100% of full-time faculty have terminal degrees. Graduate students do not teach undergraduate courses. Undergraduate student–faculty ratio: 14:1.

Student Life Student groups/activities include Art Club, Advertising Club of Baylor.

Expenses for 1998–99 Application fee: $35. One-time mandatory fee: $50. Comprehensive fee: $14,832 includes full-time tuition ($9240), mandatory fees ($1026), and college room and board ($4566). College room only: $1958. Room and board charges vary according to board plan and housing facility. Special program-related fees: $30 for studio lab fees.

Financial Aid Program-specific awards for 1997: 1 Friends of Baylor Fine Arts Award for continuing students ($1850), 12–14 Patricia Johnston Scholarships for continuing students ($500–$900), 1 C. C. and Helen Reid Scholarship for continuing students ($250), 2 Freshmen Art Scholarships for freshmen ($2500).

Application Procedures Students admitted directly into the professional program freshman year. Deadline for freshmen and transfers: April 15. Required: high school transcript, college transcript(s) for transfer students, minimum 2.0 high school GPA. Recommended: minimum 3.0 high school GPA, letter of recommendation.

Undergraduate Contact Mr. John D. McClanahan, Chair, Art Department, Baylor University, PO Box 97263, Waco, Texas 76798-7263; 254-710-1867, fax: 254-710-1566, E-mail address: dodi_holland@baylor.edu.

▼ BEAVER COLLEGE

Glenside, Pennsylvania

Independent, coed. Suburban campus. Total enrollment: 2,705. Art program established 1925.

Degrees Bachelor of Fine Arts in the areas of graphic design, interior design, painting, printmaking, ceramics, metals and jewelry, photography, art education; Bachelor of Arts in the areas of scientific illustration, art therapy. Majors and concentrations: art education, art history, art therapy, art/fine arts, ceramic art and design, graphic design, interior design, jewelry and metalsmithing, painting/drawing, photography, printmaking, scientific illustration, studio art. Program accredited by NASAD.

Enrollment Fall 1997: 149 undergraduate.

Art Student Profile 60% females, 40% males, 15% minorities, 3% international.

Art Faculty 18 total (full-time and part-time). 83% of full-time faculty have terminal degrees. Graduate students do not teach undergraduate courses. Undergraduate student–faculty ratio: 13:1.

Student Life Student groups/activities include Student Graphic Design Web Design Group (The Murphy Projects).

Expenses for 1997–98 Application fee: $30. Comprehensive fee: $22,360 includes full-time tuition ($15,560), mandatory fees ($280), and college room and board ($6520). College room only: $2450. Room and board charges vary according to board plan. Special program-related fees: $25–$100 per course for lab supplies.

Financial Aid Program-specific awards for 1997: 5–10 Achievement Awards for program majors ($1000–$5000).

Application Procedures Students admitted directly into the professional program freshman year. Deadline for freshmen and transfers: continuous. Required: essay, high school

transcript, college transcript(s) for transfer students, minimum 2.0 high school GPA, letter of recommendation, portfolio. Recommended: minimum 3.0 high school GPA, interview. Portfolio reviews held 6 times on campus and off campus in Philadelphia, PA; Baltimore, MD; New York, NY; Hartford, CT; the submission of slides may be substituted for portfolios if a campus visit is impossible.

Web Site http://www.beaver.edu.

Undergraduate Contact Office of Enrollment Management, Beaver College, 450 South Easton Road, Glenside, Pennsylvania 19038-3295; 800-776-2328, fax: 215-572-4049.

More About the College

Faculty Fine arts faculty members are practicing artists as well as gifted, caring teachers whose work is regularly exhibited and honored. Their work has been lauded in national art magazines and has been exhibited in the Philadelphia Museum of Art, The Whitney Museum, and The American Craft Museum.

Student Exhibition Opportunities Prominent in the Philadelphia area for exhibiting cutting-edge artists, the Beaver College Art Gallery is nationally known for its exhibitions and lectures. Senior art majors participate in a culminating exhibit at the Gallery.

Program Facilities The fine arts department is situated in two of the historic buildings on campus, each housing specific studio areas and equipment. Murphy Hall has a newly renovated Macintosh computer lab and a new three-dimensional design/multipurpose studio. Kilns, wheels, sand blasters, welders, and woodworking power equipment comprise the ceramics, 3-D, and metalsmith areas. The College facilities also include photographic darkrooms, printmaking facilities, painting and drawing studios, and graphic and interior design labs.

Special Programs Through Beaver's Center for Education Abroad, students can study overseas in one of the programs in Australia, Austria, England, Greece, Ireland, Hungary, Mexico, Scotland, or Wales for about the same cost as studying on the Glenside campus. Unique studio opportunities exist at the Glasgow School of Art in Scotland and the Burren College of Art in Ireland.

▼

Everybody has to do something. Why not something great? Beaver College is where students can start sketching their future in the art world. With Philadelphia's seven renowned museums and numerous galleries, and with New York, Baltimore, and Washington, D.C. within easy access by train or car, Beaver College students enjoy a distinct advantage. Students can discover firsthand what's hot in the current art world through trips, internships and co-ops.

At Beaver College, students learn the principles of design as well as the principles of problem solving. By supplementing art courses with courses in the natural sciences, social sciences, and humanities, students gain an understanding of the world around them from which they can draw ideas for creative expression.

Beaver College offers several programs to help students fulfill their artistic and career goals: The Bachelor of Fine Arts in Studio Art offers courses in basic design principles concentrating in one specific area such as ceramics, graphic design, interior design, metals and jewelry, painting, photography, or printmaking. The Bachelor of Arts in Art allows students to concentrate in art while taking a wider selection of courses outside the Fine Arts Department. Students may double major, for example, combining art with business,

English, or a foreign language. The Bachelor of Arts in Art with a concentration in art history combines liberal arts with studio courses that demonstrate creative procedures and basic techniques. Graduates often work in galleries, museums, publishing, or merchandising. The Bachelor of Fine Arts and Certification in Art Education prepare students to teach art in grades K through 12. The Bachelor of Arts in Scientific Illustration obtained in cooperation with the Biology Department prepares students for a career in scientific illustration, publication, laboratory research, or graduate work in medical illustration. The concentration in art therapy, in cooperation with the Psychology Department, combines studio art with psychology, sociology, anthropology, and art therapy. It follows guidelines approved by the National Association of Schools of Art and Design in cooperation with the American Art Therapy Association.

▼ BELLEVUE UNIVERSITY

Bellevue, Nebraska

Independent, coed. Suburban campus. Total enrollment: 2,928. Art program established 1966.

Degrees Bachelor of Fine Arts in the area of studio art. Majors and concentrations: ceramics, drawing, painting/drawing, papermaking, photography, printmaking, sculpture, watercolors.

Enrollment Fall 1997: 46 total; 40 undergraduate, 6 nonprofessional degree.

Art Student Profile 45% females, 55% males, 10% minorities, 20% international.

Art Faculty 6 total (full-time and part-time). 100% of full-time faculty have terminal degrees. Graduate students do not teach undergraduate courses. Undergraduate student–faculty ratio: 9:1.

Student Life Student groups/activities include Art Club.

Expenses for 1997–98 Application fee: $10. Tuition: $3600 full-time. Mandatory fees: $50 full-time. Special program-related fees: $30 for studio fee, supplies.

Financial Aid Program-specific awards for 1997: 4 art scholarships for art majors ($500–$1000).

Application Procedures Students admitted directly into the professional program freshman year. Deadline for freshmen and transfers: continuous. Required: high school transcript, minimum 2.0 high school GPA, SAT I or ACT test scores. Recommended: 3 letters of recommendation, interview, portfolio. Portfolio reviews held twice on campus; the submission of slides may be substituted for portfolios when distance is prohibitive.

Undergraduate Contact Admissions Office, Bellevue University, 1000 Galvin Road South, Bellevue, Nebraska 68005; 402-293-2000, fax: 402-293-2020.

▼ BELMONT UNIVERSITY

Nashville, Tennessee

Independent-Baptist, coed. Urban campus. Total enrollment: 2,986. Art program established 1994.

Degrees Bachelor of Fine Arts in the areas of studio, art education, design communications. Majors and concentrations: art education, graphic design, studio art.

Enrollment Fall 1997: 122 total; 57 undergraduate, 65 nonprofessional degree.

Art Student Profile 60% females, 40% males, 5% international.

Art Faculty 8 total (full-time and part-time). 100% of full-time faculty have terminal degrees. Graduate students do not teach undergraduate courses. Undergraduate student–faculty ratio: 12:1.

Student Life Student groups/activities include Art Association.

Expenses for 1997–98 Application fee: $25. Comprehensive fee: $14,190 includes full-time tuition ($10,050), mandatory fees ($250), and college room and board ($3890). College room only: $1990. Room and board charges vary according to board plan and housing facility. Special program-related fees: $25 per course for lab fees, model fees.

Financial Aid Program-specific awards for 1997: 5–6 Leu Art Scholarship for freshmen art majors ($2000).

Application Procedures Students admitted directly into the professional program freshman year. Deadline for freshmen: continuous. Required: high school transcript, college transcript(s) for transfer students, letter of recommendation, SAT I or ACT test scores. Recommended: minimum 2.0 high school GPA, interview, portfolio. Portfolio reviews held by arrangement on campus; the submission of slides may be substituted for portfolios whenever needed.

Web Site http://www.belmont.edu/humanities/artdept/arthome.html.

Undergraduate Contact Mr. James M. Meaders, Chair, Department of Art, Belmont University, 1900 Belmont Boulevard, Nashville, Tennessee 37212-3757; 615-460-5578, fax: 615-385-5084, E-mail address: meadersj@belmont.edu.

▼ BOSTON ARCHITECTURAL CENTER

Boston, Massachusetts

Independent, coed. Urban campus. Total enrollment: 854. Art program established 1889.

Degrees Bachelor of Interior Design; Bachelor of Architecture. Graduate degrees offered: Master of Architecture; Master of Interior Design. Cross-registration with Pro-Arts Consortium: Berklee School of Music, Boston Conservatory, Emerson College and School of the Museum of Fine Arts. Program accredited by NAAB.

Enrollment Fall 1997: 688 total; 568 undergraduate, 120 graduate.

Art Student Profile 30% females, 70% males, 10% minorities.

Art Faculty 219 total undergraduate and graduate (full-time and part-time). Graduate students do not teach undergraduate courses.

Student Life Student groups/activities include Atelier, Interior Design Student Organization.

Expenses for 1997–98 Application fee: $50. Tuition: $5616 full-time. Mandatory fees: $75 full-time.

Financial Aid Program-specific awards available.

Application Procedures Students admitted directly into the professional program freshman year. Deadline for freshmen and transfers: continuous. Required: college transcript(s) for transfer students, resume. Recommended: high school transcript, minimum 2.0 high school GPA, interview, portfolio. Portfolio reviews held twice on campus.

Web Site http://www.the-bac.edu.

Contact Valerie Nyce, Director of Admissions, Boston Architectural Center, 320 Newbury Street, Boston, Massachusetts 02115; 617-262-5000, fax: 617-536-5829, E-mail address: admissions@the-bac.edu.

▼ BOSTON UNIVERSITY

Boston, Massachusetts

Independent, coed. Urban campus. Total enrollment: 29,387. Art program established 1954.

Degrees Bachelor of Fine Arts in the areas of painting, sculpture, graphic design, art education. Graduate degrees offered: Master of Fine Arts in the areas of painting, sculpture, graphic design, art education, studio teaching. Cross-registration with Boston College, Brandeis University, Tufts University.

Enrollment Fall 1997: 306 total; 230 undergraduate, 65 graduate, 11 non-professional degree.

Art Student Profile 60% females, 40% males, 10% minorities.

Art Faculty 31 total undergraduate and graduate (full-time and part-time). 100% of full-time faculty have terminal degrees. Graduate students do not teach undergraduate courses. Undergraduate student–faculty ratio: 16:1.

Student Life Special housing available for art students.

Expenses for 1998–99 Application fee: $50. Comprehensive fee: $31,018 includes full-time tuition ($22,830), mandatory fees ($318), and college room and board ($7870). College room only: $4830. Room and board charges vary according to board plan and housing facility.

Financial Aid Program-specific awards for 1997: 160 Grants-Need/Performance Awards for enrolled program students ($17,000).

Application Procedures Students admitted directly into the professional program freshman year. Deadline for freshmen: January 15; transfers: May 1. Notification date for freshmen: April 15; transfers: May 30. Required: essay, high school transcript, portfolio. Recommended: minimum 3.0 high school GPA, 3 letters of recommendation, SAT I or ACT test scores. Portfolio reviews held continuously on campus and off campus in Washington, DC; Chicago, IL; New York, NY; Miami, FL; Los Angeles, CA; San Diego, CA; San Francisco, CA; Baltimore, MD; Louisville, KY; the submission of slides may be substituted for portfolios with permission.

Web Site http://www.bu.edu/sfa.

Undergraduate Contact Alston Purvis, Director, Visual Arts Division, School for the Arts, Boston University, 855 Commonwealth Avenue, Boston, Massachusetts 02215; 617-353-3371, fax: 617-353-7217.

More About the University

Program Facilities Painting, drawing, studios, sculpture, welding and wood shop, graphic design and computer labs; book and slide library.

Faculty, Visiting Artists, and Alumni Faculty: Hugh O'Donnell, painter; John Walker, painter; Alfred Leslie, painter; John Moore, painter; Stuart Baron, painter; Harold Reddicliffe, painter; Richard Raiselis, painter; Margaret McCann, painter; Peter Hoss, painter, Isabel McIlvain, sculptor; Nick Edmonds, sculptor; Carol Keller, sculptor; Katherine Wales, sculptor; Alston Purvis, graphic designer; Bryce Ambo, graphic designer; Robert Burns, graphic designer, Stephen Frank, photographer; Janet Olson, art educator; Judith Simpson, art educator. Visiting Artists (1995–98): Neil Welliver, painter; Greg Amenoff, painter; William Tucker, sculptor; William Bailey, painter; Lennart Anderson, painter; Lori Berenberg, educator; Jill Berger, educator; Rackstraw Downes, painter; Susan Fisher, painter; Mags Harries, sculptor; Jacqueline Kapp, educator; Jennifer Moses, painter; Deborah Muirhead, painter; Catherine Murphy, painter; Ellen Phelan, painter; Carole Robb, painter; Jonathan Shahn, sculptor; Nancy

Sheehan, educator; Jane Taylor, educator; Graham Nickson, painter; Tim Rollins, arts educator; Suzanne Coffey, painter; Andrew Forge, painter; Lisa Yuskavage, painter. Alumni: Brice Marden, painter; Nicole Hollander, cartoonist; Rick Meyerowitz, illustrator; Howardena Pindell, painter; Ira Yoffe, graphic designer; Robert Freeman, painter.

Exhibition Opportunities Continuous student exhibitions.

Special Programs Graphic design internships. Students may earn minors in liberal arts and communications or participate in the collaborative degree program and receive a second degree.

▼ BOWLING GREEN STATE UNIVERSITY

Bowling Green, Ohio

State-supported, coed. Small town campus. Total enrollment: 17,328.

Degrees Bachelor of Fine Arts in the areas of ceramics, computer art, fibers, glassworking, graphic design, jewelry/metalsmithing, photography, printmaking, sculpture, drawing, painting; Bachelor of Science in the areas of art education, art therapy. Graduate degrees offered: Master of Fine Arts in the areas of ceramics, fibers, glassworking, graphic design, jewelry/metalsmithing, photography, printmaking, sculpture, drawing, painting. Cross-registration with University of Toledo. Program accredited by NASAD.

Enrollment Fall 1997: 830 total; 600 undergraduate, 30 graduate, 200 non-professional degree.

Art Student Profile 55% females, 45% males, 5% minorities, 2% international.

Art Faculty 52 total undergraduate and graduate (full-time and part-time). 95% of full-time faculty have terminal degrees. Graduate students teach a few undergraduate courses. Undergraduate student–faculty ratio: 18:1.

Student Life Student groups/activities include Student Art Education Association, Student Art Therapy Association.

Expenses for 1997–98 Application fee: $30. State resident tuition: $4422 full-time. Nonresident tuition: $9436 full-time. College room and board: $4626. College room only: $2554. Special program-related fees: $5–$100 per course for lab fees.

Financial Aid Program-specific awards for 1997: 25–30 art scholarships for outstanding studio art majors ($1000–$1500).

Application Procedures Students admitted directly into the professional program freshman year. Deadline for freshmen and transfers: continuous. Required: high school transcript, SAT I or ACT test scores. Recommended: portfolio. Portfolio reviews held continuously on campus; the submission of slides may be substituted for portfolios when distance is prohibitive.

Undergraduate Contact Director of Admissions, Bowling Green State University, Bowling Green, Ohio 43403-0211; 419-372-2086, fax: 419-372-6955.

Graduate Contact Mr. Dennis Wojtkiewicz, Graduate Coordinator, School of Art, Bowling Green State University, Bowling Green, Ohio 43403-0211; 419-372-2640, fax: 419-372-2544.

▼ BRADLEY UNIVERSITY

Peoria, Illinois

Independent, coed. Urban campus. Total enrollment: 5,861.

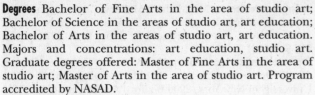

Degrees Bachelor of Fine Arts in the area of studio art; Bachelor of Science in the areas of studio art, art education; Bachelor of Arts in the areas of studio art, art education. Majors and concentrations: art education, studio art. Graduate degrees offered: Master of Fine Arts in the area of studio art; Master of Arts in the area of studio art. Program accredited by NASAD.

Enrollment Fall 1997: 172 total; 157 undergraduate, 7 graduate, 8 non-professional degree.

Art Student Profile 62% females, 38% males, 5% minorities, 2% international.

Art Faculty 17 total undergraduate and graduate (full-time and part-time). 90% of full-time faculty have terminal degrees. Graduate students do not teach undergraduate courses. Undergraduate student–faculty ratio: 11:1.

Student Life Student groups/activities include Spectrum.

Expenses for 1997–98 Application fee: $35. Comprehensive fee: $17,380 includes full-time tuition ($12,610), mandatory fees ($80), and college room and board ($4690). College room only: $2840. Room and board charges vary according to board plan. Special program-related fees: $20 per course for supplies.

Financial Aid Program-specific awards for 1997: art scholarships for art majors ($1221).

Application Procedures Students apply for admission into the professional program by sophomore year. Deadline for freshmen and transfers: continuous. Required: high school transcript, college transcript(s) for transfer students, minimum 2.0 high school GPA, portfolio, SAT I or ACT test scores. Recommended: letter of recommendation. Portfolio reviews held as needed on campus; the submission of slides may be substituted for portfolios (slides preferred for scholarship decisions).

Web Site http://gcc.bradley.edu/art/.

Undergraduate Contact Ms. Nickie Roberson, Director of Admissions, Office of Undergraduate Admissions, Bradley University, Swords Hall, Peoria, Illinois 61625; 800-447-6460, fax: 309-677-2797, E-mail address: admissions@bradley.edu.

Graduate Contact Lynne Franks, Director of Graduate Enrollment, Graduate School, Bradley University, 1501 West Bradley Avenue, Peoria, Illinois 61625; 309-677-2264.

▼ BRENAU UNIVERSITY

Gainesville, Georgia

Independent, primarily women. Small town campus. Total enrollment: 2,366. Art program established 1973.

Degrees Bachelor of Fine Arts in the areas of arts management, interior design, commercial art, studio art, fashion merchandising, art education. Majors and concentrations: ceramics, painting/drawing, sculpture. Program accredited by FIDER.

Enrollment Fall 1997: 90 total; all undergraduate.

Art Student Profile 78% females, 22% males, 19% minorities, 2% international.

Art Faculty 19 total (full-time and part-time). 100% of full-time faculty have terminal degrees. Graduate students do not teach undergraduate courses. Undergraduate student–faculty ratio: 10:1.

Student Life Student groups/activities include American Society of Interior Designers.

Expenses for 1997–98 Application fee: $30. Comprehensive fee: $17,350 includes full-time tuition ($10,740) and college

room and board ($6610). Special program-related fees: $10–$40 per per course for lab equipment fees.

Financial Aid Program-specific awards for 1997: 10 art scholarships for program majors ($1000–$3500).

Application Procedures Students admitted directly into the professional program freshman year. Deadline for freshmen and transfers: continuous. Required: high school transcript, college transcript(s) for transfer students, minimum 2.0 high school GPA, letter of recommendation, SAT I or ACT test scores (minimum combined SAT I score of 900, minimum combined ACT score of 19). Recommended: interview, portfolio. Portfolio reviews held as needed on campus; the submission of slides may be substituted for portfolios if a campus visit is impossible.

Web Site http://www.brenau.edu.

Undergraduate Contact Dr. John D. Upchurch, Dean of Admissions, Brenau University, One Centennial Circle, Gainesville, Georgia 30501; 770-534-6100, fax: 770-534-6114.

▼ BRIGHAM YOUNG UNIVERSITY

Provo, Utah

Independent, coed. Suburban campus. Total enrollment: 32,161.

Degrees Bachelor of Fine Arts in the areas of studio art, graphic design, photography, illustration, interior design, industrial design; Bachelor of Arts in the areas of art, art history, art education, design. Majors and concentrations: art education, art history, ceramics, graphic design, illustration, industrial design, interior design, painting, photography, printmaking, sculpture. Graduate degrees offered: Master of Fine Arts in the area of studio art. Program accredited by NASAD.

Enrollment Fall 1997: 272 total; 250 undergraduate, 22 graduate.

Art Student Profile 50% females, 50% males, 1% minorities, 7% international.

Art Faculty 63 total undergraduate and graduate (full-time and part-time). 78% of full-time faculty have terminal degrees. Graduate students teach more than half undergraduate courses.

Student Life Student groups/activities include Art History Student Association.

Expenses for 1997–98 Application fee: $25. Comprehensive fee: $6760 includes full-time tuition ($2630) and college room and board ($4130). Full-time tuition varies according to reciprocity agreements. Room and board charges vary according to board plan and housing facility. Special program-related fees: $200 per semester for supplies.

Financial Aid Program-specific awards for 1997: 10 Talent Awards for program majors ($1315), 1 J. Roman Andrus Printmaking Award for printmaking majors ($1000), 1 Demery Scholarship for program majors ($1000), 2–3 La Vieve Huish Earl Awards for art education majors ($1250), 4 Anna F. Sommers Scholarships for program majors ($1315), 1 Olena K. and George K. Lewis Scholarship for painting majors ($1315), 4 Betty M. and Paul J. Boshard Scholarships for program majors ($1315), 1 Cory Nathan Belleau Scholarship for program majors ($1315), 1 Max Dickson and Ruth Kimball Weaver Scholarship for ceramics majors ($1000), 2 Tanner/Ashland Oil Scholarships for industrial design majors ($1315).

Application Procedures Students apply for admission into the professional program by freshman year. Deadline for

Brigham Young University (continued)

freshmen and transfers: February 15. Notification date for freshmen and transfers: March 20. Required: high school transcript, college transcript(s) for transfer students, minimum 3.0 high school GPA, ACT test score only (minimum combined ACT score of 28), slides of portfolio. Portfolio reviews held 3 times on campus; the submission of slides may be substituted for portfolios.

Web Site http://www.byu.edu/visualarts/home.html.

Undergraduate Contact Ms. Sharon Heelis, Department Secretary, Department of Visual Arts, Brigham Young University, C-502 HFAC, Provo, Utah 84602; 801-378-4266, fax: 801-378-5964, E-mail address: heeliss@byugate.byu.edu.

Graduate Contact Ms. Jan Corallo, Graduate Secretary, Department of Visual Arts, Brigham Young University, B-509 HFAC, Provo, Utah 84602; 801-378-4429, fax: 801-378-5964, E-mail address: coralloj@byugate.byu.edu.

▼ Brooklyn College of the City University of New York

Brooklyn, New York

State and locally supported, coed. Urban campus. Total enrollment: 15,007. Art program established 1972.

Degrees Bachelor of Fine Arts in the area of art. Majors and concentrations: computer art, painting/drawing, photography, printmaking, sculpture. Graduate degrees offered: Master of Fine Arts in the area of art. Cross-registration with City University of New York System.

Enrollment Fall 1997: 90 total; 40 undergraduate, 35 graduate, 15 non-professional degree.

Art Student Profile 50% females, 50% males, 20% minorities, 15% international.

Art Faculty 22 total undergraduate and graduate (full-time and part-time). 100% of full-time faculty have terminal degrees. Graduate students teach a few undergraduate courses. Undergraduate student–faculty ratio: 10:1.

Student Life Student groups/activities include Art Group, Graduate Art Student Union.

Expenses for 1997–98 Application fee: $40. State resident tuition: $3200 full-time. Nonresident tuition: $6800 full-time. Mandatory fees: $213 full-time. Full-time tuition and fees vary according to class time and course load. Special program-related fees: $15–$20 per course for supplies and model fees.

Financial Aid Program-specific awards for 1997: 10–15 Charles G. Shaw Memorial Awards for painting students ($500–$1000), 2 Bernard Horlick Awards for program majors ($750), 2 Jerome J. Viola Memorial Awards for program majors ($350), 2 Bernard Cole Memorial Scholarships for photography students ($150), 1 Stuart Hall Zidenberg Memorial Award for program majors ($100).

Application Procedures Students apply for admission into the professional program by sophomore year. Deadline for freshmen and transfers: March 1. Notification date for freshmen and transfers: June 1. Required: high school transcript, college transcript(s) for transfer students, slides of portfolio, minimum 2.5 high school GPA. Recommended: interview, SAT I or ACT test scores. Portfolio reviews held twice on campus; the submission of slides may be substituted for portfolios.

Undergraduate Contact Mr. Michael Mallory, Chair, Department of Art, Brooklyn College of the City University of New York, 2900 Bedford Avenue, Brooklyn, New York 11210-2889; 718-951-5181.

Graduate Contact Mr. William T. Williams, Graduate Deputy Chair, Department of Art, Brooklyn College of the City University of New York, 2900 Bedford Avenue, Brooklyn, New York 11210-2889; 718-951-5181.

▼ Caldwell College

Caldwell, New Jersey

Independent-Roman Catholic, coed. Suburban campus. Total enrollment: 1,827. Art program established 1972.

Degrees Bachelor of Fine Arts in the area of studio art. Majors and concentrations: painting/drawing, photography, sculpture, visual communication.

Enrollment Fall 1997: 53 total; 47 undergraduate, 6 non-professional degree.

Art Student Profile 63% females, 37% males, 21% minorities, 12% international.

Art Faculty 6 total (full-time and part-time). 100% of full-time faculty have terminal degrees. Graduate students do not teach undergraduate courses. Undergraduate student–faculty ratio: 12:1.

Student Life Student groups/activities include Art Club.

Expenses for 1997–98 Application fee: $25. Comprehensive fee: $16,100 includes full-time tuition ($10,800) and college room and board ($5300). Special program-related fees: $40 per course for photography lab fees, $10–$40 per course for consumable supplies for studio classes.

Financial Aid Program-specific awards for 1997: 4 art scholarships for above-average students with exceptional artistic ability ($3000).

Application Procedures Students apply for admission into the professional program by sophomore year. Deadline for freshmen and transfers: August 15. Required: high school transcript, college transcript(s) for transfer students, minimum 2.0 high school GPA, letter of recommendation, SAT I or ACT test scores. Recommended: essay, portfolio. Portfolio reviews held on a case-by-case basis on campus; the submission of slides may be substituted for portfolios by prior arrangement.

Undergraduate Contact Mr. Ray Sheenan, Director of Admissions, Caldwell College, 9 Ryerson Avenue, Caldwell, New Jersey 07006; 973-228-4424, fax: 973-228-2897, E-mail address: djohnson@caldwell.edu.

▼ California College of Arts and Crafts

San Francisco, California

Independent, coed. Urban campus. Art program established 1907.

Degrees Bachelor of Fine Arts in the areas of furniture, glass, ceramics, sculpture, painting, drawing, printmaking, photography, textiles, jewelry/metal arts, graphic design, illustration, industrial design, interior architecture, fashion design, film/video; Bachelor of Architecture. Majors and concentrations: architecture, ceramic art and design, fashion design, film and video production, furniture design, glass, graphic arts, illustration, industrial design, interior architecture,

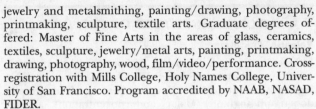

jewelry and metalsmithing, painting/drawing, photography, printmaking, sculpture, textile arts. Graduate degrees offered: Master of Fine Arts in the areas of glass, ceramics, textiles, sculpture, jewelry/metal arts, painting, printmaking, drawing, photography, wood, film/video/performance. Cross-registration with Mills College, Holy Names College, University of San Francisco. Program accredited by NAAB, NASAD, FIDER.

Enrollment Fall 1997: 1,120 total; 991 undergraduate, 82 graduate, 47 non-professional degree.

Art Student Profile 61% females, 39% males, 23% minorities, 11% international.

Art Faculty 240 total undergraduate and graduate (full-time and part-time). 62% of full-time faculty have terminal degrees. Graduate students do not teach undergraduate courses. Undergraduate student–faculty ratio: 10:1.

Student Life Student groups/activities include American Institute of Graphic Arts, American Institute of Architects, American Society of Interior Designers. Special housing available for art students.

Expenses for 1997–98 Application fee: $30. Comprehensive fee: $20,844 includes full-time tuition ($15,850), mandatory fees ($100), and college room and board ($4894). College room only: $2500. Full-time tuition and fees vary according to course load. Room and board charges vary according to housing facility. Special program-related fees: $25–$250 per year for lab fees, $170 per year for registration fee.

Financial Aid Program-specific awards for 1997: 100 Creative Achievement Awards for freshmen ($1000–$8000), 60 Faculty Honors Awards for transfer students ($1000–$7000), 30 Alumni Honors Awards for second degree students ($2000–$5000), 700 CCAC Scholarships for students demonstrating need ($1000–$10,000), 50 Named Scholarships for those demonstrating need ($1000–$10,000), 40 Diversity Scholarships for under-represented populations ($2500–$10,000).

Application Procedures Students admitted directly into the professional program freshman year. Deadline for freshmen and transfers: continuous. Required: essay, high school transcript, college transcript(s) for transfer students, minimum 2.0 high school GPA, 2 letters of recommendation, interview, portfolio, TOEFL score for international applicants. Recommended: SAT I or ACT test scores. Portfolio reviews held continuously on campus; the submission of slides may be substituted for portfolios (slides preferred).

Web Site http://www.ccac-art.edu.

Undergraduate Contact Ms. Sheri McKenzie, Director, Office of Enrollment Services, California College of Arts and Crafts, 450 Irwin Street, San Francisco, California 94107; 415-703-9523, fax: 415-703-9539, E-mail address: enroll@ccac-art.edu.

Graduate Contact Mr. Steven Goldstine, Director, Graduate Office, California College of Arts and Crafts, 5212 Broadway, Oakland, California 94618; 510-594-3667, fax: 510-428-1346, E-mail address: enroll@ccac_art.edu.

More About the College

Program Facilities From the award-winning Simpson Sculpture Studio on the Oakland campus to the spacious, light-filled design studios on the San Francisco campus, CCAC's studios and shops offer students access to a myriad of facilities that support the design and art-making process. The Oakland campus features the Treadwell Ceramic Arts Center, sculpture facilities that include one of the largest working campus foundries and jewelry/metals, textile, and extensive glass facilities. Also on this campus are painting and drawing studios, the printshop, and photography and film/video

facilities. The San Francisco campus houses the design and architecture programs and includes design studios, fashion facilities, dedicated studio space for graduate students, painting/drawing studios, and three large shops for model-making and wood/furniture design. Computer facilities are available at both campuses, including four separate image labs containing the latest Apple technology. CCAC's galleries include the Oliver Art Center on the Oakland campus, which shows work by contemporary artists; and on the San Francisco campus, the Tecoah and Thomas Bruce Galleries, which feature design and architecture exhibitions, and the new Logan Center, which serves as a forum for the presentation and discussion of leading edge contemporary culture.

Faculty, Resident Artists, and Alumni Faculty work resides in the Museum of Modern Art, New York; the Whitney Museum; the Hirshhorn Museum; the Smithsonian Institution; and other major institutions. Architecture and Design faculty members are recognized internationally. Noted alumni include painters Raymond Saunders, Manuel Neri, and Squeak Carnwath; ceramicists Robert Arneson and Peter Voulkos; filmmaker Wayne Wang; and designers Lucille Tenazas and Michael Vanderbyl. Through CCAC's Institute for Exhibitions and Public Programs Capp Street Project, acclaimed artists, designers, and architects visit CCAC each semester to enhance the studio experience.

Student Exhibitions Ongoing exhibitions show student work in the Irwin Student Center, Isabelle Percy West Gallery, and the Tecoah and Thomas Bruce Galleries. In addition, annual B.F.A. and M.F.A. shows are held in the Oliver Art Center and graduate exhibitions are shown in the Logan Center.

Special Programs CCAC students may enrich their studies abroad or through the AICAD Mobility Program with other

California College of Arts and Crafts (*continued*)

art colleges or by cross registration with the University of San Francisco, Mills College, and Holy Names College.

▼

Since 1907, California College of Arts and Crafts has educated young artists to take a leadership role in the work of art and design. Today, after completing a diversified program in the arts and the humanities, CCAC students graduate fully prepared to enter the professions of architecture and design or to begin the practice of the fine arts. The College provides in-depth training and an awareness of the broader role artists play in the shaping of culture.

Students at CCAC have an unusual opportunity to work closely in the studio with accomplished artists and designers, many of whom have attained international recognition. CCAC has strong connections to the professional arts community and helps students make the transition from school to career by offering internships in many majors. Students develop professional contacts while still in school and learn to function like working designers, architects, and artists as interns in offices, studios, museums, and arts organizations.

CCAC's location in the San Francisco Bay Area gives its students tremendous access to the arts through world-class museums, galleries, theaters, film festivals, and diverse exhibition and performance spaces. In addition, visiting artists, designers, and writers bring a fresh perspective to the CCAC campus. Stimulating lectures, symposia, studio visits, and other programs are offered throughout the year. Students also work side by side with creative, serious students from around the world who contribute to the atmosphere of camaraderie that exists at the College.

At CCAC, students tend to spend significantly more time in the studio than their counterparts at a liberal arts college or university. The flexible curriculum is designed to meet the individual needs of students preparing to become working architects, designers, and artists. Core courses introduce basic concepts and skills, enabling students to become conversant with several visual languages. Each program allows in-depth exploration of a chosen discipline, while grounding that work in the larger context of the humanities and sciences and art history, theory, and criticism. Educational technology is integrated into the studio curriculum. The College encourages students to find their own expressive voice to explore various media and to consider how theories of art and the practice of art converge.

Students find CCAC's range of interdisciplinary classes to be especially relevant and challenging. Interdisciplinary exploration is reflected through the practice of art in the real world and benefits all those involved. There are collaborations between architecture students and those majoring in glass, between filmmakers and performance artists, and between industrial designers and sculptors. Students also find that CCAC's Ethnic Studies program offers provocative discussion and an appreciation of the cultural milieu in which artists work.

Students who choose CCAC have an opportunity to work with well-known artists and designers, to find support for personal goals, and to prepare for professional achievement. The small size of the College allows for individual attention in the studio. At the same time, a wide range of approaches seeks to ensure a lively exchange of ideas in an environment where excellence is the standard.

▼ CALIFORNIA INSTITUTE OF THE ARTS
Valencia, California

Independent, coed. Suburban campus. Total enrollment: 1,140. Art program established 1971.

Degrees Bachelor of Fine Arts in the areas of art, graphic design, photography. Majors and concentrations: art/fine arts, computer graphics, graphic design, painting/drawing, photography, printmaking, sculpture, studio art, video art. Graduate degrees offered: Master of Fine Arts in the areas of art, graphic design, photography. Program accredited by NASAD.

Enrollment Fall 1997: 274 total; 179 undergraduate, 95 graduate.

Art Student Profile 50% females, 50% males, 30% minorities, 15% international.

Art Faculty 46 total undergraduate and graduate (full-time and part-time). 90% of full-time faculty have terminal degrees. Graduate students do not teach undergraduate courses. Undergraduate student–faculty ratio: 8:1.

Student Life Student groups/activities include Community Arts Partnership (CAP). Special housing available for art students.

Expenses for 1998–99 Application fee: $60. Tuition: $18,120 full-time. Mandatory fees: $65 full-time. College room only: $2800. Room charges vary according to housing facility. Special program-related fees: $65 per semester for universal access fee.

Financial Aid Program-specific awards for 1997: 1–5 Irvine Foundation Awards for minority students ($1000–$5000), 4 Philip Morris Foundation Awards for minority students ($10,000), 120 CalArts Scholarships for those demonstrating merit ($500–$5000).

Application Procedures Students admitted directly into the professional program freshman year. Deadline for freshmen and transfers: February 1. Required: college transcript(s) for transfer students, portfolio. Recommended: essay, letter of recommendation, interview, video (if applicable). Portfolio reviews held continuously on campus; the submission of slides may be substituted for portfolios (slides preferred).

Web Site http://www.calarts.edu/~art.

Undergraduate Contact Ms. Tracy Weed, Associate Director, Office of Admissions, California Institute of the Arts, 24700 McBean Parkway, Valencia, California 91355; 805-255-1050, fax: 805-254-8352.

Graduate Contact Ms. Tracy Weed, Associate Director, Office of Admissions, California Institute of the Arts, 24700 McBean Parkway, Valencia, California 91355; 805-255-1050, fax: 805-254-8352.

More About the Institute

Program Facilities CalArts is a community of approximately 1,000 performing artists, visual artists, and writers located in the suburban hills north of Los Angeles. The college was incorporated in 1961 through the vision and generosity of Walt Disney. CalArts has been at its present 60-acre campus since 1971. On the campus are the main artistic/academic building, sound stages, rehearsal spaces, art studios, recreational facilities and two residence halls. At the undergraduate level in the visual arts, CalArts offers B.F.A. degree programs in character animation, experimental animation, fine arts, graphic design, live action film and video, and photography. Admission is based on talent. The Institute requires a portfolio of recent work and a personal statement.

Portfolios are reviewed and evaluated for admission and financial aid by faculty members only.

Faculty, Resident Artists, and Alumni Contact the admissions office for a free copy of the current admissions bulletin for complete and up-to-date biographies of all faculty members along with lists of alumni and visiting artists.

Special Programs The Community Arts Partnership links CalArts students and faculty members with high school and junior high school students in Watts, East Los Angeles, Pasadena, Santa Clarita, Hollywood, and Venice. The program enables CalArts students to teach, learn, and share their talents in community settings. Other special programs include exchanges with universities in other countries as well as internships at companies and nonprofit organizations throughout southern California. Each spring the placement professionals in the Office of Student Affairs host a series of job fairs attended by companies such as Walt Disney Studios, Warner Brothers, Intel, Broderbund Software, Microsoft, Industrial Light and Magic, and Pixar Industries.

▼ CALIFORNIA STATE UNIVERSITY, CHICO

Chico, California

State-supported, coed. Small town campus. Total enrollment: 14,247.

Degrees Bachelor of Fine Arts in the areas of studio art, interior design. Majors and concentrations: ceramic art and design, computer art, glass, interior design, painting/drawing, printmaking, sculpture, weaving and fibers. Cross-registration with California State University System. Program accredited by NASAD.

Enrollment Fall 1997: 276 total; 26 undergraduate, 250 non-professional degree.

Art Student Profile 54% females, 46% males.

Art Faculty 26 total (full-time and part-time). 100% of full-time faculty have terminal degrees. Graduate students do not teach undergraduate courses. Undergraduate student–faculty ratio: 10:1.

Student Life Student groups/activities include General Student Art Club, Ceramics Student Art Club, Printmaking Club.

Expenses for 1997–98 Application fee: $55. State resident tuition: $0 full-time. Nonresident tuition: $7380 full-time. Mandatory fees: $2075 full-time. Full-time tuition and fees vary according to course load. College room and board: $5129. College room only: $3100. Special program-related fees: $10–$25 per course for materials fee.

Application Procedures Students apply for admission into the professional program by sophomore year. Deadline for freshmen: continuous. Notification date for freshmen: continuous. Required: high school transcript, portfolio, SAT I or ACT test scores. Portfolio reviews held twice on campus; the submission of slides may be substituted for portfolios whenever necessary.

Undergraduate Contact Mr. Vernon Patrick, Chairman, Department of Art and Art History, California State University, Chico, Chico, California 95929-0820; 530-898-5331, E-mail address: vpatrick@oavax.csuchico.edu.

▼ CALIFORNIA STATE UNIVERSITY, FULLERTON

Fullerton, California

State-supported, coed. Suburban campus. Total enrollment: 24,906. Art program established 1962.

Degrees Bachelor of Fine Arts in the areas of drawing/painting, printmaking, sculpture, crafts, ceramics, graphic design, illustration, creative photography. Majors and concentrations: ceramic art and design, craft design, entertainment arts, glass, graphic design, illustration, jewelry and metalsmithing, painting/drawing, photography, printmaking, sculpture. Graduate degrees offered: Master of Fine Arts in the areas of drawing/painting, printmaking, sculpture, ceramics and glass, graphic design, creative photography, illustration, jewelry and metalsmithing, exhibition design. Cross-registration with California State University System. Program accredited by NASAD.

Enrollment Fall 1997: 874 total; 753 undergraduate, 121 graduate.

Art Student Profile 57% females, 43% males, 34% minorities, 5% international.

Art Faculty 83 total undergraduate and graduate (full-time and part-time). 76% of full-time faculty have terminal degrees. Graduate students teach a few undergraduate courses. Undergraduate student–faculty ratio: 19:1.

Student Life Student groups/activities include Orange County AIDS Project, The Art Network, Graphic Design Club.

Expenses for 1997–98 Application fee: $55. State resident tuition: $0 full-time. Nonresident tuition: $7626 full-time. Mandatory fees: $1947 full-time. College room only: $3662. Special program-related fees: $10–$16 per course for lab fees, $10 per course for ceramic glaze fee.

Financial Aid Program-specific awards for 1997: 2 Mert Purkiss Awards for incoming freshmen ($1000), 2–4 Florence Arnold Awards for continuing students ($500), 1–3 John Olson Awards for design/crafts majors ($700), 2–3 Tribute Fund Awards for transfer students ($750), 1 California China Painters Association for traditional/descriptive art majors ($1000), 2 Costa Mesa Art League for juniors or seniors ($500).

Application Procedures Students apply for admission into the professional program by sophomore year. Deadline for freshmen and transfers: continuous. Required: high school transcript, college transcript(s) for transfer students, minimum 2.0 high school GPA, SAT I test score only.

Web Site http://www.arts.fullerton.edu/.

Undergraduate Contact Ms. Karen Bell, Department Secretary, Department of Visual Arts, California State University, Fullerton, Fullerton, California 92834-9480; 714-278-3471, fax: 714-278-2390.

Graduate Contact Ms. Jackie Reynolds, Graduate Secretary, Department of Visual Arts, California State University, Fullerton, Fullerton, California 92834-9480; 714-278-3471, fax: 714-278-2390.

▼ CALIFORNIA STATE UNIVERSITY, LONG BEACH

Long Beach, California

State-supported, coed. Suburban campus. Total enrollment: 27,809. Art program established 1949.

California State University, Long Beach (continued)

Degrees Bachelor of Fine Arts in the areas of art, design. Majors and concentrations: art education, art history, ceramics, fibers, graphic arts, illustration, jewelry and metalsmithing, painting/drawing, photography, printmaking, sculpture, three-dimensional studies. Graduate degrees offered: Master of Fine Arts in the areas of art, design. Cross-registration with California State University System. Program accredited by NASAD.

Enrollment Fall 1997: 1,300 total; 250 undergraduate, 150 graduate, 900 non-professional degree.

Art Student Profile 55% females, 45% males, 55% minorities, 5% international.

Art Faculty 91 total undergraduate and graduate (full-time and part-time). 95% of full-time faculty have terminal degrees. Graduate students teach a few undergraduate courses.

Student Life Student groups/activities include Student Art Association.

Expenses for 1997–98 Application fee: $55. State resident tuition: $0 full-time. Nonresident tuition: $7380 full-time. Mandatory fees: $1846 full-time. Full-time tuition and fees vary according to course load. College room and board: $5200. Room and board charges vary according to board plan. Special program-related fees: $58 per class for model fees.

Financial Aid Program-specific awards for 1997: 25 art scholarships for program majors ($1000).

Application Procedures Students admitted directly into the professional program freshman year. Required: high school transcript, college transcript(s) for transfer students, portfolio, SAT I or ACT test scores, standing in top third of graduating class. Portfolio reviews held twice and as needed on campus; the submission of slides may be substituted for portfolios for out-of-state applicants.

Undergraduate Contact Mr. John Snidecor, Undergraduate Advisor, Art Department, California State University, Long Beach, 1250 Bellflower Boulevard, Long Beach, California 90840-0119; 562-985-4376.

Graduate Contact Ms. Cynthia Osborn, Graduate Advisor, Art Department, California State University, Long Beach, 1250 Bellflower Boulevard, Long Beach, California 90840-0119; 562-985-4376.

▼ CAPITAL UNIVERSITY

Columbus, Ohio

Independent, coed. Suburban campus. Total enrollment: 3,988.

Degrees Bachelor of Fine Arts in the areas of studio art, commercial art. Majors and concentrations: art education, art therapy, art/fine arts. Cross-registration with Higher Education Council of Columbus .

Enrollment Fall 1997: 63 total; all undergraduate.

Art Faculty 7 total (full-time and part-time). 50% of full-time faculty have terminal degrees. Graduate students do not teach undergraduate courses. Undergraduate student–faculty ratio: 9:1.

Student Life Student groups/activities include Capital University Student Art Therapy Association.

Expenses for 1997–98 Application fee: $25. Comprehensive fee: $18,960 includes full-time tuition ($14,760) and college

room and board ($4200). Full-time tuition varies according to program. Room and board charges vary according to board plan.

Financial Aid Program-specific awards for 1997: Special Talent Awards for students that participate in Ohio Governor's Youth Art Exhibit ($1000).

Application Procedures Students admitted directly into the professional program freshman year. Deadline for freshmen and transfers: continuous. Required: high school transcript, letter of recommendation, SAT I or ACT test scores (minimum combined SAT I score of 870, minimum combined ACT score of 17), minimum 2.5 high school GPA. Recommended: interview, portfolio. Portfolio reviews held as needed on campus; the submission of slides may be substituted for portfolios for large works of art.

Web Site http://www.capital.edu.

Undergraduate Contact Ms. Lisa McKitrick, Associate Director of Admission, Admission Office, Capital University, 2199 East Main Street, Columbus, Ohio 43209; 614-236-6101, fax: 614-236-6820, E-mail address: admissions@capital.edu.

▼ CARDINAL STRITCH UNIVERSITY

Milwaukee, Wisconsin

Independent-Roman Catholic, coed. Suburban campus. Total enrollment: 5,316.

Degrees Bachelor of Fine Arts in the areas of art, graphic design, photography. Majors and concentrations: art education, art history, film and video production, graphic design, interdisciplinary studies, painting/drawing, photography, printmaking, three-dimensional studies.

Enrollment Fall 1997: 50 total; all undergraduate.

Art Student Profile 65% females, 35% males, 1% minorities.

Art Faculty 10 total (full-time and part-time). 100% of full-time faculty have terminal degrees. Graduate students do not teach undergraduate courses. Undergraduate student–faculty ratio: 8:1.

Student Life Student groups/activities include Student Art Club.

Expenses for 1997–98 Application fee: $20. Comprehensive fee: $14,410 includes full-time tuition ($10,080), mandatory fees ($50), and college room and board ($4280). College room only: $1560. Special program-related fees: $15–$40 per course for lab fees.

Financial Aid Program-specific awards for 1997: 5–10 art scholarships for those demonstrating talent and academic achievement ($1000–$4000).

Application Procedures Students admitted directly into the professional program freshman year. Deadline for freshmen and transfers: continuous. Required: essay, high school transcript, college transcript(s) for transfer students, minimum 2.0 high school GPA, portfolio, SAT I or ACT test scores. Recommended: interview. Portfolio reviews held as needed on campus; the submission of slides may be substituted for portfolios if a campus visit is impossible.

Web Site http://www.stritch.edu.

Undergraduate Contact David Wegener, Director of Admissions, Admissions Department, Cardinal Stritch University, 6801 North Yates Road, Milwaukee, Wisconsin 53217; 414-410-4000, fax: 414-410-4239.

▼ CARNEGIE MELLON UNIVERSITY

Pittsburgh, Pennsylvania

Independent, coed. Urban campus. Total enrollment: 7,912. Art program established 1910.

Degrees Bachelor of Fine Arts in the area of art. Graduate degrees offered: Master of Fine Arts in the area of art. Cross-registration with Chatham College, University of Pittsburgh, Duquesne University, Carlow College, Point Park College, Robert Morris College, Community College of Allegheny County, Pittsburgh Theological Seminary, LaRoche College. Program accredited by NASAD.

Enrollment Fall 1997: 182 total; 167 undergraduate, 15 graduate.

Art Student Profile 58% females, 16% minorities, 10% international.

Art Faculty 28 total undergraduate and graduate (full-time and part-time). 100% of full-time faculty have terminal degrees. Graduate students do not teach undergraduate courses. Undergraduate student–faculty ratio: 10:1.

Expenses for 1997–98 Application fee: $45. Comprehensive fee: $26,600 includes full-time tuition ($20,275), mandatory fees ($100), and college room and board ($6225). College room only: $3845. Room and board charges vary according to board plan.

Application Procedures Students admitted directly into the professional program freshman year. Deadline for freshmen and transfers: January 1. Notification date for freshmen and transfers: continuous. Required: high school transcript, college transcript(s) for transfer students, 3 letters of recommendation, portfolio, SAT I or ACT test scores. Recommended: minimum 3.0 high school GPA, interview. Portfolio reviews held 8 times on campus and off campus; the submission of slides may be substituted for portfolios (slides preferred).

Web Site http://www-art.cfa.cmu.edu.

Undergraduate Contact Admissions Office, Carnegie Mellon University, 5000 Forbes Avenue, Pittsburgh, Pennsylvania 15213-3890; 412-268-2082.

Graduate Contact Ms. Monica Palkovic, Graduate Program and Publications Assistant, School of Art, Carnegie Mellon University, College of Fine Arts, 5000 Forbes Avenue, Room 300B, Pittsburgh, Pennsylvania 15213-3890; 412-268-8001, fax: 412-268-7817, E-mail address: monicax@andrew.cmu.edu.

▼ CAZENOVIA COLLEGE

Cazenovia, New York

Independent, coed. Small town campus. Total enrollment: 897. Art program established 1993.

Degrees Bachelor of Fine Arts in the areas of visual communications, interior environmental design. Majors and concentrations: advertising graphic design, illustration.

Enrollment Fall 1997: 126 total; all undergraduate.

Art Student Profile 70% females, 30% males, 18% minorities, 1% international.

Art Faculty 20 total (full-time and part-time). 75% of full-time faculty have terminal degrees. Graduate students do not teach undergraduate courses. Undergraduate student–faculty ratio: 7:1.

Student Life Student groups/activities include Art Club, Fashion Design Club, Theater Group.

Estimated expenses for 1998–99 Application fee: $25. Comprehensive fee: $17,918 includes full-time tuition ($11,568), mandatory fees ($422), and college room and board ($5928). College room only: $3178. Room and board charges vary according to board plan. Special program-related fees: $98 per course for ceramics fee, $80 per course for photography fee.

Financial Aid Program-specific awards for 1997: merit scholarships for art majors.

Application Procedures Students admitted directly into the professional program freshman year. Deadline for freshmen and transfers: continuous. Required: high school transcript, college transcript(s) for transfer students, minimum 2.0 high school GPA. Recommended: essay, minimum 3.0 high school GPA, 2 letters of recommendation, portfolio, SAT I or ACT test scores. Portfolio reviews held as needed on campus and off campus in Lake Placid, NY and at least one other location; the submission of slides may be substituted for portfolios when distance is prohibitive or if scheduling is difficult.

Undergraduate Contact Mr. Matthew Fox, Counselor, Admissions and Financial Aid, Cazenovia College, 13 Nickerson Street, Cazenovia, New York 13035; 315-655-7208, fax: 315-655-4486, E-mail address: mfox@cazcollege.edu.

▼ CENTENARY COLLEGE

Hackettstown, New Jersey

Independent, coed. Suburban campus. Total enrollment: 959.

Degrees Bachelor of Fine Arts in the areas of interior design, art and design.

Enrollment Fall 1997: 49 total; all undergraduate.

Art Student Profile 76% females, 24% males, 5% international.

Art Faculty 6 total (full-time and part-time). 75% of full-time faculty have terminal degrees. Graduate students do not teach undergraduate courses. Undergraduate student–faculty ratio: 8:1.

Student Life Student groups/activities include American Society of Interior Designers, Art Guild, Performing Arts Guild.

Expenses for 1997–98 Application fee: $25, $50 for international students. Comprehensive fee: $19,060 includes full-time tuition ($12,900), mandatory fees ($360), and college room and board ($5800). Full-time tuition and fees vary according to program.

Application Procedures Students admitted directly into the professional program freshman year. Deadline for freshmen and transfers: continuous. Notification date for freshmen and transfers: continuous. Required: essay, high school transcript, college transcript(s) for transfer students, portfolio, SAT I or ACT test scores. Recommended: minimum 2.0 high school GPA, 2 letters of recommendation, interview. Portfolio reviews held as needed on campus; the submission of slides may be substituted for portfolios when distance is prohibitive.

Web Site http://www.centenarycollege.edu.

Undergraduate Contact Mr. Dennis Kelly, Vice President for Enrollment Management, Centenary College, 400 Jefferson Street, Hackettstown, New Jersey 07840; 800-236-8679, fax: 908-852-3454, E-mail address: admissions@centenarycollege.edu.

▼ CENTER FOR CREATIVE STUDIES— COLLEGE OF ART AND DESIGN

Detroit, Michigan

Independent, coed. Urban campus. Total enrollment: 975. Art program established 1926.

Degrees Bachelor of Fine Arts in the areas of fine arts, crafts, photography, graphic communication, industrial design, interior design, animation/digital media. Majors and concentrations: animation, art direction, art/fine arts, ceramic art and design, commercial art, computer art, furniture design, glass, illustration, interior design, jewelry and metalsmithing, painting/drawing, photography, printmaking, product design, sculpture, studio art, textile arts, transportation design. Cross-registration with Association of Independent Colleges of Art and Design. Program accredited by NASAD.

Enrollment Fall 1997: 975 total; all undergraduate.

Art Student Profile 41% females, 59% males, 21% minorities, 4% international.

Art Faculty 196 total (full-time and part-time). 45% of full-time faculty have terminal degrees. Graduate students do not teach undergraduate courses. Undergraduate student–faculty ratio: 11:1.

Student Life Student groups/activities include Student Council, Black Artists Researching Trends, Industrial Design Society of America. Special housing available for art students.

Expenses for 1998–99 Application fee: $35. Tuition: $14,280 full-time. Mandatory fees: $216 full-time. College room only: $3100. Room charges vary according to housing facility. Special program-related fees: $150–$300 for lab/material fees.

Financial Aid Program-specific awards for 1997: 1 Award of Excellence for high school seniors ($14,280), Entering Scholarships for entering students ($1500–$4000), 12 Walter B. Ford Scholarships for entering students ($8000).

Application Procedures Students admitted directly into the professional program freshman year. Deadline for freshmen and transfers: continuous. Notification date for freshmen and transfers: August 15. Required: high school transcript, college transcript(s) for transfer students, interview, portfolio, SAT I or ACT test scores (minimum combined ACT score of 20), minimum 2.5 high school GPA. Recommended: essay, 2 letters of recommendation. Portfolio reviews held throughout the year on campus; the submission of slides may be substituted for portfolios for large works of art or when distance is prohibitive.

Web Site http://www.ccscad.edu.

Undergraduate Contact Mrs. Pat Glascock, Director of Admissions, Center for Creative Studies—College of Art and Design, 201 East Kirby Street, Detroit, Michigan 48202; 800-952-ARTS, fax: 313-872-2739.

More About the College

The Center for Creative Studies—College of Art and Design is among the nation's leading colleges of art and design. Students can pursue a Bachelor of Fine Arts in twenty majors and two minors within the following departments: Crafts, Fine Arts, Graphic Communication, Industrial Design, Interior Design, Photography, and Animation/Digital Media.

At CCS, first-year students can enter their chosen department and begin to concentrate their studies in one area or spend their first semester "undeclared" and take an orientation class to learn about the three areas that interest them the most. While students are immersed in their chosen area of study upon entering CCS, they are also encouraged to take classes outside of their major to broaden their skills. For example, graphic communication students may find a printmaking or watercolor class useful to their approach to design.

Each department emphasizes four distinct components of a visual arts education: technical skill, aesthetic sensibility, conceptual ability, and practical experience. The program combines studio and academic classes with more individualized instruction. Upper-level students have the opportunity to begin working independently in private and semiprivate studio settings. Internships give students an opportunity to work side by side with art and design professionals. This educational approach prepares students for success after graduation.

Additionally, students may earn elective credit through the Institute of Music and Dance, a nondegree-granting adjunct of CCS. Dance classes include ballet, tap, and modern. Voice and music instruction is offered in private and group settings.

CCS's faculty consists of professional artists and designers who are also working and exhibiting in their field of expertise. They provide students with an immediate connection to the real world by bringing new trends, practical insights, and networking opportunities to the college, shedding a realistic light on theoretical classroom exercises. Students are assigned a faculty academic adviser in their department upon entering the school.

Studies at CCS are also fully supported by practical resources. The College has woodworking, metalsmithing, and glassblowing studios; a foundry; a visual arts library with a large collection of art and design publications; photography facilities with studios, darkrooms, film editing, and animation equipment; and an on-site digital imaging service bureau offering computerized typesetting and color laser printing.

The Academic Advising Center helps with general advising questions regarding scheduling, transfer credits, and a mobility program. The center also provides personal counseling. Students in need of academic assistance have access to the Student Success Center. Here, trained professionals help students on academic probation, or those with learning disabilities develop study skills and time management. They also help students improve their language, reading, and writing abilities. A career counselor is available to assist current students with internships and summer jobs, while also helping graduating seniors or CCS alumni secure jobs.

Computer facilities are constantly updated to adapt to rapidly changing technology. Currently, there are four Macintosh labs, running QuarkXpress, Pagemaker, Illustrator, Freehand, and Photoshop software; Silicon Graphics workstations running Alias Wavefront U4IA; and Intergraph labs with Auto CAD 3D Studio Max software. Desktop publishing, illustration, multimedia, Web page design, digital imaging, and animation are among the available computer courses.

Private and semiprivate studio space is available to many advanced students. This gives them the space to develop a serious body of work. While these students have the freedom to cultivate their own personal vision and style, they are regularly visited by faculty members for critique and guidance.

CCS students have many opportunities to exhibit their work publicly. Work is displayed in the student-run gallery, the Underground 245, and at events such as Open House and the Detroit Festival of the Arts. The annual Student Exhibition, held in conjunction with commencement, is a major public event that draws thousands of people who can view and purchase student artwork.

CCS's location is a valuable resource in itself. The campus is situated in Detroit's University Cultural Center. It is within walking distance of a number of educational institutions and museums, including the Detroit Institute of Arts (the nation's fifth-largest museum), the Museum of African-American History, the Detroit Public Library, and Wayne State University. The surrounding metropolitan area is also inspiring to art students, with theaters and cafés, eclectic neighborhoods, and galleries displaying the work of emerging and established artists.

Along with cultural resources, professional opportunities abound in the Detroit area. For example, automotive manufacturing and supply industries have a constant need for creative industrial designers, and because Detroit is the fourth-largest advertising city in the U.S., creative professionals are in constant demand.

For a visual arts education that stresses the personal development of style and vision and the practical experience needed to succeed in the real world, the Center for Creative Studies is an excellent educational option.

▼ CENTRAL MICHIGAN UNIVERSITY

Mount Pleasant, Michigan

State-supported, coed. Small town campus. Total enrollment: 24,747.

Degrees Bachelor of Fine Arts in the areas of two-dimensional studies, three-dimensional studies, graphic design. Majors and concentrations: art education, ceramics, design, fibers, graphic design, jewelry and metalsmithing, painting/drawing, photography, printmaking, sculpture. Graduate degrees offered: Master of Fine Arts in the area of studio art. Program accredited by NASAD.

Enrollment Fall 1997: 144 total; 135 undergraduate, 9 graduate.

Art Student Profile 51% females, 49% males, 1% minorities, 5% international.

Art Faculty 21 total undergraduate and graduate (full-time and part-time). 100% of full-time faculty have terminal degrees. Graduate students teach a few undergraduate courses. Undergraduate student–faculty ratio: 22:1.

Student Life Student groups/activities include Photography Club, Students in Design, Student Art League.

Expenses for 1997–98 Application fee: $25. State resident tuition: $3066 full-time. Nonresident tuition: $7961 full-time. Mandatory fees: $480 full-time. College room and board: $4320. College room only: $2004. Room and board charges vary according to board plan and housing facility. Special program-related fees: $8–$13 per course for supplies.

Financial Aid Program-specific awards for 1997: 4–8 art scholarships for art majors ($500–$1000).

Application Procedures Students apply for admission into the professional program by freshman, sophomore year. Deadline for freshmen and transfers: continuous. Required: high school transcript, college transcript(s) for transfer students, SAT I or ACT test scores.

Undergraduate Contact Mr. Richard Janis, Chair, Art Department, Central Michigan University, 132 Wightman Hall, Mount Pleasant, Michigan 48859; 517-774-3025.

Graduate Contact Mr. David Fisher, Graduate Coordinator, Art Department, Central Michigan University, 132 Wightman Hall, Mount Pleasant, Michigan 48859; 517-774-3500.

▼ CENTRAL MISSOURI STATE UNIVERSITY

Warrensburg, Missouri

State-supported, coed. Small town campus. Total enrollment: 10,320.

Degrees Bachelor of Fine Arts in the areas of commercial art, interior design, studio art. Majors and concentrations: art education, commercial art, graphic design, illustration, interior design, studio art. Program accredited by NASAD.

Enrollment Fall 1997: 325 undergraduate.

Art Student Profile 60% females, 40% males, 5% minorities, 5% international.

Art Faculty 16 total (full-time and part-time). 100% of full-time faculty have terminal degrees. Graduate students teach a few undergraduate courses. Undergraduate student–faculty ratio: 20:1.

Student Life Special housing available for art students.

Expenses for 1997–98 Application fee: $25. State resident tuition: $2640 full-time. Nonresident tuition: $5280 full-time. College room and board: $4080. Room and board charges vary according to board plan and housing facility. Special program-related fees: $5–$25 for consumable supplies.

Financial Aid Program-specific awards for 1997: 20–30 Art Achievement Awards for incoming freshmen ($200–$600).

Application Procedures Students admitted directly into the professional program freshman year. Deadline for freshmen and transfers: continuous. Required: high school transcript, college transcript(s) for transfer students, ACT test score only (minimum combined ACT score of 20). Recommended: standing in top 67% of graduating class, completion of high school core curriculum.

Undergraduate Contact Ms. Delores Hudson, Director of Admissions, Central Missouri State University, Administration Building 104, Warrensburg, Missouri 64093; 816-543-4290, fax: 816-543-8517.

▼ CLARION UNIVERSITY OF PENNSYLVANIA

Clarion, Pennsylvania

State-supported, coed. Rural campus. Total enrollment: 5,948. Art program established 1980.

Degrees Bachelor of Fine Arts in the area of art. Majors and concentrations: ceramics, drawing, graphic arts, painting, printmaking, sculpture, textile arts.

Enrollment Fall 1997: 51 undergraduate.

Art Student Profile 55% females, 45% males, 2% minorities, 1% international.

Art Faculty 9 total undergraduate (full-time and part-time). 100% of full-time faculty have terminal degrees. Graduate students do not teach undergraduate courses. Undergraduate student–faculty ratio: 6:1.

Student Life Student groups/activities include VizArts (visual arts association).

Expenses for 1997–98 Application fee: $25. State resident tuition: $3468 full-time. Nonresident tuition: $8824 full-time. Mandatory fees: $951 full-time. Full-time tuition and fees vary according to course load. College room and board: $3330. College room only: $1980.

Clarion University of Pennsylvania (continued)

Financial Aid Program-specific awards for 1997: 4–5 Lesser Scholarships for program students ($500).

Application Procedures Students admitted directly into the professional program freshman year. Deadline for freshmen and transfers: continuous. Required: high school transcript, college transcript(s) for transfer students, minimum 2.0 high school GPA, SAT I or ACT test scores, portfolio for scholarship consideration. Recommended: essay, letter of recommendation. Portfolio reviews held twice on campus; the submission of slides may be substituted for portfolios.

Web Site http://www.clarion.edu.

Undergraduate Contact Chair, Art Department, Clarion University of Pennsylvania, 114 Marwick-Boyd, Clarion, Pennsylvania 16214; 814-226-2291, fax: 814-226-2723.

▼ CLARKE COLLEGE

Dubuque, Iowa

Independent-Roman Catholic, coed. Urban campus. Total enrollment: 1,160. Art program established 1843.

Degrees Bachelor of Fine Arts in the areas of studio art, graphic design. Majors and concentrations: ceramics, drawing, graphic design, painting, printmaking, sculpture.

Enrollment Fall 1997: 46 total; 13 undergraduate, 33 non-professional degree.

Art Student Profile 72% females, 28% males, 3% minorities.

Art Faculty 9 total (full-time and part-time). 80% of full-time faculty have terminal degrees. Graduate students do not teach undergraduate courses. Undergraduate student–faculty ratio: 12:1.

Expenses for 1997–98 Application fee: $20. Comprehensive fee: $16,994 includes full-time tuition ($12,199), mandatory fees ($240), and college room and board ($4555). College room only: $2246. Full-time tuition and fees vary according to class time and reciprocity agreements.

Financial Aid Program-specific awards for 1997: 4–6 art scholarships for incoming students ($500–$2000).

Application Procedures Students apply for admission into the professional program by sophomore year. Deadline for freshmen and transfers: continuous. Required: high school transcript, college transcript(s) for transfer students, minimum 2.0 high school GPA, letter of recommendation, portfolio, SAT I or ACT test scores (minimum combined SAT I score of 1015, minimum combined ACT score of 21). Recommended: essay, interview. Portfolio reviews held by appointment from January to April on campus; the submission of slides may be substituted for portfolios when distance is prohibitive.

Undergraduate Contact Mr. John Foley, Director, Office of Admissions, Clarke College, 1550 Clarke Avenue, Dubuque, Iowa 52001; 319-588-6366, fax: 319-588-6789.

▼ CLEVELAND INSTITUTE OF ART

Cleveland, Ohio

Independent, coed. Urban campus. Total enrollment: 481. Art program established 1882.

Degrees Bachelor of Fine Arts in the areas of ceramics, drawing, enameling, fiber, glass, industrial design, interior design, graphic design, illustration, medical illustration, painting, photography, printmaking, metals, sculpture. Majors and concentrations: ceramics, drawing, enameling, fibers, glass, graphic design, illustration, industrial design, interior design, medical illustration, metals, painting, photography, printmaking, sculpture. Cross-registration with members of the Northeast Ohio Council on Higher Education. Program accredited by NASAD.

Enrollment Fall 1997: 473 total; 453 undergraduate, 20 non-professional degree.

Art Student Profile 47% females, 53% males, 18% minorities, 5% international.

Art Faculty 75 total (full-time and part-time). 99% of full-time faculty have terminal degrees. Graduate students do not teach undergraduate courses. Undergraduate student–faculty ratio: 11:1.

Student Life Student groups/activities include Industrial Design Society of America. Special housing available for art students.

Expenses for 1997–98 Application fee: $30. Comprehensive fee: $18,100 includes full-time tuition ($12,870), mandatory fees ($300), and college room and board ($4930). College room only: $2870. Special program-related fees: $57 per course for lab fees.

Financial Aid Program-specific awards for 1997: 10 Portfolio Scholarships for freshmen ($7000–$13,500), 100 Portfolio Grants ($2000–$5000), 18 Transfer Portfolio Grants for transfer students ($2000–$5000).

Application Procedures Students admitted directly into the professional program freshman year. Deadline for freshmen and transfers: continuous. Required: essay, high school transcript, college transcript(s) for transfer students, minimum 2.0 high school GPA, 2 letters of recommendation, portfolio, SAT I or ACT test scores. Recommended: interview. Portfolio reviews held bi-monthly on campus; the submission of slides may be substituted for portfolios (slides preferred).

Web Site http://www.cia.edu.

Undergraduate Contact Ms. Catherine Redhead, Director of Admissions, Cleveland Institute of Art, 11141 East Boulevard, Cleveland, Ohio 44106; 216-421-7422, fax: 216-421-7438.

More About the Institute

Program Facilities Individual studio spaces for students in a major; four computer labs for use in liberal arts and studio classes; two-story shooting studio for photography students; multimedia laboratory for photo/video production; foundry for sculpture; interdisciplinary studio space adjacent to majors' space.

Faculty, Resident Artists, and Alumni The faculty is a strong teaching group. Since CIA is exclusively undergraduate, professors—not graduate assistants—teach. But while they are teachers, faculty members are all working professionals. This shows in the awards they have received—from Emmys and IDSA Awards to the Outstanding American Educator award and the Ohio Designer Craftsman Award for Excellence. Faculty members have lectured everywhere from Alfred University to Yale University, teaching at locations ranging from Aichi University in Japan to San Diego State University to Glasgow School of Art. Faculty artwork can be seen in collections ranging from those at the Art Institute of Chicago to the Library of Congress. Clients like the Cleveland Indians, Black & Decker, and Sherwin-Williams are well served by this high-caliber assembly.

Student Performance and Exhibit Opportunities Generous student gallery space for group shows; "Coffeehouse" gallery space for majors' shows; Jessica R. Gund Memorial Library gallery

The University Circle area surrounding the Institute is a rich resource for students. The Cleveland Museum of Art, Severance Hall for the Cleveland Orchestra, and Case Western Reserve University are just a few of the educational and cultural organizations located "in the Circle." Originally the University Circle was developed in a parklike setting away from manufacturing as a center for the cultural institutions of Cleveland. Now, with a rebirth of Cleveland, the "Circle" and the Institute are minutes away by rapid transit or car from the "Flats," Jacobs Field, and the Rock and Roll Hall of Fame.

Career Services offers a monthly Jobline, which highlights potential offerings from a national and international pool of part-time, freelance, and full-time jobs. Opportunities are gleaned from many sources and also include competitions and possibilities for student and alumni shows. The Career Services office is not only for soon-to-be-graduates or recent alumni; students use the services throughout their careers at the Institute. Coordinating internships and assistance in finding the right part-time job to pay for school are just a part of a multifaceted operation. There is also a computer database of potential employers.

Sometimes, student concern about concentrating solely in the visual arts surfaces. Such students may choose to focus on particular liberal arts minors such as art and film history, literature/criticism/creative writing, multicultural studies, and art therapy. Opting for Honors in all of the liberal arts courses is also possible. If these offerings do not match the students' needs, cross-registration may be undertaken with fourteen different colleges and universities in and around Cleveland at no additional cost. Students can create a program that rivals most comprehensive universities and still includes emphasis on art.

"Quality before quantity" for those seeking "professional art careers" permeates the Cleveland Institute of Art.

▼ **THE COLLEGE OF NEW JERSEY**

Trenton, New Jersey

State-supported, coed. Suburban campus. Total enrollment: 6,780.

Degrees Bachelor of Fine Arts in the areas of fine arts, graphic design; Bachelor of Arts in the area of art education.

Enrollment Fall 1997: 325 total; all undergraduate.

Art Student Profile 65% females, 35% males, 22% minorities.

Art Faculty 34 total (full-time and part-time). 100% of full-time faculty have terminal degrees. Graduate students do not teach undergraduate courses. Undergraduate student–faculty ratio: 15:1.

Student Life Student groups/activities include Art Directors Club of New Jersey, National Art Education Association.

Expenses for 1997–98 Application fee: $50. State resident tuition: $3791 full-time. Nonresident tuition: $6620 full-time. Mandatory fees: $1052 full-time. College room and board: $5996. Room and board charges vary according to board plan. Special program-related fees: $10–$25 per semester for supplemental materials.

Application Procedures Students admitted directly into the professional program freshman year. Deadline for freshmen and transfers: March 1. Notification date for freshmen and transfers: April 1. Required: essay, high school transcript, college transcript(s) for transfer students, portfolio, SAT I test score only. Recommended: minimum 3.0 high school GPA, letter of recommendation. Portfolio reviews held 5

space for individual and group shows; annual Student Independent Show in the Reinberger Galleries; "Parade the Circle" festival in University Circle; various local restaurants, coffeehouses, and gallery connections.

Special Programs New York Studio program; extensive internship potential (students develop their own with faculty guidance or choose from a wide array of internships on file); cross-registration with fourteen other colleges and universities in and around Cleveland; nationally known artists for intensive summer workshops; wide range of tutoring possibilities in liberal arts courses; art education major in conjunction with Case Western Reserve University for undergraduates and opportunities for graduate work through Case Western; medical illustration students work with the Medical and Dental Schools of Case Western Reserve University, University Hospitals, Cleveland Clinic Foundation, and Mt. Sinai Hospital.

▼

The Cleveland Institute of Art (CIA) is not about numbers but about individual students learning and developing as artists. In its mission statement, the Institute states its aim "to provide a quality education" to those "who seek professional art careers . . . to demonstrate leadership in education in the visual arts, putting consideration of quality before quantity." This goal is evident throughout the Institute.

The College of New Jersey (*continued*)

times on campus; the submission of slides may be substituted for portfolios for international applicants or when distance is prohibitive.

Undergraduate Contact Office of Admissions, The College of New Jersey, Green Hall, Trenton, New Jersey 08650-4700; 609-771-2131.

▼ COLLEGE OF NEW ROCHELLE

New Rochelle, New York

Independent, primarily women. Suburban campus. Total enrollment: 7,065.

Degrees Bachelor of Fine Arts in the areas of studio art, art therapy, art education. Majors and concentrations: art education, art history, art therapy, art/fine arts, studio art. Cross-registration with Iona College.

Enrollment Fall 1997: 60 undergraduate.

Art Student Profile 100% females.

Art Faculty 9 total (full-time and part-time). 100% of full-time faculty have terminal degrees. Graduate students do not teach undergraduate courses. Undergraduate student–faculty ratio: 10:1.

Student Life Student groups/activities include Props and Paint, Art Student League.

Expenses for 1997–98 Application fee: $20. Comprehensive fee: $16,800 includes full-time tuition ($11,000), mandatory fees ($100), and college room and board ($5700). Full-time tuition and fees vary according to course load. Room and board charges vary according to housing facility.

Financial Aid Program-specific awards for 1997: art scholarships for program majors ($2000).

Application Procedures Students admitted directly into the professional program freshman year. Deadline for freshmen and transfers: continuous. Required: high school transcript, college transcript(s) for transfer students, minimum 2.0 high school GPA, SAT I or ACT test scores. Recommended: essay, letter of recommendation, interview, portfolio. Portfolio reviews held 10 times on campus; the submission of slides may be substituted for portfolios if a campus visit is impossible.

Web Site http://www.cnr.edu.

Undergraduate Contact Ms. Susan M. Canning, Chair, Art Department, School of Arts and Sciences, College of New Rochelle, 29 Castle Place, New Rochelle, New York 10805; 914-654-5275, fax: 914-654-5290.

▼ THE COLLEGE OF SAINT ROSE

Albany, New York

Independent, coed. Urban campus. Total enrollment: 3,973. Art program established 1995.

Degrees Bachelor of Fine Arts in the areas of studio art, graphic design. Majors and concentrations: graphic design, painting, photography, printmaking, sculpture, studio art. Graduate degrees offered: Master of Science in the area of art education. Cross-registration with University at Albany, State University of New York, Rensselaer Polytechnic Institute, Skidmore College. Program accredited by NASAD.

Enrollment Fall 1997: 248 total; 149 undergraduate, 34 graduate, 65 non-professional degree.

Art Student Profile 75% females, 25% males, 3% minorities, 1% international.

Art Faculty 21 total undergraduate and graduate (full-time and part-time). 100% of full-time faculty have terminal degrees. Graduate students do not teach undergraduate courses. Undergraduate student–faculty ratio: 16:1.

Student Life Student groups/activities include New York State Art Teachers Association, National Association of Schools of Art and Design, College Art Association.

Expenses for 1997–98 Application fee: $25. Comprehensive fee: $17,685 includes full-time tuition ($11,564), mandatory fees ($155), and college room and board ($5966). College room only: $2786. Full-time tuition and fees vary according to course load and program. Room and board charges vary according to board plan. Special program-related fees: $30–$100 per semester for material fees for some studio classes.

Financial Aid Program-specific awards for 1997: 15 art scholarships for incoming freshmen ($1000–$6000).

Application Procedures Students apply for admission into the professional program by sophomore year. Deadline for freshmen and transfers: continuous. Required: essay, high school transcript, college transcript(s) for transfer students, minimum 2.0 high school GPA, letter of recommendation, portfolio, SAT I or ACT test scores. Recommended: interview. Portfolio reviews held 4-5 times on campus and off campus in Boston, MA; Syracuse, NY; Hartford, CT; Philadelphia, PA; New York, NY on National Portfolio Days; the submission of slides may be substituted for portfolios if original work is not available.

Undergraduate Contact Ms. Mary Grondahl, Dean of Admissions, The College of Saint Rose, 432 Western Avenue, Albany, New York 12203; 518-454-5150.

Graduate Contact Ms. Karene Tarquin Faul, Head, Art Department, The College of Saint Rose, 432 Western Avenue, Albany, New York 12203; 518-485-3900, fax: 518-485-3920, E-mail address: faulk@rosnet.strose.edu.

▼ COLLEGE OF SANTA FE

Santa Fe, New Mexico

Independent, coed. Suburban campus. Total enrollment: 1,417. Art program established 1984.

Degrees Bachelor of Fine Arts in the area of studio art; Bachelor of Arts in the area of art history. Majors and concentrations: digital multi-media, multimedia, painting/drawing, photography, printmaking, sculpture.

Enrollment Fall 1997: 150 total; 120 undergraduate, 30 non-professional degree.

Art Student Profile 65% females, 35% males, 25% minorities, 5% international.

Art Faculty 12 total (full-time and part-time). 85% of full-time faculty have terminal degrees. Graduate students do not teach undergraduate courses. Undergraduate student–faculty ratio: 10:1.

Student Life Student groups/activities include Art Student Association (art club), Multimedia Art Student Association.

Expenses for 1997–98 Application fee: $25. Comprehensive fee: $17,964 includes full-time tuition ($13,000), mandatory fees ($240), and college room and board ($4724). College room only: $2308. Room and board charges vary according to board plan and housing facility. Special program-related fees: $10–$100 per course for studio fee.

Financial Aid Program-specific awards for 1997: 15–20 Talent Scholarships for entering freshmen art students ($2500), 5–10 Presidential Scholars for entering freshmen art majors ($5000), 7–12 Dean's Scholars for entering freshmen ($3000).

Application Procedures Students apply for admission into the professional program by sophomore year. Deadline for freshmen and transfers: continuous. Required: essay, high school transcript, college transcript(s) for transfer students, minimum 2.0 high school GPA, 2 letters of recommendation, portfolio, SAT I or ACT test scores. Recommended: minimum 3.0 high school GPA, interview, campus visit. Portfolio reviews held 3 times and by appointment on campus and off campus in various high schools in U.S.; the submission of slides may be substituted for portfolios (slides preferred, 20 or less).

Undergraduate Contact Mr. Dale Reinhart, Director of Admissions and Enrollment Management, Admissions Department, College of Santa Fe, 1600 Saint Michael's Drive, Santa Fe, New Mexico 87505; 505-473-6131, fax: 505-473-6127.

More About the College

The art program at the College of Santa Fe is an extraordinary blend of theory and application. Because of the school's location in Santa Fe—the arts center of the Southwest—CSF is able to offer students a tremendous variety of hands-on experiences as well as an excellent liberal arts education. Santa Fe holds a special attraction for artists. There's something about the light, colors, and intensity of nature that captures the creativity in artists and allows this creativity to flow freely. CSF wants students to be caught up in the magic that is Santa Fe and in the art that makes this community so unique. Students are encouraged to develop their talents under the direction of some of the finest artists this area has to offer. Upper-level art students are often placed in internships with local studios, galleries, foundries, museums, or printmaking shops. The curriculum is challenging, with high expectations for student performance, and the student-faculty ratio is low. Developing the talents of its students is CSF's primary concern.

CSF offers either a Bachelor of Arts or a Bachelor of Fine Arts degree and concentrated studies in drawing, painting, photography, sculpture, or printmaking. The B.A. degree is the choice for those wishing a broad-based education with serious study in the visual arts. The B.F.A. is a focused, professional degree with primary emphasis on the development of artistic skills and art history awareness.

The CSF Fine Arts Gallery provides students, faculty members, and the public the opportunity to study and view a wide range of original art on campus and offers students experience in gallery practices. Studios for painting, drawing, and sculpture are available. Facilities and equipment for the study of film, video, and art history are shared with the Moving Image Arts Department. Advanced studio majors are usually provided individual space in which to work, and all art students have access to studios anytime of day.

The new art complex, opening in late 1998, houses the college's new Marion Center for Photographic Arts, as well as a lecture hall, an art history building, studios, and classrooms. The college is also home to the Beaumont Newhall Photographic Library.

▼ COLLEGE OF VISUAL ARTS

St. Paul, Minnesota

Independent, coed. Urban campus. Total enrollment: 225. Art program established 1924.

Degrees Bachelor of Fine Arts in the areas of visual communication, fine arts. Majors and concentrations: drawing, graphic design, illustration, painting, photography, printmaking, sculpture, studio art. Program accredited by ACCSCT.

Enrollment Fall 1997: 221 total; 210 undergraduate, 11 non-professional degree.

Art Student Profile 51% females, 49% males, 10% minorities, 3% international.

Art Faculty 47 total (full-time and part-time). 71% of full-time faculty have terminal degrees. Graduate students do not teach undergraduate courses. Undergraduate student–faculty ratio: 6:1.

Student Life Student groups/activities include College of Visual Arts Design Group, The Sculpture Posse, Chasing the Sublime: A Journal of the College of Visual Arts.

Expenses for 1998–99 Application fee: $25. Tuition: $9970 full-time. Mandatory fees: $50 full-time. Special program-related fees: $10–$100 per semester for lab fees.

Financial Aid Program-specific awards for 1997: 4–5 Merit Scholarships for continuing students ($3000), College of Visual Arts Grants for those demonstrating need ($1200–$1500), Trustee and Presidential Scholarships for incoming first year and transfer students ($500–$3500).

Application Procedures Students admitted directly into the professional program freshman year. Deadline for freshmen and transfers: continuous. Notification date for freshmen and transfers: continuous. Required: essay, high school transcript, college transcript(s) for transfer students, minimum 2.0 high school GPA, interview, portfolio. Recommended: minimum 3.0 high school GPA, 2 letters of recommendation, ACT test score only. Portfolio reviews held continuously on campus; the submission of slides may be substituted for portfolios for large works of art, three-dimensional pieces, or when distance is prohibitive.

Undergraduate Contact Ms. Sherry A. Essen, Director of Admissions, College of Visual Arts, 344 Summit Avenue, St. Paul, Minnesota 55102-2124; 800-224-1536, fax: 612-224-8854.

More About the College

Program Facilities College of Visual Arts students enjoy access to the following facilities: the College's library, which offers both print and audio/visual resources, art-related books and periodicals, a slide library, as well as access to the library facilities at a neighboring private liberal arts college; the sculpture studio, which is furnished with a full metal shop, equipment for ceramic work, a complete line of woodworking tools and equipment, and full facilities to cast bronze, aluminum, and iron; a printmaking studio equipped with presses for monotype, intaglio, relief and woodblock printing, and a complete line of screenprinting equipment; a fully equipped photography studio and copy camera room for production of color slides, and darkrooms for processing both color and black-and-white film; outdoor courtyard space for exhibiting large scale sculptures; and a permanent gallery for regular student, faculty and visiting artist exhibitions. CoVA's efficient and technologically advanced computer labs are outfitted with current Macintosh hardware and the latest computer software. The College's student-to-computer ratio is 9:1.

College of Visual Arts (continued)

Faculty The College of Visual Arts views its faculty as its single greatest resource, and the strong mentoring relationships built between faculty and students have long been primary to the success of a CoVA education. In addition to teaching, CoVA faculty are working artists, illustrators, and designers in the Twin Cities, and their ability to bring the "outside inside" lends relevancy and currency to the curriculum.

Special Programs CoVA offers an internship program and career placement services, personal counseling, and individual tutoring through its Learning Resource Center.

▼

Founded in 1924, the College of Visual Arts (CoVA) is a nonprofit, four-year college of art and design, offering Bachelor of Fine Arts programs in visual communications (design, illustration, photography) and fine arts (painting, sculpture, printmaking, drawing), with 40% of the B.F.A. program consisting of general education coursework. With a 1998 enrollment of 250 students and a faculty of 45, CoVA blends a rigorous curriculum and individualized attention allowing students to realize their full creative and intellectual potential in a challenging, yet supportive, educational environment.

A CoVA education begins with a structured Foundation Program during which students develop and practice the skills on which the rest of their education will be built. During this year they draw, learn basic design and color theory, and experiment with computers, photography, and three-dimensionality. Students learn the fundamentals of visual language by engaging in artistic dialogue with their peers and faculty, and they learn how to communicate both visually and verbally while developing critical thinking skills, problem-solving abilities, and a general aesthetic awareness. At the end of their Foundation year, students engage in an intensive portfolio review during which they have an opportunity to show their work to a panel of faculty, to reflect on their first year experience, and to receive advice and guidance about their potential in a particular major area.

Following the Foundation year, the aim of each of CoVA's programs is to offer a curriculum that combines structured elements with the freedom to experiment in electives outside the major area. Students benefit from a dynamic faculty of professionals who challenge them to find new means of expression and to discover a personal artistic vision. In addition, internship opportunities, business and portfolio development classes, and contact with various visiting professionals prepares students to apply their artistic skills and conceptual knowledge to a profession. They leave with a genuine understanding of the connections between concept and practice, and a readiness to take their places as artists at work in society.

College of Visual Arts graduates have established themselves in numerous companies and nonprofit organizations across the nation, pursuing careers in graphic and advertising design, children's book illustration, art direction, package design, and photography. They are creating art at Musicland Corporation in Denver, General Mills in Minneapolis, *Minneapolis/Saint Paul* Magazine in the Twin Cities, WCCO television studio in Minneapolis, and the Walker Art Center in Minneapolis. Other graduates have had the initiative and confidence to launch their own design, illustration, and fine arts businesses, while others have gone on to attend graduate school.

The College of Visual Arts' location is a remarkable place for artists, and the Twin Cities of Minneapolis/Saint Paul are home to countless theaters, restaurants, and galleries, including the nationally renowned Walker Art Center, the Minneapolis Institute of Arts, and the Weisman Art Museum at the University of Minnesota. The Twin Cities community is an accepting, sophisticated place for artists and designers, and is one that supports the arts handsomely.

▼ COLORADO STATE UNIVERSITY

Fort Collins, Colorado

State-supported, coed. Urban campus. Total enrollment: 22,344.

Degrees Bachelor of Fine Arts in the area of art; Bachelor of Arts in the area of art education. Majors and concentrations: drawing, fibers, graphic design, metals, painting, photography, pottery, printmaking, sculpture. Graduate degrees offered: Master of Fine Arts in the areas of metalsmithing, fibers, sculpture, printmaking, graphic design, drawing, painting.

Enrollment Fall 1997: 544 total; 519 undergraduate, 25 graduate.

Art Student Profile 59% females, 41% males, 10% minorities, 1% international.

Art Faculty 36 total undergraduate and graduate (full-time and part-time). 95% of full-time faculty have terminal degrees. Graduate students teach a few undergraduate courses. Undergraduate student–faculty ratio: 20:1.

Student Life Student groups/activities include Student Organization for the Visual Arts. Special housing available for art students.

Expenses for 1997–98 Application fee: $30. State resident tuition: $2258 full-time. Nonresident tuition: $9480 full-time. Mandatory fees: $825 full-time. Full-time tuition and fees vary according to program. College room and board: $5050. Room and board charges vary according to board plan and housing facility. Special program-related fees: $50 per semester for technology fee.

Financial Aid Program-specific awards for 1997: 40 Creative and Performing Arts Awards for program students ($750), 2–3 Founding Faculty Awards for program students ($500), 3–4 Anna Lawton Printmaking Awards for printmakers ($500), 1 Tracie Noah Memorial Scholarship for painters ($500), 1 Bob Coonts Scholarship for graphic designers ($350), 1 Northern Colorado Artists Association Award for studio majors ($750).

Application Procedures Students admitted directly into the professional program freshman year. Deadline for freshmen and transfers: continuous. Notification date for freshmen and transfers: continuous. Required: high school transcript, college transcript(s) for transfer students, minimum 3.0 high school GPA, 3 letters of recommendation, SAT I or ACT test scores, portfolio for transfer students.

Web Site http://www.colostate.edu/Depts/Art/.

Undergraduate Contact Ms. Julia Morrigan, Administrative Assistant II, Art Department, Colorado State University, Fort Collins, Colorado 80523-1770; 970-491-6774, fax: 970-491-0505, E-mail address: jmorrigan@vines.colostate.edu.

Graduate Contact Ms. Sue Mohr, Administrative Assistant II, Art Department, Colorado State University, Fort Collins, Colorado 80523-1770; 970-491-6775, fax: 970-491-0505, E-mail address: smohr@vines.colostate.edu.

▼ COLUMBIA COLLEGE

Columbia, Missouri

Independent, coed. Small town campus. Total enrollment: 7,435.

Degrees Bachelor of Fine Arts in the areas of art, fashion design. Majors and concentrations: art education, art/fine arts, ceramics, computer graphics, graphic arts, illustration, painting/drawing, photography. Cross-registration with University of Missouri, Stephens College, William Woods University, Lincoln University, Westminster College.

Enrollment Fall 1997: 40 total; all undergraduate.

Art Student Profile 52% females, 48% males, 24% minorities, 48% international.

Art Faculty 6 total (full-time and part-time). 100% of full-time faculty have terminal degrees. Graduate students do not teach undergraduate courses. Undergraduate student–faculty ratio: 10:1.

Student Life Student groups/activities include The Art Club.

Expenses for 1997–98 Application fee: $25. Comprehensive fee: $13,388 includes full-time tuition ($9244) and college room and board ($4144). College room only: $2608. Special program-related fees: $20 per course for model fees, lab fees.

Financial Aid Program-specific awards for 1997: 20 Talent Awards for program majors ($500–$1000).

Application Procedures Students apply for admission into the professional program by junior year. Deadline for freshmen and transfers: continuous. Required: high school transcript, college transcript(s) for transfer students, minimum 2.0 high school GPA, SAT I or ACT test scores, portfolio for scholarship consideration. Portfolio reviews held as needed on campus; the submission of slides may be substituted for portfolios when distance is prohibitive.

Undergraduate Contact Admissions Office, Columbia College, 1001 Rogers Street, Columbia, Missouri 65216; 573-875-7352, fax: 573-875-8765, E-mail address: admissions@ccishp.ccis.edu.

▼ COLUMBUS COLLEGE OF ART AND DESIGN

Columbus, Ohio

Independent, coed. Urban campus. Art program established 1879.

Degrees Bachelor of Fine Arts in the areas of fine art, visual communication, interior design, industrial design, media studies. Majors and concentrations: art/fine arts, fashion design, fashion illustration, graphic design, illustration, industrial design, interior design, media studies, visual communication. Cross-registration with Higher Education Council of Columbus. Program accredited by NASAD.

Enrollment Fall 1997: 1,550 total; all undergraduate.

Art Student Profile 43% females, 57% males, 15% minorities, 5% international.

Art Faculty 152 total (full-time and part-time). 60% of full-time faculty have terminal degrees. Graduate students do not teach undergraduate courses. Undergraduate student–faculty ratio: 10:1.

Student Life Special housing available for art students.

Expenses for 1997–98 Application fee: $25. Comprehensive fee: $17,680 includes full-time tuition ($11,880) and college room and board ($5800). Special program-related fees: $40–$150 per class for lab fees.

Financial Aid Program-specific awards for 1997: 150 Honor Scholarships for those demonstrating talent and academic achievement ($100–$2500), 300 National Scholarship Awards for incoming freshmen ($5000–$12,600).

Application Procedures Students admitted directly into the professional program freshman year. Deadline for freshmen and transfers: continuous. Required: high school transcript, college transcript(s) for transfer students, minimum 2.0 high school GPA, letter of recommendation, portfolio. Recommended: interview, SAT I or ACT test scores. Portfolio reviews held continuously by appointment on campus and off campus; the submission of slides may be substituted for portfolios if a campus visit is impossible.

Web Site http://www.ccad.edu.

Undergraduate Contact Mr. Thomas E. Green, Director of Admissions, Columbus College of Art and Design, 107 North Ninth Street, Columbus, Ohio 43215; 614-224-9101, fax: 614-222-4040.

More About the College

The Columbus College of Art and Design is located in downtown Columbus, adjacent to the Columbus Museum of Art. The Joseph V. Canzani Center, opened in 1993, is the focal point of the seventeen-building campus and houses a large exhibition hall, library, and auditorium. A student center opened in 1996 with recreation facilities, a student-run art gallery, a lounge, and offices for student organizations.

Faculty and Alumni CCAD's faculty members include a large body of artists-designers who have extensive professional experience and hold appropriate degrees in the divisions of study offered. Faculty members are professionally oriented, practicing artist-designers with broad teaching experience in the diverse areas of the art world. In the Liberal Arts Department, experienced faculty members with graduate degrees teach a wide range of courses in the humanities and sciences. The faculty members take an active interest in the students and are involved in advising them on a one-to-one basis regarding both their careers and curricular matters. Prominent national artists Alice Schille and George Bellows attended CCAD, and Dean Mitchell, George Gaadt, Ming Fay, Jeffrey Stahler, and Robert McCall are just a few of the College's more prestigious alumni. CCAD graduates hold important creative positions in companies and organizations across the world; Xerox Corporation, Disney Studios, Hallmark, American Greetings, Saks Fifth Avenue, and General Motors are just some of the companies that have hired CCAD graduates.

Student Life Students at The Columbia College of Art and Design are immersed in a creative and productive artists' community and environment. The College takes great pride in student work; the annual student exhibition displays nearly 2,000 individual works of art from all areas of study. Seniors in the Fine Arts programs (drawing, painting, printmaking, glassblowing, ceramics, and sculpture) are each required to produce a weeklong senior thesis exhibition. In addition, the Joseph V. Canzani Center exhibition hall houses the CCAD Faculty Exhibition, the annual Student Exhibition, the Scholastic Art Awards, and various traveling exhibitions.

▼ CONCORDIA COLLEGE

Seward, Nebraska

Independent, coed. Small town campus. Total enrollment: 1,191. Art program established 1963.

Degrees Bachelor of Fine Arts in the area of commercial art.

Enrollment Fall 1997: 50 undergraduate.

Art Student Profile 60% females, 40% males, 8% international.

Art Faculty 7 total (full-time and part-time). 80% of full-time faculty have terminal degrees. Graduate students do not teach undergraduate courses. Undergraduate student–faculty ratio: 15:1.

Expenses for 1998–99 Application fee: $15. Comprehensive fee: $15,096 includes full-time tuition ($11,310) and college room and board ($3786). Special program-related fees: $35 per course for studio/materials fee.

Financial Aid Program-specific awards for 1997: 75 art scholarships for program majors ($1500).

Application Procedures Students admitted directly into the professional program freshman year. Deadline for freshmen and transfers: continuous. Notification date for freshmen and transfers: continuous. Required: high school transcript, minimum 2.0 high school GPA, SAT I or ACT test scores, health form, portfolio for scholarship consideration. Recommended: interview, portfolio. Portfolio reviews held as needed on campus; the submission of slides may be substituted for portfolios.

Undergraduate Contact Mr. William R. Wolfram, Chair, Art Department, Concordia College, 800 North Columbia Avenue, Seward, Nebraska 68434; 402-643-7499, fax: 402-643-4073.

▼ CONCORDIA UNIVERSITY

Montréal, PQ, Canada

Province-supported, coed. Urban campus. Total enrollment: 29,271. Art program established 1975.

Degrees Bachelor of Fine Arts in the areas of studio art, ceramics, fibers, interdisciplinary studies, painting and drawing, photography, print media, sculpture, women and the fine arts. Majors and concentrations: ceramics, fibers, interdisciplinary studies, painting/drawing, photography, print media, sculpture, studio art. Graduate degrees offered: Master of Fine Arts in the areas of studio arts, individual program. Doctor of Philosophy. Cross-registration with any university in Quebec.

Enrollment Fall 1997: 375 total; 306 undergraduate, 69 graduate.

Art Student Profile 4% international.

Art Faculty 72 total undergraduate and graduate (full-time and part-time). Graduate students teach a few undergraduate courses. Undergraduate student–faculty ratio: 5:1.

Expenses for 1998–99 Application fee: $40 Canadian dollars. Tuition, fee, and room only charges are reported in Canadian dollars. Province resident tuition: $1668 full-time. Canadian resident tuition: $2868 full-time. Mandatory fees: $618 full-time. College room only: $2290. Room charges vary according to housing facility. International student tuition: $8268 full-time.

Application Procedures Students admitted directly into the professional program freshman year. Deadline for freshmen and transfers: March 1. Notification date for freshmen and transfers: July 15. Required: high school transcript, college

transcript(s) for transfer students, portfolio. Portfolio reviews held 3 times in April, May, and June on campus; the submission of slides may be substituted for portfolios for large works of art and three-dimensional pieces.

Web Site http://www-fofa.concordia.ca/studio-arts/.

Undergraduate Contact Ms. Jolanta Manowska, Communications Assistant, Office of the Registrar, Concordia University, 1455 de Maisonneuve Boulevard West, LB700, Montreal, PQ H3G 1M8; 514-848-2668, fax: 514-848-2837, E-mail address: admreg@alcor.concordia.ca.

Graduate Contact Ms. Donna Mundey, Secretary/Receptionist, School of Graduate Studies, Concordia University, 1455 de Maisonneuve Boulevard West, S105, Montreal, PQ H3G 1M8; 514-848-3800, E-mail address: dmundey@alcor.concordia.ca.

▼ CONVERSE COLLEGE

Spartanburg, South Carolina

Independent, women only. Urban campus. Total enrollment: 1,474.

Degrees Bachelor of Fine Arts in the areas of studio art, interior design, textile design, graphic design; Bachelor of Arts in the areas of art history, studio art, art education, art therapy. Majors and concentrations: art education, art therapy, graphic design, interior design, studio art, textiles. Cross-registration with Wofford College.

Enrollment Fall 1997: 120 total; 100 undergraduate, 20 non-professional degree.

Art Student Profile 100% females, 5% minorities, 5% international.

Art Faculty 12 total (full-time and part-time). 100% of full-time faculty have terminal degrees. Graduate students do not teach undergraduate courses. Undergraduate student–faculty ratio: 12:1.

Student Life Student groups/activities include Student Art Club, American Society of Interior Designers. Special housing available for art students.

Expenses for 1997–98 Application fee: $35. Comprehensive fee: $18,525 includes full-time tuition ($14,445) and college room and board ($4080). Special program-related fees: $20 for drawing courses, $30–$40 for lab fees.

Financial Aid Program-specific awards for 1997: Visual Arts Scholarships for entering freshmen ($1500).

Application Procedures Students apply for admission into the professional program by sophomore year. Deadline for freshmen and transfers: continuous. Required: high school transcript, minimum 2.0 high school GPA, letter of recommendation, SAT I or ACT test scores (minimum combined SAT I score of 900). Recommended: interview, portfolio. Portfolio reviews held by appointment on campus; the submission of slides may be substituted for portfolios when distance is prohibitive.

Web Site http://www.converse.edu.

Undergraduate Contact Mr. Ray Tatem, Vice President for Enrollment Management/Dean of Admissions, Converse College, 580 East Main Street, Spartanburg, South Carolina 29302; 864-596-9040, E-mail address: ray.tatem@converse.edu.

The Cooper Union School of Art

▼ COOPER UNION FOR THE ADVANCEMENT OF SCIENCE AND ART

New York, New York

Independent, coed. Urban campus. Total enrollment: 883.

Degrees Bachelor of Fine Arts. Cross-registration with Parsons School of Design-New School for Social Research. Program accredited by NASAD.

Enrollment Fall 1997: 257 total; all undergraduate.

Art Student Profile 48% females, 52% males, 49% minorities, 3% international.

Art Faculty 58 total (full-time and part-time). 89% of full-time faculty have terminal degrees. Graduate students do not teach undergraduate courses. Undergraduate student–faculty ratio: 8:1.

Expenses for 1997–98 Application fee: $35. Special program-related fees: $500 per year for student fee.

Financial Aid Program-specific awards for 1997: full tuition scholarships for all admitted students ($25,000).

Application Procedures Students admitted directly into the professional program freshman year. Deadline for freshmen: January 10; transfers: February 10. Notification date for freshmen and transfers: April 1. Required: essay, high school transcript, college transcript(s) for transfer students, minimum 2.0 high school GPA, portfolio, SAT I or ACT test scores, home test. Recommended: 2 letters of recommendation. Portfolio reviews held 4 times during fall semester on campus and off campus; the submission of slides may be substituted for portfolios for large works of art.

Undergraduate Contact Mr. Richard Bory, Dean of Admissions and Records, Cooper Union for the Advancement of Science and Art, 30 Cooper Square, Suite 300, New York, New York 10003; 212-353-4120, fax: 212-353-4343, E-mail address: admissions@cooper.edu.

▼ THE CORCORAN SCHOOL OF ART

Washington, District of Columbia

Independent, coed. Urban campus. Total enrollment: 380. Art program established 1890.

Degrees Bachelor of Fine Arts in the areas of fine arts, graphic design, photography. Majors and concentrations: computer graphics, painting, sculpture. Program accredited by NASAD.

Enrollment Fall 1997: 340 undergraduate.

Art Student Profile 51% females, 49% males, 11% minorities, 12% international.

Art Faculty 80 total (full-time and part-time). 60% of full-time faculty have terminal degrees. Graduate students do not teach undergraduate courses. Undergraduate student–faculty ratio: 7:1.

Student Life Student groups/activities include Visual Arts Community Outreach Program. Special housing available for art students.

Expenses for 1997–98 Application fee: $30. Tuition: $12,800 full-time.

Financial Aid Program-specific awards for 1997: 40–60 Dean's Merit Scholarships for freshmen ($500–$3000), 20 departmental scholarships for program students ($1000–$2500).

Application Procedures Students admitted directly into the professional program freshman year. Deadline for freshmen and transfers: continuous. Required: high school transcript, college transcript(s) for transfer students, minimum 2.0 high school GPA, interview, portfolio, SAT I or ACT test scores. Recommended: essay, 2 letters of recommendation. Portfolio reviews held continuously by appointment on campus and off campus; the submission of slides may be substituted for portfolios when distance is prohibitive.

Web Site http://www.corcoran.edu.

Undergraduate Contact Mr. Raheel Masood, Director of Admissions, The Corcoran School of Art, 500 17th Street, NW, Washington, District of Columbia 20006; 202-639-1814, fax: 202-639-1830, E-mail address: admofc@aol.com.

More About the School

The Corcoran School of Art is one of the oldest art schools in the United States and upholds a long tradition of partnership between art schools and museums. One of the few remaining museum-schools in the country, Corcoran students are surrounded by great art and frequently by the contemporary masters whose work is regularly exhibited. The Corcoran Museum has one of the finest collections of American art in the world, which is supplemented by holdings in European painting and sculpture, classical antiquities, and the decorative arts. As Washington's first museum of art, the Corcoran has played a central role in the development of American culture for more than 125 years. The aspiring young professionals who study today at the Corcoran School of Art will join a great and long tradition of quality and impact on the development of American art and design.

Location and Program Facilities Washington is a city of monuments, set off by the classical architecture of government buildings, parks, trees, and greenery, all enhanced by a climate of long, balmy fall and spring seasons. With sixteen major colleges and universities in the metropolitan area, there exists a feeling of a giant "campus" in which restaurants, coffee shops, movie theaters, and night spots are intermingled with bookstores, clothing boutiques, and academic facilities. Within a radius of one mile, the city offers numerous museums and galleries, including the Corcoran Gallery of Art, the National Gallery of Art, the Phillips Collection, the Hirshorn Museum, the National Museum of American History, and the Smithsonian's Air and Space Museum. All students take the integrated first-year Foundation program, which includes an introduction to the many art collections of Washington. After their first year, students select a major field of study in Fine Arts, Graphic Design, or Photography.

The Corcoran School of Art and Museum of Art is located one block from the White House, with additional facilities in close proximity. The building is one of America's examples of neo-classical architecture with wings designed by Ernest Flagg and Charles Platt. Foundation students will spend most of their class time in the main building, which houses both the School and the Museum, as well as the Fine Arts and Photography departments. Juniors and seniors in Fine Arts have designated studio space as well as generous studio hours until 2 a.m. Photography majors have 24-hour access to the building.

As part of the urban campus, the Georgetown building is less than two miles away and is home to the Graphic Design department, papermaking and silkscreen facilities, and two specialized computer laboratories. Georgetown is one of Washington's best-known neighborhoods, with its tree-lined streets and historic townhomes. There is plenty of shopping, restaurants, and nightlife in this historic district.

The Corcoran School of Art (continued)

In addition to several nearby museums, a short walk from the business and government district that surrounds the Corcoran takes students to the world-famous Mall and performing art institutions such as the Kennedy Center, Ford's Theater, and the National Theater. Rock Creek Park, a 1,700-acre public park that has a golf course, bicycle path, picnic area, nature center, playgrounds, tennis center, and Horse Center, is nearby as well. Visitors to the Corcoran who have not experienced Washington, D.C., before should allow a full day or two to explore the city as well as the School and Museum.

Student and Alumni Exhibit Opportunities Students of all levels have several opportunities to exhibit work in both the main and Georgetown building galleries. In the School/Museum space, there are several exhibition areas, including the White Walls Gallery, which is also the site for the annual student work sale.

In addition, the School has two permanent exhibit spaces in the historic museum, including the Hemicycle Gallery, the site of senior thesis exhibitions for three months during each year. The Corcoran School of Art is the only college of art and design that incorporates an exhibition in a prominent museum as part of its senior curriculum. The graduating students are responsible for all aspects of these senior shows, from exhibition design to installation. Each week represents a new group of seniors' works, culminating with a final show of one piece selected from each senior exhibition by the head curator of the Corcoran Museum of Art. These exhibitions are significant milestones in the seniors' individual development. Through the formal presentation of their work in the Corcoran Museum of Art, they make the transition from students to professional artists and designers and are introduced as emerging talents to the public.

The Hemicycle Gallery also is the site of the annual juried Corcoran Alumni Association exhibition, presenting works by some of the school's most accomplished alumni, all with extensive lists of exhibitions to their credit and many with gallery affiliations. Alumni also have several opportunities to participate in juried exhibitions around Washington, D.C. Recent alumni exhibition sites include the Japanese Embassy, the Arts Club of Washington, and the Art Museum of the Americas at the Organization of American States.

In 1997, the Corcoran Gallery of Art dedicated additional space in the museum for the Corcoran School of Art Alumni Gallery, a permanent exhibition space. This exhibition area is dedicated to works by artists and designers who have received their Bachelor of Fine Arts degree from the Corcoran School of Art.

▼ CORNELL UNIVERSITY

Ithaca, New York

Independent, coed. Small town campus. Total enrollment: 18,428. Art program established 1921.

Degrees Bachelor of Fine Arts. Majors and concentrations: combined media, painting/drawing, photography, printmaking, sculpture. Graduate degrees offered: Master of Fine Arts.

Enrollment Fall 1997: 150 total; 140 undergraduate, 10 graduate.

Art Student Profile 68% females, 34% minorities, 1% international.

Art Faculty 16 total undergraduate and graduate (full-time and part-time). 85% of full-time faculty have terminal degrees. Graduate students do not teach undergraduate courses. Undergraduate student–faculty ratio: 16:1.

Student Life Student groups/activities include Images Unseen, Minority Organization of Architecture, Art, and Planning. Special housing available for art students.

Expenses for 1997–98 Application fee: $65. Comprehensive fee: $29,024 includes full-time tuition ($21,840), mandatory fees ($74), and college room and board ($7110). College room only: $4170. Room and board charges vary according to board plan and housing facility. Special program-related fees: $50–$150 for departmental fees.

Application Procedures Students admitted directly into the professional program freshman year. Deadline for freshmen: January 1; transfers: March 15. Notification date for freshmen: April 1; transfers: May 1. Required: essay, high school transcript, college transcript(s) for transfer students, minimum 3.0 high school GPA, 2 letters of recommendation, SAT I or ACT test scores, slides of portfolio. Recommended: interview. Portfolio reviews held by appointment on campus.

Web Site http://www.aap.cornell.edu.

Undergraduate Contact Ms. Elizabeth Cutter, Director of Admissions, College of Architecture, Art and Planning, Cornell University, 135 East Sibley Hall, Ithaca, New York 14853; 607-255-4376, fax: 607-254-2848, E-mail address: aap_admissions@cornell.edu.

Graduate Contact Ms. Kay WalkingStick, Associate Professor, Department of Art, Cornell University, 224 Olive Tjaden Hall, Ithaca, New York 14853; 607-255-3558, fax: 607-255-3462.

More About the University

Program Facilities Studios for painting and drawing, intaglio, lithography, and silkscreen; sculpture with bronze casting capability; multimedia labs and photography darkrooms for black-and-white, color, and alternative processes; digital imaging facilities. All facilities have been expanded with newly completed building renovation. Fine arts library contains more than 146,000 volumes. Slide library contains about 400,000 slides.

Faculty, Resident Artists, and Alumni Faculty members are practicing artists, exhibiting nationally. An art faculty exhibition is held annually in Herbert F. Johnson Museum of Art, located on campus, adjacent to the school's facilities. The Visiting Artist Lecture Series includes artists such as Gregory Amenoff, Tina Barney, Rafael Ferrer, Helen Frankenthaler, Richard Hunt, Barbara Kasten, Barbara Kruger, Michael Mazur, Philip Pearlstein, Martin Puryear, Joyce Scott, Jaune Quick-to-See Smith, William Wegman, and Jacqueline Winsor.

Student Exhibit Opportunities Opportunities for student exhibits on campus in Olive Tjaden, John Hartell, and Willard Straight galleries. A Senior Thesis Exhibit is required. Grants up to $500 available to students from Council for the Arts at Cornell encourage artists to work on projects not primarily concerned with course work.

Special Programs Access to Cornell University courses, resources, facilities, activities, etc.; dual-degree programs with Colleges of Arts and Sciences (B.F.A., B.A.), Engineering (B.F.A., B.S.), Human Ecology—Textiles and Apparel Design (B.F.A., B.S.), and junior year program in Rome to study art, architecture, urban issues. Career services available: alumni forum to discuss careers, apprenticeships with artists, internships, externships, summer employment, and portfolio development.

▼ CORNISH COLLEGE OF THE ARTS

Seattle, Washington

Independent, coed. Urban campus. Total enrollment: 621. Art program established 1914.

Degrees Bachelor of Fine Arts in the areas of fine art, painting, photography, print art, sculpture, video art. Majors and concentrations: art/fine arts, painting/drawing, photography, printmaking, sculpture, video art. Program accredited by NASAD.

Enrollment Fall 1997: 187 total; 167 undergraduate, 20 non-professional degree.

Art Student Profile 11% minorities.

Art Faculty 19 total undergraduate (full-time and part-time). 99% of full-time faculty have terminal degrees. Graduate students do not teach undergraduate courses. Undergraduate student–faculty ratio: 8:1.

Expenses for 1997–98 Application fee: $35. Tuition: $11,540 full-time. Mandatory fees: $118 full-time. Special program-related fees: $25–$75 for lab fees.

Financial Aid Program-specific awards for 1997: 1–6 Kreielsheimer Scholarships for new students from Washington, Oregon, or Alaska ($16,000), Nellie Scholarships for new students ($600–$4000), departmental scholarships for new and continuing students ($600–$4000), Presidential Scholarships for continuing students ($600–$4000).

Application Procedures Students admitted directly into the professional program freshman year. Deadline for freshmen and transfers: August 15. Required: essay, high school transcript, college transcript(s) for transfer students, minimum 2.0 high school GPA, portfolio. Recommended: letter of recommendation, interview. Portfolio reviews held 8 times and by appointment on campus and off campus; the submission of slides may be substituted for portfolios when distance is prohibitive.

Web Site http://www.cornish.edu.

Undergraduate Contact Ms. Jane Buckman, Director of Admissions, Cornish College of the Arts, 710 East Roy Street, Seattle, Washington 98102; 800-726-ARTS, fax: 206-720-1011.

More About the College

Cornish College of the Arts provides students aspiring to become practicing artists with an exclusively arts-oriented environment that nurtures creativity and intellectual curiosity and prepares them to contribute to society as artists, citizens, and innovators. Founded in 1914 as the Cornish School of Music, Cornish College of the Arts became accredited in 1977 and now offers the Bachelor of Fine Arts degree in art, dance, design, acting and performance production, and the Bachelor of Music degree. Classes are kept small so that students receive individualized attention. Cornish College instructors are practicing artists, many of national and international renown. They provide students with exposure to the professional arts arena on a daily basis. An active program of visiting artists and guest speakers, including curators, architects, composers, choreographers, and historians, enriches the curriculum. Classes in the humanities and sciences develop critical thinking and provide valuable perspective.

Cornish College of the Arts is located in Seattle, Washington. Seattle's abundant resource of professional theaters, musical groups, dance companies, galleries, and museums offers many opportunities to participate in the vibrant local arts community.

Cornish College of the Arts

The Cornish community consists of more than 650 students. Students are expected to be self-motivated and are encouraged to test the limits of their creativity. Cornish's staff and faculty members provide a supportive environment for students to realize their potential as artists.

The Cornish College Art Department curriculum leads to a B.F.A. degree in five major areas of study: painting, photography, print art, sculpture, and video art. The curriculum emphasizes contemporary intellectual and expressive art processes based on the understanding of formal skills. Through work with practicing professional artists, students discover the visual language of historical works and current elements of contemporary art. The faculty helps students develop a vision unique to each individual.

The Art Department encourages students to examine both traditional and contemporary thought and processes within the five major areas of study offered. After experiencing the introductory courses, students select two areas of concentration and pursue art-making in longer, more intensive studio classes as juniors and seniors, where classes are generally no larger than 12 students.

The Design Department offers a B.F.A. degree in design, with an emphasis on graphic, furniture or interior design, or illustration. Students learn the skills of their art as well as its business practices, trends, and history. A faculty of professional designers and visiting artists provide the art training.

Cornish College of the Arts

Cornish College of the Arts *(continued)*

During the first year, students gain a broad foundation of skill and knowledge in classes such as drawing, color theory, drafting, and perspective. Students refine their conceptualization skills in the second year and begin learning the techniques specific to their area of interest. In the third and fourth years, students apply their skills to the planning and execution of design projects, which are professionally oriented and provide students with commercially viable design solutions.

▼ CORNISH COLLEGE OF THE ARTS

Seattle, Washington

Independent, coed. Urban campus. Total enrollment: 621.
Degrees Bachelor of Fine Arts in the areas of design, interior design, graphic design, illustration, furniture design. Majors and concentrations: furniture design, graphic arts, illustration, interior design. Program accredited by NASAD.
Enrollment Fall 1997: 141 total; 129 undergraduate, 12 non-professional degree.
Art Student Profile 18% minorities.
Art Faculty 33 total undergraduate (full-time and part-time). 75% of full-time faculty have terminal degrees. Graduate students do not teach undergraduate courses. Undergraduate student–faculty ratio: 4:1.
Student Life Student groups/activities include American Society of Interior Designers, American Institute of Graphic Arts.
Expenses for 1997–98 Application fee: $35. Tuition: $11,540 full-time. Mandatory fees: $118 full-time. Special program-related fees: $15–$100 for lab fees.
Financial Aid Program-specific awards for 1997: Shannon Scholarships for interior design students ($4975), 1–6 Kreielsheimer Scholarships for new students from Washington, Oregon, or Alaska ($16,000), departmental scholarships for new and continuing students ($600–$4000), Nellie Scholarships for new students ($600–$4000), Presidential Scholarships for continuing students ($600–$4000).
Application Procedures Students admitted directly into the professional program freshman year. Deadline for freshmen and transfers: August 15. Required: essay, high school transcript, college transcript(s) for transfer students, minimum 2.0 high school GPA, portfolio. Recommended: interview, SAT I or ACT test scores. Portfolio reviews held 12 times on campus and off campus; the submission of slides may be substituted for portfolios when distance is prohibitive.
Web Site http://www.cornish.edu.
Undergraduate Contact Ms. Jane Buckman, Director of Admissions, Cornish College of the Arts, 710 East Roy Street, Seattle, Washington 98102; 800-726-ARTS, fax: 206-720-1011.

▼ CULVER-STOCKTON COLLEGE

Canton, Missouri

Independent, coed. Rural campus. Total enrollment: 994. Art program established 1900.
Degrees Bachelor of Fine Arts in the areas of studio art, graphic design, photography. Majors and concentrations: applied art, interior design.
Enrollment Fall 1997: 45 undergraduate.
Art Student Profile 60% females, 8% minorities, 4% international.
Art Faculty 4 total (full-time and part-time). 100% of full-time faculty have terminal degrees. Graduate students do not teach undergraduate courses. Undergraduate student–faculty ratio: 12:1.
Student Life Student groups/activities include Images Unlimited (art club).
Expenses for 1997–98 Comprehensive fee: $13,430 includes full-time tuition ($9200) and college room and board ($4230). College room only: $1930.
Financial Aid Program-specific awards for 1997: scholarship awards for program majors ($1000–$3000), Interest Awards for program minors ($750).
Application Procedures Students admitted directly into the professional program freshman year. Deadline for freshmen and transfers: August 31. Required: high school transcript, portfolio, SAT I or ACT test scores. Portfolio reviews held formally once in March, as needed from October–April on campus; the submission of slides may be substituted for portfolios.
Web Site http://www.culver.edu.
Undergraduate Contact Mr. Mike Mason, Director of Admissions, Culver-Stockton College, One College Hill, Canton, Missouri 63435-1299; 217-231-6466, fax: 217-231-6611, E-mail address: mmason@culver.edu.

▼ DAEMEN COLLEGE

Amherst, New York

Independent, coed. Suburban campus. Total enrollment: 1,914. Art program established 1948.
Degrees Bachelor of Fine Arts in the areas of applied design, graphic design, art; Bachelor of Science in the area of art education. Majors and concentrations: art education, drawing, graphic design, illustration, painting, printmaking, sculpture. Cross-registration with 17 area institutions.
Enrollment Fall 1997: 70 total; 59 undergraduate, 11 non-professional degree.
Art Student Profile 64% females, 36% males, 11% minorities.
Art Faculty 8 total (full-time and part-time). 100% of full-time faculty have terminal degrees. Graduate students do not teach undergraduate courses. Undergraduate student–faculty ratio: 13:1.

Student Life Student groups/activities include Student Art Organization, Art Club.

Expenses for 1997–98 Application fee: $25. Comprehensive fee: $16,480 includes full-time tuition ($10,600), mandatory fees ($380), and college room and board ($5500).

Financial Aid Program-specific awards for 1997: 2 Art Merit Scholarships for freshmen enrolling in fine arts curriculum ($5000).

Application Procedures Students admitted directly into the professional program freshman year. Deadline for freshmen and transfers: continuous. Notification date for freshmen and transfers: continuous. Required: high school transcript, college transcript(s) for transfer students, portfolio, SAT I or ACT test scores (minimum combined SAT I score of 900, minimum combined ACT score of 16). Recommended: 3 letters of recommendation, interview. Portfolio reviews held continuously on campus; the submission of slides may be substituted for portfolios.

Undergraduate Contact Admissions Office, Daemen College, 4380 Main Street, Amherst, New York 14226; 716-839-8225, fax: 716-839-8516, E-mail address: admissions@daemen.edu.

More About the College

Program Facilities Daemen College has a great deal to offer any student pursuing a degree in the arts. The Art and Graphic Design Department has twelve large and well-equipped studios that may be utilized for any of the College's various Fine Art Programs. Senior art students are given individual studio space according to their major area of study. Daemen offers instruction in many areas, including graphic design, foundation drawing and design, watercolor and illustration, painting, figure drawing, photography, sculpture, printmaking, and ceramics.

Faculty James Allen, M.F.A., Wayne State University; Dennis Barraclough, M.F.A., University of Michigan; Donna M. Stanton, M.F.A., SUNY at Buffalo.

Student Exhibit Opportunities On-campus exhibits are continuous in Daemen's Fanette Goldman and Carolyn Greenfield Art Gallery. There are annual student exhibits, and senior art majors are required to hold a Senior Thesis Exhibit in the gallery for graduation. Students' current artwork is always on display in the halls of the Art Department. The gallery holds a full schedule of exhibits each year featuring professional artists and designers from the area.

Special Programs The Art and Graphic Design Department sponsors a student art organization that allows students in the program to visit major art centers, travel to special exhibits, and bring in speakers. There are ample opportunities for students to take part in co-op arrangements in which they work in their field of interest for College credit.

▼

At Daemen, art is seen as both a lifestyle and a lifework. It calls for intense dedication, strong personal initiative and discipline, and, of course, talent. Art students at Daemen are continually challenged to find the creative solution; their understanding of the history and tradition of art-making will expand through studies and experiences at the College.

Large, well-equipped studios provide the backdrop for in-depth study in the chosen degree area. The small class size is ideal for sharing ideas and techniques and for the critique of students' work. It also ensures careful attention to individual artistic needs because it offers the opportunity for optimum interaction with faculty members, all of whom are professionally active artists and designers.

Starting in their freshman year, students work with a faculty team in the foundation program, where they develop their artistic and perceptual skills in the areas of 2- and 3-D design and drawing. Upon completion of the foundation courses, students spend their sophomore, junior, and senior years of study focusing on specific areas of interest in art and design. They take courses in their major studio area along with other studio courses in the department that will expand their vision as young artists. Daemen offers fully equipped studios in drawing, design, painting, sculpture, photography, fibers, ceramics, and life drawing and a computer center for graphic design.

Careers in the arts are numerous and diverse. Possible career opportunities include professional artist, illustrator, or craftsperson; working in an art gallery or as an art consultant; self-employment in graphic design and production; and jobs in research, art conservation, publishing, and advertising. In addition, art education students are certified to teach at the elementary or secondary level.

Daemen offers three degree options: the Bachelor of Fine Arts prepares students for careers as professional artists. Specialization in art (painting, sculpture, or drawing and illustration) and in applied design (printmaking) prepares students for professional studio work or for acceptance into graduate programs. The Bachelor of Fine Arts in graphic design integrates a solid background in basic art disciplines with the skills necessary for success in business and industry. The Bachelor of Science in Art encourages artistic growth through exposure to a variety of art experiences. The Bachelor of Science in Art Education is based upon the philosophy that competent art teachers are also practicing artists.

Upon successful completion of the degree requirements, students receive provisional New York State certification to teach at the elementary and secondary levels.

▼ DELTA STATE UNIVERSITY

Cleveland, Mississippi

State-supported, coed. Small town campus. Total enrollment: 4,012.

Degrees Bachelor of Fine Arts in the areas of graphic design, painting, interior design, crafts, sculpture, photography.

Enrollment Fall 1997: 137 undergraduate.

Art Student Profile 57% females, 43% males, 11% minorities, 1% international.

Art Faculty 12 total undergraduate (full-time and part-time). 88% of full-time faculty have terminal degrees. Graduate students do not teach undergraduate courses. Undergraduate student–faculty ratio: 10:1.

Expenses for 1997–98 Application fee: $0. State resident tuition: $2354 full-time. Nonresident tuition: $4948 full-time. College room and board: $2400.

Financial Aid Program-specific awards for 1997: 21 art scholarships for program students ($1000).

Application Procedures Students admitted directly into the professional program freshman year. Deadline for freshmen and transfers: August 2. Required: minimum 2.0 high school GPA, SAT I or ACT test scores.

Undergraduate Contact Debbie Heslep, Coordinator of Admissions, Delta State University, Kethley 105, Cleveland, Mississippi 38733; 601-846-4018, fax: 601-846-4016.

▼ DENISON UNIVERSITY

Granville, Ohio

Independent, coed. Small town campus. Total enrollment: 2,025. Art program established 1935.

Degrees Bachelor of Fine Arts in the area of studio art. Majors and concentrations: art/fine arts, photography, printmaking, sculpture. Cross-registration with Great Lakes Colleges Association.

Enrollment Fall 1997: 70 total; 46 undergraduate, 24 non-professional degree.

Art Student Profile 52% females, 48% males, 11% minorities, 5% international.

Art Faculty 8 total (full-time and part-time). 98% of full-time faculty have terminal degrees. Graduate students do not teach undergraduate courses. Undergraduate student–faculty ratio: 12:1.

Expenses for 1997–98 Application fee: $35. Comprehensive fee: $25,620 includes full-time tuition ($19,310), mandatory fees ($940), and college room and board ($5370). College room only: $2960.

Financial Aid Program-specific awards for 1997: 2 Marimac Scholarships for those demonstrating talent ($500–$2000), 2–4 Vail Performing Arts Scholarships for those demonstrating talent ($1000), 4 Foster McGraw Scholarships for those demonstrating talent ($5000).

Application Procedures Students admitted directly into the professional program freshman year. Deadline for freshmen: February 1; transfers: May 15. Notification date for freshmen: April 1; transfers: continuous. Required: essay, high school transcript, college transcript(s) for transfer students, minimum 2.0 high school GPA, 2 letters of recommendation, SAT I or ACT test scores. Recommended: minimum 3.0 high school GPA, interview, video, portfolio. Portfolio reviews held by request on campus; the submission of slides may be substituted for portfolios on a case-by-case basis.

Web Site http://www.denison.edu/art/.

Undergraduate Contact Ms. Joy Sperling, Chair, Art Department, Denison University, Granville, Ohio 43023; 740-587-6704, fax: 740-587-6417, E-mail address: sperling@cc.denison.edu.

▼ DESIGN INSTITUTE OF SAN DIEGO

San Diego, California

Proprietary, coed. Urban campus. Total enrollment: 253. Art program established 1977.

Degrees Bachelor of Fine Arts in the area of interior design. Program accredited by FIDER.

Enrollment Fall 1997: 250 total; all undergraduate.

Art Student Profile 90% females, 10% males, 16% minorities, 30% international.

Art Faculty 33 total (full-time and part-time). 96% of full-time faculty have terminal degrees. Graduate students do not teach undergraduate courses. Undergraduate student–faculty ratio: 12:1.

Student Life Student groups/activities include American Society of Interior Designers Student Chapter.

Expenses for 1997–98 Application fee: $25. Tuition: $9200 full-time.

Financial Aid Program-specific awards available.

Application Procedures Students admitted directly into the professional program freshman year. Deadline for freshmen and transfers: continuous. Required: essay, high school transcript, college transcript(s) for transfer students, 2 letters of recommendation. Recommended: interview.

Undergraduate Contact Ms. Paula Parrish, Director of Admissions, Design Institute of San Diego, 8555 Commerce Avenue, San Diego, California 92121; 619-566-1200, fax: 619-566-2711.

▼ DOMINICAN COLLEGE OF SAN RAFAEL

San Rafael, California

Independent, coed. Suburban campus. Total enrollment: 1,465.

Degrees Bachelor of Fine Arts in the area of studio art. Majors and concentrations: ceramics, drawing, painting, photography, printmaking, sculpture.

Enrollment Fall 1997: 200 total; 35 undergraduate, 165 non-professional degree.

Art Faculty 12 total (full-time and part-time). 100% of full-time faculty have terminal degrees. Graduate students do not teach undergraduate courses. Undergraduate student–faculty ratio: 17:1.

Student Life Student groups/activities include Photography Club, Student Art League, Art Career Seminar.

Expenses for 1997–98 Application fee: $35. Comprehensive fee: $22,392 includes full-time tuition ($15,120), mandatory fees ($304), and college room and board ($6968). Full-time tuition and fees vary according to program. Room and board charges vary according to board plan.

Financial Aid Program-specific awards available.

Application Procedures Students admitted directly into the professional program freshman year. Deadline for freshmen and transfers: continuous. Required: essay, high school transcript, college transcript(s) for transfer students, 2 letters of recommendation, SAT I or ACT test scores, minimum 2.5 high school GPA or 2.0 college GPA for transfer students. Recommended: interview, portfolio for transfer students. Portfolio reviews held by appointment on campus; the submission of slides may be substituted for portfolios whenever needed.

Undergraduate Contact Ms. Edythe Bresnahan, Chairperson, Art Department, Dominican College of San Rafael, 50 Acacia Avenue, San Rafael, California 94901; 415-485-3269, fax: 415-485-3205.

▼ DRAKE UNIVERSITY

Des Moines, Iowa

Independent, coed. Suburban campus. Total enrollment: 5,184.

Degrees Bachelor of Fine Arts in the areas of painting, drawing, sculpture, printmaking, graphic design, interior design; Bachelor of Art Education in the area of art education. Majors and concentrations: art education, art/fine arts, drawing, graphic arts, interior design, painting, painting/drawing, printmaking, sculpture. Cross-registration with The Institute of Italian Studies (Italy). Program accredited by NASAD.

Enrollment Fall 1997: 140 undergraduate.

Art Student Profile 60% females, 40% males, 5% minorities, 5% international.

Art Faculty 17 total undergraduate (full-time and part-time). 70% of full-time faculty have terminal degrees. Graduate students do not teach undergraduate courses. Undergraduate student–faculty ratio: 12:1.

Student Life Student groups/activities include Art Student Club.

Expenses for 1997–98 Application fee: $25. Comprehensive fee: $20,170 includes full-time tuition ($15,200) and college room and board ($4970). College room only: $2670. Full-time tuition varies according to student level. Room and board charges vary according to board plan.

Financial Aid Program-specific awards for 1997: 15–25 art scholarships for freshmen ($500–$4000).

Application Procedures Students apply for admission into the professional program by sophomore year. Deadline for freshmen and transfers: continuous. Required: essay, high school transcript, college transcript(s) for transfer students, SAT I or ACT test scores, portfolio for scholarship consideration. Portfolio reviews held as needed; the submission of slides may be substituted for portfolios.

Undergraduate Contact Prof. Ben Paskus, Chair, Art Department, Drake University, 25th and University Avenue, Des Moines, Iowa 50311; 515-271-3831, fax: 515-271-2558, E-mail address: benjamin.paskus@drake.edu.

▼ EAST CAROLINA UNIVERSITY

Greenville, North Carolina

State-supported, coed. Urban campus. Total enrollment: 18,271. Art program established 1909.

Degrees Bachelor of Fine Arts in the areas of art, art education. Majors and concentrations: art education, ceramic art and design, environmental design, graphic design, illustration, image design, jewelry and metalsmithing, painting/drawing, printmaking, sculpture, surface design, textile arts, weaving, woodworking design. Graduate degrees offered: Master of Fine Arts in the area of art. Program accredited by NASAD.

Enrollment Fall 1997: 615 total; 529 undergraduate, 37 graduate, 49 non-professional degree.

Art Student Profile 49% females, 51% males, 6% minorities, 1% international.

Art Faculty 50 total undergraduate and graduate (full-time and part-time). 90% of full-time faculty have terminal degrees. Graduate students teach a few undergraduate courses. Undergraduate student–faculty ratio: 17:1.

Student Life Student groups/activities include Visual Art Forum, North Carolina Art Education Association Student Chapter, American Institute of Architectural Students.

Expenses for 1997–98 Application fee: $35. State resident tuition: $916 full-time. Nonresident tuition: $8028 full-time. Mandatory fees: $932 full-time. College room and board: $3680. College room only: $1780. Room and board charges vary according to board plan and housing facility.

Financial Aid Program-specific awards for 1997: 2 Gravely Scholarships for program majors ($500), 1 Jenni K. Jewelry Scholarship for metal design majors ($1000), 2 University Book Exchange Scholarships for program majors ($500), 1 Richard Bean Scholarship for communication arts majors ($600), 1 Della Wade Willis Scholarship for textiles majors ($500), 1 Art Enthusiasts Scholarship for program majors ($500), 1 Tran and Marilyn Gordley Scholarship for painting majors ($500), 1 K Eastern Carolina Advertising Federation Scholarship for communication arts majors ($500), 30 out-of-state Special Talent Awards for out-of-state freshmen ($475), 1 H. Alexander III and Judith Easley Recruiting Scholarship for freshmen ($1200).

Application Procedures Students admitted directly into the professional program freshman year. Deadline for freshmen: May 15; transfers: April 15. Required: high school transcript, SAT I or ACT test scores, minimum 2.5 high school GPA.

Web Site http://www.ecu.edu/art/.

Undergraduate Contact Mr. Art Haney, Associate Dean, School of Art, East Carolina University, Jenkins Fine Arts Center, East Fifth Street, Greenville, North Carolina 27858-4353; 919-328-6563, fax: 919-328-6441, E-mail address: haneya@mail.ecu.edu.

Graduate Contact Ms. Jackie Leebrick, Director of Graduate Studies, School of Art, East Carolina University, Jenkins Fine Arts Center, East Fifth Street, Greenville, North Carolina 27858-4353; 919-328-6563, fax: 919-328-6441, E-mail address: leebrickj@mail.ecu.edu.

More About the University

Program Facilities The Leo Jenkins Fine Arts Center is the home facility for the School of Art. All art courses are taught in this building, which has 142,000 square feet. Besides containing studios, labs, classrooms, and faculty and administrative offices, the Jenkins Building also houses a media center, two computer labs, a 250-seat auditorium, and three galleries. The exhibition facilities are some of the best in the country. They include the Wellington B. Gray Gallery (6,000 square feet), the Burroughs Wellcome Senior Gallery (1,100 square feet), and the Foundations Gallery (1,350 square feet).

Faculty and Visiting Artists In order to augment the teaching of its nationally and internationally known faculty, the School of Art hosts as many as two dozen visiting artists, lecturers, and critics each year. These visiting scholars present slide lectures, workshops, demonstrations, and critiques. Their presentations are also videotaped and placed into the School's extensive collection, which is kept in the Media Center. Visiting artists during the past two years have included such noted artists as Dr. Linda C. Hults (art historian), Amie Oliver (mixed media), Charles Kraus (sculptor), Brian Wallis (art historian), Walter Liedtke (art historian), Katherine Manthorne (art historian), Chris Janney (environmental sculptor), Jean Pierre Larochette (weaver), Yael Luri (weaver), David Gamble (ceramics), Patricia Wasserboehr (sculptor), Rebecca Martin Nagy (art historian), Rob Schweiger (ceramics), Dr. Laraine Aragen (textiles), Dr. Mary Sales (art historian), Grier Carmen (textiles), Yrjo and Marja Turkka (design), six Israeli Photographers (photography), Harold Bruder (painting), Jed Perl (art critic), Sergei Isupov (ceramics), Andrei Balashov (metals), Anneli Tammik (metals), Joan McKarrell (metals), Tamar Winter (metals), Charles McNamara (curator), Michael Flecky (photography), Robin Konieczny (design), Villu Jaanisoo (sculptor), Dr. Edmund Burke Feldman (art education), John Neely (ceramics), and others. The School of Art also hires several visiting faculty persons to teach in the painting and drawing area for one year. This ensures an infusion of new ideas in teaching each and every year.

▼

Faculty members have educational backgrounds from the most prestigious universities in the world. Most possess the terminal degrees in their fields, and all have ample teaching experience. They are practicing professionals in the subjects that they teach and provide unparalleled instruction for students.

East Carolina University (*continued*)

These artists/teachers have been recognized on the regional and national levels through invitational group, solo, and competitive exhibitions. Faculty members have won numerous international art and design awards. Their work has been reproduced in major publications, and their articles have been published in leading art journals. This breadth of professional involvement, coupled with a healthy diversity of experience, provides numbrous benefits for the students.

The East Carolina University (ECU) School of Art faculty has a commitment to international interchange and program development. To that end, the school has established formal exchange agreements with the Cardiff Institute in Wales, the University of Lapland in Finland, and with Tallinn Art University in Estonia. Further arrangements are in place with various institutions and universities in Finland, Latvia, Hong Kong, New Zealand, and Germany. The School also has offered a summer program in the Baltics on a regular basis. International artists, teachers, writers, and critics are included in the School of Art's annual lecture series.

Each year the School of Art hosts from tent to twenty visiting artists. One or more teach full time for one or two semesters. Others visit the school for a few days to a week, providing a public lecture and often a show of their own work in the Wellington B. Gray Gallery. Some visiting artists offer workshops in their media, participate in individual and group critiques, and visit student and faculty studios.

The visiting artist program is an important opportunity for students, faculty members, and the public to hear varying presentations on art and to view the artwork created by artists from around the United States and, occasionally, from other countries. International artists have come from New Zealand, Great Britain, Estonia, Finland, Russia, Latvia, and Canada. All visiting artist presentations are videotaped and kept in the School's media center.

The ECU School of Art began a special project in 1997–98. The Museum without Walls project is a distance learning program that combines computer applications with flexible, interdisciplinary curriculum modules. The first of its modules will be created around images from the African art collection of the ECU School of Art. The immediate audience for the interdisciplinary program is formed by school districts in eastern North Carolina.

Anticipated outcomes of the project are (1) increased academic achievement in the arts and sciences for learners and (2) expanded instructional and technology skills for inservice and pre-service teachers. The final products of the Museum without Walls will be a distance learning program of the World Wide Web and a high resolution CD. These products will be available to students, artists, and other interested viewers around the world.

The ECU School of Art offers the following clubs and activities for its students: American Institute of Architecture Students (AIAS), Art Education Guild, Art History Society, Ceramics Guild, Craftsmen East Guild, Design Associates, Metals Guild, Painting Guild, Printmaking Guild, School of Art Graduate Alliance, Sculpture Guild, and Visual Art Forum.

▼ EASTERN NEW MEXICO UNIVERSITY

Portales, New Mexico

State-supported, coed. Rural campus. Total enrollment: 3,495.

Degrees Bachelor of Fine Arts in the areas of interdisciplinary art, graphic design. Majors and concentrations: animation, applied art, art/fine arts, ceramic art and design, computer art, graphic arts, jewelry and metalsmithing, painting/drawing, photography, sculpture, studio art.
Enrollment Fall 1997: 100 undergraduate.
Art Student Profile 50% females, 50% males, 30% minorities, 5% international.
Art Faculty 10 total (full-time and part-time). 100% of full-time faculty have terminal degrees. Graduate students do not teach undergraduate courses. Undergraduate student–faculty ratio: 12:1.
Student Life Student groups/activities include Clayhounds, Kappa Pi Art Club.
Expenses for 1997–98 Application fee: $15. State resident tuition: $1170 full-time. Nonresident tuition: $5832 full-time. Mandatory fees: $546 full-time. College room and board: $2942. College room only: $1372. Special program-related fees: $90 per course for ceramic lab fee, $60 per course for graphic design lab fee, $50 per course for photography lab fee.
Financial Aid Program-specific awards for 1997: 6–15 Lorraine Shula Awards for program majors ($500–$1000), 15 Participation Grants for freshmen program majors ($200).
Application Procedures Students apply for admission into the professional program by sophomore year. Deadline for freshmen and transfers: continuous. Required: high school transcript, minimum 2.0 high school GPA, portfolio. Portfolio reviews held by appointment on campus; the submission of slides may be substituted for portfolios when distance is prohibitive.
Undergraduate Contact Mr. Jim Bryant, Chair, Art Department, Eastern New Mexico University, Station #19, Portales, New Mexico 88130; 505-562-2778, fax: 505-562-2362.

▼ EAST TENNESSEE STATE UNIVERSITY

Johnson City, Tennessee

State-supported, coed. Small town campus. Total enrollment: 11,596. Art program established 1911.
Degrees Bachelor of Fine Arts in the areas of drawing, painting, sculpture, ceramics, metals, fibers, graphic design, photography, printmaking. Majors and concentrations: art education, art/fine arts, ceramic art and design, commercial art, computer graphics, jewelry and metalsmithing, painting/drawing, photography, printmaking, sculpture, textile arts. Graduate degrees offered: Master of Fine Arts in the areas of drawing, painting, sculpture, ceramics, metals, fibers, graphic design, photography, printmaking; Master of Arts in the area of art education. Cross-registration with Penland School of Crafts. Program accredited by NASAD.
Enrollment Fall 1997: 520 total; 200 undergraduate, 19 graduate, 301 non-professional degree.
Art Student Profile 53% females, 47% males, 7% minorities, 1% international.
Art Faculty 26 total undergraduate and graduate (full-time and part-time). 100% of full-time faculty have terminal degrees. Graduate students teach a few undergraduate courses. Undergraduate student–faculty ratio: 10:1.
Student Life Student groups/activities include Art Student League, student associations and guilds.
Expenses for 1997–98 Application fee: $15. State resident tuition: $1816 full-time. Nonresident tuition: $6412 full-time.

Mandatory fees: $284 full-time. College room and board: $2520. Room and board charges vary according to board plan and housing facility.

Financial Aid Program-specific awards for 1997: 1 Hays Scholarship for entering freshmen ($1000), 1 Adams Scholarship for rising sophomores ($1000), 1 Adams Scholarship for rising juniors ($300–$500).

Application Procedures Students apply for admission into the professional program by sophomore year. Deadline for freshmen and transfers: continuous. Required: high school transcript, college transcript(s) for transfer students, portfolio, SAT I or ACT test scores (minimum combined ACT score of 19). Recommended: minimum 3.0 high school GPA, interview. Portfolio reviews held when announced on campus.

Undergraduate Contact Mr. David G. Logan, Chairperson, Department of Art and Design, East Tennessee State University, PO Box 70708, Johnson City, Tennessee 37614-0708; 423-439-4247, fax: 423-439-4393, E-mail address: logand@etsuvax.east-tenn-st.edu.

Graduate Contact Dr. James C. Mills, Graduate Coordinator, Department of Art and Design, East Tennessee State University, PO Box 70708, Johnson City, Tennessee 37614-0708; 423-439-4247, fax: 423-439-4393, E-mail address: mills@etsuvax.east-tenn-st.edu.

▼ EDINBORO UNIVERSITY OF PENNSYLVANIA

Edinboro, Pennsylvania

State-supported, coed. Small town campus. Total enrollment: 7,083. Art program established 1920.

Degrees Bachelor of Fine Arts in the areas of crafts, applied media arts, fine arts; Bachelor of Science in the area of art education. Majors and concentrations: animation, art education, art history, ceramics, drawing, film, film and video production, furniture design, graphic design, jewelry and metalsmithing, painting, photography, printmaking, sculpture, weaving and fibers. Graduate degrees offered: Master of Fine Arts in the area of art.

Enrollment Fall 1997: 730 undergraduate, 15 graduate.

Art Faculty 40 total undergraduate and graduate (full-time and part-time). 95% of full-time faculty have terminal degrees. Graduate students do not teach undergraduate courses. Undergraduate student–faculty ratio: 15:1.

Student Life Student groups/activities include Student Art League, clubs in every studio area.

Expenses for 1997–98 Application fee: $25. State resident tuition: $3468 full-time. Nonresident tuition: $8824 full-time. Mandatory fees: $725 full-time. College room and board: $3674. College room only: $1994. Room and board charges vary according to board plan. Special program-related fees for lab fees for art studio courses.

Application Procedures Students admitted directly into the professional program freshman year. Deadline for freshmen and transfers: continuous. Required: high school transcript, college transcript(s) for transfer students, SAT I or ACT test scores. Recommended: interview, personal statement.

Undergraduate Contact Dr. Connie Mullineaux, Chair, Art Department, Edinboro University of Pennsylvania, DH 102, Edinboro, Pennsylvania 16444; 814-732-2406, fax: 814-732-2629.

Graduate Contact Dr. Philip Kerstetter, Director, School of Graduate Studies, Edinboro University of Pennsylvania, Edinboro, Pennsylvania 16444; 814-732-2856, fax: 814-732-2956.

▼ EMMANUEL COLLEGE

Boston, Massachusetts

Independent-Roman Catholic, women only. Urban campus. Total enrollment: 1,552. Art program established 1957.

Degrees Bachelor of Fine Arts in the areas of painting and printmaking, visual communications and graphic design. Majors and concentrations: art education, art history, graphic arts, painting/drawing, studio art. Cross-registration with Simmons College, Wheelock College, Wentworth Institute of Technology, Massachusetts College of Pharmacy and Allied Health Sciences.

Enrollment Fall 1997: 80 undergraduate.

Art Student Profile 99% females, 1% males, 10% international.

Art Faculty 9 total (full-time and part-time). 100% of full-time faculty have terminal degrees. Graduate students do not teach undergraduate courses. Undergraduate student–faculty ratio: 15:1.

Student Life Student groups/activities include professional gallery on campus, membership in Boston Museum of Fine Arts and Gardner Museum.

Expenses for 1997–98 Application fee: $40. Comprehensive fee: $21,335 includes full-time tuition ($14,250), mandatory fees ($300), and college room and board ($6785). Special program-related fees: $20–$50 per course for materials fee for studio classes.

Financial Aid Program-specific awards for 1997: 2 Sr. Vincent Scholarships for freshmen ($4500).

Application Procedures Students admitted directly into the professional program freshman year. Deadline for freshmen and transfers: September 1. Notification date for freshmen and transfers: September 16. Required: essay, high school transcript, minimum 2.0 high school GPA, 2 letters of recommendation, interview. Recommended: portfolio. Portfolio reviews held twice on campus; the submission of slides may be substituted for portfolios when time constraints exist.

Web Site http://www.emmanuel.edu.

Undergraduate Contact Director of Admissions, Emmanuel College, 400 The Fenway, Boston, Massachusetts 02115; 617-735-9715, fax: 617-735-9877.

▼ EMPORIA STATE UNIVERSITY

Emporia, Kansas

State-supported, coed. Small town campus. Total enrollment: 5,320. Art program established 1863.

Degrees Bachelor of Fine Arts in the areas of ceramics, commercial art, painting, photography, printmaking, sculpture and glassforming, weaving. Majors and concentrations: art education, art therapy, ceramic art and design, commercial art, glassworking, jewelry and metalsmithing, painting/drawing, photography, printmaking, sculpture, weaving. Cross-registration with Flint Hills Technical College. Program accredited by NASAD.

Enrollment Fall 1997: 145 total; 120 undergraduate, 25 non-professional degree.

Emporia State University (*continued*)

Art Student Profile 65% females, 35% males, 5% minorities, 3% international.

Art Faculty 17 total (full-time and part-time). 88% of full-time faculty have terminal degrees. Graduate students do not teach undergraduate courses. Undergraduate student–faculty ratio: 15:1.

Student Life Student groups/activities include Alpha Rho Theta, Glass Guild.

Estimated expenses for 1998–99 Application fee: $20. State resident tuition: $1536 full-time. Nonresident tuition: $5900 full-time. Mandatory fees: $446 full-time. College room and board: $3560. College room only: $1720. Special program-related fees: $5–$40 per class for expendable supplies.

Financial Aid Program-specific awards for 1997: 6 Jerry Ely Awards for art majors ($750), 1 Hazelrigg Memorial Award for metalry majors ($250), 3 Art Faculty Awards for art majors ($250), 4 Beulah Holton Memorial Awards for art education majors ($400), 1 Linda Ball Memorial Award for art majors ($250), 1 Cremer Family Memorial Award for art majors ($500), 1 Jean Hesenbart Memorial Award for art majors ($500), 1 Art 96 Award for art majors ($500), 4 Ames Family Memorial Awards for art majors ($225).

Application Procedures Students admitted directly into the professional program freshman year. Deadline for freshmen and transfers: continuous. Required: high school transcript, college transcript(s) for transfer students, ACT test score only, portfolio for scholarship consideration. Portfolio reviews held twice on campus; the submission of slides may be substituted for portfolios (slides preferred).

Web Site http://www.emporia.edu/art/arthome.htm.

Undergraduate Contact Mr. Donald Perry, Chair, Division of Art, Emporia State University, Campus Box 4015, 1200 Commercial, Emporia, Kansas 66801-5087; 316-341-5246, fax: 316-341-5681, E-mail address: perrydon@esumail.emporia.edu.

▼ Evangel College

Springfield, Missouri

Independent, coed. Urban campus. Total enrollment: 1,616.

Degrees Bachelor of Fine Arts in the areas of graphic design, sculpture, painting. Cross-registration with Drury College, Southwest Missouri State University.

Enrollment Fall 1997: 37 total; all undergraduate.

Art Student Profile 53% females, 47% males, 5% minorities, 10% international.

Art Faculty 6 total (full-time and part-time). 100% of full-time faculty have terminal degrees. Graduate students do not teach undergraduate courses.

Expenses for 1998–99 Application fee: $25. Comprehensive fee: $12,400 includes full-time tuition ($8390), mandatory fees ($460), and college room and board ($3550). Special program-related fees: $30–$80 per course for supplies.

Financial Aid Program-specific awards for 1997: 4 Humanities Awards for program students ($715), 1 Ben Messick Scholarship for program students ($950), 1 Riepma Scholarship for program students ($620), 2 Seed Scholarships for incoming freshmen ($500), 2 Young Christian Leadership Awards for incoming freshmen ($500), academic scholarships for incoming freshmen ($1000–$2000).

Application Procedures Students apply for admission into the professional program by sophomore year. Deadline for freshmen and transfers: continuous. Notification date for freshmen and transfers: continuous. Required: high school transcript, college transcript(s) for transfer students, minimum 2.0 high school GPA. Recommended: 2 letters of recommendation, interview, portfolio, SAT I or ACT test scores. Portfolio reviews held twice on campus; the submission of slides may be substituted for portfolios for large works of art.

Undergraduate Contact Mr. Stan Maples, Professor, Art Department, Evangel College, 1111 North Glenstone Avenue, Springfield, Missouri 65802; 417-865-2811 ext. 7395, fax: 417-865-9599.

▼ Fashion Institute of Technology

New York, New York

State and locally supported, coed. Urban campus. Total enrollment: 11,696. Art program established 1976.

Degrees Bachelor of Fine Arts in the areas of advertising design, fabric styling, fashion design, illustration, interior design, packaging, restoration, textile surface design, toy design. Graduate degrees offered: Master of Arts in the areas of gallery and retail art administration, museum studies: applied arts, museum studies: costume and textiles. Cross-registration with State University of New York System. Program accredited by NASAD, FIDER.

Enrollment Fall 1997: 724 undergraduate, 93 graduate.

Art Student Profile 80% females, 20% males, 50% minorities, 11% international.

Art Faculty 80 total undergraduate and graduate (full-time). 100% of full-time faculty have terminal degrees. Graduate students do not teach undergraduate courses.

Student Life Student groups/activities include Fit Theatre Ensemble club activities, literary publications, student newspaper.

Expenses for 1997–98 Application fee: $30. State resident tuition: $2500 full-time. Nonresident tuition: $5850 full-time. Mandatory fees: $210 full-time. Full-time tuition and fees vary according to degree level and program. College room and board: $5425. College room only: $3092. Room and board charges vary according to board plan and housing facility.

Financial Aid Program-specific awards for 1997: 1065 grants/scholarships for those demonstrating financial need ($1549).

Application Procedures Students admitted directly into the professional program freshman year. Deadline for freshmen and transfers: continuous. Required: essay, high school transcript, college transcript(s) for transfer students, minimum 2.0 high school GPA, portfolio. Recommended: 3 letters of recommendation, SAT I or ACT test scores. Portfolio reviews held several times on campus; the submission of slides may be substituted for portfolios with permission of the chair.

Web Site http://www.fitnyc.suny.edu.

Undergraduate Contact Mr. James Pidgeon, Director of Admissions, Fashion Institute of Technology, Seventh Avenue at 27th Street, New York, New York 10001-5992; 212-217-7675, fax: 212-217-7481, E-mail address: pidgeonj@sfitva.cc.fitsuny.edu.

Graduate Contact Bruce Chambers, Dean, Graduate Studies, Fashion Institute of Technology, Seventh Avenue at 27th Street, New York, New York 10001-5992; 212-217-5714, fax: 212-217-5156, E-mail address: chambru@sfitva.cc.fitsuny.edu.

More About the College

Program Facilities The Peter G. Scotese Computer-Aided Design and Communications facility provides art and design students with the opportunity to explore technology and its integration in the design of textiles, toys, interiors, fashion, and advertising as well as photography and computer graphics. Also located on campus is the design/research lighting laboratory, an educational and professional development facility for interior design and other academic disciplines.

The Museum at FIT is the repository for the world's largest collection of costumes, textiles, and accessories of dress (with an emphasis on 20th century apparel), and is used by students, designers, and historians for research and inspiration.

Student Opportunities The museum's galleries provide a showcase for a wide spectrum of exhibitions relevant to fashion and its satellite industries. The annual student art and design exhibition is shown here as are other student projects during the year. Student work is also displayed throughout the campus. Fashion shows of menswear, womenswear, and accessories occur each academic year.

Faculty and Alumni Those who do, teach at FIT. Members of the FIT community have considerable experience and are on the cutting edge of their various fields and industries. FIT counts among its alumni such superstars as Calvin Klein and Norma Kamali, as well as successful and talented professionals in advertising, packaging, television, the design fields, merchandising, manufacturing, public relations, and retailing.

Special Programs FIT offers semester-abroad programs and a number of international short study courses, including its own international fashion design program in New York and Florence, Italy. Internships are also offered in most majors.

Saturday Live programs are available during fall, spring, and summer. These twenty-five programs offer high school students the chance to learn in a studio environment, to explore the business and technology side of the fashion industry, and to discover natural talents and creative abilities. Classes are taught by a faculty of artists, designers, and other professionals. High school credit may be earned at the discretion of each student's school.

▼

Today, to know the Fashion Institute of Technology only by name is not to know it very well at all. The name reflects back fifty years to the college's origins when it was devoted exclusively to educating students for careers in the apparel industry. But the name no longer tells the whole story.

A "fashion college" that offers programs in interior design, jewelry design, advertising and communications, and even toy design; a community college that offers bachelor's and master's degree programs in addition to the traditional two-year associate degree, FIT is an educational institution like no other.

The campus leaves behind the rolling green lawns of the more traditional college campus in favor of the challenges and excitement of "unique New York." FIT's location in the heart of Manhattan—where the worlds of fashion, art, design, communications, and manufacturing converge—permits an exceptional two-way flow between the college and the industries and professions it serves.

FIT is rooted in industry and the world of work. Industry visits by students and lectures by many different leaders in the field provide a cooperative and creative bridge between the classroom and the actual world of work. And though the college is now associated with many industries and professions, not just one, FIT's commitment to career education is still its hallmark, and a source of pride to an institution whose industry connection is an integral part of its history.

FIT serves more than 5,600 full-time and 5,000 part-time students yearly, who come not only from within commuting distances, but also from all fifty states and sixty-five other countries.

Founded in 1944, FIT today is a college of art and design and business and technology of the State University of New York. More than fifteen majors in art and design and ten in business and technology lead to the A.A.S., B.F.A., or B.S. degree (in addition to the M.A. degree).

FIT is an accredited institutional member of the Middle States Association of Colleges and Schools, the National Association of Schools of Art and Design, and the Foundation for Interior Design Education Research.

The eight-building campus includes classrooms, studios, and labs that reflect the most advanced educational and industrial practices. Facilities include photography studios and darkrooms, painting rooms, sculpture studio, toy design workshop, a graphics laboratory, model-making workshop, printmaking room, life-sketching rooms, restoration lab, television studios, display and exhibit design rooms, and textile labs for floor, hand, and computer-aided looms. Also of importance and located on three floors is the Gladys Marcus Library, which houses more than 110,000 titles including books, periodicals, and nonprint materials. Three dormitories serve approximately 1,250 students and offer various accommodations.

At FIT, placement is the bottom line; with a consistent job placement rate of 88%, FIT graduates are well prepared to meet employers' needs. Working with both undergraduates and graduates, placement counselors develop job opportunities for full-time, part-time, freelance, and summer employment.

Student participation is encouraged through more than sixty campus clubs, organizations, and athletic teams.

Schmidt College of Arts and Letters

▼ FLORIDA ATLANTIC UNIVERSITY

Boca Raton, Florida

State-supported, coed. Suburban campus. Total enrollment: 18,823. Art program established 1961.

Florida Atlantic University *(continued)*

Degrees Bachelor of Fine Arts in the area of art. Majors and concentrations: ceramics, graphic design, painting/drawing, photography, printmaking, sculpture. Graduate degrees offered: Master of Fine Arts in the areas of ceramics, painting, graphic design, computer arts.

Enrollment Fall 1997: 314 total; 310 undergraduate, 4 graduate.

Art Student Profile 67% females, 33% males, 13% minorities, 12% international.

Art Faculty 21 total undergraduate and graduate (full-time and part-time). 100% of full-time faculty have terminal degrees. Graduate students do not teach undergraduate courses.

Student Life Student groups/activities include Potters Guild, Juried Student Show, Bachelor of Fine Arts Show.

Expenses for 1997–98 Application fee: $20. State resident tuition: $2022 full-time. Nonresident tuition: $7940 full-time. Full-time tuition varies according to course load. College room and board: $4680. College room only: $2360. Room and board charges vary according to board plan and housing facility. Special program-related fees: $15 per course per semester for studio lab fee.

Financial Aid Program-specific awards for 1997: 1 Palm Beach Water Color Society Award for art majors ($500), 1 Delray Beach Art League Award for art majors ($500), 1 Dorst Award for seniors ($500), 3 McCoy Awards for ceramics students ($500), 1 American Pen Women Award for female art majors ($500), 2 Women in the Visual Arts for female art majors ($1000).

Application Procedures Students admitted directly into the professional program freshman year. Deadline for freshmen and transfers: June 1. Required: high school transcript, minimum 2.0 high school GPA, SAT I or ACT test scores, minimum 2.0 college GPA for transfer students. Recommended: minimum 3.0 high school GPA.

Contact Dr. Kathleen Russo, Chair, Art Department, Florida Atlantic University, 777 Glades Road, Boca Raton, Florida 33431; 561-297-3870, fax: 561-297-3078, E-mail address: russok@fau.edu.

▼ FLORIDA INTERNATIONAL UNIVERSITY

Miami, Florida

State-supported, coed. Urban campus. Total enrollment: 30,012.

Degrees Bachelor of Fine Arts. Majors and concentrations: ceramics, drawing, electronic arts, jewelry and metalsmithing, painting, photography, printmaking, sculpture. Graduate degrees offered: Master of Fine Arts. Program accredited by NASAD.

Enrollment Fall 1997: 206 undergraduate.

Art Faculty 36 total undergraduate and graduate (full-time and part-time). 100% of full-time faculty have terminal degrees. Graduate students do not teach undergraduate courses. Undergraduate student–faculty ratio: 10:1.

Student Life Student groups/activities include Fine Arts Students Association.

Expenses for 1997–98 Application fee: $20. State resident tuition: $1943 full-time. Nonresident tuition: $7859 full-time. Mandatory fees: $92 full-time. College room and board: $7378. College room only: $4448. Room and board charges

vary according to board plan and housing facility. Special program-related fees: $15 per course for studio lab fee.

Application Procedures Students admitted directly into the professional program freshman year. Deadline for freshmen and transfers: April 1. Required: high school transcript, college transcript(s) for transfer students, SAT I or ACT test scores, TOEFL score for international applicants, minimum 2.0 college GPA for transfer students. Recommended: minimum 2.0 high school GPA.

Undergraduate Contact Mr. William Maguire, Head Advisor, Department of Visual Arts, Florida International University, University Park, Miami, Florida 33199; 305-348-2897, fax: 305-348-6544.

Graduate Contact James Cooper, Director of Graduate Studies, Department of Visual Arts, Florida International University, University Park, Miami, Florida 33199; 305-348-6268.

▼ FLORIDA STATE UNIVERSITY

Tallahassee, Florida

State-supported, coed. Suburban campus. Total enrollment: 30,401.

Degrees Bachelor of Fine Arts in the area of studio art. Graduate degrees offered: Master of Fine Arts in the area of studio art. Program accredited by NASAD.

Enrollment Fall 1997: 337 total; 39 undergraduate, 25 graduate, 273 non-professional degree.

Art Student Profile 50% females, 50% males, 5% minorities, 1% international.

Art Faculty 30 total undergraduate and graduate (full-time and part-time). 100% of full-time faculty have terminal degrees. Graduate students teach a few undergraduate courses. Undergraduate student–faculty ratio: 16:1.

Student Life Student groups/activities include Art Student League.

Expenses for 1997–98 Application fee: $20. State resident tuition: $1988 full-time. Nonresident tuition: $7905 full-time. College room and board: $4570. College room only: $2540. Room and board charges vary according to board plan and housing facility. Special program-related fees: $15 per course for lab fee.

Application Procedures Students apply for admission into the professional program by sophomore year. Deadline for freshmen and transfers: continuous. Required: essay, high school transcript, minimum 2.0 high school GPA, portfolio, SAT I test score only. Recommended: minimum 3.0 high school GPA, letter of recommendation. Portfolio reviews held once on campus; the submission of slides may be substituted for portfolios whenever necessary.

Undergraduate Contact Ms. Phyllis Straus, Undergraduate Admissions Coordinator, Department of Visual Arts and Dance, Florida State University, 220 FAB-2037, Tallahassee, Florida 32306-2037; 850-644-6474, fax: 850-644-8977.

Graduate Contact Ms. Patricia Kitchens, Department Secretary, Department of Art, Florida State University, 220 FAB - 2037, Tallahassee, Florida 32306-2037; 850-644-6474, fax: 850-644-8977, E-mail address: pkitchen@mailer.fsu.edu.

▼ FORT HAYS STATE UNIVERSITY

Hays, Kansas

State-supported, coed. Small town campus. Total enrollment: 5,616.

Degrees Bachelor of Fine Arts in the areas of design, graphic design, interior design, drawing, painting, printmaking, sculpture, ceramics, jewelry, art education, crafts. Majors and concentrations: art education, art/fine arts, ceramic art and design, commercial art, computer graphics, graphic arts, illustration, interior design, jewelry and metalsmithing, painting/drawing, photography, printmaking, sculpture, studio art. Graduate degrees offered: Master of Fine Arts in the areas of design, graphic design, drawing, painting, printmaking, sculpture, ceramics, jewelry, crafts.

Enrollment Fall 1997: 266 total; 232 undergraduate, 23 graduate, 11 non-professional degree.

Art Faculty 14 total undergraduate and graduate (full-time and part-time). 83% of full-time faculty have terminal degrees. Graduate students do not teach undergraduate courses. Undergraduate student–faculty ratio: 18:1.

Student Life Student groups/activities include Creative Arts Society.

Expenses for 1997–98 Application fee: $20. State resident tuition: $1992 full-time. Nonresident tuition: $6256 full-time. Full-time tuition varies according to course load, location, and reciprocity agreements. College room and board: $3400. College room only: $1766. Room and board charges vary according to board plan, housing facility, and student level. Special program-related fees: $5–$75 per semester for supplies.

Financial Aid Program-specific awards for 1997: 40 Awards of Excellence for freshmen ($400), 20 art scholarships for upperclassmen ($200).

Application Procedures Students admitted directly into the professional program freshman year. Deadline for freshmen and transfers: continuous. Required: high school transcript, college transcript(s) for transfer students. Recommended: minimum 2.0 high school GPA, portfolio. Portfolio reviews held twice on campus and off campus in various cities in Kansas; the submission of slides may be substituted for portfolios whenever needed.

Undergraduate Contact Mr. Leland W. Powers, Assistant Professor and Acting Chair, Art Department, Fort Hays State University, 600 Park Street, Hays, Kansas 67601-4099; 785-628-4247, fax: 785-628-4087, E-mail address: arlp@fhsu.edu.

Graduate Contact Colleen Taylor, Secretary, Art Department, Fort Hays State University, 600 Park Street, Hays, Kansas 67601-4099; 785-628-4247, fax: 785-628-4087, E-mail address: arct@fhsu.edu.

▼ FROSTBURG STATE UNIVERSITY

Frostburg, Maryland

State-supported, coed. Small town campus. Total enrollment: 5,199.

Degrees Bachelor of Fine Arts in the area of art and design.

Enrollment Fall 1997: 140 total; all undergraduate.

Art Student Profile 50% females, 50% males, 4% minorities.

Art Faculty 17 total (full-time and part-time). 100% of full-time faculty have terminal degrees. Graduate students do not teach undergraduate courses.

Student Life Student groups/activities include Stephanie Ann Roper Art Gallery, Art Club.

Expenses for 1997–98 Application fee: $30. State resident tuition: $2972 full-time. Nonresident tuition: $6958 full-time. Mandatory fees: $572 full-time. Full-time tuition and fees vary according to course load and program. College room

and board: $4786. College room only: $2489. Room and board charges vary according to board plan and housing facility.

Financial Aid Program-specific awards for 1997: 1 Stephanie Ann Roper Scholarship for freshmen program majors ($250), 1 Stephanie Ann Roper Scholarship for sophomore and junior program majors ($250), 1 Talent in the Arts Scholarship for entering freshmen, 1 Harry Mandell Scholarship for art education majors ($250).

Application Procedures Students apply for admission into the professional program by sophomore year. Deadline for freshmen and transfers: continuous. Required: high school transcript, college transcript(s) for transfer students, SAT I test score only. Recommended: 2 letters of recommendation, interview, portfolio. Portfolio reviews held by appointment on campus and off campus in Washington, DC; the submission of slides may be substituted for portfolios if original work is not available.

Undergraduate Contact Admissions Office, Frostburg State University, Frostburg, Maryland 21532; 301-687-4201, fax: 301-687-7074.

▼ GEORGIA SOUTHERN UNIVERSITY

Statesboro, Georgia

State-supported, coed. Small town campus. Total enrollment: 13,963.

Degrees Bachelor of Fine Arts in the area of art. Majors and concentrations: ceramics, drawing, graphic arts, painting, photography, printmaking, sculpture. Graduate degrees offered: Master of Fine Arts in the area of art. Program accredited by NASAD.

Enrollment Fall 1997: 257 total; 100 undergraduate, 17 graduate, 140 non-professional degree.

Art Student Profile 60% females, 40% males, 25% minorities, 5% international.

Art Faculty 17 total undergraduate and graduate (full-time and part-time). 100% of full-time faculty have terminal degrees. Graduate students do not teach undergraduate courses. Undergraduate student–faculty ratio: 14:1.

Student Life Student groups/activities include Club MUD, Student Art League.

Expenses for 1997–98 Application fee: $10. State resident tuition: $1680 full-time. Nonresident tuition: $6141 full-time. Mandatory fees: $576 full-time. College room and board: $3465. College room only: $1815. Room and board charges vary according to board plan and housing facility.

Application Procedures Students admitted directly into the professional program freshman year. Deadline for freshmen and transfers: continuous. Required: high school transcript, SAT I or ACT test scores.

Web Site http://www2.gasou.edu/art/.

Contact Mr. Richard Tichich, Chair, Art Department, Georgia Southern University, Landrum Box 8032, Statesboro, Georgia 30460; 912-681-5358, fax: 912-681-5104.

▼ GEORGIA SOUTHWESTERN STATE UNIVERSITY

Americus, Georgia

State-supported, coed. Small town campus. Total enrollment: 2,414.

Georgia Southwestern State University (continued)

Degrees Bachelor of Fine Arts in the area of art; Bachelor of Science in the area of art education. Majors and concentrations: ceramic art and design, commercial art, computer graphics, craft design, glassworking, graphic arts, painting/drawing, photography, sculpture. Program accredited by NASAD.
Enrollment Fall 1997: 136 total; 60 undergraduate, 76 nonprofessional degree.
Art Student Profile 44% females, 56% males, 21% minorities, 30% international.
Art Faculty 7 total (full-time and part-time). 100% of full-time faculty have terminal degrees. Graduate students do not teach undergraduate courses. Undergraduate student–faculty ratio: 15:1.
Student Life Student groups/activities include Artists Associated.
Expenses for 1997–98 Application fee: $10. State resident tuition: $1680 full-time. Nonresident tuition: $6141 full-time. Mandatory fees: $465 full-time. College room and board: $3222. College room only: $1530.
Financial Aid Program-specific awards for 1997: Rony Scholarships for freshmen and sophomore program majors, Rony Scholarships for transfer students, 9 Student Art Competition Scholarships for program majors.
Application Procedures Students apply for admission into the professional program by freshman year. Deadline for freshmen and transfers: August 1. Required: high school transcript, minimum 2.0 high school GPA, interview, portfolio, SAT I or ACT test scores. Portfolio reviews held twice on campus; the submission of slides may be substituted for portfolios when distance is prohibitive.
Undergraduate Contact Mr. Jack Lewis, Coordinator, Visual Arts Program, Department of Fine Arts, Georgia Southwestern State University, 800 Wheatley Street, Americus, Georgia 31709-4693; 912-931-2204, fax: 912-931-2927.

▼ Georgia State University
Atlanta, Georgia

State-supported, coed. Urban campus. Total enrollment: 24,276.
Degrees Bachelor of Fine Arts in the areas of studio art, art education. Majors and concentrations: ceramic art and design, graphic arts, interior design, jewelry and metalsmithing, painting/drawing, photography, printmaking, sculpture, textile arts. Graduate degrees offered: Master of Fine Arts in the area of studio art. Cross-registration with various area universities. Program accredited by NASAD.
Enrollment Fall 1997: 1,049 total; 534 undergraduate, 35 graduate, 480 non-professional degree.
Art Faculty 37 total undergraduate and graduate (full-time and part-time). 100% of full-time faculty have terminal degrees. Graduate students teach a few undergraduate courses.
Expenses for 1997–98 Application fee: $25. State resident tuition: $2250 full-time. Nonresident tuition: $9000 full-time. Mandatory fees: $423 full-time. College room only: $3789. Special program-related fees: $20–$30 per semester for art supplies.
Application Procedures Students apply for admission into the professional program by sophomore year. Deadline for freshmen and transfers: July 1. Required: high school

transcript, college transcript(s) for transfer students, minimum 2.0 high school GPA, SAT I or ACT test scores.
Web Site http://www.gsu.edu/~wwwart.
Undergraduate Contact Office of Admissions, Georgia State University, PO Box 4009, Atlanta, Georgia 30303; 404-651-2365.
Graduate Contact Office of Graduate Studies, Georgia State University, College of Arts and Sciences, University Plaza, Atlanta, Georgia 30303-3088; 404-651-2297, fax: 404-651-1032.

▼ Grand Valley State University
Allendale, Michigan

State-supported, coed. Small town campus. Total enrollment: 15,676. Art program established 1961.
Degrees Bachelor of Fine Arts in the areas of printmaking, painting, ceramics, graphic design, metalsmithing, sculpture, illustration. Majors and concentrations: ceramic art and design, graphic arts, illustration, jewelry and metalsmithing, painting/drawing, printmaking, sculpture. Program accredited by NASAD.
Enrollment Fall 1997: 1,721 total; 321 undergraduate, 1,400 non-professional degree.
Art Student Profile 71% females, 29% males, 4% minorities, 1% international.
Art Faculty 24 total (full-time and part-time). 100% of full-time faculty have terminal degrees. Graduate students do not teach undergraduate courses.
Student Life Special housing available for art students.
Expenses for 1997–98 Application fee: $20. State resident tuition: $3348 full-time. Nonresident tuition: $7238 full-time. Mandatory fees: $60 full-time. Full-time tuition and fees vary according to student level. College room and board: $4640. Room and board charges vary according to board plan and housing facility. Special program-related fees: $5–$15 per credit for studio maintenance.
Financial Aid Program-specific awards for 1997: 6 Recruitment Awards for freshmen ($1000), 2 Branstrom Awards for program majors ($1000–$1500), 2 Calder Awards for program majors ($1000–$1500), 3 Ox Bow Summer Program for program majors ($2000).
Application Procedures Students admitted directly into the professional program freshman year. Deadline for freshmen and transfers: continuous. Required: high school transcript, minimum 3.0 high school GPA, ACT test score only (minimum combined ACT score of 21), portfolio for scholarship consideration. Portfolio reviews held 4 times on campus and off campus in various cities in Michigan and contiguous states.
Web Site http://www.gvsu.edu/~art/.
Undergraduate Contact Dr. J. David McGee, Chair, Art and Design Department, Grand Valley State University, 1 College Landing, Allendale, Michigan 49401; 616-895-2575, E-mail address: mcgeed@gvsu.edu.

▼ Guilford College
Greensboro, North Carolina

Independent, coed. Suburban campus. Total enrollment: 1,402.

Degrees Bachelor of Fine Arts in the area of studio art. Majors and concentrations: ceramics, painting/drawing, photography, printmaking, sculpture. Cross-registration with University of North Carolina at Greensboro.

Enrollment Fall 1997: 53 total; 8 undergraduate, 45 non-professional degree.

Art Student Profile 60% females, 40% males, 2% minorities, 2% international.

Art Faculty 6 total (full-time and part-time). 100% of full-time faculty have terminal degrees. Graduate students do not teach undergraduate courses. Undergraduate student–faculty ratio: 12:1.

Student Life Student groups/activities include Annual Student Art Exhibition, senior thesis exhibition.

Expenses for 1997–98 Application fee: $25. Comprehensive fee: $20,020 includes full-time tuition ($14,180), mandatory fees ($570), and college room and board ($5270). College room only: $2786.

Financial Aid Program-specific awards for 1997: 1–3 J. S. Laing Scholarships for program majors ($200–$400).

Application Procedures Students apply for admission into the professional program by junior year. Deadline for freshmen: February 1; transfers: May 1. Notification date for freshmen: March 15; transfers: June 1. Required: essay, high school transcript, minimum 2.0 high school GPA, SAT I test score only. Recommended: letter of recommendation, interview, portfolio. Portfolio reviews held once at end of junior year or by appointment on campus; the submission of slides may be substituted for portfolios whenever necessary.

Undergraduate Contact Mr. Roy Nydorf, Chair, Art Department, Guilford College, 5800 West Friendly Avenue, Greensboro, North Carolina 27410; 336-316-2228.

▼ HARDING UNIVERSITY

Searcy, Arkansas

Independent, coed. Small town campus. Total enrollment: 3,754. Art program established 1936.

Degrees Bachelor of Fine Arts in the areas of graphic design, painting, three-dimensional design; Bachelor of Science in the areas of art therapy, interior design. Majors and concentrations: art therapy, graphic design, interior design. Program accredited by NCATE.

Enrollment Fall 1997: 120 total; all undergraduate.

Art Student Profile 46% females, 54% males, 5% minorities, 2% international.

Art Faculty 9 total (full-time and part-time). 83% of full-time faculty have terminal degrees. Graduate students do not teach undergraduate courses. Undergraduate student–faculty ratio: 18:1.

Student Life Student groups/activities include Kappa Pi (international honorary art fraternity), Red Brick Studio (graphic design club).

Expenses for 1997–98 Application fee: $25. Comprehensive fee: $11,698 includes full-time tuition ($6528), mandatory fees ($1184), and college room and board ($3986). College room only: $1874. Room and board charges vary according to board plan and housing facility. Special program-related fees: $10–$70 per course for supplies.

Financial Aid Program-specific awards for 1997: 15 art scholarships for program majors ($350–$700).

Application Procedures Students apply for admission into the professional program by sophomore year. Deadline for freshmen and transfers: continuous. Required: high school

transcript, college transcript(s) for transfer students, 2 letters of recommendation, SAT I or ACT test scores (minimum combined ACT score of 18). Recommended: interview, portfolio. Portfolio reviews held once on campus; the submission of slides may be substituted for portfolios for international applicants or when distance is prohibitive.

Undergraduate Contact Mr. Don Robinson, Chairman, Art Department, Harding University, Box 12253, Searcy, Arkansas 72149-0001; 501-279-4426, E-mail address: art@harding.edu.

▼ HARRINGTON INSTITUTE OF INTERIOR DESIGN

Chicago, Illinois

Proprietary, coed. Urban campus. Total enrollment: 384. Art program established 1931.

Degrees Bachelor of Fine Arts in the area of interior design. Program accredited by NASAD, FIDER.

Enrollment Fall 1997: 370 total; 195 undergraduate, 175 non-professional degree.

Art Student Profile 75% females, 25% males, 9% minorities, 9% international.

Art Faculty 31 total (full-time and part-time). 24% of full-time faculty have terminal degrees. Graduate students do not teach undergraduate courses. Undergraduate student–faculty ratio: 15:1.

Student Life Student groups/activities include American Society of Interior Designers, International Interior Design Association, Student Government.

Expenses for 1997–98 Application fee: $50. Tuition: $10,416 full-time. Mandatory fees: $50 full-time.

Financial Aid Program-specific awards for 1997: 2 Manhoff Scholarships for first semester students ($500), 2 Mallin Scholarships for first semester students ($250).

Application Procedures Students admitted directly into the professional program freshman year. Deadline for freshmen and transfers: continuous. Required: high school transcript, college transcript(s) for transfer students, interview. Recommended: minimum 2.0 high school GPA, SAT I or ACT test scores.

Web Site http://www.interiordesign.edu.

Undergraduate Contact Mr. Robert C. Marks, Dean, Harrington Institute of Interior Design, 410 South Michigan Avenue, Chicago, Illinois 60605-1496; 312-939-4975, fax: 312-939-8005.

More About the Institute

Program Facilities The Harrington Institute of Interior Design has a completely equipped CAD Lab, and a highly specialized Interior Design Library. The school's studios and classrooms offer views of Lake Michigan and Grant Park. The historic Fine Arts Building is an inspiring location for the study of design.

Faculty, Resident Artists, and Alumni The faculty consists of highly experienced, practicing designers and architects. Alumni of the Harrington Institute of Interior Design teach at and head numerous interior design programs.

Student Performance and Exhibit Opportunities Harrington students regularly enter and win regional and national design competitions.

Special Programs Harrington Institute of Interior Design is the only college in the Midwest exclusively devoted to interior design. It is also the only college in the Chicago area with

Harrington Institute of Interior Design (*continued*)

institutional accreditation by the National Association of Schools of Art and Design (NASAD), and accreditation by the Foundation for Interior Design Education Research (FIDER) for its Bachelor of Fine Arts in Interior Design program.

In addition, it is the only interior design college to offer all courses every semester. Its curriculum is designed as a unified whole, and its faculty is unsurpassed in its unity of purpose, professionalism, knowledge, and teaching accomplishment. Harrington Institute offers an exchange program with the Rotterdam College of Design in the Netherlands.

▼ HARTFORD ART SCHOOL

See University of Hartford

▼ HERRON SCHOOL OF ART

See Indiana University–Purdue University Indianapolis

▼ HOPE SCHOOL OF FINE ARTS

See Indiana University Bloomington

▼ HOWARD UNIVERSITY

Washington, District of Columbia

Independent, coed. Urban campus. Total enrollment: 10,438. Art program established 1921.

Degrees Bachelor of Fine Arts in the areas of painting, design, printmaking, photography, ceramics, sculpture, electronic studio, experimental studio. Majors and concentrations: ceramic art and design, design, electronic arts, experimental studies, painting/drawing, photography, printmaking, sculpture. Graduate degrees offered: Master of Fine Arts in the areas of painting, ceramics, printmaking/photography, design, electronic studio, experimental studio, sculpture. Cross-registration with Washington Metropolitan Area Consortium of Universities . Program accredited by NASAD.

Enrollment Fall 1997: 220 total; 190 undergraduate, 30 graduate.

Art Faculty 33 total undergraduate and graduate (full-time and part-time). 88% of full-time faculty have terminal degrees. Graduate students teach a few undergraduate courses. Undergraduate student–faculty ratio: 10:1.

Student Life Student groups/activities include American Society of Interior Designers, Fine Arts Student Council.

Expenses for 1997–98 Application fee: $45. Comprehensive fee: $13,147 includes full-time tuition ($8580), mandatory fees ($405), and college room and board ($4162).

Financial Aid Program-specific awards for 1997: 20 Special Talent Scholarships for students with outstanding portfolios ($1000–$6000).

Application Procedures Students admitted directly into the professional program freshman year. Deadline for freshmen and transfers: April 1. Notification date for freshmen and transfers: July 1. Required: essay, high school transcript, college transcript(s) for transfer students, interview, portfolio, SAT I test score only (minimum combined SAT I score of

920), minimum 2.5 high school GPA. Recommended: 2 letters of recommendation. Portfolio reviews held continuously on campus; the submission of slides may be substituted for portfolios when distance is prohibitive.

Undergraduate Contact Mrs. Richetta Johnson, Director of Admissions, Undergraduate Admissions, Howard University, 2400 Sixth Street, NW, Washington, District of Columbia 20059-0002; 202-806-2763.

Graduate Contact Mrs. Richetta Johnson, Director of Admissions, Graduate Admissions, Howard University, 2400 Sixth Street, NW, Washington, District of Columbia 20059-0002; 202-806-2755.

▼ HUNTER COLLEGE OF THE CITY UNIVERSITY OF NEW YORK

New York, New York

State and locally supported, coed. Urban campus. Total enrollment: 19,689.

Degrees Bachelor of Fine Arts in the area of in studio art. Graduate degrees offered: Master of Fine Arts in the area of in studio art; Master of Arts in the area of art history.

Enrollment Fall 1997: 2,375 total; 15 undergraduate, 210 graduate, 2,150 non-professional degree.

Art Student Profile 70% females, 30% males, 35% minorities, 2% international.

Art Faculty 63 total undergraduate and graduate (full-time and part-time). 100% of full-time faculty have terminal degrees. Graduate students teach a few undergraduate courses. Undergraduate student–faculty ratio: 40:1.

Student Life Student groups/activities include Art Club.

Expenses for 1997–98 Application fee: $40. State resident tuition: $3200 full-time. Nonresident tuition: $6800 full-time. Mandatory fees: $129 full-time. College room only: $1700. Room charges vary according to housing facility. Special program-related fees: $25–$35 per course for materials fee.

Financial Aid Program-specific awards available.

Application Procedures Students apply for admission into the professional program by junior year. Deadline for freshmen: January 15; transfers: March 15. Required: essay, high school transcript, college transcript(s) for transfer students, 2 letters of recommendation, interview, portfolio, SAT I test score only. Portfolio reviews held twice on campus; the submission of slides may be substituted for portfolios for large works of art.

Undergraduate Contact Admissions, Hunter College of the City University of New York, 695 Park Avenue, New York, New York 10021; 212-772-4490.

Graduate Contact Joel Carreiro, Graduate Advisor, Art Department, Hunter College of the City University of New York, 695 Park Avenue, New York, New York 10021; 212-772-5052.

▼ THE ILLINOIS INSTITUTE OF ART

Chicago, Illinois

Proprietary, coed. Urban campus.

Degrees Bachelor of Fine Arts in the areas of fashion design, interior design, visual communications, media arts and animation, multimedia communications; Bachelor of Arts in the area of fashion marketing and management. Majors and concentrations: animation, fashion design, fashion merchan-

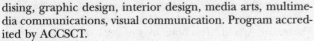

dising, graphic design, interior design, media arts, multimedia communications, visual communication. Program accredited by ACCSCT.

Enrollment Fall 1997: 1,000 undergraduate.

Art Student Profile 50% females, 50% males, 40% minorities, 10% international.

Art Faculty 85 total (full-time and part-time). 99% of full-time faculty have terminal degrees. Graduate students do not teach undergraduate courses. Undergraduate student–faculty ratio: 16:1.

Student Life Student groups/activities include American Society of Interior Designers, Fashion Group Student Chapter, Center for Design Student Chapter. Special housing available for art students.

Expenses for 1997–98 Application fee: $50. One-time mandatory fee: $50. Tuition: $9984 full-time. Special program-related fees: $300–$400 per program for art supplies.

Financial Aid Program-specific awards for 1997: 5 High School Scholarships for incoming freshmen ($21,000), 200 Merit Scholarships for those demonstrating need ($200–$2500).

Application Procedures Students admitted directly into the professional program freshman year. Deadline for freshmen and transfers: continuous. Notification date for freshmen and transfers: continuous. Required: essay, high school transcript, college transcript(s) for transfer students, interview. Recommended: minimum 2.0 high school GPA, SAT I or ACT test scores.

Undergraduate Contact Ms. Janis Anton, Director of Admissions, The Illinois Institute of Art, 350 North Orleans Street, #136, Chicago, Illinois 60654; 800-351-3450, fax: 312-280-8562, E-mail address: antonj@aii.edu.

▼ ILLINOIS STATE UNIVERSITY

Normal, Illinois

State-supported, coed. Urban campus. Total enrollment: 20,331. Art program established 1965.

Degrees Bachelor of Fine Arts in the area of art. Majors and concentrations: art/fine arts, ceramics, computer graphics, fibers, glass, graphic design, intaglio, jewelry and metalsmithing, lithography, painting/drawing, photography, printmaking, sculpture, studio art, video art. Graduate degrees offered: Master of Fine Arts; Master of Arts in the area of art history; Master of Arts/Master of Science in the area of art education and art therapy. Cross-registration with members of the National Student Exchange Program, University of Wolverhampton (United Kingdom), University of Sunderland (United Kingdom). Program accredited by NASAD.

Enrollment Fall 1997: 66 total; 16 undergraduate, 50 graduate.

Art Student Profile 55% females, 45% males, 10% minorities, 1% international.

Art Faculty 43 total undergraduate and graduate (full-time and part-time). 99% of full-time faculty have terminal degrees. Graduate students do not teach undergraduate courses.

Student Life Student groups/activities include Students in Graphic Design, National Art Education Association Student Chapter, Illinois Art Education Association Student Chapter.

Expenses for 1998–99 State resident tuition: $3038 full-time. Nonresident tuition: $9113 full-time. Mandatory fees: $1085 full-time. Full-time tuition and fees vary according to course load. College room and board: $3975. Room and board

charges vary according to board plan. Special program-related fees: $10–$50 per course for studio lab fee.

Financial Aid Program-specific awards for 1997: 25–30 departmental scholarships for program majors ($600–$3000).

Application Procedures Students apply for admission into the professional program by sophomore, junior year. Deadline for freshmen and transfers: continuous. Required: high school transcript, college transcript(s) for transfer students, interview, portfolio, SAT I or ACT test scores, minimum 3.0 college GPA. Portfolio reviews held twice on campus; the submission of slides may be substituted for portfolios.

Web Site http://www.orat.ilstu.edu/art/art.html.

Contact Dr. Ron Mottram, Chair, Department of Art, Illinois State University, Campus Box 5620, Normal, Illinois 61790-5620; 309-438-5621, fax: 309-438-8318.

▼ ILLINOIS WESLEYAN UNIVERSITY

Bloomington, Illinois

Independent, coed. Suburban campus. Total enrollment: 2,021.

Degrees Bachelor of Fine Arts in the area of art and design. Majors and concentrations: art/fine arts, ceramic art and design, commercial art, computer graphics, drawing, graphic arts, painting, photography, printmaking, sculpture, studio art. Cross-registration with Institute for European and Asian Studies.

Enrollment Fall 1997: 80 total; 65 undergraduate, 15 non-professional degree.

Art Student Profile 52% females, 48% males, 8% minorities, 5% international.

Art Faculty 7 total (full-time and part-time). 100% of full-time faculty have terminal degrees. Graduate students do not teach undergraduate courses. Undergraduate student–faculty ratio: 10:1.

Student Life Student groups/activities include Students in Design, Kappa Pi (international honorary art fraternity). Special housing available for art students.

Expenses for 1998–99 Comprehensive fee: $23,200 includes full-time tuition ($18,250), mandatory fees ($126), and college room and board ($4824). College room only: $2800. Special program-related fees: $100 for departmental fee.

Financial Aid Program-specific awards for 1997: 60 Art Talent Awards for freshmen ($2500–$7000).

Application Procedures Students admitted directly into the professional program freshman year. Deadline for freshmen and transfers: continuous. Required: essay, high school transcript, minimum 3.0 high school GPA, portfolio, SAT I or ACT test scores. Recommended: interview. Portfolio reviews held by appointment on campus; the submission of slides may be substituted for portfolios for large works of art, three-dimensional pieces, or when distance is prohibitive.

Undergraduate Contact Mr. James Routi, Director of Admissions, Illinois Wesleyan University, PO Box 2900, Bloomington, Illinois 61702-2900; 309-556-3031.

▼ INDIANA STATE UNIVERSITY

Terre Haute, Indiana

State-supported, coed. Suburban campus. Total enrollment: 10,784. Art program established 1870.

Indiana State University (continued)

Degrees Bachelor of Fine Arts in the area of studio art and design. Majors and concentrations: ceramic art and design, furniture design, graphic design, painting/drawing, photography, printmaking, sculpture, studio art, wood. Graduate degrees offered: Master of Fine Arts in the area of studio art and design. Program accredited by NASAD.
Enrollment Fall 1997: 215 total; 150 undergraduate, 50 graduate, 15 non-professional degree.
Art Student Profile 55% females, 45% males, 12% minorities, 10% international.
Art Faculty 17 total undergraduate and graduate (full-time and part-time). 83% of full-time faculty have terminal degrees. Graduate students teach a few undergraduate courses. Undergraduate student–faculty ratio: 15:1.
Student Life Student groups/activities include Student Gallery Program, Design Club, Art Club.
Expenses for 1997–98 Application fee: $20. State resident tuition: $3196 full-time. Nonresident tuition: $7916 full-time. Full-time tuition varies according to course load. College room and board: $4143. Room and board charges vary according to board plan and housing facility. Special program-related fees: $24 per course for studio lab fee.
Financial Aid Program-specific awards for 1997: 10–12 Creative and Performing Arts Scholarships for freshmen ($1200), 1 Indiana Artist-Craftsmen/Talbot Street Art Fair Scholarship for program majors ($350), 1 Violet Helen Rich Scholarship for painting majors ($1500), 1 Elmer J. Porter Scholarship for program majors ($500).
Application Procedures Students admitted directly into the professional program freshman year. Deadline for freshmen and transfers: August 15. Notification date for freshmen and transfers: continuous. Required: high school transcript, college transcript(s) for transfer students, minimum 2.0 high school GPA, SAT I or ACT test scores. Recommended: portfolio for scholarship consideration. Portfolio reviews held 6 times on campus and off campus in Vincennes, IN; Fort Wayne, IN; Louisville, KY; Indianapolis, IN; St. Louis, MO; Chicago, IL; the submission of slides may be substituted for portfolios when distance is prohibitive, if original work is unavailable, or for large works of art.
Undergraduate Contact Mr. Adrian R. Tio, Chairperson, Department of Art, Indiana State University, Fine Arts 108, Terre Haute, Indiana 47809; 812-237-3697, fax: 812-237-4369, E-mail address: artio@ruby.indstate.edu.
Graduate Contact Mr. David Erickson, Graduate Coordinator, Department of Art, Indiana State University, Fine Arts 108, Terre Haute, Indiana 47809; 812-237-3697, fax: 812-237-4369, E-mail address: armccall@ruby.indstate.edu.

Hope School of Fine Arts

▼ INDIANA UNIVERSITY BLOOMINGTON

Bloomington, Indiana

State-supported, coed. Small town campus. Total enrollment: 34,937. Art program established 1896.
Degrees Bachelor of Fine Arts in the areas of ceramics, graphic design, jewelry and metalsmithing, painting, photography, printmaking, sculpture, textiles. Majors and concentrations: ceramic art and design, graphic arts, jewelry and metalsmithing, painting/drawing, photography, printmaking, sculpture, textile arts. Graduate degrees offered: Master of Fine Arts in the areas of ceramics, graphic design, jewelry

and metalsmithing, painting, photography, printmaking, sculpture, textiles; Master of Arts in the area of art history; Master of Arts in Teaching in the area of art education. Doctor of Philosophy in the area of art history. Program accredited by NASAD.
Enrollment Fall 1997: 378 total; 65 undergraduate, 78 graduate, 235 non-professional degree.
Art Student Profile 60% females, 40% males, 7% minorities, 2% international.
Art Faculty 27 total undergraduate and graduate (full-time and part-time). 92% of full-time faculty have terminal degrees. Graduate students teach about a quarter undergraduate courses. Undergraduate student–faculty ratio: 15:1.
Student Life Student groups/activities include Fine Arts Students Association, Graphic Design Student Association.
Expenses for 1997–98 Application fee: $35. State resident tuition: $3486 full-time. Nonresident tuition: $11,410 full-time. Mandatory fees: $443 full-time. College room and board: $4900. Special program-related fees: $23–$75 per course for material fees.
Financial Aid Program-specific awards for 1997: 10–15 Hope School of Fine Arts Student Awards for program majors ($100–$800).
Application Procedures Students apply for admission into the professional program by sophomore, junior year. Deadline for freshmen: February 1; transfers: July 15. Notification date for freshmen and transfers: August 29. Required: high school transcript, college transcript(s) for transfer students, letter of recommendation, portfolio, SAT I or ACT test scores. Portfolio reviews held once on campus.
Undergraduate Contact Undergraduate Advisor, Hope School of Fine Arts, Indiana University Bloomington, Fine Arts 123, Bloomington, Indiana 47405; 812-855-1693, fax: 812-855-7498.
Graduate Contact Graduate Services Coordinator, Hope School of Fine Arts, Indiana University Bloomington, Fine Arts 123, Bloomington, Indiana 47405; 812-855-0188, fax: 812-855-7498, E-mail address: fina@indiana.edu.

▼ INDIANA UNIVERSITY OF PENNSYLVANIA

Indiana, Pennsylvania

State-supported, coed. Small town campus. Total enrollment: 13,736.
Degrees Bachelor of Fine Arts in the area of art. Majors and concentrations: ceramics, drawing, fibers, graphic design, jewelry and metalsmithing, painting, sculpture, wood. Graduate degrees offered: Master of Fine Arts in the area of art. Program accredited by NASAD.
Enrollment Fall 1997: 255 total; 110 undergraduate, 15 graduate, 130 non-professional degree.
Art Faculty 19 total undergraduate and graduate (full-time and part-time). 75% of full-time faculty have terminal degrees. Graduate students do not teach undergraduate courses. Undergraduate student–faculty ratio: 10:1.
Student Life Student groups/activities include Student Art Association.
Expenses for 1997–98 Application fee: $30. State resident tuition: $3468 full-time. Nonresident tuition: $8824 full-time. Mandatory fees: $736 full-time. Full-time tuition and fees vary according to course load. College room and board: $3408. College room only: $1952. Room and board charges vary according to board plan and housing facility. Special program-related fees: $20–$80 per course for studio lab fees.

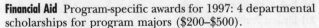

Financial Aid Program-specific awards for 1997: 4 departmental scholarships for program majors ($200–$500).

Application Procedures Deadline for freshmen and transfers: continuous. Required: high school transcript, college transcript(s) for transfer students, portfolio, SAT I or ACT test scores, standing in top 40% of graduating class. Recommended: essay, minimum 3.0 high school GPA, 3 letters of recommendation, interview. Portfolio reviews held once and as needed on campus; the submission of slides may be substituted for portfolios when distance is prohibitive.

Undergraduate Contact Chair, Art Department, Indiana University of Pennsylvania, 115 Sprowls Hall, Indiana, Pennsylvania 15705; 724-357-2530.

▼ INDIANA UNIVERSITY–PURDUE UNIVERSITY FORT WAYNE

Fort Wayne, Indiana

State-supported, coed. Urban campus. Total enrollment: 10,749.

Degrees Bachelor of Fine Arts in the areas of computer design, crafts, drawing, graphic design, painting, photography, printmaking, sculpture. Majors and concentrations: art/fine arts, ceramic art and design, commercial art, computer graphics, graphic arts, jewelry and metalsmithing, painting/drawing, photography, printmaking, sculpture.

Enrollment Fall 1997: 229 total; 219 undergraduate, 10 non-professional degree.

Art Student Profile 50% females, 50% males.

Art Faculty 90% of full-time faculty have terminal degrees. Graduate students do not teach undergraduate courses. Undergraduate student–faculty ratio: 12:1.

Student Life Student groups/activities include Art Student League.

Expenses for 1997–98 Application fee: $30. State resident tuition: $3026 full-time. Nonresident tuition: $7311 full-time. Mandatory fees: $295 full-time. Full-time tuition and fees vary according to course load.

Financial Aid Program-specific awards for 1997: 6 departmental scholarships for incoming students ($800–$1500), 8 departmental scholarships for continuing students ($800–$1500).

Application Procedures Students apply for admission into the professional program by sophomore year. Deadline for freshmen and transfers: August 1. Notification date for freshmen and transfers: continuous. Required: high school transcript, college transcript(s) for transfer students, minimum 2.0 high school GPA, 3 letters of recommendation, portfolio, SAT I or ACT test scores. Portfolio reviews held as needed on campus; the submission of slides may be substituted for portfolios for large works of art.

Undergraduate Contact Mr. Leslie P. Motz, Chair, Fine Art Department, Indiana University–Purdue University Fort Wayne, 2101 Coliseum Boulevard East, Fort Wayne, Indiana 46805; 219-481-6705.

Herron School of Art

▼ INDIANA UNIVERSITY–PURDUE UNIVERSITY INDIANAPOLIS

Indianapolis, Indiana

State-supported, coed. Urban campus. Total enrollment: 27,036. Art program established 1902.

Degrees Bachelor of Fine Arts in the areas of painting, printmaking, ceramics, woodworking, sculpture, visual communication, photography and fine arts; Bachelor of Art Education; Bachelor of Arts in the area of art history. Majors and concentrations: art education, art/fine arts, ceramic art and design, commercial art, computer graphics, graphic arts, painting/drawing, photography, printmaking, sculpture, woodworking design. Graduate degrees offered: Master of Art Education. Cross-registration with Butler University, University of Indianapolis. Program accredited by NASAD.

Enrollment Fall 1997: 631 total; 625 undergraduate, 6 graduate.

Art Student Profile 52% females, 48% males, 10% minorities, 5% international.

Art Faculty 46 total undergraduate (full-time and part-time). 98% of full-time faculty have terminal degrees. Graduate students do not teach undergraduate courses. Undergraduate student–faculty ratio: 14:1.

Student Life Student groups/activities include Herron Student Senate.

Expenses for 1997–98 Application fee: $35. State resident tuition: $3188 full-time. Nonresident tuition: $9780 full-time. Mandatory fees: $253 full-time. College room and board: $3216. Special program-related fees: $150 per year for technology fee.

Financial Aid Program-specific awards for 1997: 20 New Student Awards for program majors ($1500).

Application Procedures Students apply for admission into the professional program by sophomore year. Deadline for freshmen and transfers: June 1. Notification date for freshmen and transfers: July 15. Required: high school transcript, college transcript(s) for transfer students, minimum 2.0 high school GPA, SAT I or ACT test scores, portfolio for scholarship consideration. Portfolio reviews held once on campus; the submission of slides may be substituted for portfolios.

Web Site http://www.herron.iupui.edu/main.html.

Undergraduate Contact Ms. Nancy A. Fitzgerald, Director of Student Services, Admissions Department, Indiana University–Purdue University Indianapolis, 1701 North Pennsylvania Street, Indianapolis, Indiana 46202; 317-920-2416, fax: 317-920-2401.

Graduate Contact Ms. Cindy Borgmann, Division Coordinator, Indiana University–Purdue University Indianapolis, Indianapolis, Indiana 46202; 317-920-2450, E-mail address: cborgman@iupui.edu.

▼ INDIANA UNIVERSITY SOUTH BEND

South Bend, Indiana

State-supported, coed. Suburban campus. Total enrollment: 7,169. Art program established 1965.

Degrees Bachelor of Fine Arts in the area of visual arts. Majors and concentrations: electronic intermedia, graphic arts, painting/drawing, printmaking, sculpture. Cross-registration with Indiana University System.

Enrollment Fall 1997: 6 undergraduate.

Art Student Profile 60% females, 40% males, 10% minorities, 5% international.

Art Faculty 11 total (full-time and part-time). 100% of full-time faculty have terminal degrees. Graduate students do not teach undergraduate courses.

Student Life Student groups/activities include Student Art Show.

Indiana University South Bend (*continued*)

Expenses for 1997–98 State resident tuition: $2763 full-time. Nonresident tuition: $7562 full-time. Mandatory fees: $222 full-time. Special program-related fees: $35 per course for lab fee.

Application Procedures Students admitted directly into the professional program freshman year. Deadline for freshmen and transfers: August 15. Notification date for freshmen and transfers: September 1. Required: high school transcript, minimum 2.0 high school GPA. Recommended: interview, video, portfolio. Portfolio reviews held twice on campus; the submission of slides may be substituted for portfolios for international applicants.

Undergraduate Contact Ms. Christine Seitz, Academic Coordinator, Division of the Arts, Indiana University South Bend, 1700 Mishawaka Avenue, PO Box 7111, South Bend, Indiana 46634; 219-237-4306.

▼ INTERNATIONAL ACADEMY OF MERCHANDISING & DESIGN, INC.

Tampa, Florida

Proprietary, coed. Urban campus. Art program established 1984.

Degrees Bachelor of Fine Arts in the areas of fashion design, interior design, advertising design, digital art and technology. Program accredited by FIDER.

Enrollment Fall 1997: 672 total; all undergraduate.

Art Student Profile 70% females, 30% males, 1% international.

Art Faculty 92 total (full-time and part-time). 40% of full-time faculty have terminal degrees. Graduate students do not teach undergraduate courses. Undergraduate student–faculty ratio: 13:1.

Student Life Student groups/activities include American Society of Interior Designers Student Chapter, Student Council, Siggraph.

Expenses for 1998–99 Application fee: $50. Tuition: $10,785 full-time. Full-time tuition varies according to course level and course load.

Financial Aid Program-specific awards available.

Application Procedures Students admitted directly into the professional program freshman year. Deadline for freshmen and transfers: continuous. Required: college transcript(s) for transfer students, high school transcript or GED. Recommended: minimum 2.0 high school GPA, interview.

Web Site http://www.academy.edu.

Undergraduate Contact Scott Spitolnick, Director of Admissions, International Academy of Merchandising & Design, Inc., 5225 Memorial Highway, Tampa, Florida 33634; 813-881-0007, fax: 813-881-0008.

▼ INTERNATIONAL ACADEMY OF MERCHANDISING & DESIGN, LTD.

Chicago, Illinois

Proprietary, coed. Urban campus. Total enrollment: 815. Art program established 1977.

Degrees Bachelor of Fine Arts in the areas of interior design, fashion design, advertising and design. Program accredited by FIDER.

Enrollment Fall 1997: 815 total; all undergraduate.

Art Student Profile 54% females, 46% males, 39% minorities, 7% international.

Art Faculty 58 total (full-time and part-time). 60% of full-time faculty have terminal degrees. Graduate students do not teach undergraduate courses. Undergraduate student–faculty ratio: 15:1.

Student Life Student groups/activities include American Society of Interior Designers, Fashion Group International, Inc., The American Institute of Graphic Arts.

Expenses for 1997–98 Application fee: $50. Tuition: $9900 full-time. Full-time tuition varies according to program.

Application Procedures Students admitted directly into the professional program freshman year. Deadline for freshmen and transfers: continuous. Required: essay, high school transcript, college transcript(s) for transfer students, minimum 2.0 high school GPA, interview, SAT I or ACT test scores. Recommended: portfolio. Portfolio reviews held as needed on campus; the submission of slides may be substituted for portfolios for ease of handling.

Web Site http://www.iamd.edu.

Undergraduate Contact Mr. Roy Sokohl, Director of Admissions, International Academy of Merchandising & Design, Ltd., One North State Street, Suite 400, Chicago, Illinois 60602-3300; 312-541-3910, fax: 312-541-3929.

▼ IOWA STATE UNIVERSITY OF SCIENCE AND TECHNOLOGY

Ames, Iowa

State-supported, coed. Suburban campus. Total enrollment: 25,384. Art program established 1920.

Degrees Bachelor of Fine Arts in the areas of graphic design, interior design, art and design. Majors and concentrations: art/fine arts, craft design, graphic design, interior design, painting/drawing, printmaking, visual studies. Graduate degrees offered: Master of Fine Arts in the areas of graphic design, interior design; Master of Arts in the areas of art education, craft design, drawing/painting/printmaking, intermedia. Program accredited by FIDER.

Enrollment Fall 1997: 802 total; 700 undergraduate, 37 graduate, 65 non-professional degree.

Art Student Profile 60% females, 40% males, 1% minorities, 1% international.

Art Faculty 61 total undergraduate and graduate (full-time and part-time). 80% of full-time faculty have terminal degrees. Graduate students teach a few undergraduate courses. Undergraduate student–faculty ratio: 18:1.

Student Life Student groups/activities include Interior Design Student Association, Graphic Design Student Association, College of Design Art Club. Special housing available for art students.

Expenses for 1997–98 Application fee: $20. State resident tuition: $2566 full-time. Nonresident tuition: $8608 full-time. Mandatory fees: $200 full-time. Full-time tuition and fees vary according to class time and program. College room and board: $3647. College room only: $1879. Room and board charges vary according to board plan and housing facility. Special program-related fees: $5–$100 per course for in-studio expenses.

Financial Aid Program-specific awards for 1997: 1 Beresford/Seeds Award for incoming freshmen ($3000), 10–12 Art and Design Excellence Awards for program majors ($500–$1500),

2 Garfield/Boody Awards for fine arts majors ($1600), 3 Pickett/Kiser/Beard Awards for interior design majors ($1500), 2–4 Art and Design Minority Awards for program majors ($500–$1000).

Application Procedures Students apply for admission into the professional program by freshman year. Deadline for freshmen and transfers: continuous. Required: high school transcript, SAT I or ACT test scores, standing in top half of graduating class, minimum TOEFL score of 500 for international applicants. Recommended: minimum 2.0 high school GPA.

Web Site http://www.design.iastate.edu/.

Undergraduate Contact Director of Admissions, Iowa State University of Science and Technology, 100 Alumni Hall, Ames, Iowa 50011-2010; 515-294-5836, fax: 515-294-2592, E-mail address: admissions@iastate.edu.

Graduate Contact Graduate Admissions, Iowa State University of Science and Technology, 100 Alumni Hall, Ames, Iowa 50011-2010; 515-294-0818, fax: 515-294-2592, E-mail address: grad_admissions@iastate.edu.

▼ ITHACA COLLEGE

Ithaca, New York

Independent, coed. Small town campus. Total enrollment: 5,897. Art program established 1986.

Degrees Bachelor of Fine Arts in the areas of film, photography, visual arts. Cross-registration with Cornell University.

Enrollment Fall 1997: 76 total; all undergraduate.

Art Student Profile 40% females, 60% males, 8% minorities, 5% international.

Art Faculty 15 total (full-time and part-time). 92% of full-time faculty have terminal degrees. Graduate students do not teach undergraduate courses. Undergraduate student–faculty ratio: 6:1.

Student Life Student groups/activities include Production Unit, Radio Station, Television Station.

Expenses for 1997–98 Application fee: $40. Comprehensive fee: $24,240 includes full-time tuition ($16,900) and college room and board ($7340). College room only: $3682.

Financial Aid Program-specific awards for 1997: Kristan Landen Film Scholarships for cinema majors ($500–$1500), Mark Mazura Video Production Scholarship for video production students ($500–$2000), James B. Pendleton Filmmaking Awards for film majors ($500–$1000), James B. Pendleton Scholarships for cinema and photography majors ($1000–$8000), Rod Serling Communications Scholarships for video production students ($500–$3000), Mark Wilder Memorial Scholarships for video production students ($800).

Application Procedures Students admitted directly into the professional program freshman year. Deadline for freshmen: March 1; transfers: July 15. Notification date for freshmen: April 15; transfers: July 15. Required: essay, high school transcript, college transcript(s) for transfer students, letter of recommendation, SAT I or ACT test scores. Recommended: minimum 3.0 high school GPA, interview.

Web Site http://www.ithaca.edu.

Undergraduate Contact Ms. Paula J. Mitchell, Director, Admission Department, Ithaca College, 100 Job Hall, Ithaca, New York 14850-7020; 607-274-3124, fax: 607-274-1900, E-mail address: admission@ithaca.edu.

▼ ITHACA COLLEGE

Ithaca, New York

Independent, coed. Small town campus. Total enrollment: 5,897. Art program established 1960.

Degrees Bachelor of Fine Arts in the area of art. Cross-registration with Cornell University.

Enrollment Fall 1997: 28 total; 4 undergraduate, 24 non-professional degree.

Art Student Profile 50% females, 50% males, 1% minorities, 11% international.

Art Faculty 6 total (full-time and part-time). 100% of full-time faculty have terminal degrees. Graduate students do not teach undergraduate courses. Undergraduate student–faculty ratio: 5:1.

Student Life Student groups/activities include Ithaca College Art Club.

Expenses for 1997–98 Application fee: $40. Comprehensive fee: $24,240 includes full-time tuition ($16,900) and college room and board ($7340). College room only: $3682.

Financial Aid Program-specific awards for 1997: 1 Donald and Martha Negus Scholarship for program majors ($500–$1000).

Application Procedures Students admitted directly into the professional program freshman year. Deadline for freshmen: March 1; transfers: July 15. Notification date for freshmen: April 15; transfers: July 15. Required: essay, high school transcript, college transcript(s) for transfer students, letter of recommendation, SAT I or ACT test scores. Recommended: minimum 3.0 high school GPA, interview, portfolio. Portfolio reviews held continuously by appointment on campus; the submission of slides may be substituted for portfolios when distance is prohibitive.

Web Site http://www.ithaca.edu.

Undergraduate Contact Ms. Paula J. Mitchell, Director, Admission Department, Ithaca College, 100 Job Hall, Ithaca, New York 14850-7020; 607-274-3124, fax: 607-274-1900, E-mail address: admission@ithaca.edu.

▼ JACKSONVILLE STATE UNIVERSITY

Jacksonville, Alabama

State-supported, coed. Small town campus. Total enrollment: 7,619.

Degrees Bachelor of Fine Arts in the area of studio art. Majors and concentrations: ceramics, commercial art, painting/drawing, photography, printmaking, studio art. Program accredited by NASAD.

Enrollment Fall 1997: 210 total; 130 undergraduate, 80 non-professional degree.

Art Student Profile 41% females, 59% males, 16% minorities, 6% international.

Art Faculty 8 total (full-time and part-time). 100% of full-time faculty have terminal degrees. Graduate students do not teach undergraduate courses. Undergraduate student–faculty ratio: 18:1.

Student Life Student groups/activities include Student Art Alliance.

Expenses for 1997–98 Application fee: $20. State resident tuition: $2040 full-time. Nonresident tuition: $4080 full-time. Mandatory fees: $20 full-time. Full-time tuition and fees vary according to course load and reciprocity agreements. College

Jacksonville State University *(continued)*

room and board: $2980. Room and board charges vary according to board plan and housing facility.

Financial Aid Program-specific awards for 1997: 1 Art Department Award for incoming freshmen ($1000), 2 Art Department Awards for upperclassmen ($1000), 1 Lee Manners Scholarship for junior art major with 3.0 minimum GPA ($1000), Visual Art Society/JSU Scholarships for upperclassmen.

Application Procedures Students apply for admission into the professional program by sophomore year. Deadline for freshmen and transfers: continuous. Required: high school transcript, portfolio, SAT I or ACT test scores. Recommended: minimum 2.0 high school GPA. Portfolio reviews held twice on campus.

Undergraduate Contact Mr. Charles Groover, Head, Art Department, Jacksonville State University, 700 Pelham Road North, Jacksonville, Alabama 36265; 205-782-5626, fax: 205-782-5419.

▼ JACKSONVILLE UNIVERSITY

Jacksonville, Florida

Independent, coed. Suburban campus. Total enrollment: 2,157. Art program established 1961.

Degrees Bachelor of Fine Arts in the areas of studio art, visual communications, computer art and design; Bachelor of Art Education. Majors and concentrations: art education, art history, computer art, photography, studio art, visual communication.

Enrollment Fall 1997: 105 undergraduate.

Art Student Profile 42% females, 58% males, 14% minorities, 3% international.

Art Faculty 19 total (full-time and part-time). 75% of full-time faculty have terminal degrees. Graduate students do not teach undergraduate courses. Undergraduate student–faculty ratio: 8:1.

Student Life Student groups/activities include student group shows, student juried shows, volunteer city-wide art projects.

Expenses for 1997–98 Application fee: $25. Comprehensive fee: $18,800 includes full-time tuition ($13,360), mandatory fees ($540), and college room and board ($4900). College room only: $2260. Room and board charges vary according to board plan. Special program-related fees: $30–$135 for materials and departmental fees.

Financial Aid Program-specific awards for 1997: 10 Art Department Awards for program majors ($1000–$3000).

Application Procedures Students admitted directly into the professional program freshman year. Deadline for freshmen and transfers: continuous. Required: essay, high school transcript, minimum 2.0 high school GPA, letter of recommendation, portfolio, SAT I or ACT test scores (minimum combined SAT I score of 820). Portfolio reviews held as needed on campus and off campus in various high schools in Duval County; the submission of slides may be substituted for portfolios if a campus visit is impossible.

Undergraduate Contact Mr. Jack Turnock, Chair, Department of Art, Jacksonville University, 2800 University Boulevard North, Jacksonville, Florida 32211; 904-745-7374, fax: 904-745-7375.

More About the University

Program Facilities Classes are held in the Phillips Fine Arts Building and in a specially equipped studio art annex. Special purpose studio facilities are available for printmaking, ceramics, glassblowing, photography, painting, drawing, jewelry and metal, sculpture, graphic design, computer art, and airbrush. Classes in computer animation and video production using LightWave 3-D and Flying Toaster/Flying software are available through Computer Art & Visualization Education (CAVE). The Brest Museum houses a permanent collection of art and presents monthly exhibits of contemporary art.

Faculty Full-time and part-time adjunct art faculty members include exhibiting professional artists. The art department presents workshops each year highlighting visiting artists of regional and national reputation.

Student Exhibition Opportunities Students routinely exhibit works each year in the Brest Museum and Gallery, including an annual juried student art exhibition and senior art exhibition. Works are also displayed in the Howard Administration Building. Other opportunities are arranged each semester in alternative exhibition spaces both on and off the campus in the Jacksonville area.

Special Programs The curriculum at JU is based on guidelines prepared by the National Association of Schools of Art and Design (NASAD). Internships are required of visual communications and computer art students and encouraged for other art students. JU is accredited by the Commission on Colleges of the Southern Association of Colleges and Schools. Study-abroad programs are available.

▼ JAMES MADISON UNIVERSITY

Harrisonburg, Virginia

State-supported, coed. Small town campus. Total enrollment: 14,115. Art program established 1922.

Degrees Bachelor of Fine Arts in the areas of graphic design, interior design, general fine arts. Majors and concentrations: ceramic art and design, computer animation, computer art, graphic design, interior design, jewelry and metalsmithing, painting/drawing, papermaking, photography, printmaking, sculpture, stained glass, weaving and fibers. Graduate degrees offered: Master of Fine Arts in the area of studio art. Program accredited by NASAD, FIDER.

Enrollment Fall 1997: 430 total; 160 undergraduate, 20 graduate, 250 non-professional degree.

Art Student Profile 60% females, 40% males, 9% minorities, 1% international.

Art Faculty 45 total undergraduate and graduate (full-time and part-time). 96% of full-time faculty have terminal degrees. Graduate students teach a few undergraduate courses. Undergraduate student–faculty ratio: 16:1.

Student Life Student groups/activities include National Art Education Association Student Chapter, American Society of Interior Designers Student Chapter, Kappa Pi.

Expenses for 1997–98 Application fee: $25. State resident tuition: $4148 full-time. Nonresident tuition: $8816 full-time. College room and board: $4846. College room only: $2612.

Financial Aid Program-specific awards for 1997: 4–6 Freshman Portfolio Awards for incoming freshmen ($4000), 6 J. Binford Walford Scholarships for pre-architecture students ($1000), 10 Art Achievement Awards for continuing art students ($500), 1 Frances Grove Scholarship for continuing art students ($500), 1 Crystal Theodore Service Award for continuing art students ($500), 10 Exhibition Awards for those with artistic merit ($500).

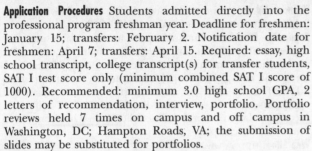

Application Procedures Students admitted directly into the professional program freshman year. Deadline for freshmen: January 15; transfers: February 2. Notification date for freshmen: April 7; transfers: April 15. Required: essay, high school transcript, college transcript(s) for transfer students, SAT I test score only (minimum combined SAT I score of 1000). Recommended: minimum 3.0 high school GPA, 2 letters of recommendation, interview, portfolio. Portfolio reviews held 7 times on campus and off campus in Washington, DC; Hampton Roads, VA; the submission of slides may be substituted for portfolios.

Web Site http://www.jmu.edu/art/.

Undergraduate Contact Dr. Cole H. Welter, Director, School of Art and Art History, James Madison University, MSC 7101, Harrisonburg, Virginia 22807; 540-568-6216, fax: 540-568-6598, E-mail address: art-arthistory@jmu.edu.

Graduate Contact Mr. Ken Szmagaj, Graduate Coordinator, School of Art and Art History, James Madison University, MSC 7101, Harrisonburg, Virginia 22807; 540-568-6312, fax: 540-568-6598, E-mail address: art-arthistory@jmu.edu.

▼ JOHNSON STATE COLLEGE

Johnson, Vermont

State-supported, coed. Rural campus. Total enrollment: 1,622. Art program established 1828.

Degrees Bachelor of Fine Arts in the area of studio art; Bachelor of Arts in the area of art education. Majors and concentrations: ceramics, drawing, multimedia, painting, photography, printmaking, sculpture. Graduate degrees offered: Master of Fine Arts in the areas of painting, sculpture, drawing, mixed media.

Enrollment Fall 1997: 60 undergraduate, 25 graduate.

Art Student Profile 50% females, 50% males, 5% minorities, 2% international.

Art Faculty 19 total undergraduate and graduate (full-time and part-time). 100% of full-time faculty have terminal degrees. Graduate students teach a few undergraduate courses. Undergraduate student–faculty ratio: 10:1.

Student Life Student groups/activities include Student Art Coalition.

Expenses for 1997–98 Application fee: $30. State resident tuition: $3780 full-time. Nonresident tuition: $8760 full-time. Mandatory fees: $861 full-time. Full-time tuition and fees vary according to reciprocity agreements. College room and board: $5086. College room only: $2928. Room and board charges vary according to board plan. Special program-related fees: $15–$35 per course for studio material fees.

Financial Aid Program-specific awards for 1997: Dibden Talent Scholarships for talented artists.

Application Procedures Students apply for admission into the professional program by sophomore year. Deadline for freshmen and transfers: continuous. Notification date for freshmen and transfers: continuous. Required: essay, high school transcript, college transcript(s) for transfer students, 2 letters of recommendation, SAT I or ACT test scores. Recommended: interview. Portfolio reviews held twice on campus.

Web Site http://www.jsc.vsc.edu.

Undergraduate Contact Mr. Jonathan H. Henry, Director of Admissions, Johnson State College, 337 College Hill, Johnson, Vermont 05656; 800-635-2356, fax: 802-635-1230, E-mail address: jscapply@badger.jsc.vsc.edu.

Graduate Contact Ms. Cathy Higley, Administrative Assistant, Graduate Studies, Johnson State College, 337 College Hill, Johnson, Vermont 05656; 802-635-1244.

▼ J. WILLIAM FULBRIGHT COLLEGE OF ARTS AND SCIENCES

See University of Arkansas

▼ KANSAS CITY ART INSTITUTE

Kansas City, Missouri

Independent, coed. Urban campus. Total enrollment: 607. Art program established 1885.

Degrees Bachelor of Fine Arts in the areas of ceramics, design, illustration, fiber, painting, printmaking, photography, sculpture, art history. Majors and concentrations: art history, ceramic art and design, design, illustration, painting/drawing, photography, printmaking, sculpture, textile arts. Cross-registration with Kansas City Area Student Exchange. Program accredited by NASAD.

Enrollment Fall 1997: 607 total; all undergraduate.

Art Student Profile 45% females, 55% males, 12% minorities, 2% international.

Art Faculty 79 total (full-time and part-time). 98% of full-time faculty have terminal degrees. Graduate students do not teach undergraduate courses. Undergraduate student–faculty ratio: 12:1.

Student Life Student groups/activities include Student Gallery Committee, Ethnic Student Association, Student Film Series Committee. Special housing available for art students.

Expenses for 1998–99 Application fee: $25. Comprehensive fee: $21,894 includes full-time tuition ($16,138), mandatory fees ($792), and college room and board ($4964). Room and board charges vary according to housing facility. Special program-related fees: $170 per course for ceramics materials.

Financial Aid Program-specific awards for 1997: 300–350 need-based scholarships for program majors ($2000–$8000), 100–125 merit-based scholarships for program majors ($2000–$8000).

Application Procedures Students admitted directly into the professional program freshman year. Deadline for freshmen and transfers: continuous. Required: essay, high school transcript, college transcript(s) for transfer students, 2 letters of recommendation, portfolio, SAT I or ACT test scores (minimum combined SAT I score of 950, minimum combined ACT score of 20), minimum 2.5 high school GPA. Recommended: interview. Portfolio reviews held continuously on campus and off campus; the submission of slides may be substituted for portfolios.

Web Site http://www.kcai.edu.

Undergraduate Contact Mr. Larry E. Stone, Vice President for Enrollment Management, Kansas City Art Institute, 4415 Warwick Boulevard, Kansas City, Missouri 64111; 800-522-5224, fax: 816-531-6296, E-mail address: admiss@kcai.edu.

▼ KANSAS STATE UNIVERSITY

Manhattan, Kansas

State-supported, coed. Suburban campus. Total enrollment: 20,306. Art program established 1964.

Kansas State University (continued)

Degrees Bachelor of Fine Arts. Majors and concentrations: art education, ceramic art and design, digital art, drawing, graphic design, illustration, jewelry and metalsmithing, painting, pre-art therapy, printmaking, sculpture. Graduate degrees offered: Master of Fine Arts. Cross-registration with Norwich School of Art and Design (England). Program accredited by NASAD.
Enrollment Fall 1997: 375 undergraduate, 25 graduate.
Art Student Profile 50% females, 50% males, 12% minorities, 8% international.
Art Faculty 26 total undergraduate and graduate (full-time and part-time). 90% of full-time faculty have terminal degrees. Graduate students teach about a quarter undergraduate courses. Undergraduate student–faculty ratio: 11:1.
Student Life Student groups/activities include exhibitions, visiting artists, workshops.
Expenses for 1997–98 Application fee: $15. State resident tuition: $1965 full-time. Nonresident tuition: $8270 full-time. Mandatory fees: $502 full-time. College room and board: $3640. Special program-related fees: $2–$147 per semester for lab fees.
Financial Aid Program-specific awards for 1997: 18 art scholarships for art majors ($150–$1000).
Application Procedures Deadline for freshmen and transfers: continuous. Required: high school transcript, college transcript(s) for transfer students, ACT test score only, portfolio for scholarship consideration. Recommended: interview. Portfolio reviews held twice on campus; the submission of slides may be substituted for portfolios when distance is prohibitive.
Web Site http://www.ksu.edu/art.
Undergraduate Contact Art Advisor, Department of Art, Kansas State University, Willard Hall 322, Manhattan, Kansas 66506; 913-532-6605, fax: 913-532-0334, E-mail address: aholcom@ksu.edu.
Graduate Contact Dr. Lou Ann Culley, Director of Graduate Studies, Department of Art, Kansas State University, Willard Hall 332, Manhattan, Kansas 66506; 913-532-1750, fax: 913-532-0334, E-mail address: lfc@ksu.edu.

▼ KEAN UNIVERSITY

Union, New Jersey

State-supported, coed. Urban campus. Total enrollment: 11,537.
Degrees Bachelor of Fine Arts in the areas of interior design, visual communications, studio art. Graduate degrees offered: Master of Arts in the areas of fine arts education, studio art. Program accredited by NASAD.
Enrollment Fall 1997: 227 undergraduate, 53 graduate.
Art Student Profile 55% females, 45% males, 28% minorities, 3% international.
Art Faculty 26 total undergraduate and graduate (full-time and part-time). 98% of full-time faculty have terminal degrees. Graduate students do not teach undergraduate courses. Undergraduate student–faculty ratio: 6:1.
Student Life Student groups/activities include Fine Arts Student Association, American Society of Interior Designers.
Expenses for 1997–98 Application fee: $35. State resident tuition: $3669 full-time. Nonresident tuition: $5140 full-time. College room only: $3920.

Financial Aid Program-specific awards for 1997: 7–8 Endowed Scholarships for program majors ($400–$1000).
Application Procedures Students apply for admission into the professional program by sophomore year. Deadline for freshmen and transfers: June 15. Required: essay, high school transcript, college transcript(s) for transfer students, portfolio, SAT I or ACT test scores, art placement exam for applicants without portfolios. Recommended: 2 letters of recommendation, interview. Portfolio reviews held once and as needed on campus.
Web Site http://www.kean.edu.
Undergraduate Contact Secretary, Fine Arts Department, Kean University, 1000 Morris Avenue, Union, New Jersey 07083; 908-527-2307, fax: 908-527-2804.
Graduate Contact Richard Buncamper, Coordinator of Graduate Programs, Fine Arts Department, Kean University, 1000 Morris Avenue, Union, New Jersey 07083; 908-527-2307, fax: 908-527-2804.

▼ KENDALL COLLEGE OF ART AND DESIGN

Grand Rapids, Michigan

Independent, coed. Urban campus. Total enrollment: 560. Art program established 1928.
Degrees Bachelor of Fine Arts in the areas of furniture design, industrial design, interior design, illustration, visual communications, fine arts. Program accredited by NASAD, FIDER.
Enrollment Fall 1997: 560 total; all undergraduate.
Art Student Profile 50% females, 50% males, 9% minorities, 3% international.
Art Faculty 66 total (full-time and part-time). 54% of full-time faculty have terminal degrees. Graduate students do not teach undergraduate courses. Undergraduate student–faculty ratio: 11:1.
Student Life Student groups/activities include Industrial Design Society of America, American Society of Interior Designers, Grand Rapids Area Furniture Designers.
Expenses for 1997–98 Application fee: $35. Tuition: $10,500 full-time. Mandatory fees: $200 full-time. Special program-related fees: $75–$100 for technology fee, $25–$50 for studio lab fee.
Financial Aid Program-specific awards for 1997: 181 Scholarships of Merit for program students ($2500).
Application Procedures Students admitted directly into the professional program freshman year. Deadline for freshmen and transfers: continuous. Required: essay, high school transcript, college transcript(s) for transfer students, minimum 2.0 high school GPA, portfolio, SAT I or ACT test scores. Recommended: letter of recommendation. Portfolio reviews held continuously on campus and off campus; the submission of slides may be substituted for portfolios.
Undergraduate Contact Ms. Amy Packard, Director of Admissions, Kendall College of Art and Design, 111 Division Avenue North, Grand Rapids, Michigan 49503; 616-451-2787, fax: 616-451-9867.

More About the College

Facilities A library with a comprehensive collection of books, periodicals, slides, and videotapes; large, fully equipped model and wood shop with on-site coordinator; extensive computer labs; printmaking lab; photography studio and darkroom; Student Gallery; and Kendall Gallery, which features a full schedule of national traveling exhibitions and faculty and student exhibits; large, roomy classrooms and studios; and individual studios for junior and senior fine arts majors.

Faculty and Alumni The KCAD faculty members are highly regarded artists, designers, and scholars, with an impressive professional record of national and international exhibitions, noted clients, and scholarly writings and activities. Alumni, most employed successfully in their chosen fields throughout the world, regularly return to give workshops and lectures.

Student Organizations and Exhibits Student chapters of professional organizations—Grand Rapids Furniture Designers Association, Industrial Designers Society of America, American Society of Interior Designers, American Center for Design—are available. The Student Gallery and the Kendall Gallery offer numerous formal exhibit opportunities, and there is an annual public Student Exhibit the first week in May. In addition, student work is exhibited throughout the building all year.

Lectures and Guest Artists Over the past several years, several artists, designers and educators have visited Kendall's campus giving lectures, critiques and demonstrations, often meeting with students in the classroom. Among the artists are Sir Terence Conran, John McQueen, Siah Armajani, Miriam Shapiro, Ed Paschke, Tom Friedman, Jeanne Dunning, Julia Fish, Margo Mensing, Gilda Snowden, Lyman Kipp, Jerry Peart; Designers P. Scott Makela, Massimo and Lella Vignelli, Katherine McCoy, Steve Frykholm, Eva Maddox, Clodagh, Martha Burns, Elizabeth McClintock, Margaret McCurry, and Carol Groh. Illustrators include Greg Spalenka, Murray Tinkelman, Ken Dallison, David Small, and Steve Brodner. Others who have visited include Rudolph Arnheim, author and theorist; Vince Carducci, critic and Michigan regional editor of *New Art Examiner*; Lambert Zuidervaart, author and philosopher; Joan Truckenbrod, author and computer artist; Kathryn Hixson, critic and associate editor of the *New Art Examiner*); Marianne Deson, gallery owner; Greg Landahl, architect; Beverly Russell, writer and editor; and Rachel Fletcher, mathematician and theater designer.

Special Programs KCAD offers Mobility Programs, a New York Studio Program, and opportunities for foreign study. Contact the Admissions Office for more information.

Scholarships and Financial Aid Kendall's Scholarship of Merit program awards more than $700,000 annually based on the creative potential and academic achievement of freshman, transfer, and currently enrolled students. Financial need is not a requirement. The College's experienced financial aid officers have helped up to 85 percent of the students receive some form of financial assistance. In addition to nearly a dozen different financial aid programs, the College offers federal and state college work-study programs and is approved for veteran's benefits.

▼

Kendall College of Art and Design, founded in 1928, offers an art and design education to a select group of students who are serious about refining their talent and who seek in-depth preparation for significant careers. Some choose Kendall for its favorable faculty-student ratio of 1:11, others for its programs' national reputation, and others because they want to be around people who share their interests.

Kendall is located in the heart of downtown Grand Rapids, Michigan, a rapidly growing metropolitan area of 750,000 people. KCAD is across the street from the Grand Rapids Art Museum and only blocks away from theaters,

galleries, and music halls, where the work of leading regional and international artists is exhibited or performed.

The faculty consists of working artists, designers, and scholars dedicated to providing students with the necessary tools to explore and pursue their own creative journey. Their experience and background create an innovative and diverse force of instructors dedicated to sharing their knowledge. The faculty continually weighs changing methods and technology, striving to provide students with meaningful, real-world experiences while maintaining a solid and proven art and design education. They are a valuable resource, and through their guidance students can take risks, based on history, that will create work that is both fresh and relevant. That rare blend of professional artists and practiced professors makes the faculty highly qualified to help students define their vision as an artist or designer.

Kendall provides individual attention for all its students. This personalized approach to education not only helps students learn the principles of visual thinking but also provides the skills necessary to achieve career success.

The College's individual majors are based on a strong Foundation program that includes intense classical training while also allowing some freedom and variety. A wide range of special lectures, exhibits, and seminars by noted artists and designers enhance the academic environment. In addition to the required courses, elective courses related to the majors can be taken in photography, computer arts, CAD/CAP and CAD/CAM, and video arts.

Of particular note is Kendall's Furniture Design program, which is recognized throughout the world and can claim nearly 90 percent of this nation's residential furniture designers as its alumni. Also, students of the Kendall Illustration program consistently place among the top winners in the Society of Illustrators' annual national scholarship competition, not only winning scholarship awards for themselves, but raising money for the College as well. The quality of Kendall's programs, combined with individual attention from its professional faculty, establishes this institution among the finest colleges of art and design.

▼ KENT STATE UNIVERSITY

Kent, Ohio

State-supported, coed. Small town campus. Total enrollment: 20,743.

Degrees Bachelor of Fine Arts in the areas of art, fine arts, visual communication design, crafts; Bachelor of Arts in the areas of art, fine arts, visual communication design, crafts, art history, art education. Majors and concentrations: art education, art history, ceramic art and design, glass, illustration, jewelry and metalsmithing, painting/drawing, printmaking, sculpture, textile arts, visual communication. Graduate degrees offered: Master of Fine Arts in the areas of art, fine arts, visual communication design, crafts; Master of Arts in the areas of art, art history, art education. Program accredited by NASAD.

Enrollment Fall 1997: 929 total; 813 undergraduate, 116 graduate.

Art Student Profile 58% females, 42% males, 5% minorities.

Art Faculty 60 total undergraduate and graduate (full-time and part-time). 77% of full-time faculty have terminal degrees. Graduate students teach a few undergraduate courses. Undergraduate student–faculty ratio: 14:1.

Kent State University *(continued)*

Student Life Student groups/activities include Art Education Council, Art Student Association, Art History Club. Special housing available for art students.

Expenses for 1997–98 Application fee: $30. State resident tuition: $4460 full-time. Nonresident tuition: $8920 full-time. Full-time tuition varies according to course load. College room and board: $4152. College room only: $2448. Special program-related fees: $10–$45 per credit hour for consumable supplies.

Financial Aid Program-specific awards for 1997: 16 art scholarships for program majors ($500), 10–20 Creative Arts Awards for incoming freshmen demonstrating academic achievement ($1000–$2000).

Application Procedures Students admitted directly into the professional program freshman year. Deadline for freshmen and transfers: continuous. Required: high school transcript, college transcript(s) for transfer students, SAT I or ACT test scores. Recommended: minimum 2.0 high school GPA, portfolio. Portfolio reviews held twice on campus.

Undergraduate Contact Mr. Joseph Fry, Assistant to the Director, School of Art, Kent State University, 211 Art Building, Kent, Ohio 44242-0001; 330-672-2192, fax: 330-672-4729.

Graduate Contact Dr. Frank D. Susi, Coordinator of Graduate Studies, School of Art, Kent State University, 211 Art Building, Kent, Ohio 44242-0001; 330-672-2192, fax: 330-672-4729.

▼ KUTZTOWN UNIVERSITY OF PENNSYLVANIA

Kutztown, Pennsylvania

State-supported, coed. Rural campus. Total enrollment: 7,920. Art program established 1924.

Degrees Bachelor of Fine Arts in the areas of fine arts, communication design, crafts. Majors and concentrations: advertising design, ceramics, fibers, graphic design, illustration, metals, painting/drawing, photography, printmaking, sculpture, woodworking design. Graduate degrees offered: Master of Art Education.

Enrollment Fall 1997: 1,150 total; 952 undergraduate, 18 graduate, 180 non-professional degree.

Art Student Profile 59% females, 41% males, 1% minorities, 1% international.

Art Faculty 90 total undergraduate and graduate (full-time and part-time). 95% of full-time faculty have terminal degrees. Graduate students do not teach undergraduate courses. Undergraduate student–faculty ratio: 11:1.

Student Life Student groups/activities include Art Student Association, Art Education Students Association. Special housing available for art students.

Expenses for 1997–98 Application fee: $25. One-time mandatory fee: $40. State resident tuition: $3468 full-time. Nonresident tuition: $8824 full-time. Mandatory fees: $751 full-time. College room and board: $3650. College room only: $2580.

Financial Aid Program-specific awards for 1997: 1 artistically talented award for talented program majors ($3224–$8198), 1 Morning Call Scholarship for minority students ($800), 1 Karen Anderson Scholarship for those demonstrating need ($500).

Application Procedures Students admitted directly into the professional program freshman year. Deadline for freshmen and transfers: continuous. Required: high school transcript, SAT I or ACT test scores, minimum 2.0 college GPA for transfer applicants, portfolio for fine arts, crafts, and art education applicants, art test for communication design applicants. Portfolio reviews held twice on campus; the submission of slides may be substituted for portfolios.

Undergraduate Contact Ms. Valerie Reidout, Director of Admission, Kutztown University of Pennsylvania, College Hill, Kutztown, Pennsylvania 19530; 610-683-4472.

Graduate Contact Dr. William Bruce Ezell, Dean of Graduate Studies and Extended Learning, Kutztown University, Kutztown University of Pennsylvania, Kutztown, Pennsylvania 19530; 610-683-4203, fax: 610-683-1393, E-mail address: ezell@kutztown.edu.

More About the University

Program Facilities Visual arts: the Sharadin Art Studio, a major University facility devoted to the visual arts; art studios open seven days a week; sixty-five–station computer design laboratory and classrooms open six days a week; continuous exhibitions in the art gallery.

Faculty, Resident Artists, and Alumni Faculty members are practicing professionals with regional, national, and international recognition, including artists whose works are in major museums and who exhibit in galleries around the country; as well as professionals who conduct national art education workshops. Visiting artists, lecturers, and alumni come to campus regularly, work with students in studios, and present master classes.

Student Performance/Exhibit Opportunities All students in the visual arts participate in gallery exhibitions; communication design students have portfolios professionally reviewed during their fourth year; senior art show, a highlight of the University cultural calendar; workshops in elementary and secondary schools conducted by art education students.

▼

The College of Visual and Performing Arts offers exceptional opportunities for students seeking training and experience in the arts in addition to a well-rounded university education. Students benefit from dedicated faculty members who are experts in drawing, painting, sculpture, printmaking, ceramics, woodworking, fibers, fine metals, graphic design, advertising design, illustration, photography, and art education. Typically, classes in the arts are small, and students receive personal attention.

Because nearly all faculty members teach full-time in the College, they are regularly available to students. In addition, all courses are taught by faculty members—not by graduate students. Even full professors may be found teaching freshman- and sophomore-year courses. Alumni who have distinguished themselves in the visual arts often return to the campus to share their ideas and experiences with students. In the past two years these have included painter Mark Innerst, scene designer David Mitchell, graphic designer Steve Frederick, jewelry designer Lisa Sorrelli, sculptor James Clarke, and Metropolitan Museum of Art photographer Robert Coscia.

Students have the advantage of receiving intensive instruction in arts disciplines in a small college as well as being part of a larger university. Outside of their major, they have the broadening experience of relating to students in the liberal arts and sciences, business, and education. In addition to the specialized facilities and equipment in the arts, they have access to the total academic, extracurricular, and career services resources of a modern regional university. Students may choose to live in campus residence halls.

Students have access to excellent equipment and facilities, such as well-equipped sculpture, painting, ceramics, woodworking, metalworking, fibers, and printmaking studios; a photography lab; and a computer design lab.

There are student clubs serving various interests in visual arts. In addition, there are more than fifty other student clubs and organizations as well as a complete student activities program at Kutztown University.

Opportunities extend beyond the campus to internships for communication design students, craft students, field work and student teaching for art education students, and study-abroad opportunities for students in all visual arts majors. Students may participate in exchange programs in three English schools in the fields of drawing, painting, sculpture, photography, ceramics, printmaking, metalworking, woodworking, graphic design, illustration, and advertising.

Kutztown University has often been described as having the ideal college campus—traditional and modern buildings in a spacious, quiet setting, nestled in beautiful Pennsylvania Dutch country—yet the major arts centers in the eastern United States are within easy driving distance: Philadelphia, 1½ hours; New York City, 2½ hours; Baltimore, 3 hours; and Washington, D.C., 3½ hours. Throughout the year, classes or student-faculty groups visit museums, art galleries, theaters, and concert halls in these locations and in nearby Allentown and Reading, Pennsylvania.

▼ LAKE ERIE COLLEGE

Painesville, Ohio

Independent, coed. Small town campus. Total enrollment: 701.

Degrees Bachelor of Fine Arts in the areas of art, interdisciplinary studies; Bachelor of Arts in the area of fine arts. Majors and concentrations: ceramics, interdisciplinary studies, photography, three-dimensional studies, two-dimensional studies, visual arts.

Enrollment Fall 1997: 5 undergraduate.

Art Student Profile 75% females, 25% males.

Art Faculty 2 undergraduate (part-time). Graduate students do not teach undergraduate courses. Undergraduate student–faculty ratio: 2:1.

Expenses for 1997–98 Application fee: $20. Comprehensive fee: $18,690 includes full-time tuition ($12,950), mandatory fees ($800), and college room and board ($4940). College room only: $2540. Special program-related fees: $30 per course for lab fees for specific courses.

Financial Aid Program-specific awards for 1997: 3 Fine Arts Scholarship Awards for program majors ($500–$3000).

Application Procedures Deadline for freshmen: July 1; transfers: August 20. Required: essay, high school transcript, college transcript(s) for transfer students, minimum 2.0 high school GPA, 2 letters of recommendation, SAT I or ACT test scores, portfolio for scholarship consideration. Recommended: interview. Portfolio reviews held as needed on campus; the submission of slides may be substituted for portfolios with permission of the chair.

Undergraduate Contact Mr. Paul Gothard, Director, Fine Arts Department, Lake Erie College, Box 354, 391 West Washington Street, Painesville, Ohio 44077; 440-639-7856.

▼ LAKEHEAD UNIVERSITY

Thunder Bay, ON, Canada

Province-supported, coed. Suburban campus. Total enrollment: 6,787. Art program established 1976.

Degrees Bachelor of Fine Arts in the area of studio art; Bachelor of Arts in the area of visual art. Majors and concentrations: ceramic art and design, drawing, painting, printmaking, sculpture, studio art. Cross-registration with Confederation College.

Enrollment Fall 1997: 56 undergraduate.

Art Student Profile 60% females, 40% males, 18% minorities, 5% international.

Art Faculty 7 total (full-time and part-time). 100% of full-time faculty have terminal degrees. Graduate students do not teach undergraduate courses. Undergraduate student–faculty ratio: 15:1.

Expenses for 1997–98 Application fee: $80 Canadian dollars. Tuition, fee, and room and board charges are reported in Canadian dollars. Canadian resident tuition: $3225 full-time. Mandatory fees: $338 full-time. College room and board: $4674. College room only: $3576. Room and board charges vary according to housing facility. International student tuition: $7000 full-time.

Financial Aid Program-specific awards for 1997: 1 Augustine 30th Anniversary Visual for 2nd or 3rd year students ($300), 1 MacAllan Munro Family Prize for awarded on the basis of competition ($450), 1 Westlake Visual Arts Bursary for students demonstrating need/B average ($750), 1 Dorothy Smith Bursary for students demonstrating need/B+ average ($750).

Application Procedures Students admitted directly into the professional program freshman year. Deadline for freshmen and transfers: continuous. Required: high school transcript, portfolio. Recommended: interview. Portfolio reviews held 3 times on campus; the submission of slides may be substituted for portfolios when distance is prohibitive.

Web Site http://www.lakeheadu.ca/~vartswww/visualarts.html.

Undergraduate Contact Mr. Mark Nisenholt, Chair, Department of Visual Arts, Lakehead University, 955 Oliver Road, Thunder Bay, ON P7B 5E1, Canada; 807-343-8787, fax: 807-345-2394.

▼ LAMAR DODD SCHOOL OF ART

See University of Georgia

▼ LA SIERRA UNIVERSITY

Riverside, California

Independent-Seventh-day Adventist, coed. Suburban campus. Total enrollment: 1,466.

Degrees Bachelor of Fine Arts in the areas of art, two-dimensional studies, three-dimensional studies. Majors and concentrations: art education, art/fine arts, graphic design, studio art.

Enrollment Fall 1997: 46 total; all undergraduate.

Art Student Profile 41% females, 59% males, 30% minorities, 24% international.

La Sierra University (continued)

Art Faculty 8 total (full-time and part-time). 100% of full-time faculty have terminal degrees. Graduate students do not teach undergraduate courses. Undergraduate student–faculty ratio: 10:1.

Student Life Student groups/activities include student exhibit in the Brandstater Gallery, internships.

Expenses for 1997–98 Application fee: $30. Comprehensive fee: $18,090 includes full-time tuition ($13,800), mandatory fees ($225), and college room and board ($4065). College room only: $2370. Full-time tuition and fees vary according to course load. Room and board charges vary according to board plan and housing facility. Special program-related fees: $20–$60 for materials fee, $25 for model fees.

Financial Aid Program-specific awards for 1997: 17 Katchamakoff Scholarships for program majors ($1500).

Application Procedures Students admitted directly into the professional program freshman year. Deadline for freshmen and transfers: continuous. Required: high school transcript, minimum 2.0 high school GPA, letter of recommendation, portfolio. Recommended: minimum 3.0 high school GPA, SAT I or ACT test scores. Portfolio reviews held twice on campus; the submission of slides may be substituted for portfolios.

Web Site http://www.lasierra.edu/art.

Undergraduate Contact University Admissions, La Sierra University, 4700 Pierce Street, Riverside, California 92515-8247; 909-785-2176, E-mail address: admissions@lasierra.edu.

▼ LAWRENCE TECHNOLOGICAL UNIVERSITY

Southfield, Michigan

Independent, coed. Suburban campus. Total enrollment: 3,645. Art program established 1991.

Degrees Bachelor of Fine Arts in the area of architectural illustration; Bachelor of Science in the area of interior architecture/design. Majors and concentrations: architectural illustration, interior architecture. Program accredited by FIDER, NASAD.

Enrollment Fall 1997: 140 total; all undergraduate.

Art Student Profile 50% females, 50% males, 10% minorities, 10% international.

Art Faculty 28 total (full-time and part-time). 100% of full-time faculty have terminal degrees. Graduate students do not teach undergraduate courses. Undergraduate student–faculty ratio: 12:1.

Student Life Student groups/activities include American Society of Architectural Perspectivists Students, American Society of Interior Designers. Special housing available for art students.

Expenses for 1997–98 Application fee: $30. Tuition: $9140 full-time. Mandatory fees: $200 full-time. Full-time tuition and fees vary according to program and student level. College room only: $2800. Room charges vary according to housing facility.

Financial Aid Program-specific awards for 1997: 6–7 LTU Scholarships for incoming freshmen ($8000–$8500), 6–7 Trustee Scholarships for incoming freshmen ($1600–$2000).

Application Procedures Students admitted directly into the professional program freshman year. Deadline for freshmen and transfers: continuous. Required: high school transcript, college transcript(s) for transfer students, minimum 3.0 high school GPA. Recommended: essay, 2 letters of recommenda-

tion, interview, portfolio. Portfolio reviews held continuously on campus; the submission of slides may be substituted for portfolios.

Undergraduate Contact Virginia North, Chair, Department of Art and Design, Lawrence Technological University, 21000 West Ten Mile Road, Southfield, Michigan 48075; 248-204-2848, E-mail address: northr@ltu.edu.

▼ LEHMAN COLLEGE OF THE CITY UNIVERSITY OF NEW YORK

Bronx, New York

State and locally supported, coed. Urban campus. Total enrollment: 9,386.

Degrees Bachelor of Fine Arts in the areas of printmaking, painting, sculpture, ceramics, photography. Majors and concentrations: art/fine arts, ceramic art and design, computer graphics, graphic arts, painting/drawing, photography, printmaking, sculpture, studio art. Graduate degrees offered: Master of Fine Arts in the areas of painting, graphics, sculpture. Cross-registration with City University of New York system.

Enrollment Fall 1997: 575 total; 50 undergraduate, 25 graduate, 500 non-professional degree.

Art Student Profile 60% females, 40% males, 75% minorities, 15% international.

Art Faculty 18 total undergraduate (full-time and part-time). 100% of full-time faculty have terminal degrees. Graduate students do not teach undergraduate courses. Undergraduate student–faculty ratio: 8:1.

Expenses for 1997–98 Application fee: $40. State resident tuition: $3200 full-time. Nonresident tuition: $6800 full-time. Mandatory fees: $120 full-time.

Financial Aid Program-specific awards available.

Application Procedures Students apply for admission into the professional program by sophomore year. Deadline for freshmen and transfers: continuous. Required: high school transcript, minimum 3.0 high school GPA, standing in top third of high school graduating class.

Contact Mr. Clarence Wilkes, Director of Admissions, 155 Shuster Hall, Lehman College of the City University of New York, 250 Bedford Park Boulevard West, Bronx, New York 10468; 718-960-8256.

▼ LINDENWOOD UNIVERSITY

St. Charles, Missouri

Independent-Presbyterian, coed. Suburban campus. Total enrollment: 4,788.

Degrees Bachelor of Fine Arts in the area of art; Bachelor of Arts in the areas of arts administration, art education. Majors and concentrations: art education, art history, art/fine arts, arts administration, ceramic art and design, computer graphics, graphic arts, painting/drawing, photography, printmaking, sculpture, studio art. Graduate degrees offered: Master of Fine Arts in the area of studio art; Master of Arts in the area of studio art. Cross-registration with Maryville University of Saint Louis, Fontbonne College, Missouri Baptist College, Webster University.

Enrollment Fall 1997: 86 total; 60 undergraduate, 26 graduate.

Art Student Profile 70% females, 30% males, 2% minorities, 7% international.

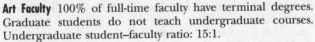

Art Faculty 100% of full-time faculty have terminal degrees. Graduate students do not teach undergraduate courses. Undergraduate student–faculty ratio: 15:1.

Student Life Student groups/activities include Student Art Association.

Expenses for 1997–98 Application fee: $25. Comprehensive fee: $15,150 includes full-time tuition ($9950), mandatory fees ($200), and college room and board ($5000). College room only: $2500.

Financial Aid Program-specific awards for 1997: art scholarships for undergraduates and transfers ($1500–$4500).

Application Procedures Deadline for freshmen and transfers: continuous. Required: essay, high school transcript, college transcript(s) for transfer students, minimum 2.0 high school GPA, interview, portfolio, SAT I or ACT test scores. Recommended: letter of recommendation. Portfolio reviews held continuously on campus; the submission of slides may be substituted for portfolios.

Contact Dr. Elaine C. Tillinger, Chair, Department of Art, Lindenwood University, 209 South Kings Highway, St. Charles, Missouri 63301; 314-949-4862, fax: 314-949-4910, E-mail address: etill@lindenwood.edu.

▼ Long Island University, C.W. Post Campus

Brookville, New York

Independent, coed. Suburban campus. Total enrollment: 8,171.

Degrees Bachelor of Fine Arts in the areas of graphic design, ceramics, painting/drawing, sculpture, photography, printmaking, art education, fine art, computer art; Bachelor of Science in the area of art therapy. Majors and concentrations: art education, art history, art therapy, art/fine arts, ceramics, computer art, graphic design, photography. Graduate degrees offered: Master of Fine Arts in the areas of graphic design, ceramics, painting/drawing, sculpture, photography, printmaking, computer art; Master of Science in the area of art education; Master of Arts in the areas of clinical art therapy, studio art. Cross-registration with Nassau Community College, Suffolk County Community College, State University of New York College of Technology at Farmingdale.

Enrollment Fall 1997: 259 total; 197 undergraduate, 62 graduate.

Art Student Profile 40% females, 60% males, 12% international.

Art Faculty 54 total undergraduate and graduate (full-time and part-time). 90% of full-time faculty have terminal degrees. Graduate students do not teach undergraduate courses.

Student Life Student groups/activities include American Association for Art Therapists.

Expenses for 1997–98 Application fee: $30. Comprehensive fee: $20,555 includes full-time tuition ($13,920), mandatory fees ($610), and college room and board ($6025). College room only: $3830. Room and board charges vary according to board plan. Special program-related fees: $30–$45 per course for supplies.

Financial Aid Program-specific awards for 1997: 15 Art Scholarships for Art Portfolio Day for freshmen and transfer students ($1000–$3000), 15 O'Malley Scholarship Fund and Posner Awards for continuing program majors ($200–$1000).

Application Procedures Students admitted directly into the professional program freshman year. Deadline for freshmen and transfers: continuous. Required: high school transcript, college transcript(s) for transfer students, portfolio, SAT I or ACT test scores (minimum combined SAT I score of 900), minimum verbal SAT score of 430. Recommended: essay, minimum 3.0 high school GPA, 2 letters of recommendation, interview. Portfolio reviews held as needed for transfer applicants on campus; the submission of slides may be substituted for portfolios for large works of art.

Web Site http://www.liu.edu.

Undergraduate Contact Ms. Christine Natali, Director of Admissions, Long Island University, C.W. Post Campus, 720 Northern Boulevard, Brookville, New York 11548-1300; 516-299-2413, fax: 516-299-2137, E-mail address: admissions@collegehall.liunet.edu.

Graduate Contact Ms. Sally Luzader, Associate Director of Graduate Admissions, Long Island University, C.W. Post Campus, 720 Northern Boulevard, Brookville, New York 11548-1300; 516-299-2417, fax: 516-299-2137, E-mail address: admissions@collegehall.liunet.edu.

More About the University

Program Facilities Tilles Center for the Performing Arts (2,200 seats); Hillwood Recital Hall (500 seats); Little Theatre MainStage (200 seats); Hillwood Cinema (330 seats); Music Rehearsal Building (100–150 seats); Great Hall (75–100 seats); Rifle Range Theatre (50 seats). The campus has two art galleries; ceramic and wood workshops; photography labs; welding, sculpture, jewelry, and graphic design studios; a dance studio; rehearsal, costume, and scene shops; a drafting room; and Long Island's largest computer graphics laboratory. The campus is home to the AAM-accredited Hillwood Art Museum. The film area includes a 50-seat movie theater/classroom, professional 16mm film, laser disc, sound editing, and video equipment. The Broadcasting program offers a state-of-the-art television and video production center, a campus radio station, and several student publications.

Faculty and Students Eighty-seven percent of the full-time faculty members hold a doctorate or the highest degree in their field. Several are international performers, working professionals in the entertainment industry, theater, music, and the media, as well as journalists and experts in their fields. Students have danced at Lincoln Center, interned at NBC television, sung across Europe, and displayed their artwork in Manhattan galleries.

Student Organizations Merriweather Consort, Madrigal and Chamber Singers, Long Island University– C.W. Post Chorus, Long Island Sound/Vocal Jazz, C.W. Post Orchestra, The Keyboard Club, Symphonic Winds, Jazz and Percussion Ensembles, Post Concert Dance Company, Post Theatre Company, Women in WCWP-FM Radio, and PTV.

The School of Visual and Performing Arts, one of six prestigious schools at Long Island University's C.W. Post Campus, provides a solid liberal arts education with professional training essential to a successful career in the arts. The suburban campus is widely recognized as one of the most beautiful college campuses in the nation. Located on 308 wooded acres, the campus is just 40 minutes from New York City.

▼ LONG ISLAND UNIVERSITY, SOUTHAMPTON COLLEGE

Southampton, New York

Independent, coed. Rural campus. Total enrollment: 1,563.

Degrees Bachelor of Fine Arts in the areas of art, graphic design, communication arts, photography, drawing/painting, mixed media.

Enrollment Fall 1997: 150 undergraduate.

Art Student Profile 60% females, 40% males.

Art Faculty 31 total (full-time and part-time). 90% of full-time faculty have terminal degrees. Graduate students do not teach undergraduate courses.

Student Life Student groups/activities include Drawing/ Painting Club, Communications Guild, Southampton Players (Theater).

Expenses for 1997–98 Application fee: $30. Comprehensive fee: $21,450 includes full-time tuition ($13,920), mandatory fees ($680), and college room and board ($6850). College room only: $3850. Room and board charges vary according to board plan and housing facility. Special program-related fees: $15–$75 per course for lab fees.

Financial Aid Program-specific awards for 1997: 6 Continuing Student Awards for upperclassmen ($2000), 30 Merit Awards for freshmen ($2000–$6000).

Application Procedures Students admitted directly into the professional program freshman year. Deadline for freshmen and transfers: continuous. Notification date for freshmen and transfers: continuous. Required: high school transcript, college transcript(s) for transfer students, portfolio, SAT I test score only. Recommended: interview, video for performance art majors. Portfolio reviews held 5-6 times on campus; the submission of slides may be substituted for portfolios when distance is prohibitive.

Undergraduate Contact Admissions Department, Long Island University, Southampton College, 239 Montauk Highway, Southampton, New York 11968; 800-LIU PLAN.

More About the University

It is hard to imagine a more beautiful or creatively stimulating environment for the study and production of art than the East End of Long Island. With its quiet farm fields and ocean vistas, Southampton offers solitude and time for contemplation. But it also reflects the excitement and culture of New York City, only 90 miles away. As many have found, Southampton is a special place for artists to work and live. The area is home to one of the most famous art communities in the country. Current residents include Robert Dash, Jane Freilicher, Roy Lichtenstein, and Larry Rivers. Southampton College's art faculty, also well known, includes Yoshi Higa, and Roy Nicholson. Two museums, several art societies and foundations, and more than thirty galleries are located in the Hamptons. Many art dealers, critics, and reviewers also have homes here. Students are linked with the cultural resources of the area in a variety of ways. Local artists participate in many of the college's programs and show their work in its Fine Arts Gallery. Some courses include visits to studios of local artists as well as trips to galleries and museums. Formal and informal contact is made with artists who are Southampton College alumni. Graduates often share their experiences with current students.

The Arts and Media Department offers a B.F.A. in fine arts and communication arts and a B.A. in art. A program leading to certification in art education is also available. To be accepted into the B.F.A. degree programs, students must present their portfolios, preferably in person. These programs offer courses in the basic techniques of art, including drawing, two- and three-dimensional design, color theory, and art history. The B.F.A. student's course work culminates in a major Directed Study Project. Students may spend a term preparing for their own exhibition in the gallery. Those interested in commercial art and graphics may choose to work for a semester at an advertising firm, design studio, or newspaper. Internships are also available at printing or graphic firms, galleries, and museums.

Facilities at the campus include studios and equipment for drawing, painting, photography, ceramics, computer graphics, printmaking, graphics, and sculpture, as well as radio and television.

Southampton offers art scholarships of $1000 to $7000 per year to students whose art portfolios show talent and promise. Students are expected to present their artwork in person. Scholarships are renewable annually if students maintain a 3.0 cumulative average. Both freshmen and transfer students may compete. Scholarships are based solely on the portfolio. Financial need and age of applicant are not considered. Students must apply for admission and must intend to major in art at Southampton.

▼ LONGWOOD COLLEGE

Farmville, Virginia

State-supported, coed. Small town campus. Total enrollment: 3,352.

Degrees Bachelor of Fine Arts in the area of art. Majors and concentrations: art education, art history, craft design, drawing, graphic design, interior architecture, painting, photography, printmaking.

Enrollment Fall 1997: 100 total; all undergraduate.

Art Student Profile 60% females, 40% males, 10% minorities.

Art Faculty 9 total (full-time and part-time). 100% of full-time faculty have terminal degrees. Graduate students do not teach undergraduate courses. Undergraduate student– faculty ratio: 13:1.

Student Life Student groups/activities include Kappa Pi.

Expenses for 1997–98 Application fee: $25. State resident tuition: $2684 full-time. Nonresident tuition: $8156 full-time. Mandatory fees: $1732 full-time. College room and board: $4280. College room only: $2506. Room and board charges vary according to board plan. Special program-related fees: $10–$60 per class for studio fee.

Financial Aid Program-specific awards for 1997: 6 departmental awards for program majors ($700).

Application Procedures Students admitted directly into the professional program freshman year. Deadline for freshmen: February 15; transfers: continuous. Required: essay, high school transcript, college transcript(s) for transfer students, minimum 2.0 high school GPA, SAT I or ACT test scores. Recommended: 3 letters of recommendation.

Undergraduate Contact Mr. Randy Edmonson, Chair, Department of Art, Longwood College, 201 High Street, Farmville, Virginia 23909; 804-395-2284, fax: 804-395-2775, E-mail address: redmonso@longwood.lwc.edu.

▼ LOUISIANA STATE UNIVERSITY AND AGRICULTURAL AND MECHANICAL COLLEGE

Baton Rouge, Louisiana

State-supported, coed. Urban campus. Total enrollment: 28,066.

Degrees Bachelor of Fine Arts in the area of studio art. Majors and concentrations: ceramics, graphic design, jewelry and metalsmithing, painting/drawing, photography, printmaking, sculpture. Graduate degrees offered: Master of Fine Arts in the area of studio art. Program accredited by NASAD.

Enrollment Fall 1997: 365 total; 300 undergraduate, 65 graduate.

Art Student Profile 57% females, 43% males, 3% minorities.

Art Faculty 32 total undergraduate and graduate (full-time and part-time). 100% of full-time faculty have terminal degrees. Graduate students teach a few undergraduate courses. Undergraduate student–faculty ratio: 20:1.

Student Life Student groups/activities include Exposure (photography club), Art League.

Expenses for 1997–98 Application fee: $25. State resident tuition: $2301 full-time. Nonresident tuition: $5901 full-time. Mandatory fees: $410 full-time. College room and board: $3772. College room only: $2020. Room and board charges vary according to board plan and housing facility.

Financial Aid Program-specific awards for 1997: 2 Supply Scholarships for talented students ($500).

Application Procedures Students admitted directly into the professional program freshman year. Deadline for freshmen and transfers: June 1. Required: high school transcript, college transcript(s) for transfer students, SAT I or ACT test scores, portfolio for graphic design applicants, minimum 2.5 high school GPA (4.0 scale). Recommended: portfolio. Portfolio reviews held twice on campus.

Undergraduate Contact Ms. Melody Guichet, Undergraduate Coordinator, School of Art, Louisiana State University and Agricultural and Mechanical College, 123 Art Building, Baton Rouge, Louisiana 70803; 504-388-5413, fax: 504-388-5424.

Graduate Contact Mr. Herb Goodman, Graduate Coordinator, School of Art, Louisiana State University and Agricultural and Mechanical College, 123 Art Building, Baton Rouge, Louisiana 70803; 504-388-5411, fax: 504-388-5424.

▼ LOUISIANA TECH UNIVERSITY

Ruston, Louisiana

State-supported, coed. Small town campus. Total enrollment: 9,500. Art program established 1894.

Degrees Bachelor of Fine Arts in the areas of studio art, photography, interior design, graphic design; Bachelor of Interior Design in the area of interior design (architecture). Majors and concentrations: art/fine arts, ceramic art and design, commercial art, computer graphics, graphic arts, illustration, painting/drawing, photography, printmaking, sculpture, studio art. Graduate degrees offered: Master of Fine Arts in the areas of studio art, photography, interior design, graphic design. Program accredited by NASAD.

Enrollment Fall 1997: 160 total; 150 undergraduate, 10 graduate.

Art Student Profile 55% females, 45% males, 5% minorities, 2% international.

Art Faculty 14 total undergraduate and graduate (full-time and part-time). 100% of full-time faculty have terminal degrees. Graduate students teach a few undergraduate courses. Undergraduate student–faculty ratio: 18:1.

Student Life Student groups/activities include Dark Horse (Graphic Design), American Society of Interior Designers, Art and Architecture Student Association. Special housing available for art students.

Expenses for 1997–98 Application fee: $20. State resident tuition: $2367 full-time. Nonresident tuition: $5367 full-time. Mandatory fees: $200 full-time. College room and board: $2805. College room only: $1605. Special program-related fees: $30 per quarter for art and architecture fee and enhancement fee for lecturers, special equipment, and workshops.

Financial Aid Program-specific awards for 1997: 3 departmental scholarships for photography majors ($1666), 3 departmental scholarships for graphic design majors ($1666), 3 departmental scholarships for studio majors ($1666).

Application Procedures Students admitted directly into the professional program freshman year. Deadline for freshmen and transfers: continuous. Required: high school transcript, college transcript(s) for transfer students, minimum 2.0 high school GPA, SAT I or ACT test scores. Recommended: interview.

Web Site http://www.art.latech.edu.

Undergraduate Contact Ms. Joanne Walker, Assistant to the Director, School of Art, Louisiana Tech University, PO Box 3175, Ruston, Louisiana 71272; 318-257-3909, fax: 318-257-4890.

Graduate Contact Mr. Peter Vones, Graduate Coordinator, School of Art, Louisiana Tech University, PO Box 3175, Ruston, Louisiana 71272; 318-257-3909, fax: 318-257-4890.

▼ LYME ACADEMY OF FINE ARTS

Old Lyme, Connecticut

Independent, coed. Small town campus. Art program established 1976.

Degrees Bachelor of Fine Arts in the areas of painting, sculpture. Cross-registration with University of Connecticut at Avery Point. Program accredited by NASAD.

Enrollment Fall 1997: 204 total; 80 undergraduate, 124 non-professional degree.

Art Student Profile 50% females, 50% males, 2% minorities, 1% international.

Art Faculty 16 total (full-time and part-time). 100% of full-time faculty have terminal degrees. Graduate students do not teach undergraduate courses. Undergraduate student–faculty ratio: 13:1.

Student Life Student groups/activities include Student Forum.

Expenses for 1997–98 Application fee: $35. Tuition: $8640 full-time. Mandatory fees: $50 full-time. Special program-related fees: $45 per semester for model/materials fees, $50 per year for student activities fee, $90 per semester for casting fee.

Financial Aid Program-specific awards for 1997: 26 Institutional Awards for program majors ($500).

Application Procedures Students admitted directly into the professional program freshman year. Deadline for freshmen and transfers: continuous. Required: essay, high school transcript, college transcript(s) for transfer students, 2 letters of recommendation, portfolio. Recommended: interview, SAT I or ACT test scores. Portfolio reviews held as needed on

Lyme Academy of Fine Arts (*continued*)

campus and off campus; the submission of slides may be substituted for portfolios if a campus visit is impossible.

Web Site http://www.lymeacademy.edu.

Undergraduate Contact Ms. Sharon Hunter, Vice President for Academic Affairs, Lyme Academy of Fine Arts, 84 Lyme Street, Old Lyme, Connecticut 06371; 860-434-5232, fax: 860-434-8725.

▼ MAHARISHI UNIVERSITY OF MANAGEMENT

Fairfield, Iowa

Independent, coed. Small town campus. Total enrollment: 1,422.

Degrees Bachelor of Fine Arts in the area of visual arts. Majors and concentrations: art/fine arts, ceramics, digital media, painting/drawing, photography, sculpture, studio art. Graduate degrees offered: Master of Fine Arts in the area of visual arts; Master of Arts in the area of visual arts.

Enrollment Fall 1997: 52 total; 30 undergraduate, 12 graduate, 10 non-professional degree.

Art Student Profile 50% females, 50% males, 10% minorities, 60% international.

Art Faculty 12 total undergraduate and graduate (full-time and part-time). 75% of full-time faculty have terminal degrees. Graduate students do not teach undergraduate courses. Undergraduate student–faculty ratio: 5:1.

Student Life Student groups/activities include Iowa wide exhibits.

Estimated expenses for 1998–99 Application fee: $25. Comprehensive fee: $19,630 includes full-time tuition ($14,670) and college room and board ($4960). College room only: $2560. Special program-related fees for lab fees for some courses.

Application Procedures Students apply for admission into the professional program by junior year. Deadline for freshmen: continuous. Notification date for freshmen: September 15. Required: essay, high school transcript, college transcript(s) for transfer students, 2 letters of recommendation, portfolio, SAT I or ACT test scores, minimum 2.5 high school GPA. Portfolio reviews held twice on campus; the submission of slides may be substituted for portfolios for transfer applicants.

Undergraduate Contact Mr. Brad Mylett, Director, Office of Admissions, Maharishi University of Management, Fairfield, Iowa 52557; 515-472-1110, fax: 515-472-1179, E-mail address: bmylett@mum.edu.

Graduate Contact Mr. Gurdon Leete, Director of Graduate Program in Art, Department of Fine Arts, Maharishi University of Management, Fairfield, Iowa 52557; 515-472-7000 ext. 5035, fax: 515-470-1387, E-mail address: gleete@mum.edu.

▼ MAINE COLLEGE OF ART

Portland, Maine

Independent, coed. Urban campus. Art program established 1882.

Degrees Bachelor of Fine Arts in the areas of ceramics, graphic design, painting, printmaking, photography, sculpture, metalsmithing and jewelry. Majors and concentrations: ceramic art and design, graphic arts, individualized major, jewelry and metalsmithing, painting, photography, printmaking, sculpture. Graduate degrees offered: Master of Fine Arts in the area of self-designed studio concentrations. Cross-registration with Bowdoin College, Greater Portland Alliance of Colleges and Universities. Program accredited by NASAD.

Enrollment Fall 1997: 322 total; all undergraduate.

Art Student Profile 56% females, 44% males, 7% minorities, 3% international.

Art Faculty 62 total undergraduate and graduate (full-time and part-time). 95% of full-time faculty have terminal degrees. Graduate students do not teach undergraduate courses. Undergraduate student–faculty ratio: 10:1.

Student Life Student groups/activities include Art in Service, America Reads. Special housing available for art students.

Expenses for 1997–98 Application fee: $40. Comprehensive fee: $20,799 includes full-time tuition ($14,850), mandatory fees ($155), and college room and board ($5794).

Financial Aid Program-specific awards for 1997: 10 half-tuition scholarships for incoming freshmen ($7800), 5 half-tuition scholarships for transfer students ($7800), 15–20 ARTS Scholarships for ARTS registrants ($1000), 250 Maine College of Art Grants for those demonstrating need ($1900).

Application Procedures Students admitted directly into the professional program freshman year. Deadline for freshmen and transfers: continuous. Notification date for freshmen and transfers: continuous. Required: essay, high school transcript, college transcript(s) for transfer students, minimum 2.0 high school GPA, 2 letters of recommendation, portfolio, SAT I or ACT test scores. Recommended: interview. Portfolio reviews held continuously on campus and off campus; the submission of slides may be substituted for portfolios when distance is prohibitive.

Undergraduate Contact Ms. Elizabeth Shea, Director of Admissions, Maine College of Art, 97 Spring Street, Portland, Maine 04101; 207-775-3052, fax: 207-772-5069, E-mail address: admissions@meca.edu.

Graduate Contact Dr. George Smith, Program Director, Maine College of Art, 97 Spring Street, Portland, Maine 04101; 207-775-3052, fax: 207-772-5069, E-mail address: gsmith@meca.edu.

More About the College

Program Facilities Departmental studios: well-equipped studios for each of the following majors: ceramics, graphic design, jewelry and metalsmithing, painting, photography, printmaking, and sculpture. Private studio space: Individual studio space is provided for all third- and fourth-year students. All MECA students are granted 24-hour studio access. Galleries: The College hosts exhibitions in three of its gallery spaces—the student and Clapp galleries and the new Institute of Contemporary Art. Works by MECA students as well as regional, national, and international artists are exhibited in these professional gallery spaces. In addition, students have opportunities to exhibit work in galleries and businesses throughout the community. Students and alumni are encouraged to put work for sale in ArtWorks, the College's sales gallery located next to the galleries in the main studio building. Library: MECA has the largest open-to-public art library in northern New England. The library's collections number 18,000 volumes, 112 periodicals, and 42,000 slides.

Special Programs Maine College of Art begins a Sister School program in September 1998 with Hanoi Fine Arts College, becoming the first college in the United States to have a reciprocal program with a college in Vietnam. The Association of Independent Colleges of Art and Design (AICAD) is a consortium of thirty-two internationally recognized colleges of art and design. The association provides opportunities such as a student mobility program, access to international study, and internships in New York City. Bowdoin College Exchange and the Greater Portland Alliance of Colleges and Universities provide cross-registration between area schools. Internships are credit-bearing employment opportunities that give students professional, hands-on experience in a business, museum, gallery, or studio environment. The College's Art in Service program matches students with nonprofit service agencies bringing art into schools, churches, outreach programs, and other areas. Visiting Artist Lecture Series: Each year, MECA hosts 10–20 well-known artists, designers, writers, and other scholars who lecture on their work and contemporary issues in the arts. In addition, the artists often meet with classes and individual students.

▼

Maine College of Art (MECA) is an independent professional art institution located in northern New England. Through a structured, four-year curriculum of studio and liberal arts courses, students grow as artists and human beings. The College fosters an environment that nurtures individual development and successfully prepares students to work in every area of the visual arts, from painting and sculpture to ceramics and jewelry, from furniture and textile design to art education and photojournalism, from video graphics and publication design to advertising and curatorial work. Graduates enter the professional world with one of the finest visual arts educations available.

One of the great attractions of MECA is its location in Portland, Maine. Portland is a small, cosmopolitan city of 65,000 situated on the Atlantic Ocean's Casco Bay. Portland consistently ranks as one of the safest and most livable cities in the United States. The city offers many of the cultural advantages of a large urban center but in a more relaxed setting. The city is home to the Portland Museum of Art, Portland Symphony Orchestra, Portland Stage Company, and numerous other cultural resources. Jazz, blues, reggae, rock, and folk music are featured in a variety of clubs in the historic Old Port district.

The College campus is located in the growing Downtown Arts District along with museums, galleries, theaters, cafes, and boutiques as well as artists' studios.

The state of Maine is well known for its extraordinary beauty, high quality of life, and rich artistic heritage. Over the past two centuries Maine has played a vital role in American art. Such renowned artists as Winslow Homer, Bernice Abbott, Edward Hopper, and Andrew Wyeth have all drawn inspiration from the Maine landscape and people. Students draw inspiration from the landscape as well. MECA is only two hours from the finest skiing and snowboarding on the East Coast and only ten minutes from beautiful beaches and island getaways.

In 1996 MECA moved five of its seven studio departments into a renovated five-story historic building in downtown Portland. The new MECA Building provides increased space, superior ventilation systems, and an inspiring location for artmaking. The renovation project has been nationally recognized as an "Energy Star Showcase" by the Environmental Protection Agency—one of only twenty-four projects in the country chosen as an outstanding model of energy efficiency and environmental sensitivity.

The professional excellence of the MECA faculty is well established, and the College seeks to ensure that students receive personal attention. All MECA instructors are accomplished, practicing artists. One example of such recognition is the prestigious Guggenheim Fellowship granted to Paul D'Amato, Associate Professor of Photography. The John Simon Guggenheim Memorial Foundation appoints Guggenheim Fellows on the basis of unusually distinguished achievement in the past and exceptional promise for future accomplishments.

Tim McCreight, Chair of the Metalsmithing and Jewelry Department, recently published a new book about the design process entitled *Design Language*. The book is the culmination of more than five years of research. *Design Language* will undoubtedly follow the precedent set by McCreight's 1982 textbook publication *The Complete Metalsmith*, considered by many to be the definitive work on the subject of metals and jewelry.

Because of its excellent reputation, Maine College of Art draws students not only from New England but also from states across the country. In addition, MECA is home to a growing number of international students. Students come from a variety of ethnic and cultural backgrounds, but all share in common the desire to study in one of the most challenging and respected art colleges in the United States.

▼ MANHATTANVILLE COLLEGE

Purchase, New York

Independent, coed. Suburban campus. Total enrollment: 1,925. Art program established 1974.

Degrees Bachelor of Fine Arts in the area of studio art. Cross-registration with Purchase College-State University of New York.

Enrollment Fall 1997: 79 undergraduate.

Art Student Profile 75% females, 25% males, 12% minorities, 6% international.

Art Faculty 15 total (full-time and part-time). 100% of full-time faculty have terminal degrees. Graduate students do not teach undergraduate courses.

Student Life Student groups/activities include Art Club, Shakespeare in the Castle, Women's Glee Club.

Expenses for 1997–98 Application fee: $35. Comprehensive fee: $25,300 includes full-time tuition ($16,760), mandatory fees ($540), and college room and board ($8000). Special program-related fees: $35 per course for lab and materials fees.

Application Procedures Students admitted directly into the professional program freshman year. Deadline for freshmen and transfers: continuous. Required: high school transcript, college transcript(s) for transfer students, minimum 2.0 high school GPA, 2 letters of recommendation, portfolio, SAT I or ACT test scores, high school transcript for transfer applicants with fewer than 45 credits. Recommended: essay, minimum 3.0 high school GPA, interview, video. Portfolio reviews held continuously as needed on campus; the submission of slides may be substituted for portfolios when distance is prohibitive.

Undergraduate Contact Mr. Jose Flores, Director of Admissions, Admissions Department, Manhattanville College, 2900 Purchase Street, Purchase, New York 10577; 800-328-4553, fax: 914-694-1732, E-mail address: jflores@mville.edu.

▼ MANKATO STATE UNIVERSITY

Mankato, Minnesota

State-supported, coed. Small town campus. Total enrollment: 12,507.

Degrees Bachelor of Fine Arts in the area of art. Majors and concentrations: ceramics, drawing, fibers, graphic arts, painting, photography, printmaking, sculpture, textile arts. Graduate degrees offered: Master of Arts in the area of studio art. Program accredited by NASAD.

Enrollment Fall 1997: 246 total; 204 undergraduate, 25 graduate, 17 non-professional degree.

Art Student Profile 55% females, 45% males, 2% minorities, 5% international.

Art Faculty 18 total undergraduate and graduate (full-time and part-time). 92% of full-time faculty have terminal degrees. Graduate students teach a few undergraduate courses. Undergraduate student–faculty ratio: 16:1.

Student Life Student groups/activities include Art League.

Expenses for 1997–98 Application fee: $20. State resident tuition: $2582 full-time. Nonresident tuition: $5769 full-time. Mandatory fees: $401 full-time. College room and board: $2965. College room only: $1880. Room and board charges vary according to board plan. Special program-related fees: $35–$50 per quarter for art supplies.

Financial Aid Program-specific awards for 1997: 6–8 Faculty Nominated Awards for program majors ($350).

Application Procedures Students apply for admission into the professional program by sophomore, junior year. Deadline for freshmen and transfers: continuous. Notification date for freshmen and transfers: continuous. Required: high school transcript, college transcript(s) for transfer students, portfolio, SAT I or ACT test scores. Portfolio reviews held 3 times on campus.

Web Site http://www.mankato.msus.edu/dept/artdept.

Contact Mr. Robert Finkler, Chairperson, Art Department, Mankato State University, South Road and Ellis Avenue, PO Box 8400, Mankato, Minnesota 56002-8400; 507-389-6412, fax: 507-389-5887, E-mail address: robert_finkler@msl.mankato.msus.edu.

▼ MARSHALL UNIVERSITY

Huntington, West Virginia

State-supported, coed. Urban campus. Total enrollment: 13,388. Art program established 1984.

Degrees Bachelor of Fine Arts in the area of art studio; Bachelor of Arts in the area of art education. Majors and concentrations: craft design, graphic design, painting, photography, printmaking, sculpture. Graduate degrees offered: Master of Arts in the area of art education. Program accredited by NCATE.

Enrollment Fall 1997: 197 total; 160 undergraduate, 25 graduate, 12 non-professional degree.

Art Student Profile 52% females, 48% males, 5% minorities, 1% international.

Art Faculty 20 total undergraduate and graduate (full-time and part-time). 100% of full-time faculty have terminal degrees. Graduate students teach a few undergraduate courses. Undergraduate student–faculty ratio: 17:1.

Student Life Student groups/activities include Art Opportunities Program (teaching elementary students in enrichment program), Keramos (Ceramics Club), Graphic Design Club-"Artatak".

Expenses for 1997–98 Application fee: $10. State resident tuition: $1798 full-time. Nonresident tuition: $5680 full-time. Mandatory fees: $386 full-time. Full-time tuition and fees vary according to reciprocity agreements. College room and board: $4420. College room only: $2266. Room and board charges vary according to board plan and housing facility. Special program-related fees: $25 per studio course for art supplies .

Financial Aid Program-specific awards for 1997: 4–5 art scholarships for program majors ($500), 10 tuition waivers for program majors ($1000), 1 Garth Brown Memorial Scholarship for program majors ($500), 1 Donald Harper Scholarship for program majors ($400), 1 College of Fine Arts Gala Scholarship for program majors ($2000), 1 John Q. Hill Memorial Scholarship for minority program majors ($1000), 1 Stewart Smith Scholarship for program majors ($800).

Application Procedures Students admitted directly into the professional program freshman year. Deadline for freshmen and transfers: August 15. Notification date for freshmen and transfers: continuous. Required: high school transcript, college transcript(s) for transfer students, minimum 2.0 high school GPA, SAT I or ACT test scores. Recommended: 3 letters of recommendation, interview, portfolio. Portfolio reviews held twice on campus; the submission of slides may be substituted for portfolios if a campus visit is impossible.

Contact Mr. Michael Cornfeld, Chairman, Department of Art, Marshall University, 400 Hal Greer Boulevard, Huntington, West Virginia 25755; 304-696-2897, fax: 304-696-6505, E-mail address: dfa003@marshall.wvnet.edu.

▼ MARYLAND INSTITUTE, COLLEGE OF ART

Baltimore, Maryland

Independent, coed. Urban campus. Total enrollment: 1,143. Art program established 1826.

Degrees Bachelor of Fine Arts in the areas of drawing, painting, sculpture, printmaking, general fine arts, ceramics, fibers, photography, illustration, interior architecture and design; Bachelor of Fine Arts/Master of Arts in Teaching; Bachelor of Fine Arts/Master of Arts in the area of digital arts. Majors and concentrations: art/fine arts, ceramic art and design, fibers, graphic arts, illustration, interior design, painting/drawing, photography, printmaking, sculpture. Graduate degrees offered: Master of Fine Arts in the areas of painting, sculpture, art education, photography, mixed media; Master of Arts in the area of digital arts. Cross-registration with Johns Hopkins University, University of Baltimore, Goucher College, Loyola College, Peabody Conservatory of Music, Notre Dame College, the Association of Independent Colleges of Art and Design. Program accredited by NASAD, FIDER.

Enrollment Fall 1997: 1,143 total; 991 undergraduate, 127 graduate, 25 non-professional degree.

Art Student Profile 56% females, 44% males, 16% minorities, 7% international.

Art Faculty 178 total undergraduate and graduate (full-time and part-time). 87% of full-time faculty have terminal degrees. Graduate students do not teach undergraduate courses. Undergraduate student–faculty ratio: 6:1.

Student Life Student groups/activities include Student Exhibitions Committee, Programming Arts Committee, American Institute of Graphic Arts. Special housing available for art students.

Expenses for 1997–98 Application fee: $45. Comprehensive fee: $21,960 includes full-time tuition ($16,590), mandatory fees ($170), and college room and board ($5200). College room only: $4100. Room and board charges vary according to board plan and housing facility.

Financial Aid Program-specific awards for 1997: 38 Thalheimer Scholarships for freshmen ($10,000–$25,000), 15 Academic Excellence Scholarships for freshmen ($10,000), 5 C.V. Starr Scholarships for international freshmen ($10,000), 40 Competitive Scholarships for transfers ($4000–$20,000), 160 Competitive Scholarships for upperclassmen/returning students ($300–$18,000).

Application Procedures Students admitted directly into the professional program freshman year. Deadline for freshmen: February 1; transfers: March 15. Notification date for freshmen: April 1; transfers: April 15. Required: essay, high school transcript, college transcript(s) for transfer students, portfolio, SAT I or ACT test scores. Recommended: 2 letters of recommendation, interview, honors and advanced placement level coursework in English and other humanities subjects. Portfolio reviews held continuously on campus and off campus in various cities; the submission of slides may be substituted for portfolios (slides preferred).

Web Site http://www.mica.edu.

Undergraduate Contact Ms. Theresa Lynch Bedoya, Vice President, Admission and Financial Aid, Admission and Financial Aid Office, Maryland Institute, College of Art, 1300 Mt. Royal Avenue, Baltimore, Maryland 21217; 410-225-2222, fax: 410-225-2337, E-mail address: admissions@mica.edu.

Graduate Contact Dr. Leslie King-Hammond, Dean of Graduate Programs, Graduate Studies, Maryland Institute, College of Art, 1300 Mt. Royal Avenue, Baltimore, Maryland 21217; 410-225-2255, fax: 410-225-2408.

More About the Institute

Program Facilities Campus of nineteen buildings; 235,000 square feet of instructional facilities designated to departments of painting, ceramics, drawing, sculpture, photography, printmaking, fibers, interior architecture, graphic design/illustration, and liberal arts; independent studio space for most seniors; seven art galleries; art-oriented library: 50,000 volumes, 300 periodicals, 120,000 slides of contemporary and historical art; intimately-sized liberal arts classrooms; 250-seat auditorium for performance art, theater, poetry readings, and lectures; 24-hour access to studios; computer facilities include 5 computer labs outfitted with 57 Power Macintosh 7100AV; 2 computer classrooms with 16 Quadra 660AV and 26 PowerMac 7200 computers with digital video capabilities; 2 3-D animation classrooms consisting of 35 Pentium 3-D and animation workstations with two rendering workstations and digital video capability; a computer writing and tutoring lab consisting of 23 486 PCs; individual workstations for each interior architecture student; 4 Avid digital video suites; computer workstations in the sculpture, fibers, ceramics, and art education departments; and Internet access stations in the Main Building and Library; equipment includes flatbed scanners, high resolution color printers, digital cameras, video capture capability, slide scanners, dye sublimation printing, a Novajet wide format printer, and CD writing capability; communications capabilities include e-mail addresses for each student, student e-mail access workstations, and classroom access to the World Wide Web.

Visiting Artists and Lecturers Each year more than 250 visiting artists, designers, critics, poets, writers, historians, and filmmakers take part in classroom/studio instruction. During the past three years, resident artists from Asia, Eastern Europe, and Latin America were included.

Faculty One hundred seventy professional artists, designers, and scholars; represented in public and private collections from MOMA to the Stedelijk; nationally recognized recipients of Fulbright, Guggenheim, MacArthur, Louis Comfort Tiffany, Prix de Rome, and National Foundation for the Arts and for the Humanities; published authors of articles, books, poetry, plays, and critical reviews: more than fifty publications published in two years; exhibit in national, regional, and international museums and galleries from Leo Castelli Galleries in New York to Galleria Tucci-Russo in Italy.

Special Programs A five-year dual degree (B.F.A/M.A.T.) combines an undergraduate degree in studio art with teaching certification at the master's level; the B.F.A./M.A. in digital arts provides a fifth year capstone experience; study abroad opportunities in Canada, England, Scotland, France, Greece, Isreal, Italy, Mexico, Japan, and the Netherlands; New York Studio program for juniors; career development programs include 800 job internship opportunities in corporations, cultural institutions, design and architectural firms, photography studios. Other reality-based programs and courses are offered in topics ranging from promoting oneself as an artist to developing business skills. Job listings and alumni referals are national.

▼

For more than 170 years, the Maryland Institute, College of Art, has brought together some of the most talented and committed students and faculty from across the nation and around the world to create art in a highly energized and intellectual environment.

The Institute offers a strong foundation in the fine arts and design, complemented by a challenging liberal arts component. Students can choose from twelve different studio majors as well as minors in art history, literature, and writing. Visual communication and interior architecture and design programs are computer based. Once students choose a major, they may opt to take electives in an array of subjects outside their major area of study in order to further develop their individual voice. The dialogue between departments and disciplines is constant. Faculty and visiting artists from all disciplines, including liberal arts, are regularly invited to take part in critiques and make studio visits to lend their diverse perspectives to the creative process.

Located in a beautiful residential neighborhood in Baltimore and surrounded by other cultural institutions, the Institute offers students the best of urban and town life. Baltimore is home to a vibrant visual and performing arts community. Its world-class museums and galleries present traditional art as well as work by contemporary and emerging artists. Additionally, Baltimore is located in the middle of the New York–Washington, D.C., arts corridor and is home to many colleges (including the Johns Hopkins University and the Peabody Conservatory of Music) that offer cooperative academic exchange programs for Institute students.

As the Maryland Institute looks toward the future, the College is planning for the influences that advances in technology and a more global society will have on the

Maryland Institute, College of Art *(continued)*

education of artists. This fall, the Maryland Institute opened a new facility that includes a multimedia center, a greatly expanded library, and a new home for all design, liberal arts, and humanities programs. Additionally, the Institute offers excellent mobility programs and extensive opportunities for students to study abroad during the summer or during their junior or senior years.

The Institute's residential campus includes the Commons, a housing complex designed especially for student artists. There, students live in apartment-style housing, complete with access to 24-hour project rooms and gallery space on site. The College Center houses the career center, dining hall, and meeting rooms for student organizations and is located next door to the art supply/bookstore.

The Institute provides an array of career services for its students. The professional career center staff prepares students for a myriad of art-related professional positions. The center helps place upperclassmen in art-related internships for academic credit and job experience as well as in part-time and freelance positions while they are in school. The career center also assists students in graduate school applications and provides national job listings for graduating seniors.

The Institute hosts more than sixty exhibitions a year by international, regional, and local artists as well as students and faculty; an extensive program of visiting artists, critics, and lecturers; an annual poetry and film series; and many special interest clubs, ranging from a multicultural club, a host-family program for international students, and a student exhibitions committee to several student publications and a variety of social and political organizations.

▼ MARYLHURST UNIVERSITY

Marylhurst, Oregon

Independent-Roman Catholic, coed. Suburban campus. Art program established 1982.

Degrees Bachelor of Fine Arts in the area of art. Majors and concentrations: art/fine arts, interior design, painting/drawing, photography, printmaking, sculpture.

Enrollment Fall 1997: 180 total; 150 undergraduate, 30 non-professional degree.

Art Student Profile 70% females, 30% males, 5% minorities, 2% international.

Art Faculty 28 total (full-time and part-time). 100% of full-time faculty have terminal degrees. Graduate students do not teach undergraduate courses. Undergraduate student–faculty ratio: 7:1.

Student Life Student groups/activities include American Society of Interior Designers Student Chapter.

Expenses for 1997–98 Application fee: $88. Comprehensive fee: $14,910 includes full-time tuition ($9765), mandatory fees ($195), and college room and board ($4950).

Financial Aid Program-specific awards for 1997: 20 Mayer Scholarships for program majors ($100).

Application Procedures Students admitted directly into the professional program freshman year. Deadline for freshmen and transfers: continuous. Required: high school transcript.

Web Site http://www.marylhurst.edu/pages/baart.htm.

Undergraduate Contact Mr. Paul Sutinen, Assistant Chair, Art Department, Marylhurst University, PO Box 261, Marylhurst, Oregon 97036; 503-699-6242, fax: 503-636-9526, E-mail address: psutinen@marylhurstl.edu.

▼ MARYVILLE UNIVERSITY OF SAINT LOUIS

St. Louis, Missouri

Independent, coed. Suburban campus. Total enrollment: 3,055. Art program established 1970.

Degrees Bachelor of Fine Arts in the areas of interior design, studio art, graphic design; Bachelor of Arts in the area of art education (K-12). Cross-registration with Webster University, Fontbonne College, Missouri Baptist College, Lindenwood University. Program accredited by NASAD, FIDER, NCATE.

Enrollment Fall 1997: 94 total; 85 undergraduate, 9 non-professional degree.

Art Student Profile 80% females, 20% males, 5% minorities, 5% international.

Art Faculty 28 total (full-time and part-time). 100% of full-time faculty have terminal degrees. Graduate students do not teach undergraduate courses.

Student Life Student groups/activities include Maryville Chapter of American Society of Interior Designers, It's Visual.

Expenses for 1997–98 Application fee: $20. Comprehensive fee: $15,910 includes full-time tuition ($10,850), mandatory fees ($60), and college room and board ($5000). Special program-related fees: $5–$30 per course for consumable supplies in studio courses, $5 per course for audiovisual teaching resources in art history courses.

Financial Aid Program-specific awards for 1997: 5–8 Art and Design Scholarships for undergraduates, first time freshmen, and outstanding transfer students ($2500–$4000).

Application Procedures Students admitted directly into the professional program freshman year. Deadline for freshmen and transfers: continuous. Required: high school transcript, college transcript(s) for transfer students, minimum 2.0 high school GPA, portfolio, SAT I or ACT test scores. Recommended: letter of recommendation, interview. Portfolio reviews held continuously on campus and off campus in St. Louis, MO; Kansas City, MO; Memphis, TN; Indianapolis, IN; Chicago, IL on National Portfolio Days; the submission of slides may be substituted for portfolios if original work is not available, for large works of art, or for three-dimensional pieces.

Web Site http://www.maryvillestl.edu/CA.html#12.

Undergraduate Contact Dr. Martha G. Wade, Dean, Admissions and Enrollment Management, Maryville University of Saint Louis, 13550 Conway Road, St. Louis, Missouri 63141-7299; 314-529-9350, fax: 314-529-9927, E-mail address: wade@maryville.edu.

More About the University

Program Facilities The new Art and Design Building (1998) is designed to accommodate growing programs and technological needs in art education, graphic design, interior design, and studio art. Features include a student gallery; two graphics studios equipped with the latest Macintosh technology; two interior design studios with AutoCAD workstations for each student; an interior design resource library and lighting lab; drawing, painting, photography, and printmaking studios; conference and critique rooms; and a workshop. An additional building houses newly renovated studios for ceramics, jewelry and metalsmithing, sculpture, and other 3-D media. The Morton J. May Foundation Gallery is located in the library and features an annual schedule of six professional exhibits, two graduating senior shows, and a student exhibit.

Faculty The faculty of artists, designers, and historians are dedicated to the primacy of teaching and to the integration of professional experiences with academic studies. A lively program of visiting artists, designers, and field trips complements the curriculum.

Student Exhibit Opportunities Work is exhibited continuously throughout the campus and in off-campus venues such as the Design Center and Art St. Louis galleries. Students have portfolio reviews at the end of each semester, and they participate in a senior exhibit to complete degree requirements.

Special Programs Seniors complete a career-related internship. Study abroad is encouraged. Affiliations include the American Institute for Foreign Study (AIFS) and the American College in London. Maryville is an accredited institutional member of the National Association of Schools of Art and Design (NASAD). Program accreditations include the Foundation for Interior Design Education Research (FIDER) and the National Council for the Accreditation of Teacher Education (NCATE).

▼ MARYWOOD UNIVERSITY

Scranton, Pennsylvania

Independent-Roman Catholic, coed. Suburban campus. Total enrollment: 2,948.

Degrees Bachelor of Fine Arts in the areas of studio art, design; Bachelor of Arts in the area of art education. Majors and concentrations: ceramic art and design, graphic arts, illustration, interior design, painting/drawing, photography, sculpture. Graduate degrees offered: Master of Fine Arts in the areas of visual arts, painting, fibers, printmaking, photography, advertising design, illustration, clay, metal; Master of Arts in the areas of studio art, art education. Cross-registration with University of Scranton. Program accredited by NASAD.

Enrollment Fall 1997: 289 total; 183 undergraduate, 65 graduate, 41 non-professional degree.

Art Student Profile 70% females, 30% males, 2% minorities, 2% international.

Art Faculty 35 total undergraduate and graduate (full-time and part-time). 100% of full-time faculty have terminal degrees. Graduate students do not teach undergraduate courses. Undergraduate student–faculty ratio: 14:1.

Student Life Student groups/activities include American Society of Interior Designers, Zeta Omicron Chapter of Kappa Pi, Pennsylvania Art Education Association.

Expenses for 1997–98 Application fee: $20. Comprehensive fee: $19,703 includes full-time tuition ($13,408), mandatory fees ($595), and college room and board ($5700). Room and board charges vary according to board plan.

Financial Aid Program-specific awards for 1997: 35 Art Talent Awards for artistically talented students ($1000).

Application Procedures Students admitted directly into the professional program freshman year. Deadline for freshmen and transfers: continuous. Required: high school transcript, college transcript(s) for transfer students, minimum 2.0 high school GPA, 2 letters of recommendation, portfolio, SAT I or ACT test scores (minimum combined SAT I score of 900, minimum combined ACT score of 19). Recommended: interview. Portfolio reviews held continuously on campus and

off campus; the submission of slides may be substituted for portfolios if a campus visit is impossible.

Undergraduate Contact Undergraduate Admissions, Marywood University, 2300 Adams Avenue, Scranton, Pennsylvania 18509; 800-346-5014, fax: 717-961-4769.

Graduate Contact Graduate School of Arts and Sciences Admissions, Marywood University, 2300 Adams Avenue, Scranton, Pennsylvania 18509; 717-348-6230, fax: 717-961-4769.

Rutgers, The State University of New Jersey

▼ MASON GROSS SCHOOL OF THE ARTS

New Brunswick, New Jersey

State-supported, coed. Small town campus. Total university enrollment: 48,341. Total unit enrollment: 770.

Degrees Bachelor of Fine Arts in the area of visual arts. Majors and concentrations: ceramics, computer graphics, film, graphic design, media arts, painting/drawing, photography, printmaking, sculpture, video production. Graduate degrees offered: Master of Fine Arts. Program accredited by NASAD.

Enrollment Fall 1997: 355 total; 304 undergraduate, 51 graduate.

Art Student Profile 55% females, 45% males, 19% minorities, 2% international.

Art Faculty 34 total undergraduate and graduate (full-time and part-time). 98% of full-time faculty have terminal degrees. Graduate students teach a few undergraduate courses. Undergraduate student–faculty ratio: 11:1.

Expenses for 1997–98 Application fee: $50. State resident tuition: $4262 full-time. Nonresident tuition: $8676 full-time. Mandatory fees: $1104 full-time. Full-time tuition and fees vary according to location. College room and board: $5314. College room only: $3112. Room and board charges vary according to board plan and housing facility. Special program-related fees: $20–$50 per class for supplies/materials.

Financial Aid Program-specific awards for 1997: 2–3 Betts Scholarships for upperclassmen ($500).

Application Procedures Students admitted directly into the professional program freshman year. Deadline for freshmen: January 15; transfers: March 15. Notification date for freshmen: June 1; transfers: July 1. Required: high school transcript, college transcript(s) for transfer students, minimum 2.0 high school GPA, portfolio, SAT I or ACT test scores. Recommended: essay. Portfolio reviews held twice on campus and off campus in various cities at College Art Recruitment Fairs; the submission of slides may be substituted for portfolios for out-of-state applicants.

Web Site http://www.rutgers.edu or http://www.mgsa.rutgers.edu/mgsa.

Undergraduate Contact Ms. Diane W. Harris, Associate Director, Undergraduate Admissions, Rutgers, The State University of New Jersey, Mason Gross School of the Arts, 65 Davidson Road, Piscataway, New Jersey 08854-8097; 732-932-INFO, fax: 732-445-0237, E-mail address: admissions@asb-ugadm.rutgers.edu.

Graduate Contact Dr. Donald J. Taylor, Director of Graduate and Professional Admissions, Graduate and Professional Admissions, Rutgers, The State University of New Jersey, Mason Gross School of the Arts, 18 Bishop Place, New Brunswick, New Jersey 08903; 732-932-7711, fax: 732-932-8231.

▼ MASSACHUSETTS COLLEGE OF ART

Boston, Massachusetts

State-supported, coed. Urban campus. Total enrollment: 2,289. Art program established 1873.

Degrees Bachelor of Fine Arts in the areas of art education, art history, fine arts, design, media and performing arts. Majors and concentrations: architectural design, art education, art history, art/fine arts, ceramic art and design, fashion design and technology, film studies, glass, graphic arts, illustration, industrial design, interrelated media, jewelry and metalsmithing, painting/drawing, photography, printmaking, sculpture, studio art, textile arts. Graduate degrees offered: Master of Fine Arts in the areas of design, fine arts, media and performing arts. Cross-registration with ProArts Consortium, College Academic Program Sharing, Public College Exchange Program. Program accredited by NASAD.

Enrollment Fall 1997: 1,442 total; 1,331 undergraduate, 111 graduate.

Art Student Profile 60% females, 40% males, 15% minorities, 6% international.

Art Faculty 159 total undergraduate and graduate (full-time and part-time). 75% of full-time faculty have terminal degrees. Graduate students teach a few undergraduate courses. Undergraduate student–faculty ratio: 12:1.

Student Life Student groups/activities include All School Show, visiting artists and professional exhibitions, Christmas Art Sale. Special housing available for art students.

Expenses for 1997–98 Application fee: $10. One-time mandatory fee: $50. State resident tuition: $1320 full-time. Nonresident tuition: $6900 full-time. Mandatory fees: $2644 full-time. Full-time tuition and fees vary according to reciprocity agreements. College room and board: $6348. Room and board charges vary according to housing facility. Special program-related fees: $20–$200 per course for course lab fees.

Financial Aid Program-specific awards available.

Application Procedures Students admitted directly into the professional program freshman year. Deadline for freshmen: March 1; transfers: April 1. Notification date for freshmen and transfers: May 15. Required: essay, high school transcript, college transcript(s) for transfer students, portfolio, SAT I or ACT test scores, minimum 2.7 high school GPA. Recommended: minimum 3.0 high school GPA, letter of recommendation. Portfolio reviews held continuously on campus; the submission of slides may be substituted for portfolios (slides preferred).

Contact Ms. Kay Ransdell, Dean for Admissions and Retention, Massachusetts College of Art, 621 Huntington Avenue, Boston, Massachusetts 02115-5882; 617-232-1555 ext. 235, fax: 617-566-4034.

▼ MEADOWS SCHOOL OF THE ARTS

See Southern Methodist University

▼ MEMPHIS COLLEGE OF ART

Memphis, Tennessee

Independent, coed. Urban campus. Art program established 1936.

Degrees Bachelor of Fine Arts in the areas of fine arts, design arts. Majors and concentrations: applied art, ceramic art and design, commercial art, computer graphics, graphic arts, illustration, jewelry and metalsmithing, painting/drawing, papermaking, photography, printmaking, sculpture, studio art, textile arts. Graduate degrees offered: Master of Fine Arts in the areas of studio art, computer arts. Cross-registration with Rhodes College, Christian Brothers University. Program accredited by NASAD.

Enrollment Fall 1997: 263 total; 218 undergraduate, 35 graduate, 10 non-professional degree.

Art Student Profile 45% females, 55% males, 21% minorities, 10% international.

Art Faculty 52 total undergraduate and graduate (full-time and part-time). 70% of full-time faculty have terminal degrees. Graduate students teach a few undergraduate courses. Undergraduate student–faculty ratio: 10:1.

Student Life Student groups/activities include Student Government, Arteli (Arts in the Schools), Children's Community Art Classes. Special housing available for art students.

Expenses for 1998–99 Application fee: $25. Tuition: $11,450 full-time. Mandatory fees: $50 full-time. College room only: $3000. Room charges vary according to housing facility. Special program-related fees: $200 per semester for studio fee.

Financial Aid Program-specific awards for 1997: 200 Portfolio Scholarships for program majors ($2500), 200 Work Study Awards for program majors ($1000).

Application Procedures Students admitted directly into the professional program freshman year. Deadline for freshmen and transfers: continuous. Required: high school transcript, college transcript(s) for transfer students, portfolio, SAT I or ACT test scores. Recommended: letter of recommendation, interview. Portfolio reviews held weekly on campus; the submission of slides may be substituted for portfolios whenever needed.

Web Site http://www.mca.edu.

Contact Ms. Susan S. Miller, Director of Admissions, Memphis College of Art, 1930 Poplar Avenue, Overton Park, Memphis, Tennessee 38104; 800-727-1088 ext. 1230, fax: 901-272-5122, E-mail address: info@mca.edu.

More About the College

Program Facilities Computer labs feature Macintosh PowerPC workstations complete with LaserWriter printers, color inkjet printers, color scanners, high-resolution film recorders, and high-end multimedia peripherals. A writing lab offers additional Macintosh computers with Internet access, e-mail, and typing tutorials. The labs also feature large computer screen projection systems for teaching purposes. MCA's shop has 4,400 square feet, with machines for woodworking, metalworking, plastic molding, glass cutting, shrink wrapping, and stretcher and frame construction. The library has 14,000 volumes, 100 art journals and periodicals, 32,000 slides, an extensive reproduction collection, audiovisual equipment, a computer writing lab, and an image file. Students have studio spaces. Conference rooms allow for slide viewing, critiques, and lectures. Sculpture, small metals, and clay have studios with foundry/welding areas for casting and metal work. Clay has wheels, handbuilding and glazing space, and a semi-enclosed firing room. Fiber/surface design has three studios, a dye room, manual and computerized looms, washer/dryer, range tops, refrigerators, and sewing machines. Printmaking, papermaking, and book arts studios provide interaction between these media. Printmaking has facilities for lithography, etching, serigraphy, and other processes. Book arts include letter presses and bindery. Papermaking has beaters, 36-square-foot vacuum table, hydraulic press, and pulper. Airbrush equipment, computerized stat cameras, darkrooms, light tables, and lucigraphs are also available.

Special Programs The New York Studio Program offers students an exciting semester in New York City with artists and students from across the country. The Mobility Program can place a student at another art college for a semester of study. Internships offer experience in fine and design arts fields, such as museum work, art therapy, set design, and advertising. Consortiums with local colleges provide a greater variety of course selection.

▼

Since 1936, Memphis College of Art has been a special community of artists. The MCA experience is organized around small classes, independent work, and one-on-one attention and guidance not usually found at a larger institution. Currently students from twenty-six states and eleven other countries attend MCA, providing a diversity often associated with larger schools.

MCA is located in a 342-acre park in midtown Memphis adjacent to the Memphis Brooks Museum of Art and the Memphis Zoo. A nearby student residence provides living space for new and returning students. Two roommates share a furnished apartment with hardwood floors, a sun porch, a kitchen, and studio space. A large variety of affordable housing is also available off-campus to suit all lifestyles and budgets.

Memphis is a great place for an aspiring artist. Known for blues, barbecue, and Elvis, Memphis is also home to Fortune 500 companies, a symphony, an opera, a theater, other colleges and universities, museums, galleries, and almost 1 million residents. Annual festivals on Beale Street and the Mississippi River are popular with students.

MCA is a close-knit community where it's easy to make friends. There are plenty of organized activities to keep students busy, such as Friday night movies, exhibition receptions, and an annual Hike and Bike and Halloween Costume Ball. Not-so-organized activities include tunnel ball and volleyball.

Tobey Exhibition Hall hosts numerous shows that expose students to a wide range of contemporary art; the Lower Gallery is a large space dedicated to student art. Students also have the opportunity to learn from visiting artists who provide a constant flow of new creative and intellectual energy. MCA organizes study trips to cities around the world renowned for their culture. In early May, a weeklong workshop is held on Horn Island off the Mississippi coast.

The Student Life Office offers job placement assistance for graduating students and part-time job placement for current students. Informative sessions are held to prepare students for career choices and for the job search/interview process. The Job Fair brings regional and national companies to MCA each spring for interviews. Internships and the student-run design agency provide students with professional experience while in school.

Faculty members have been selected for their understanding of the relationship between art and teaching. MCA's Fine Arts faculty members are professional artists who exhibit frequently and regularly execute commissions. The Design Arts faculty members stay on top of the industry through continuing professional design projects. With their knowledge of the job market and galleries at the regional and national levels, faculty members are well qualified to guide students on their career paths. Liberal Studies faculty members are chosen for their impressive credentials and their understanding of the unique nature of MCA students.

MCA is concerned about students whose financial resources are limited. More than 80 percent of the College's students receive some type of financial assistance. Financial aid programs include scholarships, loans, grants, and work-study awards. More than $700,000 is awarded by MCA in scholarship and grants each year.

▼ METROPOLITAN STATE COLLEGE OF DENVER

Denver, Colorado

State-supported, coed. Urban campus. Total enrollment: 17,343. Art program established 1965.

Degrees Bachelor of Fine Arts in the areas of fine arts, design, crafts, art history. Majors and concentrations: art education, art history, art/fine arts, ceramics, communication design, computer graphics, jewelry and metalsmithing, painting/drawing, photography, printmaking, sculpture. Cross-registration with University of Colorado at Denver, Colorado community colleges.

Enrollment Fall 1997: 500 undergraduate.

Art Student Profile 60% females, 40% males, 3% minorities.

Art Faculty 42 total (full-time and part-time). 99% of full-time faculty have terminal degrees. Graduate students do not teach undergraduate courses. Undergraduate student–faculty ratio: 18:1.

Student Life Student groups/activities include Art Club, Clay Club, Printmaking Club.

Expenses for 1997–98 Application fee: $25. State resident tuition: $1656 full-time. Nonresident tuition: $6742 full-time. Mandatory fees: $320 full-time. Full-time tuition and fees vary according to course load. Special program-related fees: $5–$65 per course for expendable materials.

Application Procedures Students admitted directly into the professional program freshman year. Deadline for freshmen and transfers: continuous. Notification date for freshmen and transfers: continuous. Required: high school transcript, college transcript(s) for transfer students, SAT I or ACT test scores, minimum 2.5 high school GPA.

Web Site http://www.mscd.edu.

Undergraduate Contact Greg Watts, Assistant Chair, Department of Art, Metropolitan State College of Denver, Campus Box 59, PO Box 173362, Denver, Colorado 80217-3362; 303-556-3090, fax: 303-556-4094.

▼ MIAMI UNIVERSITY

Oxford, Ohio

State-related, coed. Small town campus. Total enrollment: 16,328.

Degrees Bachelor of Fine Arts in the areas of painting/drawing, jewelry and metalsmithing, printmaking, sculpture, ceramic art and design, graphic arts, photography; Bachelor of Science in the area of art education. Majors and concentrations: art education, art history, ceramic art and design, computer graphics, jewelry and metalsmithing, painting/drawing, photography, printmaking, sculpture. Graduate degrees offered: Master of Fine Arts in the areas of

Miami University *(continued)*

painting, ceramics, sculpture, jewelry and metalsmithing, printmaking; Master of Arts in the area of art education. Cross-registration with John E. Dolibois European Center (Luxembourg). Program accredited by NASAD.

Enrollment Fall 1997: 309 undergraduate, 16 graduate.

Art Student Profile 66% females, 34% males, 3% minorities.

Art Faculty 30 total undergraduate and graduate (full-time and part-time). 81% of full-time faculty have terminal degrees. Graduate students teach about a quarter undergraduate courses. Undergraduate student–faculty ratio: 15:1.

Student Life Student groups/activities include Art History Association, National Art Education Association Student Chapter, Visual Arts Club.

Expenses for 1997–98 Application fee: $35. State resident tuition: $4482 full-time. Nonresident tuition: $10,582 full-time. Mandatory fees: $1030 full-time. Full-time tuition and fees vary according to course load. College room and board: $4810. Room and board charges vary according to board plan. Special program-related fees: $60–$75 per course for studio courses.

Financial Aid Program-specific awards for 1997: 1 Miami University Scholarship for program majors ($4300), 1 American Greetings Award for program majors ($1000), 1 Arthur Damon Art Award for program majors ($1500), 1 School of Fine Arts Award for program majors ($2000), 1 Marston D. Hodgin Award for program majors ($1000), 1 George R. and Galen Glasgow Hoxie Award ($890), 2 Fred and Molly Pye Awards for sophomores and juniors ($475), 1 Barbara Hershey Photo Award for female junior photo majors ($1000), 1 National Woodcarvers Award for upperclass sculpture majors ($1000), 1 Robert Wolfe Printmakers Award for junior and senior printmaking majors ($400).

Application Procedures Students admitted directly into the professional program freshman year. Deadline for freshmen: January 30; transfers: March 1. Notification date for freshmen: March 15. Required: high school transcript, college transcript(s) for transfer students, portfolio, SAT I or ACT test scores. Portfolio reviews held twice on campus; the submission of slides may be substituted for portfolios with approval from the department.

Web Site http://www.muohio.edu/~artcwis/index.htm.

Undergraduate Contact Mr. Lon Beck, Professor, Department of Art, Miami University, Art Building, Oxford, Ohio 45056; 513-529-2900, fax: 513-529-1532, E-mail address: pipernw@miamiu.muohio.edu.

Graduate Contact Mr. Ed Montgomery, Associate Professor of Art, Department of Art, Miami University, Art Building, Oxford, Ohio 45056; 513-529-2900, fax: 513-529-1532, E-mail address: pipernw@miamiu.muohio.edu.

▼ MICHIGAN STATE UNIVERSITY

East Lansing, Michigan

State-supported, coed. Suburban campus. Total enrollment: 42,603. Art program established 1931.

Degrees Bachelor of Fine Arts in the areas of studio art, art education. Majors and concentrations: art education, ceramics, computer graphics, graphic design, painting/drawing, photography, printmaking, sculpture. Graduate degrees offered: Master of Fine Arts in the area of studio art.

Enrollment Fall 1997: 355 total; 121 undergraduate, 11 graduate, 223 non-professional degree.

Art Student Profile 66% females, 34% males, 11% minorities, 4% international.

Art Faculty 28 total undergraduate and graduate (full-time and part-time). 100% of full-time faculty have terminal degrees. Graduate students teach a few undergraduate courses.

Student Life Student groups/activities include Saturday Art Program, Undergraduate Exhibit at Kresge Art Museum, Gallery 114 (student exhibition space).

Expenses for 1997–98 Application fee: $30. State resident tuition: $4223 full-time. Nonresident tuition: $11,288 full-time. Mandatory fees: $566 full-time. Full-time tuition and fees vary according to program and student level. College room and board: $4052. College room only: $1742. Room and board charges vary according to board plan and housing facility.

Financial Aid Program-specific awards for 1997: 1–4 Creative Arts Scholarships for Michigan resident studio art majors ($500–$2000).

Application Procedures Students admitted directly into the professional program freshman year. Deadline for freshmen and transfers: continuous. Required: high school transcript, college transcript(s) for transfer students, minimum 2.0 high school GPA, SAT I or ACT test scores. Recommended: minimum 3.0 high school GPA.

Web Site http://www.msu.edu/~art.

Undergraduate Contact Michelle P. Barker, Administrative Assistant, Studio Art Undergraduate Program, Michigan State University, 113 Kresge Art Center, East Lansing, Michigan 48824-1119; 517-355-7610, fax: 517-432-3938, E-mail address: mbarker@pilot.msu.edu.

Graduate Contact Dr. Phyllis Floyd, Associate Chair, Studio Art Graduate Program, Michigan State University, 113 Kresge Art Center, East Lansing, Michigan 48824-1119; 517-355-7610, fax: 517-432-3938, E-mail address: floyd@pilot.msu.edu.

▼ MIDDLE TENNESSEE STATE UNIVERSITY

Murfreesboro, Tennessee

State-supported, coed. Urban campus. Total enrollment: 18,366.

Degrees Bachelor of Fine Arts in the areas of studio art, graphic design. Majors and concentrations: ceramic art and design, graphic design, jewelry and metalsmithing, painting/drawing, printmaking, sculpture.

Enrollment Fall 1997: 320 total; all undergraduate.

Art Faculty 27 total (full-time and part-time). 100% of full-time faculty have terminal degrees. Graduate students do not teach undergraduate courses.

Expenses for 1997–98 Application fee: $15, $30 for international students. State resident tuition: $1816 full-time. Nonresident tuition: $6412 full-time. Mandatory fees: $380 full-time. College room and board: $3343. College room only: $1692. Room and board charges vary according to board plan.

Application Procedures Students admitted directly into the professional program freshman year. Deadline for freshmen and transfers: continuous. Required: high school transcript, minimum 2.0 high school GPA, SAT I or ACT test scores.

Web Site http://www.mtsu.edu/~art.

Undergraduate Contact Mr. Carlyle Johnson, Chair, Art Department, Middle Tennessee State University, PO Box 25, Murfreesboro, Tennessee 37132; 615-898-2455, fax: 615-898-2254.

▼ MIDGE KARR FINE ART DEPARTMENT

See New York Institute of Technology

▼ MIDWESTERN STATE UNIVERSITY

Wichita Falls, Texas

State-supported, coed. Urban campus. Total enrollment: 5,770.

Degrees Bachelor of Fine Arts in the area of art. Majors and concentrations: jewelry and metalsmithing, painting/drawing, printmaking, sculpture.

Enrollment Fall 1997: 72 total; all undergraduate.

Art Student Profile 53% females, 47% males, 12% minorities, 4% international.

Art Faculty 5 total (full-time and part-time). 100% of full-time faculty have terminal degrees. Graduate students do not teach undergraduate courses.

Student Life Student groups/activities include off-campus exhibitions.

Expenses for 1997–98 State resident tuition: $1054 full-time. Nonresident tuition: $7688 full-time. Mandatory fees: $1037 full-time. Full-time tuition and fees vary according to course load. College room and board: $3633. Room and board charges vary according to board plan and housing facility. Special program-related fees: $9 per credit hour for course fees.

Financial Aid Program-specific awards for 1997: 15 Endowed Scholarships for academically qualified/talented applicants ($1500).

Application Procedures Students admitted directly into the professional program freshman year. Deadline for freshmen and transfers: August 7. Required: high school transcript, college transcript(s) for transfer students, SAT I or ACT test scores. Recommended: minimum 2.0 high school GPA, portfolio. Portfolio reviews held continuously on campus; the submission of slides may be substituted for portfolios if of good quality.

Undergraduate Contact Mr. Richard Ash, Coordinator of Art Program, Division of Fine Arts, Midwestern State University, 3410 Taft Boulevard, Wichita Falls, Texas 76308; 940-397-4386.

▼ MILLIKIN UNIVERSITY

Decatur, Illinois

Independent, coed. Suburban campus. Total enrollment: 1,997.

Degrees Bachelor of Fine Arts in the areas of art education, studio art, graphic design/commercial art, art therapy, art management. Majors and concentrations: applied art, art education, art therapy, art/fine arts, arts administration, ceramic art and design, commercial art, computer graphics, graphic arts, painting/drawing, photography, printmaking, sculpture, studio art.

Enrollment Fall 1997: 100 undergraduate.

Art Student Profile 50% females, 50% males, 4% minorities.

Art Faculty 8 total (full-time and part-time). 100% of full-time faculty have terminal degrees. Graduate students do not teach undergraduate courses. Undergraduate student–faculty ratio: 16:1.

Student Life Student groups/activities include Computer Imaging Alliance.

Expenses for 1997–98 Comprehensive fee: $19,208 includes full-time tuition ($13,988), mandatory fees ($150), and college room and board ($5070). College room only: $2638. Full-time tuition and fees vary according to course load. Room and board charges vary according to board plan and housing facility. Special program-related fees: $10–$50 per semester for lab fees.

Financial Aid Program-specific awards for 1997: 20–30 Talent Awards for incoming students ($500–$3000).

Application Procedures Students apply for admission into the professional program by sophomore year. Deadline for freshmen and transfers: continuous. Required: high school transcript, college transcript(s) for transfer students, letter of recommendation, interview, SAT I or ACT test scores. Recommended: portfolio. Portfolio reviews held by appointment on campus and off campus in St. Louis, MO; Indianapolis, IN; the submission of slides may be substituted for portfolios for large works of art.

Undergraduate Contact Mr. James Schietinger, Chairman, Art Department, Millikin University, 1184 West Main Street, Decatur, Illinois 62522; 217-424-6227, fax: 217-424-3993, E-mail address: jschietinger@mail.millikin.edu.

▼ MILWAUKEE INSTITUTE OF ART & DESIGN

Milwaukee, Wisconsin

Independent, coed. Urban campus. Total enrollment: 503. Art program established 1974.

Degrees Bachelor of Fine Arts in the areas of illustration, painting, photography, printmaking, sculpture, industrial design, drawing, interior architecture and design, communication design. Cross-registration with Marquette University. Program accredited by NASAD.

Enrollment Fall 1997: 503 total; all undergraduate.

Art Student Profile 42% females, 58% males, 14% minorities, 1% international.

Art Faculty 77 total (full-time and part-time). 82% of full-time faculty have terminal degrees. Graduate students do not teach undergraduate courses.

Student Life Student groups/activities include student exhibitions, Student Government, student publication. Special housing available for art students.

Expenses for 1997–98 Application fee: $25. Comprehensive fee: $21,136 includes full-time tuition ($14,500), mandatory fees ($300), and college room and board ($6336). Full-time tuition and fees vary according to student level. Room and board charges vary according to board plan. Special program-related fees: $5–$95 per course for supplies.

Financial Aid Program-specific awards for 1997: 22–35 MIAD Scholarships for continuing students ($2000–$2200), 10–20 MIAD Admissions Scholarships for incoming students ($2500–$14,500).

Application Procedures Students admitted directly into the professional program freshman year. Deadline for freshmen and transfers: continuous. Required: essay, high school transcript, college transcript(s) for transfer students, minimum 2.0 high school GPA, interview, portfolio. Recommended: 2 letters of recommendation, SAT I or ACT test scores, minimum 3.0 GPA in high school art classes. Portfolio

Milwaukee Institute of Art & Design (continued)

reviews held continuously on campus and off campus; the submission of slides may be substituted for portfolios when distance is prohibitive.

Undergraduate Contact Ms. Mary Schopp, Executive Director of Enrollment Services, Milwaukee Institute of Art & Design, 273 East Erie Street, Milwaukee, Wisconsin 53202; 414-291-8070, fax: 414-291-8077.

More About the Institute

Program Facilities MIAD studios and classrooms are in a state-of-the-art, multi-windowed renovated 5-story warehouse half as long as a football field. It has the light necessary to artists and wide-open spaces for creating outsize paintings, sculptures, and full-size industrial prototypes. The ventilation system provides a safe environment; the studio space per student is the largest in the country.

Three computer labs, including CAD, CAID, and Alias Studio, offer the most current programs for graphic, industrial, and interior/architectural design, as well as fine art imaging. A fully equipped sculpture department and extensive photography and printmaking facilities offer fine artists wide choices and venues for expressing themselves.

Special Programs Extended academic opportunities are available to students through an affiliation with nearby Marquette University. MIAD students can choose from a wide variety of arts and sciences courses, plus use that school's excellent Recreation Center and access its full range of health services.

A mobility program allows MIAD students to study at 28 affiliated U.S. art and design schools, including an internship/study program through Parsons School of Design in New York City. MIAD offers a unique blend of international study experiences. These include trips to major European cities as part of course offerings in liberal studies. Recent courses have included journeys to Paris, Florence, and Sienna. Each summer, MIAD sponsors a 4-week exchange with the Burren College of Art in Ireland. MIAD maintains exchange opportunities for students to study with other notable art and design colleges in France, Germany, Korea, and Poland.

▼

The Milwaukee Institute of Art & Design (MIAD) is Wisconsin's only 4-year independent professional art and design college. Founded in 1974 as a successor to the Layton School of Art, MIAD offers a BFA in 5 Fine Art areas—drawing, painting, sculpture, photography, and printmaking; and 4 design areas—communication design, illustration, industrial design, and interior architecture and design. Minors can be earned in all 9 disciplines as well as in art history and writing.

All MIAD faculty members are practicing professionals recognized in their field of instruction. They share their knowledge and experience with talented, motivated students who have decided to make a career of art and/or design. Thus, the college is a community of artists with like interests, drives, and goals. Attention to individual students and their work is ensured through a small student-faculty ratio.

Curricula reflect the latest in professional needs, techniques, trends, and innovations. The ongoing emphasis is on problem solving. MIAD is a place where students learn to achieve their goals, not merely replicate the theories and processes of others.

MIAD students have a wide range of exhibition and internship opportunities each year. These include an ongoing series of shows in the MIAD Student Gallery, the annual All Student Show, the annual Senior Thesis Exhibition, the Scholarship Exhibition, and internships with many of the area's most prestigious design, architectural, and photographic studios and several of the city's professional performing art troupes. Also, MIAD students are regularly invited by local galleries to submit work for local and regional exhibitions.

While at MIAD, students succeed nationally and internationally. Industrial design students win national awards and even see their designs manufactured; communication design students have their work published internationally; and in 1996, a Foundation (first-year) student's home page received *The Net's* highest possible rating for "content, aesthetic merit, and techno smartness," which is comparable to a freshman film student receiving an Academy Award for a short film. A sculpture senior was one of 65 from nearly 1,000 international applicants to be selected for the prestigious Skowhegan Residency Program; three months after graduation, another was hired by Steven Spielberg.

Alumni own or are affiliated with local and national advertising agencies, design studios, and publishers, and design for industry throughout the world. Their fine art is in private and corporate collections; they operate their own galleries and, thanks to their education, pursue myriad other satisfying and rewarding careers.

The college is located in Milwaukee's Historic Third Ward near Lake Michigan. This clean, bright, safe neighborhood of turn-of-the-century buildings is home to artists' lofts, galleries, specialty shops, restaurants, and a live theater complex. Student housing and a Student Center are in historic buildings that offer comfort, security, and convenience in unique, artistic settings.

▼ MINNEAPOLIS COLLEGE OF ART AND DESIGN

Minneapolis, Minnesota

Independent, coed. Urban campus. Art program established 1886.

Degrees Bachelor of Fine Arts in the areas of design, fine arts, media arts. Majors and concentrations: advertising design, animation, cartooning, drawing, film, furniture design, graphic design, illustration, interactive mutli-media, painting, photography, printmaking, sculpture, studio art, video art. Graduate degrees offered: Master of Fine Arts in the area of visual studies. Cross-registration with Macalester College. Program accredited by NASAD.

Enrollment Fall 1997: 603 total; 539 undergraduate, 38 graduate, 26 non-professional degree.

Art Student Profile 44% females, 56% males, 15% minorities, 5% international.

Art Faculty 85 total undergraduate and graduate (full-time and part-time). 65% of full-time faculty have terminal degrees. Graduate students teach a few undergraduate courses. Undergraduate student–faculty ratio: 12:1.

Student Life Student groups/activities include Friday Film Series, Open Mic (poetry readings), International Association of Graphic Artists Student Chapter. Special housing available for art students.

Expenses for 1997–98 Application fee: $35. Tuition: $15,730 full-time. Mandatory fees: $80 full-time. College room only:

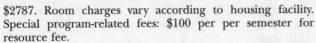

$2787. Room charges vary according to housing facility. Special program-related fees: $100 per per semester for resource fee.

Financial Aid Program-specific awards for 1997: 1 Abby Weed Grey Award for incoming students ($9000), 1 Minneapolis College of Art and Design Portfolio Award for incoming students ($9000), 1–20 Minneapolis College of Art and Design Admissions Awards for incoming students ($4000).

Application Procedures Students admitted directly into the professional program freshman year. Deadline for freshmen and transfers: continuous. Required: essay, high school transcript, college transcript(s) for transfer students, letter of recommendation, portfolio, SAT I or ACT test scores. Recommended: minimum 2.0 high school GPA, interview. Portfolio reviews held as needed on campus and off campus; the submission of slides may be substituted for portfolios for large works of art or when distance is prohibitive.

Web Site http://www.mcad.edu/.

Undergraduate Contact Ms. Rebecca Haas, Director of Admissions, Minneapolis College of Art and Design, 2501 Stevens Avenue South, Minneapolis, Minnesota 55404; 612-874-3760, fax: 612-874-3704, E-mail address: admissions@mn.mcad.edu.

Graduate Contact Rik Sferra, Graduate Program Coordinator, Admissions Department, Minneapolis College of Art and Design, 2501 Stevens Avenue South, Minneapolis, Minnesota 55404; 612-874-3760, fax: 612-874-3704, E-mail address: rik_sferra@mcad.edu.

More About the College

Program Facilities Computer Center: seven labs and a campus network (more than 120 seats), graphics design, digital media, 3-D animation, and Internet and e-mail access. Media Center: black-and-white and color photography facilities (more than fifty enlargers), two production lighting studios, super-8mm and 16mm synchronous sound films, film/video animation, video production—Hi8 or ¾-inch formats, tapeless digital suite, B-track tape suite, and computer facilities for image capturing and manipulation. 3-D Shop: fabrication facility; metals, plastic, and wood facilities: metals area—gas and arc welding; foundry for metals casting; and a gas-fired forge for blacksmithing projects. Library: 56,000 books and bound periodicals, 201 current magazine subscriptions, picture files, 133,000 slides, videos, films, laser disks, compact discs, and audiocassettes. Also featured are painting studios; a printmaking shop for intaglio, lithography, relief, serigraphy, and book arts; a papermaking studio; individual student work spaces; on-campus housing; and an on-campus bookstore.

Student Exhibition Opportunities Seven dedicated exhibition spaces; policy that permits the use of the walls, halls, and grounds of both classroom buildings for exhibiting art work and design projects; Calhoun Square Gallery; an off-campus student exhibition program; and auditoriums equipped to present media work in film and video.

Special Programs Florence Honors Program: MCAD is the only college in the United States to have an exchange with three colleges in Florence, Italy. Designs Work Center offers an on-campus design internship. The Learning Center gives advice and feedback on writing, research, and study skills.

▼

Minneapolis College of Art and Design is a private college that focuses exclusively on the education of undergraduate and graduate students in visual art and design. Founded in 1886 in a modest studio above a library, MCAD's campus shares a city block with the Minneapolis Institute of Arts and the Children's Theater Company and is located in a vibrant city that is known for its support of the arts.

MCAD offers the Bachelor of Science in visualization, the Bachelor of Fine Arts, and the Master of Fine Arts degrees. The curriculum is based on the belief that to become a professional artist or designer, one must study theory and skill as well as form and content.

MCAD's Bachelor of Fine Arts program offers majors in painting, drawing, printmaking, sculpture, advertising design, graphic design, furniture design, illustration, photography, animation, cartooning/comic illustration, interactive multimedia, film/video, and fine arts. All majors include elective courses. The electives may be taken in the student's major area of study, which provides an opportunity for in-depth, concentrated study, or used to explore the rich diversity of courses in any of the majors.

No matter what the major, the flexibility of the program provides endless potential for exciting and stimulating advanced study. At MCAD, students may also devise independent study projects, take courses through the Mobility program at other select colleges such as Macalester College in St. Paul, and earn tuition-free credits in MCAD's Continuing Studies program.

Students can study off campus through the College's special programs in New York City, Italy, Germany, France, Ireland, England, Mexico, Denmark, and Japan. And, with special approval, students can spend a semester off campus working with a specific artist or designer at another college or on the road. In the past, students have spent a semester in the Far East, London, Paris, Africa, or Russia.

MCAD prepares students for the future. The Career Development office provides assistance with resume writing and interview skills. Internships as well as job placement are available. Visiting artists, designers, and alumni are brought on campus to meet with students to share their experience and expertise.

MCAD has many advantages—a curriculum that encourages exploration, spacious studios, and state-of-the art equipment. At MCAD's core are an experienced and talented faculty, motivated and curious students, classes in which students receive much personal attention, and a rigorous liberal arts program that prepares students for their future as visual artists. The College's programs teach students how to think conceptually, to analyze and theorize, to solve problems, and to make art.

▼ MISSISSIPPI STATE UNIVERSITY

Mississippi State, Mississippi

State-supported, coed. Small town campus. Total enrollment: 15,628. Art program established 1968.

Degrees Bachelor of Fine Arts in the areas of fine arts, graphic design. Majors and concentrations: animation, ceramic art and design, graphic design, multimedia, painting/drawing, photography, printmaking, sculpture. Graduate degrees offered: Master of Fine Arts in the area of electronic visualization. Program accredited by NASAD.

Enrollment Fall 1997: 1,110 total; 272 undergraduate, 16 graduate, 822 non-professional degree.

Art Student Profile 41% females, 59% males, 8% minorities, 1% international.

Art Faculty 21 total undergraduate and graduate (full-time and part-time). 94% of full-time faculty have terminal

Mississippi State University (continued)

degrees. Graduate students teach a few undergraduate courses. Undergraduate student–faculty ratio: 12:1.

Expenses for 1997–98 Application fee: $25. State resident tuition: $1996 full-time. Nonresident tuition: $4816 full-time. Mandatory fees: $735 full-time. College room and board: $4100. College room only: $1600. Room and board charges vary according to board plan. Special program-related fees: $40–$60 per semester for lab fee.

Financial Aid Program-specific awards for 1997: 4 Gulmon Scholarships for freshmen ($1000), 1 Clifford Award for program students ($500), 1 Ferretti/Karnstedt Award for sophomores ($1000), 1 DuBoise Scholarship in Photography for juniors and seniors ($750).

Application Procedures Students admitted directly into the professional program freshman year. Deadline for freshmen and transfers: July 26. Notification date for freshmen and transfers: continuous. Required: high school transcript, college transcript(s) for transfer students, minimum 2.0 high school GPA, SAT I or ACT test scores, portfolio for transfers. Portfolio reviews held twice on campus; the submission of slides may be substituted for portfolios if of good quality.

Web Site http://www.msstate.edu.

Undergraduate Contact Mr. Brent Funderburk, Head, Art Department, Mississippi State University, PO Box 5182, Mississippi State, Mississippi 39762; 601-325-2970, fax: 601-325-3850, E-mail address: da@ra.msstate.edu.

Graduate Contact Mr. Anna Maria Chupa, Graduate Coordinator, Art Department, Mississippi State University, PO Box 5182, Mississippi State, Mississippi 39762; 601-325-2970, fax: 601-325-3850, E-mail address: da@ra.msstate.edu.

▼ MISSISSIPPI UNIVERSITY FOR WOMEN

Columbus, Mississippi

State-supported, primarily women. Small town campus. Total enrollment: 3,309.

Degrees Bachelor of Fine Arts in the area of fine arts. Majors and concentrations: art education, art/fine arts, ceramic art and design, graphic arts, interior design, painting/drawing, printmaking. Program accredited by NASAD.

Enrollment Fall 1997: 76 total; 75 undergraduate, 1 non-professional degree.

Art Student Profile 80% females, 20% males, 20% minorities, 1% international.

Art Faculty 9 total (full-time and part-time). 100% of full-time faculty have terminal degrees. Graduate students do not teach undergraduate courses. Undergraduate student–faculty ratio: 12:1.

Student Life Student groups/activities include Art Student League, American Society of Interior Designers, Kappa Pi.

Expenses for 1997–98 Application fee: $25 for nonresidents. State resident tuition: $2244 full-time. Nonresident tuition: $4746 full-time. Mandatory fees: $40 full-time. College room and board: $2557. College room only: $1260. Room and board charges vary according to board plan.

Financial Aid Program-specific awards for 1997: 5–7 specified scholarships for program majors ($250–$500), 10–12 division scholarships for program majors ($250–$500).

Application Procedures Students admitted directly into the professional program freshman year. Deadline for freshmen and transfers: continuous. Required: high school transcript, college transcript(s) for transfer students, minimum 2.0 high

school GPA, portfolio, ACT test score only. Recommended: interview. Portfolio reviews held once and by appointment on campus.

Undergraduate Contact Dr. Sue S. Coates, Head, Division of Fine and Performing Arts, Mississippi University for Women, Box W-70, Columbus, Mississippi 39701; 601-329-7341, fax: 601-329-7348.

▼ MONTCLAIR STATE UNIVERSITY

Upper Montclair, New Jersey

State-supported, coed. Suburban campus. Total enrollment: 12,808.

Degrees Bachelor of Fine Arts in the areas of studio art, painting, drawing, sculpture, ceramics, fibers, graphic design, illustration, printmaking, photography, papermaking, film/video. Program accredited by NASAD.

Enrollment Fall 1997: 368 total; 18 undergraduate, 350 non-professional degree.

Art Student Profile 60% females, 40% males, 20% minorities, 3% international.

Art Faculty 46 total (full-time and part-time). 89% of full-time faculty have terminal degrees. Graduate students do not teach undergraduate courses. Undergraduate student–faculty ratio: 15:1.

Student Life Student groups/activities include Student Gallery Committee, art publications.

Expenses for 1997–98 Application fee: $40. State resident tuition: $2912 full-time. Nonresident tuition: $4432 full-time. Mandatory fees: $782 full-time. College room and board: $5546. College room only: $3860. Special program-related fees: $35–$50 per course for studio lab fee.

Financial Aid Program-specific awards for 1997: 1 Anne Chapman Memorial Award for artistically talented ($200), 1 Ellen Mohammed Scholarship for minority student art majors ($5000), 1 Art Directors Club Scholarship for sophomore, junior, and senior graphic design and illustration majors ($1000), 3 Montclair Craft Guild Awards for competition winners ($200).

Application Procedures Deadline for freshmen: March 1; transfers: May 1. Notification date for freshmen and transfers: continuous. Required: high school transcript, interview, portfolio, SAT I or ACT test scores. Portfolio reviews held 5 times on campus and off campus in New York, NY; Philadelphia, PA; the submission of slides may be substituted for portfolios when distance is prohibitive.

Undergraduate Contact Mr. John Czerkowicz, Chairman, Fine Arts Department, Montclair State University, 1 Normal Avenue, Upper Montclair, New Jersey 07043; 973-655-7295, fax: 973-655-7833.

▼ MONTSERRAT COLLEGE OF ART

Beverly, Massachusetts

Independent, coed. Suburban campus. Total enrollment: 333. Art program established 1970.

Degrees Bachelor of Fine Arts in the areas of painting, drawing, printmaking, photography, graphic design, illustration, sculpture, art teacher certification, fine arts. Majors and concentrations: art education, art/fine arts, graphic design, illustration, painting/drawing, photography, printmaking, sculpture. Cross-registration with Northeast Consortium of

Colleges and Universities in Massachusetts, Association of Independent Colleges of Art and Design. Program accredited by NASAD.

Enrollment Fall 1997: 333 total; all undergraduate.

Art Student Profile 50% females, 50% males, 4% minorities, 8% international.

Art Faculty 60 total (full-time and part-time). 74% of full-time faculty have terminal degrees. Graduate students do not teach undergraduate courses. Undergraduate student–faculty ratio: 9:1.

Student Life Student groups/activities include Student Government, Meals-on-the-Cheap Committee, Coffee House Organization. Special housing available for art students.

Expenses for 1997–98 Application fee: $40. Tuition: $11,305 full-time. Mandatory fees: $375 full-time. College room only: $3300. Special program-related fees: $350 per year for model fees, material fees, equipment fees, $25 per year for student activity fee.

Financial Aid Program-specific awards for 1997: 99 Montserrat Grants for those demonstrating need ($1745), merit awards for program majors, 12 Dean's Merit Awards for program majors demonstrating need ($1200–$3000), 1 Presidential Award for program majors demonstrating need ($11,982).

Application Procedures Students admitted directly into the professional program freshman year. Deadline for freshmen and transfers: July 1. Notification date for freshmen and transfers: August 15. Required: essay, high school transcript, college transcript(s) for transfer students, minimum 2.0 high school GPA, 2 letters of recommendation, portfolio, SAT I or ACT test scores, minimum TOEFL score of 530 for international students. Recommended: minimum 3.0 high school GPA, interview. Portfolio reviews held continuously on campus and off campus; the submission of slides may be substituted for portfolios if a campus visit is impossible.

Web Site http://www.montserrat.edu.

Undergraduate Contact Ms. Lena Hill, Admissions Administrative Assistant, Montserrat College of Art, 23 Essex Street, Box 26, Beverly, Massachusetts 01915; 800-836-0487, fax: 978-921-4241, E-mail address: admiss@montserrat.edu.

More About the School

Additional Educational Opportunities A variety of programs provide cocurricular opportunities for Montserrat students to study abroad, or at other colleges, or to take advantage of special internship experiences tailored to individual needs. Montserrat has a number of programs that bring visiting artists and other professionals to the college to present their work and ideas to the Montserrat community. A weekly lecture series provides a diverse schedule of slide lectures, performance pieces, panel discussions, and other events. In addition, the Montserrat gallery offers gallery talks and other opportunities for discussion with artists, curators, and scholars. Academic credit may be awarded for internships completed outside the college in an approved setting. Students intern in galleries, design firms, and other art-related areas. Montserrat is a member of the Northeast Consortium of Colleges and Universities in Massachusetts (NECCUM), which allows students attending any member college to take two classes per semester and to use the library facilities at any other NECCUM institution at no additional charge. In addition, Montserrat is a member of the Association of Independent Colleges of Art and Design (AICAD). An association of internationally recognized colleges of art and design, AICAD provides numerous benefits to students, which include a student mobility program and access to international study opportunities. Montserrat also has a sister school, the Niigata

Montserrat College of Art

College of Art and Design in Niigata City, Japan, and offers a summer program in Italy. The Italian summer program focuses on painting, drawing, and photography and allows for an intensive five-week studio experience in another culture.

▼

Montserrat College of Art is a vital learning community of both student and faculty artists and scholars. Because members of this community share intense involvement in the arts and commitment to education, the atmosphere is one in which students find both support for the rigorous exploration of art and opportunity for additional study in the liberal arts. The major areas of study at Montserrat are painting and drawing, illustration, graphic design, printmaking, photography, sculpture, and teacher certification. Student interaction within the studio and the classroom is central to this experience, but the whole of student life outside of formal classes is also shaped by this passion for art.

Montserrat is located in Beverly, Massachusetts, a pleasant residential city convenient to Boston. The city has a harbor and several parks and beaches on the ocean. A number of other picturesque fishing harbors are nearby in Gloucester, Marblehead, and Rockport. The historic town of Salem, with its noted Peabody Essex Museum, is immediately adjacent to Beverly. In just 30 minutes by train or car, one can be in the

Montserrat College of Art (continued)

center of Boston, with its many galleries, museums, and libraries, and with the shopping, sports, and entertainment facilities of a great city. Students find it easy to live and work in Beverly, while enjoying convenient access to a major metropolitan area.

Montserrat provides an intensive visual arts education that enables students to sustain a lifelong involvement in art and design. After graduation, Montserrat students have the opportunity to enter a professional world that offers many possible roles. Depending upon the abilities and interests of the individual, one may work with an agency or as a freelance artist, designer, or illustrator; sell art work through a gallery; work as a designer within a business, government agency, or institution; work in a museum or gallery; operate any of a number of art-related businesses; teach visual arts; or pursue art as a personal interest for its own sake rather than as a specific career. Whatever the individual's goals or specific interest, students remark about how much they learn from Montserrat's faculty of professional artists and designers and how the advantage of being in a close-knit community has helped them define their unique role within the visual arts.

▼ MOORE COLLEGE OF ART AND DESIGN

Philadelphia, Pennsylvania

Independent, women only. Urban campus. Art program established 1848.

Degrees Bachelor of Fine Arts in the areas of general fine art with art education certification, studio art with art history emphasis. Majors and concentrations: art education, art history, fashion design, graphic design, illustration, interior design, textile arts, three-dimensional studies, two-dimensional studies. Cross-registration with Drexel University. Program accredited by NASAD, FIDER.

Enrollment Fall 1997: 408 total; all undergraduate.

Art Student Profile 100% females, 12% minorities, 3% international.

Art Faculty 90 total (full-time and part-time). 70% of full-time faculty have terminal degrees. Graduate students do not teach undergraduate courses. Undergraduate student–faculty ratio: 5:1.

Student Life Special housing available for art students.

Expenses for 1998–99 Application fee: $35. Comprehensive fee: $21,500 includes full-time tuition ($15,000), mandatory fees ($500), and college room and board ($6000).

Financial Aid Program-specific awards for 1997: 1 Evelyn A. Whittaker Award for those demonstrating need and talent ($15,000), 100 Moore College of Art and Design Presidential and Merit Awards for academically and artistically talented students ($500–$4000), 10 W. W. Smith Awards for those demonstrating talent and academic achievement ($2000), 1 Moore College of Art and Design Partnership Award for Philadelphia public school applicants demonstrating need ($15,000), 8 Sarah Peters Awards for talented freshmen ($500), 2–4 Appleman Awards for adult students demonstrating need/talent ($10,000–$12,500), 8 Fred and Naomi Hazell Awards for oil painters demonstrating need/talent ($16,000), 1 Charming Shops Scholarship for fashion/textile design juniors and seniors ($2000), 1 Kristen McCabe Memorial Award for talented junior or senior graphic design majors ($500).

Application Procedures Students apply for admission into the professional program by sophomore year. Deadline for freshmen and transfers: continuous. Required: high school transcript, college transcript(s) for transfer students, minimum 2.0 high school GPA, portfolio, SAT I or ACT test scores. Recommended: essay, letter of recommendation, interview. Portfolio reviews held continuously on campus and off campus; the submission of slides may be substituted for portfolios when distance is prohibitive.

Web Site http://www.moore.edu.

Undergraduate Contact Ms. Deborah Deery, Director of Admissions, Moore College of Art and Design, 20th and The Parkway, Philadelphia, Pennsylvania 19103-1179; 215-568-4515 ext. 1107, fax: 215-568-3547, E-mail address: admiss@digex.net.

More About the College

Program Facilities Moore's library consists of 34,000 books, catalogs, artist's books, and folios. The library subscribes to 227 periodicals and 20 newspapers and has 104,000 slides in its collection. Special resources are on women in the arts and history of design. Computer classrooms and labs are available for all students. Macintosh IIci and IIsi systems, Cubi-Comp 3-D modeling workstation, Quark XPress, Photoshop, Adobe Illustrator, Aldus PageMaker, Macromind Director, and Microsoft Word are featured. The Interior Design Department uses an AutoCADD laboratory, complete with color monitors, laser printers, and digitizing tablets. Textile design students use a computerized Macomber loom. The Goldie Paley Gallery features international exhibitions. The Levy Gallery for the Arts in Philadelphia promotes Philadelphia artists and student shows. All junior and senior fine art majors have personal studio space. There is a fully equipped wood shop and a metal-cutting and welding shop. Ceramics facilities include electric and raku kilns.

Special Programs All professional majors require internships and co-ops. An Open Majors program with emphasis in art history is available. Study-abroad programs are done collaboratively with other colleges. An exchange semester is held with Akademie Voor Beeldende Kunst in the Netherlands. Moore is a member of the Association of Independent Colleges of Art and Design Student Mobility Program. Education Support Services include advising, tutoring and advising students with special needs, and support for non-native English-speaking students.

▼

The women's college experience is even more special at Moore College of Art and Design. The only visual arts college for women in the country and one of two in the world, Moore offers women artists of all ages the experience of a comfortable, yet challenging, environment in which to develop their artistic talent and leadership skills.

At Moore students will find the combined experience of an art college, with its concentrated study in the arts and humanities, and a women's college, which gives women a voice and allows them to develop self-confidence and leadership skills. The classes are small (student-faculty ratio of 10:1) to provide individualized attention. This is very important in a visual arts college, with its emphasis on critiques and project-driven classes. In addition, students have access to a wide variety of resources. Moore's Library consists of 34,000 books, catalogs, artists books, and folios. The Learning Resources Center offers a sophisticated collection of computer graphics hardware and software. The Interior Design Department features a CAD (computer-aided design) laboratory, complete with ALR computers, color monitors, laser printers, and other equipment.

Moore's dedicated and talented faculty of professional artists, designers, and scholars are leaders in their fields who actively exhibit and/or work in the private sector. Fifty-five percent of Moore's faculty members are women and 80 percent of tenured faculty are women, thereby providing role models for women artists. Moore's president, Barbara Gillette Price, is a painter and a seasoned arts administrator who understands the concerns and challenges of women artists.

Minority students and other groups have student groups that plan social and cultural events and work to create awareness in the Moore community of each group's culture. Some of these groups are the Black Student Union (BSU), Asian Student Union, Hispanic/Latina Student group, Lesbian/Bisexual Student Union, and Re-entry Transfer Student Group. BSU has featured speakers such as poet and writer Sonia Sanchez and writer Lorene Cary.

The College's ideal location is close to all cultural institutions in Philadelphia: Philadelphia Museum of Art, Franklin Institute, Academy of Natural Sciences, Pennsylvania Academy of Fine Arts, Academy of Music, Merriam Theater, Independence Mall, and many others. Philadelphia's is a community of artists with many cultural, arts, and performing arts organizations, all working toward completing a visual artist's education. Some of these institutions include the Pennsylvania Ballet, the International House, Philadanco, and the Philadelphia Drama Guild.

Moore alumnae are accomplished artists and designers. Some of them include Adrienne Vittadini, Inc.; Alice Neel, internationally acclaimed painter; Hollis Sigler, renowned painter; Karen Daroff, interior designer and president of Daroff Design; textile designer and graphics designer Anna Russell Jones; Anne Occi, Vice President of Design for the Baseball Major League Properties; and Polly Smith, costume designer for Jim Henson productions.

Roland Dille Center for the Arts

▼ MOORHEAD STATE UNIVERSITY

Moorhead, Minnesota

State-supported, coed. Urban campus. Total enrollment: 6,466.

Degrees Bachelor of Fine Arts in the areas of ceramics, graphic design, painting, pictorial illustration, photography, printmaking, sculpture. Cross-registration with Concordia College, North Dakota State University. Program accredited by NASAD.

Enrollment Fall 1997: 260 total; all undergraduate.

Art Student Profile 60% females, 40% males, 6% minorities, 2% international.

Art Faculty 13 total (full-time and part-time). 100% of full-time faculty have terminal degrees. Graduate students do not teach undergraduate courses. Undergraduate student–faculty ratio: 18:1.

Student Life Student groups/activities include Students Involved in Visual Arts, American Institute of Graphic Arts Student Chapter, Photography Club.

Expenses for 1998–99 Application fee: $20. State resident tuition: $2484 full-time. Nonresident tuition: $5596 full-time. Mandatory fees: $424 full-time. Full-time tuition and fees vary according to reciprocity agreements. College room and board: $3256. College room only: $1874. Room and board

charges vary according to board plan. Special program-related fees: $30–$125 per course for lab fees.

Financial Aid Program-specific awards for 1997: 10 Talent Awards for freshmen program majors ($250–$500), 7 Talent Awards for upperclass program majors ($250–$750).

Application Procedures Students apply for admission into the professional program by junior year. Deadline for freshmen and transfers: August 7. Notification date for freshmen and transfers: continuous. Required: high school transcript, minimum 2.0 high school GPA, SAT I or ACT test scores (minimum combined ACT score of 21), completion of college preparatory courses, portfolio for scholarship consideration. Portfolio reviews held by appointment on campus; the submission of slides may be substituted for portfolios whenever necessary.

Undergraduate Contact Ms. Jean Lange, Admissions Director, Moorhead State University, 1104 7th Avenue South, Moorhead, Minnesota 56563; 218-236-2161, fax: 218-236-2168.

▼ MOUNT ALLISON UNIVERSITY

Sackville, NB, Canada

Province-supported, coed. Small town campus. Total enrollment: 2,474. Art program established 1937.

Degrees Bachelor of Fine Arts in the areas of painting, photography, printmaking, sculpture, mixed media, drawing. Majors and concentrations: art/fine arts, painting/drawing, photography, printmaking, sculpture, studio art. Cross-registration with Universite de Strasbourg (France), Universitat Tubingen (Germany).

Enrollment Fall 1997: 112 undergraduate.

Art Student Profile 74% females, 26% males, 1% international.

Art Faculty 8 total (full-time and part-time). 86% of full-time faculty have terminal degrees. Graduate students do not teach undergraduate courses. Undergraduate student–faculty ratio: 14:1.

Student Life Student groups/activities include Fine Arts Society. Special housing available for art students.

Expenses for 1997–98 Application fee: $40 Canadian dollars. Tuition, fee, and room and board charges are reported in Canadian dollars. Canadian resident tuition: $3850 full-time. Mandatory fees: $167 full-time. Full-time tuition and fees vary according to course load. College room and board: $5460. College room only: $3050. Room and board charges vary according to board plan and housing facility. International student tuition: $7475 full-time.

Financial Aid Program-specific awards for 1997: 1 Pulford Award for freshmen program majors ($500–$1000), 1–2 Chang Awards for senior program majors ($500–$1000), 1 Crake Award for graduating students ($500), 2 Gairdner Awards for top program majors ($1000), University Scholarships for those in top 10% of program ($750).

Application Procedures Students admitted directly into the professional program freshman year. Deadline for freshmen: April 1; transfers: July 1. Required: high school transcript, college transcript(s) for transfer students, minimum 3.0 high school GPA, 2 letters of recommendation, portfolio. Portfolio reviews held once on campus; the submission of slides may be substituted for portfolios for large works of art.

Web Site http://mta.ca/faculty/arts-letters/finearts/.

Undergraduate Contact Ms. Susan Wallace, Coordinator of Admissions, Student Administrative Services, Mount Allison

Mount Allison University *(continued)*

University, 65 York Street, Sackville, NB E4L 1E4, Canada; 506-364-2111, fax: 506-364-2272, E-mail address: swallace@mta.ca.

▼ MURRAY STATE UNIVERSITY

Murray, Kentucky

State-supported, coed. Small town campus. Total enrollment: 8,811. Art program established 1926.

Degrees Bachelor of Fine Arts in the areas of studio art, art education. Majors and concentrations: ceramics, design, graphic design, jewelry and metalsmithing, painting/drawing, photography, printmaking, sculpture, weaving/surface design, wood. Program accredited by NASAD.

Enrollment Fall 1997: 200 total; 40 undergraduate, 160 non-professional degree.

Art Student Profile 46% females, 54% males, 3% minorities, 1% international.

Art Faculty 16 total (full-time and part-time). 100% of full-time faculty have terminal degrees. Graduate students do not teach undergraduate courses. Undergraduate student–faculty ratio: 14:1.

Student Life Student groups/activities include Organization of Murray Art Students.

Expenses for 1998–99 Application fee: $20. State resident tuition: $1920 full-time. Nonresident tuition: $5760 full-time. Mandatory fees: $380 full-time. Full-time tuition and fees vary according to reciprocity agreements. College room and board: $3560. College room only: $1560. Special program-related fees: $12 per credit hour for supplies and equipment.

Financial Aid Program-specific awards for 1997: 15–20 Department of Art Scholarships for program majors ($500–$1000).

Application Procedures Students admitted directly into the professional program freshman year. Deadline for freshmen and transfers: continuous. Required: high school transcript, ACT test score only.

Undergraduate Contact Mr. Dick Dougherty, Chair, Department of Art, Murray State University, PO Box 9, Murray, Kentucky 42071; 502-762-3784, fax: 502-762-3920.

▼ THE NEW ENGLAND SCHOOL OF ART & DESIGN

See Suffolk University

▼ NEW JERSEY CITY UNIVERSITY

Jersey City, New Jersey

State-supported, coed. Urban campus. Total enrollment: 8,503. Art program established 1961.

Degrees Bachelor of Fine Arts in the areas of fine arts, design and crafts, photography, communication design. Majors and concentrations: art/fine arts, ceramic art and design, communication design, computer graphics, craft design, digital imaging, graphic design, illustration, jewelry and metalsmithing, painting/drawing, photography, printmaking, sculpture. Graduate degrees offered: Master of Fine Arts in the area of painting and drawing. Program accredited by NASAD.

Enrollment Fall 1997: 351 total; 85 undergraduate, 8 graduate, 258 non-professional degree.

Art Student Profile 58% females, 42% males, 56% minorities, 15% international.

Art Faculty 41 total undergraduate and graduate (full-time and part-time). 100% of full-time faculty have terminal degrees. Graduate students do not teach undergraduate courses. Undergraduate student–faculty ratio: 15:1.

Student Life Student groups/activities include Art Association, Juried Student Exhibition, student-curated exhibitions.

Expenses for 1997–98 Application fee: $35. State resident tuition: $2880 full-time. Nonresident tuition: $4898 full-time. Mandatory fees: $948 full-time. College room and board: $5000. College room only: $3000. Special program-related fees: $15–$35 per course for consumable supplies.

Financial Aid Program-specific awards for 1997: Prins Simons Award.

Application Procedures Students apply for admission into the professional program by junior year. Deadline for freshmen and transfers: June 1. Required: essay, high school transcript, college transcript(s) for transfer students, minimum 2.0 high school GPA, interview, portfolio, SAT I test score only. Recommended: letter of recommendation. Portfolio reviews held continuously on campus and off campus; the submission of slides may be substituted for portfolios by prior arrangement for provisional acceptance.

Web Site http://www.jcstate.edu.

Contact Ms. Denise Mullen, Chair, Art Department, New Jersey City University, 2039 Kennedy Boulevard, Jersey City, New Jersey 07305; 201-200-3241, fax: 201-200-3238, E-mail address: dmullen@jcs1.jcstate.edu.

▼ NEW MEXICO HIGHLANDS UNIVERSITY

Las Vegas, New Mexico

State-supported, coed. Small town campus. Total enrollment: 2,544.

Degrees Bachelor of Fine Arts in the areas of sculpture, printmaking, painting, foundry, ceramics, jewelry, visual communication design. Majors and concentrations: ceramic art and design, foundry, jewelry and metalsmithing, painting/drawing, printmaking, sculpture, studio art, visual communication.

Enrollment Fall 1997: 135 total; 70 undergraduate, 65 non-professional degree.

Art Student Profile 55% females, 45% males, 80% minorities, 5% international.

Art Faculty 8 total (full-time and part-time). 100% of full-time faculty have terminal degrees. Graduate students do not teach undergraduate courses. Undergraduate student–faculty ratio: 12:1.

Student Life Student groups/activities include Crossroads Art Club.

Expenses for 1997–98 Application fee: $15. One-time mandatory fee: $5. State resident tuition: $1602 full-time. Nonresident tuition: $6786 full-time. Mandatory fees: $60 full-time. Full-time tuition and fees vary according to degree level. College room and board: $2706. College room only: $1320. Room and board charges vary according to board plan and housing facility. Special program-related fees: $25–$45 per course for specific studio courses.

Financial Aid Program-specific awards for 1997: 2 Schula Awards for program majors ($1500).

Application Procedures Students admitted directly into the professional program freshman year. Deadline for freshmen and transfers: May 15. Notification date for freshmen and transfers: continuous. Required: high school transcript, college transcript(s) for transfer students, minimum 2.0 high school GPA, SAT I or ACT test scores.

Web Site http://www.nmhu.edu.

Undergraduate Contact Ms. Donna A. Martinez, Administrative Secretary, Department of Communication and Fine Arts, New Mexico Highlands University, Burris Hall, Las Vegas, New Mexico 87701; 505-454-3238, fax: 505-454-3241.

▼ NEW MEXICO STATE UNIVERSITY

Las Cruces, New Mexico

State-supported, coed. Suburban campus. Total enrollment: 15,067.

Degrees Bachelor of Fine Arts in the area of studio art. Majors and concentrations: ceramic art and design, graphic design, jewelry and metalsmithing, painting/drawing, photography, printmaking, sculpture. Graduate degrees offered: Master of Fine Arts in the area of studio art.

Enrollment Fall 1997: 160 undergraduate, 30 graduate.

Art Student Profile 55% females, 45% males, 30% minorities.

Art Faculty 12 total undergraduate and graduate (full-time and part-time). 100% of full-time faculty have terminal degrees. Graduate students teach a few undergraduate courses. Undergraduate student–faculty ratio: 15:1.

Expenses for 1997–98 Application fee: $15. State resident tuition: $2196 full-time. Nonresident tuition: $7152 full-time. College room and board: $3390. College room only: $1940. Room and board charges vary according to board plan and housing facility.

Application Procedures Students admitted directly into the professional program freshman year. Deadline for freshmen and transfers: August 14. Required: high school transcript, college transcript(s) for transfer students, SAT I or ACT test scores.

Contact Mr. Joshua Rose, Head, Art Department, New Mexico State University, Box 30001, Department 3572, Las Cruces, New Mexico 88003-0001; 505-646-1705, fax: 505-646-8036, E-mail address: artdept@nmsu.edu.

▼ NEW SCHOOL FOR SOCIAL RESEARCH

See Parsons School of Design

▼ NEW WORLD SCHOOL OF THE ARTS

Miami, Florida

State-supported, coed. Urban campus. Total enrollment: 359. Art program established 1988.

Degrees Bachelor of Fine Arts in the areas of photography, cyberarts, painting, drawing, printmaking, ceramics, communications design, sculpture (environmental public art). Mandatory cross-registration with University of Florida, Miami-Dade Community College. Program accredited by NASAD.

Enrollment Fall 1997: 138 total; all undergraduate.

Art Student Profile 54% females, 46% males, 60% minorities, 1% international.

Art Faculty 19 total (full-time and part-time). 100% of full-time faculty have terminal degrees. Graduate students do not teach undergraduate courses. Undergraduate student–faculty ratio: 12:1.

Student Life Student groups/activities include Art Club.

Estimated expenses for 1998–99 Application fee: $20. State resident tuition: $1478 full-time. Nonresident tuition: $5196 full-time. Full-time tuition varies according to course load and degree level.

Financial Aid Program-specific awards for 1997: 4 Nation's Bank Merit Scholarships for program majors ($2000), 6 Ronnie Bogaev Merit Scholarships for female in-state program majors ($2000), 18 Frances Wolfson Merit Scholarships for program majors ($2000), 15 Miami-Dade Community College Scholarships for program majors ($1000).

Application Procedures Students admitted directly into the professional program freshman year. Deadline for freshmen and transfers: continuous. Notification date for freshmen and transfers: continuous. Required: high school transcript, college transcript(s) for transfer students, portfolio. Recommended: essay, minimum 2.0 high school GPA, 2 letters of recommendation, interview, SAT I or ACT test scores. Portfolio reviews held continuously on campus and off campus; the submission of slides may be substituted for portfolios when distance is prohibitive.

Web Site http://www.mdcc.edu/nwsa.

Undergraduate Contact Ileana Gallagher, Admissions Counselor, Student Services, New World School of the Arts, 300 Northeast 2nd Avenue, Miami, Florida 33132; 305-237-7408, fax: 305-237-3794.

Midge Karr Fine Art Department

▼ NEW YORK INSTITUTE OF TECHNOLOGY

Old Westbury, New York

Independent, coed. Suburban campus. Total enrollment: 8,982.

Degrees Bachelor of Fine Arts in the areas of design graphics, computer graphics, teacher education. Majors and concentrations: art education, computer graphics, graphic arts.

Enrollment Fall 1997: 153 undergraduate.

Art Faculty 21 total undergraduate (full-time and part-time). 90% of full-time faculty have terminal degrees. Graduate students teach about a quarter undergraduate courses. Undergraduate student–faculty ratio: 8:1.

Student Life Student groups/activities include American Society of Interior Designers, Unitedartists.

Expenses for 1997–98 Application fee: $40. Comprehensive fee: $16,910 includes full-time tuition ($9750), mandatory fees ($880), and college room and board ($6280). College room only: $3260. Full-time tuition and fees vary according to program. Room and board charges vary according to board plan. Special program-related fees: $10–$40 per course for lab fees.

Financial Aid Program-specific awards for 1997: Presidential Awards for academically qualified applicants ($2200–$2600), academic achievement awards for academically qualified applicants ($1200–$1800), academic incentive awards for academically qualified applicants ($600).

Application Procedures Students admitted directly into the professional program freshman year. Deadline for freshmen and transfers: continuous. Required: essay, high school transcript, college transcript(s) for transfer students, minimum 2.0 high school GPA, interview, portfolio, SAT I or ACT

New York Institute of Technology *(continued)*

test scores. Recommended: 2 letters of recommendation. Portfolio reviews held continuously on campus and off campus in New York, NY; the submission of slides may be substituted for portfolios for out-of-state applicants.

Undergraduate Contact Ms. Louise Clemente, Administrative Assistant, Midge Karr Fine Art Department, New York Institute of Technology, PO Box 8000, Old Westbury, New York 11568-8000; 516-686-7542, fax: 516-686-7428.

▼ NEW YORK SCHOOL OF INTERIOR DESIGN

New York, New York

Independent, coed. Urban campus. Art program established 1916.

Degrees Bachelor of Fine Arts in the area of interior design. Graduate degrees offered: Master of Fine Arts in the area of interior design. Program accredited by FIDER, NASAD.

Enrollment Fall 1997: 705 total; 400 undergraduate, 5 graduate, 300 non-professional degree.

Art Student Profile 75% females, 25% males, 10% minorities, 8% international.

Art Faculty 95 total undergraduate (full-time and part-time). 40% of full-time faculty have terminal degrees. Graduate students do not teach undergraduate courses. Undergraduate student–faculty ratio: 6:1.

Student Life Student groups/activities include American Society of Interior Designers Student Chapter.

Expenses for 1998–99 Application fee: $35. Tuition: $12,600 full-time. Mandatory fees: $70 full-time. Full-time tuition and fees vary according to course load.

Financial Aid Program-specific awards for 1997: 25 Institutional and Endowed Scholarships for program majors ($1000–$5000).

Application Procedures Students admitted directly into the professional program freshman year. Deadline for freshmen and transfers: continuous. Required: essay, high school transcript, college transcript(s) for transfer students, minimum 2.0 high school GPA, 2 letters of recommendation, portfolio, SAT I or ACT test scores. Recommended: minimum 3.0 high school GPA, interview. Portfolio reviews held continuously on campus and off campus in various college fairs; the submission of slides may be substituted for portfolios when distance is prohibitive.

Web Site http://www.nysid.edu.

Contact Ms. J. Kiki Dennis, Director of Admissions, New York School of Interior Design, 170 East 70th Street, New York, New York 10021; 212-472-1500 ext. 202, fax: 212-472-1867, E-mail address: admissions@nysid.edu.

More About the School

Throughout its history, the New York School of Interior Design (NYSID) has devoted all of its resources to a single field of study—interior design. NYSID is specifically designed for those who wish to pursue a career in one or more of the various fields of interior design and wish to do so under the guidance of a faculty composed of practicing designers, architects, and art and architectural historians. The various academic programs compose an integrated curriculum covering interior design concepts, history of art, architecture, interiors and furniture, technical and communication skills, materials and methods, philosophy and theory, professional design procedures, and design problem solving.

Because of its select faculty and established reputation, the School continues to maintain a close relationship with the interior design industry. This provides an excellent means for students to develop associations that offer opportunities to move into the profession after completing their degree program at NYSID.

Many of the world's most important museums, galleries, and showrooms are within walking distance. The city is world-renowned for its cultural activities, architecture, historic districts, and cosmopolitan urban experience.

NYSID is located on a quiet, tree-lined street in Manhattan's Upper East Side Landmark District. The School has two auditorium spaces, light-filled studios and classrooms, a CAD lab, and a new lighting design lab. NYSID also has a newly renovated library containing a comprehensive collection of books, journals, periodicals, and trade and auction catalogs specifically devoted to the interior design field and related fine arts; a materials library; an atelier; two galleries; a rooftop terrace; and a café, bookstore, and student lounge.

NYSID has an active student chapter of the American Society of Interior Designers (ASID). ASID organizes lectures, tours, workshops, and other events throughout the school year, providing an inside view of the interior design industry.

One of the strengths of NYSID is its gallery exhibitions relating to architecture and design. Open to both students and the public, the gallery has mounted such acclaimed shows as *Charles Rennie Mackintosh: House for an Art Lover; Virtual Color: Light, Hue, and Form Integrated;* and *Susret/ Encounter: Artists and Refugees.* The school also sponsors lectures and symposia. Guest lecturers have included Sarah Tomerlin Lee, Alexandra Stoddard, Albert Hadley, Bunny Williams, Mark Hampton, and Arlene Dahl. Students are encouraged to attend the lecture series.

The school maintains an active placement service for graduates and current students. Many students find work while still at NYSID. Because of its reputation in the design field, many NYSID graduates are employed in the best design, architectural, and industry-related firms in New York City, across the United States, and around the world.

Tisch School of the Arts

▼ NEW YORK UNIVERSITY

New York, New York

Independent, coed. Urban campus. Total enrollment: 36,684. Art program established 1965.

Degrees Bachelor of Fine Arts in the area of photography.

Enrollment Fall 1997: 120 undergraduate.

Art Student Profile 64% females, 36% males, 19% minorities, 10% international.

Art Faculty 17 total (full-time and part-time). 80% of full-time faculty have terminal degrees. Graduate students do not teach undergraduate courses. Undergraduate student–faculty ratio: 8:1.

Student Life Student groups/activities include Artists in the Community, Out Artists, United Artists of Color.

Expenses for 1997–98 Application fee: $45. Comprehensive fee: $29,900 includes full-time tuition ($21,730) and college room and board ($8170). Full-time tuition varies according to program. Room and board charges vary according to board plan and housing facility. Special program-related fees: $174 per course for photo lab fee.

Financial Aid Program-specific awards for 1997: 3 Goddard Awards for those demonstrating financial need ($1500), 1 Wasserman Award for those demonstrating talent ($3500).

Application Procedures Students admitted directly into the professional program freshman year. Deadline for freshmen: January 15; transfers: April 1. Notification date for freshmen: April 1; transfers: May 15. Required: essay, high school transcript, college transcript(s) for transfer students, 2 letters of recommendation, portfolio, SAT I or ACT test scores, resume. Recommended: minimum 3.0 high school GPA, interview. Portfolio reviews held twice and by appointment on campus.

Web Site http://www.nyu.edu/tisch.

Undergraduate Contact Mr. Elliot Dee, Director of Recruitment, Tisch School of the Arts, New York University, 721 Broadway, 8th Floor, New York, New York 10003-6807; 212-998-1902, fax: 212-995-4060, E-mail address: eddl@is6.nyu.edu.

▼ NORTHERN ILLINOIS UNIVERSITY

De Kalb, Illinois

State-supported, coed. Small town campus. Total enrollment: 22,082.

Degrees Bachelor of Fine Arts in the areas of crafts, design, fine arts. Majors and concentrations: applied art, art/fine arts, ceramic art and design, commercial art, computer animation, computer graphics, craft design, design, graphic arts, illustration, interior design, intermedia, jewelry and metalsmithing, painting/drawing, photography, printmaking, sculpture, studio art, textile arts. Graduate degrees offered: Master of Fine Arts in the area of studio and design. Program accredited by NASAD.

Enrollment Fall 1997: 936 total; 808 undergraduate, 128 graduate.

Art Student Profile 57% females, 43% males, 11% minorities, 2% international.

Art Faculty 59 total undergraduate and graduate (full-time and part-time). 92% of full-time faculty have terminal degrees. Graduate students teach a few undergraduate courses. Undergraduate student–faculty ratio: 16:1.

Student Life Student groups/activities include National Art Education Association Student Chapter, American Center for Design Student Chapter. Special housing available for art students.

Expenses for 1997–98 State resident tuition: $2952 full-time. Nonresident tuition: $8856 full-time. Mandatory fees: $885 full-time. Full-time tuition and fees vary according to course load. College room and board: $4000. Room and board charges vary according to housing facility. Special program-related fees: $7–$76 per course for lab/materials fees.

Financial Aid Program-specific awards for 1997: 6–12 tuition waivers for high school seniors ($2520–$3136).

Application Procedures Students admitted directly into the professional program freshman year. Deadline for freshmen and transfers: continuous. Notification date for freshmen and transfers: continuous. Required: high school transcript, college transcript(s) for transfer students, ACT test score only (minimum combined ACT score of 19), standing in top half of graduating class, completion of college preparatory courses.

Web Site http://www.vpa.niu.edu/art/.

Undergraduate Contact Office of Admissions, Northern Illinois University, Williston Hall Room 101, De Kalb, Illinois 60115; 815-753-0446, fax: 815-753-1783.

Graduate Contact Yale Factor, Coordinator of Graduate Program, School of Art, Northern Illinois University, De Kalb, Illinois 60115-2883; 815-753-0292.

▼ NORTHERN KENTUCKY UNIVERSITY

Highland Heights, Kentucky

State-supported, coed. Suburban campus. Total enrollment: 11,763. Art program established 1968.

Degrees Bachelor of Fine Arts in the areas of studio art, graphic design, intermedia, art history with studio. Majors and concentrations: applied photography, art history, ceramic art and design, graphic design, intermedia, painting/drawing, photography, printmaking, sculpture, studio art. Cross-registration with Northern Kentucky/Greater Cincinnati Consortium of Colleges and Universities.

Enrollment Fall 1997: 308 total; 258 undergraduate, 50 non-professional degree.

Art Student Profile 55% females, 45% males, 1% minorities, 1% international.

Art Faculty 27 total (full-time and part-time). 100% of full-time faculty have terminal degrees. Graduate students teach a few undergraduate courses. Undergraduate student–faculty ratio: 17:1.

Student Life Student groups/activities include Students in Design, Mudd Club, Art for Our Sake.

Expenses for 1997–98 Application fee: $25. State resident tuition: $2120 full-time. Nonresident tuition: $5720 full-time. Full-time tuition varies according to course load. College room and board: $3439. College room only: $1769. Room and board charges vary according to board plan and housing facility. Special program-related fees: $20–$200 for incidental fee, technology fee, and support of learning surcharge.

Financial Aid Program-specific awards for 1997: 1–2 Friends of Fine Arts Awards for continuing students ($2000), 6 University Art Awards for continuing students ($2000), 1 Schiff Scholarship for continuing students ($2000).

Application Procedures Students apply for admission into the professional program by sophomore year. Deadline for freshmen: continuous; transfers: August 1. Required: high school transcript, college transcript(s) for transfer students, portfolio, ACT test score only, minimum 2.5 college GPA with a 3.0 art major GPA. Portfolio reviews held twice upon completion of 60 hours of coursework or 21 hours of art on campus.

Web Site http://www.nku.edu/~art/art_home.html.

Undergraduate Contact Dr. Donald Kelm, Chairman, Art Department, Northern Kentucky University, Fine Arts Center 312, Highland Heights, Kentucky 41099; 606-572-6952, fax: 606-572-6501, E-mail address: kelmd@nku.edu.

▼ NOVA SCOTIA COLLEGE OF ART AND DESIGN

Halifax, NS, Canada

Province-supported, coed. Urban campus. Art program established 1887.

Degrees Bachelor of Fine Arts in the areas of fine arts, studio art, crafts; Bachelor of Design in the areas of communication

Nova Scotia College of Art and Design (continued)

design, digital communication design. Majors and concentrations: art/fine arts, ceramics, communication design, digital communication design, jewelry and metalsmithing, media arts, photography, textiles. Graduate degrees offered: Master of Fine Arts in the areas of fine arts, design. Cross-registration with Dalhousie University, St. Mary's University, Mount St. Vincent University.

Enrollment Fall 1997: 665 total; 594 undergraduate, 18 graduate, 53 non-professional degree.

Art Student Profile 60% females, 40% males, 7% international.

Art Faculty 71 total undergraduate and graduate (full-time and part-time). 95% of full-time faculty have terminal degrees. Graduate students teach a few undergraduate courses. Undergraduate student–faculty ratio: 12:1.

Student Life Student groups/activities include "Rewire" (college publication), Women's Collective, Mosaic (minority ethnic group).

Expenses for 1997–98 Application fee: $25 Canadian dollars. Tuition and fee charges are reported in Canadian dollars. Province resident tuition: $3530 full-time. Canadian resident tuition: $6230 full-time. Mandatory fees: $66 full-time.

Financial Aid Program-specific awards for 1997: 50 Merit Scholarships for those demonstrating talent and academic achievement ($700), 10 Joseph Beuys Memorial Scholarships for those demonstrating talent and academic achievement ($1500).

Application Procedures Students admitted directly into the professional program freshman year. Deadline for freshmen: May 15; transfers: April 1. Notification date for freshmen and transfers: June 20. Required: essay, high school transcript, college transcript(s) for transfer students, slides of portfolio. Recommended: interview. Portfolio reviews held twice on campus.

Web Site http://www.nscad.ns.ca.

Contact Mr. Terry Bailey, Coordinator of Admissions, Off Campus and Recruitment, Student Services, Nova Scotia College of Art and Design, 5163 Duke Street, Halifax, NS B3J 3J6, Canada; 902-494-8129, fax: 902-425-2987, E-mail address: tbailey@nscad.ns.ca.

▼ OHIO NORTHERN UNIVERSITY

Ada, Ohio

Independent-United Methodist, coed. Small town campus. Total enrollment: 2,927. Art program established 1961.

Degrees Bachelor of Fine Arts in the area of art. Majors and concentrations: graphic design, studio art. Cross-registration with Queen Margaret College (United Kingdom), Glasgow Caledonian University (United Kingdom), St. David's University (United Kingdom), University of Science and Technology (France), Plekhanov Economic Academy (Russia).

Enrollment Fall 1997: 29 total; all undergraduate.

Art Student Profile 52% females, 48% males, 6% minorities, 2% international.

Art Faculty 6 total (full-time and part-time). 57% of full-time faculty have terminal degrees. Graduate students do not teach undergraduate courses. Undergraduate student–faculty ratio: 8:1.

Student Life Student groups/activities include Kappa Pi, Alpha Epsilon Rho, Theta Alpha Phi.

Expenses for 1998–99 Application fee: $30. Comprehensive fee: $24,690 includes full-time tuition ($19,815) and college room and board ($4875). College room only: $2130.

Full-time tuition varies according to program. Room and board charges vary according to board plan.

Financial Aid Program-specific awards for 1997: 20 Art Talent Awards for art majors ($2500–$6000).

Application Procedures Students admitted directly into the professional program freshman year. Deadline for freshmen and transfers: continuous. Notification date for freshmen and transfers: continuous. Required: high school transcript, college transcript(s) for transfer students, SAT I or ACT test scores, minimum 2.5 high school GPA. Recommended: essay, minimum 3.0 high school GPA, interview, portfolio. Portfolio reviews held by request on campus; the submission of slides may be substituted for portfolios with approval from the department.

Web Site http://www.onu.edu.

Undergraduate Contact Ms. Karen Condeni, Vice President and Dean of Admissions, Ohio Northern University, 525 South Main Street, Ada, Ohio 45810; 419-772-2260, fax: 419-772-2313, E-mail address: admissions-ug@onu.edu.

▼ THE OHIO STATE UNIVERSITY

Columbus, Ohio

State-supported, coed. Urban campus. Total enrollment: 48,278.

Degrees Bachelor of Fine Arts in the areas of ceramics, glass, sculpture, painting/drawing, printmaking, photography, art and technology. Graduate degrees offered: Master of Fine Arts in the areas of ceramics, glass, sculpture, painting/drawing, printmaking, photography, art and technology, art critical practices. Cross-registration with Columbus College of Art and Design . Program accredited by NASAD.

Enrollment Fall 1997: 282 total; 170 undergraduate, 52 graduate, 60 non-professional degree.

Art Student Profile 48% females, 52% males, 3% minorities, 8% international.

Art Faculty 34 total undergraduate and graduate (full-time and part-time). 100% of full-time faculty have terminal degrees. Graduate students teach more than half undergraduate courses.

Student Life Student groups/activities include Student League of Independent Potters, Student Printmakers Association, Undergraduate Student Art League.

Expenses for 1997–98 Application fee: $30. State resident tuition: $3660 full-time. Nonresident tuition: $10,869 full-time. College room and board: $5094. Room and board charges vary according to board plan and housing facility.

Application Procedures Students apply for admission into the professional program by junior year. Deadline for freshmen and transfers: continuous. Required: high school transcript, college transcript(s) for transfer students, portfolio, SAT I or ACT test scores. Recommended: standing in top third of graduating high school class. Portfolio reviews held twice a year upon completion of foundation year on campus; the submission of slides may be substituted for portfolios for transfer applicants when original work is no longer available or for large works of art and three-dimensional pieces.

Web Site http://www.arts.ohio-state.edu/Art/.

Undergraduate Contact University Admissions, The Ohio State University, 1800 Cannon Drive, 3rd Floor Lincoln Tower, Columbus, Ohio 43210; 614-292-5995, fax: 614-292-4818.

Graduate Contact Cathy Ellis, Assistant to Chair, Art Department, The Ohio State University, 146 Hopkins Hall, 128 North Oval Mall, Columbus, Ohio 43210; 614-292-5072, fax: 614-292-1674, E-mail address: ellis.11@postbox.acs.ohio-state.edu.

▼ OHIO UNIVERSITY

Athens, Ohio

State-supported, coed. Small town campus. Total enrollment: 19,564.

Degrees Bachelor of Fine Arts in the areas of printmaking, photography, art education, art history, ceramics, painting, graphic design, sculpture. Majors and concentrations: art education, art history, ceramic art and design, graphic arts, painting/drawing, photography, printmaking, sculpture. Graduate degrees offered: Master of Fine Arts in the areas of printmaking, photography, art history, ceramics, sculpture, painting, art history/studio.

Enrollment Fall 1997: 464 total; 384 undergraduate, 80 graduate.

Art Student Profile 64% females, 36% males, 3% minorities, 4% international.

Art Faculty 36 total undergraduate and graduate (full-time and part-time). 98% of full-time faculty have terminal degrees. Graduate students teach a few undergraduate courses. Undergraduate student–faculty ratio: 15:1.

Student Life Student groups/activities include Students in Design, Undergraduate Art League, National Art Education Association.

Expenses for 1997–98 Application fee: $30. State resident tuition: $4275 full-time. Nonresident tuition: $8994 full-time. College room and board: $4698. College room only: $2310. Room and board charges vary according to board plan. Special program-related fees: $5–$100 per course for materials fees.

Financial Aid Program-specific awards for 1997: 3–4 L. C. Mitchell Memorial Scholarships for art majors ($1000), 1 Mary Nelson Stephenson Art Memorial Award for program majors ($1500), 1 Kenneth B. Clifford Memorial Scholarship for junior/senior painting or printmaking majors ($500), 1–4 Provost Scholarship for incoming students ($1000), 1 President's Scholarship for academically qualified freshmen ($1500), 1 Third Century Scholarship for academically qualified freshmen ($3000).

Application Procedures Students apply for admission into the professional program by sophomore year. Deadline for freshmen: March 1; transfers: June 1. Required: high school transcript, college transcript(s) for transfer students, SAT I or ACT test scores (minimum combined SAT I score of 1000, minimum combined ACT score of 21), standing in top 30% of graduating class.

Web Site http://www.ohiou.edu/~artdept/soamain.html.

Undergraduate Contact Ms. Dianne Bouvier, Student Services Coordinator, School of Art, Ohio University, Seigfred 327, Athens, Ohio 45701; 614-593-0274, fax: 614-593-0457, E-mail address: bouvier@art.ohiou.edu.

Graduate Contact Mr. Michael Harper, Assistant Director of Graduate Affairs, School of Art, Ohio University, Seigfred 327, Athens, Ohio 45701; 614-593-4288, fax: 614-593-0457, E-mail address: harper@art.ohiou.edu.

▼ OHIO WESLEYAN UNIVERSITY

Delaware, Ohio

Independent-United Methodist, coed. Small town campus. Total enrollment: 1,893.

Degrees Bachelor of Fine Arts in the area of art. Majors and concentrations: ceramic art and design, computer art, graphic design, jewelry and metalsmithing, painting/drawing, photography, printmaking, sculpture.

Enrollment Fall 1997: 120 total.

Art Faculty 9 total (full-time and part-time). 100% of full-time faculty have terminal degrees. Graduate students do not teach undergraduate courses. Undergraduate student–faculty ratio: 12:1.

Student Life Special housing available for art students.

Expenses for 1998–99 Application fee: $35. Comprehensive fee: $26,410 includes full-time tuition ($20,040) and college room and board ($6370). College room only: $3230. Room and board charges vary according to board plan and location.

Application Procedures Students admitted directly into the professional program freshman year. Deadline for freshmen and transfers: May 1. Notification date for freshmen and transfers: continuous. Required: essay, high school transcript, college transcript(s) for transfer students, 2 letters of recommendation, SAT I or ACT test scores. Recommended: interview, portfolio. Portfolio reviews held by request on campus; the submission of slides may be substituted for portfolios for large works of art.

Web Site http://www.owu.edu.

Undergraduate Contact Mr. Justin Kronewetter, Chairperson, Fine Arts Department, Ohio Wesleyan University, 60 South Sandusky Street, Humphreys Hall, Delaware, Ohio 43015; 614-368-3602, fax: 614-368-3299.

▼ OKLAHOMA BAPTIST UNIVERSITY

Shawnee, Oklahoma

Independent-Southern Baptist, coed. Small town campus. Total enrollment: 2,211.

Degrees Bachelor of Fine Arts in the area of studio art. Cross-registration with St. Gregory's University.

Enrollment Fall 1997: 25 total; 25 non-professional degree.

Art Student Profile 55% females, 45% males, 15% minorities, 3% international.

Art Faculty 4 total (full-time and part-time). 33% of full-time faculty have terminal degrees. Graduate students do not teach undergraduate courses. Undergraduate student–faculty ratio: 9:1.

Expenses for 1998–99 Application fee: $25. Comprehensive fee: $11,586 includes full-time tuition ($7660), mandatory fees ($676), and college room and board ($3250). College room only: $1480. Full-time tuition and fees vary according to course load. Room and board charges vary according to board plan and housing facility. Special program-related fees: $10–$15 per course for material fees.

Financial Aid Program-specific awards for 1997: 10 Talentships for program majors ($500–$4000).

Application Procedures Students admitted directly into the professional program freshman year. Deadline for freshmen and transfers: continuous. Required: high school transcript, college transcript(s) for transfer students, minimum 2.0 high school GPA, SAT I or ACT test scores. Recommended: portfolio. Portfolio reviews held continuously on campus; the submission of slides may be substituted for portfolios when distance is prohibitive.

Web Site http://www.okbu.edu.

Undergraduate Contact Mr. Michael Cappo, Dean of Admissions, Oklahoma Baptist University, Box 61174, 500 West University, Shawnee, Oklahoma 74801; 800-654-3285, fax: 405-878-2046, E-mail address: michael_cappo@mail.okbu.edu.

▼ OKLAHOMA STATE UNIVERSITY

Stillwater, Oklahoma

State-supported, coed. Small town campus. Total enrollment: 19,350. Art program established 1924.

Degrees Bachelor of Fine Arts in the areas of graphic design, studio art. Majors and concentrations: ceramics, graphic arts, illustration, jewelry and metalsmithing, painting/drawing, printmaking, sculpture.

Enrollment Fall 1997: 193 total; 189 undergraduate, 4 non-professional degree.

Art Student Profile 58% females, 42% males, 8% minorities, 5% international.

Art Faculty 15 total (full-time and part-time). 100% of full-time faculty have terminal degrees. Graduate students do not teach undergraduate courses. Undergraduate student–faculty ratio: 20:1.

Student Life Student groups/activities include Annual Juried Student Art Exhibition, Annual Interdesign Competition.

Expenses for 1997–98 Application fee: $25. State resident tuition: $1748 full-time. Nonresident tuition: $5768 full-time. Mandatory fees: $609 full-time. Full-time tuition and fees vary according to course level and program. College room and board: $4344. College room only: $1976. Room and board charges vary according to board plan and housing facility. Special program-related fees: $5–$85 per course for consumable materials, $25 per course for model fees.

Financial Aid Program-specific awards for 1997: 5 Freshmen/Transfer Scholarships for freshmen and transfer students ($1000), 5 Medical Heritage Gallery Scholarships for continuing students ($1500).

Application Procedures Students admitted directly into the professional program freshman year. Deadline for freshmen and transfers: continuous. Required: high school transcript, college transcript(s) for transfer students, minimum 2.0 high school GPA, SAT I or ACT test scores (minimum combined ACT score of 22), portfolio for scholarship consideration. Portfolio reviews held once on campus and off campus in Tulsa, OK; the submission of slides may be substituted for portfolios for large works of art and three-dimensional pieces and for out-of-state applicants.

Web Site http://www.cas.okstate.edu/art/index.html.

Undergraduate Contact Mr. Nick Bormann, Head, Department of Art, Oklahoma State University, 108 Bartlett Center, Stillwater, Oklahoma 74078-4085; 405-744-6016, fax: 405-744-5767, E-mail address: nborman@okway.okstate.edu.

▼ OLD DOMINION UNIVERSITY

Norfolk, Virginia

State-supported, coed. Urban campus. Total enrollment: 18,557.

Degrees Bachelor of Fine Arts in the area of studio art. Majors and concentrations: art education, clay and metal, drawing, fibers, graphic design, jewelry and metalsmithing, painting, photography, printmaking, sculpture, studio art. Graduate degrees offered: Master of Fine Arts in the area of visual studies; Master of Arts in the area of visual arts. Cross-registration with Tidewater Community College, Norfolk State University. Program accredited by NASAD.

Enrollment Fall 1997: 230 total; 190 undergraduate, 15 graduate, 25 non-professional degree.

Art Student Profile 57% females, 43% males, 29% minorities, 17% international.

Art Faculty 18 total undergraduate and graduate (full-time and part-time). 100% of full-time faculty have terminal degrees. Graduate students teach a few undergraduate courses.

Student Life Student groups/activities include Student Art League, Technoart.

Expenses for 1997–98 Application fee: $30. State resident tuition: $3836 full-time. Nonresident tuition: $9940 full-time. Mandatory fees: $140 full-time. Full-time tuition and fees vary according to course load and location. College room and board: $4866. Room and board charges vary according to board plan and housing facility. Special program-related fees: $20–$30 per course for lab fees.

Financial Aid Program-specific awards for 1997: 3 Sibley Scholarships for enrolled program students by portfolio competition ($1000), 2 Margolious Scholarships for enrolled program students by portfolio competition ($700), 1–2 Gorlinsky Scholarships for enrolled program students by portfolio competition ($300–$500).

Application Procedures Students admitted directly into the professional program freshman year. Deadline for freshmen: March 15; transfers: July 1. Required: high school transcript, college transcript(s) for transfer students, minimum 2.0 high school GPA, SAT I or ACT test scores (minimum combined SAT I score of 900), portfolio for transfer students. Recommended: interview. Portfolio reviews held on a case-by-case basis on campus; the submission of slides may be substituted for portfolios at student's discretion.

Undergraduate Contact Mr. Michael Fanizza, Chair, Art Department, Old Dominion University, Visual Arts Building, 49th Street, Norfolk, Virginia 23529; 757-683-4047, fax: 757-683-5923, E-mail address: maf100f@elvis.va.odu.edu.

Graduate Contact Mr. Ron Snapp, Graduate Program Director, Visual Studies Department, Old Dominion University, Visual Arts Building, 49th Street, Norfolk, Virginia 23529; 757-683-4047, fax: 757-683-5923, E-mail address: rws200f@elvis.va.odu.edu.

▼ O'MORE COLLEGE OF DESIGN

Franklin, Tennessee

Independent, coed. Small town campus. Art program established 1970.

Degrees Bachelor of Interior Design; Bachelor of Graphic Design and Advertising; Bachelor of Fashion Design and Merchandising. Majors and concentrations: fashion design and merchandising, graphic design, interior design. Program accredited by FIDER, ACCSCT.

Enrollment Fall 1997: 150 total; 144 undergraduate, 6 non-professional degree.

Art Student Profile 92% females, 8% males, 2% minorities, 1% international.

Art Faculty 18 total (full-time and part-time). 100% of full-time faculty have terminal degrees. Graduate students do not teach undergraduate courses. Undergraduate student–faculty ratio: 10:1.

Student Life Student groups/activities include O'More Fashion and Merchandising Association, American Society of Interior Designers
American Society for Interior Design, International Interior Design Association. Special housing available for art students.

Expenses for 1997–98 Application fee: $25. Tuition: $7950 full-time. Mandatory fees: $5 full-time. Special program-related fees: $20–$50 per course for studio art courses.

Financial Aid Program-specific awards for 1997: 20–30 need-based scholarships for those demonstrating need ($1500), 4–10 Presidential Merit Scholarships for those demonstrating academic achievement ($1750).

Application Procedures Students admitted directly into the professional program freshman year. Deadline for freshmen and transfers: continuous. Required: essay, high school transcript, college transcript(s) for transfer students, 3 letters of recommendation, interview, SAT I or ACT test scores, minimum 2.5 high school GPA. Recommended: portfolio. Portfolio reviews held once on campus; the submission of slides may be substituted for portfolios if original work is not available.

Undergraduate Contact Ms. Janice Miller, Vice President for Admissions and Records, O'More College of Design, PO Box 908, Franklin, Tennessee 37064; 615-794-4254.

▼ OREGON COLLEGE OF ART AND CRAFT

Portland, Oregon

Independent, coed. Urban campus. Art program established 1994.

Degrees Bachelor of Fine Arts in the area of crafts. Majors and concentrations: book arts, ceramics, drawing, fibers, metals, photography, wood. Cross-registration with Pacific Northwest College of Art. Program accredited by NASAD.

Enrollment Fall 1997: 450 total; 100 undergraduate, 350 non-professional degree.

Art Student Profile 75% females, 25% males, 8% minorities, 2% international.

Art Faculty 21 total (full-time and part-time). 86% of full-time faculty have terminal degrees. Graduate students do not teach undergraduate courses. Undergraduate student–faculty ratio: 5:1.

Student Life Student groups/activities include Student Christmas Sale, Annual Juried Student Show.

Expenses for 1997–98 Application fee: $30. Tuition: $10,320 full-time. Mandatory fees: $105 full-time. Special program-related fees: $350–$450 per year for studio fees.

Financial Aid Program-specific awards for 1997: 15 tuition scholarships for those demonstrating need ($1465), 19 Tuition Work Study Awards for those demonstrating need ($960).

Application Procedures Students admitted directly into the professional program freshman year. Deadline for freshmen and transfers: May 1. Notification date for freshmen and transfers: August 1. Required: essay, high school transcript, college transcript(s) for transfer students, 2 letters of recommendation, interview, minimum 2.5 high school GPA, slides of portfolio, minimum 2.0 college GPA for transfer students. Recommended: minimum 3.0 high school GPA. Portfolio reviews held as needed on campus.

Web Site http://www.ocac.edu.

Undergraduate Contact Ms. Jennifer M. Green, Director of Admissions, Oregon College of Art and Craft, 8245 Southwest Barnes Road, Portland, Oregon 97225; 800-390-0632, fax: 503-297-9651, E-mail address: admissions@ocac.edu.

More About the College

Program Facilities The campus is on the site of an 8-acre orchard 3 miles west of downtown Portland; separate and specially equipped studios for each department: book arts, ceramics, drawing, fibers, metal, photography, and wood. Equipment includes papermaking Hollander beater, facilities for salt, raku, and pit firing; tapestry (including 12-foot Shamrock) and floor looms; fully equipped surface design studio; individual workbenches in metal; wood bench and machine rooms; black and white and digital photo equipment; the central building houses library (region's most extensive collection of books, slides, and periodicals on crafts), exhibition gallery, sales shop, and cafe.

Faculty, Resident Artists, and Alumni All studio faculty are exhibiting artists. Artist-in-Residence programs bring 7 to 10 emerging and midcareer artists to campus each year. The year-round workshop program has recently included these visiting faculty members: Peter Beasecker, Jim Bassler, Bob Ebendorf, Timothy Ely, Warren MacKenzie, Tim McCreight, Stephen Proctor, Buzz Spector, and Barbara Lee Smith. In recent years faculty members have helped organize national conferences of their professional associations in Portland, including the Society of North American Goldsmiths, Surface Design Association, and Handweavers Guild of America.

Student Exhibit Opportunities Annual juried student exhibition in the Hoffman Gallery each spring; group exhibition of thesis work each June; annual sale of student work each December.

Special Programs B.F.A. students take general education classes and some art history courses off campus. Departments may offer the option of an internship with a local artist as part of the final year of the program.

▼

OCAC is a place where aesthetics and function are combined. Our eight-acre campus in the hills just west of downtown Portland embodies the craft ideal of beauty in daily life. The campus buildings incorporate hand-crafted details and the studios were designed by artists to provide

Oregon College of Art and Craft *(continued)*

efficiency and serenity. The intimate size of our student body, currently at almost 100 students, combined with the energy of the work being created forms a tight-knit community of artists.

The college's Hoffman Gallery is a nationally-recognized exhibition space that shows innovative work in fine arts and craft. Students gain exposure in professional gallery practices through participation in the annual Student Show, a faculty-juried exhibition of the best student work and through their thesis exhibition. In their final year of study, students work on their thesis, an original body of work prepared for exhibition. The June Thesis Show is the highlight of the Gallery schedule.

OCAC's artists-in-residence program brings both emerging and nationally known artists to Portland, providing them with the time, resources, and equipment to push their work in new directions while also interacting with students. The program includes four-month residencies for post-graduate artists and a ten-week senior residency for mid-career artists in the summer. Applications are available by writing or calling the College. For more information visit OCAC's Web site at http://www.ocac.edu.

▼ OREGON STATE UNIVERSITY

Corvallis, Oregon

State-supported, coed. Small town campus. Total enrollment: 14,490. Art program established 1949.

Degrees Bachelor of Fine Arts in the areas of graphic design, photography, fine arts. Majors and concentrations: art/fine arts, ceramic art and design, graphic design, photography, printmaking, sculpture, studio art.

Enrollment Fall 1997: 298 total; 100 undergraduate, 198 non-professional degree.

Art Student Profile 56% females, 44% males, 5% minorities, 3% international.

Art Faculty 21 total (full-time and part-time). 100% of full-time faculty have terminal degrees. Graduate students do not teach undergraduate courses. Undergraduate student–faculty ratio: 20:1.

Student Life Student groups/activities include Montage: Art Student Union, Visions: Photography Club, American Center for Design, campus affiliation.

Expenses for 1998–99 Application fee: $50. One-time mandatory fee: $50. State resident tuition: $3540 full-time. Nonresident tuition: $11,808 full-time. College room and board: $5064. Special program-related fees: $5–$90 per course for material fees.

Financial Aid Program-specific awards for 1997: 1 Fine Arts Award in Painting for freshmen and Oregon Community College transfers ($1000), 1 Matsen-Davidson Art Scholarship for freshmen or sophomore program majors ($1500), 1 Norma Siebert Print Scholarship in Art for program majors in printmaking ($1000), 1 Yaquina Art Association Scholarship for junior or senior program majors ($1500), 1 Art Department Faculty Award for program majors ($1000), 1 Wayne Takami Memorial Scholarship for returning program students ($1000), 1 Sponenburgh Travel Grant for art history juniors ($1500).

Application Procedures Students admitted directly into the professional program freshman year. Deadline for freshmen: March 1; transfers: June 1. Required: high school transcript, minimum 2.0 high school GPA, SAT I or ACT test scores.

Web Site http://osu.orst.edu/dept/arts/.

Undergraduate Contact Director of Admissions, Oregon State University, Administration Building, 14th and Jefferson, Corvallis, Oregon 97331; 541-737-4411.

▼ OTIS COLLEGE OF ART AND DESIGN

Los Angeles, California

Independent, coed. Urban campus. Art program established 1918.

Degrees Bachelor of Fine Arts in the areas of fine arts, environmental arts, fashion design, illustration, photography, surface design, toy design, digital media design, sculpture/new genres, painting, graphic design. Majors and concentrations: art/fine arts, ceramics, digital multi-media, environmental design, fashion design and technology, graphic design, illustration, new genre, photography, printmaking, sculpture, surface design, toy design, video art. Graduate degrees offered: Master of Fine Arts in the areas of painting, ceramics, photography, sculpture/new genres. Program accredited by NASAD.

Enrollment Fall 1997: 728 total; 707 undergraduate, 19 graduate, 2 non-professional degree.

Art Student Profile 58% females, 42% males, 47% minorities, 14% international.

Art Faculty 234 total undergraduate and graduate (full-time and part-time). 60% of full-time faculty have terminal degrees. Graduate students do not teach undergraduate courses.

Estimated expenses for 1998–99 Application fee: $45. Tuition: $15,900 full-time. Mandatory fees: $400 full-time. Special program-related fees: $25–$100 per course for materials fee.

Financial Aid Program-specific awards for 1997: 537 Otis Institutional Grants for program students ($2000–$10,000), 20 International Student Scholarships for international students ($1000–$5000), 20 Transfer Student Scholarships for transfer students ($1000–$5000).

Application Procedures Students apply for admission into the professional program by sophomore year. Deadline for freshmen and transfers: continuous. Notification date for freshmen and transfers: continuous. Required: essay, high school transcript, college transcript(s) for transfer students, minimum 2.0 high school GPA, portfolio, SAT I or ACT test scores, minimum TOEFL score of 550 for international applicants. Recommended: letter of recommendation, interview. Portfolio reviews held continuously on campus and off campus; the submission of slides may be substituted for portfolios (slides preferred).

Web Site http://www.otisart.edu.

Undergraduate Contact Mr. Michael Fuller, Director of Admissions, Otis College of Art and Design, 9045 Lincoln Boulevard, Los Angeles, California 90045; 310-665-6820, fax: 310-665-6805, E-mail address: otisart@otisart.edu.

Graduate Contact Mr. Roy Dowell, Department Chair, Graduate Studies, Otis College of Art and Design, 9045 Lincoln Boulevard, Los Angeles, California 90045; 310-665-6891, fax: 310-665-6805.

Otis College of Art and Design

More About the College

Program Facilities The oldest and most renowned college fine arts press in the city; Mac lab with advanced graphics and digital technology; new digital media design lab co-sponsored by American Film Institute; specialized architecture and furniture design workshops; woodworking and metalworking shops; ceramics facilities; editorial and product photography studio; video studio and private video/sound editing labs; lithography and etching presses; individual fine art senior studios; extensive library holdings in fine art, design, art history, humanities, critical studies, and periodicals; visual resources center.

Faculty and Visiting Artists Professional faculty members include designers, architects, ceramists, photographers, and fine artists, among them Linda Burnham, Carole Caroompas, Roy Dowell, Lyle Ashton Harris, Larry Johnson, Sean Adams, Moira Cullen, Harry Mott, Mary-Ann Ray, Martin Caveza, Rosemary Brantle, Ann Field, Catherine Kanner, Aiko Beall, Lita Barrie, Parme Giuntini, Heather Joseph-Witham, Paul Vangelisti, and Simeon Wade. Guest lecturers and visiting artists include Jim Iserman, Bruce Yanemoto, Judie Bamber, Gary Indiana, Daniel Martinez, Steve Roden, Adrian Saxe, Rod Beatty and Anne Cole, Eduardo Lucero, Marie Gray and Kelly Gray, Richard Tyler, Todd Oldham, Chris Burden, Morgan Fisher, Jerry Saltz, Steven Guarnaccia, James Cross, Meryl Pollen, Jeff Morris, and Renate Kempowski.

Student Exhibit Opportunities Abe and Helen Bolsky Student Gallery, Otis Gallery, annual Senior Open Studio and M.F.A. exhibitions, critics' awards and juried fashion shows, annual literary magazine, Otis Design Group.

Special Programs Spring Paris trip for Foundation students, Fall London trip open to all students, Writing Lab, Tutoring Center, Drawing Workshops, the only menswear program on the West Coast, study abroad and a visiting/exchange student program, Summer of Art pre-college program, continuing education, and extensive internship opportunities in most departments.

▼

Otis College of Art and Design's Goldsmith Campus, located in the Westchester district, is home to the Schools of Fine Arts and Design, and is accessible to the digital media, technical film, and toy design industries. The nearby communities of Venice and Santa Monica are home to many of Los Angeles' most prominent fine art studios and galleries. This campus and the nearby Graduate Studios

place students central to the resources of the vital artistic community that fuels the Los Angeles fashion, film, fine arts, and design worlds.

Otis School of Fashion is now located inside the California Apparel Mart, headquarters for more than 10,000 collections and 1,500 vendors in California's booming apparel industry. This bold move places the College and Otis students in a pivotal position in relation to an industry that is in need of talented and well-educated designers. Students have immediate access to working designers and prominent pre-professional studio opportunities to enhance their skills.

A network of alumni includes individuals who have created such cultural icons as the first Walt Disney animated cartoons; products and promotional materials for Columbia, A & M, and Virgin Records; editorial illustrations and cover art for the *Los Angeles Times, Time, Omni, The New Yorker, Buzz,* and *American Film;* costumes for *Titanic* and *Bram Stoker's Dracula,* and a host of Academy Award-winning films costumed by alumna Edith Head; production design for Spike Lee; and the fashion-forward imagery of such industry leaders as NIKE, Guess?, Richard Tyler, Isaac Mizrahi, Mossimo, and Anne Cole swimwear. Otis alumni are featured in major museums—Whitney Museum of American Art; Museum of Modern Art, New York; Guggenheim Museum; Art Institute of Chicago; Corcoran Gallery of Art; Los Angeles County Museum of Art; and Museum of Contemporary Art, Los Angeles—and in galleries and artist-run spaces around the world.

Visiting artists, designers, lecturers, and writers bring a wealth of expertise and perspective into the classroom to share with the diverse student population. Professional training is fostered by a liberal studies curriculum that emphasizes cultural and intellectual history and cultivates a meaningful integration of traditional academic and studio skills. Studio visits, lectures, hands-on instruction, and personal critiques from the more than 150 professional faculty members facilitate the students' dynamic relationship with contemporary culture. Being committed to providing students with every opportunity to succeed, Otis provides a Tutoring Center and Writing Lab, as well as an Honors program in liberal studies and art history.

Today's Otis students are a collection of artists and designers dedicated to developing critical and technical skills to lead art and design into the next century and beyond. The unprecedented move away from Otis' historic downtown home demonstrates the momentum behind the College and its faculty members, as well as the support of the art, design, and philanthropic communities. The campus is filled with student and faculty work, as well as the work of outside professionals, and student work is prominently displayed at municipal and private galleries and businesses across the city. Campus life, though not facilitated by traditional housing, is made richer by the intensity of the studio and classroom experience, and by student-run shows, an annual magazine, and a variety of other activities.

▼ PACIFIC LUTHERAN UNIVERSITY

Tacoma, Washington

Independent, coed. Suburban campus. Total enrollment: 3,555.

Degrees Bachelor of Fine Arts in the areas of two-dimensional media, three-dimensional media, graphic design. Majors and concentrations: art/fine arts, ceramic art and design,

Pacific Lutheran University (continued)

electronic imaging, graphic arts, painting/drawing, photography, printmaking, sculpture.
Enrollment Fall 1997: 70 total; 55 undergraduate, 15 non-professional degree.
Art Student Profile 60% females, 40% males, 3% minorities, 7% international.
Art Faculty 8 total (full-time and part-time). 100% of full-time faculty have terminal degrees. Graduate students do not teach undergraduate courses. Undergraduate student–faculty ratio: 15:1.
Student Life Student groups/activities include Art Guild.
Expenses for 1998–99 Application fee: $35. Comprehensive fee: $20,570 includes full-time tuition ($15,680) and college room and board ($4890). College room only: $2400. Special program-related fees: $20–$45 per course for supplies.
Financial Aid Program-specific awards for 1997: 5–15 Talent Awards for freshmen and sophomores ($500–$3000), 1 Lila Moe Scholarship for female seniors ($1500), 1 Cheney Scholarship for juniors and seniors ($3000), 1–5 Knudsen Scholarships for juniors and seniors ($300–$1500), 1 Fellow Award for juniors and seniors ($2000), 1 Society for the Arts Scholarship for program students ($1000).
Application Procedures Students apply for admission into the professional program by freshman year. Deadline for freshmen and transfers: February 15. Notification date for freshmen and transfers: March 1. Required: essay, high school transcript, college transcript(s) for transfer students, 2 letters of recommendation, SAT I or ACT test scores. Recommended: minimum 3.0 high school GPA, portfolio. Portfolio reviews held continuously on campus; the submission of slides may be substituted for portfolios (slides preferred).
Undergraduate Contact Mr. John Hallam, Chair, Art Department, Pacific Lutheran University, Tacoma, Washington 98447; 206-535-7575, E-mail address: hallamjs@plu.edu.

▼ Pacific Northwest College of Art

Portland, Oregon

Independent, coed. Urban campus. Total enrollment: 243. Art program established 1909.
Degrees Bachelor of Fine Arts in the areas of ceramics, drawing, painting, graphic design, illustration, photography, printmaking, sculpture, general fine arts, individualized major. Cross-registration with Oregon Independent Colleges Association. Program accredited by NASAD.
Enrollment Fall 1997: 243 total; all undergraduate.
Art Student Profile 59% females, 41% males, 8% minorities, 4% international.
Art Faculty 43 total (full-time and part-time). 75% of full-time faculty have terminal degrees. Graduate students do not teach undergraduate courses. Undergraduate student–faculty ratio: 9:1.
Student Life Student groups/activities include in-house art gallery, public art gallery, Day Without Class (alternative art courses). Special housing available for art students.
Expenses for 1998–99 Application fee: $30. Tuition: $10,900 full-time. Mandatory fees: $368 full-time. College room only: $4250. Special program-related fees: $100 per course for private studio rental for third and fourth year students.
Financial Aid Program-specific awards for 1997: 1 Robert Wiener Travel Award for seniors ($1200), 1 Gamblin

Painting Award for juniors ($500), 4 Nancy Tonkin Memorial Scholarships for sophomores, juniors, seniors ($6000), 4 Leta Kennedy Scholarships for freshmen ($8000), 2 Robert C. Lee Printmaking Scholarships for sophomores and juniors ($4000), 2 Jacob and Ruth Kainen Printmaking Scholarships for sophomores and juniors ($2000), 1 Ed and Sandy Martin Award for sophomores, juniors, seniors ($1000), 2 Jane Chase Memorial Scholarship for sophomores, juniors, seniors ($1000), 3 William Jamison Scholarship for sophomores, juniors, seniors ($2500), 1 Fashion Group Scholarship for sophomores, juniors, seniors ($500).
Application Procedures Students admitted directly into the professional program freshman year. Deadline for freshmen and transfers: continuous. Notification date for freshmen and transfers: August 15. Required: essay, high school transcript, college transcript(s) for transfer students, minimum 2.0 high school GPA, 2 letters of recommendation, portfolio, documentation of high school graduation, 1 letter of recommendation for transfers. Recommended: minimum 3.0 high school GPA, interview, SAT I or ACT test scores. Portfolio reviews held continuously (student need not be present) on campus; the submission of slides may be substituted for portfolios (slides preferred).
Web Site http://www.pnca.edu.
Undergraduate Contact Enrollment Counselor, Pacific Northwest College of Art, PO Box 2725, Portland, Oregon 97208-2725; 800-818-PNCA, fax: 503-226-3587, E-mail address: pncainfo@pnca.edu.

More About the College

Program Facilities Macintosh computer lab accessible to all students, student art gallery, comprehensive art library with 22,500 volumes on art and 54 periodical subscriptions, a 14,000-square-foot sculpture/ceramic studio, individual spaces for fourth-year thesis students.
Visiting Artist/Speaker Program: The 1996–97 program included Bernadette Panek, Rodrigo Ferreira Marques, Orleonok Pitkin, Goat Island, Diana Thater, Jeffery Mitchell, Stephanie Weber, Lisa Moren, and the Raindog Playwrights.
Special Programs New York Studio School, a summer semester in New York under the aegis of the Association of Independent Colleges of Art and Design; Cooperative Training Program for Graphic Design Students, a semester program of real-world experience in design agency during the senior year; Annual American Institute of Graphic Arts (AIGA) Portfolio Evaluation Program for graphic design and illustration students.

▼

The Pacific Northwest College of Art has been providing art students a rich education in studio art since 1909. The College was started by supporters of the Portland Art Museum and continues to remain affiliated with the Museum. Through this relationship the PNCA student has firsthand acquaintance with artwork from African and Pre-Columbian art to contemporary conceptual art. The Art Museum also houses the Gilkey Print Center, which is a preservation and study facility for the Museum's noteworthy print collection and a support facility for the College's Printmaking Department. The Museum's Northwest Film Center is an added feature of the Museum that enriches the experience of PNCA students through its film programs. For the art student, the close relationship between the College and Museum provides an exceptional environment rarely found in art schools.

Community and environment are essential ingredients in the art student's experience. Portland's cultural life centers around the downtown South Park Blocks, in which are located the Pacific Northwest College of Art and Portland Art Museum; Portland's Performing Art Center, home of the Oregon Symphony and Oregon Shakespeare Theatre; the Schnitzer Concert Hall; Oregon Historical Society and its Historical Museum; the county's Main Library; and Portland State University. Within walking distance of the College are major art galleries, live theaters, movie theaters, jazz clubs, and excellent public transportation that brings the entire city within easy reach of the PNCA student.

PNCA's curriculum comes from a strong historical foundation based on structured and sequential courses and centered on the development of skills and visual intelligence. However, PNCA also offers its students the opportunity to explore options beyond the structured curriculum, to use the resources of all departments in their studies, and, in some instances, to develop individualized curricula using the strengths of the students' motivation and special interests. To further expand opportunities for its students, PNCA has an arrangement with Oregon independent colleges such as Reed College, Lewis and Clark College, and the University of Portland that allows students to cross-register. In addition, because of PNCA's membership in the Association of Independent Colleges of Art and Design, students in their junior year may also spend a semester or year at another art college elsewhere in the country. This reciprocal program also contributes to the diversity and depth of the College's student body.

PNCA has more transfer students than students directly from high school. This singular circumstance, coupled with the small size of the student body, facilitates generous exchange between students of varying experiences and backgrounds, raises the level of intellectual exchange among students and between students and faculty, and raises the faculty's level of expectations for student achievement in the classroom and studio. The Pacific Northwest College of Art expects its students to be intellectually and visually challenged and to consider their work relative to the contemporary world and to the community.

▼ PAIER COLLEGE OF ART, INC.

Hamden, Connecticut

Proprietary, coed. Suburban campus. Total enrollment: 261. Art program established 1946.

Degrees Bachelor of Fine Arts in the areas of graphic design, illustration, interior design, fine arts. Majors and concentrations: art/fine arts, graphic design, illustration, interior design.

Enrollment Fall 1997: 247 total; 225 undergraduate, 22 non-professional degree.

Art Student Profile 49% females, 51% males, 7% minorities, 7% international.

Art Faculty 34 total (full-time and part-time). 55% of full-time faculty have terminal degrees. Graduate students do not teach undergraduate courses. Undergraduate student–faculty ratio: 7:1.

Expenses for 1997–98 Application fee: $25. Tuition: $10,260 full-time. Mandatory fees: $335 full-time. Full-time tuition and fees vary according to course load, degree level, and program. Special program-related fees: $100–$250 per course for lab and model fees.

Financial Aid Program-specific awards for 1997: 1 Paier Minority Scholarship for minority students ($5000), 4 PCA Tuition Reductions for those demonstrating need ($1500).

Application Procedures Students admitted directly into the professional program freshman year. Deadline for freshmen and transfers: continuous. Required: high school transcript, college transcript(s) for transfer students, letter of recommendation, interview, portfolio, SAT I or ACT test scores. Portfolio reviews held twice and by appointment on campus; the submission of slides may be substituted for portfolios for large works of art.

Undergraduate Contact Ms. Lynn Pascale, Secretary, Admissions Department, Paier College of Art, Inc., 20 Gorham Avenue, Hamden, Connecticut 06514-3902; 203-287-3031, fax: 203-287-3021.

New School for Social Research

▼ PARSONS SCHOOL OF DESIGN

New York, New York

Independent, coed. Urban campus. Total university enrollment: 7,179. Total unit enrollment: 2,011. Art program established 1896.

Degrees Bachelor of Fine Arts in the areas of fine art, illustration, communication design, fashion design, product design, architectural design, interior design, photography. Majors and concentrations: animation, applied art, art/fine arts, ceramic art and design, commercial art, digital imaging, drafting and design, environmental design, fashion design, furniture design, glass, graphic arts, illustration, interior design, jewelry and metalsmithing, painting/drawing, photography, sculpture, studio art, textile arts. Graduate degrees offered: Master of Fine Arts in the areas of painting, sculpture, lighting design, design and technology. Cross-registration with Eugene Lang College-New School for Social Research. Program accredited by NASAD.

Enrollment Fall 1997: 2,011 total; 1,788 undergraduate, 223 graduate.

Art Student Profile 71% females, 29% males, 28% minorities, 35% international.

Art Faculty 440 total undergraduate and graduate (full-time and part-time). Graduate students teach a few undergraduate courses. Undergraduate student–faculty ratio: 15:1.

Student Life Student groups/activities include Student Gallery. Special housing available for art students.

Expenses for 1997–98 Application fee: $30. Comprehensive fee: $27,095 includes full-time tuition ($18,200), mandatory fees ($340), and college room and board ($8555). College room only: $6035. Special program-related fees for studio fees or equipment fees.

Financial Aid Program-specific awards for 1997: 750 Parsons Scholarships for those demonstrating need ($4000–$12,000), 45 University Scholars Scholarships for African-American and Latino students demonstrating need ($3000), 70 Parsons Restricted Scholarships for those demonstrating need and academic achievement ($1500–$7000).

Application Procedures Students admitted directly into the professional program freshman year. Deadline for freshmen and transfers: June 1. Notification date for freshmen and transfers: July 15. Required: high school transcript, college transcript(s) for transfer students, minimum 2.0 high school GPA, interview, portfolio, SAT I or ACT test scores, home examination, TOEFL score for all non-native speakers of English. Recommended: minimum 3.0 high school GPA.

Parsons School of Design (continued)

Portfolio reviews held continuously by appointment on campus; the submission of slides may be substituted for portfolios when distance is prohibitive.

Web Site http://www.parsons.edu.

Contact Ms. Nadine Bourgeois, Director of Admissions, Parsons School of Design, 66 Fifth Avenue, New York, New York 10011-8878; 212-229-8910, fax: 212-229-8975, E-mail address: bourgeon@newschool.edu.

More About the School

Program Facilities Black-and-white and color darkrooms; image enhancement technology; computer illustration; animation; painting, sculpture, printmaking studios; welding; fashion design studios; computer-aided fashion design; jewelry/metals, clay, mass-production, furniture/wood shops; ALIAS 3-D computer design; AutoCAD; exhibition systems; drafting studios; desktop publishing; computer graphics; Design Library; resource/materials libraries; Foundation Computing Library; Parsons Computing Center (a state-of-the-art Macintosh facility with sophisticated input and output capabilities); advanced satellite labs such as the Center for Agile Computing (modeling, rendering, animation platforms by Alias, Wavefront, Soft-Image, and Athena); Fashion Design Computing Laboratory (CDI, InfoDesign, AVL); Experimental Multimedia Workshop (including multiple dedicated World Wide Web sites). Facilities are networked via a high-speed fiber-optic WAN. Direct Internet access occurs through dedicated T1 connection.

Faculty, Critics, and Alumni Donna Karan '68, visiting critic: CDFA lifetime recipient, Coty Hall of Fame; Fred Woodward, faculty: art director, *Rolling Stone*, two gold medals—1994 Society of Publication; Isaac Mizrahi '82, visiting critic: *New York Times* 1989 leading fashion designer; Kevin Walz, faculty: cover, *Interiors* magazine, April 1994; Joan Snyder, faculty: painter, Hirschl & Adler gallery; Barbara Nessim, department chair: cover illustrator, *Time*, Levi's campaign; Jill Ciment, faculty: author, *The Law of Falling Bodies*; Adrian '22: MGM costume designer, *Wizard of Oz*; Albert Hadley '49: Parish-Hadley interior design; Michael Donovan '69 and Nancye Green '73: interior/graphic design, Ronald Reagan Presidential Library; Peter de Seve '81: cover illustrator, *New Yorker*, *New York Times Magazine*; David Spada '83: jewelry designer to performers such as Madonna.

Student Performance/Exhibition Opportunities Student gallery, senior exhibitions, Fashion Critics Awards Show.

Special Programs Internships include: Donna Karan, Andy Warhol Foundation, The Guggenheim Museum, Microsoft, Pentagram Design, Seventeen Magazine. Career placement; competitions/collaborations with Dupont, Reebok, Perry Ellis, Kodak, and Samsung; summer and freshman ESL; Summer College and High School: Paris, New York; Exchange/Mobility: Parsons Paris, U.S., Amsterdam, London, Stockholm, the Netherlands; Affiliates: Japan, Dominican Republic, Korea. HEOP: financial and tutoring support for eligible students; lecture series on contemporary art/design issues.

▼

In 1996 Parsons School of Design celebrated its 100th anniversary. Throughout its history, the School has added academic programs, students, and campuses. Parsons has responded to and anticipated shifts in art and design by changing curriculum and adding new technologies and vital faculty members.

Specialization remains a feature of the business landscape, but interdisciplinary design is gaining value. To achieve both aims from the start, freshmen are immersed in historical and contemporary ideas, visual analysis, and personal exploration, and they complete projects in various design disciplines before selecting a major.

The main campus at Greenwich Village in New York City is surrounded by brownstones, tree-lined streets, unique shops, restaurants, and galleries. Within walking distance of the campus are three residence halls that house primarily undergraduates. The Housing Office assists students in finding apartments. The Student Center Gallery and Health Clinic are recent improvements. New clubs emerge each year—such as the Student Gallery Committee, Parsons Film Society, Parson Volunteers, and ethnic and religious clubs. The Student Advisory Council meets regularly with the Dean.

Parsons has computer facilities for nearly every area of art and design offering state-of-the-art facilities with sophisticated input and output capabilities.

Parsons also has a midtown campus in the fashion district. At both locations, New York City is a main resource. The museums, galleries, exhibitions, and stores that students frequent also show the work of faculty members, who are working professionals in their field.

Internships and competitions with Reebok, Dupont, Kodak, and The Gap are typical. David Dworkin, president and CEO of Carter Hawley Hale Stores, Inc. has said, "No one unlocks that creativity—and gives it the tools that touch us—better than Parsons. It's an international treasure."

Parsons' perspective is global. The School has a Paris B.F.A. program and study-abroad option; affiliates in Japan, the Dominican Republic, and Korea; students from seventy countries; and exchange programs in London, Amsterdam, Stockholm, and Sweden. English as a second language courses are integrated with studio curricula, but Parsons' teaching method is primarily American. Students complete and pitch real-world design assignments. Summer programs in New York and Paris give college and high school students an intensive sample of this approach. In all programs, the work of artists and designers from all over the world, past and present, inspires students to find their own voices.

Many Parsons graduates become leaders in their field—some achieving brand-name status like Donna Karan, Isaac Mizrahi, and Albert Hadley. Graduates have completed prestigious design projects such as the Ronald Reagan Presidential Library and Hillary Clinton's inaugural gown. They have produced cable TV's *Nickelodeon* and designed for *Time* magazine and CBS records.

▼ PENNSYLVANIA ACADEMY OF THE FINE ARTS

Philadelphia, Pennsylvania

Independent, Art program established 1805.

Degrees Bachelor of Fine Arts in the areas of painting, sculpture, printmaking. Graduate degrees offered: Master of Fine Arts in the areas of painting, sculpture, printmaking. Cross-registration with University of Pennsylvania, University of the Arts. Program accredited by NASAD.

Enrollment Fall 1997: 282 total; 220 undergraduate, 43 graduate, 19 non-professional degree.

Art Student Profile 45% females, 55% males, 4% minorities, 9% international.

Art Faculty 67 total undergraduate and graduate (full-time and part-time). 50% of full-time faculty have terminal degrees. Graduate students teach a few undergraduate courses. Undergraduate student–faculty ratio: 10:1.

Student Life Student groups/activities include Educational Assistants Program with Museum Education Department.

Financial Aid Program-specific awards for 1997: 9 travel scholarships for juniors and seniors ($5000), 155–200 Institutional Scholarships for those demonstrating need and merit ($3550).

Application Procedures Students admitted directly into the professional program freshman year. Deadline for freshmen and transfers: August 15. Notification date for freshmen and transfers: August 30. Required: high school transcript, college transcript(s) for transfer students, 2 letters of recommendation, portfolio, TOEFL score and affidavit of support for international applicants. Recommended: minimum 2.0 high school GPA, interview. Portfolio reviews held 11 times on campus; the submission of slides may be substituted for portfolios for large works of art or when distance is prohibitive.

Contact Mr. Michael Smith, Director of Admissions, Pennsylvania Academy of the Fine Arts, 118 North Broad Street, Philadelphia, Pennsylvania 19102; 215-972-7625, fax: 215-569-0153.

More About the Academy

Almost everyone in the visual arts world knows the Academy's reputation for educating artists to achieve at the highest possible level. The Academy's objective is to assist individuals who aspire to be artists in reaching their goals. To this end, the Academy offers a two-year M.F.A. Program, a one-year Post-Baccalaureate Program, a four-year Certificate Program, and a coordinated B.F.A. program with the University of Pennsylvania. Each program has majors in painting and drawing, printmaking, and sculpture.

The Academy programs are all studio-based and require each participant to make an unequivocal commitment to the creative process. The instructional program fosters and protects the special empathy that must be struck between an instructor and student for the educational process to be meaningful.

The faculty members' professional lives as artists are considered central at the Academy and teaching schedules are created so as not to interrupt the continuity of the instructors' personal studio time. There are also twelve private studios within the Academy buildings that are reserved for faculty use, which enhances the life of the school community.

Students at the Academy come from all walks of life, all age groups, and widely varying backgrounds. This creates a high-energy, enriching community bound together by a passion for art and the creative act.

Most who seek the advantages of higher education have limited means to access the opportunity. Every student who is accepted at the Academy receives a scholarship covering more than one third of the tuition cost. The Academy is privileged to provide this support from its endowment and development efforts. For this reason, the Academy can still offer one of the lowest tuitions in the country. In addition, it has an extensive financial aid program, including fifty-two named scholarships that provide tuition assistance, and a large roster of merit prizes is awarded each spring.

The certificate program has a unique structure. In the last two years of the program, students are assigned their own private studios. Those years are devoted to the independent development of a personal approach to their work, under the guidance of faculty critics selected by the student. The first two years are characterized by rigor and discipline in the techniques and concepts on which the tradition of Western art has been built. Drawing, painting, clay modeling, and using the life model are dominant activities. Courses in portrait, still life, landscape, abstract sculpture principles, and traditional printmaking media are all required, as is the classical training embodied in anatomy, perspective, and cast drawing from the Academy's famous cast collection.

In recent years, it has become imperative to prepare graduates to manage the realities of the art world. The Academy accomplishes this in many ways. There are continuous juried student exhibitions and other opportunities for students to expose themselves to formal competition. The Visiting Artists Program contributes dimensions to the curriculum not inherent in the program. A series of lectures specifically focusing on the business of art is presented each year. But, perhaps most importantly, there is a strong tradition of mentoring at the Academy; through that system, students learn how to construct a strong, supportive environment for themselves.

The critics and instructors are often the reason students choose to study at the Academy. Students are presented with some of the most distinguished mentors available–public works artist Jody Pinto, sculptor Joel Fisher, and painters Sidney Goodman, Yvonne Jacquette, and Irving Petlin, to name a few.

Because the Academy was the first art school in the country, its alumni list reads like a "Who's Who," from painters Thomas Eakins and Mary Cassatt in the late 1800s to architect Louis Kahn and filmmaker David Lynch in the latter half of this century.

▼ PENNSYLVANIA STATE UNIVERSITY UNIVERSITY PARK CAMPUS

University Park, Pennsylvania

State-related, coed. Small town campus. Total enrollment: 40,538. Art program established 1964.

Degrees Bachelor of Fine Arts in the area of studio art; Bachelor of Science in the area of studio art. Majors and concentrations: ceramic art and design, graphic arts, metals, painting/drawing, photography, printmaking, sculpture. Graduate degrees offered: Master of Fine Arts in the area of studio art. Program accredited by NASAD.

Enrollment Fall 1997: 544 total; 522 undergraduate, 22 graduate.

Art Student Profile 59% females, 41% males, 10% minorities, 20% international.

Art Faculty 34 total undergraduate and graduate (full-time and part-time). 100% of full-time faculty have terminal degrees. Graduate students teach about a quarter undergraduate courses. Undergraduate student–faculty ratio: 17:1.

Student Life Special housing available for art students.

Expenses for 1997–98 Application fee: $40. State resident tuition: $5632 full-time. Nonresident tuition: $12,206 full-time. Mandatory fees: $200 full-time. Full-time tuition and fees vary according to course level, course load, location, and program. College room and board: $4640. College room only: $2060. Room and board charges vary according to board plan.

Pennsylvania State University University Park Campus *(continued)*

Financial Aid Program-specific awards for 1997: 1 Gallu Scholarship for incoming freshmen ($1000).

Application Procedures Students apply for admission into the professional program by sophomore year. Deadline for freshmen: November 30; transfers: March 1. Notification date for freshmen and transfers: continuous. Required: high school transcript, college transcript(s) for transfer students, minimum 2.0 high school GPA, SAT I or ACT test scores.

Contact Ms. Kitty Haupt, Staff Assistant, School of Visual Arts, Pennsylvania State University University Park Campus, 210 Paterson Building, University Park, Pennsylvania 16802; 814-865-0444, fax: 814-865-1158, E-mail address: kjh1@oas.psu.edu.

▼ PITTSBURG STATE UNIVERSITY

Pittsburg, Kansas

State-supported, coed. Small town campus. Total enrollment: 6,355.

Degrees Bachelor of Fine Arts in the area of art; Bachelor of Science Education in the areas of art education, art therapy. Majors and concentrations: art education, art therapy, art/fine arts, ceramic art and design, jewelry and metalsmithing, painting/drawing, photography, printmaking, sculpture. Graduate degrees offered: Master of Arts in the area of art.

Enrollment Fall 1997: 104 total; 86 undergraduate, 18 graduate.

Art Student Profile 60% females, 40% males, 1% minorities, 10% international.

Art Faculty 8 total undergraduate and graduate (full-time and part-time). 100% of full-time faculty have terminal degrees. Graduate students teach a few undergraduate courses. Undergraduate student–faculty ratio: 20:1.

Student Life Student groups/activities include senior and graduate exhibits, judging of art exhibits.

Expenses for 1997–98 Application fee: $15. State resident tuition: $2016 full-time. Nonresident tuition: $6280 full-time. College room and board: $3396.

Financial Aid Program-specific awards for 1997: 4 Bertha Spencer Scholarships for program majors ($100), 1 Laurence A. Wooster Scholarship for program majors ($100), 1 University Arts Association Scholarship for program majors ($100), 1 E. V. and F. B. Baxter Scholarship for program majors ($200).

Application Procedures Students admitted directly into the professional program freshman year. Deadline for freshmen and transfers: August 15. Required: high school transcript, minimum 2.0 high school GPA, GED if applicable. Portfolio reviews held once on campus; the submission of slides may be substituted for portfolios for large works of art or in case of an emergency.

Web Site http://www.pittstate.edu/art/.

Undergraduate Contact Dr. Larrie Moody, Chairperson, Art Department, Pittsburg State University, 1701 South Broadway, Pittsburg, Kansas 66762-7512; 316-235-4302, fax: 316-235-4080, E-mail address: lmoody@pittstate.edu.

▼ PRATT INSTITUTE

Brooklyn, New York

Independent, coed. Urban campus. Total enrollment: 3,640. Art program established 1887.

Degrees Bachelor of Fine Arts in the areas of communications design, fine arts, fashion design, interior design, art and design education, computer graphics, criticism and history of art, media arts; Bachelor of Industrial Design; Bachelor of Architecture. Majors and concentrations: art direction, art education, art history, ceramic art and design, commercial art, computer graphics, fashion design, film and video production, graphic design, illustration, industrial design, interior design, jewelry and metalsmithing, painting/drawing, photography, printmaking, sculpture. Graduate degrees offered: Master of Fine Arts in the areas of fine arts, computer graphics; Master of Science in the areas of communication and package design, interior design, art and design education, art history and criticism, urban design; Master of Industrial Design; Master of Professional Studies in the area of art therapy; Master of Architecture. Program accredited by NASAD, FIDER.

Enrollment Fall 1997: 3,640 total; 2,272 undergraduate, 1,368 graduate.

Art Student Profile 50% females, 50% males, 27% minorities, 27% international.

Art Faculty 627 total undergraduate and graduate (full-time and part-time). 62% of full-time faculty have terminal degrees. Graduate students do not teach undergraduate courses. Undergraduate student–faculty ratio: 13:1.

Student Life Student groups/activities include Industrial Design Society of America, American Society of Interior Designers, American Institute of Graphic Arts. Special housing available for art students.

Expenses for 1997–98 Application fee: $35. Comprehensive fee: $24,304 includes full-time tuition ($16,601), mandatory fees ($550), and college room and board ($7153). College room only: $4199.

Financial Aid Program-specific awards for 1997: Presidential Pratt Merit Awards for freshmen and transfer students ($5500).

Application Procedures Students apply for admission into the professional program by sophomore year. Deadline for freshmen: May 1; transfers: continuous. Required: essay, high school transcript, college transcript(s) for transfer students, minimum 2.0 high school GPA, letter of recommendation, portfolio, SAT I or ACT test scores. Recommended: minimum 3.0 high school GPA, interview. Portfolio reviews held continuously on campus and off campus in various locations on National Portfolio Days; the submission of slides may be substituted for portfolios when distance is prohibitive (beyond a 100-mile radius).

Web Site http://www.pratt.edu.

Undergraduate Contact Ms. Judith Aaron, Vice President for Enrollment, Admissions Department, Pratt Institute, 200 Willoughby Avenue, Brooklyn, New York 11205; 718-636-3669, fax: 718-636-3670, E-mail address: info@pratt.edu.

Graduate Contact Mr. David Jeffrey, Director of Graduate and International Admissions, Admissions Department, Pratt Institute, 200 Willoughby Avenue, Brooklyn, New York 11205; 718-636-3669, fax: 718-636-3670, E-mail address: info@pratt.edu.

Cannon Plaza at Pratt Institute

More About the Institute

Pratt Institute is located on a 25-acre tree-lined campus, with twenty-seven buildings, including landmarked Romanesque- and Renaissance Revival–style structures, in Brooklyn's historic Clinton Hill section. Approximately 75 percent of freshmen live in one of Pratt's six residence halls. On-campus parking is available for residents and commuters. Pratt's proximity to New York City, which offers a vast array of professional, cultural, and recreational opportunities, is a distinct advantage to students. Through Pratt's optional internship program, qualified students are offered challenging on-the-job experience in Manhattan's top galleries and design firms, giving them firsthand work experience as well as credit toward their professional degree. This extension of the classroom into the professional world adds a practical dimension to their education.

Pratt is one of the largest undergraduate and graduate schools for art, design, and architecture in the United States, offering a wide range of cross-disciplinary study options, dual degrees, and major concentrations. Pratt offers undergraduate degrees in art history and criticism, art and design education, communication design (advertising art direction, graphic design, and illustration), fine arts (ceramics, jewelry design, painting/drawing, printmaking, and sculpture), fashion design, industrial design, interior design, and media arts (film/video and photography). Graduate degrees are offered in art history and criticism, art and design education, art therapy, communication design (graphic and packaging design), fine art (painting/drawing, printmaking, photography, sculpture, and new forms), industrial design, and interior design.

Student services include academic advisement, career planning and placement, counseling, and academic skills development. There are more than thirty-five student-run organizations, including fraternities, sororities, professional societies, and clubs. Pratt participates in NCAA and ECAA men's and women's varsity competitions and has intramural sports teams as well.

Pratt Institute has educated professionals for productive careers in artistic and technical fields since its founding in 1887. By employing seasoned professionals as instructors; supporting its innovative programming with an extensive array of art- and design-related studios, workshops, computer labs, and galleries; and providing a rigorous liberal arts core curriculum (mandatory for all students), Pratt Institute can offer students a high-caliber professional as well as an academically well-rounded education. The fact that Pratt has one of the highest student retention rates in the country among schools of its kind confirms the satisfaction students and their families report about the quality of the education they receive here.

Pratt's faculty members, all practicing professionals, bring to the classroom a "real-world" expertise, a strong theoretical base, and the high standards of their professional work. Pratt faculty members enjoy overwhelming success and critical acclaim in their prospective fields. They have garnered prestigious academic and professional awards, including Tiffany, Fulbright, and Guggenheim grants, and have been provided with publishing contracts, travel and research scholarships, and exhibition opportunities. This intimate acquaintance with "real-world" success and high critical standards has a significant impact on Pratt students, leading them to rewarding and lucrative careers in the fields of art and design.

For more than 100 years, the Institute has produced great artists and designers. The following are just a few of Pratt's alumni and their outstanding accomplishments: Bob Giraldi, director of award-winning TV commercials, including the Michael Jackson Pepsi commercials; Morris Cousins, industrial designer and founder of Tupperware; Betsey Johnson, fashion designer; Ellsworth Kelly, painter; Robert Wilson, performance artist; Bruce Hannah, Knoll furniture designer; Paul Rand, graphic designer of IBM, Westinghouse, and NeXT computer logos; and William Boyer, automobile designer of the classic Thunderbird.

Pratt is the only school for art and design on the East Coast that has a traditional college campus containing spacious lawns and tree-lined plazas. Its numerous buildings offer an abundance of light, air, and open space—highly conducive to focused, serious studio work—and house a wealth of art and design support facilities that include exhibition galleries; printmaking, woodworking, and metalworking shops; casting forges; sculpture and ceramic studios; photo printing darkrooms; film studios; projection and editing rooms; animation stands; and computer labs.

The educational goal of the School of Art and Design is to educate whole artists and designers. A Pratt education focuses primarily on two objectives: professional training—emphasizing the learning of skills, techniques, and the methodology necessary for students to perform in the professional community as productive artists or designers—and building students' critical awareness through exposure to a strong liberal arts curriculum. Pratt students are encouraged to enroll in courses outside their major and explore the interconnectedness of art, design, technology, and human need.

At Pratt, future art teachers discover themselves by teaching classes in the Department of Art and Design Education's Saturday Art School. For almost a century, this laboratory school has provided New York City children, adolescents, and, more recently, adults and senior citizens with a high-quality art program.

By educating more than four generations of students to be creative, technically skilled, and adaptable professionals, Pratt has earned an international reputation that attracts more than 3,400 undergraduate and graduate students annually from more than forty-seven states and sixty countries.

(Photo by Sarah VanOuwerkerk)

▼ PURCHASE COLLEGE, STATE UNIVERSITY OF NEW YORK

Purchase, New York

State-supported, coed. Small town campus. Total enrollment: 3,297. Art program established 1972.

Degrees Bachelor of Fine Arts in the areas of painting/drawing, printmaking, photography, design, sculpture, art of the book. Majors and concentrations: art/fine arts, book arts, graphic design, painting/drawing, photography, printmaking, sculpture, studio art. Graduate degrees offered: Master of Fine Arts in the areas of painting/drawing, printmaking, sculpture, art of the book. Cross-registration with Manhattanville College.

Enrollment Fall 1997: 461 total; 446 undergraduate, 15 graduate.

Art Student Profile 53% females, 47% males, 12% minorities, 3% international.

Art Faculty 41 total undergraduate and graduate (full-time and part-time). 100% of full-time faculty have terminal degrees. Graduate students teach a few undergraduate courses. Undergraduate student–faculty ratio: 16:1.

Student Life Student groups/activities include Visual Artists for Visual Arts, Sonodanza (interdisciplinary performing arts/visual arts group), senior show.

Expenses for 1997–98 Application fee: $30. State resident tuition: $3400 full-time. Nonresident tuition: $8300 full-time. Mandatory fees: $479 full-time. College room and board: $5264. College room only: $1930. Room and board charges vary according to board plan and housing facility. Special program-related fees: $25–$250 per course for materials fee for some studio courses.

Financial Aid Program-specific awards for 1997: 2 Dean's Merit Scholarships for those demonstrating high academic and artistic achievement ($200–$500), 1–4 Empire Minority Scholarships for minority students from New York State ($1250), 5–10 Reed Scholarships for those demonstrating high academic and artistic achievement ($500–$750), 6 John Bendheim Scholarships for artistically talented students ($500–$1000).

Application Procedures Students admitted directly into the professional program freshman year. Deadline for freshmen and transfers: continuous. Notification date for freshmen and transfers: continuous. Required: essay, high school transcript, college transcript(s) for transfer students, minimum 2.0 high school GPA, 2 letters of recommendation, slide portfolio or personal review of original artwork, minimum TOEFL score of 550 for international applicants. Recommended: minimum 3.0 high school GPA, interview, SAT I or ACT test scores. Portfolio reviews held twice on campus; the submission of slides may be substituted for portfolios whenever needed.

Undergraduate Contact Ms. Belinda Torres, Counselor, Admissions Department, Purchase College, State University of New York, 735 Anderson Hill Road, Purchase, New York 10577-1400; 914-251-6300, fax: 914-251-6314.

Graduate Contact Mr. Robert Berlind, Coordinator, Graduate Program, Purchase College, State University of New York, 735 Anderson Hill Road, Purchase, New York 10577-1400; 914-251-6300, fax: 914-251-6314.

More About the College

Purchase College considers itself an experiment in the history of postsecondary education. Professional and conservatory programs in Fine and Performing Arts coexist with a "Public Ivy" Liberal Arts College. Philosophically as well as pragmatically, the purpose of the Art and Design program is to provide an educational atmosphere in which students and artists work together, engage in critical dialogue, experiment, test their ideas, and learn. The curriculum is based on the belief that the artist and designer who will be practicing into the twenty-first century must have both the traditional tools and emerging skills of the painter, photographer, sculptor, designer, and printmaker; an understanding of contemporary society and technology; and the educational opportunity to explore their own talents through the development of skills, the training of the eye, and the cultivation of the mind. The visual arts curriculum attempts, therefore, to remain responsive to the established traditions and categories of art and to the expanding new concepts, materials, and technologies of the contemporary world of art and design.

A core program, consisting of drawing, 2-D composition, 3-D composition, and art history, provides a common basis for students to experience the satisfaction of making, the difficulty of articulating, a deepening through shaping, awareness of community through sharing, pleasure in looking, and insight from seeing. Each student, building on the core requirements, investigates introductory courses in different visual arts disciplines (graphic design, painting/drawing, photography, printmaking, and sculpture) and either follows an established program to concentrate in one area of study or develops an individual program to pursue several media with an emphasis on synthesis and juxtaposition. Each student works closely with an assigned faculty adviser to establish a program of study that allows the student to develop particular areas of interest.

Purchase also requires that students complete a senior project. In many ways similar to a graduate thesis, the senior project is undertaken as the culminating experience of students graduating from Purchase. In the visual arts, students create a body of work of their choosing, sponsored by a faculty mentor. The work is documented and accompanied by a written thesis statement. The senior project allows for in-depth exploration of a particular content area and provides a critical focus for a student to leave their mark at Purchase. Senior projects are kept on file in the library as a reference resource for the entire campus community.

Having just celebrated its 25th anniversary, Purchase already counts major filmmakers, musicians, actors, artists, and writers among its alumni. The interaction of artists in conservatory programs and scholars in the Liberal Arts and Sciences makes for a cross-fertilization that is mutually beneficial. This then is the premise and promise of Purchase College, and the culture of the campus reflects it. On any given day one can attend a lecture on medieval literature, a dance rehearsal, a gallery opening, and more. This environment is stimulating and a springboard for the individual imagination.

▼ QUEEN'S UNIVERSITY AT KINGSTON

Kingston, ON, Canada

Province-supported, coed. Urban campus. Total enrollment: 15,973.

Degrees Bachelor of Fine Arts in the area of studio art with an art history component. Majors and concentrations: painting/drawing, printmaking, sculpture.

Enrollment Fall 1997: 120 undergraduate.

Art Faculty 6 total (full-time and part-time). 100% of full-time faculty have terminal degrees. Graduate students do not teach undergraduate courses. Undergraduate student–faculty ratio: 20:1.

Expenses for 1997–98 Application fee: $75 Canadian dollars. Tuition, fee, and room and board charges are reported in Canadian dollars. Canadian resident tuition: $3228 full-time. Mandatory fees: $550 full-time. Full-time tuition and fees vary according to program. College room and board: $5586. College room only: $3080. Room and board charges vary according to board plan and housing facility. International student tuition: $9717 full-time. Special program-related fees: $300 per trip for gallery tour to New York City.

Financial Aid Program-specific awards for 1997: 1 Robert Shotton Memorial Entrance Scholarship for freshmen art students demonstrating talent ($500).

Application Procedures Students admitted directly into the professional program freshman year. Deadline for freshmen: May 13; transfers: June 1. Required: high school transcript, college transcript(s) for transfer students, portfolio. Recommended: interview. Portfolio reviews held 6 times on campus; the submission of slides may be substituted for portfolios when distance is prohibitive.

Undergraduate Contact Art Department, Queen's University at Kingston, Ontario Hall, Kingston, ON K7L 3N6, Canada; 613-545-6166.

▼ QUINCY UNIVERSITY

Quincy, Illinois

Independent-Roman Catholic, coed. Small town campus. Total enrollment: 1,149.

Degrees Bachelor of Fine Arts in the area of art.

Enrollment Fall 1997: 30 total; all undergraduate.

Art Student Profile 50% females, 50% males, 1% minorities, 1% international.

Art Faculty 5 total (full-time and part-time). 60% of full-time faculty have terminal degrees. Graduate students do not teach undergraduate courses. Undergraduate student–faculty ratio: 10:1.

Student Life Student groups/activities include Student Show, Senior Show.

Expenses for 1997–98 Application fee: $0. Comprehensive fee: $16,830 includes full-time tuition ($12,080), mandatory fees ($330), and college room and board ($4420). College room only: $1800. Special program-related fees: $10–$25 per course for lab fees.

Financial Aid Program-specific awards for 1997: 1 de Mero Scholarship for program majors ($1025), 1 Helmer Fine Arts Scholarship for program majors ($300), 1 Mejer Visual Arts Scholarship for program majors ($100), 1 Tom Brown Art Scholarship for program majors ($500).

Application Procedures Students admitted directly into the professional program freshman year. Deadline for freshmen and transfers: continuous. Required: high school transcript, minimum 2.0 high school GPA, portfolio, SAT I or ACT test scores. Recommended: minimum 3.0 high school GPA, 2 letters of recommendation, interview. Portfolio reviews held

continuously on campus; the submission of slides may be substituted for portfolios if a campus visit is impossible, with permission of the chair.

Web Site http://www.quincy.edu.

Undergraduate Contact Mr. Jeff Van Kamp, Director of Admissions, Quincy University, 1800 College Avenue, Quincy, Illinois 62301-2699; 217-228-5210, fax: 217-228-5479, E-mail address: admissions@quincy.edu.

▼ RADFORD UNIVERSITY

Radford, Virginia

State-supported, coed. Small town campus. Total enrollment: 8,534.

Degrees Bachelor of Fine Arts in the area of art. Majors and concentrations: animation, art/fine arts, ceramics, drawing, fibers, graphic design, jewelry and metalsmithing, new genre, painting, photography, printmaking, sculpture, studio art, three-dimensional studies, two-dimensional studies, video art, watercolors. Graduate degrees offered: Master of Fine Arts in the area of art; Master of Science in the area of art education.

Enrollment Fall 1997: 180 undergraduate, 20 graduate.

Art Student Profile 55% females, 45% males, 5% minorities, 10% international.

Art Faculty 14 total undergraduate and graduate (full-time). 100% of full-time faculty have terminal degrees. Graduate students teach a few undergraduate courses. Undergraduate student–faculty ratio: 15:1.

Student Life Student groups/activities include Student Art Guild, Graduate Art Student Association. Special housing available for art students.

Expenses for 1997–98 Application fee: $20. State resident tuition: $2016 full-time. Nonresident tuition: $6788 full-time. Mandatory fees: $1164 full-time. College room and board: $4416. College room only: $2448. Room and board charges vary according to board plan and housing facility.

Financial Aid Program-specific awards for 1997: 5 Arts Society Scholarships for program students ($600–$1100), 2 De la Burdé Scholarships for program students ($600–$1100).

Application Procedures Students apply for admission into the professional program by freshman, sophomore year. Deadline for freshmen: April 1; transfers: June 1. Notification date for freshmen and transfers: continuous. Required: essay, high school transcript, college transcript(s) for transfer students, minimum 2.0 high school GPA, portfolio, SAT I or ACT test scores, minimum 2.0 college GPA for transfer students. Portfolio reviews held once on campus.

Web Site http://www.runet.edu/~art-web/.

Contact Mr. Arthur F. Jones, Chairperson, Art Department, Radford University, Box 6965, Radford, Virginia 24142; 540-831-5475, fax: 540-831-6313, E-mail address: ajones@runet.edu.

▼ RHODE ISLAND COLLEGE

Providence, Rhode Island

State-supported, coed. Suburban campus. Total enrollment: 8,622.

Degrees Bachelor of Fine Arts in the area of studio art; Bachelor of Science in the area of art education; Bachelor of Arts in the areas of studio art, art history. Majors and concentrations: art education, ceramics, fibers, graphic

Rhode Island College *(continued)*

design, jewelry and metalsmithing, painting, photography, printmaking, sculpture. Graduate degrees offered: Master of Arts in Teaching in the area of art education. Program accredited by NASAD.

Enrollment Fall 1997: 341 undergraduate, 50 graduate.

Art Student Profile 57% females, 43% males, 1% minorities, 2% international.

Art Faculty 41 total undergraduate and graduate (full-time and part-time). 100% of full-time faculty have terminal degrees. Graduate students do not teach undergraduate courses.

Student Life Student groups/activities include Art Club, Artist Cooperative, National Art Education Association-Student Chapter.

Expenses for 1997–98 Application fee: $25. State resident tuition: $2760 full-time. Nonresident tuition: $7152 full-time. Mandatory fees: $316 full-time. Full-time tuition and fees vary according to reciprocity agreements. College room and board: $5200. College room only: $2600. Room and board charges vary according to board plan and housing facility. Special program-related fees: $10 per studio course for supplies.

Financial Aid Program-specific awards for 1997: 15 Special Talent Awards for art majors ($600).

Application Procedures Students apply for admission into the professional program by sophomore year. Deadline for freshmen and transfers: April 1. Required: essay, high school transcript, college transcript(s) for transfer students, SAT I or ACT test scores, portfolio for transfer applicants and for scholarship consideration. Recommended: interview. Portfolio reviews held twice on campus; the submission of slides may be substituted for portfolios for large works of art or when distance is prohibitive.

Undergraduate Contact Stephen Fisher, Chairperson, Art Department, Rhode Island College, 600 Mount Pleasant Avenue, Providence, Rhode Island 02908; 401-456-9687, fax: 401-456-8379.

Graduate Contact Dr. Cheryl Williams, Coordinator, Art Education Department, Rhode Island College, 600 Mt. Pleasant Avenue, Providence, Rhode Island 02908; 401-456-8054, fax: 401-456-8379.

▼ RHODE ISLAND SCHOOL OF DESIGN

Providence, Rhode Island

Independent, coed. Urban campus. Total enrollment: 2,001. Art program established 1877.

Degrees Bachelor of Fine Arts in the areas of painting, sculpture, glass, jewelry/metals, textiles, apparel design, graphic design, industrial design, architecture, interior architecture, landscape architecture, printmaking, ceramics, illustration, photography, furniture design, film/animation/video. Graduate degrees offered: Master of Fine Arts in the areas of ceramics, furniture design, graphic design, glass, jewelry and metals, painting/printmaking, photography, sculpture, textiles; Master of Industrial Design; Master of Architecture; Master of Interior Architecture; Master of Landscape Architecture. Cross-registration with Brown University. Program accredited by NASAD, ASLA, NAAB.

Enrollment Fall 1997: 2,001 total; 1,786 undergraduate, 215 graduate.

Art Student Profile 60% females, 40% males, 12% minorities, 16% international.

Art Faculty 352 total undergraduate and graduate (full-time and part-time). 71% of full-time faculty have terminal degrees. Graduate students do not teach undergraduate courses. Undergraduate student–faculty ratio: 11:1.

Student Life Student groups/activities include Mixed Media Club, Ceramics Club, Industrial Design Club. Special housing available for art students.

Expenses for 1997–98 Application fee: $35. Comprehensive fee: $26,060 includes full-time tuition ($19,340), mandatory fees ($330), and college room and board ($6390). College room only: $3390. Room and board charges vary according to board plan. Special program-related fees: $10–$100 per course for lab fees for cetain courses.

Financial Aid Program-specific awards for 1997: 5–7 Trustees Scholarships for above-average students with exceptional artistic ability ($2000–$6000), 600 RISD Scholarships for those demonstrating financial need ($500–$20,000).

Application Procedures Students admitted directly into the professional program freshman year. Deadline for freshmen: February 15; transfers: March 31. Notification date for freshmen: April 1; transfers: May 1. Required: essay, high school transcript, college transcript(s) for transfer students, SAT I or ACT test scores, 3 original drawings (optional for architecture applicants), slides, prints or digital reproductions of portfolio for incoming freshmen and transfer students; except for architecture and industrial design applicants. Recommended: minimum 3.0 high school GPA, letter of recommendation, portfolio for architecture and industrial design applicants.

Contact Admissions Office, Rhode Island School of Design, 2 College Street, Providence, Rhode Island 02903; 401-454-6300, fax: 401-454-6309, E-mail address: admissions@risd.edu.

More About the School

Facilities Forty buildings with more than 500,000 square feet of space, including specialized studio spaces and equipment; access to studio spaces, with upperclass students often having a private studio space; thirteen residence halls offering a variety of living environments; Museum of Art with more than 75,000 objects frequently used for study purposes by faculty members and students; library with more than 90,000 volumes, including artist's and rare books, and an image research collection of 470,000 clippings and photographs and 145,000 slides; Nature Lab with 70,000 objects available for study and research; more than 300 computer systems available in departmental and specialized labs.

Faculty and Resident Artists RISD has 300 faculty members, 120 of them full-time and readily available to students on campus. More than 200 artists and guest critics visit the campus on average each year. Among recent visitors were Sam Gilliam, painter; Bread and Puppet Theater; Stephen J. Gould, author; Ursula Von Rydingsvard, sculptor; Sam Maloof, furniture designer; Holly Hughes, performance artist; and Frank Gehry, architect.

Student Exhibit Opportunities Two college-wide galleries and eight departmental exhibition spaces on campus, with an average of 125 shows staged each year.

Special Programs The European Honors Program allows students to study in Rome for their junior or senior year. Study-abroad exchange agreements are in place with twenty-five other art and design colleges around the world. Wintersession term provides unique study opportunities each year, including travel-abroad courses (recently to Italy,

are Phi Delta Theta International Fraternity, Sigma Sigma Sigma Sorority, Campus Activities Board, American Society of Interior Designers, Residence Hall Council, Theatre Production Guild, Outdoor Recreation, and an International Student Association.

Additionally, Ringling has a number of traditions involving the entire campus community. Annual programs include Parents' Weekend, the Goombay Festival (a Bahamian-style Mardi Gras), and Founder's Day festivities. These are supplemented by beach parties, holiday parties, and the senior graduation party.

On-campus housing is available for approximately 364 students in air-conditioned residence halls and apartments. In addition to the convenience of campus living, residents benefit from a variety of programs, residence hall support staff, and campus food service.

A weeklong orientation program is conducted prior to the start of the fall semester. The week includes opportunities to meet other students, meetings with department heads and other faculty, presentations on academic expectations, an introduction to student organizations, a parents' orientation, and a variety of social activities.

Ringling School of Art and Design welcomes applications from students with a serious commitment to the visual arts. Admission is based on a review of the student's portfolio, academic record, essay, and teacher recommendations. All applicants are reviewed individually, with special consideration given to creative ability and potential for success in college-level studies.

▼ RIVIER COLLEGE

Nashua, New Hampshire

Independent-Roman Catholic, coed. Suburban campus. Total enrollment: 2,886. Art program established 1933.

Degrees Bachelor of Fine Arts in the areas of studio art, design; Bachelor of Arts in the areas of art education, studio art. Majors and concentrations: digital imaging, graphic design, illustration, painting/drawing. Cross-registration with New Hampshire Consortium of Universities and Colleges.

Enrollment Fall 1997: 53 total; 35 undergraduate, 18 non-professional degree.

Art Student Profile 85% females, 15% males, 5% minorities.

Art Faculty 14 total (full-time and part-time). 100% of full-time faculty have terminal degrees. Graduate students do not teach undergraduate courses.

Student Life Student groups/activities include Rivier Fine Arts Society, The Rivier Theatre Company, Sweet Simplicity.

Expenses for 1998–99 Application fee: $25. Comprehensive fee: $18,715 includes full-time tuition ($12,990), mandatory fees ($200), and college room and board ($5525). College room only: $3014. Special program-related fees: $30 per course for art history field trips, $50 per course for sculpture studio materials, $75 per course for design course materials (2-D design), $70 per course for three-dimensional design and course materials, $20–$60 per course for lab fees for computer-oriented courses, $50 per course for Color I and II course fees.

Application Procedures Students admitted directly into the professional program freshman year. Deadline for freshmen and transfers: continuous. Required: essay, high school transcript, college transcript(s) for transfer students, letter of recommendation, portfolio, SAT I or ACT test scores, course catalog descriptions from other colleges attended for transfer

students, minimum TOEFL score of 500 for international students, minimum 2.3 high school GPA. Recommended: interview. Portfolio reviews held by appointment on campus; the submission of slides may be substituted for portfolios whenever needed.

Web Site http://www.rivier.edu.

Undergraduate Contact Lynn Petrillo, Director of Admissions, Rivier College, 420 Main Street, Nashua, New Hampshire 03060-5086; 603-888-1311 ext. 8560, fax: 603-888-6447, E-mail address: rivadmit@rivier.edu.

Rivier College

More About the College

Program Facilities Spacious, well-lit studios that include a Digital Imaging Studio with animation and multimedia capabilities. Excellent library and interlibrary resources for studies in aesthetics, art history, fine and applied arts, graphic design, and art education. Internet research and support services. Visual arts slide library of more than 20,000 items representing a wide range of media, periods, and cultures. A professional Art Gallery hosts regional, national, and international exhibitions.

Faculty and Alumni Studio faculty members include studio artists, designers, illustrators, photographers, digital artists, and art education specialists with advanced degrees. They contribute to Rivier's growing reputation through their continuing achievements, which include honors and awards for their work. Rivier's alumni range impressively from art educators and therapists to graphic designers, art directors, illustrators, television and digital imaging artists, and various related professionals such as art and museum administrators.

Student Exhibition Opportunities Biennial juried art student exhibition, annual senior art students' exhibition, other juried and/or invitational shows, collaboration with professional artists and designers, murals for the college and community organizations, and a wide variety of competitions.

Special Programs Credit-bearing opportunities include the art invitational honors program, design internships serving both on-campus and off-campus clients (especially nonprofit), and student teaching in art at both elementary and secondary levels. Extracurricular activities include the Adopt-a-School Program, in which student volunteers direct collaborative art projects and field trips for elementary school students. Art students may also participate in the New Hampshire Creative Club (professional artists, designers, photographers), New

Rivier College (*continued*)

Hampshire Art Association (professional artists), New Hampshire Art Educators Association, and the Nashua Artists Association. All programs include a service-learning component in one of the eight semesters. Visiting artists provide demonstrations and workshops throughout the year.

▼

Rivier College is a Catholic liberal arts institution founded in 1933 by the Sisters of the Presentation of Mary. High standards of academic excellence and professional preparation are blended in the curriculum to ensure that students receive a comprehensive education with real-world applicability. In addition, a commitment to the values of service-learning as well as to peace and social justice is woven into the curriculum, encouraging habits of service and social responsibility in contemporary society. These elements are strong in Rivier's visual arts programs, where students work closely with the artist faculty in small classes; benefit from visits by guest artists for demonstrations, talks, and critiques; and experience the vibrant artistic climate of southern New Hampshire, the entire greater Boston region, and New York City. Opportunities for credit-bearing study abroad in European centers such as London and Paris are available through the Art Department. On campus, a wide range of lectures, recitals, concerts, exhibits, seminars, and other events sponsored by the college each year offers additional enrichment. Opportunity for learning is limited only by the students' degree of enthusiasm.

Students are trained in the arts and they are also prepared to face an ever-changing and complex society. Accompanying the studio courses are classes in the humanities and sciences. This combination enables students to develop into especially well-rounded, artistically competent individuals. The intellectual, technological, and social aspects of Rivier enable students to gain a wealth of experiences that enhances the students' preparation for careers in art and design. Motivated students can go beyond the liberal arts requirements to combine work in art with electives such as creative writing, communications, psychology, business, and computer science. This academic enrichment helps create unique opportunities in the job market.

For academic support and reinforcement, students may draw on many resources. The Writing and Learning Center offers tutorial assistance in writing and core curriculum topics to help students make the most of their college experience. The Honors Program offers students academic challenges to enhance and enrich their studies. Résumé writing, interviewing skills, job search strategies, and database information on available positions are among the resources available through the Career Development and Placement Office. Recreational activities include intramural sports, individual fitness training, and varsity athletics for men and women (NCAA Division III, ECAC, GNAC, men's and women's volleyball, basketball, soccer, cross country, and women's softball). Special interest groups invite participation in student government, service, social, and professional organizations. Available individual and group counseling assists students working through personal issues. Campus Ministry offers interfaith programs and many opportunities for community outreach and service.

Rivier provides housing in its comfortable and home-like residence halls, complemented by dining and snack bar facilities in the College Center. Classrooms, studios, laboratories, and library facilities are fully equipped for academic inquiry and research. The campus itself consists of forty-one buildings on 62 landscaped acres in a residential section of Nashua, served by city bus transportation; many shopping, dining, cultural, and recreational facilities are only 5 or 10 minutes away. Boston, the seacoast, and the White Mountains recreational areas are all about an hour away.

▼ ROCHESTER INSTITUTE OF TECHNOLOGY
Rochester, New York

Independent, coed. Suburban campus. Total enrollment: 12,352. Art program established 1885.

Degrees Bachelor of Fine Arts in the areas of crafts, fine arts studio, illustration, medical illustration, graphic design, industrial design, interior design. Majors and concentrations: ceramics, furniture design, glass, graphic design, illustration, industrial design, interior design, jewelry and metalsmithing, medical illustration, studio art, woodworking design. Graduate degrees offered: Master of Fine Arts in the areas of ceramics/sculpture, metalcrafts and jewelry, woodworking and furniture design, glass, fine arts studio (sculpture, painting, new forms, printmaking), medical illustration, computer graphics design, graphic design, industrial design, interior design; Master of Science in Teaching in the areas of art education, studio (ceramics and ceramic sculpture, glass, metalcrafts and jewelry, woodworking and furniture design, graphic design, interior design, fine art (painting and printmaking), industrial design. Program accredited by NASAD, FIDER.

Enrollment Fall 1997: 1,070 total; 884 undergraduate, 186 graduate.

Art Student Profile 48% females, 52% males.

Art Faculty 111 total undergraduate and graduate (full-time and part-time). 90% of full-time faculty have terminal degrees. Graduate students teach a few undergraduate courses. Undergraduate student–faculty ratio: 7:1.

Student Life Special housing available for art students.

Expenses for 1997–98 Application fee: $40. Comprehensive fee: $22,776 includes full-time tuition ($16,083), mandatory fees ($276), and college room and board ($6417). College room only: $3486. Full-time tuition and fees vary according to course load and program. Room and board charges vary according to board plan and housing facility. Special program-related fees: $30–$60 per course for lab fees.

Financial Aid Program-specific awards for 1997: departmental awards for program majors.

Application Procedures Students admitted directly into the professional program freshman year. Deadline for freshmen and transfers: continuous. Notification date for freshmen and transfers: continuous. Required: high school transcript, portfolio, SAT I or ACT test scores. Portfolio reviews held as needed on campus and off campus; the submission of slides may be substituted for portfolios (slides preferred).

Web Site http://www.rit.edu/~651www/ART/Art.html.

Undergraduate Contact School of Art/School of Design/ School for American Crafts, Rochester Institute of Technology, 73 Lomb Memorial Drive, Rochester, New York 14623-5603; 716-475-2646, fax: 716-475-6447.

Graduate Contact School of Art/School of Design/ School for American Crafts, Rochester Institute of Technology, 73 Lamb Memorial Drive, Rochester, New York 14623-5603; 716-475-2646, fax: 716-475-6447.

▼ ROCKY MOUNTAIN COLLEGE OF ART & DESIGN

Denver, Colorado

Proprietary, coed. Urban campus. Art program established 1963.

Degrees Bachelor of Fine Arts in the areas of graphic design, illustration, interior design, painting and drawing, sculpture and drawing. Majors and concentrations: graphic design, illustration, interior design, painting/drawing, sculpture. Program accredited by ACCSCT.

Enrollment Fall 1997: 425 total; 375 undergraduate, 50 non-professional degree.

Art Student Profile 52% females, 48% males, 10% minorities, 3% international.

Art Faculty 53 total (full-time and part-time). 87% of full-time faculty have terminal degrees. Graduate students do not teach undergraduate courses. Undergraduate student–faculty ratio: 20:1.

Student Life Student groups/activities include American Society of Interior Designers, Society for Environmental Graphic Designers, Art Directors Club of Denver.

Expenses for 1997–98 Application fee: $50. Tuition: $9697 full-time. Mandatory fees: $30 full-time. Special program-related fees: $500 per trimester for supplies, $20–$80 per trimester for lab fees.

Financial Aid Program-specific awards available.

Application Procedures Students admitted directly into the professional program freshman year. Deadline for freshmen and transfers: continuous. Notification date for freshmen and transfers: continuous. Required: essay, high school transcript, college transcript(s) for transfer students, minimum 2.0 high school GPA, letter of recommendation, interview, portfolio, SAT I or ACT test scores. Portfolio reviews held continuously on campus; the submission of slides may be substituted for portfolios whenever needed.

Web Site http://www.rmcad.edu.

Undergraduate Contact Mr. Rex Whisman, Executive Director for Enrollment and Public Affairs, Admissions Office, Rocky Mountain College of Art & Design, 6875 East Evans Avenue, Denver, Colorado 80224; 800-888-2787, fax: 303-759-4970.

▼ ROLAND DILLE CENTER FOR THE ARTS

See Moorhead State University

▼ ROSEMONT COLLEGE

Rosemont, Pennsylvania

Independent-Roman Catholic, women only. Suburban campus. Total enrollment: 947.

Degrees Bachelor of Fine Arts in the areas of fine arts, graphic design. Cross-registration with Cabrini College, Villanova University, Eastern College.

Enrollment Fall 1997: 20 undergraduate.

Art Faculty 10 total (full-time and part-time). 100% of full-time faculty have terminal degrees. Graduate students do not teach undergraduate courses.

Student Life Student groups/activities include Studio Art Club.

Expenses for 1997–98 Application fee: $35. Comprehensive fee: $19,840 includes full-time tuition ($12,960), mandatory

fees ($380), and college room and board ($6500). Special program-related fees: $50 per course for supply fees for sculpture, graphics, printmaking and photography courses.

Financial Aid Program-specific awards for 1997: 1 Revere Scholarship for high school senior art students ($13,480).

Application Procedures Students apply for admission into the professional program by sophomore year. Deadline for freshmen and transfers: continuous. Required: essay, high school transcript, college transcript(s) for transfer students, letter of recommendation, interview, portfolio. Portfolio reviews held twice on campus; the submission of slides may be substituted for portfolios when distance is prohibitive.

Undergraduate Contact Amy Orr, Department Chair, Arts Division, Rosemont College, 1400 Montgomery Avenue, Rosemont, Pennsylvania 19010-1699; 610-527-0200 ext. 2311, fax: 610-527-0341, E-mail address: a.orr@rosemont.edu.

▼ RUTGERS, THE STATE UNIVERSITY OF NEW JERSEY

See Mason Gross School of the Arts

▼ ST. CLOUD STATE UNIVERSITY

St. Cloud, Minnesota

State-supported, coed. Suburban campus. Total enrollment: 13,946.

Degrees Bachelor of Fine Arts in the areas of studio art, graphic design. Majors and concentrations: ceramics, drawing, painting, photography, printmaking, sculpture. Program accredited by NASAD.

Enrollment Fall 1997: 370 total; 340 undergraduate, 30 non-professional degree.

Art Student Profile 60% females, 40% males, 10% minorities, 10% international.

Art Faculty 15 total (full-time and part-time). 80% of full-time faculty have terminal degrees. Graduate students teach a few undergraduate courses. Undergraduate student–faculty ratio: 20:1.

Student Life Student groups/activities include Art Student Union, Graphic Design Association. Special housing available for art students.

Expenses for 1997–98 Application fee: $20. State resident tuition: $2582 full-time. Nonresident tuition: $5606 full-time. Mandatory fees: $500 full-time. Full-time tuition and fees vary according to course load, location, and reciprocity agreements. College room and board: $3066. Room and board charges vary according to board plan.

Financial Aid Program-specific awards for 1997: 2–3 Bill Ellingson Awards for program majors ($500), 4 May Bowle Awards for program majors ($500), 1 Reva Reider Scholarship for new freshmen ($4000).

Application Procedures Students apply for admission into the professional program by sophomore year. Deadline for freshmen and transfers: August 15. Required: high school transcript, college transcript(s) for transfer students, minimum 2.0 high school GPA, ACT test score only, portfolio for scholarship consideration. Portfolio reviews held twice on campus and off campus in Minneapolis, MN; the submission of slides may be substituted for portfolios whenever needed.

Web Site http://www.stcloudstate.edu/~art.

St. Cloud State University (continued)

Undergraduate Contact Ms. Virginia Bradley, Chairperson, Art Department, St. Cloud State University, Kiehle Visual Arts Building, St. Cloud, Minnesota 56301; 320-255-4283, fax: 320-255-2232.

▼ ST. JOHN'S UNIVERSITY

Jamaica, New York

Independent, coed. Urban campus. Total enrollment: 18,523.

Degrees Bachelor of Fine Arts in the areas of fine arts, graphic design, photography, illustration. Mandatory cross-registration with International Center of Photography.

Enrollment Fall 1997: 94 total; all undergraduate.

Art Student Profile 40% females, 60% males, 30% minorities, 8% international.

Art Faculty 15 total (full-time and part-time). 100% of full-time faculty have terminal degrees. Graduate students do not teach undergraduate courses.

Student Life Student groups/activities include New Vision Art Society, Art Exhibits in University Gallery, Senior Citizens Art Program.

Expenses for 1997–98 Application fee: $30. Tuition: $11,800 full-time. Mandatory fees: $430 full-time. Full-time tuition and fees vary according to program and student level. Special program-related fees: $30 per course per semester for studio lab fee.

Financial Aid Program-specific awards for 1997: 2 Fine Arts Scholarships for incoming freshmen ($11,000), 3 Visual Arts Awards for incoming freshmen ($1000).

Application Procedures Students admitted directly into the professional program freshman year. Deadline for freshmen and transfers: continuous. Required: high school transcript, college transcript(s) for transfer students, 2 letters of recommendation, portfolio, SAT I or ACT test scores, minimum 3.0 high school GPA or minimum combined 1100 SAT I score. Recommended: interview. Portfolio reviews held continuously by appointment on campus; the submission of slides may be substituted for portfolios for international students and U.S. students from a great distance.

Web Site http://www.stjohns.edu/.

Undergraduate Contact Mr. Stephen Albano, Acting Director, Admissions, St. John's University, 8000 Utopia Parkway, Jamaica, New York 11439; 718-990-6240, fax: 718-990-1677, E-mail address: albanos@stjohns.edu.

▼ SAINT MARY'S COLLEGE

Notre Dame, Indiana

Independent-Roman Catholic, women only. Suburban campus. Total enrollment: 1,347.

Degrees Bachelor of Arts/Bachelor of Fine Arts in the areas of fine arts (painting, drawing, photography, printmaking, sculpture, fiber, ceramics). Majors and concentrations: art education, art/fine arts, ceramic art and design, painting/drawing, photography, printmaking, sculpture, textile arts. Cross-registration with University of Notre Dame, Indiana Technical College, Indiana University South Bend, Goshen College, Bethel College. Program accredited by NASAD.

Enrollment Fall 1997: 45 undergraduate.

Art Student Profile 100% females, 10% minorities, 10% international.

Art Faculty 8 total (full-time and part-time). 100% of full-time faculty have terminal degrees. Graduate students do not teach undergraduate courses. Undergraduate student–faculty ratio: 10:1.

Student Life Student groups/activities include Art Club, National Association of Schools of Art and Design.

Expenses for 1997–98 Application fee: $30. Comprehensive fee: $20,849 includes full-time tuition ($14,738), mandatory fees ($914), and college room and board ($5197). Special program-related fees: $35–$45 per semester for studio supplies.

Financial Aid Program-specific awards for 1997: art talent awards for art majors demonstrating need ($500), 1 Theresa McLaughlin Award for freshmen art majors demonstrating need ($1000).

Application Procedures Students admitted directly into the professional program freshman year. Deadline for freshmen: March 1; transfers: April 15. Notification date for freshmen and transfers: continuous. Required: essay, high school transcript, minimum 3.0 high school GPA, letter of recommendation, SAT I or ACT test scores. Recommended: interview, portfolio. Portfolio reviews held twice on campus; the submission of slides may be substituted for portfolios for large works of art and three-dimensional pieces.

Web Site http://www.saintmarys.edu.

Undergraduate Contact Admissions Office, Saint Mary's College, Notre Dame, Indiana 46556; 219-284-4587, fax: 219-284-4716.

▼ SALISBURY STATE UNIVERSITY

Salisbury, Maryland

State-supported, coed. Small town campus. Total enrollment: 6,022.

Degrees Bachelor of Fine Arts in the area of art; Bachelor of Science in the area of art. Majors and concentrations: art/fine arts, three-dimensional studies, two-dimensional studies, visual communication. Cross-registration with University of Maryland System, The Art Institute of Philadelphia, Art Institute of Atlanta.

Enrollment Fall 1997: 221 total; 120 undergraduate, 101 non-professional degree.

Art Faculty 18 total (full-time and part-time). 100% of full-time faculty have terminal degrees. Graduate students do not teach undergraduate courses.

Student Life Student groups/activities include Art Club, Study Abroad programs, Calumet. Special housing available for art students.

Expenses for 1997–98 Application fee: $30. State resident tuition: $2746 full-time. Nonresident tuition: $6498 full-time. Mandatory fees: $1096 full-time. Full-time tuition and fees vary according to course level and course load. College room and board: $5140. Room and board charges vary according to board plan and housing facility. Special program-related fees: $35 per year for supplies for studio courses.

Financial Aid Program-specific awards for 1997: 3 art scholarships for program majors ($500), 2–4 Art Department Meritorious Awards for program students ($50), 1 Photography Award for photography majors ($500), 1 Student Assistantship Award for program majors ($250).

Application Procedures Deadline for freshmen: February 1; transfers: March 1. Required: high school transcript, college transcript(s) for transfer students, minimum 2.0 high school

GPA, SAT I or ACT test scores, portfolio for scholarship consideration. Recommended: essay. Portfolio reviews held once and as needed on campus; the submission of slides may be substituted for portfolios when distance is prohibitive.

Undergraduate Contact Admissions Department, Salisbury State University, 1101 Camden Avenue, Salisbury, Maryland 21801; 410-543-6000, fax: 410-546-6016.

▼ SAM HOUSTON STATE UNIVERSITY

Huntsville, Texas

State-supported, coed. Small town campus. Total enrollment: 12,712. Art program established 1940.

Degrees Bachelor of Fine Arts in the areas of studio arts, advertising/graphic design. Graduate degrees offered: Master of Fine Arts in the areas of drawing, painting, printmaking, sculpture, ceramics.

Enrollment Fall 1997: 118 total; 109 undergraduate, 5 graduate, 4 non-professional degree.

Art Student Profile 65% females, 35% males, 5% minorities, 2% international.

Art Faculty 13 total undergraduate and graduate (full-time and part-time). 90% of full-time faculty have terminal degrees. Graduate students teach a few undergraduate courses. Undergraduate student–faculty ratio: 20:1.

Expenses for 1997–98 Application fee: $15. State resident tuition: $816 full-time. Nonresident tuition: $5952 full-time. Mandatory fees: $770 full-time. College room and board: $3290. College room only: $1710. Room and board charges vary according to board plan and housing facility.

Financial Aid Program-specific awards for 1997: 1 Clem Otis Memorial Scholarship for enrolled students ($700), 1 Elkins Lake/Kuntz Nelson Scholarship for enrolled students ($400), 1 Harry Ahysen Scholarship/Art Endowment for enrolled students ($600), 1 Marion St. John Baker Scholarship for enrolled students ($500).

Application Procedures Students admitted directly into the professional program freshman year. Deadline for freshmen and transfers: August 1. Required: high school transcript, SAT I or ACT test scores, minimum 2.0 college GPA for transfer students.

Undergraduate Contact Mrs. Joey Chandler, Director, Undergraduate Admissions, Sam Houston State University, Box 2418, Huntsville, Texas 77341; 409-294-1315, fax: 409-294-3668, E-mail address: adm_jbc@shsu.edu.

Graduate Contact Dr. Donald Bumpass, Director, Graduate Studies, Sam Houston State University, Box 2478, Huntsville, Texas 77341; 409-294-1971, fax: 409-294-3622, E-mail address: grs_dlb@shsu.edu.

▼ SAN FRANCISCO ART INSTITUTE

San Francisco, California

Independent, coed. Urban campus. Art program established 1871.

Degrees Bachelor of Fine Arts in the areas of painting, photography, printmaking, sculpture, new genres, filmmaking. Majors and concentrations: art/fine arts, ceramic art and design, film and video production, new genre, painting/drawing, photography, printmaking, sculpture, studio art. Graduate degrees offered: Master of Fine Arts in the areas of painting, photography, printmaking, sculpture, new genres, filmmaking. Program accredited by NASAD.

Enrollment Fall 1997: 728 total; 533 undergraduate, 148 graduate, 47 non-professional degree.

Art Student Profile 50% females, 50% males, 15% minorities, 11% international.

Art Faculty 83 total undergraduate and graduate (full-time and part-time). 100% of full-time faculty have terminal degrees. Graduate students do not teach undergraduate courses. Undergraduate student–faculty ratio: 9:1.

Student Life Student groups/activities include Multicultural Art Students, Gay and Lesbian Students, Artists for Social Responsibility.

Expenses for 1997–98 Application fee: $60. Tuition: $17,400 full-time.

Financial Aid Program-specific awards for 1997: 40 Merit Scholarships for program students ($4500), 24 Community College Scholarships for program students ($4000), 359 need-based grants for program students ($5980).

Application Procedures Students admitted directly into the professional program freshman year. Deadline for freshmen and transfers: continuous. Notification date for freshmen and transfers: September 1. Required: essay, high school transcript, college transcript(s) for transfer students, portfolio, SAT I or ACT test scores. Recommended: minimum 2.0 high school GPA, letter of recommendation, interview. Portfolio reviews held continuously on campus and off campus; the submission of slides may be substituted for portfolios for out-of-state or international applicants.

Contact Ms. Joelle Hallowell, Director of Admissions, San Francisco Art Institute, 800 Chestnut Street, San Francisco, California 94133; 415-749-4500, fax: 415-749-4590.

More About the Institute

For more than 125 years the San Francisco Art Institute, with a singular commitment to the fine arts, has educated the leading artists of our times: Richard Diebenkorn, Karen Finley, Annie Liebovitz, and David Ireland. Many more benefited from the uniquely personal and challenging experience only the Art Institute offers. Art Institute alumni and faculty members play a central role in the contemporary art world, comprising 13 percent of the artists selected for the 1997 Whitney Biennial, 20 percent of the final National Endowment for the Arts Visual Arts Grants recipients, and representing Korea and Venezuela in the last Venice Biennale.

With its unique location on the Pacific Rim, great physical beauty, and cultural diversity, San Francisco boasts a vibrant arts community open to influences from around the globe. Art Institute students frequently collaborate with local artists and nonprofit organizations. Current Art Institute students founded many of today's most adventurous galleries and performance venues in San Francisco. San Francisco Art Institute faculty members are uniquely qualified to guide students since all regularly exhibit in museums and galleries worldwide and are active in local, national, and international art communities.

Students at the San Francisco Art Institute enjoy an unparalleled degree of freedom in pursuing their personal visions as artists. At the Art Institute students may major in painting, photography, film, printmaking, sculpture, or new genres or explore a wider variety of interests through the interdisciplinary program. The Art Institute is also home to the first college computer facility exclusively dedicated to digital imaging as fine art.

▼ SAN JOSE STATE UNIVERSITY

San Jose, California

State-supported, coed. Urban campus. Total enrollment: 26,897.

Degrees Bachelor of Fine Arts in the area of art; Bachelor of Science in the areas of graphic design, interior design, industrial design, illustration. Majors and concentrations: art/fine arts, computer graphics, design, graphic design, illustration, industrial design, interior design, photography, pictorial arts, spatial arts. Graduate degrees offered: Master of Fine Arts in the area of art; Master of Arts in the areas of art/multimedia computing, art/design. Cross-registration with California State University System. Program accredited by NASAD.

Enrollment Fall 1997: 1,380 total; 1,280 undergraduate, 100 graduate.

Art Student Profile 55% females, 45% males, 55% minorities, 5% international.

Art Faculty 87 total undergraduate and graduate (full-time and part-time). 92% of full-time faculty have terminal degrees. Graduate students teach a few undergraduate courses. Undergraduate student–faculty ratio: 16:1.

Student Life Student groups/activities include American Society of Interior Designers, Industrial Design Society of America, Society of Illustrators.

Expenses for 1997–98 Application fee: $55. State resident tuition: $0 full-time. Nonresident tuition: $7380 full-time. Mandatory fees: $2017 full-time. College room and board: $5306. Room and board charges vary according to board plan. Special program-related fees: $15–$25 per course for materials fee.

Financial Aid Program-specific awards for 1997: 10–15 Speddy Urban Awards for program students ($500–$1000), 5–10 Dooley Awards for program students ($500–$1000), 15–25 art scholarships for artistically talented program majors ($300).

Application Procedures Students apply for admission into the professional program by junior year. Deadline for freshmen and transfers: August 1. Required: high school transcript, college transcript(s) for transfer students, portfolio, SAT I or ACT test scores, standing in upper 30% of graduating class, minimum 2.0 GPA from community college for transfers, minimum 2.0 high school GPA for state residents, minimum 2.45 high school GPA for out-of-state residents, minimum SAT I or ACT score dependent on high school grade point average. Portfolio reviews held twice on campus; the submission of slides may be substituted for portfolios whenever needed.

Web Site http://www.sjsu.edu/depts/art_design/.

Undergraduate Contact Office of Admissions and Records, San Jose State University, One Washington Square, San Jose, California 95192-0009; 408-924-2080.

Graduate Contact Ms. Marie Meacham, Graduate Secretary, School of Art and Design, San Jose State University, One Washington Square, San Jose, California 95192-0089; 408-924-4346, fax: 408-924-4326, E-mail address: meacham@email.sjsu.edu.

▼ SAVANNAH COLLEGE OF ART AND DESIGN

Savannah, Georgia

Independent, coed. Urban campus. Total enrollment: 3,464. Art program established 1978.

Degrees Bachelor of Fine Arts in the areas of architectural history, art history, computer art, fashion, fibers, furniture design, graphic design, historic preservation, illustration, industrial design, interior design, metals and jewelry, painting, photography, sequential art, video/film; Bachelor of Architecture. Majors and concentrations: architectural history, architecture, art history, cartooning, computer graphics, fashion design and technology, fibers, film and video production, furniture design, graphic design, historical preservation, illustration, industrial design, interior design, jewelry and metalsmithing, painting, photography. Graduate degrees offered: Master of Fine Arts in the areas of architectural history, art history, computer art, fashion, fibers, furniture design, graphic design, historic preservation, illustration, industrial design, interior design, metals and jewelry, painting, photography, sequential art, video/film; Master of Arts in the areas of architectural history, art history, computer art, fashion, fibers, furniture design, graphic design, historic preservation, illustration, industrial design, interior design, metals and jewelry, painting, photography, sequential art, video/film; Master of Architecture in the area of architecture. Program accredited by NAAB.

Enrollment Fall 1997: 3,464 total; 2,947 undergraduate, 517 graduate.

Art Student Profile 43% females, 57% males, 10% minorities, 14% international.

Art Faculty 212 total undergraduate and graduate (full-time and part-time). 81% of full-time faculty have terminal degrees. Graduate students do not teach undergraduate courses. Undergraduate student–faculty ratio: 12:1.

Student Life Student groups/activities include Society of Computer Artists, Society of Illustrators, American Institute of Architecture Students.

Expenses for 1998–99 Application fee: $50. One-time mandatory fee: $500. Comprehensive fee: $19,875 includes full-time tuition ($13,500) and college room and board ($6375). College room only: $3900.

Financial Aid Program-specific awards for 1997: Henderson Scholarships for program students ($6000), Whelan Scholarships for program students ($10,000), Friedman Scholarships for program students ($20,000), portfolio scholarships for program students ($10,000), Dorsey Scholarships for selected Governors' Program participants ($10,000), Effing Scholarships for transfer students ($10,000), Fleming Scholarships for international students ($10,000), McCommon/White Scholarships for International Competition for Student Artists contest winners ($10,000), Trustees Scholarships for program students ($10,000), Williams Scholarship ($10,000).

Application Procedures Students admitted directly into the professional program freshman year. Deadline for freshmen and transfers: continuous. Notification date for freshmen and transfers: continuous. Required: high school transcript, college transcript(s) for transfer students, minimum 2.0 high school GPA, 3 letters of recommendation, SAT I or ACT test scores. Recommended: interview, portfolio. Portfolio reviews held by request on campus and off campus in various cities; the submission of slides may be substituted for portfolios when distance is prohibitive and for international applicants.

Web Site http://www.scad.edu.

Undergraduate Contact Margaret Kross, Dean of Undergraduate Admissions, Savannah College of Art and Design, PO Box 3146, Savannah, Georgia 31402-3146; 912-238-2483, fax: 912-238-2456, E-mail address: admissions@scad.edu.

Graduate Contact Marie Vea, Dean, International and Graduate Admissions, Savannah College of Art and Design, PO Box

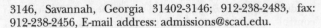

3146, Savannah, Georgia 31402-3146; 912-238-2483, fax: 912-238-2456, E-mail address: admissions@scad.edu.

More About the College

Program Facilities Fully equipped studios and classrooms are available in each major: for computer art, Silicon Graphics, Macintosh, and IBM-compatible workstations and other platforms; for fashion, the Lectra System for design and pattern technology; for fibers, traditional floor looms for computer-aided woven design, and newly installed Nedgraphics workstations; for graphic design, multiple computer labs and production equipment; for metals and jewelry, casting and finishing rooms; for painting, spacious well-lit studio areas; for photography, a digital imaging computer lab and multiple darkrooms; for sequential art, computers for computer coloring classes; and for video, editing suites, a Super Panther dolly, a Steadicam, a 72-monitor video wall, a Mozart 24-track sound editing board and recording studio, a chromakey/bluescreen studio, a sound stage, an audio production suite, and a large concentration of AVID equipment. Architecture, furniture design, historic preservation, industrial design, and interior design share a 71,000-square-foot facility that houses a computer-aided design (CAD) lab, metals conservation and paint analysis labs, a wood shop, a model shop, and traditional design studios equipped with computers. The College library contains 40,000 volumes, 175,000 slides, more than 500 serials, and more than 1,000 videotapes.

Student Performance/Exhibit Opportunities The College maintains twelve on-campus gallery spaces that feature changing exhibits of works by internationally recognized professional artists in every discipline and medium. The work of students and faculty members is displayed continuously in a number of the galleries and at annual student-faculty shows. In addition, faculty and student work is exhibited in off-campus venues, locally and abroad. The College also has an 1,100-seat Trustees Theater, an outdoor amphitheater, and an indoor studio for student performances.

Special Programs SCAD faculty direct off-campus studies in various locations throughout North America, Europe, Latin America, and Asia. Special on-campus programming includes exhibits of renowned artists such as Robert Rauschenberg, Jasper Johns, and Helen Frankenthaler. A distinguished lecturer series recently brought Dr. Henry Louis Gates Jr., Wilma Mankiller, B.D. Wong, Maurice Sendak, Arlene Raven, and Hal Rubenstein to the campus. Other opportunities for student enrichment include the Sidewalk Arts Festival and student exhibits.

▼

The College's philosophy is based on the premise that talent in the visual arts is best nurtured through an education focused on the individual, one providing that individual with intellectual diversity that enriches, a learning experience that challenges, and an environment that is creatively centered. The College's mission is to prepare talented students for careers in the visual arts, design, building arts, and the history of art and architecture, emphasizing individual attention in a positively oriented environment. A uniquely balanced curriculum has attracted students from every state and from more than eighty countries, making SCAD one of the largest art and design colleges in the United States, with a current enrollment of approximately 3,500 students.

The College is located in the heart of Savannah's picturesque National Historic Landmark District, providing a stimulating environment for the visually oriented student of art and design. Savannah is a living laboratory of architecturally and historically significant buildings. Only minutes from the Atlantic Ocean, Savannah's mild climate allows for many outdoor activities. Normal mean temperatures range from 81 degrees in July to 51 degrees in December. Because of its history as a thriving coastal port, Savannah has a cultural diversity unique among Southern cities. The city calendar is full of cultural events offering a variety of local and ethnic cuisine, musical performances, and artistic exhibitions, including Arts on the River and Savannah Onstage, and one of the nation's largest St. Patrick's Day parades. Charleston, Jacksonville, Orlando, Atlanta, and Hilton Head Island are within easy driving distance.

Study trips to major centers of artistic activity are made each quarter and provide further opportunities for enrichment. The College offers supportive academic counseling, with special programs for first-year students and tutors for all students available at no charge.

Residence hall accommodations, with meal plans, are available for students who wish to reside in the College area. While students are not required to live in College housing, some consider the camaraderie and intellectual stimulation of residence hall life a highlight of their college experience. The housing fee includes furnishings (including drafting tables) and utilities and is payable in advance for the entire academic year. Early reservations are strongly recommended.

Competing as a Division III level member of the NCAA, the College offers the following intercollegiate sports for both men and women: basketball, tennis, soccer; for women only, volleyball and softball; for men only, baseball and golf. Rowing, cheerleading, sailing, and rugby are offered as club sports. A seasonal intramural program is also available and an equestrian program is under development.

▼ SCHMIDT COLLEGE OF ARTS AND LETTERS

See Florida Atlantic University

▼ SCHOOL OF THE ART INSTITUTE OF CHICAGO

Chicago, Illinois

Independent, coed. Urban campus.

Degrees Bachelor of Fine Arts in the area of studio art; Bachelor of Interior Architecture. Majors and concentrations: art and technology, art education, ceramic art and design, fashion design and technology, fibers, film, graphic arts, interior architecture, painting/drawing, performance art, photography, printmaking, sculpture, sound design, textile arts, video art. Graduate degrees offered: Master of Fine Arts in the areas of studio art, writing; Master of Science in the area of historic preservation; Master of Arts in the areas of art education, arts administration, art history, art therapy. Cross-registration with Roosevelt University. Program accredited by NASAD.

Enrollment Fall 1997: 2,251 total; 1,468 undergraduate, 571 graduate, 212 non-professional degree.

Art Student Profile 63% females, 37% males, 17% minorities, 10% international.

School of the Art Institute of Chicago (continued)

Art Faculty 419 total undergraduate and graduate (full-time and part-time). 85% of full-time faculty have terminal degrees. Graduate students teach a few undergraduate courses.

Student Life Student groups/activities include Student Government, "F" Student Newspaper, SAIC TV. Special housing available for art students.

Expenses for 1997–98 Application fee: $45. Tuition: $17,160 full-time. College room only: $5150.

Financial Aid Program-specific awards for 1997: 24 Presidential Scholarships for academically qualified applicants ($7000), 100 Recognition Scholarships for academically qualified applicants ($3500), 101 Incentive Scholarships for academically qualified applicants ($2000), 30 Minority Scholarships for minority students ($3500), 1025 School of the Art Institute of Chicago Grants for those demonstrating need ($4197).

Application Procedures Students admitted directly into the professional program freshman year. Deadline for freshmen and transfers: continuous. Required: essay, high school transcript, college transcript(s) for transfer students, letter of recommendation, portfolio, SAT I or ACT test scores. Recommended: minimum 3.0 high school GPA, interview. Portfolio reviews held continuously on campus and off campus; the submission of slides may be substituted for portfolios and are required for transfer credit evaluation.

Web Site http://www.artic.edu/saic/saichome.html.

Undergraduate Contact Carolyn Lagerman, Associate Director of Admissions, Admissions, School of the Art Institute of Chicago, 37 South Wabash Avenue, Chicago, Illinois 60603; 312-899-5219, fax: 312-899-1840, E-mail address: admiss@artic.edu.

Graduate Contact Ms. Jennifer Stein, Associate Director of Graduate Admissions, School of the Art Institute of Chicago, 37 South Wabash Avenue, Chicago, Illinois 60603; 312-899-5219, fax: 312-899-1840, E-mail address: admiss@artic.edu.

More About the School

Program Facilities The Painting and Drawing department has many well-lit studio classrooms, individual space for undergraduate and graduate students, and space for exhibition and critiques. Facilities in the Sculpture department include separate, well-equipped shops for clay/stone, wood, and metal work. In addition, there is a foundry for casting bronze and aluminum and a light metals foundry. Students also enjoy access to a metal shop containing facilities for welding with oxyacetylene, MIG, and TIG and for fabricating metal, as well as access to a complete woodshop complex. The Printmaking department has five etching presses, six stone lithography presses, a process camera, a professional photo-mechanical darkroom, Macintosh computers, computer scanners, and an 11" x 17" laser printer.

The Art and Technology department supports several computer labs including two Macintosh-based labs, as well as a Silicon Graphics lab equipped with ten SoftImage systems. All labs are networked together and are connected to the Internet via a high-speed link. The department also maintains a high-end video editing suite, a multimedia authoring suite, an electronics construction shop, a fully equipped neon studio, a holography studio, and MIDI and digital sound systems. The Video department currently has eight editing suites, using both Hi-8 and ¾-inch formats, an Imaging lab containing Macintosh graphics computers and a Sandin Image Processing system, and a shooting studio with control room, switcher, character generator, cameras, and a controlled light grid.

The Filmmaking department provides sync and non-sync cameras, tripods, recorders, and microphones, lighting and editing equipment, optical printers, sound transfer and mix facilities, and a hand-processing lab for individual student use. Department facilities include a seventy-seat film theater, a shooting studio, and a 16mm black-and-white reversal film-processing laboratory. The Photography department has three large darkrooms for black-and-white film, ten individual darkrooms for color film, a nonsilver room, eight full-color computers with color scanner and film recorder, and three lecture-critique rooms. Equipment checkout privileges give students access to photography equipment, supplies, and chemicals.

The Ceramics department facilities include clay mixers, extruder, slab roller, and several styles of wheels. Bulk materials (clay, slip, and glazes) are provided, and diverse firing options in various kiln styles, including high and low-fire oxidation and reduction, soda, and raku, are available. The Visual Communication department facilities include a state-of-the-art computer lab, a type shop, a copy stand, and spacious studios. The Fashion department houses a resource center containing a library on fashion and the history of costume, including both foreign and domestic publications; videotapes of American, European, and Japanese collections; and a growing collection of international designer garments and accessories. Facilities include excellent industrial grade equipment and access to all shops and studios at the School. The Fiber department has thirty-five looms, a large area for hand construction, a computer lab with five stations, two computer looms, and a kitchen with industrial washers and dryers used for the setting of dyes.

The John M. Flaxman Library collections include approximately 53,000 volumes on art and the liberal arts and sciences, 635 periodical subscriptions, as well as films, videos, audio tapes, CDs, microforms, and picture files. The Joan Flasch Artists' Book Collection contains more than 3,000 artists' books along with a research collection of exhibition catalogs and other related materials. Students may also utilize the research collections at the Art Institute of Chicago Ryerson and Burnham Libraries, one of the oldest, largest, and finest art museum libraries in the country. Its non-circulating, closed-stack collections include more than 220,000 volumes and 2,225 periodicals, constituting an invaluable resource for students of the history of art and architecture. The MacLean Visual Resource center maintains a non-circulating collection of 420,000 slides.

The Video Data Bank houses more than 1,500 titles by and about contemporary artists, including experimental tapes spanning the history of video as an art form. The Film Center is a theater, research center, and archive, screening more than 500 films per year and offering premieres, extensive retrospectives, thematic series, frequent filmmaker appearances, lectures, panel discussions, and seminars. The Poetry Center at the School provides a forum for public readings by local, national, and international poets and writers.

Faculty, Resident Artists, and Alumni Faculty members are selected for their effectiveness and dedication as teachers and for their professional activity and commitment as artists, designers, and scholars. There are currently 419 full and part-time faculty members, amongst them 7 Guggenheim recipients and numerous NEA and NEH grant recipients. Each year, a hundred or more well-known visiting artists, including poets and political activists, as well as visual artists, present workshops and provide individual student critiques. Notable alumni: Grant Wood, Claes Oldenburg, Ivan Albright, Vincente Minnelli, Georgia O'Keeffe, Elizabeth Murray.

Student Performance/Exhibit Opportunities The School's exhibition spaces include the Betty Rymer Gallery, which highlights work from departments and presents special exhibitions, and Gallery 2, an off-campus student center with exhibition space, a performance space, and a space designed for site-specific installations. Additionally, Gallery X and the Lounge Gallery, sponsored by the Student Union Galleries, provide exhibition space for currently enrolled students. The Fashion Department hosts a fashion show, in late spring, for students in their second, third, and fourth year.

Off-Campus Arrangements Students can participate in the Individual Off-Campus Study Program, which includes apprenticeships, internships, and independent studies domestically and abroad. In recent years, students have studied such subjects as architecture in Vermont, drawings at the Louvre, walled cities in Italy and Greece, and engraving techniques in Italy. These projects have resulted in projects ranging from exhibitions to a documentary film. The School also sponsors a number of study trips annually; recent destinations have included Brazil, England, Mexico, and South Africa.

▼

The School of the Art Institute of Chicago, founded in 1866, is an accredited college of the visual-related arts whose primary purpose is to foster the conceptual and technical education of the artist in a highly professional and studio-oriented environment. Believing that the artist's success is dependent on both creative vision and technical expertise, the School encourages excellence, critical inquiry, and experimentation.

Graduate and undergraduate students and the faculty of artists and scholars work closely, sharing resources and establishing a forum for critiquing and refining technical abilities and conceptual concerns.

The first-year program is the beginning of an art education that encourages exploration of various concepts and media. Along with 2-D and 3-D design, students explore areas of 4-D design, including filmmaking, performance, video, and electronics and kinetics. With no declared majors, the student is allowed and encouraged to continue exploration throughout the four years of study. The teaching of studio art; the complementary program in art history, theory and criticism, and liberal arts; the visiting artists; and the collections and exhibitions of the Art Institute of Chicago all contribute to the variety, the challenge, and the resonance of the educational experience.

The School of the Art Institute of Chicago is located in the heart of downtown Chicago, the nation's third largest city and home of the nation's second largest art scene, including museums, more than 140 galleries, alternative spaces, and organizations supporting the arts. Students have a wide variety of cultural and recreational resources from which to choose: ballet, opera, theater, orchestra halls, cinemas, libraries, architecture, blues and jazz clubs, professional sports teams, parks, ethnic restaurants, and street festivals and fairs. An extensive public transportation system allows students access not only to citywide events, but to outlying communities as well.

Chicago offers a wide variety of housing choices to serve the diverse needs of students at the School. Many students spend their first few years at the School living in one of the School's two residence facilities: Wolberg Hall, which opened in 1993, and the Chicago Building, a national historic landmark that opened in 1997. Residents in the halls can truly immerse themselves in a community of fellow artists, live right in the heart of Chicago's loop, and enjoy conveniences not found in most student apartments. In addition, many students choose to live off-campus in Chicago's many interesting and diverse neighborhoods. Interested students can request a copy of the *Community Area Booklet,* a guide to living options within the city, by contacting the Student Life office at 312-899-7460.

▼ SCHOOL OF THE MUSEUM OF FINE ARTS

Boston, Massachusetts

Independent, coed. Urban campus. Total enrollment: 1,133. Art program established 1876.

Degrees Bachelor of Arts/Bachelor of Fine Arts in the area of fine arts. Majors and concentrations: animation, art education, art of Africa, art/fine arts, ceramic art and design, computer graphics, electronic arts, illustration, jewelry and metalsmithing, painting/drawing, performance, photography, printmaking, sculpture, stained glass, studio art, video art. Graduate degrees offered: Master of Fine Arts. Cross-registration with ProArts Consortium, Association of Independent Colleges of Art and Design. Program accredited by NASAD.

Enrollment Fall 1997: 729 total; 638 undergraduate, 91 graduate.

Art Student Profile 11% minorities, 11% international.

Art Faculty 184 total undergraduate and graduate (full-time and part-time). Graduate students teach a few undergraduate courses. Undergraduate student–faculty ratio: 9:1.

Student Life Student groups/activities include School Senate.

Expenses for 1997–98 Application fee: $35. Tuition: $15,490 full-time. Mandatory fees: $400 full-time. Special program-related fees: $90 per semester for materials fee for studio classes.

Financial Aid Program-specific awards for 1997: 15–20 Art Merit Scholarships for freshmen ($1000–$5000), 230 School of the Museum of Fine Arts Grants for those demonstrating need ($3749), 2 full tuition scholarships for highly advanced freshmen.

Application Procedures Students apply for admission into the professional program by freshman year. Deadline for freshmen and transfers: continuous. Required: essay, high school transcript, portfolio, interview for applicants within 150 miles of Boston. Recommended: 2,3 letters of recommendation, interview. Portfolio reviews held weekly on campus and off campus; the submission of slides may be substituted for portfolios for large works of art.

Contact John Williamson, Dean of Admissions, School of the Museum of Fine Arts, 230 The Fenway, Boston, Massachusetts 02115; 617-369-3626, E-mail address: info@smfa.edu.

More About the School

Program Facilities A formal gallery, auditorium, lobby, and corridors are used as exhibition spaces for students of all levels and from every area of study during the academic year. Under special circumstances, students have twenty-four hour access to the studio facilities.

School of the Museum of Fine Arts *(continued)*

Faculty, Visiting Artists, and Alumni All studio faculty members are practicing professional artists with regional, national, and international reputations. The Visiting Artists Program encourages students to interact with prominent artists who have included John Baldessari, Karen Finley, Yvonne Rainer, The Guerrilla Girls, Bill Viola, Lorna Simpson, Janine Antoni, and Lari Pittman.

Exhibition Opportunities A number of annual exhibitions give students the opportunity to present their work in a public forum. The school also sponsors a number of special prize funds, offering students the chance to win travel grants, cash awards, and exhibition opportunities. These exhibitions include the Boit Competition, Dana Pond Competition, Student Annual, Graduating Student Exhibition, Fifth Year Competition, and the Traveling Scholars Exhibition.

Special Programs The School is a division of the Museum of Fine Arts and is affiliated with Tufts University; special mobility programs are available with Massachusetts Institute of Technology and Wheaton College. As a member of the ProArts Consortium in Boston and the Association of Independent Colleges of Art and Design (AICAD), students have the opportunity to study at colleges throughout the United States and abroad. The Fifth Year Program is a one-year program of independent study for graduates of the School's Diploma Program; participants have a chance to win substantial travel grants and to exhibit their work at the Museum of Fine Arts.

▼

The Museum School offers students the opportunity to design their own individualized course of study and to tailor a program that best suits their needs and goals. A division of the Museum of Fine Arts and affiliated with Tufts University, the Museum School offers a diverse curriculum with a full range of studio and academic resources.

The portfolio for admission can consist of one or a number of techniques or media, depending on the interests and background of the applicant. The diversity of the faculty and the range of facilities allow the student to develop a very personal and individual means of expression. Course teaching methods range from structured classes, with regular attendance, to individual instruction for work done independently outside the School. Class sizes are generally small, and every area of study is supported by an accomplished, professional faculty; extensive visiting artists programs; and an energetic exhibitions schedule. At the end of each semester the student presents a body of art work at a review board consisting of faculty members and students. There is a discussion of the total semester experience, and suggestions are made for future study. A block of credits is awarded, appropriate to the term's accomplishments, and a written evaluation is made.

Boston is home to many educational and cultural institutions. The Museum School is a vital member of the art community, presenting a dynamic schedule of exhibitions, lectures, and panel discussions throughout the academic year. As a division of the Museum of Fine Arts, students also have special access to the educational resources, collections, curatorial departments, and special programs of one of the most comprehensive and outstanding collections of art in the world.

▼ SCHOOL OF VISUAL ARTS

New York, New York

Proprietary, coed. Urban campus. Total enrollment: 5,195. Art program established 1947.

Degrees Bachelor of Fine Arts in the areas of advertising and graphic design, art education, illustration and cartooning, interior design, photography, computer art, animation, fine arts, film and video. Majors and concentrations: advertising design, animation, applied art, art education, art/fine arts, cartooning, commercial art, computer art, computer graphics, film and video production, graphic arts, illustration, interior design, painting/drawing, photography, printmaking, sculpture, studio art. Graduate degrees offered: Master of Fine Arts in the areas of computer art, fine arts, illustration as visual essay, photography and related media, design. Program accredited by NASAD.

Enrollment Fall 1997: 5,195 total; 2,800 undergraduate, 292 graduate, 2,103 non-professional degree.

Art Student Profile 48% females, 52% males, 17% minorities, 11% international.

Art Faculty 753 total undergraduate and graduate (full-time and part-time). 36% of full-time faculty have terminal degrees. Graduate students do not teach undergraduate courses. Undergraduate student–faculty ratio: 9:1.

Student Life Student groups/activities include Visual Arts Student Association, Photography Club, Visual Opinion (magazine). Special housing available for art students.

Expenses for 1997–98 Application fee: $35. Tuition: $13,650 full-time. Mandatory fees: $240 full-time. College room only: $6100. Room charges vary according to location. Special program-related fees: $150–$750 per semester for departmental fee.

Financial Aid Program-specific awards for 1997: 1237 Institutional Scholarships for program students ($2280), 246 wages for program students ($3330).

Application Procedures Students admitted directly into the professional program freshman year. Required: essay, high school transcript, college transcript(s) for transfer students, portfolio, SAT I or ACT test scores. Recommended: minimum 2.0 high school GPA, interview. Portfolio reviews held 6 times and by appointment on campus; the submission of slides may be substituted for portfolios for large works of art.

Web Site http://www.schoolofvisualarts.edu.

Undergraduate Contact Mr. Richard M. Longo, Director of Admissions, School of Visual Arts, 209 East 23rd Street, New York, New York 10010; 212-592-2100, fax: 212-592-2116, E-mail address: admissions@adm.schoolofvisualarts.edu.

Graduate Contact Ms. Brenda Hanegan, MFA Coordinator, School of Visual Arts, 209 East 23rd Street, New York, New York 10010; 212-592-2109, fax: 212-592-2116, E-mail address: bhanegan@adm.schoolofvisualarts.edu.

More About the School

Program Facilities The College operates five student galleries and a professional gallery in SoHo at 137 Wooster Street for the exhibition and sale of advanced student work. Studio space and equipment are offered in different departments, varying in availability upon such factors as class seniority and the major of study. The SVA Library holds approximately 64,500 books, 95,000 35mm slides, and a picture file of 230,000 pieces. Other significant resources include a videotape collection and more than 50 original film scripts. The library subscribes to 255 periodicals.

Faculty, Resident Artists, and Alumni The School's roster of more than 700 faculty members, all of whom are working professionals, includes award-winning designers, critics, scholars, and artists. SVA's Alumni Society provides information, support services, and programs of general interest to artists.

Exhibit Opportunities Besides the SoHo gallery space and five student galleries affording SVA students the opportunity to exhibit their work 12 months a year, there are several possibilities for students to have their work included in Visual Arts Press publications. Students are encouraged to show their work outside of SVA's framework by participating in exhibits and competitions held in New York City and throughout the United States.

Special Programs SVA offers summer painting programs abroad in Barcelona, Spain, and an archaeological tour in Greece.

▼

Celebrating its fiftieth anniversary, the School of Visual Arts has grown steadily and is, today, one of the largest and best-equipped undergraduate colleges of art in the country. This growth is due principally to SVA's pioneering role in bringing outstanding working professionals to the classroom to teach what they know best. In addition, SVA's student advisement system not only adds close personal contact and strengthens its flexible programs but also seeks to ensure that the School will always have the best attributes of a small college. Taken together, these structures and the

commitment to professionalism enable the School to bring to students some of the very best artists and designers in the world, directly from their studios, offices, and agencies in Manhattan. Students have a broad choice of faculty within a curriculum that allows for many electives. At the same time the programs require that all students master the core of each of the disciplines taught. SVA also offers a broad range of course offerings not only in the arts, as might be expected, but also in art history, the humanities, and even computer science. SVA's faculty and courses foster that spirit of independence that is so necessary for creative work. But freedom requires self-discipline. Consequently, SVA expects the same commitment from its entering freshmen as from the most advanced graduate students.

SVA strives to prepare its students for professional careers in their field of study. In addition to offering the benefits of size, the vast faculty brings to the college a direct linkage to the professional art and design industry—a linkage that often translates to internships and job opportunities for SVA's students and graduates. Then, the Visual Arts Museum at 209 East 23rd Street, used at times to display student work, actively undertakes to improve visual awareness and increase aesthetic understanding by presenting the work of noted professionals working in the applied arts. Taken together, the attributes of the faculty and the breadth of the Museum result in more than 87 percent of SVA's alumni employed in their major field within 1 year of graduation. As noted in *Advertising Age* magazine, SVA's foresight in staffing the School with professionals helps to prepare students for the real-life professional world. Many prominent artists have graduated with degrees from SVA, including graphic designer Paul Davis, fine artist Keith Haring, and the well-known painter of 60's psychedelia, Peter Max.

SVA offers workshops, one-week seminars, concentrated studio residencies, public lectures, panel discussion series, professional symposiums, international study programs, and a one-year Asian student program which serves as a vehicle for Chinese, Japanese, and Korean art students to make an effective transition into our education culture.

▼ SETON HALL UNIVERSITY

South Orange, New Jersey

Independent–Roman Catholic, coed. Suburban campus. Total enrollment: 10,114. Art program established 1968.

Degrees Bachelor of Science in the area of art education; Bachelor of Arts in the areas of art history, fine arts, graphic design/advertising art. Graduate degrees offered: Master of Arts in the area of museum professions.

Enrollment Fall 1997: 80 undergraduate, 70 graduate.

Art Student Profile 60% females, 40% males, 15% minorities, 5% international.

Art Faculty 24 total undergraduate and graduate (full-time and part-time). 100% of full-time faculty have terminal degrees. Graduate students do not teach undergraduate courses. Undergraduate student–faculty ratio: 15:1.

Student Life Student groups/activities include student exhibitions.

Expenses for 1997–98 Application fee: $25. Comprehensive fee: $20,620 includes full-time tuition ($13,050), mandatory fees ($550), and college room and board ($7020). College room only: $4940. Full-time tuition and fees vary according to course load. Room and board charges vary according to board plan and housing facility.

Seton Hall University (*continued*)

Financial Aid Program-specific awards for 1997: 1 Henry Gasser for art majors demonstrating talent and/or academic achievement ($1800).

Application Procedures Students admitted directly into the professional program freshman year. Deadline for freshmen and transfers: continuous. Required: essay, high school transcript, college transcript(s) for transfer students, minimum 2.0 high school GPA, 3 letters of recommendation, SAT I or ACT test scores. Recommended: interview, portfolio. Portfolio reviews held as needed on campus; the submission of slides may be substituted for portfolios for large works of art.

Web Site http://www.shu.edu.

Undergraduate Contact Admissions Office, Seton Hall University, 400 South Orange Avenue, South Orange, New Jersey 07079-2696; 973-761-9000 ext. 9332.

Graduate Contact Barbara Cate, Director, MA Program in Museum Professions, Department of Art and Music, Seton Hall University, 400 South Orange Avenue, South Orange, New Jersey 07079-2696; 973-761-7966, fax: 973-275-2368, E-mail address: catebarb@shu.edu.

▼ SETON HILL COLLEGE

Greensburg, Pennsylvania

Independent-Roman Catholic, primarily women. Small town campus. Total enrollment: 1,078.

Degrees Bachelor of Fine Arts in the areas of painting, sculpture, graphic design, printmaking, ceramics, metalsmithing. Majors and concentrations: art and technology, art education, art history, art/fine arts, arts management, graphic arts, interior design, sculpture, studio art. Graduate degrees offered: Master of Arts in the area of art therapy. Cross-registration with Saint Vincent College.

Enrollment Fall 1997: 120 total; 15 undergraduate, 20 graduate, 85 non-professional degree.

Art Student Profile 80% females, 20% males, 10% minorities, 10% international.

Art Faculty 15 total undergraduate and graduate (full-time and part-time). 85% of full-time faculty have terminal degrees. Graduate students do not teach undergraduate courses. Undergraduate student–faculty ratio: 8:1.

Student Life Student groups/activities include Student Art Society.

Expenses for 1997–98 Application fee: $30. Comprehensive fee: $17,370 includes full-time tuition ($12,640) and college room and board ($4730). Special program-related fees: $15–$140 per semester for supplies.

Financial Aid Program-specific awards for 1997: 1–2 Hensler-Irwin Scholarships for freshmen program majors ($1000), 1 Art Department Award of Excellence for sophomores and juniors ($500).

Application Procedures Students admitted directly into the professional program freshman year. Deadline for freshmen and transfers: July 30. Notification date for freshmen and transfers: continuous. Required: high school transcript, college transcript(s) for transfer students, minimum 2.0 high school GPA, 3 letters of recommendation, portfolio, SAT I or ACT test scores. Recommended: essay, minimum 3.0 high school GPA, interview. Portfolio reviews held continuously on campus; the submission of slides may be substituted for portfolios when distance is prohibitive.

Web Site http://www.setonhill.edu.

Undergraduate Contact Ms. Barbara Hinkle, Director, Admissions Office, Seton Hill College, College Avenue, Greensburg, Pennsylvania 15601; 724-838-4255, fax: 724-830-4611, E-mail address: hinkle@is.setonhill.edu.

Graduate Contact Ms. Nina Denninger, Director, Graduate Program in Art Technology, Art Department, Seton Hill College, Greensburg, Pennsylvania 15601; 724-830-1047, fax: 724-830-4611.

▼ SHEPHERD COLLEGE

Shepherdstown, West Virginia

State-supported, coed. Small town campus. Total enrollment: 4,025.

Degrees Bachelor of Fine Arts in the areas of graphic design, photography/computer digital imagery, painting, printmaking, sculpture. Majors and concentrations: art/fine arts, digital imaging, graphic design, painting/drawing, photography, printmaking, sculpture.

Enrollment Fall 1997: 235 total; 210 undergraduate, 25 non-professional degree.

Art Student Profile 55% females, 45% males, 5% minorities, 5% international.

Art Faculty 19 total (full-time and part-time). 100% of full-time faculty have terminal degrees. Graduate students do not teach undergraduate courses. Undergraduate student–faculty ratio: 15:1.

Student Life Student groups/activities include Art Alliance Exhibits, Performing and Visual Arts Series, AIGA.

Expenses for 1997–98 Application fee: $25. State resident tuition: $2228 full-time. Nonresident tuition: $5348 full-time. College room and board: $4139. Room and board charges vary according to board plan and housing facility. Special program-related fees: $25 per course for studio fee.

Financial Aid Program-specific awards for 1997: 7 art scholarships for West Virginia resident program majors ($1800), 2 Blundell Award for first year students ($500), 2 Bridgeforth Awards for photo/computer imaging students ($500–$1000).

Application Procedures Students admitted directly into the professional program freshman year. Deadline for freshmen and transfers: April 1. Required: high school transcript, college transcript(s) for transfer students, minimum 2.0 high school GPA, portfolio, SAT I or ACT test scores. Portfolio reviews held 6 times on campus; the submission of slides may be substituted for portfolios (slides preferred).

Web Site http://www.shepherd.wvnet.edu.

Undergraduate Contact Mr. Karl Wolf, Director of Admissions, Art Department, Shepherd College, Shepherdstown, West Virginia 25443; 304-876-5212, fax: 304-876-3101, E-mail address: kwolf@shepherd.wvnet.edu.

▼ SHORTER COLLEGE

Rome, Georgia

Independent-Baptist, coed. Small town campus. Total enrollment: 1,639. Art program established 1994.

Degrees Bachelor of Fine Arts in the area of art. Majors and concentrations: art education, ceramics, painting/drawing, sculpture.

Enrollment Fall 1997: 16 total; all undergraduate.

Art Student Profile 60% females, 40% males.

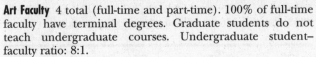

Art Faculty 4 total (full-time and part-time). 100% of full-time faculty have terminal degrees. Graduate students do not teach undergraduate courses. Undergraduate student–faculty ratio: 8:1.

Student Life Student groups/activities include Art Student League.

Expenses for 1997–98 Application fee: $25. Comprehensive fee: $12,510 includes full-time tuition ($8150), mandatory fees ($110), and college room and board ($4250).

Financial Aid Program-specific awards for 1997: 10 Art Scholarships for art majors ($500).

Application Procedures Students admitted directly into the professional program freshman year. Deadline for freshmen and transfers: continuous. Required: essay, high school transcript, college transcript(s) for transfer students, minimum 2.0 high school GPA, letter of recommendation, interview, portfolio, SAT I or ACT test scores. Portfolio reviews held 4 times on campus.

Undergraduate Contact Dr. Alan B. Wingard, Dean, School of the Arts, Shorter College, 315 Shorter Avenue, Rome, Georgia 30165; 706-233-7247, fax: 706-236-1515.

▼ Siena Heights University

Adrian, Michigan

Independent-Roman Catholic, coed. Small town campus. Total enrollment: 1,287. Art program established 1930.

Degrees Bachelor of Fine Arts in the area of art. Majors and concentrations: ceramics, drawing, graphic arts, metals, painting, photography, printmaking, sculpture. Program accredited by NASAD.

Enrollment Fall 1997: 98 total; all undergraduate.

Art Student Profile 60% females, 40% males, 10% minorities.

Art Faculty 8 total (full-time and part-time). 100% of full-time faculty have terminal degrees. Graduate students do not teach undergraduate courses. Undergraduate student–faculty ratio: 16:1.

Student Life Student groups/activities include Studio Angelico Artist League, Lambda Iota Tau Literary/Art Society.

Expenses for 1997–98 Application fee: $25. Comprehensive fee: $15,030 includes full-time tuition ($10,450), mandatory fees ($250), and college room and board ($4330). Room and board charges vary according to board plan. Special program-related fees: $50 per course for lab fee.

Financial Aid Program-specific awards for 1997: 2 Wacker Scholarships for those demonstrating merit ($2000), 2 Klemm Scholarships for female art students demonstrating need and merit ($2000), 1 Krakker Scholarship for continuing program students ($1000–$2000).

Application Procedures Students apply for admission into the professional program by sophomore year. Deadline for freshmen and transfers: continuous. Required: high school transcript, college transcript(s) for transfer students, SAT I or ACT test scores (minimum combined ACT score of 17), minimum 2.3 high school GPA. Recommended: interview, portfolio. Portfolio reviews held once and as needed on campus.

Web Site http://www.sienahts.edu.

Undergraduate Contact Director of Admissions, Siena Heights University, 1247 East Siena Heights Drive, Adrian, Michigan 49221; 517-264-7183, fax: 517-264-7704.

▼ Simon Fraser University

Burnaby, BC, Canada

Province-supported, coed. Suburban campus. Total enrollment: 18,759. Art program established 1992.

Degrees Bachelor of Fine Arts in the area of visual arts. Graduate degrees offered: Master of Fine Arts in the area of interdisciplinary studies.

Enrollment Fall 1997: 63 total.

Art Faculty 3 total undergraduate and graduate (full-time and part-time). 100% of full-time faculty have terminal degrees. Graduate students teach a few undergraduate courses. Undergraduate student–faculty ratio: 21:1.

Expenses for 1997–98 Application fee: $25 Canadian dollars. Tuition, fee, and room only charges are reported in Canadian dollars. Canadian resident tuition: $2310 full-time. Mandatory fees: $207 full-time. College room only: $2830. Room charges vary according to housing facility. International student tuition: $6930 full-time. Special program-related fees: $50–$100 per semester for studio lab fee.

Financial Aid Program-specific awards for 1997: 1 Murray Farr Scholarship for program majors ($500), 1 Adaline May Clark Scholarship for program majors ($500), 1 SCA Scholarship for program majors, 1 Helen Pitt Scholarship for program majors.

Application Procedures Students admitted directly into the professional program freshman year. Deadline for freshmen and transfers: May 1. Required: high school transcript, minimum 3.0 high school GPA, interview, video, portfolio. Portfolio reviews held twice or portfolio may be sent by mail on campus; the submission of slides may be substituted for portfolios for international applicants and for large works of art.

Web Site http://www.sfu.ca/sca.

Undergraduate Contact Admissions Office, Simon Fraser University, 8888 University Drive, Burnaby, BC V5A 1S6, Canada; 604-291-3224, fax: 604-291-4969.

Graduate Contact Chair, MFA Program, School for the Contemporary Arts, Simon Fraser University, 8888 University Drive, Burnaby, BC V5A 1S6, Canada; 604-291-3492, fax: 604-291-5907, E-mail address: mfa_grad_office@sfu.ca.

▼ Slippery Rock University of Pennsylvania

Slippery Rock, Pennsylvania

State-supported, coed. Rural campus. Total enrollment: 7,038.

Degrees Bachelor of Fine Arts in the area of art. Majors and concentrations: ceramics, design, digital art, digital imaging, drawing, metals, painting, photography, printmaking, sculpture, textiles.

Enrollment Fall 1997: 75 undergraduate.

Art Student Profile 60% females, 40% males, 10% minorities, 10% international.

Art Faculty 11 total (full-time and part-time). 100% of full-time faculty have terminal degrees. Graduate students do not teach undergraduate courses. Undergraduate student–faculty ratio: 7:1.

Student Life Student groups/activities include International Art Student Exchange, Art Student Internship. Special housing available for art students.

Slippery Rock University of Pennsylvania (continued)

Expenses for 1997–98 State resident tuition: $3468 full-time. Nonresident tuition: $8824 full-time. Mandatory fees: $834 full-time. College room and board: $3590. College room only: $1972.

Financial Aid Program-specific awards for 1997: 2 departmental scholarships for program majors ($1000), 2 Craig Succop Scholarships for metalsmithing majors ($1000), 2 Faculty Scholarships for program majors ($500), 2 John and Martha Gault Scholarships for junior or senior studio majors ($800), 4 Mihal Skarupa Memorial Scholarships for International Study for program majors, 2 Printmaking Foundation Scholarships for printmaking majors ($250).

Application Procedures Students admitted directly into the professional program freshman year. Deadline for freshmen and transfers: continuous. Required: essay, high school transcript, college transcript(s) for transfer students, SAT I or ACT test scores, minimum 2.5 high school GPA. Recommended: 3 letters of recommendation, interview.

Undergraduate Contact Mr. Glen Brunken, Chair, Art Department, Slippery Rock University of Pennsylvania, Slippery Rock, Pennsylvania 16057; 412-738-2338, fax: 412-738-4485, E-mail address: glen.brunken@sru.edu.

▼ SONOMA STATE UNIVERSITY

Rohnert Park, California

State-supported, coed. Small town campus. Total enrollment: 7,050. Art program established 1967.

Degrees Bachelor of Fine Arts in the areas of painting, printmaking, sculpture, photography. Majors and concentrations: art/fine arts, painting/drawing, photography, printmaking, sculpture. Cross-registration with San Francisco State University. Program accredited by NASAD.

Enrollment Fall 1997: 14 total; all undergraduate.

Art Student Profile 50% females, 50% males, 5% international.

Art Faculty 8 total (full-time and part-time). 100% of full-time faculty have terminal degrees. Graduate students do not teach undergraduate courses.

Student Life Student groups/activities include BFA Student Exhibition, Student Art Exhibition.

Expenses for 1997–98 Application fee: $55. State resident tuition: $0 full-time. Nonresident tuition: $7626 full-time. Mandatory fees: $2130 full-time. College room and board: $5769. College room only: $3699. Room and board charges vary according to board plan and housing facility. Special program-related fees: $25–$50 per course for supplies.

Financial Aid Program-specific awards for 1997: 1 William Smith Award for ceramics majors ($500), 1 William Smith Award for studio art majors ($500), 1 Brooks Award for art history majors ($400), 1 John Bolles Scholarship for program majors ($750), 2 Art Department Scholarships for program majors ($300).

Application Procedures Students apply for admission into the professional program by sophomore, junior year. Deadline for freshmen and transfers: November 30. Required: essay, college transcript(s) for transfer students, minimum 3.0 high school GPA, 2 letters of recommendation, portfolio. Portfolio reviews held twice on campus; the submission of slides may be substituted for portfolios (slides preferred).

Web Site http://www.sonoma.edu/art/.

Undergraduate Contact Mr. William Guynn, Chair, Art Department, Sonoma State University, 1801 East Cotati Avenue, Rohnert Park, California 94928; 707-664-2151, fax: 707-664-4333, E-mail address: william.guynn@sonoma.edu.

▼ SOUTHERN ILLINOIS UNIVERSITY AT CARBONDALE

Carbondale, Illinois

State-supported, coed. Small town campus. Total enrollment: 21,908.

Degrees Bachelor of Fine Arts in the area of art. Majors and concentrations: art education, ceramic art and design, industrial design, jewelry and metalsmithing, painting/drawing, printmaking, sculpture, visual communication, weaving and fibers. Graduate degrees offered: Master of Fine Arts in the area of art. Program accredited by NASD.

Enrollment Fall 1997: 470 total; 47 undergraduate, 57 graduate, 366 non-professional degree.

Art Student Profile 40% females, 60% males, 7% minorities, 10% international.

Art Faculty 32 total undergraduate and graduate (full-time and part-time). 100% of full-time faculty have terminal degrees. Graduate students teach about a quarter undergraduate courses. Undergraduate student–faculty ratio: 5:1.

Student Life Student groups/activities include League of Art and Design, Industrial Design Society of America Student Chapter.

Expenses for 1997–98 State resident tuition: $2700 full-time. Nonresident tuition: $8100 full-time. Mandatory fees: $720 full-time. Full-time tuition and fees vary according to course load. College room and board: $3649. Room and board charges vary according to board plan and housing facility. Special program-related fees: $50 per course for model fees, $3–$75 per course for studio materials.

Financial Aid Program-specific awards for 1997: 5–7 Talent Scholarships for incoming students ($1000), 2 Mitchell Scholarships for incoming students from Southern Illinois ($1000).

Application Procedures Students apply for admission into the professional program by sophomore year. Deadline for freshmen and transfers: continuous. Notification date for freshmen and transfers: continuous. Required: high school transcript, college transcript(s) for transfer students, portfolio, SAT I or ACT test scores (minimum combined ACT score of 20), Minimum 2.0 GPA for transfer students. Portfolio reviews held twice on campus; the submission of slides may be substituted for portfolios (slides preferred for scholarship consideration).

Web Site http://www.siu.edu/~artdesn.

Undergraduate Contact Ms. Joyce Jolliff, Academic Adviser, School of Art and Design, Southern Illinois University at Carbondale, Carbondale, Illinois 62901-4301; 618-453-4313, fax: 618-453-7710, E-mail address: jjolliff@siu.edu.

Graduate Contact Mr. Michael Onken, Graduate Program Head, School of Art and Design, Southern Illinois University at Carbondale, Carbondale, Illinois 62901-4301; 618-453-4313, fax: 618-453-7710.

▼ SOUTHERN ILLINOIS UNIVERSITY AT EDWARDSVILLE

Edwardsville, Illinois

State-supported, coed. Suburban campus. Total enrollment: 11,207. Art program established 1958.

Degrees Bachelor of Fine Arts in the area of art studio. Majors and concentrations: art education, art/fine arts, ceramic art and design, computer graphics, glassworking, graphic arts, jewelry and metalsmithing, painting/drawing, photography, printmaking, sculpture, studio art, textile arts. Graduate degrees offered: Master of Fine Arts in the area of art studio; Master of Arts in the area of art therapy.
Enrollment Fall 1997: 380 total; 270 undergraduate, 60 graduate, 50 non-professional degree.
Art Student Profile 55% females, 45% males, 20% minorities, 10% international.
Art Faculty 29 total undergraduate and graduate (full-time and part-time). 100% of full-time faculty have terminal degrees. Graduate students teach about a quarter undergraduate courses. Undergraduate student–faculty ratio: 17:1.
Student Life Special housing available for art students.
Expenses for 1998–99 Application fee: $0. State resident tuition: $2081 full-time. Nonresident tuition: $6242 full-time. Mandatory fees: $584 full-time. College room and board: $4066. College room only: $2536. Room and board charges vary according to board plan and housing facility. Special program-related fees: $12–$22 per course for studio fee.
Application Procedures Students apply for admission into the professional program by sophomore year. Deadline for freshmen and transfers: continuous. Notification date for freshmen and transfers: continuous. Required: essay, high school transcript, college transcript(s) for transfer students, minimum 3.0 high school GPA, 3 letters of recommendation, portfolio. Portfolio reviews held twice on campus; the submission of slides may be substituted for portfolios (slides preferred).
Web Site http://www.siue.edu/ART/.
Undergraduate Contact Director of Admission, Southern Illinois University at Edwardsville, Campus Box 1047, Edwardsville, Illinois 62026; 618-692-3705.
Graduate Contact Graduate Advisor, Art and Design Department, Southern Illinois University at Edwardsville, Campus Box 1774, Edwardsville, Illinois 62026; 618-692-3071, fax: 618-692-3096.

Meadows School of the Arts

▼ SOUTHERN METHODIST UNIVERSITY

Dallas, Texas

Independent, coed. Suburban campus. Total enrollment: 9,708.
Degrees Bachelor of Fine Arts in the area of art. Majors and concentrations: studio art. Graduate degrees offered: Master of Fine Arts in the area of art.
Enrollment Fall 1997: 96 total; 63 undergraduate, 8 graduate, 25 non-professional degree.
Art Student Profile 59% females, 41% males, 22% minorities, 5% international.
Art Faculty 15 total undergraduate and graduate (full-time and part-time). 100% of full-time faculty have terminal degrees. Graduate students do not teach undergraduate courses. Undergraduate student–faculty ratio: 7:1.
Student Life Student groups/activities include Student Art Association, Meadows Graduate Council, Pollock Gallery. Special housing available for art students.
Expenses for 1997–98 Application fee: $40. Comprehensive fee: $23,244 includes full-time tuition ($14,896), mandatory fees ($1894), and college room and board ($6454). College room only: $3600. Room and board charges vary according

to board plan and housing facility. Special program-related fees: $12 per credit hour for model and supply fees.
Financial Aid Program-specific awards for 1997: 10–15 Meadows Artistic Scholarships for talented program majors ($1000–$6000).
Application Procedures Students admitted directly into the professional program freshman year. Deadline for freshmen and transfers: continuous. Required: high school transcript, college transcript(s) for transfer students, letter of recommendation, portfolio, SAT I or ACT test scores, personal statement. Recommended: interview. Portfolio reviews held once on campus; the submission of slides may be substituted for portfolios (slides preferred).
Web Site http://www.smu.edu/~art.
Undergraduate Contact Ms. Jean Cherry, Associate Dean for Student Affairs, Meadows School of the Arts, Southern Methodist University, PO Box 750356, Dallas, Texas 75275-0356; 214-768-3765, fax: 214-768-3272.
Graduate Contact Ms. Jean Cherry, Director of Graduate Admissions, Meadows School of the Arts, Southern Methodist University, PO Box 750356, Dallas, Texas 75275-0356; 214-768-3765, fax: 214-768-3272.

▼ SOUTHERN OREGON UNIVERSITY

Ashland, Oregon

State-supported, coed. Small town campus. Total enrollment: 5,426. Art program established 1983.
Degrees Bachelor of Fine Arts in the areas of painting, printmaking, photography, ceramics, sculpture, fibers, digital media, mixed media. Majors and concentrations: ceramics, computer art, digital multi-media, fibers, interrelated media, painting/drawing, photography, printmaking, sculpture, studio art. Cross-registration with members of the National Student Exchange Program.
Enrollment Fall 1997: 220 total; 20 undergraduate, 200 non-professional degree.
Art Student Profile 50% females, 50% males, 10% minorities, 10% international.
Art Faculty 14 total (full-time and part-time). 90% of full-time faculty have terminal degrees. Graduate students do not teach undergraduate courses. Undergraduate student–faculty ratio: 12:1.
Student Life Student groups/activities include Schneider Museum of Art, student gallery management programs, Southern Oregon Fine Art Students.
Expenses for 1997–98 Application fee: $50. State resident tuition: $3204 full-time. Nonresident tuition: $9153 full-time. Full-time tuition varies according to course load and reciprocity agreements. College room and board: $4380. Room and board charges vary according to board plan and housing facility. Special program-related fees: $5–$50 per course for lab/materials fees.
Financial Aid Program-specific awards for 1997: 1 Mulling Award in Art for art majors demonstrating artistic ability ($500), 1 Schneider Merit Award in Art for art majors demonstrating artistic ability ($1000), 4 John Humbird Dickey Memorial Scholarships for art majors demonstrating artistic ability and financial need ($500), 1 Clifford Fowell Memorial Art Award for art majors demonstrating artistic ability ($100), 1 Anonymous Art Award for art majors demonstrating artistic ability ($100), 2 Sam and Helen

Southern Oregon University (*continued*)

Bernstein Awards for artistically talented ($100), 1 Art History Scholarship for art major with minor in art history ($1000).

Application Procedures Students apply for admission into the professional program by junior year. Deadline for freshmen and transfers: continuous. Notification date for freshmen and transfers: continuous. Required: high school transcript, college transcript(s) for transfer students, minimum 3.0 high school GPA, portfolio, SAT I or ACT test scores. Recommended: 3 letters of recommendation, interview. Portfolio reviews held twice during junior year on campus; the submission of slides may be substituted for portfolios for transfer applicants.

Undergraduate Contact Mr. Allen Blaszak, Director, Admissions and Records Department, Southern Oregon University, 1250 Siskiyou Boulevard, Ashland, Oregon 97520; 541-552-6411, fax: 541-552-6329.

▼ SOUTHWEST MISSOURI STATE UNIVERSITY
Springfield, Missouri

State-supported, coed. Suburban campus. Total enrollment: 16,468.

Degrees Bachelor of Fine Arts in the areas of design, fine arts. Majors and concentrations: ceramics, computer animation, digital imaging, drawing, graphic design, illustration, jewelry and metalsmithing, painting, photography, printmaking, sculpture.

Enrollment Fall 1997: 334 undergraduate.

Art Student Profile 55% females, 45% males, 10% minorities, 5% international.

Art Faculty 41 total (full-time and part-time). 100% of full-time faculty have terminal degrees. Graduate students do not teach undergraduate courses.

Student Life Student groups/activities include Design Student Club, Student Artist Association, clubs in various areas of emphasis.

Expenses for 1998–99 Application fee: $15. State resident tuition: $2940 full-time. Nonresident tuition: $5880 full-time. Mandatory fees: $274 full-time. Full-time tuition and fees vary according to course load. College room and board: $3594. College room only: $2396. Room and board charges vary according to board plan and housing facility. Special program-related fees: $25 per course for lab fees for specific courses.

Financial Aid Program-specific awards for 1997: 10 departmental awards for program majors ($500–$800).

Application Procedures Students apply for admission into the professional program by sophomore year. Deadline for freshmen and transfers: August 1. Notification date for freshmen and transfers: continuous. Required: high school transcript, minimum 2.0 high school GPA, portfolio for scholarship consideration.

Undergraduate Contact Bruce West, Recruitment Coordinator, Southwest Missouri State University, 901 South National, Springfield, Missouri 65804; 417-836-5110.

▼ SOUTHWEST TEXAS STATE UNIVERSITY
San Marcos, Texas

State-supported, coed. Small town campus. Total enrollment: 20,652. Art program established 1940.

Degrees Bachelor of Fine Arts in the areas of studio art, communication design, art education. Majors and concentrations: art history, ceramics, communication design, fibers, jewelry and metalsmithing, painting/drawing, photography, printmaking, sculpture, watercolors.

Enrollment Fall 1997: 520 total; 450 undergraduate, 70 non-professional degree.

Art Student Profile 56% females, 44% males, 26% minorities, 1% international.

Art Faculty 35 total (full-time and part-time). 100% of full-time faculty have terminal degrees. Graduate students do not teach undergraduate courses. Undergraduate student–faculty ratio: 18:1.

Student Life Student groups/activities include Metals Guild, CASA-Ceramics Organization, AIGA-National Communication Design Organization.

Expenses for 1997–98 Application fee: $25. State resident tuition: $816 full-time. Nonresident tuition: $5952 full-time. Mandatory fees: $1398 full-time. Full-time tuition and fees vary according to course load. College room and board: $3901. Room and board charges vary according to board plan and housing facility. Special program-related fees: $15–$55 per course for material fees.

Financial Aid Program-specific awards for 1997: 2 Dr. Francis Henry Scholarships for art education majors ($500), 1 Louise Eckerd McGehee Scholarship for program majors ($500), 8–12 Student Services Fee Scholarships for program majors ($200–$400), 1 Presidential Upper Level Scholarship for program majors ($1200), 1 Turner Endowed Scholarship for painting majors ($500), 1 Department of Art and Design Scholarship for program majors ($500), 1 Barbara Shimkus Endowed Scholarship for communication design majors ($500).

Application Procedures Students admitted directly into the professional program freshman year. Deadline for freshmen and transfers: July 1. Required: high school transcript, college transcript(s) for transfer students, minimum 2.0 high school GPA, SAT I or ACT test scores.

Undergraduate Contact Mr. Brian Row, Chair, Department of Art and Design, Southwest Texas State University, 601 University Drive, San Marcos, Texas 78666; 512-245-2611, fax: 512-245-3040, E-mail address: br01@swt.edu.

▼ STATE UNIVERSITY OF NEW YORK AT BUFFALO
Buffalo, New York

State-supported, coed. Suburban campus. Total enrollment: 23,429. Art program established 1954.

Degrees Bachelor of Fine Arts in the area of fine art. Majors and concentrations: communication design, computer art, illustration, painting/drawing, photography, printmaking, sculpture. Graduate degrees offered: Master of Fine Arts in the area of fine art. Program accredited by NASAD.

Enrollment Fall 1997: 386 total; 312 undergraduate, 17 graduate, 57 non-professional degree.

Art Student Profile 50% females, 50% males, 10% minorities, 10% international.

Art Faculty 27 total undergraduate and graduate (full-time and part-time). 90% of full-time faculty have terminal degrees. Graduate students teach a few undergraduate courses. Undergraduate student–faculty ratio: 18:1.

Student Life Student groups/activities include Art Department Gallery exhibits, University Gallery exhibits.

Expenses for 1997–98 Application fee: $30. State resident tuition: $3400 full-time. Nonresident tuition: $8300 full-time. Mandatory fees: $940 full-time. College room and board: $5604. College room only: $3224. Room and board charges vary according to housing facility. Special program-related fees: $15–$75 per course for lab fees, supplies, models.

Application Procedures Students admitted directly into the professional program freshman year. Deadline for freshmen and transfers: January 1. Notification date for freshmen and transfers: March 20. Required: college transcript(s) for transfer students, portfolio, SAT I or ACT test scores. Recommended: essay, letter of recommendation. Portfolio reviews held twice and continuously during summer on campus and off campus in Syracuse, NY on National Portfolio Day; the submission of slides may be substituted for portfolios if a campus visit is impossible.

Undergraduate Contact Ms. Kathleen Glaser, Academic Advisor, Art Department, State University of New York at Buffalo, 202 Center for the Arts, Buffalo, New York 14260-6010; 716-645-6000 ext. 1371, fax: 716-645-6970.

Graduate Contact Mr. Willard Harris, Director of Graduate Studies, Art Department, State University of New York at Buffalo, 202 Center for the Arts, Buffalo, New York 14260-6010; 716-645-6878 ext. 1360, fax: 716-645-6970.

▼ STATE UNIVERSITY OF NEW YORK AT NEW PALTZ

New Paltz, New York

State-supported, coed. Small town campus. Total enrollment: 7,641. Art program established 1960.

Degrees Bachelor of Fine Arts in the areas of ceramics, metals, painting, photography, printmaking, sculpture, graphic design. Majors and concentrations: art education, ceramic art and design, graphic design, jewelry and metalsmithing, painting/drawing, photography, printmaking, sculpture. Graduate degrees offered: Master of Fine Arts in the areas of ceramics, metals, painting, photography, printmaking, sculpture, interdisciplinary studies; Master of Science in the area of art education; Master of Arts in the areas of ceramics, sculpture, printmaking, metals, photography, painting. Cross-registration with State University of New York System. Program accredited by NASAD.

Enrollment Fall 1997: 537 total; 466 undergraduate, 71 graduate.

Art Student Profile 65% females, 35% males, 20% minorities.

Art Faculty 36 total undergraduate and graduate (full-time and part-time). 89% of full-time faculty have terminal degrees. Graduate students teach a few undergraduate courses. Undergraduate student–faculty ratio: 19:1.

Student Life Student groups/activities include Student Art Alliance, National Art Education Association, clubs in every studio area.

Estimated expenses for 1998–99 Application fee: $30. State resident tuition: $3400 full-time. Nonresident tuition: $8300 full-time. Mandatory fees: $485 full-time. College room and board: $5020. College room only: $3000. Room and board charges vary according to board plan. Special program-related fees: $45–$80 per course for lab fees.

Financial Aid Program-specific awards for 1997: 1 Resnick Scholarship for incoming freshmen.

Application Procedures Students apply for admission into the professional program by sophomore year. Deadline for freshmen: May 1; transfers: June 1. Required: high school transcript, college transcript(s) for transfer students, portfolio, SAT I or ACT test scores. Recommended: minimum 3.0 high school GPA. Portfolio reviews held 10 times on campus and off campus in Albany, NY; Rochester, NY; New York, NY; the submission of slides may be substituted for portfolios if of good quality.

Web Site http://www.newpaltz.edu.

Undergraduate Contact Ms. Dorothy Howitt, Secretary, Art Department, State University of New York at New Paltz, SAB 106, 75 South Manheim Boulevard, New Paltz, New York 12561-2499; 914-257-3830, fax: 914-257-3848.

Graduate Contact Graduate Office, State University of New York at New Paltz, HAB Room 804, New Paltz, New York 12561-2499; 914-257-3285.

▼ STATE UNIVERSITY OF NEW YORK COLLEGE AT FREDONIA

Fredonia, New York

State-supported, coed. Small town campus. Total enrollment: 4,593.

Degrees Bachelor of Fine Arts in the area of art. Majors and concentrations: ceramics, drawing, graphic design, illustration, painting, photography, sculpture.

Enrollment Fall 1997: 130 total; 30 undergraduate, 100 non-professional degree.

Art Student Profile 55% females, 45% males, 1% minorities.

Art Faculty 12 total (full-time and part-time). 100% of full-time faculty have terminal degrees. Graduate students do not teach undergraduate courses. Undergraduate student–faculty ratio: 14:1.

Student Life Student groups/activities include Art Forum.

Expenses for 1997–98 Application fee: $30. State resident tuition: $3400 full-time. Nonresident tuition: $8300 full-time. Mandatory fees: $675 full-time. College room and board: $4650. College room only: $3000. Room and board charges vary according to board plan and housing facility. Special program-related fees: $10–$70 per course for lab fees.

Financial Aid Program-specific awards for 1997: 5 departmental scholarships for talented students ($350).

Application Procedures Students apply for admission into the professional program by junior year. Deadline for freshmen and transfers: continuous. Required: high school transcript, college transcript(s) for transfer students, portfolio, SAT I or ACT test scores. Recommended: 3 letters of recommendation, interview. Portfolio reviews held by appointment on campus; the submission of slides may be substituted for portfolios (slides preferred).

Undergraduate Contact Ms. Mary Lee Lunde, Chair, Department of Art, State University of New York College at Fredonia, Rockefeller Center, Fredonia, New York 14063; 716-673-3537, E-mail address: lundem@fredonia.edu.

▼ STATE UNIVERSITY OF NEW YORK COLLEGE AT PURCHASE

See Purchase College, State University of New York

▼ STATE UNIVERSITY OF WEST GEORGIA

Carrollton, Georgia

State-supported, coed. Small town campus. Total enrollment: 8,422. Art program established 1972.

Degrees Bachelor of Fine Arts in the area of art. Majors and concentrations: art education, ceramics, graphic design, interior design, painting/drawing, photography, printmaking, sculpture. Graduate degrees offered: Master of Education in the area of art education. Program accredited by NASAD.

Enrollment Fall 1997: 156 total; 130 undergraduate, 14 graduate, 12 non-professional degree.

Art Student Profile 60% females, 40% males, 15% minorities, 1% international.

Art Faculty 13 total undergraduate and graduate (full-time and part-time). 100% of full-time faculty have terminal degrees. Graduate students do not teach undergraduate courses.

Student Life Student groups/activities include Georgia Art Education Association Student Chapter, professional artists organizations, Art Student League.

Expenses for 1997–98 Application fee: $15. State resident tuition: $1680 full-time. Nonresident tuition: $4461 full-time. Mandatory fees: $408 full-time. College room and board: $3399. College room only: $1728. Room and board charges vary according to board plan. Special program-related fees: $15 per course for ceramics fee, $20 per course for photography fee, $10–$25 per course for life drawing fee.

Financial Aid Program-specific awards for 1997: 20–30 departmental awards for those demonstrating talent and need ($500).

Application Procedures Students admitted directly into the professional program freshman year. Deadline for freshmen and transfers: continuous. Notification date for freshmen and transfers: continuous. Required: high school transcript, SAT I or ACT test scores.

Contact Mr. Bruce Bobick, Chairman, Department of Art, State University of West Georgia, 1600 Maple Street, Carrollton, Georgia 30118; 770-836-6521, fax: 770-836-4392, E-mail address: bbobick@westga.edu.

▼ STEPHEN F. AUSTIN STATE UNIVERSITY

Nacogdoches, Texas

State-supported, coed. Small town campus. Total enrollment: 12,041.

Degrees Bachelor of Fine Arts in the area of art. Majors and concentrations: studio art. Graduate degrees offered: Master of Fine Arts in the area of art. Program accredited by NASAD.

Enrollment Fall 1997: 180 undergraduate, 24 graduate.

Art Student Profile 45% females, 55% males.

Art Faculty 17 total undergraduate and graduate (full-time and part-time). 93% of full-time faculty have terminal degrees. Graduate students teach a few undergraduate courses.

Student Life Student groups/activities include Art Alliance (student art group), Ad Hoc Student Advertising Design Group.

Expenses for 1997–98 Application fee: $0. One-time mandatory fee: $10. State resident tuition: $1020 full-time. Nonresident tuition: $7440 full-time. Mandatory fees: $1168 full-time. Full-time tuition and fees vary according to course load and reciprocity agreements. College room and board: $3682. Room and board charges vary according to board plan and housing facility. Special program-related fees: $5–$40 per course for supplies.

Financial Aid Program-specific awards for 1997: 6–10 art scholarships for program majors ($200–$600).

Application Procedures Students admitted directly into the professional program freshman year. Deadline for freshmen and transfers: August 15. Required: high school transcript, college transcript(s) for transfer students, SAT I or ACT test scores.

Contact Mr. Jon D. Wink, Chairman, Art Department, Stephen F. Austin State University, Box 13001 SFA Station, Nacogdoches, Texas 75962-3001; 409-468-4804, fax: 409-468-4041, E-mail address: f_priceep@titan.sfasu.edu.

▼ STEPHENS COLLEGE

Columbia, Missouri

Independent, women only. Urban campus. Total enrollment: 819.

Degrees Bachelor of Fine Arts in the area of fashion design and product development. Cross-registration with University of Missouri-Columbia, Columbia College, William Woods University, Westminster College, Lincoln University.

Enrollment Fall 1997: 65 undergraduate.

Art Student Profile 100% females, 6% minorities, 5% international.

Art Faculty 6 total (full-time and part-time). 75% of full-time faculty have terminal degrees. Graduate students do not teach undergraduate courses. Undergraduate student–faculty ratio: 12:1.

Student Life Student groups/activities include Pi Phi Rho (fashion honorary society), Innovative Fashion Association (all fashion majors). Special housing available for art students.

Expenses for 1997–98 Application fee: $25. Comprehensive fee: $20,530 includes full-time tuition ($14,830) and college room and board ($5700). College room only: $2990. Room and board charges vary according to board plan and housing facility.

Financial Aid Program-specific awards for 1997: 1 Jeannene Booher Scholarship for fashion design majors ($3000), 1 Jill Kasten Memorial Scholarship for fashion majors ($1200).

Application Procedures Students admitted directly into the professional program freshman year. Deadline for freshmen and transfers: continuous. Required: essay, high school transcript, college transcript(s) for transfer students, minimum 2.0 high school GPA, letter of recommendation, SAT I or ACT test scores. Recommended: minimum 3.0 high school GPA, interview, portfolio. Portfolio reviews held as needed on campus; the submission of slides may be substituted for portfolios if original work is not available.

Undergraduate Contact Margaret Herron, Assistant Director of Enrollment Services, Stephens College, Columbia, Missouri 65215; 800-876-7207, fax: 573-876-7237, E-mail address: apply@sc.stephens.edu.

The New England School of Art & Design

▼ SUFFOLK UNIVERSITY

Boston, Massachusetts

Independent, coed. Urban campus. Total enrollment: 6,290. Art program established 1923.

Degrees Bachelor of Fine Arts in the areas of graphic design, interior design, fine arts. Cross-registration with Berklee College of Music, Emerson College. Program accredited by NASAD, FIDER.

Enrollment Fall 1997: 163 undergraduate.

Art Student Profile 72% females, 28% males, 5% minorities, 15% international.

Art Faculty 40 total (full-time and part-time). 78% of full-time faculty have terminal degrees. Graduate students do not teach undergraduate courses. Undergraduate student–faculty ratio: 8:1.

Student Life Student groups/activities include American Society of Interior Designers Student Chapter.

Expenses for 1997–98 Application fee: $40. Comprehensive fee: $21,270 includes full-time tuition ($12,840), mandatory fees ($80), and college room and board ($8350). Special program-related fees: $120 per course for studio fee.

Financial Aid Program-specific awards for 1997: 2 J.W.S. Cox Scholarships for those demonstrating talent ($2000).

Application Procedures Students admitted directly into the professional program freshman year. Deadline for freshmen and transfers: continuous. Required: essay, high school transcript, college transcript(s) for transfer students, minimum 2.0 high school GPA, 2 letters of recommendation, portfolio, SAT I or ACT test scores. Recommended: interview. Portfolio reviews held continuously on campus; the submission of slides may be substituted for portfolios whenever needed.

Undergraduate Contact Ms. Anne M. Blevins, Associate Director of Admission, Undergraduate Admission, Suffolk University, 8 Ashburton Place, Boston, Massachusetts 02108; 617-573-8460, fax: 617-742-4291, E-mail address: ablevins@admin.suffolk.edu.

Suffolk University

More About the University

The B.F.A. programs at Suffolk University are housed in the New School of Art and Design at Suffolk University (NESADSU). NESADSU was established in 1996 by joining The New England School of Art and Design (NESAD) and Suffolk University. NESAD has more than seventy years of providing practical, personalized education to generations of aspiring artists and designers. Combined with Suffolk's ninety-year tradition in the liberal arts, its academic resources, ideal location, and facilities, the art and design programs offered by NESADSU inspire and prepare students for careers in the arts.

NESADSU students explore their talents while learning to communicate through art. Experimentation and creativity are essential to study as well as professional success. Equally important are a clearly defined sense of purpose and a comprehensive education. A NESADSU education offers the instruction, facilities, and resources students need to become successful working professionals. NESADSU is part of Boston's cultural and creative community. Located in the city's Park Square, the art building is within walking distance of world-class museums, galleries, theaters, libraries, and other important resources. It is also a short walk to the main University campus on Beacon Hill and to the residence hall in downtown Boston. The art programs occupy approximately 18,000 square feet of newly renovated space, designed and furnished to meet the specific needs of art and design majors. Equipment includes Power Macs, CD-ROM drives, 15-inch monitors, two Quadras, six Mac IIci's, one Hewlett Packard plotter and two color scanners, one slide scanner, one Tektronix thermal wax color printer, one inkjet color printer, and three black-and-white laser printers. The software available is Adobe Dimensions, Adobe Illustrator, Adobe Photoshop, Macromedia Director, Quark Xpress, Fractal Painter, Microsoft Word, AutoCAD, and Microsoft Office.

Library resources are both at the main campus and the NESADSU building, with a focused collection of materials to support and enhance the study of graphic design, interior design, and fine arts. Of particular interest to interior design students are NCIDQ study guides and videos, ADA handbooks, Sweet's Catalogues, and a file of interior design product brochures providing comprehensive information on product sources and manufacturers' offerings. Type specimen books, paper samples, and picture reference files provide graphic designers with additional information, while fine artists have access to auction catalogs in the fine and decorative arts. The separate Materials Library provides interior design students with a comprehensive collection of fabric samples, wall and floor coverings, plastic laminates, and paints.

Along with a comprehensive, sequential curriculum, the academic program is built on a system of portfolio reviews. At the end of the first year and periodically thereafter, program directors and faculty members review a student's work to date, evaluating strengths and weaknesses and planning strategies for improvement. Senior year students use the review experience to present a final selection of work to a panel of designers unaffiliated with the School. Portfolio reviews and compulsory internships prepare students for the rigors of the employment market and help develop techniques for successful job placement.

Art students may access all of the University's resources as well, including computer, science, and language labs; the Ballotti Learning Center; gymnasium; fitness center; student advising; and extensive activities programming. An exhibit space features the work of students, faculty members, and alumni as well as outside artists and designers.

Career services, cooperative education, and internship programs allow students to gain valuable work experience related to their career goals. The University's career services

Suffolk University *(continued)*

office helps students investigate career choices and offers placement assistance as a lifetime benefit to graduates.

Suffolk University is regionally accredited by NEASC, holds AACSB–The International Association for Management Education accreditation for business programs, and is FIDER-accredited for interior design.

▼ SUL ROSS STATE UNIVERSITY

Alpine, Texas

State-supported, coed. Small town campus.

Degrees Bachelor of Fine Arts in the areas of art, art education. Majors and concentrations: art education, art/fine arts, ceramic art and design, painting/drawing, printmaking, sculpture, studio art. Graduate degrees offered: Master of Education in the areas of art, art education. Cross-registration with University of Texas at El Paso, University of Texas of the Permian Basin, Odessa College, South Plains College, El Paso Community College.

Enrollment Fall 1997: 39 total; 24 undergraduate, 15 graduate.

Art Student Profile 47% females, 53% males, 45% minorities, 1% international.

Art Faculty 5 total undergraduate and graduate (full-time and part-time). 100% of full-time faculty have terminal degrees. Graduate students do not teach undergraduate courses.

Student Life Student groups/activities include Art Club, Student Art Show, Kappa Pi (art fraternity).

Expenses for 1997–98 Application fee: $0. State resident tuition: $1020 full-time. Nonresident tuition: $6660 full-time. Mandatory fees: $660 full-time. Special program-related fees: $35 per 3 credits for clay and glazes for ceramics classes, $35 per 3 credits for plaster and clay for sculpture classes.

Financial Aid Program-specific awards for 1997: 6 Boatright Scholarships for program students ($100–$300), 3 Art Excellence Awards for program students ($300).

Application Procedures Students admitted directly into the professional program freshman year. Deadline for freshmen and transfers: continuous. Required: high school transcript, college transcript(s) for transfer students, minimum 2.0 high school GPA, portfolio, SAT I or ACT test scores (minimum combined SAT I score of 800, minimum combined ACT score of 20). Recommended: interview. Portfolio reviews held once on campus; the submission of slides may be substituted for portfolios with some original work.

Undergraduate Contact Director of Admissions, Sul Ross State University, Box C-2, Alpine, Texas 79832; 915-837-8050.

Graduate Contact Linda Coleman, Director of Graduate Admissions, Sul Ross State University, Box C-2, Alpine, Texas 79832; 915-837-8050.

▼ SYRACUSE UNIVERSITY

Syracuse, New York

Independent, coed. Urban campus. Total enrollment: 14,557. Art program established 1873.

Degrees Bachelor of Fine Arts in the areas of advertising design, art education, ceramics, computer graphics, communications design, fibers, history of art, interior design, metalsmithing, painting, photography, printmaking, sculpture, surface pattern design, illustration, film, video art; Bachelor of Industrial Design in the area of industrial design. Majors and concentrations: advertising design, art education, art history, ceramics, communication design, computer graphics, fibers, film, illustration, industrial design, interior design, jewelry and metalsmithing, painting/drawing, photography, printmaking, sculpture, surface design, video art. Graduate degrees offered: Master of Fine Arts in the areas of advertising design, ceramics, computer graphics, fibers, film, illustration, interior design, metalsmithing, museum studies, painting, photography, printmaking, sculpture, surface pattern design, video; Master of Industrial Design in the area of industrial design. Program accredited by NASAD, FIDER.

Enrollment Fall 1997: 1,227 total; 1,124 undergraduate, 103 graduate.

Art Student Profile 48% females, 52% males, 14% minorities, 2% international.

Art Faculty 103 total undergraduate and graduate (full-time and part-time). 88% of full-time faculty have terminal degrees. Graduate students teach a few undergraduate courses. Undergraduate student–faculty ratio: 18:1.

Student Life Student groups/activities include American Society of Interior Designers, Industrial Design Society of America, New York Society of Illustrators.

Expenses for 1997–98 Application fee: $40. Comprehensive fee: $25,816 includes full-time tuition ($17,550), mandatory fees ($506), and college room and board ($7760). College room only: $4090. Room and board charges vary according to board plan and housing facility. Special program-related fees: $10–$130 per semester for lab fees to cover costs of models and special supplies.

Financial Aid Program-specific awards for 1997: 15 Art Merit Scholarships for incoming freshmen ($1000), 50 Chancellor's Awards for incoming freshmen ($6000), 160 Dean's Awards for incoming freshmen ($4000), 1 National Scholastic Award for Art National Scholarship winner ($2000).

Application Procedures Students admitted directly into the professional program freshman year. Deadline for freshmen: January 15; transfers: July 1. Notification date for freshmen: March 15; transfers: August 15. Required: essay, high school transcript, college transcript(s) for transfer students, minimum 2.0 high school GPA, 2 letters of recommendation, portfolio, SAT I or ACT test scores, high school counselor evaluation. Recommended: minimum 3.0 high school GPA, interview. Portfolio reviews held continuously on campus and off campus in New York, NY; Boston, MA; Chicago, IL; Philadelphia, PA; Baltimore, MD; Hartford, CT; Miami, FL; Washington, DC; the submission of slides may be substituted for portfolios when distance is prohibitive.

Web Site http://vpa.syr.edu.

Undergraduate Contact Coordinator of Recruiting, College of Visual and Performing Arts, Syracuse University, 202P Crouse College, Syracuse, New York 13244-1010; 315-443-2769, fax: 315-443-1935, E-mail address: admissu@vpa.syr.edu.

Graduate Contact Graduate School, Syracuse University, Suite 303 Bowne Hall, Syracuse, New York 13244; 315-443-3028, fax: 315-443-3423, E-mail address: gradschl@suadmin.syr.edu.

More About the University

Program Facilities Comstock Art Facility: studios for ceramics, fibers, metalsmithing, printmaking, and sculpture and three-dimensional design studios; Crouse College: drawing and design studios and classrooms; Dorothea Ilgen Shaffer Art Building: Joe and Emily Lowe Art Gallery; Shemin auditorium (300 seats); Green & Seifter Lecture Hall (60 seats); facilities for advertising design, communications design, illustration, art photography, art video, computer graphics, film, drawing, and painting; and studios for undergraduates; Smith Hall (Center for Design): studios for industrial, interior, and surface pattern design; and M-17 Skytop Building: art education program facilities.

Faculty, Resident Artists, and Alumni Faculty members are well-established professional artists and designers who are active locally, nationally, and internationally; several are Guggenheim, Pulitzer, and Fulbright fellows and recipients of grants from the National Endowment for the Arts, Ford Foundation, and the Rockefeller Foundation. Alumni are prestigious figures in the museum and gallery world who exhibit locally, nationally, and internationally as well as professionals and executives in prominent agencies, firms, and corporations in the areas of industrial design, interior design, surface pattern design, advertising, and filmmaking.

Student Exhibit Opportunities Exhibit space is in the Joe and Emily Lowe Art Gallery, the Comstock Art Facility, the Schine Student Center, Smith Hall, the Shaffer Art Building, and Crouse College.

Special Programs Weekly visiting artist programs in painting and visual communication feature lectures and critiques of student work and are open to all; students may study abroad in Florence through SU's Division of International Programs Abroad (DIPA); internships through the School, the Syracuse University Internship Program, and the Career Services Center at galleries, museums, newspapers and magazines, design agencies, and local television stations; honors program available for students who desire a rigorous academic challenge.

▼

The School of Art and Design encourages students to reach their creative and intellectual potential and prepares them as professional artists, designers, and educators. All students in the School of Art and Design start with a one-year foundation program that offers studio work in drawing, two- and three-dimensional problem solving, academic courses in art history and issues in art, and a writing studio. In the sophomore year, students begin specialization toward their major; typically, each semester, they take studio courses in their major, studio electives, and academic electives. The studio electives allow them to experiment in disciplines and media outside the major. The academic electives may be selected from the broad range of courses offered by the University. All degree paths are accredited by the National Association of Schools of Art and Design.

Students benefit from a faculty of practicing professionals whose work is included in the permanent collections of the Smithsonian; the Art Institute of Chicago; the International Polaroid Collection in Cambridge, Massachusetts; the Museum of Fine Art in Houston; the Museum of Modern Art in New York City; the National Gallery of Canada in Ottawa, Ontario; the Gallerie Degli Uffici in Florence, Italy; and the Museo Nacional Centro de Arte Reina Sofia in Madrid, Spain. Faculty members have also contributed to such publications as *Time, Esquire, Life, the New York Times, The Washington Post, Audubon Magazine,* and *National Lampoon.* Their work is commissioned by clients in the United States and abroad, and many publish and exhibit in Europe and Asia.

Several features set SU's School of Art and Design apart from other schools and increase students' contact with the professional art and design world. An extensive network of active and successful alumni, comprehensive visiting artist programs, well-known faculty members, and University programs and organizations all contribute to the internship and professional opportunities for students.

The creative activities of the School of Art and Design are an integral part of the College of Visual and Performing Arts, which also governs programs in drama, music, and speech communication. The College serves as the center of SU's cultural life, on a campus whose lively and diverse schedule of events could only be found at a large university.

The city of Syracuse itself offers a rich culture of its own. The Everson Museum of Art, designed by architect I. M. Pei, houses one of the foremost ceramic collections in the United States and offers a diverse exhibition schedule. The Syracuse Symphony Orchestra, the Syracuse Opera, and the Society for New Music, as well as nationally known comedians, rock groups, and dance companies, perform frequently. Nestled between the Finger Lakes, the Adirondacks, and the many historical and natural landmarks in central New York State, Syracuse is within a day's drive of New York City and Boston and of Toronto, Ottawa, and Montreal in Canada.

▼ TEMPLE UNIVERSITY
See Tyler School of Art of Temple University

▼ TEXAS A&M UNIVERSITY–COMMERCE
Commerce, Texas

State-supported, coed. Small town campus. Total enrollment: 7,693. Art program established 1920.

Degrees Bachelor of Fine Arts in the areas of sculpture and metals, painting, ceramics, photography, illustration, experimental studies, graphic arts. Majors and concentrations: art direction, art education, art/fine arts, ceramic art and design, commercial art, experimental studies, graphic arts, graphic design, illustration, jewelry and metalsmithing, painting/drawing, photography, printmaking, sculpture, studio art. Graduate degrees offered: Master of Fine Arts in the areas of sculpture and metals, painting, ceramics, illustration, experimental studies, photography. Cross-registration with University of North Texas, Texas Woman's University.

Enrollment Fall 1997: 242 total; 232 undergraduate, 10 graduate.

Art Student Profile 60% females, 40% males, 10% minorities, 2% international.

Art Faculty 18 total undergraduate and graduate (full-time and part-time). 90% of full-time faculty have terminal degrees. Graduate students teach a few undergraduate courses. Undergraduate student–faculty ratio: 14:1.

Student Life Student groups/activities include Students Art Association, Photo Society. Special housing available for art students.

Expenses for 1997–98 Application fee: $0. State resident tuition: $1740 full-time. Nonresident tuition: $8160 full-time. Mandatory fees: $546 full-time. Full-time tuition and fees vary according to course load. College room and board: $3816. College room only: $1942. Room and board charges vary according to board plan and housing facility. Special program-related fees: $10 per semester for course materials in ceramic classes.

Financial Aid Program-specific awards for 1997: 7–12 Endowed Scholarships for program majors ($200–$500).

Texas A&M University–Commerce *(continued)*

Application Procedures Students admitted directly into the professional program freshman year. Deadline for freshmen and transfers: August 6. Required: high school transcript, college transcript(s) for transfer students, SAT I or ACT test scores, portfolio for transfer students. Portfolio reviews held by request on campus; the submission of slides may be substituted for portfolios if of good quality.

Web Site http://www.tamu-commerce.edu/artsg/index.html.

Undergraduate Contact Dr. William Wadley, Head, Department of Art, Texas A&M University–Commerce, East Texas Station, Commerce, Texas 75429-3011; 903-886-5208, fax: 903-886-5987.

Graduate Contact Mr. Jerry Dodd, Graduate Coordinator, Department of Art, Texas A&M University–Commerce, East Texas Station, Commerce, Texas 75429-3011; 903-886-5208, fax: 903-886-5987, E-mail address: jerry_dodd@tamu-commerce.edu.

▼ Texas A&M University–Corpus Christi

Corpus Christi, Texas

State-supported, coed. Suburban campus. Total enrollment: 6,024.

Degrees Bachelor of Fine Arts in the area of art. Majors and concentrations: studio art.

Enrollment Fall 1997: 99 total; 28 undergraduate, 71 non-professional degree.

Art Student Profile 55% females, 45% males, 38% minorities.

Art Faculty 8 total (full-time and part-time). 95% of full-time faculty have terminal degrees. Graduate students do not teach undergraduate courses. Undergraduate student–faculty ratio: 12:1.

Student Life Student groups/activities include Student Art Association.

Expenses for 1997–98 Application fee: $10. State resident tuition: $816 full-time. Nonresident tuition: $5952 full-time. Mandatory fees: $1138 full-time. Special program-related fees: $25–$33 per course for art material fees.

Financial Aid Program-specific awards for 1997: 6 Ben Vaughn Scholarships for program majors ($600), 9 Dougherty-Carr Fund for the Arts Awards for program majors ($1000), 5 Fine Arts Studio Scholarships for program majors ($1000).

Application Procedures Students apply for admission into the professional program by junior year. Deadline for freshmen and transfers: continuous. Required: high school transcript, college transcript(s) for transfer students, portfolio, SAT I or ACT test scores, completion of college preparatory courses. Recommended: letter of recommendation. Portfolio reviews held twice on campus; the submission of slides may be substituted for portfolios if accompanied by a slide list and descriptions.

Web Site http://maclab.tamucc.edu/dvpa/.

Undergraduate Contact Mr. Mark Anderson, Chairman, Department of Visual and Performing Arts, Texas A&M University–Corpus Christi, 6300 Ocean Drive, Corpus Christi, Texas 78412; 512-994-5835, fax: 512-994-6097, E-mail address: anderson@falcon.tamucc.edu.

▼ Texas A&M University–Kingsville

Kingsville, Texas

State-supported, coed. Small town campus. Total enrollment: 6,050. Art program established 1959.

Degrees Bachelor of Fine Arts in the areas of art, art education. Graduate degrees offered: Master of Science in the area of studio art.

Enrollment Fall 1997: 110 total; 80 undergraduate, 10 graduate, 20 non-professional degree.

Art Student Profile 55% females, 45% males, 70% minorities.

Art Faculty 6 total undergraduate and graduate (full-time). 83% of full-time faculty have terminal degrees. Graduate students do not teach undergraduate courses. Undergraduate student–faculty ratio: 16:1.

Student Life Student groups/activities include Association of Fine Artists. Special housing available for art students.

Expenses for 1997–98 Application fee: $15. State resident tuition: $1054 full-time. Nonresident tuition: $7688 full-time. Mandatory fees: $1126 full-time. College room and board: $3484. College room only: $1784. Room and board charges vary according to board plan. Special program-related fees: $10 per course for lab fee.

Application Procedures Students admitted directly into the professional program freshman year. Deadline for freshmen and transfers: continuous. Required: high school transcript, college transcript(s) for transfer students, minimum 2.0 high school GPA, SAT I or ACT test scores (minimum combined SAT I score of 810, minimum combined ACT score of 15). Recommended: minimum 3.0 high school GPA.

Contact Mr. Richard Scherpereel, Chair, Art Department, Texas A&M University–Kingsville, Kingsville, Texas 78363; 512-593-2619, fax: 512-593-2662.

▼ Texas Christian University

Fort Worth, Texas

Independent, coed. Suburban campus. Total enrollment: 7,273. Art program established 1884.

Degrees Bachelor of Fine Arts in the areas of art education, graphic design, studio art. Majors and concentrations: art education, graphic design, painting/drawing, photography, printmaking, sculpture. Graduate degrees offered: Master of Fine Arts in the areas of painting, printmaking, sculpture; Master of Arts in the areas of art history, museum studies. Cross-registration with Universidad de las Americas (Mexico).

Enrollment Fall 1997: 98 undergraduate, 7 graduate.

Art Student Profile 57% females, 43% males, 14% minorities, 4% international.

Art Faculty 19 total undergraduate and graduate (full-time and part-time). 100% of full-time faculty have terminal degrees. Graduate students do not teach undergraduate courses. Undergraduate student–faculty ratio: 18:1.

Student Life Student groups/activities include Visual Arts Committee of the Student Programming Council.

Expenses for 1997–98 Application fee: $30. One-time mandatory fee: $200. Comprehensive fee: $14,950 includes full-time tuition ($9900), mandatory fees ($1190), and college room and board ($3860). College room only: $2460. Room and board charges vary according to housing facility. Special program-related fees: $65 per semester for computer use.

Financial Aid Program-specific awards for 1997: 2 Nordan Scholarships for freshmen ($3000).

Application Procedures Students admitted directly into the professional program freshman year. Deadline for freshmen and transfers: April 15. Required: essay, high school transcript, college transcript(s) for transfer students, minimum 3.0 high school GPA, 3 letters of recommendation, SAT I or ACT test scores. Recommended: interview.

Web Site http://www.tcu.edu.

Contact Mr. Ronald Watson, Chairman, Department of Art and Art History, Texas Christian University, 2800 South University Drive, TCU Box 298000, Fort Worth, Texas 76129; 817-257-7643, fax: 817-257-7399, E-mail address: r.watson@tcu.edu.

▼ TEXAS SOUTHERN UNIVERSITY

Houston, Texas

State-supported, coed. Urban campus. Total enrollment: 7,282. Art program established 1948.

Degrees Bachelor of Arts in the area of fine arts. Majors and concentrations: art history, ceramics, design, painting/drawing, printmaking, sculpture.

Enrollment Fall 1997: 47 total; all undergraduate.

Art Student Profile 40% females, 60% males, 95% minorities, 10% international.

Art Faculty 8 total (full-time and part-time). 82% of full-time faculty have terminal degrees. Graduate students do not teach undergraduate courses. Undergraduate student–faculty ratio: 9:1.

Student Life Student groups/activities include Art Club.

Expenses for 1997–98 Application fee: $25. State resident tuition: $1054 full-time. Nonresident tuition: $7688 full-time. Mandatory fees: $1010 full-time. Full-time tuition and fees vary according to course load. College room and board: $4000.

Financial Aid Program-specific awards for 1997: 2–3 Selgary Scholarships for art majors ($200–$500).

Application Procedures Students admitted directly into the professional program freshman year. Deadline for freshmen and transfers: June 20. Notification date for freshmen and transfers: August 20. Required: high school transcript, college transcript(s) for transfer students, minimum 2.0 high school GPA, interview, portfolio, SAT I or ACT test scores. Portfolio reviews held twice on campus; the submission of slides may be substituted for portfolios for out-of-state applicants.

Undergraduate Contact Dr. Sarah Trotty, Chair, Department of Fine Arts, Texas Southern University, 3100 Cleburne Avenue, Houston, Texas 77004; 713-313-7337, fax: 713-313-7539.

▼ TEXAS TECH UNIVERSITY

Lubbock, Texas

State-supported, coed. Urban campus. Total enrollment: 25,022. Art program established 1967.

Degrees Bachelor of Fine Arts in the areas of studio art, design communication, art education. Majors and concentrations: art education, ceramics, communication design, jewelry and metalsmithing, painting/drawing, photography, printmaking, sculpture. Graduate degrees offered: Master of Fine Arts in the area of art. Doctor of Arts in the area of fine arts. Program accredited by NASAD.

Enrollment Fall 1997: 362 total; 320 undergraduate, 42 graduate.

Art Student Profile 51% females, 49% males, 12% minorities, 1% international.

Art Faculty 37 total undergraduate and graduate (full-time and part-time). 92% of full-time faculty have terminal degrees. Graduate students teach a few undergraduate courses. Undergraduate student–faculty ratio: 11:1.

Student Life Student groups/activities include National Art Education Association Student Chapter, Design Communication Association, Metalsmithing Club.

Expenses for 1997–98 Application fee: $25. State resident tuition: $1020 full-time. Nonresident tuition: $7440 full-time. Mandatory fees: $1587 full-time. Full-time tuition and fees vary according to course load. College room and board: $4290. Room and board charges vary according to board plan. Special program-related fees: $5–$100 per course for art supplies.

Financial Aid Program-specific awards for 1997: 20–25 art scholarships for program students ($200–$500), 3–5 H.Y. Price Scholarships for program students ($2000).

Application Procedures Students admitted directly into the professional program freshman year. Deadline for freshmen and transfers: continuous. Notification date for freshmen and transfers: continuous. Required: high school transcript, minimum 2.0 high school GPA, SAT I or ACT test scores, minimum TOEFL score of 550 for international applicants, slides or videotape of portfolio. Portfolio reviews held 4 times on campus and off campus in Junction, TX.

Web Site http://www.art.ttu.edu.

Undergraduate Contact Don Wickard, Interim Director, Undergraduate Admissions, Texas Tech University, Box 45015, Lubbock, Texas 79409-5015; 806-742-3661, fax: 806-742-0355, E-mail address: a5cdw@ttuvml.ttu.edu.

Graduate Contact Penny McLaughlin, Graduate Admissions, Texas Tech University, Box 41030, Lubbock, Texas 79409-1030; 806-742-2787, fax: 806-742-1746, E-mail address: n4prm@ttacs.ttu.edu.

▼ TEXAS WOMAN'S UNIVERSITY

Denton, Texas

State-supported, primarily women. Suburban campus. Total enrollment: 9,378. Art program established 1920.

Degrees Bachelor of Fine Arts in the areas of painting, photography, ceramics, sculpture, jewelry/metalsmithing, fibers, advertising design. Majors and concentrations: art/fine arts, ceramic art and design, commercial art, fibers, graphic arts, jewelry and metalsmithing, painting/drawing, photography, sculpture. Graduate degrees offered: Master of Fine Arts in the areas of painting, photography, ceramics, sculpture, jewelry/metalsmithing, fibers. Cross-registration with University of North Texas, East Texas State University.

Enrollment Fall 1997: 217 total; 120 undergraduate, 65 graduate, 32 non-professional degree.

Art Student Profile 85% females, 15% males, 11% minorities, 15% international.

Art Faculty 12 total undergraduate and graduate (full-time and part-time). 100% of full-time faculty have terminal degrees. Graduate students teach about a quarter undergraduate courses. Undergraduate student–faculty ratio: 13:1.

Texas Woman's University (continued)

Student Life Student groups/activities include Delta Phi Delta, American Advertising Federation Student Chapter, Photographic Artists Coalition. Special housing available for art students.

Expenses for 1998–99 Application fee: $25. State resident tuition: $864 full-time. Nonresident tuition: $5976 full-time. Mandatory fees: $1116 full-time. Full-time tuition and fees vary according to course load. College room and board: $3360. College room only: $1800. Room and board charges vary according to board plan and housing facility. Special program-related fees: $20–$30 per semester for studio courses.

Financial Aid Program-specific awards for 1997: 2–5 Marie Delleney Awards for art majors ($200–$500), 2 Helen Thomas Perry Awards for junior or senior art majors ($1000), 1–3 Hazel Snodgrass Awards for art majors ($200–$300), 1–2 Ludie Clark Thompson Awards for art majors ($200–$300), 2–4 Noreen Kitsinger Awards for art education majors ($200–$300), 2–5 Sue Comer Awards for art majors ($200–$300), 1–3 Dorothy Laselle Awards for freshmen or sophomore art majors ($300–$400), 6–12 Coreen Spellman Awards for Delta Phi Delta members ($100–$200), 1 J. Brough Miller Scholarship for art majors ($400), 1 Weller-Washmon Scholarship for painting majors ($400).

Application Procedures Students admitted directly into the professional program freshman year. Deadline for freshmen and transfers: July 15. Notification date for freshmen and transfers: August 1. Required: high school transcript, college transcript(s) for transfer students, minimum 2.0 high school GPA, portfolio, SAT I or ACT test scores, artist's statement or letter of intent. Recommended: 3 letters of recommendation, interview. Portfolio reviews held twice on campus and off campus in various high schools in Texas; the submission of slides may be substituted for portfolios.

Contact Mr. Gary Washmon, Interim Chair, Department of Visual Arts, Texas Woman's University, PO Box 425469, TWU Station, Denton, Texas 76204; 817-898-2530, fax: 817-898-2496.

▼ Tisch School of the Arts

See New York University

▼ Truman State University

Kirksville, Missouri

State-supported, coed. Small town campus. Total enrollment: 6,421.

Degrees Bachelor of Fine Arts in the areas of studio art, visual communications. Majors and concentrations: art history, ceramic art and design, commercial art, painting, photography, printmaking, sculpture, textile arts. Graduate degrees offered: Master of Art Education.

Enrollment Fall 1997: 141 total; all undergraduate.

Art Student Profile 56% females, 44% males, 1% minorities, 1% international.

Art Faculty 13 total undergraduate and graduate (full-time and part-time). 99% of full-time faculty have terminal degrees. Graduate students do not teach undergraduate courses. Undergraduate student–faculty ratio: 13:1.

Student Life Student groups/activities include Student Art History Society, Missouri Art Education Association, Art Club.

Expenses for 1997–98 Application fee: $0. State resident tuition: $3256 full-time. Nonresident tuition: $5736 full-time. Mandatory fees: $18 full-time. College room and board: $3992. Special program-related fees: $10–$30 per semester for art supplies.

Financial Aid Program-specific awards for 1997: 5 Endowed Scholarships for outstanding program majors ($300–$1000), 30 Service Scholarships for program majors ($400–$700).

Application Procedures Students admitted directly into the professional program freshman year. Deadline for freshmen: November 15; transfers: May 1. Notification date for freshmen: December 15. Required: essay, high school transcript, college transcript(s) for transfer students, minimum 3.0 high school GPA, portfolio, SAT I or ACT test scores. Portfolio reviews held twice on campus; the submission of slides may be substituted for portfolios when distance is prohibitive.

Web Site http://www.truman.edu.

Undergraduate Contact Mr. Robert L. Jones, Head, Division of Fine Arts, Truman State University, 100 East Normal, Baldwin Hall #118, Kirksville, Missouri 63501; 660-785-4417, fax: 660-785-7463.

Graduate Contact Dr. Susan Shoaff-Ballanger, Chair of Art Department, Division of Fine Arts, Truman State University, 100 East Normal, Baldwin Hall #118, Kirksville, Missouri 63501; 660-785-4417, fax: 660-785-7463, E-mail address: sshoaf@truman.edu.

Temple University

▼ Tyler School of Art of Temple University

Elkins Park, Pennsylvania

State-related, coed. Urban campus. Total enrollment: 27,670. Art program established 1935.

Degrees Bachelor of Fine Arts in the areas of ceramics/glass, fibers/fabric design, graphic design/illustration, jewelry/metals, painting/drawing, photography, printmaking, sculpture, art education. Majors and concentrations: art education, CAD/CAM, ceramic art and design, commercial art, computer graphics, glass, graphic arts, graphic design, illustration, jewelry and metalsmithing, painting/drawing, photography, printmaking, sculpture, textile arts. Graduate degrees offered: Master of Fine Arts in the areas of ceramics/glass, fibers/fabric design, graphic design/illustration, jewelry/metals, painting/drawing, photography, printmaking, sculpture; Master of Education in the area of art education. Program accredited by NASAD.

Enrollment Fall 1997: 799 total; 704 undergraduate, 80 graduate, 15 non-professional degree.

Art Student Profile 52% females, 48% males, 14% minorities, 4% international.

Art Faculty 82 total undergraduate and graduate (full-time and part-time). 95% of full-time faculty have terminal degrees. Graduate students teach a few undergraduate courses. Undergraduate student–faculty ratio: 11:1.

Student Life Special housing available for art students.

Expenses for 1997–98 Application fee: $35. State resident tuition: $5870 full-time. Nonresident tuition: $10,752 full-time. Mandatory fees: $280 full-time. Full-time tuition and fees vary according to course load and program. College room and board: $5772. Room and board charges vary according to board plan and housing facility. Special program-related fees: $25–$50 per course for lab fees.

Financial Aid Program-specific awards for 1997: 10–25 Merit Scholarships for program students ($1000–$3500), 10–40 academic scholarships for program students ($500–$8000).

Application Procedures Students admitted directly into the professional program freshman year. Deadline for freshmen and transfers: continuous. Notification date for freshmen and transfers: continuous. Required: essay, high school transcript, college transcript(s) for transfer students, minimum 2.0 high school GPA, portfolio, SAT I or ACT test scores (minimum combined SAT I score of 1000, minimum combined ACT score of 21), slides for transfer applicants, self-portrait. Recommended: minimum 3.0 high school GPA, interview. Portfolio reviews held 25 times on campus and off campus; the submission of slides may be substituted for portfolios for freshmen applicants, for large works of art, or if distance is prohibitive.

Web Site http://www.temple.edu/tyler.

Contact Ms. Carmina Cianciulli, Assistant Dean for Admissions, Tyler School of Art of Temple University, Temple University, 7725 Penrose Avenue, Elkins Park, Pennsylvania 19027; 215-782-2875, fax: 215-782-2711, E-mail address: tylerart@vm.temple.edu.

Tyler School of Art

More About the School

Faculty, Resident Artists, and Alumni Tyler has a faculty of practicing artists, many of whom have been granted prestigious awards and fellowships through such foundations as the National Endowment for the Humanities, the Guggenheim Foundation, the Fulbright Foundation, and others. The careers of Tyler faculty members are recognized throughout the professional art and design world. An extensive lecture series by visiting and exhibiting artists is an important part of a Tyler education. Invitations to lectures and exhibitions are extended to the School's alumni/ae population, a diverse group of arts professionals living throughout the country and abroad.

Program Facilities All studio facilities at Tyler are designed for extensive research and the creation of works in each major. Facilities include computer labs for graphic design/ illustration, metals/jewelry/CAD-CAM, digital imaging, a fully equipped offset printing facility, and modern studios for each major. Tyler has two on-campus galleries, a gallery on the main campus of Temple University, and one in central Philadelphia. These galleries not only show student work, but also exhibit work from important national and international artists. Additional spaces include an auditorium that functions as a lecture hall, exhibition space, and theater. The campus also provides a dormitory.

Special Programs Temple University's Rome, Italy, program, with its outstanding faculty, staff and facilities, attracts students from colleges and universities throughout the country and abroad. In conjunction with the Glasgow School of Art, Tyler offers a summer program in Great Britain. Temple University also has a campus in Japan.

▼

For more than sixty years, Tyler School of Art has offered the combination of a world-renowned faculty and the resources of a major university within a small-school atmosphere. Because Tyler is situated on an independent campus in the Philadelphia suburb of Elkins Park, students experience the intimacy of the School's art community while benefiting from the facilities, curriculum, and activities of Temple University. A Tyler education is one that distinguishes each student as an artist who is both visually and intellectually prepared for diverse opportunities in the visual arts.

Tyler alumni are recipients of many prestigious awards and fellowships; are writers and critics; own galleries and businesses; teach in schools, colleges, and universities; and are involved in much more. Tyler's graduates have produced a collective record of achievement that is one of the prime reasons for the School's excellent reputation among institutions of higher learning.

The Bachelor of Fine Arts program is divided into a four-year sequence of planned study that provides a solid base in the fundamentals, the opportunity to explore a variety of curricular options, and an intensive and professional major concentration. Intensive studio work is complemented by an academic education with strong art history and liberal arts components in the belief that artists should be grounded in a broad base of knowledge. A highly motivated and talented student body, an extensive visiting artist and exhibitions program, and access to museums and galleries contribute to this challenging educational experience. The School's graduate program is highly competitive and draws students from all fifty states and abroad. More information about all Tyler programs can be found in the Tyler catalog.

In addition to the B.F.A., M.F.A., and M.Ed. programs on the Elkins Park campus, students may also wish to investigate the programs available on the main campus of Temple University. These include the B.A. in studio art, the B.S. in art education, and the B.A., M.A., and Ph.D. in art history.

Exposure to different philosophies and cultures is particularly valuable for the art student, and Tyler encourages its students to diversify their experiences and explore other artistic environments through study in special programs. In addition to the full complement of studio and academic courses offered at Tyler, the School also provides many opportunities to attend other programs and colleges both in this country and abroad. Programs are offered during the summer as well as during the academic year.

An important resource for Tyler students is Philadelphia's great wealth of museums and galleries. Students have an easy commute to the Philadelphia Museum of Art, the Pennsylvania Academy of the Fine Arts, the Rodin Museum, the Barnes Foundation, and the Institute of Contemporary Art. Philadel-

Tyler School of Art of Temple University (continued)

phia has many prestigious galleries, art spaces, and artists' cooperatives, as well as the largest number of public art works in the country. Students also have easy access to the art collections, galleries, and cultural events in New York and Washington, D.C.

It is the combination of exceptional faculty members, dedicated students, and a richly diverse setting that make Tyler School of Art an excellent choice for a professional education in art.

▼ THE UNIVERSITY OF AKRON

Akron, Ohio

State-supported, coed. Urban campus. Total enrollment: 23,538. Art program established 1970.

Degrees Bachelor of Fine Arts in the areas of drawing, painting, photography, printmaking, metalsmithing, graphics, sculpture, ceramics. Majors and concentrations: ceramic art and design, graphic design, jewelry and metalsmithing, painting/drawing, photography, printmaking, sculpture. Program accredited by NASAD.

Enrollment Fall 1997: 665 total; 481 undergraduate, 184 non-professional degree.

Art Student Profile 54% females, 46% males, 12% minorities, 1% international.

Art Faculty 55 total (full-time and part-time). 100% of full-time faculty have terminal degrees. Graduate students do not teach undergraduate courses. Undergraduate student–faculty ratio: 13:1.

Student Life Student groups/activities include Student Art League.

Expenses for 1997–98 Application fee: $25. State resident tuition: $3312 full-time. Nonresident tuition: $8772 full-time. Mandatory fees: $348 full-time. College room and board: $4490. College room only: $2820. Room and board charges vary according to board plan. Special program-related fees: $25 for ceramics supplies, $35 for photography supplies, $35 for printmaking materials, $30 for metalsmithing materials.

Financial Aid Program-specific awards for 1997: 1–4 Scholastics Art and Writing Awards for incoming freshmen program majors ($3000–$12,000), 1–4 Governor's Art Youth Awards for Ohio resident program majors ($1000), 3–7 Incoming Freshmen Awards for incoming freshmen program majors ($500–$2000), 13–15 School of Art Scholarships for continuing program majors based on portfolio and GPA ($250–$3500).

Application Procedures Students apply for admission into the professional program by sophomore year. Deadline for freshmen: June 30; transfers: July 30. Required: high school transcript, college transcript(s) for transfer students, minimum 2.0 high school GPA, SAT I or ACT test scores, portfolio for transfer students, minimum 3.0 college GPA in art courses for transfer students. Recommended: portfolio. Portfolio reviews held as needed on campus; the submission of slides may be substituted for portfolios whenever needed.

Web Site http://www.uakron.edu/art/.

Undergraduate Contact Office of Admissions, The University of Akron, 381 Buchtel Common, Akron, Ohio 44325-2001; 330-972-7100.

▼ THE UNIVERSITY OF ALABAMA

Tuscaloosa, Alabama

State-supported, coed. Suburban campus. Total enrollment: 18,324. Art program established 1946.

Degrees Bachelor of Fine Arts in the areas of painting, printmaking, graphic design, ceramics, sculpture, photography. Majors and concentrations: art/fine arts, ceramic art and design, graphic design, painting/drawing, photography, printmaking, sculpture. Graduate degrees offered: Master of Fine Arts in the areas of painting, printmaking, ceramics, sculpture, photography. Program accredited by NASAD.

Enrollment Fall 1997: 838 total; 130 undergraduate, 28 graduate, 680 non-professional degree.

Art Student Profile 56% females, 44% males, 16% minorities, 3% international.

Art Faculty 15 total undergraduate and graduate (full-time and part-time). 100% of full-time faculty have terminal degrees. Graduate students teach a few undergraduate courses. Undergraduate student–faculty ratio: 20:1.

Student Life Student groups/activities include Art Student League.

Expenses for 1997–98 Application fee: $25. State resident tuition: $2594 full-time. Nonresident tuition: $6808 full-time. Full-time tuition varies according to course load. College room and board: $3610. College room only: $2060. Room and board charges vary according to board plan and housing facility. Special program-related fees: $20–$40 per semester for studio fees.

Financial Aid Program-specific awards for 1997: 3 Mary M. Morgan Scholarships for program students ($1141), 2 Bradley Endowed Scholarships for program students ($1141), 2 Society for the Fine Arts Scholarships for program students ($1141), 1 Ann Lary Scholarship for program students ($1000), 1 Ruth Larcom S.F.A. Scholarship for entering freshmen ($1247), 1 Joseph and Alvin Sella Scholarship for program students ($800), 8 Julie Peake Holaday Scholarships for program and incoming students ($2200).

Application Procedures Students apply for admission into the professional program by sophomore year. Deadline for freshmen and transfers: continuous. Required: high school transcript, college transcript(s) for transfer students, minimum 2.0 high school GPA, SAT I or ACT test scores (minimum combined SAT I score of 1030, minimum combined ACT score of 22), high school transcript for transfer applicants with fewer than 24 semester hours.

Undergraduate Contact Mr. W. Lowell Baker, Chairman, Art and Art History Department, The University of Alabama, Box 870270, Tuscaloosa, Alabama 35487-0270; 205-348-5967, fax: 205-348-9642, E-mail address: wbaker@woodsquad.as.ua.edu.

Graduate Contact Mr. W. Lowell Baker, Chairman, Art and Art History Department, The University of Alabama, PO Box 870270, Tuscaloosa, Alabama 35487-0270; 205-348-5967, fax: 205-348-9642, E-mail address: wbaker@woodsquad.as.ua.edu .

▼ THE UNIVERSITY OF ALABAMA AT BIRMINGHAM

Birmingham, Alabama

State-supported, coed. Urban campus. Total enrollment: 14,933.

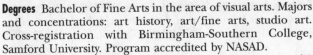

Degrees Bachelor of Fine Arts in the area of visual arts. Majors and concentrations: art history, art/fine arts, studio art. Cross-registration with Birmingham-Southern College, Samford University. Program accredited by NASAD.

Enrollment Fall 1997: 501 total; 431 undergraduate, 70 non-professional degree.

Art Student Profile 75% females, 25% males, 13% minorities, 2% international.

Art Faculty 16 total (full-time and part-time). 100% of full-time faculty have terminal degrees. Graduate students do not teach undergraduate courses. Undergraduate student–faculty ratio: 15:1.

Student Life Student groups/activities include The Art Guild.

Expenses for 1997–98 Application fee: $25, $30 for international students. State resident tuition: $2520 full-time. Nonresident tuition: $5040 full-time. Mandatory fees: $330 full-time. College room only: $3090. Special program-related fees: $40 per course for lab fees, $4 per credit for learning resources fee.

Financial Aid Program-specific awards for 1997: 1 Senior Scholarship for seniors ($2000), 1 Frohock Scholarship for juniors ($500), 1 Hulsey Prize for seniors ($100), 1 Senior Scholarship for seniors ($1000), 3 Outstanding Students Award ($100).

Application Procedures Students apply for admission into the professional program by sophomore year. Deadline for freshmen and transfers: continuous. Notification date for freshmen and transfers: continuous. Required: high school transcript, minimum 2.0 high school GPA, portfolio, SAT I or ACT test scores. Portfolio reviews held twice on campus; the submission of slides may be substituted for portfolios for large works of art.

Undergraduate Contact Mr. Bert Brouwer, Chair, Department of Art and Art History, The University of Alabama at Birmingham, 900 13th Street South, Birmingham, Alabama 35294-1260; 205-934-4941, fax: 205-975-6639, E-mail address: bbrouwer@uab.edu.

▼ UNIVERSITY OF ALASKA ANCHORAGE

Anchorage, Alaska

State-supported, coed. Urban campus. Total enrollment: 14,765. Art program established 1988.

Degrees Bachelor of Fine Arts in the area of art. Majors and concentrations: art/fine arts, ceramic art and design, graphic arts, illustration, jewelry and metalsmithing, painting/drawing, photography, printmaking, sculpture, textile arts. Program accredited by NASAD.

Enrollment Fall 1997: 111 total; 51 undergraduate, 60 non-professional degree.

Art Student Profile 60% females, 40% males, 6% minorities, 2% international.

Art Faculty 16 total (full-time and part-time). 90% of full-time faculty have terminal degrees. Graduate students do not teach undergraduate courses.

Student Life Student groups/activities include Art Student Association, organizations for printmaking, photography and ceramics.

Expenses for 1998–99 Application fee: $35. State resident tuition: $2168 full-time. Nonresident tuition: $6428 full-time. Mandatory fees: $298 full-time. Full-time tuition and fees vary according to class time, course level, and course load. College room and board: $6591. College room only: $3490. Room and board charges vary according to board plan and

housing facility. Special program-related fees: $20–$100 per course for lab fees for materials, equipment maintenance, and models.

Financial Aid Program-specific awards for 1997: 2 Saradell Ard Scholarships for upper-division program majors ($850), 2 Muriel Hannah Scholarships for program majors with preference to Native-American Alaskans ($750), 4 tuition waivers for upper-division program majors ($800–$1000), 1 Kimura Award for illustration and photography majors, 1 Ken Gray Scholarship for juniors and seniors.

Application Procedures Students apply for admission into the professional program by junior year. Deadline for freshmen and transfers: continuous. Notification date for freshmen and transfers: continuous. Required: college transcript(s) for transfer students, portfolio. Recommended: SAT I or ACT test scores. Portfolio reviews held twice on campus; the submission of slides may be substituted for portfolios.

Undergraduate Contact Office of Enrollment Services, University of Alaska Anchorage, 3211 Providence Drive, Anchorage, Alaska 99508; 907-786-1480, fax: 907-786-4888.

▼ THE UNIVERSITY OF ARIZONA

Tucson, Arizona

State-supported, coed. Urban campus. Total enrollment: 33,737.

Degrees Bachelor of Fine Arts in the area of art. Majors and concentrations: art education, art history, ceramic art and design, computer graphics, new genre, painting/drawing, photography, printmaking, sculpture, studio art, textile arts, visual communication. Graduate degrees offered: Master of Fine Arts in the area of art; Master of Arts in the areas of art education, art history. Cross-registration with Pima Community College. Program accredited by NASAD.

Enrollment Fall 1997: 724 total; 650 undergraduate, 74 graduate.

Art Faculty 70 total undergraduate and graduate (full-time and part-time). 95% of full-time faculty have terminal degrees. Graduate students teach about a quarter undergraduate courses. Undergraduate student–faculty ratio: 17:1.

Student Life Student groups/activities include Art Club, Committee for Advancement of Art Students (student committee).

Expenses for 1997–98 Application fee: $40 for nonresidents. State resident tuition: $1988 full-time. Nonresident tuition: $8640 full-time. Mandatory fees: $70 full-time. College room and board: $4930. College room only: $2480. Room and board charges vary according to board plan and housing facility. Special program-related fees: $5–$25 per semester for supplies for some studio courses.

Financial Aid Program-specific awards for 1997: 1 Robert C. Brown Memorial Scholarship for program majors ($750), Edward Francis Dunn Scholarships for program majors ($4600), Albert and Kathryn Haldeman Scholarships for program majors ($3600), 1 Hudson Foundation Scholarship for program majors ($1200), Samuel Latta Kingan Scholarships for program majors ($2300), 1 Stephen Langmade Scholarship for program majors ($950), 8 Regents In-State Registration Scholarships for state resident program majors ($922), 5 Regents In-State Registration Scholarships for state resident program majors demonstrating need ($922), 10 Regents Non-Resident Tuition Scholarships for out-of-state program majors ($3675), 1 Sandy Truett Memorial Scholarship for program majors ($1050).

The University of Arizona *(continued)*

Application Procedures Deadline for freshmen: March 1; transfers: May 1. Required: high school transcript, college transcript(s) for transfer students, 3 letters of recommendation, minimum 2.5 high school GPA for state residents, minimum 3.0 high school GPA for out-of-state residents.

Undergraduate Contact Ms. Lisa Kreamer, Undergraduate Advisor, Art Department, The University of Arizona, Art Building, Room 101D, Tucson, Arizona 85721; 520-621-7570, fax: 520-621-2955, E-mail address: lms@ccit.arizona.edu.

Graduate Contact Ms. Suzanna Ruiz, Graduate Specialist, Art Department, The University of Arizona, Art Building, Room 108, Tucson, Arizona 85721; 520-621-8518, fax: 520-621-2955.

J. William Fulbright College of Arts and Sciences

▼ UNIVERSITY OF ARKANSAS

Fayetteville, Arkansas

State-supported, coed. Small town campus. Total enrollment: 14,322. Art program established 1874.

Degrees Bachelor of Fine Arts in the areas of art, art education. Majors and concentrations: art/fine arts, ceramic art and design, graphic arts, painting/drawing, photography, printmaking, sculpture. Graduate degrees offered: Master of Fine Arts in the area of art.

Enrollment Fall 1997: 180 total; 22 undergraduate, 14 graduate, 144 non-professional degree.

Art Student Profile 62% females, 38% males, 5% minorities, 5% international.

Art Faculty 12 total undergraduate and graduate (full-time and part-time). 98% of full-time faculty have terminal degrees. Graduate students teach a few undergraduate courses. Undergraduate student–faculty ratio: 15:1.

Student Life Student groups/activities include Fine Arts League, University Union Programs Fine Arts Committee.

Expenses for 1997–98 Application fee: $15. State resident tuition: $2470 full-time. Nonresident tuition: $6418 full-time. Mandatory fees: $191 full-time. Full-time tuition and fees vary according to program. College room and board: $3867. Special program-related fees: $4 per credit hour for teaching equipment.

Financial Aid Program-specific awards for 1997: 1 David Durst Award for college sophomores ($250), 5 Blanche Elliot Awards for juniors and seniors ($300–$400), 1 Tom Turpin Award for freshmen ($100), 1 Neppie Lonner Award for sophomores ($100), 1 Collier Photo Award for juniors and seniors ($100), 1 Bedford Camera Award for juniors and seniors ($100), 1 Pauline G. West Watercolor Award ($125).

Application Procedures Students apply for admission into the professional program by sophomore year. Deadline for freshmen and transfers: August 15. Required: high school transcript, college transcript(s) for transfer students, minimum 3.0 high school GPA, 3 letters of recommendation, portfolio, SAT I or ACT test scores (minimum combined ACT score of 30). Portfolio reviews held once on campus.

Web Site http://www.uark.edu/~artinfo/art.html.

Undergraduate Contact Mr. Michael Peven, Chairman, Art Department, University of Arkansas, 116 Fine Arts Center, Fayetteville, Arkansas 72701; 501-575-5202, fax: 501-575-2062, E-mail address: mpeven@comp.uark.edu.

Graduate Contact Ms. Kristin Musgnug, MFA Coordinator, Art Department, University of Arkansas, 116 Fine Arts Center, Fayetteville, Arkansas 72701; 501-575-5202, fax: 501-575-2062.

▼ UNIVERSITY OF BRIDGEPORT

Bridgeport, Connecticut

Independent, coed. Urban campus. Total enrollment: 2,427.

Degrees Bachelor of Fine Arts in the areas of fine art, graphic design, illustration; Bachelor of Science in the areas of interior design, industrial design, fine arts, graphic design, illustration; Bachelor of Arts in the areas of fine arts, graphic design, illustration. Program accredited by NASAD.

Enrollment Fall 1997: 64 total; all undergraduate.

Art Student Profile 41% females, 59% males, 22% minorities, 56% international.

Art Faculty 12 total (full-time and part-time). 100% of full-time faculty have terminal degrees. Graduate students do not teach undergraduate courses.

Student Life Student groups/activities include art shows.

Expenses for 1997–98 Application fee: $40. Comprehensive fee: $20,454 includes full-time tuition ($13,000), mandatory fees ($644), and college room and board ($6810). College room only: $3700. Full-time tuition and fees vary according to course load and program. Room and board charges vary according to board plan.

Application Procedures Students admitted directly into the professional program freshman year. Deadline for freshmen and transfers: continuous. Required: essay, high school transcript, college transcript(s) for transfer students, portfolio, SAT I or ACT test scores. Recommended: minimum 2.0 high school GPA, interview. Portfolio reviews held as needed on campus; the submission of slides may be substituted for portfolios for international applicants.

Undergraduate Contact Dr. Suzanne D. Wilcox, Dean of Admissions and Financial Aid, University of Bridgeport, 380 University Avenue, Bridgeport, Connecticut 06601; 800-EXCEL-UB, fax: 203-576-4941, E-mail address: admit@cse.bridgeport.edu.

More About the University

Eighty-six acres in southern New England on Long Island Sound offer the perfect setting to explore and develop creative talents. The University of Bridgeport is a comprehensive university offering a variety of degree programs in design and music. Resources for these programs include the nine-story Bernhard Center equipped with art, sculpture, ceramic, and photo studios; darkrooms; state-of-the-art computer graphic facilities; a professional theater (950 seats); auditorium (250 seats); practice rooms; and the University Art Gallery. The University of Bridgeport is an accredited institutional member of the National Association of Schools of Art and Design (N.A.S.A.D.). The School of Arts, Humanities, and Social Sciences offers the following undergraduate programs in art and design: Graphic Design (B.F.A.) and Illustration (B.F.A.) with a curriculum that includes foundation drawing and composition skills, computer graphics, desktop publishing, and interactive media, concentrating on creativity, integration, and communication skills, and providing contact with professional designers and design firms in the New York metropolitan area; Industrial Design (B.S.), with a curriculum (approved by the Industrial Designers Society of America) covering conceptual and creative problem solving, traditional and computer aided 2D and 3D skill development, and relevant support subjects such as human factors and materials and manufacturing, involving experienced professional faculty supervising projects in all areas of design, including corporate sponsored projects and a summer internship program; Interior Design (B.S.), with a curriculum that allows students to experience residential design, historic preservation, and commercial and contract design including space planning and speciality areas such as lighting, furniture, and exhibition design.

▼ UNIVERSITY OF BRITISH COLUMBIA

Vancouver, BC, Canada

Province-supported, coed. Urban campus. Total enrollment: 32,110. Art program established 1955.

Degrees Bachelor of Fine Arts in the area of visual arts; Bachelor of Arts in the area of art history. Majors and concentrations: art history, art/fine arts, painting/drawing, photography, printmaking, sculpture, studio art. Graduate degrees offered: Master of Fine Arts in the area of visual arts; Master of Arts in the area of art history. Doctor of Philosophy in the area of art history.

Enrollment Fall 1997: 149 total; 90 undergraduate, 44 graduate, 15 non-professional degree.

Art Faculty 25 total undergraduate and graduate (full-time and part-time). 90% of full-time faculty have terminal degrees. Graduate students teach a few undergraduate courses.

Student Life Student groups/activities include Graduate Student Art History Symposium, Alma Mater Drawing Club.

Expenses for 1997–98 Application fee: $72 Canadian dollars. Tuition, fee, and room and board charges are reported in Canadian dollars. Canadian resident tuition: $2333 full-time. Mandatory fees: $218 full-time. College room and board: $4516. College room only: $2600. Room and board charges vary according to board plan and housing facility. International student tuition: $13,830 full-time.

Financial Aid Program-specific awards for 1997: 1 Faculty Women's Club Ida Green Award for academically qualified applicants ($2500), 1 Florence Muriel Meltzer Scholarship for academically qualified applicants ($2000), 1 Helen Pitt Graduating Award for academically qualified applicants ($1000), 1 IODE Fine Arts Foundation Scholarship for academically qualified applicants ($1000), 1 Sharon Yacawer Frohlinger Memorial Scholarship for academically qualified applicants ($325), 1 Koerner Memorial Scholarship for academically qualified applicants ($1650).

Application Procedures Students apply for admission into the professional program by junior year. Deadline for freshmen and transfers: March 31. Required: college transcript(s) for transfer students, minimum 3.0 high school GPA, portfolio and interview to enter third year studio program. Recommended: high school transcript. Portfolio reviews held once in April on campus; the submission of slides may be substituted for portfolios for out-of-town applicants.

Undergraduate Contact Ms. Patsi Longmire, Secretary to the Head and Undergraduate Secretary, Department of Fine Arts, University of British Columbia, 6333 Memorial Road #403, Vancouver, BC V6T 1Z2, Canada; 604-822-2757, fax: 604-822-9003.

Graduate Contact Ms. Nancy Vered, Graduate Administrator, Department of Fine Arts, University of British Columbia, 6333 Memorial Road #403, Vancouver, BC V6T 1Z2, Canada; 604-822-3281, fax: 604-822-9003, E-mail address: nvered@unixg. ubc.ca.

▼ THE UNIVERSITY OF CALGARY

Calgary, AB, Canada

Province-supported, coed. Urban campus. Total enrollment: 23,737.

Degrees Bachelor of Fine Arts in the areas of art, developmental art. Majors and concentrations: developmental art, painting/drawing, photography, printmaking, sculpture. Graduate degrees offered: Master of Fine Arts in the area of art.

Enrollment Fall 1997: 175 undergraduate, 15 graduate.

Art Student Profile 63% females, 37% males, 2% international.

Art Faculty 28 total undergraduate and graduate (full-time and part-time). 100% of full-time faculty have terminal degrees. Graduate students do not teach undergraduate courses.

Student Life Student groups/activities include on campus exhibitions in two venues.

Expenses for 1997–98 Application fee: $65 Canadian dollars. Tuition, fee, and room and board charges are reported in Canadian dollars. Canadian resident tuition: $3180 full-time. Mandatory fees: $186 full-time. Full-time tuition and fees vary according to course load. College room and board: $3153. College room only: $1228. Room and board charges vary according to board plan and housing facility. International student tuition: $6360 full-time.

Financial Aid Program-specific awards for 1997: 1 Alberta Printmakers Society Award for printmakers ($100), 1 Continuing Arts Association Travel Scholarship for those demonstrating academic achievement ($700), 1 Bow Fort Chapter I.O.D.E. Bursary for those demonstrating academic achievement ($250), 1 Heinz Jordan Memorial Scholarship for those demonstrating academic achievement ($500), 2 Santo Mignosa Awards for printmakers ($500), 1 George Milne Award for printmakers ($1000), 1 Sadie M. Nelson Bursary in Art for those demonstrating need and academic merit ($500), 1 Western Silk Screen Prize for silk screen majors ($300).

Application Procedures Students admitted directly into the professional program freshman year. Deadline for freshmen and transfers: June 1. Required: high school transcript, standing in top 70% of graduating class. Recommended: SAT I test score only, portfolio for transfer students. Portfolio reviews held as needed for transfer applicants on campus; the submission of slides may be substituted for portfolios for large works of art or when distance is prohibitive.

Web Site http://www.ucalgary.ca.

Undergraduate Contact Ms. Karen Lyons, Academic Advisor, Department of Art, The University of Calgary, 2500 University Drive, NW, Calgary, AB T2N 1N4, Canada; 403-220-6260, fax: 403-289-7333, E-mail address: lyons@ ucalgary.ca.

Graduate Contact Ms. Helen Miller, Graduate Secretary, Department of Art, The University of Calgary, 2500 University Drive, NW, Calgary, AB T2N 1N4, Canada; 403-220-3299, fax: 403-289-7333, E-mail address: hmiller@ucalgary.ca.

▼ UNIVERSITY OF CENTRAL ARKANSAS

Conway, Arkansas

State-supported, coed. Small town campus. Total enrollment: 8,938. Art program established 1927.

Degrees Bachelor of Fine Arts in the area of studio art. Program accredited by NASAD.

Enrollment Fall 1997: 141 total; all undergraduate.

Art Student Profile 55% females, 45% males, 13% minorities, 5% international.

Art Faculty 17 total (full-time and part-time). 100% of full-time faculty have terminal degrees. Graduate students do not teach undergraduate courses.

Expenses for 1997–98 State resident tuition: $2258 full-time. Nonresident tuition: $4478 full-time. Mandatory fees: $434 full-time. College room and board: $2920.

Financial Aid Program-specific awards for 1997: 6–12 Performance in Art Scholarships for art majors ($1000–$2000), 1 Disterheft Scholarship for art majors ($1000), 1 Curtis Scholarship for art majors ($1000).

Application Procedures Students apply for admission into the professional program by sophomore year. Deadline for freshmen and transfers: continuous. Required: high school transcript, college transcript(s) for transfer students, ACT test score only. Recommended: minimum 3.0 high school GPA.

Web Site http://www.uca.edu/art/index.htm.

Undergraduate Contact Dr. Kenneth E. Burchett, Chair, Department of Art, University of Central Arkansas, Conway, Arkansas 72032; 501-450-3113, fax: 501-450-5958, E-mail address: kenb@mail.uca.edu.

▼ UNIVERSITY OF CENTRAL FLORIDA

Orlando, Florida

State-supported, coed. Suburban campus. Total enrollment: 28,685.

Degrees Bachelor of Fine Arts in the area of art. Majors and concentrations: animation, ceramic art and design, computer animation, fibers, graphic design, painting/drawing, photography, printmaking, sculpture. Program accredited by NASAD.

Enrollment Fall 1997: 400 total; 50 undergraduate, 350 non-professional degree.

Art Faculty 27 total (full-time and part-time). 100% of full-time faculty have terminal degrees. Graduate students do not teach undergraduate courses. Undergraduate student–faculty ratio: 15:1.

Student Life Student groups/activities include Arts Alliance, Pottery Guild.

Expenses for 1997–98 Application fee: $20. State resident tuition: $1930 full-time. Nonresident tuition: $7846 full-time. Mandatory fees: $95 full-time. Full-time tuition and fees vary according to course load. College room and board: $4370. College room only: $2720. Room and board charges vary according to housing facility. Special program-related fees: $10 per course for lab fees.

Financial Aid Program-specific awards for 1997: 2 San Miguel Awards for Hispanic art students ($600), 2 Altrusa Club Awards for art students ($500).

Application Procedures Students apply for admission into the professional program by sophomore year. Deadline for freshmen and transfers: July 15. Notification date for freshmen and transfers: continuous. Required: high school transcript, college transcript(s) for transfer students, minimum 2.0 high school GPA, SAT I or ACT test scores, minimum 2.0 college GPA for transfer students, TOEFL score for international applicants, portfolio for animation and graphic design applicants. Portfolio reviews held once on campus; the submission of slides may be substituted for portfolios whenever needed.

Undergraduate Contact Dr. Joyce Lilie, Interim Chair, Art Department, University of Central Florida, VAB117, Orlando, Florida 32816; 407-823-2676, fax: 407-823-6470.

▼ UNIVERSITY OF CINCINNATI

Cincinnati, Ohio

State-supported, coed. Urban campus. Total enrollment: 28,161.

Degrees Bachelor of Fine Arts. Majors and concentrations: ceramics, electronic arts, fibers, painting/drawing, photography, printmaking, sculpture. Graduate degrees offered: Master of Fine Arts. Cross-registration with The Ohio Valley Consortium of Colleges and Universities.

Enrollment Fall 1997: 348 total; 248 undergraduate, 40 graduate, 60 non-professional degree.

Art Student Profile 55% females, 45% males, 3% minorities, 2% international.

Art Faculty 21 total undergraduate and graduate (full-time and part-time). 100% of full-time faculty have terminal degrees. Graduate students teach about a quarter undergraduate courses. Undergraduate student–faculty ratio: 11:1.

Expenses for 1997–98 Application fee: $30. State resident tuition: $3879 full-time. Nonresident tuition: $10,986 full-time. Mandatory fees: $480 full-time. College room and board: $5643.

Financial Aid Program-specific awards for 1997: 1–5 Wolf Stein Travel Scholarships for junior art majors ($1500–$2500), 1 Rockwood Production Grant for art majors ($1000), 1 Dean Tatgenhorst Conrad Scholarship for art/art history majors ($1000), 6 art scholarships for art majors ($500).

Application Procedures Students admitted directly into the professional program freshman year. Deadline for freshmen: December 31; transfers: continuous. Required: high school transcript, SAT I or ACT test scores (minimum combined SAT I score of 990, minimum combined ACT score of 21), minimum 2.5 high school GPA, standing in top third of graduating class.

Web Site http://www.daap.uc.edu/SOA/soa.html.

Undergraduate Contact Mr. Wayne Enstice, Director, School of Art, University of Cincinnati, Mail Location 0016, Cincinnati, Ohio 45221; 513-556-2962, fax: 513-556-2887, E-mail address: carol.norris@uc.edu.

Graduate Contact Ms. Kimberly Burleigh, Director of Graduate Studies, School of Art, University of Cincinnati, Mail Location 0016, Cincinnati, Ohio 45221; 513-556-2075, fax: 513-556-2887.

▼ UNIVERSITY OF COLORADO AT BOULDER

Boulder, Colorado

State-supported, coed. Suburban campus. Total enrollment: 25,109.

Degrees Bachelor of Fine Arts in the area of studio art. Majors and concentrations: art/fine arts, ceramic art and design,

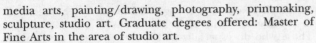

media arts, painting/drawing, photography, printmaking, sculpture, studio art. Graduate degrees offered: Master of Fine Arts in the area of studio art.

Enrollment Fall 1997: 443 undergraduate, 55 graduate.

Art Student Profile 50% females, 50% males, 15% minorities, 3% international.

Art Faculty 24 total undergraduate and graduate (full-time and part-time). 100% of full-time faculty have terminal degrees. Graduate students teach about a quarter undergraduate courses. Undergraduate student–faculty ratio: 20:1.

Student Life Student groups/activities include Art Student League.

Expenses for 1997–98 Application fee: $40. One-time mandatory fee: $35. State resident tuition: $2356 full-time. Nonresident tuition: $14,400 full-time. Mandatory fees: $583 full-time. Full-time tuition and fees vary according to program. College room and board: $4566. Room and board charges vary according to board plan, housing facility, and location. Special program-related fees: $10 per credit hour for lab fees.

Financial Aid Program-specific awards for 1997: 20 scholarships for program majors ($500).

Application Procedures Students admitted directly into the professional program freshman year. Deadline for freshmen and transfers: continuous. Required: high school transcript, minimum 2.0 high school GPA.

Web Site http://spot.colorado.edu/~finearts/.

Undergraduate Contact Office of Admissions, University of Colorado at Boulder, Campus Box 30, Boulder, Colorado 80309; 303-492-6301, fax: 303-492-7115.

Graduate Contact Ms. Dona Uyeno, Program Assistant, Fine Arts Department, University of Colorado at Boulder, Campus Box 318, Boulder, Colorado 80309-0318; 303-492-6504, fax: 303-492-4886.

▼ UNIVERSITY OF COLORADO AT DENVER

Denver, Colorado

State-supported, coed. Urban campus. Total enrollment: 13,092.

Degrees Bachelor of Fine Arts in the area of creative arts; Bachelor of Arts in the area of fine arts. Majors and concentrations: art history, art/fine arts, painting/drawing, photography, sculpture, studio art. Cross-registration with Metropolitan State College of Denver.

Enrollment Fall 1997: 160 total; all undergraduate.

Art Student Profile 60% females, 40% males, 10% minorities, 1% international.

Art Faculty 22 total (full-time and part-time). 100% of full-time faculty have terminal degrees. Graduate students do not teach undergraduate courses. Undergraduate student–faculty ratio: 8:1.

Student Life Student groups/activities include Student Art Alliance.

Expenses for 1997–98 Application fee: $40, $50 for international students. State resident tuition: $1944 full-time. Nonresident tuition: $10,416 full-time. Mandatory fees: $260 full-time. Full-time tuition and fees vary according to program. Special program-related fees: $45 per course for photography lab fee, $40 per course for general sculpture fee, $5 per course for studio class fee, $2 per course for slide/art history fee.

Financial Aid Program-specific awards for 1997: 3 Directors Fellowship Awards for upperclass program majors ($1000).

Application Procedures Students admitted directly into the professional program freshman year. Deadline for freshmen and transfers: July 22. Notification date for freshmen and transfers: August 18. Required: high school transcript, college transcript(s) for transfer students, minimum 2.0 high school GPA, SAT I or ACT test scores, standing in top 50% of graduating class. Recommended: essay, minimum 3.0 high school GPA, 2 letters of recommendation.

Undergraduate Contact Mr. John Hull, Chair, Department of Fine Arts, University of Colorado at Denver, Campus Box 177, PO Box 173364, Denver, Colorado 80217; 303-556-2809, fax: 303-556-2335.

▼ UNIVERSITY OF CONNECTICUT

Storrs, Connecticut

State-supported, coed. Rural campus. Total enrollment: 18,205.

Degrees Bachelor of Fine Arts in the area of art. Majors and concentrations: art/fine arts, graphic design, illustration, individualized major, painting/drawing, photography, printmaking, sculpture. Graduate degrees offered: Master of Fine Arts in the area of art. Program accredited by NASAD.

Enrollment Fall 1997: 246 undergraduate, 8 graduate.

Art Student Profile 58% females, 42% males, 7% minorities.

Art Faculty 32 total undergraduate and graduate (full-time and part-time). 100% of full-time faculty have terminal degrees. Graduate students teach a few undergraduate courses. Undergraduate student–faculty ratio: 16:1.

Expenses for 1997–98 Application fee: $40. State resident tuition: $4158 full-time. Nonresident tuition: $12,676 full-time. Mandatory fees: $1084 full-time. College room and board: $5462. College room only: $2776. Room and board charges vary according to board plan and housing facility.

Financial Aid Program-specific awards for 1997: 1 Victor Borge Scholarship for incoming freshmen ($1000), 8 University Scholarships for program students ($3000), 1 Anniversary Scholarship for program students ($1400), 1 Alaimo Scholarship for program students ($1000), 2 University Scholarships for incoming freshmen ($3000), 1 University Scholarship for incoming freshmen ($1000).

Application Procedures Students admitted directly into the professional program freshman year. Deadline for freshmen: April 1; transfers: May 1. Required: essay, high school transcript, college transcript(s) for transfer students, SAT I or ACT test scores. Recommended: letter of recommendation.

Undergraduate Contact Gina Werfel, Head, Department of Art and Art History, University of Connecticut, Box U-99, 875 Coventry Road, Storrs, Connecticut 06269-1099; 860-486-3930, fax: 860-486-3869.

Graduate Contact Mr. John Craig, Graduate Program Coordinator, Department of Art and Art History, University of Connecticut, Box U-99, 875 Coventry Road, Storrs, Connecticut 06269-1099; 860-486-3930, fax: 860-486-3869.

▼ UNIVERSITY OF DAYTON

Dayton, Ohio

Independent-Roman Catholic, coed. Suburban campus. Total enrollment: 10,208. Art program established 1960.

Degrees Bachelor of Fine Arts in the areas of art education, studio art, visual communication design, photography.

University of Dayton (continued)

Majors and concentrations: art education, art history, art/fine arts, computer graphics, graphic arts, illustration, photography, studio art. Cross-registration with Miami Valley Consortium.

Enrollment Fall 1997: 192 undergraduate.

Art Student Profile 67% females, 33% males, 5% minorities, 3% international.

Art Faculty 29 total (full-time and part-time). 100% of full-time faculty have terminal degrees. Graduate students do not teach undergraduate courses. Undergraduate student–faculty ratio: 5:1.

Student Life Student groups/activities include Horvath Student Art Show, Stander Symposium, American Center for Design Student Chapter.

Expenses for 1998–99 Application fee: $30. Comprehensive fee: $19,340 includes full-time tuition ($14,170), mandatory fees ($500), and college room and board ($4670). College room only: $2480. Full-time tuition and fees vary according to program. Room and board charges vary according to board plan, housing facility, and student level. Special program-related fees: $20–$60 per semester for studio/lab fees.

Financial Aid Program-specific awards for 1997: 5–10 Visual Arts Scholarships for freshmen ($2500), 1 Gordon Richardson Scholarship for juniors ($1500), 1 Horvath Scholarship for sophomores ($1250), 1 Anne Perman Scholarship for upperclassmen ($1000), 1 Rose Foreign Study Grant for program students ($800).

Application Procedures Students admitted directly into the professional program freshman year. Deadline for freshmen: continuous; transfers: August 1. Required: essay, high school transcript, college transcript(s) for transfer students, minimum 2.0 high school GPA, SAT I or ACT test scores. Recommended: interview, portfolio. Portfolio reviews held as needed on campus and off campus in various cities in Indiana, Ohio, Kentucky; the submission of slides may be substituted for portfolios if original work is not available.

Web Site http://www.as.udayton.edu/var/.

Undergraduate Contact Office of Admission, University of Dayton, 300 College Park, Dayton, Ohio 45469-1611; 937-229-4411.

More About the University

Program Facilities The Visual Arts Computing Center is a state-of-the-art facility that provides optimum access to hardware, software, and instructional assistance. The spacious Photography Lab includes several darkrooms, a large studio, an abundance of equipment, and a video lab. Studios in painting, sculpture, printmaking, and ceramics are excellent. The slide library has more than 75,000 slides and scores of videos on art and artists. The department operates two galleries that feature work from around the country in addition to faculty and student exhibitions.

Faculty and Alumni Faculty members are professional artists with extensive experience and exhibition records. The University provides small classes that afford students the opportunity for individual attention. Alumni have outstanding records of accomplishment; they are successful in virtually every field within the visual arts. They are designers, painters, photographers, filmmakers, curators, educators, illustrators, multimedia experts, and much more.

Student Exhibition Opportunities The annual Horvath Exhibition presents student work selected by an outside juror and features several substantial prizes. The Second Year and Scholarship Reviews challenge students to present their work in professional contexts before teams of faculty members. Those who do especially well in these reviews are awarded scholarships. All students participate in Senior Shows and/or Portfolio Days, opportunities to demonstrate their accomplishments as they conclude their undergraduate educations.

Special Programs Internships are strongly recommended and supported as ideal opportunities to bring together formal education with practical experience. Students are also encouraged to participate in the University's Study Abroad Program, and they are active in local chapters of national professional organizations in design, art education, photography, and art history.

▼ UNIVERSITY OF DELAWARE

Newark, Delaware

State-related, coed. Small town campus. Total enrollment: 18,230.

Degrees Bachelor of Fine Arts in the areas of ceramics, painting, photography, printmaking, sculpture, advertising design, applied photography, fibers, graphic design, illustration, metals. Majors and concentrations: advertising design, applied photography, art/fine arts, ceramics, fibers, graphic design, illustration, jewelry and metalsmithing, painting/drawing, photography, printmaking, sculpture. Graduate degrees offered: Master of Fine Arts in the areas of ceramics, painting, photography, printmaking, sculpture.

Enrollment Fall 1997: 450 total; 125 undergraduate, 25 graduate, 300 non-professional degree.

Art Student Profile 59% females, 41% males, 11% minorities, 5% international.

Art Faculty 20 total undergraduate and graduate (full-time and part-time). 100% of full-time faculty have terminal degrees. Graduate students teach about a quarter undergraduate courses. Undergraduate student–faculty ratio: 15:1.

Student Life Student groups/activities include Art History Club, university newspaper.

Expenses for 1997–98 Application fee: $45. State resident tuition: $4120 full-time. Nonresident tuition: $11,750 full-time. Mandatory fees: $454 full-time. College room and board: $4770. College room only: $2590. Room and board charges vary according to housing facility. Special program-related fees: $20–$60 per course for studio materials and supplies.

Financial Aid Program-specific awards for 1997: 4–8 Calloway Awards for those demonstrating talent, academic achievement, and financial need ($1000–$3000).

Application Procedures Students apply for admission into the professional program by sophomore year. Deadline for freshmen and transfers: March 1. Required: high school transcript, college transcript(s) for transfer students, SAT I test score only. Recommended: essay.

Web Site http://seurat.art.udel.edu.

Contact Ms. Martha Carothers, Chair, Department of Art, University of Delaware, 104 Recitation Hall, Newark, Delaware 19716; 302-831-2244, fax: 302-831-0505, E-mail address: martha.carothers@mvs.udel.edu.

▼ UNIVERSITY OF DENVER

Denver, Colorado

Independent, coed. Suburban campus. Total enrollment: 8,667. Art program established 1929.

Degrees Bachelor of Fine Arts in the areas of printmaking, ceramics, sculpture, photography, painting, graphic design, pre-conservation. Majors and concentrations: art education, ceramic art and design, commercial art, painting/drawing, photography, pre-conservation, printmaking, sculpture. Graduate degrees offered: Master of Fine Arts in the areas of printmaking, ceramics, sculpture, photography, painting, graphic design; Master of Arts in the areas of art history, museum studies.

Enrollment Fall 1997: 145 total; 70 undergraduate, 25 graduate, 50 non-professional degree.

Art Student Profile 50% females, 50% males, 12% minorities, 20% international.

Art Faculty 15 total undergraduate and graduate (full-time and part-time). 100% of full-time faculty have terminal degrees. Graduate students teach a few undergraduate courses. Undergraduate student–faculty ratio: 10:1.

Expenses for 1997–98 Application fee: $45. Comprehensive fee: $23,629 includes full-time tuition ($17,532), mandatory fees ($354), and college room and board ($5743). Full-time tuition and fees vary according to class time, course load, and program. Room and board charges vary according to board plan and housing facility. Special program-related fees: $10–$75 per course for lab fees.

Financial Aid Program-specific awards for 1997: 2–4 Harrison Scholarships for those demonstrating talent and need ($5000–$12,000), 2–4 art scholarships for those demonstrating talent and academic achievement ($5000–$12,000).

Application Procedures Students admitted directly into the professional program freshman year. Deadline for freshmen and transfers: continuous. Notification date for freshmen and transfers: continuous. Required: essay, high school transcript, college transcript(s) for transfer students, minimum 2.0 high school GPA, 2 letters of recommendation, SAT I or ACT test scores. Recommended: interview, portfolio. Portfolio reviews held as needed on campus; the submission of slides may be substituted for portfolios (slides preferred).

Web Site http://www.du.edu/art/.

Undergraduate Contact Mr. Michael L. Griffin, Director of Student Recruitment, School of Art and Art History, University of Denver, 2121 East Asbury, Denver, Colorado 80208; 303-871-2846, fax: 303-871-4112, E-mail address: mgriffin@du.edu.

Graduate Contact Ms. Bethany Kriegsman, Director, School of Art and Art History, University of Denver, 2121 East Asbury, Denver, Colorado 80208; 303-871-2846, fax: 303-871-4112, E-mail address: bkriegsm@du.edu.

▼ UNIVERSITY OF EVANSVILLE

Evansville, Indiana

Independent, coed. Suburban campus. Total enrollment: 3,023.

Degrees Bachelor of Fine Arts in the areas of ceramics, graphic design, painting, sculpture.

Enrollment Fall 1997: 76 undergraduate.

Art Student Profile 73% females, 27% males, 1% minorities, 10% international.

Art Faculty 9 total (full-time and part-time). 100% of full-time faculty have terminal degrees. Graduate students do not teach undergraduate courses.

Student Life Student groups/activities include Student Art Association.

Expenses for 1997–98 Application fee: $35. Comprehensive fee: $18,780 includes full-time tuition ($13,600), mandatory fees ($280), and college room and board ($4900). College room only: $2060. Room and board charges vary according to board plan and housing facility. Special program-related fees: $25–$50 for ceramics, photography, and printmaking fees.

Financial Aid Program-specific awards for 1997: 18 art scholarships for freshmen program majors ($500–$9000).

Application Procedures Students apply for admission into the professional program by sophomore year. Deadline for freshmen: March 1; transfers: June 1. Notification date for freshmen and transfers: continuous. Required: essay, high school transcript, college transcript(s) for transfer students, minimum 2.0 high school GPA, SAT I or ACT test scores. Recommended: minimum 3.0 high school GPA, letter of recommendation, interview, portfolio. Portfolio reviews held 7 times on campus and off campus in Louisville, KY; New Albany, IN; the submission of slides may be substituted for portfolios whenever needed.

Undergraduate Contact Mr. Les Miley, Chairman, Department of Art, University of Evansville, 1800 Lincoln Avenue, Evansville, Indiana 47722; 812-479-2043, fax: 812-479-2320.

▼ UNIVERSITY OF FLORIDA

Gainesville, Florida

State-supported, coed. Suburban campus. Total enrollment: 41,713.

Degrees Bachelor of Fine Arts in the areas of ceramics, drawing, graphic design, painting, creative photography, printmaking, sculpture, electronic intermedia; Bachelor of Arts in the areas of art history, art education. Majors and concentrations: art education, art history, ceramics, electronic intermedia, graphic design, painting/drawing, photography, printmaking, sculpture. Graduate degrees offered: Master of Fine Arts in the areas of ceramics, drawing, graphic design, painting, creative photography, printmaking, sculpture, electronic intermedia. Cross-registration with Penland School of Crafts, New World School of the Arts. Program accredited by NASAD.

Enrollment Fall 1997: 475 total; 426 undergraduate, 49 graduate.

Art Faculty 39 total undergraduate and graduate (full-time and part-time). 100% of full-time faculty have terminal degrees. Graduate students teach about a quarter undergraduate courses.

Student Life Student groups/activities include Departure: GNV publication, Fine Arts - College Council, student art exhibit.

Expenses for 1997–98 Application fee: $20. State resident tuition: $1930 full-time. Nonresident tuition: $7570 full-time. College room and board: $4610. College room only: $2270. Room and board charges vary according to board plan and housing facility. Special program-related fees: $15 per course for lab fee for studio courses.

Financial Aid Program-specific awards for 1997: 2 Amy DeGrove Scholarships for freshmen and juniors ($2500), 1 Ann Marston Scholarship for female art students ($500).

Application Procedures Students admitted directly into the professional program freshman year. Deadline for freshmen: January 30. Notification date for freshmen and transfers: continuous. Required: high school transcript, college transcript(s) for transfer students, minimum 2.0 high school

University of Florida (continued)

GPA, SAT I or ACT test scores (minimum combined SAT I score of 970, minimum combined ACT score of 20), completion of preprofessional courses Drawing I and II, Design I and II, Survey Art History I and II, slides of portfolio, two sequential courses of a foreign language. Portfolio reviews held twice on campus.
Web Site http://www.arts.ufl.edu/art.
Undergraduate Contact Leslie A. Cannon, Undergraduate Coordinator/Academic Advisor, School of Art and Art History, University of Florida, FAC 302, PO Box 115801, Gainesville, Florida 32611-5801; 352-392-0201, fax: 352-392-8453, E-mail address: lac@ufl.edu.
Graduate Contact Linda Arbuckle, Graduate Coordinator, School of Art and Art History, University of Florida, FAC 302, PO box 115801, Gainsville, Florida 32611-5801; 352-392-0201 ext. 219, fax: 352-392-8453, E-mail address: arbuck@ufl.edu.

Lamar Dodd School of Art

▼ UNIVERSITY OF GEORGIA

Athens, Georgia

State-supported, coed. Suburban campus. Total enrollment: 29,693.
Degrees Bachelor of Fine Arts in the area of art. Majors and concentrations: art education, ceramics, computer art, fabric design, graphic design, interior design, jewelry and metalsmithing, painting/drawing, photography, printmaking, scientific illustration, sculpture. Graduate degrees offered: Master of Fine Arts in the area of art. Cross-registration with 19 area institutions. Program accredited by NASAD.
Enrollment Fall 1997: 1,020 total; 296 undergraduate, 44 graduate, 680 non-professional degree.
Art Student Profile 50% females, 50% males, 8% minorities, 4% international.
Art Faculty 68 total undergraduate and graduate (full-time and part-time). 98% of full-time faculty have terminal degrees. Graduate students teach a few undergraduate courses. Undergraduate student–faculty ratio: 18:1.
Student Life Student groups/activities include American Society of Interior Designers Student Chapter, National Art Education Association Student Chapter.
Expenses for 1997–98 Application fee: $25. State resident tuition: $2838 full-time. Nonresident tuition: $8790 full-time. Full-time tuition varies according to program. College room and board: $4323. College room only: $2271. Room and board charges vary according to board plan and housing facility. Special program-related fees: $10–$75 per course for supplies.
Financial Aid Program-specific awards for 1997: 16 art awards for program students ($500–$1000).
Application Procedures Students apply for admission into the professional program by sophomore year. Deadline for freshmen: March 1; transfers: July 1. Notification date for freshmen: March 31. Required: high school transcript, minimum 2.0 high school GPA, portfolio, SAT I or ACT test scores. Portfolio reviews held once on campus.
Undergraduate Contact Dr. Nancy G. McDuff, Director of Admissions, Lamar Dodd School of Art, University of Georgia, 114 Academic Building, Athens, Georgia 30602; 706-542-8776, fax: 706-542-1466.

Graduate Contact Ms. Betty Andrews, Degree Program Specialist, Lamar Dodd School of Art, University of Georgia, Visual Arts Building, Athens, Georgia 30602; 706-542-1636, fax: 706-542-0226.

Hartford Art School

▼ UNIVERSITY OF HARTFORD

West Hartford, Connecticut

Independent, coed. Suburban campus. Total enrollment: 7,089. Art program established 1877.
Degrees Bachelor of Fine Arts in the area of art. Majors and concentrations: ceramics, experimental studies, graphic design, illustration, painting/drawing, photography, printmaking, sculpture, video art. Graduate degrees offered: Master of Fine Arts in the area of art. Cross-registration with Trinity College, St. Joseph's College, Hartford Seminary. Program accredited by NASAD.
Enrollment Fall 1997: 396 total; 357 undergraduate, 15 graduate, 24 non-professional degree.
Art Student Profile 50% females, 50% males, 5% minorities, 5% international.
Art Faculty 32 total undergraduate and graduate (full-time and part-time). 86% of full-time faculty have terminal degrees. Graduate students teach a few undergraduate courses. Undergraduate student–faculty ratio: 15:1.
Student Life Student groups/activities include Student Association, student newspaper and yearbook staff, professional fraternities and sororities. Special housing available for art students.
Expenses for 1998–99 Application fee: $35. Comprehensive fee: $25,424 includes full-time tuition ($17,190), mandatory fees ($1034), and college room and board ($7200). College room only: $4440. Room and board charges vary according to board plan and housing facility.
Financial Aid Program-specific awards for 1997: 25 Endowed Scholarships for those demonstrating need ($2000), 15–20 Artistic Merit Awards for artistically talented ($2000–$9000), 15–25 Academic Talent Awards for those with high SAT scores, high GPA, in top 10% of class ($8000–$9000).
Application Procedures Students admitted directly into the professional program freshman year. Deadline for freshmen and transfers: continuous. Notification date for freshmen and transfers: continuous. Required: high school transcript, college transcript(s) for transfer students, minimum 2.0 high school GPA, 2 letters of recommendation, portfolio, SAT I or ACT test scores. Recommended: essay, interview. Portfolio reviews held by appointment on campus and off campus in Hartford, CT; Philadelphia, PA; Miami, FL; New York, NY; Boston, MA; Syracuse, NY; Washington, DC; Baltimore, MD on National Portfolio Days; the submission of slides may be substituted for portfolios when distance is prohibitive.
Web Site http://www.hartford.edu.
Undergraduate Contact Ms. Jenni Ferney, Coordinator of Admissions, Hartford Art School, University of Hartford, 200 Bloomfield Avenue, West Hartford, Connecticut 06117; 860-768-4827, fax: 860-768-5296.
Graduate Contact Ms. Jenni Ferney, Coordinator of Admissions, Hartford Art School, University of Hartford, 200 Bloomfield Avenue, West Hartford, Connecticut 06117; 860-768-4396, fax: 860-768-5296.

▼ UNIVERSITY OF HAWAII AT MANOA

Honolulu, Hawaii

State-supported, coed. Urban campus. Total enrollment: 17,356. Art program established 1907.

Degrees Bachelor of Fine Arts in the area of art. Majors and concentrations: ceramics, fibers, glass, graphic design, intermedia, painting/drawing, photography, printmaking, sculpture. Graduate degrees offered: Master of Fine Arts in the area of art.

Enrollment Fall 1997: 408 total; 92 undergraduate, 42 graduate, 274 non-professional degree.

Art Student Profile 55% females, 45% males, 78% minorities, 8% international.

Art Faculty 47 total undergraduate and graduate (full-time and part-time). 93% of full-time faculty have terminal degrees. Graduate students teach a few undergraduate courses.

Student Life Student groups/activities include art shows, juried exhibitions.

Expenses for 1997–98 Application fee: $25 for nonresidents. State resident tuition: $2832 full-time. Nonresident tuition: $9312 full-time. Mandatory fees: $118 full-time. College room and board: $4740. College room only: $2660. Room and board charges vary according to board plan and housing facility. Special program-related fees: $20–$100 for material fees.

Financial Aid Program-specific awards for 1997: 1 tuition waiver for above-average students with exceptional artistic ability ($1500).

Application Procedures Students apply for admission into the professional program by junior year. Deadline for freshmen and transfers: May 1. Required: portfolio. Recommended: college transcript(s) for transfer students. Portfolio reviews held twice on campus; the submission of slides may be substituted for portfolios (slides preferred).

Web Site http://www2.hawaii.edu/art/.

Undergraduate Contact Mr. Frank Beaver II, Associate Chair, Department of Art, University of Hawaii at Manoa, 2535 The Mall, Honolulu, Hawaii 96822; 808-956-8251, fax: 808-956-9043, E-mail address: frank@hawaii.edu.

Graduate Contact Ms. Helen Gilbert, Graduate Chair, Department of Art, University of Hawaii at Manoa, 2535 The Mall, Honolulu, Hawaii 96822; 808-956-8251, fax: 808-956-9043.

▼ UNIVERSITY OF HOUSTON

Houston, Texas

State-supported, coed. Urban campus. Total enrollment: 31,602.

Degrees Bachelor of Fine Arts in the areas of graphic communication, interior design, photography, sculpture, painting; Bachelor of Arts in the areas of art, art history. Majors and concentrations: graphic design, interior design, painting/drawing, photography, sculpture. Graduate degrees offered: Master of Fine Arts in the areas of graphic communication, interior design, photography, painting, sculpture.

Enrollment Fall 1997: 613 total; 492 undergraduate, 36 graduate, 85 non-professional degree.

Art Student Profile 63% females, 37% males, 35% minorities, 4% international.

Art Faculty 28 total undergraduate and graduate (full-time and part-time). 72% of full-time faculty have terminal degrees. Graduate students teach a few undergraduate courses. Undergraduate student–faculty ratio: 22:1.

Estimated expenses for 1998–99 Application fee: $30. State resident tuition: $864 full-time. Nonresident tuition: $5952 full-time. Mandatory fees: $1129 full-time. Full-time tuition and fees vary according to program. College room and board: $4405. College room only: $1960. Room and board charges vary according to board plan and housing facility. Special program-related fees: $20–$50 per course for equipment maintenance and supplies fee.

Financial Aid Program-specific awards for 1997: 5 Flaxman Scholarships for seniors ($1000–$1500), 3 Flaxman Competitive Scholarships for sophomores and juniors ($1000–$1500), 1–2 George Bunker Scholarships for program majors ($2000), 2–4 LaRuth Blaine Scholarships for interior design majors ($1000–$2000).

Application Procedures Students admitted directly into the professional program freshman year. Deadline for freshmen and transfers: July 1. Notification date for freshmen and transfers: continuous. Required: high school transcript, college transcript(s) for transfer students, SAT I or ACT test scores.

Web Site http://www.art.uh.edu/.

Undergraduate Contact Admission Office, University of Houston, 4800 Calhoun, Houston, Texas 77204-2161; 713-743-1010.

Graduate Contact Graduate Advisor, Art Department, University of Houston, Houston, Texas 77204-4893; 713-743-2830, fax: 713-743-2823.

▼ UNIVERSITY OF ILLINOIS AT CHICAGO

Chicago, Illinois

State-supported, coed. Urban campus. Total enrollment: 24,578. Art program established 1966.

Degrees Bachelor of Fine Arts in the areas of studio arts, graphic design, industrial design, photo/film/electronic media, art education. Majors and concentrations: animation, art education, electronic arts, film, graphic arts, industrial design, painting/drawing, photography, printmaking, sculpture, studio art, video art. Graduate degrees offered: Master of Fine Arts in the areas of studio arts, photography, graphic design, industrial design, film/animation/video, electronic visualization; Master of Arts in the area of art therapy. Program accredited by NASAD.

Enrollment Fall 1997: 716 total; 609 undergraduate, 107 graduate.

Art Faculty 50 total undergraduate and graduate (full-time and part-time). 100% of full-time faculty have terminal degrees. Graduate students teach a few undergraduate courses.

Student Life Student groups/activities include American Center for Design Student Chapter, Industrial Design Society of America Student Chapter.

Expenses for 1997–98 Application fee: $30. State resident tuition: $2956 full-time. Nonresident tuition: $8868 full-time. Mandatory fees: $942 full-time. Full-time tuition and fees vary according to program. College room and board: $5526. Room and board charges vary according to housing facility. Special program-related fees: $10–$100 per class for models, equipment, darkroom facilities.

University of Illinois at Chicago *(continued)*

Financial Aid Program-specific awards for 1997: 10–12 Talent/ Tuition Waivers for academically qualified program majors ($1987–$4553).

Application Procedures Students apply for admission into the professional program by sophomore year. Deadline for freshmen and transfers: June 7. Required: high school transcript, college transcript(s) for transfer students, SAT I or ACT test scores, minimum TOEFL score of 520 for international applicants, minimum 3.5 college GPA for transfer students, portfolio for graphic design majors, portfolio review for transfer students in certain areas, class rank-upper 50 percent. Recommended: interview. Portfolio reviews held by arrangement on campus; the submission of slides may be substituted for portfolios (slides preferred).

Web Site http://www.uic.edu/aa/artd/.

Undergraduate Contact Office of Admissions and Records, University of Illinois at Chicago, Box 5220, M/C 018, Chicago, Illinois 60607-7161; 312-996-4350, fax: 312-413-7628.

Graduate Contact Mr. Klindt Houlberg, Director of Graduate Studies, School of Art and Design, University of Illinois at Chicago, 929 West Harrison, 106 Jefferson Hall M/C 036, Chicago, Illinois 60607-7038; 312-996-3337, fax: 312-413-2333, E-mail address: klindt@aol.com.

▼ University of Illinois at Urbana–Champaign

Champaign, Illinois

State-supported, coed. Small town campus. Total enrollment: 36,019.

Degrees Bachelor of Fine Arts in the areas of art education, art history, ceramics, glass, graphic design, industrial design, metals, painting, photography, sculpture. Graduate degrees offered: Master of Fine Arts in the areas of ceramics, glass, graphic design, industrial design, metals, painting, photography, printmaking, sculpture. Doctor of Arts in the areas of art education, art history. Program accredited by NASAD.

Enrollment Fall 1997: 4,260 total; 700 undergraduate, 160 graduate, 3,400 non-professional degree.

Art Student Profile 52% females, 48% males, 23% minorities, 18% international.

Art Faculty 72 total undergraduate and graduate (full-time and part-time). 100% of full-time faculty have terminal degrees. Graduate students teach a few undergraduate courses. Undergraduate student–faculty ratio: 15:1.

Student Life Student groups/activities include organizations for crafts, photography, industrial design, graphic design.

Expenses for 1997–98 Application fee: $40, $50 for international students. State resident tuition: $3308 full-time. Nonresident tuition: $9924 full-time. Mandatory fees: $812 full-time. Full-time tuition and fees vary according to program and student level. College room and board: $5078. College room only: $1958. Room and board charges vary according to board plan and housing facility. Special program-related fees: $100–$200 per semester for equipment and materials fees.

Financial Aid Program-specific awards for 1997: 60–70 tuition waivers for program majors ($1000).

Application Procedures Students admitted directly into the professional program freshman year. Deadline for freshmen:

January 1; transfers: March 15. Required: essay, high school transcript, college transcript(s) for transfer students, SAT I or ACT test scores, slide portfolio for tuition waiver program, slide portfolio for transfer applicants to the graphic design, industrial design, and photography programs. Portfolio reviews held twice on campus.

Web Site http://www.art.uiuc.edu.

Contact Ms. Robin Douglas, Associate Director, School of Art and Design, University of Illinois at Urbana–Champaign, 408 East Peabody Drive, Champaign, Illinois 61820; 217-333-7261, fax: 217-244-7688.

▼ The University of Iowa

Iowa City, Iowa

State-supported, coed. Small town campus. Total enrollment: 28,409.

Degrees Bachelor of Fine Arts in the area of studio arts. Majors and concentrations: art education, art history, art/fine arts, ceramics, design, intermedia, jewelry and metalsmithing, painting/drawing, photography, printmaking, sculpture, studio art, video art. Graduate degrees offered: Master of Fine Arts in the area of performance; Master of Arts in the area of art history. Doctor of Philosophy in the area of art history.

Enrollment Fall 1997: 724 undergraduate, 171 graduate.

Art Student Profile 61% females, 39% males, 6% minorities, 4% international.

Art Faculty 39 total undergraduate and graduate (full-time and part-time). 86% of full-time faculty have terminal degrees. Graduate students teach a few undergraduate courses.

Student Life Student groups/activities include Art History Society, College Art Association, art exhibitions.

Expenses for 1997–98 Application fee: $20. State resident tuition: $2566 full-time. Nonresident tuition: $9422 full-time. Mandatory fees: $194 full-time. Full-time tuition and fees vary according to course load. College room and board: $4046. Room and board charges vary according to board plan. Special program-related fees: $3–$55 per course for model fees, $10 per semester for props, $3–$150 per semester for material fees.

Financial Aid Program-specific awards for 1997: 1 Iowa Center for Art Scholarship for freshmen program majors ($3000), 1 Mary Sue Miller Memorial Award for freshmen program majors ($600–$1000), 1 Emma McAllister Novel Award for minority program majors ($1000), 1–3 Schumacher Awards for program majors ($1600–$1800).

Application Procedures Students admitted directly into the professional program freshman year. Deadline for freshmen and transfers: continuous. Required: high school transcript, college transcript(s) for transfer students, SAT I or ACT test scores, minimum 2.25 high school GPA. Recommended: interview, portfolio for transfer students. Portfolio reviews held twice on campus; the submission of slides may be substituted for portfolios for three-dimensional works of art.

Web Site http://www.uiowa.edu/~music/.

Undergraduate Contact Elizabeth VanArragon, Academic Adviser, School of Art and Art History, The University of Iowa, E100 Art Building, Iowa City, Iowa 52242; 319-335-1779, fax: 319-335-1774.

Graduate Contact Ms. Laura Jorgensen, Academic Secretary, School of Art and Art History, The University of Iowa, E100 Art Building, Iowa City, Iowa 52242; 319-335-1758, fax: 319-335-1774.

▼ UNIVERSITY OF KANSAS

Lawrence, Kansas

State-supported, coed. Suburban campus. Total enrollment: 27,567.

Degrees Bachelor of Fine Arts in the areas of painting, sculpture, printmaking. Graduate degrees offered: Master of Fine Arts in the areas of painting, sculpture, printmaking.

Enrollment Fall 1997: 168 total; 150 undergraduate, 13 graduate, 5 non-professional degree.

Art Faculty 17 total undergraduate and graduate (full-time). 100% of full-time faculty have terminal degrees. Graduate students teach a few undergraduate courses. Undergraduate student–faculty ratio: 9:1.

Expenses for 1997–98 Application fee: $20. State resident tuition: $1965 full-time. Nonresident tuition: $8270 full-time. Mandatory fees: $420 full-time. Full-time tuition and fees vary according to course load. College room and board: $3736. Room and board charges vary according to board plan and housing facility.

Financial Aid Program-specific awards for 1997: 9 Creative and Performing Arts Scholarships for incoming freshmen ($2100), 5 Basic Studies Scholarships for sophomores ($1500), 45 departmental scholarships and awards for program majors ($2000), 16 Hollander Foundation Scholarships and Awards for program majors ($2000).

Application Procedures Deadline for freshmen: April 1; transfers: June 1. Required: high school transcript, SAT I or ACT test scores. Recommended: portfolio for transfer applicants. Portfolio reviews held 3 times in Chicago, IL; St. Louis, MO; Kansas City, MO; the submission of slides may be substituted for portfolios for large works of art.

Undergraduate Contact Ms. Judith McCrea, Chairperson, Department of Art, University of Kansas, 300 Art and Design Building, Lawrence, Kansas 66045; 913-864-4401, fax: 913-864-4404.

Graduate Contact Ms. Cima Katz, Graduate Director, Department of Art, University of Kansas, 300 Art and Design Building, Lawrence, Kansas 66045; 913-864-4401, fax: 913-864-4404.

Allen R. Hite Art Institute

▼ UNIVERSITY OF LOUISVILLE

Louisville, Kentucky

State-supported, coed. Urban campus. Total enrollment: 20,283. Art program established 1981.

Degrees Bachelor of Fine Arts in the areas of painting, drawing, printmaking, sculpture, ceramics, fibers, photography, graphic design; Bachelor of Science in the area of interior design; Bachelor of Arts in the area of art education. Majors and concentrations: art education, art/fine arts, ceramic art and design, graphic arts, interior design, painting/drawing, photography, printmaking, sculpture, textile arts. Cross-registration with Metroversity.

Enrollment Fall 1997: 418 total; all undergraduate.

Art Student Profile 71% females, 29% males, 6% minorities, 5% international.

Art Faculty 37 total (full-time and part-time). 100% of full-time faculty have terminal degrees. Graduate students teach a few undergraduate courses. Undergraduate student–faculty ratio: 13:1.

Student Life Student groups/activities include Student Art League, American Society of Interior Designers, Louisville Graphic Design Association.

Expenses for 1997–98 Application fee: $25. State resident tuition: $2400 full-time. Nonresident tuition: $7200 full-time. Mandatory fees: $230 full-time. College room and board: $4982. College room only: $2338. Room and board charges vary according to board plan and housing facility. Special program-related fees: $13–$18 per course for supplies.

Financial Aid Program-specific awards for 1997: 26 Hite Scholarships for enrolled students ($500–$1500), 1 Hendershot Scholarship for incoming freshmen ($3200), 1 Nay Scholarship for incoming freshmen ($3200), 1 Kaden Scholarship for enrolled students ($1000).

Application Procedures Deadline for freshmen and transfers: continuous. Required: high school transcript, minimum 2.0 high school GPA, SAT I or ACT test scores, portfolio for transfer students and graphic design applicants. Portfolio reviews held as needed on campus; the submission of slides may be substituted for portfolios (slides preferred).

Web Site http://www.louisville.edu/a-s/finearts.

Undergraduate Contact Mr. Matt Landrus, Public Information Officer, Fine Arts Department, University of Louisville, 104 Schneider Hall, Louisville, Kentucky 40292; 502-852-6794, fax: 502-852-6791, E-mail address: mhland01@ulkyvm.louisville.edu.

▼ UNIVERSITY OF MANITOBA

Winnipeg, MB, Canada

Province-supported, coed. Suburban campus. Total enrollment: 21,083.

Degrees Bachelor of Fine Arts in the areas of studio art, art history. Majors and concentrations: ceramic art and design, graphic design, painting/drawing, photography, printmaking, sculpture.

Enrollment Fall 1997: 350 total; all undergraduate.

Art Student Profile 52% females, 48% males.

Art Faculty 28 total (full-time and part-time). 82% of full-time faculty have terminal degrees. Graduate students do not teach undergraduate courses.

Expenses for 1997–98 Application fee: $25 Canadian dollars. Tuition, fee, and room and board charges are reported in Canadian dollars. Canadian resident tuition: $3094 full-time. Mandatory fees: $1086 full-time. Full-time tuition and fees vary according to program. College room and board: $3344. Room and board charges vary according to board plan, housing facility, and location. International student tuition: $5433 full-time.

Financial Aid Program-specific awards available.

Application Procedures Students admitted directly into the professional program freshman year. Deadline for freshmen and transfers: May 1. Notification date for freshmen and transfers: continuous. Required: high school transcript, portfolio, letter of intent. Portfolio reviews held once on campus; the submission of slides may be substituted for portfolios for large works of art.

Web Site http://www.umanitoba.ca/schools/art/.

University of Manitoba (continued)

Undergraduate Contact Mrs. Shawn Anderson, Administrative Assistant, School of Art, University of Manitoba, 203 Fitz-Gerald Building, Fort Garry Campus, Winnipeg, MB R3T 2N2, Canada; 204-474-9367, fax: 204-474-7605.

▼ UNIVERSITY OF MARY HARDIN-BAYLOR

Belton, Texas

Independent-Southern Baptist, coed. Small town campus. Total enrollment: 2,313. Art program established 1930.
Degrees Bachelor of Fine Arts in the area of art. Majors and concentrations: advertising design, art education, art/fine arts, computer imaging.
Enrollment Fall 1997: 320 total; 40 undergraduate, 280 non-professional degree.
Art Student Profile 55% females, 45% males, 10% minorities, 33% international.
Art Faculty 5 total (full-time and part-time). 100% of full-time faculty have terminal degrees. Graduate students do not teach undergraduate courses. Undergraduate student–faculty ratio: 50:1.
Student Life Student groups/activities include Kappa Pi (art fraternity).
Expenses for 1997–98 Application fee: $35. Comprehensive fee: $10,194 includes full-time tuition ($6510), mandatory fees ($434), and college room and board ($3250). College room only: $1500. Room and board charges vary according to housing facility. Special program-related fees: $25 per course for lab fees/studio courses.
Financial Aid Program-specific awards for 1997: 2 Lucile Land Lacy Art Scholarships for art majors demonstrating artistic ability ($600), 2 Edna Bassel Wilson Memorial Scholarships for art majors demonstrating financial need ($800).
Application Procedures Students admitted directly into the professional program freshman year. Deadline for freshmen and transfers: continuous. Required: high school transcript, SAT I or ACT test scores, portfolio for scholarship consideration. Portfolio reviews held once on campus; the submission of slides may be substituted for portfolios for scholarship consideration.
Web Site http://www.umhb.edu.
Undergraduate Contact Mr. Hershall Seals, Chair, Art Department, University of Mary Hardin-Baylor, UMHB-Station Box 8413, 900 College Street, Belton, Texas 76513; 254-295-4675, fax: 254-295-4943, E-mail address: bjohnson@umhb.edu.

▼ UNIVERSITY OF MASSACHUSETTS

AMHERST

Amherst, Massachusetts

State-supported, coed. Small town campus. Total enrollment: 24,884. Art program established 1958.
Degrees Bachelor of Fine Arts in the area of studio art. Majors and concentrations: architectural design, art education, ceramics, computer art, graphic design, interior design, painting, photography, printmaking, sculpture. Graduate degrees offered: Master of Fine Arts in the area of studio art; Master of Science in the areas of interior design, architectural studies; Master of Arts in the areas of art education, art history. Cross-registration with Smith College, Amherst College, Mount Holyoke College, Hampshire College. Program accredited by FIDER.
Enrollment Fall 1997: 460 total; 400 undergraduate, 60 graduate.
Art Student Profile 70% females, 30% males, 11% minorities, 4% international.
Art Faculty 36 total undergraduate and graduate (full-time and part-time). 100% of full-time faculty have terminal degrees. Graduate students teach about a quarter undergraduate courses. Undergraduate student–faculty ratio: 15:1.
Student Life Student groups/activities include Design Students Organization, American Society of Interior Designers Student Chapter.
Expenses for 1997–98 Application fee: $25, $40 for nonresidents. One-time mandatory fee: $143. State resident tuition: $2004 full-time. Nonresident tuition: $9017 full-time. Mandatory fees: $3568 full-time. Full-time tuition and fees vary according to reciprocity agreements. College room and board: $4520. Room and board charges vary according to board plan and student level. Special program-related fees.
Financial Aid Program-specific awards for 1997: 10 Chancellor Talent Awards for in-state students showing academic and artistic merit ($2280).
Application Procedures Students admitted directly into the professional program freshman year. Deadline for freshmen: February 1; transfers: May 1. Required: essay, high school transcript, college transcript(s) for transfer students, minimum 3.0 high school GPA, portfolio, SAT I or ACT test scores. Recommended: letter of recommendation. Auditions held continuously on campus. Portfolio reviews held continuously on campus; the submission of slides may be substituted for portfolios (slides preferred).
Web Site http://www.umass.edu/art/.
Undergraduate Contact Mr. Paul Berube, Director of Undergraduate Studies, Department of Art, University of Massachusetts Amherst, Room 357, Fine Arts Center, Amherst, Massachusetts 01003; 413-545-0866, fax: 413-545-3929, E-mail address: peb@art.umass.edu.
Graduate Contact Ms. Jeanette Cole, Director of Graduate Study, Department of Art, University of Massachusetts Amherst, Room 362, Fine Arts Center, Amherst, Massachusetts 01003; 413-545-6940, fax: 413-545-3929.

▼ UNIVERSITY OF MASSACHUSETTS

DARTMOUTH

North Dartmouth, Massachusetts

State-supported, coed. Suburban campus. Total enrollment: 6,366. Art program established 1964.
Degrees Bachelor of Fine Arts in the areas of visual design, painting, printmaking, sculpture, textile design/fibers, art education. Majors and concentrations: art education, ceramics, electronic imaging, fibers, graphic design, illustration, jewelry and metalsmithing, painting/drawing, photography, printmaking, sculpture, textile arts, visual arts. Graduate degrees offered: Master of Fine Arts in the areas of design, artisanry; Master of Art Education in the area of art education. Cross-registration with University of Massachusetts System, Southeastern Association for Cooperation in Higher Education in Massachusetts. Program accredited by NASAD.
Enrollment Fall 1997: 653 total; 536 undergraduate, 93 graduate, 24 non-professional degree.

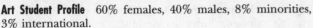
Art Student Profile 60% females, 40% males, 8% minorities, 3% international.

Art Faculty 33 total undergraduate and graduate (full-time and part-time). 94% of full-time faculty have terminal degrees. Graduate students teach a few undergraduate courses. Undergraduate student–faculty ratio: 16:1.

Student Life Student groups/activities include Illustration Club, Campus Design: Omni Ad, Ceramics Club.

Expenses for 1998–99 Application fee: $20, $40 for nonresidents. State resident tuition: $1657 full-time. Nonresident tuition: $7192 full-time. Mandatory fees: $2597 full-time. College room and board: $4828. College room only: $2734. Room and board charges vary according to board plan and housing facility. Special program-related fees: $15–$60 per semester for studio lab fees.

Financial Aid Program-specific awards for 1997: 25 Art Auction Awards for studio majors ($150–$400), 3–4 Neugebauer Awards for studio majors ($200).

Application Procedures Students admitted directly into the professional program freshman year. Deadline for freshmen and transfers: continuous. Notification date for freshmen and transfers: continuous. Required: essay, high school transcript, college transcript(s) for transfer students, SAT I or ACT test scores, slides of portfolio. Recommended: minimum 3.0 high school GPA, letter of recommendation. Portfolio reviews held continuously on campus and off campus in Dartmouth, MA and Hartford, CT on National Portfolio Days; the submission of slides may be substituted for portfolios (slides preferred).

Web Site http://www.umassd.edu/gladyouasked/gyafinearts.html.

Undergraduate Contact Mr. Jeffrey Feroce, Assistant Director of Admissions, University of Massachusetts Dartmouth, Old Westport Road, North Dartmouth, Massachusetts 02747-2300; 508-999-8613, fax: 508-999-8755, E-mail address: admissions@umassd.edu.

Graduate Contact Ms. Carol Novo, Clerk, Graduate Admissions, University of Massachusetts Dartmouth, Old Westport Road, North Dartmouth, Massachusetts 02747-2300; 508-999-8604, fax: 508-999-8183.

More About the School

Program Facilities The College of Visual and Performing Arts occupies 225,000 square feet, with buildings on the Dartmouth campus (designed by architect Paul Rudolph) and the New Bedford campus. This space encompasses studios and classrooms for eleven areas of sustained study in the visual arts—supplemented by the University's general educational facilities, such as the library and gymnasium, and the dormitories. Students have access to studio and work hours seven days a week; advanced students in the fine arts and artisanry programs are assigned large individual work spaces. All studios have the specialized equipment and tools to support a wide range of artistic creation, and the College has a slide library of 100,000 items and two galleries for showing student work and curated exhibits. Recently, the College has developed computer labs to support its courses, with a large design/electronic imaging laboratory and a dedicated, industry-specific textile design installation.

Faculty UMass Dartmouth visual arts faculty members have national and international reputations in their fields. Typified by Chris Gustin, ceramics; Laurie Kaplowitz, painting; Peter London, art education; and Dietmar Winkler, design, the College's 50 artists/designers have received numerous awards from the National Endowment for the Arts, the Massachusetts Cultural Council, the Society for Arts and Crafts, and professional groups. They are dedicated to teaching. In addition, every year more than 60 visiting artists/professionals bring their expertise to the programs.

Exhibition Opportunities The University Gallery and Gallery 210, both housed in the College, exhibit student work as well as invited shows. These are supplemented by mini-exhibitions in studio areas and the opportunity to exhibit at several spaces in New Bedford, Fall River, and surrounding towns.

Special Programs The College and University have a good range of exchange programs with foreign institutions; specifically for the visual arts are exchange programs with AR.CO in Lisbon and the Nova Scotia College of Art and Design. Internships are encouraged; recent placements have included Graphics Express, WGBH, the Museum of Fine Arts–Boston, the Smithsonian, and Guilford of Maine. In 1995, several painting students earned college credits in Brittany, and ceramics students participated in an expense-paid workshop in the Azores.

▼

Students who come to CVPA at UMass Dartmouth get the advantages of an accredited art college and a full-scale university recognized by *U.S. News & World Report* as being in the top tier of its peers in New England. As art/design majors, students pursue specialized, professionally oriented study in photography/electronic imaging, illustration, graphic design/letterform, art education, textile design/fiber arts, painting, sculpture, ceramics, metals, and art history; graduate students specialize in the above and wood/furniture design and printmaking as well. As members of the wider UMass Dartmouth community, they have a full range of opportunities across the campus. Graduate and undergraduate art students have participated in mathematical and marine biological research, they have been named All-Stars in NCAA Division III track and swimming, and they have led the University's student government. Their friends are their visual arts colleagues and students from the University's other professional and arts and sciences programs.

Visual arts undergraduates have a common freshman year in which they are introduced to the University and the multiple possibilities for advanced work. They learn traditional artistic skills, especially figure drawing, and develop a foundation for advanced work. As they progress, they are part of a strong community in which they receive individual attention from a concerned and accessible faculty.

CVPA aims to strike a balance between skills and ideas important for industry and the professions and the conceptual and expressive skills appropriate to personal artistic expression. Last year, a typical one, textile design students won prizes in the CITDA competition, wood students visited the studio of Judy McKie, and design students interned at dibs and Ziff-Davis Interactive. Art education students participated in a large Eisenhower grant–funded project with area schools, art history students developed practical skills in curating a faculty-directed inaugural exhibition at the New Bedford Art Museum, and sculptors created a site-specific outdoor exhibition.

Graduate students come to CVPA from across the U.S. and from several other countries. Each has a primary faculty adviser, and, usually, an individual committee reviews their work on a regular basis. Through common seminars, students develop rich personal relationships with colleagues within the areas of their immediate interests and across the College. Their work is supported by the College's very ample space for personal studios and the well-equipped general

University of Massachusetts Dartmouth *(continued)*

work areas; the ceramics studio is state-of-the-art. As important as space and equipment are, it is the personal attention to artistic development that is most important to the College faculty.

The success of CVPA's bachelor's and master's graduates is a source of College pride. Design students, knowledgeable of current computer-based animation and graphics, have found positions at Envision, Planet Interactive, the Beta Group, and many other leading firms; textile design/fiber arts graduates may be found at Burlington, Milliken, and Sunbury as well as in an *American Craft* feature article; art education graduates network across Massachusetts schools. Painters and sculptors have been welcomed by first-rate graduate programs. M.F.A. graduates have been offered positions at the University of Wisconsin, the University of Texas, Washington University, San Diego State University, the California College of Arts and Crafts, and Hampshire College.

▼ UNIVERSITY OF MASSACHUSETTS LOWELL
Lowell, Massachusetts

State-supported, coed. Urban campus. Total enrollment: 12,322. Art program established 1982.

Degrees Bachelor of Fine Arts in the areas of fine arts, graphic design. Cross-registration with The 15 Massachusetts Community Colleges. Program accredited by NASAD.

Enrollment Fall 1997: 130 total; all undergraduate.

Art Student Profile 48% females, 52% males, 4% minorities, 2% international.

Art Faculty 8 total (full-time and part-time). 100% of full-time faculty have terminal degrees. Graduate students do not teach undergraduate courses. Undergraduate student–faculty ratio: 17:1.

Student Life Student groups/activities include Art History Club, Art Co-Op Club.

Expenses for 1997–98 Application fee: $20. State resident tuition: $1700 full-time. Nonresident tuition: $7347 full-time. Mandatory fees: $2722 full-time. College room and board: $4580. College room only: $2580.

Financial Aid Program-specific awards for 1997: 5 Fine Art Scholarships ($500).

Application Procedures Students admitted directly into the professional program freshman year. Deadline for freshmen and transfers: continuous. Required: high school transcript, college transcript(s) for transfer students, minimum 2.0 high school GPA, portfolio, SAT I test score only (minimum combined SAT I score of 890). Portfolio reviews held twice on campus; the submission of slides may be substituted for portfolios when distance is prohibitive.

Web Site http://www.uml.edu/dept/Art/.

Undergraduate Contact Dr. Gerald J. Lloyd, Dean, College of Fine Arts, University of Massachusetts Lowell, Durgin Hall, South Campus, Lowell, Massachusetts 01854; 508-934-3850, fax: 508-934-3034, E-mail address: lloydg@woods.uml.edu.

▼ THE UNIVERSITY OF MEMPHIS
Memphis, Tennessee

State-supported, coed. Urban campus. Total enrollment: 19,851.

Degrees Bachelor of Fine Arts in the areas of art education, graphic design, interior design, ceramics, painting, printmaking, photography, sculpture; Bachelor of Arts in the area of art history. Majors and concentrations: art education, art/fine arts, ceramic art and design, graphic design, interior design, painting/drawing, photography, printmaking, sculpture. Graduate degrees offered: Master of Fine Arts in the areas of ceramics, graphic design, interior design, painting, printmaking/photography; Master of Arts in the areas of art history, Egyptian art and archaeology. Program accredited by NASAD.

Enrollment Fall 1997: 374 undergraduate, 43 graduate.

Art Student Profile 62% females, 38% males, 11% minorities, 3% international.

Art Faculty 50 total undergraduate and graduate (full-time and part-time). 100% of full-time faculty have terminal degrees. Graduate students teach about a quarter undergraduate courses.

Student Life Student groups/activities include Art History Student Organization, Photography Club, Clay Club.

Expenses for 1997–98 Application fee: $10. State resident tuition: $2344 full-time. Nonresident tuition: $6940 full-time. Mandatory fees: $68 full-time. College room and board: $3500. Special program-related fees: $5–$125 for material fees.

Financial Aid Program-specific awards for 1997: 3 Visual Arts Performance Awards for incoming freshmen ($2000–$5975), 1 Dana D. Johnson Scholarship for program majors ($500), 1 M. M. Ross Art Alumni Award for program majors ($1000), 1 Interior Design Alumni Scholarship for program majors ($500), 1 Art Directors Club of Memphis Award for graphic design majors ($500).

Application Procedures Students apply for admission into the professional program by sophomore year. Deadline for freshmen and transfers: August 1. Required: high school transcript, minimum 3.0 high school GPA, portfolio, SAT I or ACT test scores. Portfolio reviews held twice on campus; the submission of slides may be substituted for portfolios for three-dimensional work.

Web Site http://www.people.memphis.edu/~artdept/artdept.html.

Undergraduate Contact Ms. Brenda Landman, Assistant to the Chairman, Art Department, The University of Memphis, Caampus Box 526715, Memphis, Tennessee 38152-6715; 901-678-2216, fax: 901-678-2735, E-mail address: blandman@adminl.memst.edu.

Graduate Contact Mr. R. Steve Langdon, Graduate Program Coordinator, Art Department, The University of Memphis, Campus Box 526715, Memphis, Tennessee 38152-6715; 901-678-2216, fax: 901-678-2735, E-mail address: rslangdon@admin1.memst.edu.

▼ UNIVERSITY OF MIAMI
Coral Gables, Florida

Independent, coed. Suburban campus. Total enrollment: 13,651. Art program established 1954.

Degrees Bachelor of Fine Arts in the areas of ceramics, graphic design/illustration, painting, photography/digital imaging, sculpture, printmaking. Majors and concentrations: ceramic art and design, digital imaging, graphic arts, illustration, painting/drawing, photography, printmaking, sculpture. Graduate degrees offered: Master of Fine Arts in

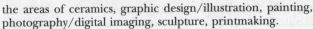

the areas of ceramics, graphic design/illustration, painting, photography/digital imaging, sculpture, printmaking.

Enrollment Fall 1997: 271 total; 34 undergraduate, 22 graduate, 215 non-professional degree.

Art Student Profile 47% females, 53% males, 35% minorities, 12% international.

Art Faculty 31 total undergraduate and graduate (full-time and part-time). 100% of full-time faculty have terminal degrees. Graduate students teach a few undergraduate courses. Undergraduate student–faculty ratio: 15:1.

Student Life Student groups/activities include Annual Student Exhibition, fall semester B.F.A. exhibition, spring semester B.F.A. exhibition.

Expenses for 1997–98 Application fee: $40. Comprehensive fee: $26,864 includes full-time tuition ($19,140), mandatory fees ($372), and college room and board ($7352). College room only: $4194. Room and board charges vary according to board plan and housing facility.

Financial Aid Program-specific awards for 1997: 6–10 art scholarships for those demonstrating talent ($6000).

Application Procedures Students apply for admission into the professional program by sophomore year. Deadline for freshmen: March 1; transfers: continuous. Notification date for freshmen: April 15; transfers: continuous. Required: essay, high school transcript, college transcript(s) for transfer students, letter of recommendation, SAT I or ACT test scores, portfolio of slides for scholarship consideration. Recommended: minimum 3.0 high school GPA. Portfolio reviews held continuously until March 15 deadline on campus.

Web Site http://www.miami.edu/art.

Contact Ms. Telma Estrada, Senior Secretary, Art and Art History Department, University of Miami, PO Box 248106, Coral Gables, Florida 33124-4410; 305-284-2542, fax: 305-284-2115, E-mail address: testrada@umiami.ir.miami.edu.

More About the University

The Department of Art and Art History is part of the University of Miami, which is recognized among the nation's best private research universities. It is located in the lush tropical paradise of Coral Gables, the "City Beautiful," minutes away from dynamic Miami and exotic Miami Beach.

Miami has one of the best foundation programs in the country. When students finish the 100-level courses, they know how to draw and design in two and three dimensions. They learn the principles of painting and have a good grasp of western art history. On the 200 levels, each area offers systematic, thorough instruction on the basics of the craft. Students begin to evolve under the guidance of talented and devoted instructors, many of them internationally recognized artists and scholars. Several young, dynamic new faculty members have come on board recently. Every art major studies with full-time, tenured faculty. There is continuous creative interchange with a large group of excellent graduate students, especially in the intense weekly critiques, open to everyone.

Facilities are first-rate and getting better. Recently the University added glassblowing and digital imaging to the curriculum. A new art library has been built. Both photography and graphic design students use computer labs with state-of-the-art software, scanners, and color printers. The Lowe Art Museum, one of the top university museums in the country, is host to the annual student and M.F.A. exhibitions. The department also has its own gallery, which shows work by nationally prominent artists as well as students and faculty members. The visiting artist/lecturer program is very active. The department annually awards more than $50,000 in art scholarships. Museum and professional internships are also offered.

Take a look at the department's Web site: Department of Art & Art History, School of Arts & Sciences, University of Miami (http://www.miami.edu/art), or e-mail mjefferson@umiami.ir.miami.edu

▼ UNIVERSITY OF MICHIGAN

Ann Arbor, Michigan

State-supported, coed. Suburban campus. Total enrollment: 36,995. Art program established 1954.

Degrees Bachelor of Fine Arts in the area of graphic and industrial design. Majors and concentrations: art/fine arts, ceramics, fibers, graphic design, industrial design, jewelry and metalsmithing, painting/drawing, photography, printmaking, scientific illustration, sculpture. Graduate degrees offered: Master of Fine Arts in the area of medical and biological illustration. Program accredited by NASAD.

Enrollment Fall 1997: 605 total; 547 undergraduate, 51 graduate, 7 non-professional degree.

Art Student Profile 62% females, 38% males, 3% international.

Art Faculty 50 total undergraduate and graduate (full-time and part-time). 95% of full-time faculty have terminal degrees. Graduate students teach a few undergraduate courses. Undergraduate student–faculty ratio: 18:1.

Student Life Student groups/activities include Art Student League, Industrial Design Society of America Student Chapter, AIGA.

Expenses for 1997–98 Application fee: $40. State resident tuition: $5694 full-time. Nonresident tuition: $18,260 full-time. Mandatory fees: $184 full-time. Full-time tuition and fees vary according to program and student level. College room and board: $5342. Room and board charges vary according to board plan and housing facility. Special program-related fees: $30–$90 per semester for lab fees for studio classes.

Financial Aid Program-specific awards for 1997: 2 Scholastic Art Awards for participants in the Scholastic Art Awards in New York ($2000), 1 National Art Honor Society Award for Michigan high school seniors belonging to Michigan Art Honor Society ($1000).

Application Procedures Students admitted directly into the professional program freshman year. Deadline for freshmen: February 1; transfers: April 1. Notification date for freshmen and transfers: May 1. Required: essay, high school transcript, college transcript(s) for transfer students, minimum 3.0 high school GPA, portfolio, SAT I or ACT test scores (minimum combined SAT I score of 1090, minimum combined ACT score of 24). Recommended: interview. Portfolio reviews held continuously on campus and off campus; the submission of slides may be substituted for portfolios if accompanied by an index sheet detailing each piece and sufficient return postage.

Web Site http://www.umich.edu/~webteam/soad/.

Undergraduate Contact Mr. Gene Pijanowski, Associate Dean for Undergraduate Education, School of Art and Design, University of Michigan, 2000 Bonisteel Boulevard, Ann Arbor, Michigan 48109-2069; 734-763-5247, fax: 734-936-0469, E-mail address: soad.ug@umich.edu.

Graduate Contact Mrs. Wendy Dignan, Graduate Program Assistant, School of Art and Design, University of Michigan,

University of Michigan *(continued)*

2000 Bonisteel Boulevard, Ann Arbor, Michigan 48109-2069; 734-936-0667, E-mail address: soad.gradinfo@umich.edu.

More About the University

Program Facilities The University of Michigan School of Art and Design is located in the Art & Architecture Building on North Campus. Opened in 1974, the spacious building houses programs in art, design, architecture, and urban planning. Studios enjoy natural light and air conditioning, and an interior courtyard provides a place to relax outdoors. The Jean Paul Slusser Gallery is a handsome showcase for exhibitions. Resources include individual and group dark-rooms and facilities for lithography and intaglio, ceramics, wood, metal, plastic, bronze casting, rapid prototyping, and electronic imaging. Specialized art and design library materials, including books, journals, slides, and video tapes are located in the Media Union library across the street. In addition, the 6 million–volume University Library network includes the History of Fine Arts Library and Undergraduate and Graduate Libraries. Computers are widely available, with easy access to extensive software and research databases.

Faculty, Visiting Artists, and Alumni Distinguished faculty members include international printmaker Takeshi Takahara, metalsmiths Hiroko and Eugene Pijanowski, photographer Joanne Leonard, fiber artist Sherri Smith, ceramist Georgette Zirbes, painter Al Hinton, and conceptual artist Joseph Grigely. Gerome Kamrowski, professor emeritus, is considered one of this century's more important artists of the Surrealist school. Between 1995 and 1998, visiting artists included Francoise Gilot, Steve Currie, Donald Lipski, Steve Frykholm, Frank Stella, Elen Feinberg, Ellen Lupton, Jan van der Marck, Ellen Driscoll, Robert Storrs, and Patrick Dougherty. Significant alumni are Michele Oka Doner, Richard Mock, and Pat Oleszko of New York City and Ruth Weisberg and Mike Kelley of Los Angeles. Christopher Van Allsburg, of "Jumanji" fame, was honored as Distinguished Alumnus of the Year.

Student Exhibit Opportunities The Jean Paul Slusser Gallery and numerous exhibition areas throughout the building provide interesting display spaces. In addition, galleries in the Media Union and Rackham Graduate School are available for student work.

Special Programs International programs are available in Kyoto, Japan, and Florence, Italy. Kyoto Seika University offers ceramics, papermaking, and wood block printing, and students experience cultural opportunities—festivals, gardens, shrines, and temples. In Florence, students sketch and paint in the picturesque gardens of Villa Corsi-Salviati and explore the surrounding Tuscany landscape.

▼ UNIVERSITY OF MICHIGAN–FLINT

Flint, Michigan

State-supported, coed. Urban campus. Total enrollment: 6,488. Art program established 1990.

Degrees Bachelor of Fine Arts in the area of studio art; Bachelor of Science in the area of art education. Mandatory cross-registration with Charles Stewart Mott Community College.

Enrollment Fall 1997: 120 total; 70 undergraduate, 50 non-professional degree.

Art Student Profile 60% females, 40% males, 15% minorities.

Art Faculty 9 total (full-time and part-time). 100% of full-time faculty have terminal degrees. Graduate students do not teach undergraduate courses. Undergraduate student–faculty ratio: 18:1.

Student Life Student groups/activities include Annual Student Exhibition, BFA Exhibits.

Expenses for 1997–98 State resident tuition: $3409 full-time. Nonresident tuition: $10,121 full-time. Mandatory fees: $150 full-time. Full-time tuition and fees vary according to program and student level.

Application Procedures Students admitted directly into the professional program freshman year. Deadline for freshmen and transfers: August 21. Notification date for freshmen: September 18; transfers: September 1. Required: high school transcript, college transcript(s) for transfer students, minimum 2.0 high school GPA, SAT I or ACT test scores, portfolio for transfer students. Portfolio reviews held as needed on campus; the submission of slides may be substituted for portfolios by prior arrangement.

Web Site http://www.flint.umich.edu/.

Undergraduate Contact Mr. Andrew Flagel, Director, Admissions, University of Michigan–Flint, University Pavillion, Flint, Michigan 48502; 810-762-3300, fax: 810-762-3687, E-mail address: aflagel@flint.umich.edu.

▼ UNIVERSITY OF MINNESOTA, DULUTH

Duluth, Minnesota

State-supported, coed. Suburban campus. Total enrollment: 9,653. Art program established 1947.

Degrees Bachelor of Fine Arts in the areas of general studio art, pregraduate studio art, graphic design, art history, art education. Majors and concentrations: art education, art history, graphic design, studio art. Graduate degrees offered: Master of Fine Arts in the area of graphic design. Cross-registration with University of Wisconsin-Superior, College of St. Scholastica.

Enrollment Fall 1997: 246 total; 244 undergraduate, 2 non-professional degree.

Art Student Profile 50% females, 50% males, 1% minorities.

Art Faculty 15 total undergraduate and graduate (full-time and part-time). 92% of full-time faculty have terminal degrees. Graduate students teach a few undergraduate courses. Undergraduate student–faculty ratio: 19:1.

Student Life Student groups/activities include American Institute of Graphic Arts.

Expenses for 1997–98 Application fee: $25. State resident tuition: $3708 full-time. Nonresident tuition: $10,588 full-time. Mandatory fees: $608 full-time. Full-time tuition and fees vary according to course level, course load, reciprocity agreements, and student level. College room and board: $3912. Room and board charges vary according to board plan and housing facility. Special program-related fees: $3–$35 per course for expendable supplies, computer lab fees.

Financial Aid Program-specific awards for 1997: 10–15 Raymond W. Darland Art Awards for program majors ($250–$1200), 2 Gershgol Awards for program majors ($1000), 1–2 Mitchell and Schissell Awards for program majors ($250), 1 Edith M. Nelson Award for program majors ($750).

Application Procedures Deadline for freshmen: continuous; transfers: June 15. Required: high school transcript, college transcript(s) for transfer students, ACT test score only.

Web Site http://www.d.umn.edu/finearts/art/art.html.

Undergraduate Contact Mr. Gerald Allen, Director, Admissions, University of Minnesota, Duluth, 184 Darland Administration Building, Duluth, Minnesota 55812; 218-726-7171, E-mail address: admis@d.umn.edu.

Graduate Contact Dr. Robyn Roslak, Director of Graduate Studies, Art Department, University of Minnesota, Duluth, H317, 10 University Drive, Duluth, Minnesota 55812; 218-726-7920, fax: 218-726-6532, E-mail address: rroslak@d.umn.edu.

▼ UNIVERSITY OF MINNESOTA, TWIN CITIES CAMPUS

Minneapolis, Minnesota

State-supported, coed. Urban campus. Total enrollment: 45,410. Art program established 1950.

Degrees Bachelor of Fine Arts in the area of art. Majors and concentrations: ceramic art and design, electronic arts, painting/drawing, photography, printmaking, sculpture. Graduate degrees offered: Master of Fine Arts in the area of art.

Enrollment Fall 1997: 1,390 total; 350 undergraduate, 40 graduate, 1,000 non-professional degree.

Art Student Profile 52% females, 48% males, 6% minorities.

Art Faculty 34 total undergraduate and graduate (full-time and part-time). 90% of full-time faculty have terminal degrees. Graduate students teach a few undergraduate courses. Undergraduate student–faculty ratio: 20:1.

Student Life Student groups/activities include Studio Arts Student Society.

Expenses for 1997–98 Application fee: $25. State resident tuition: $3976 full-time. Nonresident tuition: $11,378 full-time. Mandatory fees: $474 full-time. Full-time tuition and fees vary according to program, reciprocity agreements, and student level. College room and board: $4311. Room and board charges vary according to board plan, housing facility, and location.

Financial Aid Program-specific awards for 1997: 25 Department of Art Scholarships for program majors ($200–$1000).

Application Procedures Students apply for admission into the professional program by junior year. Deadline for freshmen: December 15; transfers: June 1. Notification date for freshmen: January 15; transfers: July 15. Required: high school transcript, SAT I or ACT test scores, minimum 2.8 high school GPA, slides of portfolio. Portfolio reviews held 3 times in junior year on campus.

Web Site http://artdept.umn.edu.

Undergraduate Contact Office of Admissions, University of Minnesota, Twin Cities Campus, 240 Williamson, 231 Pillsbury Avenue SE, Minneapolis, Minnesota 55455; 800-752-1000.

Graduate Contact Director of Graduate Studies, Department of Art, University of Minnesota, Twin Cities Campus, 216 21st Avenue South, Minneapolis, Minnesota 55455; 612-625-1848, fax: 612-625-7881.

▼ UNIVERSITY OF MISSISSIPPI

University, Mississippi

State-supported, coed. Small town campus. Total enrollment: 11,179. Art program established 1948.

Degrees Bachelor of Fine Arts in the area of art. Majors and concentrations: art education, art history, ceramic art and design, computer graphics, graphic design, painting/drawing, printmaking, sculpture, visual communication. Graduate degrees offered: Master of Fine Arts in the area of art; Master of Arts in the areas of art history, art education. Program accredited by NASAD.

Enrollment Fall 1997: 240 total; 20 graduate.

Art Student Profile 43% females, 57% males, 13% minorities, 3% international.

Art Faculty 17 total undergraduate and graduate (full-time and part-time). 100% of full-time faculty have terminal degrees. Graduate students teach a few undergraduate courses. Undergraduate student–faculty ratio: 18:1.

Student Life Student groups/activities include Student Art Association, Mud Daubers, American Society of Interior Designers Student Chapter.

Expenses for 1997–98 Application fee: $25 for nonresidents. State resident tuition: $1996 full-time. Nonresident tuition: $4816 full-time. Mandatory fees: $735 full-time. College room and board: $3186. College room only: $1786. Room and board charges vary according to board plan and housing facility. Special program-related fees: $8–$12 per credit hour for materials fee for some studio courses.

Financial Aid Program-specific awards for 1997: 10–15 Art Merit Scholarships for portfolio students ($4750–$6000).

Application Procedures Students apply for admission into the professional program by sophomore, junior year. Deadline for freshmen and transfers: July 25. Notification date for freshmen and transfers: continuous. Required: high school transcript, college transcript(s) for transfer students, minimum 2.0 high school GPA, ACT test score only (minimum combined ACT score of 18), portfolio for transfer applicants and for acceptance into the BFA program upon completion of 18 semester hours in studio art. Portfolio reviews held twice on campus.

Contact Janice W. Murray, Chair, Art Department, University of Mississippi, Bryant 205, University, Mississippi 38677; 601-232-7193, fax: 601-232-5013, E-mail address: art@olemiss.edu.

▼ UNIVERSITY OF MISSOURI–COLUMBIA

Columbia, Missouri

State-supported, coed. Small town campus. Total enrollment: 22,552.

Degrees Bachelor of Fine Arts in the area of art. Majors and concentrations: ceramics, drawing, fibers, graphic design, jewelry and metalsmithing, painting, photography, printmaking, sculpture, watercolors. Graduate degrees offered: Master of Fine Arts in the area of art. Cross-registration with Mid-Missouri Associated Colleges and Universities.

Enrollment Fall 1997: 180 total; 36 undergraduate, 12 graduate, 132 non-professional degree.

Art Student Profile 50% females, 50% males, 8% minorities, 1% international.

Art Faculty 14 total undergraduate and graduate (full-time and part-time). 100% of full-time faculty have terminal degrees. Graduate students teach a few undergraduate courses. Undergraduate student–faculty ratio: 10:1.

Student Life Student groups/activities include Imprint (graphics club), Muck (ceramics club), Student Art Community.

Expenses for 1997–98 Application fee: $25. State resident tuition: $3744 full-time. Nonresident tuition: $11,187 full-

University of Missouri–Columbia (continued)

time. Mandatory fees: $536 full-time. College room and board: $4290. Room and board charges vary according to board plan and housing facility. Special program-related fees: $10–$45 per course for lab fees.

Application Procedures Deadline for freshmen: May 1; transfers: July 1. Notification date for freshmen and transfers: continuous. Required: high school transcript, college transcript(s) for transfer students, portfolio, SAT I or ACT test scores. Portfolio reviews held once per semester on campus; the submission of slides may be substituted for portfolios.

Undergraduate Contact Mr. Jerry Berneche, Director of Undergraduate Studies, Department of Art, University of Missouri–Columbia, A 126 Fine Arts, Columbia, Missouri 65211; 573-882-3555, fax: 573-884-6807.

Graduate Contact Ms. Brooke Cameron, Director of Graduate Studies, Department of Art, University of Missouri–Columbia, A 126 Fine Arts, Columbia, Missouri 65211; 573-882-3555, fax: 573-884-6807, E-mail address: artbbc@showme.missouri.edu.

▼ University of Missouri–St. Louis

St. Louis, Missouri

State-supported, coed. Suburban campus. Total enrollment: 15,576. Art program established 1996.

Degrees Bachelor of Fine Arts in the area of art. Majors and concentrations: art/fine arts, drawing, graphic design, painting, photography, printmaking. Cross-registration with St. Louis Community Colleges. Program accredited by NASAD.

Enrollment Fall 1997: 98 total; all undergraduate.

Art Faculty 24 total (full-time and part-time). 100% of full-time faculty have terminal degrees. Graduate students do not teach undergraduate courses.

Expenses for 1997–98 State resident tuition: $3744 full-time. Nonresident tuition: $11,187 full-time. Mandatory fees: $652 full-time. College room and board: $4845. College room only: $3445. Special program-related fees: $16 per credit hour for lab fees.

Application Procedures Students admitted directly into the professional program freshman year. Deadline for freshmen and transfers: continuous. Required: high school transcript, college transcript(s) for transfer students, SAT I or ACT test scores.

Undergraduate Contact Mr. Dan Younger, BFA Coordinator, Department of Art and Art History, University of Missouri–St. Louis, 8001 Natural Bridge Road, St. Louis, Missouri 63121; 314-516-6967, fax: 314-516-6103, E-mail address: sdyoung@umslvma.umsl.edu.

▼ The University of Montana–Missoula

Missoula, Montana

State-supported, coed. Urban campus. Total enrollment: 12,124. Art program established 1957.

Degrees Bachelor of Fine Arts in the area of art. Majors and concentrations: art/fine arts, ceramics, painting/drawing, photography, printmaking, sculpture. Graduate degrees offered: Master of Fine Arts in the area of art; Master of Arts in the area of art history. Program accredited by NASAD.

Enrollment Fall 1997: 1,100 total; 245 undergraduate, 19 graduate, 836 non-professional degree.

Art Student Profile 63% females, 37% males, 3% minorities, 5% international.

Art Faculty 16 total undergraduate and graduate (full-time and part-time). 92% of full-time faculty have terminal degrees. Graduate students teach a few undergraduate courses. Undergraduate student–faculty ratio: 14:1.

Student Life Student groups/activities include Artists Collective.

Expenses for 1997–98 Application fee: $30. State resident tuition: $2630 full-time. Nonresident tuition: $7192 full-time. Full-time tuition varies according to program and student level. College room and board: $3917. Room and board charges vary according to board plan and housing facility. Special program-related fees: $35 per credit hour for materials, student aides, minor tools, and repairs for ceramics and sculpture courses, $55 per course for chemicals, lab monitors, minor tools, and repairs for printmaking and photography courses, $30 per course for basic supplies, models, photo development, studio upkeep for art fundamentals courses, $30 per course for models, equipment, studio upkeep for painting courses, $25 per course for slide replacement, library monitoring, copying for art history courses.

Financial Aid Program-specific awards for 1997: 2 Wallace Awards for sophomore or junior program majors ($500), 1 Pat Williams Scholarship for sophomore or junior program majors ($450), 1 Christopher Parker Scholarship for sophomore or junior program majors ($500), 1 Walter Hook Scholarship for sophomore or junior program majors ($600), 1 Briggs Scholarship for sophomore or junior program majors ($500), 1 Thomas Wickes Award for art majors ($2000).

Application Procedures Students apply for admission into the professional program by sophomore year. Deadline for freshmen and transfers: continuous. Required: high school transcript, SAT I or ACT test scores (minimum combined SAT I score of 920), minimum 2.5 high school GPA.

Undergraduate Contact New Student Services, The University of Montana–Missoula, The Lodge, Missoula, Montana 59812; 406-243-6266, fax: 406-243-4087, E-mail address: admiss@selway.umt.edu.

Graduate Contact Graduate School, The University of Montana–Missoula, University Hall, Missoula, Montana 59812; 406-243-2572, fax: 406-243-4593, E-mail address: gradschl@selway.umt.edu.

▼ University of Montevallo

Montevallo, Alabama

State-supported, coed. Small town campus. Total enrollment: 3,125.

Degrees Bachelor of Fine Arts in the area of studio art. Majors and concentrations: ceramic art and design, graphic design, painting/drawing, photography, printmaking, sculpture. Program accredited by NASAD.

Enrollment Fall 1997: 151 total; 146 undergraduate, 5 non-professional degree.

Art Student Profile 65% females, 35% males, 5% minorities, 2% international.

Art Faculty 9 total undergraduate (full-time and part-time). 100% of full-time faculty have terminal degrees. Graduate students do not teach undergraduate courses. Undergraduate student–faculty ratio: 17:1.

Student Life Student groups/activities include Kappa Pi, "College Night" Performance.

Expenses for 1997–98 Application fee: $25. State resident tuition: $3040 full-time. Nonresident tuition: $6080 full-time. Mandatory fees: $140 full-time. College room and board: $3116. Room and board charges vary according to board plan and housing facility.

Financial Aid Program-specific awards for 1997: 1–2 Dean's Fine Arts Awards for freshmen and transfers ($2000), 2 Endowed Scholarships for juniors and seniors ($700).

Application Procedures Deadline for freshmen and transfers: July 26. Required: high school transcript, minimum 2.0 high school GPA, SAT I or ACT test scores, minimum 2.0 college GPA for transfer students, portfolio for scholarship consideration and for transfers. Recommended: minimum 3.0 high school GPA, 3 letters of recommendation, interview. Portfolio reviews held 3 times on campus and off campus in Atlanta, GA; the submission of slides may be substituted for portfolios whenever needed.

Undergraduate Contact Kenneth J. Procter, Chairperson, Art Department, University of Montevallo, Station 6400, Montevallo, Alabama 35115; 205-665-6400, fax: 205-665-6383, E-mail address: procter@um.montevallo.edu.

▼ UNIVERSITY OF NEBRASKA–LINCOLN

Lincoln, Nebraska

State-supported, coed. Urban campus. Total enrollment: 22,827. Art program established 1918.

Degrees Bachelor of Fine Arts in the area of studio art. Majors and concentrations: art/fine arts, ceramic art and design, commercial art, computer graphics, drawing, graphic arts, illustration, painting, photography, printmaking, sculpture, studio art. Graduate degrees offered: Master of Fine Arts in the area of studio art. Cross-registration with University of Nebraska at Omaha, University of Nebraska at Kearney. Program accredited by NASAD.

Enrollment Fall 1997: 1,690 total; 309 undergraduate, 22 graduate, 1,359 non-professional degree.

Art Student Profile 52% females, 48% males.

Art Faculty 28 total undergraduate and graduate (full-time and part-time). 100% of full-time faculty have terminal degrees. Graduate students teach a few undergraduate courses.

Expenses for 1997–98 Application fee: $25. State resident tuition: $2355 full-time. Nonresident tuition: $6398 full-time. Mandatory fees: $474 full-time. Full-time tuition and fees vary according to course load. College room and board: $3700. College room only: $1638. Special program-related fees: $5–$50 per semester for lab fees.

Financial Aid Program-specific awards available.

Application Procedures Students admitted directly into the professional program freshman year. Deadline for freshmen and transfers: July 15. Notification date for freshmen and transfers: August 7. Required: high school transcript, college transcript(s) for transfer students, minimum 2.0 high school GPA.

Web Site http://www.unl.edu.

Undergraduate Contact Admission Office, University of Nebraska–Lincoln, Alexander Building, 1410 O Street, Lincoln, Nebraska 68588-0417; 402-472-2023, fax: 402-472-0670.

Graduate Contact Martha Horvay, Chairperson, Graduate Committe, Department of Art and Art History, University of Nebraska–Lincoln, 207 Nelle Cochrane Woods Hall, Lincoln, Nebraska 68588-0114; 402-472-2631, fax: 402-472-9746.

▼ UNIVERSITY OF NEVADA, LAS VEGAS

Las Vegas, Nevada

State-supported, coed. Urban campus. Total enrollment: 19,249. Art program established 1964.

Degrees Bachelor of Fine Arts in the area of art. Majors and concentrations: ceramic art and design, painting/drawing, photography, printmaking, sculpture. Graduate degrees offered: Master of Fine Arts in the area of art. Program accredited by NASAD.

Enrollment Fall 1997: 860 total; 165 undergraduate, 15 graduate, 680 non-professional degree.

Art Student Profile 70% females, 30% males, 30% minorities, 15% international.

Art Faculty 21 total undergraduate and graduate (full-time and part-time). 81% of full-time faculty have terminal degrees. Graduate students teach a few undergraduate courses.

Student Life Student groups/activities include Art Club.

Expenses for 1997–98 Application fee: $40. State resident tuition: $1596 full-time. Nonresident tuition: $8627 full-time. Mandatory fees: $46 full-time. Full-time tuition and fees vary according to course level, course load, and reciprocity agreements. College room and board: $5300. Room and board charges vary according to board plan. Special program-related fees: $15–$50 per course for lab fee.

Financial Aid Program-specific awards for 1997: 16 Devos Scholarships for program students ($1500), 12 Don King-Showtime Scholarships for minorities ($1250), 2 Agassi-Bunker Scholarships for program students ($500), 1 Harry Knudson Scholarship for program students ($500).

Application Procedures Students apply for admission into the professional program by sophomore year. Deadline for freshmen and transfers: continuous. Required: high school transcript, college transcript(s) for transfer students, minimum 2.5 high school GPA, portfolio for scholarship consideration. Portfolio reviews held once on campus; the submission of slides may be substituted for portfolios when distance is prohibitive or for large works of art.

Contact Department of Art, University of Nevada, Las Vegas, 4505 Maryland Parkway, Las Vegas, Nevada 89154-5002; 702-895-3237, fax: 702-895-4346.

▼ UNIVERSITY OF NEW HAMPSHIRE

Durham, New Hampshire

State-supported, coed. Small town campus. Total enrollment: 13,960.

Degrees Bachelor of Fine Arts in the area of studio arts. Majors and concentrations: ceramics, furniture design, painting/drawing, photography, printmaking, sculpture, studio art.

Enrollment Fall 1997: 135 total; 105 undergraduate, 30 non-professional degree.

University of New Hampshire (continued)

Art Student Profile 60% females, 40% males, 1% minorities, 1% international.

Art Faculty 22 total (full-time and part-time). 100% of full-time faculty have terminal degrees. Graduate students do not teach undergraduate courses. Undergraduate student–faculty ratio: 10:1.

Student Life Student groups/activities include Student Art Association.

Expenses for 1997–98 Application fee: $25. State resident tuition: $4600 full-time. Nonresident tuition: $13,460 full-time. Mandatory fees: $1289 full-time. College room and board: $4524. College room only: $2644. Room and board charges vary according to board plan.

Financial Aid Program-specific awards for 1997: 4 Elizabeth Jones Scholarships for junior or senior program majors ($1000–$2000), 1 Tripetti Scholarship for junior or senior program majors ($1000).

Application Procedures Students apply for admission into the professional program by sophomore year. Deadline for freshmen: February 1; transfers: March 1. Notification date for freshmen and transfers: April 15. Required: essay, high school transcript, college transcript(s) for transfer students, letter of recommendation, portfolio, SAT I or ACT test scores. Recommended: minimum 3.0 high school GPA, interview. Portfolio reviews held as needed on campus; the submission of slides may be substituted for portfolios when distance is prohibitive.

Undergraduate Contact Mr. Scott Schnepf, Chair, Department of Art and Art History, University of New Hampshire, Paul Creative Arts Center, 30 College Road, Durham, New Hampshire 03824; 603-862-2190.

▼ UNIVERSITY OF NEW MEXICO

Albuquerque, New Mexico

State-supported, coed. Urban campus. Total enrollment: 23,956.

Degrees Bachelor of Fine Arts in the area of studio art. Majors and concentrations: art/fine arts. Graduate degrees offered: Master of Fine Arts in the area of studio art. Doctor of Philosophy in the area of art history.

Enrollment Fall 1997: 426 total; 301 undergraduate, 125 graduate.

Art Student Profile 55% females, 45% males.

Art Faculty 45 total undergraduate and graduate (full-time and part-time). 100% of full-time faculty have terminal degrees. Graduate students teach about a quarter undergraduate courses.

Student Life Student groups/activities include Art Student Association Gallery.

Expenses for 1997–98 Application fee: $15. State resident tuition: $2165 full-time. Nonresident tuition: $8174 full-time. College room and board: $4119. Room and board charges vary according to board plan and housing facility. Special program-related fees: $10–$100 per studio for course materials.

Financial Aid Program-specific awards for 1997: 12 art scholarships ($500).

Application Procedures Students apply for admission into the professional program by junior year. Deadline for freshmen and transfers: July 26. Required: high school transcript, college transcript(s) for transfer students, portfolio, SAT I or

ACT test scores, minimum 2.25 high school GPA. Portfolio reviews held continuously by appointment on campus.

Undergraduate Contact Office of Admissions, University of New Mexico, Albuquerque, New Mexico 87131; 505-277-2446.

Graduate Contact Ms. Emily Griffith, Graduate Advisor, Department of Art and Art History, University of New Mexico, Albuquerque, New Mexico 87131; 505-277-6672, fax: 505-277-5955.

▼ UNIVERSITY OF NORTH ALABAMA

Florence, Alabama

State-supported, coed. Urban campus. Total enrollment: 5,575. Art program established 1930.

Degrees Bachelor of Fine Arts in the area of art. Majors and concentrations: ceramics, graphic design, painting/drawing, photography, printmaking, sculpture. Program accredited by NASAD.

Enrollment Fall 1997: 520 total; 95 undergraduate, 425 non-professional degree.

Art Student Profile 60% females, 40% males, 5% minorities, 2% international.

Art Faculty 8 total (full-time and part-time). 90% of full-time faculty have terminal degrees. Graduate students do not teach undergraduate courses. Undergraduate student–faculty ratio: 12:1.

Student Life Student groups/activities include Student Art Association, W.C. Handy Music Festival Poster Competition, Floala (student newspaper) and Diorama (yearbook).

Expenses for 1997–98 Application fee: $25. State resident tuition: $2064 full-time. Nonresident tuition: $4128 full-time. Mandatory fees: $120 full-time. College room and board: $3260. College room only: $1520. Special program-related fees: $30 per semester for studio lab fee.

Financial Aid Program-specific awards for 1997: 4 Endowed Scholarships for program majors ($300–$1500), 6 Leadership-Fine Arts Scholarships for talented program majors ($1000–$6000), 4 Academic-Fine Arts Scholarships for talented program majors ($1000–$6000).

Application Procedures Students apply for admission into the professional program by sophomore year. Deadline for freshmen and transfers: August 30. Notification date for freshmen and transfers: continuous. Required: high school transcript, college transcript(s) for transfer students, portfolio, SAT I or ACT test scores. Recommended: minimum 2.0 high school GPA. Portfolio reviews held twice on campus.

Web Site http://www.una.edu.

Undergraduate Contact Dr. Sue Wilson, Dean of Enrollment Management, Admissions Office, University of North Alabama, Box 5058, Florence, Alabama 35632-0001; 256-765-4680, fax: 256-765-4329, E-mail address: swilson@unanov.una.edu.

▼ UNIVERSITY OF NORTH CAROLINA AT ASHEVILLE

Asheville, North Carolina

State-supported, coed. Suburban campus. Total enrollment: 3,179. Art program established 1966.

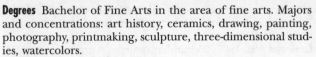

Degrees Bachelor of Fine Arts in the area of fine arts. Majors and concentrations: art history, ceramics, drawing, painting, photography, printmaking, sculpture, three-dimensional studies, watercolors.
Enrollment Fall 1997: 50 total.
Art Student Profile 55% females, 45% males, 1% minorities, 1% international.
Art Faculty 10 total (full-time and part-time). 100% of full-time faculty have terminal degrees. Graduate students do not teach undergraduate courses.
Student Life Student groups/activities include Art Front (student group), Annual Juried Student Exhibition.
Expenses for 1997–98 Application fee: $35. State resident tuition: $752 full-time. Nonresident tuition: $7046 full-time. Mandatory fees: $1082 full-time. College room and board: $3826. College room only: $1816. Room and board charges vary according to board plan and housing facility.
Financial Aid Program-specific awards for 1997: 1 Otto Feistmann Memorial Scholarship for declared art major ($500), 1 Biltmore Iron and Metal Scholarship for declared art major/sculpture ($500), 1 Millspaugh Scholarship for declared art major ($500), 1 Walter E. Ogilvie Scholarship for declared art major ($500), 1 W. H. Tucker Scholarship for declared art major ($500), 1 Norman Sultan Scholarship for declared art major ($500), 1 Krivatsy Award for Excellence in Painting for declared art major/painting ($300), 1 Ryan Patrick Jones Award for Excellence in Photography for photo students ($300).
Application Procedures Students apply for admission into the professional program by sophomore year. Deadline for freshmen and transfers: continuous. Notification date for freshmen and transfers: continuous. Required: high school transcript, college transcript(s) for transfer students, portfolio, SAT I test score only. Portfolio reviews held as needed on campus; the submission of slides may be substituted for portfolios on a case-by-case basis.
Web Site http://bulldog.unca.edu/art.
Undergraduate Contact Mr. Robert Dunning, Admissions Office Liaison, Art Department, University of North Carolina at Asheville, One University Heights, Asheville, North Carolina 28804; 704-251-6559, fax: 704-251-6142, E-mail address: rdunning@unca.edu.

▼ UNIVERSITY OF NORTH CAROLINA AT CHARLOTTE

Charlotte, North Carolina

State-supported, coed. Urban campus. Total enrollment: 16,511. Art program established 1965.
Degrees Bachelor of Fine Arts in the area of art. Majors and concentrations: art education, art history, art/fine arts, ceramic art and design, commercial art, computer graphics, electronic intermedia, fibers, graphic arts, illustration, museum studies, painting/drawing, photography, printmaking, sculpture, studio art, textile arts. Cross-registration with area universities.
Enrollment Fall 1997: 400 total; all undergraduate.
Art Student Profile 54% females, 46% males, 11% minorities, 2% international.
Art Faculty 28 total (full-time and part-time). 100% of full-time faculty have terminal degrees. Graduate students do not teach undergraduate courses. Undergraduate student–faculty ratio: 15:1.

Student Life Student groups/activities include National Art Education Association Student Chapter, Art Student Association.
Expenses for 1997–98 Application fee: $35. State resident tuition: $900 full-time. Nonresident tuition: $8028 full-time. Mandatory fees: $877 full-time. Full-time tuition and fees vary according to course load. College room and board: $3446. Room and board charges vary according to board plan and housing facility.
Financial Aid Program-specific awards for 1997: 6 art scholarships for freshmen and transfers ($500–$1000).
Application Procedures Students admitted directly into the professional program freshman year. Deadline for freshmen and transfers: continuous. Required: high school transcript, college transcript(s) for transfer students, minimum 3.0 high school GPA, interview, portfolio, SAT I or ACT test scores. Portfolio reviews held once for BA applicants and throughout the year for entrance into BFA program on campus.
Undergraduate Contact Department of Art, University of North Carolina at Charlotte, 173 Rowe Building, Charlotte, North Carolina 28223; 704-547-2473, fax: 704-547-3795.

▼ UNIVERSITY OF NORTH CAROLINA AT GREENSBORO

Greensboro, North Carolina

State-supported, coed. Urban campus. Total enrollment: 12,308. Art program established 1936.
Degrees Bachelor of Fine Arts in the areas of studio art, art education. Majors and concentrations: art education, ceramic art and design, computer art, design, painting/drawing, sculpture. Graduate degrees offered: Master of Fine Arts in the area of studio art.
Enrollment Fall 1997: 365 total; 350 undergraduate, 15 graduate.
Art Student Profile 60% females, 40% males, 10% minorities, 2% international.
Art Faculty 23 total undergraduate and graduate (full-time and part-time). 99% of full-time faculty have terminal degrees. Graduate students do not teach undergraduate courses. Undergraduate student–faculty ratio: 22:1.
Student Life Student groups/activities include Student Art Alliance, Student Government, Coraddi Art Magazine.
Expenses for 1997–98 Application fee: $35. State resident tuition: $1016 full-time. Nonresident tuition: $9304 full-time. Mandatory fees: $1015 full-time. College room and board: $3661. College room only: $2011.
Financial Aid Program-specific awards for 1997: 3 Reeves/Howard/Falk Awards for junior program majors ($500–$1500).
Application Procedures Students admitted directly into the professional program freshman year. Deadline for freshmen and transfers: continuous. Required: high school transcript, college transcript(s) for transfer students, minimum 2.0 high school GPA, SAT I or ACT test scores (minimum combined SAT I score of 800, minimum combined ACT score of 15), portfolio for scholarship consideration. Recommended: portfolio for transfer students. Portfolio reviews held continuously by appointment on campus.
Web Site http://www.uncg.edu/art.
Undergraduate Contact Patricia Wasserboehr, Head, Art Department, University of North Carolina at Greensboro, PO Box

University of North Carolina at Greensboro (continued)

26170, Greensboro, North Carolina 27402-6170; 336-334-5248, fax: 336-334-5270, E-mail address: trsoule@hamlet.uncg.edu.

Graduate Contact Mr. John Maggio, Graduate Coordinator, Art Department, University of North Carolina at Greensboro, PO Box 26170, Greensboro, North Carolina 27402-6170; 336-334-5248, fax: 336-334-5270, E-mail address: trsoule@hamlet.uncg.edu.

▼ UNIVERSITY OF NORTH DAKOTA

Grand Forks, North Dakota

State-supported, coed. Small town campus. Total enrollment: 10,363. Art program established 1978.

Degrees Bachelor of Fine Arts in the area of visual arts. Majors and concentrations: ceramic art and design, jewelry and metalsmithing, painting/drawing, photography, printmaking, sculpture. Graduate degrees offered: Master of Fine Arts in the area of visual arts. Program accredited by NASAD.

Enrollment Fall 1997: 307 total; 89 undergraduate, 18 graduate, 200 non-professional degree.

Art Student Profile 50% females, 50% males, 3% minorities, 1% international.

Art Faculty 13 total undergraduate and graduate (full-time and part-time). 93% of full-time faculty have terminal degrees. Graduate students teach a few undergraduate courses. Undergraduate student–faculty ratio: 10:1.

Student Life Student groups/activities include Annual Juried Student Show, Art Student Collective, League of Metalsmiths.

Expenses for 1997–98 Application fee: $25. State resident tuition: $2677 full-time. Nonresident tuition: $6144 full-time. Mandatory fees: $441 full-time. Full-time tuition and fees vary according to program and reciprocity agreements. College room and board: $3117. College room only: $1216. Room and board charges vary according to board plan and housing facility.

Application Procedures Students apply for admission into the professional program by sophomore year. Deadline for freshmen and transfers: continuous. Required: high school transcript, college transcript(s) for transfer students, portfolio, ACT test score only. Portfolio reviews held as needed on campus; the submission of slides may be substituted for portfolios for large works of art or when distance is prohibitive.

Contact Ms. Jacquelyn McElroy-Edwards, Chair, Department of Visual Arts, University of North Dakota, Box 7099, Grand Forks, North Dakota 58202; 701-777-2257, fax: 701-777-3395, E-mail address: mcelroye@badlands.nodak.edu.

▼ UNIVERSITY OF NORTHERN IOWA

Cedar Falls, Iowa

State-supported, coed. Small town campus. Total enrollment: 13,503. Art program established 1895.

Degrees Bachelor of Fine Arts in the area of studio arts. Majors and concentrations: art history, ceramics, drawing, graphic design, jewelry and metalsmithing, painting, photography, printmaking, sculpture. Graduate degrees offered: Master of Arts. Cross-registration with institutions of the International Student Exchange Program . Program accredited by NASAD.

Enrollment Fall 1997: 250 undergraduate, 8 graduate.

Art Faculty 22 total undergraduate and graduate (full-time and part-time). 94% of full-time faculty have terminal degrees. Graduate students do not teach undergraduate courses.

Student Life Student groups/activities include ARTS-UNI, Student Art Education Association.

Expenses for 1997–98 Application fee: $20. State resident tuition: $2566 full-time. Nonresident tuition: $6950 full-time. Mandatory fees: $186 full-time. College room and board: $3452. Special program-related fees: $35 per course for lab fee.

Financial Aid Program-specific awards for 1997: 3–6 Art Department Scholarships for incoming freshmen ($2566), Art Department scholarships for undergraduate art majors ($1283–$2566), 1 Tostlebe Ray Scholarship for undergraduate art majors ($2600).

Application Procedures Students apply for admission into the professional program by junior year. Deadline for freshmen and transfers: continuous. Required: high school transcript, college transcript(s) for transfer students, portfolio, SAT I or ACT test scores, TOEFL score for international applicants, minimum 2.0 college GPA for transfer students. Recommended: standing in top half of graduating class. Portfolio reviews held twice on campus; the submission of slides may be substituted for portfolios whenever needed.

Web Site http://www.uni.edu/artdept.

Undergraduate Contact Dr. William Lew, Head, Department of Art, University of Northern Iowa, 104 Kamerick Building, Cedar Falls, Iowa 50614-0362; 319-273-2077, fax: 319-273-7333, E-mail address: lew.william@uni.edu.

Graduate Contact Mr. Jeffery Byrd, Graduate Coordinator, Department of Art, University of Northern Iowa, 104 Kamerick Building, Cedar Falls, Iowa 50614-0362; 319-273-2077, fax: 319-273-7333, E-mail address: jeffery.byrd@uni.edu.

▼ UNIVERSITY OF NORTH FLORIDA

Jacksonville, Florida

State-supported, coed. Urban campus. Total enrollment: 11,389. Art program established 1972.

Degrees Bachelor of Fine Arts in the areas of painting, drawing, ceramics, sculpture, graphic design. Cross-registration with Florida State University System.

Enrollment Fall 1997: 195 total; 52 undergraduate, 143 non-professional degree.

Art Student Profile 60% females, 40% males, 5% minorities, 5% international.

Art Faculty 25 total (full-time and part-time). 100% of full-time faculty have terminal degrees. Graduate students do not teach undergraduate courses.

Expenses for 1997–98 Application fee: $20. State resident tuition: $2006 full-time. Nonresident tuition: $7923 full-time. College room and board: $3492. College room only: $2342. Room and board charges vary according to board plan and housing facility. Special program-related fees: $15 per course for materials.

Financial Aid Program-specific awards for 1997: 1–4 Neil Gray Scholarships for junior and senior program majors ($2000).

Application Procedures Students apply for admission into the professional program by junior year. Deadline for freshmen and transfers: July 5. Notification date for freshmen and transfers: continuous. Required: high school transcript, college transcript(s) for transfer students, SAT I test score only. Recommended: portfolio. Portfolio reviews held 3 times on campus; the submission of slides may be substituted for portfolios for large works of art and when the slides are of adequate quality.

Web Site http://www.unf.edu/coas/cva.

Undergraduate Contact Registrar, University of North Florida, 4567 St. Johns Bluff Road South, Jacksonville, Florida 32224; 904-646-2624.

▼ University of North Texas

Denton, Texas

State-supported, coed. Urban campus. Total enrollment: 25,013. Art program established 1894.

Degrees Bachelor of Fine Arts in the areas of communication design, art history, ceramics, drawing and painting, fashion design, fibers, interior design, metalsmithing and jewelry, photography, printmaking, sculpture, visual arts studies. Majors and concentrations: art history, art/fine arts, ceramic art and design, communication design, fashion design and technology, fibers, interior design, jewelry and metalsmithing, painting/drawing, photography, printmaking, sculpture, visual arts. Graduate degrees offered: Master of Fine Arts in the areas of art education, art history, ceramics, communication design, drawing and painting, fashion design, fibers, interior design, metalsmithing and jewelry, photography, printmaking, sculpture. Program accredited by FIDER.

Enrollment Fall 1997: 1,559 total; 1,439 undergraduate, 120 graduate.

Art Student Profile 60% females, 40% males, 16% minorities, 4% international.

Art Faculty 79 total undergraduate and graduate (full-time and part-time). 100% of full-time faculty have terminal degrees. Graduate students teach about a quarter undergraduate courses. Undergraduate student–faculty ratio: 16:1.

Expenses for 1997–98 Application fee: $25. State resident tuition: $1666 full-time. Nonresident tuition: $8300 full-time. Mandatory fees: $521 full-time. College room and board: $3842. Special program-related fees: $25–$75 per course for materials fee.

Financial Aid Program-specific awards for 1997: 3–6 John D. Murchison Scholarships for program majors ($500), 2–6 Helen Voertman Scholarships for program majors ($500), 1–4 Nelda Lee Scholarships for program majors ($250), 2–4 Cora Stafford Scholarships for program majors ($250), 2 Roger Thomason Scholarships for fibers majors ($500), 3–6 Jean Andrews Awards for program majors ($500), 2 Edward and Betty Mattil Scholarships for program students ($500), 1 Mozelle Rawson Brown Scholarship for program students ($250), 2 J. Robert Egan Scholarships for photography majors ($500), 3 Mac Mathis Scholarships for program majors ($500).

Application Procedures Students admitted directly into the professional program freshman year. Deadline for freshmen and transfers: June 15. Required: high school transcript, college transcript(s) for transfer students, SAT I or ACT test scores, minimum 2.5 high school GPA.

Web Site http://www.art.unt.edu.

Undergraduate Contact Ms. Mickey McCarter, Director of Undergraduate Programs, School of Visual Arts, University of North Texas, PO Box 305100, Denton, Texas 76203-5100; 940-565-2216, fax: 940-565-4717.

Graduate Contact Dr. Diane Taylor, Director of Graduate Programs, School of Visual Arts, University of North Texas, PO Box 305100, Denton, Texas 76203-5100; 940-565-2216, fax: 940-565-4717.

▼ University of Notre Dame

Notre Dame, Indiana

Independent-Roman Catholic, coed. Suburban campus. Total enrollment: 10,275.

Degrees Bachelor of Fine Arts in the areas of studio art, design. Majors and concentrations: art/fine arts, ceramic art and design, computer graphics, graphic arts, industrial design, painting/drawing, photography, printmaking, sculpture, studio art. Graduate degrees offered: Master of Fine Arts in the areas of studio art, design; Master of Arts in the area of art history.

Enrollment Fall 1997: 150 total; 125 undergraduate, 25 graduate.

Art Student Profile 50% females, 50% males, 15% minorities, 5% international.

Art Faculty 25 total undergraduate and graduate (full-time and part-time). 100% of full-time faculty have terminal degrees. Graduate students teach about a quarter undergraduate courses. Undergraduate student–faculty ratio: 15:1.

Student Life Student groups/activities include student exhibitions.

Expenses for 1997–98 Application fee: $40. Comprehensive fee: $25,007 includes full-time tuition ($19,800), mandatory fees ($147), and college room and board ($5060). Full-time tuition and fees vary according to program. Room and board charges vary according to housing facility. Special program-related fees: $15–$50 per course for studio materials.

Application Procedures Students admitted directly into the professional program freshman year. Deadline for freshmen and transfers: January 4. Notification date for freshmen and transfers: April 10. Required: essay, high school transcript, minimum 3.0 high school GPA, 2 letters of recommendation. Recommended: slide portfolio. Portfolio reviews held by request on campus; the submission of slides may be substituted for portfolios (slides preferred).

Undergraduate Contact Admissions Office, University of Notre Dame, 113 Main Building, Notre Dame, Indiana 46556; 219-631-7505.

Graduate Contact Mr. Richard Gray, Graduate Director, Department of Art, Art History and Design, University of Notre Dame, 132 O'Shaughnessy Hall, Notre Dame, Indiana 46556; 219-631-4272, fax: 219-631-6312.

▼ University of Oklahoma

Norman, Oklahoma

State-supported, coed. Suburban campus. Total enrollment: 25,975. Art program established 1903.

Degrees Bachelor of Fine Arts in the area of art. Majors and concentrations: art history, ceramic art and design, film and video production, metals, painting/drawing, photography,

University of Oklahoma *(continued)*

printmaking, sculpture, video art, visual communication. Graduate degrees offered: Master of Fine Arts in the area of art.

Enrollment Fall 1997: 394 total; 319 undergraduate, 35 graduate, 40 non-professional degree.

Art Student Profile 54% females, 46% males, 24% minorities, 8% international.

Art Faculty 21 total undergraduate and graduate (full-time and part-time). 90% of full-time faculty have terminal degrees. Graduate students teach a few undergraduate courses. Undergraduate student–faculty ratio: 20:1.

Student Life Student groups/activities include student art exhibits.

Expenses for 1997–98 Application fee: $25. State resident tuition: $1745 full-time. Nonresident tuition: $5785 full-time. Mandatory fees: $566 full-time. Full-time tuition and fees vary according to course level, course load, location, program, and reciprocity agreements. College room and board: $3800. College room only: $1884. Room and board charges vary according to board plan, housing facility, and student level. Special program-related fees: $10–$90 per semester for material fees/ facilities or lab fees.

Financial Aid Program-specific awards for 1997: 8–12 Ben Barnett Scholarships for program students ($500), 1–2 DeLoe Memorial Awards for program students ($250–$500), 1–2 Selma Naifeh Scholarships for painting students ($250–$500).

Application Procedures Students apply for admission into the professional program by freshman, sophomore year. Deadline for freshmen and transfers: continuous. Required: high school transcript, college transcript(s) for transfer students, minimum 3.0 high school GPA, SAT I or ACT test scores, portfolio for visual communication applicants. Portfolio reviews held 4 times on campus and off campus; the submission of slides may be substituted for portfolios (slides preferred).

Web Site http://www.ou.edu/finearts/.

Undergraduate Contact Dr. Andrew L. Phelan, Director, School of Art, University of Oklahoma, 520 Parrington Oval, Room 202, Norman, Oklahoma 73019-0550; 405-325-2691, fax: 405-325-1668.

Graduate Contact Mr. Andrew Strout, Graduate Liaison, School of Art, University of Oklahoma, 520 Parrington Oval, Room 202, Norman, Oklahoma 73019-0550; 405-325-2691.

More About the University

Program Facilities The School of Art occupies 42,500 square feet in the modern Fred Jones Jr. Memorial Art Center, which also contains the Art Museum. It contains offices; classrooms; studios for painting and drawing; sculpture, ceramics, and metal design studios; a comprehensive printmaking studio for etching, lithography, serigraphy, and relief printing; photography darkrooms and color printing facilities; and several digital media and computer graphics labs with Internet connections and with a wide variety of software, input and output devices, extensive film and video equipment, and linear and nonlinear editing facilities.

The 3,600-square-foot Old Faculty Club is being renovated to house the Charles M. Russell Center for Study of Art of the American West and will also contain a sculpture studio for an artist-in-residence. A new ceramics building is under construction on the South Campus. Other facilities used by the School of Art include several buildings on the North (Research) Campus, where graduate students and faculty members maintain studios.

Faculty, Visiting Artists, and Alumni The faculty members are exhibiting artists, publishing scholars, working designers, or active film/video makers. Thoroughly professional, many have national or international reputations. They're augmented by a program of guest artists and scholars. Distinguished alumni include the legendary Kiowa Five, the late Allen Houser, and others whose art hangs in major museums or who work as professionals, artists, or faculty members. The first Charles M. Russell Scholar in the Art of the American West, Peter Hassrick, has been appointed for the coming year. An artist-in-residence program has begun with the appointment of Paul Moore, a sculptor who specializes in monumental pieces.

Student Exhibition Opportunities Students exhibit regularly in the School's Lightwell Gallery or in the annual exhibition in the Fred Jones Jr. Museum of Art.

Special Programs The School has programs in Santa Fe and exchanges (in place or under development) at such places as the University of Birmingham in England and the University of Newcastle in Australia.

▼ UNIVERSITY OF OREGON

Eugene, Oregon

State-supported, coed. Urban campus. Total enrollment: 17,530.

Degrees Bachelor of Fine Arts in the areas of painting, sculpture, ceramics, fibers, metals and jewelry, printmaking, visual design. Majors and concentrations: animation, ceramics, computer graphics, fibers, graphic design, jewelry and metalsmithing, painting/drawing, photography, printmaking, sculpture. Graduate degrees offered: Master of Fine Arts in the areas of painting, sculpture, ceramics, fibers, metals and jewelry, printmaking, visual design.

Enrollment Fall 1997: 571 total; 64 undergraduate, 43 graduate, 464 non-professional degree.

Art Student Profile 50% females, 50% males, 10% minorities, 3% international.

Art Faculty 24 total undergraduate and graduate (full-time and part-time). 90% of full-time faculty have terminal degrees. Graduate students teach a few undergraduate courses. Undergraduate student–faculty ratio: 20:1.

Student Life Student groups/activities include American Institute of Graphic Arts, Society for Photographic Educators, Association for Computer Machinery.

Expenses for 1997–98 Application fee: $50. State resident tuition: $2694 full-time. Nonresident tuition: $11,145 full-time. Mandatory fees: $714 full-time. College room and board: $4646. Special program-related fees: $5–$80 per term for material fees.

Financial Aid Program-specific awards for 1997: 4 Phillip Johnson Scholarships for continuing painting and printmaking students ($200–$400), 1 LaVerne Krause Scholarship for continuing printmaking students ($500–$750), 1 Merz Memorial Scholarship for continuing students ($500), 4 David McCosh Painting Scholarships for continuing painting students ($200–$400), 1 Jack Wilkinson Paint Award for continuing students ($200–$400), 2 Molly Muntzel Awards for continuing students ($200–$400).

Application Procedures Deadline for freshmen and transfers: March 1. Notification date for freshmen and transfers:

April 1. Required: letter of recommendation. Recommended: portfolio. Portfolio reviews held 3 times on campus; the submission of slides may be substituted for portfolios (slides preferred).

Undergraduate Contact Fine Arts Admissions, Fine and Applied Arts Department, University of Oregon, 5232 University of Oregon, Eugene, Oregon 97403-5232; 541-346-3610, fax: 541-346-3626, E-mail address: blawrenc@darkwing.uoregon.edu.

Graduate Contact Graduate Program, Fine and Applied Arts Department, University of Oregon, 5232 University of Oregon, Eugene, Oregon 97403-5232; 541-346-3610, fax: 541-346-3626, E-mail address: blawrenc@darkwing.uoregon.edu.

▼ UNIVERSITY OF REGINA

Regina, SK, Canada

Province-supported, coed. Urban campus. Art program established 1915.

Degrees Bachelor of Fine Arts in the areas of drawing, painting, sculpture, ceramics, printmaking, intermedia. Majors and concentrations: ceramics, intermedia, painting/drawing, printmaking, sculpture. Graduate degrees offered: Master of Fine Arts in the areas of drawing, painting, sculpture, ceramics, printmaking, intermedia.

Enrollment Fall 1997: 85 undergraduate, 6 graduate.

Art Student Profile 55% females, 45% males, 2% minorities, 5% international.

Art Faculty 90% of full-time faculty have terminal degrees. Graduate students teach a few undergraduate courses. Undergraduate student–faculty ratio: 15:1.

Expenses for 1997–98 Application fee: $25. Canadian resident tuition: $2813 full-time. Mandatory fees: $229 full-time. College room and board: $3680. International student tuition: $5625 full-time.

Financial Aid Program-specific awards for 1997: 3 Endowed Scholarships for program majors ($50–$250), 4 Funded Scholarships for program majors ($250–$1000).

Application Procedures Students admitted directly into the professional program freshman year. Deadline for freshmen and transfers: April 1. Notification date for freshmen and transfers: April 15. Required: high school transcript, college transcript(s) for transfer students, minimum 2.0 high school GPA, interview, portfolio. Recommended: letter of recommendation. Portfolio reviews held twice on campus; the submission of slides may be substituted for portfolios for large works of art or when distance is prohibitive.

Web Site http://www.uregina.ca.

Contact Mr. Roger Lee, Chairperson, Department of Visual Arts, University of Regina, University Center, Room 247, Regina, SK S4S 0A2, Canada; 306-585-5552, fax: 306-585-5526, E-mail address: roger.lee@uregina.ca.

▼ UNIVERSITY OF SOUTH ALABAMA

Mobile, Alabama

State-supported, coed. Suburban campus.

Degrees Bachelor of Fine Arts in the area of studio art. Majors and concentrations: ceramics, graphic design, painting/drawing, printmaking, sculpture. Program accredited by NASAD.

Enrollment Fall 1997: 142 total; all undergraduate.

Art Student Profile 46% females, 54% males, 2% minorities, 5% international.

Art Faculty 19 total (full-time and part-time). 90% of full-time faculty have terminal degrees. Graduate students do not teach undergraduate courses. Undergraduate student–faculty ratio: 12:1.

Student Life Student groups/activities include Student Art Association, Art History Association.

Expenses for 1997–98 Application fee: $25. State resident tuition: $2640 full-time. Nonresident tuition: $5280 full-time. Mandatory fees: $198 full-time. Special program-related fees: $10–$50 per quarter for lab fees.

Application Procedures Students admitted directly into the professional program freshman year. Deadline for freshmen and transfers: continuous. Required: high school transcript, college transcript(s) for transfer students, SAT I or ACT test scores. Recommended: portfolio for transfer students. Portfolio reviews held continuously on campus; the submission of slides may be substituted for portfolios if of good quality.

Undergraduate Contact Mr. Larry B. Simpson, Acting Chair, Art and Art History Department, University of South Alabama, 172 Visual Arts Building, Mobile, Alabama 36688; 334-460-6335, fax: 334-414-8294.

▼ UNIVERSITY OF SOUTH CAROLINA

Columbia, South Carolina

State-supported, coed. Urban campus. Total enrollment: 25,447.

Degrees Bachelor of Fine Arts in the area of studio art. Majors and concentrations: ceramics, graphic design, painting/drawing, photography, printmaking, three-dimensional studies. Graduate degrees offered: Master of Fine Arts in the area of studio art.

Enrollment Fall 1997: 200 undergraduate, 25 graduate.

Art Student Profile 50% females, 50% males.

Art Faculty 44 total undergraduate and graduate (full-time and part-time). 100% of full-time faculty have terminal degrees. Graduate students teach a few undergraduate courses. Undergraduate student–faculty ratio: 10:1.

Expenses for 1997–98 Application fee: $35. One-time mandatory fee: $25. State resident tuition: $3434 full-time. Nonresident tuition: $8840 full-time. Mandatory fees: $100 full-time. College room and board: $3830.

Financial Aid Program-specific awards for 1997: 3 Katherine Heyward Scholarships for academically qualified entering and continuing students ($800), 2 Delores Cauthen Scholarships for academically qualified entering and continuing students ($800), 5 Yaghjian Chair in Painting Awards for academically qualified entering and continuing students ($800).

Application Procedures Students admitted directly into the professional program freshman year. Deadline for freshmen and transfers: continuous. Required: college transcript(s) for transfer students, minimum 3.0 high school GPA.

Undergraduate Contact Mr. Harry Hansen, Director of Undergraduate Studies, Art Department, University of South Carolina, Columbia, South Carolina 29208; 803-777-4236, fax: 803-777-0535.

University of South Carolina (continued)

Graduate Contact Dr. Philip Dunn, Director of Graduate Studies, Art Department, University of South Carolina, Columbia, South Carolina 29208; 803-777-4236, fax: 803-777-0535.

▼ UNIVERSITY OF SOUTH DAKOTA
Vermillion, South Dakota

State-supported, coed. Small town campus. Total enrollment: 7,392. Art program established 1882.

Degrees Bachelor of Fine Arts in the areas of graphic design, photography, ceramics, painting, sculpture, printmaking, art education. Graduate degrees offered: Master of Fine Arts in the areas of painting, printmaking, sculpture, studio art. Program accredited by NASAD.

Enrollment Fall 1997: 622 total; 85 undergraduate, 17 graduate, 520 non-professional degree.

Art Student Profile 51% females, 49% males, 8% minorities, 2% international.

Art Faculty 11 total undergraduate and graduate (full-time and part-time). 100% of full-time faculty have terminal degrees. Graduate students teach a few undergraduate courses.

Student Life Student groups/activities include Art Student Organization, Art Student Co-op.

Expenses for 1997–98 Application fee: $15. State resident tuition: $1728 full-time. Nonresident tuition: $5496 full-time. Mandatory fees: $1284 full-time. Full-time tuition and fees vary according to reciprocity agreements. College room and board: $2912. College room only: $1322. Room and board charges vary according to board plan. Special program-related fees: $15–$85 per course for consumable materials, $95 per course for computer graphic design course fees.

Financial Aid Program-specific awards for 1997: 5–6 Oscar Howe Scholarships for high school juniors and seniors with preference to Native Americans from South Dakota ($400), 1 A.B. Gunderson Fine Arts Scholarship for seniors ($750), 4 Louise Hansen Art Scholarships for freshmen ($235), 1 Lance Hyde Memorial Art Scholarship for art education majors ($250).

Application Procedures Students admitted directly into the professional program freshman year. Deadline for freshmen and transfers: continuous. Required: high school transcript, college transcript(s) for transfer students, minimum 2.0 high school GPA, standing in top 50% of graduating class or minimum ACT score of 22 if high school GPA is less than 2.0. Recommended: portfolio. Portfolio reviews held as needed on campus; the submission of slides may be substituted for portfolios on a case-by-case basis.

Web Site http://www.usd.edu/cfa/Art/art.html.

Undergraduate Contact Director, Admissions Office, University of South Dakota, Slagle 12, 414 East Clark Street, Vermillion, South Dakota 57069-2390; 605-677-5434, fax: 605-677-5073, E-mail address: admiss@sunflower.usd.edu.

Graduate Contact Mr. Lawrence P. Anderson, Chair, Department of Art, University of South Dakota, CFA 179, 414 East Clark Street, Vermillion, South Dakota 57069-2390; 605-677-5636, fax: 605-677-5988, E-mail address: artdept@usd.edu.

▼ UNIVERSITY OF SOUTHERN CALIFORNIA
Los Angeles, California

Independent, coed. Urban campus. Total enrollment: 28,342. Art program established 1985.

Degrees Bachelor of Fine Arts in the area of studio arts. Majors and concentrations: art/fine arts, ceramic art and design, computer imaging, new genre, painting/drawing, photography, printmaking, sculpture, studio art. Graduate degrees offered: Master of Fine Arts in the area of studio arts.

Enrollment Fall 1997: 174 total; 96 undergraduate, 14 graduate, 64 non-professional degree.

Art Student Profile 65% females, 35% males, 17% minorities, 20% international.

Art Faculty 30 total undergraduate and graduate (full-time and part-time). 80% of full-time faculty have terminal degrees. Graduate students do not teach undergraduate courses. Undergraduate student–faculty ratio: 10:1.

Student Life Student groups/activities include Annual Student Art Exhibition, Animation Club.

Expenses for 1997–98 Application fee: $55. Comprehensive fee: $27,228 includes full-time tuition ($20,078), mandatory fees ($402), and college room and board ($6748). College room only: $3716. Room and board charges vary according to board plan and housing facility. Special program-related fees: $55 per course for lab/studio materials fee.

Financial Aid Program-specific awards for 1997: 30 Fine Art Scholarships for program majors ($2000).

Application Procedures Students admitted directly into the professional program freshman year. Deadline for freshmen: February 1; transfers: March 1. Notification date for freshmen: May 1; transfers: June 1. Required: essay, high school transcript, college transcript(s) for transfer students, 3 letters of recommendation, SAT I or ACT test scores, slides for transfer applicants, minimum 2.8 college GPA for transfer applicants, portfolio for transfer students. Recommended: minimum 3.0 high school GPA, interview, portfolio. Portfolio reviews held continuously on campus; the submission of slides may be substituted for portfolios.

Web Site http://www.usc.edu/dept/finearts.

Contact Ms. Penelope Jones, Director of Admissions, School of Fine Arts, University of Southern California, Watt Hall 103, Los Angeles, California 90089-0292; 213-740-9153, fax: 213-740-8938, E-mail address: finearts@mizar.usc.edu.

▼ UNIVERSITY OF SOUTHERN MAINE
Portland, Maine

State-supported, coed. Suburban campus. Total enrollment: 10,236. Art program established 1976.

Degrees Bachelor of Fine Arts in the areas of studio art, art education. Majors and concentrations: art education, ceramics, drawing, painting, photography, printmaking, sculpture. Cross-registration with Maine College of Art, University of New England, St. Joseph's College, Westbrook College, Southern Maine Technical College. Program accredited by NASAD.

Enrollment Fall 1997: 290 total; all undergraduate.

Art Student Profile 55% females, 45% males, 5% minorities, 1% international.

Art Faculty 24 total (full-time and part-time). 92% of full-time faculty have terminal degrees. Graduate students do not teach undergraduate courses.

Student Life Student groups/activities include Association of Visual Artists.

Expenses for 1997–98 Application fee: $25. One-time mandatory fee: $15. State resident tuition: $3450 full-time. Nonresident tuition: $9540 full-time. Mandatory fees: $488 full-time. Full-time tuition and fees vary according to course load and reciprocity agreements. College room and board: $4646. College room only: $2406. Special program-related fees: $20–$40 per semester for supplies for some studio courses.

Application Procedures Deadline for freshmen and transfers: continuous. Notification date for freshmen and transfers: July 15. Required: essay, high school transcript, letter of recommendation, portfolio. Recommended: minimum 2.0 high school GPA, interview. Portfolio reviews held twice on campus.

Web Site http://macweb.acs.usm.maine.edu/art/.

Undergraduate Contact Ms. Deborah Jordan, Director of Admissions, University of Southern Maine, 37 College Avenue, Gorham, Maine 04038; 207-780-5670, fax: 207-780-5640.

▼ University of Southern Mississippi

Hattiesburg, Mississippi

State-supported, coed. Suburban campus. Total enrollment: 14,599. Art program established 1947.

Degrees Bachelor of Fine Arts in the area of art. Majors and concentrations: art education, graphic communication, painting/drawing, three-dimensional studies. Graduate degrees offered: Master of Fine Arts in the areas of drawing, painting; Master of Art Education. Program accredited by NASAD.

Enrollment Fall 1997: 160 total; 150 undergraduate, 10 graduate.

Art Student Profile 30% females, 70% males, 27% minorities, 4% international.

Art Faculty 18 total undergraduate and graduate (full-time and part-time). 100% of full-time faculty have terminal degrees. Graduate students teach a few undergraduate courses.

Student Life Student groups/activities include Student Art Club, American Institute of Graphic Arts Student Chapter.

Expenses for 1997–98 State resident tuition: $2590 full-time. Nonresident tuition: $5410 full-time. College room and board: $2565. Room and board charges vary according to board plan and housing facility.

Financial Aid Program-specific awards for 1997: 7 Endowed Scholarships for program majors ($1250), 1 Mississippi Gulf Coast Scholarship for program majors ($600–$900), 1 Maude Sherrod Scholarship for program majors ($700).

Application Procedures Students admitted directly into the professional program freshman year. Deadline for freshmen and transfers: continuous. Notification date for freshmen and transfers: continuous. Required: high school transcript, ACT test score only, portfolio for scholarship consideration. Portfolio reviews held by appointment on campus; the submission of slides may be substituted for portfolios (slides preferred).

Web Site http://www.arts.usm.edu/.

Undergraduate Contact Admissions Office, University of Southern Mississippi, Box 5011, Hattiesburg, Mississippi 39406-5011; 601-266-5000, fax: 601-266-5186.

Graduate Contact Graduate Admissions, University of Southern Mississippi, Box 10066, Hattiesburg, Mississippi 39406; 601-266-5137, fax: 601-266-5138.

▼ University of Tennessee at Chattanooga

Chattanooga, Tennessee

State-supported, coed. Urban campus. Total enrollment: 8,528.

Degrees Bachelor of Fine Arts in the areas of graphic design, painting and drawing, sculpture; Bachelor of Science in the area of art education. Majors and concentrations: art education, graphic design, painting/drawing, sculpture. Program accredited by NASAD.

Enrollment Fall 1997: 742 total; 146 undergraduate, 596 non-professional degree.

Art Student Profile 53% females, 47% males, 8% minorities.

Art Faculty 18 total (full-time and part-time). 100% of full-time faculty have terminal degrees. Graduate students do not teach undergraduate courses. Undergraduate student–faculty ratio: 45:1.

Student Life Student groups/activities include Student Art Cooperative.

Expenses for 1997–98 Application fee: $25. State resident tuition: $2200 full-time. Nonresident tuition: $6796 full-time. College room only: $1900.

Financial Aid Program-specific awards for 1997: 1 Wayne Hannah Award for freshmen graphic design majors ($1800), 1 Doug Griffith Award for continuing student graphic design majors ($1800), 2 Lillian B. Fernstein Awards for program majors ($1800).

Application Procedures Students admitted directly into the professional program freshman year. Deadline for freshmen and transfers: continuous. Notification date for freshmen and transfers: continuous. Required: high school transcript, college transcript(s) for transfer students, minimum 2.0 high school GPA, SAT I or ACT test scores.

Undergraduate Contact Ms. Patsy Reynolds, Admissions Director, University of Tennessee at Chattanooga, 615 Mc Callie Avenue, Chattanooga, Tennessee 37403; 423-755-4662, fax: 423-755-4157, E-mail address: patsy-reynolds@utc.edu.

▼ The University of Tennessee at Martin

Martin, Tennessee

State-supported, coed. Small town campus. Total enrollment: 5,997. Art program established 1989.

Degrees Bachelor of Fine Arts in the area of fine and performing arts. Majors and concentrations: art education.

Enrollment Fall 1997: 44 undergraduate.

Art Student Profile 60% females, 40% males, 5% minorities, 5% international.

Art Faculty 3 total (full-time). 100% of full-time faculty have terminal degrees. Graduate students do not teach undergraduate courses. Undergraduate student–faculty ratio: 12:1.

Student Life Student groups/activities include Visual Arts Society.

Expenses for 1997–98 Application fee: $25. State resident tuition: $2240 full-time. Nonresident tuition: $6706 full-time.

The University of Tennessee at Martin (*continued*)

College room and board: $3104. College room only: $1600. Room and board charges vary according to board plan and housing facility.

Financial Aid Program-specific awards for 1997: 1 Endowment for the Arts Scholarship for art design majors ($750).

Application Procedures Students admitted directly into the professional program freshman year. Deadline for freshmen and transfers: continuous. Required: high school transcript, minimum 2.0 high school GPA, SAT I or ACT test scores, portfolio for visual arts applicants. Portfolio reviews held by appointment on campus; the submission of slides may be substituted for portfolios whenever needed.

Web Site http://www.utm.edu/departments/finearts/dfpa.htm.

Undergraduate Contact Dr. Earl Norwood, Director, Division of Fine and Performing Arts, The University of Tennessee at Martin, 102 Fine Arts Building, Martin, Tennessee 38238; 901-587-7400, fax: 901-587-7415, E-mail address: norwood@utm.edu.

▼ UNIVERSITY OF TENNESSEE, KNOXVILLE

Knoxville, Tennessee

State-supported, coed. Urban campus. Total enrollment: 25,397. Art program established 1947.

Degrees Bachelor of Fine Arts in the areas of studio art, graphic design. Majors and concentrations: ceramics, graphic arts, media arts, painting/drawing, photography, printmaking, sculpture, watercolors. Graduate degrees offered: Master of Fine Arts in the area of studio art. Cross-registration with Arrowmont School of Art and Crafts. Program accredited by NASAD.

Enrollment Fall 1997: 405 total; 380 undergraduate, 25 graduate.

Art Faculty 32 total undergraduate and graduate (full-time and part-time). 100% of full-time faculty have terminal degrees. Graduate students teach a few undergraduate courses. Undergraduate student–faculty ratio: 12:1.

Student Life Student groups/activities include University of Tennessee Potters, Student Art History Association, Art Department Student Advisory Committee.

Expenses for 1997–98 Application fee: $25. State resident tuition: $2096 full-time. Nonresident tuition: $6778 full-time. Mandatory fees: $480 full-time. College room and board: $3802. College room only: $1890. Room and board charges vary according to board plan and housing facility. Special program-related fees: $10–$100 per course for lab fees.

Financial Aid Program-specific awards for 1997: 1 Buck Ewing Undergraduate Scholarship for juniors and seniors ($2000), 1 Community College Transfer Award for transfer students ($1000), 1 Department of Art Materials Award for program students ($500), Department of Art Travel Awards for program students ($1000), Mary Louise Seilaz Awards for program students ($750), T. H. Jeanette Gillespie Awards for juniors and seniors ($300), 1 Mary Lynn Glustoff Memorial Scholarship for program students ($750), 1 Rod Norman Memorial Scholarship for program students ($500).

Application Procedures Students admitted directly into the professional program freshman year. Deadline for freshmen and transfers: June 1. Required: high school transcript, college transcript(s) for transfer students, minimum 2.0 high

school GPA, SAT I or ACT test scores. Recommended: minimum 3.0 high school GPA.

Web Site http://funnelweb.utcc.utk.edu/~art/.

Undergraduate Contact Dr. Norman Magden, Head, Department of Art, University of Tennessee, Knoxville, 1715 Volunteer Boulevard, Knoxville, Tennessee 37996-2410; 423-974-3407, fax: 423-974-3198, E-mail address: nmagden@utk.edu.

Graduate Contact Beauvais Lyons, Graduate Coordinator, Department of Art, University of Tennessee, Knoxville, 1715 Volunteer Boulevard, Knoxville, Tennessee 37996-2410; 423-974-3407, fax: 423-974-3198, E-mail address: blyons@utk.edu.

▼ THE UNIVERSITY OF TEXAS AT ARLINGTON

Arlington, Texas

State-supported, coed. Suburban campus. Total enrollment: 19,286.

Degrees Bachelor of Fine Arts in the areas of studio art, media art. Majors and concentrations: art history, art/fine arts, ceramic art and design, glass, graphic arts, jewelry and metalsmithing, painting/drawing, photography, printmaking, screenwriting, sculpture, studio art, video art.

Enrollment Fall 1997: 380 total; all undergraduate.

Art Student Profile 60% females, 40% males, 5% minorities, 2% international.

Art Faculty 29 total (full-time and part-time). 100% of full-time faculty have terminal degrees. Graduate students do not teach undergraduate courses. Undergraduate student–faculty ratio: 18:1.

Student Life Student groups/activities include Student Art Association, Student Film and Video Association.

Expenses for 1997–98 Application fee: $25. State resident tuition: $816 full-time. Nonresident tuition: $5952 full-time. Mandatory fees: $1272 full-time. Full-time tuition and fees vary according to course load. College room only: $1600. Room charges vary according to housing facility. Special program-related fees: $25–$75 per course for materials fee.

Financial Aid Program-specific awards for 1997: 5 departmental scholarships for talented majors ($350).

Application Procedures Students apply for admission into the professional program by sophomore year. Deadline for freshmen and transfers: June 1. Required: high school transcript, college transcript(s) for transfer students, minimum 2.0 high school GPA, SAT I or ACT test scores.

Undergraduate Contact Office of Admissions, The University of Texas at Arlington, Box19111, Arlington, Texas 76019-0111; 817-272-2118, fax: 817-272-3435.

▼ THE UNIVERSITY OF TEXAS AT AUSTIN

Austin, Texas

State-supported, coed. Urban campus. Total enrollment: 48,857.

Degrees Bachelor of Fine Arts in the areas of design, studio art. Majors and concentrations: ceramic art and design, design, intaglio, jewelry and metalsmithing, lithography, painting/drawing, performance art, photography, printmaking, sculpture, seriography, studio art, video art. Graduate degrees offered: Master of Fine Arts in the area of studio art.

Enrollment Fall 1997: 1,000 total; 383 undergraduate, 30 graduate, 587 non-professional degree.

Art Student Profile 54% females, 46% males, 21% minorities, 1% international.

Art Faculty 43 total undergraduate and graduate (full-time and part-time). 99% of full-time faculty have terminal degrees. Graduate students teach a few undergraduate courses. Undergraduate student–faculty ratio: 18:1.

Expenses for 1997–98 Application fee: $40. State resident tuition: $2040 full-time. Nonresident tuition: $8460 full-time. Mandatory fees: $826 full-time. Full-time tuition and fees vary according to course load and program. College room and board: $3901. College room only: $1950. Room and board charges vary according to board plan. Special program-related fees: $48–$191 per course for lab fees.

Application Procedures Deadline for freshmen and transfers: February 1. Required: essay, high school transcript, college transcript(s) for transfer students, SAT I or ACT test scores.

Web Site http://www.utexas.edu/cofa/a_ah/index.html.

Undergraduate Contact Ms. Rachel Hinshaw, Student Development Specialist II, Department of Art and Art History, The University of Texas at Austin, Art 3.342, Austin, Texas 78712-1285; 512-475-7718, fax: 512-471-7801, E-mail address: r.hinshaw@mail.utexas.edu.

Graduate Contact Ms. Judy Franchow, Graduate Coordinator, Department of Art and Art History, The University of Texas at Austin, Art 3.328, Austin, Texas 78712-1285; 512-471-3377, fax: 512-471-7801, E-mail address: jfranchow@mail.utexas.edu.

▼ THE UNIVERSITY OF TEXAS AT EL PASO

El Paso, Texas

State-supported, coed. Urban campus. Total enrollment: 15,176. Art program established 1947.

Degrees Bachelor of Fine Arts in the areas of painting, sculpture, ceramics, drawing, metals, graphic design, printmaking. Graduate degrees offered: Master of Arts in the areas of painting, sculpture, ceramics, drawing, metals, graphic design, printmaking.

Enrollment Fall 1997: 260 total.

Art Student Profile 55% females, 45% males, 80% minorities, 2% international.

Art Faculty 22 total undergraduate and graduate (full-time and part-time). 92% of full-time faculty have terminal degrees. Graduate students teach a few undergraduate courses. Undergraduate student–faculty ratio: 16:1.

Expenses for 1997–98 Application fee: $0. State resident tuition: $1020 full-time. Nonresident tuition: $7440 full-time. Mandatory fees: $1246 full-time. Full-time tuition and fees vary according to course load and reciprocity agreements. Special program-related fees: $4–$45 per course for lab fees.

Financial Aid Program-specific awards for 1997: 10 Endowed Awards for program majors ($500–$2500).

Application Procedures Students admitted directly into the professional program freshman year. Deadline for freshmen and transfers: May 1. Required: high school transcript, college transcript(s) for transfer students, minimum 2.0 high school GPA, SAT I or ACT test scores.

Web Site http://www.utep.edu/arts/.

Contact Mr. Jim Quinnan, Advisor, Department of Art, The University of Texas at El Paso, 500 West University Avenue, El Paso, Texas 79968; 915-747-7839, fax: 915-747-6749, E-mail address: jquinnan@mail.utep.edu.

▼ THE UNIVERSITY OF TEXAS AT SAN ANTONIO

San Antonio, Texas

State-supported, coed. Suburban campus. Total enrollment: 17,494. Art program established 1974.

Degrees Bachelor of Fine Arts in the area of art. Majors and concentrations: ceramics, digital imaging, drawing, painting, photography, printmaking, sculpture. Graduate degrees offered: Master of Fine Arts in the area of art. Program accredited by NASAD.

Enrollment Fall 1997: 200 undergraduate, 32 graduate.

Art Student Profile 60% females, 40% males, 39% minorities, 2% international.

Art Faculty 18 total undergraduate and graduate (full-time and part-time). 100% of full-time faculty have terminal degrees. Graduate students teach a few undergraduate courses. Undergraduate student–faculty ratio: 18:1.

Student Life Student groups/activities include Art Guild, Printmaking Club, Art History Association.

Expenses for 1998–99 Application fee: $20. State resident tuition: $2010 full-time. Nonresident tuition: $8400 full-time. Mandatory fees: $734 full-time. Full-time tuition and fees vary according to course load. College room only: $3000. Room charges vary according to housing facility. Special program-related fees: $25 per semester for lab fees.

Application Procedures Students admitted directly into the professional program freshman year. Deadline for freshmen and transfers: July 1. Required: high school transcript, college transcript(s) for transfer students, minimum 2.0 high school GPA, SAT I or ACT test scores (minimum combined SAT I score of 970, minimum combined ACT score of 22), Texas Academic Skills Program test, portfolio for transfer students with junior standing and above. Portfolio reviews held as needed on campus; the submission of slides may be substituted for portfolios when original work is not available or for large works of art.

Web Site http://altamira.arts.utsa.edu/.

Undergraduate Contact Mr. James Broderick, Director, Division of Visual Arts, The University of Texas at San Antonio, 6900 North Loop 1604 West, San Antonio, Texas 78249-1130; 210-458-4352, fax: 210-458-4356, E-mail address: artinfo@lonestar.utsa.edu.

Graduate Contact Mr. Ken Little, Graduate Advisor of Record, Division of Visual Arts, The University of Texas at San Antonio, 6900 North Loop 1604 West, San Antonio, Texas 78249-1130; 210-458-4352, fax: 201-458-4356, E-mail address: klittle@lonestar.utsa.edu.

▼ THE UNIVERSITY OF TEXAS AT TYLER

Tyler, Texas

State-supported, coed. Urban campus. Total enrollment: 3,393. Art program established 1970.

Degrees Bachelor of Fine Arts in the area of art. Majors and concentrations: art history, ceramics, drawing, painting, photography, printmaking, sculpture.

Enrollment Fall 1997: 50 total; all undergraduate.

Art Student Profile 60% females, 40% males, 2% minorities, 2% international.

The University of Texas at Tyler *(continued)*

Art Faculty 9 total (full-time and part-time). 95% of full-time faculty have terminal degrees. Graduate students do not teach undergraduate courses. Undergraduate student–faculty ratio: 9:1.

Student Life Student groups/activities include Art Club.

Expenses for 1997–98 State resident tuition: $816 full-time. Nonresident tuition: $5952 full-time. Mandatory fees: $1268 full-time. Full-time tuition and fees vary according to course load. College room and board: $6029. Room and board charges vary according to board plan and housing facility. Special program-related fees: $5–$40 per course for course fees.

Financial Aid Program-specific awards for 1997: 25 departmental awards for program majors ($200–$2000).

Application Procedures Students apply for admission into the professional program by junior year. Deadline for freshmen and transfers: continuous. Required: college transcript(s) for transfer students, portfolio, SAT I or ACT test scores, Texas Academic Skills Program test if SAT I or ACT scores do not qualify, 30 hours of college credit with a minimum 2.0 college GPA for transfer students. Recommended: 2 letters of recommendation. Portfolio reviews held twice on campus; the submission of slides may be substituted for portfolios when distance is prohibitive.

Undergraduate Contact Mr. James Pace, Chairman, Department of Art, The University of Texas at Tyler, Tyler, Texas 75799; 903-566-7384, fax: 903-566-7287, E-mail address: jpace@mail.uttyl.edu.

▼ THE UNIVERSITY OF TEXAS–PAN AMERICAN
Edinburg, Texas

State-supported, coed. Rural campus. Art program established 1970.

Degrees Bachelor of Fine Arts in the areas of studio art, advertising design, secondary art education. Majors and concentrations: advertising design, art education, ceramic art and design, jewelry and metalsmithing, lithography, painting/drawing, printmaking, sculpture. Graduate degrees offered: Master of Fine Arts in the area of studio art. Cross-registration with University of Texas System.

Enrollment Fall 1997: 188 total; 181 undergraduate, 7 non-professional degree.

Art Student Profile 50% females, 50% males, 80% minorities, 10% international.

Art Faculty 13 total undergraduate and graduate (full-time and part-time). 90% of full-time faculty have terminal degrees. Graduate students do not teach undergraduate courses.

Student Life Student groups/activities include Visual Arts Society.

Expenses for 1997–98 Application fee: $0. State resident tuition: $1612 full-time. Nonresident tuition: $8246 full-time. Mandatory fees: $361 full-time. College room and board: $2250. Special program-related fees: $4 per course for equipment maintenance and supplies.

Financial Aid Program-specific awards for 1997: 4 Lamont-Wilcox Art Scholarships for freshmen and sophomores ($800).

Application Procedures Students admitted directly into the professional program freshman year. Deadline for freshmen: July 1; transfers: continuous. Required: high school transcript, college transcript(s) for transfer students, minimum 2.0 high school GPA, SAT I or ACT test scores (minimum combined SAT I score of 930, minimum combined ACT score of 20). Recommended: portfolio. Portfolio reviews held once on campus; the submission of slides may be substituted for portfolios for large works of art.

Web Site http://www.panam.edu/dept/art.

Undergraduate Contact Dr. Nancy Moyer, Chair, Art Department, The University of Texas–Pan American, 1201 West University Drive, Edinburg, Texas 78539; 956-381-3480, fax: 956-384-5072, E-mail address: nmoyer@panam.edu.

Graduate Contact Mr. Philip Field, Graduate Coordinator, Art Department, The University of Texas–Pan American, 1201 West University Drive, Edinburg, Texas 78539; 956-381-3482, fax: 956-384-5072.

▼ UNIVERSITY OF THE ARTS
Philadelphia, Pennsylvania

Independent, coed. Urban campus. Total enrollment: 1,624. Art program established 1876.

Degrees Bachelor of Fine Arts in the areas of graphic design, painting, printmaking, sculpture, illustration, photography, animation, film, ceramics, jewelry/metals, fibers, wood multimedia; Bachelor of Science in the area of industrial design. Majors and concentrations: animation, applied art, art education, art/fine arts, ceramic art and design, film studies, graphic arts, illustration, industrial design, jewelry and metalsmithing, multimedia, painting/drawing, photography, printmaking, sculpture, studio art, textile arts, wood. Graduate degrees offered: Master of Fine Arts in the areas of museum exhibition planning and design, book arts/printmaking, painting, sculpture, ceramics; Master of Industrial Design; Master of Arts in the areas of art education, museum education; Master of Arts in Teaching in the area of art education. Program accredited by NASAD.

Enrollment Fall 1997: 728 undergraduate, 100 graduate.

Art Student Profile 45% females, 55% males, 18% minorities, 10% international.

Art Faculty 135 total undergraduate and graduate (full-time and part-time). 60% of full-time faculty have terminal degrees. Graduate students teach a few undergraduate courses. Undergraduate student–faculty ratio: 9:1.

Student Life Special housing available for art students.

Expenses for 1997–98 Application fee: $40. Tuition: $14,570 full-time. Mandatory fees: $500 full-time. College room only: $4100.

Financial Aid Program-specific awards for 1997: 50 Merit Scholarships for program students ($500–$5000).

Application Procedures Students admitted directly into the professional program freshman year. Deadline for freshmen and transfers: continuous. Required: essay, high school transcript, college transcript(s) for transfer students, minimum 2.0 high school GPA, letter of recommendation, portfolio, SAT I or ACT test scores. Recommended: minimum 3.0 high school GPA, interview, resume. Portfolio reviews held continuously by appointment on campus and off campus; the submission of slides may be substituted for portfolios when distance is prohibitive.

Web Site http://www.uarts.edu.

Contact Ms. Barbara Elliott, Director of Admissions, University of the Arts, 320 South Broad Street, Philadelphia, Pennsylvania 19102; 800-616-ARTS, fax: 215-875-5458.

More About the University

Program Facilities Music: new recording studio, three MIDI studios, editing suites, chamber music studios, Challis harpsichords, Moog synthesizer, computer music calligraphy facility, grand piano studios, music library; Theatre/Dance: several theaters, including the 1,668-seat Merriam: light-filled studios with barres, mirrors, resilient 4-inch suspended floors; Art: public galleries maintained by UArts include the Rosenwald-Wolf, Dorrance Hamilton Hall, the Great Hall galleries, and the Mednick.

Faculty, Resident Artists, and Alumni Faculty members (334) are professionals, most with advanced degrees, who perform and exhibit regularly. Visiting artists have included dance: Edward Villela, Donna McKechnie, Oleg Briansky, Gabriella Darvash, James Truitt, Meredith Monk, Ronnie Favors; music: Andre Watts, Jack Elliott, Wynton Marsalis, Pierre Boulez, Billy Joel, George Crumb, Eddie Gomez, Placido Domingo, Klaus Tennstedt, Ricardo Muti, Thad Joones, Mel Lewis, Peter Erskine, Stanley Clarke; theater: Elizabeth Ashley, Laurie Anderson, Tommy Hicks, David Henry Hwang. Alumni include Philadelphia orchestra violinist Michael Ludwig, Alvin Ailey Dance member Antonio Carlos Scott, artist Sidney Goodman, Tony-Award-nominated dancer/actress Rhonda LaChanze Sapp, illustrator Arnold Roth, jazz artist/composer Stanley Clarke, director Joe Dante, illustrator Charles Santore, dancer/choreographer Judith Jamison, actress Irene Bedard, concert pianist Lydia Artymiw, childrens' book authors/illustrators Jan and Stan Berenstain, and the Quay Brothers.

Student Performance/Exhibit Opportunities Ensemble productions, student composition concerts featuring original choreography, repertory concerts, an annual freshmen inter-arts project, exhibitions in University galleries, recitals, appearances with visiting artists.

Special Programs Student exchange with other schools and colleges, foreign and summer studies, career planning and placement, personal counseling, academic support, professional and peer tutoring, services for the disabled, international student services.

▼

The University of the Arts sits in the heart of Philadelphia's professional arts community and is surrounded by everything a major city should offer: theaters, museums, galleries, night life, and restaurants. The city, long a supporter of the arts, is urban and sophisticated, yet also features a diversity of small neighborhoods and ethnic enclaves.

UArts is among a few universities in the nation devoted exclusively to education and training in design and in the visual and performing arts. Composed of the Philadelphia College of Art and Design, the Philadelphia College of Performing Arts, and the College of Media and Communication, UArts offers intensive concentration within its major and other creative possibilities for exploration and growth. Nearly 1,400 undergraduate and graduate students from thirty-seven states and thirty countries are enrolled, coming to Philadelphia for an educational atmosphere dedicated to the aesthetic experience.

College of Art and Design faculty members are practicing professionals and are deeply committed to the development of their students. As active participants in the arts, they have achieved recognition in their specific fields of study. Members of the art and design faculty regularly exhibit their work in galleries and museums across the country. It is this real-world experience, in a most demanding environment, that gives them the knowledge and understanding so vital in the training of young, emerging artists–not just professionally but also in terms of personal growth. The faculty has 178 full- and part-time members. The majority hold advanced degrees. The faculty-student ratio is approximately 1:9.

Members of the music faculty of the College of Performing Arts have international reputations as concert soloists and jazz artists. Members of the dance faculty have distinguished careers in ballet and modern, jazz, and tap dance. Members of the theater faculty have acting and directing experience that ranges from Broadway shows to European companies. There are 156 full- and part-time members. Again, the faculty-student ratio is about 1:9.

The newly formed College of Media and Communication explores new ideas and new concepts in a changing world. Video games, the Internet, CD-ROM, interactive television, and virtual reality are just a few examples of the emerging forms that are changing communication. Offering majors in Writing for Media and Performance and Multimedia, the College stresses the interdisciplinary nature of these new forms. A new major in Mass Media Communications will be introduced in Fall 1999.

UArts is a different kind of university, defined by students with a passion for what they want to do and where they want to go. The University is looking for student talent and potential; it provides formal exposure to the great ideas that shape the arts, focused practice and coaching in a student's chosen discipline, and an environment that frees imagination, stimulates creativity, and encourages change. The University of the Arts is a member of the New Media Centers, a group of the nation's leading academic institutions and technology corporations dedicated to the advancement of technology in education.

Student housing, with coed apartment-style accommodations, complete kitchen and bath facilities, and laundry rooms on the premises, is available. Resident advisers are on each floor.

Please see the University of the Art's other programs listed under Dance, Music, and Theater.

▼ University of the Pacific

Stockton, California

Independent, coed. Suburban campus. Total enrollment: 5,585.

Degrees Bachelor of Fine Arts in the areas of studio art, graphic design. Program accredited by NASAD.

Enrollment Fall 1997: 80 undergraduate.

Art Student Profile 65% females, 35% males, 45% minorities, 5% international.

Art Faculty 10 total (full-time and part-time). 90% of full-time faculty have terminal degrees. Graduate students do not teach undergraduate courses. Undergraduate student-faculty ratio: 9:1.

Expenses for 1998–99 Application fee: $50. One-time mandatory fee: $100. Comprehensive fee: $25,135 includes full-time tuition ($19,000), mandatory fees ($365), and college room and board ($5770). Full-time tuition and fees vary according

University of the Pacific (*continued*)

to program. Room and board charges vary according to board plan and housing facility. Special program-related fees: $10–$30 for studio materials.

Financial Aid Program-specific awards for 1997: 10 Endowed Scholarships for art majors ($1000).

Application Procedures Students admitted directly into the professional program freshman year. Deadline for freshmen: March 1. Notification date for freshmen: April 15. Required: essay, high school transcript, minimum 2.0 high school GPA, letter of recommendation, SAT I or ACT test scores. Recommended: minimum 3.0 high school GPA.

Web Site http://www.uop.edu/cop/art/index.html.

Undergraduate Contact Office of Admissions, University of the Pacific, 3601 Pacific Avenue, Stockton, California 95211-0197; 800-959-2867.

▼ UNIVERSITY OF UTAH

Salt Lake City, Utah

State-supported, coed. Urban campus. Total enrollment: 25,883.

Degrees Bachelor of Fine Arts in the area of art. Majors and concentrations: art education, ceramic art and design, graphic design, illustration, painting/drawing, photography, printmaking, sculpture. Graduate degrees offered: Master of Fine Arts in the area of art.

Enrollment Fall 1997: 799 total; 442 undergraduate, 7 graduate, 350 non-professional degree.

Art Student Profile 53% females, 47% males, 5% minorities, 2% international.

Art Faculty 39 total undergraduate and graduate (full-time and part-time). 90% of full-time faculty have terminal degrees. Graduate students teach a few undergraduate courses. Undergraduate student–faculty ratio: 20:1.

Student Life Student groups/activities include student exhibitions, intercollegiate exhibitions, interdepartmental collaborative classes.

Expenses for 1997–98 Application fee: $30. State resident tuition: $2601 full-time. Nonresident tuition: $7,998 full-time. Full-time tuition varies according to course load. College room and board: $4620. College room only: $1708. Room and board charges vary according to board plan. Special program-related fees: $20 per course for models, $30–$45 per course for materials, tools and equipment maintenance.

Financial Aid Program-specific awards for 1997: 4 Special Departmental Scholarships for incoming freshmen ($7515), 5 Continuing Student Scholarships for continuing students ($9393), 2 Ann Cannon Scholarships for continuing students ($1000), 1 Ethel A. Rolapp Award for graduating students ($2000), 1 Speess Memorial Award for continuing students ($1000).

Application Procedures Students apply for admission into the professional program by freshman year. Deadline for freshmen and transfers: continuous. Notification date for freshmen and transfers: continuous. Required: high school transcript, college transcript(s) for transfer students, portfolio, SAT I or ACT test scores (minimum combined ACT score of 20). Recommended: minimum 2.0 high school GPA. Portfolio reviews held as needed on campus; the submission of slides may be substituted for portfolios for large works of art and three-dimensional pieces.

Undergraduate Contact Mrs. Nevon Bruschke, Undergraduate Counselor, Art Department, University of Utah, 161 AAC, Salt Lake City, Utah 84112; 801-581-8677, fax: 801-585-6171, E-mail address: nevon.bruschke@m.cc.utah.edu.

Graduate Contact Mrs. Nevon Bruschke, Undergraduate Counselor, Art Department, University of Utah, 161 ACC, Salt Lake City, Utah 84112; 801-581-8677, fax: 801-585-6171, E-mail address: nevon.bruschke@m.cc.utah.edu.

▼ UNIVERSITY OF WASHINGTON

Seattle, Washington

State-supported, coed. Urban campus. Total enrollment: 35,367.

Degrees Bachelor of Fine Arts in the area of art. Majors and concentrations: ceramics, fibers, graphic design, industrial design, interdisciplinary studies, metals, painting, photography, printmaking, sculpture. Graduate degrees offered: Master of Fine Arts in the area of art.

Enrollment Fall 1997: 950 undergraduate, 50 graduate.

Art Student Profile 65% females, 35% males, 10% minorities, 10% international.

Art Faculty 41 total undergraduate and graduate (full-time). 95% of full-time faculty have terminal degrees. Graduate students teach a few undergraduate courses. Undergraduate student–faculty ratio: 22:1.

Expenses for 1997–98 Application fee: $35. State resident tuition: $3366 full-time. Nonresident tuition: $10,656 full-time. College room and board: $4671. College room only: $2556. Part-time tuition per term ranges from $226 to $1010 for state residents, $712 to $3197 for nonresidents. Special program-related fees: $35–$95 per course for materials fee.

Financial Aid Program-specific awards for 1997: 51 School of Art Scholarships for program majors ($800).

Application Procedures Students admitted directly into the professional program freshman year. Deadline for freshmen: February 1; transfers: April 1. Notification date for freshmen: March 15. Required: high school transcript, SAT I or ACT test scores, portfolio for transfer applicants. Portfolio reviews held continuously on campus; the submission of slides may be substituted for portfolios whenever needed.

Undergraduate Contact Admissions Office, University of Washington, Box 355840, Seattle, Washington 98195-5840; 206-543-9686.

Graduate Contact Pat Dougherty, Program Coordinator, University of Washington, Box 353440, Seattle, Washington 98195-3440; 206-685-1714, fax: 206-685-1657, E-mail address: patd@u.washington.edu.

▼ UNIVERSITY OF WEST FLORIDA

Pensacola, Florida

State-supported, coed. Suburban campus. Total enrollment: 8,038. Art program established 1980.

Degrees Bachelor of Fine Arts in the area of studio arts. Majors and concentrations: art/fine arts, studio art.

Enrollment Fall 1997: 160 total; 31 undergraduate, 129 non-professional degree.

Art Student Profile 75% females, 25% males, 4% minorities, 3% international.

Art Faculty 17 total (full-time and part-time). 100% of full-time faculty have terminal degrees. Graduate students teach a few undergraduate courses.

Expenses for 1997–98 Application fee: $20. State resident tuition: $1985 full-time. Nonresident tuition: $7902 full-time. College room only: $2144. Room charges vary according to housing facility.

Financial Aid Program-specific awards for 1997: 8 Talent Scholarships for incoming students ($1000).

Application Procedures Students apply for admission into the professional program by junior year. Deadline for freshmen and transfers: July 1. Required: high school transcript, college transcript(s) for transfer students, minimum 2.0 high school GPA, SAT I or ACT test scores.

Web Site http://www.uwf.edu/~art.

Undergraduate Contact Mr. Jim Jipson, Chair, Department of Art, University of West Florida, 11000 University Parkway, Pensacola, Florida 32514; 904-474-2045, E-mail address: jjipson@uwf.cc.uwf.edu.

▼ University of Wisconsin–Eau Claire

Eau Claire, Wisconsin

State-supported, coed. Urban campus. Total enrollment: 10,484.

Degrees Bachelor of Fine Arts in the areas of graphic design, illustration, painting, drawing and printmaking, photography, sculpture, ceramics. Cross-registration with members of the National Student Exchange Program.

Enrollment Fall 1997: 274 total; 121 undergraduate, 153 non-professional degree.

Art Faculty 16 total (full-time and part-time). 95% of full-time faculty have terminal degrees. Graduate students do not teach undergraduate courses. Undergraduate student–faculty ratio: 18:1.

Student Life Student groups/activities include Art Student Association, None of the Above (arts magazine).

Expenses for 1997–98 Application fee: $28. State resident tuition: $2870 full-time. Nonresident tuition: $8812 full-time. Mandatory fees: $2 full-time. Full-time tuition and fees vary according to reciprocity agreements. College room and board: $2986. College room only: $1720. Special program-related fees: $20 per semester for studio materials, lab fees.

Financial Aid Program-specific awards for 1997: 1 Patrick Danen Memorial Scholarship for upper-division photography majors ($350), 1 Edward Fish Art Scholarship for academically qualified juniors or seniors ($450), 1 Ruth Foster Scholarship for academically qualified upperclassmen ($125), 3 Gerald Newton Scholarships for academically qualified seniors ($50), 1 Sigrid Rasmussen Memorial Art Scholarship for academically qualified program majors ($100), 1 Charles Campbell Scholarship for academically qualified program majors ($300), 3 Gretchen Grimm Memorial Scholarships for academically qualified art education majors ($450).

Application Procedures Deadline for freshmen: February 1; transfers: April 1. Required: high school transcript, college transcript(s) for transfer students, minimum 3.0 high school GPA, portfolio, ACT score for state residents, SAT or ACT score for out-of-state residents. Portfolio reviews held twice on campus; the submission of slides may be substituted for portfolios for large works of art, three-dimensional pieces, or when distance is prohibitive.

Undergraduate Contact Admissions Office, University of Wisconsin–Eau Claire, PO Box 4004, Eau Claire, Wisconsin 54702-4004; 715-836-5415, fax: 715-836-2380.

▼ University of Wisconsin–Madison

Madison, Wisconsin

State-supported, coed. Urban campus. Total enrollment: 40,196.

Degrees Bachelor of Fine Arts in the area of art; Bachelor of Science in the area of art. Majors and concentrations: art/fine arts, graphic design. Graduate degrees offered: Master of Fine Arts in the area of art. Program accredited by NASAD.

Enrollment Fall 1997: 566 total; 439 undergraduate, 127 graduate.

Art Student Profile 60% females, 40% males, 10% minorities, 1% international.

Art Faculty 42 total undergraduate and graduate (full-time and part-time). 100% of full-time faculty have terminal degrees. Graduate students teach about a quarter undergraduate courses. Undergraduate student–faculty ratio: 23:1.

Student Life Student groups/activities include Friends of Art Metal, Friends of Typography, Clay Club.

Estimated expenses for 1998–99 Application fee: $35. State resident tuition: $3242 full-time. Nonresident tuition: $10,552 full-time. Full-time tuition varies according to reciprocity agreements. College room and board: $4880. Special program-related fees: $10–$300 per course for consumable supplies.

Financial Aid Program-specific awards for 1997: 2 Edith Gilbertson Scholarships for continuing program students ($1000), 2 Ethel Odegaard Scholarships for continuing program students ($1250), 1 Carrie Jones Cady Scholarship for continuing program students ($350).

Application Procedures Students admitted directly into the professional program freshman year. Deadline for freshmen and transfers: February 1. Required: high school transcript, college transcript(s) for transfer students, minimum 3.0 high school GPA, SAT I test score only.

Undergraduate Contact Mr. Keith White, Assistant Director, Undergraduate Admissions, University of Wisconsin–Madison, 750 University Avenue, Madison, Wisconsin 53706; 608-262-3961, E-mail address: keith.white@mail.admin.wisc.edu.

Graduate Contact Ms. Carla Leskinen, Graduate Advisor, Art Department, University of Wisconsin–Madison, 455 North Park Street, 6241 Humanities Building, Madison, Wisconsin 53706; 608-262-1660.

▼ University of Wisconsin–Milwaukee

Milwaukee, Wisconsin

State-supported, coed. Urban campus. Total enrollment: 21,525. Art program established 1961.

Degrees Bachelor of Fine Arts in the area of art. Majors and concentrations: art education, ceramic art and design, fibers, graphic design, jewelry and metalsmithing, painting/drawing, photography, printmaking, sculpture. Graduate degrees offered: Master of Fine Arts in the area of art.

Enrollment Fall 1997: 732 total; 640 undergraduate, 85 graduate, 7 non-professional degree.

University of Wisconsin–Milwaukee *(continued)*

Art Student Profile 50% females, 50% males, 2% minorities, 3% international.

Art Faculty 63 total undergraduate and graduate (full-time and part-time). 99% of full-time faculty have terminal degrees. Graduate students teach a few undergraduate courses. Undergraduate student–faculty ratio: 15:1.

Expenses for 1997–98 Application fee: $28. State resident tuition: $3327 full-time. Nonresident tuition: $10,790 full-time. Full-time tuition varies according to reciprocity agreements. College room only: $2457.

Financial Aid Program-specific awards for 1997: 3–4 Layton Scholarships for incoming program majors, 1–2 Harold A. Levin Memorial Scholarships for incoming program majors.

Application Procedures Students admitted directly into the professional program freshman year. Deadline for freshmen and transfers: continuous. Required: high school transcript, college transcript(s) for transfer students, SAT I or ACT test scores (minimum combined ACT score of 21), ACT score for state residents.

Web Site http://www.uwm.edu/Dept/SFA/.

Undergraduate Contact Ms. Patricia Busalacchi, Administrative Assistant, Art Department, University of Wisconsin–Milwaukee, PO Box 413, 2400 East Kenwood Boulevard, Milwaukee, Wisconsin 53201; 414-229-6054, fax: 414-229-6154, E-mail address: pats@csd.uwm.edu.

Graduate Contact Ms. Vicki Grafentin, Head, Graduate Studies, Art Department, University of Wisconsin–Milwaukee, PO Box 413, 2400 East Kenwood Boulevard, Milwaukee, Wisconsin 53201; 414-229-6053, fax: 414-229-6154.

▼ UNIVERSITY OF WISCONSIN–OSHKOSH

Oshkosh, Wisconsin

State-supported, coed. Suburban campus. Total enrollment: 10,960.

Degrees Bachelor of Fine Arts in the areas of art education, studio/fine arts. Majors and concentrations: applied design, art education, ceramic art and design, drawing, fibers, graphic communication, jewelry and metalsmithing, painting, photography, printmaking, sculpture.

Enrollment Fall 1997: 300 total; all undergraduate.

Art Faculty 19 total (full-time and part-time). 100% of full-time faculty have terminal degrees. Graduate students do not teach undergraduate courses. Undergraduate student–faculty ratio: 12:1.

Expenses for 1997–98 Application fee: $35. State resident tuition: $2607 full-time. Nonresident tuition: $8549 full-time. Mandatory fees: $2 full-time. Full-time tuition and fees vary according to reciprocity agreements. College room and board: $2658. College room only: $1628. Room and board charges vary according to board plan and housing facility. Special program-related fees: $15–$20 per course per semester for lab fees.

Financial Aid Program-specific awards for 1997: 1 Charles Charonis Scholarship for junior or senior art education majors, 1 Milton Gardener Sculpture Scholarship for junior or senior sculpture students, 1 Bill Neiderberger Scholarship for junior or senior art students, 1–4 Willcoxon Scholarships for incoming freshmen.

Application Procedures Students admitted directly into the professional program freshman year. Deadline for freshmen and transfers: continuous. Notification date for freshmen and transfers: continuous. Required: high school transcript, college transcript(s) for transfer students, standing in top half of graduating class or minimum ACT score of 22, ACT score for state residents, SAT I or ACT score for out-of-state residents.

Web Site http://www.uwosh.edu.

Undergraduate Contact Dr. Arthur Pontynen, Chair, Department of Art, University of Wisconsin–Oshkosh, 900 Algoma Boulevard, Oshkosh, Wisconsin 54901, 414; 920-424-0492, E-mail address: pontynen@vaxa.cis.uwosh.edu.

▼ UNIVERSITY OF WISCONSIN–STEVENS POINT

Stevens Point, Wisconsin

State-supported, coed. Small town campus. Total enrollment: 8,446.

Degrees Bachelor of Fine Arts in the area of art. Majors and concentrations: ceramics, graphic design, painting, photography, printmaking, sculpture. Program accredited by NASAD.

Enrollment Fall 1997: 310 total; 260 undergraduate, 50 non-professional degree.

Art Student Profile 60% females, 40% males, 6% minorities, 5% international.

Art Faculty 15 total (full-time and part-time). 100% of full-time faculty have terminal degrees. Graduate students do not teach undergraduate courses. Undergraduate student–faculty ratio: 18:1.

Student Life Student groups/activities include Student Art League and Designers, National Student Graphic Design Organization.

Expenses for 1997–98 Application fee: $35. State resident tuition: $2790 full-time. Nonresident tuition: $8732 full-time. Full-time tuition varies according to course load and reciprocity agreements. College room and board: $3188. College room only: $1861. Room and board charges vary according to board plan. Special program-related fees: $15–$40 per course for studio fees.

Financial Aid Program-specific awards available.

Application Procedures Students admitted directly into the professional program freshman year. Deadline for freshmen and transfers: continuous. Required: high school transcript, ACT test score only. Recommended: interview, portfolio. Portfolio reviews held 3 times on campus; the submission of slides may be substituted for portfolios if original work is not available.

Web Site http://www.uwsp.edu/acad/art.

Undergraduate Contact Mr. Gary Hagen, Chair, Department of Art and Design, University of Wisconsin–Stevens Point, College of Fine Arts and Communication, Stevens Point, Wisconsin 54481; 715-346-2669, fax: 715-346-2718.

▼ UNIVERSITY OF WISCONSIN–STOUT

Menomonie, Wisconsin

State-supported, coed. Small town campus. Total enrollment: 7,418.

Degrees Bachelor of Fine Arts in the area of art; Bachelor of Science in the area of art education. Majors and concentrations: graphic design, industrial design, interior design, multimedia, studio art. Program accredited by NASAD.

Enrollment Fall 1997: 824 total; all undergraduate.

Art Student Profile 57% females, 43% males, 4% minorities, 1% international.
Art Faculty 36 total (full-time and part-time). Graduate students do not teach undergraduate courses. Undergraduate student–faculty ratio: 14:1.
Student Life Student groups/activities include Industrial Design Society of America Student Chapter, American Society of Interior Designers Student Chapter, Graphic Design Association Student Chapter.
Expenses for 1997–98 Application fee: $35. State resident tuition: $2806 full-time. Nonresident tuition: $8748 full-time. Full-time tuition varies according to reciprocity agreements. College room and board: $3062. College room only: $1618. Room and board charges vary according to board plan.
Financial Aid Program-specific awards for 1997: 2 John and Frances Furlong Art Scholarships for art/art education majors ($250), 2 Bud and Betty Micheels Student Artist-in-Residence Grants for program students ($1300).
Application Procedures Students admitted directly into the professional program freshman year. Deadline for freshmen and transfers: continuous. Notification date for freshmen and transfers: continuous. Required: high school transcript, college transcript(s) for transfer students, ACT test score only. Recommended: letter of recommendation.
Undergraduate Contact Dr. Cynthia Jenkins, Director of Admissions, University of Wisconsin–Stout, 124 Bowman Hall, Menomonie, Wisconsin 54751; 715-232-1232, fax: 715-232-1667, E-mail address: jenkinsc@uwstout.edu.

▼ UNIVERSITY OF WISCONSIN–SUPERIOR

Superior, Wisconsin

State-supported, coed. Small town campus. Total enrollment: 2,574. Art program established 1922.
Degrees Bachelor of Fine Arts in the area of art; Bachelor of Science in the areas of art therapy, art education. Majors and concentrations: art education, art history, art therapy, ceramics, fibers, painting, photography, printmaking, sculpture. Graduate degrees offered: Master of Arts in the areas of art therapy, art education. Cross-registration with University of Minnesota-Duluth.
Enrollment Fall 1997: 100 undergraduate, 24 graduate.
Art Student Profile 65% females, 35% males, 3% minorities, 3% international.
Art Faculty 9 total undergraduate and graduate (full-time and part-time). 100% of full-time faculty have terminal degrees. Graduate students do not teach undergraduate courses. Undergraduate student–faculty ratio: 15:1.
Student Life Student groups/activities include Art Student Club, Ceramic Invitational Golf Tournament.
Expenses for 1997–98 Application fee: $35. State resident tuition: $2652 full-time. Nonresident tuition: $8600 full-time. Full-time tuition varies according to course load and reciprocity agreements. College room and board: $3200. College room only: $1600. Special program-related fees: $50 per semester for lab fees.
Financial Aid Program-specific awards for 1997: 10 departmental awards for program majors ($400).
Application Procedures Students apply for admission into the professional program by sophomore year. Deadline for freshmen and transfers: continuous. Required: high school transcript, college transcript(s) for transfer students, minimum 3.0 high school GPA, portfolio, SAT I or ACT test scores, standing in top 50% of graduating class. Recom-

mended: interview. Portfolio reviews held once and as needed on campus; the submission of slides may be substituted for portfolios for transfer applicants from non-accredited schools.
Undergraduate Contact Mr. James Grittner, Chair, Visual Arts Department, University of Wisconsin–Superior, Superior, Wisconsin 54880; 715-394-8391, E-mail address: jgrittne@staff.uwsuper.edu.
Graduate Contact Nancy Minahan, Dean of Graduate School, University of Wisconsin–Superior, Superior, Wisconsin 54880; 715-394-6504, E-mail address: nminahan@staff.uwsuper.edu.

▼ UNIVERSITY OF WISCONSIN–WHITEWATER

Whitewater, Wisconsin

State-supported, coed. Small town campus. Total enrollment: 10,563.
Degrees Bachelor of Fine Arts in the area of art. Majors and concentrations: art education, art/fine arts, computer graphics, studio art. Cross-registration with University of Wisconsin Center System.
Enrollment Fall 1997: 328 undergraduate.
Art Student Profile 54% females, 46% males, 7% minorities, 1% international.
Art Faculty 17 total (full-time and part-time). 100% of full-time faculty have terminal degrees. Graduate students do not teach undergraduate courses. Undergraduate student–faculty ratio: 13:1.
Student Life Student groups/activities include Juried Student Art Exhibition, Student Design Association, Student Art Association.
Expenses for 1997–98 Application fee: $35. State resident tuition: $2772 full-time. Nonresident tuition: $8714 full-time. Full-time tuition varies according to reciprocity agreements. College room and board: $2812. College room only: $1620. Special program-related fees: $5–$300 per course for studio materials.
Financial Aid Program-specific awards for 1997: 1 Roberta Fiskum Award for returning program majors, graphic design ($600), 10 Art Department Scholarships for artistically talented returning program majors ($100), 1 Mary Weiser Award for returning program majors, excellence in ceramics ($100).
Application Procedures Students apply for admission into the professional program by sophomore year. Deadline for freshmen and transfers: continuous. Required: high school transcript, college transcript(s) for transfer students, minimum 2.0 high school GPA. Recommended: interview.
Web Site http://www.uww.edu.
Undergraduate Contact Dr. William Chandler, Chair, Art Department, University of Wisconsin–Whitewater, College of Arts and Communications, Whitewater, Wisconsin 53190; 414-472-1324, fax: 414-472-2808.

▼ UTAH STATE UNIVERSITY

Logan, Utah

State-supported, coed. Urban campus. Total enrollment: 21,234. Art program established 1908.
Degrees Bachelor of Fine Arts in the area of art. Majors and concentrations: art education, art history, ceramic art and design, graphic design, illustration, painting/drawing, pho-

Utah State University *(continued)*

tography, printmaking, sculpture. Graduate degrees offered: Master of Fine Arts in the area of art.

Enrollment Fall 1997: 320 undergraduate, 32 graduate.

Art Student Profile 40% females, 60% males, 10% minorities, 2% international.

Art Faculty 18 total undergraduate and graduate (full-time and part-time). 100% of full-time faculty have terminal degrees. Graduate students teach a few undergraduate courses. Undergraduate student–faculty ratio: 14:1.

Student Life Student groups/activities include Student Art Guild.

Expenses for 1997–98 Application fee: $35. State resident tuition: $1767 full-time. Nonresident tuition: $6207 full-time. Mandatory fees: $408 full-time. Full-time tuition and fees vary according to course load. College room and board: $3510. College room only: $1440. Room and board charges vary according to board plan and housing facility. Special program-related fees: $15–$75 per semester for lab fees.

Financial Aid Program-specific awards for 1997: 8 Endowed Scholarships for studio art or art education majors, 5 University Scholarships for incoming freshmen ($1700).

Application Procedures Students admitted directly into the professional program freshman year. Deadline for freshmen and transfers: continuous. Required: high school transcript, college transcript(s) for transfer students, minimum 2.0 high school GPA, SAT I or ACT test scores.

Undergraduate Contact Mr. Christopher Terry, Director of Undergraduate Curriculum, Department of Art, Utah State University, Logan, Utah 84322-4000; 801-797-3460, fax: 801-797-3412.

Graduate Contact Mr. John Neely, Director of Graduate Curriculum, Department of Art, Utah State University, Logan, Utah 84322-4000; 801-797-3460, fax: 801-797-3412.

▼ VALDOSTA STATE UNIVERSITY

Valdosta, Georgia

State-supported, coed. Small town campus. Total enrollment: 9,779.

Degrees Bachelor of Fine Arts in the areas of art, art education. Graduate degrees offered: Master of Art Education. Program accredited by NASAD.

Enrollment Fall 1997: 205 total; 180 undergraduate, 8 graduate, 17 non-professional degree.

Art Student Profile 56% females, 44% males, 16% minorities, 4% international.

Art Faculty 16 total undergraduate and graduate (full-time and part-time). 100% of full-time faculty have terminal degrees. Graduate students teach a few undergraduate courses. Undergraduate student–faculty ratio: 14:1.

Student Life Student groups/activities include Art Student League, National Art Education Association Student Chapter.

Expenses for 1997–98 Application fee: $10. State resident tuition: $1680 full-time. Nonresident tuition: $6141 full-time. Mandatory fees: $294 full-time. College room and board: $3465. College room only: $1665. Room and board charges vary according to board plan. Special program-related fees: $10–$50 per course for materials purchase in lab classes.

Financial Aid Program-specific awards for 1997: 5 Freshman Art Scholarships for incoming majors ($300–$500), 3 Fortner Scholarships for continuing majors ($1275), 1 Art Depart-

ment Assistantship for program majors ($1000), 2 Lee Bennet Scholarships for continuing majors ($1275).

Application Procedures Students admitted directly into the professional program freshman year. Deadline for freshmen and transfers: continuous. Required: high school transcript, college transcript(s) for transfer students, SAT I or ACT test scores, completion of college preparatory curriculum or equivalent, minimum re-centered SAT I scores of 430 verbal and 400 math. Recommended: minimum 2.0 high school GPA, portfolio. Portfolio reviews held once on campus; the submission of slides may be substituted for portfolios whenever needed.

Undergraduate Contact Mr. Walter Peacock, Director, Admissions Office, Valdosta State University, 1500 North Patterson Street, Valdosta, Georgia 31698; 912-333-5791, E-mail address: wpeacock@valdosta.edu.

Graduate Contact Dr. J. Stephen Lahr, Professor/Art Education, Department of Art, Valdosta State University, Valdosta, Georgia 31698; 912-333-5835, fax: 912-245-3799, E-mail address: jslahr@valdosta.edu.

▼ VIRGINIA COMMONWEALTH UNIVERSITY

Richmond, Virginia

State-supported, coed. Urban campus. Total enrollment: 22,702. Art program established 1928.

Degrees Bachelor of Fine Arts in the areas of art education, art history, communications, crafts, fashion, interior design, painting/printmaking, sculpture. Majors and concentrations: art education, commercial art, computer graphics, craft design, drafting and design, fashion design and technology, furniture design, glassworking, graphic arts, illustration, interior design, jewelry and metalsmithing, painting/drawing, printmaking, sculpture, textile arts, woodworking design. Graduate degrees offered: Master of Fine Arts in the areas of art education, art history, communications, crafts, interior design, painting/printmaking, photography, sculpture. Doctor of Philosophy in the area of art history. Program accredited by NASAD, FIDER.

Enrollment Fall 1997: 2,643 total; 2,367 undergraduate, 276 graduate.

Art Student Profile 61% females, 39% males, 18% minorities, 11% international.

Art Faculty 288 total undergraduate and graduate (full-time and part-time). 97% of full-time faculty have terminal degrees. Graduate students teach a few undergraduate courses. Undergraduate student–faculty ratio: 17:1.

Expenses for 1997–98 Application fee: $25. State resident tuition: $3125 full-time. Nonresident tuition: $11,382 full-time. Mandatory fees: $986 full-time. Full-time tuition and fees vary according to program. College room and board: $4540. College room only: $2715. Room and board charges vary according to board plan and housing facility. Special program-related fees: $150 per semester for comprehensive arts fee.

Application Procedures Students apply for admission into the professional program by sophomore year. Deadline for freshmen: February 1; transfers: May 1. Notification date for freshmen and transfers: continuous. Required: essay, high school transcript, college transcript(s) for transfer students, letter of recommendation, SAT I test score only, portfolio of six drawing/design exercises or slide portfolio of 12 to 16 works. Recommended: interview. Portfolio reviews held

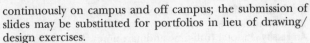

continuously on campus and off campus; the submission of slides may be substituted for portfolios in lieu of drawing/ design exercises.

Web Site http://www.vcu.edu/artweb/.

Undergraduate Contact Ms. Lydia Thompson, Assistant Dean of Student Affairs, School of the Arts, Virginia Commonwealth University, PO Box 842519, Richmond, Virginia 23284-2519; 804-828-2787, fax: 804-828-6469, E-mail address: lcthomps@ saturn.vcu.edu.

Graduate Contact Dr. Daniel Reeves, Assistant Dean and Director of Graduate Studies, School of the Arts, Virginia Commonwealth University, PO Box 842519, Richmond, Virginia 23284-2519; 804-828-2787, fax: 804-828-6469, E-mail address: dreeves@saturn.vcu.edu.

More About the School

The School of the Arts at Virginia Commonwealth University, with more than 2,600 full-time students, is one of the largest art schools in the nation. The School hosts more than 300 on-campus performances and exhibitions in the visual and performing arts each year, and its faculty members and students are involved in hundreds more throughout metropolitan Richmond. *U.S. News and World Report* has ranked the School of the Arts in the top 19 in the nation.

Students invest many hours in serious creative pursuit of the arts disciplines. Artistic freedom is stressed, and students are exposed to a wide variety of artistic sensibilities and techniques. All students experience artistic applications using computers, and departments have fully equipped multistation laboratories. The Department of Communication Arts and Design houses a virtual reality lab.

VCU's School of the Arts offers degrees in virtually every visual and performing arts discipline. The School is organized into 12 departments: Communication Arts and Design, Crafts, Dance and Choreography, Art Education, Interior Design, Art History, Music, Painting and Printmaking, Photography and Film, Sculpture, and Theatre. Within the departments are various tracks of study. For example, crafts students can major in any of the 5 areas: clay, fibers, metal, wood, and glass. Painting and Printmaking students can major in lithography, screenprinting, etching, and various paint and mixed mediums.

Among the School's strengths is its Sculpture Department whose graduate program was recently named as one of the top five in the nation by *U.S. News and World Report*, and the Department of Interior Design recognized in the top 5 in the country by *Interior Design Magazine*. The Student Jazz Orchestra I has recorded three acclaimed albums and was named Outstanding Big Band 3 times at the Notre Dame Intercollegiate Jazz Festival.

There are 130 full-time and 158 part-time faculty members. Many are recognized for significant accomplishments both nationally and internationally. Philip B. Meggs is the author of *A History of Graphic Design*, and his students were featured in *USA Today* for their "new dollar bill" design project. Martha Curtis' video performance, "Three Dances with Martha Curtis," has been seen by PBS audiences in every major national market. Art history professor Dr. Babatunde Lawal serves on the editorial board of the *Art Bulletin*, and Dr. David Burton of the Department of Art Education has been awarded the National Art Education Student Chapter Sponsor Award for 1997.

The School's alumni include Kenneth Smith, Oscar winner for visual effects for *E.T.* and *Innerspace*; Phil Jordan, art director for *Smithsonian Air and Space Magazine*; and Thomas Moser, soloist for New York's Metropolitan Opera

Company. Tony Coke is a three-time exhibitor at the Whitney Museum of American Art and a Guggenheim Fellow. Jon Kuhn's glass creations are in the collections of the Metropolitan Museum of Art in New York, the Smithsonian Institution, Switzerland's Musée Des Artes Décoratifs, and Denmark's Ebeltoft International Glass Museum. Chris Murray has designed furniture for Knoll Associates Venturi Collection, and Tinnakorm Rujinarong has designed commercial and residential interiors throughout the Far East and Europe.

The School of the Arts is a part of Virginia Commonwealth University, one of 84 Research I universities in the nation, with more than 20,000 students located on two campuses in Richmond, Virginia: the Medical College of Virginia and the Academic Campus. The University's schools include such areas of study as medicine, dentistry, pharmacy, mass communication, social work, education, nursing, humanities and sciences, business, and engineering.

The University has on-campus housing facilities, and there are additional housing opportunities throughout the historic fan residential district, which borders the campus. The majority of students come from Virginia, but students from all states and dozens of countries also attend. The School has initiated cooperative educational agreements and/or on-site study in Russia, Germany, Italy, England, China, Africa, and Latin America.

The School's Anderson Gallery is recognized internationally as a major exhibitor of contemporary art. It has a record of grants from the National Endowment for the Arts and the Institute of Museum Services. The Yoko Ono FLY exhibition, opened by Ms. Ono, the paintings of Arnaldo Roche-Rabell, and the large scale photographs of Gregory Crewdson are recent exhibitions at the Anderson.

The city of Richmond has a great number of art galleries and clubs, music and theater performance groups, ballet, symphony, opera, and museums. Richmond is a two-hour drive from Washington, D.C., and one hour from historic Williamsburg.

▼ VIRGINIA INTERMONT COLLEGE

Bristol, Virginia

Independent, coed. Small town campus. Total enrollment: 848.

Degrees Bachelor of Fine Arts in the areas of fine arts, photography, graphic design. Majors and concentrations: art education, art/fine arts, graphic arts, photography. Cross-registration with King College.

Enrollment Fall 1997: 33 total; all undergraduate.

Art Faculty 14 total (full-time and part-time). 83% of full-time faculty have terminal degrees. Graduate students do not teach undergraduate courses. Undergraduate student–faculty ratio: 6:1.

Student Life Student groups/activities include Society for Photographic Arts, Society for Photographic Education, Collegiate Arts Association.

Expenses for 1997–98 Application fee: $15. Comprehensive fee: $15,350 includes full-time tuition ($10,650) and college room and board ($4700). Special program-related fees: $40 per course for computer lab use, $60 per course for advanced color and professional courses, $20–$95 for photography workshop fee, $40 per course for lab fees.

Financial Aid Program-specific awards for 1997: 60 departmental awards for program majors ($1200).

Virginia Intermont College (continued)

Application Procedures Deadline for freshmen and transfers: continuous. Notification date for freshmen and transfers: continuous. Required: high school transcript, college transcript(s) for transfer students, minimum 2.0 high school GPA, SAT I or ACT test scores, portfolio for scholarship consideration. Recommended: letter of recommendation, portfolio. Portfolio reviews held by request on campus; the submission of slides may be substituted for portfolios for large works of art or when a campus visit is impossible.

Undergraduate Contact Ms. Robin Cozart, Director of Admissions, Virginia Intermont College, Box D-460, Bristol, Virginia 24201; 540-669-6101, fax: 540-466-7855, E-mail address: viadmit@vic.edu.

▼ Virginia State University

Petersburg, Virginia

State-supported, coed. Suburban campus. Total enrollment: 4,200.

Degrees Bachelor of Fine Arts in the areas of art education, visual communications arts and design, studio arts. Program accredited by NASAD.

Enrollment Fall 1997: 65 undergraduate.

Art Student Profile 40% females, 60% males, 90% minorities, 3% international.

Art Faculty 8 total (full-time and part-time). 72% of full-time faculty have terminal degrees. Graduate students do not teach undergraduate courses. Undergraduate student–faculty ratio: 10:1.

Student Life Student groups/activities include Art Club, Cartoon Club.

Expenses for 1997–98 State resident tuition: $1951 full-time. Nonresident tuition: $6430 full-time. Mandatory fees: $1356 full-time. Full-time tuition and fees vary according to course level, course load, and program. College room and board: $4910. College room only: $2800. Room and board charges vary according to board plan and housing facility.

Financial Aid Program-specific awards for 1997: 1 Meredith Award for highest ranking student ($150), 4 Joyner Academic Award for highest GPA in each class ($100).

Application Procedures Students admitted directly into the professional program freshman year. Deadline for freshmen and transfers: May 1. Required: high school transcript, college transcript(s) for transfer students, minimum 2.0 high school GPA, SAT I or ACT test scores. Recommended: essay, letter of recommendation, interview.

Undergraduate Contact Ms. Lisa Winn, Director of Admissions, Virginia State University, PO Box 9018, Petersburg, Virginia 23806; 804-524-5902.

▼ Washburn University of Topeka

Topeka, Kansas

City-supported, coed. Urban campus. Total enrollment: 6,281. Art program established 1897.

Degrees Bachelor of Fine Arts in the areas of arts/fine arts, art education. Program accredited by NASAD.

Enrollment Fall 1997: 90 total; 40 undergraduate, 50 non-professional degree.

Art Student Profile 56% females, 44% males, 2% minorities, 2% international.

Art Faculty 12 total (full-time and part-time). 100% of full-time faculty have terminal degrees. Graduate students do not teach undergraduate courses.

Student Life Student groups/activities include Washburn Art Student Association, Mulvane Art Museum.

Expenses for 1997–98 State resident tuition: $3100 full-time. Nonresident tuition: $6758 full-time. Mandatory fees: $50 full-time. College room and board: $3300.

Financial Aid Program-specific awards for 1997: 1 Jolee Houx Award for art majors ($300), 1 Grace Dean Award for art majors ($600), 1 Anton Award for art majors ($700), 3 Coutts Awards for art majors ($1200), 1 Fitzgibbons Award for art majors ($600), 1 Jostens Printing Award for graphic design majors ($600), 1 Wise Award for graphic design majors ($1000), 1 Tebben Award for art education majors ($500), 1 Pollak Award for junior or senior art majors ($1000).

Application Procedures Students apply for admission into the professional program by sophomore year. Deadline for freshmen and transfers: continuous. Required: high school transcript, college transcript(s) for transfer students, ACT test score only, minimum 2.0 high school GPA for out-of-state applicants. Recommended: portfolio for transfer applicants. Portfolio reviews held twice during sophomore year on campus; the submission of slides may be substituted for portfolios for transfer applicants.

Web Site http://www.washburn.edu/cas/art/index.html.

Undergraduate Contact Ms. Glenda Taylor, Chair, Department of Art, Washburn University of Topeka, 1700 College Street, Topeka, Kansas 66621; 785-231-1010 ext. 1639, fax: 785-231-1089, E-mail address: zztayl@washburn.edu.

▼ Washington State University

Pullman, Washington

State-supported, coed. Rural campus. Total enrollment: 20,243. Art program established 1910.

Degrees Bachelor of Fine Arts in the areas of painting, sculpture, printmaking, ceramics, photography, computer art, drawing. Majors and concentrations: art/fine arts, ceramics, computer graphics, painting/drawing, photography, printmaking, sculpture, studio art. Graduate degrees offered: Master of Fine Arts in the areas of painting, sculpture, printmaking, ceramics, photography, computer art, drawing. Cross-registration with institutions in the state of Washington, University of Idaho.

Enrollment Fall 1997: 197 total; 178 undergraduate, 19 graduate.

Art Student Profile 60% females, 40% males, 30% minorities, 10% international.

Art Faculty 18 total undergraduate and graduate (full-time and part-time). 100% of full-time faculty have terminal degrees. Graduate students teach a few undergraduate courses.

Expenses for 1997–98 Application fee: $35. State resident tuition: $2989 full-time. Nonresident tuition: $9871 full-time. Mandatory fees: $405 full-time. College room and board: $4426. Room and board charges vary according to board plan and housing facility. Special program-related fees: $25–$60 for materials.

Financial Aid Program-specific awards for 1997: 1 John Ludwig Memorial Scholarship for program majors ($300–$500), 2–3 James Balyeat Awards for program majors ($200–$300), 3

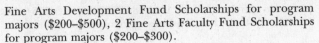

Fine Arts Development Fund Scholarships for program majors ($200–$500), 2 Fine Arts Faculty Fund Scholarships for program majors ($200–$300).

Application Procedures Students apply for admission into the professional program by sophomore, junior year. Deadline for freshmen and transfers: continuous. Required: high school transcript, college transcript(s) for transfer students, minimum 2.0 high school GPA.

Web Site http://www.wsu.edu:8080/~finearts/.

Undergraduate Contact Chris Watts, Chair, Fine Arts Department, Washington State University, 5072 Fine Arts Center, Pullman, Washington 99164-7450; 509-335-8686.

Graduate Contact Sharon Wells, Program Coordinator, Fine Arts Department, Washington State University, 5072 Fine Arts Center, Pullman, Washington 99164-7450; 509-335-8686, E-mail address: swells@mail.wsu.edu.

▼ WASHINGTON UNIVERSITY IN ST. LOUIS

St. Louis, Missouri

Independent, coed. Suburban campus. Total enrollment: 11,606.

Degrees Bachelor of Fine Arts in the areas of ceramics, fashion design, graphic communications, painting, photography, sculpture, printmaking/drawing. Majors and concentrations: advertising design, ceramics, fashion design, graphic design, illustration, painting, photography, printmaking, sculpture. Graduate degrees offered: Master of Fine Arts in the areas of ceramics, painting, photography,sculpture,printmaking/drawing. Program accredited by NASAD.

Enrollment Fall 1997: 343 total; 300 undergraduate, 39 graduate, 4 non-professional degree.

Art Student Profile 67% females, 33% males, 14% minorities, 1% international.

Art Faculty 44 total undergraduate and graduate (full-time and part-time). 92% of full-time faculty have terminal degrees. Graduate students teach a few undergraduate courses. Undergraduate student–faculty ratio: 11:1.

Student Life Student groups/activities include American Institute for Graphic Arts Student Chapter, Mid-America College Art Association.

Expenses for 1998–99 Application fee: $55. Comprehensive fee: $29,344 includes full-time tuition ($22,200), mandatory fees ($222), and college room and board ($6922). College room only: $4142. Room and board charges vary according to board plan and housing facility. Special program-related fees: $3–$150 per semester for material fees.

Financial Aid Program-specific awards for 1997: 1 Conway/Proetz Award for high academic and artistic achievement ($21,000).

Application Procedures Students admitted directly into the professional program freshman year. Deadline for freshmen: January 15; transfers: June 1. Notification date for freshmen: April 1; transfers: August 1. Required: essay, high school transcript, college transcript(s) for transfer students, minimum 2.0 high school GPA, 2 letters of recommendation, SAT I or ACT test scores, portfolio for transfer students. Recommended: minimum 3.0 high school GPA, portfolio. Portfolio reviews held once on campus and off campus; the submission of slides may be substituted for portfolios when distance is prohibitive.

Undergraduate Contact MaryAnne Modzelewski, Assistant Director, Undergraduate Admissions, Washington University in St.

Louis, Campus Box 1089, One Brookings Drive, St. Louis, Missouri 63130; 314-935-7354, fax: 314-935-4949, E-mail address: maryanne@wuvmd.wustl.edu.

Graduate Contact Sabina Ott, Director of Graduate Studies, School of Art, Washington University in St. Louis, Campus Box 1031, One Brookings Drive, St. Louis, Missouri 63130; 314-935-5884, fax: 314-935-6462, E-mail address: sdott@art. wustl.edu.

More About the University

Program Facilities The School of Art is housed in two buildings, Bixby Hall and Lewis Center. Combined, these facilities offer approximately 49,000 square feet of studio space, including Bixby Gallery. Each of the School's major areas has a studio space equipped with professional tools and equipment. Majors work in their own studio space. The Carolyne Roehm Electronic Media Center serves all areas and contains sophisticated hardware and software, video cameras, and editing equipment. Next door to Bixby Hall is Steinberg Hall, which contains the Gallery of Art and the Art and Architecture Library. The Art and Architecture Library, part of the University's library system, contains more than 60,000 volumes, 457 periodicals, and a rare book room.

Faculty and Alumni Faculty artists have received fellowship and grant support from the NEA and the Guggenheim Foundation, among others. Two emeritus professors are elected members of the prestigious American Academy of Arts and Letters. Selected School of Art alumni include Erika Beckman, Mike Peters, Bernie Fuchs, Carolyne Roehm, Judy Pfaff, Jack Unruh, Adam Niklewicz, and Jay Krueger. Quondam visiting artists: Susan Crile, Frida Baranek, Tom Nakashima, Robert Andrew Parker, and Catherine Wagner.

Student Exhibit Opportunities Student Fine Arts Council Juried Show; Junior Major, Core, B.F.A., Annual Fashion, and Major shows; the University City Sculpture Project Show.

Special Programs Study-abroad, internship, and volunteer opportunities are offered. Special programs in learning, health, counseling, and career development are all available.

▼ WAYNE STATE UNIVERSITY

Detroit, Michigan

State-supported, coed. Urban campus. Total enrollment: 30,729.

Degrees Bachelor of Fine Arts in the area of art. Majors and concentrations: ceramic art and design, electronic arts, fibers, graphic design, industrial design, interior design, jewelry and metalsmithing, painting/drawing, photography, printmaking, sculpture. Graduate degrees offered: Master of Fine Arts in the area of art; Master of Arts in the area of fine arts. Cross-registration with University of Windsor (Canada).

Enrollment Fall 1997: 504 total.

Art Student Profile 60% females, 40% males, 25% minorities, 5% international.

Art Faculty 68 total undergraduate and graduate (full-time and part-time). 100% of full-time faculty have terminal degrees. Graduate students teach a few undergraduate courses.

Student Life Student groups/activities include American Society of Interior Designers, American Ceramic Design, Fashion Design and Merchandising Club.

Expenses for 1997–98 Application fee: $20. State resident tuition: $3348 full-time. Nonresident tuition: $7471 full-time. Mandatory fees: $138 full-time. Full-time tuition and fees

Wayne State University (*continued*)

vary according to student level. College room only: $3875. Room charges vary according to housing facility.

Financial Aid Program-specific awards for 1997: 5 Talent Awards for program majors ($1000), 1 Becker Award for program majors ($1500), 12–15 Endowed Scholarships for program majors ($1000).

Application Procedures Students admitted directly into the professional program freshman year. Deadline for freshmen and transfers: continuous. Required: high school transcript, college transcript(s) for transfer students, minimum 2.0 high school GPA.

Undergraduate Contact Ms. Carolyn J. Hooper, Associate Chair, Art and Art History Department, Wayne State University, 150 Art Building, Detroit, Michigan 48202; 313-577-2980, fax: 313-577-3491.

Graduate Contact Mr. Stanley Rosenthal, Graduate Officer, Art and Art History Department, Wayne State University, 150 Art Building, Detroit, Michigan 48202; 313-577-2980, fax: 313-577-3491.

▼ WEBER STATE UNIVERSITY

Ogden, Utah

State-supported, coed. Urban campus. Total enrollment: 14,613. Art program established 1990.

Degrees Bachelor of Fine Arts in the areas of two-dimensional art, three-dimensional art, photography, visual communication/design, visual communications/illustration, general art.

Enrollment Fall 1997: 209 total; 25 undergraduate, 184 non-professional degree.

Art Student Profile 51% females, 49% males, 6% minorities, 5% international.

Art Faculty 30 total (full-time and part-time). 100% of full-time faculty have terminal degrees. Graduate students teach a few undergraduate courses. Undergraduate student–faculty ratio: 17:1.

Expenses for 1997–98 Application fee: $35. State resident tuition: $1518 full-time. Nonresident tuition: $5313 full-time. Mandatory fees: $417 full-time. College room and board: $3810. College room only: $1500. Room and board charges vary according to board plan and housing facility. Special program-related fees: $10 per class for painting supplies, $20 per class for weaving supplies, $20 per class for metals/jewelry supplies, $30 per class for ceramics supplies, $35–$45 per class for printmaking supplies, $5–$25 per class for sculpture supplies, $35–$45 per class for photography supplies.

Financial Aid Program-specific awards for 1997: 5 State Activity Scholarships for incoming and continuing art majors ($1500), 7 Sponsor Scholarships for incoming and continuing art majors ($1100).

Application Procedures Students apply for admission into the professional program by sophomore, junior year. Deadline for freshmen and transfers: continuous. Notification date for freshmen and transfers: continuous. Required: college transcript(s) for transfer students, interview, portfolio. Recommended: SAT I or ACT test scores. Portfolio reviews held 3 times on campus.

Web Site http://dova.weber.edu.

Undergraduate Contact Mr. James C. Jacobs, Chairman, Department of Visual Arts, Weber State University, Room 104, 2001 University Circle, Ogden, Utah 84408-2001; 801-626-6455, fax: 801-626-6976, E-mail address: jcjacobs@weber.edu.

▼ WEBSTER UNIVERSITY

St. Louis, Missouri

Independent, coed. Suburban campus. Total enrollment: 11,756.

Degrees Bachelor of Fine Arts in the areas of studio art, graphic design; Bachelor of Arts in the areas of studio art, art history and criticism. Majors and concentrations: art history, ceramic art and design, graphic design, media performance, painting/drawing, photography, printmaking, sculpture. Graduate degrees offered: Master of Arts in the areas of studio art, art history and criticism. Cross-registration with various colleges in St. Louis.

Enrollment Fall 1997: 202 total; 182 undergraduate, 20 graduate.

Art Student Profile 60% females, 40% males, 11% minorities, 2% international.

Art Faculty 30 total undergraduate and graduate (full-time and part-time). 100% of full-time faculty have terminal degrees. Graduate students do not teach undergraduate courses.

Student Life Student groups/activities include Art Council, Graduate Art Council.

Expenses for 1997–98 Application fee: $25. Comprehensive fee: $15,940 includes full-time tuition ($10,860), mandatory fees ($50), and college room and board ($5030). College room only: $3080. Room and board charges vary according to board plan and housing facility. Special program-related fees: $50–$125 per course for studio lab fee.

Financial Aid Program-specific awards for 1997: 1 Sr. Gabriel Mary Hoare Scholarship for visual arts students.

Application Procedures Students apply for admission into the professional program by junior year. Deadline for freshmen and transfers: continuous. Required: essay, high school transcript, college transcript(s) for transfer students, minimum 3.0 high school GPA, 2 letters of recommendation, interview, portfolio, SAT I or ACT test scores. Portfolio reviews held 10 times on campus; the submission of slides may be substituted for portfolios when distance is prohibitive.

Web Site http://www.websteruniv.edu/depts/finearts/art.

Undergraduate Contact Ms. Amy Storey, Auditions Coordinator, Office of Admissions, Webster University, 470 East Lockwood Avenue, St. Louis, Missouri 63119-3194; 314-968-7001, fax: 314-968-7115.

Graduate Contact Dr. Jeffrey Hughes, Graduate Program Coordinator, Department of Art, Webster University, 470 East Lockwood Avenue, St. Louis, Missouri 63119-3194; 314-968-7159, fax: 314-968-7139, E-mail address: hughesja@websteruniv.edu.

▼ WEST CHESTER UNIVERSITY OF PENNSYLVANIA

West Chester, Pennsylvania

State-supported, coed. Small town campus. Total enrollment: 11,430.

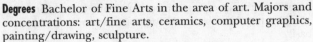

Degrees Bachelor of Fine Arts in the area of art. Majors and concentrations: art/fine arts, ceramics, computer graphics, painting/drawing, sculpture.

Enrollment Fall 1997: 150 undergraduate.

Art Student Profile 60% females, 40% males.

Art Faculty 13 total (full-time and part-time). 100% of full-time faculty have terminal degrees. Graduate students do not teach undergraduate courses. Undergraduate student–faculty ratio: 10:1.

Student Life Student groups/activities include Print Club, Art Association.

Expenses for 1997–98 Application fee: $25. State resident tuition: $3468 full-time. Nonresident tuition: $8824 full-time. Mandatory fees: $694 full-time. College room and board: $4376. College room only: $2776. Room and board charges vary according to board plan, housing facility, and location.

Financial Aid Program-specific awards for 1997: 2 McKinney Scholarships for junior painting majors ($1000).

Application Procedures Students admitted directly into the professional program freshman year. Deadline for freshmen and transfers: continuous. Required: essay, high school transcript, college transcript(s) for transfer students, minimum 2.0 high school GPA, SAT I or ACT test scores (minimum combined SAT I score of 1000). Recommended: minimum 3.0 high school GPA.

Undergraduate Contact Mr. John Baker, Chair, Art Department, West Chester University of Pennsylvania, Mitchell Hall, West Chester, Pennsylvania 19383; 610-436-2755, E-mail address: jbaker@wcupa.edu.

▼ WESTERN CAROLINA UNIVERSITY

Cullowhee, North Carolina

State-supported, coed. Rural campus.

Degrees Bachelor of Fine Arts in the areas of studio art, graphic design. Majors and concentrations: book arts, ceramic art and design, graphic arts, painting/drawing, photography, printmaking, sculpture. Cross-registration with Penland School of Crafts.

Enrollment Fall 1997: 400 total; 100 undergraduate, 300 non-professional degree.

Art Student Profile 50% females, 50% males, 3% minorities, 1% international.

Art Faculty 25 total (full-time and part-time). 100% of full-time faculty have terminal degrees. Graduate students do not teach undergraduate courses. Undergraduate student–faculty ratio: 15:1.

Student Life Student groups/activities include Annual Student Exhibition, Nomad (student art and literature publication), Cullowhee Arts Festival.

Financial Aid Program-specific awards for 1997: 1 Lorraine Stone Scholarship for non-traditional students ($500).

Application Procedures Students admitted directly into the professional program freshman year. Deadline for freshmen and transfers: continuous. Notification date for freshmen and transfers: August 1. Required: high school transcript, minimum 2.0 high school GPA, letter of recommendation, SAT I or ACT test scores. Recommended: interview, portfolio. Portfolio reviews held continuously on campus; the submission of slides may be substituted for portfolios (slides preferred).

Undergraduate Contact Mr. Robert Godfrey, Head, Department of Art, Western Carolina University, Cullowhee, North Carolina 28723; 704-227-7210, fax: 704-227-7505, E-mail address: wcuart@wcu.edu.

▼ WESTERN ILLINOIS UNIVERSITY

Macomb, Illinois

State-supported, coed. Small town campus. Total enrollment: 12,200. Art program established 1938.

Degrees Bachelor of Fine Arts in the area of art. Majors and concentrations: art/fine arts, ceramic art and design, commercial art, painting/drawing, printmaking, sculpture, studio art, watercolors.

Enrollment Fall 1997: 155 total; 97 undergraduate, 58 non-professional degree.

Art Student Profile 44% females, 56% males, 11% minorities, 15% international.

Art Faculty 18 total (full-time and part-time). 100% of full-time faculty have terminal degrees. Graduate students do not teach undergraduate courses. Undergraduate student–faculty ratio: 11:1.

Student Life Student groups/activities include Student Art League, National Art Education Association Student Chapter, Clay Club. Special housing available for art students.

Expenses for 1997–98 Application fee: $0. State resident tuition: $2119 full-time. Nonresident tuition: $6358 full-time. Mandatory fees: $918 full-time. College room and board: $3838. College room only: $2278. Special program-related fees: $10–$55 for material fees.

Financial Aid Program-specific awards for 1997: 4 Bulkeley Scholarships for program majors ($800), 7 Talent Grants for program majors ($500), 8 tuition waivers for program majors ($550), 2 freshman scholarships for incoming freshmen program majors ($500), 1 Purdum Scholarship for art education majors ($1000).

Application Procedures Students admitted directly into the professional program freshman year. Deadline for freshmen and transfers: August 10. Notification date for freshmen and transfers: continuous. Required: high school transcript, college transcript(s) for transfer students, minimum 2.0 high school GPA, SAT I or ACT test scores. Recommended: portfolio. Portfolio reviews held continuously on campus; the submission of slides may be substituted for portfolios when distance is prohibitive.

Undergraduate Contact Mr. Ed Gettinger, Chair, Department of Art, Western Illinois University, 32 Garwood Hall, Macomb, Illinois 61455; 309-298-1549, fax: 309-298-2695, E-mail address: ew-gettinger@wiu.edu.

▼ WESTERN KENTUCKY UNIVERSITY

Bowling Green, Kentucky

State-supported, coed. Suburban campus. Total enrollment: 14,543. Art program established 1960.

Degrees Bachelor of Fine Arts in the areas of fine arts, graphic design; Bachelor of Arts in the areas of studio art, art education. Majors and concentrations: ceramics, painting, printmaking, sculpture, weaving. Program accredited by NASAD.

Enrollment Fall 1997: 177 total; all undergraduate.

Western Kentucky University (continued)

Art Student Profile 50% females, 50% males, 3% minorities, 1% international.

Art Faculty 15 total (full-time and part-time). 100% of full-time faculty have terminal degrees. Graduate students do not teach undergraduate courses. Undergraduate student–faculty ratio: 15:1.

Expenses for 1997–98 Application fee: $15. State resident tuition: $1800 full-time. Nonresident tuition: $5400 full-time. Mandatory fees: $340 full-time. College room and board: $2700.

Financial Aid Program-specific awards for 1997: 13 departmental awards for art majors ($500–$1000).

Application Procedures Students admitted directly into the professional program freshman year. Deadline for freshmen and transfers: continuous. Notification date for freshmen and transfers: continuous. Required: high school transcript, minimum 2.4 high school GPA, minimum ACT score of 19 for state residents, minimum combined SAT I score of 890 (re-centered) or minimum ACT score of 19 for out-of-state residents.

Web Site http://www.wku.edu/Dept/Academic/AHSS/Art/art.html.

Undergraduate Contact Dr. James Flynn, Interim Head, Department of Art, Western Kentucky University, Bowling Green, Kentucky 42101; 502-745-3944, fax: 502-745-5932, E-mail address: james.flynn@wku.edu.

▼ WESTERN MICHIGAN UNIVERSITY

Kalamazoo, Michigan

State-supported, coed. Urban campus. Total enrollment: 26,132.

Degrees Bachelor of Fine Arts in the areas of painting, ceramics, sculpture, photography, graphic design, printmaking. Majors and concentrations: art education, art/fine arts, ceramic art and design, graphic design, painting/drawing, photography, printmaking, sculpture. Graduate degrees offered: Master of Fine Arts in the areas of painting, printmaking, graphic design, sculpture. Cross-registration with Michigan colleges and universities. Program accredited by NASAD.

Enrollment Fall 1997: 527 undergraduate, 13 graduate.

Art Faculty 39 total undergraduate and graduate (full-time and part-time). 100% of full-time faculty have terminal degrees. Graduate students teach a few undergraduate courses. Undergraduate student–faculty ratio: 25:1.

Student Life Student groups/activities include Students in Design.

Expenses for 1997–98 Application fee: $25. State resident tuition: $3061 full-time. Nonresident tuition: $7770 full-time. Mandatory fees: $594 full-time. Full-time tuition and fees vary according to course load and student level. College room and board: $4398. College room only: $1815. Room and board charges vary according to board plan.

Application Procedures Students apply for admission into the professional program by freshman, sophomore year. Deadline for freshmen and transfers: continuous. Required: high school transcript, college transcript(s) for transfer students, minimum 2.0 high school GPA, portfolio, ACT test score only. Recommended: minimum 3.0 high school GPA. Portfolio reviews held once for graphic design majors and 2 times for other program majors on campus; the submission of slides may be substituted for portfolios on a case-by-case basis.

Web Site http://www.wmich.edu/art.

Contact Academic Advisor, Art Department, Western Michigan University, 1201 Oliver Street, Kalamazoo, Michigan 49008; 616-387-2440, fax: 616-387-2477.

▼ WEST TEXAS A&M UNIVERSITY

Canyon, Texas

State-supported, coed. Small town campus. Total enrollment: 6,489.

Degrees Bachelor of Fine Arts in the areas of studio art, graphic design. Majors and concentrations: ceramics, computer art, graphic design, jewelry and metalsmithing, painting/drawing, printmaking, sculpture. Graduate degrees offered: Master of Fine Arts in the area of studio art; Master of Arts in the area of art.

Enrollment Fall 1997: 89 total; 57 undergraduate, 12 graduate, 20 non-professional degree.

Art Student Profile 48% females, 52% males, 10% minorities, 1% international.

Art Faculty 7 total undergraduate and graduate (full-time and part-time). 99% of full-time faculty have terminal degrees. Graduate students teach a few undergraduate courses. Undergraduate student–faculty ratio: 16:1.

Student Life Student groups/activities include Art History Club.

Expenses for 1997–98 State resident tuition: $1296 full-time. Nonresident tuition: $6432 full-time. Mandatory fees: $448 full-time. Full-time tuition and fees vary according to course load. College room and board: $2969. College room only: $1308. Room and board charges vary according to board plan and housing facility. Special program-related fees: $7–$20 per course for lab fees.

Financial Aid Program-specific awards for 1997: 2 Levi Margaret Cole Endowment Awards for program majors ($200–$500), 1 Charles Hohmann Endowment Award for graphic design majors ($400), 30 Mary Moody Northen Endowment Awards for program majors ($200–$500), 1 Isabel Robinson Scholarship for program majors ($200–$500), 1 Emmit Smith Art Scholarship for studio art students ($200–$500).

Application Procedures Students admitted directly into the professional program freshman year. Deadline for freshmen and transfers: continuous. Required: high school transcript, college transcript(s) for transfer students, SAT I or ACT test scores. Recommended: letter of recommendation, portfolio. Portfolio reviews held once and as needed on campus; the submission of slides may be substituted for portfolios when distance is prohibitive.

Undergraduate Contact Mr. Royal Brantley, Head, Department of Art, Communication and Theater, West Texas A&M University, WTAMU Box 60747, Canyon, Texas 79016; 806-651-2799, fax: 806-651-2818, E-mail address: rbrantley@faculty.wtamu.edu.

Graduate Contact Mr. David Rindlisbacher, Graduate Program Coordinator, Department of Art, Communication and Theater, West Texas A&M University, WTAMU BOX 60747, Canyon, Texas 79016; 806-651-2792, fax: 806-651-2818, E-mail address: drindlisbacher@faculty.wtamu.edu.

▼ WEST VIRGINIA UNIVERSITY

Morgantown, West Virginia

State-supported, coed. Small town campus. Total enrollment: 22,238. Art program established 1897.

Degrees Bachelor of Fine Arts in the areas of painting, printmaking, sculpture, ceramics, graphic design, art education. Majors and concentrations: art education, art/fine arts, ceramic art and design, graphic arts, painting/drawing, printmaking, sculpture. Graduate degrees offered: Master of Fine Arts in the areas of painting, printmaking, sculpture, ceramics, new forms (experimental); Master of Arts in the area of art education. Program accredited by NASAD.

Enrollment Fall 1997: 239 undergraduate, 18 graduate.

Art Student Profile 49% females, 6% minorities, 4% international.

Art Faculty 17 total undergraduate and graduate (full-time). 95% of full-time faculty have terminal degrees. Graduate students teach a few undergraduate courses. Undergraduate student–faculty ratio: 17:1.

Student Life Student groups/activities include Women's Caucus for the Arts, Student Art Association.

Expenses for 1997–98 Application fee: $15, $35 for nonresidents. State resident tuition: $2336 full-time. Nonresident tuition: $7356 full-time. Full-time tuition varies according to location, program, and reciprocity agreements. College room and board: $4832. Room and board charges vary according to board plan, housing facility, and location. Special program-related fees: $50 per course for expendable supplies for studio courses.

Financial Aid Program-specific awards for 1997: 16 Performance Grants for program students ($2000–$6000), 3 Loyalty Permanent Endowment Awards for state residents ($1000), 1 Gabriel Fellowship for state residents ($1000), 6 Mesaros Scholarships for junior and senior art majors ($1000).

Application Procedures Students admitted directly into the professional program freshman year. Deadline for freshmen and transfers: continuous. Notification date for freshmen and transfers: continuous. Required: high school transcript, college transcript(s) for transfer students, minimum 2.0 high school GPA, SAT I or ACT test scores. Recommended: portfolio. Portfolio reviews held twice on campus; the submission of slides may be substituted for portfolios if original work is not available.

Undergraduate Contact Ms. Victoria Fergus, Undergraduate Advisor, Division of Art, West Virginia University, College of Creative Arts, PO Box 6111, Morgantown, West Virginia 26506-6111; 304-293-2140 ext. 3138, fax: 304-293-3550.

Graduate Contact Mr. Paul Krainak, Graduate Advisor, Division of Art, West Virginia University, College of Creative Arts, PO Box 6111, Morgantown, West Virginia 26506-6111; 304-293-2140 ext. 3137, fax: 304-293-3550, E-mail address: krainak@ wvnvm.wvnet.edu.

▼ WICHITA STATE UNIVERSITY

Wichita, Kansas

State-supported, coed. Urban campus. Total enrollment: 14,061.

Degrees Bachelor of Fine Arts in the areas of ceramics, painting/drawing, printmaking, sculpture, graphic design, art history; Bachelor of Art Education; Bachelor of Arts in the area of studio arts. Majors and concentrations: art education, art history, ceramic art and design, graphic design, painting/drawing, printmaking, sculpture, studio art. Graduate degrees offered: Master of Fine Arts in the areas of ceramics, painting/drawing, printmaking, sculpture; Master of Arts in the area of art education.

Enrollment Fall 1997: 387 total; 320 undergraduate, 30 graduate, 37 non-professional degree.

Art Student Profile 58% females, 42% males, 11% minorities, 9% international.

Art Faculty 35 total undergraduate and graduate (full-time and part-time). 100% of full-time faculty have terminal degrees. Graduate students teach a few undergraduate courses.

Student Life Student groups/activities include Visual Arts Guild, Potters Guild, National Art Education Association Student Chapter. Special housing available for art students.

Expenses for 1997–98 Application fee: $20. State resident tuition: $1486 full-time. Nonresident tuition: $6414 full-time. Mandatory fees: $500 full-time. College room and board: $3760. Room and board charges vary according to board plan. Special program-related fees: $15–$70 per course for lab fees.

Financial Aid Program-specific awards for 1997: 20 Miller Trust Awards for program students ($500), 1 Budge Trust Award for program majors ($350), 1 Lair Trust Award for junior painters ($1200), 2 Paulson Endowment Awards for sculpture majors ($600), 1 Sawallace Award for program majors ($500), 1 Heriford Scholarship for program majors ($600).

Application Procedures Students apply for admission into the professional program by freshman, sophomore year. Deadline for freshmen and transfers: continuous. Notification date for freshmen and transfers: continuous. Required: high school transcript, college transcript(s) for transfer students, minimum 2.0 high school GPA. Recommended: interview, portfolio. Portfolio reviews held 4 times on campus and off campus in various locations in Kansas; the submission of slides may be substituted for portfolios whenever needed.

Undergraduate Contact Dr. Donald R. Byrum, Chair, School of Art and Design, Wichita State University, 1845 Fairmount, Wichita, Kansas 67260-0067; 316-978-3555, fax: 316-978-3951.

Graduate Contact Mr. Ronald W. Christ, Graduate Coordinator, School of Art and Design, Wichita State University, 1845 Fairmount, Wichita, Kansas 67260-0067; 316-978-3555, fax: 316-978-3951, E-mail address: christ@twsuvm.uc.twsu.edu.

▼ WILLIAMS BAPTIST COLLEGE

Walnut Ridge, Arkansas

Independent-Southern Baptist, coed. Rural campus. Total enrollment: 708. Art program established 1994.

Degrees Bachelor of Fine Arts in the areas of painting, printmaking, ceramics.

Enrollment Fall 1997: 10 undergraduate.

Art Student Profile 60% females, 40% males, 10% minorities, 10% international.

Art Faculty 3 total (full-time and part-time). 100% of full-time faculty have terminal degrees. Graduate students do not teach undergraduate courses. Undergraduate student–faculty ratio: 5:1.

Student Life Student groups/activities include Art Club.

Expenses for 1997–98 Application fee: $20. Comprehensive fee: $8182 includes full-time tuition ($5000), mandatory fees

Williams Baptist College *(continued)*

($260), and college room and board ($2922). Special program-related fees: $50 per course for lab fees.

Financial Aid Program-specific awards for 1997: 1 art scholarship for program majors ($4000).

Application Procedures Students admitted directly into the professional program freshman year. Deadline for freshmen and transfers: May 1. Required: high school transcript, college transcript(s) for transfer students, 2 letters of recommendation, portfolio, SAT I or ACT test scores, minimum 2.5 college GPA for transfer students. Recommended: minimum 2.0 high school GPA, interview. Portfolio reviews held once per semester after completion of foundation courses on campus; the submission of slides may be substituted for portfolios when distance is prohibitive.

Web Site http://wbc2.wbcoll.edu.

Undergraduate Contact Dr. David Midkiff, Chairman, Department of Art, Williams Baptist College, PO Box 3536 WBC, Walnut Ridge, Arkansas 72476; 870-886-6741 ext. 157, fax: 870-886-3924, E-mail address: dmidkiff@wbclab.wbcoll.edu.

▼ WINTHROP UNIVERSITY

Rock Hill, South Carolina

State-supported, coed. Suburban campus. Total enrollment: 5,574. Art program established 1984.

Degrees Bachelor of Fine Arts in the area of art; Bachelor of Arts in the area of art education. Majors and concentrations: ceramics, graphic design, interior design, jewelry and metalsmithing, painting/drawing, photography, printmaking, sculpture, studio art. Graduate degrees offered: Master of Fine Arts in the area of art; Master of Arts in the areas of art education (studio), art education (research). Cross-registration with York Technical College. Program accredited by NASAD, FIDER, NCATE.

Enrollment Fall 1997: 337 total; 312 undergraduate, 16 graduate, 9 non-professional degree.

Art Student Profile 63% females, 37% males, 10% minorities.

Art Faculty 35 total undergraduate and graduate (full-time and part-time). 100% of full-time faculty have terminal degrees. Graduate students do not teach undergraduate courses. Undergraduate student–faculty ratio: 15:1.

Student Life Student groups/activities include American Society of Interior Designers Student Chapter, National Art Education Association Student Chapter, Union of Student Artists.

Expenses for 1997–98 Application fee: $35. State resident tuition: $3918 full-time. Nonresident tuition: $7046 full-time. Mandatory fees: $20 full-time. College room and board: $3764. College room only: $2260. Special program-related fees: $10–$35 per course for lab fees.

Financial Aid Program-specific awards for 1997: 1 Clara Barres Strait Award for incoming freshmen ($500), 1 Hovermale Award for interior design majors ($500), 1 Bell Theodore Award for juniors ($500), 1–2 Chesterfield Manufacturers Awards for interior design majors ($1500).

Application Procedures Students admitted directly into the professional program freshman year. Deadline for freshmen and transfers: continuous. Notification date for freshmen and transfers: continuous. Required: high school transcript, SAT I or ACT test scores, minimum 2.2 college GPA for transfer students, portfolio for transfer applicants and scholarship consideration. Recommended: interview. Portfo-

lio reviews held by appointment on campus; the submission of slides may be substituted for portfolios (no fewer than 10 slides).

Undergraduate Contact Mr. Jerry Walden, Chair, Art and Design Department, Winthrop University, 140 McLaurin, Rock Hill, South Carolina 29733; 803-323-2126, E-mail address: waldenr@winthrop.edu.

Graduate Contact Dr. Margaret Johnson, Associate Chair and Graduate Coordinator, Art and Design Department, Winthrop University, 140 McLaurin, Rock Hill, South Carolina 29733; 803-323-2126, fax: 803-323-2323, E-mail address: johnsonm@winthrop.edu.

▼ WRIGHT STATE UNIVERSITY

Dayton, Ohio

State-supported, coed. Suburban campus. Total enrollment: 15,343. Art program established 1964.

Degrees Bachelor of Fine Arts. Majors and concentrations: painting, photography, printmaking, sculpture.

Enrollment Fall 1997: 113 total; 49 undergraduate, 64 non-professional degree.

Art Student Profile 65% females, 35% males, 12% minorities, 5% international.

Art Faculty 15 total (full-time and part-time). 100% of full-time faculty have terminal degrees. Graduate students do not teach undergraduate courses. Undergraduate student–faculty ratio: 12:1.

Expenses for 1997–98 Application fee: $30. State resident tuition: $3708 full-time. Nonresident tuition: $7416 full-time. College room and board: $4500. Room and board charges vary according to board plan and housing facility. Special program-related fees: $20–$100 per course for materials fee.

Financial Aid Program-specific awards for 1997: 10–20 Art Department Merit Scholarships for program majors ($1500).

Application Procedures Students apply for admission into the professional program by sophomore year. Deadline for freshmen and transfers: continuous. Required: high school transcript, college transcript(s) for transfer students, SAT I or ACT test scores.

Undergraduate Contact Dr. Linda Caron, Chair, Department of Art and Art History, Wright State University, Creative Arts Center A-226, Colonel Glenn Highway, Dayton, Ohio 45435; 937-775-2896, fax: 937-775-3049.

▼ XAVIER UNIVERSITY

Cincinnati, Ohio

Independent-Roman Catholic, coed. Suburban campus. Total enrollment: 6,504. Art program established 1988.

Degrees Bachelor of Fine Arts in the area of art; Bachelor of Arts in the area of art. Majors and concentrations: art education, art history, art/fine arts, ceramic art and design, graphic arts, painting/drawing, pre-art therapy, printmaking, sculpture, studio art, textile arts. Cross-registration with Greater Cincinnati Consortium of Colleges and Universities.

Enrollment Fall 1997: 55 undergraduate.

Art Student Profile 55% females, 45% males, 3% minorities, 3% international.

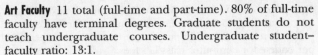

Art Faculty 11 total (full-time and part-time). 80% of full-time faculty have terminal degrees. Graduate students do not teach undergraduate courses. Undergraduate student–faculty ratio: 13:1.

Expenses for 1998–99 Application fee: $25. Comprehensive fee: $20,420 includes full-time tuition ($14,400), mandatory fees ($120), and college room and board ($5900). College room only: $3220. Full-time tuition and fees vary according to course load and program. Room and board charges vary according to board plan and housing facility. Special program-related fees: $20–$30 per semester for studio fees.

Financial Aid Program-specific awards for 1997: 3 McAuley Scholarships for incoming freshmen ($6475–$12,950).

Application Procedures Students apply for admission into the professional program by sophomore year. Deadline for freshmen: May 1; transfers: continuous. Required: high school transcript, college transcript(s) for transfer students, minimum 3.0 high school GPA, letter of recommendation, SAT I or ACT test scores, portfolio for scholarship consideration. Recommended: interview. Portfolio reviews held 4 times on campus; the submission of slides may be substituted for portfolios for scholarship consideration.

Undergraduate Contact Marsha Karagheusian, Chair, Department of Art, Xavier University, 3800 Victory Parkway, Cincinnati, Ohio 45207-7311; 513-745-3811, fax: 513-745-4301.

▼ YORK UNIVERSITY

North York, ON, Canada

Province-supported, coed. Urban campus. Total enrollment: 37,900. Art program established 1969.

Degrees Bachelor of Fine Arts in the area of visual arts. Majors and concentrations: design, drawing, new media, painting, photography, printmaking, sculpture. Graduate degrees offered: Master of Fine Arts in the area of visual arts.

Enrollment Fall 1997: 831 total; 755 undergraduate, 16 graduate, 60 non-professional degree.

Art Student Profile 70% females, 30% males, 5% international.

Art Faculty 62 total undergraduate and graduate (full-time and part-time). 60% of full-time faculty have terminal degrees. Graduate students teach a few undergraduate courses. Undergraduate student–faculty ratio: 13:1.

Student Life Student groups/activities include Visual Arts Student Council, Creative Arts Students Association.

Expenses for 1997–98 Application fee: $60 Canadian dollars. Tuition, fee, and room and board charges are reported in Canadian dollars. Canadian resident tuition: $3750 full-time. Full-time tuition varies according to course load, degree level, and program. College room and board: $5000. Room and board charges vary according to board plan and housing facility. International student tuition: $10,800 full-time. Special program-related fees: $20–$100 for lab fees for photography, sculpture, and printmaking.

Financial Aid Program-specific awards for 1997: 4 Talent Awards for applicants with outstanding portfolios ($1000), 1 International Talent Award for international applicants with outstanding portfolios ($2000), 1 Harry Rowe Bursary for demonstrated achievement or potential in artistic or scholarly work ($2000), 25 Fine Arts Bursary for academically qualified applicants demonstrating financial need ($250–$1500), 1 Ferdous Akhter Memorial Bursary for female sophomores, juniors or seniors, demonstrating need ($500), 5 Jack Bush Scholarships for those demonstrating merit in studio work ($800), 1 L.L. Odette Sculpture Scholarship for juniors or seniors showing excellence in sculpture ($500), 1 Carl Dair Memorial Scholarship for applicants demonstrating excellence in studio work ($300), 1 Elaine Newton/Alan Wilder Achievement Bursary for applicants with a minimum B average demonstrating need ($1000).

Application Procedures Students admitted directly into the professional program freshman year. Deadline for freshmen and transfers: March 1. Notification date for freshmen: June 30; transfers: July 15. Required: essay, high school transcript, college transcript(s) for transfer students, minimum 3.0 high school GPA, portfolio, SAT I, ACT or Canadian equivalent, interview for applicants within a reasonable distance. Recommended: 2 letters of recommendation. Portfolio reviews held once on campus; the submission of slides may be substituted for portfolios when distance is prohibitive or for large works of art.

Web Site http://www.yorku.ca/faculty/finearts/visa/.

Undergraduate Contact Mr. Don Murdoch, Liaison Officer, Liaison and Advising, Faculty of Fine Arts, York University, 213 CFA, 4700 Keele Street, Toronto, ON M3J 1P3, Canada; 416-736-5135, fax: 416-736-5447, E-mail address: donm@yorku.ca.

Graduate Contact Dr. Janet Jones, Graduate Director, Department of Visual Arts, York University, 232 CFA, 4700 Keele Street, Toronto, ON M3J 1P3, Canada; 416-736-5533, fax: 416-736-5875, E-mail address: jjones@yorku.ca.

More About the Department

Program Facilities York's Centre for Fine Arts is one of the largest and best-equipped teaching complexes of its kind in Canada, with dedicated space, facilities, and technical support staff for a wide variety of media. Extended studio access outside of regular class time is available, and, in some areas, upper-level students are given their own personal work stations. M.F.A. candidates are assigned their own private studio space. Additional resources include one of the largest art history slide collections in the country, a reference center dedicated to the study of sculpture, and a student-run art supply store.

Faculty York visual arts faculty members are among Canada's leading artists, designers, art educators, theorists, and historians. Their work can be found around the world in private and public collections such as the National Art Gallery in Ottawa and the Canadian Chancellory in Tokyo.

Exhibition Opportunities Students have ample opportunity to formally exhibit their work in any of the six student-run and two professionally staffed galleries on campus. Designers and multimedia artists make their work available on the Internet. The academic year regularly concludes with an Open House exhibition of the work of graduating students.

Special Programs Students benefit from being part of one of the largest faculties of fine arts in North America. Combined-degree programs are available with the Departments of Dance, Film & Video, Music, and Theatre and through an interdisciplinary program in fine arts cultural studies. Combined-degree programs are also available with the Faculties of Arts, Education, and Environmental Studies.

▼ YOUNGSTOWN STATE UNIVERSITY

Youngstown, Ohio

State-supported, coed. Urban campus. Total enrollment: 12,324. Art program established 1927.

Youngstown State University (*continued*)

Degrees Bachelor of Fine Arts in the areas of painting, photography, printmaking, spatial arts, studio arts, graphic design, art and technology. Program accredited by NASAD.

Enrollment Fall 1997: 330 total; 300 undergraduate, 30 non-professional degree.

Art Student Profile 50% females, 50% males, 8% minorities, 1% international.

Art Faculty 40 total (full-time and part-time). 90% of full-time faculty have terminal degrees. Graduate students do not teach undergraduate courses. Undergraduate student–faculty ratio: 12:1.

Student Life Student groups/activities include Student Art Association.

Expenses for 1997–98 Application fee: $25. State resident tuition: $2826 full-time. Nonresident tuition: $6609 full-time. Mandatory fees: $732 full-time. Full-time tuition and fees vary according to course load and reciprocity agreements.

College room and board: $4350. Room and board charges vary according to board plan and housing facility. Special program-related fees: $20 per course for studio lab fees, $35 per course for computer class lab fees.

Financial Aid Program-specific awards for 1997: 4 Beecher Talent Scholarships for freshmen ($1000).

Application Procedures Students admitted directly into the professional program freshman year. Deadline for freshmen and transfers: continuous. Required: high school transcript, college transcript(s) for transfer students, portfolio for scholarship consideration. Recommended: SAT I or ACT test scores. Portfolio reviews held once in April on campus; the submission of slides may be substituted for portfolios for large works of art.

Web Site http://cc.ysu.edu.

Undergraduate Contact Ms. Susan Russo, Chairperson, Department of Art, Youngstown State University, One University Plaza, Youngstown, Ohio 44555; 330-742-3627, fax: 330-742-7183, E-mail address: scrusso@cc.ysu.edu.

DANCE PROGRAMS

Dance programs differ greatly in terms of what is offered and what is required. Many colleges/universities offer one or two kinds of programs in dance: a Bachelor of Arts (B.A.), a Bachelor of Science (B.S.), and a Bachelor of Fine Arts (B.F.A.). These degrees are offered as part of the larger four-year university program.

For a B.A., students usually take 30–45 credits (out of a total of 120) in their major. These degrees offer a broad curriculum that emphasizes dance while the student pursues a general liberal arts education.

A university Bachelor of Fine Arts program is more specialized and often emphasizes professional training. It usually requires somewhere between 45 and 60 credits in the major as well as a general education component—some science, social science, humanities, and so on. In a B.F.A. program, more studio work is required than for a B.A. or B.S., and there is a more

---

REPORT FROM THE FIELD

Interview with dance teacher Penny Frank

Penny Frank, senior modern dance teacher at New York City's Fiorello H. La Guardia High School of Music and Art, is in her third decade of grooming young dancers for the future—for careers with professional dance companies as well as for college.

While admitting that she herself may never have finished college ("at that time we finished school because our parents said we had to,"), Frank thinks quite differently today. In light of fierce competition for jobs in a dwindling dance market, Frank now stresses the need for even her most talented students to complete their college education.

Beginning her freshman year at Sarah Lawrence College as a dance major, she ultimately graduated with a degree in literature—in part to please her parents, who did not support the idea of their daughter pursuing dance as her life's work . However, Frank—a relative late bloomer who had never taken a dance class until her freshman year in high school—had other ideas for her future.

Frank had a successful performance career with modern dance pioneer Martha Graham and numerous other companies, including Joyce Trisler's and the Juilliard Dance Theatre. When her grueling performance schedule became too much of a conflict with marriage and family, Frank focused exclusively on teaching her craft and today is one of the most respected dance educators in the country. She has garnered several awards along the way, including a Distinguished Teacher Award from the National Foundation for Advancement in the Arts in 1993, and three citations from the White House Commission on Presidential Scholars. She also was voted Outstanding Teacher by the Performing Arts School's parents association in 1995.

Awards and honors, however, don't give Frank as much satisfaction in her work as do the students who return year after year to thank her. "My pleasure and joy, my kind of self-reassurance that what I'm doing is right, is in the number of kids who succeed," she says. "It's a very profound relationship that occurs and it's based on what happens in the classroom."

Frank deplores what she calls the "lousy arts situation in this country," which has led to the relocation of many American dancers to Europe and elsewhere overseas, where jobs are more plentiful. At the same time, she says that the current arts climate has allowed numerous quality regional dance companies to grow and develop and that this bodes well for young dancers. "The facilities and funds are there and available for the regional companies. Regional audiences are much more educated and sophisticated than before. There are careers to be had that do not necessitate [working in a] city."

Even so, regardless of a student's talent or desire, Frank advises the majority of her dancers to pursue a college degree just as seriously as a professional dance career. "I do feel very strongly, more than I used to, about getting a degree. Those who were very gifted I used to encourage to go into the field right away. Now you must think in terms of going to school; with the state of the arts situation in this country, you must have something to fall back on."

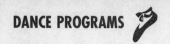

HOW DO YOU KNOW A PROGRAM IS RIGHT FOR YOU?

With all the dance programs described in this guide, how will you choose the one that will be best for you? The key is to think of the school search as a research project and start asking questions. Here's our list of the ones you'll want to ask:

- What is the focus of the program? Is this program going to help get you where you want to go? For example, some programs focus exclusively on modern dance, others primarily on ballet, and still others on both. It's important to understand that there are differences and to inquire about them.
- What kinds of classes are offered? What are the requirements, outside of dance? How many technique classes will you have each week? How does the program determine in which technique class students will be?
- Find out which repertory you'll perform. Will the works of students, faculty, or guest artists be included? Major American and international choreographers?
- How much performing will you be able to do? How are performers selected?
- Is a final project required? It is very important for students to do a senior project that synthesizes and pulls together their four years of education.
- How many professional companies come to the school or a nearby venue that you will be able to see?
- Does the program feature guest artists, artists-in-residence, or industry visitors so you can meet practicing professionals and learn the latest theories and techniques? How long do they stay on campus? Do they give lectures, teach classes, or offer workshops? Do they work with all students or advanced students only?
- Does the program allow time off for professional leave or internships?
- What kind of facilities are available to you? Is there adequate rehearsal space? Is the equipment state-of-the-art?
- How large is the school or university? How many people are in the program in which you're interested? What's the student-faculty ratio in your area of study?
- Who is on the faculty? Are faculty members practicing in their field?
- Are alumni of the program working in their chosen field? If most of the alumni of a performance program are teaching instead of performing, this tells you something. Speak to some alumni of the program, if possible, to find out how they feel about their experiences.
- What kind of placement help does the program or school offer?

stringent process of leveling—that is, putting students in classes based on their level of ability. The advanced class will be much more rigorous, and the school's performing group is usually chosen from the B.F.A. students (although some schools also audition B.A. students). B.F.A. programs usually require students to complete a senior project in their area of specialization.

Many B.F.A. programs have a very defined focus. It may be performance, the physiology of movement, dance notation, or the body sciences (such as the Alexander technique). Some schools emphasize learning something about all kinds of dance—jazz, tap, ethnic, modern, ballet, and more—and others concentrate on just one or two types.

The B.F.A. programs in some schools are set up as conservatory programs offering professional training in different performing arts (such as dance, music, theater, and film) as well as visual arts. These schools

for the arts are accredited degree-granting institutions that may or may not be part of a larger university. They require that about 90 of the 120 required credits be taken in the professional field. These conservatory dance programs primarily focus on ballet and modern dance.

Evaluating Programs and Your Goals

If you think you want to be a performer, audition for B.F.A. programs. Whether you are accepted is one of the very first steps to finding out whether your professional goals are realistic. You might also get guidance from your own dance teachers, who know about how you work and something about the range of differences that exist in the various B.F.A. programs. If you have the passion to become a professional performer, as well as positive evaluations by your current teachers and successful auditions for major

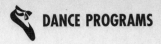

performing institutions, a B.F.A. program may be the route you wish to pursue. If a dance program is doing its job, it will evaluate students and their potential honestly and help them make this decision.

Dance requires commitment at a very young age. If you are interested in becoming a performing artist, you must begin the process now. Choose a school where you have opportunities to go in the direction you wish to pursue. Once you are accepted at such a school, it is your daily and annual progress, initiative, and ability to absorb the technique and the connections between all of these courses that will help you to succeed.

At the end of their junior year of high school, students interested in pursuing a dance career should participate in a top-flight summer program and have their potential to become a professional assessed. In the ballet world, fewer dancers have degrees. In the modern dance world, more dancers have degrees. Most have attended at least a couple of years of school because it allows them to work in a professional training program where everything is in one place, progressively and sequentially organized—access to studios, musicians who accompany class, a curriculum that surrounds the studio work, ongoing evaluation by the faculty—rather than having to go from studio to studio putting together a schedule of classes on their own.

The Admissions Process: B.A. and B.F.A. Programs

For most B.A. programs, students apply through the office of admissions to be accepted by the university or the college. The procedure would be the same as that for any other discipline—there aren't any special criteria. When you get there, you will go to the dance department and enroll in classes. Every department has its own standards in accepting majors. Some let you declare yourself a major right away, some require the student to wait two years, and sometimes you must go through a pre–dance curriculum for a year.

Admission procedures for university B.F.A. programs vary. Some schools use the process just described—you're admitted to the university, and then you enter the dance department. (In some schools you eventually have to audition to become a major.) Others have a dual admission process—you have to audition to be accepted into the program, and you must be accepted by the university as well.

Auditions

The audition process itself usually includes taking one technique class (sometimes two) in ballet and/or modern dance. Some schools may also require a performance, a showing of your choreographic work, improvisations, an essay, and/or an interview. Every school has a different combination. You must be able to demonstrate how much training you have had, your ability to take correction, and your ability to phrase musically.

There is usually a panel of dance faculty members who judge the students. How much weight the audition carries depends on the program. For the performance-oriented programs, the admissions officers go out and talk to students and distribute or collect material, but it is usually the dance faculty that makes the admission determination. Most schools will try, if possible, to have U.S. students come to campus for an audition; many schools travel around and either hold regional auditions or attend various high school dance festivals to look at students. Most (but not all) schools accept videotapes from international students or from those who can't afford to travel; each school has its own requirements for videotapes. It is very important for students to find out what each school requires. If you can possibly audition in person, it is by far the best choice.

There are a few factors that schools—conservatory and B.F.A. programs in particular—consider when they look at dancers: What are your physical proportions? How fit are you? Are you injury-free?

For more tips on what to expect at a dance audition, see the "Words of Wisdom" column within this article.

Contacts and Networking

If you are in the performance field, it's a distinct handicap to attend a college or university where you don't have an opportunity to see professional companies perform and to take classes and interact with professional dancers. It is a great advantage to be near a major metropolitan area. If you are not, try to get there during the summer.

There are schools that do a very good job of developing a network, especially through faculty members. And there are pockets outside of New York—in Utah, California, Arizona, and Texas, for example—where a lot of networking is going on.

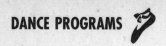

Performance Majors and Internships

Some companies have apprentices chosen solely by company audition. Usually apprenticeships are not arranged by the school—the student must take the initiative. In many cases students will take a leave of absence from school to work with a professional company. In a few instances, apprenticeships may be incorporated into the program of study. In administration, an internship may be required as part of the degree program.

Career Paths After Performance Programs

Most students begin their careers by auditioning for companies immediately following graduation. Very lucky students will already have something by the time they graduate. In the dance world, as in theater and music, there is very intense competition for jobs.

Many students have fears about choosing a performing career. Some worry about having their careers cut short by injuries. Fortunately, this does not happen frequently today because many medical procedures for care and prevention now exist. Others may believe that their dance career will be over in ten years. This is also a misconception. Some ballerinas have been performing with the same company for twenty or twenty-five years. Longevity is no longer the issue it used to be.

When there are an abundance of companies and a diversity of techniques and styles in one area, there are many more options. In areas with only a few companies, a student's job prospects depend largely on whether a company has vacancies. Since dance is such a dynamic profession, dancers must be flexible in terms of going where the jobs are—and that means around the world, not only in the United States.

Options for Performance Graduates

In addition to performing or while they are preparing for a performing career, some graduates produce their own concerts—they find space, make a budget, choreograph a work, and select their dancers. Dancers can work for arts councils, in the box office in performing spaces, or as assistant managers in dance companies in exchange for taking classes. Some have opened their own schools or founded their own companies.

Beyond that, performance majors who have a degree can do practically anything. Studying the arts is one of the best preparations for the rest of life because students learn how to evaluate themselves, meet deadlines, develop a sense of responsibility, work with groups, develop skills in creative thinking and "thinking on their feet," and locate information that they need. Performance students also have degrees—they've learned how to write papers, they speak well—they have acquired various skills outside of dance. Depending on your area of specialization in dance, many other career options are available. Arts administration and dance production (lighting and costuming) are two popular areas right now. In numerous areas—history, notation, sports medicine, dance ethnology (documenting dances indigenous to different cultures), dance or movement therapy, and body therapies—a master's degree or the equivalent is usually required. In the field of dance history, there are quite a few part-time jobs available at universities, but there are very few full-time jobs. Some of these positions will require a Ph.D. If you get a teacher's certification as part of your undergraduate work, that entitles you to teach in the public school system. If you want to proceed in the educational world, you should have a professional performing career. Some university positions require this as well as an M.F.A. degree to qualify as a faculty member. Conservatory programs primarily hire professionals of the highest caliber in dance, choreography, music, history, and other fields. To open your own studio, you need initiative, knowledge of dance training, and administrative skills.

WORDS OF WISDOM

Dance Audition Advice

- Dance auditions are often "dog eat dog;" the competition is very stiff. There may be a large panel of judges or only a few. Be prepared for either situation.
- Be noticed for positive attention. Be aggressive to the point of becoming noticeable; however, don't go to the other extreme and become aggressive to the point of becoming obnoxious.
- Your behavior is as important as your technique. Be a team player.
- Be sure to ask about the dress code for auditions.

▼ Arizona State University

Tempe, Arizona

State-supported, coed. Suburban campus. Total enrollment: 44,255.

Degrees Bachelor of Fine Arts in the areas of dance, dance education. Majors and concentrations: choreography and performance, dance education. Graduate degrees offered: Master of Fine Arts in the area of dance.

Enrollment Fall 1997: 147 total; 127 undergraduate, 20 graduate.

Dance Student Profile 92% females, 8% males, 2% minorities, 3% international.

Dance Faculty 16 total undergraduate and graduate (full-time and part-time). 67% of full-time faculty have terminal degrees. Graduate students teach more than half undergraduate courses. Undergraduate student–faculty ratio: 16:1.

Student Life Student groups/activities include Dance Arizona Repertory Theatre.

Expenses for 1997–98 Application fee: $40 for nonresidents. State resident tuition: $1988 full-time. Nonresident tuition: $8640 full-time. Mandatory fees: $71 full-time. College room and board: $4500. College room only: $2700. Room and board charges vary according to board plan and housing facility.

Financial Aid Program-specific awards for 1997: 10 in-state tuition scholarships for those demonstrating need/talent ($994), 5 Friends of Dance Scholarships for those demonstrating need/talent ($800), 1 Sun Angel Scholarship for those demonstrating need/talent ($1000), 8 out-of-state tuition scholarships for those demonstrating need/talent ($3326).

Application Procedures Students apply for admission into the professional program by sophomore year. Deadline for freshmen and transfers: continuous. Required: high school transcript, college transcript(s) for transfer students, minimum 2.0 high school GPA, SAT I or ACT test scores. Recommended: minimum 3.0 high school GPA.

Undergraduate Contact Ms. Rose Welsh, Undergraduate Advisor, Dance Department, Arizona State University, PO Box 870304, Tempe, Arizona 85287-0304; 602-965-6807, fax: 602-965-2247, E-mail address: rwelsh@asuvm.inre.asu.edu.

Graduate Contact Ms. Ann Ludwig, Graduate Advisor, Dance Department, Arizona State University, PO Box 870304, Tempe, Arizona 85287-0304; 602-965-5029, fax: 602-965-2247, E-mail address: icabl@asuvm.inre.asu.edu.

▼ Barat College

Lake Forest, Illinois

Independent-Roman Catholic, coed. Suburban campus. Total enrollment: 749. Dance program established 1970.

Degrees Bachelor of Fine Arts in the area of performance and choreography. Majors and concentrations: ballet, modern dance. Cross-registration with Lake Forest College.

Enrollment Fall 1997: 240 total; 40 undergraduate, 200 non-professional degree.

Dance Student Profile 85% females, 15% males, 30% minorities, 5% international.

Dance Faculty 14 total (full-time and part-time). 100% of full-time faculty have terminal degrees. Graduate students do not teach undergraduate courses. Undergraduate student–faculty ratio: 10:1.

Student Life Student groups/activities include The Repertory Dance Company, Choreographers Showcase, "Dance Chicago" festival. Special housing available for dance students.

Expenses for 1997–98 Application fee: $20. Comprehensive fee: $17,536 includes full-time tuition ($12,570) and college room and board ($4966). Full-time tuition varies according to course load.

Financial Aid Program-specific awards for 1997: 8–10 Dance Talent Awards for dance majors ($2500–$5000).

Application Procedures Students apply for admission into the professional program by sophomore year. Deadline for freshmen and transfers: continuous. Required: essay, high school transcript, college transcript(s) for transfer students, minimum 2.0 high school GPA, 2 letters of recommendation, audition, SAT I or ACT test scores, minimum 2.0 college GPA for transfer students. Recommended: minimum 3.0 high school GPA. Auditions held 4 times and by appointment on campus; videotaped performances are permissible as a substitute for live auditions if a campus visit is impossible.

Undergraduate Contact Mr. Doug Schacke, Admissions Office, Barat College, 700 East Westleigh Road, Lake Forest, Illinois 60045; 847-295-4260, fax: 847-604-6300.

▼ Boston Conservatory

Boston, Massachusetts

Independent, coed. Urban campus. Total enrollment: 501. Dance program established 1943.

Degrees Bachelor of Fine Arts in the area of dance. Graduate degrees offered: Master of Fine Arts in the areas of performance, choreography. Cross-registration with Emerson College, Massachusetts College of Art, Berklee College of Music, Boston Architectural Center, School of the Museum of Fine Arts.

Enrollment Fall 1997: 59 undergraduate, 6 graduate.

Dance Student Profile 85% females, 15% males, 25% minorities, 27% international.

Dance Faculty 30 total undergraduate and graduate (full-time and part-time). Graduate students teach a few undergraduate courses. Undergraduate student–faculty ratio: 2:1.

Student Life Student groups/activities include Boston Dance Theater. Special housing available for dance students.

Expenses for 1997–98 Application fee: $60. Comprehensive fee: $23,075 includes full-time tuition ($15,300), mandatory fees ($625), and college room and board ($7150). Full-time tuition and fees vary according to course load, degree level, and program.

Financial Aid Program-specific awards for 1997: 44 Conservatory Scholarships for those passing audition evaluations ($7000), 5 Jan Veen Memorial Scholarships for continuing students ($2000), 1 Ruth S. Ambrose Award for juniors ($3000).

Application Procedures Students admitted directly into the professional program freshman year. Deadline for freshmen and transfers: continuous. Notification date for freshmen and transfers: September 1. Required: essay, high school transcript, college transcript(s) for transfer students, 3 letters of recommendation, interview, audition, minimum 2.7 high school GPA. Recommended: video, SAT I or ACT test scores. Auditions held 10 times on campus and off campus in St. Petersburg, FL; Washington, DC; San Diego, CA; Los Angeles, CA; Dallas, TX; Houston, TX; San Francisco, CA; videotaped performances are permissible as a substitute for live auditions when distance is prohibitive.

Boston Conservatory (*continued*)

Contact Mr. Richard Wallace, Director of Admissions, Boston Conservatory, 8 The Fenway, Boston, Massachusetts 02215; 617-536-6340 ext. 9153, fax: 617-536-3176, E-mail address: admissions@bostonconservatory.edu.

More About the Conservatory

Program Facilities Five dance studios plus annex studios, Mainstage Proscenium arch theater (400 seats), Seully Hall (200 seats), costume shop, computer lab (Apple), library of 60,000 volumes and scores, and interlibrary loan availability with college network of Boston.

Faculty and Alumni Professional artist faculty represents all styles of dance and teaching methods. Alumni can be seen in professional dance companies in the United States and Europe, Broadway companies, industrials, and television.

Student Performance Opportunities Three mainstage concerts yearly, studio recitals (various), student choreographed recitals, road company performances in greater Boston area, guest appearances with Boston Pops and Boston Symphony Open House.

Special Programs Gig office providing performance opportunities throughout the greater Boston area, career seminar series, counseling and health services, international student ESL classes/orientation program, academic year ESL course work, and tutorial assistance.

▼

The Boston Conservatory, founded in 1867, is one of the oldest colleges offering training to serious students of the performing arts. The three divisions of the college—Music, Dance, and Theater—take full advantage of the wealth of cultural and academic offerings Boston has to offer. Guest artists, master classes, performance opportunities, and professional contacts and networking are provided to all students of the college. These experiences seek to ensure that each student receives a varied and professional level of education to augment the intensive study of the prescribed curriculum.

The Boston Conservatory Dance Division is the oldest degree-granting dance program in the United States. Founded in 1943 by the dance innovator and teacher, Jan Veen, the Dance Division was the first to offer ballet and modern training as a core curriculum of study. This tradition continues today with additional study in all styles of dance performance.

Daily technique classes provide professional training in ballet and modern dance. In addition, dancers study choreography, pedagogy, music, laban, jazz, tap, and ethnic dance styles.

Versatility for a dancer translates into work and performance opportunities; therefore, the Boston Conservatory curriculum requires students to extend themselves and be knowledgeable about music, literature, dance repertory, danced history, and anatomy. To support the inner dancer, seminars in health and nutrition are scheduled throughout the academic year.

Faculty members are current or former members of some of the most prestigious dance organizations in the United States. Their artistry and professional qualifications offer students a full range of dance technique and teaching methods. Faculty members serve as mentors to a core of dancers, forming a nurturing and supportive relationship. Students are thus able to grow and achieve their dreams within a caring, artistic environment.

Performance experience is provided in both studio and mainstage concerts. The range of work performed runs the gamut of dance repertory, in addition to frequent premieres of new works choreographed by artist faculty members or commissioned by the school. Mainstage concerts are held in collaboration with the Music Division, offering a unique opportunity to interact with musicians as part of the performance preparation.

Boston is a major center of higher education in America, with more than fifty major colleges and universities. This provides a diverse student population and an endless array of courses, lectures, concerts, and social opportunities. The Conservatory is in the Pro-Arts Consortium with five area colleges (Emerson College, Berklee College of Music, Museum School, Massachusetts College of Art, and Boston Architectural Center), which offers extensive cross-registration course possibilities to all students.

On-campus housing is provided to all interested students, offering brownstone-style living accommodations just a few steps from the main training and rehearsal buildings. For those students interested in off-campus housing, Boston offers a wide range of architectural styles and rent prices in neighborhoods throughout the city, which are all within easy access to the school by public transportation.

The Boston Conservatory strives to meet each student's needs, musically and personally, and provides a nurturing, safe environment in which to study, learn, and grow. The supportive atmosphere of the college extends to student life areas as well. More than a dozen special interest groups and organizations exist on campus, with new ones developing constantly as the student population grows and needs change. As part of the student services, a number of career seminars are given each year ranging from resume writing and audition anxiety to grant writing and tax laws for the performing artist. In addition, there is an active student government and a student-run newspaper.

▼ BRENAU UNIVERSITY

Gainesville, Georgia

Independent, primarily women. Small town campus. Total enrollment: 2,366. Dance program established 1978.

Degrees Bachelor of Fine Arts in the areas of arts management, dance pedagogy, dance performance, dance education. Majors and concentrations: dance education, pedagogy, performance.

Enrollment Fall 1997: 39 total; 30 undergraduate, 9 nonprofessional degree.

Dance Student Profile 100% females, 20% minorities, 6% international.

Dance Faculty 4 total (full-time and part-time). 100% of full-time faculty have terminal degrees. Graduate students do not teach undergraduate courses. Undergraduate student–faculty ratio: 10:1.

Student Life Student groups/activities include Tau Sigma, Brenau Opera Company, Gainesville Theatre Alliance.

Expenses for 1997–98 Application fee: $30. Comprehensive fee: $17,350 includes full-time tuition ($10,740) and college room and board ($6610).

Financial Aid Program-specific awards for 1997: dance scholarships for program majors ($1000–$3000).

Application Procedures Students admitted directly into the professional program freshman year. Deadline for freshmen and transfers: continuous. Notification date for freshmen and transfers: continuous. Required: high school transcript, letter of recommendation, audition, SAT I or ACT test scores (minimum combined SAT I score of 900, minimum combined ACT score of 19), minimum 2.5 high school GPA. Recommended: minimum 3.0 high school GPA, interview. Auditions held 3 times on campus; videotaped performances are permissible as a substitute for live auditions when distance is prohibitive.

Undergraduate Contact Dr. John D. Upchurch, Dean of Admissions, Brenau University, One Centennial Circle, Gainesville, Georgia 30501; 800-252-5119, fax: 770-538-4306.

Jordan College of Fine Arts

▼ BUTLER UNIVERSITY

Indianapolis, Indiana

Independent, coed. Urban campus. Total enrollment: 3,911. Dance program established 1913.

Degrees Bachelor of Fine Arts in the area of dance performance. Majors and concentrations: ballet, dance. Cross-registration with Consortium for Urban Education. Program accredited by NASD.

Enrollment Fall 1997: 225 total; 100 undergraduate, 125 non-professional degree.

Dance Student Profile 88% females, 12% males, 9% minorities, 4% international.

Dance Faculty 12 total (full-time and part-time). 50% of full-time faculty have terminal degrees. Graduate students do not teach undergraduate courses. Undergraduate student–faculty ratio: 10:1.

Student Life Student groups/activities include Butler Ballet, senior production concerts, summer dance concert.

Expenses for 1997–98 Application fee: $25. Comprehensive fee: $21,120 includes full-time tuition ($15,570), mandatory fees ($120), and college room and board ($5430). Full-time tuition and fees vary according to program. Room and board charges vary according to board plan and housing facility.

Financial Aid Program-specific awards for 1997: 8–12 Talent Awards for freshmen ($2000–$10,000).

Application Procedures Students admitted directly into the professional program freshman year. Deadline for freshmen and transfers: April 15. Notification date for freshmen and transfers: August 20. Required: essay, high school transcript, college transcript(s) for transfer students, minimum 2.0 high school GPA, SAT I or ACT test scores, audition in ballet. Recommended: minimum 3.0 high school GPA. Auditions held 23 times on campus and off campus in Hartford, CT; Miami, FL; San Francisco, CA; St. Petersburg, FL; Los Angeles, CA; New York, NY; videotaped performances are permissible as a substitute for live auditions for international applicants.

Web Site http://butler.edu/dance/.

Undergraduate Contact Ms. Maggie Hayworth, Admissions Secretary, Jordan College of Fine Arts, Butler University, 4600 Sunset Avenue, Indianapolis, Indiana 46208; 317-940-9656, fax: 317-940-9658, E-mail address: mhayworth@thomas.butler.edu.

More About the College

Program Facilities Because computers play an increasingly important role for Butler fine arts majors, a computer lab especially for fine arts students is located in Lilly Hall. Clowes Memorial Hall, a 2,200-seat multifaceted performing arts center, the hub of the performing arts at Butler, offers its own season of varied performing arts events. Dance studios and rehearsal space are state-of-the-art, with resilient flooring designed to meet the specific needs of dancers. Most of the works produced by the theater department take place in Butler's Studio Theatre, a large black box theater located in Lilly Hall, the University's performing arts complex, or in a small proscenium theater in Robertson Hall. Additional facilities include a rehearsal room, which serves as a studio classroom for courses in acting and directing; a costume shop; a scenery studio; and a makeup room. Butler operates WTBU-TV Channel 69, a full-power educational television station affiliated with the Corporation for Public Broadcasting. The department also operates a radio station, WRBU, a campus-limited station serving the Butler community.

Faculty and Resident Artists Faculty-in-Residence: Panayis Lyras, artist-in-residence (piano); Laurence Shapiro, artist-in-residence (violin); Michael Schelle, composer-in-residence, Pulitzer Price nominee (composition).

Student Performance Opportunities The Butler Ballet, a pre-professional company, performs a full season with a number of local professional music organizations, notably the Indianapolis Chamber Orchestra. Past performances of full-length classical ballets include *Swan Lake, The Sleeping Beauty, Cinderella*, and an annual performance of *The Nutcracker* that draws more than 15,000 patrons a year. Butler's instrumental and vocal groups—18 in all—perform professional-level works for campus concerts in Clowes Memorial Hall. Freshman through seniors join together to perform popular annual events such as the "Rejoice!" concert, the Butler Symphony Orchestra's Halloween concert, and the student concerto competition. Theater students are encouraged to write, produce, and direct works of their own choice in the department's laboratory theater. As many as twenty-six student productions have been presented in one year. Most of the faculty-produced works are performed by students in a large black box theater.

Special Programs Each year students take advantage of Butler's opportunities abroad. Dancers can spend a semester at an institution such as the Laban Center or Middlesex University in London, the Centre de Danse in Cannes, France, or the Vaganova Academy in St. Petersburg, Russia. The dancers traveled to Taipei, Taiwan, in the summer of 1997 to perform in conjunction with the Su-Hwei-Suh Ballet Company as part of a cultural exchange program. Music opportunities for performance touring and study abroad give students valuable exposure to the music and cultures of the world.

▼

Butler University's Jordan College of Fine Arts (JCFA) continues a 100-year tradition of educating students as emerging professionals in the arts. JCFA has established its educational tradition in the arts through a dynamic faculty, creative and talented students from around the nation, and outstanding facilities, including Clowes Memorial Hall, a 2,200-seat multifaceted performing arts center. The Butler Ballet, Butler Symphony Orchestra, Symphonic Band and Wind Ensemble, Chorale, Jazz Ensemble, and Jordan Jazz Singers perform annually in Clowes Memorial Hall and enjoy the benefits of professional stagehands and box office staff members.

As freshmen, students are admitted to JCFA and make the transition into the academic area of their choice with a wide range of programs within the Departments of Dance, Music, Theatre, and Telecommunication Arts. Programs in these areas include arts administration, dance/pedagogy concen-

Butler University (*continued*)

tration, dance performance, music, music business, music education, music performance, music theory and composition, performing arts, piano pedagogy, telecommunication arts, theater performance, and theater/pedagogy concentration.

The Department of Dance is counted among the nation's leading dance schools. Butler dance alumni are currently with the Boston Ballet, Paris Opera Ballet, and Joffrey Ballet; in Broadway shows; and on the faculty of leading dance departments and studios around the country. Among the first in the nation to offer a university dance program centered on classical ballet technique, Butler continues to offer professional-level training combined with a liberal arts education. In addition, faculty members of the Department of Dance are highly qualified artists whose range of experience contributes to the diversity of the dance program. With rigorous classes in dance studios, theoretical studies, and a strong choreography program, the serious dance student is prepared for a professional career in dance.

Within the Department of Music, Butler offers extensive programs in both instrumental and vocal music. All students have the opportunity to study one-on-one with recognized artist-teachers who teach throughout the music curriculum, including the freshman year. The highly diversified music faculty, mixed with a wide range of curricular offerings, attracts students in the performance areas of voice, piano, orchestral instruments, organ, guitar, piano pedagogy, conducting, music education, music theory, and composition. In addition, students may request a specific instructor for their private study, and freshmen often have more contact with their primary teacher than any other faculty member.

The Department of Theatre offers programs in performance, technical theater, arts administration, theater pedagogy, and theater studies. Faculty members within the theater department have extensive experience, and the performance faculty members maintain active professional careers. In addition to classroom study, theater majors are required to have firsthand experience creating theater, since all students are required to audition and accept crew assignments for all major productions. The department produces at least four faculty-directed shows each year. Some of the past productions have included *Oh Coward!*, *Noises Off*, *Hedda Gabler*, *Oklahoma*, *Over a Glass of Wine*, *Equus*, *1959 Pink Thunderbird*, and *A Midsummer Night's Dream*. Additional productions during the year give juniors and seniors valuable directing experience and give faculty the opportunity to present works in progress.

The Department of Telecommunication Arts offers students hands-on experience in electronic media production, management, and news. With a television station and radio station owned and operated by Butler, students may begin work in video and audio as early as their freshman year. Telecommunication Arts operates WTBU-TV Channel 69, a full-power educational television station, which airs many student-produced programs. WTBU-TV is also affiliated with the Corporation for Public Broadcasting and is carried by most cable systems in central Indiana. In addition, students have access to professional studios and remote production equipment, including a live remote truck. Students learn audio production using new digital workstations that harness computer technology and spend 360 hours on the job, as part of the department's internship program, at a broadcast, cable, or other telecommunications facility in a major-market city. Indianapolis has network affiliate, independent, and

public television stations and is the twenty-sixth-largest television market in the nation. In addition, Indianapolis is home to twenty-two radio stations and various production facilities.

The performing arts are a vital part of the Indianapolis community, and the city is developing its niche as a growing arts center. JCFA enjoys a cooperative relationship with the Indianapolis arts community, including the American Pianists Association, the Indianapolis Chamber Orchestra, and the Indianapolis Opera.

Butler University is an independent, coeducational, nonsectarian university with a total enrollment of about 4,000 students. Students at Butler are exposed to both breadth and depth in academic programs, and a core curriculum encourages students to gain a broad knowledge in government, the arts, social sciences, natural sciences, humanities, and mathematics. Butler students can take advantage of more than 100 different activities, which include but are not limited to social groups, service clubs, honorary societies, performance groups, fraternities and sororities, intramural sports, and varsity teams.

▼ CALIFORNIA INSTITUTE OF THE ARTS

Valencia, California

Independent, coed. Suburban campus. Total enrollment: 1,140. Dance program established 1971.

Degrees Bachelor of Fine Arts in the area of dance. Graduate degrees offered: Master of Fine Arts in the areas of dance, integrated media. Program accredited by NASD.

Enrollment Fall 1997: 66 total; 54 undergraduate, 10 graduate, 2 non-professional degree.

Dance Student Profile 91% females, 9% males, 13% minorities, 21% international.

Dance Faculty 13 total undergraduate and graduate (full-time and part-time). 100% of full-time faculty have terminal degrees. Graduate students do not teach undergraduate courses. Undergraduate student–faculty ratio: 6:1.

Student Life Student groups/activities include American College Dance Festival Association. Special housing available for dance students.

Expenses for 1998–99 Application fee: $60. Tuition: $18,120 full-time. Mandatory fees: $65 full-time. College room only: $2800. Room charges vary according to housing facility.

Financial Aid Program-specific awards for 1997: 30–35 Sharon Lund Scholarships for program majors ($2000–$10,000).

Application Procedures Deadline for freshmen and transfers: September 2. Required: essay, high school transcript, college transcript(s) for transfer students, audition. Auditions held 15 times on campus and off campus in New York, NY; Baltimore, MD; Dallas, TX; Houston, TX; Atlanta, GA; San Francisco, CA; Chicago, IL; Minneapolis, MN; Portland,OR; San Diego, CA; Seattle, WA; videotaped performances are permissible as a substitute for live auditions with approval from the department and for international students.

Contact Mr. Stuart Horn, Admissions Officer, California Institute of the Arts, 24700 McBean Parkway, Valencia, California 91355; 805-255-1050.

More About the Institute

Program Facilities CalArts is a community of approximately 1,000 performing artists, visual artists, and writers located in the suburban hills north of Los Angeles. The college was incorporated in 1961 through the vision and generosity of

Walt Disney. CalArts has been at its present 60-acre campus since 1971. On the campus are the main artistic/academic building, sound stages, rehearsal spaces, art studios, recreational facilities and two residence halls. At the undergraduate level in dance, CalArts offers a B.F.A. degree designed to enable dancers to exist as choreographer/performer/producers. Each dancer is expected to make satisfactory progress in all aspects of the total program. The School of Dance requires that all students enroll in modern and ballet technique classes every semester. Admission is based on talent. Auditions are conducted each winter in major cities in the United States.

Faculty, Resident Artists, and Alumni Contact the admissions office for a free copy of the current admissions bulletin for complete and up-to-date biographies of all faculty members along with lists of alumni and visiting artists.

Special Programs The Community Arts Partnership links CalArts students and faculty members with high school and junior high school students in Watts, East Los Angeles, Pasadena, Santa Clarita, Hollywood, and Venice. The program enables CalArts students to teach, learn, and share their talents in community settings. Other special programs include exchanges with universities in other countries as well as internships at companies and nonprofit organizations throughout southern California. Each spring the placement professionals in the Office of Student Affairs host a series of job fairs attended by companies well known in the world of entertainment and the arts.

▼ CALIFORNIA STATE UNIVERSITY, LONG BEACH

Long Beach, California

State-supported, coed. Suburban campus. Total enrollment: 27,809.

Degrees Bachelor of Fine Arts in the area of dance. Graduate degrees offered: Master of Fine Arts in the area of dance: performance and/or choreography. Program accredited by NASD.

Enrollment Fall 1997: 624 total; 120 undergraduate, 4 graduate, 500 non-professional degree.

Dance Student Profile 85% females, 15% males, 25% minorities, 10% international.

Dance Faculty 22 total undergraduate and graduate (full-time and part-time). 50% of full-time faculty have terminal degrees. Graduate students do not teach undergraduate courses. Undergraduate student–faculty ratio: 15:1.

Student Life Student groups/activities include Off 7th Dancers.

Expenses for 1997–98 Application fee: $55. State resident tuition: $0 full-time. Nonresident tuition: $7380 full-time. Mandatory fees: $1846 full-time. Full-time tuition and fees vary according to course load. College room and board: $5200. Room and board charges vary according to board plan.

Financial Aid Program-specific awards for 1997: 1 Fine Arts Affiliates Award for program majors ($1000), 1 Dramatic Allied Arts Guild Award for program majors ($1000), 10–15 Adopt-A-Dancer Scholarships for all dancers demonstrating need ($200–$500), 2 Rotating Awards for program majors ($1000–$1200), 1 Lana Alper Award for program majors ($2000).

Application Procedures Students admitted directly into the professional program freshman year. Deadline for freshmen: March 15; transfers: June 1. Required: high school transcript, college transcript(s) for transfer students, minimum 2.0 high school GPA, audition, SAT I or ACT test scores. Auditions held 4 times on campus; videotaped performances are permissible as a substitute for live auditions for out-of-state and international applicants.

Web Site http://www.csulb.edu/~dance.

Undergraduate Contact Tryntje Shapli, Professor/ BFA Advisor, California State University, Long Beach, 1250 Bellflower Boulevard, Long Beach, California 90840; 562-985-4747, fax: 562-985-7896.

Graduate Contact Ms. Judith Allen, Chair, Department of Dance, California State University, Long Beach, 1250 Bellflower Boulevard, Long Beach, California 90840; 562-985-4747, fax: 562-985-7896.

▼ CHAPMAN UNIVERSITY

Orange, California

Independent, coed. Suburban campus. Total enrollment: 3,806.

Degrees Bachelor of Fine Arts in the areas of dance performance, dance theater. Majors and concentrations: dance performance, dance theater.

Enrollment Fall 1997: 50 undergraduate.

Dance Student Profile 65% females, 35% males, 36% minorities, 4% international.

Dance Faculty 10 total (full-time and part-time). 100% of full-time faculty have terminal degrees. Graduate students do not teach undergraduate courses. Undergraduate student–faculty ratio: 10:1.

Student Life Student groups/activities include Orange County Choreographers Showcase, American Celebration, Performing Arts Society of Chapman.

Expenses for 1997–98 Application fee: $30. Comprehensive fee: $25,556 includes full-time tuition ($18,510), mandatory fees ($240), and college room and board ($6806). Room and board charges vary according to board plan and housing facility.

Financial Aid Program-specific awards for 1997: 20 Talent Awards for incoming students ($10,000).

Application Procedures Students admitted directly into the professional program freshman year. Deadline for freshmen and transfers: continuous. Required: high school transcript, college transcript(s) for transfer students, minimum 2.0 high school GPA, 2 letters of recommendation, audition. Recommended: essay, interview. Auditions held twice on campus; videotaped performances are permissible as a substitute for live auditions with permission of the program director.

Web Site http://www.chapman.edu/comm/td/.

Undergraduate Contact Mr. Cyrus Parker-Jeannette, Dance Director, Theatre and Dance Department, Chapman University, 333 North Glassell Street, Orange, California 92666; 714-744-7839, fax: 714-997-6700, E-mail address: cyparker@chapman.edu.

▼ COLUMBIA COLLEGE

Columbia, South Carolina

Independent-United Methodist, women only. Suburban campus. Total enrollment: 1,368. Dance program established 1986.

Columbia College *(continued)*

Degrees Bachelor of Fine Arts in the area of dance performance and choreography. Program accredited by NASD.

Enrollment Fall 1997: 48 total; 45 undergraduate, 3 non-professional degree.

Dance Student Profile 100% females, 10% minorities.

Dance Faculty 9 total (full-time and part-time). 100% of full-time faculty have terminal degrees. Graduate students do not teach undergraduate courses. Undergraduate student–faculty ratio: 10:1.

Student Life Student groups/activities include American College Dance Festival Association, Dance Majors Club, SoSoHo Performance Series.

Expenses for 1997–98 Application fee: $20. Comprehensive fee: $16,450 includes full-time tuition ($12,050), mandatory fees ($100), and college room and board ($4300). Room and board charges vary according to board plan.

Financial Aid Program-specific awards for 1997: 35 dance scholarships for program majors ($1000–$2500).

Application Procedures Students apply for admission into the professional program by freshman, sophomore year. Deadline for freshmen and transfers: continuous. Required: high school transcript, college transcript(s) for transfer students, 3 letters of recommendation, audition, SAT I or ACT test scores. Recommended: essay, interview. Auditions held once and by appointment on campus; videotaped performances are permissible as a substitute for live auditions for out-of-state applicants.

Web Site http://www.colacoll.edu.

Undergraduate Contact Ms. Patty Graham, Associate Professor, Dance Department, Columbia College, 1301 Columbia College Drive, Columbia, South Carolina 29203; 803-786-3668, fax: 803-786-3868, E-mail address: pgraham@colacoll.edu.

▼ CONCORDIA UNIVERSITY

Montréal, PQ, Canada

Province-supported, coed. Urban campus. Total enrollment: 29,271. Dance program established 1979.

Degrees Bachelor of Fine Arts in the area of contemporary dance. Cross-registration with any university in Quebec.

Enrollment Fall 1997: 52 total; all undergraduate.

Dance Student Profile 4% international.

Dance Faculty 14 total (full-time and part-time). Graduate students teach a few undergraduate courses. Undergraduate student–faculty ratio: 4:1.

Expenses for 1998–99 Application fee: $40 Canadian dollars. Tuition, fee, and room only charges are reported in Canadian dollars. Province resident tuition: $1668 full-time. Canadian resident tuition: $2868 full-time. Mandatory fees: $618 full-time. College room only: $2290. Room charges vary according to housing facility. International student tuition: $8268 full-time.

Application Procedures Students admitted directly into the professional program freshman year. Deadline for freshmen and transfers: June 1. Notification date for freshmen and transfers: August 31. Required: high school transcript, college transcript(s) for transfer students, audition. Auditions held 3 times in April, May, and August on campus; videotaped performances are permissible as a substitute for live auditions if a campus visit is impossible.

Web Site http://www-fofa.concordia.ca/dance/.

Undergraduate Contact Ms. Jolanta Manowska, Communications Assistant, Office of the Registrar, Concordia University, 1455 de Maisonneuve Boulevard West, LB700, Montreal, PQ H3G 1M8; 514-848-2668, fax: 514-848-2837, E-mail address: admreg@alcor.concordia.ca.

▼ CORNISH COLLEGE OF THE ARTS

Seattle, Washington

Independent, coed. Urban campus. Total enrollment: 621. Dance program established 1914.

Degrees Bachelor of Fine Arts in the area of dance. Majors and concentrations: ballet, choreography and performance, modern dance.

Enrollment Fall 1997: 82 total; 80 undergraduate, 2 non-professional degree.

Dance Student Profile 80% females, 20% males, 14% minorities.

Dance Faculty 16 total (full-time and part-time). 70% of full-time faculty have terminal degrees. Graduate students do not teach undergraduate courses. Undergraduate student–faculty ratio: 5:1.

Student Life Student groups/activities include Northwest Regional American College Dance Festival Association, Cornish Dance Theatre.

Expenses for 1997–98 Application fee: $35. Tuition: $11,540 full-time. Mandatory fees: $118 full-time.

Financial Aid Program-specific awards for 1997: Presidential Scholarships for continuing students ($600–$4000), Nellie Scholarships for new students ($600–$4000), 1–6 Kreielsheimer Scholarships for new students from Washington, Oregon, or Alaska ($16,000), departmental scholarships for program students ($600–$4000).

Application Procedures Students admitted directly into the professional program freshman year. Deadline for freshmen and transfers: August 15. Required: essay, high school transcript, college transcript(s) for transfer students, minimum 2.0 high school GPA, audition. Recommended: letter of recommendation, interview, SAT I or ACT test scores. Auditions held 10 times on campus and off campus in various sites in northern and southern California, Texas, Michigan; videotaped performances are permissible as a substitute for live auditions when distance is prohibitive.

Web Site http://www.cornish.edu.

Undergraduate Contact Ms. Jane Buckman, Director of Admissions, Cornish College of the Arts, 710 East Roy Street, Seattle, Washington 98102; 800-726-ARTS, fax: 206-720-1011.

More About the College

The Dance Department at Cornish College of the Arts provides demanding but nurturing training for professional artists to create graduates with proficient technique, creative voice, self-assurance, and a willingness to take risks. The training is designed to give students a thorough knowledge of the craft of the past while preparing them to become artistic innovators of the twenty-first century.

Students pursuing a B.F.A. in dance will participate in daily ballet and modern dance classes, which form the core of the technique curriculum. Other courses offered include pointe, partnering, character, and African dance. Strength and flexibility exercises are incorporated into all technique classes to prevent injuries. A three-year sequence of courses in composition and improvisation develops choreographic craft. A senior project, typically involving an advanced level of choreography and a public performance, is the final requirement of the B.F.A. program.

Faculty members and guest artists choreograph for Cornish Dance Theatre, the department's performing ensemble, which presents two concert seasons each year. Additional performance and choreographic opportunities arise from an annual concert of student choreography, senior projects, and collaborations with the Theatre and Music departments.

There is a two-way dialogue between the professional dance community and the department. Students have the chance to intern with several local companies. Seattle offers many opportunities to present choreography, while visiting artists such as Mark Morris, and members of the Martha Graham, Merce Cunningham, and Paul Taylor Dance companies provide a vital connection to the national dance world.

▼ EAST CAROLINA UNIVERSITY

Greenville, North Carolina

State-supported, coed. Urban campus. Total enrollment: 18,271. Dance program established 1962.

Degrees Bachelor of Fine Arts in the area of dance. Majors and concentrations: ballet, dance, jazz dance, modern dance.

Enrollment Fall 1997: 150 total; all undergraduate.

Dance Student Profile 70% females, 30% males, 4% minorities.

Dance Faculty 6 total (full-time). 95% of full-time faculty have terminal degrees. Graduate students do not teach undergraduate courses. Undergraduate student–faculty ratio: 25:1.

Expenses for 1997–98 Application fee: $35. State resident tuition: $916 full-time. Nonresident tuition: $8028 full-time. Mandatory fees: $932 full-time. College room and board: $3680. College room only: $1780. Room and board charges vary according to board plan and housing facility.

Financial Aid Program-specific awards available.

Application Procedures Students apply for admission into the professional program by sophomore year. Deadline for freshmen: March 15; transfers: April 15. Required: high school transcript, SAT I test score only. Recommended: minimum 2.0 high school GPA, 3 letters of recommendation, audition. Auditions held once on campus.

Web Site http://www.theatre-dance.ecu.edu.

Undergraduate Contact Undergraduate Admissions, East Carolina University, Wichard Building, Greenville, North Carolina 27858-4353; 252-328-6640.

▼ FLORIDA STATE UNIVERSITY

Tallahassee, Florida

State-supported, coed. Suburban campus. Total enrollment: 30,401. Dance program established 1965.

Degrees Bachelor of Fine Arts in the area of dance. Graduate degrees offered: Master of Fine Arts in the area of dance. Cross-registration with Florida Agricultural and Mechanical University. Program accredited by NASD.

Enrollment Fall 1997: 630 total; 59 undergraduate, 11 graduate, 560 non-professional degree.

Dance Student Profile 91% females, 9% males, 11% minorities, 1% international.

Dance Faculty 23 total undergraduate and graduate (full-time and part-time). 58% of full-time faculty have terminal degrees. Graduate students teach about a quarter undergraduate courses. Undergraduate student–faculty ratio: 5:1.

Student Life Student groups/activities include American College Dance Festival Association, Florida Dance Association.

Expenses for 1997–98 Application fee: $20. State resident tuition: $1988 full-time. Nonresident tuition: $7905 full-time. College room and board: $4570. College room only: $2540. Room and board charges vary according to board plan and housing facility.

Financial Aid Program-specific awards for 1997: 31 out-of-state tuition waivers for program majors ($1200–$1500).

Application Procedures Students admitted directly into the professional program freshman year. Deadline for freshmen: March 1; transfers: June 20. Required: high school transcript, college transcript(s) for transfer students, minimum 2.0 high school GPA, audition, SAT I or ACT test scores. Recommended: minimum 3.0 high school GPA, letter of recommendation. Auditions held 3 times on campus; videotaped performances are permissible as a substitute for live auditions for international applicants or in special circumstances.

Undergraduate Contact Mrs. Patricia Phillips, Assistant Chairperson, Department of Dance, Florida State University, Room 404 Montgomery Gym, Tallahassee, Florida 32306-2120; 904-644-1023, fax: 904-644-1277.

Graduate Contact Ms. Elizabeth Patenaude, Chairperson, Department of Dance, Florida State University, Room 404 Montgomery Gym, Tallahassee, Florida 32306-2120; 904-644-1023, fax: 904-644-1277.

More About the School

The Florida State University Dance Department has long been recognized as one of the country's outstanding professional programs. Offering only the BFA and MFA degrees, the department is clearly focused on the professional preparation of dance performers and choreographers.

Program Facilities Florida State University has four dance studios, a multimedia resource lab, and the department's own fully equipped proscenium theater seating 216. The department houses valuable historical materials, including an extensive collection of Denishawn costumes (the Killinger Collection) and the Honya Holm costumes. Ruby Diamond Auditorium, with a seating capacity of 2,000, is one of several larger performance venues available to the department annually.

Faculty and Resident Artists The resident faculty is composed of outstanding professionals in the fields of performance, choreography, and theory. This produces an active community of artist-teachers who provide the education and direction of young dancers and who also actively pursue their own artistic and intellectual lives. Excellent professional staff in the areas of production, lighting, costuming, and promotion provide artistic and technical instruction and guidance. Resident faculty and staff members are augmented by some of the most exciting dance artists in the field today. Artists scheduled for residencies and performances for 1998–99 include Urban Bush Women, Buglisi/Foreman, and Garth Fagan Dance.

Student Performance Opportunities There are more than twenty full, formal concerts annually. Numerous informal performance opportunities are available. The Dance Repertory Theatre, directed by Lynda Davis, is open to exceptionally gifted students who are interested in the touring company experience.

Florida State University *(continued)*

Special Programs The Summer Dance Institute: A New Dancer for a New Society is a special offering in partnership with Urban Bush Women.

▼ FRIENDS UNIVERSITY

Wichita, Kansas

Independent, coed. Urban campus. Total enrollment: 2,729.
Degrees Bachelor of Fine Arts in the area of ballet. Cross-registration with Kansas Newman College.
Enrollment Fall 1997: 16 undergraduate.
Dance Student Profile 55% females, 5% minorities, 10% international.
Dance Faculty 100% of full-time faculty have terminal degrees. Graduate students do not teach undergraduate courses. Undergraduate student–faculty ratio: 15:1.
Student Life Student groups/activities include Wichita Ballet Theater.
Expenses for 1997–98 Application fee: $15. One-time mandatory fee: $40. Comprehensive fee: $13,225 includes full-time tuition ($9885), mandatory fees ($90), and college room and board ($3250). College room only: $1400. Full-time tuition and fees vary according to course load. Room and board charges vary according to student level.
Financial Aid Program-specific awards for 1997: 5 Miller Scholarships for program majors ($1500), 15 departmental scholarships for program majors ($1000).
Application Procedures Students admitted directly into the professional program freshman year. Deadline for freshmen: August 1; transfers: August 15. Required: high school transcript, minimum 2.0 high school GPA, audition. Auditions held 4 times on campus; videotaped performances are permissible as a substitute for live auditions if a campus visit is impossible.
Undergraduate Contact Mr. Stan Rogers, Director, Department of Dance, Friends University, 2100 University Drive, Wichita, Kansas 67213; 316-295-5848.

▼ GEORGE MASON UNIVERSITY

Fairfax, Virginia

State-supported, coed. Suburban campus. Total enrollment: 23,826.
Degrees Bachelor of Fine Arts in the area of dance. Majors and concentrations: choreography, performance. Graduate degrees offered: Master of Fine Arts in the area of dance.
Enrollment Fall 1997: 70 total; 40 undergraduate, 10 graduate, 20 non-professional degree.
Dance Student Profile 92% females, 8% males, 15% minorities, 8% international.
Dance Faculty 19 total undergraduate and graduate (full-time and part-time). 71% of full-time faculty have terminal degrees. Graduate students teach a few undergraduate courses. Undergraduate student–faculty ratio: 10:1.
Student Life Student groups/activities include George Mason University Dance Company.
Expenses for 1997–98 Application fee: $30. State resident tuition: $4296 full-time. Nonresident tuition: $12,240 full-time. Full-time tuition varies according to course load.

College room and board: $5120. College room only: $3300. Room and board charges vary according to board plan and housing facility.
Financial Aid Program-specific awards for 1997: 1 Joanne Johnson Arts Scholarship for program majors ($1000).
Application Procedures Students admitted directly into the professional program freshman year. Deadline for freshmen: February 1; transfers: March 15. Notification date for freshmen: April 1; transfers: April 15. Required: essay, high school transcript, college transcript(s) for transfer students, interview, audition, SAT I or ACT test scores. Recommended: minimum 3.0 high school GPA. Auditions held twice on campus.
Undergraduate Contact Ms. Marjorie Summerall, Program Coordinator, Division of Dance, George Mason University, MS 3D4, Fairfax, Virginia 22030-4444; 703-993-1114, fax: 703-993-1366.
Graduate Contact Ms. Karen Studd, Graduate Program Coordinator, Division of Dance, George Mason University, MS 3D4, Fairfax, Virginia 22030-4444; 703-993-1114, fax: 703-993-1366.

▼ THE HARTT SCHOOL

See University of Hartford

▼ JACKSONVILLE UNIVERSITY

Jacksonville, Florida

Independent, coed. Suburban campus. Total enrollment: 2,157. Dance program established 1982.
Degrees Bachelor of Fine Arts in the area of dance. Program accredited by NASD.
Enrollment Fall 1997: 48 total; all undergraduate.
Dance Student Profile 96% females, 4% males, 2% minorities, 2% international.
Dance Faculty 9 total (full-time and part-time). 100% of full-time faculty have terminal degrees. Graduate students do not teach undergraduate courses. Undergraduate student–faculty ratio: 12:1.
Student Life Student groups/activities include Jacksonville University Dance Theatre, Jacksonville University Dance Ensemble.
Expenses for 1997–98 Application fee: $25. Comprehensive fee: $18,800 includes full-time tuition ($13,360), mandatory fees ($540), and college room and board ($4900). College room only: $2260. Room and board charges vary according to board plan. Special program-related fees: $15 per course per semester for materials, $50 per course per semester for student choreography production fees.
Financial Aid Program-specific awards for 1997: 20 dance scholarships for those demonstrating need/talent ($1000).
Application Procedures Students admitted directly into the professional program freshman year. Deadline for freshmen and transfers: continuous. Notification date for freshmen and transfers: continuous. Required: essay, high school transcript, college transcript(s) for transfer students, minimum 2.0 high school GPA, 3 letters of recommendation, audition, SAT I or ACT test scores (minimum combined SAT I score of 850). Recommended: minimum 3.0 high school GPA. Auditions held by appointment on campus; videotaped performances are permissible as a substitute for live auditions if a campus visit is impossible.

Undergraduate Contact Mrs. Angelus Hollis, Director, Dance Studies, Jacksonville University, 2800 University Boulevard North, Jacksonville, Florida 32211; 904-745-7374, fax: 904-745-7375, E-mail address: ahollis@junix.ju.edu.

More About the University

Program Facilities Classes are held in studios specifically designed for dance in the Brest Dance Pavilion. JU's dance studio complex was built in 1987 and contains two large, airy studios with professionally designed dance flooring, floor-to-ceiling windows and extensive mirrors, and dressing rooms with showers and lockers. All ballet technique and modern classes have live musical accompaniment.

Faculty, Resident Artists, and Alumni The faculty emphasizes the best in academic and performing traditions in classical ballet, modern dance, and jazz. Guest faculty members and visiting artists include Donlin Forman, Ernestine Stodelle, Bojan Spassoff, Phyllis Lamhut, Rachel Lampert, Edward Villela, Russel Sultzback, Carl Ratcliff, Twyla Tharp, Alvin Ailey, and others.

Student Performance Opportunities Performance opportunities are offered each semester, including the Student Choreography Concert, Spring Dance Concert, special choreography set by guest artists, and opportunities to perform in Jacksonville's First Coast *Nutcracker*. The JU Dance Theatre performing ensemble performs on and off campus.

Special Programs Dance programs at JU are accredited by the National Association of Schools of Dance (NASD). JU is accredited by the Commission on Colleges of the Southern Association of Colleges and Schools. Internships and study-abroad programs are available.

▼ JORDAN COLLEGE OF FINE ARTS

See Butler University

▼ THE JUILLIARD SCHOOL

New York, New York

Independent, coed. Urban campus. Total enrollment: 782.
Degrees Bachelor of Fine Arts in the area of dance. Majors and concentrations: ballet, modern dance.
Enrollment Fall 1997: 78 total; all undergraduate.
Dance Student Profile 58% females, 42% males, 46% minorities, 15% international.
Dance Faculty 32 total (full-time and part-time). Graduate students do not teach undergraduate courses.
Student Life Student groups/activities include dance performances. Special housing available for dance students.
Expenses for 1997–98 Application fee: $85. Comprehensive fee: $21,500 includes full-time tuition ($14,400), mandatory fees ($600), and college room and board ($6500). Room and board charges vary according to housing facility.
Financial Aid Program-specific awards for 1997: 59 The Juilliard Scholarship Fund Awards for program majors ($9745).
Application Procedures Students admitted directly into the professional program freshman year. Deadline for freshmen and transfers: December 1. Notification date for freshmen and transfers: April 1. Required: essay, high school transcript, 2 letters of recommendation, audition, health form, photo. Recommended: video. Auditions held once on campus and off campus in San Francisco, CA; Dallas, TX; St. Petersburg, FL.

Undergraduate Contact Ms. Mary K. Gray, Director of Admissions, The Juilliard School, 60 Lincoln Center Plaza, New York, New York 10023-6590; 212-799-5000 ext. 223, fax: 212-769-6420.

More About the College

The Juilliard Dance Division was established in 1951 by William Schuman during his tenure as President of The Juilliard School. Under the guidance of the late Martha Hill, founding director of the division, Juilliard became the first major teaching institution ever to combine equal dance instruction in both modern and ballet techniques, an idea that was considered heretical in its day. Her program was a forecast of the future of dance in America, where ballet and modern dance companies routinely cross into one another's territory. Ms. Hill became Artistic Director Emeritus with the appointment of Muriel Topaz as Director in 1985. Since 1992, noted choreographer and artistic director Benjamin Harkarvy has been Director of the Juilliard Dance Division.

Graduates of the division have gone on to dance with professional dance companies in the United States and abroad. Among its alumni are noted dancers, choreographers, and company directors such as Pina Bausch, Gregory Burge, Martha Clarke, Bruce Marks, Susan Marshall, Dennis Nahat, Paul Taylor, and Michael Uthoff.

The Dance Division offers a four-year course of study; its goal is to give dancers the essential tools enabling them to cross the bridge from dance studio to stage. Students may choose between pursuing a Bachelor of Fine Arts degree or a diploma. The core curriculum requires intensive technical study in ballet and modern dance and includes courses in repertory, pas de deux, point or men's class, dance composition, contemporary partnering, anatomy, dance history, stagecraft, production, and the study of musical theory. The dancers work in an enormous variety of repertory styles and techniques. Electives such as acting, voice, and tap are also offered. Juilliard dancers are expected to develop versatility, a keen stylistic sense, and an ease when working with choreographers, which makes them inspiring and desirable collaborators. Of particular note is the School's choreographic training, which begins with improvisational studies and finally advances to fully wrought works. Many of these reach the stage of the Juilliard Theater in a theatrically produced performance. The facilities at Juilliard include four specialized performance halls, two-story studios, classrooms, and teaching studios.

Throughout their four-year program, students participate in approximately seventy-five performances a year, including eight fully-staged concerts and workshop presentations in the Juilliard Theater, informal workshops, and tours with the Lincoln Center and Juilliard Students Programs. Masterworks are performed frequently, and students are encouraged to present their own choreographed works in informal concerts and workshop showings as well as in Juilliard's *Wednesdays at One* series presented in Alice Tully Hall at Lincoln Center.

Each season, the Juilliard Dance Division presents a concert performance series in the Juilliard Theater performed by the students enrolled in the Division. These concert series often feature major repertory works in addition to world premieres created for the Dance Division by noted choreographers, many of whom are Juilliard alumni. The 1997–98 season's series featured the American premiere of Jiří Kylián's *Stoolgame*, the world premieres of Igan Perry's *Mourning Song* and Charlotte Griffin's *In Time Taken*, as well as a staging of Paul Taylor's lyrical *Roses*.

The Juilliard School (continued)

Student Performance Opportunities On the basis of capacity and achievement, students audition or are assigned to participate in several performances throughout the year. Each year there are fully staged public dance concerts, monthly workshop performances, and special projects. Students also tour local schools and perform in area hospitals and community centers. Fully staged performances feature standard repertory and commissioned works by both recognized and emerging choreographers in a wide range of styles. Workshop performances are presented either on stage or in the studio, with programming selected from advanced classes, student choreography, and studies prepared in composition, notation, and other classes. In addition, Juilliard may host dance companies from across the United States and other countries who participate in discussions and informal workshops with students during their visits.

▼ Kent State University

Kent, Ohio

State-supported, coed. Small town campus. Total enrollment: 20,743. Dance program established 1983.
Degrees Bachelor of Fine Arts in the area of dance.
Enrollment Fall 1997: 30 total; all undergraduate.
Dance Student Profile 95% females, 5% males, 7% minorities.
Dance Faculty 12 total (full-time and part-time). 100% of full-time faculty have terminal degrees. Graduate students do not teach undergraduate courses.
Student Life Student groups/activities include Kent Dance Ensemble, Kent Dance Association.
Expenses for 1997–98 Application fee: $30. State resident tuition: $4460 full-time. Nonresident tuition: $8920 full-time. Full-time tuition varies according to course load. College room and board: $4152. College room only: $2448.
Financial Aid Program-specific awards for 1997: 2–6 Creative Arts Awards for program majors ($1200–$2600).
Application Procedures Students admitted directly into the professional program freshman year. Deadline for freshmen and transfers: continuous. Required: high school transcript, college transcript(s) for transfer students, minimum 2.0 high school GPA, audition, SAT I or ACT test scores. Recommended: 3 letters of recommendation, interview. Auditions held 4 times on campus.
Undergraduate Contact Andrea Shearer, Dance Coordinator, School of Theatre and Dance, Kent State University, P O Box 5190, Kent, Ohio 44242; 330-672-2069, fax: 330-672-4897.

▼ Lake Erie College

Painesville, Ohio

Independent, coed. Small town campus. Total enrollment: 701.
Degrees Bachelor of Fine Arts in the areas of dance, interdisciplinary studies; Bachelor of Arts in the area of dance. Majors and concentrations: choreography and performance, dance, interdisciplinary studies.
Enrollment Fall 1997: 4 undergraduate.
Dance Student Profile 80% females, 20% males.
Dance Faculty 2 total (part-time). Graduate students do not teach undergraduate courses.

Student Life Student groups/activities include Dance/Theater Collective.
Expenses for 1997–98 Application fee: $20. Comprehensive fee: $18,690 includes full-time tuition ($12,950), mandatory fees ($800), and college room and board ($4940). College room only: $2540.
Financial Aid Program-specific awards for 1997: Fine Arts Awards for program majors ($500–$1000).
Application Procedures Deadline for freshmen: July 1; transfers: August 20. Required: essay, high school transcript, college transcript(s) for transfer students, minimum 2.0 high school GPA, 2 letters of recommendation, SAT I or ACT test scores, audition for scholarship consideration. Recommended: interview. Auditions held as needed on campus.
Undergraduate Contact Mr. Paul Gothard, Director, Fine Arts Department, Lake Erie College, Box 354, 391 West Washington Street, Painesville, Ohio 44077; 440-639-7856.

▼ Long Island University, C.W. Post Campus

Brookville, New York

Independent, coed. Suburban campus. Total enrollment: 8,171. Dance program established 1996.
Degrees Bachelor of Fine Arts in the area of dance studies.
Enrollment Fall 1997: 5 total; all undergraduate.
Dance Faculty 12 total (full-time and part-time). 80% of full-time faculty have terminal degrees. Graduate students do not teach undergraduate courses.
Student Life Student groups/activities include lecture demonstrations, Post Concert Dance Company, American College Dance Festival.
Expenses for 1997–98 Application fee: $30. Comprehensive fee: $20,555 includes full-time tuition ($13,920), mandatory fees ($610), and college room and board ($6025). College room only: $3830. Room and board charges vary according to board plan. Special program-related fees: $35 per technique class for accompanist and theater services, $35 per technical theatre for class supplies.
Financial Aid Program-specific awards for 1997: 2 Provost's Awards for dance studies majors ($2000), 8 Post Concert Dance Company Awards for dance studies majors ($2000), 4 Freshman Incentive Awards for dance studies majors ($2000).
Application Procedures Students admitted directly into the professional program freshman year. Deadline for freshmen and transfers: continuous. Required: high school transcript, college transcript(s) for transfer students, minimum 2.0 high school GPA, interview, audition, SAT I or ACT test scores. Recommended: essay, minimum 3.0 high school GPA, letter of recommendation. Auditions held continuously by appointment on campus and off campus in Miami, FL; videotaped performances are permissible as a substitute for live auditions when distance is prohibitive.
Undergraduate Contact Christine Natali, Director, Admissions, Long Island University, C.W. Post Campus, 720 Northern Boulevard, Brookville, New York 11548-1300; 516-299-2999, fax: 516-299-2137, E-mail address: admissions@collegehall.liunet.edu.
Graduate Contact Sally Luzader, Associate Director, Graduate Admissions, Long Island University, C.W. Post Campus, 720

Northern Boulevard, Brookville, New York 11548-1300; 516-299-4024, fax: 516-299-2137, E-mail address: sluzader@ john.liunet.edu.

▼ MARYMOUNT MANHATTAN COLLEGE

New York, New York

Independent, coed. Urban campus. Total enrollment: 2,140.

Degrees Bachelor of Fine Arts in the area of dance.

Enrollment Fall 1997: 83 total; all undergraduate.

Dance Student Profile 85% females, 15% males, 20% minorities, 20% international.

Dance Faculty 20 total (full-time and part-time). 5% of full-time faculty have terminal degrees. Graduate students do not teach undergraduate courses.

Expenses for 1997–98 Application fee: $40. Tuition: $11,990 full-time. Mandatory fees: $300 full-time. College room only: $3182. Room charges vary according to housing facility. Special program-related fees: $45 per course for technique/ lab fees.

Financial Aid Program-specific awards for 1997: competitive talent awards for dance majors ($1000–$5000).

Application Procedures Students admitted directly into the professional program freshman year. Deadline for freshmen and transfers: April 30. Required: high school transcript, college transcript(s) for transfer students, 2 letters of recommendation, interview, audition, SAT I or ACT test scores. Auditions held 4 times on campus; videotaped performances are permissible as a substitute for live auditions when distance is prohibitive.

Undergraduate Contact Katie Langan, Director, Department of Dance, Marymount Manhattan College, 221 East 71st Street, New York, New York 10021; 212-517-0651, fax: 212-517-0413.

Rutgers, The State University of New Jersey

▼ MASON GROSS SCHOOL OF THE ARTS

New Brunswick, New Jersey

State-supported, coed. Small town campus. Total university enrollment: 48,341. Total unit enrollment: 770. Dance program established 1981.

Degrees Bachelor of Fine Arts in the area of dance. Majors and concentrations: modern dance. Program accredited by NASD.

Enrollment Fall 1997: 104 total; 67 undergraduate, 37 non-professional degree.

Dance Student Profile 90% females, 10% males, 15% minorities, 1% international.

Dance Faculty 11 total (full-time and part-time). 100% of full-time faculty have terminal degrees. Graduate students do not teach undergraduate courses. Undergraduate student–faculty ratio: 15:1.

Student Life Student groups/activities include University Dance Works. Special housing available for dance students.

Expenses for 1997–98 Application fee: $50. State resident tuition: $4262 full-time. Nonresident tuition: $8676 full-time. Mandatory fees: $1104 full-time. Full-time tuition and fees vary according to location. College room and board: $5314. College room only: $3112. Room and board charges vary according to board plan and housing facility.

Application Procedures Students admitted directly into the professional program freshman year. Deadline for freshmen and transfers: continuous. Notification date for freshmen and transfers: continuous. Required: high school transcript, college transcript(s) for transfer students, minimum 2.0 high school GPA, interview, audition, SAT I or ACT test scores. Auditions held 4 times on campus; videotaped performances are permissible as a substitute for live auditions when distance is prohibitive.

Undergraduate Contact Office of Undergraduate Admissions, Rutgers, The State University of New Jersey, Mason Gross School of the Arts, PO Box 2101, New Brunswick, New Jersey 08903-2101; 732-445-3777.

▼ MEADOWS SCHOOL OF THE ARTS

See Southern Methodist University

▼ MONTCLAIR STATE UNIVERSITY

Upper Montclair, New Jersey

State-supported, coed. Suburban campus. Total enrollment: 12,808.

Degrees Bachelor of Fine Arts in the area of dance. Program accredited by NASD.

Enrollment Fall 1997: 47 undergraduate.

Dance Student Profile 97% females, 3% males, 3% minorities, 1% international.

Dance Faculty 8 total (full-time and part-time). 50% of full-time faculty have terminal degrees. Graduate students do not teach undergraduate courses. Undergraduate student–faculty ratio: 7:1.

Student Life Student groups/activities include Danceworks, musicals, American College Dance Festival.

Expenses for 1997–98 Application fee: $40. State resident tuition: $2912 full-time. Nonresident tuition: $4432 full-time. Mandatory fees: $782 full-time. College room and board: $5546. College room only: $3860.

Application Procedures Students admitted directly into the professional program freshman year. Deadline for freshmen: March 1; transfers: May 1. Required: essay, high school transcript, college transcript(s) for transfer students, minimum 2.0 high school GPA, interview, audition, SAT I test score only. Recommended: letter of recommendation. Auditions held continuously on campus; videotaped performances are permissible as a substitute for live auditions for international students and U.S. students when distance is prohibitive.

Undergraduate Contact Ms. Lori Katterhenry, Program Coordinator, Division of Dance, Montclair State University, Normal Avenue, Upper Montclair, New Jersey 07043; 973-655-7080, fax: 973-655-5279, E-mail address: katterhenryl@saturn. montclair.edu.

▼ NEW WORLD SCHOOL OF THE ARTS

Miami, Florida

State-supported, coed. Urban campus. Total enrollment: 359. Dance program established 1988.

Degrees Bachelor of Fine Arts in the area of dance. Majors and concentrations: performance. Mandatory cross-registration with University of Florida, Miami-Dade Community College. Program accredited by NASD.

New World School of the Arts *(continued)*

Enrollment Fall 1997: 82 total; all undergraduate.
Dance Student Profile 90% females, 10% males, 60% minorities, 1% international.
Dance Faculty 27 total (full-time and part-time). Graduate students do not teach undergraduate courses.
Student Life Student groups/activities include Florida Dance Association, local dance companies.
Estimated expenses for 1998–99 Application fee: $20. State resident tuition: $1478 full-time. Nonresident tuition: $5196 full-time. Full-time tuition varies according to course load and degree level.
Financial Aid Program-specific awards for 1997: 4 Nations Bank Merit Scholarships for program majors ($2000), 1 Lewis Dorfman Merit Scholarship for program majors ($1000), 1 Patricia Olalde Merit Scholarship for choreography majors ($1000), 10 Dr. Betty Rowen Merit Scholarships for dance education majors ($1500), 25 Miami-Dade Community College Scholarships for program majors ($1500).
Application Procedures Students admitted directly into the professional program freshman year. Deadline for freshmen and transfers: continuous. Required: high school transcript, college transcript(s) for transfer students, audition. Recommended: essay, minimum 2.0 high school GPA, 2 letters of recommendation, interview, SAT I or ACT test scores. Auditions held continuously on campus and off campus in Jacksonville, FL; Tampa, FL; West Palm Beach, FL; Orlando, FL; Ft. Lauderdale, FL; videotaped performances are permissible as a substitute for live auditions when distance is prohibitive.
Web Site http://www.mdcc.edu/nwsa.
Undergraduate Contact Ileana Gallagher, Admissions Counselor, Student Services, New World School of the Arts, 300 North East 2nd Avenue, Miami, Florida 33132; 305-237-7408, fax: 305-237-3794.

Tisch School of the Arts

▼ NEW YORK UNIVERSITY

New York, New York
Independent, coed. Urban campus. Total enrollment: 36,684. Dance program established 1965.
Degrees Bachelor of Fine Arts in the area of dance. Graduate degrees offered: Master of Fine Arts in the area of dance.
Enrollment Fall 1997: 75 undergraduate, 32 graduate.
Dance Faculty 21 total undergraduate and graduate (full-time and part-time). Graduate students do not teach undergraduate courses. Undergraduate student–faculty ratio: 5:1.
Student Life Student groups/activities include Artists in the Community, Out Artists, United Artists of Color.
Expenses for 1997–98 Application fee: $45. Comprehensive fee: $29,900 includes full-time tuition ($21,730) and college room and board ($8170). Full-time tuition varies according to program. Room and board charges vary according to board plan and housing facility.
Financial Aid Program-specific awards available.
Application Procedures Students admitted directly into the professional program freshman year. Deadline for freshmen: January 15; transfers: April 1. Notification date for freshmen: April 1; transfers: May 15. Required: essay, high school transcript, college transcript(s) for transfer students, 2 letters of recommendation, audition, SAT I or ACT test scores. Recommended: minimum 3.0 high school GPA, interview.

Auditions held continuously from November through April on campus and off campus in Chicago, IL; San Francisco, CA; videotaped performances are permissible as a substitute for live auditions for international applicants or with approval from the department.
Web Site http://www.nyu.edu/tisch.
Undergraduate Contact Mr. Elliot Dee, Director of Recruitment, Tisch School of the Arts, New York University, 721 Broadway, 8th Floor, New York, New York 10003-6807; 212-998-1902, fax: 212-995-4060, E-mail address: eddl@is6.nyu.edu.
Graduate Contact Mr. Dan Sanford, Director of Graduate Admissions, Tisch School of the Arts, New York University, 721 Broadway, 8th Floor, New York, New York 10003-6807; 212-998-1900, fax: 212-995-4060, E-mail address: dan.sandford@nyu.edu.

▼ NORTH CAROLINA SCHOOL OF THE ARTS

Winston-Salem, North Carolina
State-supported, coed. Urban campus. Total enrollment: 773. Dance program established 1965.
Degrees Bachelor of Fine Arts in the area of dance. Majors and concentrations: ballet, contemporary dance.
Enrollment Fall 1997: 64 total; all undergraduate.
Dance Student Profile 41% females, 59% males, 11% minorities, 5% international.
Dance Faculty 15 total (full-time and part-time). Graduate students do not teach undergraduate courses. Undergraduate student–faculty ratio: 9:1.
Expenses for 1997–98 Application fee: $35. State resident tuition: $1401 full-time. Nonresident tuition: $9858 full-time. Mandatory fees: $1121 full-time. Full-time tuition and fees vary according to program. College room and board: $3970. College room only: $2060. Special program-related fees: $135 per year for educational and technology fee.
Financial Aid Program-specific awards for 1997: talent scholarships for artistically talented.
Application Procedures Students admitted directly into the professional program freshman year. Deadline for freshmen and transfers: continuous. Required: high school transcript, college transcript(s) for transfer students, 2 letters of recommendation, interview, audition, SAT I or ACT test scores, two photos. Auditions held by request on campus and off campus in various cities in the U.S.; videotaped performances are permissible as a substitute for live auditions for provisional acceptance.
Web Site http://www.ncarts.edu.
Undergraduate Contact Ms. Carol J. Palm, Director of Admissions, North Carolina School of the Arts, 1533 South Main Street, Winston-Salem, North Carolina 27117-2189; 336-770-3291, fax: 336-770-3370, E-mail address: palmc@ncsavx.ncsart.edu.

More About the School

Program Facilities Dance concerts featuring ballet and contemporary dance are presented at the Stevens Center, a magnificently restored 1920s movie palace seating 1,380 in downtown Winston-Salem. On campus, Agnes de Mille Theatre is a 188-seat performance space used mainly for dance concerts. Dance classes and rehearsals are conducted in modern, clerestory-lit, air-conditioned dance studios, which feature "sprung" floors specially designed for dancers. The School of the Arts also has a dance costume shop and provides complete dance production support through its own School of Design and Production.

Faculty, Guest Artists, and Alumni The resident faculty of artist-teachers features distinguished professionals who have danced and/or choreographed for some of the world's finest companies, including American Ballet Theatre, New York City Ballet, Netherlands Dance Theatre, Martha Graham, and Murray Louis. In addition, internationally renowned guest artists frequently visit to teach, coach, choreograph, or restage works for performance by students. The Lucia Chase Endowed Fellowship supports weeklong residencies by some of the world's most respected dancers; these have included Margot Fonteyn, Agnes de Mille, Jacques d'Amboise, and Arthur Mitchell. School of Dance graduates are currently performing in major companies throughout the world and can be found at the creative vanguard of contemporary dance. Noted alumni include Mary Cochran, Taylor 11; Linnette Hitchin, principal, Pacific Northwest Ballet; Jaime Martinez, associate director, Parsons Dance Company; Keith Roberts, principal, American Ballet Theater.

Student Performance Opportunities The School of Dance has a growing repertory of classical and contemporary dance unsurpassed in its diversity and challenge. Each year, students perform more than forty workshops and public performances, including an annual tour of *The Nutcracker*. These performance opportunities develop the dance student's versatility, a trademark of the School's alumni.

▼ THE OHIO STATE UNIVERSITY

Columbus, Ohio

State-supported, coed. Urban campus. Total enrollment: 48,278.

Degrees Bachelor of Fine Arts in the areas of performance, dance education. Majors and concentrations: dance education, performance. Graduate degrees offered: Master of Fine Arts in the areas of choreography, performance, lighting, directing in lab annotation. Program accredited by NASD.

Enrollment Fall 1997: 120 total; 90 undergraduate, 30 graduate.

Dance Student Profile 90% females, 10% males, 20% minorities, 4% international.

Dance Faculty 22 total undergraduate and graduate (full-time and part-time). 75% of full-time faculty have terminal degrees. Graduate students teach a few undergraduate courses. Undergraduate student–faculty ratio: 8:1.

Expenses for 1997–98 Application fee: $30. State resident tuition: $3660 full-time. Nonresident tuition: $10,869 full-time. College room and board: $5094. Room and board charges vary according to board plan and housing facility.

Financial Aid Program-specific awards for 1997: dance scholarships for talented dance majors ($1000).

Application Procedures Students admitted directly into the professional program freshman year. Deadline for freshmen: February 15; transfers: June 25. Required: high school transcript, college transcript(s) for transfer students, minimum 2.0 high school GPA, audition, SAT I or ACT test scores. Recommended: letter of recommendation, interview. Auditions held twice on campus; videotaped performances are permissible as a substitute for live auditions for international applicants.

Web Site http://www.dance.ohio-state.edu/.

Undergraduate Contact Ms. Karen Woods, Coordinator of Auditions, Department of Dance, The Ohio State University, Sullivant Hall, 1813 North High Street, Columbus, Ohio 43210-1307; 614-292-7977, fax: 614-292-0939, E-mail address: woods.60@osu.edu.

Graduate Contact Ms. Kathleen Monegan, Graduate Secretary, Department of Dance, The Ohio State University, Sullivant Hall, 1813 North High Street, Columbus, Ohio 43210-1307; 614-292-7977, fax: 614-292-0939, E-mail address: graddance@osu.edu.

▼ OHIO UNIVERSITY

Athens, Ohio

State-supported, coed. Small town campus. Total enrollment: 19,564. Dance program established 1969.

Degrees Bachelor of Fine Arts in the area of dance. Program accredited by NASD.

Enrollment Fall 1997: 54 total; all undergraduate.

Dance Student Profile 89% females, 11% males, 9% minorities, 3% international.

Dance Faculty 9 total (full-time and part-time). 66% of full-time faculty have terminal degrees. Graduate students do not teach undergraduate courses. Undergraduate student–faculty ratio: 7:1.

Student Life Student groups/activities include The Movement (student performance organization), Dance Factory (local dance studio).

Expenses for 1997–98 Application fee: $30. State resident tuition: $4275 full-time. Nonresident tuition: $8994 full-time. College room and board: $4698. College room only: $2310. Room and board charges vary according to board plan.

Financial Aid Program-specific awards for 1997: 4–5 Provost Scholarships for talented students ($1000), 1 Ruiz-Lewis Scholarship for minorities and males ($500), 1 Bailin-Stern Scholarship for talented students ($400–$500), 1 Hazeland Carr Liggett Award for talented students ($800), 1–2 Shirley Wimmer Awards for talented students ($1000–$1200), 1 Betty Milhendler Award for talented students ($500).

Application Procedures Students admitted directly into the professional program freshman year. Deadline for freshmen: February 1; transfers: June 1. Notification date for freshmen: March 15; transfers: June 15. Required: high school transcript, college transcript(s) for transfer students, 3 letters of recommendation, audition, SAT I or ACT test scores. Recommended: essay, minimum 3.0 high school GPA, interview. Auditions held twice on campus; videotaped performances are permissible as a substitute for live auditions when distance is prohibitive.

Web Site http://www.dance.ohiou.edu.

Undergraduate Contact Ms. Teresa Holland, School Secretary, School of Dance, Ohio University, Putnam Hall 222, Athens, Ohio 45701; 740-593-1826, fax: 740-593-0749, E-mail address: dancdept@ouvaxa.cats.ohiou.edu.

▼ POINT PARK COLLEGE

Pittsburgh, Pennsylvania

Independent, coed. Urban campus. Total enrollment: 2,270. Dance program established 1968.

Degrees Bachelor of Arts/Bachelor of Fine Arts in the areas of ballet, modern dance, jazz, arts management; Bachelor of Arts in the area of dance pedagogy. Cross-registration with Carnegie Mellon University, University of Pittsburgh, Chatham

Point Park College (continued)

College, Robert Morris College, Duquesne University, Carlow College. Program accredited by NASD.

Enrollment Fall 1997: 160 total; all undergraduate.

Dance Student Profile 90% females, 10% males, 20% minorities, 10% international.

Dance Faculty 15 total (full-time and part-time). 80% of full-time faculty have terminal degrees. Graduate students do not teach undergraduate courses.

Student Life Student groups/activities include Student Choreography Showcase, American College Dance Festival.

Expenses for 1997–98 Application fee: $20. Comprehensive fee: $16,580 includes full-time tuition ($11,050), mandatory fees ($356), and college room and board ($5174). College room only: $2550. Room and board charges vary according to board plan and housing facility. Special program-related fees: $325 per term for voice/piano private lessons, $20–$60 per course for music course fees, $35–$330 per term for performing arts instructional fee.

Financial Aid Program-specific awards for 1997: academic scholarships for those demonstrating talent and academic achievement ($2000–$7500), 24–35 dance scholarships for those demonstrating talent and academic achievement ($500–$2000), 39–50 Talent Scholarships for those demonstrating academic achievement and talent ($500–$3500).

Application Procedures Students admitted directly into the professional program freshman year. Deadline for freshmen and transfers: June 1. Required: high school transcript, college transcript(s) for transfer students, minimum 2.0 high school GPA, 2 letters of recommendation, audition, SAT I or ACT test scores. Auditions held 6 times on campus and off campus in New York, NY; Chicago, IL; Philadelphia, PA; Baltimore, MD; videotaped performances are permissible as a substitute for live auditions if distance is prohibitive or in special circumstances.

Undergraduate Contact Mr. Joseph McGoldrick, Assistant to the Chair, Department of Fine, Applied and Performing Arts, Point Park College, 201 Wood Street, Pittsburgh, Pennsylvania 15222-1984; 800-321-0129.

More About the Program

Program Facilities and Features Nine dance studios; a three-theater complex at "The Playhouse" of Point Park College; performance opportunities for students in front of a subscription audience; on-site costume/set construction apprenticeships; eleven private singing and piano instructors; College Choir; art and design classes; more than 100 dance classes per week; ratio of 1 instructor to 14 students in acting classes; central to many educational arts entertainment activities; walking distance to boating, swimming, parks.

Alumni FAPA has more than 150 graduates performing in touring companies, on Broadway, in dance groups, in movies, on TV, and in other theaters, as well as many more teaching in schools, on faculties, choreographing, writing, directing, and stage managing around the world. Broadway and national touring productions of *Carousel, Cats, Joseph and the Technicolor Dreamcoat, Side Show, Tommy, Damn Yankees, The Rink, Kiss of the Spider Woman, Victor/Victoria, Les Miserables, Jekyll & Hyde, Ragtime,* and *Smokey Joe's Cafe* as well as movie and TV credits including *Pulp Fiction, NYPD Blue, Due South, The Guiding Light* and *Leaving L.A.* are just a few of the vehicles showcasing FAPA graduates of theater and dance.

The Department of Fine, Applied and Performing Arts (FAPA) offers conservatory oriented programs within a liberal arts context. Students receive intense training in their concentration as well as a thorough academic education. Because the faculty of FAPA believes that performing arts majors develop best in front of a live audience, the program offers many performing opportunities for students at The Playhouse.

Nationally renowned, The Playhouse of Point Park College (formerly The Pittsburgh Playhouse) is the performance facility for the Department of Fine, Applied and Performing Arts. Here students participate in live-theater/dance experiences before a subscription audience. Comprised of three working theaters, this 60-year-old facility is fully staffed by a production team of designers and artisans who train and supervise student apprentices in building, designing, lighting, and managing shows. The front-of-house staff, box office, and public relations personnel engage all students in the business aspect of running a theater. The season, which features student actors, dancers, designers, and stage managers, consists of five Playhouse, Jr., shows for children; four College Theatre Company dramas and musicals; and two Playhouse Theatre Company presentations for professional faculty, alumni, visiting artists and selected undergraduates.

Dance students are featured in three Playhouse Dance Theatre productions, a student choreography showcase, and a Playhouse, Jr. Children's Dance Show as well as a public school outreach program in cooperation with the Gateway to Music organization.

The B.F.A. degree in Film and Video Production is offered in collaboration with Pittsburgh Filmmakers. Students take their academic courses at Point Park College and their film and video requirements at Pittsburgh Filmmakers' newly built facility in the Oakland section of Pittsburgh. Both institutions work together to ensure students receive a challenging educational experience.

The B.A. degree in Arts Management is designed for students who wish to pursue a career in Arts Management but who are not primarily interested in pursuing a professional performance career. The departmental requirements in business, finance, and management courses along with selected art courses provide a solid base from which entry-level employment in any one of a wide variety of arts management areas (marketing, development, financial management, performing company, etc.) is possible.

The B.F.A. degree in Arts Management is designed for students who wish to pursue a dual career in arts management and in performance. The curriculum includes the same foundation requirements as the B.A. program, but students choose one artistic focus: dance, theater, or music. A Performance requirement focus is an expectation in the B.F.A. degree.

The innovative B.A. in Children's Theatre provides opportunities for majors to plan, teach, and direct creative drama activities within the Children's School of the Education Department, Playhouse, Jr., or classes offered by the Community Conservatories of Dance, Music and Theatre (non-credit classes are also offered through FAPA). An Elementary Teaching Certificate is structured into this four-year degree.

A Theater Communications Degree prepares students to teach at the high school level in Drama and English. A Secondary Teaching Certificate for Pennsylvania is part of this four-year degree.

FAPA faculty are working professionals in acting, singing, dancing, writing, composing, painting, designing, choreography, and other specialties. Guest artists and master teachers in musical theater, voice and speech, and dance are regularly

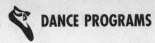

featured. Past guests include Chita Rivera, Michael Rupert, Jeff Shade, Rob Ashford, Sherry Zunker-Dow, Cicely Berry, Paul Gavert, Patricia Wilde, Albert Poland, Barbara Pontecorvo, Edward Villella, Maxine Sherman, Marshall Swiney, and Claire Bataille. The program also offers many workshops and collaborative efforts of an interdisciplinary nature with other college programs.

During the summer, FAPA offers an International Summer Dance program (open by audition) featuring renowned names in the world of dance. The International Summer Dance program offers jazz, ballet, Alexander, and modern with famous names such as Laura Alonso, Roberto Munoz, Miguel Campaneria, Alexander Filipov, Michael Uthoff, and Whilheim Burman. The program culminates in a recital performance.

The community of Pittsburgh itself is an arts and education center with the Pittsburgh Symphony, opera, ballet, Dance Council, the Pittsburgh Public Theater supplemented by eight other institutions of higher learning within a 15-minute drive. The whole city is truly the campus of our programs.

Prospective applicants must apply and be accepted by the college. An audition for and an interview with faculty is required of all prospective majors. Scholarships/Apprenticeships from $750 to $2500 are based on either talent or academics, or both. Presidential and Special academic full- and part-time awards are highly competitive.

Off-campus auditions are possible at Thespian and Dance conferences at San Juan, Puerto Rico; Chicago; New York; Ohio; Philadelphia, Pennsylvania; and Louisville, Kentucky. Videotaped auditions acceptable under special circumstances.

For more information and audition guidelines, contact Joseph McGoldrick, Assistant to the Chair, Point Park College, 201 Wood Street, Pittsburgh, Pennsylvania 15222, or call 800-321-0129.

▼ POTTER COLLEGE OF ARTS, HUMANITIES, AND SOCIAL SCIENCES

See Western Kentucky University

▼ PURCHASE COLLEGE, STATE UNIVERSITY OF NEW YORK

Purchase, New York

State-supported, coed. Small town campus. Total enrollment: 3,297.

Degrees Bachelor of Fine Arts in the area of dance. Majors and concentrations: ballet, composition, modern dance, production.

Enrollment Fall 1997: 141 total; all undergraduate.

Dance Student Profile 82% females, 18% males, 23% minorities, 9% international.

Dance Faculty 17 total (full-time and part-time). 100% of full-time faculty have terminal degrees. Graduate students do not teach undergraduate courses. Undergraduate student–faculty ratio: 19:1.

Student Life Student groups/activities include lectures/demonstrations at local schools, national and international performance tours, Purchase Dance Corps.

Expenses for 1997–98 Application fee: $30. State resident tuition: $3400 full-time. Nonresident tuition: $8300 full-time. Mandatory fees: $479 full-time. College room and board: $5264. College room only: $1930. Room and board charges vary according to board plan and housing facility.

Financial Aid Program-specific awards for 1997: 2 Bales/Fernandez Scholarships for talented students ($600), 1 Jane Falk Scholarship for talented students ($1210), 8 Harkness Scholarships for those demonstrating need/talent ($860), 23 Nutcracker Scholarships for talented students ($250–$2000), 7 Friends of Dance Awards for those demonstrating need/talent ($500–$1000), 40 college scholarships for those demonstrating need/talent ($500–$3700), 1 Bert Terborgh Award for talented students ($1000), 3 Abeles Scholarships for academically qualified/talented applicants ($1250–$2500), 2 Fay and Kenneth Gang Scholarships for talented students ($650), 1–4 Empire Minority Awards for minority students from New York State ($1250), 5 Reed Scholarship for students with high academic and artistic achievement ($750).

Application Procedures Students admitted directly into the professional program freshman year. Deadline for freshmen and transfers: April 15. Notification date for freshmen and transfers: May 1. Required: high school transcript, college transcript(s) for transfer students, audition, minimum TOEFL score of 550 for international applicants. Recommended: SAT I or ACT test scores. Auditions held 9 times on campus and off campus in Miami, FL; Chicago, IL; San Francisco, CA; Los Angeles, CA; Interlochen, MI; videotaped performances are permissible as a substitute for live auditions for international applicants and applicants from Hawaii.

Undergraduate Contact Ms. Meryl Wiener, Admissions Counselor, Office of Admissions, Purchase College, State University of New York, 735 Anderson Hill Road, Purchase, New York 10577-1400; 914-251-6300, fax: 914-251-6314.

More About the College

Facilities Award-winning dance building; largest specially built facility designed in the United States exclusively for the training and performance of dance; nine fully equipped, light-filled studios; 270-seat Dance Theatre Lab; two Pilates studios with physical therapy treatment areas. Performing Arts Center, with four theaters for Purchase Dance Corps concerts.

Faculty Faculty members have performed with Martha Graham, Merce Cunningham, Alvin Ailey, José Limôn, Viola Farber, New York City Ballet, The American Ballet Theatre, Paul Taylor Dance Company, and the Joffrey Ballet. They choreograph, teach, and/or set masterworks in Asia, Europe, and South America. They produce their own work in Manhattan. The faculty members teach the students daily. Musicians accompany every technique class. Alumni perform with major American and international companies, are founders of their own companies, or are freelance choreographers.

Performance Opportunities Students are required to perform. The Purchase Dance Corps, the performing company of the Conservatory of Dance, presents two concerts annually of major professional repertory in the Performing Arts Center, including modern works by artists such as Paul Taylor and Mark Morris, ballets by George Balanchine and Lew Christianson, reconstructions of Doris Humphrey and José Limôn, The Nutcracker Ballet, works by international choreographers Lin Hwai Min and Robert Cohan, as well as commissioned pieces by emerging choreographers and faculty works created especially for the Purchase Dance Corps. Additional performance opportunities: six weekends of senior project concerts in the Dance Theatre Lab, special fund-raising events and galas, and summer tours to Asia and Europe.

Special Programs Student exchange programs in dance in London, Amsterdam, Rotterdam, or Taipei; Arts Management certificate; physical therapist available two days per week.

▼

Purchase is a preeminent conservatory program from which to launch a career in dance. Why? Because it offers professional, comprehensive, in-depth, personalized training in modern dance, classical ballet, and composition.

Performance credits are required for graduation. Students may perform in the Purchase Dance Corps concerts, tours, senior projects, lecture demonstrations, galas and fund-raising events, student concerts, studio showings, and workshops. Performance of a major professional repertory piece is required for the senior project. Purchase Dance Corps International Tours have included Amsterdam (1991); Taiwan (1992 and 1995); Beijing, China (1994); France (1995) and Hong Kong (1987, 1990, and 1997).

The four-year composition program involves each student in performance of a sophomore and junior showing. The senior project is mentored by a faculty member and monitored by the faculty senior project committee. The senior project concerts, coproduced by 3 to 4 seniors in the Dance Theatre Lab, are culminating artistic and directorial events that serve the student as a bridge to the profession.

The Conservatory of Dance faculty members are active in the profession as choreographers, teachers, coaches, musicians, and performers. Alumni are performing or have performed in the Martha Graham Dance Co., the Merce Cunningham Dance Co., the Trisha Brown Dance Co., the Frankfurt Ballet, the Houston Ballet, the Parsons Co., the Mark Morris Dance Co., Limón Dance Co., American Ballet Theatre, the Feld Ballets N.Y., the Paul Taylor Dance Co., and the Bill T. Jones/Arnie Zane Co. An extensive listing of alumni accomplishments is available upon request.

On campus, the Performing Arts Center provides professional theaters in which the conservatory students perform, and a professional concert series of major contemporary and classical companies is mounted annually. Each company provides a master class for students. These have included the Miami City Ballet, Alvin Ailey, Dance Theatre of Harlem, Paul Taylor, Hubbard Street, Bill T. Jones, and David Parsons.

The B.F.A. degree conservatory professional training program requires 120 semester credits to graduate: 90 credits in the professional dance curriculum, 30 credits in liberal arts. The program emphasizes modern dance technique, classical ballet technique, performance, and choreography. Students take classical ballet and modern dance technique daily, anatomy for dance, music for dance, dance history, dance production, improvisation, ballet and modern partnering, ballet or modern composition, and pointe. The M.F.A. degree is a 60 credit, 2-year, residential curriculum in Choreography or Performance/Teaching.

Purchase College is 45 minutes north of New York City in a suburban setting where students have the best of both worlds. They reside on campus in residence halls or apartment complexes with students from the Music, Theatre Arts and Film, Art and Design, and liberal arts and science divisions. The ease of living in a campus setting, combined with the cultural advantages of Manhattan, informs the students' artistic stimulation and knowledge of the real challenges they will face upon graduation. They travel to the city to attend concerts, take classes, go to auditions, visit museums, and absorb the rich culture. New York City is a crucial resource in the education of these future artists. It is the reality check and the constant reminder of what students work for in their programs at the Conservatory.

"For a number of years, the Dance Division of the State University College at Purchase has been turning out more than its fair share of the most interesting and skillful professional dancers working in New York City."–Jennifer Dunning, *The New York Times*.

▼ RADFORD UNIVERSITY
Radford, Virginia

State-supported, coed. Small town campus. Total enrollment: 8,534.

Degrees Bachelor of Fine Arts in the areas of classical dance, contemporary dance. Majors and concentrations: ballet, modern dance.

Enrollment Fall 1997: 65 total; 56 undergraduate, 9 nonprofessional degree.

Dance Student Profile 98% females, 2% males, 2% international.

Dance Faculty 5 total (full-time and part-time). 100% of full-time faculty have terminal degrees. Graduate students do not teach undergraduate courses. Undergraduate student–faculty ratio: 15:1.

Student Life Student groups/activities include Harmony in Motion. Special housing available for dance students.

Expenses for 1997–98 Application fee: $20. State resident tuition: $2016 full-time. Nonresident tuition: $6788 full-time. Mandatory fees: $1164 full-time. College room and board: $4416. College room only: $2448. Room and board charges vary according to board plan and housing facility.

Financial Aid Program-specific awards for 1997: 5 Arts Society Scholarships for talented program students ($500–$1000), 5 Horth Scholarships for upperclassmen demonstrating need/talent ($300–$1000).

Application Procedures Students admitted directly into the professional program freshman year. Deadline for freshmen and transfers: continuous. Required: essay, high school transcript, college transcript(s) for transfer students, minimum 2.0 high school GPA, interview, audition, SAT I or ACT test scores (minimum combined SAT I score of 940). Auditions held continuously by appointment on campus; videotaped performances are permissible as a substitute for live auditions when distance is prohibitive.

Undergraduate Contact Mr. David Kraus, Director, Office of Admissions, Radford University, PO Box 6903, Radford, Virginia 24142; 540-831-5371, fax: 540-831-5138, E-mail address: dwkraus@runet.edu.

▼ RUTGERS, THE STATE UNIVERSITY OF NEW JERSEY
See Mason Gross School of the Arts

▼ SAM HOUSTON STATE UNIVERSITY

Huntsville, Texas

State-supported, coed. Small town campus. Total enrollment: 12,712. Dance program established 1975.

Degrees Bachelor of Fine Arts in the areas of dance, musical theater. Majors and concentrations: dance. Graduate degrees offered: Master of Fine Arts in the area of dance.

Enrollment Fall 1997: 55 undergraduate, 6 graduate.

Dance Student Profile 95% females, 5% males, 37% minorities, 1% international.

Dance Faculty 6 total undergraduate and graduate (full-time and part-time). 100% of full-time faculty have terminal degrees. Graduate students teach about a quarter undergraduate courses.

Student Life Student groups/activities include Chi Tau Epsilon (dance honor society), Swing Kids (swing dance performance group).

Expenses for 1997–98 Application fee: $15. State resident tuition: $816 full-time. Nonresident tuition: $5952 full-time. Mandatory fees: $770 full-time. College room and board: $3290. College room only: $1710. Room and board charges vary according to board plan and housing facility.

Financial Aid Program-specific awards for 1997: 10 dance scholarships for students with outstanding auditions ($250–$1000).

Application Procedures Students admitted directly into the professional program freshman year. Deadline for freshmen and transfers: continuous. Required: high school transcript, minimum 2.0 high school GPA, SAT I or ACT test scores (minimum combined SAT I score of 1050), standing in top half of graduating class. Recommended: audition. Auditions held twice on campus; videotaped performances are permissible as a substitute for live auditions when distance is prohibitive.

Web Site http://www.shsu.edu/~drm_www/dance.htm.

Contact Mr. Dane Eugene Nicolay, Dance Program Coordinator, Department of Theatre and Dance, Sam Houston State University, PO Box 2269, Huntsville, Texas 77341-2269; 409-294-1875, fax: 409-294-3954, E-mail address: dnc_dxn@shsu.edu.

▼ SHENANDOAH UNIVERSITY

Winchester, Virginia

Independent-United Methodist, coed. Small town campus. Total enrollment: 1,927.

Degrees Bachelor of Fine Arts in the areas of dance, dance education. Majors and concentrations: dance, dance education. Graduate degrees offered: Master of Fine Arts in the area of dance choreography and performance.

Enrollment Fall 1997: 48 total; 42 undergraduate, 2 graduate, 4 non-professional degree.

Dance Student Profile 88% females, 12% males, 15% minorities, 6% international.

Dance Faculty 10 total undergraduate and graduate (full-time and part-time). 75% of full-time faculty have terminal degrees. Graduate students teach a few undergraduate courses. Undergraduate student–faculty ratio: 5:1.

Student Life Student groups/activities include American College Dance Festival Association, Shenandoah Dance Ensembles on tour, Shenandoah University Dance Association.

Expenses for 1997–98 Application fee: $30. Comprehensive fee: $19,450 includes full-time tuition ($14,400) and college room and board ($5050). Full-time tuition varies according to course load, degree level, and program. Room and board charges vary according to board plan.

Financial Aid Program-specific awards for 1997: 30 Talent Scholarships for program majors ($250–$3000).

Application Procedures Students admitted directly into the professional program freshman year. Deadline for freshmen and transfers: continuous. Required: high school transcript, college transcript(s) for transfer students, minimum 2.0 high school GPA, interview, video, audition, SAT I or ACT test scores. Recommended: letter of recommendation. Auditions held 8 times on campus and off campus in various cities; videotaped performances are permissible as a substitute for live auditions if a campus visit is impossible.

Contact Mr. Michael Carpenter, Director, Admissions Office, Shenandoah University, 1460 University Drive, Winchester, Virginia 22601-5195; 540-665-4581, fax: 540-665-4627, E-mail address: admit@su.edu.

▼ SIMON FRASER UNIVERSITY

Burnaby, BC, Canada

Province-supported, coed. Suburban campus. Total enrollment: 18,759. Dance program established 1993.

Degrees Bachelor of Fine Arts in the area of contemporary dance. Graduate degrees offered: Master of Fine Arts in the area of interdisciplinary studies.

Enrollment Fall 1997: 46 total.

Dance Faculty 3 total undergraduate and graduate (full-time). 33% of full-time faculty have terminal degrees. Graduate students teach a few undergraduate courses.

Student Life Student groups/activities include Off Centre Dance Company.

Expenses for 1997–98 Application fee: $25 Canadian dollars. Tuition, fee, and room only charges are reported in Canadian dollars. Canadian resident tuition: $2310 full-time. Mandatory fees: $207 full-time. College room only: $2830. Room charges vary according to housing facility. International student tuition: $6930 full-time.

Financial Aid Program-specific awards for 1997: 5 Adaline May Clark Scholarships for program majors ($100–$500), 1 Murray Farr Award for program majors ($500).

Application Procedures Students apply for admission into the professional program by sophomore year. Deadline for freshmen and transfers: May 1. Required: high school transcript, minimum 3.0 high school GPA, interview, audition. Auditions held twice on campus; videotaped performances are permissible as a substitute for live auditions for international applicants.

Web Site http://www.sfu.ca/sca.

Undergraduate Contact Admissions Office, Simon Fraser University, 8888 University Drive, Burnaby, BC V5A 1S6, Canada; 604-291-3224, fax: 604-291-4969.

Graduate Contact Chair, MFA Program, School for the Contemporary Arts, Simon Fraser University, 8888 University Drive, Burnaby, BC V5A 1S6, Canada; 604-291-3492, fax: 604-291-5907, E-mail address: mfa_grad_office@sfu.ca.

Meadows School of the Arts

▼ SOUTHERN METHODIST UNIVERSITY

Dallas, Texas

Independent, coed. Suburban campus. Total enrollment: 9,708.

Degrees Bachelor of Fine Arts in the area of dance performance. Majors and concentrations: ballet, jazz dance, modern dance. Graduate degrees offered: Master of Fine Arts in the area of choreographic theory and practice. Program accredited by NASD.

Enrollment Fall 1997: 89 total; 87 undergraduate, 2 graduate.

Dance Student Profile 85% females, 15% males, 21% minorities.

Dance Faculty 12 total undergraduate and graduate (full-time and part-time). 85% of full-time faculty have terminal degrees. Graduate students do not teach undergraduate courses. Undergraduate student–faculty ratio: 10:1.

Student Life Student groups/activities include American Dance Festival, Dallas Morning News Dance Festival, Dance for the Planet. Special housing available for dance students.

Expenses for 1997–98 Application fee: $40. Comprehensive fee: $23,244 includes full-time tuition ($14,896), mandatory fees ($1894), and college room and board ($6454). College room only: $3600. Room and board charges vary according to board plan and housing facility.

Financial Aid Program-specific awards for 1997: 20 Meadows Artistic Scholarships for talented program majors ($1000–$5000).

Application Procedures Students apply for admission into the professional program by sophomore year. Deadline for freshmen and transfers: continuous. Required: essay, high school transcript, letter of recommendation, audition, SAT I or ACT test scores. Recommended: interview. Auditions held 20 times on campus and off campus in various locations; videotaped performances are permissible as a substitute for live auditions when distance is prohibitive.

Web Site http://www.smu.edu/~dance.

Undergraduate Contact Dr. Robert Stroker, Associate Dean for Student Affairs, Meadows School of the Arts, Southern Methodist University, PO Box 750356, Dallas, Texas 75275-0356; 214-768-3217, fax: 214-768-3272, E-mail address: rstroker@mail.smu.edu.

Graduate Contact Dr. Shelley C. Berg, Chair, Dance Division, Southern Methodist University, PO Box 750356, Dallas, Texas 75275-0356; 214-768-2718, fax: 214-768-4669, E-mail address: sberg@mail.smu.edu.

▼ SOUTHWEST MISSOURI STATE UNIVERSITY

Springfield, Missouri

State-supported, coed. Suburban campus. Total enrollment: 16,468.

Degrees Bachelor of Fine Arts in the area of dance.

Enrollment Fall 1997: 35 undergraduate.

Dance Student Profile 90% females, 10% males, 5% minorities, 1% international.

Dance Faculty 6 total (full-time and part-time). 67% of full-time faculty have terminal degrees. Graduate students do not teach undergraduate courses. Undergraduate student–faculty ratio: 12:1.

Student Life Student groups/activities include Inertia Dance Company, Footnotes Entertainment Troupe.

Expenses for 1998–99 Application fee: $15. State resident tuition: $2940 full-time. Nonresident tuition: $5880 full-time. Mandatory fees: $274 full-time. Full-time tuition and fees vary according to course load. College room and board: $3594. College room only: $2396. Room and board charges vary according to board plan and housing facility.

Financial Aid Program-specific awards for 1997: 4 Dance Activity Awards for program majors ($2000), 2 out-of-state waivers for program majors ($2000), 6 Footnotes Entertainment Troupe Awards for program majors ($2000).

Application Procedures Students apply for admission into the professional program by sophomore year. Deadline for freshmen and transfers: August 1. Notification date for freshmen and transfers: continuous. Required: high school transcript, college transcript(s) for transfer students, minimum 2.0 high school GPA, ACT test score only, standing in top 67% of graduating class.

Web Site http://www.smsu.edu/contrib/the_dan/.

Undergraduate Contact Dr. Robert H. Bradley, Head, Department of Theatre and Dance, Southwest Missouri State University, 901 South National, Springfield, Missouri 65804; 417-836-5268, fax: 417-836-6940, E-mail address: rhb072f@vma.smsu.edu.

▼ STATE UNIVERSITY OF NEW YORK COLLEGE AT BROCKPORT

Brockport, New York

State-supported, coed. Small town campus. Total enrollment: 8,492. Dance program established 1970.

Degrees Bachelor of Fine Arts in the area of dance. Graduate degrees offered: Master of Fine Arts in the area of dance. Cross-registration with members of the National Student Exchange Program. Program accredited by NASD.

Enrollment Fall 1997: 100 total; 35 undergraduate, 15 graduate, 50 non-professional degree.

Dance Student Profile 90% females, 10% males, 15% minorities, 10% international.

Dance Faculty 14 total undergraduate and graduate (full-time and part-time). 75% of full-time faculty have terminal degrees. Graduate students teach about a quarter undergraduate courses. Undergraduate student–faculty ratio: 15:1.

Student Life Student groups/activities include Dance Club, Scholars Day, Freshman Convocation.

Expenses for 1997–98 Application fee: $30. State resident tuition: $3400 full-time. Nonresident tuition: $8300 full-time. Mandatory fees: $515 full-time. College room and board: $4960. College room only: $3050. Room and board charges vary according to board plan.

Financial Aid Program-specific awards for 1997: 2 Friars Scholarships for talented students ($1000), 1 Pylyshenko-Strasser Award for sophomores ($200).

Application Procedures Students admitted directly into the professional program freshman year. Deadline for freshmen and transfers: continuous. Required: high school transcript, minimum 2.0 high school GPA, audition, SAT I or ACT test scores. Recommended: minimum 3.0 high school GPA, letter of recommendation, interview. Auditions held on campus; videotaped performances are permissible as a substitute for live auditions for international applicants.

Web Site http://www.brockport.edu.

Undergraduate Contact Ms. Jacqueline Davis, Undergraduate Program Director, Dance Department, State University of New York College at Brockport, Neff Hall, Brockport, New York 14420; 716-395-2153, fax: 716-395-5134.
Graduate Contact Ms. Susannah Newman, Graduate Program Director, Dance Department, State University of New York College at Brockport, Neff Hall, Brockport, New York 14420; 716-395-5302, fax: 716-395-5134.

▼ STATE UNIVERSITY OF NEW YORK COLLEGE AT PURCHASE

See Purchase College, State University of New York

▼ STEPHENS COLLEGE

Columbia, Missouri

Independent, women only. Urban campus. Total enrollment: 819. Dance program established 1965.
Degrees Bachelor of Fine Arts in the areas of dance, performance. Cross-registration with Mid-Missouri Area Consortium of Colleges and Universities.
Enrollment Fall 1997: 27 total.
Dance Student Profile 95% females, 5% males, 2% international.
Dance Faculty 5 total (full-time and part-time). 40% of full-time faculty have terminal degrees. Graduate students do not teach undergraduate courses. Undergraduate student–faculty ratio: 7:1.
Student Life Student groups/activities include Chi Tau Epsilon, Stephens College Repertory Dance Theatre. Special housing available for dance students.
Expenses for 1997–98 Application fee: $25. Comprehensive fee: $20,530 includes full-time tuition ($14,830) and college room and board ($5700). College room only: $2990. Room and board charges vary according to board plan and housing facility. Special program-related fees: $45 per semester for physical therapy evaluation (weekly consultation).
Financial Aid Program-specific awards for 1997: Stephens Leadership Award ($1000–$3000).
Application Procedures Students admitted directly into the professional program freshman year. Deadline for freshmen and transfers: June 1. Notification date for freshmen and transfers: August 1. Required: essay, high school transcript, college transcript(s) for transfer students, minimum 2.0 high school GPA, 2 letters of recommendation, interview, audition, SAT I or ACT test scores. Auditions held once on campus; videotaped performances are permissible as a substitute for live auditions when distance is prohibitive.
Undergraduate Contact John F. Fluke, Dean of Enrollment Services, Admission Department, Stephens College, Box 2121, Columbia, Missouri 65215-0002; 800-876-7207, fax: 573-876-7237, E-mail address: apply@sc.stephens.edu.

▼ SYBIL B. HARRINGTON COLLEGE OF FINE ARTS AND HUMANITIES

See West Texas A&M University

▼ TEMPLE UNIVERSITY

Philadelphia, Pennsylvania

State-related, coed. Urban campus. Total enrollment: 27,670.
Degrees Bachelor of Fine Arts in the area of dance. Majors and concentrations: choreography, dance, performance. Graduate degrees offered: Master of Fine Arts in the area of dance; Master of Education in the area of dance education. Doctor of Philosophy in the areas of dance history, dance education. Program accredited by NASD.
Enrollment Fall 1997: 157 total; 62 undergraduate, 60 graduate, 35 non-professional degree.
Dance Student Profile 92% females, 8% males, 25% minorities, 7% international.
Dance Faculty 14 total undergraduate and graduate (full-time and part-time). 100% of full-time faculty have terminal degrees. Graduate students teach a few undergraduate courses. Undergraduate student–faculty ratio: 10:1.
Expenses for 1997–98 Application fee: $35. State resident tuition: $5870 full-time. Nonresident tuition: $10,752 full-time. Mandatory fees: $280 full-time. Full-time tuition and fees vary according to course load and program. College room and board: $5772. Room and board charges vary according to board plan and housing facility. Special program-related fees: $10 per course for lab fees.
Financial Aid Program-specific awards for 1997: 3 departmental scholarships for freshmen and returning students ($1500).
Application Procedures Students admitted directly into the professional program freshman year. Deadline for freshmen and transfers: June 15. Notification date for freshmen and transfers: August 1. Required: essay, high school transcript, minimum 2.0 high school GPA, letter of recommendation, interview, audition, SAT I or ACT test scores. Recommended: minimum 3.0 high school GPA. Auditions held 5 times on campus; videotaped performances are permissible as a substitute for live auditions for international applicants.
Web Site http://www.temple.edu/HPERD/dance/.
Undergraduate Contact Mr. Philip Grosser, Coordinator, BFA Program, Dance Department, Temple University, 309 Vivacqua Hall, Philadelphia, Pennsylvania 19122; 215-204-8710, E-mail address: lkahlich@nimbus.temple.edu.
Graduate Contact Dance Admissions Office, Dance Department, Temple University, 309 Vivacqua Hall, Philadelphia, Pennsylvania 19122; 215-204-8710, E-mail address: lkahlich@nimbus.temple.edu.

▼ TEXAS CHRISTIAN UNIVERSITY

Fort Worth, Texas

Independent, coed. Suburban campus. Total enrollment: 7,273. Dance program established 1949.
Degrees Bachelor of Fine Arts in the areas of modern dance, ballet. Graduate degrees offered: Master of Fine Arts in the areas of modern dance, ballet.
Enrollment Fall 1997: 60 undergraduate, 4 graduate.
Dance Student Profile 90% females, 10% males, 6% minorities, 2% international.
Dance Faculty 8 total undergraduate and graduate (full-time and part-time). 80% of full-time faculty have terminal degrees. Graduate students do not teach undergraduate courses.
Expenses for 1997–98 Application fee: $30. One-time mandatory fee: $200. Comprehensive fee: $14,950 includes full-time

Texas Christian University (continued)

tuition ($9900), mandatory fees ($1190), and college room and board ($3860). College room only: $2460. Room and board charges vary according to housing facility.

Financial Aid Program-specific awards for 1997: 2 Nordan Awards for dance majors ($4000).

Application Procedures Students admitted directly into the professional program freshman year. Deadline for freshmen: February 5; transfers: August 1. Notification date for freshmen: April 1; transfers: continuous. Required: essay, high school transcript, college transcript(s) for transfer students, 2 letters of recommendation, audition, SAT I or ACT test scores. Recommended: interview. Auditions held 4 times on campus; videotaped performances are permissible as a substitute for live auditions for international applicants.

Web Site http://www.tcu.edu.

Undergraduate Contact Ms. Ellen Page Garrison, Chair, Ballet and Modern Dance Department, Texas Christian University, PO Box 297910, Fort Worth, Texas 76129; 817-921-7615, fax: 817-921-7333, E-mail address: e.garrison@gamma.is.tcu.edu.

Graduate Contact Ms. Ellen Page Page Garrison, Chair, Ballet and Modern Dance Department, Texas Christian University, PO Box 297910, Fort Worth, Texas 76129; 817-921-7615, fax: 817-921-7333, E-mail address: e.garrison@gamma.is.tcu.edu.

▼ TISCH SCHOOL OF THE ARTS

See New York University

▼ TOWSON UNIVERSITY

Towson, Maryland

State-supported, coed. Suburban campus. Total enrollment: 15,524.

Degrees Bachelor of Fine Arts in the areas of dance performance, dance performance and education. Program accredited by NASD.

Dance Faculty 11 total (full-time and part-time). 100% of full-time faculty have terminal degrees. Graduate students do not teach undergraduate courses.

Student Life Student groups/activities include dance company.

Expenses for 1997–98 Application fee: $30. State resident tuition: $3080 full-time. Nonresident tuition: $8158 full-time. Mandatory fees: $1040 full-time. College room and board: $5044. College room only: $2924.

Financial Aid Program-specific awards for 1997: dance scholarships for program majors.

Application Procedures Students admitted directly into the professional program freshman year. Deadline for freshmen and transfers: May 1. Notification date for freshmen and transfers: continuous. Required: high school transcript, college transcript(s) for transfer students, audition, SAT I or ACT test scores (minimum combined SAT I score of 1100, minimum combined ACT score of 22). Recommended: minimum 3.0 high school GPA, letter of recommendation. Auditions held twice on campus; videotaped performances are permissible as a substitute for live auditions with permission of the chair.

Web Site http://www.towson.edu/dance.

Undergraduate Contact Mr. Dennis Price, Chairperson, Department of Dance, Towson University, Burdick Hall, Room 101B, Towson, Maryland 21252; 410-830-2760, fax: 410-830-3752, E-mail address: dprice@towson.edu.

▼ THE UNIVERSITY OF AKRON

Akron, Ohio

State-supported, coed. Urban campus. Total enrollment: 23,538. Dance program established 1970.

Degrees Bachelor of Fine Arts in the areas of dance, musical theater-dance. Program accredited by NASD.

Enrollment Fall 1997: 78 total; 28 undergraduate, 50 non-professional degree.

Dance Student Profile 95% females, 5% males, 5% minorities.

Dance Faculty 13 total (full-time and part-time). 75% of full-time faculty have terminal degrees. Graduate students do not teach undergraduate courses. Undergraduate student–faculty ratio: 10:1.

Student Life Student groups/activities include Ohio Association of Health, Physical Education, Recreation and Dance, American College Dance Festival, OHIODANCE.

Expenses for 1997–98 Application fee: $25. State resident tuition: $3312 full-time. Nonresident tuition: $8772 full-time. Mandatory fees: $348 full-time. College room and board: $4490. College room only: $2820. Room and board charges vary according to board plan. Special program-related fees: $5 per course for trainer and supplies.

Financial Aid Program-specific awards for 1997: 1–10 Muehlstein Awards for applicants living within 100 miles of New York City ($7000), 1 Mary Schiller Myers Award for male dancers ($500).

Application Procedures Students admitted directly into the professional program freshman year. Deadline for freshmen and transfers: continuous. Required: high school transcript, college transcript(s) for transfer students, SAT I or ACT test scores. Recommended: interview, video, audition. Auditions held twice on campus; videotaped performances are permissible as a substitute for live auditions if a campus visit is impossible.

Web Site http://www.uakron.edu/faa/schools/dance.html.

Undergraduate Contact Ms. Lucinda Lavelli, Director, School of Dance, Theatre, and Arts Administration, The University of Akron, 354 East Market Street, Akron, Ohio 44325-2502; 330-972-7948, E-mail address: lsl@uakron.edu.

▼ THE UNIVERSITY OF ARIZONA

Tucson, Arizona

State-supported, coed. Urban campus. Total enrollment: 33,737. Dance program established 1984.

Degrees Bachelor of Fine Arts in the area of dance. Majors and concentrations: ballet, jazz dance, modern dance. Graduate degrees offered: Master of Arts/Master of Fine Arts in the area of theater arts (with concentration in dance). Program accredited by NASD.

Enrollment Fall 1997: 145 total; 100 undergraduate, 15 graduate, 30 non-professional degree.

Dance Student Profile 89% females, 11% males, 12% minorities, 4% international.

Dance Faculty 9 total undergraduate and graduate (full-time and part-time). 57% of full-time faculty have terminal degrees. Graduate students teach about a quarter undergraduate courses. Undergraduate student–faculty ratio: 15:1.

Student Life Student groups/activities include Dancers' Consort.

Expenses for 1997–98 Application fee: $40 for nonresidents. State resident tuition: $1988 full-time. Nonresident tuition: $8640 full-time. Mandatory fees: $70 full-time. College room and board: $4930. College room only: $2480. Room and board charges vary according to board plan and housing facility.

Financial Aid Program-specific awards for 1997: 6–12 out-of-state tuition waivers for program majors ($3500), 7–14 in-state fee waivers for program majors ($1000), 18–20 Dance Performance Scholarships for program majors ($250–$500).

Application Procedures Students admitted directly into the professional program freshman year. Deadline for freshmen: April 1; transfers: June 1. Required: high school transcript, college transcript(s) for transfer students, SAT I or ACT test scores, minimum 2.8 high school GPA, video or audition. Auditions held continuously by appointment on campus; videotaped performances are permissible as a substitute for live auditions if a live audition is impossible.

Undergraduate Contact Ms. Melissa Lowe, Undergraduate Advisor, Dance Division, School of Music and Dance, The University of Arizona, Ina Gittings Building, Room 121, Tucson, Arizona 85721; 520-621-1387, fax: 520-621-6981.

Graduate Contact Dr. Suzanne Knosp, Graduate Advisor, Dance Division, School of Music and Dance, The University of Arizona, Ina Gittings Building, Room 121, Tucson, Arizona 85721; 520-621-2923, fax: 520-621-6981.

▼ UNIVERSITY OF CALIFORNIA, IRVINE

Irvine, California

State-supported, coed. Suburban campus.

Degrees Bachelor of Fine Arts in the areas of dance, choreography, performance. Graduate degrees offered: Master of Fine Arts in the area of dance.

Enrollment Fall 1997: 159 total; 7 undergraduate, 22 graduate, 130 non-professional degree.

Dance Student Profile 91% females, 9% males, 30% minorities.

Dance Faculty 21 total undergraduate and graduate (full-time and part-time). 50% of full-time faculty have terminal degrees. Graduate students teach a few undergraduate courses.

Student Life Special housing available for dance students.

Application Procedures Students apply for admission into the professional program by sophomore year. Deadline for freshmen and transfers: November 30. Notification date for freshmen: March 15; transfers: May 1. Required: essay, high school transcript, college transcript(s) for transfer students, audition, SAT I or ACT test scores. Recommended: minimum 3.5 high school GPA. Auditions held once in January on campus; videotaped performances are permissible as a substitute for live auditions when distance is prohibitive.

Undergraduate Contact Mr. Donald Bradburn, Undergraduate Advisor, Department of Dance, University of California, Irvine, School of the Arts, Irvine, California 92717; 949-824-7284, fax: 949-824-4563.

Graduate Contact Mr. Alan Terricciano, Graduate Advisor, Department of Dance, University of California, Irvine, School of the Arts, Irvine, California 92717; 949-824-7284, fax: 949-824-4563.

▼ UNIVERSITY OF CALIFORNIA, SANTA BARBARA

Santa Barbara, California

State-supported, coed. Suburban campus. Total enrollment: 18,940.

Degrees Bachelor of Fine Arts in the areas of performance, choreography. Majors and concentrations: choreography and performance. Program accredited by NASD.

Enrollment Fall 1997: 10 total; all undergraduate.

Dance Student Profile 90% females, 10% males.

Dance Faculty 9 total (full-time and part-time). 28% of full-time faculty have terminal degrees. Graduate students do not teach undergraduate courses.

Student Life Student groups/activities include American College Dance Festival, Intercampus Arts Festival.

Expenses for 1997–98 Application fee: $40. State resident tuition: $0 full-time. Nonresident tuition: $8989 full-time. Mandatory fees: $4098 full-time. College room and board: $6407. Room and board charges vary according to housing facility.

Financial Aid Program-specific awards for 1997: 1–2 M. Plaskett Scholarships for incoming males ($1000), 1 Drama and Dance Affiliate Scholarship for seniors ($200–$400).

Application Procedures Students apply for admission into the professional program by sophomore year. Deadline for freshmen and transfers: November 30. Notification date for freshmen: March 15; transfers: April 1. Required: essay, high school transcript, college transcript(s) for transfer students, minimum 3.0 high school GPA, audition. Auditions held twice on campus; videotaped performances are permissible as a substitute for live auditions if a campus visit is impossible.

Web Site http://humanitas.ucsb.edu/depts/drama_art/.

Undergraduate Contact Ms. Marilyn Romine, Undergraduate Advisor, Department of Dramatic Art and Dance, University of California, Santa Barbara, Snidecor 2645, Santa Barbara, California 93106; 805-893-3241, fax: 805-893-7029, E-mail address: romine@humanitas.ucsb.edu.

University of Cincinnati

▼ UNIVERSITY OF CINCINNATI COLLEGE CONSERVATORY OF MUSIC

Cincinnati, Ohio

State-supported, coed. Urban campus. Total enrollment: 28,161. Dance program established 1964.

Degrees Bachelor of Fine Arts in the area of dance. Majors and concentrations: ballet. Cross-registration with Greater Cincinnati Consortium of Colleges and Universities. Program accredited by NASD.

Enrollment Fall 1997: 26 undergraduate.

Dance Student Profile 96% females, 4% males, 3% minorities, 3% international.

Dance Faculty 7 total (full-time and part-time). 25% of full-time faculty have terminal degrees. Graduate students do not teach undergraduate courses. Undergraduate student–faculty ratio: 7:1.

Student Life Student groups/activities include Choreographers Showcase.

University of Cincinnati College Conservatory of Music
(continued)

Expenses for 1997–98 Application fee: $30. State resident tuition: $3879 full-time. Nonresident tuition: $10,986 full-time. Mandatory fees: $480 full-time. College room and board: $5643.

Financial Aid Program-specific awards for 1997: Honor Awards for program majors ($890–$8000).

Application Procedures Students admitted directly into the professional program freshman year. Deadline for freshmen and transfers: continuous. Notification date for freshmen and transfers: continuous. Required: high school transcript, college transcript(s) for transfer students, minimum 2.0 high school GPA, letter of recommendation, audition, SAT I or ACT test scores. Recommended: minimum 3.0 high school GPA. Auditions held 9 times on campus and off campus in Interlochen, MI; Washington, DC; Cleveland, OH; Louisville, KY; Orlando, FL; videotaped performances are permissible as a substitute for live auditions when distance is prohibitive with approval from the division head.

Web Site http://www.uc.edu/www/ccm/dance/.

Undergraduate Contact Mrs. Angela K. Vaubel, Admissions Officer, College-Conservatory of Music, University of Cincinnati, PO Box 210003, Cincinnati, Ohio 45221-0003; 513-556-5463, fax: 513-556-1028, E-mail address: angela.vaubel@uc.edu.

▼ UNIVERSITY OF COLORADO AT BOULDER

Boulder, Colorado

State-supported, coed. Suburban campus. Total enrollment: 25,109. Dance program established 1948.

Degrees Bachelor of Fine Arts in the area of dance. Majors and concentrations: modern dance. Graduate degrees offered: Master of Fine Arts in the area of dance.

Enrollment Fall 1997: 68 total; 6 undergraduate, 14 graduate, 48 non-professional degree.

Dance Student Profile 92% females, 8% males, 3% minorities.

Dance Faculty 8 total undergraduate and graduate (full-time and part-time). 85% of full-time faculty have terminal degrees. Graduate students teach a few undergraduate courses. Undergraduate student–faculty ratio: 7:1.

Student Life Student groups/activities include American College Dance Festival, Onstage.

Expenses for 1997–98 Application fee: $40. One-time mandatory fee: $35. State resident tuition: $2356 full-time. Nonresident tuition: $14,400 full-time. Mandatory fees: $583 full-time. Full-time tuition and fees vary according to program. College room and board: $4566. Room and board charges vary according to board plan, housing facility, and location. Special program-related fees: $25 per course for accompanist fee, $15 per course for tapes and compact discs.

Financial Aid Program-specific awards for 1997: 10–12 University Dance Awards for program majors ($250–$500), 1 Redmond Scholarship for upperclass program majors demonstrating talent and academic achievement ($1300), 1 Katherine J. Lamont Scholarship for program majors ($450).

Application Procedures Students apply for admission into the professional program by freshman year. Deadline for freshmen: February 15; transfers: April 1. Notification date for freshmen and transfers: continuous. Required: high school transcript, college transcript(s) for transfer students, minimum 2.0 high school GPA, SAT I or ACT test scores.

Web Site http://www.colorado.edu/TheatreDance/.

Undergraduate Contact Office of Admissions, University of Colorado at Boulder, Box 30, Boulder, Colorado 80309; 303-492-6301, fax: 303-492-7115.

Graduate Contact Ms. Marcia Richardson, Graduate Secretary, Department of Theatre and Dance, University of Colorado at Boulder, Box 261, Boulder, Colorado 80309; 303-492-7356, fax: 303-492-7722, E-mail address: marcia.richardson@colorado.edu.

▼ UNIVERSITY OF FLORIDA

Gainesville, Florida

State-supported, coed. Suburban campus. Total enrollment: 41,713. Dance program established 1997.

Degrees Bachelor of Fine Arts in the area of dance. Majors and concentrations: choreography and performance, dance, dance in medicine, theater arts/drama. Cross-registration with New World School of the Arts.

Enrollment Fall 1997: 17 total; all undergraduate.

Dance Student Profile 100% females, 11% minorities.

Dance Faculty 7 total (full-time and part-time). 100% of full-time faculty have terminal degrees. Graduate students do not teach undergraduate courses. Undergraduate student–faculty ratio: 4:1.

Student Life Student groups/activities include Alpha Psi Omega, Florida Players, Floridance Company (includes performance ensemble).

Expenses for 1997–98 Application fee: $20. State resident tuition: $1930 full-time. Nonresident tuition: $7570 full-time. College room and board: $4610. College room only: $2270. Room and board charges vary according to board plan and housing facility. Special program-related fees: $5–$15 per course for expendable supplies.

Financial Aid Program-specific awards for 1997: departmental scholarships for program majors ($500).

Application Procedures Students admitted directly into the professional program freshman year. Deadline for freshmen and transfers: January 31. Required: high school transcript, college transcript(s) for transfer students, minimum 2.0 high school GPA, interview, audition, SAT I or ACT test scores (minimum combined SAT I score of 950, minimum combined ACT score of 19). Recommended: essay. Auditions held twice a year and by appointment on campus; videotaped performances are permissible as a substitute for live auditions if a live audition is impossible.

Undergraduate Contact Dr. Louise Rothman, Undergraduate Coordinator, Department of Theatre and Dance, University of Florida, PO Box 115900, Gainesville, Florida 32611-5900; 352-392-2038, fax: 352-392-5114, E-mail address: lrothman@ufl.edu.

The Hartt School

▼ UNIVERSITY OF HARTFORD

West Hartford, Connecticut

Independent, coed. Suburban campus. Total enrollment: 7,089. Dance program established 1994.

Degrees Bachelor of Fine Arts in the areas of dance performance, dance pedagogy, children's dance. Majors and concentrations: ballet pedagogy, children's dance, perfor-

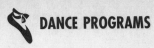

mance. Cross-registration with Trinity College, Saint Joseph College, Hartford Seminary. Program accredited by NASD.
Enrollment Fall 1997: 40 total; all undergraduate.
Dance Student Profile 90% females, 10% males, 1% international.
Dance Faculty 12 total (full-time and part-time). 80% of full-time faculty have terminal degrees. Graduate students do not teach undergraduate courses. Undergraduate student–faculty ratio: 6:1.
Student Life Special housing available for dance students.
Expenses for 1998–99 Application fee: $35. Comprehensive fee: $25,424 includes full-time tuition ($17,190), mandatory fees ($1034), and college room and board ($7200). College room only: $4440. Room and board charges vary according to board plan and housing facility.
Financial Aid Program-specific awards for 1997: 20 Performing Arts Scholarships for students passing audition evaluations ($6000).
Application Procedures Students admitted directly into the professional program freshman year. Deadline for freshmen and transfers: continuous. Required: high school transcript, college transcript(s) for transfer students, minimum 2.0 high school GPA, 3 letters of recommendation, interview, audition, SAT I or ACT test scores. Recommended: essay, minimum 3.0 high school GPA. Auditions held 12 times on campus and off campus in Hartford, CT; Boston, MA; New York, NY; Dallas, TX; Houston, TX; Interlochen, MI; Boca Raton, FL; Miami, FL; Seattle, WA; Los Angeles, CA; New Orleans, LA; Columbus, OH; videotaped performances are permissible as a substitute for live auditions when distance is prohibitive.
Undergraduate Contact Mr. James Jacobs, Director of Admissions, The Hartt School, University of Hartford, 200 Bloomfield Avenue, West Hartford, Connecticut 06117-1500; 860-768-4465, fax: 860-768-4441.

▼ UNIVERSITY OF HAWAII AT MANOA

Honolulu, Hawaii

State-supported, coed. Urban campus. Total enrollment: 17,356. Dance program established 1965.
Degrees Bachelor of Fine Arts in the areas of dance, theater. Graduate degrees offered: Master of Fine Arts in the area of dance.
Enrollment Fall 1997: 35 undergraduate, 14 graduate.
Dance Student Profile 92% females, 8% males, 70% minorities, 10% international.
Dance Faculty 15 total undergraduate and graduate (full-time and part-time). 80% of full-time faculty have terminal degrees. Graduate students teach a few undergraduate courses. Undergraduate student–faculty ratio: 4:1.
Student Life Student groups/activities include American College Dance Festival Association, Council of Dance Administrators.
Expenses for 1997–98 Application fee: $25 for nonresidents. State resident tuition: $2832 full-time. Nonresident tuition: $9312 full-time. Mandatory fees: $118 full-time. College room and board: $4740. College room only: $2660. Room and board charges vary according to board plan and housing facility.
Application Procedures Students apply for admission into the professional program by sophomore year. Deadline for freshmen and transfers: May 1. Required: college transcript(s) for transfer students, minimum 3.0 high school

GPA, audition, SAT I or ACT test scores (minimum combined SAT I score of 1120), minimum TOEFL score of 540 for international applicants. Recommended: 3 letters of recommendation, video. Auditions held once on campus; videotaped performances are permissible as a substitute for live auditions for the MFA degree.
Undergraduate Contact Ms. Peggy Gaither Adams, Undergraduate Advisor, Department of Theatre and Dance, University of Hawaii at Manoa, 1770 East West Road, Honolulu, Hawaii 96822; 808-956-3264, fax: 808-956-4234, E-mail address: adams@hawaii.edu.
Graduate Contact Mr. Gregg Lizenbery, Director of Dance, Department of Theatre and Dance, University of Hawaii at Manoa, 1770 East West Road, Honolulu, Hawaii 96822; 808-956-2464, fax: 808-956-4234, E-mail address: lgreg@hawaii.edu.

▼ UNIVERSITY OF ILLINOIS AT URBANA–CHAMPAIGN

Champaign, Illinois

State-supported, coed. Small town campus. Total enrollment: 36,019.
Degrees Bachelor of Fine Arts in the area of dance. Majors and concentrations: choreography and performance. Graduate degrees offered: Master of Fine Arts in the area of dance. Program accredited by NASD.
Enrollment Fall 1997: 62 total; 50 undergraduate, 12 graduate.
Dance Student Profile 87% females, 13% males, 2% minorities, 8% international.
Dance Faculty 11 total undergraduate and graduate (full-time and part-time). 100% of full-time faculty have terminal degrees. Graduate students teach about a quarter undergraduate courses. Undergraduate student–faculty ratio: 7:1.
Student Life Student groups/activities include Illinois Dance Theatre.
Expenses for 1997–98 Application fee: $40, $50 for international students. State resident tuition: $3308 full-time. Nonresident tuition: $9924 full-time. Mandatory fees: $812 full-time. Full-time tuition and fees vary according to program and student level. College room and board: $5078. College room only: $1958. Room and board charges vary according to board plan and housing facility.
Financial Aid Program-specific awards for 1997: Talented Student Awards for talented students ($1500).
Application Procedures Students admitted directly into the professional program freshman year. Deadline for freshmen and transfers: continuous. Notification date for freshmen and transfers: continuous. Required: high school transcript, college transcript(s) for transfer students, minimum 3.0 high school GPA, interview, audition, SAT I or ACT test scores. Auditions held 5 times on campus and off campus in Louisville, KY; Chicago, IL; videotaped performances are permissible as a substitute for live auditions when distance is prohibitive.
Web Site http://www.dance.uiuc.edu/dance/.
Undergraduate Contact Ms. Rebecca Nettl-Fiol, Associate Professor, Department of Dance, University of Illinois at Urbana-Champaign, 907 1/2 West Nevada, Urbana, Illinois 61801-3810; 217-244-4307, fax: 217-333-3000, E-mail address: rnettl@uiuc.edu.
Graduate Contact Ms. Kimberly Mattingly, Administrative Secretary, Department of Dance, University of Illinois at Urbana-

University of Illinois at Urbana–Champaign (continued)

Champaign, 907 1/2 West Nevada, Urbana, Illinois 61801-3810; 217-333-1011, fax: 217-333-3000, E-mail address: kmatting@uiuc.edu.

▼ THE UNIVERSITY OF IOWA

Iowa City, Iowa

State-supported, coed. Small town campus. Total enrollment: 28,409.

Degrees Bachelor of Fine Arts in the area of dance. Majors and concentrations: ballet, choreography, modern dance. Graduate degrees offered: Master of Fine Arts in the area of dance.

Enrollment Fall 1997: 861 total; 145 undergraduate, 16 graduate, 700 non-professional degree.

Dance Student Profile 80% females, 20% males, 6% minorities, 2% international.

Dance Faculty 8 total undergraduate and graduate (full-time and part-time). 95% of full-time faculty have terminal degrees. Graduate students teach more than half undergraduate courses.

Student Life Student groups/activities include American College Dance Festival Association.

Expenses for 1997–98 Application fee: $20. State resident tuition: $2566 full-time. Nonresident tuition: $9422 full-time. Mandatory fees: $194 full-time. Full-time tuition and fees vary according to course load. College room and board: $4046. Room and board charges vary according to board plan.

Financial Aid Program-specific awards for 1997: 1 Iowa Center for the Arts Scholarship for incoming freshmen ($3000), 1 T. J. Myers Memorial Scholarship for male incoming freshmen ($1000), 1 dance scholarship for freshmen program majors ($1000).

Application Procedures Students apply for admission into the professional program by freshman year. Deadline for freshmen and transfers: May 13. Required: high school transcript, college transcript(s) for transfer students, minimum 2.0 high school GPA, letter of recommendation, interview, SAT I or ACT test scores, audition or video. Recommended: essay, minimum 3.0 high school GPA, resume. Auditions held 6 times on campus; videotaped performances are permissible as a substitute for live auditions when distance is prohibitive or for financial reasons.

Undergraduate Contact Ms. Helen Chadima, Chair, Dance Department, The University of Iowa, E114 Halsey Hall, Iowa City, Iowa 52242; 319-335-2228, fax: 319-335-3246.

Graduate Contact Linda Crist, Dance Department, The University of Iowa, E114 Halsey Hall, Iowa City, Iowa 52242; 319-335-2183, fax: 319-335-3246.

▼ UNIVERSITY OF MASSACHUSETTS AMHERST

Amherst, Massachusetts

State-supported, coed. Small town campus. Total enrollment: 24,884.

Degrees Bachelor of Fine Arts in the area of dance. Cross-registration with Amherst College, Hampshire College, Mount Holyoke College, Smith College.

Enrollment Fall 1997: 60 total; all undergraduate.

Dance Student Profile 99% females, 1% males, 1% minorities.

Dance Faculty 4 total (full-time and part-time). 100% of full-time faculty have terminal degrees. Graduate students do not teach undergraduate courses. Undergraduate student–faculty ratio: 20:1.

Student Life Student groups/activities include Alive With Dance, Dance Team, Music Guild.

Expenses for 1997–98 Application fee: $25, $40 for nonresidents. One-time mandatory fee: $143. State resident tuition: $2004 full-time. Nonresident tuition: $9017 full-time. Mandatory fees: $3568 full-time. Full-time tuition and fees vary according to reciprocity agreements. College room and board: $4520. Room and board charges vary according to board plan and student level.

Financial Aid Program-specific awards for 1997: 4–6 Chancellor's Talent Awards for program students ($2200), 2 cash awards for program students ($1000).

Application Procedures Deadline for freshmen: February 1; transfers: May 1. Notification date for freshmen: April 15; transfers: June 1. Required: essay, high school transcript, college transcript(s) for transfer students, audition, SAT I or ACT test scores. Auditions held 4 times on campus; videotaped performances are permissible as a substitute for live auditions when distance is prohibitive, if auditions are full, or in special circumstances.

Undergraduate Contact Ms. Mariah Lilly, Acting Director of Dance Admissions, Dance Program, University of Massachusetts Amherst, 11 Totman, Amherst, Massachusetts 01003; 413-545-6064, fax: 413-545-0220, E-mail address: mariahl@dance.umass.edu.

▼ UNIVERSITY OF MICHIGAN

Ann Arbor, Michigan

State-supported, coed. Suburban campus. Total enrollment: 36,995. Dance program established 1929.

Degrees Bachelor of Fine Arts in the areas of dance performance, dance performance with K-12 certification; Bachelor of Dance Arts in the area of dance. Majors and concentrations: choreography and performance, modern dance. Graduate degrees offered: Master of Fine Arts in the area of dance.

Enrollment Fall 1997: 394 total; 64 undergraduate, 5 graduate, 325 non-professional degree.

Dance Student Profile 90% females, 10% males, 7% minorities, 2% international.

Dance Faculty 12 total undergraduate and graduate (full-time and part-time). 90% of full-time faculty have terminal degrees. Graduate students do not teach undergraduate courses.

Student Life Student groups/activities include community outreach in public schools (teaching and guest choreography), "Life Forms" software consultations in the media union, "Video Dance" in conjunction with Film and Video Department.

Expenses for 1997–98 Application fee: $40. State resident tuition: $5694 full-time. Nonresident tuition: $18,260 full-time. Mandatory fees: $184 full-time. Full-time tuition and fees vary according to program and student level. College room and board: $5342. Room and board charges vary according to board plan and housing facility.

Financial Aid Program-specific awards for 1997: 26 Dance Merit Scholarships for incoming students ($1500).

Application Procedures Students admitted directly into the professional program freshman year. Deadline for freshmen and transfers: continuous. Required: essay, high school transcript, college transcript(s) for transfer students, minimum 3.0 high school GPA, audition, SAT I or ACT test scores, written personal statement. Auditions held 5 times on campus and off campus in New York, NY; videotaped performances are permissible as a substitute for live auditions with permission of the chair.

Web Site http://www.music.umich.edu/departments/dance/.

Undergraduate Contact Ms. Laura Strozeski, Senior Admissions Counselor, School of Music, University of Michigan, Moore Building, Ann Arbor, Michigan 48109-2085; 734-764-0593, fax: 734-763-5097, E-mail address: music.admissions@umich.edu.

Graduate Contact Ms. Gay Delanghe, Chair, Dance Department, University of Michigan, 1310 North University Court, Ann Arbor, Michigan 48109-2217; 734-763-5460, fax: 734-763-5962, E-mail address: delanghe@umich.edu.

▼ UNIVERSITY OF MINNESOTA, TWIN CITIES CAMPUS

Minneapolis, Minnesota

State-supported, coed. Urban campus. Total enrollment: 45,410. Dance program established 1987.

Degrees Bachelor of Fine Arts in the area of dance. Program accredited by NASD.

Enrollment Fall 1997: 1,170 total; 70 undergraduate, 1,100 non-professional degree.

Dance Student Profile 95% females, 5% males, 9% minorities, 5% international.

Dance Faculty 23 total (full-time and part-time). 75% of full-time faculty have terminal degrees. Graduate students do not teach undergraduate courses.

Student Life Student groups/activities include Student Dance Coalition.

Expenses for 1997–98 Application fee: $25. State resident tuition: $3976 full-time. Nonresident tuition: $11,378 full-time. Mandatory fees: $474 full-time. Full-time tuition and fees vary according to program, reciprocity agreements, and student level. College room and board: $4311. Room and board charges vary according to board plan, housing facility, and location.

Financial Aid Program-specific awards for 1997: 1 Nadine Jette-Sween Scholarship for dance majors ($800), 1 Marion Haynes Andrus Scholarship for dance majors ($800), 1 Advisory Council Scholarship for dance majors ($800), 1 Tom and Ellie Crosby Scholarship for incoming freshmen or newly declared dance majors ($800), 2 Robert Moulton Memorial Scholarships for dance majors ($800).

Application Procedures Students admitted directly into the professional program freshman year. Deadline for freshmen and transfers: continuous. Required: essay, high school transcript, college transcript(s) for transfer students, audition, SAT I or ACT test scores. Recommended: minimum 3.0 high school GPA, letter of recommendation. Auditions held 4 times on campus; videotaped performances are permissible as a substitute for live auditions if a campus visit is impossible.

Web Site http://cla.umn.edu/theater/index.html.

Undergraduate Contact Mr. Paul Meierant, Coordinator, Office of Admissions, University of Minnesota, Twin Cities Campus, 240 Williamson Hall, 231 Pillsbury Drive, SE, Minneapolis, Minnesota 55455; 612-625-2008, E-mail address: meier010@gold.tc.umn.edu.

More About the University

Faculty, Resident Artists, and Alumni The University Dance Program is particularly proud of its distinguished faculty, the latest addition being the choreographic team of Danial Shapiro and Joanie Smith. All technique teachers are national award-winning professional artists, many of whom have been or are directors of dance companies. In addition, the Dance Program annually hosts an average of five internationally renowned dance artists in residencies as an integral component of its performance, creative, and academic training. Past guest artists include Sally Banes, Merce Cunningham, Bill T. Jones, Ralph Lemon, Barbara Mahler, Bebe Miller, Shapiro & Smith, Bill Siegenfeld, Doug Varone, Dan Wagoner, David White, Mel Wong, and Sali Ann and Alan M. Kriegsman. Dance graduates have entered the professional companies of Creach and Koester, Ralph Lemon, José Limon, and Shapiro & Smith.

Student Performance Students give close to two dozen performances per year, including informal workshop showings, self-produced events by the Student Dance Coalition, and fully produced concerts by the University Dance Theatre (UDT). In addition, UDT annually collaborates with a major presenter and/or guest artists on a work of national significance. Examples include Bill T. Jones's "The Promised Land," Susan Marshall's "Spectators at an Event," and Kei Takei's "24 Hours of Light."

Program Facilities/Environment The program has four studios, classrooms, video equipment, and full production facilities shared with the Theatre Program. In 1999, the Dance Program will move into a new facility. The campus is situated in a major metropolitan area minutes away from the downtown districts of Minneapolis and St. Paul. Both cities are noted for their extraordinary arts communities. Professional dance companies include Zenon, 45 CHARTREUSE, Paula Mann & Dancers, Danny Buraczeski's JAZZDANCE, Corning Dancers & Company, Ethnic Dance Theatre, Shapiro & Smith Dance, and the Flying Foot Forum. Current dance majors and past graduates are performing with all of these companies.

▼ UNIVERSITY OF MISSOURI–KANSAS CITY

Kansas City, Missouri

State-supported, coed. Urban campus. Total enrollment: 10,445.

Degrees Bachelor of Fine Arts in the area of dance.

Enrollment Fall 1997: 90 total; 40 undergraduate, 50 non-professional degree.

Dance Student Profile 90% females, 10% males, 5% minorities, 15% international.

Dance Faculty 6 total (full-time and part-time). 75% of full-time faculty have terminal degrees. Graduate students do not teach undergraduate courses. Undergraduate student–faculty ratio: 8:1.

Student Life Student groups/activities include Dance Student Association.

University of Missouri–Kansas City (*continued*)

Expenses for 1997–98 Application fee: $25. State resident tuition: $4278 full-time. Nonresident tuition: $11,721 full-time. College room and board: $4270.

Financial Aid Program-specific awards for 1997: 20 Endowed Scholarships for program majors ($700–$2500).

Application Procedures Students admitted directly into the professional program freshman year. Deadline for freshmen and transfers: continuous. Notification date for freshmen and transfers: continuous. Required: high school transcript, 3 letters of recommendation, audition, ACT score for state residents, SAT I or ACT score for out-of-state residents. Auditions held by appointment on campus; videotaped performances are permissible as a substitute for live auditions for provisional acceptance.

Web Site http://www.umkc.edu.

Undergraduate Contact Mr. James T. Elswick, Admissions Coordinator, University of Missouri–Kansas City, 4949 Cherry, Kansas City, Missouri 64110-2229; 816-235-2900, fax: 816-235-5264, E-mail address: cadmissions@cctr.umkc.edu.

▼ THE UNIVERSITY OF MONTANA–MISSOULA

Missoula, Montana

State-supported, coed. Urban campus. Total enrollment: 12,124.

Degrees Bachelor of Fine Arts in the area of dance. Majors and concentrations: choreography and performance, dance education.

Enrollment Fall 1997: 230 total; 30 undergraduate, 200 non-professional degree.

Dance Student Profile 90% females, 10% males, 1% minorities, 2% international.

Dance Faculty 9 total (full-time and part-time). 100% of full-time faculty have terminal degrees. Graduate students do not teach undergraduate courses. Undergraduate student–faculty ratio: 20:1.

Student Life Student groups/activities include Associated Students of the University of Montana.

Expenses for 1997–98 Application fee: $30. State resident tuition: $2630 full-time. Nonresident tuition: $7192 full-time. Full-time tuition varies according to program and student level. College room and board: $3917. Room and board charges vary according to board plan and housing facility. Special program-related fees: $20–$60 for class materials/accompanist fee.

Financial Aid Program-specific awards for 1997: 2 departmental scholarships for program majors ($500), 2 Alexander Dean Awards for program majors ($600).

Application Procedures Students admitted directly into the professional program freshman year. Deadline for freshmen and transfers: March 1. Required: essay, high school transcript, audition, SAT I test score only. Auditions held once at the end of freshman year on campus.

Undergraduate Contact Terri Denney, Administrative Assistant, Department of Drama/Dance, The University of Montana–Missoula, Missoula, Montana 59812; 406-243-4481, fax: 406-243-5726.

▼ UNIVERSITY OF NEBRASKA–LINCOLN

Lincoln, Nebraska

State-supported, coed. Urban campus. Total enrollment: 22,827. Dance program established 1927.

Degrees Bachelor of Fine Arts in the area of dance. Majors and concentrations: ballet, modern dance.

Enrollment Fall 1997: 25 undergraduate.

Dance Student Profile 98% females, 2% males, 2% minorities.

Dance Faculty 5 total (full-time and part-time). 100% of full-time faculty have terminal degrees. Graduate students do not teach undergraduate courses.

Student Life Student groups/activities include Arts Festival.

Expenses for 1997–98 Application fee: $25. State resident tuition: $2355 full-time. Nonresident tuition: $6398 full-time. Mandatory fees: $474 full-time. Full-time tuition and fees vary according to course load. College room and board: $3700. College room only: $1638.

Financial Aid Program-specific awards for 1997: 20 departmental awards for program majors ($50–$400).

Application Procedures Students admitted directly into the professional program freshman year. Deadline for freshmen and transfers: July 15. Required: high school transcript, audition, SAT I or ACT test scores. Auditions held once on campus; videotaped performances are permissible as a substitute for live auditions if a campus visit is impossible.

Undergraduate Contact Ms. Charlotte Adams, Director, Dance Department, University of Nebraska–Lincoln, 215 Temple Building, PO Box 880201, Lincoln, Nebraska 68588-0201; 402-472-1713, fax: 402-472-1712.

▼ UNIVERSITY OF NORTH CAROLINA AT GREENSBORO

Greensboro, North Carolina

State-supported, coed. Urban campus. Total enrollment: 12,308. Dance program established 1948.

Degrees Bachelor of Fine Arts in the area of dance choreography and performance; Bachelor of Science in the area of dance education. Majors and concentrations: dance, dance education. Graduate degrees offered: Master of Fine Arts in the area of dance; Master of Arts in the area of dance. Cross-registration with North Carolina Agricultural and Technical State University, Guilford College, Greensboro College, Bennett College, Guilford Technical Community College. Program accredited by NCATE.

Enrollment Fall 1997: 135 total; 80 undergraduate, 15 graduate, 40 non-professional degree.

Dance Student Profile 90% females, 10% males, 15% minorities, 3% international.

Dance Faculty 12 total undergraduate and graduate (full-time and part-time). 89% of full-time faculty have terminal degrees. Graduate students teach a few undergraduate courses. Undergraduate student–faculty ratio: 10:1.

Student Life Student groups/activities include Prime Movers (student dance association). Special housing available for dance students.

Expenses for 1997–98 Application fee: $35. State resident tuition: $1016 full-time. Nonresident tuition: $9304 full-time. Mandatory fees: $1015 full-time. College room and board: $3661. College room only: $2011.

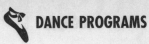
Financial Aid Program-specific awards for 1997: 1–2 Virginia Moomaw Scholarships for continuing program students ($400), 1 Feinstein Scholarship for minority students ($750), 1–3 Burns Scholarships for continuing students with career interest in musical theater ($750).

Application Procedures Students apply for admission into the professional program by sophomore year. Deadline for freshmen and transfers: August 1. Notification date for freshmen and transfers: continuous. Required: high school transcript, college transcript(s) for transfer students, SAT I or ACT test scores, minimum 2.0 college GPA for transfer students. Recommended: minimum 3.0 high school GPA, letter of recommendation.

Undergraduate Contact Dr. Sue Stinson, Head, Department of Dance, University of North Carolina at Greensboro, UNCG Box 26169, Greensboro, North Carolina 27402-6169; 336-334-5570, fax: 336-334-3238, E-mail address: swstinso@hamlet.uncg.edu.

Graduate Contact Dr. Jan Van Dyke, Graduate Coordinator, Department of Dance, University of North Carolina at Greensboro, UNCG Box 26169, Greensboro, North Carolina 27402-6169; 336-334-5570, fax: 336-334-3238, E-mail address: jevandyk@hamlet.uncg.edu.

▼ UNIVERSITY OF OKLAHOMA

Norman, Oklahoma

State-supported, coed. Suburban campus. Total enrollment: 25,975. Dance program established 1963.

Degrees Bachelor of Fine Arts in the area of dance. Majors and concentrations: ballet, modern dance. Graduate degrees offered: Master of Fine Arts in the area of dance.

Enrollment Fall 1997: 75 total; 65 undergraduate, 10 graduate.

Dance Student Profile 82% females, 18% males, 10% minorities, 11% international.

Dance Faculty 12 total undergraduate and graduate (full-time and part-time). 67% of full-time faculty have terminal degrees. Graduate students teach a few undergraduate courses.

Student Life Student groups/activities include Drama and Dance Student Association, Student Advisory Council.

Expenses for 1997–98 Application fee: $25. State resident tuition: $1745 full-time. Nonresident tuition: $5785 full-time. Mandatory fees: $566 full-time. Full-time tuition and fees vary according to course level, course load, location, program, and reciprocity agreements. College room and board: $3800. College room only: $1884. Room and board charges vary according to board plan, housing facility, and student level. Special program-related fees: $50 per course for accompanist's salary.

Financial Aid Program-specific awards for 1997: 15–20 tuition waivers for out-of-state program students ($1500–$3000), 10–20 Barnett Foundation Scholarships for excellent dancers ($300–$800), 2–6 Everett Foundation Scholarships for male ballet majors ($1000), 4–6 fee waivers for state residents ($500–$800), 1 Busken Scholarship for junior/senior ballet majors.

Application Procedures Students admitted directly into the professional program freshman year. Deadline for freshmen and transfers: continuous. Notification date for freshmen and transfers: continuous. Required: high school transcript, minimum 3.0 high school GPA, 2 letters of recommendation, audition, SAT I or ACT test scores. Recommended: interview. Auditions held 3 times and by appointment on campus and

off campus in Dallas, TX; Houston, TX; Louisville, KY; videotaped performances are permissible as a substitute for live auditions when distance is prohibitive.

Undergraduate Contact Martha Cornelison, Administrative Secretary, Dance Department, University of Oklahoma, 563 Elm Avenue, Room 209, Norman, Oklahoma 73019; 405-325-4051.

Graduate Contact Allan Kinzie, Assistant Professor, Dance Department, University of Oklahoma, 563 Elm Avenue, Room 209, Norman, Oklahoma 73019; 405-325-5328, E-mail address: akinzie@ou.edu.

More About the University

The Department of Dance is performance oriented, with a special focus on class work and the performance experience. Students are, for the most part, interested in pursuing performing, teaching, or choreographic careers. All students take from eight to fourteen technique classes per week, with placement determined by ability. Undergraduates must complete 124 semester hours, while the 54 credit hours for M.F.A. students are influenced by the students' needs, abilities, and interests. Also, a graduate project and thesis are required for degree completion.

The department's resources include four full-time studios, equipped with pianos and sound and videotape technology, all housed in the University's Fine Arts Center along with complete theater and design facilities. Guest artists hosted by the school have included Patricia McBride, Jean-Pierre Bonnefoux, Louis Fuente, Jack Anderson of the *New York Times*, Dr. Camille Hardy of *Dance Magazine*, Denise Jefferson, Cynthia Harvey, Takako Asakawa, Bruce Wells, Jacqulyn Bug, Bolshoi principal dancer Vyacheslav Gordeyev, Margaret and Kathleen Tracey, Earl Mosley, and Dennis Po.

Two resident companies, the Oklahoma Festival Ballet and the Modern Repertory Dance Theatre, present more than 20 performances annually. Lecture-demonstrations, operas, and musicals provide additional performance opportunities. Performance repertoire is drawn from faculty choreography, and reconstructions of classics. An additional concert is composed entirely of adjudicated student choreography. Student choreography has been performed at Regional American College Dance Festivals, and also in the National Festival at the Kennedy Center. Both companies schedule yearly tours throughout the region and nation, and regularly accept international invitations to perform in countries such as Japan, Mexico, Ecuador, France, Paraguay, and Taiwan. A five-week summer session offers intensive work in technique and performances in the SummerWind arts festival. Scholarships and assistantships are available.

▼ UNIVERSITY OF SOUTHERN MISSISSIPPI

Hattiesburg, Mississippi

State-supported, coed. Suburban campus. Total enrollment: 14,599. Dance program established 1971.

Degrees Bachelor of Fine Arts in the area of dance. Majors and concentrations: choreography and performance. Program accredited by NASD.

Enrollment Fall 1997: 55 total; all undergraduate.

Dance Student Profile 97% females, 3% males, 6% minorities.

Dance Faculty 5 total (full-time and part-time). 75% of full-time faculty have terminal degrees. Graduate students do not teach undergraduate courses. Undergraduate student–faculty ratio: 14:1.

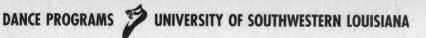

University of Southern Mississippi (continued)

Student Life Student groups/activities include Southern Arts Pro Musica, Opera Theatre, theatre productions.

Expenses for 1997–98 State resident tuition: $2590 full-time. Nonresident tuition: $5410 full-time. College room and board: $2565. Room and board charges vary according to board plan and housing facility.

Financial Aid Program-specific awards for 1997: 1–2 Dean's Endowment Awards for those demonstrating talent ($250–$500), 20–25 Service Awards for program majors ($100–$600), 10–15 Out-of-State Awards for program majors ($1410–$2820), 1–2 Myers Scholarships for program majors ($500–$1000), 1–2 J. Clinton Endowment Awards for those demonstrating talent ($380–$500).

Application Procedures Students admitted directly into the professional program freshman year. Deadline for freshmen and transfers: continuous. Required: essay, high school transcript, college transcript(s) for transfer students, minimum 2.0 high school GPA, 2 letters of recommendation, interview, SAT I or ACT test scores. Recommended: video, audition. Auditions held twice on campus; videotaped performances are permissible as a substitute for live auditions if a campus visit is impossible.

Undergraduate Contact Ms. Janet Prieur, Assistant Chair/Associate Professor, Department of Theatre and Dance, University of Southern Mississippi, Box 5052, Hattiesburg, Mississippi 39406-5052; 601-266-4161, fax: 601-266-4161.

▼ University of Southwestern Louisiana

Lafayette, Louisiana

State-supported, coed. Urban campus. Total enrollment: 17,020. Dance program established 1994.

Degrees Bachelor of Fine Arts in the area of performing arts. Majors and concentrations: dance, theater arts/drama.

Enrollment Fall 1997: 30 total; all undergraduate.

Dance Faculty 7 total (full-time and part-time). 100% of full-time faculty have terminal degrees. Graduate students do not teach undergraduate courses.

Student Life Student groups/activities include dance fraternity and sorority.

Expenses for 1997–98 Application fee: $5, $15 for international students. State resident tuition: $1947 full-time. Nonresident tuition: $6075 full-time. College room and board: $2592. Room and board charges vary according to board plan.

Financial Aid Program-specific awards for 1997: 4 departmental scholarships for program majors ($500–$1500).

Application Procedures Students admitted directly into the professional program freshman year. Deadline for freshmen and transfers: continuous. Required: high school transcript, minimum 2.0 high school GPA, SAT I or ACT test scores, minimum 2.75 high school GPA and audition for scholarship consideration. Auditions held once in the spring or by appointment on campus; videotaped performances are permissible as a substitute for live auditions for provisional scholarship consideration.

Web Site http://www.usl.edu.

Undergraduate Contact Dr. Stephen Taft, Chairman, Performing Arts Department, University of Southwestern Louisiana, Box 43850, Lafayette, Louisiana 70504; 318-482-6357, fax: 318-482-5089.

▼ The University of Tennessee at Martin

Martin, Tennessee

State-supported, coed. Small town campus. Total enrollment: 5,997. Dance program established 1989.

Degrees Bachelor of Fine Arts in the area of fine and performing arts. Majors and concentrations: dance.

Enrollment Fall 1997: 8 undergraduate.

Dance Student Profile 100% females.

Dance Faculty 1 total (full-time). 100% of full-time faculty have terminal degrees. Graduate students do not teach undergraduate courses.

Student Life Student groups/activities include UTM Dance Ensemble.

Expenses for 1997–98 Application fee: $25. State resident tuition: $2240 full-time. Nonresident tuition: $6706 full-time. College room and board: $3104. College room only: $1600. Room and board charges vary according to board plan and housing facility.

Financial Aid Program-specific awards for 1997: 3 Carolyn Byrum Scholarships for dance majors ($150).

Application Procedures Students admitted directly into the professional program freshman year. Deadline for freshmen and transfers: continuous. Required: high school transcript, minimum 2.0 high school GPA, audition, SAT I or ACT test scores. Auditions held once on campus; videotaped performances are permissible as a substitute for live auditions whenever needed.

Web Site http://www.utm.edu/departments/finearts/dfpa.htm.

Undergraduate Contact Dr. Earl Norwood, Director, Division of Fine and Performing Arts, The University of Tennessee at Martin, 102 Fine Arts Building, Martin, Tennessee 38238; 901-587-7400, fax: 901-587-7415, E-mail address: norwood@utm.edu.

▼ The University of Texas at Austin

Austin, Texas

State-supported, coed. Urban campus. Total enrollment: 48,857. Dance program established 1938.

Degrees Bachelor of Fine Arts in the area of dance. Majors and concentrations: ballet, choreography and performance, dance, modern dance. Program accredited by NASD.

Enrollment Fall 1997: 79 total; all undergraduate.

Dance Student Profile 96% females, 4% males, 10% minorities, 1% international.

Dance Faculty 11 total (full-time and part-time). 71% of full-time faculty have terminal degrees. Graduate students do not teach undergraduate courses. Undergraduate student–faculty ratio: 7:1.

Student Life Student groups/activities include Dance Repertory Theatre, community outreach programs.

Expenses for 1997–98 Application fee: $40. State resident tuition: $2040 full-time. Nonresident tuition: $8460 full-time. Mandatory fees: $826 full-time. Full-time tuition and fees vary according to course load and program. College room and board: $3901. College room only: $1950. Room and board charges vary according to board plan. Special program-related fees: $115 per per semester for performance and production fee.

Financial Aid Program-specific awards for 1997: 2 McGriff Scholarships for program students ($2000), 3 Danielian Scholarships for program students ($2000).

Application Procedures Students apply for admission into the professional program by freshman year. Deadline for freshmen: March 1; transfers: February 1. Notification date for freshmen and transfers: continuous. Required: essay, high school transcript, college transcript(s) for transfer students, 3 letters of recommendation, audition, SAT I or ACT test scores. Auditions held 3 times on campus; videotaped performances are permissible as a substitute for live auditions for out-of-state applicants with permission from the faculty.

Web Site http://www.utexas.edu/cofa/theatre.

Undergraduate Contact Ms. Sharon Vasquez, Chair, Department of Theatre and Dance, The University of Texas at Austin, WIN 1.142, Austin, Texas 78712-1168; 512-471-5793, fax: 512-471-0824.

▼ UNIVERSITY OF THE ARTS

Philadelphia, Pennsylvania

Independent, coed. Urban campus. Total enrollment: 1,624. Dance program established 1947.

Degrees Bachelor of Fine Arts in the area of dance. Majors and concentrations: ballet, dance education, jazz dance, modern dance.

Enrollment Fall 1997: 256 total; 156 undergraduate, 100 non-professional degree.

Dance Student Profile 93% females, 7% males, 22% minorities, 3% international.

Dance Faculty 29 total (full-time and part-time). 33% of full-time faculty have terminal degrees. Graduate students do not teach undergraduate courses. Undergraduate student–faculty ratio: 5:1.

Student Life Special housing available for dance students.

Expenses for 1997–98 Application fee: $40. Tuition: $14,570 full-time. Mandatory fees: $500 full-time. College room only: $4100.

Financial Aid Program-specific awards for 1997: 25 Merit Scholarships for incoming students ($500–$6500).

Application Procedures Students admitted directly into the professional program freshman year. Deadline for freshmen and transfers: continuous. Required: essay, high school transcript, college transcript(s) for transfer students, minimum 2.0 high school GPA, letter of recommendation, audition, SAT I or ACT test scores, resume. Recommended: minimum 3.0 high school GPA, interview. Auditions held 8 times on campus; videotaped performances are permissible as a substitute for live auditions if student lives more than 200 miles from Philadelphia.

Web Site http://www.uarts.edu.

Undergraduate Contact Ms. Barbara Elliott, Director of Admissions, University of the Arts, 320 South Broad Street, Philadelphia, Pennsylvania 19102; 800-616-ARTS, fax: 215-875-5458.

▼ UNIVERSITY OF UTAH

Salt Lake City, Utah

State-supported, coed. Urban campus. Total enrollment: 25,883. Dance program established 1951.

Degrees Bachelor of Fine Arts in the area of ballet. Majors and concentrations: ballet, ballet pedagogy, ethnic dance, performance. Graduate degrees offered: Master of Fine Arts in the area of ballet; Master of Arts in the area of ballet.

Enrollment Fall 1997: 120 total; 112 undergraduate, 8 graduate.

Dance Student Profile 90% females, 10% males, 10% minorities, 5% international.

Dance Faculty 13 total undergraduate and graduate (full-time and part-time). 50% of full-time faculty have terminal degrees. Graduate students teach a few undergraduate courses. Undergraduate student–faculty ratio: 15:1.

Student Life Student groups/activities include collaborative concerts, student guest artist opportunities.

Expenses for 1997–98 Application fee: $30. State resident tuition: $2601 full-time. Nonresident tuition: $7,998 full-time. Full-time tuition varies according to course load. College room and board: $4620. College room only: $1708. Room and board charges vary according to board plan. Special program-related fees: $8 for hydrostatic weighing of students.

Financial Aid Program-specific awards for 1997: 3 William F. Christensen Scholarships for resident incoming freshmen ($2000), 25–40 departmental scholarships for program students ($600–$6000), 1–2 Honors at entrance/Presidential Scholarships for high academic achievement - ballet major ($2280–$7000).

Application Procedures Students admitted directly into the professional program freshman year. Deadline for freshmen and transfers: March 30. Notification date for freshmen and transfers: April 30. Required: high school transcript, college transcript(s) for transfer students, minimum 2.0 high school GPA, 2 letters of recommendation, audition, SAT I or ACT test scores, 2 photographs in ballet poses - women on pointe, application form (ballet majors). Recommended: essay, minimum 3.0 high school GPA. Auditions held once or as needed on campus; videotaped performances are permissible as a substitute for live auditions when distance is prohibitive or time constraints exist.

Web Site http://www.ballet.utah.edu.

Undergraduate Contact Ms. Valerie Horton, Administrative Secretary, Ballet Department, University of Utah, 330 S 1500 E, Room 110, Salt Lake City, Utah 84112-0280; 801-581-8231, fax: 801-581-5442, E-mail address: v.horton@m.cc.utah.edu.

Graduate Contact Bene Arnold, Graduate Advisor, Ballet Department, University of Utah, 330 S 1500 E, Room 110, Salt Lake City, Utah 84112-0280; 801-581-8231, fax: 801-581-5442, E-mail address: v.horton@m.cc.utah.edu.

▼ UNIVERSITY OF UTAH

Salt Lake City, Utah

State-supported, coed. Urban campus. Total enrollment: 25,883. Dance program established 1940.

Degrees Bachelor of Fine Arts in the area of modern dance. Graduate degrees offered: Master of Fine Arts in the area of modern dance.

Enrollment Fall 1997: 75 undergraduate, 15 graduate.

Dance Student Profile 94% females, 6% males, 3% minorities, 6% international.

Dance Faculty 16 total undergraduate and graduate (full-time and part-time). 90% of full-time faculty have terminal degrees. Graduate students teach a few undergraduate courses. Undergraduate student–faculty ratio: 6:1.

University of Utah (continued)

Student Life Student groups/activities include American College Dance Festival, Associated Student Organization, Student Dance Company.

Expenses for 1997–98 Application fee: $30. State resident tuition: $2601 full-time. Nonresident tuition: $7,998 full-time. Full-time tuition varies according to course load. College room and board: $4620. College room only: $1708. Room and board charges vary according to board plan. Special program-related fees: $7–$15 per class for equipment use fee, musicians.

Financial Aid Program-specific awards for 1997: 2 Hayes Scholarships for state residents, 10 departmental scholarships for program students.

Application Procedures Students admitted directly into the professional program freshman year. Deadline for freshmen and transfers: April 1. Required: high school transcript, college transcript(s) for transfer students, minimum 3.0 high school GPA, audition for transfer applicants. Auditions held twice on campus and off campus in various cities; videotaped performances are permissible as a substitute for live auditions.

Web Site http://www.dance.utah.edu.

Undergraduate Contact Ms. Neva Borden, Administrative Assistant, Modern Dance Department, University of Utah, 330 S 1500 E, Room 110, Salt Lake City, Utah 84112-0280; 801-581-7327, fax: 801-581-5442, E-mail address: neva.borden@m.cc.utah.edu.

Graduate Contact Mr. Ed Groff, Director of Graduate Studies, Modern Dance Department, University of Utah, 330 S 1500 E, Room 110, Salt Lake City, Utah 84112-0280; 801-581-7327, fax: 801-581-5442, E-mail address: egroff@m.cc.utah.edu.

▼ UNIVERSITY OF WISCONSIN–MILWAUKEE

Milwaukee, Wisconsin

State-supported, coed. Urban campus. Total enrollment: 21,525.

Degrees Bachelor of Fine Arts in the area of dance. Majors and concentrations: modern dance. Graduate degrees offered: Master of Fine Arts in the area of dance.

Enrollment Fall 1997: 60 total; 50 undergraduate, 10 graduate.

Dance Faculty 7 total undergraduate and graduate (full-time and part-time). Graduate students teach a few undergraduate courses.

Expenses for 1997–98 Application fee: $28. State resident tuition: $3327 full-time. Nonresident tuition: $10,790 full-time. Full-time tuition varies according to reciprocity agreements. College room only: $2457.

Application Procedures Students admitted directly into the professional program freshman year. Deadline for freshmen and transfers: continuous. Required: high school transcript, ACT score for state residents, SAT or ACT score for out-of-state residents.

Undergraduate Contact Undergraduate Admissions, University of Wisconsin–Milwaukee, PO Box 413, Milwaukee, Wisconsin 53201-0413; 414-229-3800.

Graduate Contact Graduate Admissions, University of Wisconsin–Milwaukee, PO Box 340, Milwaukee, Wisconsin 53201; 414-229-4982.

▼ UNIVERSITY OF WYOMING

Laramie, Wyoming

State-supported, coed. Small town campus. Total enrollment: 11,094.

Degrees Bachelor of Fine Arts in the area of dance. Majors and concentrations: ballet, jazz dance, modern dance.

Enrollment Fall 1997: 40 total; 20 undergraduate, 20 non-professional degree.

Dance Student Profile 99% females, 1% males, 1% minorities, 1% international.

Dance Faculty 11 total (full-time and part-time). 90% of full-time faculty have terminal degrees. Graduate students do not teach undergraduate courses. Undergraduate student–faculty ratio: 10:1.

Student Life Student groups/activities include Association of the Performing Arts.

Expenses for 1997–98 Application fee: $30. State resident tuition: $1944 full-time. Nonresident tuition: $7032 full-time. Mandatory fees: $386 full-time. College room and board: $4278. College room only: $1758. Room and board charges vary according to board plan.

Financial Aid Program-specific awards for 1997: 21 departmental awards for program majors ($2144).

Application Procedures Students admitted directly into the professional program freshman year. Deadline for freshmen and transfers: August 31. Required: high school transcript, college transcript(s) for transfer students, minimum 3.0 high school GPA, SAT I or ACT test scores, audition for scholarship consideration, minimum 2.75 high school GPA for Wyoming residents. Recommended: letter of recommendation, interview. Auditions held twice on campus and off campus in Rocky Mountain Theatre Association Festival locations; videotaped performances are permissible as a substitute for live auditions if a campus visit is impossible.

Undergraduate Contact Dr. Rebecca Hilliker, Head, Department of Theatre and Dance, University of Wyoming, Box 3951 University Station, Laramie, Wyoming 82071-3951; 307-766-2198, fax: 307-766-2197, E-mail address: hilliker@uwyo.edu.

▼ VIRGINIA COMMONWEALTH UNIVERSITY

Richmond, Virginia

State-supported, coed. Urban campus. Total enrollment: 22,702. Dance program established 1981.

Degrees Bachelor of Fine Arts in the area of dance and choreography. Majors and concentrations: modern dance.

Enrollment Fall 1997: 80 undergraduate.

Dance Student Profile 80% females, 20% males, 25% minorities, 2% international.

Dance Faculty 18 total (full-time and part-time). 65% of full-time faculty have terminal degrees. Graduate students do not teach undergraduate courses. Undergraduate student–faculty ratio: 11:1.

Expenses for 1997–98 Application fee: $25. State resident tuition: $3125 full-time. Nonresident tuition: $11,382 full-time. Mandatory fees: $986 full-time. Full-time tuition and fees vary according to program. College room and board: $4540. College room only: $2715. Room and board charges vary according to board plan and housing facility. Special program-related fees: $5 for musician/accompanists fees.

Financial Aid Program-specific awards for 1997: departmental awards for continuing students, 4 Carpenter Fellow Awards for incoming students ($2500–$12,000).

Application Procedures Students admitted directly into the professional program freshman year. Deadline for freshmen and transfers: June 1. Notification date for freshmen and transfers: June 1. Required: essay, high school transcript, college transcript(s) for transfer students, minimum 2.0 high school GPA, 2 letters of recommendation, audition, SAT I or ACT test scores (minimum combined SAT I score of 800). Recommended: interview. Auditions held 8 times on campus and off campus in various performing arts high schools in the U.S.; videotaped performances are permissible as a substitute for live auditions when distance is prohibitive.

Undergraduate Contact Ms. Martha Curtis, Chair, Department of Dance, Virginia Commonwealth University, 1315 Floyd Avenue, Richmond, Virginia 23284-3007; 804-828-1711, fax: 804-828-7356.

▼ VIRGINIA INTERMONT COLLEGE

Bristol, Virginia

Independent, coed. Small town campus. Total enrollment: 848.

Degrees Bachelor of Fine Arts in the area of performing arts/dance. Cross-registration with King College.

Enrollment Fall 1997: 14 total; all undergraduate.

Dance Faculty 7 total (full-time and part-time). 100% of full-time faculty have terminal degrees. Graduate students do not teach undergraduate courses. Undergraduate student–faculty ratio: 4:1.

Student Life Student groups/activities include American College Dance Festival, Visiting Artists Workshop.

Expenses for 1997–98 Application fee: $15. Comprehensive fee: $15,350 includes full-time tuition ($10,650) and college room and board ($4700). Special program-related fees: $300 per course for instruction fee.

Financial Aid Program-specific awards for 1997: 15 Room Grants for program majors ($1800), 15 departmental awards for program majors ($1200), performance scholarships for program majors ($500–$1500).

Application Procedures Deadline for freshmen and transfers: continuous. Notification date for freshmen and transfers: continuous. Required: high school transcript, college transcript(s) for transfer students, minimum 2.0 high school GPA, audition, SAT I or ACT test scores. Recommended: letter of recommendation. Auditions held by request on campus.

Undergraduate Contact Ms. Robin Cozart, Director of Admissions, Virginia Intermont College, Box D-460, Bristol, Virginia 24201; 540-669-6101, fax: 540-466-7855, E-mail address: viadmit@vic.edu.

▼ WEBSTER UNIVERSITY

St. Louis, Missouri

Independent, coed. Suburban campus. Total enrollment: 11,756. Dance program established 1970.

Degrees Bachelor of Fine Arts in the area of dance; Bachelor of Arts in the area of dance. Cross-registration with various colleges in St. Louis.

Enrollment Fall 1997: 186 total; 36 undergraduate, 150 non-professional degree.

Dance Student Profile 90% females, 10% males, 5% minorities, 15% international.

Dance Faculty 7 total (full-time and part-time). 50% of full-time faculty have terminal degrees. Graduate students do not teach undergraduate courses.

Student Life Student groups/activities include Dance Club, Fine Arts Club.

Expenses for 1997–98 Application fee: $25. Comprehensive fee: $15,940 includes full-time tuition ($10,860), mandatory fees ($50), and college room and board ($5030). College room only: $3080. Room and board charges vary according to board plan and housing facility.

Application Procedures Students admitted directly into the professional program freshman year. Deadline for freshmen and transfers: continuous. Required: essay, high school transcript, college transcript(s) for transfer students, 2 letters of recommendation, audition, SAT I or ACT test scores. Recommended: minimum 2.0 high school GPA. Auditions held 8 times on campus; videotaped performances are permissible as a substitute for live auditions when distance is prohibitive. Portfolio reviews held on campus.

Web Site http://www.webster.edu.

Undergraduate Contact Ms. Bethany Wood, Auditions Coordinator, Office of Admissions, Webster University, 470 East Lockwood Avenue, St. Louis, Missouri 63119-3194; 314-968-7001, fax: 314-968-7115.

Potter College of Arts, Humanities, and Social Sciences

▼ WESTERN KENTUCKY UNIVERSITY

Bowling Green, Kentucky

State-supported, coed. Suburban campus. Total enrollment: 14,543. Dance program established 1987.

Degrees Bachelor of Fine Arts in the area of performing arts/dance. Majors and concentrations: ballet, jazz dance, music theater, tap dance.

Enrollment Fall 1997: 30 undergraduate.

Dance Student Profile 71% females, 29% males, 3% minorities.

Dance Faculty 8 total (full-time and part-time). 86% of full-time faculty have terminal degrees. Graduate students do not teach undergraduate courses.

Student Life Student groups/activities include Dance Company, Musical Theatre Ensemble.

Expenses for 1997–98 Application fee: $15. State resident tuition: $1800 full-time. Nonresident tuition: $5400 full-time. Mandatory fees: $340 full-time. College room and board: $2700.

Financial Aid Program-specific awards for 1997: 10 Governor's School of the Arts Award for students who complete Governor's School of the Arts ($1130–$3050).

Application Procedures Students apply for admission into the professional program by sophomore year. Deadline for freshmen and transfers: June 1. Required: high school transcript, minimum 2.0 high school GPA. Recommended: audition. Auditions held once on campus; recorded music is permissible as a substitute for live auditions and videotaped performances are permissible as a substitute for live auditions.

Web Site http://www.wku.edu/Dept/Academic/AHSS/Theatre/.

Western Kentucky University (continued)

Undergraduate Contact Office of Admissions, Western Kentucky University, 101 Cravens Center, One Big Red Way, Bowling Green, Kentucky 42101-3576; 502-745-5422.

▼ WESTERN MICHIGAN UNIVERSITY

Kalamazoo, Michigan

State-supported, coed. Urban campus. Total enrollment: 26,132. Dance program established 1972.

Degrees Bachelor of Fine Arts in the area of dance. Program accredited by NASD.

Enrollment Fall 1997: 64 total; 5 undergraduate, 59 non-professional degree.

Dance Student Profile 97% females, 3% males, 6% minorities.

Dance Faculty 14 total (full-time and part-time). 57% of full-time faculty have terminal degrees. Graduate students do not teach undergraduate courses. Undergraduate student–faculty ratio: 10:1.

Student Life Student groups/activities include Orchesis Dance Society, Children's Repertory Dance Theatre, University musicals and operas.

Expenses for 1997–98 Application fee: $25. State resident tuition: $3061 full-time. Nonresident tuition: $7770 full-time. Mandatory fees: $594 full-time. Full-time tuition and fees vary according to course load and student level. College room and board: $4398. College room only: $1815. Room and board charges vary according to board plan. Special program-related fees: $10–$40 per technique course for accompanying fee, $10 per technique course for enrichment fee.

Financial Aid Program-specific awards for 1997: 1–4 Dalton New Dance Major Scholarships for incoming students ($500), 1–2 Male Dance Major Scholarships for male program students ($300–$1000), 1–2 Cultural Diversity Dance Major Scholarships for under-represented groups ($200–$1000), 1–6 Exceptional Dance Major Scholarships for talented program majors ($750), 4–6 Outstanding Dance Major Scholarships for outstanding program majors ($1000–$2000).

Application Procedures Students apply for admission into the professional program by sophomore year. Notification date for freshmen and transfers: continuous. Required: high school transcript, college transcript(s) for transfer students, minimum 2.0 high school GPA, audition, SAT I or ACT test scores, high school transcripts for transfer students with fewer than 26 transferable credit hours. Auditions held 3 times in November, February, and April on campus; videotaped performances are permissible as a substitute for live auditions for international applicants.

Web Site http://www.wmich.edu/dance.

Undergraduate Contact Ms. Wendy Cornish, Professor of Dance and Academic Advisor, Department of Dance, Western Michigan University, Kalamazoo, Michigan 49008-3833; 616-387-5845, fax: 616-387-5809, E-mail address: wendy.cornish@wmich.edu.

Sybil B. Harrington College of Fine Arts and Humanities

▼ WEST TEXAS A&M UNIVERSITY

Canyon, Texas

State-supported, coed. Small town campus. Total enrollment: 6,489.

Degrees Bachelor of Fine Arts in the area of dance. Majors and concentrations: ballet, dance, jazz dance, tap dance. Graduate degrees offered: Master of Arts in the area of interdisciplinary studies: dance emphasis.

Enrollment Fall 1997: 92 total; 28 undergraduate, 4 graduate, 60 non-professional degree.

Dance Student Profile 60% females, 40% males, 16% minorities, 1% international.

Dance Faculty 2 total undergraduate and graduate (full-time and part-time). 100% of full-time faculty have terminal degrees. Graduate students teach a few undergraduate courses. Undergraduate student–faculty ratio: 10:1.

Student Life Student groups/activities include American College Dance Festival, Dance for the Planet.

Expenses for 1997–98 State resident tuition: $1296 full-time. Nonresident tuition: $6432 full-time. Mandatory fees: $448 full-time. Full-time tuition and fees vary according to course load. College room and board: $2969. College room only: $1308. Room and board charges vary according to board plan and housing facility.

Financial Aid Program-specific awards for 1997: 20 Lone Star Ballet Scholarships for dancers ($1200).

Application Procedures Students admitted directly into the professional program freshman year. Deadline for freshmen and transfers: August 1. Notification date for freshmen and transfers: August 1. Required: high school transcript, minimum 2.0 high school GPA, SAT I or ACT test scores. Recommended: letter of recommendation, interview, audition. Auditions held at various times on campus; videotaped performances are permissible as a substitute for live auditions when distance is prohibitive.

Undergraduate Contact Mr. Neil Hess, Director, Dance Department, West Texas A&M University, Box 879, Canyon, Texas 79016-0001; 806-651-2820, fax: 806-651-2779.

▼ WICHITA STATE UNIVERSITY

Wichita, Kansas

State-supported, coed. Urban campus. Total enrollment: 14,061. Dance program established 1978.

Degrees Bachelor of Fine Arts in the area of performing arts/dance. Majors and concentrations: modern dance, music theater. Program accredited by NASD.

Enrollment Fall 1997: 22 undergraduate, 242 non-professional degree.

Dance Student Profile 90% females, 10% males, 40% minorities, 15% international.

Dance Faculty 7 total undergraduate (full-time and part-time). 100% of full-time faculty have terminal degrees. Graduate students do not teach undergraduate courses. Undergraduate student–faculty ratio: 10:1.

Student Life Student groups/activities include Kansas Dance Festival, Mid-America Dance Network, American College Dance Festival. Special housing available for dance students.

Expenses for 1997–98 Application fee: $20. State resident tuition: $1486 full-time. Nonresident tuition: $6414 full-time. Mandatory fees: $500 full-time. College room and board: $3760. Room and board charges vary according to board plan. Special program-related fees: $12 per course for live accompanying fees for specific courses.

Financial Aid Program-specific awards for 1997: 16–18 Miller Dance Scholarships for incoming students ($600–$1200).

Application Procedures Students apply for admission into the professional program by sophomore year. Deadline for freshmen and transfers: continuous. Required: high school transcript, college transcript(s) for transfer students, minimum 2.0 high school GPA, audition, SAT I or ACT test scores. Auditions held twice on campus.

Undergraduate Contact Ms. Christine Schneikart-Luebbe, Dean of Enrollment Services, Office of Undergraduate Admissions, Wichita State University, 1845 Fairmount, Wichita, Kansas 67260-0124; 316-978-3085.

▼ WRIGHT STATE UNIVERSITY

Dayton, Ohio

State-supported, coed. Suburban campus. Total enrollment: 15,343.

Degrees Bachelor of Fine Arts in the area of dance.

Enrollment Fall 1997: 40 undergraduate.

Dance Student Profile 90% females, 10% males, 7% minorities, 1% international.

Dance Faculty 6 total (full-time and part-time). 33% of full-time faculty have terminal degrees. Graduate students do not teach undergraduate courses.

Student Life Student groups/activities include Dayton Ballet II Company, Dayton Contemporary Dance Company II.

Expenses for 1997–98 Application fee: $30. State resident tuition: $3708 full-time. Nonresident tuition: $7416 full-time. College room and board: $4500. Room and board charges vary according to board plan and housing facility. Special program-related fees: $125 per quarter for private voice lessons.

Financial Aid Program-specific awards for 1997: Wright State/ Dayton Ballet, Dayton Contemporary Dance Company II Awards for program majors ($1000–$3700), Faculty Academic Scholarship.

Application Procedures Students admitted directly into the professional program freshman year. Deadline for freshmen and transfers: continuous. Required: high school transcript, video, audition, SAT I or ACT test scores, dance photograph. Auditions held by appointment on campus; videotaped performances are permissible as a substitute for live auditions when distance is prohibitive.

Undergraduate Contact Ms. Victoria Oleen, Administrative Coordinator, Department of Theatre Arts, Wright State University, 3640 Colonel Glenn Highway, T148 CAC, Dayton, Ohio 45435; 937-775-3072, fax: 937-775-3787.

More About the University

Program Facilities The Department of Theatre Arts is housed in a newly constructed, state-of-the-art facility that includes acting studios, a movement studio, a lighting lab, and motion picture production facilities. Mainstage theater productions are held in the Festival Playhouse, a 376-seat proscenium theater. Studio productions are in a 100-seat black box theater. The department has access to a comprehensive

collection of playscripts, musical theater scores and soundtracks, and a videotape library.

Faculty, Resident Artists, and Alumni Chair W. Stuart McDowell is the founder and former artistic director of the Riverside Shakespeare Company in New York City and stage director of numerous professional productions in New York and across the country. Faculty members have worked professionally at the New York Shakespeare Festival, the Alabama Shakespeare Festival, the Milwaukee Repertory Theatre, the Cincinnati Playhouse in the Park, the Dayton Ballet, the Dayton Contemporary Dance Company, and the Human Race Theatre Company. Motion picture professors have been nominated for the Academy Award, and student-directed films have received recognition at leading film festivals internationally.

Student Performance Opportunities Students may work on six mainstage and three studio productions as actors, designers, dancers, or technicians. Students are also offered directing, design, choreography, acting, and dance opportunities in student productions in the directing lab and studio theater. Motion picture production majors are required to complete two fully realized films prior to graduation. Performance opportunities are also offered with the Human Race Theatre Company, Dayton's professional Equity theater, the Victoria Theatre, the Dayton Ballet, and the Dayton Contemporary Dance Company.

▼ YORK UNIVERSITY

North York, ON, Canada

Province-supported, coed. Urban campus. Total enrollment: 37,900. Dance program established 1970.

Degrees Bachelor of Fine Arts in the areas of dance performance, composition, modern dance. Majors and concentrations: ballet, composition, modern dance.

Enrollment Fall 1997: 187 total; 167 undergraduate, 20 non-professional degree.

Dance Student Profile 95% females, 5% males, 5% international.

Dance Faculty 21 total (full-time and part-time). 82% of full-time faculty have terminal degrees. Graduate students do not teach undergraduate courses. Undergraduate student–faculty ratio: 8:1.

Student Life Student groups/activities include Dance Students Association, Creative Arts Students Association.

Expenses for 1997–98 Application fee: $60 Canadian dollars. Tuition, fee, and room and board charges are reported in Canadian dollars. Canadian resident tuition: $3750 full-time. Full-time tuition varies according to course load, degree level, and program. College room and board: $5000. Room and board charges vary according to board plan and housing facility. International student tuition: $10,800 full-time. Special program-related fees: $20 per year for studio/ conditioning equipment/lockers.

Financial Aid Program-specific awards for 1997: 2 Talent Awards for applicants with outstanding auditions ($1000), 1 International Talent Award for international applicants with outstanding auditions ($2000), 1 Harry Rowe Bursary for demonstrated achievement or potential in artistic or scholarly work ($2000), 25 Fine Arts Bursary for academically qualified students demonstrating financial need ($250–$1500), 2 Lynda and Brian Wilson Memorial Awards for exceptional talent in studio or choreography work with children ($300), 3 Dance Department Awards for those demonstrating exceptional talent ($200), 1 Elaine Newton/

York University *(continued)*

Alan Wilder Achievement Bursary for students with a minimum B average demonstrating need ($1000), 1 Dance Scholar's Award for senior demonstrating excellence in scholarship/need ($350), 1 Dance Education Award for applicants demonstrating strength in the field and need ($300), 1 Spedding Memorial Award for applicants showing excellence in choreography and need ($350), 1 Lynda and Brian Wilson Memorial Award for junior or senior demonstrating exceptional talent ($300).

Application Procedures Students admitted directly into the professional program freshman year. Deadline for freshmen and transfers: March 1. Notification date for freshmen: June 30; transfers: July 15. Required: essay, high school transcript, college transcript(s) for transfer students, minimum 3.0 high school GPA, interview, audition, SAT I, ACT or Canadian equivalent, letters of recommendation and video if applicant cannot audition in person. Recommended: 3 letters of recommendation. Auditions held 3 times on campus; videotaped performances are permissible as a substitute for live auditions when distance is prohibitive.

Web Site http://www.yorku.ca/faculty/finearts/dance/.

Undergraduate Contact Mr. Don Murdoch, Liaison Officer, Liaison and Advising, Faculty of Fine Arts, York University, 213 CFA, 4700 Keele Street, Toronto, ON M3J 1P3, Canada; 416-736-5135, fax: 416-736-5447, E-mail address: donm@yorku.ca.

More About the Department

Program Facilities Three spacious rehearsal studios; Pilates equipment; costume collection; audio and video recording facilities; extensive library collection of dance books and periodicals; dance-specific computer software and peripherals. Formal performance spaces include Burton Auditorium, the Grant Strate Dance Studio Theatre, and the Joseph G. Green Studio Theatre.

Faculty and Alumni York dance faculty members are among Canada's leading dance scholars, educators, and choreographers. Adjunct faculty members include classical East Indian dancer Menaka Thakkar, choreographer Danny Grossman, and former principal dancer of the National Ballet of Canada Veronica Tennant. Alumni include Andrea Nann of the Danny Grossman Dance Company; Tedd Robinson, artistic director of Le Groupe de la Place Royale; Debra Brown, choreographer for Cirque du Soleil; and Christopher House, artistic director of Toronto Dance Theatre. Independent dancers and choreographers include Jennifer Mascall, Conrad Alexandrowicz, Daniel Bélanger, Denise Fujiwara, Carol Anderson, and Susan McKenzie.

Performance Opportunities The work of student dancers and choreographers is regularly showcased in public concerts on and off campus. Upper-level students also have the opportunity to join the York Dance Ensemble, the department's repertory touring company.

Special Programs Daily technique classes in ballet and modern dance are complemented by special workshops in jazz and tap, as well as world performance traditions such as African, East Indian, and Aboriginal dance.

Students also benefit from being part of one of the largest faculties of fine arts in North America. Combined-degree programs are available with the Departments of Film & Video, Music, Theatre, and Visual Arts and through an interdisciplinary program in fine arts cultural studies.

MUSIC PROGRAMS

I f you are interested in pursuing a music degree, your first step will be to decide which type of program and setting is right for you. Professional degree programs, which are the main subject of this book, most often lead to the Bachelor of Music (B.M.) or the Bachelor of Music Education (B.M.E.). Offered at conservatories, liberal arts colleges, and universities, these programs emphasize acquiring professional skills in either performance or education. Enroll in one of them and you can expect to devote about 75 percent of your time to music and 25 percent to other areas.

If you go the liberal arts route, on the other hand, you'll earn a Bachelor of Arts (B.A.) in music. About half your course work will be in music and half will be spent on other subjects. Consult *Peterson's Guide to Four-Year Colleges* for information on B.A. programs.

Once you know the type of degree you'd like to earn, you'll need to consider the setting in which you'll live, study, and grow as an artist. Curriculum alone won't tell you whether you'll be happiest at a conservatory, small liberal arts college, or a large urban campus of a major university. What you really need to think about is the overall environment that different schools offer.

Where to Study

Conservatories focus on preparing students for careers in music. Often located in large cities, conservatories offer students the chance to study in an environment devoted to music. Their professors are usually working professionals who teach part-time.

Music programs at liberal arts colleges and universities are located in a range of settings—from cities, to small towns, to rural areas. Students with diverse interests are often better served by university programs. The teaching also differs from the conservatory approach. In university programs, faculties tend to be made up of full-time teachers. Faculty members are probably more available to students in a university setting, since they are committed full-time to teaching.

Whatever program you choose, keep in mind that the vast majority of people with careers in music have extensive formal training. Music is much more

REPORT FROM THE FIELD

Interview with composer Frances White

Composer Frances White, currently a doctoral candidate at Princeton University, received her bachelor's degree in composition from the University of Maryland and her master's degree from Brooklyn College.

The daughter of parents who instilled in her an early and lifelong appreciation of music, White grew up playing the piano and says "I've probably been composing since I was 8 or 9 years old." The idea of turning this passion into her life's work, however, didn't seriously occur to White until high school. "As a little kid, I never really thought being a composer was an option; I didn't think that was something that women did. All the composers I knew about were men."

White works part-time at Princeton's Recording for the Blind and Dyslexic. When she is not working, she composes as much as she can. She recorded a piece for traditional Chinese instruments and a CD at Princeton University's studios. White will receive her doctorate once she completes her dissertation; however, she claims the degree in itself is not the primary reason for her continuing study. "The most important aspects of my education have been to establish relationships with performers and other composers; to have a chance to meet people who were living as composers, and to learn technically how you put a piece of music together," says White. "Getting professional experience was the main goal for me."

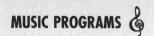

HOW DO YOU KNOW A MUSIC PROGRAM IS RIGHT FOR YOU?

Choosing a degree program is never easy, but you greatly increase your odds of making the right choice by researching your options thoroughly. Here's a list of questions to ask before you select a program:

- What is the focus of the program? Every program has a different emphasis. One school may be more rooted in a nineteenth-century tradition, while another may be avant-garde in its approach. Each institution has a very different bent, and you'll want to find out what that is.
- What kind of social atmosphere does the school have? Is it intensely competitive? Supportive and nurturing? The best school for you is the one that will enable you to grow as thoroughly and quickly as possible.
- Find out about the opportunities you'll have to perform. How many student performance groups are there? How many concerts or recitals do students take part in each semester? How many recitals are required for graduation?
- Consider enrollment size. How many people are in the program in which you're interested? In your instrument? What's the student-faculty ratio in your area of study?
- Does the school's location suit your needs and preferences?
- Does the program feature guest artists, artists-in-residence, or industry visitors so you can meet practicing professionals and learn the latest theories and techniques? How long do they stay on campus? Do they give lectures, teach classes, or offer workshops? Do they work with all students or advanced students only?
- Research the faculty. Are they practicing in their field? Who teaches your instrument?
- Ask about the program's alumni. How many are working in their chosen field?
- Tour the facilities. Which ones are available to you? Is there adequate practice space? Is the equipment state-of-the-art?
- Does the school offer an internship program? Are there regional symphonies, jazz bands, or other music ensembles in the area that welcome student enrollment?
- Check into the placement help the program or school offers. Is there a career placement center to help you assess your skills and find work?

structured than many of the other arts. Theoretical studies provide the structure that puts music together. Pursuing a degree will not only make you a better, more well-rounded musician, it also provides an automatic connection to the arts world that is much more difficult to obtain on your own.

Auditions

In addition to transcripts, test scores, and the usual forms, music students have to audition. Of course, every school is different and the importance of the audition in the admissions process varies. But in general, the more selective the institution, the more important the audition. Students who apply to a conservatory will likely find that the audition will be the critical factor, followed by grades and test scores or interviews. When looking at a university or liberal arts college, by contrast, you will usually find that the admission criteria are more equally weighted—you'll need to pass both academic and performance requirements to get in.

Some schools hold regional auditions in different cities, while others require students to go to them. When schools hold auditions in different cities, a representative—either an admissions officer or faculty member—makes a videotape or audiotape to bring back for review.

Auditions are usually judged by teachers of your instrument. Whether the audition panel consists of 1 person or 10 depends on the institution's philosophy and the size of the faculty. Suppose, for example, that you are auditioning in flute. Here are three examples of what might happen: At a conservatory, the flute faculty will all listen to the audition. At a college or university with a much smaller faculty—say with only one flute teacher—the whole woodwind faculty will listen. At yet another college, only one teacher will listen to tapes and/or auditions.

As a rule, the more applicants a school has, the shorter the audition. An audition at most high-powered schools can be as short as 5 to 15 minutes. A liberal arts college with a smaller applicant pool is often able to take a more personal approach. They may take a half-hour with you, listening to you play and then interviewing you. When you go in, the judges will ask for your first piece. They will probably stop you somewhere along the way and ask you for a second piece. They may stop you again and, if time permits, ask you for part of a third piece. The school will usually let applicants know if the audition will include sight reading (playing a piece you haven't prepared).

The audition repertoire is usually stated in general terms, such as: "Perform a piece from the eighteenth, nineteenth, and twentieth centuries in contrasting styles." However, some schools ask for very specific things, like a Mozart concerto, for example.

Will I Get a Job?

With 300 or 500 people auditioning for one spot in an orchestra, competition is often incredibly intense. Some instruments, such as the flute, the trumpet, and the clarinet, are more popular and more competitive than others. The bassoon, viola, and double bass are not as competitive, yet a bassoon position may still have 100 applicants. And that holds true with getting into college, too. If you are a flutist, you will most likely have a more difficult time getting into a selective school than if you are a bassoonist. When a school says it accepts a certain percentage of the number of people who apply, it is stating an overall figure. It may accept 100 percent of the double bassists and 5 percent of the flutists.

In the area of jazz and commercial music, the pathway to jobs is not quite as structured. Most often there are no formal auditions. You may be recommended by other professionals or a contractor may call you for a particular gig. You may audition for a contractor and he/she may call you to do a Broadway show. Through contacts you have made on other jobs, you may do a European tour with a group for six months. Following that, you may be back in the United States substituting for someone in the Radio City Music Hall Orchestra.

Besides performance, music students can prepare for careers in teaching, sound engineering, music therapy, and arts administration. With an undergraduate degree in music education, you can teach elementary and secondary school. To teach at the college level, however, you'll probably need performance and/or music education training up through a doctoral degree.

When considering the future, don't rule out nonmusic career opportunities. The analytical skills

---

WORDS OF WISDOM

Advice for Music Auditions

- In auditions, judges are first looking for raw talent and second, technique. They are also listening for something special—a musicality and artistry that sets you apart from other candidates.

- Never play pieces that are technically too difficult for you to perform well. Teachers are much more impressed with seeing what you can do rather than what you can't. It's better to pick an easier piece that you play extremely well. And don't play something that you dislike even though you may be able to play it technically well and you think the teacher is going to like it. When auditioning, the rule is that if you can't sell it, don't play it.

- If possible, prepare for your audition programs in advance by playing a couple of concerts or recitals in the weeks leading up to the audition, if possible. This may help you to feel more comfortable playing the music in front of a live audience as well as give you more experience with the particular pieces of music you plan to play.

- Be prepared for anything in terms of which, and how many, faculty members will be judging your performance. You never know what you're going to find—some students may be auditioning before the entire music faculty of a school; others may have to contend with only two adjudicators.

- Judges will make decisions based on what they hear and what they see; dress very professionally for an audition. Let the faculty see that you are serious about your craft.

---

music students acquire are often quite useful in other fields, including computer science, medicine, or law.

Advice for Studying Music

Students should be involved as much as they can not only in their own high school music activities but also in local, district, and state youth orchestras and performance ensembles. The more you perform and study, the deeper and richer your musical experience becomes and the more confident you will be on stage. These experiences will clearly show in your auditions and you'll be a better candidate for admission at your schools of choice.

▼ AARON COPLAND SCHOOL OF MUSIC

See Queens College of the City University of New York

▼ ABILENE CHRISTIAN UNIVERSITY

Abilene, Texas

Independent, coed. Urban campus. Total enrollment: 4,507.
Degrees Bachelor of Music in the areas of voice performance, piano performance, vocal music education, instrumental music education; Bachelor of Arts in the areas of vocal, piano, instrumental. Majors and concentrations: piano, stringed instruments, voice, wind and percussion instruments. Cross-registration with Hardin-Simmons University. Program accredited by NASM.
Enrollment Fall 1997: 63 total; all undergraduate.
Music Student Profile 53% females, 47% males, 10% international.
Music Faculty 24 total undergraduate (full-time and part-time). 60% of full-time faculty have terminal degrees. Graduate students do not teach undergraduate courses.
Student Life Student groups/activities include Children's Theater, Sing Song, Homecoming Musical.
Expenses for 1997–98 Application fee: $25, $45 for international students. Comprehensive fee: $12,990 includes full-time tuition ($8730), mandatory fees ($450), and college room and board ($3810). College room only: $1610. Room and board charges vary according to board plan and housing facility. Special program-related fees: $90–$225 per credit hour for private lessons.
Financial Aid Program-specific awards for 1997: 10–15 budgeted awards for musically qualified students ($750), 5 endowed awards for program majors ($800).
Application Procedures Students admitted directly into the professional program freshman year. Deadline for freshmen and transfers: continuous. Required: high school transcript, college transcript(s) for transfer students, 2 letters of recommendation, audition, SAT I or ACT test scores. Recommended: interview. Auditions held twice on campus; recorded music is permissible as a substitute for live auditions when distance is prohibitive and videotaped performances are permissible as a substitute for live auditions when scheduling is difficult.
Undergraduate Contact Dr. Paul Piersall, Chair, Music Department, Abilene Christian University, ACU Station, Box 28274, Abilene, Texas 79699; 915-674-2199.

▼ ACADIA UNIVERSITY

Wolfville, NS, Canada

Province-supported, coed. Small town campus. Total enrollment: 3,964.
Degrees Bachelor of Music in the areas of performance, composition, music theory/history, music education; Bachelor of Arts in Music in the areas of music business, music (in combination with an outside field). Majors and concentrations: composition, harpsichord, music, music business, music education, music history, music theory, piano/organ, stringed instruments, voice, wind and percussion instruments. Program accredited by CUMS.
Enrollment Fall 1997: 124 total; 94 undergraduate, 30 non-professional degree.

Music Student Profile 75% females, 25% males, 5% minorities, 4% international.
Music Faculty 27 total (full-time and part-time). 100% of full-time faculty have terminal degrees. Graduate students do not teach undergraduate courses. Undergraduate student–faculty ratio: 11:1.
Expenses for 1997–98 Application fee: $25 Canadian dollars. Tuition, fee, and room and board charges are reported in Canadian dollars. Canadian resident tuition: $5055 full-time. Mandatory fees: $147 full-time. Full-time tuition and fees vary according to student level. College room and board: $4465. College room only: $2470. Room and board charges vary according to board plan and housing facility. International student tuition: $8770 full-time.
Financial Aid Program-specific awards for 1997: 40 Endowed Awards for program majors ($400–$7500), 12 Alumni Awards for program majors ($400–$5000).
Application Procedures Students admitted directly into the professional program freshman year. Deadline for freshmen and transfers: continuous. Notification date for freshmen and transfers: continuous. Required: high school transcript, college transcript(s) for transfer students, 2 letters of recommendation, interview, audition, music theory test, minimum 2.5 high school GPA. Recommended: minimum 3.0 high school GPA. Auditions held 6 times on campus; recorded music is permissible as a substitute for live auditions when distance is prohibitive and videotaped performances are permissible as a substitute for live auditions when distance is prohibitive.
Web Site http://ace.acadiau.ca/arts/music/home.htm.
Undergraduate Contact Director, School of Music, Acadia University, Wolfville, NS B0P 1X0, Canada; 902-542-2201 ext. 1512, E-mail address: bjordan@acadiau.ca.

▼ ALABAMA STATE UNIVERSITY

Montgomery, Alabama

State-supported, coed. Urban campus. Total enrollment: 5,273.
Degrees Bachelor of Music Education. Majors and concentrations: choral music education, instrumental music education. Graduate degrees offered: Master of Music Education. Program accredited by NASM.
Enrollment Fall 1997: 98 total; 70 undergraduate, 22 graduate, 6 non-professional degree.
Music Student Profile 40% females, 16% minorities, 1% international.
Music Faculty 16 total undergraduate and graduate (full-time and part-time). 54% of full-time faculty have terminal degrees. Graduate students do not teach undergraduate courses. Undergraduate student–faculty ratio: 8:1.
Student Life Student groups/activities include professional fraternities and sororities, Music Educators National Conference Student Chapter.
Expenses for 1997–98 State resident tuition: $1800 full-time. Nonresident tuition: $3600 full-time. Mandatory fees: $230 full-time. Full-time tuition and fees vary according to course load, degree level, and student level. College room and board: $3300. Room and board charges vary according to housing facility.
Financial Aid Program-specific awards for 1997: 80 Band Grants for band majors ($500–$2000), 15 Choral Grants for vocal music majors ($500–$200), 15 School of Music Scholarships for program majors ($1000–$2500).

Application Procedures Students admitted directly into the professional program freshman year. Deadline for freshmen and transfers: continuous. Required: high school transcript, college transcript(s) for transfer students, minimum 2.0 high school GPA, 3 letters of recommendation, audition, ACT test score only. Auditions held twice and by appointment on campus; recorded music is permissible as a substitute for live auditions when distance is prohibitive and videotaped performances are permissible as a substitute for live auditions when distance is prohibitive.

Web Site http://www.alasu.edu.

Contact Dr. Horace Lamar, Dean, School of Music, Alabama State University, PO Box 271, Montgomery, Alabama 36101-0271; 334-229-4341, fax: 334-229-4901, E-mail address: hlamar@asunet.alasu.edu.

▼ ALCORN STATE UNIVERSITY

Lorman, Mississippi

State-supported, coed. Rural campus. Total enrollment: 2,847.

Degrees Bachelor of Music in the area of performance; Bachelor of Music Education. Majors and concentrations: brass, guitar, music education, piano/organ, voice, wind and percussion instruments. Program accredited by NASM.

Enrollment Fall 1997: 53 undergraduate.

Music Student Profile 60% females, 40% males, 100% minorities.

Music Faculty 12 total (full-time and part-time). 42% of full-time faculty have terminal degrees. Graduate students do not teach undergraduate courses. Undergraduate student–faculty ratio: 4:1.

Student Life Student groups/activities include Music Educators National Conference, Kappa Kappa Psi, Tau Beta Sigma.

Expenses for 1997–98 State resident tuition: $2429 full-time. Nonresident tuition: $4931 full-time. College room and board: $2324.

Financial Aid Program-specific awards for 1997: 25–30 music scholarships for program majors, 100–125 Band Grants for talented band members.

Application Procedures Students admitted directly into the professional program freshman year. Deadline for freshmen and transfers: July 31. Required: high school transcript, college transcript(s) for transfer students, minimum 2.0 high school GPA, audition, SAT I or ACT test scores. Auditions held as needed on campus and off campus in various sites in southern United States; recorded music is permissible as a substitute for live auditions when distance is prohibitive and videotaped performances are permissible as a substitute for live auditions when distance is prohibitive.

Undergraduate Contact Dr. Joyce J. Bolden, Chair, Department of Fine Arts, Alcorn State University, 1000 ASU Drive #29, Lorman, Mississippi 39096-9402; 601-877-6261, fax: 601-877-6262, E-mail address: jbolden@academic.alcorn.edu.

▼ ALMA COLLEGE

Alma, Michigan

Independent-Presbyterian, coed. Small town campus. Total enrollment: 1,407. Music program established 1886.

Degrees Bachelor of Music in the areas of performance, education. Cross-registration with American University,

Stillman College, University of Aberdeen (Scotland). Program accredited by NASM.

Enrollment Fall 1997: 40 total; all undergraduate.

Music Student Profile 56% females, 44% males, 4% minorities, 1% international.

Music Faculty 18 total (full-time and part-time). 85% of full-time faculty have terminal degrees. Graduate students do not teach undergraduate courses.

Student Life Student groups/activities include Phi Mu Alpha, Sigma Alpha Iota, Music Educators National Conference.

Expenses for 1997–98 Application fee: $20. Comprehensive fee: $19,290 includes full-time tuition ($14,100), mandatory fees ($138), and college room and board ($5052). College room only: $2478. Special program-related fees: $75 per term for private lessons, accompanist fee, piano maintenance.

Financial Aid Program-specific awards for 1997: 50 Performance Awards for ensemble participants ($1250).

Application Procedures Students apply for admission into the professional program by sophomore year. Deadline for freshmen and transfers: continuous. Notification date for freshmen and transfers: continuous. Required: high school transcript, college transcript(s) for transfer students, minimum 3.0 high school GPA, audition, SAT I or ACT test scores (minimum combined SAT I score of 1025, minimum combined ACT score of 22). Recommended: essay, 2 letters of recommendation, interview. Auditions held by appointment on campus; recorded music is permissible as a substitute for live auditions when distance is prohibitive with teacher recommendation and videotaped performances are permissible as a substitute for live auditions when distance is prohibitive with teacher recommendation.

Undergraduate Contact Mr. Mark Nazario, Director of Admissions, Alma College, Alma, Michigan 48801; 800-321-ALMA, fax: 517-463-7277.

▼ ALVERNO COLLEGE

Milwaukee, Wisconsin

Independent-Roman Catholic, women only. Suburban campus. Total enrollment: 2,072.

Degrees Bachelor of Music in the areas of music education, music therapy, music performance and pedagogy. Program accredited by NASM.

Enrollment Fall 1997: 37 total; all undergraduate.

Music Student Profile 100% females, 5% minorities.

Music Faculty 17 total (full-time and part-time). 50% of full-time faculty have terminal degrees. Graduate students do not teach undergraduate courses. Undergraduate student–faculty ratio: 3:1.

Student Life Student groups/activities include Music Therapy Club, Music Educators National Conference Student Chapter.

Expenses for 1997–98 Application fee: $20. Comprehensive fee: $13,612 includes full-time tuition ($9672), mandatory fees ($50), and college room and board ($3890). Full-time tuition and fees vary according to program. Room and board charges vary according to board plan. Special program-related fees: $100–$200 per credit for private lessons.

Financial Aid Program-specific awards for 1997: 1 Beihoff Scholarship for music majors ($300), 2 Ermenc Scholarship for music and dance students ($250), 3 Hytrek Scholarship for music majors ($700), 3 Zeyen Scholarship for music majors ($600), 5 Lampe Scholarship for music and art majors ($400), 1 Steffen Scholarship for music majors

Alverno College (continued)

($200), 1 Stoecker Scholarship for music majors ($200), 2 Samudio for music therapy majors ($400), 1 Milwaukee Music Teachers Association for music majors ($400), 1 Rosbach Scholarship for music majors ($600).

Application Procedures Students admitted directly into the professional program freshman year. Deadline for freshmen and transfers: continuous. Required: high school transcript, college transcript(s) for transfer students, interview, audition, ACT test score only. Auditions held 5 times on campus; recorded music is permissible as a substitute for live auditions for out-of-state applicants and videotaped performances are permissible as a substitute for live auditions for out-of-state applicants.

Undergraduate Contact Mr. Owen Smith, Director, Admissions Department, Alverno College, 3401 South 39th Street, Milwaukee, Wisconsin 53234-3922; 414-382-6100, fax: 414-382-6354.

▼ American Conservatory of Music

Chicago, Illinois

Independent, coed. Urban campus. Music program established 1886.

Degrees Bachelor of Music in the areas of jazz, classical music. Majors and concentrations: arranging, composition, guitar, harpsichord, jazz, music theory, organ, piano, stringed instruments, voice, wind and percussion instruments. Graduate degrees offered: Master of Music in the areas of jazz, classical music. Doctor of Musical Arts in the areas of jazz, classical music. Program accredited by NASM.

Enrollment Fall 1997: 83 total.

Music Student Profile 51% females, 49% males, 64% international.

Music Faculty 52 total undergraduate an graduate (part-time). Graduate students do not teach undergraduate courses. Undergraduate student–faculty ratio: 3:1.

Student Life Student groups/activities include Choir, Jazz Band.

Expenses for 1997–98 Application fee: $50. Tuition: $9000 full-time. Mandatory fees: $600 full-time. Full-time tuition and fees vary according to course load.

Financial Aid Program-specific awards for 1997: Leo Heim Presidential Scholarships for talented program students ($500–$6000).

Application Procedures Students admitted directly into the professional program freshman year. Deadline for freshmen and transfers: continuous. Required: essay, high school transcript, college transcript(s) for transfer students, 2 letters of recommendation, interview, audition, affidavit of support (international students), certificate of immunization (international students). Recommended: minimum 2.0 high school GPA, video, portfolio for composition transfer students. Auditions held by appointment on campus; recorded music is permissible as a substitute for live auditions when distance is prohibitive and videotaped performances are permissible as a substitute for live auditions when distance is prohibitive. Portfolio reviews held whenever needed on campus.

Web Site http://members.aol.com/amerconsmu/index.html.

Undergraduate Contact Ms. Mary Ellen Newsom, Registrar, American Conservatory of Music, 36 South Wabash, Suite 800, Chicago, Illinois 60603; 312-263-4161, fax: 312-263-5832.

Graduate Contact Ms. Mary Ellen Newsom, Registrar, American Conservatory of Music, 36 South Wabash, Suite 800, Chicago, Illinois 60603; 312-263-4161, fax: 312-263-5832.

▼ Anderson College

Anderson, South Carolina

Independent-Baptist, coed. Suburban campus. Total enrollment: 1,012. Music program established 1911.

Degrees Bachelor of Music Education in the areas of vocal/choral music education, instrumental music education. Majors and concentrations: music education. Program accredited by NASM.

Enrollment Fall 1997: 27 undergraduate.

Music Student Profile 70% females, 30% males, 15% minorities, 4% international.

Music Faculty 11 total (full-time and part-time). 75% of full-time faculty have terminal degrees. Graduate students do not teach undergraduate courses. Undergraduate student–faculty ratio: 11:1.

Student Life Student groups/activities include Music Educators National Conference Student Chapter, Anderson College Playhouse, National Association of Teachers of Singing student auditions.

Expenses for 1997–98 Application fee: $20. Comprehensive fee: $13,620 includes full-time tuition ($8680), mandatory fees ($795), and college room and board ($4145). College room only: $2086. Special program-related fees: $225 per credit hour for private music lessons.

Financial Aid Program-specific awards for 1997: merit scholarships for program majors ($1500–$6000).

Application Procedures Students apply for admission into the professional program by freshman year. Deadline for freshmen and transfers: continuous. Notification date for freshmen and transfers: continuous. Required: essay, high school transcript, college transcript(s) for transfer students, minimum 2.0 high school GPA, interview, audition, SAT I or ACT test scores. Recommended: minimum 3.0 high school GPA. Auditions held continuously on campus; recorded music is permissible as a substitute for live auditions when distance is prohibitive and videotaped performances are permissible as a substitute for live auditions in special circumstances.

Undergraduate Contact Mr. David Larson, Division Head, Fine Arts Department, Anderson College, 316 Boulevard, Anderson, South Carolina 29621; 864-231-2002, fax: 864-231-2004.

▼ Andrews University

Berrien Springs, Michigan

Independent-Seventh-day Adventist, coed. Small town campus. Total enrollment: 3,152.

Degrees Bachelor of Music in the areas of music education, performance. Majors and concentrations: music, music education, piano/organ, stringed instruments, voice, wind and percussion instruments. Graduate degrees offered: Master of Music in the areas of music education, performance. Program accredited by NASM.

Enrollment Fall 1997: 42 total; 19 undergraduate, 7 graduate, 16 non-professional degree.

Music Student Profile 74% females, 26% males, 40% minorities, 48% international.

Music Faculty 23 total undergraduate and graduate (full-time and part-time). 38% of full-time faculty have terminal degrees. Graduate students teach a few undergraduate courses. Undergraduate student–faculty ratio: 8:1.

Student Life Student groups/activities include Collegiate Music Educators National Conference, Composers Club.

Expenses for 1997–98 Application fee: $30. Comprehensive fee: $15,087 includes full-time tuition ($11,340), mandatory fees ($237), and college room and board ($3510). College room only: $2070. Special program-related fees: $40 per term for private lessons, $125 per year for ensemble uniform fee.

Financial Aid Program-specific awards for 1997: 15 Named Scholarships for program majors ($500–$1000), 20–30 Performance Scholarships for Ensembles for ensemble performers ($500–$1000).

Application Procedures Students apply for admission into the professional program by freshman year. Deadline for freshmen and transfers: continuous. Required: high school transcript, 2 letters of recommendation, audition. Auditions held by request on campus; recorded music is permissible as a substitute for live auditions when distance is prohibitive and videotaped performances are permissible as a substitute for live auditions when distance is prohibitive.

Contact Dr. Peter Cooper, Chairman, Department of Music, Andrews University, Berrien Springs, Michigan 49104-0230; 616-471-3128, fax: 616-471-9751, E-mail address: pcooper@andrews.edu.

▼ ANGELO STATE UNIVERSITY

San Angelo, Texas

State-supported, coed. Urban campus. Total enrollment: 6,234.

Degrees Bachelor of Music in the area of music education. Majors and concentrations: music, music education, piano/organ, voice, wind and percussion instruments. Program accredited by NASM.

Enrollment Fall 1997: 107 total; 77 undergraduate, 30 non-professional degree.

Music Student Profile 50% females, 50% males, 10% minorities.

Music Faculty 14 total (full-time and part-time). 82% of full-time faculty have terminal degrees. Graduate students do not teach undergraduate courses. Undergraduate student–faculty ratio: 7:1.

Student Life Student groups/activities include Kappa Kappa Psi, Phi Mu Alpha, Sigma Alpha Iota.

Estimated expenses for 1998–99 State resident tuition: $1080 full-time. Nonresident tuition: $7470 full-time. Mandatory fees: $1162 full-time. Full-time tuition and fees vary according to course load. College room and board: $3908. College room only: $2468. Room and board charges vary according to board plan and housing facility. Special program-related fees: $20–$40 per semester for private lessons.

Financial Aid Program-specific awards for 1997: Carr Academic Scholarships for academically qualified applicants ($3000), band awards for instrumentalists ($300–$500), choral awards for vocalists ($300–$500), 10 Carr Performing Arts Scholarships ($1500), 20 Fame Scholarships ($500–$1000).

Application Procedures Students admitted directly into the professional program freshman year. Deadline for freshmen and transfers: August 5. Notification date for freshmen and transfers: August 15. Required: high school transcript, college transcript(s) for transfer students, audition, SAT I or ACT test scores. Recommended: minimum 2.0 high school GPA, letter of recommendation. Auditions held continuously on campus; recorded music is permissible as a substitute for live auditions for out-of-state applicants and videotaped performances are permissible as a substitute for live auditions for out-of-state applicants.

Undergraduate Contact Dean of Admissions, Angelo State University, Administration and Journalism Building, San Angelo, Texas 76909; 915-942-2042, E-mail address: monique.cossich@angelo.edu.

▼ ANNA MARIA COLLEGE

Paxton, Massachusetts

Independent-Roman Catholic, coed. Rural campus. Total enrollment: 1,668. Music program established 1947.

Degrees Bachelor of Music in the areas of music education, music therapy, music education and music therapy, piano performance, vocal performance. Majors and concentrations: music, piano/organ, voice. Cross-registration with Worcester Consortium. Program accredited by NASM, NAMT.

Enrollment Fall 1997: 65 total; all undergraduate.

Music Student Profile 84% females, 16% males, 1% minorities, 1% international.

Music Faculty 19 total (full-time and part-time). 50% of full-time faculty have terminal degrees. Graduate students do not teach undergraduate courses.

Student Life Student groups/activities include Music Club, Music Educators National Conference, Music Therapy Club. Special housing available for music students.

Expenses for 1997–98 Application fee: $30. Comprehensive fee: $17,496 includes full-time tuition ($11,600), mandatory fees ($640), and college room and board ($5256). Special program-related fees: $415 per course for private lessons, $50 per course for instrument rental.

Financial Aid Program-specific awards for 1997: 4 music scholarships for program majors ($1500).

Application Procedures Students admitted directly into the professional program freshman year. Deadline for freshmen and transfers: continuous. Required: essay, high school transcript, college transcript(s) for transfer students, minimum 2.0 high school GPA, 3 letters of recommendation, audition, SAT I or ACT test scores. Recommended: interview. Auditions held by appointment on campus; recorded music is permissible as a substitute for live auditions when distance is prohibitive and videotaped performances are permissible as a substitute for live auditions when distance is prohibitive.

Web Site http://www.anna-maria.edu.

Undergraduate Contact Ms. Christine Soverow, Director of Admissions, Admissions Office, Anna Maria College, Box 78, Paxton, Massachusetts 01612-1198; 508-849-3360, fax: 508-849-3362, E-mail address: csoverow@anna-maria.edu.

▼ APPALACHIAN STATE UNIVERSITY

Boone, North Carolina

State-supported, coed. Small town campus. Total enrollment: 12,108.

Degrees Bachelor of Music in the areas of music education, performance, composition, sacred music, music therapy. Majors and concentrations: classical music, composition,

Appalachian State University (*continued*)

music, music education, music therapy, musical instrument technology, piano/organ, sacred music, stringed instruments, voice, wind and percussion instruments. Graduate degrees offered: Master of Music in the areas of music education, performance, composition. Program accredited by NASM.

Enrollment Fall 1997: 417 total; 401 undergraduate, 16 graduate.

Music Student Profile 47% females, 53% males, 5% minorities, 2% international.

Music Faculty 47 total undergraduate and graduate (full-time and part-time). 74% of full-time faculty have terminal degrees. Graduate students teach a few undergraduate courses. Undergraduate student–faculty ratio: 10:1.

Student Life Student groups/activities include Music Educators National Conference, Music and Entertainment Industry Student Association, music fraternities and sororities.

Expenses for 1997–98 Application fee: $25. State resident tuition: $900 full-time. Nonresident tuition: $8028 full-time. Mandatory fees: $940 full-time. College room and board: $3008. College room only: $1740. Room and board charges vary according to board plan and housing facility. Special program-related fees: $18 per semester hour for applied music fee.

Financial Aid Program-specific awards for 1997: 20 School of Music Awards for program majors ($750–$1000), 6 Fletcher Scholarships for program majors ($1000–$5000), 1 Presser Award for program majors ($2250), 9 Appal PIE Awards for program majors ($2500).

Application Procedures Students admitted directly into the professional program freshman year. Deadline for freshmen and transfers: April 1. Notification date for freshmen and transfers: July 1. Required: high school transcript, college transcript(s) for transfer students, audition, SAT I or ACT test scores (minimum combined SAT I score of 800). Recommended: minimum 3.0 high school GPA. Auditions held 4 times on campus; recorded music is permissible as a substitute for live auditions when distance is prohibitive and videotaped performances are permissible as a substitute for live auditions when distance is prohibitive.

Web Site http://www.acs.appstate.edu/dept/music.

Undergraduate Contact Ms. Cara Osborne, Receptionist, School of Music, Appalachian State University, Rivers Street, Boone, North Carolina 28608; 704-262-3020, fax: 704-262-6446.

Graduate Contact Dr. William Harbinson, Associate Dean, School of Music, Appalachian State University, Rivers Street, Boone, North Carolina 28608; 704-262-3020, fax: 704-262-6446.

▼ AQUINAS COLLEGE

Grand Rapids, Michigan

Independent-Roman Catholic, coed. Suburban campus. Total enrollment: 2,458.

Degrees Bachelor of Music in the areas of choral supervision, instrumental supervision, liturgical music. Majors and concentrations: guitar, liturgical music, music education, organ, piano, voice.

Enrollment Fall 1997: 70 total; 20 undergraduate, 50 non-professional degree.

Music Student Profile 50% females, 50% males, 7% international.

Music Faculty 18 total (full-time and part-time). 100% of full-time faculty have terminal degrees. Graduate students do not teach undergraduate courses. Undergraduate student–faculty ratio: 12:1.

Student Life Student groups/activities include Music Educators National Conference, National Pastoral Musicians, National Association of Jazz Educators.

Expenses for 1997–98 Application fee: $25. Comprehensive fee: $17,274 includes full-time tuition ($12,910), mandatory fees ($40), and college room and board ($4324). Full-time tuition and fees vary according to course load. Special program-related fees: $100 per term for lab fees.

Financial Aid Program-specific awards for 1997: 20 departmental awards for program majors ($150–$200).

Application Procedures Students admitted directly into the professional program freshman year. Deadline for freshmen and transfers: continuous. Notification date for freshmen and transfers: continuous. Required: high school transcript, letter of recommendation, SAT I or ACT test scores. Recommended: audition for scholarship consideration. Auditions held 3 times on campus.

Undergraduate Contact Ms. Paula Meehan, Dean of Admissions, Aquinas College, 1607 Robinson Road, SE, Grand Rapids, Michigan 49506; 616-459-8281 ext. 5205, fax: 616-732-4435.

▼ ARIZONA STATE UNIVERSITY

Tempe, Arizona

State-supported, coed. Suburban campus. Total enrollment: 44,255.

Degrees Bachelor of Music in the areas of choral music, general music, instrumental music, music theater, performance, music theory and composition, music therapy, jazz performance, piano accompanying. Majors and concentrations: accompanying, jazz, music education, music history and literature, music theater, music theory and composition, music therapy, piano/organ, stringed instruments, voice, wind and percussion instruments. Graduate degrees offered: Master of Music in the areas of choral music, general music, instrumental music, music theater, performance, music theater direction, performance pedagogy, music theory, composition, piano accompanying. Doctor of Musical Arts in the areas of choral music, instrumental music, performance. Program accredited by NASM.

Enrollment Fall 1997: 764 total; 483 undergraduate, 281 graduate.

Music Student Profile 53% females, 47% males, 11% minorities, 7% international.

Music Faculty 71 total undergraduate and graduate (full-time and part-time). 75% of full-time faculty have terminal degrees. Graduate students teach a few undergraduate courses. Undergraduate student–faculty ratio: 16:1.

Expenses for 1997–98 Application fee: $40 for nonresidents. State resident tuition: $1988 full-time. Nonresident tuition: $8640 full-time. Mandatory fees: $71 full-time. College room and board: $4500. College room only: $2700. Room and board charges vary according to board plan and housing facility. Special program-related fees: $60 per semester for studio lesson fee.

Financial Aid Program-specific awards for 1997: 165 tuition waivers for out-of-state program students ($8000), 167 tuition waivers for state residents ($2000), 100 Cash Awards for program students ($500).

Application Procedures Students admitted directly into the professional program freshman year. Deadline for freshmen and transfers: June 15. Required: high school transcript, audition, SAT I or ACT test scores. Auditions held 3 times on campus; recorded music is permissible as a substitute for live auditions when distance is prohibitive or in special circumstances and videotaped performances are permissible as a substitute for live auditions if distance is prohibitive or in special circumstances.

Undergraduate Contact Ms. Delores Thompson, Admissions Officer and Advisor, School of Music, Arizona State University, Box 870405, Tempe, Arizona 85287-0405; 602-965-2816, fax: 602-965-2659.

▼ ARKANSAS STATE UNIVERSITY
State University, Arkansas

State-supported, coed. Small town campus. Total enrollment: 10,012. Music program established 1945.

Degrees Bachelor of Music in the areas of vocal music, instrumental music, keyboard performance, composition; Bachelor of Music Education in the areas of vocal music, instrumental music. Majors and concentrations: composition, music, music education, piano/organ, stringed instruments, voice, wind and percussion instruments. Graduate degrees offered: Master of Music in the areas of performance, composition; Master of Music Education. Program accredited by NASM.

Enrollment Fall 1997: 150 total; 135 undergraduate, 10 graduate, 5 non-professional degree.

Music Student Profile 30% females, 70% males, 5% minorities.

Music Faculty 21 total undergraduate and graduate (full-time and part-time). 55% of full-time faculty have terminal degrees. Graduate students do not teach undergraduate courses.

Expenses for 1997–98 Application fee: $15. State resident tuition: $2000 full-time. Nonresident tuition: $5090 full-time. Mandatory fees: $280 full-time. College room and board: $2840. Room and board charges vary according to board plan and housing facility. Special program-related fees: $35–$55 per semester for private lessons.

Financial Aid Program-specific awards for 1997: 130 grants-in-aid for instrumentalists ($250–$1000), 10 Keyboard Scholarships for keyboardists ($500–$1000), 30 grants-in-aid for vocalists ($250–$1000).

Application Procedures Students admitted directly into the professional program freshman year. Deadline for freshmen and transfers: August 15. Required: high school transcript, college transcript(s) for transfer students, audition, SAT I or ACT test scores. Recommended: minimum 2.0 high school GPA. Auditions held twice and by appointment on campus; recorded music is permissible as a substitute for live auditions by request and videotaped performances are permissible as a substitute for live auditions by request.

Web Site http://www.astate.edu.

Contact Dr. Dale Miller, Chair, Music Department, Arkansas State University, PO Box 779, State University, Arkansas 72467; 870-972-2094, fax: 870-972-3932, E-mail address: rdmiller@aztec.astate.edu.

▼ ARMSTRONG ATLANTIC STATE UNIVERSITY
Savannah, Georgia

State-supported, coed. Suburban campus. Total enrollment: 5,696. Music program established 1935.

Degrees Bachelor of Music Education in the areas of instrumental music education, choral music education, general music education. Program accredited by NASM.

Enrollment Fall 1997: 70 total; 55 undergraduate, 15 non-professional degree.

Music Student Profile 15% minorities.

Music Faculty 28 total (full-time and part-time). 75% of full-time faculty have terminal degrees. Graduate students do not teach undergraduate courses.

Student Life Student groups/activities include Collegiate Music Educators National Conference.

Expenses for 1997–98 Application fee: $15. State resident tuition: $1680 full-time. Nonresident tuition: $6141 full-time. Mandatory fees: $282 full-time. College room and board: $4116.

Financial Aid Program-specific awards for 1997: 30 departmental awards for program majors ($600).

Application Procedures Students admitted directly into the professional program freshman year. Deadline for freshmen and transfers: continuous. Required: high school transcript, college transcript(s) for transfer students, minimum 2.0 high school GPA, audition, SAT I or ACT test scores, music theory placement test. Recommended: minimum 3.0 high school GPA, video. Auditions held by appointment on campus; recorded music is permissible as a substitute for live auditions for out-of-state applicants and videotaped performances are permissible as a substitute for live auditions for out-of-state applicants.

Web Site http://www.music.armstrong.edu.

Undergraduate Contact Dr. Jim Anderson, Head, Department of Art and Music, Armstrong Atlantic State University, 11935 Abercorn Street, Savannah, Georgia 31419; 912-927-5325, fax: 912-921-5492, E-mail address: jim_anderson@mailgate.armstrong.edu.

▼ ASHLAND UNIVERSITY
Ashland, Ohio

Independent, coed. Small town campus. Total enrollment: 5,737.

Degrees Bachelor of Music in the area of music education. Majors and concentrations: composition, music education, music history, music theory, piano/organ, stringed instruments, voice, wind and percussion instruments. Program accredited by NASM.

Enrollment Fall 1997: 55 total; all undergraduate.

Music Student Profile 56% females, 44% males, 12% minorities, 3% international.

Music Faculty 25 total (full-time and part-time). 100% of full-time faculty have terminal degrees. Graduate students do not teach undergraduate courses.

Student Life Student groups/activities include Music Educators National Conference, National Association of Schools of Music, Kappa Kappa Psi.

Expenses for 1997–98 Application fee: $25. Comprehensive fee: $18,717 includes full-time tuition ($13,293), mandatory

Ashland University (continued)

fees ($308), and college room and board ($5116). College room only: $2715. Room and board charges vary according to board plan and housing facility. Special program-related fees: $205 per semester for private music lessons and instrument lab fees.

Financial Aid Program-specific awards for 1997: 20 scholarships for program majors ($1800).

Application Procedures Students admitted directly into the professional program freshman year. Deadline for freshmen and transfers: continuous. Required: high school transcript, college transcript(s) for transfer students, letter of recommendation, audition, SAT I or ACT test scores. Recommended: minimum 3.0 high school GPA, interview. Auditions held on campus; recorded music is permissible as a substitute for live auditions when distance is prohibitive and videotaped performances are permissible as a substitute for live auditions when distance is prohibitive.

Web Site http://www.ashland.edu.

Undergraduate Contact Mr. Leonard Salvo, Chair, Department of Music, Ashland University, 401 College Avenue, Ashland, Ohio 44805; 419-289-5100, fax: 419-289-5329, E-mail address: lsalvo@ashland.edu.

▼ ATLANTIC UNION COLLEGE

South Lancaster, Massachusetts

Independent-Seventh-day Adventist, coed. Small town campus. Total enrollment: 722.

Degrees Bachelor of Music in the areas of performance, music education. Majors and concentrations: guitar, music education, piano/organ, stringed instruments, voice, wind and percussion instruments. Program accredited by NASM.

Enrollment Fall 1997: 21 total; 2 undergraduate, 19 nonprofessional degree.

Music Student Profile 33% females, 67% males, 40% minorities, 10% international.

Music Faculty 30 total (full-time and part-time). 50% of full-time faculty have terminal degrees. Graduate students do not teach undergraduate courses. Undergraduate student–faculty ratio: 3:1.

Expenses for 1997–98 Application fee: $15. Comprehensive fee: $15,900 includes full-time tuition ($11,330), mandatory fees ($670), and college room and board ($3900). College room only: $2100. Special program-related fees: $35–$70 per semester for piano/organ maintenance fee.

Financial Aid Program-specific awards for 1997: Music Department Scholarships for program majors ($500).

Application Procedures Students apply for admission into the professional program by freshman year. Deadline for freshmen and transfers: August 15. Required: high school transcript, minimum 2.0 high school GPA, 2 letters of recommendation, audition, SAT I or ACT test scores, 3 musical references. Auditions held as needed on campus and off campus in Providence, RI; New York, NY; Boston, MA; Hartford, CT; recorded music is permissible as a substitute for live auditions if a campus visit is impossible.

Undergraduate Contact Enrollment Management Office, Atlantic Union College, PO Box 1000, South Lancaster, Massachusetts 01561-1000; 978-368-2255, fax: 978-368-2015.

▼ AUBURN UNIVERSITY

Auburn University, Alabama

State-supported, coed. Small town campus. Total enrollment: 21,505. Music program established 1935.

Degrees Bachelor of Music Education in the areas of choral music, band. Majors and concentrations: band, choral music. Graduate degrees offered: Doctor of Philosophy in the area of music education. Program accredited by NASM.

Enrollment Fall 1997: 80 total; 65 undergraduate, 15 graduate.

Music Student Profile 57% females, 43% males, 4% minorities, 2% international.

Music Faculty 29 total undergraduate and graduate (full-time and part-time). 80% of full-time faculty have terminal degrees. Graduate students teach a few undergraduate courses.

Student Life Student groups/activities include Phi Mu Alpha, Kappa Kappa Psi, Auburn Women of Music.

Expenses for 1997–98 Application fee: $25, $50 for international students. State resident tuition: $2610 full-time. Nonresident tuition: $7830 full-time. Full-time tuition varies according to program. College room only: $1905. Room charges vary according to housing facility. Part-time mandatory fees per term: $145 for state residents, $435 for nonresidents. Special program-related fees: $82 per quarter for private lessons.

Application Procedures Students apply for admission into the professional program by sophomore year. Deadline for freshmen and transfers: September 1. Required: high school transcript, college transcript(s) for transfer students, SAT I or ACT test scores.

Undergraduate Contact Nancy Barry, Curriculum and Teaching, College of Education, Auburn University, 5040 Haley Center, Auburn University, Alabama 36849; 334-844-6877, E-mail address: barrynh@duc.auburn.edu.

Graduate Contact Mr. Joseph Stephenson, Head, Department of Music, Auburn University, 101 Goodwin Music Building, Auburn University, Alabama 36849-5420; 334-844-4164, fax: 334-844-3168, E-mail address: stephjb@mail.auburn.edu.

▼ AUGSBURG COLLEGE

Minneapolis, Minnesota

Independent-Lutheran, coed. Urban campus. Total enrollment: 2,817. Music program established 1922.

Degrees Bachelor of Music in the area of performance; Bachelor of Music Education; Bachelor of Science in the area of music therapy; Bachelor of Arts in the area of music. Majors and concentrations: music, music education, music performance, music therapy. Cross-registration with Associated Colleges of the Twin Cities - Hamline University, Macalester College, College of St. Catherine, University of St. Thomas. Program accredited by NASM.

Enrollment Fall 1997: 25 total; all undergraduate.

Music Student Profile 70% females, 30% males, 1% minorities, 1% international.

Music Faculty 28 total (full-time and part-time). 70% of full-time faculty have terminal degrees. Graduate students do not teach undergraduate courses.

Estimated expenses for 1998–99 Application fee: $20. Comprehensive fee: $19,750 includes full-time tuition ($14,470), mandatory fees ($146), and college room and board ($5134). College room only: $2624.

Financial Aid Program-specific awards for 1997: 35 scholarships for program majors ($200–$1500).

Application Procedures Students apply for admission into the professional program by sophomore year. Deadline for freshmen and transfers: continuous. Required: essay, high school transcript, college transcript(s) for transfer students, minimum 2.0 high school GPA, SAT I or ACT test scores, audition for scholarship consideration. Recommended: 2 letters of recommendation. Auditions held once on campus; recorded music is permissible as a substitute for live auditions when distance is prohibitive and videotaped performances are permissible as a substitute for live auditions when distance is prohibitive.

Web Site http://www.augsburg.edu.

Undergraduate Contact Admissions, Augsburg College, 2211 Riverside Avenue, Minneapolis, Minnesota 55454; 612-330-1001, fax: 612-330-1590.

▼ AUGUSTA STATE UNIVERSITY

Augusta, Georgia

State-supported, coed. Urban campus. Total enrollment: 5,479. Music program established 1971.

Degrees Bachelor of Music in the area of performance; Bachelor of Music Education. Majors and concentrations: music, music education, piano/organ, stringed instruments, voice, wind and percussion instruments. Program accredited by NASM.

Enrollment Fall 1997: 85 undergraduate.

Music Student Profile 58% females, 42% males, 13% minorities.

Music Faculty 25 total undergraduate (full-time and part-time). 100% of full-time faculty have terminal degrees. Graduate students do not teach undergraduate courses.

Expenses for 1997–98 Application fee: $10. State resident tuition: $1680 full-time. Nonresident tuition: $6141 full-time. Mandatory fees: $246 full-time. Special program-related fees: $25–$45 per instrument per quarter for applied music fee.

Financial Aid Program-specific awards for 1997: 12–15 Maxwell Fund Awards for program majors ($300–$600), 2 Storyland Theater Awards for music theater participants ($2000), 4–6 Church Scholarships for choir singers ($1200–$1650), 2 Mary Byrd Scholarships for students from Columbia County, Georgia ($1000), 4–8 Pamplin Scholarships for program majors ($1000).

Application Procedures Students admitted directly into the professional program freshman year. Deadline for freshmen and transfers: August 15. Required: high school transcript, minimum 2.0 high school GPA, 2 letters of recommendation. Recommended: audition. Auditions held 6 times on campus; recorded music is permissible as a substitute for live auditions when distance is prohibitive and videotaped performances are permissible as a substitute for live auditions when distance is prohibitive.

Undergraduate Contact Dr. Clayton Shotwell, Chairman, Fine Arts Department, Augusta State University, 2500 Walton Way, Augusta, Georgia 30904-2200; 706-737-1453, fax: 706-737-1773, E-mail address: cshotwel@aug.edu.

▼ BAKER UNIVERSITY

Baldwin City, Kansas

Independent-United Methodist, coed. Small town campus. Total enrollment: 796.

Degrees Bachelor of Music in the area of performance; Bachelor of Music Education. Majors and concentrations: music, music education, piano/organ, voice, wind and percussion instruments. Program accredited by NASM, NCATE.

Enrollment Fall 1997: 30 undergraduate.

Music Faculty 12 total (full-time and part-time). 83% of full-time faculty have terminal degrees. Graduate students do not teach undergraduate courses.

Student Life Student groups/activities include Collegiate Music Educators National Conference.

Expenses for 1997–98 Application fee: $20. Comprehensive fee: $15,500 includes full-time tuition ($10,900) and college room and board ($4600). Special program-related fees: $155 per credit for applied music fee.

Financial Aid Program-specific awards for 1997: 6 Music Department Scholarships for program majors ($4000).

Application Procedures Students admitted directly into the professional program freshman year. Deadline for freshmen and transfers: continuous. Required: high school transcript, letter of recommendation, interview, audition, SAT I or ACT test scores, minimum 2.7 high school GPA. Recommended: minimum 3.0 high school GPA. Auditions held 3 times and by appointment on campus; recorded music is permissible as a substitute for live auditions when distance is prohibitive and videotaped performances are permissible as a substitute for live auditions when distance is prohibitive.

Undergraduate Contact Dr. John Buehler, Chairman, Department of Music, Baker University, PO Box 65, Baldwin City, Kansas 66006-0065; 913-594-6451, fax: 913-594-4546.

▼ BALDWIN-WALLACE COLLEGE

Berea, Ohio

Independent-Methodist, coed. Suburban campus. Total enrollment: 4,539. Music program established 1898.

Degrees Bachelor of Music in the areas of performance, musical theater, music therapy, composition, music history and literature, music theory; Bachelor of Music Education in the area of integrated instrumental/vocal music education. Majors and concentrations: brass, classical guitar, composition, music, music education, music history and literature, music theater, music theory, music therapy, piano/organ, stringed instruments, voice, wind and percussion instruments. Cross-registration with Case-Western Reserve University, Cleveland Institute of Music, Cleveland State University, John Carroll University, Notre-Dame College of Ohio, David N. Meyers College, and several community colleges. Program accredited by NASM, NCATE.

Enrollment Fall 1997: 278 total; 240 undergraduate, 38 non-professional degree.

Music Student Profile 60% females, 40% males, 4% minorities, 1% international.

Music Faculty 54 total (full-time and part-time). 75% of full-time faculty have terminal degrees. Graduate students do not teach undergraduate courses.

Student Life Student groups/activities include Northcoast Student Music Therapists, Ohio Collegiate Music Educators Association, Student Chapter, American String Teachers' Association.

Expenses for 1997–98 Application fee: $15. Comprehensive fee: $18,156 includes full-time tuition ($13,275) and college room and board ($4881). College room only: $2415.

Baldwin-Wallace College *(continued)*

Financial Aid Program-specific awards for 1997: 40–70 Talent Scholarships for program majors ($1000–$3000).

Application Procedures Students admitted directly into the professional program freshman year. Deadline for freshmen: May 1; transfers: June 1. Notification date for freshmen: June 1; transfers: August 15. Required: essay, high school transcript, college transcript(s) for transfer students, 2 letters of recommendation, audition, SAT I or ACT test scores, minimum 2.5 high school GPA. Recommended: minimum 3.0 high school GPA, interview. Auditions held 7 times on campus and off campus in Chicago, IL; Tampa, FL; videotaped performances are permissible as a substitute for live auditions if all application materials are complete; voice and musical theater applicants must attend a live audition.

Web Site http://www.bw.edu.

Undergraduate Contact Ms. Anita S. Evans, Assistant Director of Admission, Conservatory of Music, Baldwin-Wallace College, 275 Eastland Road, Berea, Ohio 44017; 440-826-2367, fax: 440-826-3239, E-mail address: aevans@bw.edu.

More About the Conservatory

The reputation of The Conservatory at Baldwin-Wallace College is due in large part to an exceptional faculty of performing artists, conductors, scholars, and composers who are committed to developing the highest performance standards in students. The faculty of more than 50 includes members of both The Cleveland Orchestra and Ohio Chamber Orchestra.

Celebrating one hundred years of professional music tradition, the Baldwin-Wallace College Conservatory of Music assumes an established position among the nation's finest conservatories and schools of music. A sincere commitment to provide undergraduate students with the very best training within a supportive and highly personalized environment is the foundation upon which all degree programs are based.

The Conservatory offers the Bachelor of Music degree with concentration in performance, musical theater, music therapy, history and literature, composition, and theory. The Bachelor of Music Education degree offers integrated vocal and instrumental music study. Students desiring a liberal arts emphasis may elect the Bachelor of Arts music degree or music management program.

Of special note are the programs in music therapy and musical theater. B-W is the home site of the Cleveland Music Therapy Consortium and maintains one of the most highly respected undergraduate music therapy programs in the United States. Therapy majors benefit from the fact that Cleveland leads the nation in the development and implementation of this discipline, and students have opportunities to work with many board-certified Music Therapists in a variety of clinical settings. The musical theater program is a Bachelor of Music degree with collaborative course work in music, dance, and theater. Performance opportunities are abundant, including musical, drama, opera, and dance productions.

Performance is an integral part of all Conservatory degree programs. Ensembles include orchestra, symphonic wind ensemble, motetchoir, college choir, women's choir, stage choir, jazz ensemble, brass choir, percussion ensemble, collegium musicum, and guitar ensemble. Professional faculty ensembles in residence are Battu (percussion), the Elysian Trio, and the B-W Reed Trio.

The Baldwin-Wallace Conservatory truly is "more than a music school." A Conservatory student body of approximately 240 is enriched through interaction with professional musicians, scholars, and peers within the Conservatory as well as faculty and students from the Liberal Arts College. It is this greater College community that fosters individual growth—not just as a musician, but as a complete person.

At the B-W Conservatory, students do not compete with graduate students for performance opportunities, nor do they receive instruction from graduate teaching assistants. The faculty has a passion for teaching and working with undergraduate students, and the College is committed to providing the finest resources for its undergraduate students.

The Conservatory facilities have been extensively renovated in keeping with this institutional commitment. Kulas Musical Arts Building houses two concert halls, a 650-seat air-conditioned hall of superb acoustical design, and a 100-seat chamber hall. Kulas also houses a choral rehearsal room, faculty studios, classrooms, and an electronic music studio. Fifty practice rooms are well-maintained, many with grand pianos. The adjoining Merner-Pfeiffer Hall houses administrative offices, faculty studios, the Jones Music Library, classrooms, the Music Therapy Center, and The Riemenschneider Bach Institute, one of the finest Bach research centers in the western hemisphere. A multimedia computer lab features twelve student Power Mac computers with Kurzweil keyboards, MIDI capability, a teacher workstation, and a projection system.

Two music festivals offer Conservatory students the opportunity to collaborate with prominent guest artists. The annual Bach Festival is the oldest collegiate Bach festival in the United States, with a high standard of performance that has resulted in worldwide recognition. Each spring world-renowned soloists come to B-W, joining with students to present two days of concerts. The biennial FOCUS Festival of Contemporary Music features the music of a contemporary composer who has a weeklong residency on the B-W campus. Past featured composers have included John Corigliano, Witold Lutoslawski, Karel Husa, Gunther Schuller, Lukas Foss, and Loris Chobanian.

Students find that B-W's location is a tremendous asset. Although situated in the small college town of Berea, Ohio, the picturesque campus is just 20 minutes away from the cultural wealth of Cleveland. Proximity to The Cleveland Orchestra, Ohio Chamber Orchestra, Cleveland Opera, Lyric Opera Cleveland, Cleveland Ballet, Ohio Ballet, The Cleveland Museum of Art, Great Lakes Theater Festival, The Cleveland Play House, and many other arts organizations has clear advantages for music students. Whether studying privately with members of The Cleveland Orchestra or Ohio Chamber Orchestra, attending cultural events with tickets made available through the Conservatory, or enjoying the beauty, serenity, and security of the campus and surrounding metroparks system, students truly benefit from the best of both worlds.

▼ BALL STATE UNIVERSITY

Muncie, Indiana

State-supported, coed. Suburban campus. Total enrollment: 19,419.

Degrees Bachelor of Music in the areas of guitar, composition, organ, piano, music engineering technology, symphonic instruments, voice; Bachelor of Science in the area of music education. Majors and concentrations: composition, music education, music technology, piano/organ, stringed instruments, voice, wind and percussion instruments. Graduate degrees offered: Master of Music in the areas of performance, conducting, woodwinds, piano chamber music/accompanying, music history and musicology, music education, music theory, music composition. Doctor of Arts in the areas of performance, conducting, woodwinds, piano chamber music/accompanying, music history and musicology, music education, music theory, music composition. Program accredited by NASM.

Enrollment Fall 1997: 480 undergraduate, 84 graduate.

Music Student Profile 34% females, 8% minorities, 3% international.

Music Faculty 60 total undergraduate and graduate (full-time and part-time). Graduate students teach a few undergraduate courses. Undergraduate student–faculty ratio: 20:1.

Student Life Student groups/activities include Music Educators National Conference.

Expenses for 1997–98 Application fee: $25. State resident tuition: $3316 full-time. Nonresident tuition: $8872 full-time. Mandatory fees: $98 full-time. College room and board: $4120. Special program-related fees: $8 per semester for instrument rental, $40 per credit hour for applied music lesson fee.

Financial Aid Program-specific awards for 1997: 72 Young Artist Scholarships for program students ($1500), 60 general music scholarships for program students ($800), 20 Meloy Scholarships for program students ($1000).

Application Procedures Students admitted directly into the professional program freshman year. Deadline for freshmen: April 1; transfers: June 1. Required: high school transcript, college transcript(s) for transfer students, audition, SAT I or ACT test scores. Recommended: 2 letters of recommendation, interview. Auditions held 7 times on campus; recorded music is permissible as a substitute for live auditions when distance is prohibitive and videotaped performances are permissible as a substitute for live auditions when distance is prohibitive.

Undergraduate Contact Dr. Lawrence Waters, Director of Admissions, Office of Admissions, Ball State University, Lucina Hall 130, Muncie, Indiana 47306; 317-285-8279.

Graduate Contact Dr. Kirby Koriath, Coordinator, Graduate Programs in Music, School of Music, Ball State University, Muncie, Indiana 47306; 317-285-5502, fax: 317-285-5401, E-mail address: 00klkoriath@bsuvc.bsu.edu.

▼ BARRY UNIVERSITY

Miami Shores, Florida

Independent-Roman Catholic, coed. Suburban campus. Total enrollment: 6,899. Music program established 1997.

Degrees Bachelor of Music in the area of performance. Majors and concentrations: guitar, music theater, piano, voice.

Enrollment Fall 1997: 20 undergraduate.

Music Faculty 13 total (full-time and part-time). 100% of full-time faculty have terminal degrees. Graduate students do not teach undergraduate courses. Undergraduate student–faculty ratio: 8:1.

Student Life Student groups/activities include theater productions, Music Educators National Conference Student Chapter.

Expenses for 1997–98 Application fee: $30. Comprehensive fee: $19,400 includes full-time tuition ($13,290), mandatory fees ($260), and college room and board ($5850). Full-time tuition and fees vary according to location. Room and board charges vary according to board plan. Special program-related fees: $120 per 2 credits for studio rehearsal space for applied music students.

Financial Aid Program-specific awards for 1997: 2 Evelyn and Phil Spitalny Scholarships for female program majors ($1000).

Application Procedures Students admitted directly into the professional program freshman year. Deadline for freshmen and transfers: continuous. Required: essay, high school transcript, college transcript(s) for transfer students, 2 letters of recommendation, interview, audition, SAT I or ACT test scores (minimum combined SAT I score of 1000), minimum 2.5 high school GPA. Recommended: video. Auditions held once on campus; recorded music is permissible as a substitute for live auditions for out-of-state applicants if a campus visit is impossible and videotaped performances are permissible as a substitute for live auditions for out-of-state applicants if a campus visit is impossible.

Undergraduate Contact Ms. Derna M. Ford, Chair, Department of Fine Arts, Barry University, 11300 Northeast Second Avenue, Miami Shores, Florida 33161; 305-899-3422, fax: 305-899-2972, E-mail address: dford@buaxp1.barry.edu.

▼ BAYLOR UNIVERSITY

Waco, Texas

Independent-Baptist, coed. Urban campus. Total enrollment: 12,472. Music program established 1903.

Degrees Bachelor of Music in the area of classical music; Bachelor of Music Education in the area of classical music. Majors and concentrations: classical music, music, music education, opera, piano/organ, sacred music, stringed instruments, voice, wind and percussion instruments. Graduate degrees offered: Master of Music in the area of classical music. Program accredited by NASM.

Enrollment Fall 1997: 391 total; 312 undergraduate, 61 graduate, 18 non-professional degree.

Music Student Profile 57% females, 43% males, 14% minorities, 3% international.

Music Faculty 62 total undergraduate and graduate (full-time and part-time). 57% of full-time faculty have terminal degrees. Graduate students teach a few undergraduate courses. Undergraduate student–faculty ratio: 6:1.

Student Life Student groups/activities include professional fraternities and sororities, Music Educators National Conference Student Chapter, Baylor Association of Church Musicians.

Expenses for 1998–99 Application fee: $35. One-time mandatory fee: $50. Comprehensive fee: $14,832 includes full-time tuition ($9240), mandatory fees ($1026), and college room and board ($4566). College room only: $1958. Room and board charges vary according to board plan and housing facility. Special program-related fees: $25 per course for lab fees, $90 per credit hour for applied music fee.

Financial Aid Program-specific awards for 1997: 1 Competitive Scholarship for organ majors, 29 general scholarships for program majors, 100 incentive scholarships for program majors.

Application Procedures Students admitted directly into the professional program freshman year. Deadline for freshmen

Baylor University *(continued)*

and transfers: continuous. Required: high school transcript, college transcript(s) for transfer students, minimum 2.0 high school GPA, audition, SAT I or ACT test scores. Recommended: minimum 3.0 high school GPA. Auditions held 4 times on campus; recorded music is permissible as a substitute for live auditions if a campus visit is impossible.
Web Site http://www.baylor.edu/~music/.
Undergraduate Contact Ms. Celia Austin, Secretary, School of Music, Baylor University, PO Box 97408, Waco, Texas 76798-7408; 254-710-1161, fax: 254-710-1191, E-mail address: celia_austin@baylor.edu.
Graduate Contact Dr. Harry Elzinga, Director of Graduate Studies, School of Music, Baylor University, PO Box 97408, Waco, Texas 76798-7408; 254-710-2360, fax: 254-710-1191, E-mail address: harry_elzinga@baylor.edu.

▼ BELMONT UNIVERSITY

Nashville, Tennessee

Independent-Baptist, coed. Urban campus. Total enrollment: 2,986. Music program established 1951.
Degrees Bachelor of Music in the areas of church music, commercial music, composition, performance, piano pedagogy, music theory, music education, musical theater. Majors and concentrations: church music, classical performance, commercial music, composition, music, music education, music theater, music theory, piano pedagogy. Graduate degrees offered: Master of Music in the areas of performance, pedagogy, church music; Master of Music Education. Program accredited by NASM.
Enrollment Fall 1997: 342 total; 324 undergraduate, 18 graduate.
Music Student Profile 54% females, 46% males, 1% international.
Music Faculty 75 total undergraduate and graduate (full-time and part-time). 64% of full-time faculty have terminal degrees. Graduate students do not teach undergraduate courses. Undergraduate student–faculty ratio: 11:1.
Student Life Student groups/activities include International Association of Jazz Educators, Phi Mu Alpha, Sigma Alpha Iota.
Expenses for 1997–98 Application fee: $25. Comprehensive fee: $14,190 includes full-time tuition ($10,050), mandatory fees ($250), and college room and board ($3890). College room only: $1990. Room and board charges vary according to board plan and housing facility. Special program-related fees: $60–$200 per semester for applied lessons, $30–$100 per semester for material fees.
Financial Aid Program-specific awards for 1997: 6–16 Endowed Scholarships for talented applicants ($1000–$2000), 20–25 music scholarships for talented applicants ($1000–$2000).
Application Procedures Students admitted directly into the professional program freshman year. Deadline for freshmen and transfers: June 1. Required: high school transcript, college transcript(s) for transfer students, minimum 2.0 high school GPA, letter of recommendation, audition, SAT I or ACT test scores (minimum combined SAT I score of 1000, minimum combined ACT score of 21). Auditions held 6 times on campus; recorded music is permissible as a substitute for live auditions if a campus visit is impossible and videotaped performances are permissible as a substitute for live auditions if a campus visit is impossible.

Web Site http://www.belmont.edu/Music/Musichome.html.
Undergraduate Contact Dr. Jean Fallis, Admissions Counselor, School of Music, Belmont University, 1900 Belmont Boulevard, Nashville, Tennessee 37212-3757, 3757; 615-460-6408, fax: 615-386-0239, E-mail address: fallisjt.belmont.edu.
Graduate Contact Mrs. Lisa Grubbs, Adjunct Faculty Coordinator, School of Music, Belmont University, 1900 Belmont Boulevard, Nashville, Tennessee 37212-3757; 615-460-6408, fax: 615-386-0239, E-mail address: grubbsl@belmont.edu.

More About the University

Program Facilities The newly renovated School of Music Wilson and Massey Buildings provide ample rehearsal and practice rooms; spacious teaching studios; fully equipped classrooms; and computer, piano, and music technology labs. Multiple performance areas include a recital hall, a large theater, and a historic antebellum mansion. Guest artists frequently perform and hold master classes.
Faculty Music students from thirty states and five countries prepare at Belmont for careers as performers, church musicians, composers, music teachers, and studio musicians. Faculty are graduates of some of the most prestigious institutions and hold such honors as Composer of the Year awards, listings in *Who's Who in Music,* Outstanding Educator of America, Nashville Composer of the Year, Grammy Award nominations, professionally released recordings, and Metropolitan Opera Regional Finalist.
Student Performance Ensemble opportunities include Oratorio Chorus, Chorale, Chamber Singers, Women's Choir and Men's Chorus, Company, Jazzmin, Southbound (country ensemble), Phoenix (top 40 ensemble), Opera and Musical Theater workshops, University Band and Orchestra, Jazz Ensemble and small groups, Brass and Woodwind Quintets, String Quartet, Rock Combo, New Music Ensembles, Pops, and Bluegrass Ensemble. Belmont's proximity to downtown Nashville and Music Row allows for involvement in professional recording projects and productions of leading arts organizations.
Special Programs International music opportunities are growing with The Russian Academy of Music in Moscow and with Germany's Hochschule für Musik Dresden, Karl Maria von Weber. The Commercial Music Program, a unique approach to the study of popular styles, continues to develop course work in music technology to stay current with developing technological advances as they impact music composition, copying, and performance. A vocal arts lab utilizing state-of-the-art technology to assist students in the development of proper technique has just opened.

▼ BENJAMIN T. ROME SCHOOL OF MUSIC
See The Catholic University of America

▼ BERKLEE COLLEGE OF MUSIC

Boston, Massachusetts

Independent, coed. Urban campus. Total enrollment: 2,933. Music program established 1945.
Degrees Bachelor of Music in the areas of performance, music writing, music technology, music business, music education. Majors and concentrations: composition, contemporary writing and production, film scoring, jazz composition, music business, music education, music engineering,

music synthesis, music therapy, performance, professional music, songwriting. Cross-registration with ProArts Consortium: Boston Architectural Center, School of the Museum of Fine Arts, Massachusetts College of Art, Boston Conservatory, Emerson College, Art Institute of Boston.

Enrollment Fall 1997: 2,933 total; all undergraduate.

Music Student Profile 22% females, 78% males, 8% minorities, 39% international.

Music Faculty 359 total (full-time and part-time). Graduate students do not teach undergraduate courses. Undergraduate student–faculty ratio: 8:1.

Student Life Student groups/activities include Public Service through Music Club, Music Business Association, Audio Engineering Society. Special housing available for music students.

Expenses for 1998–99 Application fee: $65. Comprehensive fee: $22,990 includes full-time tuition ($14,950), mandatory fees ($150), and college room and board ($7890). Special program-related fees: $50–$395 for lab fees for courses in recording studios; music business/management/synthesizer labs.

Financial Aid Program-specific awards for 1997: United States and European Scholarship Tour Awards for incoming freshmen ($1500–$14,950), Berklee Entering Student Talent (BEST) Scholarships for incoming freshmen ($1500–$14,950), Berklee Achievement Scholarships (BAS) for upperclassmen.

Application Procedures Students admitted directly into the professional program freshman year. Deadline for freshmen and transfers: continuous. Notification date for freshmen and transfers: continuous. Required: essay, high school transcript, college transcript(s) for transfer students, 2 letters of recommendation, SAT I or ACT test scores, English reference letter for international applicants, Audition for scholarship consideration. Recommended: minimum 2.0 high school GPA, interview, TOEFL score for international applicants. Auditions held 24 times on campus and off campus in domestic and international sites; recorded music is permissible as a substitute for live auditions.

Web Site http://www.berklee.edu.

Undergraduate Contact Ms. Yvette Agan, Director of Admissions, Admissions Office, Berklee College of Music, 1140 Boylston Street, Boston, Massachusetts 02215-3693; 617-266-1400, fax: 617-536-2632.

Graduate Contact Mr. Steven Lipman, Assistant Dean of Students, Berklee College of Music, 1140 Boylston Street, Boston, Massachusetts 02215-3693; 617-266-1400, fax: 617-536-2632.

More About the College

Performance Facilities Berklee Performance Center, a 1,200-seat concert hall servicing more than 300 student, faculty, and other concerts each year; four recital halls equipped with a variety of sound reinforcement systems; more than 40 ensemble rooms; 75 private instruction studios; 250 private practice rooms; and an outdoor concert pavilion.

Technological Facilities Recording Studio Complex consisting of ten studio facilities that include 8-, 16-, and 24-track digital and analog recording capability, automated mixdown, digital editing, video postproduction, and comprehensive signal processing facilities; Synthesis Labs featuring more than 250 MIDI and digitally equipped synthesizers, expanders, drum machines, sequencers, and computers, including hard-disk recording; Learning Center equipped with forty computer-based MIDI workstations; Professional Writing Division MIDI Lab, offering the ability to produce high-quality demos of compositions, arrangements, and songs at individual workstations; and Film Scoring Labs providing professional training in the areas of film music composition, editing, sequencing, and computer applications.

Faculty, Visiting Artists, Alumni, and More Faculty members are all experienced musicians and educators who bring to the classroom a thorough knowledge of music and the wisdom that comes from professional music experience. Through the Visiting Artist Series, students are exposed to valuable firsthand career insights from every sector of the industry. Berklee alumni can be found in every facet of the music profession: in education, business, technology, film, and television—to name just a few. *The Berklee Prospectus* lists some of the renowned faculty, visiting artists, and alumni who have contributed to the college over the years, as well as information on housing, financial aid, student activities, counseling services, and more.

▼

Students come to a music school to master instrumental skills and to develop creative abilities. They need a place that offers numerous opportunities to pursue their own paths across a vast musical landscape, a place that will help them excel in whatever musical field they choose to explore—a place like Berklee College of Music.

Whether it be performance, production and synthesis, composition, songwriting and arranging, business and management, music education, or music theory, there is a wealth of possibilities for the contemporary musician, all of which can be studied at Berklee.

The broad-based contemporary curriculum includes majors in performance, music production and engineering, songwriting, music business/management, film scoring, music education, jazz composition, contemporary writing and producing, music synthesis, composition, music therapy, and professional music. The dual major allows students to combine two majors and graduate with a more marketable degree that expands their career options in the music industry.

More than 350 ensembles rehearse each semester and perform throughout the year, offering students countless opportunities to play or sing lead or provide instrumental or vocal support for their classmates and friends. Berklee students at all levels of ability have the chance to participate in instrumental labs, ensembles, public performances, special college musical events, recording sessions, informal jam sessions, and student-led groups.

While at Berklee, students have the chance to work in the College's state-of-the-art music technology facilities, using some of the most sophisticated recording and synthesis equipment currently available, in addition to facilities specially designed for the areas of composition, arranging, and film scoring. The facilities at Berklee are equipped with the instruments and equipment that are being used in the world beyond the classroom.

Berklee students learn from the professionals. Like the technology, the faculty at Berklee is highly regarded. Professionals from every field of music make up the faculty, most of whom teach on a full-time basis.

Berklee is located in Boston, Massachusetts, in the heart of historic Back Bay. An international hub of intellectual and creative activity, Boston hosts many of the world's finest colleges and universities (and an estimated 240,000 stu-

Berklee College of Music (continued)

dents), a lively club and concert scene, treasure-filled museums and avant-garde galleries, and world-class performing arts centers.

For more than fifty years, Berklee has prepared students for the many challenges presented in the contemporary music industry. The Berklee mission is to provide the best possible academic and professional career preparation for its students. That preparation includes teaching students to be ethical, global citizens. Berklee celebrates human diversity, nurtures the artistic spirit, and encourages intellectual curiosity as the rest of that preparation, for each student brings to Berklee something new—a new sound, a new idea, a new song.

▼ BERNICE YOUNG JONES SCHOOL OF FINE ARTS

See Ouachita Baptist University

▼ BERRY COLLEGE

Mount Berry, Georgia

Independent, coed. Small town campus. Total enrollment: 2,070. Music program established 1969.

Degrees Bachelor of Music in the areas of music education, music business, musical arts performance. Majors and concentrations: brass, music and business, music education, piano/organ, voice, wind and percussion instruments. Program accredited by NASM.

Enrollment Fall 1997: 72 total; all undergraduate.

Music Student Profile 55% females, 45% males, 5% minorities, 5% international.

Music Faculty 13 total (full-time and part-time). 60% of full-time faculty have terminal degrees. Graduate students do not teach undergraduate courses. Undergraduate student–faculty ratio: 10:1.

Student Life Student groups/activities include Music to the People Projects, Church Concerts, Kindermusik program.

Expenses for 1997–98 Application fee: $25. Comprehensive fee: $14,746 includes full-time tuition ($10,210) and college room and board ($4536). College room only: $2600. Room and board charges vary according to board plan. Special program-related fees: $90–$175 per semester for weekly lessons.

Financial Aid Program-specific awards for 1997: 60 music scholarships for performers/program majors ($2000), 20 Performance Grants for performers/program minors ($750).

Application Procedures Students admitted directly into the professional program freshman year. Deadline for freshmen: February 1; transfers: April 1. Required: high school transcript, college transcript(s) for transfer students, minimum 3.0 high school GPA, 2 letters of recommendation, interview, audition, SAT I or ACT test scores (minimum combined SAT I score of 1000, minimum combined ACT score of 19). Auditions held 3 times on campus; recorded music is permissible as a substitute for live auditions when distance is prohibitive and videotaped performances are permissible as a substitute for live auditions when distance is prohibitive.

Undergraduate Contact Mr. George Gaddie, Dean of Admissions, Berry College, 159 Mount Berry Station, Mount Berry, Georgia 30149-0159; 706-236-2215, fax: 706-290-2178, E-mail address: admissions@berry.edu.

▼ BETHEL COLLEGE

St. Paul, Minnesota

Independent, coed. Suburban campus. Total enrollment: 2,612.

Degrees Bachelor of Music in the areas of applied performance, composition; Bachelor of Music Education in the areas of vocal music education, instrumental music education. Majors and concentrations: composition, music education, piano/organ, stringed instruments, voice, wind and percussion instruments.

Enrollment Fall 1997: 80 total; 50 undergraduate, 30 non-professional degree.

Music Student Profile 65% females, 35% males, 5% minorities, 3% international.

Music Faculty 26 total (full-time and part-time). 75% of full-time faculty have terminal degrees. Graduate students do not teach undergraduate courses.

Student Life Student groups/activities include Music Educators National Conference, National Association of Teachers of Singing, American Choral Directors Association.

Expenses for 1998–99 Application fee: $20. Comprehensive fee: $18,790 includes full-time tuition ($13,840) and college room and board ($4950). College room only: $2800. Room and board charges vary according to board plan. Special program-related fees: $30 per year for music purchase, $15 per year for robe rental.

Financial Aid Program-specific awards for 1997: 6 music scholarships for performers ($1000), 100 Paid Lesson Stipends for freshmen and sophomore members of performance organizations ($550).

Application Procedures Students apply for admission into the professional program by sophomore year. Deadline for freshmen and transfers: continuous. Required: essay, high school transcript, 2 letters of recommendation, SAT I or ACT test scores. Recommended: audition. Auditions held once on campus; recorded music is permissible as a substitute for live auditions when distance is prohibitive.

Web Site http://www.bethel.edu/college/acad/dept/music.htm.

Undergraduate Contact Dr. Dennis Port, Chair, Department of Music, Bethel College, 3900 Bethel Drive, St. Paul, Minnesota 55112; 612-638-6486, fax: 612-638-6001, E-mail address: d-port@bethel.edu.

▼ BIOLA UNIVERSITY

La Mirada, California

Independent-interdenominational, coed. Suburban campus. Total enrollment: 3,257. Music program established 1955.

Degrees Bachelor of Music in the areas of performance, composition, music education. Majors and concentrations: music education, piano/organ, stringed instruments, voice, wind and percussion instruments. Program accredited by NASM.

Enrollment Fall 1997: 101 undergraduate.

Music Student Profile 65% females, 30% minorities, 10% international.

Music Faculty 15 total (full-time and part-time). 55% of full-time faculty have terminal degrees. Graduate students do not teach undergraduate courses. Undergraduate student–faculty ratio: 9:1.

Student Life Student groups/activities include American Choral Directors Association, Music Educators National Conference.

Expenses for 1997–98 Application fee: $35. Comprehensive fee: $19,188 includes full-time tuition ($14,286) and college room and board ($4902). College room only: $2580. Room and board charges vary according to board plan and housing facility. Special program-related fees: $220 for private applied lessons.

Financial Aid Program-specific awards for 1997: 100 Biola Music Awards for program majors, music ensemble members ($2500–$6000).

Application Procedures Students admitted directly into the professional program freshman year. Deadline for freshmen and transfers: June 1. Notification date for freshmen and transfers: August 15. Required: high school transcript, college transcript(s) for transfer students, 2 letters of recommendation, interview, audition, SAT I or ACT test scores. Auditions held continuously on campus; recorded music is permissible as a substitute for live auditions when distance is prohibitive and videotaped performances are permissible as a substitute for live auditions when distance is prohibitive.

Undergraduate Contact Ms. Gail Neal, Admissions Counselor, Music Department, Biola University, 13800 Biola Avenue, LaMirada, California 90639; 310-903-4892, fax: 310-903-4746.

▼ BIRMINGHAM-SOUTHERN COLLEGE

Birmingham, Alabama

Independent-Methodist, coed. Urban campus. Total enrollment: 1,531. Music program established 1922.

Degrees Bachelor of Music in the areas of classical performance, composition, music history, church music; Bachelor of Music Education. Majors and concentrations: church music, classical music, composition, guitar, music history, opera, piano/organ, stringed instruments, voice, wind and percussion instruments. Cross-registration with University of Alabama at Birmingham. Program accredited by NASM.

Enrollment Fall 1997: 304 total; 62 undergraduate, 242 non-professional degree.

Music Student Profile 60% females, 40% males, 20% minorities, 10% international.

Music Faculty 24 total (full-time and part-time). 100% of full-time faculty have terminal degrees. Graduate students do not teach undergraduate courses. Undergraduate student–faculty ratio: 8:1.

Student Life Student groups/activities include GALA, Opera Productions, Music Theater Productions.

Expenses for 1997–98 Application fee: $25. Comprehensive fee: $19,160 includes full-time tuition ($13,750), mandatory fees ($210), and college room and board ($5200). Room and board charges vary according to board plan and housing facility. Special program-related fees: $160–$300 per course for private lessons.

Financial Aid Program-specific awards for 1997: 2–3 Music Theater Scholarships for program majors and minors ($3000–$6000), 7–8 Music Performance Scholarships for

program majors and minors ($4000–$8000), 1–2 Music Composition Awards for program majors ($4000–$8000).

Application Procedures Students admitted directly into the professional program freshman year. Deadline for freshmen and transfers: May 1. Required: essay, high school transcript, college transcript(s) for transfer students, minimum 2.0 high school GPA, SAT I or ACT test scores. Recommended: letter of recommendation, interview, audition, portfolio for composition majors. Auditions held twice on campus; recorded music is permissible as a substitute for live auditions when distance is prohibitive and videotaped performances are permissible as a substitute for live auditions when distance is prohibitive. Portfolio reviews held once on campus.

Web Site http://www.bsc.edu.

Undergraduate Contact Ms. DeeDee Barnes Bruns, Dean of Admissions, Birmingham-Southern College, 900 Arkadelphia Road, Birmingham, Alabama 35254; 205-226-4686, fax: 205-226-4696, E-mail address: dbruns@bsc.edu.

▼ BLAIR SCHOOL OF MUSIC

See Vanderbilt University

▼ BOISE STATE UNIVERSITY

Boise, Idaho

State-supported, coed. Urban campus. Total enrollment: 15,433.

Degrees Bachelor of Music in the area of performance; Bachelor of Music Education in the areas of elementary music education, secondary music education. Majors and concentrations: classical music, jazz, music, music and business, music education, opera, piano/organ, stringed instruments, voice, wind and percussion instruments. Graduate degrees offered: Master of Music in the areas of pedagogy, performance; Master of Music Education in the areas of elementary music education, secondary music education. Program accredited by NASM.

Enrollment Fall 1997: 272 total; 212 undergraduate, 38 graduate, 22 non-professional degree.

Music Student Profile 70% females, 30% males, 2% minorities, 3% international.

Music Faculty 36 total undergraduate and graduate (full-time and part-time). 55% of full-time faculty have terminal degrees. Graduate students teach a few undergraduate courses.

Student Life Student groups/activities include Music Educators National Conference, Kappa Kappa Psi.

Expenses for 1997–98 Application fee: $20. State resident tuition: $0 full-time. Nonresident tuition: $5880 full-time. Mandatory fees: $2294 full-time. College room and board: $3264. Room and board charges vary according to board plan and housing facility.

Financial Aid Program-specific awards for 1997: 104 music scholarships for those demonstrating talent and academic achievement ($200–$1200), 55 band scholarships for band members ($500).

Application Procedures Students admitted directly into the professional program freshman year. Deadline for freshmen and transfers: April 2. Required: high school transcript, minimum 2.0 high school GPA, 2 letters of recommendation, audition, portfolio, SAT I or ACT test scores. Recommended: minimum 3.0 high school GPA, interview. Auditions held

Boise State University (continued)

once or by appointment on campus and off campus in various cities in Idaho; recorded music is permissible as a substitute for live auditions when distance is prohibitive and videotaped performances are permissible as a substitute for live auditions when distance is prohibitive. Portfolio reviews held once or by appointment on campus.

Undergraduate Contact Dr. James D. Cook, Chair, Department of Music, Boise State University, 1910 University Drive, Boise, Idaho 83725; 208-385-1773, fax: 208-385-1771, E-mail address: amucook@idbsu.idbsu.edu.

Graduate Contact Dr. Jeanne Belfy, Graduate Advisor, Department of Music, Boise State University, 1910 University Drive, Boise, Idaho 83725; 208-385-1216, fax: 208-385-1771.

▼ BOSTON CONSERVATORY

Boston, Massachusetts

Independent, coed. Urban campus. Total enrollment: 501. Music program established 1867.

Degrees Bachelor of Music in the areas of composition, performance, music education; Bachelor of Music Education. Majors and concentrations: brass, composition, guitar, music, music education, opera, piano/organ, stringed instruments, voice, wind and percussion instruments. Graduate degrees offered: Master of Music in the areas of composition, choral conducting, performance, music education, jazz studies, musical theater, opera. Cross-registration with ProArts Consortium. Program accredited by NASM.

Enrollment Fall 1997: 287 total; 127 undergraduate, 160 graduate.

Music Student Profile 70% females, 30% males, 9% minorities, 20% international.

Music Faculty 115 total undergraduate and graduate (full-time and part-time). 10% of full-time faculty have terminal degrees. Graduate students do not teach undergraduate courses. Undergraduate student–faculty ratio: 5:1.

Student Life Student groups/activities include Music Educators National Conference, Phi Mu Alpha Sinfonia, Sigma Alpha Iota. Special housing available for music students.

Expenses for 1997–98 Application fee: $60. Comprehensive fee: $23,075 includes full-time tuition ($15,300), mandatory fees ($625), and college room and board ($7150). Full-time tuition and fees vary according to course load, degree level, and program. Special program-related fees: $60 per year for music education lab fees, $500 per year for opera studio surcharge for part-time students.

Financial Aid Program-specific awards for 1997: 45–70 Merit Scholarships for artistically talented students ($2000–$10,500).

Application Procedures Students admitted directly into the professional program freshman year. Deadline for freshmen and transfers: March 1. Notification date for freshmen and transfers: April 1. Required: essay, high school transcript, college transcript(s) for transfer students, 4 letters of recommendation, audition, SAT I or ACT test scores, minimum 2.7 high school GPA, portfolio for composition majors. Recommended: minimum 3.0 high school GPA. Auditions held on campus and off campus in Chicago, IL; St. Louis, MO; Minneapolis, MN; Seattle, WA; Los Angeles, CA; Houston, TX; Tampa, FL; Washington, DC; Pittsburgh, PA; Boston, MA; Tokyo, Japan; Kyoto, Japan; Osaka, Japan; Hong Kong; Sydney, Australia; Adelaide, Australia; Melbourne,

Australia; Brisbane, Australia; Perth, Australia; Wellington, New Zealand; Auckland, New Zealand; recorded music is permissible as a substitute for live auditions when distance is prohibitive and videotaped performances are permissible as a substitute for live auditions when distance is prohibitive. Portfolio reviews held continuously on campus.

Web Site http://www.bostonconservatory.edu.

Contact Mr. Richard Wallace, Director of Admissions, Boston Conservatory, 8 The Fenway, Boston, Massachusetts 02215; 617-536-6340 ext. 9153, fax: 617-536-3176, E-mail address: admissions@bostonconservatory.edu.

More About the Conservatory

Program Facilities Two recital halls (400 and 75 seats); computer lab (Apple and print stations); library of 60,000 volumes and scores, and interlibrary loan availability with college network of Boston; twenty-five practice rooms.

Faculty and Alumni Faculty are members of the Boston Symphony Orchestra, Boston Pops, and Boston Ballet orchestras as well as concert, chamber, and recording artists. The Atlantic Brass Quintet is in residence. Alumni are represented in major orchestras, opera companies, and faculty of college and university music programs in the United States and Europe.

Student Performance Opportunities Orchestra, wind ensemble, opera orchestra, musical theater orchestra, dance orchestra, chorale, festival chorus, women's chorus, opera theater, percussion ensemble, chamber music groups (numerous), jazz ensembles (with Berklee College of Music).

Special Programs Gig office providing performance opportunities throughout the greater Boston area, career seminar series, counseling and health services, international student ESL classes/orientation program, academic year ESL course work, and tutorial assistance.

▼

The Boston Conservatory, founded in 1867, is one of the oldest colleges offering training to serious students of the performing arts. The three divisions of the college—Music, Dance, and Theater—take full advantage of the wealth of cultural and academic offerings Boston has to offer. Guest artists, master classes, performance opportunities, and professional contacts and networking are provided to all students of the college. These experiences seek to ensure that each student receives a varied and professional level of education to augment the intensive study of the prescribed curriculum.

Music students work with artist faculty members and teachers who are truly interested in working to develop students' musical abilities to their utmost potential. With more than 300 concerts being offered each year, performance experience is a core part of the curriculum. Students participate in orchestra, wind ensemble, chamber ensembles, choral ensembles, and pit work for the dance, opera, and musical theater mainstage productions produced several times throughout the academic year. Pianists are involved with accompanying and can choose to expand their skills and work with dance and/or musical theater studio classes.

In addition to the school's performance opportunities, the greater Boston area provides numerous playing possibilities for solo, small chamber, and orchestral musicians that students may choose to further expand both their performance experience and knowledge of the repertory.

Boston is a major center of higher education in America, with more than fifty major colleges and universities. The city provides a diverse student population and an endless array of courses, lectures, concerts, and social opportunities. The Conservatory is in the Pro-Arts Consortium with five area colleges (Emerson College, Berklee College of Music, Museum School, Massachusetts College of Art, and Boston Architectural Center), which offers extensive cross-registration course possibilities to all students.

On-campus housing is provided to all interested students, offering brownstone-style living accommodations just a few steps from the main training and rehearsal buildings. For those students interested in off-campus housing, Boston offers a wide range of architectural styles and rent prices in neighborhoods throughout the city, which are all within easy access to the school by public transportation.

The Boston Conservatory strives to meet each student's needs, musically and personally, and provides a nurturing, safe environment in which to study, learn, and grow. The supportive atmosphere of the college extends to student life areas as well. More than a dozen special interest groups and organizations exist on campus, with new ones developing constantly as the student population grows and needs change. As part of the student services, a number of career seminars are given each year ranging from resume writing and audition anxiety to grant writing and tax laws for the performing artist. In addition, there is an active student government and a student-run newspaper.

▼ BOSTON UNIVERSITY

Boston, Massachusetts

Independent, coed. Urban campus. Total enrollment: 29,387.

Degrees Bachelor of Music in the areas of performance, music education, music theory and composition, music history and literature. Majors and concentrations: brass, music education, music history and literature, music theory and composition, percussion, piano/organ, stringed instruments, voice, wind instruments. Graduate degrees offered: Master of Music in the areas of performance, music education, music theory and composition, music history and literature, orchestral and choral conducting, historical performance, collaborative piano. Doctor of Musical Arts in the areas of performance, music education, music theory and composition, music history and literature, orchestral and choral conducting, historical performance, collaborative piano. Program accredited by NASM.

Enrollment Fall 1997: 600 total; 250 undergraduate, 300 graduate, 50 non-professional degree.

Music Student Profile 50% females, 50% males, 15% minorities, 30% international.

Music Faculty 110 total undergraduate and graduate (full-time and part-time). 100% of full-time faculty have terminal degrees. Graduate students teach a few undergraduate courses. Undergraduate student–faculty ratio: 7:1.

Student Life Student groups/activities include Jazz Ensemble, Symphonic Chorus, Marching Band. Special housing available for music students.

Expenses for 1998–99 Application fee: $50. Comprehensive fee: $31,018 includes full-time tuition ($22,830), mandatory fees ($318), and college room and board ($7870). College room only: $4830. Room and board charges vary according to board plan and housing facility.

Financial Aid Program-specific awards for 1997: 55 Grants-Performance Awards for freshmen ($6000–$22,900).

Application Procedures Students admitted directly into the professional program freshman year. Deadline for freshmen: January 15; transfers: May 1. Notification date for freshmen: March 8; transfers: June 1. Required: essay, high school transcript, college transcript(s) for transfer students, 2 letters of recommendation, audition, SAT I or ACT test scores, portfolio for composition majors. Recommended: minimum 3.0 high school GPA, interview, resume. Auditions held 24 times on campus and off campus in various cities; recorded music is permissible as a substitute for live auditions when distance is prohibitive (beyond a 250-mile radius) and videotaped performances are permissible as a substitute for live auditions when distance is prohibitive (beyond a 250-mile radius). Portfolio reviews held as needed on campus.

Undergraduate Contact Ms. Halley Shefler, Director of Admissions, Music Division, Boston University, 855 Commonwealth Avenue, Boston, Massachusetts 02215; 617-353-3341, fax: 617-353-7455, E-mail address: hshefler@bu.edu.

Graduate Contact Ms. Patricia Mitro, Assistant Dean for Enrollment Services, School for the Arts, Boston University, 855 Commonwealth Avenue, Boston, Massachusetts 02215; 617-353-3350, fax: 617-353-7455, E-mail address: arts@bu.edu.

More About the University

Program Facilities Performance spaces include a 485-seat concert hall in the School for the Arts and the 650-seat Tsai Performance Center on the Boston University campus. There are three rehearsal halls for orchestra, wind ensemble, band, and choral groups; more than 100 soundproof practice rooms; a recording studio; and three electronic music studios. Opera rehearsal and coaching studios are adjacent to the School for the Arts.

Faculty, Resident Artists, and Alumni Bruce MacCombie, a noted composer and former Dean of the Juilliard School, has served as Dean of the Boston University School for the Arts since 1992. The faculty includes many members of the Boston Symphony Orchestra. Phyllis Curtin, one of the world's leading sopranos, is Dean Emerita of the School for the Arts and founder of the Opera Institute at Boston University. Artists-in-residence include the Muir String Quartet, the Atlantic Brass Quintet, and Alea III, a contemporary music ensemble.

Student Performance Opportunities Ensembles include the Symphony Orchestra, Chamber Orchestra, Wind Ensemble, Symphonic Chorus, Chamber Chorus, Women's Chorus, New Music Ensemble, Collegium in Early Music, Baroque Chamber Music, and Opera Theatre. All-University organizations include the Jazz Ensemble, Concert Band, Pep Band, and Marching Band.

Special Programs Students at the Boston University School for the Arts may take advantage of a wide range of academic and extracurricular activities. Through the Collaborative Degree Program (BUCOP), students may obtain a dual degree in two of the University's schools and colleges. Boston University also offers intensive English programs for international students.

▼ BOWLING GREEN STATE UNIVERSITY

Bowling Green, Ohio

State-supported, coed. Small town campus. Total enrollment: 17,328. Music program established 1917.

Bowling Green State University (continued)

Degrees Bachelor of Music in the areas of music education, performance, music history and literature, composition, jazz studies. Majors and concentrations: jazz, literature, music, music education, piano pedagogy, piano/organ, stringed instruments, voice, wind and percussion instruments. Graduate degrees offered: Master of Music in the areas of music education, performance, composition, music theory, music history. Cross-registration with University of Toledo. Program accredited by NASM.

Enrollment Fall 1997: 484 total; 363 undergraduate, 114 graduate, 7 non-professional degree.

Music Student Profile 51% females, 49% males, 5% minorities, 4% international.

Music Faculty 64 total undergraduate and graduate (full-time and part-time). 100% of full-time faculty have terminal degrees. Graduate students teach a few undergraduate courses. Undergraduate student–faculty ratio: 7:1.

Student Life Student groups/activities include Ohio Collegiate Music Educators Association, professional music fraternities and sororities, American Choral Directors Association. Special housing available for music students.

Expenses for 1997–98 Application fee: $30. State resident tuition: $4422 full-time. Nonresident tuition: $9436 full-time. College room and board: $4626. College room only: $2554. Special program-related fees: $70 per year for music equipment fee, $180 per year for applied music lesson fee.

Financial Aid Program-specific awards for 1997: 180 Music Talent Awards for top musicians ($1340).

Application Procedures Students admitted directly into the professional program freshman year. Deadline for freshmen and transfers: continuous. Notification date for freshmen and transfers: continuous. Required: high school transcript, college transcript(s) for transfer students, minimum 2.0 high school GPA, audition, SAT I or ACT test scores. Recommended: essay, minimum 3.0 high school GPA, 2 letters of recommendation, interview. Auditions held 6 times on campus; recorded music is permissible as a substitute for live auditions when distance is prohibitive and videotaped performances are permissible as a substitute for live auditions when distance is prohibitive.

Web Site http://www.bgsu.edu/welcome/music.html.

Contact Dr. Richard Kennell, Associate Dean, College of Musical Arts, Bowling Green State University, 1031 Moore Musical Arts Center, Bowling Green, Ohio 43403-0290; 419-372-2182, fax: 419-372-2938, E-mail address: kennel@bgnet.bgsu.edu.

▼ BRADLEY UNIVERSITY

Peoria, Illinois

Independent, coed. Urban campus. Total enrollment: 5,861.

Degrees Bachelor of Music in the areas of performance, music education, composition. Majors and concentrations: composition, music education, music performance. Program accredited by NASM.

Enrollment Fall 1997: 66 total; 50 undergraduate, 16 non-professional degree.

Music Student Profile 51% females, 49% males, 5% minorities.

Music Faculty 25 total (full-time and part-time). 75% of full-time faculty have terminal degrees. Graduate students do not teach undergraduate courses.

Student Life Student groups/activities include Music Educators National Conference, Phi Mu Alpha Sinfonia, Sigma Alpha Iota.

Expenses for 1997–98 Application fee: $35. Comprehensive fee: $17,380 includes full-time tuition ($12,610), mandatory fees ($80), and college room and board ($4690). College room only: $2840. Room and board charges vary according to board plan. Special program-related fees: $140 per hour for applied music fee.

Financial Aid Program-specific awards for 1997: music scholarships for program majors ($833).

Application Procedures Deadline for freshmen and transfers: continuous. Required: high school transcript, college transcript(s) for transfer students, minimum 2.0 high school GPA, audition, SAT I or ACT test scores. Recommended: letter of recommendation. Auditions held continuously on campus; recorded music is permissible as a substitute for live auditions when distance is prohibitive and videotaped performances are permissible as a substitute for live auditions when distance is prohibitive.

Undergraduate Contact Ms. Nickie Roberson, Director of Admissions, Office of Undergraduate Admissions, Bradley University, Swords Hall, Peoria, Illinois 61625; 800-447-6460, fax: 309-677-2797, E-mail address: admissions@bradley.edu.

▼ BRENAU UNIVERSITY

Gainesville, Georgia

Independent, primarily women. Small town campus. Total enrollment: 2,366. Music program established 1878.

Degrees Bachelor of Music in the areas of performance, music education. Majors and concentrations: music education, piano, voice.

Enrollment Fall 1997: 35 undergraduate.

Music Student Profile 100% females, 20% minorities, 3% international.

Music Faculty 8 total (full-time and part-time). 100% of full-time faculty have terminal degrees. Graduate students do not teach undergraduate courses. Undergraduate student–faculty ratio: 10:1.

Student Life Student groups/activities include Opera Company.

Expenses for 1997–98 Application fee: $30. Comprehensive fee: $17,350 includes full-time tuition ($10,740) and college room and board ($6610).

Financial Aid Program-specific awards for 1997: music scholarships for program majors ($1000–$4000).

Application Procedures Students admitted directly into the professional program freshman year. Deadline for freshmen and transfers: continuous. Required: high school transcript, letter of recommendation, interview, audition, SAT I or ACT test scores (minimum combined SAT I score of 900, minimum combined ACT score of 19). Auditions held 6 times and by appointment on campus; recorded music is permissible as a substitute for live auditions when distance is prohibitive and videotaped performances are permissible as a substitute for live auditions when distance is prohibitive.

Undergraduate Contact Dr. John D. Upchurch, Dean of Admissions, Brenau University, One Centennial Circle, Gainesville, Georgia 30501; 800-252-5119, fax: 770-538-4306.

▼ BREWTON-PARKER COLLEGE

Mt. Vernon, Georgia

Independent-Southern Baptist, coed. Rural campus. Total enrollment: 1,652. Music program established 1964.

Degrees Bachelor of Music in the area of music education. Majors and concentrations: brass, music education, piano/organ, voice, wind and percussion instruments. Program accredited by NASM.

Enrollment Fall 1997: 39 undergraduate.

Music Student Profile 54% females, 46% males, 5% minorities, 1% international.

Music Faculty 8 total (full-time and part-time). 83% of full-time faculty have terminal degrees. Graduate students do not teach undergraduate courses.

Student Life Student groups/activities include Students Professional Association of Georgia Educators.

Expenses for 1997–98 Application fee: $15. Comprehensive fee: $8430 includes full-time tuition ($5490), mandatory fees ($270), and college room and board ($2670). Full-time tuition and fees vary according to reciprocity agreements. Room and board charges vary according to housing facility.

Financial Aid Program-specific awards for 1997: 50–60 music scholarships for ensemble participants ($300–$600).

Application Procedures Students apply for admission into the professional program by freshman year. Deadline for freshmen and transfers: continuous. Required: high school transcript, college transcript(s) for transfer students, letter of recommendation, audition, SAT I or ACT test scores. Auditions held 3 times on campus.

Undergraduate Contact Mr. Don Buckner, Director of Admissions, Brewton-Parker College, Highway 280, Mt. Vernon, Georgia 30445; 912-583-2241, fax: 912-583-4498.

▼ BRIGHAM YOUNG UNIVERSITY

Provo, Utah

Independent, coed. Suburban campus. Total enrollment: 32,161. Music program established 1903.

Degrees Bachelor of Music in the areas of composition, music education (K-12), elementary music specialist, performance. Majors and concentrations: brass, composition, music, music education, piano/organ, sound recording technology, stringed instruments, voice, wind and percussion instruments. Graduate degrees offered: Master of Music in the areas of composition, conducting, music education, performance, pedagogy. Program accredited by NASM.

Enrollment Fall 1997: 826 total; 750 undergraduate, 76 graduate.

Music Student Profile 65% females, 35% males, 4% international.

Music Faculty 89 total undergraduate and graduate (full-time and part-time). 100% of full-time faculty have terminal degrees. Graduate students teach a few undergraduate courses. Undergraduate student–faculty ratio: 12:1.

Expenses for 1997–98 Application fee: $25. Comprehensive fee: $6760 includes full-time tuition ($2630) and college room and board ($4130). Full-time tuition varies according to reciprocity agreements. Room and board charges vary according to board plan and housing facility. Special program-related fees: $250 for private lessons.

Financial Aid Program-specific awards for 1997: 225 Performance Scholarships for program majors ($800), 225 Service Awards for marching band students ($400), 45 Service Awards for pep band students ($300).

Application Procedures Students apply for admission into the professional program by freshman year. Deadline for freshmen: February 15; transfers: March 15. Required: essay, high school transcript, minimum 3.0 high school GPA, letter of recommendation, audition, ACT test score only, music theory examination. Auditions held twice on campus; recorded music is permissible as a substitute for live auditions if a campus visit is impossible; video tape preferred and videotaped performances are permissible as a substitute for live auditions if a campus visit is impossible; video tape preferred.

Web Site http://www.byu.edu/music/.

Undergraduate Contact Dr. J. Arden Hopkin, Associate Director of Undergraduate Studies, School of Music, Brigham Young University, C-550 HFAC, Provo, Utah 84602; 801-378-3083, fax: 801-378-5973.

Graduate Contact Mr. Thomas L. Durham, Associate Director - Graduate Studies, School of Music, Brigham Young University, C-550 HFAC, Provo, Utah 84602; 801-378-3083, fax: 801-378-5973.

▼ BROCK UNIVERSITY

St. Catharines, ON, Canada

Province-supported, coed. Urban campus. Total enrollment: 11,135. Music program established 1975.

Degrees Bachelor of Music. Majors and concentrations: music. Program accredited by CUMS.

Enrollment Fall 1997: 50 total; 30 undergraduate, 20 non-professional degree.

Music Student Profile 65% females, 35% males, 2% minorities, 3% international.

Music Faculty 19 total (full-time and part-time). 100% of full-time faculty have terminal degrees. Graduate students do not teach undergraduate courses.

Student Life Student groups/activities include choral ensembles, music society, fine arts festival.

Expenses for 1997–98 Tuition, fee, and room and board charges are reported in Canadian dollars. One-time mandatory fee: $30. Canadian resident tuition: $3458 full-time. Full-time tuition varies according to course load. College room and board: $5400. College room only: $2800. Room and board charges vary according to board plan and housing facility. International student tuition: $9456 full-time. Mandatory fees per year for nonresidents: $570. Special program-related fees: $40 per year for practice room rental, $800 per year for music lesson fee.

Financial Aid Program-specific awards for 1997: 1 Sir Isaac Brock Scholarship for junior and senior program majors ($475), 1 Senior Scholarship in Music I for junior program majors ($250), 1 Senior Scholarship in Music II for senior program majors ($250).

Application Procedures Students admitted directly into the professional program freshman year. Deadline for freshmen and transfers: June 1. Notification date for freshmen and transfers: June 30. Required: high school transcript, college transcript(s) for transfer students, minimum 3.0 high school GPA, interview, audition, 2 years of theory study, photograph. Recommended: 4 years of keyboard study. Auditions held by appointment on campus; recorded music is permissible as a substitute for live auditions for international applicants and

Brock University (continued)

videotaped performances are permissible as a substitute for live auditions for international applicants.

Web Site http://www.brocku.ca/music.

Undergraduate Contact Dr. Harris Loewen, Chair, Department of Music, Brock University, 500 Glenridge Avenue, St. Catharines, ON L2S 3A1, Canada; 905-688-5550 ext. 3817, fax: 905-688-2789, E-mail address: hloewen@spartan.ac.brocku.ca.

▼ BROOKLYN COLLEGE OF THE CITY UNIVERSITY OF NEW YORK

Brooklyn, New York

State and locally supported, coed. Urban campus. Total enrollment: 15,007. Music program established 1963.

Degrees Bachelor of Music in the areas of performance, composition. Majors and concentrations: classical music, composition, music, music education, opera, performance, stringed instruments, voice, wind and percussion instruments. Graduate degrees offered: Master of Music in the areas of performance, composition. Cross-registration with City University of New York System.

Enrollment Fall 1997: 210 total; 100 undergraduate, 90 graduate, 20 non-professional degree.

Music Student Profile 60% females, 40% males, 20% minorities, 25% international.

Music Faculty 36 total undergraduate and graduate (full-time and part-time). 100% of full-time faculty have terminal degrees. Graduate students teach a few undergraduate courses. Undergraduate student–faculty ratio: 6:1.

Student Life Student groups/activities include music for convocations and commencements.

Expenses for 1997–98 Application fee: $40. State resident tuition: $3200 full-time. Nonresident tuition: $6800 full-time. Mandatory fees: $213 full-time. Full-time tuition and fees vary according to class time and course load.

Financial Aid Program-specific awards for 1997: 20 music scholarships for qualified students ($300–$1200).

Application Procedures Students admitted directly into the professional program freshman year. Deadline for freshmen and transfers: continuous. Required: high school transcript, college transcript(s) for transfer students, minimum 3.0 high school GPA, audition, minimum TOEFL score of 500 for international students. Recommended: letter of recommendation, interview, video, SAT I test score only (minimum combined SAT I score of 1100), portfolio for composition students. Auditions held 4 times on campus; recorded music is permissible as a substitute for live auditions when distance is prohibitive and videotaped performances are permissible as a substitute for live auditions when distance is prohibitive. Portfolio reviews held continuously on campus.

Web Site http://www.brooklyn.cuny.edu/.

Undergraduate Contact Dr. Bruce Mac Intyre, Deputy Chairman, Conservatory of Music, Brooklyn College of the City University of New York, 2900 Bedford Avenue, Brooklyn, New York 11210; 718-951-5286, fax: 718-951-4502, E-mail address: bmacintyre@brooklyn.cuny.edu.

Graduate Contact Dr. Paul Shelden, Deputy Chairman, Conservatory of Music, Brooklyn College of the City University of New York, 2900 Bedford Avenue, Brooklyn, New York 11210; 718-951-5286, fax: 718-951-4502, E-mail address: bmacintyre@brooklyn.cuny.edu.

More About the Conservatory of Music

Young musicians from all over the world come to Brooklyn College's Conservatory of Music to study with an exceptional professional faculty, to learn in a liberal arts environment, and to experience the dynamic and diverse cultural life of New York City—at a fraction of the tuition of private institutions.

In addition to intense, focused music study, Conservatory students are encouraged to collaborate with fellow students in the College's fine programs in film and video, theater, and television/radio. Among the stellar faculty are violinist Itzhak Perlman, composer/conductor Tania León, pianist Agustin Anievas, and former New York Philharmonic percussionist Morris Lang. Richard Barrett heads the Brooklyn College Opera Theater, the only comprehensive opera program in the City University system.

A calendar of more than 100 performances by students and faculty is integral to the life of the Conservatory, and has featured critically acclaimed premieres of operas by Darius Milhaud and Francis Thorne. Off-campus performances have included a Taiwan tour by the Conservatory Orchestra, two European tours and a visit to Korea by the percussion ensemble, a brass ensemble exchange with London's Royal Academy of Music, and award-winning appearances by the jazz ensemble at the Villanova Jazz Festival in Pennsylvania.

Special features include a performing arts center, state-of-the-art Center for Computer Music, Institute for Studies in American Music with comprehensive research library, and professional recording studio. Unique opportunities for networking and professional growth include internships at local public and private schools and performance opportunities at area museums and public spaces arranged through the Conservatory Concert Office.

▼ BUCKNELL UNIVERSITY

Lewisburg, Pennsylvania

Independent, coed. Small town campus. Total enrollment: 3,543. Music program established 1892.

Degrees Bachelor of Music in the areas of performance, music education, music history, music composition. Majors and concentrations: composition, music education, music history, piano/organ, stringed instruments, voice, wind instruments. Program accredited by NASM.

Enrollment Fall 1997: 40 undergraduate.

Music Student Profile 52% females, 48% males, 7% minorities.

Music Faculty 18 total (full-time and part-time). 88% of full-time faculty have terminal degrees. Graduate students do not teach undergraduate courses.

Expenses for 1997–98 Application fee: $45. Comprehensive fee: $26,410 includes full-time tuition ($21,080), mandatory fees ($130), and college room and board ($5200). College room only: $2785. Room and board charges vary according to board plan and housing facility. Special program-related fees: $240 per semester for lessons for non-majors.

Financial Aid Program-specific awards for 1997: preferential awards for program majors demonstrating need ($2000).

Application Procedures Students admitted directly into the professional program freshman year. Deadline for freshmen: January 1; transfers: April 1. Notification date for freshmen: April 1; transfers: July 1. Required: essay, high school transcript, college transcript(s) for transfer students, minimum 3.0 high school GPA, audition, SAT I or ACT test scores. Recommended: 3 letters of recommendation, interview. Auditions held 4 times on campus; recorded music is permissible as a substitute for live auditions if a campus visit is impossible and videotaped performances are permissible as a substitute for live auditions if a campus visit is impossible.

Web Site http://www.bucknell.edu/departments/music.

Undergraduate Contact Mr. Christopher Para, Associate Professor of Music, Department of Music, Bucknell University, Lewisburg, Pennsylvania 17837; 717-524-3191, fax: 717-524-1215, E-mail address: para@bucknell.edu.

Jordan College of Fine Arts

▼ BUTLER UNIVERSITY

Indianapolis, Indiana

Independent, coed. Urban campus. Total enrollment: 3,911. Music program established 1896.

Degrees Bachelor of Music in the areas of performance, piano pedagogy, music theory/composition; Bachelor of Music Education in the areas of choral music education, instrumental music education. Majors and concentrations: music, music education, music theory and composition, piano pedagogy, piano/organ, stringed instruments, voice, wind and percussion instruments. Graduate degrees offered: Master of Music in the areas of performance, composition, conducting, music theory, music history, piano pedagogy; Master of Music Education. Cross-registration with Indianapolis Consortium for Urban Education. Program accredited by NASM.

Enrollment Fall 1997: 225 undergraduate, 40 graduate.

Music Student Profile 57% females, 43% males, 9% minorities, 3% international.

Music Faculty 73 total undergraduate and graduate (full-time and part-time). 90% of full-time faculty have terminal degrees. Graduate students do not teach undergraduate courses.

Student Life Student groups/activities include Music Educators National Conference Student Chapter, American String Teachers Association Student Chapter, music fraternities and sororities.

Expenses for 1997–98 Application fee: $25. Comprehensive fee: $21,120 includes full-time tuition ($15,570), mandatory fees ($120), and college room and board ($5430). Full-time tuition and fees vary according to program. Room and board charges vary according to board plan and housing facility.

Financial Aid Program-specific awards for 1997: 40 Performance Audition Awards for program majors ($1500–$10,000).

Application Procedures Students admitted directly into the professional program freshman year. Deadline for freshmen and transfers: continuous. Required: essay, high school transcript, college transcript(s) for transfer students, letter of recommendation, audition, SAT I or ACT test scores. Auditions held 2onces on campus; recorded music is permissible as a substitute for live auditions when distance is prohibitive and videotaped performances are permissible as a substitute for live auditions when distance is prohibitive.

Contact Ms. Margaret Hayworth, Admissions Secretary, Jordan College of Fine Arts, Butler University, 4600 Sunset Avenue, Indianapolis, Indiana 46208; 317-940-9656, fax: 317-940-9658.

▼ CALIFORNIA INSTITUTE OF THE ARTS

Valencia, California

Independent, coed. Suburban campus. Total enrollment: 1,140. Music program established 1961.

Degrees Bachelor of Fine Arts in the areas of music composition, musical arts, performance, world music, composition/new media. Majors and concentrations: classical music, composition, jazz, music, new media, piano, stringed instruments, voice, wind and percussion instruments, world music. Graduate degrees offered: Master of Fine Arts in the areas of music composition, musical arts, performance, world music, composition/new media. Program accredited by NASM.

Enrollment Fall 1997: 131 undergraduate, 67 graduate.

Music Student Profile 23% females, 77% males, 21% minorities, 9% international.

Music Faculty 57 total undergraduate and graduate (full-time and part-time). 80% of full-time faculty have terminal degrees. Graduate students do not teach undergraduate courses. Undergraduate student–faculty ratio: 5:1.

Student Life Student groups/activities include Community Arts Partnership (CAP), off-campus performance groups. Special housing available for music students.

Expenses for 1998–99 Application fee: $60. Tuition: $18,120 full-time. Mandatory fees: $65 full-time. College room only: $2800. Room charges vary according to housing facility.

Financial Aid Program-specific awards available.

Application Procedures Students admitted directly into the professional program freshman year. Deadline for freshmen and transfers: February 1. Required: essay, high school transcript, college transcript(s) for transfer students, audition, portfolio. Recommended: letter of recommendation, interview. Auditions held by appointment on campus; recorded music is permissible as a substitute for live auditions whenever needed and videotaped performances are permissible as a substitute for live auditions whenever needed. Portfolio reviews held on campus.

Web Site http://www.calarts.edu.

Undergraduate Contact Mr. Kenneth Young, Director of Admissions, California Institute of the Arts, 24700 McBean Parkway, Valencia, California 91355; 805-253-7863, fax: 805-254-8352, E-mail address: kyoung@muse.calarts.edu.

More About the Institute

Program Facilities CalArts is a community of approximately 1,000 performing artists, visual artists, and writers located in the suburban hills north of Los Angeles. The college was incorporated in 1961 through the vision and generosity of Walt Disney. CalArts has been at its present 60-acre campus since 1971. On the campus are the main artistic/academic building, sound stages, rehearsal spaces, art studios, recreational facilities and two residence halls. At the undergraduate level in music, CalArts offers B.F.A. degree programs in music composition, music technology and new media, instrumental music, voice performance, jazz and African-American music, and world music–African music and dance, Indonesian music and dance, and North Indian music. Admission is based on talent. An audition, either in-person or on tape, or a portfolio of recent composition work is required.

Faculty, Resident Artists, and Alumni Please contact the admissions office for a free copy of the current admissions bulletin for complete and up-to-date biographies of all faculty members along with lists of alumni and visiting artists.

California Institute of the Arts *(continued)*

Special Programs The Community Arts Partnership links CalArts students and faculty members with high school and junior high school students in Watts, East Los Angeles, Pasadena, Santa Clarita, Hollywood, and Venice. The program enables CalArts students to teach, learn, and share their talents in community settings. Other special programs include exchanges with universities in other countries as well as internships at companies and nonprofit organizations throughout southern California. Each spring the placement professionals in the Office of Student Affairs host a series of job fairs attended by companies well known in the world of entertainment and the arts.

▼ CALIFORNIA STATE UNIVERSITY, FULLERTON

Fullerton, California

State-supported, coed. Suburban campus. Total enrollment: 24,906. Music program established 1960.

Degrees Bachelor of Music in the areas of voice, piano/organ, stringed instruments, wind/percussion instruments, composition. Majors and concentrations: composition, music education, piano/organ, stringed instruments, voice, wind and percussion instruments. Graduate degrees offered: Master of Music in the areas of performance, composition. Cross-registration with California State University System, California community colleges. Program accredited by NASM.

Enrollment Fall 1997: 305 total; 260 undergraduate, 35 graduate, 10 non-professional degree.

Music Student Profile 55% females, 45% males, 40% minorities, 5% international.

Music Faculty 57 total undergraduate and graduate (full-time and part-time). 85% of full-time faculty have terminal degrees. Graduate students do not teach undergraduate courses.

Student Life Student groups/activities include American Choral Directors Association Student Chapter, Phi Mu Alpha Sinfonia, Mu Phi Epsilon.

Expenses for 1997–98 Application fee: $55. State resident tuition: $0 full-time. Nonresident tuition: $7626 full-time. Mandatory fees: $1947 full-time. College room only: $3662. Special program-related fees: $25 per semester for piano maintenance fee, $25 per semester for instrument use fee.

Financial Aid Program-specific awards for 1997: 15–20 departmental scholarships for performers ($1000).

Application Procedures Students apply for admission into the professional program by sophomore year. Deadline for freshmen and transfers: June 1. Required: essay, high school transcript, college transcript(s) for transfer students, minimum 2.0 high school GPA, SAT I or ACT test scores, audition for access to private lessons. Auditions held 3 times on campus; recorded music is permissible as a substitute for live auditions when distance is prohibitive and videotaped performances are permissible as a substitute for live auditions when distance is prohibitive. Portfolio reviews held on campus.

Web Site http://www.music.fullerton.edu.

Undergraduate Contact Mr. David Grines, Vice Chair, Music Department, California State University, Fullerton, Box 6850, Fullerton, California 92834-6850; 714-278-3598, fax: 714-278-5956, E-mail address: dgrines@fullerton.edu.

Graduate Contact Mr. Leo Kreter, Coordinator of Graduate Studies, Music Department, California State University, Fullerton, PO Box 34080, Fullerton, California 92834-6850; 714-278-3511, fax: 714-278-5956, E-mail address: lkreter@fullerton.edu.

▼ CALIFORNIA STATE UNIVERSITY, LONG BEACH

Long Beach, California

State-supported, coed. Suburban campus. Total enrollment: 27,809.

Degrees Bachelor of Music in the areas of performance, music history and literature, composition; Bachelor of Music Education. Majors and concentrations: classical music, composition, jazz, music, music education, music history, opera, piano, stringed instruments, voice, wind and percussion instruments. Graduate degrees offered: Master of Music in the areas of composition, conducting, performance, music history, music theory, opera, jazz studies; Master of Music Education. Cross-registration with California State University System. Program accredited by NASM.

Enrollment Fall 1997: 350 total; 260 undergraduate, 65 graduate, 25 non-professional degree.

Music Student Profile 52% females, 48% males, 40% minorities, 5% international.

Music Faculty 68 total undergraduate and graduate (full-time and part-time). 85% of full-time faculty have terminal degrees. Graduate students teach a few undergraduate courses. Undergraduate student–faculty ratio: 15:1.

Student Life Student groups/activities include American Choral Directors Association, Music Educators National Conference, professional music fraternities.

Expenses for 1997–98 Application fee: $55. State resident tuition: $0 full-time. Nonresident tuition: $7380 full-time. Mandatory fees: $1846 full-time. Full-time tuition and fees vary according to course load. College room and board: $5200. Room and board charges vary according to board plan. Special program-related fees: $20 per semester for practice room and instrument fee.

Financial Aid Program-specific awards for 1997: 60 music scholarships for program majors ($750).

Application Procedures Students apply for admission into the professional program by sophomore year. Deadline for freshmen and transfers: March 15. Required: high school transcript, minimum 3.0 high school GPA, audition, SAT I or ACT test scores. Auditions held 4 times on campus; recorded music is permissible as a substitute for live auditions when distance is prohibitive and videotaped performances are permissible as a substitute for live auditions when distance is prohibitive.

Web Site http://www.csulb.edu/~music.

Undergraduate Contact Dr. Lee Vail, Coordinator of Undergraduate Studies, Department of Music, California State University, Long Beach, 1250 Bellflower Boulevard, Long Beach, California 90840-7101; 562-985-4399, fax: 562-985-2490.

Graduate Contact Dr. Kristine Forney, Director of Graduate Studies, Department of Music, California State University, Long Beach, 1250 Bellflower Boulevard, Long Beach, California 90840-7101; 562-984-4788, fax: 562-985-2490.

▼ CALIFORNIA STATE UNIVERSITY, LOS ANGELES

Los Angeles, California

State-supported, coed. Urban campus. Total enrollment: 19,160.

Degrees Bachelor of Music in the areas of performance, composition, jazz studies; Bachelor of Arts in the area of music education. Majors and concentrations: composition, jazz, music, music education, piano/organ, stringed instruments, voice, wind and percussion instruments. Graduate degrees offered: Master of Music in the areas of commercial music, composition, performance, conducting; Master of Arts in the area of music education. Cross-registration with California State University System. Program accredited by NASM.

Enrollment Fall 1997: 110 undergraduate, 70 graduate.

Music Student Profile 40% females, 60% males, 75% minorities, 10% international.

Music Faculty 49 total undergraduate and graduate (full-time and part-time). 80% of full-time faculty have terminal degrees. Graduate students do not teach undergraduate courses.

Student Life Student groups/activities include Music Educators National Conference, American Choral Directors Association, International Association of Jazz Educators.

Expenses for 1997–98 Application fee: $55. State resident tuition: $0 full-time. Nonresident tuition: $7661 full-time. Mandatory fees: $1757 full-time. College room only: $2915. Special program-related fees: $25 per quarter for practice room fee.

Financial Aid Program-specific awards for 1997: 15 Friends of Music Scholarships for music majors ($600–$1200), 12 general music scholarships for music majors ($600–$1200).

Application Procedures Students apply for admission into the professional program by freshman year. Deadline for freshmen and transfers: June 30. Required: essay, high school transcript, minimum 2.0 high school GPA, audition, portfolio. Recommended: SAT I or ACT test scores. Auditions held by appointment on campus; recorded music is permissible as a substitute for live auditions when distance is prohibitive and videotaped performances are permissible as a substitute for live auditions when distance is prohibitive. Portfolio reviews held once on campus.

Web Site http://web.calstatela.edu/academic/music/index. htm.

Contact Mr. H. David Caffey, Chair, Department of Music, California State University, Los Angeles, 5151 State University Drive, Los Angeles, California 90032; 213-343-4060, fax: 213-343-4063, E-mail address: dcaffey@calstatela.edu.

▼ CALIFORNIA STATE UNIVERSITY, NORTHRIDGE

Northridge, California

State-supported, coed. Urban campus. Total enrollment: 27,653. Music program established 1958.

Degrees Bachelor of Music in the areas of performance, jazz, choral performance, composition/music theory. Majors and concentrations: guitar, jazz, music theory and composition, orchestral instruments, performance, piano/organ, voice, wind and percussion instruments. Graduate degrees offered:

Master of Music in the areas of performance, conducting, composition. Cross-registration with California State University System. Program accredited by NASM.

Enrollment Fall 1997: 610 total; 500 undergraduate, 60 graduate, 50 non-professional degree.

Music Student Profile 44% females, 56% males, 30% minorities, 1% international.

Music Faculty 69 total undergraduate and graduate (full-time and part-time). 42% of full-time faculty have terminal degrees. Graduate students teach a few undergraduate courses. Undergraduate student–faculty ratio: 15:1.

Student Life Student groups/activities include Sigma Alpha Iota, California Music Educators Association Student Chapter, American Association of Music Therapy Student Chapter.

Expenses for 1997–98 Application fee: $55. State resident tuition: $0 full-time. Nonresident tuition: $7626 full-time. Mandatory fees: $1980 full-time. College room only: $4190. Special program-related fees: $10 per semester for piano classes, piano lessons, use of instruments.

Financial Aid Program-specific awards for 1997: 25 University Scholarships for program students ($1000), 70 departmental scholarships for program students ($750).

Application Procedures Students admitted directly into the professional program freshman year. Deadline for freshmen and transfers: continuous. Required: essay, high school transcript, college transcript(s) for transfer students, minimum 2.0 high school GPA, letter of recommendation, audition. Auditions held 3 times on campus; recorded music is permissible as a substitute for live auditions when distance is prohibitive and videotaped performances are permissible as a substitute for live auditions when distance is excessive.

Contact Ms. Mary Shamrock, Assistant Chair, Department of Music, California State University, Northridge, 18111 Nordhoff Street, Northridge, California 91330-8314; 818-677-3181, fax: 818-885-3164, E-mail address: mshamrock@huey.csun.edu.

▼ CALIFORNIA STATE UNIVERSITY, SACRAMENTO

Sacramento, California

State-supported, coed. Urban campus. Total enrollment: 23,481.

Degrees Bachelor of Music in the areas of voice, piano, organ, orchestral instruments, guitar, music theory/composition. Majors and concentrations: guitar, music, music theory and composition, piano/organ, stringed instruments, voice, wind and percussion instruments. Graduate degrees offered: Master of Music in the areas of conducting, composition, music education, music history and literature, performance. Cross-registration with Sacramento City College, American River College, Cosumnes River College, Sierra College, University of California-Davis. Program accredited by NASM.

Enrollment Fall 1997: 220 total; 155 undergraduate, 35 graduate, 30 non-professional degree.

Music Student Profile 59% females, 41% males, 36% minorities, 5% international.

Music Faculty 37 total undergraduate and graduate (full-time and part-time). 100% of full-time faculty have terminal degrees. Graduate students do not teach undergraduate courses. Undergraduate student–faculty ratio: 12:1.

Student Life Student groups/activities include Music Educators National Conference, Mu Phi Epsilon, Pi Kappa Lambda.

California State University, Sacramento (continued)

Expenses for 1997–98 Application fee: $55. State resident tuition: $0 full-time. Nonresident tuition: $7626 full-time. Mandatory fees: $1982 full-time. Full-time tuition and fees vary according to course load. College room and board: $5100. Room and board charges vary according to board plan and housing facility. Special program-related fees: $20 per semester for practice room fee.

Financial Aid Program-specific awards for 1997: 30–50 various awards for program majors ($500–$1500).

Application Procedures Deadline for freshmen and transfers: continuous. Required: high school transcript, college transcript(s) for transfer students, minimum 2.0 high school GPA, audition, SAT I or ACT test scores, portfolio for theory/composition applicants. Recommended: essay, minimum 3.0 high school GPA, video. Auditions held 4 times on campus; recorded music is permissible as a substitute for live auditions if a campus visit is impossible and videotaped performances are permissible as a substitute for live auditions if a campus visit is impossible. Portfolio reviews held 4 times on campus.

Web Site http://www.csus.edu/musc/.

Undergraduate Contact Mr. Mark Allen, Admissions Counselor, Department of Music, California State University, Sacramento, 6000 J Street, Sacramento, California 95819-6015; 916-278-6543, fax: 916-278-7217, E-mail address: mallen@csus.edu.

Graduate Contact Dr. Carole Delaney, Professor, Department of Music, California State University, Sacramento, 6000 J Street, Sacramento, California 95819-6015; 916-278-6558, fax: 916-278-7217.

▼ CALVARY BIBLE COLLEGE AND THEOLOGICAL SEMINARY

Kansas City, Missouri

Independent-religious, coed. Suburban campus. Total enrollment: 613. Music program established 1955.

Degrees Bachelor of Music Education in the areas of keyboard, voice, conducting. Majors and concentrations: music education.

Enrollment Fall 1997: 4 undergraduate.

Music Student Profile 50% females, 50% males.

Music Faculty 3 total undergraduate (full-time and part-time). 100% of full-time faculty have terminal degrees. Graduate students do not teach undergraduate courses. Undergraduate student–faculty ratio: 2:1.

Student Life Student groups/activities include musicals.

Expenses for 1997–98 Application fee: $25. Comprehensive fee: $7520 includes full-time tuition ($4200), mandatory fees ($370), and college room and board ($2950). College room only: $1200. Special program-related fees: $100 per semester for private lessons.

Application Procedures Students admitted directly into the professional program freshman year. Deadline for freshmen and transfers: continuous. Required: high school transcript, college transcript(s) for transfer students, 2 letters of recommendation, SAT I or ACT test scores. Recommended: audition. Auditions held whenever needed on campus; recorded music is permissible as a substitute for live auditions if a campus visit is impossible and videotaped

performances are permissible as a substitute for live auditions if a campus visit is impossible.

Undergraduate Contact Mr. John Bryden, Director of Admissions, Calvary Bible College and Theological Seminary, 15800 Calvary Road, Kansas City, Missouri 64147; 816-322-0110 ext. 1326, fax: 816-331-4474.

▼ CALVIN COLLEGE

Grand Rapids, Michigan

Independent, coed. Suburban campus. Total enrollment: 4,071. Music program established 1995.

Degrees Bachelor of Music Education. Majors and concentrations: choral music education, instrumental music education. Program accredited by NASM.

Enrollment Fall 1997: 50 total; all undergraduate.

Music Student Profile 65% females, 35% males, 1% minorities, 5% international.

Music Faculty 32 total (full-time and part-time). 80% of full-time faculty have terminal degrees. Graduate students do not teach undergraduate courses. Undergraduate student–faculty ratio: 7:1.

Student Life Student groups/activities include Music Educators National Conference.

Expenses for 1997–98 Application fee: $35. Comprehensive fee: $16,590 includes full-time tuition ($12,225), mandatory fees ($25), and college room and board ($4340). College room only: $2360. Room and board charges vary according to board plan. Special program-related fees: $180–$360 per semester for private lessons.

Financial Aid Program-specific awards for 1997: 1 DeJonge Award for program majors ($720), 1 Holtvluwer Award for program majors ($720), 1 DeVries Church Music Award for program majors ($720), 1 Henry Bruinsma Family Scholarship for program majors/non-majors ($600), 1 Leo Cayuan Award for program majors/non-majors ($720), 1 Geerdes String Award for program majors/non-majors ($720), 2 Gezon Voice Awards for program majors/non-majors ($720), 1 Houskamp Organ Scholarship for program majors/non-majors ($1500), 1 Scripps Wind Award for program majors/non-majors ($720), 2 Van Dellen Music Awards for program majors/non-majors ($1200).

Application Procedures Students apply for admission into the professional program by sophomore year. Deadline for freshmen and transfers: continuous. Required: essay, high school transcript, college transcript(s) for transfer students, letter of recommendation, interview, audition, SAT I or ACT test scores (minimum combined SAT I score of 940, minimum combined ACT score of 20), minimum 2.5 high school GPA. Auditions held once on campus.

Undergraduate Contact Dr. Dale Topp, Director of Music Education, Department of Music, Calvin College, 3201 Burton Street, SE, Grand Rapids, Michigan 49546; 616-957-6260, fax: 616-957-6266, E-mail address: jcza@ursa.calvin.edu.

▼ CAMERON UNIVERSITY

Lawton, Oklahoma

State-supported, coed. Suburban campus. Total enrollment: 5,147.

Degrees Bachelor of Music in the areas of vocal music education, instrumental music education, composition, performance. Majors and concentrations: composition, music education, performance, piano, stringed instruments, voice, wind and percussion instruments. Mandatory cross-registration with Oklahoma University, State Board of Regents University System. Program accredited by NASM.

Enrollment Fall 1997: 72 total; all undergraduate.

Music Student Profile 55% females, 45% males, 20% minorities.

Music Faculty 16 total (full-time and part-time). 100% of full-time faculty have terminal degrees. Graduate students do not teach undergraduate courses.

Student Life Student groups/activities include Kappa Kappa Psi, Tau Beta Sigma.

Expenses for 1997–98 Application fee: $15. State resident tuition: $1880 full-time. Nonresident tuition: $4490 full-time. Mandatory fees: $300 full-time. Full-time tuition and fees vary according to course level, course load, degree level, and student level. College room and board: $2600. College room only: $1200. Room and board charges vary according to board plan. Special program-related fees: $18–$36 per credit hour for private music lessons.

Financial Aid Program-specific awards for 1997: Leslie Powell Scholarship for above-average students with exceptional artistic ability ($1000), 1 Presser Scholarship for above-average students with exceptional artistic ability ($2200), 18 McMahon Scholarships for academically qualified applicants ($1000).

Application Procedures Students apply for admission into the professional program by sophomore year. Deadline for freshmen and transfers: continuous. Required: essay, high school transcript, college transcript(s) for transfer students, minimum 2.0 high school GPA, audition, SAT I or ACT test scores. Auditions held twice on campus; recorded music is permissible as a substitute for live auditions when distance is prohibitive and videotaped performances are permissible as a substitute for live auditions when distance is prohibitive.

Web Site http://www.cameron.edu.

Undergraduate Contact Ms. Tammy Johnson, Secretary, Department of Music, Cameron University, 2800 West Gore Boulevard, Lawton, Oklahoma 73505; 405-581-2440, fax: 405-581-5764, E-mail address: tammyj@cameron.edu.

▼ CAMPBELLSVILLE UNIVERSITY

Campbellsville, Kentucky

Independent, coed. Small town campus. Total enrollment: 1,521. Music program established 1957.

Degrees Bachelor of Music in the areas of church music, music education. Majors and concentrations: music education, piano/organ, sacred music, stringed instruments, voice, wind and percussion instruments. Graduate degrees offered: Master of Music in the area of music education. Program accredited by NASM.

Enrollment Fall 1997: 65 undergraduate, 25 non-professional degree.

Music Student Profile 55% females, 1% minorities, 1% international.

Music Faculty 17 total undergraduate and graduate (full-time and part-time). 90% of full-time faculty have terminal degrees. Graduate students do not teach undergraduate courses.

Student Life Student groups/activities include Fall Drama, Spring Musical Drama, Children's Theater.

Expenses for 1997–98 Application fee: $20. Comprehensive fee: $10,742 includes full-time tuition ($7200), mandatory

fees ($102), and college room and board ($3440). College room only: $1560. Room and board charges vary according to board plan and housing facility. Special program-related fees: $100 per credit hour for applied lesson fees.

Financial Aid Program-specific awards for 1997: 3 Competitive Music Scholarships for program majors ($2400), 60 Music Performance Grants for program majors/minors ($1400), 50 Band Grants for band members ($600).

Application Procedures Students apply for admission into the professional program by sophomore year. Deadline for freshmen and transfers: continuous. Required: high school transcript, college transcript(s) for transfer students, audition, SAT I or ACT test scores (minimum combined SAT I score of 890, minimum combined ACT score of 19). Recommended: essay, minimum 2.0 high school GPA, letter of recommendation. Auditions held by request on campus; recorded music is permissible as a substitute for live auditions when distance is prohibitive and videotaped performances are permissible as a substitute for live auditions when distance is prohibitive.

Web Site http://www.campbellsvil.edu/music.

Contact Dr. Robert Gaddis, Dean, School of Music, Campbellsville University, 1 University Drive, CPO 1314, Campbellsville, Kentucky 42718; 502-789-5237, fax: 502-789-5524, E-mail address: music@campbellsvil.edu.

▼ CAPITAL UNIVERSITY

Columbus, Ohio

Independent, coed. Suburban campus. Total enrollment: 3,988. Music program established 1918.

Degrees Bachelor of Music in the areas of music education, composition, jazz studies, music industry, performance, keyboard pedagogy, music theater, music merchandising, music media; Bachelor of Arts in the area of music. Majors and concentrations: composition, jazz, keyboard pedagogy, music education, music industry, music media, music performance, performance. Program accredited by NASM.

Enrollment Fall 1997: 200 total; all undergraduate.

Music Student Profile 51% females, 49% males, 5% minorities, 2% international.

Music Faculty 46 total (full-time and part-time). 37% of full-time faculty have terminal degrees. Graduate students do not teach undergraduate courses. Undergraduate student–faculty ratio: 5:1.

Student Life Student groups/activities include Ohio Student Music Educators Association, Phi Mu Alpha, Phi Beta.

Expenses for 1997–98 Application fee: $25. Comprehensive fee: $18,960 includes full-time tuition ($14,760) and college room and board ($4200). Full-time tuition varies according to program. Room and board charges vary according to board plan. Special program-related fees: $225–$300 per semester for private lessons, $100 per semester for group lesson.

Financial Aid Program-specific awards for 1997: music scholarships for program majors ($500–$10,000), participation awards for non-music majors ($500–$1000), music grants for program majors needing instruments ($500–$1000).

Application Procedures Students admitted directly into the professional program freshman year. Deadline for freshmen and transfers: continuous. Required: high school transcript, college transcript(s) for transfer students, audition, SAT I or ACT test scores, minimum 2.5 high school GPA. Recommended: minimum 3.0 high school GPA, letter of recommen-

Capital University *(continued)*

dation, interview. Auditions held 5 times on campus; recorded music is permissible as a substitute for live auditions when distance is prohibitive and videotaped performances are permissible as a substitute for live auditions when distance is prohibitive.

Web Site http://www.capital.edu.

Undergraduate Contact Ms. Marla Jones, Admission Counselor, Admission Office, Capital University, 2199 East Main Street, Columbus, Ohio 43209; 614-236-6101, fax: 614-236-6820, E-mail address: admissions@capital.edu.

▼ CARLETON UNIVERSITY

Ottawa, ON, Canada

Province-supported, coed. Urban campus. Total enrollment: 17,541. Music program established 1967.

Degrees Bachelor of Music in the areas of performance, composition, musical research. Majors and concentrations: classical music, ethnomusicology, jazz, music, piano/organ, popular music, sociology of music, stringed instruments, voice, wind and percussion instruments. Cross-registration with University of Ottawa. Program accredited by CUMS.

Enrollment Fall 1997: 157 total; 37 undergraduate, 120 non-professional degree.

Music Student Profile 46% females, 54% males.

Music Faculty 11 total (full-time and part-time). 85% of full-time faculty have terminal degrees. Graduate students teach a few undergraduate courses. Undergraduate student–faculty ratio: 18:1.

Student Life Student groups/activities include Art Gallery Concert Series performers.

Expenses for 1997–98 Application fee: $50 Canadian dollars. Tuition, fee, and room and board charges are reported in Canadian dollars. Canadian resident tuition: $3170 full-time. Mandatory fees: $358 full-time. Full-time tuition and fees vary according to program. College room and board: $4965. Room and board charges vary according to board plan. International student tuition: $8800 full-time. Special program-related fees: $2 for practice room key rental.

Financial Aid Program-specific awards for 1997: 3 Jack Barwick Awards for program majors ($350), 2 MacDonald Club Awards for upperclassmen ($500), 2 Bettina Oppenheimer Awards for seniors ($600), 1 music award for sophomores ($185).

Application Procedures Students admitted directly into the professional program freshman year. Deadline for freshmen and transfers: April 1. Notification date for freshmen: June 15. Required: high school transcript, college transcript(s) for transfer students, audition, Canadian OAC of 6. Recommended: essay, interview. Auditions held once on campus; recorded music is permissible as a substitute for live auditions when distance is prohibitive and videotaped performances are permissible as a substitute for live auditions when distance is prohibitive.

Web Site http://www.carleton.ca.

Undergraduate Contact Mr. Victor Chapman, Director of Admissions, Office of Admissions and Academic Records, Carleton University, 1125 Colonel By Drive, Ottawa, ON K1S 5B6, Canada; 613-520-3663, fax: 613-520-3517, E-mail address: vic_chapman@carleton.ca.

▼ CARNEGIE MELLON UNIVERSITY

Pittsburgh, Pennsylvania

Independent, coed. Urban campus. Total enrollment: 7,912. Music program established 1913.

Degrees Bachelor of Fine Arts in the areas of music performance, composition. Majors and concentrations: composition, instrumental music, piano/organ, voice. Graduate degrees offered: Master of Music in the areas of composition, conducting, performance, music education. Cross-registration with Pittsburgh Council on Higher Education. Program accredited by NASM.

Enrollment Fall 1997: 225 total; 140 undergraduate, 60 graduate, 25 non-professional degree.

Music Student Profile 55% females, 45% males, 4% minorities, 20% international.

Music Faculty 90 total undergraduate and graduate (full-time and part-time). 33% of full-time faculty have terminal degrees. Graduate students do not teach undergraduate courses. Undergraduate student–faculty ratio: 4:1.

Student Life Student groups/activities include Greek Sing, Carnival, Scotch 'n Soda (student-run theater group).

Expenses for 1997–98 Application fee: $45. Comprehensive fee: $26,600 includes full-time tuition ($20,275), mandatory fees ($100), and college room and board ($6225). College room only: $3845. Room and board charges vary according to board plan.

Financial Aid Program-specific awards for 1997: 20–40 music scholarships for program majors ($1000–$20,275).

Application Procedures Students admitted directly into the professional program freshman year. Deadline for freshmen and transfers: January 1. Notification date for freshmen and transfers: March 15. Required: essay, high school transcript, college transcript(s) for transfer students, 3 letters of recommendation, audition, SAT I or ACT test scores. Recommended: minimum 3.0 high school GPA, interview, video. Auditions held 22 times on campus and off campus in Atlanta, GA; Boston, MA; Chicago, IL; Dallas, TX; Houston, TX; Interlochen, MI; Miami, FL; New York, NY; Philadelphia, PA; Washington, DC; Los Angeles, CA; San Francisco, CA; recorded music is permissible as a substitute for live auditions if a campus visit is impossible and videotaped performances are permissible as a substitute for live auditions if a campus visit is impossible.

Web Site http://www.cmu.edu/cfa/music/.

Contact Ms. Annette Valenti, Director of Admissions, School of Music, Carnegie Mellon University, 5000 Forbes Avenue, Pittsburgh, Pennsylvania 15213-3890; 412-268-4118, fax: 412-268-1431, E-mail address: valenti@andrew.cmu.edu.

▼ CARSON-NEWMAN COLLEGE

Jefferson City, Tennessee

Independent-Southern Baptist, coed. Small town campus. Total enrollment: 2,308. Music program established 1888.

Degrees Bachelor of Music in the areas of applied music, church music, music education, performance. Majors and concentrations: music education, music theory, piano/organ, sacred music, voice. Program accredited by NASM.

Enrollment Fall 1997: 91 total; 84 undergraduate, 7 non-professional degree.

Music Student Profile 67% females, 33% males, 2% international.

Music Faculty 21 total (full-time and part-time). 60% of full-time faculty have terminal degrees. Graduate students do not teach undergraduate courses. Undergraduate student–faculty ratio: 8:1.

Student Life Student groups/activities include Delta Omicron benefit recitals, American Guild of Organists projects, Center for Church Music workshops.

Expenses for 1998–99 Application fee: $25. Comprehensive fee: $14,440 includes full-time tuition ($10,000), mandatory fees ($610), and college room and board ($3830). College room only: $1530. Full-time tuition and fees vary according to class time. Room and board charges vary according to board plan. Special program-related fees: $90–$170 per semester for applied music lesson fees.

Financial Aid Program-specific awards for 1997: 1 Ersa Davis Organ Scholarship for organists ($2000), 50–60 Performance Scholarships for program majors ($1412).

Application Procedures Students admitted directly into the professional program freshman year. Deadline for freshmen and transfers: continuous. Required: high school transcript, college transcript(s) for transfer students, minimum 2.0 high school GPA, 2 letters of recommendation, audition, SAT I or ACT test scores, 24 hours of credit and minimum 2.0 college GPA for transfer students. Auditions held 3 times and by appointment on campus; recorded music is permissible as a substitute for live auditions when distance is prohibitive and videotaped performances are permissible as a substitute for live auditions when distance is prohibitive.

Web Site http://www.cn.edu/academics/departments/music/MusicDep.html.

Undergraduate Contact Ms. Sheryl Gray, Director, Undergraduate Admissions, Carson-Newman College, Box 72025, Jefferson City, Tennessee 37760; 800-678-9061, fax: 423-471-3502, E-mail address: sgray@cncadm.cn.edu.

Benjamin T. Rome School of Music

▼ THE CATHOLIC UNIVERSITY OF AMERICA
Washington, District of Columbia

Independent, coed. Urban campus. Total enrollment: 5,616. Music program established 1965.

Degrees Bachelor of Music in the areas of vocal performance, instrumental performance, composition, musical theater, general-choral music education, instrumental music education, combined general choral and instrumental music education, music history and literature. Graduate degrees offered: Master of Music in the areas of vocal performance, instrumental performance, accompanying, chamber music, pedagogy, composition, instrumental conducting, music education; Master of Liturgical Music; Master of Arts in the areas of music history, music theory. Doctor of Musical Arts in the areas of vocal performance, instrumental performance, accompanying, chamber music, composition, instrumental conducting, liturgical music, music education, pedagogy. Cross-registration with Consortium of Universities of the Washington Metropolitan Area. Program accredited by NASM.

Enrollment Fall 1997: 346 total; 155 undergraduate, 168 graduate, 23 non-professional degree.

Music Student Profile 67% females, 33% males, 12% minorities, 20% international.

Music Faculty 128 total undergraduate and graduate (full-time and part-time). 71% of full-time faculty have terminal degrees. Graduate students teach a few undergraduate courses.

Student Life Student groups/activities include drama department productions and student-run productions, Music Educators National Conference Student Chapter, Sigma Alpha Iota.

Expenses for 1997–98 Application fee: $50. Comprehensive fee: $24,146 includes full-time tuition ($16,500), mandatory fees ($610), and college room and board ($7036). College room only: $3978. Full-time tuition and fees vary according to program. Room and board charges vary according to board plan and housing facility. Special program-related fees for applied music fee.

Financial Aid Program-specific awards for 1997: 45 University Scholarships for academically qualified applicants ($6500), 80 Music Performance Scholarships for musically qualified applicants ($4500).

Application Procedures Students admitted directly into the professional program freshman year. Deadline for freshmen: February 15; transfers: April 1. Required: essay, high school transcript, college transcript(s) for transfer students, minimum 3.0 high school GPA, letter of recommendation, audition, SAT I or ACT test scores. Recommended: interview, SAT II. Auditions held approximately once per month on campus; recorded music is permissible as a substitute for live auditions if a campus visit is impossible and videotaped performances are permissible as a substitute for live auditions if a campus visit is impossible.

Web Site http://www.cua.edu/musu/welcome.htm.

Undergraduate Contact Dr. Amy Antonelli, Assistant Dean of Undergraduate Studies, Benjamin T. Rome School of Music, The Catholic University of America, Washington, District of Columbia 20064; 202-319-5414, fax: 202-319-6280.

Graduate Contact Dr. Paul Taylor, Assistant Dean of Graduate Studies, Benjamin T. Rome School of Music, The Catholic University of America, Washington, District of Columbia 20064; 202-319-5414, fax: 202-319-6280.

More About the University

Special Programs Qualified CUA students may enroll in dual-degree (double major) programs within the School of Music or between the School of Music and other schools of the University. The University is part of a consortium of universities in the Washington, D.C., area, and students may elect to take courses at any of these universities as well. The Summer Opera Theatre Company, a professional company national in scope, resides at the University and hires many qualified students annually.

Faculty, Resident Artists, and Alumni The 100-member full-time/part-time faculty of artists and scholars includes members of The National Symphony Orchestra, Kennedy Center Orchestra, Philadelphia Orchestra, Baltimore Symphony Orchestra, and The Metropolitan Opera. Piano faculty members perform internationally in solo, chamber, and orchestral programs. Many of the world's greatest concert performers and conductors visit Washington, D.C., and The Catholic University of America on their concert tours. Alberto Ginastera, Horacio Gutierrez, Mstislav Rostropovich, Gian Carlo Menotti, Lorin Hollander, Andre Watts, Joseph Kalichstein, and Renata Scotto are among the artists who have performed or given master classes at the School. Alumni hold positions in many of the major orchestras and opera houses in the world.

The Catholic University of America (*continued*)

Student Performance Opportunities The CUA Symphony Orchestra and Chorus, Concert Choir, Chamber Winds, Jazz Ensemble, and other ensembles perform throughout the academic year. These concerts are highlighted annually by a nationally televised Christmas Concert, a concerto/vocal competition (which entitles the winner to solo with the CUA Symphony Orchestra), and opera and musical theater performances. More than 200 student solo and chamber recitals are presented each year in addition to performances by faculty members, resident and visiting artists, and alumni.

Program Facilities Performance spaces include Ward Recital Hall (120 seats), Hartke Theatre (590 seats), and St. Vincent's Chapel (400 seats), as well as access to the Kennedy Center, Basilica of The National Shrine, and other churches; recording studio; electronic piano lab; thirty practice rooms; classrooms; and studios. An on-line catalog combines the music library's collection of approximately 25,000 books, scores, CDs, and videotapes with the collection of the consortium of university libraries in the Washington, D.C., metropolitan area. Students may borrow materials from any of the libraries in the consortium system.

▼ CEDARVILLE COLLEGE

Cedarville, Ohio

Independent-Baptist, coed. Rural campus. Total enrollment: 2,559. Music program established 1887.

Degrees Bachelor of Music Education in the areas of choral music education, instrumental music education. Majors and concentrations: church music, music education, music theory and composition, piano/organ, stringed instruments, voice, wind and percussion instruments.

Enrollment Fall 1997: 105 total; 92 undergraduate, 13 non-professional degree.

Music Student Profile 64% females, 36% males, 3% minorities.

Music Faculty 27 total (full-time and part-time). 73% of full-time faculty have terminal degrees. Graduate students do not teach undergraduate courses. Undergraduate student–faculty ratio: 3:1.

Student Life Student groups/activities include Music Educators National Conference.

Expenses for 1997–98 Application fee: $30. Comprehensive fee: $14,028 includes full-time tuition ($9168), mandatory fees ($144), and college room and board ($4716). College room only: $2532. Special program-related fees: $25 per quarter for practice room, $75 per quarter for lab fee.

Financial Aid Program-specific awards for 1997: 33 music scholarships for those demonstrating musical achievement ($900).

Application Procedures Students admitted directly into the professional program freshman year. Deadline for freshmen and transfers: continuous. Required: essay, high school transcript, college transcript(s) for transfer students, minimum 2.0 high school GPA, 2 letters of recommendation, audition, SAT I or ACT test scores (minimum combined ACT score of 21). Recommended: minimum 3.0 high school GPA. Auditions held 4 times and by appointment on campus; recorded music is permissible as a substitute for live auditions (video tape or signed affidavit preferred) and videotaped performances are permissible as a substitute for live auditions if a campus visit is impossible.

Undergraduate Contact Ms. Pam Miller, Secretary, Music Department, Cedarville College, PO Box 601, Cedarville, Ohio 45314; 937-766-7728, fax: 937-766-7661, E-mail address: millerp@cedarville.edu.

Hurley School of Music

▼ CENTENARY COLLEGE OF LOUISIANA

Shreveport, Louisiana

Independent-United Methodist, coed. Suburban campus. Total enrollment: 986.

Degrees Bachelor of Music in the areas of performance, sacred music, music theory/composition; Bachelor of Music Education in the areas of vocal music education, instrumental music education. Majors and concentrations: music education, music theory and composition, piano/organ, sacred music, stringed instruments, voice, wind and percussion instruments. Program accredited by NASM.

Enrollment Fall 1997: 58 total; all undergraduate.

Music Student Profile 57% females, 43% males, 5% minorities, 2% international.

Music Faculty 20 total (full-time and part-time). 88% of full-time faculty have terminal degrees. Graduate students do not teach undergraduate courses. Undergraduate student–faculty ratio: 11:1.

Student Life Student groups/activities include Sigma Alpha Iota, Music Educators National Conference, Music Teachers National Association.

Expenses for 1997–98 Application fee: $30. Comprehensive fee: $15,300 includes full-time tuition ($11,050), mandatory fees ($350), and college room and board ($3900). College room only: $1650. Full-time tuition and fees vary according to course load. Room and board charges vary according to housing facility. Special program-related fees: $125 per semester for applied music fee.

Financial Aid Program-specific awards for 1997: 50–70 Hurley Foundation Scholarships for incoming freshmen and program majors ($3500–$10,000), 1–4 Mary C. White Awards for program majors ($12,000–$16,000).

Application Procedures Students admitted directly into the professional program freshman year. Deadline for freshmen and transfers: continuous. Required: essay, high school transcript, college transcript(s) for transfer students, minimum 2.0 high school GPA, letter of recommendation, interview, audition, SAT I or ACT test scores (minimum combined ACT score of 21). Auditions held 4 times on campus; recorded music is permissible as a substitute for live auditions when distance is prohibitive and videotaped performances are permissible as a substitute for live auditions when distance is prohibitive.

Web Site http://www.centenary.edu/centenar/academic/music/music.html.

Undergraduate Contact Director of Admissions, Centenary College of Louisiana, PO Box 41188, Shreveport, Louisiana 71134; 318-869-5208, fax: 318-869-5026.

The Swinney Conservatory of Music

▼ CENTRAL METHODIST COLLEGE

Fayette, Missouri

Independent-Methodist, coed. Small town campus. Total enrollment: 1,292.

WRIGHT STATE UNIVERSITY

"One of the finest theatre arts
programs in America."
Martin Sheen

Undergraduate Study Only
Offering a B.F.A. in

ACTING

ACTING/MUSICAL THEATRE

DESIGN TECHNOLOGY

STAGE MANAGEMENT

MOTION PICTURES

DANCE

CHICAGO—part of WSU Theatre's 1997-98 season

T H E A T R E

Degrees Bachelor of Music in the areas of piano, organ, voice; Bachelor of Music Education in the area of instrumental and vocal music. Majors and concentrations: classical music, music education, piano/organ, voice. Program accredited by NASM.

Enrollment Fall 1997: 51 undergraduate.

Music Student Profile 55% females, 45% males, 4% minorities.

Music Faculty 17 total undergraduate (full-time and part-time). 67% of full-time faculty have terminal degrees. Graduate students do not teach undergraduate courses.

Student Life Student groups/activities include Phi Mu Alpha, Music Educators National Conference, Sigma Alpha Iota.

Expenses for 1998–99 Application fee: $20. Comprehensive fee: $14,860 includes full-time tuition ($10,440), mandatory fees ($270), and college room and board ($4150). College room only: $1930. Special program-related fees: $75 per per person for applied lesson fee.

Financial Aid Program-specific awards for 1997: 20–40 music scholarships for program majors, music ensemble members ($5500).

Application Procedures Students apply for admission into the professional program by freshman year. Deadline for freshmen and transfers: continuous. Required: high school transcript, college transcript(s) for transfer students, minimum 2.0 high school GPA, interview, audition, SAT I or ACT test scores. Recommended: letter of recommendation. Auditions held continuously on campus; recorded music is permissible as a substitute for live auditions when distance is prohibitive or if a campus visit is impossible and videotaped performances are permissible as a substitute for live auditions when distance is prohibitive or if a campus visit is impossible.

Undergraduate Contact Vice President for Enrollment Management, Central Methodist College, Fayette, Missouri 65248; 816-248-3391 ext. 251.

▼ CENTRAL MICHIGAN UNIVERSITY

Mount Pleasant, Michigan

State-supported, coed. Small town campus. Total enrollment: 24,747. Music program established 1900.

Degrees Bachelor of Music in the areas of performance, music theory/composition; Bachelor of Music Education. Majors and concentrations: music, music education, piano/organ, stringed instruments, voice, wind and percussion instruments. Graduate degrees offered: Master of Music in the areas of music education, performance. Program accredited by NASM.

Enrollment Fall 1997: 344 total; 315 undergraduate, 29 graduate.

Music Student Profile 55% females, 45% males, 8% minorities, 3% international.

Music Faculty 40 total undergraduate and graduate (full-time and part-time). 80% of full-time faculty have terminal degrees. Graduate students do not teach undergraduate courses. Undergraduate student–faculty ratio: 9:1.

Student Life Student groups/activities include Music Educators National Conference Student Chapter, Phi Mu Alpha Sinfonia, music fraternity and sorority.

Expenses for 1997–98 Application fee: $25. State resident tuition: $3066 full-time. Nonresident tuition: $7961 full-time. Mandatory fees: $480 full-time. College room and board: $4320. College room only: $2004. Room and board charges

vary according to board plan and housing facility. Special program-related fees: $40–$70 per semester for private lessons.

Financial Aid Program-specific awards for 1997: 85–125 music scholarships for program majors ($800–$1600).

Application Procedures Students admitted directly into the professional program freshman year. Deadline for freshmen and transfers: May 1. Required: high school transcript, college transcript(s) for transfer students, minimum 2.0 high school GPA, audition, SAT I or ACT test scores. Recommended: minimum 3.0 high school GPA. Auditions held 4 times on campus; recorded music is permissible as a substitute for live auditions for out-of-state applicants and videotaped performances are permissible as a substitute for live auditions for out-of-state applicants.

Web Site http://www.mus.cmich.edu.

Undergraduate Contact Mr. Roger Rehm, Assistant Director, School of Music, Central Michigan University, Mount Pleasant, Michigan 48859; 517-774-3281, fax: 517-774-3766, E-mail address: roger.rehm@cmich.edu.

Graduate Contact Dr. Daniel Steele, Graduate Coordinator, School of Music, Central Michigan University, Mount Pleasant, Michigan 48859; 517-774-3281, fax: 517-774-3766, E-mail address: daniel.steele@cmich.edu.

▼ CENTRAL MISSOURI STATE UNIVERSITY

Warrensburg, Missouri

State-supported, coed. Small town campus. Total enrollment: 10,320. Music program established 1920.

Degrees Bachelor of Music in the areas of instrumental music, jazz/commercial music, piano, piano pedagogy, voice; Bachelor of Music Education in the areas of instrumental music education, vocal music education. Majors and concentrations: commercial music, jazz, music education, piano pedagogy, piano/organ, stringed instruments, voice, wind and percussion instruments. Graduate degrees offered: Master of Arts in the areas of theory and composition, history and literature, music education, performance, piano pedagogy. Program accredited by NASM.

Enrollment Fall 1997: 149 total; 132 undergraduate, 17 graduate.

Music Student Profile 50% females, 50% males, 3% minorities, 2% international.

Music Faculty 22 total undergraduate and graduate (full-time and part-time). 95% of full-time faculty have terminal degrees. Graduate students do not teach undergraduate courses. Undergraduate student–faculty ratio: 8:1.

Student Life Student groups/activities include Phi Mu Alpha Sinfonia, Sigma Alpha Iota, Music Educators National Conference.

Expenses for 1997–98 Application fee: $25. State resident tuition: $2640 full-time. Nonresident tuition: $5280 full-time. College room and board: $4080. Room and board charges vary according to board plan and housing facility.

Financial Aid Program-specific awards for 1997: 10–12 Achievement Awards for program majors ($300), 30–35 Foundation Awards for program majors and minors ($200–$500), 150–175 Service Awards for ensemble performers ($150–$350).

Application Procedures Students admitted directly into the professional program freshman year. Deadline for freshmen and transfers: continuous. Required: high school transcript, college transcript(s) for transfer students, minimum 2.0 high

Central Missouri State University (continued)

school GPA, ACT test score only (minimum combined ACT score of 20). Recommended: letter of recommendation, audition. Auditions held at student's convenience on campus and off campus in St. Louis, MO; Jefferson City, MO; Springfield, MO; recorded music is permissible as a substitute for live auditions if a campus visit is impossible and videotaped performances are permissible as a substitute for live auditions if a campus visit is impossible.

Web Site http://www.cmsu.edu/music.

Undergraduate Contact Director of Admissions, Central Missouri State University, Administration Building 104, Warrensburg, Missouri 64093; 660-543-4290, fax: 660-543-8517.

Graduate Contact Dr. Franklin Fenley, Graduate Coordinator, Department of Music, Central Missouri State University, Warrensburg, Missouri 64093; 660-543-4974, fax: 660-543-8271.

▼ CENTRAL STATE UNIVERSITY

Wilberforce, Ohio

State-supported, coed. Rural campus. Total enrollment: 1,051. Music program established 1947.

Degrees Bachelor of Music in the areas of music education, performance, jazz studies. Cross-registration with Consortium of Ohio State Universities. Program accredited by NASM.

Enrollment Fall 1997: 640 total; 40 undergraduate, 600 non-professional degree.

Music Student Profile 95% minorities, 2% international.

Music Faculty 10 total (full-time and part-time). 60% of full-time faculty have terminal degrees. Graduate students do not teach undergraduate courses.

Student Life Student groups/activities include Phi Mu Alpha, Kappa Kappa Psi.

Expenses for 1997–98 Application fee: $15. State resident tuition: $3318 full-time. Nonresident tuition: $7293 full-time. College room and board: $4695. College room only: $2415.

Financial Aid Program-specific awards for 1997: 60 music scholarships for above-average students with exceptional artistic ability ($300–$6000).

Application Procedures Students admitted directly into the professional program freshman year. Deadline for freshmen and transfers: continuous. Notification date for freshmen and transfers: continuous. Required: high school transcript, college transcript(s) for transfer students, audition, ACT test score only, placement test in theory. Recommended: minimum 2.0 high school GPA. Auditions held 3 times on campus; recorded music is permissible as a substitute for live auditions when distance is prohibitive and videotaped performances are permissible as a substitute for live auditions when distance is prohibitive.

Undergraduate Contact Admissions Department, Central State University, Wilberforce, Ohio 45384; 937-376-6011.

▼ CENTRAL WASHINGTON UNIVERSITY

Ellensburg, Washington

State-supported, coed. Small town campus. Total enrollment: 8,438.

Degrees Bachelor of Music in the areas of music education, performance, composition, conducting, music theory, pedagogy, music business. Majors and concentrations: classical music, guitar, jazz, music, music business, music education, piano/organ, stringed instruments, voice, wind and percussion instruments. Graduate degrees offered: Master of Music in the areas of music education, performance, composition, conducting, music theory, pedagogy. Program accredited by NASM.

Enrollment Fall 1997: 276 total; 264 undergraduate, 12 graduate.

Music Student Profile 50% females, 50% males, 5% minorities, 1% international.

Music Faculty 30 total undergraduate and graduate (full-time and part-time). 75% of full-time faculty have terminal degrees. Graduate students teach a few undergraduate courses. Undergraduate student–faculty ratio: 24:1.

Student Life Student groups/activities include Music Educators National Conference Student Chapter, Pi Kappa Lambda (music honorary fraternity), International Association of Jazz Educators.

Expenses for 1997–98 Application fee: $35. State resident tuition: $2526 full-time. Nonresident tuition: $8961 full-time. Mandatory fees: $300 full-time. Full-time tuition and fees vary according to location. College room and board: $4269. Room and board charges vary according to board plan and housing facility. Special program-related fees: $15 per course for lab fee, $30 per quarter for recital fee.

Financial Aid Program-specific awards for 1997: 12 Music Department Scholarships for program majors ($600).

Application Procedures Students admitted directly into the professional program freshman year. Deadline for freshmen and transfers: May 1. Required: high school transcript, college transcript(s) for transfer students, minimum 2.0 high school GPA, 2 letters of recommendation, audition, SAT I or ACT test scores. Auditions held throughout the school year on campus; recorded music is permissible as a substitute for live auditions when distance is prohibitive and videotaped performances are permissible as a substitute for live auditions when distance is prohibitive.

Undergraduate Contact Dr. Russ Schultz, Chair, Music Department, Central Washington University, 400 East Eighth Avenue, Ellensburg, Washington 98926-7458; 509-963-1216, fax: 509-963-1239, E-mail address: schultz@cwu.edu.

Graduate Contact Dr. Russ Schultz, Chair, Music Department, Central Washington University, 400 East Eighth Avenue, Ellensburg, Washington 98926-7458; 509-963-1216, fax: 509-963-1239, E-mail address: schultz@cwu.edu.

▼ CHAPMAN UNIVERSITY

Orange, California

Independent, coed. Suburban campus. Total enrollment: 3,806.

Degrees Bachelor of Music in the areas of performance, conducting, composition, music therapy; Bachelor of Music Education. Majors and concentrations: composition, conducting, music education, music therapy, piano/organ, stringed instruments, voice, wind and percussion instruments. Program accredited by NASM.

Enrollment Fall 1997: 150 total; 140 undergraduate, 10 non-professional degree.

Music Student Profile 60% females, 40% males, 15% minorities, 10% international.

Music Faculty 44 total (full-time and part-time). 70% of full-time faculty have terminal degrees. Graduate students do not teach undergraduate courses. Undergraduate student–faculty ratio: 4:1.

Student Life Student groups/activities include American Choral Directors Association Student Chapter, American Association of Music Therapy Student Chapter.

Expenses for 1997–98 Application fee: $30. Comprehensive fee: $25,556 includes full-time tuition ($18,510), mandatory fees ($240), and college room and board ($6806). Room and board charges vary according to board plan and housing facility. Special program-related fees: $210 for private lessons.

Financial Aid Program-specific awards for 1997: 75 Talent Awards for talented students ($10,000).

Application Procedures Students admitted directly into the professional program freshman year. Deadline for freshmen and transfers: March 1. Required: essay, high school transcript, college transcript(s) for transfer students, letter of recommendation, audition, SAT I or ACT test scores. Auditions held by appointment on campus; recorded music is permissible as a substitute for live auditions when distance is prohibitive and videotaped performances are permissible as a substitute for live auditions when distance is prohibitive.

Web Site http://www.chapman.edu/music/index.html.

Undergraduate Contact Mr. Michael Drummy, Director of Admissions, Chapman University, Orange, California 92866; 714-997-6711.

▼ CHICAGO MUSICAL COLLEGE

See Roosevelt University

▼ CHRISTOPHER NEWPORT UNIVERSITY

Newport News, Virginia

State-supported, coed. Suburban campus. Total enrollment: 4,878. Music program established 1984.

Degrees Bachelor of Music in the areas of performance, music history and literature, music theory, composition, instrumental music education, choral music education. Majors and concentrations: choral music education, instrumental music education, music history and literature, music theory and composition, piano/organ, stringed instruments, voice, wind and percussion instruments. Mandatory cross-registration with any state university in Virginia. Program accredited by NASM.

Enrollment Fall 1997: 70 total; 65 undergraduate, 5 non-professional degree.

Music Student Profile 60% females, 40% males, 19% minorities.

Music Faculty 27 total (full-time and part-time). 100% of full-time faculty have terminal degrees. Graduate students do not teach undergraduate courses.

Student Life Student groups/activities include Phi Mu Alpha Sinfonia, Sigma Alpha Iota, Music Educators National Conference.

Expenses for 1997–98 Application fee: $25. State resident tuition: $3426 full-time. Nonresident tuition: $8100 full-time. Mandatory fees: $40 full-time. College room and board: $4650. Special program-related fees: $105 per course (1 credit) for applied music fees.

Financial Aid Program-specific awards for 1997: 1 Ed D'Alfonso Scholarship for instrumental majors ($500), 5 Friends of Music Scholarships for program majors ($500), 1 Arts and Communication Scholarship for program majors ($1000), 1 David Reynolds Scholarship for vocal majors ($1000), 1 J. Archie and Wilma Handy Cornette Scholarship for keyboard majors ($400).

Application Procedures Students apply for admission into the professional program by sophomore year. Deadline for freshmen and transfers: August 1. Required: essay, high school transcript, college transcript(s) for transfer students, minimum 2.0 high school GPA, 2 letters of recommendation, interview, audition, SAT I or ACT test scores (minimum combined SAT I score of 920, minimum combined ACT score of 20). Auditions held 4 times on campus; recorded music is permissible as a substitute for live auditions when distance is prohibitive and videotaped performances are permissible as a substitute for live auditions when distance is prohibitive (beyond a 250-mile radius).

Undergraduate Contact Dr. Mark Reimer, Director of Music, Arts and Communication Department, Christopher Newport University, 50 Shoe Lane, Newport News, Virginia 23606; 757-594-7074, fax: 757-594-7389, E-mail address: mreimer@cnu.edu.

▼ CINCINNATI BIBLE COLLEGE AND SEMINARY

Cincinnati, Ohio

Independent, coed. Urban campus. Total enrollment: 915.

Degrees Bachelor of Music in the area of church music. Majors and concentrations: brass, composition, piano/organ, voice. Cross-registration with College of Mount St. Joseph, Miami University, Northern Kentucky University, University of Cincinnati, Xavier University.

Enrollment Fall 1997: 50 undergraduate.

Music Student Profile 38% females, 62% males, 6% minorities, 4% international.

Music Faculty 6 total (full-time and part-time). 33% of full-time faculty have terminal degrees. Graduate students do not teach undergraduate courses. Undergraduate student–faculty ratio: 8:1.

Expenses for 1998–99 Application fee: $35. Comprehensive fee: $9890 includes full-time tuition ($5940), mandatory fees ($250), and college room and board ($3700). College room only: $1825. Room and board charges vary according to board plan. Special program-related fees: $127 for applied fees.

Financial Aid Program-specific awards for 1997: 8 Music Fest Scholarships for high school students ($700).

Application Procedures Students admitted directly into the professional program freshman year. Deadline for freshmen and transfers: August 10. Required: essay, high school transcript, college transcript(s) for transfer students, 3 letters of recommendation, audition, SAT I or ACT test scores (minimum combined SAT I score of 810, minimum combined ACT score of 17). Recommended: interview, minimum 2.5 high school GPA. Auditions held by appointment on campus; recorded music is permissible as a substitute for live auditions if a campus visit is impossible and videotaped performances are permissible as a substitute for live auditions if a campus visit is impossible.

Undergraduate Contact Ms. Jeannine Geans, Administrative Assistant, Music Department, Cincinnati Bible College and

Cincinnati Bible College and Seminary *(continued)*

Seminary, 2700 Glenway Avenue, Cincinnati, Ohio 45204; 513-244-8165, fax: 513-244-8140, E-mail address: jeannine. geans@cincybible.edu.

Division of the Arts: The Leonard Davis Center

▼ CITY COLLEGE OF THE CITY UNIVERSITY OF NEW YORK

New York, New York

State and locally supported, coed. Urban campus. Total enrollment: 12,061.

Degrees Bachelor of Fine Arts in the areas of jazz performance, classical performance. Majors and concentrations: classical music, jazz, music, music technology, performance. Graduate degrees offered: Master of Arts in the areas of musicology, theory, composition, performance (classical and jazz).

Enrollment Fall 1997: 122 total; 90 undergraduate, 32 graduate.

Music Student Profile 40% females, 60% males, 60% minorities, 30% international.

Music Faculty 34 total undergraduate and graduate (full-time and part-time). 90% of full-time faculty have terminal degrees. Graduate students teach a few undergraduate courses. Undergraduate student–faculty ratio: 8:1.

Student Life Student groups/activities include Friends of Music.

Expenses for 1997–98 Application fee: $35. State resident tuition: $3200 full-time. Nonresident tuition: $6800 full-time. Mandatory fees: $109 full-time. Special program-related fees: $200–$400 per semester for off-campus private instruction.

Financial Aid Program-specific awards for 1997: 2 Friar Foundation Awards for BFA applicants passing audition evaluation ($750), 2 Rosalind Joel Scholarships for talented performers ($3000).

Application Procedures Students admitted directly into the professional program freshman year. Deadline for freshmen and transfers: continuous. Required: high school transcript, minimum 3.0 high school GPA, audition for performance majors. Auditions held twice on campus; recorded music is permissible as a substitute for live auditions when distance is prohibitive and videotaped performances are permissible as a substitute for live auditions when distance is prohibitive.

Undergraduate Contact Mr. Allen Sabal, Associate Director of Admissions, City College of the City University of New York, Admissions A100B, 138th Street and Convent Avenue, New York, New York 10031; 212-650-6977, fax: 212-650-5428.

Graduate Contact Dr. John Graziano, Professor, Music Department, City College of the City University of New York, Shepard Hall 72, 138th Street and Convent Avenue, New York, New York 10031; 212-650-7654, E-mail address: jrgcc@cunyvm.cuny.edu.

▼ CLARION UNIVERSITY OF PENNSYLVANIA

Clarion, Pennsylvania

State-supported, coed. Rural campus. Total enrollment: 5,948. Music program established 1965.

Degrees Bachelor of Music in the areas of music performance, music marketing; Bachelor of Science in the area of music education. Program accredited by NASM.

Enrollment Fall 1997: 68 total; all undergraduate.

Music Student Profile 56% females, 44% males, 3% minorities.

Music Faculty 13 total (full-time and part-time). 80% of full-time faculty have terminal degrees. Graduate students do not teach undergraduate courses. Undergraduate student–faculty ratio: 5:1.

Student Life Student groups/activities include Pennsylvania Collegiate Music Educators Association, professional fraternities and sororities.

Expenses for 1997–98 Application fee: $25. State resident tuition: $3468 full-time. Nonresident tuition: $8824 full-time. Mandatory fees: $951 full-time. Full-time tuition and fees vary according to course load. College room and board: $3330. College room only: $1980.

Financial Aid Program-specific awards for 1997: 1 Dr. John A. Mooney Scholarship for upperclassmen ($1000), 1 Mary L. Seifert Scholarship for program majors ($500), 4 Trunzo Memorial Scholarships for freshmen ($700), 1 Presser Foundation Award for program seniors ($2000).

Application Procedures Students admitted directly into the professional program freshman year. Deadline for freshmen and transfers: continuous. Required: high school transcript, college transcript(s) for transfer students, minimum 2.0 high school GPA, audition, SAT I or ACT test scores. Recommended: letter of recommendation, interview. Auditions held 7 times and by appointment on campus; recorded music is permissible as a substitute for live auditions when distance is prohibitive and videotaped performances are permissible as a substitute for live auditions when distance is prohibitive.

Web Site http://wwwartsci.clarion.edu/music/index.htm.

Undergraduate Contact Dr. Lawrence J. Wells, Chair, Music Department, Clarion University of Pennsylvania, 215 Fine Arts, Clarion, Pennsylvania 16214; 814-226-2287, fax: 814-226-2723, E-mail address: wells@mail.clarion.edu.

▼ CLAYTON COLLEGE & STATE UNIVERSITY

Morrow, Georgia

State-supported, coed. Suburban campus. Total enrollment: 4,713. Music program established 1992.

Degrees Bachelor of Music in the areas of performance, composition. Majors and concentrations: composition, early instruments, keyboard, stringed instruments, voice, wind and percussion instruments. Cross-registration with all eighteen schools affiliated with The University Center in Georgia.

Enrollment Fall 1997: 94 total; all undergraduate.

Music Student Profile 55% females, 45% males, 10% minorities, 5% international.

Music Faculty 26 total (full-time and part-time). 86% of full-time faculty have terminal degrees. Graduate students do not teach undergraduate courses.

Student Life Student groups/activities include Music Club, Sigma Alpha Iota.

Expenses for 1997–98 Application fee: $20. State resident tuition: $1680 full-time. Nonresident tuition: $6141 full-time. Mandatory fees: $488 full-time.

Financial Aid Program-specific awards for 1997: 45 Spivey Scholarships for program majors ($2000).

Application Procedures Students apply for admission into the professional program by sophomore year. Deadline for freshmen and transfers: August 25. Notification date for freshmen and transfers: continuous. Required: high school transcript, college transcript(s) for transfer students, minimum 2.0 high school GPA, SAT I or ACT test scores (minimum combined SAT I score of 830). Recommended: audition. Auditions held 3 times and by arrangement on campus; recorded music is permissible as a substitute for live auditions for out-of-state applicants and videotaped performances are permissible as a substitute for live auditions for out-of-state applicants.

Web Site http://www.clayton.edu.

Undergraduate Contact Dr. John Schuster-Craig, Chair, Music Department, Clayton College & State University, 5900 North Lee Street, Morrow, Georgia 30260; 770-961-3609, fax: 770-961-3700, E-mail address: schuster-craig@gg.clayton.edu.

▼ CLEVELAND INSTITUTE OF MUSIC

Cleveland, Ohio

Independent, coed. Urban campus. Total enrollment: 360. Music program established 1920.

Degrees Bachelor of Music in the areas of piano, harpsichord, organ, voice, violin, viola, cello, double bass, harp, classical guitar, flute, oboe, clarinet, bassoon, trumpet, horn, trombone, bass trombone, tuba, percussion, audio recording, composition, music theory, eurythmics. Majors and concentrations: audio recording technology, classical music, composition, eurythmics, music theory, piano/organ, stringed instruments, voice, wind and percussion instruments. Graduate degrees offered: Master of Music in the areas of piano, harpsichord, organ, accompanying, voice, violin, viola, cello, double bass, harp, classical guitar, flute, oboe, clarinet, bassoon, trumpet, horn, trombone, bass trombone, tuba, Suzuki violin pedagogy, percussion, composition, orchestral conducting. Doctor of Musical Arts in the areas of piano, organ, accompanying, voice, violin, viola, cello, double bass, harp, classical guitar, flute, oboe, clarinet, bassoon, trombone, bass trombone, tuba, timpani, percussion, composition, horn, trumpet. Mandatory cross-registration with Case Western Reserve University. Program accredited by NASM.

Enrollment Fall 1997: 360 total; 220 undergraduate, 140 graduate.

Music Student Profile 54% females, 46% males, 12% minorities, 26% international.

Music Faculty 93 total undergraduate and graduate (full-time and part-time). 15% of full-time faculty have terminal degrees. Graduate students do not teach undergraduate courses. Undergraduate student–faculty ratio: 7:1.

Student Life Special housing available for music students.

Expenses for 1997–98 Application fee: $60. One-time mandatory fee: $460. Comprehensive fee: $22,249 includes full-time tuition ($16,365), mandatory fees ($664), and college room and board ($5220). College room only: $3250.

Financial Aid Program-specific awards for 1997: 140 Cleveland Institute of Music Scholarships for program students ($1000–$15,000), 110 Cleveland Institute of Music Loans for program students ($1000–$2000).

Application Procedures Students admitted directly into the professional program freshman year. Deadline for freshmen and transfers: December 1. Notification date for freshmen and transfers: April 1. Required: essay, high school transcript, college transcript(s) for transfer students, 2 letters of recommendation, audition, SAT I or ACT test scores. Recommended: minimum 3.0 high school GPA, interview. Auditions held several times on campus; recorded music is permissible as a substitute for live auditions with approval from the department and videotaped performances are permissible as a substitute for live auditions with approval from the department.

Undergraduate Contact Mr. William Fay, Director of Admission, Cleveland Institute of Music, 11021 East Boulevard, Cleveland, Ohio 44106; 216-795-3107, fax: 216-791-1530, E-mail address: ewf3@po.cwru.edu.

More About the Institute

Program Facilities CIM's main building includes two concert and recital halls, classrooms, teaching studios, practice rooms, a library, a eurhythmics studio, an orchestra library, an opera theater workshop and studio, electronic music studios, a conference room, a performers' lounge, and a music store. Through connection of the entire facility to Case Western Reserve University's fiber-optic computer network, CWRUnet, CIM also provides a Technology Learning Center that enables students to become aware of and accustomed to the ways in which music and technology go hand in hand. The library contains 47,500 books and scores, 110 periodical subscriptions, and an audiovisual collection of 18,000 items. Through the Institute's relationship with CWRU, CIM students have access to additional library resources, especially those at the CWRU Music Department. CWRU holdings include approximately 1 million volumes, 500,000 microforms, and 10,000 current serial subscriptions. A shared on-line system permits access to public catalogs in the CIM library and to OhioLink, a statewide information network. The dormitory, Cutter House, is adjacent to CIM's main building. In addition to the usual amenities, each room is connected to CWRUnet. Adjacent to CIM's main building is the Hazel Road Annex, an additional facility for individual practice, chamber music, rehearsal and coaching, master classes, and class recitals.

Faculty The distinguished faculty includes the principals and many section players of The Cleveland Orchestra, with which CIM has a close relationship. All collegiate-level music instruction is conducted by CIM faculty members and not by teaching assistants; however, there are occasional opportunities for graduate students to teach within CIM's Preparatory and Continuing Education Department. Liberal arts, music education, and music history courses are taught by the faculty of Case Western Reserve University.

▼

The mission of the Cleveland Institute of Music (CIM) is to provide its students with a thoroughly professional, world-class education in instrumental and vocal performance, composition, music theory, and audio technology. The Institute challenges its students to achieve the ultimate within their potential and provides an outstanding setting in which they may prepare for success. Ranked as one of the foremost schools of music in the United States, CIM bases its curriculum on solid, traditional musical values while incorporating substantial liberal arts instruction and new technologies designed to equip students to meet the challenges of the twenty-first century. Graduates routinely attend other leading graduate schools, are winners of major competitions, and occupy important performance and teaching positions throughout the world.

Founded in 1920, the Cleveland Institute of Music maintains its current size of approximately 350 undergradu-

Cleveland Institute of Music (continued)

ate and graduate students and 90 full- and part-time faculty members by controlling enrollment through carefully balanced admission policies. In admitting the optimum rather than an unlimited number of students to each performance area, CIM seeks to provide personal, individual attention for each student and to maximize performance opportunities.

The unusually intense performance environment encourages students to develop multifaceted skills that include solo, chamber, orchestral, and operatic literature. This approach leads students to focus on solo expertise as well as to develop the collaborative abilities necessary for small and large ensemble work. The key is access to faculty members and visiting artists in a challenging but supportive atmosphere of private lessons, master classes, repertoire classes, concerts, and recitals.

Orchestral studies are designed to develop and maintain the discipline and skill necessary to make the smoothest possible transition from school to professional life. Regularly scheduled sectional rehearsals and orchestral repertoire classes are conducted by principals of The Cleveland Orchestra. The Institute's two symphony orchestras present approximately twenty concerts during the academic year, including multiple performances of two fully staged operas. These ensembles also provide a vehicle through which student composers may hear and record readings of their works.

CIM is located in University Circle, a cultural, educational, and scientific research center situated approximately 3 miles east of downtown Cleveland. University Circle comprises more than thirty institutions that together constitute one of the largest diversified cultural complexes in the world. Located within easy walking distance of CIM are Case Western Reserve University, where CIM students have access to all facilities and liberal arts course offerings, and Severance Hall, home of The Cleveland Orchestra, the rehearsals of which are open to CIM students by special arrangement. Also easily accessible are numerous other University Circle institutions, such as the Cleveland Museum of Art, Cleveland Institute of Art, Cleveland Playhouse, Cleveland Museum of Natural History, Western Reserve Historical Society, and Cleveland Botanical Garden.

▼ CLEVELAND STATE UNIVERSITY

Cleveland, Ohio

State-supported, coed. Urban campus. Total enrollment: 15,655.

Degrees Bachelor of Music in the areas of performance, education, composition, history. Majors and concentrations: composition, music education, piano/organ, stringed instruments, voice, wind and percussion instruments. Graduate degrees offered: Master of Music in the areas of performance, education, composition, history. Program accredited by NASM.

Enrollment Fall 1997: 158 total; 110 undergraduate, 48 graduate.

Music Student Profile 43% females, 57% males, 12% minorities, 3% international.

Music Faculty 58 total undergraduate and graduate (full-time and part-time). 100% of full-time faculty have terminal degrees. Graduate students do not teach undergraduate courses. Undergraduate student–faculty ratio: 15:1.

Student Life Student groups/activities include Ohio Collegiate Music Educators Association, Mu Phi Epsilon, American Choral Directors Association.

Expenses for 1997–98 Application fee: $25. State resident tuition: $3456 full-time. Nonresident tuition: $6912 full-time. Mandatory fees: $72 full-time. College room and board: $4410. Room and board charges vary according to board plan. Special program-related fees: $165 for music lessons.

Financial Aid Program-specific awards for 1997: 60 music scholarships for program majors ($1500).

Application Procedures Students admitted directly into the professional program freshman year. Deadline for freshmen and transfers: continuous. Notification date for freshmen and transfers: continuous. Required: high school transcript, college transcript(s) for transfer students, interview, audition. Recommended: minimum 2.0 high school GPA. Auditions held by appointment on campus; recorded music is permissible as a substitute for live auditions when distance is prohibitive and videotaped performances are permissible as a substitute for live auditions when distance is prohibitive.

Undergraduate Contact Mr. Howard Meeker, Chair, Department of Music, Cleveland State University, Euclid Avenue at East 24th Street, Cleveland, Ohio 44115; 216-687-2301, fax: 216-687-9279.

Graduate Contact Dr. Judith Eckelmeyer, Associate Professor, Department of Music, Cleveland State University, Euclid Avenue at East 24th Street, Cleveland, Ohio 44115; 216-687-2035, fax: 216-687-9279.

▼ COE COLLEGE

Cedar Rapids, Iowa

Independent, coed. Urban campus. Total enrollment: 1,318.

Degrees Bachelor of Music in the areas of performance, music education, music theory/composition. Majors and concentrations: classical music, guitar, harpsichord, music, music education, music theory and composition, piano/organ, stringed instruments, voice, wind and percussion instruments. Cross-registration with Mount Mercy College. Program accredited by NASM.

Enrollment Fall 1997: 75 total; 43 undergraduate, 32 non-professional degree.

Music Student Profile 50% females, 50% males, 3% minorities.

Music Faculty 28 total (full-time and part-time). 80% of full-time faculty have terminal degrees. Graduate students do not teach undergraduate courses.

Student Life Student groups/activities include Music Educators National Conference, Mu Phi Epsilon, Phi Mu Alpha.

Expenses for 1997–98 Comprehensive fee: $20,890 includes full-time tuition ($16,170), mandatory fees ($150), and college room and board ($4570). College room only: $2030. Room and board charges vary according to board plan. Special program-related fees: $150–$400 for private lessons.

Financial Aid Program-specific awards for 1997: 3 Bachelor of Music Full Tuition Scholarships for program majors ($13,000), 20–30 music scholarships for program majors ($4500).

Application Procedures Students apply for admission into the professional program by sophomore year. Deadline for freshmen and transfers: March 1. Notification date for freshmen and transfers: March 15. Required: essay, high school transcript, college transcript(s) for transfer students, minimum 2.0 high school GPA, 2 letters of recommendation, SAT I or ACT test scores, minimum 2.75 high school GPA. Recommended: minimum 3.0 high school GPA, interview, audition. Auditions held twice on campus; recorded music is permissible as a substitute for live auditions when distance is prohibitive and videotaped performances are permissible as a substitute for live auditions when distance is prohibitive.

Undergraduate Contact Ms. Sharon K. Stang, Recruiting Coordinator, Music Department, Coe College, 1220 1st Avenue, NE, Cedar Rapids, Iowa 52402; 319-399-8640, fax: 319-399-8830, E-mail address: sstang@coe.edu.

▼ COKER COLLEGE

Hartsville, South Carolina

Independent, coed. Small town campus. Total enrollment: 970. Music program established 1908.

Degrees Bachelor of Music Education. Program accredited by NASM.

Enrollment Fall 1997: 8 total; all undergraduate.

Music Student Profile 70% females, 30% males, 38% minorities.

Music Faculty 6 total (full-time and part-time). 100% of full-time faculty have terminal degrees. Graduate students do not teach undergraduate courses.

Student Life Student groups/activities include Music Educators National Conference, National Association of Teachers of Singing, Music Teachers National Association.

Expenses for 1997–98 Application fee: $15. Comprehensive fee: $17,916 includes full-time tuition ($13,200), mandatory fees ($200), and college room and board ($4516). College room only: $1846. Special program-related fees: $10 per hour for accompanist fee (vocal only).

Financial Aid Program-specific awards for 1997: 5–10 Wilds Music Awards for music majors ($1000), 1 Vaughan Music Award for academically qualified/talented applicants ($1000–$2000), 2 Goodson Music Awards for musically talented performers ($1000–$2000), 1–2 Anna White Hill Scholarships for non-music major/chorale singers ($2500).

Application Procedures Students admitted directly into the professional program freshman year. Deadline for freshmen and transfers: continuous. Required: high school transcript, college transcript(s) for transfer students, minimum 2.0 high school GPA, 2 letters of recommendation, audition, SAT I or ACT test scores (minimum combined SAT I score of 850). Recommended: essay, minimum 3.0 high school GPA, interview, portfolio. Auditions held by arrangement on campus; recorded music is permissible as a substitute for live auditions when distance is prohibitive and videotaped performances are permissible as a substitute for live auditions when distance is prohibitive. Portfolio reviews held by appointment on campus.

Web Site http://www.coker.edu.

Undergraduate Contact Ms. Susannah Whitener, Admissions Counselor, Office of Admissions, Coker College, 300 East College Avenue, Hartsville, South Carolina 29550; 843-383-8050, fax: 843-383-8056.

▼ THE COLLEGE OF NEW JERSEY

Trenton, New Jersey

State-supported, coed. Suburban campus. Total enrollment: 6,780. Music program established 1916.

Degrees Bachelor of Music in the areas of performance, music education. Majors and concentrations: classical music, music, music education, piano/organ, stringed instruments, voice, wind and percussion instruments. Graduate degrees offered: Master of Music Education. Program accredited by NASM, NCATE.

Enrollment Fall 1997: 187 total; 161 undergraduate, 26 graduate.

Music Student Profile 4% minorities, 3% international.

Music Faculty 33 total undergraduate and graduate (full-time and part-time). 84% of full-time faculty have terminal degrees. Graduate students do not teach undergraduate courses. Undergraduate student–faculty ratio: 5:1.

Student Life Student groups/activities include Music Educators National Conference, Delta Omicron, American String Teachers Association.

Expenses for 1997–98 Application fee: $50. State resident tuition: $3791 full-time. Nonresident tuition: $6620 full-time. Mandatory fees: $1052 full-time. College room and board: $5996. Room and board charges vary according to board plan.

Financial Aid Program-specific awards for 1997: 5–10 Talent Scholarships for those demonstrating talent ($750–$1500), 1 Hy Frank Music Scholarship for music education students (non voice/keyboard) ($1500), 1 George and Christine Krauss Music Scholarship for music education students (non voice/keyboard) ($500).

Application Procedures Students admitted directly into the professional program freshman year. Deadline for freshmen and transfers: February 15. Notification date for freshmen: April 1; transfers: April 15. Required: essay, high school transcript, college transcript(s) for transfer students, minimum 2.0 high school GPA, 2 letters of recommendation, interview, audition, SAT I or ACT test scores. Recommended: minimum 3.0 high school GPA. Auditions held 5 times on campus.

Web Site http://www.tcnj.edu/~music.

Undergraduate Contact Dr. Robert E. Parrish, Chairperson, Department of Music, The College of New Jersey, PO Box 7718, Ewing, New Jersey 08628-0718; 609-771-2551, fax: 609-637-5182, E-mail address: rparrish@tcnj.edu.

Graduate Contact Dr. Robert E. Parrish, Graduate Coordinator, Department of Music, The College of New Jersey, PO Box 7718, Ewing, New Jersey 08628-0718; 609-771-2551, fax: 609-637-5182, E-mail address: rparrish@tcnj.edu.

▼ COLLEGE OF NOTRE DAME

Belmont, California

Independent-Roman Catholic, coed. Suburban campus. Total enrollment: 1,782. Music program established 1851.

Degrees Bachelor of Music in the area of performance. Majors and concentrations: harp, piano/organ, stringed instruments, voice, wind and percussion instruments. Graduate degrees offered: Master of Music in the areas of performance, pedagogy. Cross-registration with Trinity College, Emmanuel College. Program accredited by NASM.

Enrollment Fall 1997: 31 total; 21 undergraduate, 10 graduate.

Music Student Profile 66% females, 34% males, 26% international.

Music Faculty 17 total undergraduate and graduate (full-time and part-time). 100% of full-time faculty have terminal degrees. Graduate students teach a few undergraduate courses. Undergraduate student–faculty ratio: 9:1.

Expenses for 1997–98 Application fee: $35. Comprehensive fee: $21,476 includes full-time tuition ($14,976) and college room and board ($6500). Room and board charges vary

College of Notre Dame *(continued)*

according to board plan and housing facility. Special program-related fees: $395–$450 per semester for private applied lessons.

Financial Aid Program-specific awards for 1997: 6 Brooks Memorial Scholarships for those demonstrating need/talent ($1400), 21 Music Assistance Grants for those demonstrating need/talent ($700), 1 La Ratta Scholarship for those demonstrating need/talent ($840), Presidential Scholarships for those demonstrating academic excellence, 1 Sr. Anthony Marie Herzo Scholarship for musically talented students ($2500).

Application Procedures Students admitted directly into the professional program freshman year. Deadline for freshmen: July 1; transfers: August 1. Notification date for freshmen: August 1; transfers: September 1. Required: essay, high school transcript, college transcript(s) for transfer students, letter of recommendation, audition, SAT I or ACT test scores, TOEFL score of 450 for international students. Recommended: minimum 3.0 high school GPA. Auditions held twice on campus and off campus in Carmel, CA; Sacramento, CA; recorded music is permissible as a substitute for live auditions when distance is prohibitive and videotaped performances are permissible as a substitute for live auditions when distance is prohibitive.

Web Site http://www.cndarts.com.

Undergraduate Contact Undergraduate Admissions, College of Notre Dame, 1500 Ralston Avenue, Belmont, California 94002-1997; 650-508-3607, fax: 650-637-0493.

Graduate Contact Graduate Office, College of Notre Dame, 1500 Ralston Avenue, Belmont, California 94002-1997; 650-508-3524, fax: 650-637-0493.

▼ COLLEGE OF SANTA FE

Santa Fe, New Mexico

Independent, coed. Suburban campus. Total enrollment: 1,417. Music program established 1992.

Degrees Bachelor of Fine Arts in the area of contemporary music. Majors and concentrations: composition, music technology, performance.

Enrollment Fall 1997: 57 undergraduate.

Music Student Profile 62% females, 38% males, 27% minorities, 2% international.

Music Faculty 23 total (full-time and part-time). 100% of full-time faculty have terminal degrees. Graduate students do not teach undergraduate courses. Undergraduate student–faculty ratio: 12:1.

Student Life Student groups/activities include Music Club.

Expenses for 1997–98 Application fee: $25. Comprehensive fee: $17,964 includes full-time tuition ($13,000), mandatory fees ($240), and college room and board ($4724). College room only: $2308. Room and board charges vary according to board plan and housing facility. Special program-related fees: $30–$40 per semester for conducting practicum and orchestration, $160 per credit for private lessons, $20–$50 per semester for music technology classes.

Financial Aid Program-specific awards for 1997: 6 Talent Scholarships for freshmen ($1000–$1500).

Application Procedures Students admitted directly into the professional program freshman year. Deadline for freshmen and transfers: continuous. Required: essay, high school transcript, college transcript(s) for transfer students, minimum 2.0 high school GPA, letter of recommendation, interview, audition,

SAT I or ACT test scores (minimum combined SAT I score of 900, minimum combined ACT score of 20). Recommended: minimum 3.0 high school GPA. Auditions held as needed on campus; recorded music is permissible as a substitute for live auditions with approval from the department and videotaped performances are permissible as a substitute for live auditions with approval from the department.

Web Site http://www.csf.edu.

Undergraduate Contact Mr. Steven M. Miller, Director, Contemporary Music Program, College of Santa Fe, 1600 Saint Michael's Drive, Santa Fe, New Mexico 87505; 505-473-6196, fax: 505-473-6127, E-mail address: cmp@unix.nets.com.

More About the College

The Contemporary Music Program at the College of Santa Fe explores music tradition and innovation while exposing today's students to the global languages of music. The program embraces the merits of all musical traditions. Students choose the scope and focus of the musical lineages they wish to explore under intensive and highly personalized instruction. The program requires extensive study of Western theory and common practice, and yet includes much that is not classical and/or non-Western as integral components. What is created is a blend of traditional principles combined, confirmed, enhanced, and updated by contemporary issues, practices, techniques, and tools from around the world.

The College of Santa Fe's Contemporary Music Program, begun in 1991, combines the best elements of music education with a focus on individual expression in a highly personalized and supportive environment. Bachelor of Fine Arts and Bachelor of Arts degrees are offered in contemporary music, with concentrations in performance or music and technology. Course work includes a variety of theoretical studies, practica, individual private lessons, and hands-on projects.

The program's core is the Contemporary Music Forum, a weekly performance and lecture/demonstration event. As a student, faculty, and staff performance venue, the forum serves to model professional situations that students will face in their careers. On a weekly basis, students hear presentations by faculty members and guest speakers and artists, as well as schedule their own performances throughout each semester. The Contemporary Music Program also sponsors the Collaborations Concert Series each semester as a venue for professional music performances. Regional, national, and internationally recognized musicians from all genres are presented, and often lead seminars and workshops, all at no cost for CMP students. Contemporary Music students are integrally involved in the production of these concerts, assisting in the technical, production, and managerial aspects of the series. In addition to the Collaborations series, CMP students work closely with other departments and programs of the College, including the theater and dance divisions of Performing Arts, the Moving Image Arts Department, and the Visual Arts Department. Many CMP students are also involved in on- and off-campus ensembles of various sorts, and participate in the production of an annual all-day music festival, produced entirely by students every spring. In this way CMP students gain first-hand experience in approaching the larger role that music takes in contemporary culture.

▼ THE COLLEGE OF WOOSTER

Wooster, Ohio

Independent, coed. Small town campus. Total enrollment: 1,714.

Degrees Bachelor of Music in the areas of performance, music theory/composition, music history; Bachelor of Music Education in the areas of public school teaching, music therapy. Majors and concentrations: composition, music education, music therapy, piano/organ, stringed instruments, voice, wind and percussion instruments. Mandatory cross-registration with Baldwin-Wallace College (music therapy courses only). Program accredited by NASM.
Enrollment Fall 1997: 43 total; all undergraduate.
Music Student Profile 50% females, 50% males, 5% minorities, 10% international.
Music Faculty 21 total undergraduate (full-time and part-time). 67% of full-time faculty have terminal degrees. Graduate students do not teach undergraduate courses.
Student Life Student groups/activities include Student Music Association.
Expenses for 1997–98 Application fee: $35. Comprehensive fee: $24,300 includes full-time tuition ($19,230) and college room and board ($5070). College room only: $2310. Special program-related fees: $450 per semester for music lessons (if exceed credit limit).
Financial Aid Program-specific awards for 1997: 4–6 Music Performance Scholarships for program majors ($6000).
Application Procedures Students apply for admission into the professional program by sophomore year. Deadline for freshmen: February 15; transfers: June 1. Notification date for freshmen: March 25. Required: essay, high school transcript, college transcript(s) for transfer students, 2 letters of recommendation, SAT I or ACT test scores. Recommended: minimum 2.0 high school GPA, interview.
Undergraduate Contact Carol Wheatley, Dean of Admissions, The College of Wooster, 1101 North Bever Street, Wooster, Ohio 44691; 800-877-9905.

▼ COLORADO CHRISTIAN UNIVERSITY
Lakewood, Colorado

Independent-interdenominational, coed. Suburban campus. Total enrollment: 1,910.
Degrees Bachelor of Music in the area of performance; Bachelor of Music Education in the areas of choral music education, instrumental music education, general music education; Bachelor of Church Music in the area of music ministry. Majors and concentrations: classical music, contemporary Christian music, jazz, music, piano/organ, sound recording technology, stringed instruments, voice, wind and percussion instruments.
Enrollment Fall 1997: 75 total; 45 undergraduate, 30 non-professional degree.
Music Student Profile 67% females, 33% males, 7% minorities, 2% international.
Music Faculty 22 total (full-time and part-time). 66% of full-time faculty have terminal degrees. Graduate students do not teach undergraduate courses.
Student Life Student groups/activities include Music Ministry in local churches, music theater productions, contemporary Christian music ensembles.
Expenses for 1997–98 Application fee: $35. Comprehensive fee: $14,570 includes full-time tuition ($9360), mandatory fees ($650), and college room and board ($4560). College room only: $2960. Room and board charges vary according to board plan. Special program-related fees: $65 per semester for vocal accompanying fee, $35 per semester for instrumental accompanying fee.

Financial Aid Program-specific awards for 1997: 41 music scholarships for program students ($750), 22 Ensemble Scholarships for program students ($300).
Application Procedures Students apply for admission into the professional program by sophomore year. Deadline for freshmen and transfers: continuous. Notification date for freshmen and transfers: continuous. Required: high school transcript, college transcript(s) for transfer students, minimum 2.0 high school GPA, 3 letters of recommendation, audition, SAT I or ACT test scores. Recommended: minimum 3.0 high school GPA, interview, video. Auditions held 3 times on campus; videotaped performances are permissible as a substitute for live auditions if a campus visit is impossible.
Undergraduate Contact Ms. Kim Myrick, Director of Admissions, Colorado Christian University, 180 South Garrison Street, Lakewood, Colorado 80226; 800-44-FAITH, fax: 303-274-7560.

More About the University

A unique, progressive, creative, and distinctively Christian philosophy guides the music program. Integrated offerings combine all aspects of classical, jazz, folk, cross-cultural, popular, and contemporary Christian music with a blend of musical development, Biblical ethics, and Christian living.

The music program provides world-class preparation for life, the opportunity for performance tours, on- and off-campus recording studios, computer-assisted instruction, an emphasis on Christian ministry, and personal attention by an exceptional, creative, and caring faculty.

CCU provides state-of-the-art course offerings such as Computers in Music and Sound Recording Technology balanced with first-rate traditions in Music Theory, Music History, and Music Performance.

The Music Center houses a music information technologies laboratory with Power Macintosh color computers and multi-timbral synthesizers using the latest software for music composition and transcription, as well as a keyboard laboratory with *Roland* full 88-key keyboards.

Annual tours are taken by the larger ensembles. The smaller chamber and jazz ensembles are frequent performers in the Denver area. Membership in ensembles is by audition only. Ensembles include University Choir, University Wind Ensemble, Orchestra and Chamber Ensembles, as well as Mainstream (instrumental jazz ensemble), Profile (vocal jazz ensemble), Music Theatre Ensemble, Tapestry (Praise and Worship), and Chronicle (a Contemporary Christian band).

Majors offered in the School of Music, Theatre, and Arts provide an integrated, life-enriching, well-rounded education. Weekly concerts, recitals, and music convocations provide ample performing and listening opportunities throughout the year. Graduates excel in a wide variety of careers.

▼ COLORADO STATE UNIVERSITY
Fort Collins, Colorado

State-supported, coed. Urban campus. Total enrollment: 22,344. Music program established 1937.
Degrees Bachelor of Music in the areas of music therapy, music education, performance. Majors and concentrations: composition, music, music education, music therapy, piano pedagogy, piano/organ, string pedagogy, stringed instruments, voice, wind and percussion instruments. Graduate

Colorado State University *(continued)*

degrees offered: Master of Music in the areas of conducting, music theory, music history and literature, music therapy, music education, performance. Program accredited by NASM.

Enrollment Fall 1997: 230 total; 193 undergraduate, 27 graduate.

Music Student Profile 57% females, 43% males, 14% minorities, 1% international.

Music Faculty 35 total undergraduate and graduate (full-time and part-time). 90% of full-time faculty have terminal degrees. Graduate students teach a few undergraduate courses.

Student Life Student groups/activities include Music Therapy Student Association, Music Educators National Conference Student Chapter, Phi Mu Alpha Sinfonia. Special housing available for music students.

Expenses for 1997–98 Application fee: $30. State resident tuition: $2258 full-time. Nonresident tuition: $9480 full-time. Mandatory fees: $825 full-time. Full-time tuition and fees vary according to program. College room and board: $5050. Room and board charges vary according to board plan and housing facility. Special program-related fees: $17 for practice room fee, $25 for instrument fee, $5 for locker fee.

Financial Aid Program-specific awards for 1997: 1 Walter Charles Scholarship for cello majors ($1000), 1 Wendel Diebel Scholarship for pianists ($1000), 2 Sallee Performance Awards for program majors ($1500), Creative and Performing Arts Awards for program majors ($250–$1500).

Application Procedures Students apply for admission into the professional program by freshman year. Deadline for freshmen and transfers: July 1. Required: essay, high school transcript, college transcript(s) for transfer students, audition, SAT I or ACT test scores. Recommended: minimum 3.0 high school GPA, 2 letters of recommendation. Auditions held 4 times on campus; recorded music is permissible as a substitute for live auditions when distance is prohibitive or scheduling is difficult and videotaped performances are permissible as a substitute for live auditions when distance is prohibitive or scheduling is difficult.

Web Site http://www.colostate.edu/Depts/Music/.

Undergraduate Contact Ms. Paulette Rudolf, Administrative Assistant, Department of Music, Theatre, and Dance, Colorado State University, Fort Collins, Colorado 80523-1778; 970-491-5529, fax: 970-491-7541.

Graduate Contact Mr. Michael H. Thaut, Director of Graduate Studies, Department of Music, Theatre, and Dance, Colorado State University, Fort Collins, Colorado 80523-1778; 970-491-7384, fax: 970-491-7541, E-mail address: mthaut@lamar.colostate.edu.

▼ COLUMBIA COLLEGE

Columbia, South Carolina

Independent-United Methodist, women only. Suburban campus. Total enrollment: 1,368.

Degrees Bachelor of Music in the areas of music education, sacred music, piano/voice pedagogy, performance. Majors and concentrations: music education, piano/organ, sacred music, stringed instruments, voice, wind and percussion instruments. Program accredited by NASM.

Enrollment Fall 1997: 75 total; 40 undergraduate, 35 non-professional degree.

Music Student Profile 100% females.

Music Faculty 27 total (full-time and part-time). 63% of full-time faculty have terminal degrees. Graduate students do not teach undergraduate courses.

Student Life Student groups/activities include Music Educators National Conference Student Chapter.

Expenses for 1997–98 Application fee: $20. Comprehensive fee: $16,450 includes full-time tuition ($12,050), mandatory fees ($100), and college room and board ($4300). Room and board charges vary according to board plan. Special program-related fees: $100 per semester for private lessons for music majors.

Financial Aid Program-specific awards for 1997: 40 Talent Scholarships for music majors ($2000).

Application Procedures Students admitted directly into the professional program freshman year. Deadline for freshmen and transfers: continuous. Required: high school transcript, 3 letters of recommendation, audition, SAT I or ACT test scores. Auditions held 3 times and by appointment on campus; recorded music is permissible as a substitute for live auditions when distance is prohibitive and videotaped performances are permissible as a substitute for live auditions when distance is prohibitive.

Web Site http://www.colacoll.edu.

Undergraduate Contact Dr. James Caldwell, Chair, Music Department, Columbia College, 1301 Columbia College Drive, Columbia, South Carolina 29203; 803-786-3810.

▼ COLUMBUS STATE UNIVERSITY

Columbus, Georgia

State-supported, coed. Suburban campus. Total enrollment: 5,405. Music program established 1969.

Degrees Bachelor of Music in the areas of performance, piano pedagogy, music education. Majors and concentrations: music education, piano pedagogy, piano/organ, stringed instruments, voice, wind and percussion instruments. Graduate degrees offered: Master of Music in the areas of music education, piano pedagogy. Program accredited by NASM, NCATE.

Enrollment Fall 1997: 126 total; 109 undergraduate, 10 graduate, 7 non-professional degree.

Music Student Profile 58% females, 27% minorities, 18% international.

Music Faculty 32 total undergraduate and graduate (full-time and part-time). 43% of full-time faculty have terminal degrees. Graduate students do not teach undergraduate courses. Undergraduate student–faculty ratio: 4:1.

Student Life Student groups/activities include Music Educators National Conference Student Chapter, Mu Phi Epsilon, Pi Kappa Lambda.

Expenses for 1997–98 Application fee: $20. State resident tuition: $1941 full-time. Nonresident tuition: $6402 full-time. Mandatory fees: $522 full-time. College room and board: $3825. Room and board charges vary according to board plan, gender, and housing facility. Special program-related fees: $30–$55 per quarter for lessons.

Financial Aid Program-specific awards for 1997: 100 Patrons of Music Awards ($2000).

Application Procedures Students apply for admission into the professional program by sophomore year. Deadline for freshmen and transfers: August 5. Required: high school transcript, college transcript(s) for transfer students, interview, audition, SAT I or ACT test scores (minimum combined

SAT I score of 830, minimum combined ACT score of 34), college preparatory curriculum. Recommended: minimum 3.0 high school GPA, 2 letters of recommendation. Auditions held 3 times and by appointment on campus; recorded music is permissible as a substitute for live auditions for out-of-state applicants and videotaped performances are permissible as a substitute for live auditions for out-of-state applicants.

Web Site http://www.colstate.edu/coa/music.

Undergraduate Contact Ms. Diane E. Andrae, Admissions Secretary for Music, Schwob Department of Music, Columbus State University, 4225 University Avenue, Columbus, Georgia 31907-5645; 706-568-2049, fax: 706-568-2409, E-mail address: andrae_diane@colstate.edu.

Graduate Contact Dr. William J. Bullock, Graduate Studies Coordinator, Schwob Department of Music, Columbus State University, 4225 University Avenue, Columbus, Georgia 31907-5645; 706-568-2049, fax: 706-568-2409, E-mail address: bullock_william@colstate.edu.

▼ CONCORDIA COLLEGE
Moorhead, Minnesota

Independent, coed. Suburban campus. Total enrollment: 2,931. Music program established 1932.

Degrees Bachelor of Music in the areas of music education, performance, music theory. Majors and concentrations: music education, music theory, piano/organ, stringed instruments, voice, wind and percussion instruments. Cross-registration with Moorhead State University, North Dakota State University. Program accredited by NASM.

Enrollment Fall 1997: 175 total; all undergraduate.

Music Student Profile 58% females, 42% males, 3% minorities, 2% international.

Music Faculty 38 total (full-time and part-time). 56% of full-time faculty have terminal degrees. Graduate students do not teach undergraduate courses. Undergraduate student–faculty ratio: 5:1.

Student Life Student groups/activities include Music Educators National Conference Student Chapter, American Choral Directors Association Student Chapter.

Expenses for 1998–99 Application fee: $20. Comprehensive fee: $16,300 includes full-time tuition ($12,550), mandatory fees ($105), and college room and board ($3645). College room only: $1600. Room and board charges vary according to board plan. Special program-related fees: $225 per credit for private lessons.

Financial Aid Program-specific awards for 1997: 30 Music Performance Scholarships for freshmen ($9000).

Application Procedures Students admitted directly into the professional program freshman year. Deadline for freshmen and transfers: continuous. Notification date for freshmen and transfers: September 1. Required: high school transcript, minimum 2.0 high school GPA, SAT I or ACT test scores, proficiency exams for transfer students.

Web Site http://www1.cord.edu/dept/music/frontpage.html.

Undergraduate Contact Mr. Lee E. Johnson, Director of Admissions, Concordia College, 901 8th Street South, Moorhead, Minnesota 56562; 218-299-3004.

▼ CONCORDIA COLLEGE
Bronxville, New York

Independent-Lutheran, coed. Suburban campus. Total enrollment: 599.

Degrees Bachelor of Music in the area of church music.

Enrollment Fall 1997: 28 total; 3 undergraduate, 25 non-professional degree.

Music Faculty 5 total (full-time and part-time). 100% of full-time faculty have terminal degrees. Graduate students do not teach undergraduate courses. Undergraduate student–faculty ratio: 5:1.

Expenses for 1997–98 Comprehensive fee: $17,540 includes full-time tuition ($11,990) and college room and board ($5550). College room only: $2550. Special program-related fees: $30 per semester for practice fees, $320 per semester for applied music fee.

Application Procedures Students admitted directly into the professional program freshman year. Deadline for freshmen and transfers: continuous. Required: essay, high school transcript, college transcript(s) for transfer students, interview, audition. Recommended: minimum 2.0 high school GPA, SAT I or ACT test scores. Auditions held by appointment on campus; recorded music is permissible as a substitute for live auditions when distance is prohibitive and videotaped performances are permissible as a substitute for live auditions when distance is prohibitive.

Undergraduate Contact Mr. Tom Weede, Dean of Enrollment Management, Admissions Office, Concordia College, South Building, Bronxville, New York 10708; 914-337-9300 ext. 2150, E-mail address: tdw@concordia-ny.edu.

▼ CONCORDIA UNIVERSITY
Montréal, PQ, Canada

Province-supported, coed. Urban campus. Total enrollment: 29,271. Music program established 1975.

Degrees Bachelor of Fine Arts in the areas of music, jazz studies, music performance studies, music theory/composition, selected music studies, integrative music studies. Cross-registration with any university in Quebec.

Enrollment Fall 1997: 261 undergraduate.

Music Student Profile 4% international.

Music Faculty 55 total (full-time and part-time). Graduate students teach a few undergraduate courses. Undergraduate student–faculty ratio: 5:1.

Expenses for 1998–99 Application fee: $40 Canadian dollars. Tuition, fee, and room only charges are reported in Canadian dollars. Province resident tuition: $1668 full-time. Canadian resident tuition: $2868 full-time. Mandatory fees: $618 full-time. College room only: $2290. Room charges vary according to housing facility. International student tuition: $8268 full-time. Special program-related fees: $190 per 3 credits for private studies.

Application Procedures Students admitted directly into the professional program freshman year. Deadline for freshmen and transfers: March 1. Notification date for freshmen and transfers: June 15. Required: high school transcript, college transcript(s) for transfer students, audition. Auditions held 3 times in April, May, and June on campus; recorded music is permissible as a substitute for live auditions if a campus visit is impossible.

Web Site http://www-fofa.concordia.ca/music/.

Concordia University *(continued)*

Undergraduate Contact Ms. Jolanta Manowska, Communications Assistant, Office of the Registrar, Concordia University, 1455 de Maisonneuve Boulevard West, LB700, Montreal, PQ H3G 1M8; 514-848-2668, fax: 514-848-2837, E-mail address: admreg@alcor.concordia.ca.

▼ CONVERSE COLLEGE

Spartanburg, South Carolina

Independent, women only. Urban campus. Total enrollment: 1,474. Music program established 1889.

Degrees Bachelor of Music in the areas of performance (vocal, instrumental), music theory, composition, music history, music education, piano pedagogy. Majors and concentrations: music education, music history, music theory and composition, piano pedagogy, piano/organ, stringed instruments, voice, wind and percussion instruments. Graduate degrees offered: Master of Music in the areas of performance (vocal, instrumental), music theory, composition, piano pedagogy, music education, music history. Cross-registration with Wofford College. Program accredited by NASM.

Enrollment Fall 1997: 109 total; 73 undergraduate, 14 graduate, 22 non-professional degree.

Music Student Profile 95% females, 5% males, 10% minorities, 2% international.

Music Faculty 27 total undergraduate and graduate (full-time and part-time). 67% of full-time faculty have terminal degrees. Graduate students teach a few undergraduate courses. Undergraduate student–faculty ratio: 6:1.

Student Life Student groups/activities include Delta Omicron, Pi Kappa Lambda.

Expenses for 1997–98 Application fee: $35. Comprehensive fee: $18,525 includes full-time tuition ($14,445) and college room and board ($4080). Special program-related fees: $500 per year for private lessons .

Financial Aid Program-specific awards for 1997: Music Dean's Honor Scholarships ($1000–$13,000).

Application Procedures Students admitted directly into the professional program freshman year. Deadline for freshmen and transfers: continuous. Notification date for freshmen and transfers: September 1. Required: high school transcript, college transcript(s) for transfer students, minimum 2.0 high school GPA, letter of recommendation, audition, SAT I or ACT test scores. Recommended: minimum 3.0 high school GPA, interview. Auditions held 3 times or by appointment on campus and off campus in various cities in the Southeast; recorded music is permissible as a substitute for live auditions when distance is prohibitive and videotaped performances are permissible as a substitute for live auditions when distance is prohibitive.

Undergraduate Contact Ms. Alice Eanes, Assistant to the Dean, School of Music, Converse College, 580 East Main, Spartanburg, South Carolina 29302-0006; 864-596-9166, fax: 864-596-9167, E-mail address: alice.eanes@converse.edu.

Graduate Contact Ms. Alice Eanes, Assistant to the Dean, School of Music, Converse College, 580 East Main, Spartanburg, South Carolina 29302-0006; 864-596-9166, fax: 864-596-9167, E-mail address: alice.eanes@converse.edu.

▼ CORNELL COLLEGE

Mount Vernon, Iowa

Independent-Methodist, coed. Small town campus. Total enrollment: 1,079. Music program established 1853.

Degrees Bachelor of Music in the area of performance; Bachelor of Music Education. Program accredited by NASM.

Enrollment Fall 1997: 40 total; 30 undergraduate, 10 non-professional degree.

Music Student Profile 60% females, 40% males, 10% minorities.

Music Faculty 21 total (full-time and part-time). 100% of full-time faculty have terminal degrees. Graduate students teach a few undergraduate courses. Undergraduate student–faculty ratio: 5:1.

Expenses for 1997–98 Application fee: $25. Comprehensive fee: $22,690 includes full-time tuition ($17,700), mandatory fees ($140), and college room and board ($4850). College room only: $2220. Full-time tuition and fees vary according to reciprocity agreements. Room and board charges vary according to board plan.

Financial Aid Program-specific awards for 1997: 10 Trustees Music Scholar Awards for music majors and minors ($15,000).

Application Procedures Students apply for admission into the professional program by sophomore year. Deadline for freshmen and transfers: continuous. Required: essay, high school transcript, letter of recommendation, audition, SAT I or ACT test scores. Recommended: interview. Auditions held twice and by appointment on campus; recorded music is permissible as a substitute for live auditions if a campus visit is impossible and videotaped performances are permissible as a substitute for live auditions if a campus visit is impossible.

Web Site http://www.cornell-iowa.edu/.

Undergraduate Contact Dean of Admissions, Cornell College, 600 First Street West, Mount Vernon, Iowa 52314-1098; 319-895-4477.

▼ CORNERSTONE COLLEGE

Grand Rapids, Michigan

Independent-Baptist, coed. Suburban campus. Total enrollment: 1,160. Music program established 1945.

Degrees Bachelor of Music in the areas of performance, church music, composition, electronic music; Bachelor of Music Education in the areas of vocal music education, instrumental music education. Majors and concentrations: church music, composition, electronic music, music education, piano/organ, voice, wind and percussion instruments. Cross-registration with Calvin College. Program accredited by NASM.

Enrollment Fall 1997: 181 total; 81 undergraduate, 100 non-professional degree.

Music Student Profile 60% females, 40% males, 2% minorities, 1% international.

Music Faculty 32 total undergraduate (full-time and part-time). 85% of full-time faculty have terminal degrees. Graduate students do not teach undergraduate courses.

Expenses for 1998–99 Application fee: $25. Comprehensive fee: $14,418 includes full-time tuition ($9376), mandatory fees ($650), and college room and board ($4392). College room only: $2116. Special program-related fees: $15–$35 per semester for practice room fee, ensemble fee.

Financial Aid Program-specific awards for 1997: 89 music scholarships for talented instrumentalists and vocalists ($750–$3000).

Application Procedures Students apply for admission into the professional program by sophomore year. Deadline for freshmen and transfers: continuous. Required: high school transcript, college transcript(s) for transfer students, minimum 2.0 high school GPA, letter of recommendation, interview, audition, ACT test score only (minimum combined ACT score of 18). Recommended: essay, minimum 3.0 high school GPA, portfolio. Auditions held continuously on campus; recorded music is permissible as a substitute for live auditions when distance is prohibitive and videotaped performances are permissible as a substitute for live auditions when distance is prohibitive. Portfolio reviews held continuously on campus.

Web Site http://www.cornerstone.edu.

Undergraduate Contact Dr. W. Bruce Curlette, Chair, Division of Fine Arts, Cornerstone College, 1001 East Beltline Avenue, NE, Grand Rapids, Michigan 49505; 616-222-1522, E-mail address: bcurlette@cornerstone.edu.

▼ CORNISH COLLEGE OF THE ARTS

Seattle, Washington

Independent, coed. Urban campus. Total enrollment: 621. Music program established 1914.

Degrees Bachelor of Music in the areas of jazz performance, classical and new music performance, composition. Majors and concentrations: classical music, composition, electronic music, instrumental music, jazz, new genre, voice, world music.

Enrollment Fall 1997: 101 total; 95 undergraduate, 6 non-professional degree.

Music Student Profile 12% minorities.

Music Faculty 36 total (full-time and part-time). 11% of full-time faculty have terminal degrees. Graduate students do not teach undergraduate courses. Undergraduate student–faculty ratio: 4:1.

Expenses for 1997–98 Application fee: $35. Tuition: $11,540 full-time. Mandatory fees: $118 full-time. Special program-related fees: $120–$220 for private lessons.

Financial Aid Program-specific awards for 1997: Presidential Scholarships for continuing students ($600–$4000), departmental scholarships for program students ($600–$4000), Nellie Scholarships for new students ($600–$4000), 1–6 Kreielsheimer Scholarships for new students from Washington, Oregon, or Alaska ($16,000).

Application Procedures Students admitted directly into the professional program freshman year. Deadline for freshmen and transfers: August 15. Required: essay, high school transcript, college transcript(s) for transfer students, minimum 2.0 high school GPA, audition. Recommended: letter of recommendation, interview. Auditions held 7 times on campus and off campus in San Francisco, CA; Los Angeles, CA; recorded music is permissible as a substitute for live auditions when distance is prohibitive.

Web Site http://www.cornish.edu.

Undergraduate Contact Ms. Jane Buckman, Director of Admissions, Cornish College of the Arts, 710 East Roy Street, Seattle, Washington 98102; 800-726-ARTS, fax: 206-720-1011.

More About the College

Cornish College of the Arts is an exciting place for musicians who want to play a role in shaping the music of the twenty-first century. Students can pursue a Bachelor of Music degree with a major emphasis in jazz vocal or instrumental performance, classical/new music vocal performance, instrumental performance, or composition, with additional emphases in world music and electro-acoustic music. The Music Department is alive with fresh musical influences from around the world, which build on a solid understanding of tradition and past masters.

The Music Department provides individualized instruction and a flexible curriculum that encourages students to become fluent in a variety of musical dialects. Students work with a renowned faculty of professional musicians who are leaders in their fields on a regional, national, and international level. The Music Department also maintains an active visiting artist program, which in recent years has brought George Cables, Larry Coryell, Rinde Eckert, Lou Harrison, Tania León, Bud Shank, Joseph Schwantner, Jane Ira Bloom, Jin Hi Kim, Jerry Granelli, and Chinary Ung.

Each year students are featured in more than 100 music performances. These include twice-weekly noon concerts, junior and senior recitals, an annual opera, and evening performances for ensemble classes and student composers.

Cornish College music facilities include twelve teaching studios, five classrooms with grand pianos, and an electronic music studio. Most Music Department performances take place in the 230-seat PONCHO Concert hall. Eight additional practice rooms with pianos and a state-of-the-art electronic piano lab are also available. A percussion building houses the gamelan, percussion instruments, the Chinese instrument collection, and a grand piano.

▼ COVENANT COLLEGE

Lookout Mountain, Georgia

Independent, coed. Suburban campus. Total enrollment: 945.

Degrees Bachelor of Music in the area of performance. Majors and concentrations: piano/organ, stringed instruments, voice, wind and percussion instruments. Cross-registration with University of Tennessee at Chattanooga.

Enrollment Fall 1997: 25 total; 7 undergraduate, 18 non-professional degree.

Music Student Profile 50% females, 50% males.

Music Faculty 16 total (full-time and part-time). 66% of full-time faculty have terminal degrees. Graduate students do not teach undergraduate courses. Undergraduate student–faculty ratio: 7:1.

Student Life Student groups/activities include Madrigal Singers Group, Brass Choir, Symphonette.

Expenses for 1997–98 Application fee: $20. Comprehensive fee: $17,020 includes full-time tuition ($12,550), mandatory fees ($350), and college room and board ($4120). Special program-related fees: $60–$120 per semester for lessons.

Financial Aid Program-specific awards for 1997: 4 Keyboard Scholarships for musically qualified students ($825), 34 Instrument Scholarships for musically qualified students ($875), 35 Vocal Scholarships for musically qualified students ($791).

Application Procedures Deadline for freshmen and transfers: continuous. Required: essay, high school transcript, 2 letters of recommendation, interview, audition, SAT I or ACT test

Covenant College (*continued*)

scores, minimum 2.5 high school GPA. Auditions held by appointment on campus; recorded music is permissible as a substitute for live auditions when distance is prohibitive and videotaped performances are permissible as a substitute for live auditions when distance is prohibitive.

Undergraduate Contact Admissions Office, Covenant College, Lookout Mountain, Georgia 30750; 706-820-1560, fax: 706-820-2165.

State University of New York College at Potsdam

▼ CRANE SCHOOL OF MUSIC

Potsdam, New York

State-supported, coed. Small town campus. Total enrollment: 4,038. Music program established 1886.

Degrees Bachelor of Music in the areas of music education, musical studies, performance, business of music. Majors and concentrations: classical music, early music, harp, jazz, keyboard, music, music and business, music education, music theater, opera, piano pedagogy, piano/organ, special music education, stringed instruments, voice, wind and percussion instruments. Graduate degrees offered: Master of Music in the areas of music education, performance, composition, music theory, music history. Cross-registration with State University of New York College of Technology at Canton, St. Lawrence University, Clarkson University. Program accredited by NASM.

Enrollment Fall 1997: 569 undergraduate, 20 graduate.

Music Student Profile 42% females, 58% males, 8% minorities, 1% international.

Music Faculty 60 total undergraduate and graduate (full-time and part-time). 95% of full-time faculty have terminal degrees. Graduate students do not teach undergraduate courses. Undergraduate student–faculty ratio: 12:1.

Student Life Student groups/activities include Music Educators National Conference, Phi Mu Alpha Sinfonia, Sigma Alpha Iota.

Expenses for 1997–98 Application fee: $30. State resident tuition: $3400 full-time. Nonresident tuition: $8300 full-time. Mandatory fees: $499 full-time. College room and board: $4900. College room only: $3000. Room and board charges vary according to board plan and housing facility. Special program-related fees: $183 for instrument maintenance, $60 for community performance series fee.

Financial Aid Program-specific awards for 1997: 100 Endowed Scholarships for program students ($851).

Application Procedures Students admitted directly into the professional program freshman year. Deadline for freshmen and transfers: continuous. Required: high school transcript, college transcript(s) for transfer students, letter of recommendation, interview, audition, SAT I or ACT test scores, 80% average out of 100% in high school. Auditions held 10 times on campus and off campus in Mt. Sinai, NY; Rochester, NY; Buffalo, NY; Albany, NY; recorded music is permissible as a substitute for live auditions for out-of-state and international applicants and videotaped performances are permissible as a substitute for live auditions for out-of-state and international applicants.

Undergraduate Contact Ms. Karen O'Brien, Interim Director, Admissions Office, State University of New York College at Potsdam, Potsdam, New York 13676; 315-267-2180.

Graduate Contact Mr. James Madeja, Graduate Advisor, The Crane School of Music, State University of New York College at Potsdam, Potsdam, New York 13676; 315-267-2418, fax: 315-267-2413.

More About the School

Program Facilities The five-building music complex includes a 1,400-seat concert hall, 450-seat music theater, 130-seat lecture/recital hall, expansive music library, rehearsal halls, classrooms, electronic music studio, MIE lab, fully equipped computer lab, and seventy practice rooms. The library, classrooms, and studios are sound equipped, and the School has available more than 1,500 instruments, including 150 pianos. All equipment is maintained by a full-time professional staff.

Faculty, Visiting Artists, and Alumni The School of Music's full-time staff of artist-teachers are all active performers as well as leaders in the field of music education. Recent visiting artists include Arturo Sandoval, Richard Stolzman, the Canadian Brass and Empire Brass Quintets, Emanuel Ax, David Burge, Bobbie McFerrin, the Beaux Arts Trio, Gregg Smith Singers, Juilliard String Quartet, Mark O'Connor, Tokyo String Quartet, and Claude Frank. It is estimated that more than 50 percent of New York State music teachers are Crane alumni; graduates perform across the country from regional ensembles to the stage at the Metropolitan Opera and teach nationwide.

Student Performance Opportunities The Crane School of Music at SUNY College at Potsdam has more than fifty performing ensembles that present more than 250 concerts each year, including Orchestra, String Orchestra, Opera Orchestra, Wind Ensemble, two bands, three jazz ensembles, six choirs, Opera/Music Theater, Opera Ensemble, like-ensembles, and woodwind, brass, and string chamber ensembles.

Special Programs Degree minors and concentrations include business of music, piano pedagogy, jazz and commercial music, and special education. Double majors include music education and performance, music education and elementary education, and music education and secondary education. Cross-registration is available with Clarkson University, St. Lawrence University, and SUNY Canton. Study abroad includes sites in England, Germany, and Australia.

▼ CROWN COLLEGE

St. Bonifacius, Minnesota

Independent, coed. Suburban campus. Total enrollment: 713.

Degrees Bachelor of Music Education in the areas of vocal music education, instrumental music education; Bachelor of Church Music. Majors and concentrations: conducting, music, music education, piano/organ, voice. Graduate degrees offered: Master of Arts in the area of ethnomusicology.

Enrollment Fall 1997: 31 total; 22 undergraduate, 7 graduate, 2 non-professional degree.

Music Student Profile 64% females, 36% males, 8% minorities, 10% international.

Music Faculty 25 total undergraduate and graduate (full-time and part-time). 66% of full-time faculty have terminal degrees. Graduate students do not teach undergraduate courses.

Student Life Student groups/activities include American Choral Directors Association Student Chapter, Music Educators National Conference Student Chapter, Minnesota Music Educators Association Student Chapter. Special housing available for music students.

Expenses for 1997–98 Application fee: $35. Comprehensive fee: $13,355 includes full-time tuition ($8640), mandatory fees ($695), and college room and board ($4020). College room only: $1996. Special program-related fees: $25 per semester for practice room rental, $50 per semester for music computer center fee, $15 per course for concert tickets for classes, $15 per semester for printed musical scores.

Financial Aid Program-specific awards for 1997: 130 Music Participation Grants for music performers ($200–$1000), 12 scholarships for program majors ($200–$4000).

Application Procedures Students apply for admission into the professional program by sophomore year. Deadline for freshmen and transfers: continuous. Notification date for freshmen and transfers: continuous. Required: high school transcript, minimum 2.0 high school GPA, 4 letters of recommendation, interview, audition for scholarship consideration. Recommended: minimum 3.0 high school GPA, audition. Auditions held as needed on campus; recorded music is permissible as a substitute for live auditions when distance is prohibitive and videotaped performances are permissible as a substitute for live auditions when distance is prohibitive.

Undergraduate Contact Ms. Janelle Wood, Director of Admissions, Admissions Department, Crown College, 6425 County Road 30, St. Bonifacius, Minnesota 55375; 612-446-4142, fax: 612-446-4149.

Graduate Contact Dr. John Benham, Director of Music in World Cultures, Music Department, Crown College, 6425 County Road 30, St. Bonifacius, Minnesota 55375; 612-446-4246, fax: 612-446-4250, E-mail address: benhamj@gw.crown.edu.

▼ CULVER-STOCKTON COLLEGE

Canton, Missouri

Independent, coed. Rural campus. Total enrollment: 994. Music program established 1980.

Degrees Bachelor of Music Education in the areas of vocal music education, instrumental and vocal music education, instrumental music education. Majors and concentrations: music, music education, piano/organ, voice, wind and percussion instruments.

Enrollment Fall 1997: 49 total; 43 undergraduate, 6 nonprofessional degree.

Music Student Profile 60% females, 40% males, 5% minorities, 2% international.

Music Faculty 10 total (full-time and part-time). 80% of full-time faculty have terminal degrees. Graduate students do not teach undergraduate courses.

Student Life Student groups/activities include Music Educators National Conference, Sigma Phi Zeta (honorary music fraternity).

Expenses for 1997–98 Comprehensive fee: $13,430 includes full-time tuition ($9200) and college room and board ($4230). College room only: $1930.

Financial Aid Program-specific awards for 1997: 130 Music Grants for program majors and non-majors ($500–$2000).

Application Procedures Students admitted directly into the professional program freshman year. Deadline for freshmen: May 1; transfers: June 1. Notification date for freshmen: June

1; transfers: July 1. Required: high school transcript, college transcript(s) for transfer students, minimum 2.0 high school GPA, interview, audition, SAT I or ACT test scores. Auditions held as needed on campus; recorded music is permissible as a substitute for live auditions if a campus visit is impossible and videotaped performances are permissible as a substitute for live auditions if a campus visit is impossible.

Undergraduate Contact Mr. Terry Taylor, Director of Admissions, Culver-Stockton College, #1 College Hill, Canton, Missouri 63435-1299; 217-231-6466, fax: 217-231-6611.

▼ CUMBERLAND COLLEGE

Williamsburg, Kentucky

Independent-Kentucky Baptist, coed. Rural campus. Total enrollment: 1,698. Music program established 1968.

Degrees Bachelor of Music in the areas of music education, church music. Majors and concentrations: instrumental music, piano, vocal music.

Enrollment Fall 1997: 63 total; 51 undergraduate, 12 nonprofessional degree.

Music Student Profile 2% minorities, 2% international.

Music Faculty 12 total (full-time and part-time). 50% of full-time faculty have terminal degrees. Graduate students do not teach undergraduate courses.

Student Life Student groups/activities include Collegiate Music Educators National Conference, American Choral Directors Association.

Expenses for 1997–98 Application fee: $25. Comprehensive fee: $12,206 includes full-time tuition ($8398), mandatory fees ($32), and college room and board ($3776). Special program-related fees: $75 per semester for applied lesson fee, $5 per semester for locker rental, $50 for instrument maintenance.

Financial Aid Program-specific awards for 1997: 10–15 music scholarships for program majors ($400–$1300).

Application Procedures Students admitted directly into the professional program freshman year. Deadline for freshmen and transfers: continuous. Required: essay, high school transcript, college transcript(s) for transfer students, minimum 2.0 high school GPA, 3 letters of recommendation, SAT I or ACT test scores. Recommended: interview, audition. Auditions held continuously on campus and off campus in Louisville, KY; recorded music is permissible as a substitute for live auditions when distance is prohibitive and videotaped performances are permissible as a substitute for live auditions when distance is prohibitive.

Undergraduate Contact Dr. Jeff Smoak, Chair, Music Department, Cumberland College, 7525 College Station Drive, Williamsburg, Kentucky 40769; 606-539-4332, fax: 606-539-4317, E-mail address: jsmoak@cc.cumber.edu.

▼ THE CURTIS INSTITUTE OF MUSIC

Philadelphia, Pennsylvania

Independent, coed. Urban campus. Total enrollment: 162. Music program established 1924.

Degrees Bachelor of Music in the area of performance. Majors and concentrations: composition, conducting, piano/organ, stringed instruments, voice, wind and percussion instruments. Graduate degrees offered: Master of Music in

The Curtis Institute of Music (continued)

the area of opera. Cross-registration with University of Pennsylvania. Program accredited by NASM.

Enrollment Fall 1997: 162 total; 120 undergraduate, 12 graduate, 30 non-professional degree.

Music Student Profile 46% females, 54% males, 53% international.

Music Faculty 54 total undergraduate and graduate (full-time and part-time). Graduate students do not teach undergraduate courses. Undergraduate student–faculty ratio: 2:1.

Expenses for 1997–98 Application fee: $60. Tuition: $0 full-time. Mandatory fees: $695 full-time.

Financial Aid Program-specific awards for 1997: 158 tuition scholarships for program students, 50–75 Supplemental Financial Assistance for those demonstrating need.

Application Procedures Students admitted directly into the professional program freshman year. Deadline for freshmen and transfers: January 15. Required: high school transcript, college transcript(s) for transfer students, 4 letters of recommendation, audition, SAT I test score only. Auditions held once on campus.

Contact Mr. Chris Hodges, Director of Admissions, The Curtis Institute of Music, 1726 Locust Street, Philadelphia, Pennsylvania 19103; 215-893-5262, fax: 215-893-0194.

▼ DALHOUSIE UNIVERSITY

Halifax, NS, Canada

Province-supported, coed. Urban campus. Total enrollment: 12,387. Music program established 1977.

Degrees Bachelor of Music in the areas of composition, history, church music, performance, music education; Bachelor of Arts in the area of music and theater. Majors and concentrations: brass, church music, classical guitar, early instruments, electronic music, harpsichord, jazz, music education, music history, music theory and composition, opera, piano/organ, stringed instruments, voice, wind and percussion instruments. Mandatory cross-registration with Atlantic School of Theology (for church music majors only); University of Kings College.

Enrollment Fall 1997: 325 total; 125 undergraduate, 200 non-professional degree.

Music Student Profile 60% females, 40% males, 5% minorities, 1% international.

Music Faculty 34 total (full-time and part-time). 100% of full-time faculty have terminal degrees. Graduate students do not teach undergraduate courses. Undergraduate student–faculty ratio: 5:1.

Student Life Student groups/activities include Canadian Music Educators Association, Symphony Nova Scotia, Nova Scotia Choral Federation.

Expenses for 1997–98 Application fee: $35 Canadian dollars. Tuition, fee, and room and board charges are reported in Canadian dollars. Canadian resident tuition: $3655 full-time. Mandatory fees: $195 full-time. Full-time tuition and fees vary according to course load, degree level, program, and student level. College room and board: $4875. Room and board charges vary according to board plan and housing facility. International student tuition: $6355 full-time. Special program-related fees: $750 per year for applied skills class.

Financial Aid Program-specific awards for 1997: 2 Don Wright Scholarships for music education majors ($1000), 1 Halifax Ladies Musical Club Scholarship for first year students ($300), 8 Incentive Awards for first year students ($500–$1500), 10 Effie Mae Ross and Campbell Scholarships for in course studies ($200–$1500), 2 Women's Alumni Association Medal and Prize for graduating year ($100), 1 L.D. Currie Memorial Scholarship for in course students ($750), 1 Elizabeth Meyerhof Scholarship for fourth year student ($1500), 1 Bornoff/Ganami Scholarship for string majors ($200), 1 "Sing Sunrise" Prize for choral majors ($100), 1 Lorne Huben Memorial Prize for brass majors ($100).

Application Procedures Students admitted directly into the professional program freshman year. Deadline for freshmen and transfers: June 1. Notification date for freshmen: August 1; transfers: September 1. Required: high school transcript, college transcript(s) for transfer students, minimum 3.0 high school GPA, interview, audition, SAT I test score only. Recommended: letter of recommendation, video for music education majors, portfolio for composition majors. Auditions held 6 times from March through June on campus; recorded music is permissible as a substitute for live auditions when distance is prohibitive and videotaped performances are permissible as a substitute for live auditions when distance is prohibitive. Portfolio reviews held as needed on campus.

Web Site http://www.dal.ca.

Undergraduate Contact Dr. Walter H. Kemp, Chair, Music Department, Dalhousie University, Room 514 Arts Center, Halifax, NS B3H 3J5, Canada; 902-494-2418, fax: 902-494-2801.

▼ DALLAS BAPTIST UNIVERSITY

Dallas, Texas

Independent-Southern Baptist, coed. Urban campus. Total enrollment: 3,493. Music program established 1965.

Degrees Bachelor of Music in the areas of performance, church music, music education. Majors and concentrations: music education, piano/organ, sacred music, voice.

Enrollment Fall 1997: 75 total; all undergraduate.

Music Student Profile 50% females, 50% males, 2% minorities, 4% international.

Music Faculty 22 total (full-time and part-time). 85% of full-time faculty have terminal degrees. Graduate students do not teach undergraduate courses.

Student Life Student groups/activities include American Choral Directors Association Student Chapter, National Association of Teachers of Singing, Southern Baptist Church Music Conference.

Expenses for 1997–98 Application fee: $25. Comprehensive fee: $11,222 includes full-time tuition ($7800) and college room and board ($3422). College room only: $1410. Special program-related fees: $90 per semester for practice room fee.

Financial Aid Program-specific awards for 1997: 14–16 Boettcher Awards for vocalists ($2000), 6 Leonore Kirk Awards for minority program majors ($4000), 53 Music Department Scholarships for those demonstrating need/talent ($2000).

Application Procedures Students admitted directly into the professional program freshman year. Deadline for freshmen and transfers: continuous. Required: essay, high school transcript, college transcript(s) for transfer students, audition, standing in top half of graduating class. Recommended: letter of recommendation, interview. Auditions held twice on campus; recorded music is permissible as a substitute for live auditions if a campus visit is impossible and videotaped performances are permissible as a substitute for live auditions if a campus visit is impossible.

Undergraduate Contact Mr. John Plotts, Director, Admissions Department, Dallas Baptist University, 3000 Mountain Creek Parkway, Dallas, Texas 75211; 214-333-5360.

▼ DANA SCHOOL OF MUSIC

See Youngstown State University

▼ DELTA STATE UNIVERSITY

Cleveland, Mississippi

State-supported, coed. Small town campus. Total enrollment: 4,012.

Degrees Bachelor of Music Education in the areas of vocal music education, instrumental music education. Majors and concentrations: piano/organ, voice, wind and percussion instruments. Graduate degrees offered: Master of Music Education in the areas of vocal music education, instrumental music education. Program accredited by NASM.

Enrollment Fall 1997: 94 total; 90 undergraduate, 4 graduate.

Music Student Profile 49% females, 51% males, 3% minorities.

Music Faculty 18 total undergraduate and graduate (full-time and part-time). 73% of full-time faculty have terminal degrees. Graduate students do not teach undergraduate courses.

Expenses for 1997–98 Application fee: $0. State resident tuition: $2354 full-time. Nonresident tuition: $4948 full-time. College room and board: $2400.

Financial Aid Program-specific awards for 1997: 150 music scholarships for members of ensembles ($1333).

Application Procedures Students admitted directly into the professional program freshman year. Deadline for freshmen and transfers: continuous. Required: high school transcript, audition, SAT I or ACT test scores. Auditions held by appointment on campus; recorded music is permissible as a substitute for live auditions when distance is prohibitive.

Web Site http://www.deltast.edu.

Contact Mr. Douglas Wheeler, Chair, Department of Music, Delta State University, PO Box 3256, Cleveland, Mississippi 38733; 601-846-4606, fax: 601-846-4605, E-mail address: dwheeler@dsu.deltast.edu.

▼ DEPAUL UNIVERSITY

Chicago, Illinois

Independent-Roman Catholic, coed. Urban campus. Total enrollment: 17,804.

Degrees Bachelor of Music in the areas of composition, jazz studies, music/business, music education, performance. Majors and concentrations: piano, stringed instruments, voice, wind and percussion instruments. Graduate degrees offered: Master of Music in the areas of composition, music education, performance, jazz studies. Program accredited by NASM.

Enrollment Fall 1997: 389 total; 300 undergraduate, 80 graduate, 9 non-professional degree.

Music Student Profile 44% females, 15% minorities, 4% international.

Music Faculty 104 total undergraduate and graduate (full-time and part-time). 88% of full-time faculty have terminal degrees. Graduate students do not teach undergraduate courses.

Student Life Student groups/activities include Music Educators National Conference.

Expenses for 1997–98 Application fee: $25. Comprehensive fee: $19,331 includes full-time tuition ($13,460), mandatory fees ($30), and college room and board ($5841). College room only: $4251. Full-time tuition and fees vary according to program. Room and board charges vary according to board plan and housing facility. Special program-related fees: $20 for music education instrument rental.

Financial Aid Program-specific awards for 1997: 250 Music Performance Awards for program majors ($3000).

Application Procedures Students apply for admission into the professional program by sophomore year. Deadline for freshmen and transfers: January 15. Notification date for freshmen: March 15. Required: essay, high school transcript, college transcript(s) for transfer students, minimum 2.0 high school GPA, letter of recommendation, interview, audition, SAT I or ACT test scores (minimum combined SAT I score of 1040, minimum combined ACT score of 22). Recommended: minimum 3.0 high school GPA. Auditions held continuously on campus; recorded music is permissible as a substitute for live auditions when distance is prohibitive and with approval from Admissions and videotaped performances are permissible as a substitute for live auditions when distance is prohibitive and with approval from Admissions.

Contact Mr. Ross Beacraft, Coordinator of Admissions, School of Music, DePaul University, 804 West Belden Avenue, Chicago, Illinois 60614-3296; 773-325-7444, fax: 773-325-7264, E-mail address: rbeacraf@wppost.depaul.edu.

▼ DEPAUW UNIVERSITY

Greencastle, Indiana

Independent, coed. Small town campus. Total enrollment: 2,334. Music program established 1884.

Degrees Bachelor of Music in the areas of performance, composition, music/business; Bachelor of Music Education; Bachelor of Musical Arts in the areas of music, music/business, music in conjunction with an outside field. Majors and concentrations: classical music, composition, music, music and business, music education, piano/organ, stringed instruments, voice, wind and percussion instruments. Program accredited by NASM.

Enrollment Fall 1997: 140 undergraduate.

Music Student Profile 60% females, 40% males, 12% minorities, 3% international.

Music Faculty 47 total (full-time and part-time). 50% of full-time faculty have terminal degrees. Graduate students do not teach undergraduate courses. Undergraduate student–faculty ratio: 5:1.

Student Life Student groups/activities include Music Educators National Conference, Pi Kappa Lambda, Mu Phi Epsilon. Special housing available for music students.

Expenses for 1997–98 Application fee: $40. Comprehensive fee: $22,666 includes full-time tuition ($16,815), mandatory fees ($235), and college room and board ($5616).

Financial Aid Program-specific awards for 1997: Music Honor Performance Awards for enrolled students ($1000–$17,500).

Application Procedures Students apply for admission into the professional program by sophomore year. Deadline for

DePauw University (continued)

freshmen: February 15; transfers: March 1. Notification date for freshmen and transfers: April 1. Required: essay, high school transcript, college transcript(s) for transfer students, 2 letters of recommendation, audition, SAT I or ACT test scores. Recommended: minimum 3.0 high school GPA, interview. Auditions held 4 times or by appointment on campus and off campus in Interlochen, MI; recorded music is permissible as a substitute for live auditions when distance is prohibitive and videotaped performances are permissible as a substitute for live auditions if distance is prohibitive.

Undergraduate Contact Robert Garcia, Assistant Director of Music Admission, School of Music, DePauw University, Performing Arts Center, 600 South Locust, Greencastle, Indiana 46135; 800-447-2495, fax: 365-658-4042, E-mail address: rgarcia@depauw.edu.

▼ DIVISION OF THE ARTS: THE LEONARD DAVIS CENTER

See City College of the City University of New York

▼ DRAKE UNIVERSITY

Des Moines, Iowa

Independent, coed. Suburban campus. Total enrollment: 5,184.

Degrees Bachelor of Music in the area of performance; Bachelor of Music Education in the areas of choral music education, instrumental music education. Majors and concentrations: church music, classical music, music and business, piano pedagogy, piano/organ, stringed instruments, voice, wind and percussion instruments. Graduate degrees offered: Master of Music in the areas of performance, conducting; Master of Music Education. Program accredited by NASM.

Enrollment Fall 1997: 140 total; 115 undergraduate, 15 graduate, 10 non-professional degree.

Music Student Profile 60% females, 40% males, 10% minorities, 2% international.

Music Faculty 28 total undergraduate and graduate (full-time and part-time). 65% of full-time faculty have terminal degrees. Graduate students do not teach undergraduate courses. Undergraduate student–faculty ratio: 10:1.

Student Life Student groups/activities include Music Educators National Conference Student Chapter, Phi Mu Alpha, Sigma Alpha Iota.

Expenses for 1997–98 Application fee: $25. Comprehensive fee: $20,170 includes full-time tuition ($15,200) and college room and board ($4970). College room only: $2670. Full-time tuition varies according to student level. Room and board charges vary according to board plan. Special program-related fees: $105 per semester for applied music lesson fee.

Financial Aid Program-specific awards for 1997: 57 Fine Arts Scholarships for program majors ($2000–$6000).

Application Procedures Students admitted directly into the professional program freshman year. Deadline for freshmen and transfers: continuous. Required: high school transcript, minimum 2.0 high school GPA, 2 letters of recommendation, audition, SAT I or ACT test scores. Auditions held continuously on campus; recorded music is permissible as a substitute for live auditions when distance is prohibitive and videotaped performances are permissible as a substitute for live auditions when distance is prohibitive.

Web Site http://www.drake.edu/artsci/Music_Dept/music_home.html.

Undergraduate Contact Dr. William Dougherty, Chair, Department of Music, Drake University, FAC 260, 25th and Carpenter, Des Moines, Iowa 50311; 515-271-3975, fax: 515-271-2558, E-mail address: william.dougherty@drake.edu.

Graduate Contact Dr. David Harris, Graduate Studies Coordinator, Department of Music, Drake University, FAC 234,, 25th and Carpenter, Des Moines, Iowa 50311; 515-271-3104, fax: 515-271-2558, E-mail address: david.harris@drake.edu.

▼ DUQUESNE UNIVERSITY

Pittsburgh, Pennsylvania

Independent-Roman Catholic, coed. Urban campus. Total enrollment: 9,500. Music program established 1926.

Degrees Bachelor of Music in the areas of performance, recording arts and sciences, music technology; Bachelor of Science in the areas of music education, music therapy. Majors and concentrations: guitar, jazz, music education, music technology, music therapy, piano/organ, sacred music, sound recording technology, stringed instruments, voice, wind and percussion instruments. Graduate degrees offered: Master of Music in the areas of performance, sacred music, music theory/composition; Master of Music Education. Cross-registration with Pittsburgh Council of Higher Education. Program accredited by NASM.

Enrollment Fall 1997: 1,000 total; 225 undergraduate, 125 graduate, 650 non-professional degree.

Music Student Profile 50% females, 50% males, 20% minorities, 10% international.

Music Faculty 92 total undergraduate and graduate (full-time and part-time). 90% of full-time faculty have terminal degrees. Graduate students do not teach undergraduate courses. Undergraduate student–faculty ratio: 8:1.

Student Life Student groups/activities include Mu Phi Epsilon, Music Educators National Conference, Music Therapy Club.

Expenses for 1997–98 Application fee: $45. Comprehensive fee: $20,044 includes full-time tuition ($13,041), mandatory fees ($1025), and college room and board ($5978). Full-time tuition and fees vary according to program. Room and board charges vary according to board plan.

Financial Aid Program-specific awards for 1997: 70 School of Music Talent Awards for program students ($6000).

Application Procedures Students admitted directly into the professional program freshman year. Deadline for freshmen and transfers: May 1. Notification date for freshmen and transfers: August 15. Required: essay, high school transcript, college transcript(s) for transfer students, minimum 2.0 high school GPA, 2 letters of recommendation, audition, SAT I or ACT test scores, theory examination, musicianship examination, compositions (for composition majors). Recommended: minimum 3.0 high school GPA, interview. Auditions held 12 times on campus and off campus in Washington, DC area; recorded music is permissible as a substitute for live auditions if a campus visit is impossible and a recorded video performance is impossible and videotaped performances are permissible as a substitute for live auditions if a campus visit is impossible.

Web Site http://www.duq.edu/music/music.html.

Undergraduate Contact Rev. Thomas G. Schaefer, Dean of Admissions, Duquesne University, 600 Forbes Avenue, Pittsburgh, Pennsylvania 15282; 412-396-6222, fax: 412-396-5644, E-mail address: schaefer@duq2.cc.duq.edu.

Graduate Contact Mr. Nicholas Jordanoff, Director of Music Admissions, School of Music, Duquesne University, 600 Forbes Avenue, Pittsburgh, Pennsylvania 15282; 412-396-5983, fax: 412-396-5479, E-mail address: jordanof@duq2.cc. duq.edu.

▼ EAST CAROLINA UNIVERSITY

Greenville, North Carolina

State-supported, coed. Urban campus. Total enrollment: 18,271. Music program established 1909.

Degrees Bachelor of Music in the areas of performance, music education, piano pedagogy, church music, theory/composition, music therapy, music theater. Majors and concentrations: music education, music theater, music theory and composition, music therapy, piano pedagogy, piano/organ, sacred music, stringed instruments, voice, wind and percussion instruments. Graduate degrees offered: Master of Music in the areas of accompanying, church music, music education, composition, performance, piano pedagogy, Suzuki pedagogy, music therapy, choral conducting, jazz performance, theory, voice pedagogy, instrumental conducting. Program accredited by NASM, NAMT.

Enrollment Fall 1997: 367 total; 302 undergraduate, 45 graduate, 20 non-professional degree.

Music Student Profile 48% females, 52% males, 10% minorities, 1% international.

Music Faculty 54 total undergraduate and graduate (full-time and part-time). 100% of full-time faculty have terminal degrees. Graduate students teach a few undergraduate courses. Undergraduate student–faculty ratio: 7:1.

Student Life Student groups/activities include music sororities and fraternities, Music Educators National Conference, American Choral Directors Association.

Expenses for 1997–98 Application fee: $35. State resident tuition: $916 full-time. Nonresident tuition: $8028 full-time. Mandatory fees: $932 full-time. College room and board: $3680. College room only: $1780. Room and board charges vary according to board plan and housing facility. Special program-related fees: $30 per credit hour for applied music fee.

Financial Aid Program-specific awards for 1997: 74 music scholarships for music majors ($1600).

Application Procedures Students admitted directly into the professional program freshman year. Deadline for freshmen: March 15; transfers: April 15. Required: high school transcript, college transcript(s) for transfer students, minimum 2.0 high school GPA, audition, SAT I or ACT test scores (minimum combined SAT I score of 900), minimum combined SAT I score of 1000 for out-of-state applicants. Recommended: minimum 3.0 high school GPA, 2 letters of recommendation. Auditions held 8 times on campus; recorded music is permissible as a substitute for live auditions if a campus visit is impossible and videotaped performances are permissible as a substitute for live auditions if a campus visit is impossible.

Web Site http://www.music.ecu.edu.

Undergraduate Contact Mr. Robert Hause, Assistant Dean, Undergraduate Studies, School of Music, East Carolina University, A.J. Fletcher Music Center, Greenville, North

Carolina 27858-4353; 252-328-6331, fax: 252-328-6258, E-mail address: hauser@mail.ecu.edu.

Graduate Contact Dr. Rodney Schmidt, Assistant Dean, Graduate Studies, School of Music, East Carolina University, A.J. Fletcher Music Center, Greenville, North Carolina 27858-4353; 252-328-6282, fax: 252-328-6258, E-mail address: schmidtr@mail.ecu.edu.

▼ EAST CENTRAL UNIVERSITY

Ada, Oklahoma

State-supported, coed. Small town campus. Total enrollment: 4,087. Music program established 1909.

Degrees Bachelor of Science in the areas of music, music education. Majors and concentrations: music education, piano/organ, voice, wind and percussion instruments. Program accredited by NASM.

Enrollment Fall 1997: 78 total; all undergraduate.

Music Student Profile 50% females, 50% males, 1% minorities.

Music Faculty 16 total (full-time and part-time). 90% of full-time faculty have terminal degrees.

Student Life Student groups/activities include Music Educators National Conference Student Chapter, Kappa Kappa Psi.

Expenses for 1997–98 State resident tuition: $1773 full-time. Nonresident tuition: $4117 full-time. Mandatory fees: $39 full-time. Full-time tuition and fees vary according to course level and student level. College room and board: $2066. Room and board charges vary according to board plan and housing facility. Special program-related fees: $18 per credit hour for private lessons, $3 per semester for studio rental, $10 per semester for organ rental, $3 per credit hour for class instrument rental fee.

Application Procedures Students admitted directly into the professional program freshman year. Deadline for freshmen and transfers: continuous. Required: high school transcript, college transcript(s) for transfer students, audition, ACT test score only (minimum combined ACT score of 19). Auditions held continuously on campus; recorded music is permissible as a substitute for live auditions if a campus visit is impossible.

Undergraduate Contact Dr. Dennis Silkebakken, Chair, Music Department, East Central University, Box P-6, Ada, Oklahoma 74820; 405-332-8000 ext. 390, fax: 405-332-3042.

▼ EASTERN ILLINOIS UNIVERSITY

Charleston, Illinois

State-supported, coed. Small town campus. Total enrollment: 11,777.

Degrees Bachelor of Music in the areas of music education, performance, jazz studies, composition. Majors and concentrations: classical music, jazz, music, music education, piano/organ, stringed instruments, voice, wind and percussion instruments. Graduate degrees offered: Master of Music in the areas of performance, conducting.

Enrollment Fall 1997: 207 total; 185 undergraduate, 22 graduate.

Music Student Profile 51% females, 49% males, 6% minorities.

Music Faculty 35 total undergraduate (full-time and part-time). 40% of full-time faculty have terminal degrees. Graduate students teach a few undergraduate courses. Undergraduate student–faculty ratio: 4:1.

Eastern Illinois University (*continued*)

Student Life Student groups/activities include professional music fraternities and sororities.

Expenses for 1998–99 Application fee: $25. State resident tuition: $2190 full-time. Nonresident tuition: $6564 full-time. Mandatory fees: $922 full-time. College room and board: $3919. Room and board charges vary according to board plan. Special program-related fees: $15 per per season for marching band equipment.

Financial Aid Program-specific awards for 1997: 25 Endowed Scholarships for program majors ($250–$1900).

Application Procedures Students admitted directly into the professional program freshman year. Deadline for freshmen and transfers: continuous. Required: high school transcript, college transcript(s) for transfer students, minimum 2.0 high school GPA, audition, SAT I or ACT test scores. Recommended: interview. Auditions held 6 times on campus; recorded music is permissible as a substitute for live auditions if a campus visit is impossible and videotaped performances are permissible as a substitute for live auditions if a campus visit is impossible.

Undergraduate Contact Dr. Herman D. Taylor, Chair, Music Department, Eastern Illinois University, 600 Lincoln Avenue, Charleston, Illinois 61920; 217-581-3010, fax: 217-581-7137, E-mail address: cfhdt@ux1.cts.eiu.edu.

Graduate Contact Dr. Peter Hesterman, Director of Graduate Studies, Music Department, Eastern Illinois University, 600 Lincoln Avenue, Charleston, Illinois 61920; 217-581-3611, fax: 217-581-7137.

▼ Eastern Kentucky University

Richmond, Kentucky

State-supported, coed. Small town campus. Total enrollment: 15,424. Music program established 1930.

Degrees Bachelor of Music in the area of performance; Bachelor of Music Education. Majors and concentrations: instrumental music, keyboard, voice. Graduate degrees offered: Master of Music in the areas of choral conducting, performance, theory/composition, music education. Program accredited by NASM.

Enrollment Fall 1997: 630 total; 150 undergraduate, 30 graduate, 450 non-professional degree.

Music Faculty 23 total undergraduate and graduate (full-time and part-time). 80% of full-time faculty have terminal degrees. Graduate students teach a few undergraduate courses. Undergraduate student–faculty ratio: 20:1.

Student Life Student groups/activities include Phi Mu Alpha Sinfonia, Sigma Alpha Iota, Delta Omicron.

Expenses for 1997–98 State resident tuition: $2060 full-time. Nonresident tuition: $5660 full-time. College room and board: $3240. College room only: $1316. Room and board charges vary according to board plan and housing facility. Special program-related fees: $50 per semester for music lessons.

Financial Aid Program-specific awards for 1997: 82 departmental awards for talented program students ($600).

Application Procedures Students admitted directly into the professional program freshman year. Deadline for freshmen and transfers: continuous. Required: high school transcript, audition, ACT test score only (minimum combined ACT score of 17). Auditions held 3 times on campus and off campus in Louisville, KY; Cincinnati, OH; recorded music is

permissible as a substitute for live auditions and videotaped performances are permissible as a substitute for live auditions.

Undergraduate Contact Admissions Office, Eastern Kentucky University, 203 Jones Building, Richmond, Kentucky 40475-3101; 606-622-1000.

Graduate Contact Dr. Karen Sehmann, Coordinator of Graduate Studies, Department of Music, Eastern Kentucky University, 203 Jones Building, Richmond, Kentucky 40475-3101; 606-622-3266.

▼ Eastern Michigan University

Ypsilanti, Michigan

State-supported, coed. Suburban campus. Total enrollment: 22,730.

Degrees Bachelor of Music in the area of performance; Bachelor of Music Education in the areas of vocal music education, instrumental music education; Bachelor of Music Therapy. Majors and concentrations: conducting, guitar, music education, music therapy, piano/organ, stringed instruments, voice, wind and percussion instruments. Graduate degrees offered: Master of Arts in the areas of performance, piano pedagogy, theory/literature. Program accredited by NASM.

Enrollment Fall 1997: 340 total; 240 undergraduate, 70 graduate, 30 non-professional degree.

Music Student Profile 60% females, 40% males, 5% international.

Music Faculty 41 total undergraduate (full-time and part-time). 60% of full-time faculty have terminal degrees. Graduate students teach a few undergraduate courses. Undergraduate student–faculty ratio: 10:1.

Expenses for 1997–98 Application fee: $25. State resident tuition: $2984 full-time. Nonresident tuition: $7874 full-time. Mandatory fees: $545 full-time. Full-time tuition and fees vary according to course level and reciprocity agreements. College room and board: $4528. Room and board charges vary according to board plan, housing facility, and location. Special program-related fees: $30–$60 per semester for applied music fee, $10 per course for instrument maintenance.

Financial Aid Program-specific awards for 1997: 10 Alexander Talent Awards for music majors ($500–$3000), endowed awards for music majors ($200–$1700).

Application Procedures Students admitted directly into the professional program freshman year. Deadline for freshmen and transfers: continuous. Required: high school transcript, college transcript(s) for transfer students, minimum 2.0 high school GPA, audition, SAT I or ACT test scores. Auditions held 5 times and by special arrangement on campus; recorded music is permissible as a substitute for live auditions when distance is prohibitive and videotaped performances are permissible as a substitute for live auditions by special arrangement.

Undergraduate Contact Dr. David Pierce, Coordinator of Undergraduate Advising, Department of Music, Eastern Michigan University, Alexander Music Building, Ypsilanti, Michigan 48197; 734-487-1044, fax: 734-487-6939.

Graduate Contact Dr. Diane Winder, Coordinator of Graduate Advising, Department of Music, Eastern Michigan University, Alexander Music Building, Ypsilanti, Michigan 48197; 734-487-1044, fax: 734-487-6939.

▼ EASTERN NEW MEXICO UNIVERSITY

Portales, New Mexico

State-supported, coed. Rural campus. Total enrollment: 3,495.

Degrees Bachelor of Music in the areas of piano performance, string performance, vocal performance, winds or percussion performance, music theater; Bachelor of Music Education in the areas of choral music education, string music education, winds music education, percussion music education. Majors and concentrations: music, music business, music education, music theater, piano/organ, stringed instruments, voice, wind and percussion instruments. Graduate degrees offered: Master of Music in the area of music education. Program accredited by NASM.

Enrollment Fall 1997: 130 total; 70 undergraduate, 10 graduate, 50 non-professional degree.

Music Student Profile 45% females, 55% males, 22% minorities.

Music Faculty 17 total undergraduate and graduate (full-time and part-time). 88% of full-time faculty have terminal degrees. Graduate students teach a few undergraduate courses. Undergraduate student–faculty ratio: 10:1.

Student Life Student groups/activities include Music Educators National Conference, American Choral Directors Association, music sorority and fraternity.

Expenses for 1997–98 Application fee: $15. State resident tuition: $1170 full-time. Nonresident tuition: $5832 full-time. Mandatory fees: $546 full-time. College room and board: $2942. College room only: $1372. Special program-related fees: $50 per semester for applied music lesson fee.

Financial Aid Program-specific awards for 1997: 6–7 Symphony League Awards for strings/winds majors ($100–$1000), 45 Participation Grants for program majors ($200), performance scholarships for performers ($100–$300).

Application Procedures Students apply for admission into the professional program by sophomore year. Deadline for freshmen and transfers: July 23. Required: high school transcript, college transcript(s) for transfer students, minimum 2.0 high school GPA, audition, SAT I or ACT test scores. Auditions held continuously on campus; recorded music is permissible as a substitute for live auditions when distance is prohibitive and videotaped performances are permissible as a substitute for live auditions when distance is prohibitive.

Undergraduate Contact Dr. David Gerig, Director, School of Music, Eastern New Mexico University, Station #16, Portales, New Mexico 88130; 505-562-2376, fax: 505-562-2500, E-mail address: gerigd@email.enmu.edu.

Graduate Contact Mr. William Wood, Graduate Coordinator, School of Music, Eastern New Mexico University, Station #16, Portales, New Mexico 88130; 505-562-2379, fax: 505-562-2500, E-mail address: woodw@email.enmu.edu.

▼ EASTERN WASHINGTON UNIVERSITY

Cheney, Washington

State-supported, coed. Small town campus. Total enrollment: 7,537.

Degrees Bachelor of Music in the areas of instrumental music, vocal performance, composition; Bachelor of Art Education in the area of music. Majors and concentrations: music, music theory and composition, piano, stringed instruments, voice, wind and percussion instruments. Graduate degrees

offered: Master of Arts in the areas of music, music education, performance, composition. Program accredited by NASM.

Enrollment Fall 1997: 160 total; 130 undergraduate, 10 graduate, 20 non-professional degree.

Music Student Profile 50% females, 50% males, 3% minorities, 2% international.

Music Faculty 21 total undergraduate and graduate (full-time and part-time). 92% of full-time faculty have terminal degrees. Graduate students do not teach undergraduate courses.

Student Life Student groups/activities include Music Educators National Conference Student Chapter, National Association of String Teachers, Music Teachers National Association.

Expenses for 1998–99 Application fee: $35. State resident tuition: $2622 full-time. Nonresident tuition: $9315 full-time. College room and board: $4294. College room only: $2188. Room and board charges vary according to board plan and housing facility. Special program-related fees: $50 for applied lesson fee.

Financial Aid Program-specific awards for 1997: Instrumental Scholars Program Awards for instrumentalists, 1 George W. Lotzenhiser Scholarship for artistically talented brass instrumentalists, 1 Lloyd and Thekla Rowles Scholarship for artistically talented vocalists, 1 Ann Harder Wyatt Scholarship for artistically talented juniors or seniors, 1 Marvin Mutchnik Scholarship for artistically talented strings students, 1 Eastern Washington University Scholarship for artistically talented woodwind students, Meritorious Music Awards for artistically talented program majors, 1 Gwendoline Harper Scholarship for artistically talented pianists, Pep Band Awards for band students ($100).

Application Procedures Students admitted directly into the professional program freshman year. Deadline for freshmen and transfers: continuous. Required: high school transcript, college transcript(s) for transfer students, audition, SAT I or ACT test scores, minimum 2.5 high school GPA. Recommended: interview. Auditions held continuously on campus and off campus in Seattle, WA; recorded music is permissible as a substitute for live auditions when distance is prohibitive and videotaped performances are permissible as a substitute for live auditions when distance is prohibitive.

Undergraduate Contact Dr. Lynn Brinckmeyer, Director of Music Education, Music Department, Eastern Washington University, MS-100, Cheney, Washington 99004; 509-359-2241, fax: 509-359-7028, E-mail address: lbrinckmeyer@ewu.edu.

Graduate Contact Dr. David Rostkoski, Professor, Music Department, Eastern Washington University, MS-100, Cheney, Washington 99004; 509-359-6119, E-mail address: drostkoski@ewu.edu.

University of Rochester

▼ EASTMAN SCHOOL OF MUSIC

Rochester, New York

Independent, coed. Suburban campus. Total enrollment: 8,451. Music program established 1921.

Degrees Bachelor of Music in the areas of composition, music education, music theory, performance, jazz studies. Majors and concentrations: classical music, composition, guitar, harpsichord, jazz, music education, music theory, piano/organ, stringed instruments, voice, wind and percussion instruments. Graduate degrees offered: Master of Music in the areas of jazz studies, composition, choral conducting,

Eastman School of Music *(continued)*

music education, performance, piano accompanying and chamber music, theory pedagogy; Master of Arts in the areas of composition, music education, music theory pedagogy; Master of Music/Doctor of Philosophy in the areas of musicology, music theory. Doctor of Musical Arts in the areas of composition, conducting, music education, performance and literature, piano accompanying and chamber music; Doctor of Philosophy in the areas of composition, music education. Program accredited by NASM.

Enrollment Fall 1997: 832 total; 491 undergraduate, 341 graduate.

Music Student Profile 53% females, 47% males, 19% minorities, 19% international.

Music Faculty 106 total undergraduate and graduate (full-time and part-time). 53% of full-time faculty have terminal degrees. Graduate students teach a few undergraduate courses. Undergraduate student–faculty ratio: 5:1.

Student Life Student groups/activities include Music Educators National Conference, professional music fraternities and sororities. Special housing available for music students.

Expenses for 1997–98 Application fee: $50. Comprehensive fee: $28,205 includes full-time tuition ($20,540), mandatory fees ($480), and college room and board ($7185). College room only: $4335. Room and board charges vary according to board plan.

Financial Aid Program-specific awards for 1997: 350 Merit-based Scholarships for those demonstrating talent and academic achievement ($2000–$7000), 425 financial aid awards for those demonstrating need ($2000–$17,000).

Application Procedures Students admitted directly into the professional program freshman year. Deadline for freshmen and transfers: January 1. Notification date for freshmen and transfers: April 15. Required: high school transcript, college transcript(s) for transfer students, 3 letters of recommendation, audition, portfolio for composition majors. Recommended: minimum 3.0 high school GPA, interview, SAT I or ACT test scores. Auditions held 23 times on campus and off campus in Atlanta, GA; Boston, MA; Chicago, IL; Dallas, TX; Houston, TX; Los Angeles, CA; Minneapolis, MN; Seattle, WA; Washington, DC; New York, NY; San Francisco, CA; Singapore; Hong Kong; Taipei, Taiwan; Seoul, South Korea; recorded music is permissible as a substitute for live auditions if a campus visit is impossible and videotaped performances are permissible as a substitute for live auditions if a campus visit is impossible. Portfolio reviews held once on campus.

Contact Ms. Kathleen Tesar, Director of Admissions, Eastman School of Music, University of Rochester, 26 Gibbs Street, Rochester, New York 14604; 716-274-1060, fax: 716-274-1088, E-mail address: esmadmit@uhura.cc.rochester.edu.

More About the School

Program Facilities Performance spaces include Eastman Theatre (3,094 seats), Kilbourn Hall (459 seats), Howard Hanson Recital Hall, Schmitt Organ Recital Hall, and Ciminelli Formal Lounge. The school has professional-quality recording studios. The Eastman Computer and Electronic Music Center features two studios (one software-based, the other MIDI-based). Several fine organs are available to Eastman students. The Sibley Music Library has holdings of more than 500,000 items, including more than 50,000 recordings. The Student Living Center (opened in 1991) provides residence for 350 undergraduates as well as space for student services, including the Career Planning and Placement Office,

Eastman School of Music

Writing and Study Skills Center, and the Computing Room (IBM and MacIntosh computers with MIDI and electronic keyboards).

Faculty, Resident Artists, and Alumni Faculty members are performers, composers, and scholars. The Eastman Brass are members of the faculty. Alumni are active professionally as members of many leading American orchestras and as opera singers, composers, jazz artists, music critics, heads of music schools, managers of orchestras, school teachers, college professors, and arts administrators.

Student Performance Opportunities Students present more than 400 recitals annually. Eastman ensembles include the Philharmonia, Wind Ensemble, Chorale, Opera Theatre, Jazz Ensemble, Musica Nova, Collegium Musicum, InterMusica, Saxology, Trombone Choir, Percussion Ensemble, Marimba Ensemble, and Horn Choir. Each year, eight Composers' Forums allow composition students to hear their chamber works performed.

Special Programs Eastman Philharmonia annual summer residency, Heidelberg, Germany; Eastman Wind Ensemble biennial Japan tour; Performer's Certificate and Artist's Diploma; Concerto Competition; Kneisel German Lied Competition; Early Music Program. Career counseling is offered individually and in seminars. Volunteer and music outreach opportunities and professional performance opportunities are offered.

▼

During its seventy-six-year history, the Eastman School of Music has become one of the world's most prestigious music schools. In a 1997 *U.S. News and World Report* survey, the Eastman School received the top ranking for graduate school programs. The School's stature also is reflected in its eight Pulitzer Prize-winning composers, two of whom, Joseph Schwantner and Christopher Rouse, are current members of the composition faculty. Eastman students are guided by a renowned resident faculty. The impact of recordings, publications, compositions, performances, and research by Eastman faculty members is far-reaching.

The School is known for having fine programs in performance, scholarship, composition, and teaching and for its curricula in the liberal arts. The Humanities Department encourages students to refine their language and writing skills and to explore intellectual interests in fields as varied as visual arts and architecture, Western cultural history, ethics, educational psychology, and religion.

As Eastman is a professional school within the University of Rochester, its students may take advantage of diverse course offerings in other colleges of the University and may design personalized double-degree programs.

Nearly all Eastman students perform regularly in one of the School's more than twenty ensembles. Exceptional performance opportunities in Rochester and abroad are an Eastman hallmark. The Eastman Philharmonia has spent its summers at the Heidelberg Castle Festival since 1980. The Eastman Jazz Ensemble has played at the Montreux Jazz Festival, and the Eastman Wind Ensemble has made five major tours of Japan.

An Eastman School education is distinguished by the opportunity to work closely with some of the most influential musicians of our time. Recent guest conductors have included Sir Georg Solti, Karel Husa, Paul Sacher, Leonard Slatkin, and Robert Shaw. Yo-Yo- Ma, Marie-Claire Alain, Murray Perahia, Marilyn Horne, Martin Katz, Heinz Hollinger, Leon Fleischer, Ani Kavafian, Dawn Upshaw, John Harbison, the Beaux Arts Trio, and the Kronos Quartet have recently taught master classes at Eastman.

The School's concert life includes faculty concerts, student recitals, fully staged opera, and Eastman ensemble performances. In addition, the Kilbourn Concert Series features guest artists in solo recitals and chamber music concerts. Malcolm Bilson, Anner Bylsma, Richard Goode, William Sharp, and the Saint Lawrence Quartet are among recent performers. Non-Western music is highlighted in the World Music Series.

In recent years, students have been able to attend presentations by conductor-composer Robert Kapilow, author Joseph Horowitz, and music critics Robert Commanday, Alan Rich, and Michael Walsh.

The distinctive combination of learning experiences that creates an Eastman School education has resulted in a tradition of student excellence. The School's composition students have regularly won the Prix de Rome, the Bearns Prize, and major awards from ASCAP and BML. Eastman graduates are consistently recognized at the American Guild of Organists competitions, and the School's jazz ensembles have repeatedly won honors in *Down Beat* magazine's annual recording competition. Winners of Eastman's Cleveland Quartet Competition have claimed top prizes in the Fischoff and Portsmouth International Quartet competitions and, most recently, the Naumburg Chamber Music Award.

▼ EAST TENNESSEE STATE UNIVERSITY

Johnson City, Tennessee

State-supported, coed. Small town campus. Total enrollment: 11,596.

Degrees Bachelor of Music in the areas of music education, performance. Majors and concentrations: music education, piano/organ, stringed instruments, voice, wind and percussion instruments. Graduate degrees offered: Master of Music Education in the area of music education. Cross-registration with Milligan College. Program accredited by NASM.

Enrollment Fall 1997: 101 total; 90 undergraduate, 11 graduate.

Music Student Profile 50% females, 50% males, 7% minorities.

Music Faculty 23 total undergraduate and graduate (full-time and part-time). 77% of full-time faculty have terminal degrees. Graduate students do not teach undergraduate courses.

Student Life Student groups/activities include Pi Kappa Lambda, Music Educators National Conference, Percussive Arts Society.

Expenses for 1997–98 Application fee: $15. State resident tuition: $1816 full-time. Nonresident tuition: $6412 full-time. Mandatory fees: $284 full-time. College room and board: $2520. Room and board charges vary according to board plan and housing facility. Special program-related fees: $55 per credit hour for private music lessons.

Financial Aid Program-specific awards for 1997: Floyd Cramer Scholarships for those passing audition evaluations ($600), 7 Lamar Alexander Scholarships for those passing audition evaluations ($750), 1 Theresa Bowers Endowment Award for those passing audition evaluations ($350), 40 APS Awards for above-average students with exceptional artistic ability ($2000), 7 other endowed scholarships for those passing audition evaluations ($750).

Application Procedures Students admitted directly into the professional program freshman year. Deadline for freshmen and transfers: continuous. Required: high school transcript, college transcript(s) for transfer students, audition, SAT I or ACT test scores (minimum combined ACT score of 19), minimum 2.3 high school GPA. Auditions held 4 times on campus and off campus in high schools in northeast Tennessee; recorded music is permissible as a substitute for live auditions if a live audition is impossible and videotaped performances are permissible as a substitute for live auditions if a live audition is impossible.

Undergraduate Contact Dr. Mary Dave Blackman, Chair, Music Department, East Tennessee State University, Box 70661, Johnson City, Tennessee 37614; 423-439-6948, fax: 423-439-7088, E-mail address: blackman@etsu.edu.

Graduate Contact Dr. Ben Caton, Graduate Coordinator, Music Department, East Tennessee State University, Box 70661, Johnson City, Tennessee 37614; 423-439-4405, fax: 423-439-7088, E-mail address: caton@etsu.edu.

▼ EAST TEXAS BAPTIST UNIVERSITY

Marshall, Texas

Independent-Baptist, coed. Small town campus. Total enrollment: 1,292. Music program established 1914.

Degrees Bachelor of Music in the areas of sacred music, music education, applied voice. Program accredited by NASM.

Enrollment Fall 1997: 170 total; 70 undergraduate, 100 non-professional degree.

Music Student Profile 60% females, 40% males, 5% minorities, 5% international.

Music Faculty 18 total (full-time and part-time). 50% of full-time faculty have terminal degrees. Graduate students do not teach undergraduate courses. Undergraduate student–faculty ratio: 10:1.

Student Life Student groups/activities include Sigma Alpha Iota, Phi Mu Alpha Sinfonia.

Expenses for 1997–98 Application fee: $25. Comprehensive fee: $9848 includes full-time tuition ($6150), mandatory fees ($600), and college room and board ($3098). College room only: $1300. Room and board charges vary according to board plan and housing facility. Special program-related fees: $50 per credit hour for applied music fee.

Financial Aid Program-specific awards for 1997: 35 music scholarships for program majors ($600–$2000), 50 Ensemble Scholarships for ensemble players ($200–$800).

East Texas Baptist University (continued)

Application Procedures Students apply for admission into the professional program by sophomore year. Deadline for freshmen and transfers: August 31. Required: high school transcript, college transcript(s) for transfer students, minimum 2.0 high school GPA, interview, audition, SAT I or ACT test scores (minimum combined SAT I score of 800, minimum combined ACT score of 16). Recommended: letter of recommendation. Auditions held 5 times on campus; recorded music is permissible as a substitute for live auditions when distance is prohibitive or scheduling is difficult and videotaped performances are permissible as a substitute for live auditions when distance is prohibitive or if scheduling is difficult.

Undergraduate Contact Mr. David Howard, Director of Admissions, East Texas Baptist University, 1209 North Grove, Marshall, Texas 75670; 800-804-3828, fax: 903-938-1705, E-mail address: dhoward@etbu.edu.

▼ ELMHURST COLLEGE

Elmhurst, Illinois

Independent, coed. Suburban campus. Total enrollment: 2,842. Music program established 1938.

Degrees Bachelor of Music in the areas of music education, music business.

Enrollment Fall 1997: 100 total; 60 undergraduate, 40 non-professional degree.

Music Student Profile 53% females, 47% males, 8% minorities, 5% international.

Music Faculty 49 total (full-time and part-time). 85% of full-time faculty have terminal degrees. Graduate students do not teach undergraduate courses.

Student Life Student groups/activities include Music Educators National Conference, Music and Entertainment Industry Student Association, Student Recording Services.

Expenses for 1997–98 Application fee: $15. Comprehensive fee: $16,900 includes full-time tuition ($11,820), mandatory fees ($80), and college room and board ($5000). College room only: $2600.

Financial Aid Program-specific awards for 1997: 20–30 Music Scholarship/Talent Awards for performers ($500–$3000), 1 National Association of Music Merchants Scholarship for academically qualified/talented applicants ($1000), 1 National Academy of Recording Arts and Sciences Scholarship for academically qualified/talented applicants ($1000).

Application Procedures Students admitted directly into the professional program freshman year. Deadline for freshmen and transfers: August 1. Notification date for freshmen and transfers: August 15. Required: high school transcript, college transcript(s) for transfer students, audition, SAT I or ACT test scores, minimum 2.5 high school GPA. Auditions held continuously on campus; recorded music is permissible as a substitute for live auditions for international students and U.S. students from a great distance and videotaped performances are permissible as a substitute for live auditions for international students and U.S. students from a great distance.

Web Site http://www.elmhurst.edu.

Undergraduate Contact Mr. Kevin Olson, Director of Music Admissions, Music Department, Elmhurst College, 190 Prospect Avenue, Elmhurst, Illinois 60126; 630-617-3515, fax: 630-617-3738.

▼ EMPORIA STATE UNIVERSITY

Emporia, Kansas

State-supported, coed. Small town campus. Total enrollment: 5,320. Music program established 1947.

Degrees Bachelor of Music in the area of performance; Bachelor of Music Education in the areas of instrumental music education, vocal music education. Majors and concentrations: music education, piano/organ, stringed instruments, voice, wind and percussion instruments. Graduate degrees offered: Master of Music in the area of performance; Master of Music Education. Program accredited by NASM.

Enrollment Fall 1997: 101 total; 85 undergraduate, 16 graduate.

Music Student Profile 55% females, 45% males, 5% minorities, 3% international.

Music Faculty 20 total undergraduate and graduate (full-time and part-time). 70% of full-time faculty have terminal degrees. Graduate students teach a few undergraduate courses. Undergraduate student–faculty ratio: 6:1.

Student Life Student groups/activities include Collegiate Music Educators National Conference, Kappa Kappa Psi, Tau Beta Sigma.

Estimated expenses for 1998–99 Application fee: $20. State resident tuition: $1536 full-time. Nonresident tuition: $5900 full-time. Mandatory fees: $446 full-time. College room and board: $3560. College room only: $1720.

Financial Aid Program-specific awards for 1997: 60 Endowed Scholarships for talented students ($800–$1500).

Application Procedures Students apply for admission into the professional program by sophomore year. Deadline for freshmen and transfers: continuous. Required: high school transcript, college transcript(s) for transfer students, SAT I or ACT test scores, theory skills evaluation. Recommended: audition. Auditions held 3 times on campus; recorded music is permissible as a substitute for live auditions if a campus visit is impossible and videotaped performances are permissible as a substitute for live auditions if a campus visit is impossible.

Web Site http://www.emporia.edu/music/muhome.htm.

Undergraduate Contact Dr. Marie Miller, Chair, Division of Music, Emporia State University, Box 4029, Emporia, Kansas 66801; 316-341-5431, fax: 316-341-5073, E-mail address: millerma@esumail.emporia.edu.

Graduate Contact Dr. Penelope Speedie, Director, Graduate Studies in Music, Division of Music, Emporia State University, Box 4029, Emporia, Kansas 66801; 316-341-5438, E-mail address: speediep@esumail.emporia.edu.

Temple University

▼ ESTHER BOYER COLLEGE OF MUSIC AT TEMPLE UNIVERSITY

Philadelphia, Pennsylvania

State-related, coed. Urban campus. Total enrollment: 27,670. Music program established 1962.

Degrees Bachelor of Music in the areas of composition, jazz studies (arranging and composition, instrumental, and voice), music education, music history, music theory, music therapy, piano pedagogy, performance (instrumental, piano, voice); Bachelor of Science in the area of music. Majors and concentrations: bassoon, cello, clarinet, classical guitar,

double bass, euphonium, flute, harp, horn, jazz bass, jazz drums, jazz guitar, jazz piano, jazz saxophone, jazz trombone, jazz trumpet, jazz voice, oboe, percussion, piano, saxophone, trombone, trumpet, tuba, viola, violin, voice. Graduate degrees offered: Master of Music in the areas of choral conducting, composition, music education, music history, opera, orchestral performance (brass, percussion, strings, woodwind), piano accompanying, chamber music, opera coaching, pedagogy (piano, string), performance (guitar, piano, voice); Master of Music Therapy in the area of music therapy. Doctor of Musical Arts in the areas of composition, guitar performance, orchestral instrumental performance (brass instruments, percussion instruments, stringed instruments, woodwind instruments), piano performance, voice performance; Doctor of Philosophy in the area of music education. Program accredited by NASM.
Enrollment Fall 1997: 600 total; 350 undergraduate, 225 graduate, 25 non-professional degree.
Music Student Profile 52% females, 48% males, 32% minorities, 11% international.
Music Faculty 195 total undergraduate and graduate (full-time and part-time). 93% of full-time faculty have terminal degrees. Graduate students teach a few undergraduate courses. Undergraduate student–faculty ratio: 10:1.
Student Life Student groups/activities include music, band and honor societies, Music Educators National Conference Student Chapter. Special housing available for music students.
Expenses for 1997–98 Application fee: $35. State resident tuition: $5870 full-time. Nonresident tuition: $10,752 full-time. Mandatory fees: $280 full-time. Full-time tuition and fees vary according to course load and program. College room and board: $5772. Room and board charges vary according to board plan and housing facility. Special program-related fees: $150 per course for private lesson fee, $8–$30 per course for lab fees.
Financial Aid Program-specific awards for 1997: 40 Boyer Grants for freshmen and transfers ($250–$11,140), 100 Performance Grants for program majors ($250–$11,140).
Application Procedures Students admitted directly into the professional program freshman year. Deadline for freshmen: May 1; transfers: June 15. Notification date for freshmen and transfers: September 1. Required: essay, high school transcript, college transcript(s) for transfer students, minimum 2.0 high school GPA, audition, SAT I or ACT test scores, portfolio for composition and jazz arranging/composition applicants. Recommended: 2 letters of recommendation, interview. Auditions held 9 times on campus; recorded music is permissible as a substitute for live auditions when distance is prohibitive and videotaped performances are permissible as a substitute for live auditions when distance is prohibitive. Portfolio reviews held 9 times on campus.
Web Site http://www.temple.edu/music.
Contact Ms. Catherine Grudzinski, Coordinator of Recruitment, Esther Boyer College of Music, Temple University, Box 012-00, Philadelphia, Pennsylvania 19122; 215-204-8301, fax: 215-204-4957, E-mail address: music@blue.temple.edu.

▼ EVANGEL COLLEGE

Springfield, Missouri

Independent, coed. Urban campus. Total enrollment: 1,616. Music program established 1955.

Degrees Bachelor of Music in the areas of music education, sacred music, performance. Majors and concentrations: classical music, music, music education, piano/organ, sacred music, stringed instruments, voice, wind and percussion instruments. Program accredited by NASM, NCATE.
Enrollment Fall 1997: 106 undergraduate.
Music Student Profile 55% females, 45% males, 5% minorities, 5% international.
Music Faculty 27 total (full-time and part-time). 100% of full-time faculty have terminal degrees. Graduate students do not teach undergraduate courses. Undergraduate student–faculty ratio: 10:1.
Student Life Student groups/activities include Music Educators National Conference Student Chapter, Pi Kappa Lambda.
Expenses for 1998–99 Application fee: $25. Comprehensive fee: $12,400 includes full-time tuition ($8390), mandatory fees ($460), and college room and board ($3550). Special program-related fees: $20 per semester for techniques classes, instrument rental.
Financial Aid Program-specific awards for 1997: 50 Music Performance Awards for program students ($1500–$2000), 18 Endowed Awards for upperclassmen ($300–$1000).
Application Procedures Students admitted directly into the professional program freshman year. Deadline for freshmen and transfers: August 15. Required: high school transcript, 3 letters of recommendation, audition, ACT test score only. Recommended: minimum 2.0 high school GPA. Auditions held 4 times and by appointment on campus; recorded music is permissible as a substitute for live auditions when distance is prohibitive and videotaped performances are permissible as a substitute for live auditions when distance is prohibitive.
Undergraduate Contact Mr. John Shows, Chairman, Music Department, Evangel College, 1111 North Glenstone, Springfield, Missouri 65802; 417-865-2815 ext. 7211, fax: 417-865-9599, E-mail address: showsj@evangel.edu.

▼ FISK UNIVERSITY

Nashville, Tennessee

Independent, coed. Urban campus. Total enrollment: 765.
Degrees Bachelor of Music in the area of performance; Bachelor of Science in the area of music education; Bachelor of Arts in the area of music. Majors and concentrations: instrumental music, organ, piano, stringed instruments, voice. Cross-registration with Vanderbilt University. Program accredited by NASM.
Enrollment Fall 1997: 24 undergraduate.
Music Student Profile 100% minorities.
Music Faculty 5 total (full-time and part-time). 33% of full-time faculty have terminal degrees. Graduate students do not teach undergraduate courses. Undergraduate student–faculty ratio: 6:1.
Student Life Student groups/activities include Jazz Ensemble, Jubilee Singers, University Choir.
Expenses for 1997–98 Application fee: $25. Comprehensive fee: $12,054 includes full-time tuition ($7500), mandatory fees ($250), and college room and board ($4304). College room only: $2522. Special program-related fees: $60–$100 per course per semester for applied music lesson fee.
Financial Aid Program-specific awards for 1997: departmental scholarships for upperclassmen.
Application Procedures Students admitted directly into the professional program freshman year. Deadline for freshmen

Fisk University *(continued)*

and transfers: June 15. Required: essay, high school transcript, college transcript(s) for transfer students, minimum 2.0 high school GPA, 2 letters of recommendation, audition, SAT I or ACT test scores. Recommended: interview, video. Auditions held by appointment on campus; recorded music is permissible as a substitute for live auditions when distance is prohibitive and videotaped performances are permissible as a substitute for live auditions when distance is prohibitive.

Undergraduate Contact Admissions Office, Fisk University, 1000 17th Avenue North, Nashville, Tennessee 37208-3051; 615-329-8700.

▼ FIVE TOWNS COLLEGE

Dix Hills, New York

Independent, coed. Suburban campus. Music program established 1972.

Degrees Bachelor of Music in the area of jazz/commercial music; Bachelor of Music Education. Majors and concentrations: audio recording technology, composition/songwriting, music business, music education, performance, video music. Graduate degrees offered: Master of Music Education; Master of Music in the areas of composition arranging, music history, music performance, audio recording technology.

Enrollment Fall 1997: 611 total; 584 undergraduate, 27 graduate.

Music Student Profile 35% females, 65% males, 27% minorities, 2% international.

Music Faculty 73 total undergraduate and graduate (full-time and part-time). Graduate students do not teach undergraduate courses.

Student Life Student groups/activities include Music Theatre Production Society, Audio Recording Society, Music Educators National Conference Student Chapter.

Expenses for 1998–99 Application fee: $25. Comprehensive fee: $14,774 includes full-time tuition ($8900), mandatory fees ($320), and college room and board ($5554). Room and board charges vary according to board plan. Special program-related fees: $525 per semester for private music instruction, $10 per semester for piano lab fee, $25–$150 per semester for audio/video lab .

Financial Aid Program-specific awards for 1997: 6 Mickey Sheen Awards for percussion majors ($1200), 40 Music Program Awards for musical performers ($1200), 8 Brass and Woodwind Awards for brass/woodwind majors ($1200), 15 Long Island Superintendent Awards for music education majors ($4300), 1 Mel Fuhrman/B'nai B'rith Music Business Scholarship for those demonstrating outstanding academic achievement.

Application Procedures Students admitted directly into the professional program freshman year. Deadline for freshmen and transfers: continuous. Required: essay, high school transcript, college transcript(s) for transfer students, minimum 2.0 high school GPA, interview, audition. Recommended: minimum 3.0 high school GPA, 2 letters of recommendation, SAT I or ACT test scores. Auditions held 7 times on campus; recorded music is permissible as a substitute for live auditions for international applicants.

Web Site http://www.fivetowns.edu.

Contact Ms. Christina Kuhl, Director of Admissions, Five Towns College, 305 North Service Road, Dix Hills, New York 11746; 516-424-7000 ext. 110, fax: 516-424-7006.

More About the College

Program Facilities Performance spaces include the Dix Hills Center for the Performing Arts (500 seats), College athletic center (1,000-seat arena), and The Upbeat Café (132 seats). In addition, the College is equipped with 8-, 16-, 24-, and 48-track state-of-the-art recording studios as well as a MIDI technology laboratory. The College's television studios are equipped with both linear and nonlinear digital editing suites.

Faculty, Resident Artists, and Alumni The many gifted and talented musicians and educators who comprise the Five Towns College faculty bring a vast array of backgrounds and experiences to campus. The faculty is exemplary in both their academic and performance credentials. Artists-in-residence include the Township Theatre Group, Ray Alexander, Wes Belcamp, and Peter Rogine. Representative visiting artists include the Sea Cliff Chamber Players, the Sound Symphony Orchestra, and the Gilbert & Sullivan Light Opera Theatre Company of Long Island. John Sebastian, Ian McDonald, Steve Howe, Arvell Shaw, J.Geils, Jimmy Vivino, Sal Salvador, Arlen Roth, and Tuck and Patti are just a few of the artists/clinicians who appeared at the College the past few seasons. Alumni work throughout the music industry in numerous capacities, such as musicians, business managers, audio recording engineers, and music educators.

Student Performance Students have the opportunity to perform in ensembles of every size and instrumentation. The most popular ensembles include the Concert Choir, Stage Band, Guitar Ensemble, and Percussion Ensemble. Students are invited to participate in any of the six major theatrical productions produced on campus each year. These include two musicals, one operetta, one comedy, and two dramas. The Upbeat Café provides an informal atmosphere for students to gather, perform, and collaborate each afternoon.

Special Programs The College is a member of the Phi Sigma National Honor Society and hosts a student chapter of the Music Educators National Conference (MENC). Each spring, the College hosts the Classic American Guitar Show, which brings thousands of guitarists from around the world together for a conference and exposition. Numerous other festivals and performances are held each year, including a Stage Band Festival and Music Industry Conference.

▼

Nestled on nearly 40 rolling acres at Dix Hills, Long Island, New York, Five Towns College is a comprehensive institution of higher education with a well-rounded music and performing arts environment. Through its three major divisions—Music, Business, and Liberal Arts—the College offers more than thirty different programs of study leading to associate and bachelor degrees.

The College awards a Bachelor of Music degree in jazz/commercial music, with major areas of concentration in performance, composition/songwriting, musical theater, audio recording technology, music business, and video music. These programs are designed for students pursuing careers as professional performers, composers, recording engineers, music business executives, or producers of video music.

The College also offers a Bachelor of Music degree program in music education. The Music Education program is designed for students interested in a career as a teacher of music in a public or private school (K–12), leads to New York State Certification, and prepares students for the National Teacher Education (NTE) Core Battery Tests. In addition, the college now offers a new master degree program leading to a Master of Music (Mus.M) in jazz/commercial music or music education.

For students interested in nonperforming careers in the music industry, Five Towns College offers the Bachelor of Professional Studies (B.P.S.) degree program in business management, with major areas of concentration in audio recording technology, music business, and video arts. These programs are designed for students planning to pursue careers in management and marketing with firms in the areas of record and music production, broadcasting, concert promotion, radio, television, theater, and communications. The program is intended for students who are interested in developing their business and technical expertise.

Students who attend Five Towns College benefit from the institution's excellent reputation for preparing students for entry into the music industry. In addition to its highly qualified faculty, the College has facilities that are state-of-the-art. The College is equipped with 8-, 16-, 24-, and 48-track world-class recording studios. The College is also equipped with a television production facility and sound stages of various sizes. The Dix Hills Center for the Performing Arts has been described as "acoustically perfect." The Five Towns College library consists of over 30,000 print and nonprint materials and has a significant collection of recorded music.

Five Towns College is fully accredited by the Middle States Association and the New York State Board of Regents.

Schmidt College of Arts and Letters

▼ FLORIDA ATLANTIC UNIVERSITY

Boca Raton, Florida

State-supported, coed. Suburban campus. Total enrollment: 18,823. Music program established 1963.

Degrees Bachelor of Music in the areas of music performance, music education, jazz studies, music business. Majors and concentrations: accompanying, classical music, jazz, music education, piano, stringed instruments, voice, wind and percussion instruments. Program accredited by NASM.

Enrollment Fall 1997: 110 total; 90 undergraduate, 20 nonprofessional degree.

Music Student Profile 50% females, 50% males, 10% minorities, 2% international.

Music Faculty 36 total (full-time and part-time). 75% of full-time faculty have terminal degrees. Graduate students teach a few undergraduate courses.

Student Life Student groups/activities include Collegiate Music Educators National Conference, International Association of Jazz Educators.

Expenses for 1997–98 Application fee: $20. State resident tuition: $2022 full-time. Nonresident tuition: $7940 full-time. Full-time tuition varies according to course load. College room and board: $4680. College room only: $2360. Room and board charges vary according to board plan and housing facility.

Financial Aid Program-specific awards for 1997: 60 music scholarships for program majors and ensemble participants ($300–$1500).

Application Procedures Students admitted directly into the professional program freshman year. Deadline for freshmen and transfers: August 1. Required: high school transcript,

college transcript(s) for transfer students, minimum 2.0 high school GPA, audition, SAT I or ACT test scores. Auditions held 8 times on campus; recorded music is permissible as a substitute for live auditions when distance is prohibitive and videotaped performances are permissible as a substitute for live auditions when distance is prohibitive.

Web Site http://www.fau.edu.

Undergraduate Contact Dr. Stuart Glazer, Chair, Music Department, Florida Atlantic University, 777 Glades Road, Boca Raton, Florida 33431; 561-297-3820, fax: 561-297-2944, E-mail address: sglazer@acc.fau.edu.

▼ FLORIDA BAPTIST THEOLOGICAL COLLEGE

Graceville, Florida

Independent-Southern Baptist, coed. Small town campus. Total enrollment: 486. Music program established 1960.

Degrees Bachelor of Music in the area of church music. Majors and concentrations: sacred music. Program accredited by NASM.

Enrollment Fall 1997: 70 total; all undergraduate.

Music Student Profile 26% females, 74% males, 5% minorities, 3% international.

Music Faculty 8 total (full-time and part-time). 60% of full-time faculty have terminal degrees. Graduate students do not teach undergraduate courses. Undergraduate student–faculty ratio: 13:1.

Student Life Student groups/activities include Spring Concert, Christmas Concert, Florida Baptist Convention.

Expenses for 1997–98 Application fee: $20. Tuition: $2850 full-time. Mandatory fees: $84 full-time. College room only: $1500. Special program-related fees: $2–$3 for practice room fee, $25 for class instruction, $50–$100 for private lessons, $20–$30 for recital fee, $90–$200 for applied music fees.

Financial Aid Program-specific awards for 1997: 72 Institutional Scholarships for students demonstrating need ($500).

Application Procedures Students admitted directly into the professional program freshman year. Deadline for freshmen and transfers: August 1. Notification date for freshmen and transfers: August 15. Required: high school transcript, college transcript(s) for transfer students, minimum 2.0 high school GPA, 3 letters of recommendation, interview, audition, SAT I or ACT test scores. Auditions held twice on campus.

Undergraduate Contact Mr. Lavan Wilson, Director of Admissions, Florida Baptist Theological College, PO Box 1306, Graceville, Florida 32440; 850-263-3261, fax: 850-263-7506.

▼ FLORIDA INTERNATIONAL UNIVERSITY

Miami, Florida

State-supported, coed. Urban campus. Total enrollment: 30,012. Music program established 1973.

Degrees Bachelor of Music. Majors and concentrations: jazz, music theory and composition, performance. Graduate degrees offered: Master of Music in the areas of conducting/performance/composition/jazz studies, performance art production. Cross-registration with Florida State University System. Program accredited by NASM.

Enrollment Fall 1997: 200 total; 170 undergraduate, 30 non-professional degree.

Florida International University (continued)

Music Student Profile 50% females, 50% males, 80% minorities, 25% international.

Music Faculty 65 total undergraduate and graduate (full-time and part-time). 100% of full-time faculty have terminal degrees. Graduate students do not teach undergraduate courses.

Student Life Student groups/activities include Music Educators National Conference, American Choral Directors Association.

Expenses for 1997–98 Application fee: $20. State resident tuition: $1943 full-time. Nonresident tuition: $7859 full-time. Mandatory fees: $92 full-time. College room and board: $7378. College room only: $4448. Room and board charges vary according to board plan and housing facility.

Financial Aid Program-specific awards for 1997: 60 departmental scholarships for musically talented students ($250–$1000).

Application Procedures Students apply for admission into the professional program by sophomore year. Deadline for freshmen and transfers: continuous. Required: high school transcript, college transcript(s) for transfer students, minimum 2.0 high school GPA, audition, SAT I or ACT test scores. Recommended: 3 letters of recommendation. Auditions held 6 times on campus and off campus in Taiwan; Hong Kong; Puerto Rico; Bangkok, Thailand; recorded music is permissible as a substitute for live auditions if a campus visit is impossible and videotaped performances are permissible as a substitute for live auditions if a campus visit is impossible.

Undergraduate Contact Dr. Frederick Kaufman, Director, School of Music, Florida International University, Wertheim Performing Arts Center, Room 141, Miami, Florida 33199; 305-348-2896, fax: 305-348-4073, E-mail address: kaufmanf@servms.fiu.edu.

Graduate Contact Dr. Orlando Garcia, Graduate Director, School of Music, Florida International University, Wertheim Performing Arts Center, Room 141, Miami, Florida 33199fax: 305-348-4073, E-mail address: ogarcia@servms.fiu.edu.

▼ Florida Southern College

Lakeland, Florida

Independent, coed. Suburban campus. Total enrollment: 1,775.

Degrees Bachelor of Music in the areas of winds, percussion, voice; Bachelor of Music Education; Bachelor of Sacred Music. Majors and concentrations: classical music, composition, music, music education, piano/organ, sacred music, stringed instruments, voice, wind and percussion instruments.

Enrollment Fall 1997: 246 total; 96 undergraduate, 150 non-professional degree.

Music Student Profile 60% females, 40% males, 4% minorities, 1% international.

Music Faculty 35 total (full-time and part-time). 60% of full-time faculty have terminal degrees. Graduate students do not teach undergraduate courses. Undergraduate student–faculty ratio: 8:1.

Student Life Student groups/activities include Music Educators National Conference Student Chapter, Phi Mu Alpha Sinfonia, Delta Omicron.

Expenses for 1997–98 Application fee: $30. Comprehensive fee: $16,034 includes full-time tuition ($9818), mandatory fees ($786), and college room and board ($5430). College room only: $2400. Special program-related fees: $275 per semester for applied lesson fee, $150–$300 per semester for applied music fee for non-music majors.

Financial Aid Program-specific awards for 1997: 28 Davidson Scholarships for program majors ($2000), 1 Presser Scholarship for program majors ($2000), 1 Gannaway Award for program majors ($4000), 2 Pickard Scholarships for program majors ($2000), 4 Wolff/MacDonald Scholarships for program majors ($4000), 1 Bosendorfer Award for program majors ($1000), 1 Schimmel Award for program majors ($1000), 1 Woodard Scholarship for program majors ($650), 1 Houts Scholarship for program majors ($600).

Application Procedures Students admitted directly into the professional program freshman year. Deadline for freshmen and transfers: continuous. Required: essay, high school transcript, college transcript(s) for transfer students, minimum 2.0 high school GPA, 3 letters of recommendation, audition, SAT I or ACT test scores (minimum combined SAT I score of 1000, minimum combined ACT score of 20). Recommended: minimum 3.0 high school GPA, interview. Auditions held by appointment on campus; recorded music is permissible as a substitute for live auditions when distance is prohibitive and videotaped performances are permissible as a substitute for live auditions when distance is prohibitive.

Web Site http://www.flsouthern.edu.

Undergraduate Contact Mr. Robert Palmer, Dean of Enrollment Management, Florida Southern College, 111 Lake Hollingsworth Drive, Lakeland, Florida 33801-5698; 941-680-6212, fax: 941-680-4120.

▼ Florida State University

Tallahassee, Florida

State-supported, coed. Suburban campus. Total enrollment: 30,401. Music program established 1900.

Degrees Bachelor of Music in the areas of performance, piano pedagogy, composition, music history/literature, music theory, music theater, music therapy; Bachelor of Music Education in the areas of instrumental music education, choral music education, general music education. Majors and concentrations: classical music, jazz, music, music education, music theater, music therapy, piano/organ, stringed instruments, voice, wind and percussion instruments. Graduate degrees offered: Master of Music in the areas of performance, accompanying, piano pedagogy, choral conducting, opera, instrumental conducting, jazz, theory, composition, ethnomusicology, historical musicology, music therapy; Master of Music Education in the areas of instrumental music education, choral music education; Master of Arts in the area of arts administration. Doctor of Music in the areas of composition, performance; Doctor of Philosophy in the areas of music education, music theory, ethnomusicology, historical musicology. Cross-registration with Tallahassee Community College. Program accredited by NASM, NCATE.

Enrollment Fall 1997: 986 total; 497 undergraduate, 305 graduate, 184 non-professional degree.

Music Student Profile 52% females, 48% males, 14% minorities, 2% international.

Music Faculty 79 total undergraduate and graduate (full-time and part-time). 94% of full-time faculty have terminal

degrees. Graduate students teach about a quarter undergraduate courses. Undergraduate student–faculty ratio: 9:1.

Student Life Student groups/activities include Collegiate Music Educators National Conference, American Choral Directors Association.

Expenses for 1997–98 Application fee: $20. State resident tuition: $1988 full-time. Nonresident tuition: $7905 full-time. College room and board: $4570. College room only: $2540. Room and board charges vary according to board plan and housing facility.

Financial Aid Program-specific awards for 1997: 65 out-of-state tuition waivers for program majors ($4507), 180 general scholarships for program majors ($250–$2500).

Application Procedures Students admitted directly into the professional program freshman year. Deadline for freshmen: March 1; transfers: July 17. Required: high school transcript, college transcript(s) for transfer students, minimum 3.0 high school GPA, audition, SAT I or ACT test scores. Auditions held 7 times on campus; recorded music is permissible as a substitute for live auditions when distance is prohibitive.

Web Site http://www.music.fsu.edu.

Undergraduate Contact Dr. Ted Stanley, Program Director for Undergraduate Studies, School of Music, Florida State University, Tallahassee, Florida 32306-1180; 850-644-4833, fax: 850-644-2033, E-mail address: tstanley@garnet.acns.fsu.edu.

Graduate Contact Dr. John Deal, Assistant Dean; Director of Graduate Studies, School of Music, Florida State University, Tallahassee, Florida 32306-1180; 850-644-5848, fax: 850-644-2033, E-mail address: deal_j@otto.cmr.fsu.edu.

▼ FORT HAYS STATE UNIVERSITY

Hays, Kansas

State-supported, coed. Small town campus. Total enrollment: 5,616. Music program established 1902.

Degrees Bachelor of Music in the areas of performance, music education. Majors and concentrations: music education, piano, stringed instruments, voice, wind and percussion instruments. Program accredited by NASM.

Enrollment Fall 1997: 64 total; 59 undergraduate, 5 nonprofessional degree.

Music Student Profile 50% females, 50% males, 10% minorities, 10% international.

Music Faculty 16 total (full-time and part-time). 62% of full-time faculty have terminal degrees. Graduate students do not teach undergraduate courses. Undergraduate student–faculty ratio: 5:1.

Student Life Student groups/activities include Collegiate Music Educators National Conference, Phi Mu Alpha Sinfonia, Sigma Alpha Iota.

Expenses for 1997–98 Application fee: $20. State resident tuition: $1992 full-time. Nonresident tuition: $6256 full-time. Full-time tuition varies according to course load, location, and reciprocity agreements. College room and board: $3400. College room only: $1766. Room and board charges vary according to board plan, housing facility, and student level. Special program-related fees: $32–$64 per credit hour for applied lessons for non-majors.

Financial Aid Program-specific awards for 1997: 20–30 Awards of Excellence in Music for freshmen ($400), 40–60 music scholarships for program students ($900).

Application Procedures Deadline for freshmen and transfers: continuous. Required: high school transcript, 2 letters of recommendation, audition. Auditions held 3 times and by appointment on campus and off campus in various locations in Kansas; recorded music is permissible as a substitute for live auditions when distance is prohibitive and videotaped performances are permissible as a substitute for live auditions when distance is prohibitive.

Undergraduate Contact Mr. Joey Linn, Director, Admissions Department, Fort Hays State University, 600 Park Street, Hays, Kansas 67601; 913-628-5666, E-mail address: adpm@fhsuvm.fhsu.edu.

▼ FRIENDS UNIVERSITY

Wichita, Kansas

Independent, coed. Urban campus. Total enrollment: 2,729.

Degrees Bachelor of Music in the areas of voice, piano; Bachelor of Music Education in the areas of vocal music education, instrumental music education. Program accredited by NASM.

Enrollment Fall 1997: 280 total; all undergraduate.

Music Student Profile 50% females, 50% males, 10% minorities, 5% international.

Music Faculty 24 total (full-time and part-time). 75% of full-time faculty have terminal degrees. Graduate students do not teach undergraduate courses. Undergraduate student–faculty ratio: 15:1.

Student Life Student groups/activities include Mu Phi Epsilon, American Choral Directors Association, Music Educators National Conference.

Expenses for 1997–98 Application fee: $15. One-time mandatory fee: $40. Comprehensive fee: $13,225 includes full-time tuition ($9885), mandatory fees ($90), and college room and board ($3250). College room only: $1400. Full-time tuition and fees vary according to course load. Room and board charges vary according to student level.

Financial Aid Program-specific awards for 1997: 10 Miller Scholarships for program majors ($1000), 100 departmental scholarships for program majors ($1000–$1500).

Application Procedures Students admitted directly into the professional program freshman year. Deadline for freshmen: August 1; transfers: August 26. Required: high school transcript, college transcript(s) for transfer students, minimum 2.0 high school GPA, audition, SAT I or ACT test scores, minimum 3.0 high school GPA and ACT score of 20 for scholarship consideration. Auditions held by appointment on campus; recorded music is permissible as a substitute for live auditions if a campus visit is impossible.

Undergraduate Contact Dr. John Taylor, Director of Instrumental Music and Music Education, Fine Arts Department, Friends University, 2100 University Drive, Wichita, Kansas 67213; 316-295-5535, fax: 316-295-5593.

▼ FURMAN UNIVERSITY

Greenville, South Carolina

Independent, coed. Suburban campus. Total enrollment: 2,840.

Degrees Bachelor of Music in the areas of performance, church music, music education, music theory. Majors and concentrations: church music, music education, music

Furman University *(continued)*

theory, performance, piano/organ, stringed instruments, voice, wind and percussion instruments. Program accredited by NASM.

Enrollment Fall 1997: 149 total; 94 undergraduate, 55 non-professional degree.

Music Student Profile 56% females, 44% males, 7% minorities.

Music Faculty 34 total (full-time and part-time). 94% of full-time faculty have terminal degrees. Graduate students do not teach undergraduate courses.

Student Life Student groups/activities include Phi Mu Alpha, Sigma Alpha Iota.

Expenses for 1997–98 Application fee: $30. Comprehensive fee: $20,868 includes full-time tuition ($16,256), mandatory fees ($163), and college room and board ($4449). College room only: $2329. Room and board charges vary according to board plan and housing facility. Special program-related fees: $129–$180 per term for private music lessons.

Financial Aid Program-specific awards for 1997: 16 Daniel Scholarships for program majors ($1500–$2500), 12 Timmons Scholarships for program majors ($1000–$4000), 132 general music scholarships for program students ($1000–$3000), 6 Gunter Scholarships for program majors ($1500–$3000), 5 Lusby Scholarships for strings students ($4000–$6000).

Application Procedures Deadline for freshmen and transfers: February 1. Notification date for freshmen: March 15. Required: essay, high school transcript, college transcript(s) for transfer students, SAT I or ACT test scores, audition for scholarship consideration, audition for ensembles and/or private lessons. Recommended: 2 letters of recommendation. Auditions held 4 times on campus; recorded music is permissible as a substitute for live auditions when distance is prohibitive and videotaped performances are permissible as a substitute for live auditions when distance is prohibitive.

Web Site http://www.furman.edu.

Undergraduate Contact Mr. Carey Thompson, Admissions Director, Furman University, Greenville, South Carolina 29613; 864-294-2086, E-mail address: carey.thompson@furman.edu.

▼ GEORGE MASON UNIVERSITY

Fairfax, Virginia

State-supported, coed. Suburban campus. Total enrollment: 23,826. Music program established 1972.

Degrees Bachelor of Music in the areas of music education, performance. Graduate degrees offered: Master of Arts in the areas of conducting, performance, music education, composition. Program accredited by NASM.

Enrollment Fall 1997: 201 total; 176 undergraduate, 25 graduate.

Music Student Profile 55% females, 45% males, 6% minorities, 12% international.

Music Faculty 63 total undergraduate and graduate (full-time and part-time). 95% of full-time faculty have terminal degrees. Graduate students do not teach undergraduate courses.

Student Life Student groups/activities include Music Educators National Conference.

Expenses for 1997–98 Application fee: $30. State resident tuition: $4296 full-time. Nonresident tuition: $12,240 full-time. Full-time tuition varies according to course load. College room and board: $5120. College room only: $3300.

Room and board charges vary according to board plan and housing facility. Special program-related fees: $165 per credit hour for private instruction.

Financial Aid Program-specific awards for 1997: 2 Cook Piano Scholarships for pianists ($1000), 20–25 Music/Arts Scholarships for music majors ($1000).

Application Procedures Students apply for admission into the professional program by junior year. Deadline for freshmen: February 1; transfers: March 15. Required: essay, high school transcript, college transcript(s) for transfer students, minimum 2.0 high school GPA, interview, audition, SAT I or ACT test scores. Recommended: minimum 3.0 high school GPA, letter of recommendation. Auditions held 8 times on campus; recorded music is permissible as a substitute for live auditions for international applicants or when distance is prohibitive and videotaped performances are permissible as a substitute for live auditions for international students or when distance is prohibitive.

Web Site http://www.ido.gmu.edu/departments/music/muscont.htm.

Undergraduate Contact Dr. Joseph Kanyan, Associate Chair, Department of Music, George Mason University, Mail Stop 3E3, Fairfax, Virginia 22030-4444; 703-993-1389, fax: 703-993-1394, E-mail address: jkanyan@osf1.gmu.edu.

Graduate Contact Dr. Evelyn Orman, Graduate Coordinator, Department of Music, George Mason University, Mail Stop 3E3, Fairfax, Virginia 22030-4444; 703-993-1379, fax: 703-993-1394, E-mail address: eorman1@osf1.gmu.edu.

▼ GEORGETOWN COLLEGE

Georgetown, Kentucky

Independent, coed. Suburban campus. Total enrollment: 1,626. Music program established 1840.

Degrees Bachelor of Music in the area of church music; Bachelor of Music Education in the areas of vocal music education, instrumental music education. Majors and concentrations: music education, piano/organ, sacred music, voice, wind and percussion instruments.

Enrollment Fall 1997: 50 total; 25 undergraduate, 25 non-professional degree.

Music Student Profile 60% females, 40% males, 3% minorities.

Music Faculty 12 total (full-time and part-time). 83% of full-time faculty have terminal degrees. Graduate students do not teach undergraduate courses. Undergraduate student–faculty ratio: 13:1.

Student Life Student groups/activities include Music Educators National Conference Student Chapter, Delta Omicron.

Expenses for 1997–98 Application fee: $25. Comprehensive fee: $14,370 includes full-time tuition ($9990), mandatory fees ($200), and college room and board ($4180). College room only: $2080. Special program-related fees: $150–$240 per semester for applied fees, $120 per semester for piano class.

Financial Aid Program-specific awards for 1997: 12–15 Music Department Scholarships ($200–$2000), 25–50 College Grants in Music ($200–$2000).

Application Procedures Students admitted directly into the professional program freshman year. Deadline for freshmen and transfers: April 15. Required: essay, high school transcript, college transcript(s) for transfer students, audition, SAT I or ACT test scores. Recommended: interview. Auditions held 5 times and by appointment on campus; recorded music is permissible as a substitute for live auditions when distance is prohibitive and videotaped performances are permissible as a substitute for live auditions when distance is prohibitive.

Undergraduate Contact Dr. Sonny Burnette, Chair, Department of Music, Georgetown College, 400 East College Street, Georgetown, Kentucky 40324-1696; 502-863-8112, E-mail address: sburnett@gtc.georgetown.ky.us.

▼ THE GEORGE WASHINGTON UNIVERSITY

Washington, District of Columbia

Independent, coed. Urban campus. Total enrollment: 19,356. Music program established 1962.

Degrees Bachelor of Music in the area of performance. Majors and concentrations: brass, classical guitar, piano/organ, stringed instruments, voice, wind and percussion instruments. Cross-registration with Washington Metropolitan Area Consortium of Universities. Program accredited by NASM.

Enrollment Fall 1997: 754 total; 4 undergraduate, 750 non-professional degree.

Music Student Profile 56% females, 44% males, 3% minorities, 5% international.

Music Faculty 55 total (full-time and part-time). 60% of full-time faculty have terminal degrees. Graduate students do not teach undergraduate courses. Undergraduate student–faculty ratio: 15:1.

Student Life Student groups/activities include Creative and Performing Arts Residential Learning Program, Kappa Kappa Psi. Special housing available for music students.

Expenses for 1997–98 Application fee: $50. Comprehensive fee: $28,685 includes full-time tuition ($20,370), mandatory fees ($990), and college room and board ($7325). College room only: $4590. Room and board charges vary according to board plan and housing facility. Special program-related fees: $75 per semester for practice room facilities fee.

Financial Aid Program-specific awards for 1997: 5 Presidential Arts Scholarships for program majors and non-majors ($7500), 1 Steiner Music Scholarship for string students ($2000), University Band Scholarships for band members ($1000–$3000).

Application Procedures Students apply for admission into the professional program by freshman year. Deadline for freshmen: February 1; transfers: June 1. Notification date for freshmen: March 15; transfers: September 1. Required: essay, high school transcript, college transcript(s) for transfer students, minimum 2.0 high school GPA, 2 letters of recommendation, audition, SAT I or ACT test scores, minimum 2.7 college GPA for transfer students. Recommended: minimum 3.0 high school GPA, interview. Auditions held twice and by appointment on campus; recorded music is permissible as a substitute for live auditions when distance is prohibitive or scheduling is difficult and videotaped performances are permissible as a substitute for live auditions when distance is prohibitive or if scheduling is difficult.

Undergraduate Contact Dr. Roy J. Guenther, Chairman, Department of Music, The George Washington University, Academic Center B-144, 801 22nd Street, NW, Washington, District of Columbia 20052; 202-994-6245, fax: 202-994-9038, E-mail address: gwmusic@gwis2.circ.gwu.edu.

▼ GEORGIA COLLEGE AND STATE UNIVERSITY

Milledgeville, Georgia

State-supported, coed. Small town campus. Total enrollment: 5,512. Music program established 1957.

Degrees Bachelor of Music in the areas of intrumental music, voice; Bachelor of Music Education in the areas of choral music, instrumental music; Bachelor of Arts in the area of music. Majors and concentrations: brass, choral music education, guitar, instrumental music education, piano/organ, voice, wind and percussion instruments. Program accredited by NASM, NAMT, NCATE.

Enrollment Fall 1997: 80 total; 65 undergraduate, 15 non-professional degree.

Music Student Profile 60% females, 40% males, 1% minorities, 1% international.

Music Faculty 21 total (full-time and part-time). 43% of full-time faculty have terminal degrees. Graduate students do not teach undergraduate courses. Undergraduate student–faculty ratio: 4:1.

Student Life Student groups/activities include Music Educators National Conference Student Chapter, American Choral Directors Association Student Chapter.

Expenses for 1997–98 Application fee: $10. State resident tuition: $1680 full-time. Nonresident tuition: $6141 full-time. Mandatory fees: $384 full-time. College room and board: $4203. Room and board charges vary according to board plan and housing facility. Special program-related fees: $20–$40 per credit hour for applied music fees.

Financial Aid Program-specific awards for 1997: 7 Outstanding Student Scholarships for those demonstrating talent and academic achievement ($4000), 3 Weir Service Awards for those demonstrating financial need ($3600), 3–4 Gilbert Service Awards for music majors ($2000), alumni scholarships for music majors/minors ($2000).

Application Procedures Students admitted directly into the professional program freshman year. Deadline for freshmen and transfers: continuous. Required: high school transcript, college transcript(s) for transfer students, audition, SAT I or ACT test scores (minimum combined SAT I score of 870), completion of College Preparatory Curriculum (CPC) with no deficiencies. Recommended: minimum 2.0 high school GPA, interview. Auditions held twice and by appointment on campus; recorded music is permissible as a substitute for live auditions on a case-by-case basis and videotaped performances are permissible as a substitute for live auditions on a case-by-case basis.

Undergraduate Contact Chairman, Department of Music and Theatre, Georgia College and State University, Box 066, Milledgeville, Georgia 31061; 912-445-4226, fax: 912-445-1633.

▼ GEORGIA SOUTHERN UNIVERSITY

Statesboro, Georgia

State-supported, coed. Small town campus. Total enrollment: 13,963.

Degrees Bachelor of Music in the areas of composition, music education, performance. Graduate degrees offered: Master

Georgia Southern University (*continued*)

of Music in the areas of composition, music education, performance, music history and literature. Program accredited by NASM.

Enrollment Fall 1997: 163 total; 145 undergraduate, 8 graduate, 10 non-professional degree.

Music Student Profile 50% females, 50% males, 5% minorities, 1% international.

Music Faculty 28 total undergraduate and graduate (full-time and part-time). 95% of full-time faculty have terminal degrees. Graduate students do not teach undergraduate courses.

Student Life Student groups/activities include Collegiate Music Educators National Conference, American Choral Directors Association, professional music fraternities and sororities.

Expenses for 1997–98 Application fee: $10. State resident tuition: $1680 full-time. Nonresident tuition: $6141 full-time. Mandatory fees: $576 full-time. College room and board: $3465. College room only: $1815. Room and board charges vary according to board plan and housing facility. Special program-related fees: $13 per credit hour for applied music fee.

Financial Aid Program-specific awards for 1997: 7 Endowed Scholarships for music majors ($500–$1000), 30–40 Georgia Southern Foundation Music Scholarships for those demonstrating talent and academic merit ($600–$1000), 20 Symphony Service Awards for symphony players ($500), 130 Symphonic Wind Ensemble/Marching Band Service Awards for symphonic wind ensemble/marching band players ($400–$500), 8 Jazz Ensemble Service Awards for jazz ensemble players ($600–$1000), 25 Choral Service Awards for members of Southern Chorale ($150).

Application Procedures Students admitted directly into the professional program freshman year. Deadline for freshmen and transfers: continuous. Required: high school transcript, college transcript(s) for transfer students, minimum 2.0 high school GPA, audition, SAT I or ACT test scores (minimum combined SAT I score of 920). Auditions held 4 times and by appointment on campus; recorded music is permissible as a substitute for live auditions when distance is prohibitive and videotaped performances are permissible as a substitute for live auditions when distance is prohibitive.

Web Site http://www2.gasou.edu/music.

Undergraduate Contact Dr. David Mathew, Interim Chair, Department of Music, Georgia Southern University, LB 8052, Statesboro, Georgia 30460-8052; 912-681-5396, fax: 912-681-0583.

Graduate Contact Dr. Greg Harwood, Director of Graduate Music Studies, Department of Music, Georgia Southern University, LB 8052, Statesboro, Georgia 30460-8052; 912-681-5396, fax: 912-681-0583.

▼ GEORGIA STATE UNIVERSITY

Atlanta, Georgia

State-supported, coed. Urban campus. Total enrollment: 24,276. Music program established 1958.

Degrees Bachelor of Music in the areas of music education, performance, jazz studies, composition, music industry, music theory. Graduate degrees offered: Master of Music in the areas of music education, performance, composition, jazz studies, music theory, conducting, piano pedagogy, sacred

music. Cross-registration with Georgia State University System. Program accredited by NASM.

Enrollment Fall 1997: 405 total; 300 undergraduate, 90 graduate, 15 non-professional degree.

Music Student Profile 50% females, 50% males, 15% minorities, 10% international.

Music Faculty 88 total undergraduate and graduate (full-time and part-time). 64% of full-time faculty have terminal degrees. Graduate students teach a few undergraduate courses.

Student Life Student groups/activities include Pi Kappa Lambda.

Expenses for 1997–98 Application fee: $25. State resident tuition: $2250 full-time. Nonresident tuition: $9000 full-time. Mandatory fees: $423 full-time. College room only: $3789. Special program-related fees: $100 per semester for applied music fees, $40 per recital for use of hall.

Financial Aid Program-specific awards for 1997: 1 The Harris M. Taft Memorial Scholarship for program majors ($500–$2000), 1 The Charles Thomas Wurm Music Scholarship for program majors ($500–$2000), 1 The Friends of Rick Bell Jazz Scholarship for jazz majors ($500–$2000), 1 The Haskell Boyter Choral Scholarship for voice majors ($500–$2000), 1 The Thomas M. Brumby Keyboard Scholarship for keyboard majors ($500–$2000), 1 The Friends of Music Scholarship for program majors ($500–$2000), 1 The Montgomery Music Scholarship for program majors ($500–$2000), 1 The National Association for Recording Arts and Sciences Award for program majors ($500–$2000), 1 The Presser Foundation Music Scholarship for program majors ($500–$2000), 1 The Robert Swiatek Memorial Scholarship in Percussion for percussion majors ($500–$2000).

Application Procedures Students admitted directly into the professional program freshman year. Deadline for freshmen and transfers: continuous. Required: high school transcript, college transcript(s) for transfer students, minimum 2.0 high school GPA, audition, SAT I test score only, audition and interview for music industry applicants, portfolio review for composition applicants. Recommended: essay, minimum 3.0 high school GPA, 2 letters of recommendation, portfolio. Auditions held 4 times on campus; recorded music is permissible as a substitute for live auditions when distance is prohibitive and videotaped performances are permissible as a substitute for live auditions when distance is prohibitive. Portfolio reviews held 4 times on campus.

Undergraduate Contact Dr. David Myers, Associate Director, School of Music, Georgia State University, University Plaza, Atlanta, Georgia 30303; 404-651-1721, fax: 404-651-1583.

Graduate Contact Dr. James Lyke, Director of Graduate Program, School of Music, Georgia State University, University Plaza, Atlanta, Georgia 30303-3083; 404-651-1641, fax: 404-651-1583, E-mail address: musrst@gsusgi2.gsu.edu.

▼ GORDON COLLEGE

Wenham, Massachusetts

Independent-nondenominational, coed. Small town campus. Total enrollment: 1,375.

Degrees Bachelor of Music in the areas of music performance, music education. Majors and concentrations: classical music, music, music education, piano/organ, stringed instruments, voice, wind and percussion instruments. Cross-registration with Christian College Coalition, Northeast

Consortium of Colleges and Universities in Massachusetts. Program accredited by NASM.

Enrollment Fall 1997: 63 undergraduate.

Music Student Profile 65% females, 35% males, 10% minorities, 15% international.

Music Faculty 31 total (full-time and part-time). 70% of full-time faculty have terminal degrees. Graduate students do not teach undergraduate courses. Undergraduate student–faculty ratio: 10:1.

Student Life Student groups/activities include Music Educators National Conference Student Chapter, American Choral Directors Association Student Chapter.

Expenses for 1998–99 Application fee: $40. Comprehensive fee: $20,710 includes full-time tuition ($15,100), mandatory fees ($660), and college room and board ($4950). College room only: $3350. Room and board charges vary according to board plan and location. Special program-related fees: $405 per semester for applied music fee.

Financial Aid Program-specific awards for 1997: 40 Music Grants for program majors ($750–$3000).

Application Procedures Students admitted directly into the professional program freshman year. Deadline for freshmen and transfers: continuous. Required: essay, high school transcript, college transcript(s) for transfer students, interview, audition, SAT I or ACT test scores. Recommended: minimum 2.0 high school GPA, 2 letters of recommendation. Auditions held continuously by appointment on campus; recorded music is permissible as a substitute for live auditions when distance is prohibitive and videotaped performances are permissible as a substitute for live auditions when distance is prohibitive.

Undergraduate Contact Mr. C. Thomas Brooks, Chair, Music Department, Gordon College, 255 Grapevine Road, Wenham, Massachusetts 01984; 508-927-2300, fax: 508-524-3706.

▼ GRACE COLLEGE

Winona Lake, Indiana

Independent, coed. Small town campus. Total enrollment: 800. Music program established 1948.

Degrees Bachelor of Music. Majors and concentrations: classical music, music, piano/organ, stringed instruments, voice, wind and percussion instruments.

Enrollment Fall 1997: 30 total; all undergraduate.

Music Student Profile 60% females, 40% males.

Music Faculty 24 total (full-time and part-time). 50% of full-time faculty have terminal degrees. Graduate students do not teach undergraduate courses.

Student Life Student groups/activities include Music Educators National Conference.

Expenses for 1997–98 Application fee: $20. Comprehensive fee: $14,102 includes full-time tuition ($9820) and college room and board ($4282). College room only: $2062. Special program-related fees: $50 per credit hour for studio fee for instrumentalists, $100 per credit hour for studio fee for vocalists.

Financial Aid Program-specific awards for 1997: 5 Grace Honors Brass Quintet Scholarships for freshmen program majors ($2240), 5 Grace Honors Woodwind Quintet Scholarships for freshmen program majors ($2240), 4 Grace Honors String Quartet Scholarships for freshmen program majors ($2240), 13 Music Talent Scholarships for freshmen program majors ($500).

Application Procedures Students admitted directly into the professional program freshman year. Deadline for freshmen and transfers: August 1. Required: high school transcript, college transcript(s) for transfer students, minimum 2.0 high school GPA, 3 letters of recommendation, audition, SAT I or ACT test scores (minimum combined SAT I score of 800, minimum combined ACT score of 19). Auditions held 3 times on campus; recorded music is permissible as a substitute for live auditions when distance is prohibitive or scheduling is difficult and videotaped performances are permissible as a substitute for live auditions when distance is prohibitive.

Web Site http://www.grace.edu.

Undergraduate Contact Mr. Ron Henry, Dean of Enrollment, Admissions Office, Grace College, 200 Seminary Drive, Winona Lake, Indiana 46590; 219-372-5131, fax: 219-372-5265.

▼ GRAND VALLEY STATE UNIVERSITY

Allendale, Michigan

State-supported, coed. Small town campus. Total enrollment: 15,676.

Degrees Bachelor of Music in the area of performance; Bachelor of Music Education in the areas of vocal music education, instrumental music education; Bachelor of Arts in the areas of composition, music technology. Majors and concentrations: composition, music, music education, music technology, piano/organ, stringed instruments, voice, wind and percussion instruments. Program accredited by NASM.

Enrollment Fall 1997: 100 total; all undergraduate.

Music Student Profile 51% females, 49% males, 4% minorities, 2% international.

Music Faculty 33 total (full-time and part-time). 80% of full-time faculty have terminal degrees. Graduate students do not teach undergraduate courses. Undergraduate student–faculty ratio: 9:1.

Student Life Student groups/activities include Music Educators National Conference, Mu Phi Epsilon.

Expenses for 1997–98 Application fee: $20. State resident tuition: $3348 full-time. Nonresident tuition: $7238 full-time. Mandatory fees: $60 full-time. Full-time tuition and fees vary according to student level. College room and board: $4640. Room and board charges vary according to board plan and housing facility. Special program-related fees: $25 per semester for practice room rental, $50 per semester for recital recording programs, $25 per semester for instrument rental.

Financial Aid Program-specific awards for 1997: 1 Blodgett Piano Award for pianists ($1000), 1 Eitzen Voice Award for vocalists ($1000), 2 Arthur Hills Scholarship for musically talented juniors ($1000).

Application Procedures Students admitted directly into the professional program freshman year. Deadline for freshmen and transfers: July 30. Required: high school transcript, college transcript(s) for transfer students, minimum 3.0 high school GPA, 2 letters of recommendation, interview, audition, theory placement examination. Recommended: essay, portfolio for composition students. Auditions held 6 times on campus; recorded music is permissible as a substitute for live auditions when distance is prohibitive and videotaped performances are permissible as a substitute for live auditions when distance is prohibitive. Portfolio reviews held 6 times on campus.

Grand Valley State University (continued)

Undergraduate Contact Director of Admissions, Grand Valley State University, 1 Campus Drive, Allendale, Michigan 49401; 616-895-2025.

▼ GROVE CITY COLLEGE
Grove City, Pennsylvania

Independent-Presbyterian, coed. Small town campus. Total enrollment: 2,292.

Degrees Bachelor of Music in the areas of music education, music and religion, music and business, music and performing arts.

Enrollment Fall 1997: 96 total; all undergraduate.

Music Student Profile 60% females, 40% males.

Music Faculty 22 total (full-time and part-time). 100% of full-time faculty have terminal degrees. Graduate students do not teach undergraduate courses.

Student Life Student groups/activities include Music Educators National Conference Student Chapter.

Expenses for 1997–98 Application fee: $25. Comprehensive fee: $10,392 includes full-time tuition ($6576) and college room and board ($3816). Full-time tuition varies according to course load and program.

Financial Aid Program-specific awards for 1997: 6 music awards for upperclassmen.

Application Procedures Students apply for admission into the professional program by sophomore year. Deadline for freshmen: February 15. Notification date for freshmen: March 15. Required: essay, high school transcript, college transcript(s) for transfer students, minimum 3.0 high school GPA, 2 letters of recommendation, interview, audition, SAT I or ACT test scores. Recommended: video. Auditions held 5 times and by appointment on campus; recorded music is permissible as a substitute for live auditions when distance is prohibitive and videotaped performances are permissible as a substitute for live auditions when distance is prohibitive.

Undergraduate Contact Dr. Edwin Arnold, Chair, Department of Music and Fine Arts, Grove City College, 100 Campus Drive, Grove City, Pennsylvania 16127; 412-458-2263, fax: 412-458-2190.

▼ HARDING UNIVERSITY
Searcy, Arkansas

Independent, coed. Small town campus. Total enrollment: 3,754. Music program established 1934.

Degrees Bachelor of Music Education in the areas of instrumental music, vocal/choral music. Program accredited by NASM.

Enrollment Fall 1997: 30 undergraduate.

Music Student Profile 60% females, 40% males.

Music Faculty 13 total (full-time and part-time). 75% of full-time faculty have terminal degrees. Graduate students do not teach undergraduate courses.

Student Life Student groups/activities include Collegiate Music Educators National Conference, American Choral Directors Association, National Association of Teachers of Singing. Special housing available for music students.

Expenses for 1997–98 Application fee: $25. Comprehensive fee: $11,698 includes full-time tuition ($6528), mandatory

fees ($1184), and college room and board ($3986). College room only: $1874. Room and board charges vary according to board plan and housing facility. Special program-related fees: $200 per semester hour for private lessons.

Financial Aid Program-specific awards for 1997: 17 departmental scholarships for music majors ($750–$3500).

Application Procedures Students admitted directly into the professional program freshman year. Deadline for freshmen and transfers: continuous. Required: high school transcript, college transcript(s) for transfer students, SAT I or ACT test scores. Recommended: minimum 2.0 high school GPA, interview, audition. Auditions held once on campus; recorded music is permissible as a substitute for live auditions when distance is prohibitive and videotaped performances are permissible as a substitute for live auditions when distance is prohibitive.

Web Site http://www.harding.edu/~music/music_frame.html.

Undergraduate Contact Mr. Mike Williams, Director of Admissions, Harding University, Box 2255, Searcy, Arkansas 72149-0001; 800-477-4407.

▼ HARDIN-SIMMONS UNIVERSITY
Abilene, Texas

Independent-Baptist, coed. Urban campus. Total enrollment: 2,312.

Degrees Bachelor of Music in the areas of performance, music education, church music, music theory/composition. Majors and concentrations: church music, music education, music theory and composition, piano/organ, stringed instruments, voice, wind and percussion instruments. Graduate degrees offered: Master of Music in the areas of performance, music education, music theory/composition, church music. Cross-registration with Abilene Christian University, McMurry University. Program accredited by NASM.

Enrollment Fall 1997: 188 total; 130 undergraduate, 4 graduate, 54 non-professional degree.

Music Student Profile 55% females, 45% males, 10% minorities.

Music Faculty 25 total undergraduate and graduate (full-time and part-time). 70% of full-time faculty have terminal degrees. Graduate students do not teach undergraduate courses. Undergraduate student–faculty ratio: 10:1.

Student Life Student groups/activities include Music Educators National Conference Student Chapter, Phi Mu Alpha, Sigma Alpha Iota.

Expenses for 1997–98 Application fee: $25. Comprehensive fee: $11,370 includes full-time tuition ($7500), mandatory fees ($630), and college room and board ($3240). College room only: $1445. Room and board charges vary according to board plan and housing facility. Special program-related fees: $15 per semester for music performance facilities fee, $100 per credit hour for private instruction.

Financial Aid Program-specific awards for 1997: 1 Irl Allison Award for pianists/returning students ($400), 6 Foreman Awards for cowboy band /returning students ($1890), 1 Hamilton Award for vocalists/returning students ($1600), 1 Lacewell Award for church music majors ($2500), 4 Reeves Awards for program majors ($2475), 1 Shaw Award for church music majors ($1400).

Application Procedures Students admitted directly into the professional program freshman year. Deadline for freshmen and transfers: continuous. Required: high school transcript, college transcript(s) for transfer students, minimum 2.0 high school GPA, 2 letters of recommendation, audition, SAT I or ACT test scores (minimum combined SAT I score of 860, minimum combined ACT score of 18). Auditions held 4 times on campus; recorded music is permissible as a substitute for live auditions if a campus visit is impossible and videotaped performances are permissible as a substitute for live auditions if a campus visit is impossible.

Undergraduate Contact Shane Davidson, Associate Vice President of Enrollment Services, Hardin-Simmons University, Box 16050, Abilene, Texas 79698-6050; 915-670-1207, fax: 915-670-1527, E-mail address: lmoore.es@hsutx.edu.

Graduate Contact Dr. Andy J. Patterson, Head, Graduate Studies in Music, School of Music, Hardin-Simmons University, Box 16230, Abilene, Texas 79698-6230; 915-670-1429, fax: 915-670-5873.

▼ THE HARID CONSERVATORY

Boca Raton, Florida

Independent, coed. Suburban campus. Total enrollment: 61. Music program established 1991.

Degrees Bachelor of Music in the area of performance. Majors and concentrations: bass trombone, bassoon, cello, clarinet, double bass, flute, French horn, oboe, percussion, piano, trombone, trumpet, tuba, viola, violin. Program accredited by NASM.

Enrollment Fall 1997: 61 total; 48 undergraduate, 13 non-professional degree.

Music Student Profile 39% females, 61% males, 43% minorities, 66% international.

Music Faculty 24 total (full-time and part-time). 20% of full-time faculty have terminal degrees. Graduate students do not teach undergraduate courses. Undergraduate student–faculty ratio: 2:1.

Student Life Special housing available for music students.

Expenses for 1997–98 Application fee: $0. One-time mandatory fee: $500. Tuition: $0 full-time. All students are on full scholarship.

Financial Aid Program-specific awards for 1997: full tuition scholarships for all enrolled students, 48 Supplemental Financial Aid Awards for those demonstrating need ($2000).

Application Procedures Students admitted directly into the professional program freshman year. Deadline for freshmen and transfers: March 31. Notification date for freshmen and transfers: continuous. Required: essay, high school transcript, college transcript(s) for transfer students, 3 letters of recommendation, audition, SAT I or ACT test scores, TOEFL score for international students, CEGCEP for French Canadian students. Recommended: pre-audition tape. Auditions held for two weeks in February and March and by appointment on campus and off campus in Interlochen, MI; recorded music is permissible as a substitute for live auditions with permission of the director and videotaped performances are permissible as a substitute for live auditions with permission of the director.

Undergraduate Contact Ms. Chantal Prosperi, Administrative Assistant/Music Admissions, Music Division, The Harid Conservatory, 2285 Potomac Road, Boca Raton, Florida 33431; 561-997-2677, fax: 561-997-8920.

▼ THE HARTT SCHOOL

See University of Hartford

▼ HASTINGS COLLEGE

Hastings, Nebraska

Independent-Presbyterian, coed. Small town campus. Total enrollment: 1,059. Music program established 1882.

Degrees Bachelor of Music in the areas of performance, music education, piano pedagogy. Majors and concentrations: music, music education, piano pedagogy, piano/organ, stringed instruments, voice, wind and percussion instruments. Program accredited by NASM.

Enrollment Fall 1997: 336 total; 68 undergraduate, 268 non-professional degree.

Music Student Profile 56% females, 44% males, 2% minorities.

Music Faculty 16 total undergraduate (full-time and part-time). 50% of full-time faculty have terminal degrees. Graduate students do not teach undergraduate courses. Undergraduate student–faculty ratio: 13:1.

Student Life Student groups/activities include Sigma Alpha Iota, Music Educators National Conference, Phi Mu Alpha Sinfonia.

Expenses for 1997–98 Application fee: $20. Comprehensive fee: $15,126 includes full-time tuition ($10,908), mandatory fees ($460), and college room and board ($3758). College room only: $1584. Special program-related fees: $300 per semester for private lessons.

Financial Aid Program-specific awards for 1997: 150 music scholarships for vocalists and instrumentalists ($860).

Application Procedures Students apply for admission into the professional program by freshman year. Deadline for freshmen and transfers: August 20. Required: essay, high school transcript, college transcript(s) for transfer students, minimum 2.0 high school GPA, letter of recommendation, interview, audition, SAT I or ACT test scores. Auditions held by request on campus and off campus in Denver, CO; Kansas City, MO; Omaha, NE; Lincoln, NE; recorded music is permissible as a substitute for live auditions when distance is prohibitive and videotaped performances are permissible as a substitute for live auditions when distance is prohibitive.

Web Site http://www.hastings.edu.

Undergraduate Contact Mr. Mike Karloff, Admissions Department, Hastings College, 7th and Turner, Hastings, Nebraska 68901; 402-461-7315, fax: 402-463-3002, E-mail address: mkarloff@hastings.edu.

▼ HEIDELBERG COLLEGE

Tiffin, Ohio

Independent, coed. Small town campus. Total enrollment: 1,480. Music program established 1886.

Degrees Bachelor of Music in the areas of composition, performance, pedagogy, music industry, music education. Majors and concentrations: music, music education, music industry, piano/organ, stringed instruments, voice, wind and percussion instruments. Program accredited by NASM.

Enrollment Fall 1997: 80 undergraduate.

Music Student Profile 50% females, 50% males, 1% minorities, 2% international.

Music Faculty 21 total undergraduate (full-time and part-time). 80% of full-time faculty have terminal degrees. Graduate students do not teach undergraduate courses. Undergraduate student–faculty ratio: 6:1.

Heidelberg College (continued)

Student Life Student groups/activities include Ohio Collegiate Music Educators National Conference, National Association of Teachers of Singing, Tau Mu Sigma.

Estimated expenses for 1998–99 Application fee: $20. Comprehensive fee: $21,395 includes full-time tuition ($16,060), mandatory fees ($200), and college room and board ($5135). College room only: $2800. Room and board charges vary according to housing facility.

Financial Aid Program-specific awards for 1997: 25–30 music scholarships for program majors ($1500), 20 Ensemble Scholarships for ensemble performers ($250–$400), 10 Endowed Music Awards for program majors ($500–$1000).

Application Procedures Students admitted directly into the professional program freshman year. Deadline for freshmen and transfers: continuous. Required: high school transcript, minimum 2.0 high school GPA, letter of recommendation, interview, audition, SAT I or ACT test scores. Recommended: essay. Auditions held 3 times on campus; recorded music is permissible as a substitute for live auditions when distance is prohibitive and videotaped performances are permissible as a substitute for live auditions when distance is prohibitive.

Web Site http://www.heidelberg.edu/.

Undergraduate Contact Dr. Catherine E. Thiedt, Chair, Department of Music, Heidelberg College, 310 East Market Street, Tiffin, Ohio 44883; 419-448-2073, fax: 419-448-2124, E-mail address: cthiedt@nike.heidelberg.edu.

▼ HENDERSON STATE UNIVERSITY

Arkadelphia, Arkansas

State-supported, coed. Small town campus. Total enrollment: 3,773.

Degrees Bachelor of Music in the areas of performance, music education, composition. Majors and concentrations: music education, piano/organ, voice, wind and percussion instruments. Cross-registration with Ouachita Baptist University. Program accredited by NASM.

Enrollment Fall 1997: 95 total; 85 undergraduate, 10 non-professional degree.

Music Student Profile 47% females, 53% males, 1% minorities.

Music Faculty 17 total (full-time and part-time). 90% of full-time faculty have terminal degrees. Graduate students do not teach undergraduate courses.

Student Life Student groups/activities include Elementary Music Workshops.

Expenses for 1997–98 State resident tuition: $1980 full-time. Nonresident tuition: $3960 full-time. Mandatory fees: $186 full-time. College room and board: $2856. Room and board charges vary according to board plan and housing facility. Special program-related fees: $40–$60 per credit hour for applied music fees.

Financial Aid Program-specific awards for 1997: 55–100 Band Scholarships for band members ($1000–$1600), 30–50 music scholarships for program majors/non-majors ($1000–$1600).

Application Procedures Students admitted directly into the professional program freshman year. Deadline for freshmen and transfers: continuous. Required: high school transcript, college transcript(s) for transfer students, minimum 2.0 high school GPA, SAT I or ACT test scores (minimum combined ACT score of 19). Recommended: interview, audition. Auditions held continuously on campus and off campus in various schools in Arkansas; recorded music is permissible as

a substitute for live auditions when distance is prohibitive; must have references and videotaped performances are permissible as a substitute for live auditions when distance is prohibitive; must have references.

Web Site http://www.hsu.edu/dept/mus.

Undergraduate Contact Mr. Tom Gattin, Registrar, Admissions Office, Henderson State University, Box 7534, Arkadelphia, Arkansas 71999-0001; 501-230-5135, fax: 501-230-5144.

▼ HOLY NAMES COLLEGE

Oakland, California

Independent-Roman Catholic, coed. Urban campus. Total enrollment: 861. Music program established 1880.

Degrees Bachelor of Music in the areas of piano performance, vocal performance, instrumental performance, piano pedagogy. Majors and concentrations: classical music, harp, piano/organ, stringed instruments, voice, wind and percussion instruments. Graduate degrees offered: Master of Music in the areas of piano performance, piano pedagogy, vocal performance, music education with Kodály emphasis, vocal performance with pedagogy emphasis, piano pedagogy with Suzuki emphasis. Cross-registration with Mills College, University of California-Berkeley, California State University-Hayward, California College of Arts and Crafts, Merritt College, Laney College, Saint Mary's College of California.

Enrollment Fall 1997: 45 total; 20 undergraduate, 20 graduate, 5 non-professional degree.

Music Student Profile 90% females, 10% males, 40% minorities, 25% international.

Music Faculty 12 total undergraduate and graduate (full-time and part-time). 60% of full-time faculty have terminal degrees. Graduate students do not teach undergraduate courses.

Student Life Student groups/activities include Mu Phi Epsilon.

Expenses for 1997–98 Application fee: $35. Comprehensive fee: $19,660 includes full-time tuition ($13,870) and college room and board ($5790). Room and board charges vary according to board plan. Special program-related fees: $15 per semester for practice room fee, $490–$1050 per semester for private music lessons.

Financial Aid Program-specific awards for 1997: 10–12 Shaklee Awards for vocalists ($500–$1000), 3–4 Cotton Awards for those demonstrating need ($500–$1500), 1 Trutner Award for instrumentalists ($430), 1 Abramowitsch Award for program majors ($150), 1 Cadenasso Award for pianists ($1000), 1 Babin Award for Jewish students ($200), 1 Dufresne Award for students demonstrating need ($600), 1–2 Mason Awards for students demonstrating need ($400–$800), 1 Mullen Award for voice majors ($130), 6 Distinguished Musician Scholarships for students demonstrating need ($5000).

Application Procedures Students admitted directly into the professional program freshman year. Deadline for freshmen and transfers: continuous. Required: essay, high school transcript, college transcript(s) for transfer students, minimum 2.0 high school GPA, 2 letters of recommendation, audition, SAT I or ACT test scores (minimum combined SAT I score of 870), TOEFL score for international students. Recommended: interview. Auditions held as needed on campus; recorded music is permissible as a substitute for live auditions when distance is prohibitive and videotaped performances are permissible as a substitute for live auditions if of good quality.

Undergraduate Contact JoAnn Berridge, Admissions Director, Holy Names College, 3500 Mountain Boulevard, Oakland, California 94619-1699; 510-436-1323, fax: 510-436-1199, E-mail address: berridge@admin.hnc.edu.

Graduate Contact Ms. Jean Ann Flaherty, Graduate Admissions Director, Holy Names College, 3500 Mountain Boulevard, Oakland, California 94619-1699; 510-436-1361, fax: 510-436-1199, E-mail address: flaherty@admin.hnc.edu.

▼ HOPE COLLEGE

Holland, Michigan

Independent, coed. Small town campus. Total enrollment: 2,911.

Degrees Bachelor of Music in the areas of performance, jazz studies; Bachelor of Music Education in the areas of vocal music education, instrumental music education. Majors and concentrations: jazz, music education, piano/organ, stringed instruments, voice, wind and percussion instruments. Program accredited by NASM.

Enrollment Fall 1997: 104 undergraduate.

Music Student Profile 65% females, 35% males, 5% minorities.

Music Faculty 39 total (full-time and part-time). 75% of full-time faculty have terminal degrees. Graduate students do not teach undergraduate courses.

Student Life Student groups/activities include Music Educators National Conference, American Guild of Organists.

Expenses for 1997–98 Application fee: $25. Comprehensive fee: $19,412 includes full-time tuition ($14,788), mandatory fees ($90), and college room and board ($4534). College room only: $2142. Room and board charges vary according to board plan and housing facility. Special program-related fees: $75–$85 for lessons.

Financial Aid Program-specific awards for 1997: 15–20 Distinguished Artist Awards for program majors ($2500), 3 Swaby Awards for program majors ($2000), 1 Hughes Award for organists ($5000).

Application Procedures Students apply for admission into the professional program by sophomore year. Deadline for freshmen and transfers: continuous. Required: essay, high school transcript, college transcript(s) for transfer students, audition, SAT I or ACT test scores. Recommended: minimum 2.0 high school GPA, interview. Auditions held once on campus; recorded music is permissible as a substitute for live auditions if a campus visit is impossible and videotaped performances are permissible as a substitute for live auditions if a campus visit is impossible.

Undergraduate Contact Ms. Linda Strouf, Music Recruitment Coordinator, Music Department, Hope College, 127 East 12th Street, Holland, Michigan 49422-9000; 616-395-7106, fax: 616-395-7182, E-mail address: strouf@hope.edu.

▼ HOUGHTON COLLEGE

Houghton, New York

Independent-Wesleyan, coed. Rural campus. Total enrollment: 1,411. Music program established 1946.

Degrees Bachelor of Music in the areas of applied music, music education, music theory/composition. Majors and concentrations: brass, music education, music theory and composition, piano/organ, stringed instruments, voice, wind and percussion instruments. Program accredited by NASM.

Enrollment Fall 1997: 109 total; 95 undergraduate, 14 non-professional degree.

Music Student Profile 60% females, 40% males, 10% minorities, 5% international.

Music Faculty 32 total undergraduate (full-time and part-time). 100% of full-time faculty have terminal degrees. Graduate students do not teach undergraduate courses. Undergraduate student–faculty ratio: 7:1.

Student Life Student groups/activities include Student Music Education Association. Special housing available for music students.

Expenses for 1997–98 Application fee: $25. Comprehensive fee: $17,003 includes full-time tuition ($12,344), mandatory fees ($421), and college room and board ($4238). College room only: $2118. Full-time tuition and fees vary according to course load and program.

Financial Aid Program-specific awards for 1997: 20–30 Performance Grants for program majors ($1000–$1500), 1 Presidential Scholarship for program majors ($2500–$5000).

Application Procedures Students admitted directly into the professional program freshman year. Deadline for freshmen and transfers: continuous. Required: essay, high school transcript, college transcript(s) for transfer students, minimum 2.0 high school GPA, 2 letters of recommendation, audition, SAT I or ACT test scores. Recommended: minimum 3.0 high school GPA, interview. Auditions held 10 times on campus; recorded music is permissible as a substitute for live auditions when distance is prohibitive and videotaped performances are permissible as a substitute for live auditions when distance is prohibitive.

Web Site http://www.houghton.edu.

Undergraduate Contact Dr. George Boespflug, Director, School of Music, Houghton College, 1 Willard Avenue, Houghton, New York 14744; 716-567-9400, fax: 716-567-9517, E-mail address: music@houghton.edu.

▼ HOWARD PAYNE UNIVERSITY

Brownwood, Texas

Independent-Southern Baptist, coed. Small town campus. Total enrollment: 1,489.

Degrees Bachelor of Music in the areas of piano, organ, voice, instrumental music, piano pedagogy and accompanying, church music, choral music education, instrumental music education. Majors and concentrations: music, music education, piano/organ, sacred music, voice, wind and percussion instruments. Program accredited by NASM.

Enrollment Fall 1997: 66 total; all undergraduate.

Music Student Profile 59% females, 41% males, 3% minorities, 3% international.

Music Faculty 18 total (full-time and part-time). 50% of full-time faculty have terminal degrees. Graduate students do not teach undergraduate courses. Undergraduate student–faculty ratio: 5:1.

Student Life Student groups/activities include Music Educators National Conference, American Choral Directors Association, Southern Baptist Church Music Conference.

Expenses for 1997–98 Application fee: $25. Comprehensive fee: $11,250 includes full-time tuition ($7170), mandatory fees ($450), and college room and board ($3630). College room only: $1670. Full-time tuition and fees vary according to student level. Room and board charges vary according to housing facility. Special program-related fees: $10 per course

Howard Payne University (continued)

for computer lab use, $100 per course for piano accompanying fees, $85 per course for applied music fees.

Financial Aid Program-specific awards for 1997: 1 Turner Music Award ($500), 1 Presser Award ($2250), 1 Schubert Music Award ($100), 93 music scholarships for program majors/minors ($400–$1800).

Application Procedures Students admitted directly into the professional program freshman year. Deadline for freshmen and transfers: continuous. Required: high school transcript, college transcript(s) for transfer students, interview, audition, SAT I or ACT test scores (minimum combined SAT I score of 950, minimum combined ACT score of 19). Recommended: minimum 3.0 high school GPA, letter of recommendation. Auditions held twice and at student's convenience on campus; recorded music is permissible as a substitute for live auditions if a campus visit is impossible and videotaped performances are permissible as a substitute for live auditions if a campus visit is impossible.

Undergraduate Contact Ms. Cheryl Mangrum, Director, Recruiting and Admissions, Howard Payne University, 1000 Fisk Street, HPU Station 828, Brownwood, Texas 76801-2494; 915-649-8020, fax: 915-649-8901.

▼ Howard University

Washington, District of Columbia

Independent, coed. Urban campus. Total enrollment: 10,438. Music program established 1902.

Degrees Bachelor of Music in the areas of vocal performance, instrumental performance, music history, jazz studies, music business, music therapy, music theory and composition; Bachelor of Music Education. Graduate degrees offered: Master of Music in the areas of performance, jazz studies; Master of Music Education. Cross-registration with Consortium of Universities. Program accredited by NASM.

Enrollment Fall 1997: 153 undergraduate, 16 graduate.

Music Student Profile 70% females, 30% males, 90% minorities, 5% international.

Music Faculty 38 total undergraduate and graduate (full-time and part-time). 55% of full-time faculty have terminal degrees. Graduate students teach a few undergraduate courses. Undergraduate student–faculty ratio: 7:1.

Student Life Student groups/activities include Howard University Choir, Howard University Marching Band, Howard University Jazz Ensemble.

Expenses for 1997–98 Application fee: $45. Comprehensive fee: $13,147 includes full-time tuition ($8580), mandatory fees ($405), and college room and board ($4162).

Financial Aid Program-specific awards for 1997: Special Talent Awards for program majors, Trustee Scholarships for program majors, grant/aid awards for program majors.

Application Procedures Students admitted directly into the professional program freshman year. Deadline for freshmen and transfers: continuous. Required: high school transcript, college transcript(s) for transfer students, audition, SAT I or ACT test scores (minimum combined SAT I score of 870), GED if applicable. Auditions held 6 times and by appointment on campus; recorded music is permissible as a substitute for live auditions when distance is prohibitive and videotaped performances are permissible as a substitute for live auditions when distance is prohibitive.

Contact Dr. J. Weldon Norris, Chairman, Department of Music, Howard University, College of Arts and Sciences, Washington, District of Columbia 20059; 202-806-7082, fax: 202-806-9673.

▼ Hugh A. Glauser School of Music

See Kent State University

▼ Hunter College of the City University of New York

New York, New York

State and locally supported, coed. Urban campus. Total enrollment: 19,689.

Degrees Bachelor of Music in the area of performance. Majors and concentrations: classical music, composition, jazz, piano/organ, stringed instruments, voice, wind and percussion instruments. Graduate degrees offered: Master of Arts in the areas of music performance, music composition. Cross-registration with senior colleges of the City University of New York System.

Enrollment Fall 1997: 207 total; 11 undergraduate, 17 graduate, 179 non-professional degree.

Music Student Profile 54% females, 46% males, 32% minorities, 26% international.

Music Faculty 42 total undergraduate and graduate (full-time and part-time). 100% of full-time faculty have terminal degrees. Graduate students teach about a quarter undergraduate courses.

Student Life Student groups/activities include Music Theater Workshop, Hunter College Jazz Society, Musica Antiqua.

Expenses for 1997–98 Application fee: $40. State resident tuition: $3200 full-time. Nonresident tuition: $6800 full-time. Mandatory fees: $129 full-time. College room only: $1700. Room charges vary according to housing facility. Special program-related fees: $10 per semester for practice room fee.

Financial Aid Program-specific awards for 1997: 20 Alumni Awards for students taking private lessons ($500), 10 Music Department Awards for students taking private lessons ($500).

Application Procedures Students admitted directly into the professional program freshman year. Deadline for freshmen: November 1; transfers: March 15. Notification date for freshmen and transfers: June 1. Required: high school transcript, college transcript(s) for transfer students, audition, minimum 2.2 high school GPA, minimum 2.0 college GPA for transfer students with 24 credits, minimum 2.7 college GPA for transfer students with 28 credits. Recommended: minimum 3.0 high school GPA. Auditions held twice on campus; recorded music is permissible as a substitute for live auditions for provisional admission and videotaped performances are permissible as a substitute for live auditions for provisional acceptance.

Web Site http://sapientia.hunter.cuny.edu/~music.

Undergraduate Contact Dr. Jewel Thompson, Director of Undergraduate Studies, Department of Music, Hunter College of the City University of New York, 695 Park Avenue, New York, New York 10021; 212-772-5020, fax: 212-772-5022, E-mail address: wthompso@shiva.hunter.cuny.edu.

Graduate Contact Dr. Ruth DeFord, Director of Graduate Studies, Department of Music, Hunter College of the City

University of New York, 695 Park Avenue, New York, New York 10021; 212-772-5020, fax: 212-772-5022, E-mail address: rdeford@shiva.hunter.cuny.edu.

▼ HUNTINGTON COLLEGE

Huntington, Indiana

Independent, coed. Small town campus. Total enrollment: 814.

Degrees Bachelor of Music in the areas of music performance, music education. Majors and concentrations: music, music education. Program accredited by NASM.

Enrollment Fall 1997: 27 total; all undergraduate.

Music Student Profile 49% females, 51% males, 2% minorities, 2% international.

Music Faculty 19 total (full-time and part-time). 100% of full-time faculty have terminal degrees. Graduate students do not teach undergraduate courses.

Expenses for 1998–99 Application fee: $15. Comprehensive fee: $17,570 includes full-time tuition ($12,250), mandatory fees ($550), and college room and board ($4770). College room only: $2140. Special program-related fees: $25 per course for instrument use fee, $175 per half-hour lesson for private instruction and practice room fee.

Financial Aid Program-specific awards for 1997: 26 Performance Grants for program majors/minors ($570).

Application Procedures Students admitted directly into the professional program freshman year. Deadline for freshmen and transfers: continuous. Required: high school transcript, college transcript(s) for transfer students, minimum 2.0 high school GPA, audition, SAT I or ACT test scores. Auditions held as needed on campus.

Web Site http://www.huntcol.edu.

Undergraduate Contact Mr. Jeffrey Berggren, Executive Director of Enrollment Management, Admissions Department, Huntington College, 2303 College Avenue, Huntington, Indiana 46750; 219-356-6000, fax: 219-356-9448.

▼ HURLEY SCHOOL OF MUSIC

See Centenary College of Louisiana

▼ IDAHO STATE UNIVERSITY

Pocatello, Idaho

State-supported, coed. Small town campus. Total enrollment: 11,886. Music program established 1940.

Degrees Bachelor of Music in the area of performance; Bachelor of Music Education. Majors and concentrations: music, music education, piano, stringed instruments, voice, wind and percussion instruments. Program accredited by NASM.

Enrollment Fall 1997: 77 total; 54 undergraduate, 23 non-professional degree.

Music Student Profile 70% females, 30% males.

Music Faculty 18 total (full-time and part-time). 88% of full-time faculty have terminal degrees. Graduate students do not teach undergraduate courses.

Student Life Student groups/activities include Music Educators National Conference Student Chapter, American Choral Directors Association Student Chapter.

Expenses for 1997–98 Application fee: $20. State resident tuition: $0 full-time. Nonresident tuition: $5980 full-time. Mandatory fees: $1984 full-time. College room and board: $3580. College room only: $1520. Room and board charges vary according to board plan. Special program-related fees: $135 per half-hour lesson for applied music fee.

Financial Aid Program-specific awards for 1997: 80 Ensemble Scholarships for program majors ($350–$600), 1 Missal Band Scholarship for band majors ($1400), 5 Berryman Endowment Awards for program majors ($500), 5 Phoenix Endowment Awards for program majors ($500), 12 Department Music Endowment Awards for program majors ($500), 1 Anderson Vocal Scholarship for vocal majors ($1000), 50 Marching Band Scholarships for instrumentalists ($500), 25 Vocal Endowment for vocal majors ($500–$1000).

Application Procedures Students apply for admission into the professional program by sophomore year. Deadline for freshmen: August 1; transfers: continuous. Required: high school transcript, college transcript(s) for transfer students, minimum 2.0 high school GPA, letter of recommendation, interview, audition, SAT I or ACT test scores. Recommended: essay, minimum 3.0 high school GPA. Auditions held 3-4 times on campus and off campus in various Idaho locations; recorded music is permissible as a substitute for live auditions when distance is prohibitive and videotaped performances are permissible as a substitute for live auditions when distance is prohibitive.

Web Site http://www.isu.edu/departments/music.

Undergraduate Contact Dr. Alan E. Stanek, Chairman, Department of Music, Idaho State University, Box 8099, Pocatello, Idaho 83209-8099; 208-236-3636, fax: 208-236-4884, E-mail address: stanalan@isu.edu.

▼ ILLINOIS STATE UNIVERSITY

Normal, Illinois

State-supported, coed. Urban campus. Total enrollment: 20,331.

Degrees Bachelor of Music in the areas of performance, music therapy, music theory/composition; Bachelor of Music Education. Majors and concentrations: classical guitar, classical music, music, music education, music therapy, piano/organ, stringed instruments, voice, wind and percussion instruments. Graduate degrees offered: Master of Music in the areas of performance, music theory/composition, music therapy; Master of Music Education. Program accredited by NASM.

Enrollment Fall 1997: 240 undergraduate, 45 graduate.

Music Student Profile 54% females, 46% males, 1% minorities, 2% international.

Music Faculty 40 total undergraduate and graduate (full-time). 65% of full-time faculty have terminal degrees. Graduate students teach a few undergraduate courses. Undergraduate student–faculty ratio: 6:1.

Student Life Student groups/activities include National Association of Music Therapy, Music Educators National Conference, Tau Beta Sigma. Special housing available for music students.

Expenses for 1998–99 State resident tuition: $3038 full-time. Nonresident tuition: $9113 full-time. Mandatory fees: $1085 full-time. Full-time tuition and fees vary according to course load. College room and board: $3975. Room and board charges vary according to board plan.

Illinois State University (continued)

Financial Aid Program-specific awards for 1997: 16 tuition waivers for program majors and minors ($300–$1200), 20 Talent Grants-in-Aid for program majors and minors ($100–$500), 20 Endowed Scholarships for enrolled music majors.

Application Procedures Deadline for freshmen and transfers: continuous. Required: high school transcript, college transcript(s) for transfer students, audition, SAT I or ACT test scores. Auditions held 6 times on campus; recorded music is permissible as a substitute for live auditions for out-of-state applicants.

Web Site http://orathost.cfa.ilstu.edu/.

Undergraduate Contact Ms. Judy Thomas, Recruiting Secretary, Music Department, Illinois State University, Campus Box 5660, Normal, Illinois 61790-5660; 309-438-3566, fax: 309-438-8318, E-mail address: jrthoma@oratmail.cfa.ilstu.edu.

Graduate Contact Mr. Joe Neisler, Assistant Chair, Music Department, Illinois State University, Campus Box 5660, Normal, Illinois 61790-5660; 309-438-8960, fax: 309-438-8318, E-mail address: musadmin@oratmail.cfa.ilstu.edu.

▼ ILLINOIS WESLEYAN UNIVERSITY

Bloomington, Illinois

Independent, coed. Suburban campus. Total enrollment: 2,021. Music program established 1897.

Degrees Bachelor of Music in the areas of performance, composition; Bachelor of Music Education in the areas of vocal music education, instrumental music education; Bachelor of Fine Arts in the area of music theater. Majors and concentrations: classical music, composition, music, music education, music theater, piano/organ, stringed instruments, voice, wind and percussion instruments. Program accredited by NASM.

Enrollment Fall 1997: 151 total; all undergraduate.

Music Student Profile 53% females, 47% males, 5% minorities.

Music Faculty 39 total (full-time and part-time). 100% of full-time faculty have terminal degrees. Graduate students do not teach undergraduate courses. Undergraduate student–faculty ratio: 8:1.

Student Life Student groups/activities include Music Educators National Conference Student Chapter, Phi Mu Alpha, Sigma Alpha Iota.

Expenses for 1998–99 Comprehensive fee: $23,200 includes full-time tuition ($18,250), mandatory fees ($126), and college room and board ($4824). College room only: $2800. Special program-related fees: $230 per semester for applied music lessons for second instrument/half hour a week.

Financial Aid Program-specific awards for 1997: 16 Music Talent Awards for incoming students ($5700), 40 Music Talent Awards for upperclassmen ($4650).

Application Procedures Students apply for admission into the professional program by sophomore year. Deadline for freshmen and transfers: April 1. Notification date for freshmen and transfers: May 1. Required: essay, high school transcript, college transcript(s) for transfer students, minimum 3.0 high school GPA, interview, audition, SAT I or ACT test scores (minimum combined SAT I score of 950, minimum combined ACT score of 23), portfolio for composition majors. Recommended: 2 letters of recommendation. Auditions held by appointment on campus and off campus in Chicago, IL; recorded music is permissible as a

substitute for live auditions when distance is prohibitive and videotaped performances are permissible as a substitute for live auditions when distance is prohibitive. Portfolio reviews held by appointment on campus.

Undergraduate Contact Ms. Laura Dolan, Recruiting Coordinator, School of Music, Illinois Wesleyan University, PO Box 2900, Bloomington, Illinois 61702; 309-556-3063, fax: 309-556-3411.

▼ IMMACULATA COLLEGE

Immaculata, Pennsylvania

Independent-Roman Catholic, primarily women. Suburban campus. Total enrollment: 2,312. Music program established 1921.

Degrees Bachelor of Music in the areas of music therapy, music education. Graduate degrees offered: Master of Arts in the area of music therapy. Program accredited by NASM, AAMT.

Enrollment Fall 1997: 116 total; 42 undergraduate, 33 graduate, 41 non-professional degree.

Music Student Profile 95% females, 5% males, 5% minorities, 1% international.

Music Faculty 20 total undergraduate and graduate (full-time and part-time). 100% of full-time faculty have terminal degrees. Graduate students do not teach undergraduate courses. Undergraduate student–faculty ratio: 8:1.

Student Life Student groups/activities include Music Educators National Conference Student Chapter, American Association of Music Therapy Student Chapter, Annual Institute for Music and Healing
Annual Institute for Music and Healing.

Expenses for 1997–98 Application fee: $25. Comprehensive fee: $17,971 includes full-time tuition ($11,900), mandatory fees ($215), and college room and board ($5856). College room only: $3120. Special program-related fees: $250–$300 per course for private music lessons.

Financial Aid Program-specific awards for 1997: 19 Music Talent Scholarships for program majors ($2700), 1 Borelli Award for program juniors or seniors ($1000), 1 Almira Doutt Award for program juniors or seniors ($1000).

Application Procedures Students apply for admission into the professional program by sophomore year. Deadline for freshmen and transfers: continuous. Required: high school transcript, college transcript(s) for transfer students, minimum 2.0 high school GPA, letter of recommendation, audition, SAT I or ACT test scores. Recommended: essay, interview, video. Auditions held 6 times on campus; recorded music is permissible as a substitute for live auditions if a campus visit is impossible and videotaped performances are permissible as a substitute for live auditions if a campus visit is impossible.

Web Site http://www.immaculata.edu.

Undergraduate Contact Mr. Ken R. Rasp, Dean of Enrollment Management, Immaculata College, 1145 King Road, Immaculata, Pennsylvania 19345; 610-647-4400 ext. 3015, fax: 610-251-1668.

Graduate Contact Sr. Jean Anthony Gileno, Chair, Graduate Music Program, Music Department, Immaculata College, PO Box 697, Immaculata, Pennsylvania 19345-0697; 610-647-4400 ext. 3490, E-mail address: cphelanz@immaculata.edu.

▼ INDIANA STATE UNIVERSITY

Terre Haute, Indiana

State-supported, coed. Suburban campus. Total enrollment: 10,784.

Degrees Bachelor of Music in the area of performance; Bachelor of Music Education. Majors and concentrations: music business, music education, piano, stringed instruments, voice, wind and percussion instruments. Graduate degrees offered: Master of Music in the area of performance; Master of Music Education. Cross-registration with Saint Mary-of-the-Woods College. Program accredited by NASM.

Enrollment Fall 1997: 220 total; 208 undergraduate, 12 graduate.

Music Student Profile 50% females, 50% males, 5% minorities, 4% international.

Music Faculty 33 total undergraduate and graduate (full-time and part-time). 84% of full-time faculty have terminal degrees. Graduate students teach a few undergraduate courses. Undergraduate student–faculty ratio: 8:1.

Student Life Student groups/activities include Music Educators National Conference, Music Industry Association, Music Teachers National Association. Special housing available for music students.

Expenses for 1997–98 Application fee: $20. State resident tuition: $3196 full-time. Nonresident tuition: $7916 full-time. Full-time tuition varies according to course load. College room and board: $4143. Room and board charges vary according to board plan and housing facility. Special program-related fees: $30 per credit hour for applied music fee.

Application Procedures Deadline for freshmen and transfers: June 1. Required: high school transcript, audition, SAT I or ACT test scores, minimum 2.0 college GPA for transfer students. Recommended: essay, minimum 2.0 high school GPA. Auditions held 8 times and by appointment on campus and off campus in several cities in Indiana including Evansville, South Bend, and Fort Wayne; recorded music is permissible as a substitute for live auditions when distance is prohibitive or for international applicants and videotaped performances are permissible as a substitute for live auditions when distance is prohibitive or for international applicants.

Web Site http://www.indstate.edu/music.

Undergraduate Contact Chair, Department of Music, Indiana State University, Terre Haute, Indiana 47809; 812-237-2771, fax: 812-237-3009.

Graduate Contact Dr. Linda Damer, Director of Graduate Studies, Department of Music, Indiana State University, Terre Haute, Indiana 47809; 812-237-2790, fax: 812-237-3009.

▼ INDIANA UNIVERSITY BLOOMINGTON

Bloomington, Indiana

State-supported, coed. Small town campus. Total enrollment: 34,937.

Degrees Bachelor of Music in the areas of composition, early music, jazz studies, performance; Bachelor of Music Education in the areas of choral-general teaching, instrumental teaching, choral and instrumental teaching area; Bachelor of Music in the areas of bassoon, cello, clarinet, classical guitar, double bass, euphonium, flute, harp, horn, oboe, organ, percussion, piano, saxophone, trombone, trumpet, tuba,

viola, violin, voice. Graduate degrees offered: Master of Music in the areas of choral conducting, composition, early music, instrumental conducting, jazz studies, music theory, organ and church music, wind conducting; Master of Science in the areas of ballet, music theater scenic techniques, stage direction for opera; Master of Arts in the area of musicology; Master of Music in the areas of brass, guitar, harp, organ, percussion, piano, strings, voice, woodwinds. Doctor of Music in the areas of choral conducting, composition, early music, instrumental conducting, jazz studies, music theory, musicology, organ and church music, wind conducting. Program accredited by NASM.

Enrollment Fall 1997: 981 undergraduate, 757 graduate.

Music Student Profile 56% females, 44% males, 11% minorities, 18% international.

Music Faculty 150 total undergraduate and graduate (full-time). Graduate students teach about a quarter undergraduate courses. Undergraduate student–faculty ratio: 18:1.

Expenses for 1997–98 Application fee: $35. State resident tuition: $3486 full-time. Nonresident tuition: $11,410 full-time. Mandatory fees: $443 full-time. College room and board: $4900. Special program-related fees: $73 for applied music fee, $32 per semester for instrument rental, $27–$38 per program for recital program printing, $40 per recital for recital recording.

Financial Aid Program-specific awards for 1997: Music Merti Scholarships for those demonstrating musical ability, scholastic achievement, and financial need, minority scholarships, IU Honors Division Awards for high academic achievers, IU Dean's Awards for those demonstrating strong musical and academic skills.

Application Procedures Students admitted directly into the professional program freshman year. Deadline for freshmen and transfers: March 1. Required: essay, high school transcript, college transcript(s) for transfer students, minimum 2.0 high school GPA, 3 letters of recommendation, audition, SAT I or ACT test scores. Auditions held 3 times on campus; recorded music is permissible as a substitute for live auditions with later audition on campus and videotaped performances are permissible as a substitute for live auditions with later audition on campus.

Web Site http://www.music.indiana.edu.

Undergraduate Contact Mr. Gwyn Richards, Associate Dean of Admissions and Financial Aid, School of Music, Indiana University Bloomington, Bloomington, Indiana 47405; 812-855-7998, fax: 812-855-4936.

▼ INDIANA UNIVERSITY OF PENNSYLVANIA

Indiana, Pennsylvania

State-supported, coed. Small town campus. Total enrollment: 13,736.

Degrees Bachelor of Fine Arts in the area of music performance. Program accredited by NASM.

Enrollment Fall 1997: 26 undergraduate.

Music Student Profile 40% females, 60% males, 2% minorities, 1% international.

Music Faculty 38 total (full-time and part-time). 85% of full-time faculty have terminal degrees. Graduate students do not teach undergraduate courses.

Student Life Student groups/activities include Music Educators National Conference Student Chapter, National Association of Schools of Music, College Music Society.

Indiana University of Pennsylvania (continued)

Expenses for 1997–98 Application fee: $30. State resident tuition: $3468 full-time. Nonresident tuition: $8824 full-time. Mandatory fees: $736 full-time. Full-time tuition and fees vary according to course load. College room and board: $3408. College room only: $1952. Room and board charges vary according to board plan and housing facility.

Financial Aid Program-specific awards for 1997: 9 Freshmen Music Scholarships for program majors ($500–$1000), 1 Anne Moon Heyword Scholarship for voice majors ($500–$750), 2 Gloria Bryan Johnson Scholarship for string majors ($500–$750), 1 Gorell Scholarship for string majors ($1500–$3000).

Application Procedures Students admitted directly into the professional program freshman year. Deadline for freshmen and transfers: continuous. Required: high school transcript, interview, audition, SAT I test score only (minimum combined SAT I score of 850). Recommended: letter of recommendation. Auditions held 10 times on campus; recorded music is permissible as a substitute for live auditions for international applicants and U.S. students from a great distance and videotaped performances are permissible as a substitute for live auditions for international applicants and U.S. students from a great distance.

Web Site http://www.iup.edu/mu.

Undergraduate Contact Dr. John Scandrett, Chair, Department of Music, Indiana University of Pennsylvania, 101 Cogswell Hall, Indiana, Pennsylvania 15705; 724-357-2390, fax: 724-357-7778.

▼ INDIANA UNIVERSITY–PURDUE UNIVERSITY FORT WAYNE

Fort Wayne, Indiana

State-supported, coed. Urban campus. Total enrollment: 10,749. Music program established 1967.

Degrees Bachelor of Music in the areas of piano, voice, orchestral instruments, interdisciplinary studies; Bachelor of Music Education in the area of choral and/or instrumental teaching; Bachelor of Music Therapy. Majors and concentrations: interdisciplinary studies, music, music education, music therapy, piano/organ, stringed instruments, voice, wind and percussion instruments. Program accredited by NASM.

Enrollment Fall 1997: 98 total; 90 undergraduate, 8 non-professional degree.

Music Student Profile 55% females, 45% males, 5% minorities, 2% international.

Music Faculty 23 total (full-time and part-time). 90% of full-time faculty have terminal degrees. Graduate students do not teach undergraduate courses.

Student Life Student groups/activities include Sigma Alpha Iota, Music Educators National Conference, Music Therapy Club.

Expenses for 1997–98 Application fee: $30. State resident tuition: $3026 full-time. Nonresident tuition: $7311 full-time. Mandatory fees: $295 full-time. Full-time tuition and fees vary according to course load.

Financial Aid Program-specific awards for 1997: 1–2 Ator Scholarships for instrumental majors ($800), 1–2 Loessi Scholarships for vocal/choral majors ($800), 6–8 Whitney

Scholarships for program majors ($500), 20 departmental Merit Awards for program majors ($500).

Application Procedures Students admitted directly into the professional program freshman year. Deadline for freshmen and transfers: August 1. Notification date for freshmen and transfers: August 21. Required: high school transcript, college transcript(s) for transfer students, minimum 2.0 high school GPA, interview, audition, SAT I or ACT test scores, music theory placement exam. Auditions held continuously on campus; recorded music is permissible as a substitute for live auditions if a campus visit is impossible and videotaped performances are permissible as a substitute for live auditions if a campus visit is impossible.

Undergraduate Contact Dr. Raymond Marchionni, Chair, Department of Music, Indiana University–Purdue University Fort Wayne, 2101 Coliseum Boulevard East, Fort Wayne, Indiana 46805-1499; 219-481-6714, fax: 219-481-6985.

▼ INDIANA UNIVERSITY SOUTH BEND

South Bend, Indiana

State-supported, coed. Suburban campus. Total enrollment: 7,169. Music program established 1965.

Degrees Bachelor of Music in the areas of piano, orchestral instruments, guitar, composition, voice; Bachelor of Music Education; Bachelor of Science in the area of music and an outside field. Majors and concentrations: classical music, composition, guitar, music, music education, opera, piano/organ, stringed instruments, voice, wind and percussion instruments. Graduate degrees offered: Master of Music in the areas of piano, orchestral instruments, guitar, composition, voice; Master of Science in the area of secondary music education. Cross-registration with Indiana University System, Bethel College.

Enrollment Fall 1997: 35 total; 30 undergraduate, 5 graduate.

Music Student Profile 49% females, 51% males, 17% minorities, 23% international.

Music Faculty 28 total undergraduate and graduate (full-time and part-time). 100% of full-time faculty have terminal degrees. Graduate students do not teach undergraduate courses. Undergraduate student–faculty ratio: 8:1.

Expenses for 1997–98 State resident tuition: $2763 full-time. Nonresident tuition: $7562 full-time. Mandatory fees: $222 full-time. Special program-related fees: $156 per semester for applied music.

Financial Aid Program-specific awards for 1997: 15–20 music scholarships for pianists and string instrumentalists ($500).

Application Procedures Students admitted directly into the professional program freshman year. Deadline for freshmen and transfers: August 15. Notification date for freshmen and transfers: September 1. Required: high school transcript, minimum 2.0 high school GPA, audition. Auditions held 3 times on campus; recorded music is permissible as a substitute for live auditions for international applicants and videotaped performances are permissible as a substitute for live auditions for international applicants.

Undergraduate Contact Dr. David Barton, Director of Instruction, Division of the Arts, Indiana University South Bend, 1700 Mishawaka Avenue, PO Box 7111, South Bend, Indiana 46634; 219-237-4161.

Graduate Contact Dr. Michael J. Esselstrom, Division of the Arts, Indiana University South Bend, 1700 Mishawaka Avenue, PO Box 7111, South Bend, Indiana 46634; 219-237-4562.

▼ Iowa State University of Science and Technology

Ames, Iowa

State-supported, coed. Suburban campus. Total enrollment: 25,384. Music program established 1967.

Degrees Bachelor of Music in the areas of music education, performance, composition; Bachelor of Music Education in the areas of vocal music education, instrumental music education. Majors and concentrations: music, music education, piano/organ, stringed instruments, voice, wind and percussion instruments. Program accredited by NASM.

Enrollment Fall 1997: 122 undergraduate.

Music Student Profile 57% females, 43% males, 5% minorities, 3% international.

Music Faculty 31 total undergraduate (full-time and part-time). 60% of full-time faculty have terminal degrees. Graduate students do not teach undergraduate courses.

Student Life Student groups/activities include Phi Mu Alpha Sinfonia, Sigma Alpha Iota, Kappa Kappa Psi/Tau Beta Sigma.

Expenses for 1997–98 Application fee: $20. State resident tuition: $2566 full-time. Nonresident tuition: $8608 full-time. Mandatory fees: $200 full-time. Full-time tuition and fees vary according to class time and program. College room and board: $3647. College room only: $1879. Room and board charges vary according to board plan and housing facility. Special program-related fees: $90–$130 per semester for applied music fee.

Financial Aid Program-specific awards for 1997: 45–50 departmental scholarships for program majors ($300–$2200).

Application Procedures Students admitted directly into the professional program freshman year. Deadline for freshmen and transfers: continuous. Required: high school transcript, college transcript(s) for transfer students, minimum 2.0 high school GPA, interview, audition, SAT I or ACT test scores (minimum combined ACT score of 24). Auditions held continuously on campus; recorded music is permissible as a substitute for live auditions if a campus visit is impossible and videotaped performances are permissible as a substitute for live auditions if a campus visit is impossible.

Web Site http://www.music.iastate.edu/.

Undergraduate Contact Admissions Secretary, Department of Music, Iowa State University of Science and Technology, 149 Music Hall, Ames, Iowa 50011; 515-294-3831, fax: 515-294-6409, E-mail address: takrock@iastate.edu.

▼ Iowa Wesleyan College

Mount Pleasant, Iowa

Independent-United Methodist, coed. Small town campus. Total enrollment: 804.

Degrees Bachelor of Music Education.

Enrollment Fall 1997: 20 undergraduate.

Music Student Profile 36% females, 64% males.

Music Faculty 10 total undergraduate (full-time and part-time). 50% of full-time faculty have terminal degrees. Graduate students do not teach undergraduate courses. Undergraduate student–faculty ratio: 3:1.

Student Life Student groups/activities include Music Educators National Conference Student Chapter, American Choral Directors Association Student Chapter.

Expenses for 1998–99 Application fee: $15. Comprehensive fee: $16,310 includes full-time tuition ($12,220) and college room and board ($4090). College room only: $1780.

Financial Aid Program-specific awards for 1997: 6 Goodell Music Scholarships for incoming students ($6000).

Application Procedures Students apply for admission into the professional program by sophomore year. Deadline for freshmen and transfers: continuous. Required: essay, high school transcript, college transcript(s) for transfer students, minimum 2.0 high school GPA, letter of recommendation, SAT I or ACT test scores (minimum combined ACT score of 19), audition for scholarship consideration. Recommended: audition. Auditions held by appointment on campus; recorded music is permissible as a substitute for live auditions when distance is prohibitive and videotaped performances are permissible as a substitute for live auditions when distance is prohibitive.

Undergraduate Contact Mr. Don Hapward, Director, Admissions Department, Iowa Wesleyan College, 601 North Main Street, Mount Pleasant, Iowa 52641; 319-385-6231.

▼ Ithaca College

Ithaca, New York

Independent, coed. Small town campus. Total enrollment: 5,897. Music program established 1892.

Degrees Bachelor of Music in the areas of composition, jazz studies, music education, performance, performance/music education, music theory, music in combination with an outside field, recording. Majors and concentrations: composition, guitar, jazz, music education, music theory, performance, piano/organ, recording arts and sciences, stringed instruments, voice, wind and percussion instruments. Graduate degrees offered: Master of Music in the areas of brasses, composition, conducting, music education, performance, strings, Suzuki pedagogy, music theory, woodwinds. Cross-registration with Cornell University. Program accredited by NASM.

Enrollment Fall 1997: 500 total; 439 undergraduate, 38 graduate, 23 non-professional degree.

Music Student Profile 57% females, 43% males, 6% minorities, 4% international.

Music Faculty 72 total undergraduate and graduate (full-time and part-time). 96% of full-time faculty have terminal degrees. Graduate students do not teach undergraduate courses. Undergraduate student–faculty ratio: 8:1.

Student Life Student groups/activities include American Choral Directors Association, Music Educators National Conference.

Expenses for 1997–98 Application fee: $40. Comprehensive fee: $24,240 includes full-time tuition ($16,900) and college room and board ($7340). College room only: $3682.

Financial Aid Program-specific awards for 1997: Clinton B. Ford Scholarship for talented stringed instrumentalists ($500–$1500), Ithaca Premier Talent Scholarships for program majors ($10,000), Leo A. & Frances MacArthur Keilocker Scholarships for talented stringed instrumentalists ($500–$1500), Colonel George S. Howard Scholarships for talented wind instrumentalists ($1000–$1500), Iola Angood Taylor Scholarships for students from public school music programs ($500–$1500), Robert S. Boothroyd, Sr. Scholarships for contributors to the School of Music ($200–$1000), Patrick Conway Endowed Scholarships for program majors ($200–$700), David J. Laub Memorial Scholarships for talented

Ithaca College *(continued)*

upperclassmen ($300–$700), Allan H. Treman Music Scholarships for music students who made contributions to the School of Music ($200–$1000), W. Grant Egbert Music Scholarships for students demonstrating excellence in music, scholarship, and service ($50–$500).

Application Procedures Students admitted directly into the professional program freshman year. Deadline for freshmen: March 1; transfers: July 15. Notification date for freshmen: April 15; transfers: July 15. Required: essay, high school transcript, college transcript(s) for transfer students, letter of recommendation, audition, SAT I or ACT test scores, two original music scores for composition applicants. Recommended: minimum 3.0 high school GPA, interview. Auditions held 13 times on campus and off campus in New York, NY; Interlochen, MI; Chicago, IL; Tampa, FL; Washington, DC; Philadelphia, PA; Boston, MA; Pittsburgh, PA; candidates for performance in percussion and organ must audition in Ithaca; recorded music is permissible as a substitute for live auditions when distance is prohibitive or scheduling is difficult and videotaped performances are permissible as a substitute for live auditions if distance is prohibitive or scheduling is difficult.

Web Site http://www.ithaca.edu.

Undergraduate Contact Ms. Paula J. Mitchell, Director, Admission Department, Ithaca College, 100 Job Hall, Ithaca, New York 14850-7020; 607-274-3124, fax: 607-274-1900, E-mail address: admission@ithaca.edu.

Graduate Contact Mr. Garry Brodhead, Assistant Provost and Dean of Graduate Studies, Graduate Studies and Continuing Education, Ithaca College, 111 Towers Concourse, Ithaca, New York 14850-7142; 607-274-3527, fax: 607-274-1263, E-mail address: gradstudies@ithaca.edu.

More About the College

Program Facilities Performance spaces include Ford Hall auditorium (735 seats) and Nabenhauer Recital Hall (150 seats). Three electroacoustic music studios, computer-assisted instruction facilities, and a full complement of practice instruments are available. Some ninety practice room spaces are open to students, and there are four concert grands for performances as well as seventeen practice grands included in the 141 pianos at the school. The library has extensive holdings of music and recordings. A new $11.5-million music building addition, slated for completion in the 1998–99 academic year, will nearly double the existing space and will include a new recital hall, state-of-the-art recording facilities, increased rehearsal space, a computer classroom and lab, and a music education resource center.

Faculty, Resident Artists, and Alumni Faculty members perform nationally and regionally; many are scholars in the fields of music education, theory, composition, and history. Resident faculty ensembles include the Ithaca Brass, Ithaca Wind Quintet, and Ariadne String Quartet. Alumni hold positions in major orchestras and opera companies, perform in many prestigious chamber ensembles, sing on Broadway, and are recognized jazz recording artists. They also hold teaching positions in secondary schools and universities and are successful in arts administration, music publishing, audio technology, and music business.

Student Performance Opportunities Every student is required to perform in a major ensemble; many participate in more than one. There are twenty-four student ensembles, including wind ensemble, concert band, symphony orchestra, chamber orchestra, brass choir, percussion ensemble, guitar ensemble, choir, chorus, women's chorale, madrigal singers, vocal jazz ensemble, opera workshop, and jazz workshop, as well as numerous chamber ensembles.

Special Programs Students may study abroad at the Ithaca College London Center or elsewhere. Programs in Suzuki string and piano pedagogy are available, as is a teacher certification program. The Office of Career Planning and Placement offers special assistance geared to music students, and alumni also actively serve as career opportunity resources.

▼

Since its founding in 1892 as a conservatory of music, Ithaca College has been nurturing and developing its musical character. The College remains dedicated to the goals of its founder, W. Grant Egbert, who said, "It is my plan to build a school of music second to none in the excellence of its faculty, the soundness of its educational ideals, and the superior quality of instruction."

As the conservatory evolved into a college with expanded academic offerings, the programs in music retained their position of prominence. Today, Ithaca's School of Music is counted among the nation's leading schools. In 1999, a 65,000-square foot addition will open, featuring a new recital hall, electroacoustic music suite, and increased rehearsal space.

Devoted primarily to undergraduate study, the School of Music is steadfastly committed to providing a high level of music education. Students benefit from a blend of first-class faculty members, innovative programs, and outstanding facilities.

Students in the School of Music take one quarter of their academic work in the liberal arts, primarily through the School of Humanities and Sciences. Additional electives from Ithaca's other professional schools—Business, Communications, and Health Sciences and Human Performance—are also available. The interaction among the schools is another advantage to an Ithaca education: physics majors can be found working in the electroacoustic music studios, television-radio majors take courses such as Music and the Media, and music students play in the pit orchestra for theater productions and perform on soundtracks for student filmmakers. The planned studies option allows students to create their own degree programs that take advantage of the broad array of courses and majors—some 1,900 courses and more than 100 degree programs are offered.

Students who come to the Ithaca College School of Music are already dedicated to the idea of mastering voice or any of the standard orchestral musical instruments. At Ithaca they continue their training under a faculty of performing professionals. Students prepare for their musical performances through weekly private lessons and 1-hour repertory classes with their major teachers and fellow students. Repertory classes provide opportunities for students to perform for each other, review performance techniques, and meet guest artists such as Elly Ameling, James Galway, Yefim Bronfman, the Ying Quartet, and the Stuttgart Chamber Orchestra. As soloists and with ensembles, students become part of the rich musical life of the school, where more than 300 recitals, concerts, musicals, and operas are given each year.

All degree programs emphasize performance. Each year, some 450 undergraduate and 40 graduate students are involved in live performances—on campus, in the Ithaca community, and throughout the northeastern United States.

In addition, several ensembles tour annually and have won critical acclaim for their work in New York at Lincoln Center's Alice Tully Hall, St. Patrick's Cathedral, and Carnegie Hall; in Boston and throughout New England; in Washington, D.C. and other cities; and in international venues such as London's Royal Academy of Music.

The city of Ithaca is one of the country's premier college towns, with nearly 25,000 students at Ithaca College and Cornell University. Surrounded by magnificent gorges, lakes, and countryside in the Finger Lakes region of New York State, Ithaca is a thriving cultural center. The community supports an impressive array of concerts, art galleries, movies, and theater productions. Among the artists who have performed in town recently are Itzhak Perlman, Richard Goode, Mstislav Rostropovich, James Galway, and Thomas Hampson.

Ithaca College's combination of a resident faculty, an emphasis on undergraduate performance, and access to a wide spectrum of liberal arts courses makes it an excellent choice among the major music schools in the nation.

▼ JACKSON STATE UNIVERSITY

Jackson, Mississippi

State-supported, coed. Urban campus. Total enrollment: 6,333.

Degrees Bachelor of Music in the area of piano performance; Bachelor of Music Education in the areas of instrumental music education, vocal music education, piano music education, jazz music education. Majors and concentrations: jazz, music education, piano/organ, stringed instruments, voice, wind and percussion instruments. Graduate degrees offered: Master of Music Education. Program accredited by NASM.

Enrollment Fall 1997: 114 total; 96 undergraduate, 8 graduate, 10 non-professional degree.

Music Student Profile 45% females, 55% males, 3% international.

Music Faculty 21 total undergraduate and graduate (full-time and part-time). Graduate students do not teach undergraduate courses. Undergraduate student–faculty ratio: 5:1.

Student Life Student groups/activities include Music Educators National Conference, Music Teachers National Association, Kappa Kappa Psi/Tau Beta Sigma.

Expenses for 1997–98 State resident tuition: $2380 full-time. Nonresident tuition: $4974 full-time. College room and board: $3296. College room only: $1882.

Financial Aid Program-specific awards for 1997: music scholarships for talented program majors.

Application Procedures Students admitted directly into the professional program freshman year. Deadline for freshmen and transfers: July 1. Required: high school transcript, audition, SAT I or ACT test scores (minimum combined ACT score of 17), minimum 2.5 high school GPA. Recommended: 3 letters of recommendation, video. Auditions held 3 times on campus and off campus in St. Louis, MO; East St. Louis, IL; Chicago, IL; Detroit, MI; Atlanta, GA; Hattiesburg, MS; Natchez, MS; Clarksdale, MS; Meridian, MS; recorded music is permissible as a substitute for live auditions when distance is prohibitive and videotaped performances are permissible as a substitute for live auditions when distance is prohibitive.

Undergraduate Contact Dr. Jimmie J. James Jr., Chair, Music Department, Jackson State University, PO Box 17055, Jackson, Mississippi 39217; 601-968-2141, fax: 601-968-2586, E-mail address: jjames@ccaix.jsums.edu.

Graduate Contact Dr. Johnnie Anthony, Associate Professor, Music Department, Jackson State University, PO Box 17055, Jackson, Mississippi 39217; 601-968-2141, fax: 601-968-2586.

▼ JACKSONVILLE STATE UNIVERSITY

Jacksonville, Alabama

State-supported, coed. Small town campus. Total enrollment: 7,619. Music program established 1960.

Degrees Bachelor of Music Education. Majors and concentrations: classical music, music, music education. Graduate degrees offered: Master of Music Education. Program accredited by NASM.

Enrollment Fall 1997: 185 total; 144 undergraduate, 24 graduate, 17 non-professional degree.

Music Student Profile 45% females, 55% males, 10% minorities, 5% international.

Music Faculty 19 total undergraduate and graduate (full-time and part-time). 75% of full-time faculty have terminal degrees. Graduate students do not teach undergraduate courses.

Student Life Student groups/activities include Music Educators National Conference Student Chapter, Phi Mu Alpha Sinfonia, Sigma Alpha Iota. Special housing available for music students.

Expenses for 1997–98 Application fee: $20. State resident tuition: $2040 full-time. Nonresident tuition: $4080 full-time. Mandatory fees: $20 full-time. Full-time tuition and fees vary according to course load and reciprocity agreements. College room and board: $2980. Room and board charges vary according to board plan and housing facility. Special program-related fees: $25 for individual applied music fee, $5 for class applied music fee.

Financial Aid Program-specific awards for 1997: 75–100 band scholarships for wind and percussion majors ($800–$1000), 25–50 Choral Scholarships for vocal/choral majors ($800–$1000), 10–15 Vocal Scholarships for voice majors ($800–$1000), 10–15 Piano Scholarships for piano majors ($800–$1000).

Application Procedures Students admitted directly into the professional program freshman year. Deadline for freshmen and transfers: continuous. Required: high school transcript, college transcript(s) for transfer students, minimum 2.0 high school GPA, SAT I or ACT test scores. Recommended: interview, audition. Auditions held 3 times on campus; recorded music is permissible as a substitute for live auditions if a campus visit is impossible and videotaped performances are permissible as a substitute for live auditions if a campus visit is impossible.

Undergraduate Contact Dr. Jerry D. Smith, Dean of Admissions and Records, Jacksonville State University, 700 Pelham Road North, Jacksonville, Alabama 36265; 256-782-5400.

Graduate Contact Dr. William Carr, Dean of Graduate Studies, Jacksonville State University, 700 Pelham Road North, Jacksonville, Alabama 36265; 256-782-5329.

▼ JACKSONVILLE UNIVERSITY

Jacksonville, Florida

Independent, coed. Suburban campus. Total enrollment: 2,157.

Jacksonville University *(continued)*

Degrees Bachelor of Music in the areas of performance, composition and theory; Bachelor of Music Education; Bachelor of Fine Arts in the area of music theater. Majors and concentrations: classical music, music, music education, music theater, music theory and composition, piano/organ, stringed instruments, voice, wind and percussion instruments. Program accredited by NASM.

Enrollment Fall 1997: 81 total; 57 undergraduate, 24 nonprofessional degree.

Music Student Profile 57% females, 43% males, 11% minorities.

Music Faculty 37 total (full-time and part-time). 33% of full-time faculty have terminal degrees. Graduate students do not teach undergraduate courses. Undergraduate student–faculty ratio: 5:1.

Student Life Student groups/activities include Mu Phi Epsilon, Florida National Music Educators Conference Student Chapter.

Expenses for 1997–98 Application fee: $25. Comprehensive fee: $18,800 includes full-time tuition ($13,360), mandatory fees ($540), and college room and board ($4900). College room only: $2260. Room and board charges vary according to board plan. Special program-related fees: $30 per course per semester for instrumental methods instructional material assessment, $80–$110 per semester for private music lessons, $100 per course for music technology fee.

Financial Aid Program-specific awards for 1997: 41 music grants for program students ($4042), 14 Service Awards for chorus, band, orchestra students ($1826), 14 Accompanying Grants for pianists ($3416), 20 awards for musically talented students ($1000).

Application Procedures Students admitted directly into the professional program freshman year. Deadline for freshmen and transfers: continuous. Notification date for freshmen and transfers: continuous. Required: essay, high school transcript, college transcript(s) for transfer students, minimum 2.0 high school GPA, audition, SAT I or ACT test scores (minimum combined SAT I score of 800). Recommended: minimum 3.0 high school GPA, 2 letters of recommendation. Auditions held 5 times on campus; recorded music is permissible as a substitute for live auditions if a campus visit is impossible and videotaped performances are permissible as a substitute for live auditions if a campus visit is impossible.

Web Site http://www.ju.edu.

Undergraduate Contact Dr. Susan Hallenbeck, Director of Admissions, Jacksonville University, 2800 University Boulevard North, Jacksonville, Florida 32211; 904-745-7370, fax: 904-745-7375.

More About the University

Program Facilities Terry Concert Hall, opened in 1991, is a state-of-the-art 400-seat concert hall with excellent acoustics. Swisher Auditorium seats 550 and is used for staging the dramatic and musical productions presented by College of Fine Arts students. The Phillips Fine Arts Building houses classrooms, teaching studios, practice rooms, rehearsal rooms, an electronic music studio, a recital hall/art museum, and an ear-training lab.

Faculty, Resident Artists, and Alumni A number of JU music faculty are members of the Jacksonville Symphony Orchestra and St. Johns River City Band as well as active concert artists, recitalists, and church musicians. Aaron Krosnick, violin, and Mary Lou Krosnick, piano, present more than forty recitals and master classes each year throughout Florida. Each year,

the College of Fine Arts hosts numerous master classes featuring renowned artists from the U.S. and abroad.

Student Performance Opportunities JU has eight formal student ensembles and other smaller performing groups. Students participate in the University-Community Orchestra, University Wind Ensemble, Jazz Ensemble, Percussion Ensemble, Pep Band, Concert Choir, Chamber Singers, and Dolphinaires, a vocal jazz ensemble. Open auditions are also held for musicals and operas performed on campus.

Special Programs Music programs at JU are accredited by the National Association of Schools of Music (NASM). JU is accredited by the Commission on Colleges of the Southern Association of Colleges and Schools. Internships and study-abroad programs are available.

▼ JAMES MADISON UNIVERSITY
Harrisonburg, Virginia

State-supported, coed. Small town campus. Total enrollment: 14,115. Music program established 1934.

Degrees Bachelor of Music in the areas of music industry, music education, performance, composition, musical theater. Majors and concentrations: accompanying, composition, music, music business, music education, music theater, piano/organ, stringed instruments, voice, wind and percussion instruments. Graduate degrees offered: Master of Music in the areas of performance, music education, conducting, music theory/composition. Program accredited by NASM.

Enrollment Fall 1997: 403 total; 378 undergraduate, 25 graduate.

Music Student Profile 50% females, 50% males, 8% minorities, 1% international.

Music Faculty 41 total undergraduate and graduate (full-time and part-time). 100% of full-time faculty have terminal degrees. Graduate students teach a few undergraduate courses. Undergraduate student–faculty ratio: 8:1.

Student Life Student groups/activities include Music Educators National Conference, Kappa Kappa Psi, Sigma Alpha Iota.

Expenses for 1997–98 Application fee: $25. State resident tuition: $4148 full-time. Nonresident tuition: $8816 full-time. College room and board: $4846. College room only: $2612.

Financial Aid Program-specific awards for 1997: 50 Music Performance Awards for program majors ($2000).

Application Procedures Students admitted directly into the professional program freshman year. Deadline for freshmen: January 15; transfers: February 1. Notification date for freshmen and transfers: April 1. Required: essay, high school transcript, college transcript(s) for transfer students, minimum 2.0 high school GPA, 3 letters of recommendation, audition, SAT I or ACT test scores, music aptitude test, piano placement test. Recommended: minimum 3.0 high school GPA. Auditions held 3 times on campus; recorded music is permissible as a substitute for live auditions when distance is prohibitive and videotaped performances are permissible as a substitute for live auditions when distance is prohibitive.

Web Site http://www.jmu.edu/music/.

Undergraduate Contact Music Admissions, School of Music, James Madison University, MSC 7301, Harrisonburg, Virginia 22807; 540-568-6197, fax: 540-568-7819, E-mail address: music_admit@jmu.edu.

Graduate Contact Dr. Mellasenah Y. Morris, Director, School of Music, James Madison University, MSC 7301, Harrisonburg, Virginia 22807; 540-568-6197, fax: 540-568-7819, E-mail address: morrismy@jmu.edu.

Peabody Conservatory of Music

▼ JOHNS HOPKINS UNIVERSITY

Baltimore, Maryland

Independent, coed. Urban campus. Total enrollment: 5,022.
Degrees Bachelor of Music in the areas of composition, performance, recording arts sciences, music education. Majors and concentrations: composition, early music, guitar, music education, piano/organ, recording arts and sciences, stringed instruments, voice, wind and percussion instruments. Graduate degrees offered: Master of Music in the areas of composition, performance, conducting, music education, music history, computer music, theory pedagogy, performance pedagogy. Doctor of Musical Arts in the areas of composition, performance, conducting. Cross-registration with Maryland Institute-College of Art, Loyola College. Program accredited by NASM.
Enrollment Fall 1997: 617 total; 282 undergraduate, 335 graduate.
Music Student Profile 59% females, 41% males, 10% minorities, 32% international.
Music Faculty 142 total undergraduate and graduate (full-time and part-time). 37% of full-time faculty have terminal degrees. Graduate students do not teach undergraduate courses.
Student Life Special housing available for music students.
Expenses for 1997–98 Application fee: $55. One-time mandatory fee: $500. Comprehensive fee: $29,055 includes full-time tuition ($21,700) and college room and board ($7355). College room only: $3120. Room and board charges vary according to board plan.
Application Procedures Students admitted directly into the professional program freshman year. Deadline for freshmen and transfers: April 1. Notification date for freshmen and transfers: June 10. Required: essay, high school transcript, college transcript(s) for transfer students, minimum 3.0 high school GPA, 3 letters of recommendation, audition, SAT I test score only (minimum combined SAT I score of 1010). Recommended: interview. Auditions held 12 times on campus and off campus in New York, NY; Boston, MA; Atlanta, GA; Chicago, IL; San Francisco, CA; Los Angeles, CA; recorded music is permissible as a substitute for live auditions when distance is prohibitive.
Web Site http://www.peabody.jhu.edu/.
Contact Mr. David Lane, Director of Admissions, Peabody Conservatory of Music, Johns Hopkins University, 1 East Mount Vernon Place, Baltimore, Maryland 21202; 410-659-8110.

More About the Conservatory

The Admissions office at the Peabody Institute understands how daunting the college search process can be to an aspiring artist. Readers of this guide are likely to be collecting literature from many colleges, conservatories, and universities. The college viewbooks they receive generally paint a wholly appealing picture of life at the school—no scheduling problems, an exquisite campus, incredibly talented students, and understanding faculty members—one could imagine

that a Carnegie Hall debut is only a step away. How does a student make a wise choice and separate the fantasies from realities?

As the Director of Admissions at Peabody has said, "We can't be everything to everybody. If a student and I do our jobs well, it is likely he or she will be happy with the final school selected. We need to see if what Peabody has to offer fits a student's needs."

Of course, Peabody has much to offer. The school was founded in 1857 but did not actually open its doors until 1866. The advantage of this age is that Peabody has been turning out top quality musicians for more than a century, and the music world has come to assume that anyone who graduates from Peabody is a good performer. When students are asked how they heard about the school, they often reply, "I don't know. I think I've always known about Peabody."

In 1977 the Conservatory entered into an affiliation with The Johns Hopkins University, giving Peabody students access to all the facilities and activities at the Schools of Arts and Sciences. In 1986 the Peabody Institute officially became a division of the University system. Thus, Peabody graduates are simultaneously graduates of JHU. If the Carnegie Hall fantasy doesn't work out, a Peabody/Hopkins diploma is a powerful credential to have on a résumé.

The focus of Peabody's 630 or so students is entirely "classical". However, within the field of classical music, Peabody is actually quite diverse. It is possible for interested students to include jazz and a wide variety of other subjects (via cross-registration to the Krieger School of Arts and Sciences) in their Peabody experience.

Students can write or call Peabody for application materials, or to learn details about the school's philosophy, audition requirements, faculty members, and the financial side of things. In any case, the Peabody Institute wishes every student planning to pursue a music career the best of luck in finding the right school.

▼ JORDAN COLLEGE OF FINE ARTS
See Butler University

▼ THE JUILLIARD SCHOOL

New York, New York

Independent, coed. Urban campus. Total enrollment: 782. Music program established 1905.
Degrees Bachelor of Music. Majors and concentrations: accompanying, bassoon, clarinet, composition, conducting, double bass, English horn, flute, guitar, harp, harpsichord, horn, oboe, organ, percussion, piano, trombone, trumpet, tuba, viola, violin, violoncello, voice. Graduate degrees offered: Master of Music. Doctor of Musical Arts. Cross-registration with Columbia University, Barnard College.
Enrollment Fall 1997: 782 total; 465 undergraduate, 234 graduate, 83 non-professional degree.
Music Student Profile 53% females, 47% males, 46% minorities, 30% international.
Music Faculty 241 total undergraduate and graduate (full-time and part-time). Graduate students do not teach undergraduate courses. Undergraduate student–faculty ratio: 4:1.
Student Life Special housing available for music students.
Expenses for 1997–98 Application fee: $85. Comprehensive fee: $21,500 includes full-time tuition ($14,400), mandatory

The Juilliard School *(continued)*

fees ($600), and college room and board ($6500). Room and board charges vary according to housing facility.

Financial Aid Program-specific awards for 1997: 440 The Juilliard Scholarship Fund Awards for program majors ($8554).

Application Procedures Students admitted directly into the professional program freshman year. Deadline for freshmen and transfers: December 1. Notification date for freshmen and transfers: April 1. Required: high school transcript, interview, audition, video for piano and voice applicants. Recommended: essay, letter of recommendation. Auditions held once on campus.

Contact Ms. Mary K. Gray, Director of Admissions, The Juilliard School, 60 Lincoln Center Plaza, New York, New York 10023-6590; 212-799-5000 ext. 223, fax: 212-769-6420.

▼ J. WILLIAM FULBRIGHT COLLEGE OF ARTS AND SCIENCES

See University of Arkansas

▼ KANSAS STATE UNIVERSITY

Manhattan, Kansas

State-supported, coed. Suburban campus. Total enrollment: 20,306.

Degrees Bachelor of Music in the areas of performance, composition, music theater; Bachelor of Music Education. Majors and concentrations: composition, music, music education, music theater, piano/organ, stringed instruments, voice, wind and percussion instruments. Graduate degrees offered: Master of Music in the areas of music education, performance, music history and literature, composition. Program accredited by NASM.

Enrollment Fall 1997: 180 undergraduate, 25 graduate.

Music Student Profile 55% females, 45% males, 5% minorities, 5% international.

Music Faculty 26 total undergraduate and graduate (full-time and part-time). 90% of full-time faculty have terminal degrees. Graduate students teach a few undergraduate courses.

Student Life Student groups/activities include Music Educators National Conference Student Chapter, American Choral Directors Association, music fraternity and sorority.

Expenses for 1997–98 Application fee: $15. State resident tuition: $1965 full-time. Nonresident tuition: $8270 full-time. Mandatory fees: $502 full-time. College room and board: $3640.

Financial Aid Program-specific awards for 1997: 50 Music Service Guild Awards for freshmen program majors ($400).

Application Procedures Students admitted directly into the professional program freshman year. Deadline for freshmen and transfers: continuous. Required: high school transcript. Recommended: video, audition. Auditions held 3 times on campus; recorded music is permissible as a substitute for live auditions if a campus visit is impossible and videotaped performances are permissible as a substitute for live auditions if a campus visit is impossible.

Undergraduate Contact Mr. Jack Flouer, Head, Music Department, Kansas State University, McCain 109, Manhattan, Kansas 66506; 913-532-5740, fax: 913-532-5709, E-mail address: flouer@ksu.edu.

Graduate Contact Mr. Craig Parker, Director of Graduates Studies, Music Department, Kansas State University, McCain 109, Manhattan, Kansas 66506; 913-532-5740, fax: 913-532-5709, E-mail address: cbp@ksu.edu.

▼ KEENE STATE COLLEGE

Keene, New Hampshire

State-supported, coed. Small town campus. Total enrollment: 4,409. Music program established 1971.

Degrees Bachelor of Music in the areas of music education, performance. Majors and concentrations: classical guitar, music education, piano/organ, stringed instruments, voice, wind and percussion instruments. Program accredited by NASM.

Enrollment Fall 1997: 108 total; 83 undergraduate, 25 non-professional degree.

Music Student Profile 55% females, 45% males, 3% minorities, 1% international.

Music Faculty 24 total (full-time and part-time). 85% of full-time faculty have terminal degrees. Graduate students do not teach undergraduate courses. Undergraduate student–faculty ratio: 10:1.

Student Life Student groups/activities include Music Educators National Conference Student Chapter.

Expenses for 1997–98 Application fee: $25, $35 for nonresidents. State resident tuition: $3240 full-time. Nonresident tuition: $8740 full-time. Mandatory fees: $1100 full-time. College room and board: $4660. College room only: $3120. Room and board charges vary according to board plan and housing facility. Special program-related fees: $100 per credit hour for applied music fees.

Financial Aid Program-specific awards for 1997: 3 Talent Scholarships for incoming freshmen ($2800), 1 Jesse Davis Scholarship for upperclassmen ($500).

Application Procedures Students admitted directly into the professional program freshman year. Deadline for freshmen and transfers: April 15. Notification date for freshmen and transfers: May 1. Required: essay, high school transcript, college transcript(s) for transfer students, 2 letters of recommendation, audition, SAT I or ACT test scores. Recommended: minimum 3.0 high school GPA, interview. Auditions held continuously on campus; recorded music is permissible as a substitute for live auditions if a campus visit is impossible and videotaped performances are permissible as a substitute for live auditions if a campus visit is impossible.

Undergraduate Contact Mr. Douglas A. Nelson, Coordinator, Music Department, Keene State College, Box 2402, Keene, New Hampshire 03435; 603-358-2177, fax: 603-358-2973, E-mail address: dnelson@keene.edu.

▼ KENNESAW STATE UNIVERSITY

Kennesaw, Georgia

State-supported, coed. Suburban campus. Total enrollment: 13,108.

Degrees Bachelor of Music in the area of performance; Bachelor of Music Education. Majors and concentrations:

classical guitar, jazz guitar, music education, piano, stringed instruments, voice, wind and percussion instruments. Cross-registration with University System of Georgia. Program accredited by NASM.

Enrollment Fall 1997: 165 total; all undergraduate.

Music Student Profile 50% females, 50% males, 5% minorities.

Music Faculty 30 total (full-time and part-time). 100% of full-time faculty have terminal degrees. Graduate students do not teach undergraduate courses.

Student Life Student groups/activities include Music Educators National Conference Student Chapter, Pi Kappa Lambda, Music Teachers National Association Student Chapter.

Expenses for 1997–98 Application fee: $20. State resident tuition: $1680 full-time. Nonresident tuition: $6141 full-time. Mandatory fees: $333 full-time. Special program-related fees: $150 per semester for applied music fee, $150 per semester for applied music techniques fee.

Financial Aid Program-specific awards for 1997: 1–2 Gibson Scholarships for voice/piano majors ($500), 1 Sullivan Scholarship for voice majors ($800), 1–2 Miller and Wilhoit Scholarships for program majors ($1100), 15–20 Kennesaw State College Foundation Scholarships for program majors ($300), 3–6 Cobb County Music Teachers Awards for program majors ($300), 1 Hollingsworth Scholarship for program majors ($1000), 2 Cobb County Schools for program majors ($1250), 1 H.F. Rodenhauser Scholarship for program majors ($500).

Application Procedures Students apply for admission into the professional program by junior year. Deadline for freshmen and transfers: July 17. Required: high school transcript, college transcript(s) for transfer students, minimum 2.0 high school GPA, interview, audition, SAT I or ACT test scores (minimum combined SAT I score of 980), immunization record. Auditions held 3 times and by arrangement on campus; videotaped performances are permissible as a substitute for live auditions with approval from the department.

Undergraduate Contact Department of Music, Kennesaw State University, 1000 Chastain Road, Kennesaw, Georgia 30144; 770-423-6151, fax: 770-423-6368, E-mail address: jmeeks@ksumail.kennesaw.edu.

Hugh A. Glauser School of Music

▼ KENT STATE UNIVERSITY

Kent, Ohio

State-supported, coed. Small town campus. Total enrollment: 20,743.

Degrees Bachelor of Music in the areas of performance, music theory, composition, music education. Majors and concentrations: classical music, composition, music, music education, music theory, piano/organ, stringed instruments, voice, wind and percussion instruments. Graduate degrees offered: Master of Music in the areas of performance, conducting, piano pedagogy, music education. Doctor of Philosophy in the areas of music education, theory/composition, musicology/ethnomusicology. Program accredited by NASM, NCATE.

Enrollment Fall 1997: 255 total; 130 undergraduate, 125 graduate.

Music Student Profile 50% females, 50% males, 2% minorities, 3% international.

Music Faculty 50 total undergraduate and graduate (full-time and part-time). 95% of full-time faculty have terminal degrees. Graduate students teach a few undergraduate courses. Undergraduate student–faculty ratio: 14:1.

Student Life Student groups/activities include Music Educators National Conference, music fraternities and sororities.

Expenses for 1997–98 Application fee: $30. State resident tuition: $4460 full-time. Nonresident tuition: $8920 full-time. Full-time tuition varies according to course load. College room and board: $4152. College room only: $2448. Special program-related fees: $45–$90 per semester for applied music lesson fee.

Financial Aid Program-specific awards for 1997: 20 departmental awards for program majors ($1500), 10 Orchestra Society Awards for orchestra participants ($500), 1 L. Wallach Award for program majors ($1000), 1 A. Wallach Award for program majors ($1000), 1 D. Morgan Award for program majors ($1000).

Application Procedures Students admitted directly into the professional program freshman year. Deadline for freshmen and transfers: continuous. Notification date for freshmen and transfers: continuous. Required: high school transcript, audition, minimum 2.5 high school GPA. Auditions held 4 times on campus; recorded music is permissible as a substitute for live auditions when distance is prohibitive.

Web Site http://www.kent.edu/music.

Undergraduate Contact Mr. Kent Larmee, Coordinator of Undergraduate Studies, Hugh A. Glauser School of Music, Kent State University, PO Box 5190, Kent, Ohio 44242-0001; 330-672-2172, fax: 330-672-7837, E-mail address: klarmee@kentvm.kent.edu.

Graduate Contact Dr. Donald L. Hamann, Coordinator of Graduate Studies, Hugh A. Glauser School of Music, Kent State University, PO Box 5190, Kent, Ohio 44242-0001; 330-672-2172, fax: 330-672-7837, E-mail address: ljohnso4@kent.edu.

▼ KENTUCKY STATE UNIVERSITY

Frankfort, Kentucky

State-related, coed. Small town campus. Total enrollment: 2,288.

Degrees Bachelor of Music in the areas of vocal performance, instrumental performance; Bachelor of Music Education in the areas of vocal music education, instrumental music education. Majors and concentrations: music, music education. Program accredited by NASM, NCATE.

Enrollment Fall 1997: 308 total; 64 undergraduate, 244 non-professional degree.

Music Student Profile 67% females, 33% males, 98% minorities.

Music Faculty 12 total (full-time and part-time). 78% of full-time faculty have terminal degrees. Graduate students do not teach undergraduate courses. Undergraduate student–faculty ratio: 26:1.

Student Life Student groups/activities include Music Educators National Conference Student Chapter, Tau Beta Sigma, Delta Omicron.

Expenses for 1997–98 Application fee: $15. State resident tuition: $1800 full-time. Nonresident tuition: $5400 full-time. Mandatory fees: $250 full-time. College room and board: $3190. College room only: $1454.

Financial Aid Program-specific awards for 1997: 50 Performance Scholarships for program majors ($2000), 100 Ensemble Scholarships for ensemble performers ($500).

Kentucky State University (*continued*)

Application Procedures Students apply for admission into the professional program by junior year. Deadline for freshmen and transfers: July 10. Notification date for freshmen and transfers: July 15. Required: high school transcript, college transcript(s) for transfer students, minimum 2.0 high school GPA, 3 letters of recommendation, audition, SAT I or ACT test scores. Recommended: essay, minimum 3.0 high school GPA, interview, video, portfolio. Auditions held 4 times on campus; recorded music is permissible as a substitute for live auditions for provisional admission and videotaped performances are permissible as a substitute for live auditions for provisional acceptance. Portfolio reviews held by appointment on campus.

Web Site http://www.kysu.edu.

Undergraduate Contact Dr. Roosevelt O. Shelton, Chairperson, Division of Fine Arts, Kentucky State University, G5-Bradford Hall, Frankfort, Kentucky 40601; 502-227-6496, fax: 502-227-5999, E-mail address: rshelton@gwmail.kysu.edu.

▼ KENTUCKY WESLEYAN COLLEGE

Owensboro, Kentucky

Independent-Methodist, coed. Suburban campus. Total enrollment: 777.

Degrees Bachelor of Music in the areas of performance, church music; Bachelor of Music Education. Majors and concentrations: music, music education, piano/organ, sacred music, voice. Cross-registration with Brescia College.

Enrollment Fall 1997: 46 total; 21 undergraduate, 25 nonprofessional degree.

Music Student Profile 58% females, 42% males, 4% minorities, 2% international.

Music Faculty 11 total undergraduate (full-time and part-time). 100% of full-time faculty have terminal degrees. Graduate students do not teach undergraduate courses. Undergraduate student–faculty ratio: 8:1.

Student Life Student groups/activities include Music Educators National Conference, Kentucky Wesleyan Singers, Kentucky Wesleyan Players.

Expenses for 1998–99 Application fee: $20. Comprehensive fee: $14,360 includes full-time tuition ($9480), mandatory fees ($250), and college room and board ($4630). College room only: $2130. Full-time tuition and fees vary according to course load. Special program-related fees: $50 per credit hour for applied music fee.

Financial Aid Program-specific awards for 1997: 30–35 music scholarships for program majors ($2500).

Application Procedures Students admitted directly into the professional program freshman year. Deadline for freshmen and transfers: continuous. Required: high school transcript, minimum 2.0 high school GPA, audition, SAT I or ACT test scores. Recommended: essay, minimum 3.0 high school GPA, 3 letters of recommendation, interview. Auditions held 4 times and by appointment on campus and off campus in various cities by special arrangement; recorded music is permissible as a substitute for live auditions and videotaped performances are permissible as a substitute for live auditions.

Undergraduate Contact Dr. Diane K. Earle, Professor of Music, Music Department, Kentucky Wesleyan College, 3000 Frederica Street, Owensboro, Kentucky 42302-1039; 502-926-3111 ext. 245.

▼ LAKE ERIE COLLEGE

Painesville, Ohio

Independent, coed. Small town campus. Total enrollment: 701.

Degrees Bachelor of Fine Arts in the areas of music, interdisciplinary studies; Bachelor of Arts in the area of music. Majors and concentrations: composition, instrumental music, interdisciplinary studies, music history, music theory, voice. Program accredited by NASM.

Enrollment Fall 1997: 2 total; all undergraduate.

Music Faculty 1 undergraduate (full-time). 100% of full-time faculty have terminal degrees. Graduate students do not teach undergraduate courses. Undergraduate student–faculty ratio: 2:1.

Student Life Student groups/activities include Community Chorus.

Expenses for 1997–98 Application fee: $20. Comprehensive fee: $18,690 includes full-time tuition ($12,950), mandatory fees ($800), and college room and board ($4940). College room only: $2540.

Financial Aid Program-specific awards for 1997: 1 Fine Arts Award for program majors ($500–$1000).

Application Procedures Deadline for freshmen: July 1; transfers: August 20. Required: essay, high school transcript, college transcript(s) for transfer students, minimum 2.0 high school GPA, letter of recommendation, SAT I or ACT test scores, audition for scholarship consideration. Recommended: interview. Auditions held as needed on campus.

Undergraduate Contact Mr. Paul Gothard, Director, Fine Arts Department, Lake Erie College, Box 354, 391 West Washington Street, Painesville, Ohio 44077; 440-639-7856.

▼ LAKEHEAD UNIVERSITY

Thunder Bay, ON, Canada

Province-supported, coed. Suburban campus. Total enrollment: 6,787. Music program established 1988.

Degrees Bachelor of Music. Majors and concentrations: classical music. Cross-registration with Confederation College. Program accredited by CUMS.

Enrollment Fall 1997: 75 undergraduate.

Music Student Profile 50% females, 50% males, 5% minorities.

Music Faculty 22 total (full-time and part-time). 100% of full-time faculty have terminal degrees. Graduate students do not teach undergraduate courses. Undergraduate student–faculty ratio: 4:1.

Expenses for 1997–98 Application fee: $80 Canadian dollars. Tuition, fee, and room and board charges are reported in Canadian dollars. Canadian resident tuition: $3225 full-time. Mandatory fees: $338 full-time. College room and board: $4674. College room only: $3576. Room and board charges vary according to housing facility. International student tuition: $7000 full-time.

Financial Aid Program-specific awards for 1997: 1 Munro Family Memorial Prize for program majors ($725), 5 A.L. Musselman Awards for program majors ($297–$800), 1 Westlake Music Scholarship for continuing students ($450), 1 Ranta Entrance Award for incoming students ($300), 1 Lakehead University Music Festival Scholarship for incoming students ($1226), Westlake Music Scholarships for incoming students ($450), 1 Canadian Scholars' Press Music Bursary for program majors ($500), 1 Westlake Music Bursary for continuing students ($750), 2 Wilma C. Ayre Memorial Bursaries for continuing students ($300).

Application Procedures Students admitted directly into the professional program freshman year. Deadline for freshmen and transfers: continuous. Required: high school transcript, college transcript(s) for transfer students, minimum 2.0 high school GPA, interview, audition, music theory entrance test. Auditions held by appointment on campus; recorded music is permissible as a substitute for live auditions for out-of-town applicants and videotaped performances are permissible as a substitute for live auditions for out-of-town applicants.

Undergraduate Contact Registrar's Office, Lakehead University, 955 Oliver Road, Thunder Bay, ON P7B 5E1, Canada; 807-343-8500, fax: 807-343-8156.

▼ LAMAR UNIVERSITY

Beaumont, Texas

State-supported, coed. Suburban campus. Total enrollment: 9,677.

Degrees Bachelor of Music in the areas of performance, composition, music education. Majors and concentrations: composition, music education, piano, stringed instruments, voice, wind and percussion instruments. Graduate degrees offered: Master of Music in the area of performance; Master of Music Education. Program accredited by NASM.

Enrollment Fall 1997: 108 total; 101 undergraduate, 7 graduate.

Music Student Profile 50% females, 50% males, 20% minorities, 5% international.

Music Faculty 22 total undergraduate and graduate (full-time and part-time). 92% of full-time faculty have terminal degrees. Graduate students teach a few undergraduate courses.

Student Life Student groups/activities include Delta Omicron, Phi Mu Alpha Sinfonia, International Association of Jazz Educators.

Expenses for 1997–98 State resident tuition: $1392 full-time. Nonresident tuition: $6504 full-time. Mandatory fees: $476 full-time. College room and board: $3200. College room only: $1600. Room and board charges vary according to board plan and housing facility. Special program-related fees: $50–$150 for applied music fee.

Financial Aid Program-specific awards for 1997: 45–50 band scholarships for band students ($300–$1900), 20–25 Choir Scholarships for choir students ($300–$1300), 5–10 Orchestra Scholarships for orchestra students ($700–$2000), 20–30 scholarships for program majors ($300–$1900).

Application Procedures Students admitted directly into the professional program freshman year. Deadline for freshmen and transfers: continuous. Required: high school transcript, college transcript(s) for transfer students, audition, SAT I or ACT test scores. Recommended: interview. Auditions held continuously on campus; recorded music is permissible as a substitute for live auditions when distance is prohibitive and videotaped performances are permissible as a substitute for live auditions when distance is prohibitive.

Undergraduate Contact Dr. Barry W. Johnson, Chair, Department of Music, Theatre and Dance, Lamar University, PO Box 10044, Beaumont, Texas 77710; 409-880-8144, fax: 409-880-8143, E-mail address: johnsbw@lub002.lamar.edu.

Graduate Contact Dr. Kurt Gilman, Director of Graduate Studies in Music, Department of Music, Theatre and Dance, Lamar University, PO Box 10044, Beaumont, Texas 77710; 409-880-8077, fax: 409-880-8143.

▼ LAMBUTH UNIVERSITY

Jackson, Tennessee

Independent-United Methodist, coed. Urban campus. Total enrollment: 1,012.

Degrees Bachelor of Music in the areas of church music, instrumental music education, vocal music education, performance, piano pedagogy. Cross-registration with Union University, Freed-Hardeman University.

Enrollment Fall 1997: 25 undergraduate.

Music Student Profile 54% females, 46% males, 16% minorities, 6% international.

Music Faculty 6 total undergraduate (full-time and part-time). 80% of full-time faculty have terminal degrees. Graduate students do not teach undergraduate courses.

Expenses for 1997–98 Application fee: $10. Comprehensive fee: $10,144 includes full-time tuition ($5924), mandatory fees ($270), and college room and board ($3950). College room only: $1780. Room and board charges vary according to board plan and housing facility. Special program-related fees: $100–$200 per semester for applied music lesson fee.

Financial Aid Program-specific awards for 1997: 20–25 Endowed Music Majors Awards for program majors ($250), 50–75 Student Musician Awards for band/choir majors ($200–$2000).

Application Procedures Students admitted directly into the professional program freshman year. Deadline for freshmen and transfers: continuous. Required: high school transcript, college transcript(s) for transfer students, minimum 2.0 high school GPA, 2 letters of recommendation, SAT I or ACT test scores. Recommended: audition. Auditions held 3 times and by appointment on campus; recorded music is permissible as a substitute for live auditions when distance is prohibitive and videotaped performances are permissible as a substitute for live auditions when distance is prohibitive.

Web Site http://www.lambuth.edu.

Undergraduate Contact Ms. Nancy Callis, Director of Admissions, Lambuth University, 705 Lambuth Boulevard, Jackson, Tennessee 38301; 901-425-3223, fax: 901-988-4600, E-mail address: admit@lambuth.edu.

▼ LAMONT SCHOOL OF MUSIC

See University of Denver

▼ LANDER UNIVERSITY

Greenwood, South Carolina

State-supported, coed. Small town campus. Music program established 1872.

Degrees Bachelor of Music Education in the areas of instrumental music education, vocal music education. Majors and concentrations: instrumental music, keyboard, music education, voice. Cross-registration with University of Plymouth (England), Trent Polytechnic University (England), Nene College (England). Program accredited by NASM.

Enrollment Fall 1997: 45 total; all undergraduate.

Music Student Profile 68% females, 32% males, 16% minorities.

Lander University *(continued)*

Music Faculty 9 total (full-time and part-time). 80% of full-time faculty have terminal degrees. Graduate students do not teach undergraduate courses. Undergraduate student–faculty ratio: 7:1.

Student Life Student groups/activities include Music Educators National Conference.

Expenses for 1997–98 Application fee: $25. State resident tuition: $3600 full-time. Nonresident tuition: $5832 full-time. College room and board: $3560. Special program-related fees: $40 per semester for applied music fee.

Financial Aid Program-specific awards for 1997: 1 Kerhoulas Award for incoming students ($500), 1 White Award for instrumentalists ($300), 1 Hutto Award for voice majors ($225), 2 Lenti Awards for piano majors ($225).

Application Procedures Students admitted directly into the professional program freshman year. Deadline for freshmen and transfers: continuous. Required: high school transcript, college transcript(s) for transfer students, letter of recommendation, audition, SAT I or ACT test scores (minimum combined SAT I score of 900), standing in top 50% of graduating class, music theory test, minimum 2.5 high school GPA. Recommended: minimum 3.0 high school GPA, interview. Auditions held 2-3 times on campus; recorded music is permissible as a substitute for live auditions when distance is prohibitive and videotaped performances are permissible as a substitute for live auditions when distance is prohibitive.

Undergraduate Contact Mrs. Jackie Roark, Director of Admissions, Lander University, Stanley Avenue, Greenwood, South Carolina 29649; 864-388-8307, fax: 864-388-8890.

▼ LAWRENCE UNIVERSITY

Appleton, Wisconsin

Independent, coed. Small town campus. Music program established 1874.

Degrees Bachelor of Music in the areas of music education, music theory-composition, performance; Bachelor of Arts/Bachelor of Music in the areas of liberal arts in combination with music performance, music education, theory-composition. Majors and concentrations: choral music, classical guitar, classical music, harp, harpsichord, instrumental music, jazz, music, music education, music theory and composition, performance, piano/organ, stringed instruments, voice, wind and percussion instruments. Program accredited by NASM.

Enrollment Fall 1997: 1,189 total; 261 undergraduate, 928 non-professional degree.

Music Student Profile 50% females, 50% males, 5% minorities, 10% international.

Music Faculty 42 total (full-time and part-time). 93% of full-time faculty have terminal degrees. Graduate students do not teach undergraduate courses.

Student Life Student groups/activities include Phi Mu Alpha Sinfonia, Sigma Alpha Iota, WLFM-FM (campus radio station).

Expenses for 1997–98 Application fee: $30. Comprehensive fee: $24,195 includes full-time tuition ($19,494), mandatory fees ($126), and college room and board ($4575). Room and board charges vary according to board plan.

Financial Aid Program-specific awards for 1997: 15–25 Performance Awards for top auditions ($2000–$5000), 5–8 Trustee Awards for top auditions ($10,000).

Application Procedures Students admitted directly into the professional program freshman year. Deadline for freshmen: February 1; transfers: May 15. Notification date for freshmen: April 1; transfers: June 1. Required: essay, high school transcript, college transcript(s) for transfer students, 3 letters of recommendation, audition, SAT I or ACT test scores, music theory examination. Recommended: minimum 3.0 high school GPA, interview. Auditions held 14 times on campus and off campus in Boston, MA; Denver, CO; Interlochen, MI; Los Angeles, CA; Minneapolis, MN; New York, NY; Portland, OR; San Francisco, CA; St. Louis, MO; Washington, DC; recorded music is permissible as a substitute for live auditions when distance is prohibitive to campus or a regional site and videotaped performances are permissible as a substitute for live auditions when distance is prohibitive to campus or a regional site.

Web Site http://lawrence.edu.

Undergraduate Contact Director of Conservatory Admissions, Office of Admissions, Lawrence University, PO Box 599, Appleton, Wisconsin 54912-0599; 888-556-3952, fax: 920-832-6782, E-mail address: excel@lawrence.edu.

More About the University

Program Facilities Memorial Chapel (concert hall of 1,250 seats); Harper Recital Hall (250 seats); Miller Hall (150 seats/choral rehearsal hall); orchestral rehearsal hall (315 seats); jazz rehearsal/recording studio; percussion studios; recording studio, including 16-track digital system, with compact disk recording, editing, and production capabilities; Macintosh-based computer lab, including MIDI technology in conjunction with Finale, Symphony, and Vivace programs; Cloak Theatre (experimental black box); Stansbury Theatre (proscenium theater of 500 seats); outdoor amphitheater; WLFM campus radio station affiliated with Wisconsin Public Radio; historical instruments such as forty-one-stop mechanical action organ by John Brombaugh, 1815 Broadwood piano, Guarneri violin.

Faculty and Resident Artists Thirty full-time faculty members, 6 part-time faculty members; artists-in-residence include faculty chamber ensembles and Dale Duesing ('67), Grammy award-winning lyric baritone; recent visiting artists include Richard Goode, Emanuel Ax, Joshua Bell, The Chamber Music Society of Lincoln Center, Marilyn Horne, Joe Henderson, Wynton Marsalis, and Nadja Salerno-Sonnenberg.

Student Performance Opportunities Ensembles include Symphony Orchestra, Contemporary Music Ensemble, Wind Ensemble, Percussion Ensemble, African Drumming Ensemble, Cello Ensemble, Choral Society, Low Brass Choir, Lawrence Chorale, Horn Choir, Jazz Ensemble, Concert Choir, Opera Theatre, Musical Theatre, Jazz Singers, and numerous chamber ensembles.

Special Programs Music education certification K–12; five-year double-degree (B.A./B.Mus.) program; twenty-three off-campus programs, both domestic and international; academic advising; residence hall life; counseling center; career center; writing skills lab; seventy campus clubs and organizations; twenty-three varsity sports; fifteen club and intramural sports.

The Lawrence Conservatory of Music is a nationally recognized conservatory devoted exclusively to the education of undergraduate musicians within a college of the liberal arts and sciences.

The faculty of performers, composers, scholars, and pedagogues provide individual attention and guidance to the 250 music majors and the many college students who participate in the Conservatory's activities.

Music facilities are housed within three contiguous buildings: the Music-Drama Center, the Memorial Chapel, and the Ruth Harwood Shattuck Hall of Music. The music library, located in the Media Center of the main university library, holds more than 31,000 recordings and scores as well as music reference works.

Music students choose from five degree programs: the Bachelor of Music degree in performance, the Bachelor of Music degree in music education (instrumental; general; choral/general; instrumental/general; choral/general/instrumental), the Bachelor of Music degree in theory-composition, the Bachelor of Arts degree in music, and the double degree. The Lawrence five-year program permits students to earn a Bachelor of Music degree and a Bachelor of Arts degree in a discipline other than music. The combined degree program provides both professional-level study of music and engagement in a rigorous academic program of study. A challenging program, it is one that many students find rewarding. In addition, students may design their own majors with the approval of faculty and also may pursue a double major within the Bachelor of Music degree. The curriculum in the Conservatory of Music seeks to ensure that all music students, regardless of major, graduate with a thorough and firm grounding in music theory and analysis, music history and literature, and both solo and ensemble performance.

At Lawrence, music is not isolated from the other disciplines. All music majors complete a core curriculum in the college in addition to their Conservatory course work. Conservatory students live in the same residence halls and dine with college students, taking full advantage of the residential nature of the liberal arts institution. While the degree curriculum within the Conservatory is intense and focused in music, it allows students to explore the liberal arts and sciences through an array of courses taught by an accomplished faculty. The study of music at Lawrence occurs within the context of the liberal arts, thereby providing a well-rounded, broad-based understanding of music and its place within society.

This preparation and training have allowed Lawrence's students and ensembles to receive national and international awards; major ensembles have performed at regional and national music conferences and have recorded CDs for national distribution; individual students consistently place as finalists and winners in the Metropolitan Opera auditions, the National Association of Teachers of Singing auditions, and a variety of other district, regional, and national instrumental competitions. Each summer a high percentage of conservatory students continue their studies at festivals such as Tanglewood and Aspen.

Lawrence University is committed to the development of intellect and talent, the acquisition of knowledge and understanding, and the cultivation of judgment and values. The University prepares students for lives of service, achievement, leadership, and personal fulfillment. Lawrence Conservatory graduates are counted not only among the ranks of professional orchestras and opera companies, Grammy Award winners, university faculties, elementary and high school teachers, college administrators, and composers, but also among authors, medical and law professionals, and public servants.

▼ LEBANON VALLEY COLLEGE

Annville, Pennsylvania

Independent-United Methodist, coed. Small town campus. Total enrollment: 1,856. Music program established 1932.

Degrees Bachelor of Music in the area of sound recording technology; Bachelor of Science in the area of music education. Program accredited by NASM.

Enrollment Fall 1997: 172 total; 152 undergraduate, 20 non-professional degree.

Music Student Profile 49% females, 51% males, 1% minorities, 1% international.

Music Faculty 23 total (full-time and part-time). 70% of full-time faculty have terminal degrees. Graduate students do not teach undergraduate courses.

Student Life Student groups/activities include Audio Engineering Society, Music Educators National Conference Student Chapter.

Expenses for 1997–98 Application fee: $25. Comprehensive fee: $21,090 includes full-time tuition ($15,490), mandatory fees ($490), and college room and board ($5110). College room only: $2490. Special program-related fees: $85 per half-hour for private instruction.

Financial Aid Program-specific awards for 1997: 4 Carmean String Scholarships for string players ($1000), 6 Carmean Talent Awards for musically talented students ($1000).

Application Procedures Students apply for admission into the professional program by sophomore year. Deadline for freshmen and transfers: June 1. Required: high school transcript, college transcript(s) for transfer students, audition, SAT I or ACT test scores. Recommended: essay, 2 letters of recommendation, interview. Auditions held by appointment on campus; recorded music is permissible as a substitute for live auditions for international applicants or when distance is prohibitive and videotaped performances are permissible as a substitute for live auditions for international applicants or when distance is prohibitive.

Web Site http://www.lvc.edu.

Undergraduate Contact Mr. Barry Hill, Director, Sound Recording Technology, Music Department, Lebanon Valley College, Blair Music Center, Annville, Pennsylvania 17003; 717-867-6285, fax: 717-867-6390, E-mail address: hill@lvc.edu.

▼ LEE UNIVERSITY

Cleveland, Tennessee

Independent, coed. Small town campus. Total enrollment: 2,870.

Degrees Bachelor of Music Education in the areas of vocal/general music education, instrumental music education. Majors and concentrations: piano, sacred music, voice, wind and percussion instruments. Graduate degrees offered: Master of Church Music in the area of church music. Program accredited by NASM.

Enrollment Fall 1997: 260 total; 123 undergraduate, 27 graduate, 110 non-professional degree.

Lee University (*continued*)

Music Student Profile 55% females, 45% males, 12% minorities, 12% international.

Music Faculty 41 total undergraduate and graduate (full-time and part-time). 40% of full-time faculty have terminal degrees. Graduate students teach a few undergraduate courses.

Student Life Student groups/activities include Music Drama Workshop.

Expenses for 1997–98 Application fee: $25. Comprehensive fee: $9318 includes full-time tuition ($5496), mandatory fees ($142), and college room and board ($3680). College room only: $1850. Full-time tuition and fees vary according to program. Special program-related fees: $150 per semester for practice room rental, lesson fee.

Financial Aid Program-specific awards for 1997: 20 Endowed Scholarships for program majors ($500).

Application Procedures Students apply for admission into the professional program by sophomore year. Deadline for freshmen and transfers: continuous. Required: high school transcript, college transcript(s) for transfer students, audition, SAT I or ACT test scores. Recommended: 3 letters of recommendation, interview. Auditions held 4 times on campus; recorded music is permissible as a substitute for live auditions when distance is prohibitive and videotaped performances are permissible as a substitute for live auditions when distance is prohibitive.

Undergraduate Contact Ms. Mary Beth Wickes, Coordinator, School of Music, Lee University, PO Box 3450, Cleveland, Tennessee 37320-3450; 423-614-8240, fax: 423-614-8242, E-mail address: mwickes@leeuniversity.edu.

Graduate Contact Ms. Debbie Daniels, Secretary for Graduate Studies, School of Music, Lee University, PO Box 3450, Cleveland, Tennessee 37320-3450; 423-614-8240, fax: 423-614-8242.

▼ LENOIR-RHYNE COLLEGE

Hickory, North Carolina

Independent-Lutheran, coed. Small town campus. Total enrollment: 1,616. Music program established 1900.

Degrees Bachelor of Music Education in the areas of vocal music education, choral music education, keyboard music education, instrumental music education. Majors and concentrations: piano/organ, voice, wind and percussion instruments.

Enrollment Fall 1997: 30 total; all undergraduate.

Music Student Profile 70% females, 30% males, 1% minorities.

Music Faculty 10 total (full-time and part-time). 75% of full-time faculty have terminal degrees. Graduate students do not teach undergraduate courses. Undergraduate student–faculty ratio: 5:1.

Student Life Student groups/activities include Suzuki Program, Youth Percussion Program, sacred music program.

Expenses for 1998–99 Application fee: $25. Comprehensive fee: $16,886 includes full-time tuition ($12,386) and college room and board ($4500). Special program-related fees: $85 per half-hour lesson for applied music fee.

Financial Aid Program-specific awards for 1997: 15 Talent Scholarships for program majors ($5000), 5 Music Minor Scholarships for music minors ($2000), 10–15 Ensemble Scholarships for ensemble participants ($1000).

Application Procedures Students admitted directly into the professional program freshman year. Deadline for freshmen and transfers: continuous. Required: essay, high school transcript, college transcript(s) for transfer students, 2 letters of recommendation, audition, SAT I or ACT test scores (minimum combined SAT I score of 800, minimum combined ACT score of 20), minimum 2.5 high school GPA. Recommended: interview. Auditions held 4 times and by appointment on campus and off campus in various locations in North Carolina and Florida; recorded music is permissible as a substitute for live auditions when distance is prohibitive or scheduling is difficult and videotaped performances are permissible as a substitute for live auditions if distance is prohibitive or scheduling is difficult.

Web Site http://www.lrc.edu.

Undergraduate Contact Mr. Daniel Kaiser, Director of Music Recruiting, Music Department, Lenoir-Rhyne College, Box 7355, Hickory, North Carolina 28603; 704-328-1741, fax: 704-328-7368, E-mail address: kiserd@lrc.edu.

▼ LIBERTY UNIVERSITY

Lynchburg, Virginia

Independent-nondenominational, coed. Suburban campus. Total enrollment: 6,646. Music program established 1971.

Degrees Bachelor of Music in the areas of choral music, instrumental music, instrumental music education, choral music education. Majors and concentrations: music, music education.

Enrollment Fall 1997: 120 undergraduate.

Music Student Profile 51% females, 49% males, 10% minorities, 2% international.

Music Faculty 23 total (full-time and part-time). 75% of full-time faculty have terminal degrees. Graduate students do not teach undergraduate courses.

Student Life Student groups/activities include Music Educators National Conference, American Choral Directors Association, Kappa Kappa Psi.

Expenses for 1998–99 Application fee: $35. Comprehensive fee: $13,300 includes full-time tuition ($8400), mandatory fees ($100), and college room and board ($4800). Full-time tuition and fees vary according to course load. Special program-related fees: $15 for practice room rental, $300 for concert band tour.

Financial Aid Program-specific awards for 1997: Fine Arts Scholarships for program majors ($500–$1000), Marching Band Service Awards for marching band members ($500–$1000), Concert Band Service Awards for concert band members ($500).

Application Procedures Students apply for admission into the professional program by sophomore year. Deadline for freshmen and transfers: August 1. Required: high school transcript, college transcript(s) for transfer students, 3 letters of recommendation, audition, SAT I test score only. Recommended: interview. Auditions held 4 times on campus; recorded music is permissible as a substitute for live auditions when distance is prohibitive and videotaped performances are permissible as a substitute for live auditions when distance is prohibitive.

Undergraduate Contact Dr. Raymond S. Locy, Chairman, Department of Fine Arts, Liberty University, 1971 University Boulevard, Lynchburg, Virginia 24502; 804-582-2318, fax: 804-582-2280.

▼ LINCOLN UNIVERSITY

Jefferson City, Missouri

State-supported, coed. Small town campus. Total enrollment: 3,041. Music program established 1951.

Degrees Bachelor of Music Education in the areas of instrumental music, vocal music, piano. Majors and concentrations: instrumental music, music education, voice. Program accredited by NASM.

Enrollment Fall 1997: 31 total; all undergraduate.

Music Student Profile 55% females, 45% males, 71% minorities.

Music Faculty 6 total (full-time and part-time). 60% of full-time faculty have terminal degrees. Graduate students do not teach undergraduate courses. Undergraduate student–faculty ratio: 10:1.

Student Life Student groups/activities include Music Educators National Conference, Kappa Kappa Psi.

Expenses for 1997–98 Application fee: $17. State resident tuition: $2016 full-time. Nonresident tuition: $4032 full-time. Mandatory fees: $60 full-time. College room and board: $3276. Special program-related fees: $69 per semester for applied lab fees.

Financial Aid Program-specific awards for 1997: 10 music scholarships for program majors ($1200), 30 Service Awards for ensemble players ($500).

Application Procedures Students apply for admission into the professional program by sophomore year. Deadline for freshmen and transfers: July 15. Required: high school transcript, college transcript(s) for transfer students, audition, ACT test score only, theory test, performance on piano, minimum 2.0 high school GPA for out-of state students. Auditions held 4 times on campus and off campus in St. Louis, MO; Kansas City, MO; recorded music is permissible as a substitute for live auditions for provisional acceptance and videotaped performances are permissible as a substitute for live auditions for provisional acceptance.

Undergraduate Contact Office of Admissions, Lincoln University, 820 Chestnut Street, Jefferson City, Missouri 65102-0029; 573-681-5599, fax: 573-681-5566.

▼ LIONEL HAMPTON SCHOOL OF MUSIC

See University of Idaho

▼ LOCK HAVEN UNIVERSITY OF PENNSYLVANIA

Lock Haven, Pennsylvania

State-supported, coed. Small town campus. Total enrollment: 3,538.

Degrees Bachelor of Fine Arts in the area of music performance; Bachelor of Arts in the area of music. Majors and concentrations: music, piano, stringed instruments, voice, wind and percussion instruments. Cross-registration with Clarion University of Pennsylvania.

Enrollment Fall 1997: 55 total; 15 undergraduate, 40 non-professional degree.

Music Student Profile 50% females, 50% males.

Music Faculty 10 total (full-time and part-time). 60% of full-time faculty have terminal degrees. Graduate students do not teach undergraduate courses.

Student Life Student groups/activities include Kappa Kappa Psi, Tau Beta Sigma.

Expenses for 1997–98 Application fee: $25. State resident tuition: $3468 full-time. Nonresident tuition: $8824 full-time. Mandatory fees: $594 full-time. College room and board: $3880. Room and board charges vary according to board plan.

Financial Aid Program-specific awards for 1997: 2–3 Miriam Claster Awards for music majors ($400–$600), 1–2 Mary Ulmer Awards for music majors ($400–$600), 7 Band Awards for freshmen band members ($100–$500), 1 Allen E. & Howard Z. Lamey Memorial Scholarship for student in program with jazz emphasis ($500), 1 John Ross Memorial Award for male with outstanding commitment to band ($300), 1 Mark Groner Memorial Scholarship for rising junior or senior instrumental/minimum GPA 3.0 ($500), 4 Band Alumni Service Award for juniors and seniors/outstanding service to band programs ($100), 1 Florentina J. Caimi Excellence in Music Award for rising senior marching band member and other major ensemble ($500).

Application Procedures Students admitted directly into the professional program freshman year. Deadline for freshmen and transfers: continuous. Required: high school transcript, college transcript(s) for transfer students, audition, SAT I or ACT test scores, minimum 3.0 college GPA and 24 credits for transfer students. Recommended: minimum 3.0 high school GPA, standing in top 40% of graduating class. Auditions held 4 times on campus.

Undergraduate Contact Dr. Florentino J. Caimi, Chairman, Music Department, Lock Haven University of Pennsylvania, 208 Price Performance Center, Lock Haven, Pennsylvania 17745; 717-893-2143, fax: 717-893-2432, E-mail address: fcaimi@eagle.lhup.edu.

▼ LONG ISLAND UNIVERSITY, C.W. POST CAMPUS

Brookville, New York

Independent, coed. Suburban campus. Total enrollment: 8,171.

Degrees Bachelor of Fine Arts in the areas of music, music education. Graduate degrees offered: Master of Arts in the areas of music, music education.

Enrollment Fall 1997: 120 total; 80 undergraduate, 40 graduate.

Music Student Profile 50% females, 50% males, 15% minorities, 10% international.

Music Faculty 76 total undergraduate and graduate (full-time and part-time). 20% of full-time faculty have terminal degrees. Graduate students do not teach undergraduate courses.

Expenses for 1997–98 Application fee: $30. Comprehensive fee: $20,555 includes full-time tuition ($13,920), mandatory fees ($610), and college room and board ($6025). College room only: $3830. Room and board charges vary according to board plan.

Financial Aid Program-specific awards for 1997: 80 music scholarships for music students ($2500).

Application Procedures Students admitted directly into the professional program freshman year. Required: high school transcript, college transcript(s) for transfer students, interview, audition, SAT I test score only. Auditions held 3 times and by appointment on campus; recorded music is permis-

Long Island University, C.W. Post Campus *(continued)*

sible as a substitute for live auditions if a live audition is impossible and videotaped performances are permissible as a substitute for live auditions if a live audition is impossible.

Web Site http://www.liu.edu/cwis/cwp/svpa/music/music.htm.

Undergraduate Contact Undergraduate Admissions, Long Island University, C.W. Post Campus, 720 Northern Boulevard, Brookville, New York 11548; 516-299-2413.

Graduate Contact Graduate Admissions, Long Island University, C.W. Post Campus, 720 Northern Boulevard, Brookville, New York 11548; 516-299-2413.

▼ LONGWOOD COLLEGE

Farmville, Virginia

State-supported, coed. Small town campus. Total enrollment: 3,352.

Degrees Bachelor of Music in the areas of performance, composition, education. Majors and concentrations: brass, composition, music education, piano/organ, stringed instruments, voice, wind and percussion instruments. Program accredited by NASM.

Enrollment Fall 1997: 35 undergraduate.

Music Student Profile 60% females, 40% males, 10% minorities.

Music Faculty 13 total (full-time and part-time). 90% of full-time faculty have terminal degrees. Graduate students do not teach undergraduate courses. Undergraduate student–faculty ratio: 5:1.

Expenses for 1997–98 Application fee: $25. State resident tuition: $2684 full-time. Nonresident tuition: $8156 full-time. Mandatory fees: $1732 full-time. College room and board: $4280. College room only: $2506. Room and board charges vary according to board plan. Special program-related fees: $50 per semester for applied music fee.

Financial Aid Program-specific awards for 1997: 4 Hull Scholarships for music majors ($1200–$1500), 1 Haga Scholarship for juniors and seniors ($600), 3 Christmas Dinner Scholarships for music majors ($500), Foundation Scholarships for music majors, 7 Band Talentships for program majors and non-majors ($300).

Application Procedures Students admitted directly into the professional program freshman year. Deadline for freshmen and transfers: March 1. Required: essay, high school transcript, college transcript(s) for transfer students, minimum 2.0 high school GPA, audition, SAT I or ACT test scores (minimum combined SAT I score of 920). Recommended: letter of recommendation, interview. Auditions held 6 times and by appointment on campus; recorded music is permissible as a substitute for live auditions for out-of-state applicants and videotaped performances are permissible as a substitute for live auditions for out-of-state applicants.

Web Site http://web.lwc.edu/academic/LAS/Music/DEPTMUSC.HTM.

Undergraduate Contact Dr. Donald Trott, Chair, Music Department, Longwood College, 201 High Street, Wygal Building, Farmville, Virginia 23909; 804-395-2504, fax: 804-395-2149, E-mail address: dtrott@longwood.lwc.edu.

▼ LOUISIANA COLLEGE

Pineville, Louisiana

Independent-Southern Baptist, coed. Small town campus. Total enrollment: 925.

Degrees Bachelor of Music in the areas of voice performance, piano performance, church music, music education. Majors and concentrations: music education, piano, sacred music, voice. Program accredited by NASM.

Enrollment Fall 1997: 35 undergraduate.

Music Student Profile 70% females, 30% males, 3% minorities, 1% international.

Music Faculty 8 total (full-time and part-time). 90% of full-time faculty have terminal degrees. Graduate students do not teach undergraduate courses. Undergraduate student–faculty ratio: 7:1.

Expenses for 1997–98 Application fee: $25. Comprehensive fee: $9799 includes full-time tuition ($6272), mandatory fees ($491), and college room and board ($3036). College room only: $1300. Room and board charges vary according to board plan. Special program-related fees: $85 per course for applied music fee, $40 per course for accompanying fee, $15 per course for materials fee.

Financial Aid Program-specific awards for 1997: 10 music scholarships for freshmen ($750), 2 Piano Majors Scholarships for freshmen ($2000).

Application Procedures Students admitted directly into the professional program freshman year. Deadline for freshmen: April 24; transfers: continuous. Notification date for freshmen and transfers: continuous. Required: high school transcript, college transcript(s) for transfer students, minimum 2.0 high school GPA, 3 letters of recommendation, audition, SAT I or ACT test scores (minimum combined ACT score of 20). Auditions held 3 times on campus; recorded music is permissible as a substitute for live auditions when distance is prohibitive and videotaped performances are permissible as a substitute for live auditions when distance is prohibitive.

Undergraduate Contact Admissions, Louisiana College, Pineville, Louisiana 71359; 318-487-7259, fax: 318-487-7191, E-mail address: gregorczyk@andria.lacollege.edu.

▼ LOUISIANA STATE UNIVERSITY AND AGRICULTURAL AND MECHANICAL COLLEGE

Baton Rouge, Louisiana

State-supported, coed. Urban campus. Total enrollment: 28,066.

Degrees Bachelor of Music in the areas of performance, composition; Bachelor of Music Education in the areas of instrumental music education, vocal music education. Majors and concentrations: composition, harp, piano, piano pedagogy, stringed instruments, voice, wind and percussion instruments. Graduate degrees offered: Master of Music in the areas of performance, theory, musicology, music education, piano pedagogy, conducting. Doctor of Musical Arts in the areas of performance, composition. Cross-registration with Southern University and Agricultural and Mechanical College. Program accredited by NASM.

Enrollment Fall 1997: 430 total; 280 undergraduate, 145 graduate, 5 non-professional degree.

Music Student Profile 52% females, 48% males, 8% minorities, 12% international.
Music Faculty 51 total undergraduate and graduate (full-time and part-time). 100% of full-time faculty have terminal degrees. Graduate students teach a few undergraduate courses. Undergraduate student–faculty ratio: 10:1.
Student Life Student groups/activities include music fraternities and sororities.
Expenses for 1997–98 Application fee: $25. State resident tuition: $2301 full-time. Nonresident tuition: $5901 full-time. Mandatory fees: $410 full-time. College room and board: $3772. College room only: $2020. Room and board charges vary according to board plan and housing facility. Special program-related fees: $75 for senior recital fee, $10 per year for locker rental fee, $5 per credit hour for technology fee.
Financial Aid Program-specific awards for 1997: 110 School of Music Scholarships for talented students ($600–$7000).
Application Procedures Students admitted directly into the professional program freshman year. Deadline for freshmen and transfers: June 1. Required: high school transcript, audition, SAT I or ACT test scores (minimum combined ACT score of 19), minimum 2.3 high school GPA. Recommended: 2 letters of recommendation. Auditions held 3 times and by appointment on campus; recorded music is permissible as a substitute for live auditions if a live audition is impossible and videotaped performances are permissible as a substitute for live auditions if a live audition is impossible.
Undergraduate Contact Dr. Sara Lynn Baird, Assistant Dean, School of Music, Louisiana State University and Agricultural and Mechanical College, 102 School of Music, Baton Rouge, Louisiana 70803; 504-388-3261, fax: 504-388-2562, E-mail address: sbaird@lsu.edu.
Graduate Contact Dr. Kathleen Rountree, Associate Dean, School of Music, Louisiana State University and Agricultural and Mechanical College, 102 School of Music, Baton Rouge, Louisiana 70803; 504-388-3261, fax: 504-388-2562, E-mail address: muroun@lsuvm.sncc.lsu.edu.

▼ LOUISIANA TECH UNIVERSITY

Ruston, Louisiana

State-supported, coed. Small town campus. Total enrollment: 9,500. Music program established 1959.
Degrees Bachelor of Fine Arts in the areas of voice, keyboard, instruments of symphony orchestra or band; Bachelor of Arts in the area of music education. Majors and concentrations: instrumental music, keyboard, voice. Cross-registration with Grambling State University. Program accredited by NASM.
Enrollment Fall 1997: 67 total; 62 undergraduate, 5 non-professional degree.
Music Student Profile 46% females, 54% males, 15% minorities, 1% international.
Music Faculty 15 total (full-time and part-time). 43% of full-time faculty have terminal degrees. Graduate students do not teach undergraduate courses. Undergraduate student–faculty ratio: 5:1.
Student Life Student groups/activities include Phi Mu Alpha, Sigma Alpha Iota, Music Educators National Conference.
Expenses for 1997–98 Application fee: $20. State resident tuition: $2367 full-time. Nonresident tuition: $5367 full-time. Mandatory fees: $200 full-time. College room and board: $2805. College room only: $1605.
Financial Aid Program-specific awards for 1997: 40–60 departmental scholarships for program majors ($100–$5200),

out-of-state fee waivers for academically qualified students ($6000), 20–30 Dorm Scholarships for program majors ($650–$1300).
Application Procedures Students apply for admission into the professional program by sophomore year. Deadline for freshmen and transfers: August 1. Required: high school transcript, college transcript(s) for transfer students, minimum 2.0 high school GPA, interview, audition, SAT I or ACT test scores (minimum combined ACT score of 22). Recommended: letter of recommendation. Auditions held as needed on campus and off campus in high schools of prospective students; recorded music is permissible as a substitute for live auditions when distance is prohibitive and videotaped performances are permissible as a substitute for live auditions when distance is prohibitive.
Undergraduate Contact Admissions Office, Louisiana Tech University, PO Box 3178 Tech Station, Ruston, Louisiana 71272; 318-257-3036.

▼ LOYOLA UNIVERSITY NEW ORLEANS

New Orleans, Louisiana

Independent-Roman Catholic (Jesuit), coed. Urban campus. Total enrollment: 5,079. Music program established 1932.
Degrees Bachelor of Music in the areas of performance, piano pedagogy, jazz studies, theory and composition; Bachelor of Music Education; Bachelor of Music Therapy. Majors and concentrations: classical music, jazz, music education, music therapy, piano/organ, stringed instruments, voice, wind and percussion instruments. Graduate degrees offered: Master of Music in the areas of performance, piano pedagogy; Master of Music Education; Master of Music Therapy. Cross-registration with Xavier University of Louisiana. Program accredited by NASM.
Enrollment Fall 1997: 262 total; 239 undergraduate, 19 graduate, 4 non-professional degree.
Music Student Profile 55% females, 45% males, 15% minorities, 2% international.
Music Faculty 52 total undergraduate and graduate (full-time and part-time). 57% of full-time faculty have terminal degrees. Graduate students do not teach undergraduate courses. Undergraduate student–faculty ratio: 6:1.
Student Life Student groups/activities include Loyola Association of Music Therapy Students, Music Educators National Conference Student Chapter, Loyola University Community Action Program.
Expenses for 1997–98 Application fee: $20. Comprehensive fee: $19,184 includes full-time tuition ($12,948), mandatory fees ($406), and college room and board ($5830). College room only: $2570. Room and board charges vary according to board plan and housing facility.
Financial Aid Program-specific awards for 1997: 50 music scholarships for music majors ($4500).
Application Procedures Students admitted directly into the professional program freshman year. Deadline for freshmen and transfers: continuous. Required: essay, high school transcript, college transcript(s) for transfer students, letter of recommendation, audition, SAT I or ACT test scores, minimum 2.25 high school GPA. Recommended: portfolio. Auditions held twice and by appointment on campus and off campus in Las Vegas, NV; Fairfield, CT; Chicago, IL; recorded music is permissible as a substitute for live auditions when distance is prohibitive and videotaped

Loyola University New Orleans (continued)

performances are permissible as a substitute for live auditions when distance is prohibitive. Portfolio reviews held as needed on campus.

Web Site http://www.loyno.edu/music/.

Undergraduate Contact Dr. Anthony Decuir, Associate Dean, College of Music, Loyola University New Orleans, 6363 Saint Charles Avenue, New Orleans, Louisiana 70118; 504-865-3037.

▼ MANHATTAN SCHOOL OF MUSIC

New York, New York

Independent, coed. Urban campus. Total enrollment: 835. Music program established 1917.

Degrees Bachelor of Music in the areas of classical performance, classical composition, jazz/commercial music. Majors and concentrations: classical music, jazz, piano/organ, stringed instruments, voice, wind and percussion instruments. Graduate degrees offered: Master of Music in the areas of classical performance, classical composition, jazz/commercial music. Doctor of Musical Arts in the areas of classical performance, classical composition. Cross-registration with Barnard College .

Enrollment Fall 1997: 804 total; 408 undergraduate, 394 graduate, 2 non-professional degree.

Music Student Profile 56% females, 44% males, 18% minorities, 40% international.

Music Faculty 277 total undergraduate and graduate (full-time and part-time). 70% of full-time faculty have terminal degrees. Graduate students teach a few undergraduate courses. Undergraduate student–faculty ratio: 10:1.

Student Life Special housing available for music students.

Expenses for 1997–98 Application fee: $90. Comprehensive fee: $26,900 includes full-time tuition ($17,300), mandatory fees ($600), and college room and board ($9000).

Financial Aid Program-specific awards for 1997: 130–170 scholarships ($4500–$18,000).

Application Procedures Students admitted directly into the professional program freshman year. Deadline for freshmen and transfers: March 15. Notification date for freshmen and transfers: July 1. Required: essay, high school transcript, college transcript(s) for transfer students, minimum 2.0 high school GPA, audition. Recommended: minimum 3.0 high school GPA, 2 letters of recommendation, interview, SAT I or ACT test scores. Auditions held twice on campus; recorded music is permissible as a substitute for live auditions for applicants living outside North America and for cello, double bass, and tuba applicants and videotaped performances are permissible as a substitute for live auditions for applicants living outside North America and for cello, double bass, and tuba applicants.

Web Site http://www.msmnyc.edu.

Contact Lee Cioppa, Director of Admission, Office of Admission and Financial Aid, Manhattan School of Music, 120 Claremont Avenue, New York, New York 10027-4698; 212-749-2802 ext. 2, fax: 212-749-5471, E-mail address: admission@msmnyc.edu.

More About the School

Program Facilities Borden Auditorium (1,000 seats), Hubbard Hall (300 seats), Pforzheimer Hall (75 seats), Myers Hall and

Recording Studio (35 seats); library with 21,000 recordings, 61,000 volumes, 125 periodical subscriptions; two electronic music studios.

Faculty, Resident Artists, and Alumni Faculty are members of the New York Philharmonic, Metropolitan Opera and Orchestra, New York City Opera, Chamber Music Society of Lincoln Center, and Orpheus Chamber Orchestra, as well as concert, chamber, jazz, and recording artists. Artists-in-residence: American String Quartet, Saturday Brass Quintet, New Music Consort. 1996–98 master classes: Robert Mann, violin; Kiri Te Kanawa, voice; John Corigliano, composition; Shlomo Mintz, violin and chamber music; John Graham, viola; Beata Huang, guitar; Elvin Jones, jazz drum set; Midori, violin; Dr. Anthony Jahn, vocal health; Gunther Schuller, interpretation and artistry; Yfrah Neaman, violin; John Soroka, orchestral percussion; Hermann Prey, voice; Dave Weckl, jazz drum set; Byron Janis, piano; Charles Reicker, voice and auditioning; Joseph Seiger, sonatas; Sarah Bullen, orchestral harp; Alex Klein, orchestral oboe; David Tanenbaum, guitar; The Vanguard Orchestra, jazz ensembles; Licia Albanese, voice; Sergio & Odair Assad, guitar; Matthew Guilford, orchestral double bass; Janet Bookspan, voice; Floyd Cooley, tuba; Robert Dick, flute; Simon Dinnigan, guitar; John Engelkes, trombone; Wenzel Fuchs, clarinet; Franz Halasz, guitar; Martin Katz, voice and accompanying; Benny Waters, jazz saxophone; Glenn Dicterow, violin; Betty Allen, voice; The L.A. Guitar Quartet; Michael Leiter, bass; Sherrill Milnes, voice; Debu Chaudhuri, Indian music; Duncan Patton, percussion; the Raphael Trio, chamber music; J.R. Robinson, jazz drum set; Mignon Dunn, voice; Dr. Emil Pascarelli, repetitive strain injuries; George Tsontakis, composition; Jeanne Baxtresser, orchestral flute; Glen Velez, percussion; Claude Williams and John Blake, jazz strings; Bill Watrous, jazz trombone.

Student Performance Opportunities Classical ensembles: Symphony, Philharmonia, Chamber Sinfonia, Opera Theater, Handel Project (opera), American Musical Theater Ensemble, Contemporary Ensemble, Baroque Aria Ensemble, Percussion Ensemble, Brass Ensemble, Guitar Ensemble, Early Music Ensemble, numerous chamber ensembles. Jazz/commercial music ensembles: Jazz Orchestra, Jazz Lab Band, Jazz Ensemble, Jazz Choir, numerous jazz combos.

Special Programs The Office of Career Planning offers students gig information throughout the metro area, information about summer festivals, competitions and graduate schools, and one-on-one counseling regarding career preparation and marketing.

▼

Since 1917 Manhattan School of Music has prepared gifted young musicians to assume their place on the world's stages.

In selecting MSM, students choose to work with faculty who are themselves performers with international reputations. They choose to be with students from around the world who come together to create an environment remarkable not just for its intensity but for genuine friendliness and cooperation. And, of course, they choose New York itself, a major center of music and art in America.

While many fine music conservatories are acknowledged for their ability to develop talents and skills, MSM has a particular combination of strengths that make it an excellent place from which to launch a career.

With extensive performance opportunities on campus as well as the chance to freelance and begin to develop a network of professional contacts, students undergo remarkable changes here: they start to function as professional musicians while they are still in school. It is this powerful convergence of opportunity and training that gives students the chance to go as far as their talent, intelligence, and courage can take them.

Alumni are the School's best examples of this training. Here are just a few of MSM alumni from 1970 to the present: Laura Albeck, Metropolitan Opera Orchestra; Robert Anderson, Minnesota Orchestra; Gerald Appleman, New York Philharmonic; Karen Beardsley, soprano, New York City Opera; Elizabeth Burkhardt, Atlanta Symphony; John Carabella, New York Philharmonic; Todd Coolman, jazz bassist; Harry Connick Jr., singer; Alison Dalton, Chicago Symphony; Jacqui Danilow, Metropolitan Opera Orchestra; Garry Dial, jazz pianist; James Dooley, San José Symphony; Desiree Elsevier, Metropolitan Opera Orchestra; Mary Ewing, New York Philharmonic; Lauren Flannigan, soprano, Metropolitan Opera; Susan Graham, mezzo-soprano, Metropolitan Opera; Andrea Gruber, soprano, Metropolitan Opera; Laura Hamilton, Metropolitan Opera Orchestra; Herbie Hancock, jazz pianist; Louella Hasbun, San José Symphony; Douglas Hedwig, Metropolitan Opera Orchestra; Donald Hilsberg, Denver Chamber Orchestra; Christina Hinton, Louisville Orchestra; Frank Hosticka, Metropolitan Opera Orchestra; Simon James, Seattle Symphony; Richard Jensen, Cincinnati Symphony; Henry Kao, New Jersey Symphony; Gilad Karni, New York Philharmonic; Motti Kaston, baritone; Kemal Khan, Assistant Conductor, Metropolitan Opera; Christopher Komer, New Jersey Symphony; Dawn Kotoski, soprano, Metropolitan Opera; Morris Lang, New York Philharmonic; Michael Leonhart, Grammy Award winner; Roy Lewis, Manhattan String Quartet; Douglas Lindsay, Cincinnati Symphony; George Manahan, Music Director, Minnesota Opera; Marvis Martin, soprano, Metropolitan Opera; Kerri McDermott, New York Philharmonic; Peter McGinnis, jazz trombonist; Sharon Meekins, Metropolitan Opera Orchestra; Warren Mok, tenor, Berlin Opera; Frank Morelli, Orpheus Chamber Orchestra; June Morganstern, Chicago Lyric Opera Orchestra; Elmar Oliveira, concert violinist; Susan Quittmeyer, mezzo-soprano, Metropolitan Opera; Mary Kay Robinson, New Jersey Symphony; Bruce Smith, Detroit Symphony; Dawn Stahler, Dallas Symphony; James Stubbs, Metropolitan Opera Orchestra; Stewart Taylor, Israel Philharmonic; Dawn Upshaw, soprano, Metropolitan Opera; Roland Vasquez, jazz drummer; Rosa Vento, soprano, Vienna State Opera; Bing Wang, Cincinnati Symphony; Mark Wells, Canadian Opera Orchestra; Virginia Chen Wells, Toronto Symphony; Thomas Wetzel, Milwaukee Symphony; Timothy Wilson, San Francisco Opera Orchestra; Carol Wincenc, concert flutist; Naomi Youngstein, New Jersey Symphony; and Dolara Zajick, mezzo-soprano, Metropolitan Opera.

▼ MANHATTANVILLE COLLEGE

Purchase, New York

Independent, coed. Suburban campus. Total enrollment: 1,925. Music program established 1937.

Degrees Bachelor of Music in the area of music education; Bachelor of Arts in the areas of music management, music. Majors and concentrations: music, music education, music management. Graduate degrees offered: Master of Arts in Teaching in the area of music education. Cross-registration with Purchase College-State University of New York.

Enrollment Fall 1997: 56 total; 50 undergraduate, 6 graduate.
Music Faculty 35 total undergraduate and graduate (full-time and part-time). 100% of full-time faculty have terminal degrees. Graduate students do not teach undergraduate courses. Undergraduate student–faculty ratio: 10:1.
Student Life Student groups/activities include Music Educators National Conference, Music Teachers National Association.
Expenses for 1997–98 Application fee: $35. Comprehensive fee: $25,300 includes full-time tuition ($16,760), mandatory fees ($540), and college room and board ($8000). Special program-related fees: $400 per semester for instrumental and vocal instruction, $35 per semester for practice rooms.
Financial Aid Program-specific awards for 1997: departmental awards ($2000–$5000).
Application Procedures Students admitted directly into the professional program freshman year. Deadline for freshmen and transfers: continuous. Required: high school transcript, college transcript(s) for transfer students, minimum 2.0 high school GPA, letter of recommendation, audition, SAT I or ACT test scores, high school transcript for transfer applicants with fewer than 45 credits. Recommended: essay, minimum 3.0 high school GPA, interview. Auditions held 6 times on campus; recorded music is permissible as a substitute for live auditions for international applicants and in special circumstances and videotaped performances are permissible as a substitute for live auditions for international applicants and in special circumstances.
Undergraduate Contact Mr. Jose Flores, Director of Admissions, Admissions Department, Manhattanville College, 2900 Purchase Street, Purchase, New York 10577; 800-328-4553, fax: 914-694-1732, E-mail address: admissions@mville.edu.
Graduate Contact Dr. Anthony Lamagra, Director/Chair, Music Department, Manhattanville College, 2900 Purchase Street, Purchase, New York 10577; 914-323-5260.

▼ MANKATO STATE UNIVERSITY

Mankato, Minnesota

State-supported, coed. Small town campus. Total enrollment: 12,507.
Degrees Bachelor of Music in the areas of voice, piano, winds, strings, percussion, organ; Bachelor of Science in the areas of music education, instrumental, choral/vocal, music management. Majors and concentrations: music, music education, music management, piano/organ, stringed instruments, voice, wind and percussion instruments. Graduate degrees offered: Master of Music in the areas of performance, music education. Program accredited by NASM.
Enrollment Fall 1997: 130 total; 110 undergraduate, 10 graduate, 10 non-professional degree.
Music Student Profile 30% females, 70% males, 8% minorities, 4% international.
Music Faculty 20 total undergraduate and graduate (full-time and part-time). 81% of full-time faculty have terminal degrees. Graduate students teach a few undergraduate courses. Undergraduate student–faculty ratio: 15:1.
Student Life Student groups/activities include Music Educators National Conference, American Choral Directors Association, International Association of Jazz Educators.
Expenses for 1997–98 Application fee: $20. State resident tuition: $2582 full-time. Nonresident tuition: $5769 full-time. Mandatory fees: $401 full-time. College room and board: $2965. College room only: $1880. Room and board charges

Mankato State University *(continued)*

vary according to board plan. Special program-related fees: $10–$30 per term for instrument rental.

Financial Aid Program-specific awards for 1997: 1 Stewart Ross Band Scholarship for band instrumentalists ($600), 1 Nancy Cora Williams Scholarship for music education majors ($500), 1 Hickory Tech Award for music majors ($1000), 1 President's Scholarship for program majors ($1000), 1 Van Sickle Endowment for string or voice majors ($600), 1 Een Endowment for program majors ($470), 16 Talent Grants for incoming freshmen ($9600), 7 Stein Scholarships for music majors ($2400), 7 Music Foundation Awards for music majors ($3190), 4 Mankato Symphony Awards for orchestra students ($5000).

Application Procedures Students admitted directly into the professional program freshman year. Deadline for freshmen and transfers: continuous. Required: high school transcript, college transcript(s) for transfer students, minimum 2.0 high school GPA, 3 letters of recommendation, interview, audition. Recommended: minimum 3.0 high school GPA. Auditions held as needed on campus; recorded music is permissible as a substitute for live auditions when distance is prohibitive and videotaped performances are permissible as a substitute for live auditions when distance is prohibitive.

Web Site http://www.mankato.msus.edu/dept/music.

Undergraduate Contact Mr. John Lindberg, Undergraduate Coordinator, Music Department, Mankato State University, Mankato State University 6, Mankato, Minnesota 56002-8400; 507-389-1523, fax: 507-389-2922, E-mail address: bassoon@vax1.mankato.msus.edu.

Graduate Contact Mr. Stewart Ross, Graduate Coordinator, Music Department, Mankato State University, Mankato State University 6, Mankato, Minnesota 56002-8400; 507-389-5800, fax: 507-389-2922, E-mail address: stewart_ross@ms1.mankato.msus.edu.

New School for Social Research

▼ MANNES COLLEGE OF MUSIC

New York, New York

Independent, coed. Urban campus. Total university enrollment: 7,179. Total unit enrollment: 864. Music program established 1916.

Degrees Bachelor of Music in the areas of orchestral instruments, piano, organ, voice, composition, music theory, orchestral and choral conducting, historical performance, guitar. Majors and concentrations: classical music, composition, conducting, guitar, music, music theory, performance, piano/organ, stringed instruments, voice, wind and percussion instruments. Graduate degrees offered: Master of Music in the areas of orchestral instruments, piano, organ, voice, composition, music theory, orchestral and choral conducting, historical performance, guitar. Cross-registration with New School for Social Research.

Enrollment Fall 1997: 278 total; 140 undergraduate, 84 graduate, 54 non-professional degree.

Music Student Profile 55% females, 45% males, 13% minorities, 42% international.

Music Faculty 150 total undergraduate and graduate (full-time and part-time). 100% of full-time faculty have terminal degrees. Graduate students do not teach undergraduate courses. Undergraduate student–faculty ratio: 8:1.

Student Life Special housing available for music students.

Expenses for 1997–98 Application fee: $75. Tuition: $15,520 full-time. Mandatory fees: $150 full-time. College room only: $6500. Part-time students pay a minimum of $4800 for lessons.

Application Procedures Students admitted directly into the professional program freshman year. Deadline for freshmen and transfers: continuous. Required: high school transcript, letter of recommendation, interview, audition. Auditions held 5 times on campus.

Contact Ms. Lisa C. Wright, Director of Admissions, Mannes College of Music, New School for Social Research, 150 West 85th Street, New York, New York 10024; 212-580-0210, fax: 212-580-1738.

More About the College

Founded in 1916 by David and Clara Mannes, world renowned as a violin-piano duo, the Mannes College of Music is recognized internationally as being among the finest professional music conservatories.

Throughout its existence, Mannes has taken a leading role with programs known for broad musical training and the encouragement of artistic growth. Its distinguished faculty includes some of the world's most prominent musicians and ensembles. Current faculty members include Peter Serkin, Richard Goode, Vladimir Feltsman, Grant Johannesen, Felix Galimir, Walter Trampler, Timothy Eddy, Ruth Falcon, Theodor Uppman, and principal players from the New York Philharmonic, Metropolitan Opera Orchestra, and New York City Opera and Ballet orchestras. Mannes graduates include Frederica von Stade, Julius Rudel, Murray Perahia, Eugene Istomin, Richard Goode, Semyon Bychkov, and Myung Whun Chung.

Mannes offers the Bachelor of Music, Bachelor of Science, and Master of Music degrees and a Professional Studies Diploma. Major instructional fields include all keyboard and orchestral instruments, guitar, voice, theory, composition, orchestral and choral conducting, and historical performance.

Performance is the main activity of Mannes students, and the training of aspirant professional musicians is the College's mission. Mannes has developed a distinctive approach and environment in which to implement it. Through an intensive curriculum in ear-training, dictation, theory, harmony, composition, and analysis, Mannes students are provided with a thorough understanding of the theory, structure, and history of music. The enrollment limit of about 250 students seeks to ensure highly personalized instruction and close interaction among students, faculty members, and administrators. Students receive individual lessons from their major teachers and participate in small performance groups. Class size is kept small to maximize individual attention. Mannes prides itself on being a community of musicians dedicated to advancing art through a personal and humanistic approach to education.

The Mannes Orchestra gives four to five concerts yearly in Symphony Space, a major New York City facility; performs at Lincoln Center; and takes part in choral concerts and opera presentations. Each concert features a student performance of a solo work with orchestra.

Participation in chamber music ensembles is an essential part of the performance training of any musician, and Mannes activities include performances for all standard instrumental groups as well as Percussion Ensemble, Piano Ensemble, Guitar Ensemble, Baroque Chamber Players, and the Contemporary Ensemble. Student chamber music groups regularly perform works by student composers.

The Opera Department presents programs of opera scenes and excerpts, and, in the spring, a full chamber opera production is mounted. A concert presentation of vocal repertory is included in one orchestral concert.

Mannes's location is particularly well suited for students and musicians. Manhattan's West Side is one of the most vibrant areas of New York and is the site of most of the city's major musical and cultural activities. Within blocks of the College are Lincoln Center, Merkin Hall, Symphony Space, the Museum of Natural History, and the New York Historical Society as well as recreational centers such as Central Park and Riverside Park.

In an age of mass education, Mannes maintains an intimate atmosphere that permits a close and sustained contact among all members of the College. In the larger context, students have the benefit of full access to the richness of New York City's musical and cultural life.

New School for Social Research

▼ MANNES JAZZ AND CONTEMPORARY MUSIC PROGRAM

New York, New York

Music program established 1986.

Degrees Bachelor of Fine Arts in the area of jazz; Bachelor of Arts/Bachelor of Fine Arts in the area of liberal arts/jazz. Majors and concentrations: composition, jazz.

Enrollment Fall 1997: 219 total; all undergraduate.

Music Student Profile 18% females, 82% males, 15% minorities, 32% international.

Music Faculty 83 total (full-time and part-time). 33% of full-time faculty have terminal degrees. Graduate students do not teach undergraduate courses. Undergraduate student–faculty ratio: 3:1.

Student Life Student groups/activities include Mannes Jazz Student Council, university committees.

Financial Aid Program-specific awards for 1997: 97 Jazz Scholarships for those demonstrating need and talent ($4200), 15 University Scholar Awards for minority students ($3500).

Application Procedures Students admitted directly into the professional program freshman year. Deadline for freshmen and transfers: June 1. Notification date for freshmen and transfers: August 1. Required: essay, high school transcript, college transcript(s) for transfer students, minimum 2.0 high school GPA, audition. Auditions held 15 times on campus; recorded music is permissible as a substitute for live auditions when distance is prohibitive.

Web Site http://www.newschool.edu/academic/mannes/jazz.

Undergraduate Contact Ms. L. E. Howell, Director of Admissions, The Mannes Jazz and Contemporary Music Program, New School Jazz and Contemporary Music, 55 West 13th Street, New York, New York 10011; 212-229-5896 ext. 301, fax: 212-229-8936, E-mail address: howelll@newschool.edu.

More About the School

Program Facilities Includes a MIDI computer lab, a 110-seat Performance Space with recording capabilities, and a B-3 Hammond Organ room. Multiple practice rooms. All classrooms are equipped with Yamaha grand pianos, drum kits, professional P.A. systems, and complete stereo systems.

Faculty, Resident Artists, and Alumni Mannes Jazz Program alumni include Joe Ascione, Peter Bernstein, Walter Blanding Jr.,

Adam Cruz, Jesse Davis, Rebecca Coupe Franks, Larry Goldings, Roy Hargrove, Virginia Mayhew, Carlos McKinney, Brad Mehldau, and John Popper.

Student Performance/Exhibit Opportunities Elective student ensembles perform each semester. These may include but are not limited to the Thelonius Monk Ensemble, the Miles Davis Ensemble, the Duke Ellington Ensemble, the Composers Ensemble workshop, the vocal rhythm section ensemble, the James Brown Ensemble, the Afro–Cuban Orchestra, and the Art Blakey Ensemble. All seniors are required to offer a senior recital in the semester in which they are scheduled to graduate. Students also perform at various independent and school-sponsored events.

▼

The metropolitan New York region is home to most of the great jazz artists in the world. It is also one of America's two centers for the recording and television industry, and as a consequence, is the most active environment, internationally, for jazz and related contemporary music. The Mannes Jazz Program's Bachelor of Fine Arts curriculum in jazz performing and/or composing and arranging draws both its faculty members and its inspiration from this extraordinary resource. It provides a comprehensive musical education, coupled with specialized work in the performance, writing, and recording of jazz and its related musical forms. Students work in the classroom and private studio with world-class professionals, and they are able to follow the great tradition of jazz at first hand, learning through intense exposure to the finest musicians, as they perform throughout the New York metropolitan area, live in concert, in jazz clubs, and in recording studios.

Students of jazz and contemporary music at Mannes find themselves in an energetic and diversified college community, offering many opportunities to learn from instructors and students in a variety of disciplines and areas of inquiry. Mannes College of Music is one of the academic divisions of the New School University. Mannes, as one of New York's three major classical conservatories, provides curricular depth, enhanced credibility for instruction in musicianship, and dialogue between musicians with distinctly different professional experiences. All of this takes place within the context of New York City itself, whose vast cultural resources offer endless opportunities for intellectual and creative development.

In the fall of 1995, the program opened new facilities that offer greatly expanded space and services, including the addition of an intimate performance/recording space and MIDI/computer facilities. This state-of-the-art facility, located within the jazz environs of Greenwich Village, constitutes a direct investment in the future of jazz and contemporary music, and affords students a new level of artistic opportunity and excellence.

Performance, and the artist as educator and mentor, are the heart of the program's philosophy. The curriculum begins with a comprehensive musical foundation that becomes more flexible as the student advances to graduation. Advanced students have the opportunity to apprentice with one or more jazz masters, gaining a realistic view of the art form, not only through its daily practice, but also through close observation of the art, its working environment, and lifestyle.

The key to this program's success, however, lies in its use of the finest professionals available anywhere to supervise an intense involvement in small group playing. Students work

Mannes Jazz and Contemporary Music Program (continued)

closely with the creators, not the interpreters, of jazz—an art form that is continually reaching toward, and achieving, new technical and conceptual horizons.

Faculty: Classroom and Ensemble Junko Arita, Richie Beirach, Richard Boukas, Joanne Brackeen, Cecil Bridgewater, Brian Camelio, Jeff Carney, Joe Chambers, Gloria Cooper, Haim Cotton, Andrew Cyrille, Gerard D'Angelo, Jon Davis, Garry Dial, Armen Donelian, Mario Escalera, Chico Freeman, Hal Galper, George Garzone, David Glasser, Ron Gonzalez, Jamey Haddad, Chico Hamilton, Billy Harper, Richard Harper Adam Holzman, Satoshi Inoue, Sonia Jacobsen, Christopher Johnson, Vic Juris, Kristina Kanders, Michael Karn, Bill Kirchner, Janet Lawson, Lee Ann Ledgerwood, Julie Lyonn Lieberman, Amy London, David Lopato, Arun Luthra, Ed MacEachen, Junior Mance, Phil Markowitz, Cecil McBee, Makanda McIntyre, Andy McKee, Ed Neumeister, Jimmy Owens, Velibor Pedevski, Charli Persip, Ron Petrides, Benny Powell, John Riley, Ted Rosenthal, Bob Sadin, Bobby Sanabria, David Schnitter, Loren Schoenberg, David Schroeder, Rich Shemaria, Jim Snidero, Joan Stiles, Rory Stuart, Francesca Tanksley, Charles Tolliver, Elina Vassiltchikova, Oliver von Essen, Johannes Weidenmueller, Doug Weiss, Buster Williams, Reggie Workman, Peter Zak.

Instrumental Faculty (partial list): **Trombone** Urbie Green, Slide Hampton, Conrad Herwig, Ed Neumeister, Benny Powell, **Trumpet** Cecil Bridgewater, Jimmy Owens, Valery Ponomarev, Charles Tolliver, **Saxophone and Woodwinds** Charles Davis, George Garzone, Frank Foster, Billy Harper, Vincent Herring, **Bass** Eddie Gomez, Andy McKee, Reggie Workman, Buster Williams, **Guitar** John Abercrombie, Peter Bernstein, Vic Juris, Jack Wilkins, **Percussion** Horacee Arnold, Joe Ascione, Michael Carvin, Joe Chambers, Lewis Nash, **Piano** Richie Bierach, Harold Danko, Herman Foster, Hilton Ruiz, **Composition and Arranging** Bill Kirchner, Ed Neumeister, Bob Sadin, Maria Schneider, **Vocals** Sheila Jordan, Janet Lawson, Anne Marie Moss, Jackie Paris, **Master Class and Special Guests** (partial list): Toshiko Akiyoshi, Victor Bailey, Lester Bowie, Randy Brecker, Ray Brown, Benny Carter, Art Farmer, Tommy Flanagan, Frank Foster, Benny Golson, Sir Roland Hanna, Billy Hart, Jon Hendricks, Milt Hinton, Milt Jackson, Etta James, Roger Kellaway, Steve Lacey, John Lewis, Branford Marsalis, Hugh Maskela, Jay McShann, Charlie Palmieri, Wallace Roney, Badal Roy, Clark Terry, Cedar Walton, Joe Williams.

▼ MANSFIELD UNIVERSITY OF PENNSYLVANIA

Mansfield, Pennsylvania

State-supported, coed. Small town campus. Total enrollment: 2,907. Music program established 1880.

Degrees Bachelor of Music in the areas of music education, music therapy, performance, elective studies in business. Majors and concentrations: music, music business, music education, music therapy, piano, stringed instruments, voice, wind and percussion instruments. Graduate degrees offered: Master of Music in the area of music education. Program accredited by NASM.

Enrollment Fall 1997: 188 total; 168 undergraduate, 20 graduate.

Music Student Profile 60% females, 40% males, 1% minorities, 1% international.

Music Faculty 26 total undergraduate and graduate (full-time and part-time). 75% of full-time faculty have terminal degrees. Graduate students do not teach undergraduate courses. Undergraduate student–faculty ratio: 8:1.

Student Life Student groups/activities include Music Educators National Conference Student Chapter, Mid-Atlantic Regional Association of Music Therapy Students, Music Entertainment and Industry Education Association.

Expenses for 1997–98 Application fee: $25. State resident tuition: $3468 full-time. Nonresident tuition: $8824 full-time. Mandatory fees: $936 full-time. College room and board: $3704. College room only: $2080. Room and board charges vary according to board plan.

Financial Aid Program-specific awards for 1997: 5 Kreuscher Awards for program majors ($1000), 1 Darrin-Dye Award for freshmen program majors ($1000), 1 Doud Award for freshmen program majors ($3400), 7 Music Department Scholarships for freshmen program majors ($1000), 5 Jones Awards for voice program majors ($2000).

Application Procedures Students admitted directly into the professional program freshman year. Deadline for freshmen and transfers: continuous. Required: high school transcript, college transcript(s) for transfer students, minimum 2.0 high school GPA, interview, audition, SAT I or ACT test scores. Auditions held 8 times on campus; recorded music is permissible as a substitute for live auditions when distance is prohibitive and videotaped performances are permissible as a substitute for live auditions when distance is prohibitive.

Web Site http://www.mnsfld.edu.

Contact Dr. Joseph Murphy, Chairperson, Music Department, Mansfield University of Pennsylvania, Butler Center 110, Mansfield, Pennsylvania 16933; 717-662-4710, fax: 717-662-4114.

▼ MARGARET E. PETREE SCHOOL OF MUSIC AND PERFORMING ARTS

See Oklahoma City University

▼ MARSHALL UNIVERSITY

Huntington, West Virginia

State-supported, coed. Urban campus. Total enrollment: 13,388. Music program established 1980.

Degrees Bachelor of Fine Arts in the area of music. Majors and concentrations: music history and literature, music theory and composition, piano/organ, stringed instruments, voice, wind and percussion instruments. Graduate degrees offered: Master of Arts in the areas of music education, performance, theory/composition, and music history and literature.

Enrollment Fall 1997: 176 total; 134 undergraduate, 30 graduate, 12 non-professional degree.

Music Student Profile 48% females, 3% minorities, 1% international.

Music Faculty 24 total undergraduate and graduate (full-time and part-time). 75% of full-time faculty have terminal degrees. Graduate students teach a few undergraduate courses. Undergraduate student–faculty ratio: 11:1.

Student Life Student groups/activities include Kappa Kappa Psi, Music Educators National Conference Student Chapter.

Expenses for 1997–98 Application fee: $10. State resident tuition: $1798 full-time. Nonresident tuition: $5680 full-time. Mandatory fees: $386 full-time. Full-time tuition and fees vary according to reciprocity agreements. College room and board: $4420. College room only: $2266. Room and board charges vary according to board plan and housing facility.

Financial Aid Program-specific awards for 1997: 32 tuition waivers for program majors ($520–$5146), 6 Endowed Scholarships for program majors ($400–$600), 5 Marching Band Tuition Awards for marching band members ($520–$5146), 25 Marching Band Awards for marching band members ($200).

Application Procedures Students admitted directly into the professional program freshman year. Deadline for freshmen and transfers: continuous. Notification date for freshmen and transfers: continuous. Required: high school transcript, college transcript(s) for transfer students, minimum 2.0 high school GPA, audition, SAT I or ACT test scores. Recommended: letter of recommendation, interview. Auditions held 7 times on campus; recorded music is permissible as a substitute for live auditions with approval from the department and videotaped performances are permissible as a substitute for live auditions if a campus visit is impossible.

Undergraduate Contact Dr. Donald A. Williams, Chairman, Music Department, Marshall University, 400 Hal Greer Boulevard, Huntington, West Virginia 25755; 304-696-3117, fax: 304-696-3333, E-mail address: dfa004@marshall.wvnet. edu.

Graduate Contact Dr. Paul Balshaw, Distinguished Professor of Music, Department of Music, Marshall University, 400 Hal Greer Boulevard, Huntington, West Virginia 25755; 304-696-2399, fax: 304-696-3232, E-mail address: balshaw@marshall. edu.

▼ MARS HILL COLLEGE

Mars Hill, North Carolina

Independent-Baptist, coed. Small town campus. Total enrollment: 1,244.

Degrees Bachelor of Music in the areas of music education, performance; Bachelor of Fine Arts in the area of music theater. Majors and concentrations: classical guitar, music education, piano/organ, voice, wind and percussion instruments. Program accredited by NASM.

Enrollment Fall 1997: 74 total; all undergraduate.

Music Student Profile 55% females, 45% males, 5% minorities, 5% international.

Music Faculty 24 total (full-time and part-time). 25% of full-time faculty have terminal degrees. Graduate students do not teach undergraduate courses. Undergraduate student–faculty ratio: 8:1.

Student Life Student groups/activities include Music Educators National Conference Student Chapter, American Choral Directors Association Student Chapter, Phi Mu Alpha Sinfonia.

Expenses for 1997–98 Application fee: $15. Comprehensive fee: $12,700 includes full-time tuition ($8350), mandatory fees ($550), and college room and board ($3800). College room only: $1700. Full-time tuition and fees vary according to course load. Room and board charges vary according to board plan and housing facility. Special program-related fees: $150 per credit hour for private instruction.

Financial Aid Program-specific awards for 1997: 2–3 Corbett Awards for upperclassmen ($1000), 1 Alexander Award for program students ($1000), 1 Cornwell Award for program students ($1000), 2 Gentile Awards for percussion majors ($500), 1 Strom Award for upperclassmen ($500), 6 Hoyle Scholarships for program students ($1000).

Application Procedures Students admitted directly into the professional program freshman year. Deadline for freshmen and transfers: continuous. Notification date for freshmen and transfers: continuous. Required: essay, high school transcript, college transcript(s) for transfer students, minimum 2.0 high school GPA, 3 letters of recommendation, audition, SAT I or ACT test scores (minimum combined SAT I score of 850). Recommended: interview. Auditions held 4 times on campus; recorded music is permissible as a substitute for live auditions when distance is prohibitive and videotaped performances are permissible as a substitute for live auditions when distance is prohibitive.

Undergraduate Contact Office of Admissions, Mars Hill College, Mars Hill, North Carolina 28754; 704-689-1201, fax: 704-689-1474.

▼ MARYGROVE COLLEGE

Detroit, Michigan

Independent-Roman Catholic, coed. Urban campus. Total enrollment: 3,603.

Degrees Bachelor of Music in the areas of performance (voice, program or piano), piano pedagogy, music education, sacred music (choral or organ emphasis), theory and composition. Majors and concentrations: electronic music, music education, music theory and composition, performance, piano pedagogy, sacred music. Cross-registration with University of Detroit Mercy.

Enrollment Fall 1997: 41 total; all undergraduate.

Music Student Profile 75% females, 25% males, 80% minorities, 1% international.

Music Faculty 10 total undergraduate (full-time and part-time). 100% of full-time faculty have terminal degrees. Graduate students do not teach undergraduate courses. Undergraduate student–faculty ratio: 9:1.

Student Life Student groups/activities include Music Teachers National Association Student Chapter, Marygrove College Chorale, Marygrove College Chamber Singers.

Expenses for 1997–98 Application fee: $25. Tuition: $9190 full-time. Mandatory fees: $220 full-time. Special program-related fees: $65 per credit hour for private lessons, $20 per semester for choir fee.

Financial Aid Program-specific awards for 1997: 2 Choral Leadership Awards for talented students ($6000), 2–4 music scholarships for talented students ($500–$1000), Distinguished Student Awards for talented students ($2000–$9000).

Application Procedures Students admitted directly into the professional program freshman year. Deadline for freshmen and transfers: continuous. Required: high school transcript, college transcript(s) for transfer students, SAT I or ACT test scores, minimum 2.7 high school GPA, minimum 2.0 college GPA for transfer applicants, audition for scholarship consideration. Recommended: interview, audition. Auditions held 3 times on campus; recorded music is permissible as a substitute for live auditions for international applicants and videotaped performances are permissible as a substitute for live auditions for international applicants.

Marygrove College *(continued)*

Undergraduate Contact Ms. Carla Mathews, Director of Admissions, Marygrove College, 8425 West McNichols Road, Detroit, Michigan 48221; 313-927-1200, fax: 313-864-6670.

▼ MARYLHURST UNIVERSITY

Marylhurst, Oregon

Independent-Roman Catholic, coed. Suburban campus. Music program established 1972.

Degrees Bachelor of Music. Majors and concentrations: composition, performance, sacred music. Program accredited by NASM.

Enrollment Fall 1997: 60 total; 20 undergraduate, 40 nonprofessional degree.

Music Student Profile 65% females, 35% males, 5% minorities.

Music Faculty 30 total undergraduate (full-time and part-time). 25% of full-time faculty have terminal degrees. Graduate students do not teach undergraduate courses.

Expenses for 1997–98 Application fee: $88. Comprehensive fee: $14,910 includes full-time tuition ($9765), mandatory fees ($195), and college room and board ($4950). Special program-related fees: $82 per credit for music lessons.

Financial Aid Program-specific awards for 1997: 6 departmental scholarships for freshmen and sophomore music majors ($1000–$3000).

Application Procedures Students apply for admission into the professional program by sophomore year. Deadline for freshmen and transfers: continuous. Required: high school transcript, college transcript(s) for transfer students, interview, ACT test score only. Recommended: audition, portfolio. Auditions held as needed on campus; recorded music is permissible as a substitute for live auditions when distance is prohibitive or in special circumstances and videotaped performances are permissible as a substitute for live auditions when distance is prohibitive or in special circumstances. Portfolio reviews held as needed on campus.

Web Site http://www.marylhurst.edu/pages/bamusic.htm.

Undergraduate Contact Dr. Del Aebischer, Chair, Department of Music, Marylhurst University, PO Box 261, Marylhurst, Oregon 97036; 503-636-8141 ext. 3361, fax: 503-636-9526.

▼ MARYVILLE COLLEGE

Maryville, Tennessee

Independent-Presbyterian, coed. Suburban campus. Total enrollment: 955.

Degrees Bachelor of Music in the areas of vocal music education, instrumental music education, piano performance, vocal performance. Majors and concentrations: music education, piano/organ, voice. Program accredited by NASM.

Enrollment Fall 1997: 45 total; 18 undergraduate, 27 nonprofessional degree.

Music Student Profile 62% females, 38% males, 9% minorities, 2% international.

Music Faculty 17 total undergraduate (full-time and part-time). 80% of full-time faculty have terminal degrees. Graduate students do not teach undergraduate courses.

Student Life Student groups/activities include Delta Omicron.

Expenses for 1997–98 Application fee: $25. Comprehensive fee: $19,145 includes full-time tuition ($14,200), mandatory fees ($225), and college room and board ($4720). College room only: $2290. Room and board charges vary according to board plan and housing facility. Special program-related fees: $160–$340 for applied music lesson fees.

Financial Aid Program-specific awards for 1997: 20–45 Music Performance Scholarships for program majors ($3500–$4000).

Application Procedures Students apply for admission into the professional program by freshman year. Deadline for freshmen and transfers: February 15. Notification date for freshmen and transfers: August 1. Required: high school transcript, college transcript(s) for transfer students, minimum 2.0 high school GPA, letter of recommendation, audition, SAT I or ACT test scores. Recommended: essay. Auditions held on a case-by-case basis on campus; recorded music is permissible as a substitute for live auditions if a campus visit is impossible and videotaped performances are permissible as a substitute for live auditions if a campus visit is impossible.

Web Site http://www.maryvillecollege.edu.

Undergraduate Contact Ms. Donna Davis, Vice President of Admissions and Enrollment, Maryville College, Anderson 210, 502 East Lamar Alexander Parkway, Maryville, Tennessee 37804-5907; 423-981-8111, fax: 423-981-8010, E-mail address: davis@maryvillecollege.edu.

▼ MARYWOOD UNIVERSITY

Scranton, Pennsylvania

Independent-Roman Catholic, coed. Suburban campus. Total enrollment: 2,948. Music program established 1915.

Degrees Bachelor of Music in the areas of performance, music therapy, church music, music education. Graduate degrees offered: Master of Arts in the areas of church music, music education, musicology. Cross-registration with University of Scranton. Program accredited by NASM.

Enrollment Fall 1997: 100 total; 62 undergraduate, 21 graduate, 17 non-professional degree.

Music Student Profile 80% females, 20% males, 2% international.

Music Faculty 18 total undergraduate and graduate (full-time and part-time). 50% of full-time faculty have terminal degrees. Graduate students do not teach undergraduate courses. Undergraduate student–faculty ratio: 9:1.

Student Life Student groups/activities include Music Educators National Conference Student Chapter, American Music Therapy Association Student Chapter, American Choral Association.

Expenses for 1997–98 Application fee: $20. Comprehensive fee: $19,703 includes full-time tuition ($13,408), mandatory fees ($595), and college room and board ($5700). Room and board charges vary according to board plan. Special program-related fees: $100–$350 per credit for applied music lesson fees and practice room rental.

Financial Aid Program-specific awards for 1997: 15 Presidential Scholarships for those demonstrating academic achievement and talent ($14,208), 15 Marywood Talent Award for those demonstrating talent ($1500).

Application Procedures Students admitted directly into the professional program freshman year. Deadline for freshmen and transfers: continuous. Required: high school transcript, letter of recommendation, interview, audition. Recommended: minimum 2.5 high school GPA. Auditions held continuously on campus; recorded music is permissible as a substitute for live auditions when distance is prohibitive and videotaped performances are permissible as a substitute for live auditions when distance is prohibitive.

Contact Sr. Miriam Joseph Reinhardt, IHM, Chairperson, Music Department, Marywood University, 2300 Adams Avenue, Scranton, Pennsylvania 18509; 717-348-6268, fax: 717-961-4768, E-mail address: reinhardt@marywood1. marywood.edu.

Rutgers, The State University of New Jersey

▼ MASON GROSS SCHOOL OF THE ARTS

New Brunswick, New Jersey

State-supported, coed. Small town campus. Total university enrollment: 48,341. Total unit enrollment: 770. Music program established 1976.

Degrees Bachelor of Music in the areas of music education, jazz, performance. Majors and concentrations: classical music, jazz, music education. Graduate degrees offered: Master of Music in the areas of performance, jazz. Doctor of Musical Arts in the area of performance. Program accredited by NASM.

Enrollment Fall 1997: 301 total; 159 undergraduate, 97 graduate, 45 non-professional degree.

Music Student Profile 40% females, 60% males, 10% minorities, 15% international.

Music Faculty 55 total undergraduate and graduate (full-time and part-time). 100% of full-time faculty have terminal degrees. Graduate students teach a few undergraduate courses. Undergraduate student–faculty ratio: 3:1.

Student Life Student groups/activities include National Association of Teachers.

Expenses for 1997–98 Application fee: $50. State resident tuition: $4262 full-time. Nonresident tuition: $8676 full-time. Mandatory fees: $1104 full-time. Full-time tuition and fees vary according to location. College room and board: $5314. College room only: $3112. Room and board charges vary according to board plan and housing facility.

Financial Aid Program-specific awards for 1997: 12 Benefit Series Awards for those with artistic merit ($500–$3000), 20 Nicholas Awards for those with artistic merit ($500–$4000), 9 Naumberg Awards for those with artistic merit ($2000–$5000), 1 Pee Wee Russell Award for those with artistic merit ($2500), 9 Douglass Noe Awards for those with artistic merit ($500–$2100), 2 Douglass Shaw Awards for those with artistic merit ($500–$1000), 3 Douglass Waxman Awards for those with artistic merit ($500–$1000), 1 Lockfeld Award in Jazz for those with artistic merit ($800), 2 Jean Hooper Awards for those with artistic merit ($2500).

Application Procedures Students admitted directly into the professional program freshman year. Deadline for freshmen: continuous; transfers: March 15. Notification date for freshmen and transfers: May 1. Required: high school transcript, college transcript(s) for transfer students, minimum 2.0 high school GPA, interview, audition, SAT I or ACT test scores. Auditions held 5 times on campus; recorded music is permissible as a substitute for live auditions when distance is prohibitive or scheduling is difficult and videotaped performances are permissible as a substitute for live auditions when distance is prohibitive or scheduling is difficult.

Web Site http://www.rutgers.edu.

Undergraduate Contact Mr. William Benz, Chairman, Music Department, Rutgers, The State University of New Jersey, Mason Gross School of the Arts, Marryott Music Building, PO Box 270, New Brunswick, New Jersey 08903; 732-932-8860, fax: 732-932-1517.

Graduate Contact Ms. Judith Civitano, Graduate Director, Music Department, Rutgers, The State University of New Jersey, Mason Gross School of the Arts, Marryott Music Building, PO Box 270, New Brunswick, New Jersey 08903; 732-932-8462, fax: 732-932-1517.

▼ McNEESE STATE UNIVERSITY

Lake Charles, Louisiana

State-supported, coed. Suburban campus. Total enrollment: 8,117. Music program established 1939.

Degrees Bachelor of Music in the area of performance; Bachelor of Music Education in the areas of vocal school music, instrumental school music. Majors and concentrations: jazz, music education, piano pedagogy, piano/organ, stringed instruments, voice, wind and percussion instruments. Graduate degrees offered: Master of Music Education in the areas of vocal school music, instrumental school music (elementary emphasis). Program accredited by NCATE, NASM.

Enrollment Fall 1997: 101 total; 96 undergraduate, 3 graduate, 2 non-professional degree.

Music Student Profile 34% females, 66% males, 14% minorities, 3% international.

Music Faculty 21 total undergraduate and graduate (full-time and part-time). 37% of full-time faculty have terminal degrees. Graduate students teach a few undergraduate courses. Undergraduate student–faculty ratio: 7:1.

Student Life Student groups/activities include Phi Mu Alpha Sinfonia, Music Educators National Conference, Sigma Alpha Iota.

Expenses for 1997–98 Application fee: $10. State resident tuition: $2012 full-time. Nonresident tuition: $6452 full-time. College room and board: $2310. Room and board charges vary according to board plan.

Financial Aid Program-specific awards for 1997: 160 Band Service Awards for musically talented students ($4800), 50 Choir Service Awards for musically talented students ($4200), 4 Orchestra Awards for musically talented students ($5100), 7 Piano Scholarships for musically talented students ($3850–$4800).

Application Procedures Students apply for admission into the professional program by sophomore year. Deadline for freshmen and transfers: continuous. Required: high school transcript, college transcript(s) for transfer students, audition, SAT I or ACT test scores. Recommended: letter of recommendation. Auditions held continuously on campus and off campus in selected locations; recorded music is permissible as a substitute for live auditions for provisional acceptance and videotaped performances are permissible as a substitute for live auditions for provisional acceptance.

Contact Ms. Michele Martin, Head, Department of Music, McNeese State University, PO Box 92175, Lake Charles, Louisiana 70609-2175; 318-475-5028, fax: 318-475-5922.

▼ MEADOWS SCHOOL OF THE ARTS

See Southern Methodist University

▼ MERCER UNIVERSITY

Macon, Georgia

Independent-Baptist, coed. Suburban campus. Total enrollment: 6,801. Music program established 1981.

Degrees Bachelor of Music in the areas of performance, sacred music; Bachelor of Music Education. Majors and concentrations: music education, piano/organ, sacred music, stringed instruments, voice, wind and percussion instruments. Cross-registration with Wesleyan College. Program accredited by NASM.

Enrollment Fall 1997: 305 total; 55 undergraduate, 250 non-professional degree.

Music Student Profile 50% females, 50% males, 12% minorities.

Music Faculty 23 total (full-time and part-time). 90% of full-time faculty have terminal degrees. Graduate students do not teach undergraduate courses. Undergraduate student–faculty ratio: 10:1.

Student Life Student groups/activities include Phi Mu Alpha Sinfonia, Delta Omicron, Music Educators National Conference Student Chapter.

Expenses for 1997–98 Application fee: $25. Comprehensive fee: $19,538 includes full-time tuition ($14,656) and college room and board ($4882). College room only: $2272. Full-time tuition varies according to course load, location, and program. Room and board charges vary according to board plan and housing facility. Special program-related fees: $210 per semester for lesson fee.

Financial Aid Program-specific awards for 1997: 40 music scholarships for music majors ($1000–$5000).

Application Procedures Students admitted directly into the professional program freshman year. Deadline for freshmen and transfers: continuous. Notification date for freshmen and transfers: continuous. Required: high school transcript, letter of recommendation, audition, SAT I or ACT test scores, list of extracurricular activities. Auditions held 3 times and by appointment on campus; recorded music is permissible as a substitute for live auditions when distance is prohibitive and videotaped performances are permissible as a substitute for live auditions when distance is prohibitive.

Undergraduate Contact Office of Undergraduate Admission, Mercer University, 1400 Coleman Avenue, Macon, Georgia 31207; 912-752-2650, fax: 912-752-4120.

▼ MEREDITH COLLEGE

Raleigh, North Carolina

Independent, women only. Urban campus. Total enrollment: 2,552. Music program established 1899.

Degrees Bachelor of Music in the areas of performance, music education. Majors and concentrations: classical music, composition, music, music education, piano pedagogy, piano/organ, stringed instruments, voice, wind and percussion instruments. Graduate degrees offered: Master of Music in the area of performance/pedagogy. Cross-registration with North Carolina State University and Cooperating Raleigh Colleges Consortium. Program accredited by NASM.

Enrollment Fall 1997: 105 total; 50 undergraduate, 15 graduate, 40 non-professional degree.

Music Student Profile 100% females, 2% minorities, 2% international.

Music Faculty 50 total undergraduate and graduate (full-time and part-time). 90% of full-time faculty have terminal

degrees. Graduate students do not teach undergraduate courses. Undergraduate student–faculty ratio: 5:1.

Student Life Student groups/activities include Sigma Alpha Iota, Pi Kappa Lambda, Collegiate Music Educators National Conference.

Expenses for 1997–98 Application fee: $35. Comprehensive fee: $12,240 includes full-time tuition ($8490) and college room and board ($3750). Special program-related fees: $115–$230 per half-hour lesson for applied music fee.

Financial Aid Program-specific awards for 1997: 1 A.J. Fletcher Award for incoming freshmen ($7500), 1 Robert H. Lewis Award for incoming freshmen ($2000), 3 Music Talent Scholarships for incoming freshmen ($500–$1500), 1 Mary Perry Beddingfield Award for incoming freshmen ($350–$400).

Application Procedures Students apply for admission into the professional program by sophomore year. Deadline for freshmen and transfers: continuous. Required: high school transcript, college transcript(s) for transfer students, minimum 2.0 high school GPA, 2 letters of recommendation, interview, audition, SAT I test score only. Recommended: essay. Auditions held at various times on campus; recorded music is permissible as a substitute for live auditions when distance is prohibitive or scheduling is difficult and videotaped performances are permissible as a substitute for live auditions when distance is prohibitive or scheduling is difficult.

Web Site http://www.meredith.edu.

Undergraduate Contact Ms. Carol Kercheval, Director, Office of Admissions, Meredith College, 3800 Hillsborough Street, Raleigh, North Carolina 27607-5298; 800-637-3348, fax: 919-760-2348, E-mail address: admissions@meredith.edu.

Graduate Contact Dr. W. David Lynch, Chairman, John E. Weems Graduate School, Meredith College, 3800 Hillsborough Street, Raleigh, North Carolina 27607-5298; 919-760-8423, fax: 919-760-2898, E-mail address: snodgrassc@meredith.edu.

▼ METHODIST COLLEGE

Fayetteville, North Carolina

Independent-United Methodist, coed. Suburban campus. Total enrollment: 1,720. Music program established 1960.

Degrees Bachelor of Music in the areas of music education, performance. Majors and concentrations: classical music, music education, piano/organ, stringed instruments, voice, wind and percussion instruments.

Enrollment Fall 1997: 22 total; 18 undergraduate, 4 non-professional degree.

Music Student Profile 68% females, 32% males, 17% minorities, 1% international.

Music Faculty 7 total (full-time and part-time). 50% of full-time faculty have terminal degrees. Graduate students do not teach undergraduate courses. Undergraduate student–faculty ratio: 5:1.

Student Life Student groups/activities include American Choral Directors Association, Intercollegiate Choral Festival, Music Educators National Conference.

Estimated expenses for 1998–99 Application fee: $25. Comprehensive fee: $16,480 includes full-time tuition ($11,900) and college room and board ($4580). College room only: $2150. Full-time tuition varies according to program. Room and board charges vary according to board plan.

Financial Aid Program-specific awards for 1997: 13 Vocal Ensemble Scholarships for recent high school graduates

($3000), 4–5 endowed scholarships for recent high school graduates and returning music majors ($1500).

Application Procedures Students apply for admission into the professional program by sophomore year. Deadline for freshmen and transfers: continuous. Notification date for freshmen and transfers: August 15. Required: high school transcript, college transcript(s) for transfer students, minimum 2.0 high school GPA, audition, SAT I or ACT test scores. Recommended: essay, letter of recommendation, interview. Auditions held 3 times and by appointment on campus; recorded music is permissible as a substitute for live auditions when distance is prohibitive and videotaped performances are permissible as a substitute for live auditions when distance is prohibitive.

Undergraduate Contact Mrs. Jane Weekes Gardiner, Head, Department of Music, Methodist College, 5400 Ramsey Street, Fayetteville, North Carolina 28311; 910-630-7158, fax: 910-630-2123, E-mail address: gardiner@methodist.edu.

▼ Miami University

Oxford, Ohio

State-related, coed. Small town campus. Total enrollment: 16,328. Music program established 1929.

Degrees Bachelor of Music in the areas of performance, music education. Majors and concentrations: music, music education, piano/organ, stringed instruments, voice, wind and percussion instruments. Graduate degrees offered: Master of Music in the areas of performance, music education. Cross-registration with Luxembourg Conservatory of Music (Luxembourg). Program accredited by NASM, NCATE.

Enrollment Fall 1997: 220 total; 200 undergraduate, 20 graduate.

Music Student Profile 50% females, 50% males, 5% minorities, 1% international.

Music Faculty 43 total undergraduate and graduate (full-time and part-time). 50% of full-time faculty have terminal degrees. Graduate students teach a few undergraduate courses. Undergraduate student–faculty ratio: 6:1.

Student Life Student groups/activities include Music Educators National Conference, American Choral Directors Association, professional music fraternities and sororities. Special housing available for music students.

Expenses for 1997–98 Application fee: $35. State resident tuition: $4482 full-time. Nonresident tuition: $10,582 full-time. Mandatory fees: $1030 full-time. Full-time tuition and fees vary according to course load. College room and board: $4810. Room and board charges vary according to board plan.

Financial Aid Program-specific awards available.

Application Procedures Students admitted directly into the professional program freshman year. Deadline for freshmen: January 31; transfers: May 1. Notification date for freshmen: March 15; transfers: June 1. Required: essay, high school transcript, college transcript(s) for transfer students, minimum 2.0 high school GPA, audition, SAT I or ACT test scores. Recommended: minimum 3.0 high school GPA, 3 letters of recommendation, interview. Auditions held 15 times on campus; recorded music is permissible as a substitute for live auditions when distance is prohibitive and videotaped performances are permissible as a substitute for live auditions when distance is prohibitive.

Web Site http://www.muohio.edu/music/.

Undergraduate Contact Department of Music, Miami University, 119 Center for the Performing Arts, Oxford, Ohio 45056; 513-529-3014, fax: 513-529-3027, E-mail address: brandeji@muohio.edu.

Graduate Contact Dr. William Albin, Director of Graduate Studies, Department of Music, Miami University, 119 Center for the Performing Arts, Oxford, Ohio 45056; 513-529-3014, fax: 513-529-3027, E-mail address: albinwr@miavx1.muohio.edu.

▼ Michigan State University

East Lansing, Michigan

State-supported, coed. Suburban campus. Total enrollment: 42,603.

Degrees Bachelor of Music in the areas of performance, theory/composition, conducting. Majors and concentrations: composition, music education, music theory, music therapy, piano, piano pedagogy, stringed instruments, voice, wind and percussion instruments. Graduate degrees offered: Master of Music in the areas of composition, conducting, music education, music theory, music therapy, performance. Doctor of Musical Arts in the areas of performance, conducting, composition; Doctor of Philosophy in the areas of music education, music theory. Program accredited by NASM.

Enrollment Fall 1997: 560 total; 360 undergraduate, 200 graduate.

Music Student Profile 55% females, 45% males, 10% minorities, 10% international.

Music Faculty 65 total undergraduate and graduate (full-time and part-time). 70% of full-time faculty have terminal degrees. Graduate students teach a few undergraduate courses. Undergraduate student–faculty ratio: 10:1.

Student Life Student groups/activities include Music Educators National Conference, American Choral Directors Association, American String Teachers Association.

Expenses for 1997–98 Application fee: $30. State resident tuition: $4223 full-time. Nonresident tuition: $11,288 full-time. Mandatory fees: $566 full-time. Full-time tuition and fees vary according to program and student level. College room and board: $4052. College room only: $1742. Room and board charges vary according to board plan and housing facility.

Financial Aid Program-specific awards for 1997: 200 scholarships for those passing audition evaluations ($500–$10,000).

Application Procedures Students admitted directly into the professional program freshman year. Deadline for freshmen and transfers: continuous. Required: high school transcript, college transcript(s) for transfer students, 3 letters of recommendation, audition, SAT I or ACT test scores. Auditions held 5 times on campus and off campus in Interlochen, MI; Philadelphia, PA; recorded music is permissible as a substitute for live auditions when distance is prohibitive and videotaped performances are permissible as a substitute for live auditions when distance is prohibitive.

Web Site http://www.music.msu.edu.

Undergraduate Contact Ms. Dorothy Bartholic, Admissions Secretary, School of Music, Michigan State University, 102 Music Building, East Lansing, Michigan 48824-1043; 517-355-2140, fax: 517-432-2880, E-mail address: barthol3@pilot.msu.edu.

Graduate Contact Ms. Dorothy Bartholic, Secretary, School of Music, Michigan State University, 102 Music Building, East

Michigan State University (continued)

Lansing, Michigan 48824-1043; 517-355-2140, fax: 517-432-2880, E-mail address: barthol3@pilot.msu.edu.

More About the University

Program Facilities The School of Music consists of two buildings, which include classrooms, computer music studios, computer-assisted instruction classroom, music education resource room, music therapy clinic, psychology of music laboratory, recording facilities, rehearsal and practice rooms, and teaching studios. The School of Music is adjacent to the main library, which houses the Fine Arts Library, and near the University Auditorium, which houses an early childhood music classroom and research facility. On-campus performances (more than 350 each year) are given in the Music Auditorium, Hart Recital Hall, Fairchild Theatre, Kellogg Center Auditorium, and Wharton Center for Performing Arts.

Faculty, Guest Artists, and Alumni Faculty appear in solo and chamber recitals and as soloists with orchestras throughout the United States and abroad. They also serve as consultants, publish in scholarly journals, and present at national and international conferences. Guest artists present recitals and master classes and have included the Chamber Music Society of Lincoln Center, Pinchas Zukerman, Samuel Adler, Max Roach, Marcus Roberts, and Milt Hinton. Alumni are found on the concert stage, on faculties of leading schools of music, in professional symphony orchestras, directing some of the most successful school music programs, and as practicing music therapy clinicians.

Student Performance Opportunities Students have a wide variety of performing opportunities, and ensembles have appeared in concert from Boston to Los Angeles, from Tokyo to New York's Alice Tully Hall. Ensembles include: Symphony Orchestra, Chamber Orchestra, Campus Orchestra, Wind Symphony, Symphony Band, Concert Band, Campus Band, Jazz Bands, Jazz Combos, Spartan Marching Band, Opera and Opera Workshop, University Chorale, State Singers, Collegiate Choir, Chamber Choir, Men's Glee Club, Women's Glee Club, Choral Union, New Music Ensemble, Chamber Music Ensembles, and Percussion Ensemble.

▼

The School of Music is known throughout the United States and in many parts of the world as a leading professional training ground for composers, music educators, performers, scholars, and therapists. An outstanding faculty of more than 65 resident artists and scholars and more than 40 graduate assistants serve a talented student body. The faculty is noted for devotion to teaching, for excellence in performance, for innovative and imaginative curricula, and for the production of creative works and meaningful research in all areas of music. The School's graduate program, according to U.S. News & World Report, continues to rank among the best twenty-five in the country.

Students compete favorably with those from leading conservatories and universities around the nation. The School's students have been invited to compete in the Van Cliburn International Piano Competition and Leeds International Piano Competition; winners of the Grace Welsh Award; and winners of such awards as the Houston Symphony Concerto Competition, Coleman Chamber Music Competition (CA), Fishoff National Chamber Music Competition, the New York Concert Artists Guild, and the Pro Musicis International Music Competition.

Students have many performance and teaching opportunities within the University and in the community. Many students perform in regional professional orchestras. The Community Music School (CMS), a division of the School of Music with a weekly enrollment of 1,400, offers comprehensive music education to interested individuals of all ages. Many School of Music students work in CMS as teachers and in laboratory teaching settings, in cooperation with faculty, to develop their skills in teaching and research.

The School of Music has a successful Faculty Artist Recital series, in addition to the many student ensemble and solo recitals given each year. Guest artist recitals and master classes by prominent teachers and performers are arranged frequently, providing rich interaction with students.

MSU School of Music alumni perform with renowned orchestras and teach at prestigious colleges and universities around the world, including Atlanta Symphony, Australian Chamber Orchestra, Chicago Lyric Opera, Chicago Symphony, Columbus Symphony, Detroit Symphony, Florida Symphony, Grand Rapids Symphony, Honolulu Symphony, Indianapolis Symphony, Ismir State Symphony, Korean Philharmonic, Maracaibo Symphony, Milwaukee Symphony, Naples Philharmonic, Nashville Symphony, National Orchestra of Puerto Rico, New World Symphony, Prague Chamber Orchestra, Royal Concertgebow Orchestra, Seattle Symphony, Shanghai Symphony, State Philharmonic Orchestra of Mexico, State Symphony Orchestra of São Paulo, U.S. Air Force Band, U.S. Army Band, U.S. Coast Guard Band, U.S. Marine Band, U.S. Navy Band, Xian Symphony Orchestra, Zagreb Philharmonic Orchestra, California State University at Bakersfield, Juilliard School, Louisiana State University, North Dakota University, Shanghai Conservatory of Music, University of Akron, University of Arizona, University of Miami–Florida, University of São Paulo, University of Virginia, and Xian Conservatory of Music.

▼ MIDDLE TENNESSEE STATE UNIVERSITY

Murfreesboro, Tennessee

State-supported, coed. Urban campus. Total enrollment: 18,366.

Degrees Bachelor of Music in the areas of music education, performance, music industry, music theory/composition. Majors and concentrations: music education, music industry, music theory and composition, piano/organ, stringed instruments, voice, wind and percussion instruments. Program accredited by NASM.

Enrollment Fall 1997: 323 undergraduate.

Music Student Profile 46% females, 54% males, 3% minorities.

Music Faculty 46 total (full-time and part-time). 65% of full-time faculty have terminal degrees. Graduate students teach a few undergraduate courses. Undergraduate student–faculty ratio: 5:1.

Student Life Student groups/activities include American Guild of Organists, Music Educators National Conference Student Chapter, International Association of Jazz Educators Student Chapter.

Expenses for 1997–98 Application fee: $15, $30 for international students. State resident tuition: $1816 full-time. Nonresident tuition: $6412 full-time. Mandatory fees: $380 full-time. College room and board: $3343. College room only: $1692. Room and board charges vary according to board plan. Special program-related fees: $55 per credit hour for lab fee.

Financial Aid Program-specific awards for 1997: 80 music scholarships for music majors ($800–$1850).

Application Procedures Students admitted directly into the professional program freshman year. Deadline for freshmen and transfers: continuous. Required: high school transcript, college transcript(s) for transfer students, minimum 2.0 high school GPA, audition, SAT I or ACT test scores, theory placement test. Auditions held 5 times and by appointment on campus; recorded music is permissible as a substitute for live auditions if a campus visit is impossible and videotaped performances are permissible as a substitute for live auditions if a campus visit is impossible.

Undergraduate Contact Dr. Roger Kugler, Chair, Department of Music, Middle Tennessee State University, Box 47, Murfreesboro, Tennessee 37132; 615-898-2469.

▼ MIDWESTERN STATE UNIVERSITY

Wichita Falls, Texas

State-supported, coed. Urban campus. Total enrollment: 5,770.

Degrees Bachelor of Music in the areas of performance, music education. Majors and concentrations: music, music education, piano/organ, voice, wind and percussion instruments. Program accredited by NASM.

Enrollment Fall 1997: 86 total; all undergraduate.

Music Student Profile 60% females, 40% males, 5% minorities, 5% international.

Music Faculty 13 total (full-time and part-time). 80% of full-time faculty have terminal degrees. Graduate students do not teach undergraduate courses. Undergraduate student–faculty ratio: 10:1.

Student Life Student groups/activities include Mu Phi Epsilon, Kappa Kappa Psi, Tau Beta Sigma.

Expenses for 1997–98 State resident tuition: $1054 full-time. Nonresident tuition: $7688 full-time. Mandatory fees: $1037 full-time. Full-time tuition and fees vary according to course load. College room and board: $3633. Room and board charges vary according to board plan and housing facility. Special program-related fees: $70 per credit hour for private lesson fee.

Financial Aid Program-specific awards for 1997: 50 music scholarships for program majors ($1600).

Application Procedures Students admitted directly into the professional program freshman year. Deadline for freshmen and transfers: April 1. Notification date for freshmen and transfers: August 15. Required: high school transcript, minimum 2.0 high school GPA, audition, SAT I or ACT test scores. Recommended: 3 letters of recommendation, interview. Auditions held 5 times on campus; recorded music is permissible as a substitute for live auditions when distance is prohibitive and videotaped performances are permissible as a substitute for live auditions when distance is prohibitive.

Web Site http://www.mwsu.edu/htmldocs/departments/fine_arts/.

Undergraduate Contact Dr. Dan White, Coordinator, Department of Music, Midwestern State University, 3410 Taft Boulevard, Wichita Falls, Texas 76308; 940-397-4268, fax: 940-397-4511, E-mail address: fwhited@nexus.mwsu.edu.

▼ MILLIKIN UNIVERSITY

Decatur, Illinois

Independent, coed. Suburban campus. Total enrollment: 1,997. Music program established 1901.

Degrees Bachelor of Music in the areas of performance, church music, music education, commercial music; Bachelor of Music Education in the areas of instrumental music education, vocal music education; Bachelor of Fine Arts in the area of musical theater. Majors and concentrations: commercial music, guitar, instrumental music, jazz, music, music education, music performance, piano/organ, sacred music, stringed instruments, voice, wind and percussion instruments. Program accredited by NASM.

Enrollment Fall 1997: 319 total; all undergraduate.

Music Student Profile 60% females, 40% males, 10% minorities, 5% international.

Music Faculty 56 total (full-time and part-time). 100% of full-time faculty have terminal degrees. Graduate students do not teach undergraduate courses. Undergraduate student–faculty ratio: 8:1.

Student Life Student groups/activities include Music Educators National Conference Student Chapter, music fraternity and sorority, Music and Entertainment Industry Educators Association. Special housing available for music students.

Expenses for 1997–98 Comprehensive fee: $19,208 includes full-time tuition ($13,988), mandatory fees ($150), and college room and board ($5070). College room only: $2638. Full-time tuition and fees vary according to course load. Room and board charges vary according to board plan and housing facility.

Financial Aid Program-specific awards for 1997: talent awards for those passing audition evaluations ($1000–$6000).

Application Procedures Students admitted directly into the professional program freshman year. Deadline for freshmen and transfers: continuous. Required: high school transcript, college transcript(s) for transfer students, minimum 2.0 high school GPA, 2 letters of recommendation, interview, audition, SAT I or ACT test scores. Auditions held 9 times on campus and off campus in St. Louis, MO; Indianapolis, IN; Chicago, IL; recorded music is permissible as a substitute for live auditions when distance is prohibitive and videotaped performances are permissible as a substitute for live auditions when distance is prohibitive.

Web Site http://www.millikin.edu.

Undergraduate Contact Mr. Lin Stoner, Dean of Admissions, Millikin University, 1184 West Main Street, Decatur, Illinois 62522; 800-373-7733, fax: 217-424-2711.

▼ MISSISSIPPI COLLEGE

Clinton, Mississippi

Independent-Southern Baptist, coed. Suburban campus. Total enrollment: 3,532. Music program established 1948.

Degrees Bachelor of Music in the areas of vocal performance, piano, organ, instrumental music, church music, composition; Bachelor of Music Education in the areas of vocal music education, instrumental music education. Majors and concentrations: composition, music, music education, piano/organ, sacred music, stringed instruments, voice, wind and percussion instruments. Graduate degrees offered: Master of Music in the areas of performance, composition, vocal pedagogy, music education, conducting. Program accredited by NASM.

Mississippi College (continued)

Enrollment Fall 1997: 91 total; 73 undergraduate, 18 graduate.
Music Student Profile 50% females, 50% males, 1% minorities, 1% international.
Music Faculty 19 total undergraduate and graduate (full-time and part-time). 85% of full-time faculty have terminal degrees. Graduate students teach a few undergraduate courses.
Student Life Student groups/activities include Music Educators National Conference Student Chapter, American Choral Directors Association Student Chapter.
Expenses for 1998–99 Application fee: $25. Comprehensive fee: $11,994 includes full-time tuition ($7890), mandatory fees ($474), and college room and board ($3630). College room only: $1810. Full-time tuition and fees vary according to course load. Room and board charges vary according to board plan and housing facility. Special program-related fees: $160–$200 per year for private studio fee.
Financial Aid Program-specific awards for 1997: 30 Endowed Scholarships for program majors ($2000), 110 Ensemble Scholarships for ensemble performers ($1000).
Application Procedures Students apply for admission into the professional program by sophomore year. Deadline for freshmen and transfers: continuous. Notification date for freshmen and transfers: continuous. Required: essay, high school transcript, college transcript(s) for transfer students, minimum 2.0 high school GPA, 3 letters of recommendation, interview, audition, SAT I or ACT test scores. Auditions held at various times on campus; recorded music is permissible as a substitute for live auditions when distance is prohibitive and videotaped performances are permissible as a substitute for live auditions when distance is prohibitive.
Undergraduate Contact Dr. Jim Turcotte, Admissions Director, Mississippi College, Box 4203, Clinton, Mississippi 39058; 601-925-3240, fax: 601-925-3804, E-mail address: turcotte@mc.edu.
Graduate Contact Dr. Edward MacMillan, Vice President for Graduate Studies, Graduate School, Mississippi College, Box 4185, Clinton, Mississippi 39058; 601-925-3260, fax: 601-925-3889, E-mail address: mcmillan@mc.edu.

▼ MISSISSIPPI STATE UNIVERSITY
Mississippi State, Mississippi

State-supported, coed. Small town campus. Total enrollment: 15,628. Music program established 1957.
Degrees Bachelor of Music Education in the areas of instrumental music education, vocal music education, vocal music education with an emphasis in keyboard, piano pedagogy. Majors and concentrations: instrumental music education, vocal music education. Program accredited by NASM.
Enrollment Fall 1997: 76 total; all undergraduate.
Music Student Profile 50% females, 50% males, 13% minorities, 1% international.
Music Faculty 21 total (full-time and part-time). 67% of full-time faculty have terminal degrees. Graduate students do not teach undergraduate courses. Undergraduate student–faculty ratio: 4:1.
Student Life Student groups/activities include Music Educators National Conference, Phi Mu Alpha Sinfonia, Sigma Alpha Iota.

Expenses for 1997–98 Application fee: $25. State resident tuition: $1996 full-time. Nonresident tuition: $4816 full-time. Mandatory fees: $735 full-time. College room and board: $4100. College room only: $1600. Room and board charges vary according to board plan.
Financial Aid Program-specific awards available.
Application Procedures Students admitted directly into the professional program freshman year. Deadline for freshmen and transfers: continuous. Required: high school transcript, college transcript(s) for transfer students, audition, SAT I or ACT test scores. Auditions held twice on campus; recorded music is permissible as a substitute for live auditions when distance is prohibitive.
Undergraduate Contact Dr. Randi L'Hommedieu, Professor and Head, Music Education Department, Mississippi State University, Box 9734, Mississippi State, Mississippi 39762; 601-325-3070, fax: 601-325-0250.

▼ MISSISSIPPI UNIVERSITY FOR WOMEN
Columbus, Mississippi

State-supported, primarily women. Small town campus. Total enrollment: 3,309. Music program established 1935.
Degrees Bachelor of Music in the area of music education. Cross-registration with Mississippi State University. Program accredited by NASM, NCATE.
Enrollment Fall 1997: 41 total; 13 undergraduate, 28 nonprofessional degree.
Music Student Profile 60% females, 40% males, 30% minorities.
Music Faculty 7 total (full-time and part-time). 60% of full-time faculty have terminal degrees. Graduate students do not teach undergraduate courses. Undergraduate student–faculty ratio: 7:1.
Student Life Student groups/activities include Music Educators National Conference.
Expenses for 1997–98 Application fee: $25 for nonresidents. State resident tuition: $2244 full-time. Nonresident tuition: $4746 full-time. Mandatory fees: $40 full-time. College room and board: $2557. College room only: $1260. Room and board charges vary according to board plan.
Financial Aid Program-specific awards for 1997: 30 Service Awards for ensemble performers ($400), 12 scholarships for program majors ($500).
Application Procedures Students admitted directly into the professional program freshman year. Deadline for freshmen and transfers: continuous. Required: high school transcript, college transcript(s) for transfer students, ACT test score only (minimum combined ACT score of 18). Recommended: minimum 2.0 high school GPA, interview, audition. Auditions held 4 times and by appointment on campus.
Web Site http://www.muw.edu/fine_arts.
Undergraduate Contact Office of Admissions, Mississippi University for Women, W-1613, Columbus, Mississippi 39701; 601-329-7106.

▼ MISSISSIPPI VALLEY STATE UNIVERSITY
Itta Bena, Mississippi

State-supported, coed. Small town campus. Total enrollment: 2,234.

Degrees Bachelor of Music Education in the areas of vocal music education, instrumental music education, keyboard music education. Program accredited by NASM.

Enrollment Fall 1997: 22 undergraduate.

Music Student Profile 36% females, 64% males, 100% minorities.

Music Faculty 10 total (full-time and part-time). 44% of full-time faculty have terminal degrees. Graduate students do not teach undergraduate courses. Undergraduate student–faculty ratio: 3:1.

Student Life Student groups/activities include Music Educators National Conference, senior recitals, local/state/national competitions and programs.

Expenses for 1997–98 State resident tuition: $1739 full-time. Nonresident tuition: $4241 full-time. Mandatory fees: $614 full-time. College room and board: $2350. College room only: $1200.

Financial Aid Program-specific awards for 1997: 130 Band/Choir Scholarships for those demonstrating need/talent ($2500).

Application Procedures Students apply for admission into the professional program by sophomore year. Deadline for freshmen and transfers: continuous. Required: high school transcript, minimum 2.0 high school GPA, interview, audition, SAT I or ACT test scores (minimum combined ACT score of 16), minimum composite ACT score of 18 for out-of-state applicants. Recommended: 2 letters of recommendation. Auditions held 3 times and as needed on campus and off campus in Jackson, MS; Greenville, MS; Greenwood, MS; Indianola, MS; recorded music is permissible as a substitute for live auditions when distance is prohibitive and videotaped performances are permissible as a substitute for live auditions when distance is prohibitive.

Undergraduate Contact Mr. Lawrence Horn, Acting Head, Fine Arts Department, Mississippi Valley State University, 14000 Highway 82 West, #1301, Itta Bena, Mississippi 38941-1400; 601-254-3682, fax: 601-254-3485.

▼ Montana State University–Bozeman

Bozeman, Montana

State-supported, coed. Small town campus. Total enrollment: 11,603. Music program established 1967.

Degrees Bachelor of Music Education. Majors and concentrations: music education, piano/organ, stringed instruments, voice, wind and percussion instruments. Program accredited by NASM.

Enrollment Fall 1997: 85 total; all undergraduate.

Music Student Profile 53% females, 47% males.

Music Faculty 17 total (full-time and part-time). 100% of full-time faculty have terminal degrees. Graduate students do not teach undergraduate courses. Undergraduate student–faculty ratio: 5:1.

Student Life Student groups/activities include Kappa Kappa Psi, College Music Educators National Conference, American Choral Directors Association.

Expenses for 1997–98 Application fee: $30. State resident tuition: $1954 full-time. Nonresident tuition: $6969 full-time. Mandatory fees: $723 full-time. Full-time tuition and fees vary according to course load and reciprocity agreements. College room and board: $4025. Room and board charges vary according to board plan and housing facility. Special program-related fees: $60 per semester for applied music fee, $10 per course for lab fee/instrument maintenance.

Financial Aid Program-specific awards for 1997: 30 fee waivers for program majors ($1000), 5 Intermountain Opera Awards for state resident program majors ($1000), 20 Music Performance Awards for program majors ($100–$500).

Application Procedures Students admitted directly into the professional program freshman year. Deadline for freshmen and transfers: continuous. Required: high school transcript, audition for scholarship consideration. Auditions held continuously on campus; recorded music is permissible as a substitute for live auditions when distance is prohibitive and videotaped performances are permissible as a substitute for live auditions when distance is prohibitive.

Web Site http://www.montana.edu/wwwdt/music.

Undergraduate Contact Ms. Carole Oeschger, Administrative Assistant, Department of Music, Montana State University–Bozeman, Howard Hall, Bozeman, Montana 59717-0342; 406-994-3561, fax: 406-994-3680, E-mail address: zmu7001@msu.maia.montana.edu.

▼ Montclair State University

Upper Montclair, New Jersey

State-supported, coed. Suburban campus. Total enrollment: 12,808. Music program established 1963.

Degrees Bachelor of Music in the areas of performance, music theory/composition; Bachelor of Arts in the areas of music education, music therapy. Majors and concentrations: classical music, music, music education, music theory and composition, music therapy, performance, piano/organ, stringed instruments, voice, wind and percussion instruments. Graduate degrees offered: Master of Arts in the areas of performance, theory/composition, music education, music therapy. Program accredited by NASM.

Enrollment Fall 1997: 230 total; 150 undergraduate, 50 graduate, 30 non-professional degree.

Music Student Profile 60% females, 40% males, 30% minorities, 10% international.

Music Faculty 60 total undergraduate and graduate (full-time and part-time). 100% of full-time faculty have terminal degrees. Graduate students teach a few undergraduate courses. Undergraduate student–faculty ratio: 2:1.

Student Life Student groups/activities include Sigma Alpha Iota, Phi Mu Alpha Sinfonia, Music Educators National Conference.

Expenses for 1997–98 Application fee: $40. State resident tuition: $2912 full-time. Nonresident tuition: $4432 full-time. Mandatory fees: $782 full-time. College room and board: $5546. College room only: $3860. Special program-related fees: $300 per semester for applied music fees, $30 per semester for instrument rental, $100 per recital for recital recording fee.

Financial Aid Program-specific awards for 1997: 1–10 Griffiths Piano Scholarships for piano majors ($100–$500), 1–10 Ravina Strings Awards for strings majors ($100–$500), 1–10 Howe Scholarships for music majors ($100–$500).

Application Procedures Students apply for admission into the professional program by sophomore year. Deadline for freshmen: March 1; transfers: May 1. Notification date for freshmen and transfers: continuous. Required: high school transcript, college transcript(s) for transfer students, interview, audition, SAT I test score only, portfolio for theory/composition applicants. Recommended: essay, 2 letters of recommendation. Auditions held 4 times on campus; recorded music is permissible as a substitute for live

Montclair State University *(continued)*

auditions when distance is prohibitive or scheduling is difficult and videotaped performances are permissible as a substitute for live auditions when distance is prohibitive or scheduling is difficult. Portfolio reviews held 4 times and by appointment on campus.

Web Site http://www.montclair.edu/pages/music/music.html.

Undergraduate Contact Mr. Kevin O'Brien, Admissions Chairperson, Department of Music, Montclair State University, 1 Normal Avenue, Upper Montclair, New Jersey 07043; 973-655-7610, E-mail address: balestracci@saturn.montclair.edu.

Graduate Contact Dr. Donald Mintz, Graduate Advisor, Department of Music, Montclair State University, 1 Normal Avenue, Upper Montclair, New Jersey 07043; 973-655-7219, E-mail address: mintz@saturn.montclair.edu.

▼ MOODY BIBLE INSTITUTE

Chicago, Illinois

Independent-nondenominational, coed. Urban campus. Total enrollment: 1,404.

Degrees Bachelor of Music in the area of sacred music. Program accredited by NASM.

Enrollment Fall 1997: 74 total; all undergraduate.

Music Student Profile 45% females, 55% males, 10% minorities, 10% international.

Music Faculty 17 total (full-time and part-time). 66% of full-time faculty have terminal degrees. Graduate students do not teach undergraduate courses. Undergraduate student–faculty ratio: 5:1.

Student Life Student groups/activities include Campus Radio Station, National Association of Teachers of Singing. Special housing available for music students.

Expenses for 1997–98 Application fee: $35. Comprehensive fee: $5310 includes full-time tuition ($0), mandatory fees ($830), and college room and board ($4480). Special program-related fees: $25 per half-hour lesson for piano practice room.

Financial Aid Program-specific awards for 1997: 1 Wilfred Burton Award for upperclassmen ($500), 1 Howard Hermansen Award for upperclassmen ($300).

Application Procedures Students admitted directly into the professional program freshman year. Deadline for freshmen and transfers: March 1. Notification date for freshmen and transfers: May 1. Required: high school transcript, college transcript(s) for transfer students, minimum 2.0 high school GPA, 3 letters of recommendation, audition, ACT test score only (minimum combined ACT score of 24). Recommended: minimum 3.0 high school GPA. Auditions held twice on campus; recorded music is permissible as a substitute for live auditions when distance is prohibitive and videotaped performances are permissible as a substitute for live auditions when distance is prohibitive.

Undergraduate Contact Ms. Annette Moy, Administrator of Admissions, Enrollment Management, Moody Bible Institute, 820 North LaSalle Boulevard, Chicago, Illinois 60610; 312-329-4265, fax: 312-329-8987.

▼ MOORES SCHOOL OF MUSIC

See University of Houston

Roland Dille Center for the Arts

▼ MOORHEAD STATE UNIVERSITY

Moorhead, Minnesota

State-supported, coed. Urban campus. Total enrollment: 6,466.

Degrees Bachelor of Music in the areas of voice, keyboard, instrumental music, composition, music industry; Bachelor of Science in the area of music education. Majors and concentrations: composition, music, music education, music industry, performance. Graduate degrees offered: Master of Science in the area of music education; Master of Arts in the area of music. Cross-registration with Concordia College, North Dakota State University. Program accredited by NASM.

Enrollment Fall 1997: 148 total; 140 undergraduate, 8 graduate.

Music Student Profile 60% females, 40% males, 6% minorities, 2% international.

Music Faculty 25 total undergraduate and graduate (full-time and part-time). 87% of full-time faculty have terminal degrees. Graduate students do not teach undergraduate courses.

Student Life Student groups/activities include Music and Entertainment Industry Club, International Association of Jazz Educators and Music Educators Student Chapters, jazz ensembles.

Expenses for 1998–99 Application fee: $20. State resident tuition: $2484 full-time. Nonresident tuition: $5596 full-time. Mandatory fees: $424 full-time. Full-time tuition and fees vary according to reciprocity agreements. College room and board: $3256. College room only: $1874. Room and board charges vary according to board plan. Special program-related fees: $85 per credit for performance study fee.

Financial Aid Program-specific awards for 1997: 40–50 Talent Awards for program majors ($300–$500).

Application Procedures Students admitted directly into the professional program freshman year. Deadline for freshmen and transfers: continuous. Required: high school transcript, college transcript(s) for transfer students, SAT I or ACT test scores (minimum combined ACT score of 21), completion of college preparatory courses, standing in top 50% of graduating class. Recommended: audition. Auditions held continuously on campus; recorded music is permissible as a substitute for live auditions with permission of the chair and videotaped performances are permissible as a substitute for live auditions with permission of the chair.

Undergraduate Contact Ms. Jean Butler, Director of Admissions, Moorhead State University, 1104 7th Avenue South, Moorhead, Minnesota 56563; 218-236-2161, fax: 218-236-2168.

Graduate Contact Mr. Larry Reed, Dean of Academic Services, Library, Moorhead State University, 1104 7th Avenue South, Moorhead, Minnesota 56563; 218-236-2923, fax: 218-236-2168.

▼ MORAVIAN COLLEGE

Bethlehem, Pennsylvania

Independent, coed. Suburban campus. Total enrollment: 1,830. Music program established 1982.

Degrees Bachelor of Music in the areas of performance, composition, music education. Majors and concentrations: composition, instrumental music, jazz, music education, performance, voice. Cross-registration with Lehigh University, Lafayette College, Muhlenberg College, Allentown College, Cedar Crest. Program accredited by NASM.

Enrollment Fall 1997: 56 total; all undergraduate.

Music Student Profile 69% females, 31% males, 1% minorities, 1% international.

Music Faculty 49 total (full-time and part-time). 60% of full-time faculty have terminal degrees. Graduate students do not teach undergraduate courses. Undergraduate student–faculty ratio: 11:1.

Student Life Student groups/activities include Music Educators National Conference, Delta Omicron.

Expenses for 1997–98 Application fee: $30. Comprehensive fee: $22,856 includes full-time tuition ($17,140), mandatory fees ($136), and college room and board ($5580). College room only: $3035.

Financial Aid Program-specific awards for 1997: 15 Ina Love Thursby Scholarships for those demonstrating need ($1000).

Application Procedures Students admitted directly into the professional program freshman year. Deadline for freshmen: September 1; transfers: continuous. Required: essay, high school transcript, college transcript(s) for transfer students, minimum 2.0 high school GPA, 3 letters of recommendation, audition. Recommended: interview. Auditions held continuously at student's convenience on campus.

Web Site http://www.moravian.edu.

Undergraduate Contact Mr. James Earl Barnes, Director of Instrumental Music, Music Department, Moravian College, 1200 Main Street, Bethlehem, Pennsylvania 18018; 610-861-1672, fax: 610-861-1657, E-mail address: mejeb01@moravian.edu.

▼ MOREHEAD STATE UNIVERSITY

Morehead, Kentucky

State-supported, coed. Small town campus. Total enrollment: 8,200. Music program established 1937.

Degrees Bachelor of Music in the areas of voice, piano, organ, strings, winds, music theory/composition, jazz; Bachelor of Music Education. Majors and concentrations: jazz, music education, music theory and composition, piano/organ, stringed instruments, voice, wind and percussion instruments. Graduate degrees offered: Master of Music in the areas of performance, music education. Program accredited by NASM, NCATE.

Enrollment Fall 1997: 183 total; 166 undergraduate, 7 graduate, 10 non-professional degree.

Music Student Profile 58% females, 42% males, 4% minorities, 3% international.

Music Faculty 26 total undergraduate and graduate (full-time and part-time). 52% of full-time faculty have terminal degrees. Graduate students do not teach undergraduate courses.

Student Life Special housing available for music students.

Expenses for 1997–98 State resident tuition: $2150 full-time. Nonresident tuition: $5750 full-time. College room and board: $3200. Room and board charges vary according to housing facility. Special program-related fees: $45–$75 for private lessons, $11–$16 for instrument rental.

Financial Aid Program-specific awards for 1997: 60 music scholarships for program majors ($700).

Application Procedures Students admitted directly into the professional program freshman year. Deadline for freshmen and transfers: June 15. Notification date for freshmen: August 1. Required: high school transcript, SAT I or ACT test

scores. Recommended: 2 letters of recommendation, interview, audition. Auditions held 4 times on campus; recorded music is permissible as a substitute for live auditions when distance is prohibitive and videotaped performances are permissible as a substitute for live auditions when distance is prohibitive.

Web Site http://www.morehead-st.edu/colleges/humanities/music.

Contact Dr. Christopher Gallaher, Chair, Music Department, Morehead State University, Baird Music Hall #106, Morehead, Kentucky 40351; 606-783-2473, fax: 606-783-5447, E-mail address: c.gallaher@morehead-st.edu.

▼ MORNINGSIDE COLLEGE

Sioux City, Iowa

Independent-United Methodist, coed. Suburban campus. Total enrollment: 1,166.

Degrees Bachelor of Music in the areas of piano, voice, instrumental music; Bachelor of Music Education; Bachelor of Arts in the area of music. Majors and concentrations: classical music, music education, piano/organ, stringed instruments, voice, wind and percussion instruments. Cross-registration with Western Iowa Tech Community College. Program accredited by NASM, NCATE.

Enrollment Fall 1997: 67 total; 50 undergraduate, 17 non-professional degree.

Music Student Profile 55% females, 45% males, 2% international.

Music Faculty 14 total (full-time and part-time). 90% of full-time faculty have terminal degrees. Graduate students do not teach undergraduate courses. Undergraduate student–faculty ratio: 15:1.

Student Life Student groups/activities include Phi Mu Alpha, Mu Phi Epsilon.

Expenses for 1998–99 Application fee: $15. Comprehensive fee: $16,696 includes full-time tuition ($12,110), mandatory fees ($196), and college room and board ($4390). College room only: $2280. Room and board charges vary according to board plan. Special program-related fees: $165 per semester for lessons.

Financial Aid Program-specific awards for 1997: 10–12 Talent Grants for freshmen ($4500–$6000), 7–8 Endowed Scholarships for program majors ($50–$2000).

Application Procedures Students admitted directly into the professional program freshman year. Deadline for freshmen and transfers: continuous. Notification date for freshmen and transfers: September 1. Required: essay, high school transcript, college transcript(s) for transfer students, interview, audition, SAT I or ACT test scores (minimum combined ACT score of 21). Recommended: minimum 2.0 high school GPA. Auditions held 3 times on campus; recorded music is permissible as a substitute for live auditions when distance is prohibitive and videotaped performances are permissible as a substitute for live auditions when distance is prohibitive and with approval from the department.

Undergraduate Contact Mr. Lance Lehmberg, Chair, Music Department, Morningside College, 1501 Morningside Avenue, Sioux City, Iowa 51106; 712-274-5218, fax: 712-274-5280, E-mail address: hll001@alpha.morningside.edu.

▼ MOUNT ALLISON UNIVERSITY

Sackville, NB, Canada

Province-supported, coed. Small town campus. Total enrollment: 2,474. Music program established 1874.

Degrees Bachelor of Music. Program accredited by CUMS.

Enrollment Fall 1997: 110 undergraduate.

Music Student Profile 55% females, 45% males, 2% international.

Music Faculty 16 total (full-time and part-time). 81% of full-time faculty have terminal degrees. Graduate students do not teach undergraduate courses. Undergraduate student–faculty ratio: 10:1.

Student Life Student groups/activities include Symphonic Band, Garnet and Gold, Ethel Peak Memorial Society. Special housing available for music students.

Expenses for 1997–98 Application fee: $40 Canadian dollars. Tuition, fee, and room and board charges are reported in Canadian dollars. Canadian resident tuition: $3850 full-time. Mandatory fees: $167 full-time. Full-time tuition and fees vary according to course load. College room and board: $5460. College room only: $3050. Room and board charges vary according to board plan and housing facility. International student tuition: $7475 full-time.

Financial Aid Program-specific awards for 1997: 3 Blakie Scholarship for freshmen program majors ($500), 1 Blair Scholarship for freshmen program majors ($200), 1 Robert Marsh Scholarship for freshmen program majors ($500), 1 Gladys Muttart Scholarship for freshmen program majors ($1250), 5 Pickard Scholarship for freshmen program majors ($1500–$2000).

Application Procedures Students admitted directly into the professional program freshman year. Deadline for freshmen: April 25; transfers: May 1. Required: high school transcript, college transcript(s) for transfer students, minimum 3.0 high school GPA, interview, audition, music theory examination, completion of college preparatory courses. Recommended: essay, 2 letters of recommendation, SAT I or ACT test scores. Auditions held twice and by appointment on campus; recorded music is permissible as a substitute for live auditions if a campus visit is impossible and videotaped performances are permissible as a substitute for live auditions if a campus visit is impossible.

Web Site http://www.mta.ca/faculty/arts-letters/music/.

Undergraduate Contact Head, Department of Music, Mount Allison University, Sackville, NB E0A 3C0, Canada; 506-364-2374, fax: 506-364-2376.

▼ MOUNT ST. MARY'S COLLEGE

Los Angeles, California

Independent-Roman Catholic, primarily women. Suburban campus. Total enrollment: 1,984. Music program established 1925.

Degrees Bachelor of Music in the areas of vocal performance, instrumental performance, liturgical music, theory and composition. Majors and concentrations: music theory and composition, performance, piano, sacred music, voice. Cross-registration with University of California-Los Angeles. Program accredited by NASM.

Enrollment Fall 1997: 30 undergraduate.

Music Student Profile 96% females, 4% males, 33% minorities.

Music Faculty 9 total (full-time and part-time). 50% of full-time faculty have terminal degrees. Graduate students do not teach undergraduate courses. Undergraduate student–faculty ratio: 11:1.

Student Life Student groups/activities include Campus Liturgies in Mary Chapel, Spring Sing, trips to off campus concerts.

Expenses for 1997–98 Application fee: $30. Comprehensive fee: $20,554 includes full-time tuition ($14,716), mandatory fees ($500), and college room and board ($5338). Room and board charges vary according to housing facility.

Financial Aid Program-specific awards for 1997: 16 music scholarships for those demonstrating talent and need ($3000).

Application Procedures Students admitted directly into the professional program freshman year. Deadline for freshmen and transfers: continuous. Required: essay, high school transcript, minimum 3.0 high school GPA, SAT I or ACT test scores, audition for scholarship consideration. Auditions held twice on campus; recorded music is permissible as a substitute for live auditions when distance is prohibitive and videotaped performances are permissible as a substitute for live auditions when distance is prohibitive.

Undergraduate Contact Admissions Office, Mount St. Mary's College, 12001 Chalon Road, Los Angeles, California 90049; 310-471-9546.

▼ MOUNT UNION COLLEGE

Alliance, Ohio

Independent-United Methodist, coed. Suburban campus. Total enrollment: 1,935.

Degrees Bachelor of Music in the area of performance; Bachelor of Music Education. Majors and concentrations: classical music, music education, piano/organ, stringed instruments, voice, wind and percussion instruments.

Enrollment Fall 1997: 48 total; 40 undergraduate, 8 nonprofessional degree.

Music Student Profile 55% females, 45% males, 10% minorities, 10% international.

Music Faculty 30 total (full-time and part-time). 83% of full-time faculty have terminal degrees. Graduate students do not teach undergraduate courses.

Student Life Student groups/activities include Kappa Kappa Psi, Mu Phi Epsilon.

Expenses for 1997–98 Application fee: $1.50. Comprehensive fee: $18,160 includes full-time tuition ($13,520), mandatory fees ($770), and college room and board ($3870). College room only: $1540. Special program-related fees: $150 for private music lessons.

Financial Aid Program-specific awards for 1997: 40 Music Proficiency Awards for those demonstrating musical achievement ($1000–$3000).

Application Procedures Deadline for freshmen and transfers: continuous. Required: essay, high school transcript, minimum 2.0 high school GPA, letter of recommendation, interview, audition, SAT I or ACT test scores. Auditions held 5 times on campus; recorded music is permissible as a substitute for live auditions when distance is prohibitive and videotaped performances are permissible as a substitute for live auditions when distance is prohibitive.

Undergraduate Contact Dr. James E. Perone, Chairperson, Department of Music, Mount Union College, 1972 Clark

Avenue, Alliance, Ohio 44601; 330-823-2180, fax: 330-823-2144, E-mail address: peroneje@muc.edu.

▼ MURRAY STATE UNIVERSITY

Murray, Kentucky

State-supported, coed. Small town campus. Total enrollment: 8,811.

Degrees Bachelor of Music in the area of performance; Bachelor of Music Education. Majors and concentrations: classical music, jazz, music, music education, opera, piano/organ, stringed instruments, voice, wind and percussion instruments. Graduate degrees offered: Master of Music Education. Program accredited by NASM.

Enrollment Fall 1997: 200 total; 137 undergraduate, 31 graduate, 32 non-professional degree.

Music Student Profile 55% females, 45% males, 2% minorities, 3% international.

Music Faculty 26 total undergraduate and graduate (full-time and part-time). 55% of full-time faculty have terminal degrees. Graduate students teach a few undergraduate courses. Undergraduate student–faculty ratio: 8:1.

Student Life Student groups/activities include Music Educators National Conference, Phi Mu Alpha Sinfonia, Sigma Alpha Iota.

Expenses for 1998–99 Application fee: $20. State resident tuition: $1920 full-time. Nonresident tuition: $5760 full-time. Mandatory fees: $380 full-time. Full-time tuition and fees vary according to reciprocity agreements. College room and board: $3560. College room only: $1560. Special program-related fees: $50–$100 per semester for lesson fees.

Financial Aid Program-specific awards for 1997: 30–88 Music/University Scholarships for program majors ($200–$2000).

Application Procedures Students apply for admission into the professional program by sophomore year. Deadline for freshmen and transfers: continuous. Required: high school transcript, college transcript(s) for transfer students, audition, ACT test score only, interview for scholarship consideration. Recommended: letter of recommendation. Auditions held 4 times on campus; recorded music is permissible as a substitute for live auditions when distance is prohibitive and videotaped performances are permissible as a substitute for live auditions when distance is prohibitive.

Web Site http://www.murraystate.edu.

Undergraduate Contact Dr. Brian D. Runnels, Chair, Department of Music, Murray State University, Box 9, Murray, Kentucky 42071-0009; 502-762-6339, fax: 502-762-3965, E-mail address: brian.runnels@murraystate.edu.

Graduate Contact Dr. Pamela Wurgler, Graduate Coordinator, Department of Music, Murray State University, Box 9, Murray, Kentucky 42071-0009; 502-762-6452, fax: 502-762-3965, E-mail address: pamela.wurgler@murraystate.edu.

▼ MUSICIANS INSTITUTE

Hollywood, California

Proprietary, coed. Music program established 1994.

Degrees Bachelor of Music in the area of commercial music. Majors and concentrations: bass, guitar, keyboard, percussion, voice. Program accredited by NASM.

Enrollment Fall 1997: 56 undergraduate.

Music Student Profile 30% females, 70% males, 15% minorities, 40% international.

Music Faculty 40 total (full-time and part-time). 75% of full-time faculty have terminal degrees. Graduate students do not teach undergraduate courses. Undergraduate student–faculty ratio: 5:1.

Student Life Student groups/activities include Career Development Center, Music Industry Internship Programs.

Expenses for 1997–98 Application fee: $100. Tuition: $12,000 full-time. Special program-related fees: $50–$200 per quarter for lab fees.

Application Procedures Students admitted directly into the professional program freshman year. Deadline for freshmen and transfers: August 1. Notification date for freshmen and transfers: September 1. Required: essay, high school transcript, college transcript(s) for transfer students, minimum 2.0 high school GPA, 2 letters of recommendation, SAT I or ACT test scores (minimum combined SAT I score of 1000), minimum TOEFL score of 500 for international applicants, taped video or audition. Recommended: interview, video. Auditions held as needed on campus; recorded music is permissible as a substitute for live auditions if video is not available.

Web Site http://www.mi.edu.

Undergraduate Contact Mr. Masta Edwards, Student Advisor, Degree Program, Musicians Institute, 1655 North McCadden Place, Hollywood, California 90028; 800-255-PLAY, fax: 213-462-6978.

▼ NAZARETH COLLEGE OF ROCHESTER

Rochester, New York

Independent, coed. Suburban campus. Total enrollment: 2,782. Music program established 1924.

Degrees Bachelor of Music in the areas of music education, music therapy, performance, music theory, music history. Cross-registration with State University of New York College at Brockport, University of Rochester, St. John Fisher College. Program accredited by NASM.

Enrollment Fall 1997: 105 undergraduate.

Music Student Profile 60% females, 40% males, 1% minorities.

Music Faculty 26 total (full-time and part-time). 100% of full-time faculty have terminal degrees. Graduate students do not teach undergraduate courses. Undergraduate student–faculty ratio: 10:1.

Expenses for 1997–98 Application fee: $40. Comprehensive fee: $18,970 includes full-time tuition ($12,560), mandatory fees ($425), and college room and board ($5985). College room only: $3475. Full-time tuition and fees vary according to course load. Room and board charges vary according to board plan. Special program-related fees: $190 per course for voice or instrument lessons for majors, $105 per course for voice or instrument lessons for minors, $105 per course for group lessons, $33 per course for music therapy clinic fee.

Financial Aid Program-specific awards for 1997: 15 Honors Music Scholarships for incoming freshmen passing audition evaluations ($2500), 5 Gerald Wilmot Music Scholarships for honors juniors or seniors ($1000–$2500), 2 Lewis Dollinger Scholarships for honors juniors or seniors ($1000), 1 Presser Scholarship for seniors ($2000).

Application Procedures Students apply for admission into the professional program by sophomore year. Deadline for freshmen and transfers: continuous. Required: essay, high school transcript, college transcript(s) for transfer students,

Nazareth College of Rochester (*continued*)

minimum 2.0 high school GPA, 2 letters of recommendation, interview, audition, SAT I or ACT test scores. Auditions held 7 times on campus; videotaped performances are permissible as a substitute for live auditions when distance is prohibitive or in special circumstances.

Web Site http://naz.edu.

Undergraduate Contact Mr. Tom DaRin, Director of Admissions, Nazareth College of Rochester, 4245 East Avenue, Rochester, New York 14618; 716-389-2860, fax: 716-586-2452.

▼ NEBRASKA WESLEYAN UNIVERSITY

Lincoln, Nebraska

Independent-United Methodist, coed. Suburban campus. Total enrollment: 1,709.

Degrees Bachelor of Music in the areas of applied music, music education. Program accredited by NASM.

Enrollment Fall 1997: 60 undergraduate.

Music Student Profile 50% females, 50% males, 2% minorities.

Music Faculty 17 total (full-time and part-time). 90% of full-time faculty have terminal degrees. Graduate students do not teach undergraduate courses.

Student Life Student groups/activities include Mu Phi Epsilon, Music Educators National Conference, Nebraska Music Educators Association.

Expenses for 1997–98 Application fee: $20. One-time mandatory fee: $80. Comprehensive fee: $14,834 includes full-time tuition ($10,898), mandatory fees ($322), and college room and board ($3614). Room and board charges vary according to board plan.

Financial Aid Program-specific awards for 1997: 10 Bennett Music Scholarships for program majors ($500–$2000).

Application Procedures Students admitted directly into the professional program freshman year. Deadline for freshmen and transfers: continuous. Required: high school transcript, audition, SAT I or ACT test scores. Auditions held once on campus; recorded music is permissible as a substitute for live auditions if a campus visit is impossible and videotaped performances are permissible as a substitute for live auditions.

Web Site http://music.nebrwesleyan.edu/.

Undergraduate Contact Mr. Ken Sieg, Director of Admissions, Nebraska Wesleyan University, 5000 St. Paul Avenue, Lincoln, Nebraska 68504; 402-465-2141, fax: 402-465-2179.

▼ NEWBERRY COLLEGE

Newberry, South Carolina

Independent-Lutheran, coed. Small town campus. Total enrollment: 716. Music program established 1933.

Degrees Bachelor of Music in the area of music performance; Bachelor of Music Education in the areas of choral music, instrumental music. Majors and concentrations: music education, piano/organ, voice, wind and percussion instruments. Program accredited by NASM.

Enrollment Fall 1997: 21 total; all undergraduate.

Music Student Profile 33% females, 67% males, 14% minorities, 1% international.

Music Faculty 8 total undergraduate (full-time and part-time). 20% of full-time faculty have terminal degrees.

Student Life Student groups/activities include Phi Mu Alpha, Delta Omicron.

Expenses for 1997–98 Application fee: $25. Comprehensive fee: $15,544 includes full-time tuition ($11,996), mandatory fees ($330), and college room and board ($3218). College room only: $1364. Special program-related fees: $75 per course for instrument maintenance, $100 per credit hour for private lessons.

Financial Aid Program-specific awards for 1997: 40 music scholarships for program majors ($1500).

Application Procedures Students admitted directly into the professional program freshman year. Deadline for freshmen and transfers: continuous. Required: college transcript(s) for transfer students, minimum 2.0 high school GPA, audition, SAT I or ACT test scores, high school transcript or GED, high school transcript for transfer applicants with fewer than 30 credits. Auditions held 4 times on campus; recorded music is permissible as a substitute for live auditions if a campus visit is impossible and videotaped performances are permissible as a substitute for live auditions if a campus visit is impossible.

Web Site http://www.newberry.edu.

Undergraduate Contact Dr. John W. Wagner, Chairman, Music Department, Newberry College, 2100 College Street, Newberry, South Carolina 29108; 803-321-5174, fax: 803-321-5232.

▼ NEW ENGLAND CONSERVATORY OF MUSIC

Boston, Massachusetts

Independent, coed. Urban campus. Total enrollment: 800. Music program established 1867.

Degrees Bachelor of Music in the areas of composition, historical performance, music history, music theory, performance. Majors and concentrations: classical music, composition, improvisation, jazz, music theory, performance, piano/organ, stringed instruments, voice, wind and percussion instruments. Graduate degrees offered: Master of Music in the areas of composition, historical performance, music history, music theory, accompaniment, conducting, musicology, vocal pedagogy, performance; Master of Music Education. Doctor of Musical Arts in the areas of performance, composition, music education. Cross-registration with Northeastern University, Tufts University, Simmons College. Program accredited by NASM.

Enrollment Fall 1997: 800 total; 387 undergraduate, 413 graduate.

Music Student Profile 50% females, 50% males, 16% minorities, 37% international.

Music Faculty 212 total undergraduate and graduate (full-time and part-time). 100% of full-time faculty have terminal degrees. Graduate students teach a few undergraduate courses. Undergraduate student–faculty ratio: 4:1.

Student Life Special housing available for music students.

Expenses for 1997–98 Application fee: $75. Comprehensive fee: $26,375 includes full-time tuition ($17,900), mandatory fees ($100), and college room and board ($8375). College room only: $5375. Full-time tuition and fees vary according to program. Room and board charges vary according to housing facility. Tuition for studio instruction: $4475 per term. Special program-related fees: $100 per year for practice room fee for collaborative piano, piano, organ, and harpsicord majors only, $50 per semester for registration fee for any electronic music course.

Application Procedures Students admitted directly into the professional program freshman year. Deadline for freshmen and transfers: January 2. Notification date for freshmen and transfers: April 1. Required: essay, high school transcript, college transcript(s) for transfer students, 2 letters of recommendation, audition, SAT I or ACT test scores, portfolio for composition majors, resume, repertoire listing. Auditions held 35 times on campus; recorded music is permissible as a substitute for live auditions when distance is prohibitive and videotaped performances are permissible as a substitute for live auditions when distance is prohibitive. Portfolio reviews held as needed on campus.

Web Site http://www.newenglandconservatory.edu.

Contact Ms. Allison Ball, Dean of Enrollment Services, Office of Admissions, New England Conservatory of Music, 290 Huntington Avenue, Boston, Massachusetts 02115; 617-262-1120 ext. 430, fax: 617-262-0500.

▼ NEW MEXICO STATE UNIVERSITY

Las Cruces, New Mexico

State-supported, coed. Suburban campus. Total enrollment: 15,067. Music program established 1905.

Degrees Bachelor of Music in the areas of performance, music theory/composition, piano pedagogy; Bachelor of Music Education in the areas of vocal music education, instrumental music education. Majors and concentrations: music, music business, music education, music theory and composition, piano/organ, stringed instruments, voice, wind and percussion instruments. Graduate degrees offered: Master of Music in the areas of accompanying, music theory/composition, music history, performance, music education, conducting. Program accredited by NASM.

Enrollment Fall 1997: 161 total; 142 undergraduate, 19 graduate.

Music Student Profile 45% females, 55% males, 36% minorities, 1% international.

Music Faculty 22 total undergraduate and graduate (full-time and part-time). 85% of full-time faculty have terminal degrees. Graduate students teach a few undergraduate courses. Undergraduate student–faculty ratio: 15:1.

Student Life Student groups/activities include Phi Mu Alpha.

Expenses for 1997–98 Application fee: $15. State resident tuition: $2196 full-time. Nonresident tuition: $7152 full-time. College room and board: $3390. College room only: $1940. Room and board charges vary according to board plan and housing facility.

Financial Aid Program-specific awards for 1997: 1 Theodore Presser Scholarship for program majors ($1500), 3 Jack Ward Scholarships for wind or percussion students ($600), 2 Vivien B. Head Scholarships for program majors ($1500), 1 Ray Tross Scholarship for woodwind majors ($300), 300 Band, Choir, and Orchestra Service Grants for musically talented performers ($500).

Application Procedures Students admitted directly into the professional program freshman year. Deadline for freshmen and transfers: April 15. Notification date for freshmen and transfers: July 1. Required: high school transcript, college transcript(s) for transfer students, audition, SAT I or ACT test scores. Recommended: minimum 3.0 high school GPA, 3

letters of recommendation, interview. Auditions held continuously on campus and off campus in various New Mexico cities.

Contact Dr. William Clark, Head, Music Department, New Mexico State University, Box 3F, Las Cruces, New Mexico 88003; 505-646-1290, fax: 505-646-8199, E-mail address: music@nmsu.edu.

▼ NEW SCHOOL FOR SOCIAL RESEARCH

See Mannes College of Music

▼ NEW SCHOOL FOR SOCIAL RESEARCH

See Mannes Jazz and Contemporary Music Program

▼ NEW WORLD SCHOOL OF THE ARTS

Miami, Florida

State-supported, coed. Urban campus. Total enrollment: 359. Music program established 1988.

Degrees Bachelor of Music in the areas of instrumental studies, vocal studies, composition/electronic music. Cross-registration with Miami-Dade Community College, University of Florida.

Enrollment Fall 1997: 55 total; all undergraduate.

Music Student Profile 50% females, 50% males, 45% minorities, 50% international.

Music Faculty 33 total (full-time and part-time). 85% of full-time faculty have terminal degrees. Graduate students do not teach undergraduate courses. Undergraduate student–faculty ratio: 5:1.

Estimated expenses for 1998–99 Application fee: $20. State resident tuition: $1478 full-time. Nonresident tuition: $5196 full-time. Full-time tuition varies according to course load and degree level.

Financial Aid Program-specific awards for 1997: 25–30 NWSA Music Scholarships for talented music students ($2500).

Application Procedures Students admitted directly into the professional program freshman year. Deadline for freshmen and transfers: continuous. Required: high school transcript, college transcript(s) for transfer students, audition. Recommended: essay, minimum 2.0 high school GPA, 2 letters of recommendation, interview, SAT I or ACT test scores. Auditions held 4 times on campus; recorded music is permissible as a substitute for live auditions when distance is prohibitive or if a campus visit is impossible and videotaped performances are permissible as a substitute for live auditions when distance is prohibitive or if a campus visit is impossible.

Undergraduate Contact Dean of Music, New World School of the Arts, 300 North East 2nd Avenue, Miami, Florida 33132; 305-237-3539, fax: 305-237-3512.

New York University

▼ NEW YORK UNIVERSITY SCHOOL OF EDUCATION

New York, New York

Independent, coed. Urban campus. Total enrollment: 36,684.

New York University School of Education *(continued)*

Degrees Bachelor of Music in the areas of performance, composition, music business, music technology, piano, voice; Bachelor of Science in the area of music education. Majors and concentrations: classical music, composition, instrumental music, jazz, music business, music education, music performance, music technology, music theater, music theory and composition, orchestral instruments, performance, piano/organ, stringed instruments, voice, wind and percussion instruments. Graduate degrees offered: Master of Music in the area of music technology; Master of Arts in the areas of music performance and composition, music education, music therapy, music entertainment professions. Doctor of Arts in the area of music therapy; Doctor of Philosophy in the areas of music performance and composition, music education. Program accredited by NASM, AAMT.

Enrollment Fall 1997: 673 total; 371 undergraduate, 302 graduate.

Music Student Profile 60% females, 40% males, 30% minorities, 34% international.

Music Faculty 204 total undergraduate and graduate (full-time and part-time). 100% of full-time faculty have terminal degrees. Graduate students teach a few undergraduate courses.

Student Life Student groups/activities include New York State Music Association, Music Educators National Conference, Music Business Association.

Expenses for 1997–98 Application fee: $45. Comprehensive fee: $29,900 includes full-time tuition ($21,730) and college room and board ($8170). Full-time tuition varies according to program. Room and board charges vary according to board plan and housing facility. Special program-related fees: $60 per course for private instruction fee, $75 per course for recital fee.

Application Procedures Students admitted directly into the professional program freshman year. Deadline for freshmen: January 15; transfers: April 1. Notification date for freshmen: April 1; transfers: continuous. Required: essay, high school transcript, college transcript(s) for transfer students, minimum 3.0 high school GPA, 3 letters of recommendation, interview, audition, portfolio, SAT I test score only. Auditions held 12 times on campus; recorded music is permissible as a substitute for live auditions when distance is prohibitive and videotaped performances are permissible as a substitute for live auditions when distance is prohibitive. Portfolio reviews held continuously on campus.

Undergraduate Contact Ms. Nicole Scrofani, Director of Undergraduate Admissions, School of Education, New York University, 22 Washington Square North, New York, New York 10012; 212-998-4500, fax: 212-995-4902.

Graduate Contact Mr. Stan Greidus, Director of Enrollment Services, Office of Graduate Admissions, School of Education, New York University, 82 Washington Square East, 2nd Floor, New York, New York 10003; 212-998-5030, fax: 212-995-4328, E-mail address: ed.gradadmissions@nyu.edu.

More About the University

Facilities and resources include the education building (private practice rooms, ensemble rehearsal rooms, teaching studios, Frederick Lowe Theatre); computer music studios (MacIntosh-based computer music, audio for video, film music studios; multimedia laboratories using IBM, NeXT, SGI, and Apple computers; digital recording and editing rooms featuring Digidesign Pro Tools and Sonic Solutions multitrack systems. Rollnick Recording Studios (multitrack facility featuring analog and digital recording, automated inline console, outboard effects, and MIDI processing for live and studio performance); Village Records (a full-service NYU-based record company providing experience in all aspects of record production and promotion); Nordoff-Robbins Center for Music Therapy (an international outreach and training center for music therapists); NYU Arts and Media Studio (advanced hardware platforms for computer music, graphics, and animation); Elmer Holmes Bobst Library (open-stack; over 2.5 million volumes; includes the Avery Fisher Center for Music and Media).

Faculty, Resident Artists, and Alumni Faculty members are internationally acclaimed artists, composers, scholars, industry executives, and members of such renowned music organizations as the New York Philharmonic and the Metropolitan Opera Company. Currently in residence: The Brentano String Quartet, The Dorian Woodwind Quintet and Reimann Opera Theatre, and composors in residence. Guest artists have included George Perle, Milton Babbitt, John Corigliano, Ned Rorem, Roger Reynolds, Allen Menken, Lukas Foss, Emil Sein, and George Crumb.

Student Performance Opportunities Student composers and performers are involved in national and international tours and are regularly featured in concerts and recitals at NYU, Carnegie Recital Hall, Merkin Hall, Lincoln Center and landmark jazz clubs and new music venues in Greenwich Village and SoHo. Performance ensembles include: Chamber Music Ensemble; Symphony Orchestra; Concert Band; Washington Square Woodwind Ensemble; Jazz Ensembles; New Music Ensemble; Percussion Ensembles; Choral Arts Society; Opera Workshop; All-University Gospel Choir, University Singers. The Center for Music Performance sponsors music events and serves as a referral service for the entire NYU musical community. An active NYU composers' forum features visiting composers and provides ongoing opportunities for students' work to be performed.

Special Programs Interactive Performance Series; Stephen F. Temmer Tonmeister Studies (advanced recording technology); Annual Summer Composers Seminar; Summer Musical Theatre and Opera, Music, and Dance in Pisa, Italy, a summer study abroad program, includes participation in an international music festival and study with distinguished NYU faculty and Italian performers and composers.

The Department of Music and Performing Arts Professions at New York University's School of Education offers the finest professional training for your career combined with academic studies at a preeminent, internationally acclaimed university. Alongside the music programs described above, our department also offers: dance education (B.S., M.A., Ed.D, Ph.D), educational theater (B.S., M.A., Ed.D, Ph.D), drama therapy (M.A.), and performing arts administration (M.A.). Baccalaureate programs combine intense professional training in music, technology, music business, dance, or theater with a solid liberal arts core in the humanities and the social and natural sciences. In seminars, master classes, and selected classes, undergraduate students join advanced master's and doctoral degree students and faculty members in a collaborative environment that fosters creativity of the highest order.

Studies in music performance and composition prepare students for the demands of a professional career in music by providing them with the breadth of skills to perform in a wide range of styles and contexts. Whatever their musical interests, students benefit from being part of a department that thrives on a variety of styles–from the Western musical tradition to contemporary multicultural music.

Added to this are the excitement and opportunities of New York City, which enable students to build important career alliances and professional opportunities. World-class artists regularly provide seminars and master classes and often join students in performances on- and off-campus. Music business and technology students as well as performance and composition majors gain hands-on experience through internships at leading recording companies, publishing houses, and concert management, and public relations firms. Students in music education gain the finest student experiences in the country's largest public school system.

NYU attracts talented high achievers from across the country and around the world. The diverse course offerings of NYU's 13 schools and colleges provide unparalleled opportunities to pursue many academic interests. For those interested in careers in the visual arts, the Department of Art and Art Professions at NYU's School of Education offers: studio art (B.S., M.F.A., M.A.), including painting, drawing, sculpture, printmaking, photography, and art and media; art education (B.S., M.A., Ed.D, Ph.D); visual arts administration, including for-profit studies (M.A.); visual culture (M.A.), including folk art studies and costume studies; and art therapy (M.A.).

▼ NICHOLLS STATE UNIVERSITY

Thibodaux, Louisiana

State-supported, coed. Small town campus. Total enrollment: 7,173. Music program established 1967.

Degrees Bachelor of Music Education in the areas of instrumental music, vocal music. Cross-registration with Loyola University-New Orleans. Program accredited by NASM.

Enrollment Fall 1997: 53 total; all undergraduate.

Music Student Profile 55% females, 45% males, 7% minorities.

Music Faculty 13 total (full-time and part-time). 45% of full-time faculty have terminal degrees. Graduate students do not teach undergraduate courses. Undergraduate student–faculty ratio: 5:1.

Student Life Student groups/activities include Phi Mu Alpha Sinfonia, Sigma Alpha Iota.

Expenses for 1997–98 Application fee: $10. State resident tuition: $2136 full-time. Nonresident tuition: $5376 full-time. Mandatory fees: $371 full-time. College room and board: $2720. Special program-related fees: $10 per lab course for laboratory fees.

Financial Aid Program-specific awards for 1997: 105 Band Service Awards for instrumental ensemble members ($300), 20 Choir Service Awards for choir members ($100), 25 Music Department Scholarships for program majors ($600), academic scholarships for program majors ($500).

Application Procedures Students admitted directly into the professional program freshman year. Deadline for freshmen and transfers: continuous. Notification date for freshmen and transfers: August 15. Required: high school transcript, college transcript(s) for transfer students, audition, ACT test score only. Recommended: 3 letters of recommendation. Auditions held 4 times on campus; recorded music is permissible as a substitute for live auditions if a campus visit is impossible and videotaped performances are permissible as a substitute for live auditions if a campus visit is impossible.

Undergraduate Contact Mr. Greg Torres, Director of Bands, Department of Music, Nicholls State University, PO Box 2017, Thibodaux, Louisiana 70310; 504-448-4600, E-mail address: mus-gjt@nich-nsunet.nich.edu.

▼ NORFOLK STATE UNIVERSITY

Norfolk, Virginia

State-supported, coed. Urban campus. Total enrollment: 7,659.

Degrees Bachelor of Music in the areas of media, music education. Majors and concentrations: piano/organ, stringed instruments, voice, wind and percussion instruments. Graduate degrees offered: Master of Music in the areas of performance, theory and composition, music education. Cross-registration with Old Dominion University. Program accredited by NASM.

Enrollment Fall 1997: 175 total; 150 undergraduate, 15 graduate, 10 non-professional degree.

Music Student Profile 40% females, 60% males, 90% minorities.

Music Faculty 24 total undergraduate and graduate (full-time and part-time). 60% of full-time faculty have terminal degrees. Graduate students do not teach undergraduate courses.

Student Life Student groups/activities include Music Educators National Conference, American Choral Directors Association, Intercollegiate Music Association.

Expenses for 1997–98 Application fee: $20. One-time mandatory fee: $35. State resident tuition: $3000 full-time. Nonresident tuition: $6802 full-time. College room and board: $4166. Special program-related fees: $35 for miscellaneous music fees.

Financial Aid Program-specific awards for 1997: 100 band scholarships for band students ($500), 20 Choir Scholarships for choir students ($500), 20 Jazz Ensemble Scholarships for jazz players ($500).

Application Procedures Students admitted directly into the professional program freshman year. Deadline for freshmen and transfers: continuous. Required: high school transcript, college transcript(s) for transfer students, minimum 2.0 high school GPA, audition, SAT I or ACT test scores. Auditions held 4 times on campus.

Contact Dr. B. Dexter Allgood, Head, Department of Music, Norfolk State University, 2401 Corprew Avenue, Norfolk, Virginia 23504; 757-683-8544, fax: 757-683-8213.

▼ NORTH CAROLINA AGRICULTURAL AND TECHNICAL STATE UNIVERSITY

Greensboro, North Carolina

State-supported, coed. Urban campus. Total enrollment: 7,468. Music program established 1950.

Degrees Bachelor of Arts in the area of musical performance. Cross-registration with Greater Greensboro Area Consortium of Programs. Program accredited by NASM.

Enrollment Fall 1997: 45 total; all undergraduate.

Music Faculty 9 total (full-time and part-time). 55% of full-time faculty have terminal degrees. Graduate students do not teach undergraduate courses. Undergraduate student–faculty ratio: 5:1.

Student Life Student groups/activities include Kappa Kappa Psi, Tau Beta Sigma, Phi Mu Alpha Sinfonia of America.

Expenses for 1997–98 Application fee: $35. State resident tuition: $900 full-time. Nonresident tuition: $8028 full-time.

North Carolina Agricultural and Technical State University *(continued)*

Mandatory fees: $722 full-time. Full-time tuition and fees vary according to course load. College room and board: $3850. College room only: $2420. Room and board charges vary according to board plan.

Financial Aid Program-specific awards available.

Application Procedures Students admitted directly into the professional program freshman year. Deadline for freshmen and transfers: continuous. Required: high school transcript, college transcript(s) for transfer students, minimum 2.0 high school GPA, audition, SAT I or ACT test scores (minimum combined SAT I score of 850, minimum combined ACT score of 21). Recommended: 3 letters of recommendation, interview. Auditions held by appointment on campus; recorded music is permissible as a substitute for live auditions if applicant is unable to visit campus and videotaped performances are permissible as a substitute for live auditions if applicant is unable to visit campus.

Web Site http://www.ncat.edu/~music.

Undergraduate Contact Mr. John Smith, Director of Admissions, Admissions Office, North Carolina Agricultural and Technical State University, Webb Hall, Greensboro, North Carolina 27411; 336-334-7946, fax: 336-334-7478, E-mail address: smithjl@ncat.edu.

▼ North Carolina Central University

Durham, North Carolina

State-supported, coed. Urban campus. Total enrollment: 5,664.

Degrees Bachelor of Music in the areas of jazz studies, sacred music; Bachelor of Arts in the area of music education. Majors and concentrations: jazz, piano/organ, sacred music, stringed instruments, voice, wind and percussion instruments.

Enrollment Fall 1997: 61 undergraduate.

Music Student Profile 8% minorities.

Music Faculty 17 total (full-time and part-time). Graduate students do not teach undergraduate courses.

Student Life Student groups/activities include Tau Beta Sigma, Kappa Kappa Psi, Collegiate Music Educators Association.

Expenses for 1997–98 Application fee: $30. State resident tuition: $874 full-time. Nonresident tuition: $8028 full-time. Mandatory fees: $1070 full-time. College room and board: $3384. College room only: $1808.

Application Procedures Students admitted directly into the professional program freshman year. Deadline for freshmen and transfers: continuous. Required: high school transcript, college transcript(s) for transfer students, audition, SAT I or ACT test scores. Recommended: minimum 2.0 high school GPA. Auditions held twice on campus; recorded music is permissible as a substitute for live auditions if a campus visit is impossible.

Undergraduate Contact Dr. Marva Cooper, Chair, Department of Music, North Carolina Central University, 1801 Fayetteville Street, Durham, North Carolina 27707; 919-560-6319, fax: 919-560-3340.

▼ North Carolina School of the Arts

Winston-Salem, North Carolina

State-supported, coed. Urban campus. Total enrollment: 773. Music program established 1965.

Degrees Bachelor of Music in the area of music performance. Majors and concentrations: classical music, composition, guitar, harp, performance, piano/organ, saxophone, stringed instruments, voice, wind and percussion instruments. Graduate degrees offered: Master of Music in the areas of music performance, opera, film music composition, voice performance.

Enrollment Fall 1997: 178 total; 142 undergraduate, 36 graduate.

Music Student Profile 40% females, 60% males, 11% minorities, 5% international.

Music Faculty 43 total undergraduate and graduate (full-time and part-time). Graduate students do not teach undergraduate courses. Undergraduate student–faculty ratio: 9:1.

Student Life Special housing available for music students.

Expenses for 1997–98 Application fee: $35. State resident tuition: $1401 full-time. Nonresident tuition: $9858 full-time. Mandatory fees: $1121 full-time. Full-time tuition and fees vary according to program. College room and board: $3970. College room only: $2060. Special program-related fees: $135 per year for educational and technology fee, $150 for music course fee.

Financial Aid Program-specific awards for 1997: talent scholarships for artistically talented.

Application Procedures Students admitted directly into the professional program freshman year. Deadline for freshmen and transfers: continuous. Required: high school transcript, 2 letters of recommendation, interview, audition, SAT I or ACT test scores, portfolio for composition applicants. Auditions held several times on campus and off campus in various cities in the U.S.; recorded music is permissible as a substitute for live auditions for provisional acceptance and videotaped performances are permissible as a substitute for live auditions for provisional acceptance. Portfolio reviews held several times on campus.

Web Site http://www.ncarts.edu.

Contact Ms. Carol J. Palm, Director of Admissions, North Carolina School of the Arts, 1533 South Main Street, Winston-Salem, North Carolina 27117-2189; 336-770-3291, fax: 336-770-3370, E-mail address: palmc@ncsavx.ncsart.edu.

More About the School

Program Facilities A major performance center for the School of Music is the Stevens Center, a magnificently restored 1920s movie palace seating 1,380 in downtown Winston-Salem. Crawford Hall, a 590-seat auditorium, houses the Sarah Graham Kenan organ (designed specifically for the hall by Charles Fisk), a Dowd harpsichord, a Hamburg Steinway, and a Baldwin concert grand. Chamber and solo recitals are presented in the more intimate Recital Hall, which accommodates 60 people. Reference materials are found in the Semans Library, which contains a growing selection of 2,000 CDs, 24,000 LPs, and 700 videocassettes, as well as more than 100,000 volumes on music and the other arts. The music school also maintains two electronic studios, including a composite analog/MIDI digital studio.

Faculty, Guest Artists, and Alumni The resident faculty is composed of outstanding artist-teachers who actively pursue

North Carolina School of the Arts

professional careers while offering individual attention and personal guidance to students. Their careers have spanned the New York City Opera Orchestra to the Crackow Philharmonic of Poland to the Saugatuck Chamber Music Festival to the recording studios of 20th Century Fox. Throughout the year, distinguished guest artists visit the campus for performances and master classes. They have included Leonard Bernstein, John Cage, Itzhak Perlman, Menahem Pressler, and William Schuman. The standard of training at the School is reflected in the accomplishments of the alumni, who are currently employed by such institutions as the Berlin Philharmonic, Metropolitan Opera, San Francisco Symphony, and Solisti New York. Noted alumni include soloist John Cheek, flutist/conductor Ransom Wilson, and composer Kenneth Frazelle.

Student Performance Opportunities The music program is designed to provide the broadest possible performance opportunities for each student. The Symphony Orchestra, Cantata Singers, Jazz Ensemble, Percussion Ensemble, Contemporary Ensemble, opera productions, and chamber groups in every medium provide ensemble performance opportunities through rehearsals and frequent public performances.

Special Programs Music ensembles and soloists are often involved in performance tours throughout the southeastern United States and beyond. The School of the Arts is the only American school that offers students a chance to perform in a multiweek European tour (International Music Program) each summer.

▼

Since it opened in 1965 as the first state-assisted residential conservatory in the nation, the North Carolina School of the Arts has provided students with solid professional training for careers as performing artists. Today, the school's mission has grown to encompass not only the performing arts, but the moving image and visual arts as well.

At the School of the Arts, students of all arts disciplines live, learn, practice, and perform together on one campus. A musician's roommate may be a dancer or filmmaker. Scene designers and actors and cellists debate philosophical points or work calculus problems in the same classes. Interdisciplinary collaborations, both structured and spontaneous, are part of daily life at the School of the Arts. The inclusion of all the arts makes for a unique vitality and richness of creative expression.

The relationship between students and their teachers, that of apprentice to master, is the heart of the School of the Arts. Students and teachers are engaged in classes, rehearsals, and shoots from morning to late evening six days a week, and weekends are filled with performances and screenings. The resident faculty of 100 artists have had successful careers on Broadway, in Hollywood, as members of the great orchestras and dance companies and theaters of the world. Most continued to perform, direct, choreograph, coach, write, and produce professionally. In the tradition of artists throughout human history, they pass on their knowledge and experience to their students, one-on-one, face-to-face. Their close, sustained work with students is supplemented with residencies by more than 150 guest artists each year.

For aspiring performers, there is no substitute for performing. The 300 performances presented each year by students provide an unparalleled learning experience. Music students participate in jazz ensemble and orchestral performances, operas, solo recitals, and chamber groups in every medium. Dance students perform a repertory of ballet and contemporary works that is unsurpassed in its diversity. Actors are cast in challenging works from the world's repertory of classical and contemporary plays. Theatrical design and production students light the shows, design and build costumes and sets, and manage the productions.

As the School's alumni know, there is no better preparation for careers in the arts than performing in professionally mounted productions, in performance places designed to professional standards. Graduates emerge ready to go on stage because they have been on stage all through their training.

Students are intimately connected to the professional world that awaits them through many channels, including their faculty, guest artists, and touring performances around the country and abroad. Also vital to the emerging artist is the professional network of thousands of successful North Carolina School of the Arts alumni who are putting their training to work on the stages and screens of the world.

School of the Arts alumni have distinguished themselves from the Metropolitan Opera to the Houston Ballet, from the Great Lakes Theater Festival to Merce Cunningham Dance Company, from Broadway to Hollywood. Virtually every orchestra in this country has had a School of the Arts alumnus in its ranks. Some of the finest ballet, theater, and opera companies the world over feature School alumni in the corps, the chorus, in starring roles, and behind the scenes. Alumni continually enrich the lives of the people in the communities where they perform, live, or work as artists in residence.

The School of the Arts is located in Winston-Salem, a medium-sized city in the central Piedmont of scenic North Carolina. The city has a tradition of appreciation for the arts dating back to the eighteenth century, when the area was settled by European members of the Moravian church, many of whom were highly skilled classical musicians, artisans, and craftsmen. The first arts council in America was established in Winston-Salem, and the city relied on its strong support of the arts in its quest to become the home of the School of the Arts.

Today, the North Carolina School of the Arts enrolls more than 1,000 students—from middle school through graduate school—in the Schools of Dance, Design and Production, Drama, Filmmaking, and Music. A high school Visual Arts Program is part of the School of Design and Production. Long considered part of the School's mission, filmmaking

North Carolina School of the Arts (continued)

was added in 1993; this unique program focuses on creative rather than technical aspects of the industry.

At the School of the Arts, arts courses are balanced with academic courses to give students a solid grounding in the humanities and sciences, and to deepen their understanding of the role of the artist in society. The School is part of the highly regarded sixteen-campus University of North Carolina. Both the high school and the college programs are accredited.

(Photo by Lenny Cohen)

▼ NORTHEAST LOUISIANA UNIVERSITY

Monroe, Louisiana

State-supported, coed. Urban campus. Total enrollment: 10,942.

Degrees Bachelor of Music in the areas of performance, pedagogy, music theory/composition, music history/literature, music theater; Bachelor of Music Education. Majors and concentrations: classical music, music, music education, music history and literature, music theater, music theory and composition, piano pedagogy, piano/organ, stringed instruments, voice, wind and percussion instruments. Graduate degrees offered: Master of Music in the areas of performance, music education, music theory/composition, conducting. Program accredited by NASM.

Enrollment Fall 1997: 99 total; 86 undergraduate, 13 graduate.

Music Student Profile 55% females, 45% males, 5% minorities, 10% international.

Music Faculty 26 total undergraduate and graduate (full-time and part-time). 55% of full-time faculty have terminal degrees. Graduate students do not teach undergraduate courses. Undergraduate student–faculty ratio: 4:1.

Student Life Student groups/activities include Music Educators National Conference Student Chapter, music sorority, band fraternity and sorority.

Expenses for 1997–98 Application fee: $15. State resident tuition: $1644 full-time. Nonresident tuition: $4044 full-time. Mandatory fees: $308 full-time. College room only: $1140.

Financial Aid Program-specific awards for 1997: 220 Music Talent Grants for members of major ensembles ($900).

Application Procedures Students admitted directly into the professional program freshman year. Deadline for freshmen and transfers: continuous. Notification date for freshmen and transfers: continuous. Required: high school transcript, college transcript(s) for transfer students, audition, ACT test score only. Recommended: interview. Auditions held throughout the year on campus; recorded music is permissible as a substitute for live auditions when distance is prohibitive or scheduling is difficult and videotaped performances are permissible as a substitute for live auditions when distance is prohibitive or scheduling is difficult.

Contact Dr. Larry W. Edwards, Director, School of Music, Northeast Louisiana University, 700 University Avenue, Monroe, Louisiana 71209-0250; 318-342-1570, fax: 318-342-1369, E-mail address: muedwards@alpha.nlu.edu.

▼ NORTHERN ARIZONA UNIVERSITY

Flagstaff, Arizona

State-supported, coed. Small town campus. Total enrollment: 19,618.

Degrees Bachelor of Music in the area of performance; Bachelor of Music Education. Majors and concentrations: choral music education, instrumental music, instrumental music education, voice. Graduate degrees offered: Master of Music in the areas of performance, music education, music history/musicology, music theory/composition. Program accredited by NASM.

Enrollment Fall 1997: 301 total; 259 undergraduate, 42 graduate.

Music Student Profile 60% females, 40% males, 20% minorities, 5% international.

Music Faculty 47 total undergraduate and graduate (full-time and part-time). 90% of full-time faculty have terminal degrees. Graduate students teach a few undergraduate courses.

Student Life Student groups/activities include music fraternities and sororities, Music Educators National Conference Student Chapter, American Choral Directors Association.

Expenses for 1997–98 Application fee: $40. State resident tuition: $2008 full-time. Nonresident tuition: $7754 full-time. Mandatory fees: $72 full-time. College room and board: $3500. College room only: $1750. Room and board charges vary according to board plan and housing facility. Special program-related fees: $74 per semester for private lessons.

Financial Aid Program-specific awards for 1997: tuition waiver scholarships for program majors and minors ($1300–$5516).

Application Procedures Students admitted directly into the professional program freshman year. Deadline for freshmen and transfers: continuous. Required: high school transcript, college transcript(s) for transfer students, minimum 2.0 high school GPA, audition, SAT I or ACT test scores. Recommended: 3 letters of recommendation, video. Auditions held 3 times and in special circumstances with approval from the department on campus; recorded music is permissible as a substitute for live auditions when distance is prohibitive and videotaped performances are permissible as a substitute for live auditions when distance is prohibitive.

Undergraduate Contact Band and Choral Departments, Northern Arizona University, PO Box 6040, Flagstaff, Arizona 86011-6040; 520-523-3413, fax: 520-523-5111.

Graduate Contact Dr. C. T. Aufdemberge, Graduate Music Studies, Department of Music, Northern Arizona University, PO Box 6040, Flagstaff, Arizona 86011-6040; 520-523-3731, fax: 520-523-5111.

▼ NORTHERN ILLINOIS UNIVERSITY

De Kalb, Illinois

State-supported, coed. Small town campus. Total enrollment: 22,082.

Degrees Bachelor of Music in the areas of performance, music education, composition, jazz studies. Majors and concentrations: composition, jazz, music education, piano/organ, stringed instruments, voice, wind and percussion instruments. Graduate degrees offered: Master of Music in the areas of performance, music education, individualized studies. Program accredited by NASM.

Enrollment Fall 1997: 333 total; 258 undergraduate, 75 graduate.

Music Student Profile 44% females, 56% males, 10% minorities, 8% international.

Music Faculty 60 total undergraduate and graduate (full-time and part-time). 100% of full-time faculty have terminal

degrees. Graduate students do not teach undergraduate courses. Undergraduate student–faculty ratio: 5:1.

Student Life Student groups/activities include professional fraternities and sororities, Music Educators National Conference, International Association of Jazz Educators. Special housing available for music students.

Expenses for 1997–98 State resident tuition: $2952 full-time. Nonresident tuition: $8856 full-time. Mandatory fees: $885 full-time. Full-time tuition and fees vary according to course load. College room and board: $4000. Room and board charges vary according to housing facility. Special program-related fees: $20–$50 for applied fees.

Financial Aid Program-specific awards for 1997: 80 scholarships for program majors ($300–$3400).

Application Procedures Students admitted directly into the professional program freshman year. Deadline for freshmen: August 1; transfers: July 15. Required: high school transcript, college transcript(s) for transfer students, audition, ACT test score only. Auditions held 3 times on campus; recorded music is permissible as a substitute for live auditions by request and videotaped performances are permissible as a substitute for live auditions by request.

Web Site http://www.vpa.niu.edu/music.

Undergraduate Contact Ms. Lynn Slater, Coordinator of Undergraduate Admissions, School of Music, Northern Illinois University, De Kalb, Illinois 60115; 815-753-1546, fax: 815-753-1759, E-mail address: lslater@niu.edu.

Graduate Contact Dr. C. T. Blickhan, Coordinator of Graduate Studies, School of Music, Northern Illinois University, De Kalb, Illinois 60115-2889; 815-753-0394, fax: 815-753-1759, E-mail address: blickhan@niu.edu.

▼ NORTHERN KENTUCKY UNIVERSITY

Highland Heights, Kentucky

State-supported, coed. Suburban campus. Total enrollment: 11,763. Music program established 1969.

Degrees Bachelor of Music in the areas of performance, music education. Majors and concentrations: composition, guitar, harp, music education, music theory, piano, piano pedagogy, stringed instruments, voice, wind and percussion instruments. Cross-registration with Greater Cincinnati Consortium of Colleges and Universities. Program accredited by NASM.

Enrollment Fall 1997: 130 total; all undergraduate.

Music Student Profile 50% females, 50% males, 1% minorities, 1% international.

Music Faculty 34 total (full-time and part-time). 100% of full-time faculty have terminal degrees. Graduate students do not teach undergraduate courses. Undergraduate student–faculty ratio: 12:1.

Student Life Student groups/activities include Sigma Alpha Iota, Phi Mu Alpha, Music Educators National Conference Student Chapter.

Expenses for 1997–98 Application fee: $25. State resident tuition: $2120 full-time. Nonresident tuition: $5720 full-time. Full-time tuition varies according to course load. College room and board: $3439. College room only: $1769. Room and board charges vary according to board plan and housing facility. Special program-related fees: $180 per semester for private music lessons.

Financial Aid Program-specific awards for 1997: 18 University Scholarships for musically talented students ($1500), 6 Private Scholarships for musically talented students ($2200).

Application Procedures Students apply for admission into the professional program by freshman year. Deadline for freshmen and transfers: continuous. Required: high school transcript, college transcript(s) for transfer students, SAT I or ACT test scores, audition (for transfers), music theory test (for transfers), music history test (for transfers). Recommended: 2 letters of recommendation, audition. Auditions held 4 times on campus; recorded music is permissible as a substitute for live auditions and videotaped performances are permissible as a substitute for live auditions if a live audition is impossible.

Web Site http://www.nku.edu/~music.

Undergraduate Contact David Dunevant, Chairman, Department of Music, Northern Kentucky University, Fine Arts Center, Room 253, Highland Heights, Kentucky 41099-1005; 606-572-6399, fax: 606-572-6076, E-mail address: dunevant@nku.edu.

▼ NORTHERN MICHIGAN UNIVERSITY

Marquette, Michigan

State-supported, coed. Small town campus. Total enrollment: 7,787. Music program established 1969.

Degrees Bachelor of Music Education in the areas of choral music education, instrumental music education. Majors and concentrations: music, music education. Program accredited by NASM.

Enrollment Fall 1997: 33 undergraduate.

Music Student Profile 55% females, 45% males, 3% international.

Music Faculty 10 undergraduate (full-time). 90% of full-time faculty have terminal degrees. Graduate students do not teach undergraduate courses. Undergraduate student–faculty ratio: 3:1.

Student Life Student groups/activities include Music Educators National Conference.

Expenses for 1997–98 Application fee: $25. State resident tuition: $2880 full-time. Nonresident tuition: $5160 full-time. Mandatory fees: $106 full-time. College room and board: $4340. College room only: $2102.

Financial Aid Program-specific awards for 1997: 12 scholarships for talented program majors ($800).

Application Procedures Students apply for admission into the professional program by freshman year. Deadline for freshmen and transfers: continuous. Required: high school transcript, college transcript(s) for transfer students, SAT I or ACT test scores (minimum combined SAT I score of 800, minimum combined ACT score of 19), minimum 2.25 high school GPA. Recommended: letter of recommendation, audition. Auditions held as needed for voice and instrumental applicants on campus; recorded music is permissible as a substitute for live auditions if a campus visit is impossible and videotaped performances are permissible as a substitute for live auditions if a campus visit is impossible.

Web Site http://www.nmu.edu/music_dept/!music.htm.

Undergraduate Contact Dr. Donald Grant, Head, Music Department, Northern Michigan University, 1401 Presque Isle Avenue, Marquette, Michigan 49855; 906-227-2563, fax: 906-227-2165.

▼ NORTHERN STATE UNIVERSITY

Aberdeen, South Dakota

State-supported, coed. Small town campus. Total enrollment: 2,646.

Northern State University (continued)

Degrees Bachelor of Music Education in the areas of instrumental music, vocal music. Majors and concentrations: instrumental music, piano/organ, stringed instruments, voice. Program accredited by NASM.

Enrollment Fall 1997: 86 total; 80 undergraduate, 6 non-professional degree.

Music Student Profile 64% females, 36% males, 1% international.

Music Faculty 13 total (full-time and part-time). 54% of full-time faculty have terminal degrees. Graduate students do not teach undergraduate courses. Undergraduate student–faculty ratio: 5:1.

Student Life Student groups/activities include Music Educators National Conference, Sigma Alpha Iota, Phi Mu Alpha Sinfonia.

Expenses for 1997–98 Application fee: $15. State resident tuition: $1620 full-time. Nonresident tuition: $5152 full-time. Mandatory fees: $915 full-time. Full-time tuition and fees vary according to reciprocity agreements. College room and board: $2750. College room only: $1232. Room and board charges vary according to board plan.

Financial Aid Program-specific awards for 1997: 35 music scholarships for incoming freshmen/transfers ($533).

Application Procedures Students admitted directly into the professional program freshman year. Deadline for freshmen and transfers: August 15. Notification date for freshmen and transfers: continuous. Required: high school transcript, college transcript(s) for transfer students, minimum 2.0 high school GPA, audition, ACT test score only. Auditions held 4 times and by appointment on campus and off campus in Sioux Falls, SD; Rapid City, SD; recorded music is permissible as a substitute for live auditions when distance is prohibitive and videotaped performances are permissible as a substitute for live auditions when distance is prohibitive.

Undergraduate Contact Admissions Office, Northern State University, 1200 South Jay Street, Aberdeen, South Dakota 57401-7198; 605-626-2544, fax: 605-626-2587.

▼ NORTH PARK UNIVERSITY

Chicago, Illinois

Independent, coed. Urban campus. Total enrollment: 2,004. Music program established 1944.

Degrees Bachelor of Music in the area of performance; Bachelor of Music Education. Majors and concentrations: brass, piano, stringed instruments, voice, wind instruments. Program accredited by NASM.

Enrollment Fall 1997: 31 total; 14 undergraduate, 17 non-professional degree.

Music Student Profile 67% females, 33% males, 13% minorities, 3% international.

Music Faculty 30 total (full-time and part-time). 50% of full-time faculty have terminal degrees. Graduate students do not teach undergraduate courses. Undergraduate student–faculty ratio: 15:1.

Student Life Student groups/activities include Student Performance Awards Competition, Chicago-area competitions.

Expenses for 1997–98 Application fee: $20. Comprehensive fee: $19,510 includes full-time tuition ($14,690) and college room and board ($4820). College room only: $2680. Full-time tuition varies according to program. Room and board charges vary according to board plan, housing facility, and student level.

Financial Aid Program-specific awards for 1997: 15 music scholarships for freshmen and transfer students ($1000–$4000), 14 Named Music Scholarships for continuing students ($300–$1500).

Application Procedures Students apply for admission into the professional program by sophomore year. Deadline for freshmen and transfers: continuous. Required: essay, high school transcript, college transcript(s) for transfer students, letter of recommendation, interview, audition, SAT I or ACT test scores (minimum combined SAT I score of 800, minimum combined ACT score of 17). Auditions held at least twice and by appointment on campus; recorded music is permissible as a substitute for live auditions if a campus visit is impossible and videotaped performances are permissible as a substitute for live auditions if a campus visit is impossible.

Undergraduate Contact Mr. Joseph Lill, Admissions Coordinator, School of Music, North Park University, 3225 West Foster Avenue, Chicago, Illinois 60625; 773-244-5634, fax: 773-583-0858.

▼ NORTHWESTERN OKLAHOMA STATE UNIVERSITY

Alva, Oklahoma

State-supported, coed. Small town campus. Total enrollment: 1,871.

Degrees Bachelor of Music in the area of performance; Bachelor of Music Education in the areas of vocal music education, instrumental music education. Majors and concentrations: music education, piano/organ, voice, wind and percussion instruments.

Enrollment Fall 1997: 25 undergraduate.

Music Student Profile 60% females, 40% males, 5% minorities.

Music Faculty 6 total (full-time and part-time). 100% of full-time faculty have terminal degrees. Graduate students do not teach undergraduate courses.

Expenses for 1997–98 State resident tuition: $1772 full-time. Nonresident tuition: $4205 full-time. Mandatory fees: $30 full-time. Full-time tuition and fees vary according to course load, location, and student level. College room and board: $2316. Room and board charges vary according to board plan. Special program-related fees: $8 per credit hour for practice room fees, $18 per credit hour for private lessons.

Financial Aid Program-specific awards for 1997: Foundation Scholarships for music majors ($200–$1000), tuition waivers for ensemble participants ($200–$1000).

Application Procedures Students apply for admission into the professional program by sophomore year. Deadline for freshmen and transfers: continuous. Required: high school transcript, college transcript(s) for transfer students, ACT test score only (minimum combined ACT score of 19). Recommended: letter of recommendation, interview, audition. Auditions held twice in February and April and by appointment on campus; recorded music is permissible as a substitute for live auditions when distance is prohibitive and videotaped performances are permissible as a substitute for live auditions when distance is prohibitive.

Undergraduate Contact Dr. Mike Knedler, Chair, Music Department, Northwestern Oklahoma State University, 709 Oklahoma Boulevard, Alva, Oklahoma 73717; 580-327-8590, fax: 580-327-1881, E-mail address: jmknedle@ranger2.nwalva.edu.

▼ NORTHWESTERN STATE UNIVERSITY OF LOUISIANA

Natchitoches, Louisiana

State-supported, coed. Small town campus. Total enrollment: 8,873.

Degrees Bachelor of Music in the area of performance; Bachelor of Music Education in the areas of instrumental music education, vocal music education, piano music education. Majors and concentrations: music, music education, piano/organ, voice, wind and percussion instruments. Graduate degrees offered: Master of Music in the areas of instrumental music, vocal music, piano. Cross-registration with Louisiana State University in Shreveport, Louisiana State University and Agricultural and Mechanical College. Program accredited by NASM.

Enrollment Fall 1997: 151 undergraduate, 15 graduate.

Music Student Profile 40% females, 60% males, 10% minorities, 1% international.

Music Faculty 27 total undergraduate and graduate (full-time and part-time). 80% of full-time faculty have terminal degrees. Graduate students teach a few undergraduate courses.

Student Life Student groups/activities include professional fraternities and sororities, Music Educators National Conference.

Expenses for 1997–98 Application fee: $15. State resident tuition: $2000 full-time. Nonresident tuition: $5336 full-time. Mandatory fees: $177 full-time. College room and board: $2416. College room only: $1180. Room and board charges vary according to board plan and housing facility.

Financial Aid Program-specific awards for 1997: 200–250 Band Awards for incoming freshmen ($800–$1200), 75–100 music awards for incoming freshmen ($800–$1200).

Application Procedures Students admitted directly into the professional program freshman year. Deadline for freshmen and transfers: August 27. Notification date for freshmen: August 27. Required: high school transcript, college transcript(s) for transfer students, minimum 2.0 high school GPA, 3 letters of recommendation, audition, SAT I or ACT test scores. Recommended: interview, video, portfolio. Auditions held by appointment on campus; recorded music is permissible as a substitute for live auditions with approval from the department and videotaped performances are permissible as a substitute for live auditions with approval from the department. Portfolio reviews held by appointment on campus.

Web Site http://www.nsula.edu/departments/capa/.

Undergraduate Contact Mr. Chris Maggio, Director, Office of Admissions, Northwestern State University of Louisiana, College Avenue, Natchitoches, Louisiana 71497; 318-357-4503, fax: 318-357-5906, E-mail address: maggio@alpha.nsula.edu.

Graduate Contact Dr. Tom Hanson, Dean, Graduate Studies, Northwestern State University of Louisiana, College Avenue, Natchitoches, Louisiana 71497; 318-357-5851, fax: 318-357-5019, E-mail address: hanson@alpha.nsula.edu.

▼ NORTHWESTERN UNIVERSITY

Evanston, Illinois

Independent, coed. Suburban campus. Total enrollment: 15,487. Music program established 1895.

Degrees Bachelor of Music in the areas of church music, composition, music history, music education, music technology, percussion, piano, strings, music theory, voice, winds, organ; Bachelor of Arts/Bachelor of Music in the area of music and liberal arts; Bachelor of Music/Bachelor of Science in the area of music and engineering. Majors and concentrations: classical music, composition, jazz studies, music, music education, music history and literature, music technology, music theory, opera, piano/organ, stringed instruments, voice, wind and percussion instruments. Graduate degrees offered: Master of Music in the areas of church music, composition, conducting, musicology, jazz pedagogy, music education, music technology, percussion, piano, strings, music theory, voice, winds, organ, piano pedagogy, string pedagogy. Doctor of Music in the areas of composition, conducting, percussion, piano, strings, voice, winds, organ; Doctor of Philosophy in the areas of music education, musicology, music theory, music technology. Program accredited by NASM.

Enrollment Fall 1997: 586 total; 379 undergraduate, 207 graduate.

Music Student Profile 53% females, 47% males, 22% minorities, 8% international.

Music Faculty 110 total undergraduate and graduate (full-time and part-time). 98% of full-time faculty have terminal degrees. Graduate students teach a few undergraduate courses. Undergraduate student–faculty ratio: 3:1.

Student Life Student groups/activities include Phi Mu Alpha Sinfonia, Sigma Alpha Iota, Pi Kappa Lambda. Special housing available for music students.

Expenses for 1998–99 Application fee: $55. Comprehensive fee: $29,133 includes full-time tuition ($22,392), mandatory fees ($66), and college room and board ($6675). Room and board charges vary according to board plan.

Application Procedures Students admitted directly into the professional program freshman year. Deadline for freshmen: January 1; transfers: June 1. Notification date for freshmen: April 15; transfers: July 1. Required: essay, high school transcript, college transcript(s) for transfer students, minimum 3.0 high school GPA, letter of recommendation, audition, SAT I or ACT test scores, portfolio for composition, music education, music theory, music history, music technology. Recommended: interview, SAT II, 1 additional letter of recommendation from music teacher. Auditions held 26 times on campus and off campus in Kansas City, MO; Denver, CO; Boston, MA; Seattle, WA; Minneapolis, MN; Orlando, FL; Atlanta, GA; Philadelphia, PA; New York, NY; Washington, DC; Houston, TX; Albuquerque, NM; Interlochen, MI; Cleveland, OH; Portland, OR; San Francisco, CA; Los Angeles, CA; Dallas, TX; Louisville, KY; recorded music is permissible as a substitute for live auditions if a live audition is impossible and videotaped performances are permissible as a substitute for live auditions if a live audition is impossible.

Web Site http://nuinfo.nwu.edu/musicschool/.

Contact Ms. Heather Landes, Director of Music Admissions and Financial Aid, School of Music, Northwestern University, 711 Elgin Road, Evanston, Illinois 60208-1200; 847-491-3141, fax: 847-491-5260, E-mail address: hlandes@nwu.edu.

More About the University

Established in 1895, the School of Music ranks among the nation's most prestigious music schools, providing an environment in which musicians can dedicate themselves to their art. Committed to educating students toward highly proficient performance coupled with comprehensive musicianship, the School has developed distinctive programs that meet the artistic and professional needs of those seeking

Northwestern University (continued)

careers in classical, jazz, and music theater performance, education, composition, conducting, music theory, music history, technology, criticism, arts administration, and other fields requiring specialized knowledge of music. These programs are responsive to new directions, recognizing that a thriving curriculum should preserve the riches of tradition while encouraging the exploration and advancement of practices to produce the music of the future.

School of Music faculty members endeavor to expand musical knowledge through research and scholarship; to prepare students meticulously as performers, composers, teachers, scholars, and audience members; and to enrich their communities through their own artistry. Undergraduate programs give students a comprehensive musical grounding through an education centered on musical production, informed by scholarly study of theory and history, and complemented by broad study in the humanities. Graduate programs emphasize scholarly performance and include concentrated work and research in specific fields of interest, producing informed performers, independent scholars, and inspired teachers. Besides providing instruction in voice and all principal instruments and academic areas of music, the School supports a variety of large and small ensembles and staged musical productions that give students high-quality experience in all areas of musical expression. Being part of an eminent research university, the School of Music offers students the unique advantage of pursuing academic study outside music through a variety of courses with distinguished faculty in all disciplines.

Several celebrated artists visit the School each year. Guests have included Grace Bumbry, Pierre Boulez, John Cage, Renee Fleming, James Galway, Erich Leinsdorf, Witold Lutoslowski, Wynton Marsalis, Bobby McFerrin, Sherrill Milnes, James Moody, Dmitri Shostakovich, Sir Georg Solti, and Pinchas Zukerman. An annual performing arts series presents artists such as these in concerts, recitals, and master classes. The School also is uniquely situated to allow excellent opportunities for professional associations in the Chicago metropolitan area.

The School of Music occupies six buildings on Northwestern's lakefront campus: the Music Administration Building, Regenstein Hall, Pick-Staiger Concert Hall, the Practice Hall, Lutkin Hall, and the Deering Music Library. These facilities provide classrooms, offices, computer labs, an electronic music studio, a computer music studio, numerous practice rooms, and three recital halls. Pick-Staiger Concert Hall, an acoustically superb 1,000-seat concert hall, offers the campus and surrounding community top-level student and professional performances year-round. Deering Music Library, recognized internationally for its contemporary music collection, is also a leader in library automation. Housed within the Cambridge-inspired structure are a multimedia listening center; holdings of 142,000 books, musical scores, journals, and microforms, as well as 53,000 discs and tapes; a manuscript collection documenting contemporary notation compiled by John Cage for use in his book, *Notations*; holograph scores, sketches, and letters of musicians; the Fritz Reiner Library; and other rare printed resources.

▼ Nyack College

Nyack, New York

Independent, coed. Suburban campus. Total enrollment: 1,433. Music program established 1947.

Degrees Bachelor of Music in the areas of performance, music education, composition; Bachelor of Sacred Music. Majors and concentrations: classical music, composition, music, music education, piano/organ, sacred music, stringed instruments, voice, wind and percussion instruments. Cross-registration with Sarah Lawrence College, Rockland Community College. Program accredited by NASM.
Enrollment Fall 1997: 70 total; all undergraduate.
Music Student Profile 60% females, 40% males, 40% minorities, 16% international.
Music Faculty 25 total (full-time and part-time). 75% of full-time faculty have terminal degrees. Graduate students do not teach undergraduate courses.
Student Life Student groups/activities include Music Educators National Conference, American Guild of Organists, American Choral Directors Association.
Expenses for 1997–98 Application fee: $15. Comprehensive fee: $15,960 includes full-time tuition ($10,400), mandatory fees ($700), and college room and board ($4860). Full-time tuition and fees vary according to location. Room and board charges vary according to housing facility. Special program-related fees: $195 per credit for private lessons.
Financial Aid Program-specific awards for 1997: 6 Music Achievement Grants for talented performers ($3000).
Application Procedures Students admitted directly into the professional program freshman year. Deadline for freshmen and transfers: continuous. Notification date for freshmen: continuous. Required: essay, high school transcript, college transcript(s) for transfer students, 3 letters of recommendation, interview, audition, SAT I or ACT test scores, portfolio for composition majors. Recommended: minimum 2.0 high school GPA. Auditions held 4 times and by appointment on campus; recorded music is permissible as a substitute for live auditions when distance is prohibitive (beyond a 200-mile radius) and videotaped performances are permissible as a substitute for live auditions when distance is prohibitive (beyond a 200-mile radius). Portfolio reviews held continuously on campus.
Undergraduate Contact Mr. Miguel Sanchez, Head, Admissions Office, Nyack College, 1 South Boulevard, Nyack, New York 10960; 800-366-9225.

▼ Oakland City University

Oakland City, Indiana

Independent-General Baptist, coed. Rural campus.
Degrees Bachelor of Music Education in the area of choral/general music education; Bachelor of Arts in the areas of church music, music performance. Majors and concentrations: church music, guitar, music, music education, music performance, piano/organ, sacred music, voice.
Enrollment Fall 1997: 32 total; 26 undergraduate, 6 non-professional degree.
Music Student Profile 55% females, 45% males, 5% minorities.
Music Faculty 4 total (full-time and part-time). 50% of full-time faculty have terminal degrees. Graduate students do not teach undergraduate courses. Undergraduate student–faculty ratio 6:1.
Student Life Student groups/activities include Music Educators National Conference, Music Club.
Financial Aid Program-specific awards for 1997: 1 Voice Scholarship for vocalists ($300), 1 Instrumental Scholarship for piano, organ, guitar, or flute players ($300), 6 tuition

scholarships for program majors and minors ($1700–$5100), 1 Piano Accompanying Scholarship for pianists ($6800).

Application Procedures Students admitted directly into the professional program freshman year. Deadline for freshmen and transfers: continuous. Notification date for freshmen and transfers: continuous. Required: high school transcript, college transcript(s) for transfer students, SAT I or ACT test scores, audition for scholarship consideration. Recommended: minimum 2.0 high school GPA, 3 letters of recommendation, interview, video. Auditions held by appointment on campus; recorded music is permissible as a substitute for live auditions when distance is prohibitive and videotaped performances are permissible as a substitute for live auditions when distance is prohibitive.

Undergraduate Contact Dr. Jean Cox, Associate Professor, Department of Music, Oakland City University, Lucretia Street, Oakland City, Indiana 47660; 812-749-1427.

▼ OAKLAND UNIVERSITY

Rochester, Michigan

State-supported, coed. Suburban campus. Total enrollment: 14,379. Music program established 1972.

Degrees Bachelor of Music in the areas of music education, sacred music, voice performance, piano performance, composition. Majors and concentrations: composition, music education, piano, sacred music, voice. Graduate degrees offered: Master of Music in the areas of music education, conducting, performance, composition, pedagogy.

Enrollment Fall 1997: 200 undergraduate, 29 graduate.

Music Student Profile 52% females, 48% males, 6% minorities, 1% international.

Music Faculty 50 total undergraduate and graduate (full-time and part-time). 87% of full-time faculty have terminal degrees. Graduate students do not teach undergraduate courses. Undergraduate student–faculty ratio: 16:1.

Student Life Student groups/activities include Music Educators National Conference.

Expenses for 1997–98 Application fee: $25. State resident tuition: $3472 full-time. Nonresident tuition: $10,199 full-time. Mandatory fees: $262 full-time. Full-time tuition and fees vary according to student level. College room and board: $4250. Special program-related fees: $13–$85 per credit for applied music lessons or classes.

Financial Aid Program-specific awards for 1997: music scholarships for talented students ($750–$2000).

Application Procedures Students apply for admission into the professional program by sophomore year. Deadline for freshmen and transfers: July 15. Required: high school transcript, SAT I or ACT test scores, minimum 2.5 high school GPA, audition for scholarship consideration. Auditions held once and by appointment on campus; recorded music is permissible as a substitute for live auditions if a campus visit is impossible.

Undergraduate Contact Dr. Carol Halsted, Chairperson, Department of Music, Theatre, and Dance, Oakland University, 315 Varner, Rochester, Michigan 48309; 248-370-2030, fax: 248-370-2041, E-mail address: halsted@oakland.edu.

Graduate Contact Ms. Claire Ramel, Director, Office of Graduate Studies, Oakland University, 420 O'Dowd Hall, Rochester, Michigan 48309; 248-370-3167, fax: 248-370-4114, E-mail address: ramel@oakland.edu.

▼ OBERLIN COLLEGE

Oberlin, Ohio

Independent, coed. Small town campus. Total enrollment: 2,904. Music program established 1865.

Degrees Bachelor of Music in the areas of performance, music education, composition, music history, electronic and computer music, jazz studies, music theory, accompanying. Majors and concentrations: accompanying, brass, classical music, composition, electronic music, historical performance, jazz, music education, music theory, musicology, piano/organ, stringed instruments, voice, wind and percussion instruments. Graduate degrees offered: Master of Music in the areas of historical performance, opera theater, conducting; Master of Music Education. Program accredited by NASM.

Enrollment Fall 1997: 592 total; 575 undergraduate, 5 graduate, 12 non-professional degree.

Music Student Profile 52% females, 48% males, 16% minorities, 13% international.

Music Faculty 82 total undergraduate and graduate (full-time and part-time). 90% of full-time faculty have terminal degrees. Graduate students do not teach undergraduate courses. Undergraduate student–faculty ratio: 8:1.

Expenses for 1997–98 Application fee: $45. Comprehensive fee: $28,796 includes full-time tuition ($22,282), mandatory fees ($156), and college room and board ($6358). College room only: $3166. Room and board charges vary according to housing facility.

Financial Aid Program-specific awards for 1997: 220 Oberlin College Scholarships for those demonstrating need ($2000–$24,000), 120 Oberlin Conservatory Dean's Scholarships for those demonstrating talent and academic achievement ($4000–$24,000), 10 Oberlin College Prize Funds for those with academic merit ($50–$4000), 15 Oberlin Conservatory/Aspen-John H. Stern Scholarships for enrolled students ($1500), 220 Work Study Awards for program majors ($500–$1500).

Application Procedures Students admitted directly into the professional program freshman year. Deadline for freshmen and transfers: February 15. Notification date for freshmen and transfers: April 1. Required: essay, high school transcript, college transcript(s) for transfer students, minimum 2.0 high school GPA, 2 letters of recommendation, audition, SAT I or ACT test scores, transfer release form (for transfer applicants coming from a NASM school). Recommended: minimum 3.0 high school GPA, interview, video. Auditions held 28 times on campus and off campus in Atlanta, GA; Boston, MA; Chicago, IL; Denver, CO; Houston, TX; Interlochen, MI; Los Angeles, CA; Miami, FL; Minneapolis, MN; New York, NY; Portland, OR; San Diego, CA; San Francisco, CA; Seattle, WA; Washington, DC; Hong Kong; Seoul, South Korea; Singapore; Taipei, Taiwan; Tokyo, Japan; recorded music is permissible as a substitute for live auditions if of good quality and videotaped performances are permissible as a substitute for live auditions if of good quality.

Web Site http://www.oberlin.edu/.

Contact Mr. Michael Manderen, Director of Conservatory Admissions, Conservatory of Music, Oberlin College, 77 West College Street, Oberlin, Ohio 44074; 440-775-8413, fax: 440-775-6972, E-mail address: conservatory.admissions@oberlin.edu.

Oberlin College (continued)

More About the College

Facilities Within the Conservatory, which is housed in a modern complex designed by Minoru Yamasaki, are ensemble rehearsal rooms, two excellent concert halls, and 153 individual practice rooms. The Conservatory houses the largest collection of Steinway pianos in the world, and the campus is also home to twenty-five organs. Other features include numerous instrument collections, seven acoustically isolated and optimized electronic music studios, and a library that rivals those in the nation's largest university music schools.

Special Programs The Conservatory of Music and the College of Arts and Sciences share the same campus. As a result, Conservatory students can take courses in both the College and the Conservatory in the same semester and can simultaneously pursue majors in both divisions, completing majors leading to both the B.Mus. and the B.A. degrees after five years. Twenty-five to 30 percent of the Conservatory's students are in the Double Degree Program. Additionally, the Conservatory offers four dual-degree programs, open only to Oberlin's own undergraduates, which combine bachelor's degree study in performance or music education with graduate study leading to the master's degree in conducting, opera theater, music education, or music teaching.

The Oberlin Conservatory is one of the few major music schools in the country devoted primarily to the education of undergraduate musicians. As a division of Oberlin College, the Conservatory is also recognized for being paired with a preeminent college of the liberal arts and sciences. These factors allow the conservatory to offer its students the essential components of excellent musical training: an accomplished faculty, outstanding facilities, an extensive curriculum drawing on both divisions of Oberlin College, and an active cultural life centered on campus and drawing on Cleveland as well.

"You're at Oberlin? What do you play?" Every Oberlinian has heard this question even though the Conservatory of Music is but one fourth the size of its partner, the College of Arts and Sciences. Yet it is natural that the name Oberlin should evoke thoughts of music. Built up by an amateur cellist (Charles Grandison Finney) and funded mainly by a former piano student (Charles Martin Hall), Oberlin College created America's first professorship in music in 1835. Oberlin's Conservatory of Music, established in 1865, is the country's first continuously operating conservatory. Even before the Civil War, a visitor, Thomas Hastings, pronounced the Oberlin choir "the finest in the land." A century later Igor Stravinsky was similarly effusive over the Conservatory's young instrumentalists.

Oberlin has been the source of much innovation in American musical education. It established the country's first full-time chair in music history (1892), offered the country's first four-year degree program in public school music (1921), introduced to the United States the renowned Suzuki method of string pedagogy (1958), pioneered a program in electronic music (1969), and created the American-Soviet Youth Orchestra, composed of 100 young musicians from the United States and the former U.S.S.R., the first arts exchange produced jointly by the two countries (1988).

Conservatory alumni include well-known composers, conductors, performers, and teachers. Some, like David Zinman, conductor of the Baltimore Orchestra, have gained public renown. Others, like jazz pioneer Will Marion Cook—whom Duke Ellington called "my conservatory"—are revered mainly by specialists. Today's Oberlin graduates are to be found in virtually every major American orchestra as well as in foreign orchestras from Berlin to Hong Kong. Its singers and pianists are no less ubiquitous, as are Oberlinians in the many new allied fields of music.

The Oberlin Conservatory of Music has taken great pains to both educate and train its students. More than ever, technical proficiency is essential to success in music; however, the day when a pianist could simply perfect a limited repertoire of classics in order to launch a career is past. Increasingly, musicians will have to master worlds of sound that were scarcely imaginable when they were students. Only the most well-educated minds will attain such flexibility. Oberlin is committed to providing its students a balanced combination of professional training and deep education.

▼ OHIO NORTHERN UNIVERSITY

Ada, Ohio

Independent-United Methodist, coed. Small town campus. Total enrollment: 2,927. Music program established 1871.

Degrees Bachelor of Music in the areas of performance, composition, music education. Program accredited by NASM, NCATE.

Enrollment Fall 1997: 65 total; all undergraduate.

Music Student Profile 67% females, 33% males.

Music Faculty 22 total (full-time and part-time). 57% of full-time faculty have terminal degrees. Graduate students do not teach undergraduate courses. Undergraduate student–faculty ratio: 3:1.

Student Life Student groups/activities include Ohio Music Educators Association, National Association of Teachers of Singing, National Federation of Music Clubs.

Expenses for 1998–99 Application fee: $30. Comprehensive fee: $24,690 includes full-time tuition ($19,815) and college room and board ($4875). College room only: $2130. Full-time tuition varies according to program. Room and board charges vary according to board plan. Special program-related fees: $50 per quarter for private lessons.

Financial Aid Program-specific awards for 1997: 8 Snyder Scholarships for top musicians ($7000–$10,000), 30 Dean's Talent Awards for top musicians ($3000–$3500).

Application Procedures Students admitted directly into the professional program freshman year. Deadline for freshmen and transfers: continuous. Required: high school transcript, college transcript(s) for transfer students, minimum 2.0 high school GPA, audition, SAT I or ACT test scores. Auditions held 4 times on campus; recorded music is permissible as a substitute for live auditions for out-of-state applicants and videotaped performances are permissible as a substitute for live auditions for out-of-state applicants.

Undergraduate Contact Dr. Edwin L. Williams, Chairman, Music Department, Ohio Northern University, 525 South Main Street, Ada, Ohio 45810; 419-772-2151, fax: 419-772-2488, E-mail address: e-williams@onu.edu.

▼ THE OHIO STATE UNIVERSITY

Columbus, Ohio

State-supported, coed. Urban campus. Total enrollment: 48,278. Music program established 1921.

Degrees Bachelor of Music in the areas of performance, music theory, composition, jazz studies, music history; Bachelor of Music Education. Majors and concentrations: composition, jazz, music, music education, music history, music theory, piano, stringed instruments, voice, wind and percussion instruments. Graduate degrees offered: Master of Music in the areas of composition, conducting, performance; Master of Arts in the areas of music education, musicology, music theory, pedagogy. Doctor of Musical Arts in the areas of performance, composition, conducting; Doctor of Philosophy in the areas of music education, musicology, music theory. Cross-registration with Capital University, Columbus State Community College, Ohio Dominican College, Otterbein College. Program accredited by NASM.

Enrollment Fall 1997: 530 total; 350 undergraduate, 180 graduate.

Music Student Profile 55% females, 45% males, 10% minorities, 5% international.

Music Faculty 65 total undergraduate and graduate (full-time and part-time). Graduate students teach about a quarter undergraduate courses. Undergraduate student–faculty ratio: 6:1.

Student Life Student groups/activities include Ohio Collegiate Music Education Association, Sigma Alpha Iota, Phi Mu Alpha Sinfonia.

Expenses for 1997–98 Application fee: $30. State resident tuition: $3660 full-time. Nonresident tuition: $10,869 full-time. College room and board: $5094. Room and board charges vary according to board plan and housing facility.

Financial Aid Program-specific awards for 1997: 30 Music Achievement Scholarships for program majors ($1500).

Application Procedures Students admitted directly into the professional program freshman year. Deadline for freshmen and transfers: continuous. Required: high school transcript, college transcript(s) for transfer students, audition. Recommended: essay, SAT I or ACT test scores. Auditions held 9 days for group auditions and by appointment on campus; recorded music is permissible as a substitute for live auditions for out-of-state and international applicants and videotaped performances are permissible as a substitute for live auditions for out-of-state and international applicants.

Web Site http://www.arts.ohio-state.edu/Music/.

Undergraduate Contact Dr. Judith K. Delzell, Assistant Director, School of Music, The Ohio State University, 1866 College Road, Columbus, Ohio 43210-1170; 614-292-2870, fax: 614-292-1102, E-mail address: delzell.1@osu.edu.

Graduate Contact Dr. Patricia Flowers, Chair, Graduate Studies, School of Music, The Ohio State University, 1866 College Road, Columbus, Ohio 43210-1170; 614-292-6389, fax: 614-292-1102, E-mail address: flowers.1@osu.edu.

▼ OHIO UNIVERSITY

Athens, Ohio

State-supported, coed. Small town campus. Total enrollment: 19,564.

Degrees Bachelor of Music in the areas of performance, composition, theory, history, education, therapy. Majors and concentrations: classical music, music, music education, music history and literature, music theory and composition, music therapy, piano/organ, stringed instruments, voice, wind and percussion instruments. Graduate degrees offered: Master of Music in the areas of performance, composition,

theory, history, education, therapy, conducting, and pedagogy. Program accredited by NASM.

Enrollment Fall 1997: 252 total; 200 undergraduate, 52 graduate.

Music Student Profile 46% females, 54% males, 4% minorities, 3% international.

Music Faculty 34 total undergraduate and graduate (full-time and part-time). 100% of full-time faculty have terminal degrees. Graduate students do not teach undergraduate courses.

Student Life Student groups/activities include Music Educators National Conference Student Chapter, American Association of Music Therapy Student Chapter, Honorary Music Fraternities.

Expenses for 1997–98 Application fee: $30. State resident tuition: $4275 full-time. Nonresident tuition: $8994 full-time. College room and board: $4698. College room only: $2310. Room and board charges vary according to board plan. Special program-related fees: $12 per credit hour for applied music lesson fee.

Financial Aid Program-specific awards for 1997: 15–20 Talent Scholarships for artistically talented ($1000–$3600).

Application Procedures Students admitted directly into the professional program freshman year. Deadline for freshmen and transfers: February 1. Notification date for freshmen and transfers: March 15. Required: high school transcript, college transcript(s) for transfer students, minimum 2.0 high school GPA, letter of recommendation, audition, portfolio for composition majors, interview for music education and music therapy majors. Recommended: minimum 3.0 high school GPA, interview, SAT I or ACT test scores. Auditions held 4-6 times on campus; videotaped performances are permissible as a substitute for live auditions when distance is prohibitive. Portfolio reviews held once on campus.

Web Site http://www.cats.ohiou.edu/~musdept/.

Undergraduate Contact Dr. Harold Robison, Associate Director, School of Music, Ohio University, Music Building, Athens, Ohio 45701-2979; 740-593-4244, fax: 740-593-1429, E-mail address: hrobison1@ohiou.edu.

Graduate Contact Mr. Roger L. Stephens, Director, School of Music, Ohio University, Music Building, Athens, Ohio 45701-2979; 740-593-4244, fax: 740-593-1429, E-mail address: rstephens1@ohiou.edu.

▼ OHIO WESLEYAN UNIVERSITY

Delaware, Ohio

Independent-United Methodist, coed. Small town campus. Total enrollment: 1,893. Music program established 1877.

Degrees Bachelor of Music in the areas of performance, music education. Majors and concentrations: music, music education, piano/organ, stringed instruments, voice, wind and percussion instruments. Program accredited by NASM.

Enrollment Fall 1997: 42 total; all undergraduate.

Music Student Profile 49% females, 51% males, 1% minorities.

Music Faculty 14 total (full-time and part-time). 100% of full-time faculty have terminal degrees. Graduate students do not teach undergraduate courses. Undergraduate student–faculty ratio: 6:1.

Student Life Student groups/activities include Mu Phi Epsilon Student Chapter, Music Educators National Conference Student Chapter.

Expenses for 1998–99 Application fee: $35. Comprehensive fee: $26,410 includes full-time tuition ($20,040) and college

Ohio Wesleyan University (*continued*)

room and board ($6370). College room only: $3230. Room and board charges vary according to board plan and location.

Financial Aid Program-specific awards for 1997: 1 Ruth Wilson Music Scholarship for program majors ($2000–$15,000), 1 Edward D. and Laura Rich Cleary Music Education Memorial Scholarship for music education majors ($1000), 1 Edith Mahon Davis Music Education Scholarship for music education majors ($500), 10 Ohio Wesleyan University Merit Scholarships for program majors ($5000–$19,000), 1–2 Edith M. Keller Scholarship in Music Educations for music education majors ($2500), 1 Col. George Howard Instrumental Music Scholarship for instrumental majors ($1500).

Application Procedures Students admitted directly into the professional program freshman year. Deadline for freshmen and transfers: March 1. Required: essay, high school transcript, college transcript(s) for transfer students, letter of recommendation, audition, SAT I or ACT test scores. Recommended: interview, video. Auditions held 4 scheduled times and by appointment on campus; recorded music is permissible as a substitute for live auditions when distance is prohibitive and videotaped performances are permissible as a substitute for live auditions when distance is prohibitive.

Web Site http://www.owu.edu/~musiweb.

Undergraduate Contact Dean of Admission, Ohio Wesleyan University, Slocum Hall, Delaware, Ohio 43015; 740-368-3020, fax: 740-368-3314.

▼ OKLAHOMA BAPTIST UNIVERSITY

Shawnee, Oklahoma

Independent-Southern Baptist, coed. Small town campus. Total enrollment: 2,211. Music program established 1917.

Degrees Bachelor of Music in the areas of voice/keyboard, music performance, church music, theory/composition; Bachelor of Music Education in the areas of vocal music education, instrumental music education. Majors and concentrations: music education, piano/organ, sacred music, stringed instruments, voice, wind and percussion instruments. Cross-registration with St. Gregory's University. Program accredited by NASM.

Enrollment Fall 1997: 137 total; all undergraduate.

Music Student Profile 55% females, 45% males, 15% minorities, 3% international.

Music Faculty 32 total (full-time and part-time). 59% of full-time faculty have terminal degrees. Graduate students do not teach undergraduate courses. Undergraduate student–faculty ratio: 9:1.

Student Life Student groups/activities include Music Educators National Conference, Sigma Alpha Iota, Phi Mu Alpha Sinfonia.

Expenses for 1998–99 Application fee: $25. Comprehensive fee: $11,586 includes full-time tuition ($7660), mandatory fees ($676), and college room and board ($3250). College room only: $1480. Full-time tuition and fees vary according to course load. Room and board charges vary according to board plan and housing facility. Special program-related fees: $900 per course for applied music fees.

Financial Aid Program-specific awards for 1997: 83 Talentships for program majors ($500–$4000).

Application Procedures Students admitted directly into the professional program freshman year. Deadline for freshmen

and transfers: continuous. Required: high school transcript, college transcript(s) for transfer students, minimum 2.0 high school GPA, audition, SAT I or ACT test scores. Auditions held 4 times on campus; recorded music is permissible as a substitute for live auditions when distance is prohibitive and videotaped performances are permissible as a substitute for live auditions when distance is prohibitive.

Web Site http://www.okbu.edu.

Undergraduate Contact Mr. Michael Cappo, Dean of Admissions, Oklahoma Baptist University, Box 61174, 500 West University, Shawnee, Oklahoma 74801; 800-654-3285, fax: 405-878-2046, E-mail address: michael_cappo@mail.okbu.edu.

▼ OKLAHOMA CHRISTIAN UNIVERSITY OF SCIENCE AND ARTS

Oklahoma City, Oklahoma

Independent, coed. Suburban campus. Total enrollment: 1,904. Music program established 1972.

Degrees Bachelor of Music Education in the areas of vocal music education, instrumental music education. Cross-registration with University of Central Oklahoma. Program accredited by NASM.

Enrollment Fall 1997: 37 total; 25 undergraduate, 12 non-professional degree.

Music Student Profile 57% females, 43% males, 5% minorities.

Music Faculty 19 total (full-time and part-time). 25% of full-time faculty have terminal degrees. Graduate students do not teach undergraduate courses. Undergraduate student–faculty ratio: 10:1.

Student Life Student groups/activities include Collegiate Music Educators National Conference.

Expenses for 1997–98 Application fee: $25. Comprehensive fee: $12,118 includes full-time tuition ($7600), mandatory fees ($678), and college room and board ($3840). Special program-related fees: $200 per credit hour for private instruction, $50 per semester for ensemble tour expenses.

Financial Aid Program-specific awards for 1997: Distinguished Performer Awards for program majors and non-majors ($3000–$6300), music performance scholarships for vocalists/instrumentalists and non-majors ($1000).

Application Procedures Students apply for admission into the professional program by sophomore year. Deadline for freshmen and transfers: continuous. Required: high school transcript, college transcript(s) for transfer students, SAT I or ACT test scores, placement exam. Recommended: interview, audition. Auditions held twice and by appointment on campus; videotaped performances are permissible as a substitute for live auditions if a campus visit is impossible.

Undergraduate Contact Mr. Kyle Wray, Admissions Coordinator, Oklahoma Christian University of Science and Arts, Box 11000, Oklahoma City, Oklahoma 73136-1100; 800-577-5010, fax: 405-425-5208.

Margaret E. Petree School of Music and Performing Arts

▼ OKLAHOMA CITY UNIVERSITY

Oklahoma City, Oklahoma

Independent-United Methodist, coed. Urban campus. Total enrollment: 4,323.

Degrees Bachelor of Music in the areas of performance, musical theater, composition, piano pedagogy; Bachelor of Music Education in the areas of vocal music education, instrumental music education. Majors and concentrations: composition, music, music education, music theater, piano/organ, stringed instruments, voice, wind and percussion instruments. Graduate degrees offered: Master of Music in the areas of performance, composition, music theater, opera performance. Program accredited by NASM.

Enrollment Fall 1997: 225 undergraduate, 35 graduate.

Music Faculty 48 total undergraduate and graduate (full-time and part-time). 40% of full-time faculty have terminal degrees. Graduate students do not teach undergraduate courses. Undergraduate student–faculty ratio: 25:1.

Student Life Student groups/activities include American String Teachers Association, Sigma Alpha Iota, Music Educators National Conference.

Expenses for 1997–98 Application fee: $20. Comprehensive fee: $12,502 includes full-time tuition ($8380), mandatory fees ($132), and college room and board ($3990). College room only: $1900. Room and board charges vary according to board plan. Special program-related fees: $40 per semester for practice room fee, $165 per credit for accompanist fee.

Financial Aid Program-specific awards for 1997: 30 Endowed Scholarships for program majors and performers ($500–$7000), 100–150 general music scholarships for program majors and performers ($500–$7000).

Application Procedures Students admitted directly into the professional program freshman year. Deadline for freshmen and transfers: continuous. Notification date for freshmen and transfers: August 15. Required: high school transcript, audition, SAT I or ACT test scores (minimum combined SAT I score of 900, minimum combined ACT score of 20), minimum 2.5 high school GPA, standing in top 50% of graduating class. Recommended: minimum 3.0 high school GPA. Auditions held 5 times on campus; recorded music is permissible as a substitute for live auditions if a campus visit is impossible and videotaped performances are permissible as a substitute for live auditions if a campus visit is impossible.

Undergraduate Contact Mr. Mark Blakeman, Director of Student Services, School of Music and Performing Arts, Oklahoma City University, 2501 North Blackwelder, Oklahoma City, Oklahoma 73106; 800-633-7242 ext. 5980, fax: 405-521-5971.

▼ OKLAHOMA STATE UNIVERSITY

Stillwater, Oklahoma

State-supported, coed. Small town campus. Total enrollment: 19,350.

Degrees Bachelor of Music in the areas of performance, music education, music business. Majors and concentrations: piano/organ, stringed instruments, voice, wind and percussion instruments. Program accredited by NASM.

Enrollment Fall 1997: 137 total; all undergraduate.

Music Student Profile 52% females, 48% males, 10% minorities, 4% international.

Music Faculty 28 total (full-time and part-time). 30% of full-time faculty have terminal degrees. Graduate students do not teach undergraduate courses. Undergraduate student–faculty ratio: 5:1.

Student Life Student groups/activities include professional music fraternities and sororities.

Expenses for 1997–98 Application fee: $25. State resident tuition: $1748 full-time. Nonresident tuition: $5768 full-time.

Mandatory fees: $609 full-time. Full-time tuition and fees vary according to course level and program. College room and board: $4344. College room only: $1976. Room and board charges vary according to board plan and housing facility. Special program-related fees: $25 per credit for applied lessons, $10 per credit for organ rental.

Financial Aid Program-specific awards for 1997: music scholarships for program majors ($100–$2000).

Application Procedures Students admitted directly into the professional program freshman year. Deadline for freshmen and transfers: continuous. Required: high school transcript, minimum 3.0 high school GPA, audition, SAT I or ACT test scores. Auditions held continuously on campus and off campus in various locations in Oklahoma; recorded music is permissible as a substitute for live auditions if a campus visit is impossible and videotaped performances are permissible as a substitute for live auditions if a campus visit is impossible.

Undergraduate Contact Dr. William Ballenger, Head, Music Department, Oklahoma State University, 132 Seratean Center, Stillwater, Oklahoma 74078-4077; 405-744-6133, fax: 405-744-9324.

▼ OLD DOMINION UNIVERSITY

Norfolk, Virginia

State-supported, coed. Urban campus. Total enrollment: 18,557.

Degrees Bachelor of Music in the areas of performance, composition; Bachelor of Music Education; Bachelor of Arts in the area of music history. Majors and concentrations: classical music, music education, piano/organ, stringed instruments, voice, wind and percussion instruments. Cross-registration with Norfolk State University, Hampton University, Tidewater Community College, College of William and Mary, Virginia Wesleyan College, Christopher Newport University. Program accredited by NASM.

Enrollment Fall 1997: 120 total; 100 undergraduate, 20 non-professional degree.

Music Student Profile 50% females, 50% males, 10% minorities, 5% international.

Music Faculty 30 total (full-time and part-time). 100% of full-time faculty have terminal degrees. Graduate students do not teach undergraduate courses.

Student Life Student groups/activities include Phi Mu Alpha, Sigma Alpha Iota, Music Educators National Conference.

Expenses for 1997–98 Application fee: $30. State resident tuition: $3836 full-time. Nonresident tuition: $9940 full-time. Mandatory fees: $140 full-time. Full-time tuition and fees vary according to course load and location. College room and board: $4866. Room and board charges vary according to board plan and housing facility. Special program-related fees: $85 per semester for applied music fee.

Financial Aid Program-specific awards for 1997: 16–50 Ensemble Scholarships for performers ($500–$750), 5–7 Stamos Scholarships for vocalists ($300–$600), 1 Vogan Scholarship for keyboard players ($1800).

Application Procedures Students admitted directly into the professional program freshman year. Deadline for freshmen: May 1; transfers: July 5. Required: high school transcript, college transcript(s) for transfer students, minimum 2.0 high school GPA, 2 letters of recommendation, audition, SAT I or ACT test scores (minimum combined SAT I score of 950). Recommended: minimum 3.0 high school GPA. Auditions held 4 times on campus; recorded music is permissible as a

Old Dominion University (continued)

substitute for live auditions when distance is prohibitive and videotaped performances are permissible as a substitute for live auditions when distance is prohibitive.

Undergraduate Contact Mr. Dennis Zeisler, Chair, Department of Music, Old Dominion University, Room 244 Fine Arts Building, Norfolk, Virginia 23529-0187; 757-683-4061, fax: 757-683-5056, E-mail address: dzeisler@odu.edu.

▼ ORAL ROBERTS UNIVERSITY

Tulsa, Oklahoma

Independent-interdenominational, coed. Urban campus. Total enrollment: 3,966. Music program established 1963.

Degrees Bachelor of Music in the areas of sacred music, composition, performance, composition/technology; Bachelor of Music Education in the areas of vocal music education, instrumental music education. Majors and concentrations: composition, music education, music technology, piano, sacred music, stringed instruments, voice, wind and percussion instruments. Program accredited by NASM.

Enrollment Fall 1997: 160 undergraduate.

Music Student Profile 60% females, 40% males, 30% minorities, 10% international.

Music Faculty 43 total (full-time and part-time). 70% of full-time faculty have terminal degrees. Graduate students do not teach undergraduate courses.

Student Life Student groups/activities include Franco Autori Concert, Family Christmas Concert.

Expenses for 1998–99 Application fee: $35. Comprehensive fee: $15,188 includes full-time tuition ($10,160), mandatory fees ($300), and college room and board ($4728). College room only: $2208. Special program-related fees: $30 per course for music equipment, $50 per semester for applied music lesson fee.

Financial Aid Program-specific awards for 1997: talent awards for music majors or participants ($500).

Application Procedures Students admitted directly into the professional program freshman year. Deadline for freshmen and transfers: continuous. Required: essay, high school transcript, college transcript(s) for transfer students, minimum 2.0 high school GPA, 2 letters of recommendation, audition, SAT I or ACT test scores. Auditions held by appointment on campus; recorded music is permissible as a substitute for live auditions when distance is prohibitive and videotaped performances are permissible as a substitute for live auditions when distance is prohibitive.

Web Site http://www.oru.edu/programs/arts.

Undergraduate Contact Music Department, Oral Roberts University, 7777 South Lewis Avenue, Tulsa, Oklahoma 74171; 918-495-7500, fax: 918-495-7502, E-mail address: melmoore@oru.edu.

▼ OTTERBEIN COLLEGE

Westerville, Ohio

Independent-United Methodist, coed. Suburban campus. Total enrollment: 2,697. Music program established 1847.

Degrees Bachelor of Music Education in the area of vocal and instrumental music education; Bachelor of Fine Arts in the area of musical theater. Majors and concentrations: classical

music, music, music and business, music education, music history, music theater, music theory and composition, piano/organ, stringed instruments, voice, wind and percussion instruments. Cross-registration with Ohio State University, Capital University, Columbus State Community College. Program accredited by NASM.

Enrollment Fall 1997: 110 total; all undergraduate.

Music Student Profile 55% females, 45% males, 2% minorities, 1% international.

Music Faculty 33 total (full-time and part-time). 75% of full-time faculty have terminal degrees. Graduate students do not teach undergraduate courses. Undergraduate student–faculty ratio: 4:1.

Student Life Student groups/activities include Ohio Student Music Educators Association, Delta Omicron.

Expenses for 1997–98 Application fee: $20. Comprehensive fee: $19,747 includes full-time tuition ($14,997) and college room and board ($4750). College room only: $2100. Special program-related fees: $570–$1380 for private applied music lessons.

Financial Aid Program-specific awards for 1997: 20–30 Music Talent Grants for program majors ($1250–$3000).

Application Procedures Students admitted directly into the professional program freshman year. Deadline for freshmen and transfers: continuous. Required: high school transcript, college transcript(s) for transfer students, minimum 2.0 high school GPA, audition, SAT I or ACT test scores. Recommended: interview. Auditions held continuously on campus; recorded music is permissible as a substitute for live auditions when distance is prohibitive and videotaped performances are permissible as a substitute for live auditions when distance is prohibitive.

Web Site http://www.otterbein.edu/admission/music.html.

Undergraduate Contact Dr. Morton Achter, Chairperson, Department of Music, Otterbein College, Battelle Fine Arts Center, Westerville, Ohio 43081; 614-823-1508, fax: 614-823-1118, E-mail address: machter@otterbein.edu.

Bernice Young Jones School of Fine Arts

▼ OUACHITA BAPTIST UNIVERSITY

Arkadelphia, Arkansas

Independent-Baptist, coed. Small town campus. Total enrollment: 1,619. Music program established 1886.

Degrees Bachelor of Music in the areas of performance, musical theater, church music, music theory/composition; Bachelor of Music Education in the areas of choral music education, instrumental music education. Majors and concentrations: classical music, music, music education, music theater, piano/organ, sacred music, voice, wind and percussion instruments. Cross-registration with Henderson State University. Program accredited by NASM.

Enrollment Fall 1997: 145 total.

Music Student Profile 51% females, 49% males, 2% minorities, 2% international.

Music Faculty 30 total (full-time and part-time). 81% of full-time faculty have terminal degrees. Graduate students do not teach undergraduate courses. Undergraduate student–faculty ratio: 6:1.

Student Life Student groups/activities include Phi Mu Alpha Sinfonia, Sigma Alpha Iota, Music Educators National Conference Student Chapter. Special housing available for music students.

Expenses for 1997–98 Application fee: $25. Comprehensive fee: $11,130 includes full-time tuition ($7970), mandatory fees ($120), and college room and board ($3040). College room only: $1390. Room and board charges vary according to board plan and housing facility. Special program-related fees: $100–$200 per credit hour for private instruction.

Financial Aid Program-specific awards for 1997: 125 music scholarships for program majors ($2000–$4000), 1 Presidential Scholarship for freshmen program majors ($6500).

Application Procedures Students admitted directly into the professional program freshman year. Deadline for freshmen and transfers: continuous. Notification date for freshmen and transfers: continuous. Required: high school transcript, college transcript(s) for transfer students, letter of recommendation, audition, SAT I or ACT test scores (minimum combined ACT score of 20), minimum 2.5 high school GPA (4.0 scale). Auditions held twice and by appointment on campus; recorded music is permissible as a substitute for live auditions if a campus visit is impossible and videotaped performances are permissible as a substitute for live auditions if a campus visit is impossible.

Undergraduate Contact Mr. Charles W. Wright, Dean, Bernice Young Jones School of Fine Arts, Ouachita Baptist University, Box 3771, Arkadelphia, Arkansas 71998-0001; 501-245-5129, E-mail address: wrightc@alpha.obu.edu.

▼ PACIFIC LUTHERAN UNIVERSITY

Tacoma, Washington

Independent, coed. Suburban campus. Total enrollment: 3,555. Music program established 1891.

Degrees Bachelor of Music in the area of performance; Bachelor of Music Education in the areas of choral music, band, orchestra; Bachelor of Musical Arts in the area of music combined with an outside field. Majors and concentrations: composition, music education, performance. Program accredited by NASM.

Enrollment Fall 1997: 150 total; all undergraduate.

Music Student Profile 50% females, 50% males, 8% minorities, 10% international.

Music Faculty 45 total (full-time and part-time). 33% of full-time faculty have terminal degrees. Graduate students do not teach undergraduate courses. Undergraduate student–faculty ratio: 15:1.

Student Life Student groups/activities include Music Educators National Conference, American Choral Directors Association, Mu Phi Epsilon.

Expenses for 1998–99 Application fee: $35. Comprehensive fee: $20,570 includes full-time tuition ($15,680) and college room and board ($4890). College room only: $2400. Special program-related fees: $150–$225 per semester for private lessons, $75–$250 per year for ensemble tours.

Financial Aid Program-specific awards for 1997: music scholarships for incoming freshmen demonstrating need and talent ($1000–$4000), 30 music scholarships for continuing program students.

Application Procedures Students admitted directly into the professional program freshman year. Deadline for freshmen and transfers: continuous. Required: essay, high school transcript, college transcript(s) for transfer students, 2 letters of recommendation, SAT I or ACT test scores, minimum 2.5 high school GPA.

Web Site http://www.plu.edu/.

Undergraduate Contact Ms. Pam Deacon, Administrative Assistant, Department of Music, Pacific Lutheran University, Tacoma, Washington 98447; 253-535-7603, fax: 253-535-8669.

▼ PACIFIC UNION COLLEGE

Angwin, California

Independent-Seventh-day Adventist, coed. Rural campus. Total enrollment: 1,570. Music program established 1967.

Degrees Bachelor of Music in the areas of music education, performance. Majors and concentrations: classical music, music, music education, piano/organ, stringed instruments, voice, wind and percussion instruments. Program accredited by NASM.

Enrollment Fall 1997: 39 total; all undergraduate.

Music Student Profile 65% females, 35% males, 45% minorities, 15% international.

Music Faculty 19 total (full-time and part-time). 57% of full-time faculty have terminal degrees. Graduate students do not teach undergraduate courses. Undergraduate student–faculty ratio: 6:1.

Student Life Student groups/activities include California Music Educators Association.

Expenses for 1998–99 Comprehensive fee: $18,360 includes full-time tuition ($14,055) and college room and board ($4305). College room only: $2580.

Financial Aid Program-specific awards for 1997: 5 Proficiency in Performance Scholarships for ensemble participants ($500–$1000), 6 Loye Scholarships for organists ($1000–$3000), 1–2 Mayes Music Ministry Scholarships for organ/voice majors ($500–$1000), 1–2 Coltrin Lewis Scholarships for musicians ($500–$1000), 1–2 Edward Mackett Scholarships for brass musicians ($500–$1000).

Application Procedures Students admitted directly into the professional program freshman year. Deadline for freshmen and transfers: continuous. Notification date for freshmen and transfers: September 30. Required: high school transcript, college transcript(s) for transfer students, 3 letters of recommendation, audition, ACT test score only, minimum 2.3 high school GPA. Auditions held 3 times on campus; recorded music is permissible as a substitute for live auditions when distance is prohibitive and videotaped performances are permissible as a substitute for live auditions when distance is prohibitive.

Web Site http://www.puc.edu.

Undergraduate Contact Mr. Al Trace, Admissions Director, Pacific Union College, 100 Howell Mountain Road, Angwin, California 94508; 707-965-6336, fax: 707-965-6432.

▼ PALM BEACH ATLANTIC COLLEGE

West Palm Beach, Florida

Independent-nondenominational, coed. Urban campus. Total enrollment: 1,932. Music program established 1994.

Degrees Bachelor of Music in the areas of performance, church music, music education, music composition. Majors and concentrations: church music, composition, keyboard, music education, performance, voice. Program accredited by NASM.

Enrollment Fall 1997: 100 undergraduate.

Music Student Profile 55% females, 45% males, 16% minorities, 7% international.

Palm Beach Atlantic College (continued)

Music Faculty 20 total (full-time and part-time). 63% of full-time faculty have terminal degrees. Graduate students do not teach undergraduate courses. Undergraduate student–faculty ratio: 17:1.

Student Life Student groups/activities include Collegiate Music Educators National Conference.

Expenses for 1997–98 Application fee: $25. Comprehensive fee: $14,538 includes full-time tuition ($9900) and college room and board ($4638). College room only: $2453. Room and board charges vary according to board plan and housing facility. Special program-related fees: $75–$150 per course for applied fees.

Financial Aid Program-specific awards for 1997: 50–80 music scholarships for program majors ($1000–$2000), 1 Brown Vargas Scholarship for music theater students ($400), 1 Sylvia Brainen Piano Quartet Scholarship for piano students ($300).

Application Procedures Students admitted directly into the professional program freshman year. Deadline for freshmen and transfers: continuous. Required: essay, high school transcript, college transcript(s) for transfer students, minimum 2.0 high school GPA, 2 letters of recommendation, audition, SAT I or ACT test scores. Recommended: minimum 3.0 high school GPA, interview, video. Auditions held continuously on campus; recorded music is permissible as a substitute for live auditions when distance is prohibitive and videotaped performances are permissible as a substitute for live auditions when distance is prohibitive.

Undergraduate Contact Mr. Buckley A. James, Dean, Admissions Department, Palm Beach Atlantic College, PO Box 24708, West Palm Beach, Florida 33416; 800-238-3998, fax: 561-803-2115.

▼ PEABODY CONSERVATORY OF MUSIC

See Johns Hopkins University

▼ PENNSYLVANIA STATE UNIVERSITY UNIVERSITY PARK CAMPUS

University Park, Pennsylvania

State-related, coed. Small town campus. Total enrollment: 40,538. Music program established 1929.

Degrees Bachelor of Music in the areas of performance, composition; Bachelor of Science in the area of music education; Bachelor of Musical Arts in the area of performance. Majors and concentrations: classical music, composition, music education, music history, music theory, piano/organ, stringed instruments, voice, wind and percussion instruments. Graduate degrees offered: Master of Music in the areas of performance, composition, conducting, piano pedagogy and performance, voice pedagogy and performance; Master of Arts in the areas of musicology, theory and history (integrative); Master of Education in the area of music education. Doctor of Philosophy in the area of music education. Program accredited by NASM.

Enrollment Fall 1997: 340 total; 280 undergraduate, 60 graduate.

Music Student Profile 47% females, 53% males, 5% minorities, 2% international.

Music Faculty 46 total undergraduate and graduate (full-time and part-time). 100% of full-time faculty have terminal degrees. Graduate students teach a few undergraduate courses.

Expenses for 1997–98 Application fee: $40. State resident tuition: $5632 full-time. Nonresident tuition: $12,206 full-time. Mandatory fees: $200 full-time. Full-time tuition and fees vary according to course level, course load, location, and program. College room and board: $4640. College room only: $2060. Room and board charges vary according to board plan. Special program-related fees: $100–$150 per semester for applied music lesson fee.

Financial Aid Program-specific awards for 1997: 110 music scholarships for program majors ($1500).

Application Procedures Students admitted directly into the professional program freshman year. Deadline for freshmen: April 1; transfers: June 1. Notification date for freshmen and transfers: continuous. Required: high school transcript, college transcript(s) for transfer students, minimum 2.0 high school GPA, audition, SAT I or ACT test scores. Recommended: letter of recommendation, interview. Auditions held 4 times on campus; recorded music is permissible as a substitute for live auditions when distance is prohibitive and videotaped performances are permissible as a substitute for live auditions when distance is prohibitive.

Web Site http://www.music.psu.edu/.

Undergraduate Contact Ms. Irene Lucas, Staff Assistant V, School of Music, Pennsylvania State University University Park Campus, 233 Music Building, University Park, Pennsylvania 16802-1503; 814-865-0431, fax: 814-865-7140, E-mail address: music-ug-adm@psu.edu.

Graduate Contact Ms. Sue Spaugh, Graduate Admissions Secretary, School of Music, Pennsylvania State University University Park Campus, 201 Music Building, University Park, Pennsylvania 16802; 814-865-0431, E-mail address: music-gr-adm@psu.edu.

▼ PHILADELPHIA COLLEGE OF BIBLE

Langhorne, Pennsylvania

Independent-nondenominational, coed. Suburban campus. Total enrollment: 1,280. Music program established 1969.

Degrees Bachelor of Music in the areas of performance, music education, church music, composition. Majors and concentrations: composition, guitar, music education, piano/organ, sacred music, stringed instruments, voice, wind and percussion instruments. Program accredited by NASM.

Enrollment Fall 1997: 60 total; all undergraduate.

Music Student Profile 67% females, 33% males, 28% minorities, 27% international.

Music Faculty 23 total (full-time and part-time). 57% of full-time faculty have terminal degrees. Graduate students do not teach undergraduate courses.

Student Life Student groups/activities include Music Educators National Conference, American Choral Directors Association, Pennsylvania Music Teachers Association.

Expenses for 1998–99 Application fee: $15. Comprehensive fee: $14,410 includes full-time tuition ($9250), mandatory fees ($270), and college room and board ($4890). College room only: $2290. Full-time tuition and fees vary according to course load, location, and program. Room and board charges vary according to board plan, housing facility, and location.

Financial Aid Program-specific awards for 1997: 50 music scholarships for freshmen ($3000–$8000).

Application Procedures Students admitted directly into the professional program freshman year. Deadline for freshmen and transfers: continuous. Required: high school transcript, college transcript(s) for transfer students, minimum 2.0 high school GPA, interview, audition, SAT I or ACT test scores (minimum combined SAT I score of 920, minimum combined ACT score of 19). Auditions held continuously on campus; recorded music is permissible as a substitute for live auditions when distance is prohibitive (over 300 miles) and videotaped performances are permissible as a substitute for live auditions when distance is prohibitive (beyond 300 miles).

Web Site http://www.pcb.edu.

Undergraduate Contact Dr. Paul S. Jones, Chair, Music Department, Philadelphia College of Bible, 200 Manor Avenue, Langhorne, Pennsylvania 19047; 215-702-4330, fax: 215-702-4342, E-mail address: pjones@pcb.edu.

▼ PHILLIPS UNIVERSITY

Enid, Oklahoma

Independent, coed. Small town campus. Total enrollment: 584. Music program established 1907.

Degrees Bachelor of Music Education in the areas of instrumental music education, vocal music education; Bachelor of Music Therapy. Cross-registration with Regent's College (United Kingdom). Program accredited by NASM.

Enrollment Fall 1997: 34 total; 25 undergraduate, 9 non-professional degree.

Music Student Profile 60% females, 40% males, 10% minorities, 7% international.

Music Faculty 14 total undergraduate (full-time and part-time). 50% of full-time faculty have terminal degrees. Graduate students do not teach undergraduate courses. Undergraduate student–faculty ratio: 6:1.

Student Life Student groups/activities include Mu Phi Epsilon, Music Therapy Club, Music Educators National Conference Student Chapter.

Expenses for 1998–99 Application fee: $20. Comprehensive fee: $11,204 includes full-time tuition ($6685), mandatory fees ($615), and college room and board ($3904). College room only: $1700. Full-time tuition and fees vary according to course load. Room and board charges vary according to board plan and housing facility. Special program-related fees: $150 per semester for private music lessons.

Financial Aid Program-specific awards for 1997: 15 Music Major Scholarships for music majors ($1500–$6000), 20 Music Participant Scholarships for ensemble participants ($500–$3000).

Application Procedures Students admitted directly into the professional program freshman year. Deadline for freshmen and transfers: continuous. Notification date for freshmen and transfers: continuous. Required: essay, high school transcript, college transcript(s) for transfer students, audition. Recommended: interview, SAT I or ACT test scores, minimum 2.75 high school GPA. Auditions held 6 times on campus; recorded music is permissible as a substitute for live auditions if a campus visit is impossible and videotaped performances are permissible as a substitute for live auditions if a campus visit is impossible.

Web Site http://www.phillips.edu/bromusic.htm.

Undergraduate Contact Mr. Bill LaFrance, Vice President for Enrollment Management, Undergraduate Admissions, Phillips University, 100 South University Avenue, Enid, Oklahoma 73701; 800-238-1185, fax: 405-237-1607.

▼ PITTSBURG STATE UNIVERSITY

Pittsburg, Kansas

State-supported, coed. Small town campus. Total enrollment: 6,355. Music program established 1914.

Degrees Bachelor of Music in the areas of classical, music performance; Bachelor of Music Education in the area of instrumental and vocal music education (grades K-12). Majors and concentrations: classical music, music education, piano pedagogy, piano/organ, stringed instruments, voice, wind and percussion instruments. Graduate degrees offered: Master of Music in the areas of music theory/composition, performance, music history/literature, vocal music education, instrumental music education, piano pedagogy, instrumental conducting, choral conducting. Program accredited by NASM, NCATE.

Enrollment Fall 1997: 119 total; 60 undergraduate, 11 graduate, 48 non-professional degree.

Music Student Profile 55% females, 45% males, 7% minorities, 10% international.

Music Faculty 19 total undergraduate and graduate (full-time and part-time). 100% of full-time faculty have terminal degrees. Graduate students do not teach undergraduate courses. Undergraduate student–faculty ratio: 6:1.

Student Life Student groups/activities include Music Educators National Conference Student Chapter, International Association of Jazz Educators, Pi Kappa Lambda (music honorary society).

Expenses for 1997–98 Application fee: $15. State resident tuition: $2016 full-time. Nonresident tuition: $6280 full-time. College room and board: $3396.

Financial Aid Program-specific awards for 1997: 100 music scholarships for program majors and minors ($300–$2000).

Application Procedures Students admitted directly into the professional program freshman year. Deadline for freshmen and transfers: July 1. Required: high school transcript, college transcript(s) for transfer students, minimum 2.0 high school GPA, audition. Recommended: SAT I or ACT test scores. Auditions held continuously on campus; recorded music is permissible as a substitute for live auditions when distance is prohibitive and videotaped performances are permissible as a substitute for live auditions when distance is prohibitive.

Web Site http://pittstate.edu/music/.

Undergraduate Contact Dr. Keith Ward, Chair, Department of Music, Pittsburg State University, 1701 South Broadway, Pittsburg, Kansas 66762; 316-235-4466, fax: 316-232-7515, E-mail address: kward@pittstate.edu.

Graduate Contact Dr. Russell Jones, Director, Graduate Studies in Music, Department of Music, Pittsburg State University, 1701 South Broadway, Pittsburg, Kansas 66762; 316-235-4466, E-mail address: rjones@pittstate.edu.

▼ PORTLAND STATE UNIVERSITY

Portland, Oregon

State-supported, coed. Urban campus. Total enrollment: 16,997. Music program established 1954.

Portland State University *(continued)*

Degrees Bachelor of Music in the areas of classical performance, jazz studies. Majors and concentrations: classical music, jazz studies, music performance, piano/organ, stringed instruments, voice, wind and percussion instruments. Graduate degrees offered: Master of Music in the areas of classical performance, conducting. Program accredited by NASM.
Enrollment Fall 1997: 290 total.
Music Student Profile 55% females, 45% males, 5% minorities, 5% international.
Music Faculty 21 total undergraduate and graduate (full-time and part-time). 67% of full-time faculty have terminal degrees. Graduate students teach a few undergraduate courses. Undergraduate student–faculty ratio: 13:1.
Student Life Student groups/activities include Music Educators National Conference, Mu Phi Epsilon.
Expenses for 1997–98 Application fee: $50. One-time mandatory fee: $30. State resident tuition: $2694 full-time. Nonresident tuition: $10,260 full-time. Mandatory fees: $663 full-time. College room and board: $5850. College room only: $4050. Room and board charges vary according to housing facility. Special program-related fees: $40 per credit hour for applied music fee.
Financial Aid Program-specific awards for 1997: 14 Laurel Awards for program majors ($3000), 50 departmental awards for program majors ($500–$1000).
Application Procedures Students apply for admission into the professional program by freshman year. Deadline for freshmen and transfers: June 1. Notification date for freshmen and transfers: continuous. Required: high school transcript, college transcript(s) for transfer students, audition, minimum 2.5 high school GPA. Recommended: letter of recommendation, interview. Auditions held 2-3 times on campus; recorded music is permissible as a substitute for live auditions when distance is prohibitive and videotaped performances are permissible as a substitute for live auditions when distance is prohibitive.
Undergraduate Contact Music Department, Portland State University, PO Box 751, Portland, Oregon 97207-0751; 503-725-3011, fax: 503-725-3351.
Graduate Contact Dr. Marilyn Shotola, Graduate Coordinator, Music Department, Portland State University, PO Box 751, Portland, Oregon 97207-0751; 503-725-3010, fax: 503-725-3351, E-mail address: marilyn@fpa.lh.pdx.edu.

▼ POTTER COLLEGE OF ARTS, HUMANITIES, AND SOCIAL SCIENCES

See Western Kentucky University

▼ PRAIRIE VIEW A&M UNIVERSITY

Prairie View, Texas

State-supported, coed. Small town campus. Total enrollment: 6,004. Music program established 1920.
Degrees Bachelor of Music in the areas of applied music, music education. Majors and concentrations: music, music education, piano/organ, voice, wind and percussion instruments.
Enrollment Fall 1997: 86 total; 80 undergraduate, 6 graduate.

Music Student Profile 50% females, 50% males, 90% minorities, 3% international.
Music Faculty 11 total (full-time and part-time). 50% of full-time faculty have terminal degrees. Graduate students do not teach undergraduate courses. Undergraduate student–faculty ratio: 10:1.
Student Life Student groups/activities include Music Educators National Conference Student Chapter, Kappa Kappa Psi, Tau Beta Sigma.
Expenses for 1997–98 Application fee: $10. State resident tuition: $1020 full-time. Nonresident tuition: $7440 full-time. Mandatory fees: $1344 full-time. Full-time tuition and fees vary according to course load. College room and board: $3953. College room only: $1774. Room and board charges vary according to board plan and housing facility. Special program-related fees: $12 per semester for applied music fees, $10 per semester for lab fees.
Financial Aid Program-specific awards for 1997: 3 University Talent Scholarships for program majors ($1000–$2500), 1 Bobby J. Baldwin Scholarship for piano majors ($500–$3000).
Application Procedures Students admitted directly into the professional program freshman year. Deadline for freshmen and transfers: May 1. Notification date for freshmen and transfers: August 1. Required: high school transcript, college transcript(s) for transfer students, minimum 2.0 high school GPA, letter of recommendation, interview, audition, SAT I or ACT test scores. Auditions held 4 times on campus and off campus in Dallas, TX; Houston, TX; Fort Worth, TX; San Antonio, TX; recorded music is permissible as a substitute for live auditions when distance is prohibitive and videotaped performances are permissible as a substitute for live auditions when distance is prohibitive.
Undergraduate Contact Director of Admissions, Prairie View A&M University, PO Box 3089, Prairie View, Texas 77446; 409-857-2618.

▼ PURCHASE COLLEGE, STATE UNIVERSITY OF NEW YORK

Purchase, New York

State-supported, coed. Small town campus. Total enrollment: 3,297.
Degrees Bachelor of Fine Arts in the areas of performance, composition. Majors and concentrations: classical music, composition, jazz, opera, piano/organ, production, stringed instruments, studio composition, voice, wind and percussion instruments. Graduate degrees offered: Master of Fine Arts in the areas of performance, composition.
Enrollment Fall 1997: 275 total; 212 undergraduate, 63 graduate.
Music Student Profile 38% females, 62% males, 15% minorities, 22% international.
Music Faculty 110 total undergraduate and graduate (full-time and part-time). 90% of full-time faculty have terminal degrees. Graduate students do not teach undergraduate courses.
Student Life Student groups/activities include Ballet and Arts in Education performances, performances in the community.
Expenses for 1997–98 Application fee: $30. State resident tuition: $3400 full-time. Nonresident tuition: $8300 full-time. Mandatory fees: $479 full-time. College room and board:

$5264. College room only: $1930. Room and board charges vary according to board plan and housing facility. Special program-related fees: $1600 per year for applied music fees, $50 for audition.

Financial Aid Program-specific awards for 1997: 55 scholarships for program students ($500–$8000), 1–4 Empire Minority Awards for minority students from New York State ($1250), 7 Reed Scholarships for students with high academic and artistic achievement ($750–$4500), 1 John Bendheim Scholarship for art majors ($500).

Application Procedures Students admitted directly into the professional program freshman year. Deadline for freshmen and transfers: June 1. Notification date for freshmen and transfers: July 1. Required: high school transcript, college transcript(s) for transfer students, audition, SAT I or ACT test scores, minimum TOEFL score of 550 for international applicants, portfolio for composition majors. Recommended: essay, minimum 3.0 high school GPA, 2 letters of recommendation, interview. Auditions held 4 times on campus; recorded music is permissible as a substitute for live auditions when distance is prohibitive or in special circumstances and videotaped performances are permissible as a substitute for live auditions when distance is prohibitive or in special circumstances. Portfolio reviews held 4 times on campus.

Undergraduate Contact Ms. Janicemarie Hamm, Admissions Counselor, Conservatory of Theatre, Purchase College, State University of New York, 735 Anderson Hill Road, Purchase, New York 10577-1400; 914-251-6300, fax: 914-251-6314.

Graduate Contact Ms. Jody Strong, Conservatory Coordinator, Conservatory of Music, Purchase College, State University of New York, 735 Anderson Hill Road, Purchase, New York 10577-1400; 914-251-6700, fax: 914-251-6739.

More About the College

The Conservatory of Music at Purchase College offers a comprehensive musical education at both the undergraduate and graduate level for a limited number of gifted students who wish to pursue the art of music at a professional level. It is a small community of about 260 students and faculty members dedicated to professional training in performance and composition in a conservatory setting. Music students have the opportunity to work very closely on an individual basis with many wonderful musicians who care deeply about them and who are passionately committed to teaching. Faculty members have active professional careers as performers and composers, and the Conservatory's performance affiliates include some of the most prestigious artist-teachers in the metropolitan area. Programs—instrumental (including jazz), voice/opera, piano, organ, composition, and studio composition—are designed to prepare students for a professional career.

The young artist aspiring to master the craft of musical performance or composition soon discovers the need for knowledge, insight, and imagination in addition to technical skill. The core undergraduate curriculum is similar throughout the four years for all areas of study: all students are required to take private or small-group study; ensemble; a set of courses in music theory, history, and musicianship; and courses specific to their area—all this, with sufficient time to practice. Further effort is made, in cooperation with programs in the letters and sciences, to acquaint students with landmarks of cultural and social history as well as of scientific and philosophical thought. It is assumed that musical and cultural studies can be realistically undertaken together, given both desire and discipline. The Master of

Fine Arts degree is an intensive program of approximately 60 credits designed to provide advanced training for students clearly destined for professional careers.

Each curriculum has a strong and vital component of specialized professional training; for example, the voice/opera program has courses in song repertoire, diction, languages (Italian, French, and German), acting, body movement, modern dance, dance improvisation and composition, opera history, opera workshop, and coaching. The jazz and studio composition curricula have courses in jazz harmony and arranging; jazz improvisation and repertoire, ensemble, and chorus; the history of recorded music; world music survey and ensemble; AfroCuban dialogues; songwriting; orchestration; commercial arranging; advanced studio production; film scoring; and hard drive digital recording.

Private lessons are taken with a faculty member or an affiliate artist-teacher selected by agreement of the student, the private teacher, and the Dean. Guidance in the choice of teacher is available from the resident faculty, in particular the head of the student's discipline area. In most areas, the student may choose, subject to approval by the Dean, any established teacher in the New York City metropolitan area. Many students take their lessons with teachers in the city and use the opportunity to attend concerts and rehearsals and to taste the extraordinary richness that this cultural center has to offer.

▼ QUEENS COLLEGE

Charlotte, North Carolina

Independent-Presbyterian, coed. Suburban campus. Total enrollment: 1,652. Music program established 1857.

Degrees Bachelor of Music in the areas of music therapy, applied music performance. Majors and concentrations: classical music, guitar, harp, music therapy, piano/organ, stringed instruments, voice, wind and percussion instruments. Cross-registration with 13 member colleges of the Charlotte Area Educational Consortium. Program accredited by NASM, NAMT.

Enrollment Fall 1997: 135 total; 35 undergraduate, 100 non-professional degree.

Music Student Profile 96% females, 4% males, 8% minorities, 4% international.

Music Faculty 19 total (full-time and part-time). 80% of full-time faculty have terminal degrees. Graduate students do not teach undergraduate courses. Undergraduate student–faculty ratio: 5:1.

Student Life Student groups/activities include Music Therapy Club, Drama Club.

Expenses for 1998–99 Application fee: $25. Comprehensive fee: $15,240 includes full-time tuition ($9410) and college room and board ($5830). Special program-related fees: $75 per semester hour for private music instruction.

Financial Aid Program-specific awards for 1997: 15 music major awards for freshmen program majors ($1000), 8 music minor awards for freshmen program minors ($500), 1 Stegner Music Scholarship for program students ($5000), 1 Lammers Music Scholarship for program majors ($5000), 1 McDorman Scholarship for vocal students ($5000), 2 McMahon Scholarships for music majors ($5000–$10,000).

Application Procedures Students admitted directly into the professional program freshman year. Deadline for freshmen and transfers: continuous. Required: essay, high school transcript, college transcript(s) for transfer students, mini-

Queens College (continued)

mum 2.0 high school GPA, 2 letters of recommendation, SAT I or ACT test scores (minimum combined SAT I score of 750), audition for music therapy and performance majors. Recommended: interview, audition, portfolio. Auditions held 4 times and by appointment on campus; recorded music is permissible as a substitute for live auditions if student has already visited the campus or when distance is prohibitive and videotaped performances are permissible as a substitute for live auditions if student has already visited the campus or when distance is prohibitive. Portfolio reviews held as needed on campus.

Undergraduate Contact Ms. Eileen Dills, Dean of Enrollment Management, Queens College, 1900 Selwyn Avenue, Charlotte, North Carolina 28274; 800-849-0202, fax: 704-337-2503.

Aaron Copland School of Music

▼ QUEENS COLLEGE OF THE CITY UNIVERSITY OF NEW YORK

Flushing, New York

State and locally supported, coed. Urban campus. Total enrollment: 16,381. Music program established 1937.

Degrees Bachelor of Music in the area of performance. Majors and concentrations: brass, early music, piano/organ, stringed instruments, voice, wind and percussion instruments. Graduate degrees offered: Master of Science in the area of music education; Master of Arts in the areas of performance, composition, musicology, music theory.

Enrollment Fall 1997: 271 total; 100 undergraduate, 171 graduate.

Music Student Profile 50% females, 50% males, 35% minorities, 35% international.

Music Faculty 73 total undergraduate and graduate (full-time and part-time). 85% of full-time faculty have terminal degrees. Graduate students teach a few undergraduate courses. Undergraduate student–faculty ratio: 15:1.

Student Life Student groups/activities include Music Educators National Conference, Music Students Association.

Expenses for 1997–98 Application fee: $40. State resident tuition: $3200 full-time. Nonresident tuition: $6800 full-time. Mandatory fees: $193 full-time.

Financial Aid Program-specific awards for 1997: 1–3 Boris Schwarz Scholarships for string majors ($250–$500), 2 Zatkin Scholarships-Opera Awards for voice majors ($250–$500), 1 Edward Downes Scholarship for voice majors ($250–$500), 25 departmental scholarships for those demonstrating talent/financial need ($200–$4000).

Application Procedures Students admitted directly into the professional program freshman year. Deadline for freshmen and transfers: March 15. Notification date for freshmen and transfers: continuous. Required: essay, high school transcript, college transcript(s) for transfer students, minimum 3.0 high school GPA, audition. Recommended: portfolio, SAT I or ACT test scores. Auditions held twice on campus; recorded music is permissible as a substitute for live auditions when distance is prohibitive and videotaped performances are permissible as a substitute for live auditions when distance is prohibitive. Portfolio reviews held twice on campus.

Undergraduate Contact Dr. Jonathan Irving, Special Assistant to the Director, Aaron Copland School of Music, Queens College of the City University of New York, 65-30 Kissena Boulevard, Flushing, New York 11367; 718-997-3800, fax: 718-997-3849.

▼ RADFORD UNIVERSITY

Radford, Virginia

State-supported, coed. Small town campus. Total enrollment: 8,534.

Degrees Bachelor of Music in the areas of music education, music business, performance, composition, music therapy, music and technology. Majors and concentrations: composition, music business, music education, music technology, music therapy, performance. Graduate degrees offered: Master of Science in the areas of music therapy, music education. Program accredited by NASM.

Enrollment Fall 1997: 178 total; 144 undergraduate, 11 graduate, 23 non-professional degree.

Music Student Profile 55% females, 45% males, 2% minorities, 2% international.

Music Faculty 32 total undergraduate and graduate (full-time and part-time). 53% of full-time faculty have terminal degrees. Graduate students teach a few undergraduate courses. Undergraduate student–faculty ratio: 5:1.

Student Life Student groups/activities include Music Therapy Club, Music Educators National Conference Student Chapter, Arts and Entertainment Association. Special housing available for music students.

Expenses for 1997–98 Application fee: $20. State resident tuition: $2016 full-time. Nonresident tuition: $6788 full-time. Mandatory fees: $1164 full-time. College room and board: $4416. College room only: $2448. Room and board charges vary according to board plan and housing facility.

Financial Aid Program-specific awards for 1997: 2–4 Arts Society Awards for freshmen ($4000), 3 Ingram-Lee Awards for program majors ($750), 1 Presser Award for seniors ($2250).

Application Procedures Students apply for admission into the professional program by freshman year. Deadline for freshmen: April 1; transfers: June 1. Notification date for freshmen and transfers: continuous. Required: high school transcript, college transcript(s) for transfer students, minimum 2.0 high school GPA, audition, SAT I or ACT test scores. Recommended: minimum 3.0 high school GPA. Auditions held continuously by appointment on campus; recorded music is permissible as a substitute for live auditions if unedited and videotaped performances are permissible as a substitute for live auditions if unedited.

Web Site http://www.runet.edu/~musc-web/.

Undergraduate Contact Mr. David Kraus, Director, Office of Admissions, Radford University, PO Box 6903, Radford, Virginia 24142; 540-831-5371, fax: 540-831-5138, E-mail address: dwkraus@runet.edu.

Graduate Contact Dr. Wilbur W. Stanton, Dean, College of Graduate and Extended Education, Radford University, PO Box 6928, Radford, Virginia 24142; 540-831-5431, fax: 540-831-6061, E-mail address: gradcou@runet.edu.

▼ RHODE ISLAND COLLEGE

Providence, Rhode Island

State-supported, coed. Suburban campus. Total enrollment: 8,622. Music program established 1967.

Degrees Bachelor of Music in the area of performance; Bachelor of Science in the area of music education. Graduate degrees offered: Master of Music Education. Program accredited by NASM, NCATE.

Enrollment Fall 1997: 115 total; 80 undergraduate, 20 graduate, 15 non-professional degree.

Music Student Profile 58% females, 42% males, 2% minorities.

Music Faculty 29 total undergraduate and graduate (full-time and part-time). 90% of full-time faculty have terminal degrees. Graduate students do not teach undergraduate courses. Undergraduate student–faculty ratio: 15:1.

Student Life Student groups/activities include Collegiate Chapter-Music Educators National Conference.

Expenses for 1997–98 Application fee: $25. State resident tuition: $2760 full-time. Nonresident tuition: $7152 full-time. Mandatory fees: $316 full-time. Full-time tuition and fees vary according to reciprocity agreements. College room and board: $5200. College room only: $2600. Room and board charges vary according to board plan and housing facility. Special program-related fees: $320 per semester for applied music lesson fee.

Financial Aid Program-specific awards for 1997: 25 Special Talent Awards for program majors ($640–$2500).

Application Procedures Students apply for admission into the professional program by sophomore year. Deadline for freshmen and transfers: continuous. Required: essay, high school transcript, college transcript(s) for transfer students, audition, SAT I or ACT test scores. Recommended: minimum 3.0 high school GPA, 3 letters of recommendation. Auditions held 3 times on campus; recorded music is permissible as a substitute for live auditions if a campus visit is impossible and videotaped performances are permissible as a substitute for live auditions if a campus visit is impossible.

Web Site http://www.ric.edu.

Contact Dr. Philip McClintock, Assistant Chair, Performing Arts - Music, Rhode Island College, 600 Mt. Pleasant Avenue, Providence, Rhode Island 02908; 401-456-8244, fax: 401-456-8379.

Shepherd School of Music

▼ RICE UNIVERSITY

Houston, Texas

Independent, coed. Urban campus. Total enrollment: 4,209. Music program established 1974.

Degrees Bachelor of Music in the areas of performance, music theory, composition, musicology. Majors and concentrations: classical music, composition, music, music history, music theory, piano/organ, stringed instruments, voice, wind and percussion instruments. Graduate degrees offered: Master of Music in the areas of performance, music theory, composition, musicology. Doctor of Musical Arts in the areas of performance, composition.

Enrollment Fall 1997: 271 total; 119 undergraduate, 152 graduate.

Music Student Profile 51% females, 49% males, 6% minorities, 10% international.

Music Faculty 55 total undergraduate and graduate (full-time and part-time). 99% of full-time faculty have terminal degrees. Graduate students teach a few undergraduate courses. Undergraduate student–faculty ratio: 5:1.

Expenses for 1997–98 Application fee: $35. Comprehensive fee: $20,506 includes full-time tuition ($13,900), mandatory fees ($406), and college room and board ($6200). College

room only: $3500. Full-time tuition and fees vary according to student level. Room and board charges vary according to board plan. Part-time mandatory fees per term: $379.35 for the first term, $181 for the second term.

Financial Aid Program-specific awards for 1997: merit awards for program majors ($1000–$15,300).

Application Procedures Students admitted directly into the professional program freshman year. Deadline for freshmen: January 2; transfers: April 1. Notification date for freshmen: April 1; transfers: May 1. Required: essay, high school transcript, college transcript(s) for transfer students, 2 letters of recommendation, interview, audition, SAT I or ACT test scores, SAT II, portfolio for composition students. Recommended: minimum 3.0 high school GPA. Auditions held as needed on campus; recorded music is permissible as a substitute for live auditions if a live audition is impossible and videotaped performances are permissible as a substitute for live auditions if a live audition is impossible. Portfolio reviews held as needed on campus.

Web Site http://www.ruf.rice.edu/~musi/.

Undergraduate Contact Mr. Gary Smith, Assistant Dean, Shepherd School of Music, Rice University, 6100 Main, Houston, Texas 77005; 713-527-4047, fax: 713-285-5317.

Graduate Contact Graduate Admissions, Shepherd School of Music, Rice University, 6100 Main, Houston, Texas 77005; 713-527-4854, fax: 713-285-5317.

▼ RIDER UNIVERSITY

See Westminster Choir College of Rider University

▼ ROLAND DILLE CENTER FOR THE ARTS

See Moorhead State University

Chicago Musical College

▼ ROOSEVELT UNIVERSITY

Chicago, Illinois

Independent, coed. Urban campus. Total enrollment: 6,605. Music program established 1867.

Degrees Bachelor of Music in the areas of jazz performance, classical performance, music education, composition, theory, music history, piano pedagogy, music business, jazz composition, orchestral studies. Majors and concentrations: classical music, composition, harpsichord, jazz, music business, music education, music history, music theory, piano pedagogy, piano/organ, stringed instruments, vocal pedagogy, voice, wind and percussion instruments. Graduate degrees offered: Master of Music in the areas of classical performance, music education, theory, composition, musicology, vocal pedagogy, piano pedagogy, orchestral studies. Cross-registration with School of the Art Institute of Chicago. Program accredited by NASM.

Enrollment Fall 1997: 358 total; 250 undergraduate, 92 graduate, 16 non-professional degree.

Music Student Profile 48% females, 52% males, 47% minorities, 30% international.

Music Faculty 93 total undergraduate and graduate (full-time and part-time). 59% of full-time faculty have terminal degrees. Graduate students do not teach undergraduate courses. Undergraduate student–faculty ratio: 11:1.

Roosevelt University *(continued)*

Student Life Student groups/activities include Music Educators National Conference, Mu Phi Epsilon (music honorary fraternity). Special housing available for music students.

Expenses for 1997–98 Application fee: $25. Comprehensive fee: $16,530 includes full-time tuition ($10,830), mandatory fees ($200), and college room and board ($5500). Special program-related fees: $40 per semester for practice room rental.

Financial Aid Program-specific awards for 1997: 100 music scholarships for music majors ($3000), 60 Roosevelt Tuition Grants for those demonstrating need ($1200).

Application Procedures Students admitted directly into the professional program freshman year. Deadline for freshmen and transfers: continuous. Required: essay, high school transcript, college transcript(s) for transfer students, minimum 2.0 high school GPA, interview, audition, SAT I or ACT test scores (minimum combined ACT score of 20). Auditions held 10 times on campus; recorded music is permissible as a substitute for live auditions when distance is prohibitive and videotaped performances are permissible as a substitute for live auditions when distance is prohibitive.

Web Site http://www.roosevelt.edu.

Contact Mr. Bryan Shilander, Assistant Dean, Chicago Musical College, Roosevelt University, 430 South Michigan Avenue, Chicago, Illinois 60605; 312-341-3789, fax: 312-341-6358, E-mail address: bdsmusic@insnet.com.

More About the College

Program Facilities Chicago Musical College was founded in 1867 and joined Roosevelt University in 1954. Students make the most of the city's vast musical and cultural activities. Within walking distance are the Chicago Symphony Orchestra, the Lyric Opera of Chicago, the Grant Park Symphony, the Auditorium Theatre, Jazz Showcase, theaters, museums, and parks. Located in Roosevelt University's landmark Auditorium Building, the College features air conditioned practice studios, MIDI instruments and computers, the historic Ganz Recital Hall, well-equipped studios and classrooms, and a large music library. Secure modern dormitory, dining, meeting, and recreational facilities. Special unlimited practice privileges for resident students.

Faculty, Resident Artists, and Alumni Many faculty members perform on national and international concert stages. Notables include Ludmila Lazar and Pawel Checinski, piano; Bruce Berr, piano pedagogy; David Schrader, organ and harpsichord; Cyrus Forough, violin; Natalia Khoma, cello; Paul Henry, classical guitar; Gregory Smith, clarinet; Judith Haddon, Maria Lagios, and Patryk Wroblewski, voice; Rob Parton, jazz; Edward Poremba, percussion; Robert Lombardo, composition; and Anne Heider, choral conducting. Many faculty members of the Chicago Symphony Orchestra are faculty members, including Richard Graef, flute; Alex Klein and Michael Henoch, oboe; Gregory Smith, clarinet; William Buchman, bassoon; Dale Clevenger, horn; Jay Friedman and Charles Vernon, trombone; Gene Pokorny, tuba; Sarah Bullen, harp; Joseph Golan, violin; Li-Kuo Chang and Richard Ferrin, viola; John Sharp, cello; and Stephen Lester, bass.

Student Performance/Exhibit Opportunities More than 140 concerts, recitals, operas, and musicals presented each year. Ensembles include Chorus, Chamber Singers, Symphony, Wind Ensemble, Opera, Jazz Ensembles, Chamber Music, Early Music,

New Music, Two-Piano, Guitar Ensemble, and Collegium Musicum. Off-campus performance opportunities for advanced students.

Special Programs A diverse student body from 19 states and 23 foreign countries. Particularly accommodating to international students. Admission with or without TOEFL and TWE scores. Roosevelt University offers extensive ESL preparation for students without TOEFL. Music scholarship program open to both U.S. and international applicants. Music business internship, MENC, and Mu Phi Epsilon chapters.

▼ ROWAN UNIVERSITY

Glassboro, New Jersey

State-supported, coed. Small town campus. Total enrollment: 9,367.

Degrees Bachelor of Music. Majors and concentrations: composition, jazz, music education, performance. Program accredited by NASM.

Enrollment Fall 1997: 147 total; 110 undergraduate, 37 non-professional degree.

Music Student Profile 50% females, 50% males, 10% minorities, 5% international.

Music Faculty 45 total (full-time and part-time). 100% of full-time faculty have terminal degrees. Graduate students do not teach undergraduate courses. Undergraduate student–faculty ratio: 8:1.

Student Life Student groups/activities include Music Educators National Conference Student Chapter, Pi Kappa Lambda, Phi Mu Alpha.

Expenses for 1997–98 Application fee: $50. State resident tuition: $3130 full-time. Nonresident tuition: $6260 full-time. Mandatory fees: $1111 full-time. College room and board: $5326. College room only: $3326. Room and board charges vary according to board plan and housing facility.

Financial Aid Program-specific awards for 1997: 25 Department of Music Scholarships for music students ($1000).

Application Procedures Students admitted directly into the professional program freshman year. Deadline for freshmen: March 15; transfers: April 15. Required: high school transcript, college transcript(s) for transfer students, audition, SAT I or ACT test scores, portfolio for composition applicants. Auditions held 4 times on campus; recorded music is permissible as a substitute for live auditions when distance is prohibitive and videotaped performances are permissible as a substitute for live auditions when distance is prohibitive. Portfolio reviews held throughout the year on campus.

Web Site http://www.rowan.edu.

Undergraduate Contact Mr. Dean Witten, Chair, Music Department, Rowan University, 201 Mullica Hill Road, Glassboro, New Jersey 08028-1702; 609-256-4555, E-mail address: witten@heroes.rowan.edu.

▼ RUTGERS, THE STATE UNIVERSITY OF NEW JERSEY

See Mason Gross School of the Arts

▼ St. Cloud State University

St. Cloud, Minnesota

State-supported, coed. Suburban campus. Total enrollment: 13,946. Music program established 1869.

Degrees Bachelor of Music in the areas of performance, piano pedagogy; Bachelor of Science in the area of music education; Bachelor of Arts in the area of music. Majors and concentrations: classical music, composition, jazz, music education, piano/organ, stringed instruments, voice, wind and percussion instruments. Graduate degrees offered: Master of Music in the areas of education, conducting, piano pedagogy. Program accredited by NASM.

Enrollment Fall 1997: 370 total; 90 undergraduate, 30 graduate, 250 non-professional degree.

Music Student Profile 50% females, 50% males, 3% minorities, 4% international.

Music Faculty 26 total undergraduate and graduate (full-time and part-time). 90% of full-time faculty have terminal degrees. Graduate students do not teach undergraduate courses. Undergraduate student–faculty ratio: 13:1.

Student Life Student groups/activities include Sigma Alpha Iota, Music Educators National Conference Student Chapter, American String Teachers Association Student Chapter.

Expenses for 1997–98 Application fee: $20. State resident tuition: $2582 full-time. Nonresident tuition: $5606 full-time. Mandatory fees: $500 full-time. Full-time tuition and fees vary according to course load, location, and reciprocity agreements. College room and board: $3066. Room and board charges vary according to board plan. Special program-related fees: $60 per year for instrument rental .

Financial Aid Program-specific awards for 1997: 40 Endowed/Foundation Scholarships for talented students ($650), 5 May Bowle Scholarships for talented students ($400), 8 David Swenson Memorial Awards for percussion students ($2000).

Application Procedures Students apply for admission into the professional program by sophomore year. Deadline for freshmen and transfers: continuous. Required: high school transcript, minimum 2.0 high school GPA, ACT test score only, audition for scholarship consideration. Auditions held once on campus; recorded music is permissible as a substitute for live auditions by arrangement with department and videotaped performances are permissible as a substitute for live auditions by arrangement with department.

Web Site http://www.stcloudstate.edu/~music.

Undergraduate Contact Mr. Sherwood Reid, Director of Admissions, St. Cloud State University, 720 4th Avenue South, St. Cloud, Minnesota 56301-4498; 320-255-2244, fax: 320-654-5367.

Graduate Contact Mr. Dennis Nunes, Dean, School of Graduate Studies, St. Cloud State University, 720 4th Avenue South, St. Cloud, Minnesota 56301-4498; 320-255-2113, fax: 320-654-5371.

▼ St. Francis Xavier University

Antigonish, NS, Canada

Independent-Roman Catholic, coed. Small town campus. Total enrollment: 4,048.

Degrees Bachelor of Music in the areas of jazz performance, jazz composition/arranging. Majors and concentrations: bass, brass, classical music, jazz, jazz guitar, music, piano, voice, wind and percussion instruments.

Enrollment Fall 1997: 375 total; 100 undergraduate, 275 non-professional degree.

Music Student Profile 20% females, 80% males, 5% minorities, 1% international.

Music Faculty 11 total (full-time and part-time). 100% of full-time faculty have terminal degrees. Graduate students do not teach undergraduate courses. Undergraduate student–faculty ratio: 25:1.

Student Life Student groups/activities include Nova Scotia Music Educators Association.

Expenses for 1997–98 Application fee: $30 Canadian dollars. Tuition, fee, and room and board charges are reported in Canadian dollars. Canadian resident tuition: $3775 full-time. Mandatory fees: $123 full-time. Full-time tuition and fees vary according to course load. College room and board: $4985. Room and board charges vary according to board plan and housing facility. International student tuition: $6775 full-time.

Financial Aid Program-specific awards for 1997: 3 music scholarships for program majors ($1000), 8 music bursaries for program majors ($250–$500).

Application Procedures Deadline for freshmen and transfers: June 30. Notification date for freshmen and transfers: August 1. Required: high school transcript, college transcript(s) for transfer students, audition. Recommended: 2 letters of recommendation. Auditions held continuously on campus; recorded music is permissible as a substitute for live auditions if certified by a teacher and videotaped performances are permissible as a substitute for live auditions if certified by a teacher.

Undergraduate Contact Director of Admissions, St. Francis Xavier University, PO Box 5000, Antigonish, NS B2G 2W5, Canada; 902-867-2219, fax: 902-867-2329.

▼ Saint Mary's College

Notre Dame, Indiana

Independent-Roman Catholic, women only. Suburban campus. Total enrollment: 1,347.

Degrees Bachelor of Music in the areas of performance, music education. Cross-registration with University of Notre Dame. Program accredited by NASM, NCATE.

Enrollment Fall 1997: 20 total; 11 undergraduate, 9 non-professional degree.

Music Student Profile 100% females, 15% minorities.

Music Faculty 25 total (full-time and part-time). 100% of full-time faculty have terminal degrees. Graduate students do not teach undergraduate courses. Undergraduate student–faculty ratio: 4:1.

Student Life Student groups/activities include Music Educators National Conference Student Chapter, Arts Club, NATS Competitions (National Association of Teachers of Singing).

Expenses for 1997–98 Application fee: $30. Comprehensive fee: $20,849 includes full-time tuition ($14,738), mandatory fees ($914), and college room and board ($5197). Special program-related fees: $195 per 1/2 hour for private lessons, $325 per 50-minute for private lessons, $5 per key for practice room key deposit.

Financial Aid Program-specific awards for 1997: 1–3 Presidential Merit Scholarships for exceptionally talented students ($4000).

Application Procedures Students admitted directly into the professional program freshman year. Deadline for freshmen and transfers: continuous. Required: essay, high school

Saint Mary's College (*continued*)

transcript, college transcript(s) for transfer students, minimum 3.0 high school GPA, letter of recommendation, audition, SAT I or ACT test scores, minimum 3.0 college GPA for transfer students. Recommended: interview. Auditions held continuously on campus; recorded music is permissible as a substitute for live auditions when distance is prohibitive and videotaped performances are permissible as a substitute for live auditions when distance is prohibitive.
Web Site http://www.saintmarys.edu.
Undergraduate Contact Dr. Nancy Menk, Chair, Department of Music, Saint Mary's College, 313 Moreau Center for the Arts, Notre Dame, Indiana 46556-5001; 219-284-4632, fax: 219-284-4716, E-mail address: nmenk@saintmarys.edu.

▼ St. Norbert College

De Pere, Wisconsin

Independent-Roman Catholic, coed. Suburban campus. Total enrollment: 2,000.
Degrees Bachelor of Music in the areas of performance, music education. Majors and concentrations: music, music education, music liberal arts, piano/organ, voice, wind and percussion instruments.
Enrollment Fall 1997: 57 total; all undergraduate.
Music Student Profile 58% females, 42% males, 4% minorities, 1% international.
Music Faculty 13 total (full-time and part-time). 66% of full-time faculty have terminal degrees. Graduate students do not teach undergraduate courses. Undergraduate student–faculty ratio: 7:1.
Student Life Student groups/activities include Music Educators National Conference.
Expenses for 1997–98 Application fee: $25. Comprehensive fee: $19,554 includes full-time tuition ($14,234), mandatory fees ($200), and college room and board ($5120). College room only: $2675. Full-time tuition and fees vary according to course load. Room and board charges vary according to board plan and housing facility.
Financial Aid Program-specific awards for 1997: 20–25 Music Merit Scholarships for program majors/minors ($2500).
Application Procedures Deadline for freshmen and transfers: continuous. Required: essay, high school transcript, college transcript(s) for transfer students, letter of recommendation, SAT I or ACT test scores, minimum 2.5 high school GPA. Recommended: interview, audition. Auditions held 4 times and by request on campus; recorded music is permissible as a substitute for live auditions when distance is prohibitive and videotaped performances are permissible as a substitute for live auditions when distance is prohibitive.
Web Site http://www.snc.edu.
Undergraduate Contact Mr. Dan Meyer, Dean of Admission, St. Norbert College, 316 Third Street, De Pere, Wisconsin 54115; 920-403-3005, fax: 920-403-4072, E-mail address: admit@sncac.snc.edu.

▼ St. Olaf College

Northfield, Minnesota

Independent-Lutheran, coed. Small town campus. Total enrollment: 2,975.

Degrees Bachelor of Music in the areas of performance, music education, church music, theory/composition. Majors and concentrations: classical guitar, piano/organ, stringed instruments, voice, wind and percussion instruments. Program accredited by NASM.
Enrollment Fall 1997: 1,031 total; 180 undergraduate, 851 non-professional degree.
Music Student Profile 61% females, 39% males, 2% minorities, 1% international.
Music Faculty 67 total (full-time and part-time). 85% of full-time faculty have terminal degrees. Graduate students do not teach undergraduate courses. Undergraduate student–faculty ratio: 11:1.
Expenses for 1997–98 Application fee: $35. Comprehensive fee: $20,520 includes full-time tuition ($16,500) and college room and board ($4020). College room only: $1820. Room and board charges vary according to board plan.
Financial Aid Program-specific awards for 1997: 10 Winston Cassler Scholarships for music and non-music majors ($3000), 15 Music Merit Scholarships for music majors ($1000).
Application Procedures Students apply for admission into the professional program by freshman year. Deadline for freshmen: June 1; transfers: July 1. Notification date for freshmen and transfers: continuous. Required: essay, high school transcript, college transcript(s) for transfer students, 2 letters of recommendation, audition, SAT I or ACT test scores. Recommended: portfolio for theory/composition applicants. Auditions held once on campus; recorded music is permissible as a substitute for live auditions for provisional acceptance and videotaped performances are permissible as a substitute for live auditions if a live audition is impossible. Portfolio reviews held by request on campus.
Web Site http://www.stolaf.edu/depts/music/.
Undergraduate Contact Ms. Anna Lisa Hembre Rustad, Music Admissions Coordinator, Department of Music, St. Olaf College, 1520 St. Olaf Avenue, Northfield, Minnesota 55057-1098; 507-646-3297, fax: 507-646-3527, E-mail address: music@stolaf.edu.

▼ Saint Xavier University

Chicago, Illinois

Independent-Roman Catholic, coed. Urban campus. Total enrollment: 3,719. Music program established 1990.
Degrees Bachelor of Music in the areas of performance, music education. Majors and concentrations: music education, piano/organ, stringed instruments, voice, wind and percussion instruments. Program accredited by NASM.
Enrollment Fall 1997: 235 total; 35 undergraduate, 200 non-professional degree.
Music Student Profile 60% females, 40% males, 5% minorities, 1% international.
Music Faculty 21 total (full-time and part-time). 100% of full-time faculty have terminal degrees. Graduate students do not teach undergraduate courses. Undergraduate student–faculty ratio: 5:1.
Student Life Student groups/activities include Collegiate Music Educators National Conference.
Expenses for 1997–98 Application fee: $25. One-time mandatory fee: $30. Comprehensive fee: $17,744 includes full-time tuition ($12,450), mandatory fees ($110), and college room and board ($5184). Special program-related fees: $100 per semester for accompanist fee, $45 per semester for computer

lab fee for theory courses, $45 per semester for piano lab fee for keyboard musicianship courses, $45 per semester for instrument rental fee for methods courses, $100 per credit for applied practicum fee.

Financial Aid Program-specific awards for 1997: 3 Sinon Catherine O'Donohue Keyboard Scholarships for keyboard students ($2000), 7 Sister Gabrielle McShane Awards for vocalists/instrumentalists ($2000), band scholarships for ensemble performers ($750–$5000), 8 Talent Awards for voice/string students ($1000–$2000).

Application Procedures Students apply for admission into the professional program by sophomore year. Deadline for freshmen and transfers: continuous. Required: essay, high school transcript, college transcript(s) for transfer students, minimum 2.0 high school GPA, letter of recommendation, interview, audition, SAT I or ACT test scores. Auditions held 4-5 times and by appointment on campus; videotaped performances are permissible as a substitute for live auditions for out-of-state and international applicants.

Web Site http://www.sxu.edu.

Undergraduate Contact Dr. Greg Coutts, Chair, Music Department, Saint Xavier University, 3700 West 103rd Street, Chicago, Illinois 60655; 773-298-3424, fax: 773-779-9061, E-mail address: coutts@sxu.edu.

▼ SALEM COLLEGE

Winston-Salem, North Carolina

Independent-Moravian, primarily women. Urban campus. Total enrollment: 1,002. Music program established 1879.

Degrees Bachelor of Music in the areas of piano, organ, voice, flute. Cross-registration with Wake Forest University. Program accredited by NASM.

Enrollment Fall 1997: 37 total; 29 undergraduate, 8 non-professional degree.

Music Student Profile 100% females, 8% minorities.

Music Faculty 9 total (full-time and part-time). 100% of full-time faculty have terminal degrees. Graduate students do not teach undergraduate courses. Undergraduate student–faculty ratio: 7:1.

Student Life Student groups/activities include Pierrette's Players (drama club).

Expenses for 1997–98 Application fee: $25. Comprehensive fee: $19,735 includes full-time tuition ($12,200), mandatory fees ($215), and college room and board ($7320). Special program-related fees: $170–$340 per semester for private lessons.

Financial Aid Program-specific awards for 1997: 3 Dunford Scholarships for program majors ($2500–$3000), 3 Christian Gregor Awards for program majors ($5000–$6000), 3 Fletcher Foundation Awards for program majors ($7000), 5 Vardell Music Scholarships for program majors ($1000–$1500), 1 Mueller Scholarship for organ majors, 1 Pfohl Scholarship for program majors.

Application Procedures Students admitted directly into the professional program freshman year. Deadline for freshmen and transfers: continuous. Required: essay, high school transcript, college transcript(s) for transfer students, minimum 2.0 high school GPA, 2 letters of recommendation, audition, SAT I or ACT test scores. Recommended: interview. Auditions held 3-4 times and by appointment on campus; recorded music is permissible as a substitute for live auditions if a campus visit is impossible and videotaped

performances are permissible as a substitute for live auditions if a campus visit is impossible.

Undergraduate Contact Ms. Katherine Knapp Watts, Dean of Admissions and Financial Aid, Salem College, PO Box 10548, Winston-Salem, North Carolina 27108; 336-721-2621, fax: 336-721-2683.

▼ SAMFORD UNIVERSITY

Birmingham, Alabama

Independent-Baptist, coed. Suburban campus. Total enrollment: 4,485.

Degrees Bachelor of Music in the areas of performance, church music, music theory/composition; Bachelor of Music Education in the areas of vocal music education, instrumental music education. Majors and concentrations: church music, music education, music theory and composition, piano/organ, stringed instruments, voice, wind and percussion instruments. Graduate degrees offered: Master of Music in the areas of church music, music education. Program accredited by NASM.

Enrollment Fall 1997: 132 total; 122 undergraduate, 10 graduate.

Music Student Profile 55% females, 45% males.

Music Faculty 26 total undergraduate and graduate (full-time and part-time). 68% of full-time faculty have terminal degrees. Graduate students do not teach undergraduate courses. Undergraduate student–faculty ratio: 8:1.

Student Life Student groups/activities include Phi Mu Alpha Sinfonia, Delta Omicron, Music Educators National Conference Student Chapter.

Expenses for 1997–98 Application fee: $25. Comprehensive fee: $13,828 includes full-time tuition ($9432) and college room and board ($4396). Special program-related fees: $35 per credit hour for applied music fee.

Financial Aid Program-specific awards for 1997: 30–40 music scholarships for program majors ($500–$2000), 20 band scholarships for band members ($400–$1500).

Application Procedures Students admitted directly into the professional program freshman year. Deadline for freshmen and transfers: continuous. Notification date for freshmen and transfers: May 1. Required: essay, high school transcript, college transcript(s) for transfer students, 2 letters of recommendation, audition, SAT I or ACT test scores. Recommended: minimum 3.0 high school GPA. Auditions held 4 times on campus; videotaped performances are permissible as a substitute for live auditions in special circumstances and when scheduling is difficult.

Web Site http://www.samford.edu/schools/music/music.html.

Undergraduate Contact Dr. Billy Strickland, Assistant Dean for Undergraduate Studies, School of Music, Samford University, PO Box 292242, 800 Lakeshore Drive, Birmingham, Alabama 35229; 205-870-2826, fax: 205-870-2165.

Graduate Contact Dr. Paul Richardson, Assistant Dean for Graduate Studies, School of Music, Samford University, PO Box 292242, 800 Lakeshore Drive, Birmingham, Alabama 35229; 205-870-2496, fax: 205-870-2165.

▼ SAM HOUSTON STATE UNIVERSITY

Huntsville, Texas

State-supported, coed. Small town campus. Total enrollment: 12,712. Music program established 1938.

Sam Houston State University *(continued)*

Degrees Bachelor of Music in the areas of performance, music theory/composition, music literature, music therapy; Bachelor of Music Education. Majors and concentrations: classical music, music, music education, music therapy, opera, piano/organ, stringed instruments, voice, wind and percussion instruments. Graduate degrees offered: Master of Music in the areas of performance, music theory/composition, conducting, musicology, Kodály pedagogy; Master of Music Education. Program accredited by NASM.

Enrollment Fall 1997: 369 total; 285 undergraduate, 19 graduate, 65 non-professional degree.

Music Student Profile 45% females, 55% males, 30% minorities, 10% international.

Music Faculty 45 total undergraduate and graduate (full-time and part-time). 85% of full-time faculty have terminal degrees. Graduate students teach a few undergraduate courses. Undergraduate student–faculty ratio: 10:1.

Student Life Student groups/activities include American Association of Music Therapy Student Chapter, Sigma Alpha Iota, Kappa Kappa Psi.

Expenses for 1997–98 Application fee: $15. State resident tuition: $816 full-time. Nonresident tuition: $5952 full-time. Mandatory fees: $770 full-time. College room and board: $3290. College room only: $1710. Room and board charges vary according to board plan and housing facility. Special program-related fees: $20 for recital recording fee, $30 for recital hall rental fee.

Financial Aid Program-specific awards for 1997: 120 scholarships for program students ($200–$1700).

Application Procedures Students admitted directly into the professional program freshman year. Deadline for freshmen and transfers: continuous. Required: high school transcript, 2 letters of recommendation, interview, audition. Recommended: minimum 2.0 high school GPA. Auditions held a minimum of 6 times on campus and off campus in various locations; recorded music is permissible as a substitute for live auditions with permission of the chair and videotaped performances are permissible as a substitute for live auditions when distance is prohibitive.

Web Site http://www.shsu.edu.

Undergraduate Contact Mr. Rodney M. Cannon, Chair, Music Department, Sam Houston State University, PO Box 2208, Huntsville, Texas 77341-2208; 409-294-1360, fax: 409-294-3765, E-mail address: mus_rmc@shsu.edu.

Graduate Contact Dr. Alan Strong, Graduate Student Advisor, Music Department, Sam Houston State University, PO Box 2208, Huntsville, Texas 77341-2208; 409-294-1360, fax: 409-294-3765, E-mail address: mus_rmc@shsu.edu.

▼ SAN DIEGO STATE UNIVERSITY

San Diego, California

State-supported, coed. Urban campus. Total enrollment: 29,898. Music program established 1898.

Degrees Bachelor of Music in the areas of performance, jazz studies, composition, general music, music education. Majors and concentrations: classical music, composition, early instruments, jazz, music, music education, piano/organ, stringed instruments, voice, wind and percussion instruments, world music instruments. Graduate degrees offered: Master of Music in the areas of performance, jazz studies, composition, conducting; Master of Arts in the area of music.

Cross-registration with University of California-San Diego. Program accredited by NASM.

Enrollment Fall 1997: 190 undergraduate, 60 graduate.

Music Student Profile 55% females, 45% males, 40% minorities, 5% international.

Music Faculty 52 total undergraduate and graduate (full-time and part-time). 12% of full-time faculty have terminal degrees. Graduate students teach a few undergraduate courses. Undergraduate student–faculty ratio: 17:1.

Student Life Student groups/activities include Phi Mu Alpha, Kappa Kappa Psi, Sigma Alpha Iota.

Expenses for 1997–98 Application fee: $55. State resident tuition: $0 full-time. Nonresident tuition: $7626 full-time. Mandatory fees: $1854 full-time. College room and board: $6730. Room and board charges vary according to board plan. Special program-related fees: $20 per semester for piano practice room, $20 per semester for instrument use fee.

Financial Aid Program-specific awards for 1997: 40–50 scholarships for music majors ($500–$3000).

Application Procedures Students admitted directly into the professional program freshman year. Deadline for freshmen and transfers: continuous. Notification date for freshmen and transfers: continuous. Required: high school transcript, college transcript(s) for transfer students, minimum 2.0 high school GPA, audition, SAT I or ACT test scores. Auditions held twice on campus.

Web Site http://apple.sdsu.edu/music_dance/music_dance.html.

Undergraduate Contact Dr. Marian Liebowitz, Undergraduate Advisor - Music, School of Music and Dance, San Diego State University, San Diego, California 92182-7902; 619-594-6031, fax: 619-594-1692, E-mail address: music.dance@sdsu.edu.

Graduate Contact Dr. Eddie Meadows, Graduate Advisor - Music, School of Music and Dance, San Diego State University, San Diego, California 92182-7902; 619-594-6031, fax: 619-594-1692, E-mail address: music.dance@sdsu.edu.

▼ SAN FRANCISCO CONSERVATORY OF MUSIC

San Francisco, California

Independent, coed. Urban campus. Total enrollment: 261. Music program established 1917.

Degrees Bachelor of Music in the areas of classical guitar, composition, keyboard instruments, orchestral instruments, voice. Majors and concentrations: classical guitar, classical music, composition, piano/organ, stringed instruments, voice, wind and percussion instruments. Graduate degrees offered: Master of Music in the areas of chamber music, classical guitar, composition, instrumental conducting, keyboard instruments, orchestral instruments, piano accompanying, voice. Program accredited by NASM.

Enrollment Fall 1997: 261 total; 154 undergraduate, 100 graduate, 7 non-professional degree.

Music Student Profile 57% females, 43% males, 26% minorities, 21% international.

Music Faculty 77 total undergraduate and graduate (full-time and part-time). 30% of full-time faculty have terminal degrees. Graduate students do not teach undergraduate courses. Undergraduate student–faculty ratio: 6:1.

Student Life Student groups/activities include Student Government Organization.

Expenses for 1997–98 Application fee: $60. Tuition: $16,300 full-time. Mandatory fees: $250 full-time. Full-time tuition and fees vary according to program.

Financial Aid Program-specific awards for 1997: 85–120 Conservatory Scholarships for undergraduates ($8000).

Application Procedures Students admitted directly into the professional program freshman year. Deadline for freshmen and transfers: March 1. Notification date for freshmen and transfers: June 15. Required: high school transcript, college transcript(s) for transfer students, minimum 2.0 high school GPA, 2 letters of recommendation, audition, SAT I or ACT test scores, video tape for voice applicants. Auditions held 6 times on campus and off campus in Boston, MA; New York, NY; Chicago, IL; Oberlin, OH; Interlochen, MI; Los Angeles, CA; Houston, TX; Portland, OR; Seattle, WA; recorded music is permissible as a substitute for live auditions for applicants residing outside of northern California and international applicants and videotaped performances are permissible as a substitute for live auditions for applicants residing outside of northern California and international applicants.

Web Site http://www.sfcm.edu.

Contact Ms. Joan Gordon, Admission Officer, Office of Student Services, San Francisco Conservatory of Music, 1201 Ortega Street, San Francisco, California 94122-4498; 415-759-3431, fax: 415-759-3499, E-mail address: jgordon@sirius.com.

San Francisco Conservatory of Music

More About the Conservatory

Program Facilities Hellman Hall (333 seats), considered one of the finest concert halls of its size in northern California, and Agnes Albert Hall (sixty seats), a multiuse performance/teaching space; Bothin Library, offering more than 35,000 volumes, scores, and periodicals and more than 9,000 recordings; E. L. Wieland Computer Laboratory and the Electronic Composition Studio; additional features, including a professional recording studio, bookstore, and sixty-three practice rooms.

Faculty, Visiting Artists, and Alumni SFCM faculty are members of the San Francisco Symphony, San Francisco Opera, San Francisco Ballet, and Philharmonia Baroque orchestras and perform internationally as soloists and chamber musicians. Recent visiting artists include Isaac Stern, Elliott Carter, John Adams, Leon Fleisher, Thomas Hampson, Richard Goode, Frederica von Stade, and the Juilliard String Quartet. Nationally known alumni include pianists Jeffrey Kahane and Robin Sutherland, guitarist David Tanenbaum, mezzo-

soprano Wendy Hillhouse, and Naumburg Award–winning cellist Hai-Ye Ni. Isaac Stern and Yehudi Menuhin studied at the Conservatory as children.

Student Performance Opportunities Approximately 400 events are presented at SFCM each year, featuring solo recitals by students and faculty members, small ensembles, a fully staged opera, and symphonic programs. Ensembles: the Conservatory Orchestra, Conservatory Opera Theatre, Cantata Singers, Conservatory Baroque, and special ensembles focusing on brass and woodwinds, new music, guitar, and percussion. Concentrated studies: chamber music and baroque performance.

▼

The San Francisco Conservatory of Music was founded in 1917 as a small piano school and has become a nationally prominent conservatory with an international reputation. The Conservatory enrolls approximately 270 students from all over the United States and the world in the undergraduate and graduate programs each year. Students work both one-on-one with their major instrument teacher and in small classes with other faculty members. In addition to their teaching, faculty members coach students for their recitals and often perform with alumni and students in concerts throughout the year. The Conservatory offers a great deal of personal attention for each student, in part because of a low student-teacher ratio of 6:1. In the school's friendly and intimate atmosphere, students receive an intense and intellectually rigorous preparation for a career in music.

Most students live near the Conservatory, which is in a quiet, affordable residential neighborhood near Golden Gate Park about 2 miles from the Pacific Ocean. Convenient public transportation provides access to downtown San Francisco and the Civic Center, the city's performing arts center.

San Francisco's performing arts offerings range from world-class symphony, opera, and ballet to avant-garde music, theater, dance, and performance. Free tickets to many performances are available to Conservatory students. Museums, galleries, and the great physical beauty of San Francisco—its parks, beaches, views, and neighborhoods—provide much to explore.

Performing is a major aspect of student life at the Conservatory. Students perform recitals required for their degrees and perform with the orchestra, opera theater, and numerous ensembles based at the Conservatory.

Every year, the Conservatory's Community Service Program sends students out into the community to perform concerts at convalescent homes, hospitals and other institutions, while the Music To Go! program offers approximately 1,000 paid performance opportunities. Outside the Conservatory, students can augment their studies by performing with a wide range of professional groups including many regional symphony orchestras, chamber music ensembles, opera companies, and choruses in the San Francisco Bay Area. With this opportunity to build a professional network while still in school, students from the Conservatory have a head start in the highly competitive field of music. Students at the Conservatory fulfill their early promise by going on to work directly in the music profession. Conservatory alumni have distinguished themselves in many facets of music. Alumni perform with a wide range of music organizations, including the following: Arditti String Quartet, Chicago Symphony, Glyndebourne Festival Opera, Israel Philhar-

San Francisco Conservatory of Music *(continued)*

monic, Los Angeles Philharmonic, Metropolitan Opera, Minnesota Orchestra, National Symphony Orchestra, New York City Opera, New Zealand String Quartet, Sausalito String Quartet, New York Philharmonic, Oslo Philharmonic, Peabody Trio, Philadelphia Orchestra, Philharmonia Baroque, Philip Glass Ensemble, San Diego Symphony, San Francisco Ballet Orchestra, San Francisco Opera and Opera Orchestra, San Francisco Symphony, Santa Fe Opera, Stuttgart Staatsoper, and Tokyo Philharmonic Orchestra.

The San Francisco Conservatory was the first conservatory in the United States to offer a graduate degree program in chamber music and also offers a significant undergraduate experience in chamber music.

The Conservatory travels to many U.S. cities to hear auditions. The 1998–99 regional audition tours include stops in Boston, New York City, Chicago, Oberlin, Interlochen, Los Angeles, Houston, Portland, and Seattle.

(Photo by Terence McCarthy)

▼ San Francisco State University

San Francisco, California

State-supported, coed. Urban campus. Total enrollment: 27,420. Music program established 1930.

Degrees Bachelor of Music in the areas of music education, performance, composition, music history and literature. Majors and concentrations: composition, instrumental music, instrumental performance, music education, music history, organ, piano, voice. Graduate degrees offered: Master of Music in the areas of solo performance, chamber music, conducting, music; Master of Arts in the area of music. Program accredited by NASM.

Enrollment Fall 1997: 875 total; 275 undergraduate, 50 graduate, 550 non-professional degree.

Music Student Profile 54% females, 46% males, 25% minorities, 5% international.

Music Faculty 52 total undergraduate and graduate (full-time and part-time). 100% of full-time faculty have terminal degrees. Graduate students teach a few undergraduate courses. Undergraduate student–faculty ratio: 18:1.

Student Life Student groups/activities include California Music Educators Association.

Expenses for 1997–98 Application fee: $55. State resident tuition: $0 full-time. Nonresident tuition: $5904 full-time. Mandatory fees: $1982 full-time. College room and board: $5935. Room and board charges vary according to board plan and housing facility. Special program-related fees: $25 per year for ear lab fee.

Financial Aid Program-specific awards for 1997: music scholarships for academically and artistically talented program majors.

Application Procedures Students admitted directly into the professional program freshman year. Deadline for freshmen and transfers: continuous. Required: high school transcript, college transcript(s) for transfer students, minimum 3.0 high school GPA, audition, SAT I or ACT test scores, minimum TOEFL score of 500 for international applicants, theory and ear training placement exam. Auditions held 4 times on campus; recorded music is permissible as a substitute for live auditions when distance is prohibitive and videotaped performances are permissible as a substitute for live auditions when distance is prohibitive.

Undergraduate Contact Enrollment Services, San Francisco State University, 1600 Holloway Avenue, San Francisco, California 94132-1722; 415-338-1431, fax: 415-338-3294.

Graduate Contact Graduate Division, San Francisco State University, 1600 Holloway Avenue, San Francisco, California 94132-1722; 415-338-2233.

▼ San Jose State University

San Jose, California

State-supported, coed. Urban campus. Total enrollment: 26,897.

Degrees Bachelor of Music in the area of performance. Program accredited by NASM.

Enrollment Fall 1997: 275 total; 50 undergraduate, 225 non-professional degree.

Music Student Profile 50% females, 50% males, 30% minorities, 10% international.

Music Faculty 55 total (full-time and part-time). 90% of full-time faculty have terminal degrees. Graduate students do not teach undergraduate courses. Undergraduate student–faculty ratio: 4:1.

Student Life Student groups/activities include Music Educators National Conference Student Chapter, Mu Phi Epsilon.

Expenses for 1997–98 Application fee: $55. State resident tuition: $0 full-time. Nonresident tuition: $7380 full-time. Mandatory fees: $2017 full-time. College room and board: $5306. Room and board charges vary according to board plan. Special program-related fees: $20 per semester for equipment use fee.

Financial Aid Program-specific awards for 1997: 25–50 music scholarships for freshmen and transfer students ($750–$850).

Application Procedures Students apply for admission into the professional program by freshman year. Deadline for freshmen and transfers: continuous. Notification date for freshmen and transfers: continuous. Required: essay, high school transcript, college transcript(s) for transfer students, minimum 2.0 high school GPA, audition, SAT I or ACT test scores, TOEFL score for international applicants. Auditions held twice on campus; recorded music is permissible as a substitute for live auditions when distance is prohibitive and videotaped performances are permissible as a substitute for live auditions when distance is prohibitive.

Undergraduate Contact Director of Admissions, San Jose State University, One Washington Square, San Jose, California 95192-0009; 408-283-7500, fax: 408-924-2050, E-mail address: contact@anrnet.sjsu.edu.

▼ Schmidt College of Arts and Letters

See Florida Atlantic University

▼ Seton Hall University

South Orange, New Jersey

Independent-Roman Catholic, coed. Suburban campus. Total enrollment: 10,114. Music program established 1968.

Degrees Bachelor of Music in the areas of voice, piano, classical instruments, historical musicology; Bachelor of

Music Education in the areas of vocal music education, instrumental music education. Majors and concentrations: applied music, music, music education, music history.

Enrollment Fall 1997: 50 undergraduate.

Music Student Profile 50% females, 50% males, 10% minorities, 1% international.

Music Faculty 31 total (full-time and part-time). 100% of full-time faculty have terminal degrees. Graduate students do not teach undergraduate courses. Undergraduate student–faculty ratio: 10:1.

Student Life Student groups/activities include musical theatre.

Expenses for 1997–98 Application fee: $25. Comprehensive fee: $20,620 includes full-time tuition ($13,050), mandatory fees ($550), and college room and board ($7020). College room only: $4940. Full-time tuition and fees vary according to course load. Room and board charges vary according to board plan and housing facility.

Financial Aid Program-specific awards for 1997: 1 O'Connor Award for those demonstrating talent and academic achievement ($1000).

Application Procedures Students admitted directly into the professional program freshman year. Deadline for freshmen and transfers: continuous. Required: essay, high school transcript, minimum 2.0 high school GPA, 3 letters of recommendation, audition, SAT I or ACT test scores. Recommended: interview. Auditions held by appointment on campus; recorded music is permissible as a substitute for live auditions for out-of-state applicants and videotaped performances are permissible as a substitute for live auditions for out-of-state applicants.

Undergraduate Contact Ms. Jeanette Hile, Professor of Applied Music, Music Department, Seton Hall University, 400 South Orange Avenue, South Orange, New Jersey 07079; 973-761-9417, fax: 973-275-2368, E-mail address: hilejean@shu.edu.

▼ SETON HILL COLLEGE

Greensburg, Pennsylvania

Independent-Roman Catholic, primarily women. Small town campus. Total enrollment: 1,078. Music program established 1918.

Degrees Bachelor of Music in the areas of performance, music education, sacred music. Majors and concentrations: music, music education, sacred music. Cross-registration with Saint Vincent College. Program accredited by NASM.

Enrollment Fall 1997: 72 total; 60 undergraduate, 12 non-professional degree.

Music Student Profile 50% females, 50% males, 3% minorities, 3% international.

Music Faculty 22 total (full-time and part-time). 100% of full-time faculty have terminal degrees. Graduate students do not teach undergraduate courses.

Student Life Student groups/activities include Music Educators National Conference, Pennsylvania Music Educators Association Student Chapter, American Guild of Organists.

Expenses for 1997–98 Application fee: $30. Comprehensive fee: $17,370 includes full-time tuition ($12,640) and college room and board ($4730). Special program-related fees: $12–$50 for music education methods course fee, $12 for large ensembles, $170 for private instruction on a major instrument, $85 for private instruction on a secondary instrument.

Financial Aid Program-specific awards for 1997: 2 Gabriel Burda Scholarships for incoming students ($4000), 4 String Quartet Scholarships for string players ($1500), 1 Highberger Scholarship for incoming students ($1000), 1 Choral Society Scholarship for incoming students ($500), 1 Symphonic Winds Scholarship for incoming students ($1000), 1–4 Mildred Gardner Music Scholarships for incoming students from Westmoreland County, PA ($1000–$4000).

Application Procedures Students admitted directly into the professional program freshman year. Deadline for freshmen and transfers: continuous. Notification date for freshmen and transfers: continuous. Required: high school transcript, college transcript(s) for transfer students, minimum 2.0 high school GPA, audition, SAT I or ACT test scores. Recommended: essay, minimum 3.0 high school GPA, letter of recommendation, interview. Auditions held by appointment on campus; recorded music is permissible as a substitute for live auditions if a campus visit is impossible and videotaped performances are permissible as a substitute for live auditions if a campus visit is impossible.

Web Site http://www.setonhill.edu.

Undergraduate Contact Ms. Barbara Hinkle, Director, Admissions Office, Seton Hill College, College Avenue, Greensburg, Pennsylvania 15601; 724-838-4255, fax: 724-830-4611, E-mail address: hinkle@is.setonhill.edu.

▼ SHENANDOAH UNIVERSITY

Winchester, Virginia

Independent-United Methodist, coed. Small town campus. Total enrollment: 1,927.

Degrees Bachelor of Music in the areas of church music, commercial music, composition, jazz studies, music education, pedagogy, performance, piano accompanying; Bachelor of Science in the area of arts management; Bachelor of Music Therapy. Majors and concentrations: arts management, commercial music, composition, jazz, music education, music therapy, pedagogy, piano/organ, sacred music, stringed instruments, voice, wind and percussion instruments. Graduate degrees offered: Master of Music in the areas of composition, conducting, performance, church music, dance accompanying, piano accompanying; Master of Music Education in the area of music education; Master of Science in the area of arts management. Doctor of Musical Arts in the area of music education. Program accredited by NASM.

Enrollment Fall 1997: 391 total; 292 undergraduate, 83 graduate, 16 non-professional degree.

Music Student Profile 61% females, 39% males, 20% minorities, 10% international.

Music Faculty 79 total undergraduate and graduate (full-time and part-time). 52% of full-time faculty have terminal degrees. Graduate students do not teach undergraduate courses. Undergraduate student–faculty ratio: 5:1.

Student Life Student groups/activities include music fraternities and sororities, Music Educators National Conference Student Chapter, Student Association of Music Therapy.

Expenses for 1997–98 Application fee: $30. Comprehensive fee: $19,450 includes full-time tuition ($14,400) and college room and board ($5050). Full-time tuition varies according to course load, degree level, and program. Room and board charges vary according to board plan. Special program-related fees: $250 per 1 hour lesson for private music lessons for majors, $125 per 1/2 hour lesson for private voice and piano lessons.

Financial Aid Program-specific awards for 1997: 115 Talent Scholarships for program students ($250–$14,400).

Shenandoah University (*continued*)

Application Procedures Students admitted directly into the professional program freshman year. Deadline for freshmen and transfers: continuous. Required: high school transcript, college transcript(s) for transfer students, minimum 2.0 high school GPA, interview, video, audition, SAT I or ACT test scores, portfolio for composition majors. Recommended: letter of recommendation, portfolio. Auditions held 15 times on campus and off campus in various cities; recorded music is permissible as a substitute for live auditions if a campus visit is impossible and videotaped performances are permissible as a substitute for live auditions if a campus visit is impossible. Portfolio reviews held throughout the year on campus and off campus in various cities.

Contact Mr. Michael Carpenter, Director, Admissions Office, Shenandoah University, 1460 University Drive, Winchester, Virginia 22601-5195; 540-665-4581, fax: 540-665-4627, E-mail address: admit@su.edu.

▼ SHEPHERD SCHOOL OF MUSIC

See Rice University

▼ SHORTER COLLEGE

Rome, Georgia

Independent-Baptist, coed. Small town campus. Total enrollment: 1,639.

Degrees Bachelor of Music in the areas of voice, piano, organ, piano pedagogy; Bachelor of Music Education; Bachelor of Fine Arts in the area of musical theater; Bachelor of Church Music. Majors and concentrations: church music, music education, music theater, organ, piano, piano pedagogy, voice. Program accredited by NASM.

Enrollment Fall 1997: 101 undergraduate.

Music Student Profile 75% females, 25% males, 5% minorities, 1% international.

Music Faculty 14 total (full-time and part-time). 50% of full-time faculty have terminal degrees. Graduate students do not teach undergraduate courses. Undergraduate student–faculty ratio: 13:1.

Student Life Student groups/activities include Mu Phi Epsilon, Phi Mu Alpha Sinfonia.

Expenses for 1997–98 Application fee: $25. Comprehensive fee: $12,510 includes full-time tuition ($8150), mandatory fees ($110), and college room and board ($4250). Special program-related fees: $230 per instrument per semester for private applied lessons.

Financial Aid Program-specific awards for 1997: music scholarships for music majors.

Application Procedures Students admitted directly into the professional program freshman year. Deadline for freshmen and transfers: continuous. Required: essay, high school transcript, minimum 2.0 high school GPA, interview, audition, SAT I or ACT test scores, music theory examination, minimum 2.0 college GPA for transfer students. Recommended: letter of recommendation. Auditions held 4 times and by appointment on campus; recorded music is permissible as a substitute for live auditions for international students and U.S. students from a great distance and

videotaped performances are permissible as a substitute for live auditions for international students and U.S. students from a great distance.

Undergraduate Contact School of the Arts, Shorter College, 315 Shorter Avenue, Rome, Georgia 30165; 706-233-7247, fax: 706-236-1515, E-mail address: awingard@shorter.peachnet.edu.

▼ SILVER LAKE COLLEGE

Manitowoc, Wisconsin

Independent-Roman Catholic, coed. Rural campus. Total enrollment: 1,050.

Degrees Bachelor of Music in the areas of music education, music. Majors and concentrations: choral music education, instrumental music education, music education. Graduate degrees offered: Master of Music in the area of music education. Program accredited by NASM.

Enrollment Fall 1997: 27 total; 6 undergraduate, 17 graduate, 4 non-professional degree.

Music Student Profile 96% females, 4% males.

Music Faculty 12 total undergraduate and graduate (full-time and part-time). 80% of full-time faculty have terminal degrees. Graduate students do not teach undergraduate courses.

Student Life Student groups/activities include sophomore and senior recitals.

Expenses for 1998–99 Comprehensive fee: $14,212 includes full-time tuition ($9986) and college room and board ($4226). College room only: $2300. Full-time tuition varies according to location and program. Room and board charges vary according to board plan and housing facility.

Financial Aid Program-specific awards available.

Application Procedures Students apply for admission into the professional program by sophomore year. Deadline for freshmen and transfers: continuous. Required: high school transcript, college transcript(s) for transfer students, minimum 2.0 high school GPA, audition, SAT I or ACT test scores (minimum combined SAT I score of 1200, minimum combined ACT score of 19), high school transcript for transfer applicants with fewer than 30 credits. Auditions held 3 times on campus; recorded music is permissible as a substitute for live auditions when distance is prohibitive and videotaped performances are permissible as a substitute for live auditions when distance is prohibitive.

Contact Admissions Office, Silver Lake College, 2406 South Alverno Road, Manitowoc, Wisconsin 54220-9319; 920-684-5955, fax: 920-684-7082, E-mail address: admslc@sl.edu.

▼ SIMON FRASER UNIVERSITY

Burnaby, BC, Canada

Province-supported, coed. Suburban campus. Total enrollment: 18,759. Music program established 1992.

Degrees Bachelor of Fine Arts in the area of music. Graduate degrees offered: Master of Fine Arts in the area of interdisciplinary studies.

Enrollment Fall 1997: 39 total.

Music Faculty 3 total undergraduate and graduate (full-time). 100% of full-time faculty have terminal degrees. Graduate students teach a few undergraduate courses.

Expenses for 1997–98 Application fee: $25 Canadian dollars. Tuition, fee, and room only charges are reported in Canadian dollars. Canadian resident tuition: $2310 full-time. Mandatory fees: $207 full-time. College room only: $2830. Room charges vary according to housing facility. International student tuition: $6930 full-time.

Financial Aid Program-specific awards for 1997: 5 Adaline May Clark Scholarships for program majors ($100–$500), 1 Murray Farr Award for program majors ($500).

Application Procedures Students admitted directly into the professional program freshman year. Deadline for freshmen and transfers: May 1. Required: high school transcript, minimum 3.0 high school GPA, interview. Recommended: audition. Auditions held twice on campus; recorded music is permissible as a substitute for live auditions for international applicants.

Web Site http://www.sfu.ca/sca.

Undergraduate Contact Admissions Office, Simon Fraser University, 8888 University Drive, Burnaby, BC V5A 1S6, Canada; 604-291-3224, fax: 604-291-4969.

Graduate Contact Chair, MFA Program, School for the Contemporary Arts, Simon Fraser University, 8888 University Drive, Burnaby, BC V5A 1S6, Canada; 604-291-3492, fax: 604-291-5907, E-mail address: mfa_grad_office@cfu.ca.

▼ Simpson College

Indianola, Iowa

Independent-United Methodist, coed. Small town campus. Total enrollment: 1,958. Music program established 1900.

Degrees Bachelor of Music in the areas of classical music, piano/organ, voice, winds and percussion music, vocal music education, instrumental music education. Majors and concentrations: classical guitar, classical music, music education, piano/organ, voice, wind and percussion instruments. Program accredited by NASM.

Enrollment Fall 1997: 105 total; 98 undergraduate, 7 non-professional degree.

Music Student Profile 60% females, 40% males, 4% minorities, 1% international.

Music Faculty 23 total (full-time and part-time). 75% of full-time faculty have terminal degrees. Graduate students do not teach undergraduate courses. Undergraduate student–faculty ratio: 7:1.

Student Life Student groups/activities include Phi Mu Alpha Sinfonia, Mu Phi Epsilon, Music Educators National Conference.

Expenses for 1997–98 Comprehensive fee: $17,385 includes full-time tuition ($12,975), mandatory fees ($120), and college room and board ($4290). Room and board charges vary according to board plan and housing facility. Special program-related fees: $40 for accompanist fee, $180 for lesson fee, $50 for recital fee.

Financial Aid Program-specific awards for 1997: 70–80 music scholarships for program majors ($2000–$4000).

Application Procedures Students apply for admission into the professional program by sophomore year. Deadline for freshmen and transfers: August 1. Notification date for freshmen and transfers: August 15. Required: essay, high school transcript, college transcript(s) for transfer students, minimum 2.0 high school GPA, letter of recommendation, audition, SAT I or ACT test scores (minimum combined ACT score of 19). Recommended: minimum 3.0 high school GPA, interview, video. Auditions held twice plus special auditions

on campus; recorded music is permissible as a substitute for live auditions if a campus visit is impossible and videotaped performances are permissible as a substitute for live auditions if a campus visit is impossible.

Web Site http://storm.simpson.edu/academics/catalog/music.html.

Undergraduate Contact Dr. Robert L. Larsen, Chairman, Department of Music, Simpson College, 701 North Street, Indianola, Iowa 50125-1297; 515-961-1637, fax: 515-961-1498, E-mail address: terry@storm.simpson.edu.

Simpson College

More About the College

The Simpson College Conservatory of Music was founded in 1891. In 1940 it became the Music Department at Simpson and has developed and maintained a position of preeminence among schools offering serious musical training in the Midwest.

Simpson combines the atmosphere of a fine small liberal arts college with a distinguished program in music education and musical performance. Students at Simpson are given the opportunity of working with superior teachers in private study and small classes and are given extraordinary opportunities for both ensemble and solo performance. Here, every student is an individual and treated as such, often having the opportunity for upper division directed studies in such areas as conducting, vocal repertory, ethnomusicology, Kodaly and Orff techniques, and opera coaching.

Instrumentalists sing and singers play instruments, if they choose. The Middle Ages, the Renaissance, the great operatic repertory of the nineteenth century, and the vitality of twentieth-century musical thought and American jazz are living, breathing, exciting, and viable entities in the music department. Visiting artists such as Russian pianist Oleg Volkov and soprano Evelyn Lear give recitals and master classes. Alumni artists like Brad Cresswell, tenor with the New York City Opera and the Sante Fe Festival, and Kimm Julian, well-known baritone with regional opera companies and in Europe, also return for recitals and master classes each season. Distinguished music educators on the national scene appear regularly in seminars for students and area teachers.

Indianola and the Blank Performing Arts Center are the home of the Des Moines Metro Opera, one of America's leading regional opera companies, and a number of students become a part of its staff each summer.

Simpson is a remarkable place for a young musician to watch, listen, and grow. It is a place where each student is

Simpson College (continued)

challenged to develop his or her musical and artistic gifts to the fullest and counseled carefully on realistic career goals and the steps to be taken beyond the Simpson years.

▼ SLIPPERY ROCK UNIVERSITY OF PENNSYLVANIA

Slippery Rock, Pennsylvania

State-supported, coed. Rural campus. Total enrollment: 7,038.

Degrees Bachelor of Music in the areas of music theory, performance; Bachelor of Science in the areas of music education, music therapy. Majors and concentrations: band, orchestral instruments, piano, voice. Program accredited by NASM, NAMT.

Enrollment Fall 1997: 87 total; all undergraduate.

Music Student Profile 60% females, 40% males, 1% minorities, 1% international.

Music Faculty 17 total (full-time and part-time). 38% of full-time faculty have terminal degrees. Graduate students do not teach undergraduate courses. Undergraduate student–faculty ratio: 5:1.

Student Life Student groups/activities include Pennsylvania Collegiate Music Educators Association, National Association of Music Therapy Regional Association Student Chapter, Mu Phi Epsilon. Special housing available for music students.

Expenses for 1997–98 State resident tuition: $3468 full-time. Nonresident tuition: $8824 full-time. Mandatory fees: $834 full-time. College room and board: $3590. College room only: $1972.

Financial Aid Program-specific awards for 1997: 1 Swope Scholarship for sophomores and juniors ($500), 10 Madrigal Scholarships for vocal majors ($400), 1 Winder Scholarship for freshmen ($500), 1 Chapin Scholarship for flutists ($500), 1 Williamson Scholarship for vocal majors ($500), 1 Kevin Woods Memorial Scholarship for sophomore, junior, or senior instrumental majors ($500), 1 Dwight Baker Memorial Scholarship for instrumental majors ($250).

Application Procedures Students admitted directly into the professional program freshman year. Deadline for freshmen and transfers: May 1. Required: college transcript(s) for transfer students, minimum 2.0 high school GPA, interview, audition, Seashore Musical Aptitude Test. Auditions held 5 times and by appointment on campus; recorded music is permissible as a substitute for live auditions when distance is prohibitive or scheduling is difficult and videotaped performances are permissible as a substitute for live auditions when distance is prohibitive or scheduling is difficult.

Web Site http://www.sru.edu.

Undergraduate Contact Stacey Steele, Audition Committee Chairperson, Department of Music, Slippery Rock University of Pennsylvania, Swope Music Hall, Slippery Rock, Pennsylvania 16057; 724-738-2440, fax: 724-738-4469, E-mail address: stacey.steele@sru.edu.

▼ SOUTH DAKOTA STATE UNIVERSITY

Brookings, South Dakota

State-supported, coed. Small town campus. Total enrollment: 8,867. Music program established 1906.

Degrees Bachelor of Music Education in the areas of vocal music education, instrumental music education, general music education; Bachelor of Science in the area of music merchandising. Majors and concentrations: music education, music marketing. Program accredited by NASM.

Enrollment Fall 1997: 821 total; 101 undergraduate, 720 non-professional degree.

Music Student Profile 56% females, 44% males, 2% minorities, 2% international.

Music Faculty 14 total (full-time and part-time). 46% of full-time faculty have terminal degrees. Graduate students do not teach undergraduate courses. Undergraduate student–faculty ratio: 15:1.

Student Life Student groups/activities include Music Educators National Conference, Music Industry Club. Special housing available for music students.

Expenses for 1997–98 Application fee: $15. State resident tuition: $1728 full-time. Nonresident tuition: $5496 full-time. Mandatory fees: $1184 full-time. Full-time tuition and fees vary according to location and reciprocity agreements. College room and board: $2482. College room only: $1282. Room and board charges vary according to board plan and housing facility.

Financial Aid Program-specific awards for 1997: 20–30 music scholarships for music majors and minors ($600–$1000).

Application Procedures Students admitted directly into the professional program freshman year. Deadline for freshmen and transfers: June 23. Notification date for freshmen and transfers: continuous. Required: high school transcript, college transcript(s) for transfer students, ACT test score only (minimum combined ACT score of 18), minimum 2.6 high school GPA or standing in top 60% of graduating class. Recommended: 2 letters of recommendation, audition. Auditions held 3 times on campus and off campus in Rapid City, SD; recorded music is permissible as a substitute for live auditions when distance is prohibitive and videotaped performances are permissible as a substitute for live auditions when distance is prohibitive.

Undergraduate Contact Dr. Corliss Johnson, Head, Department of Music, South Dakota State University, LMH Box 2212, Brookings, South Dakota 57007; 605-688-5188, fax: 605-688-4307, E-mail address: johnsoc@ur.sdstate.edu.

▼ SOUTHEASTERN LOUISIANA UNIVERSITY

Hammond, Louisiana

State-supported, coed. Small town campus. Total enrollment: 15,241.

Degrees Bachelor of Music in the areas of instrumental music, vocal music, keyboard; Bachelor of Music Education in the areas of instrumental music education, vocal music education. Majors and concentrations: band, music education, piano/organ, voice. Graduate degrees offered: Master of Music in the areas of theory, performance. Program accredited by NASM.

Enrollment Fall 1997: 116 total; 101 undergraduate, 15 graduate.

Music Student Profile 54% females, 46% males, 5% minorities, 5% international.

Music Faculty 29 total undergraduate and graduate (full-time and part-time). 50% of full-time faculty have terminal degrees. Graduate students teach a few undergraduate courses. Undergraduate student–faculty ratio: 4:1.

Estimated expenses for 1998–99 Application fee: $10. State resident tuition: $2030 full-time. Nonresident tuition: $4296 full-time. Mandatory fees: $125 full-time. College room and board: $2400. Room and board charges vary according to board plan and housing facility.

Financial Aid Program-specific awards for 1997: 72 Performance Grants for music majors ($1000).

Application Procedures Students admitted directly into the professional program freshman year. Deadline for freshmen and transfers: July 15. Required: high school transcript, audition, ACT test score only. Auditions held 10 times on campus and off campus in various locations; recorded music is permissible as a substitute for live auditions when distance is prohibitive and videotaped performances are permissible as a substitute for live auditions when distance is prohibitive.

Undergraduate Contact Dr. David Evenson, Head, Department of Music, Southeastern Louisiana University, SLU Box 815, Hammond, Louisiana 70402; 504-549-2184, fax: 504-549-2892, E-mail address: devenson@admin.selu.edu.

Graduate Contact Dr. Willis Delony, Graduate Coordinator, Department of Music, Southeastern Louisiana University, SLU Box 815, Hammond, Louisiana 70402; 504-549-3991, fax: 504-549-2892, E-mail address: wdelony@admin.selu.edu.

▼ SOUTHEASTERN OKLAHOMA STATE UNIVERSITY

Durant, Oklahoma

State-supported, coed. Small town campus. Total enrollment: 3,946. Music program established 1978.

Degrees Bachelor of Music in the areas of performance, sacred music; Bachelor of Music Education in the areas of vocal music education, instrumental music education. Majors and concentrations: music education, sacred music, voice, wind and percussion instruments. Program accredited by NASM.

Enrollment Fall 1997: 73 total; all undergraduate.

Music Student Profile 60% females, 40% males, 25% minorities, 4% international.

Music Faculty 18 total (full-time and part-time). 66% of full-time faculty have terminal degrees. Graduate students do not teach undergraduate courses. Undergraduate student–faculty ratio: 8:1.

Student Life Student groups/activities include Music Educators National Conference Student Chapter, Kappa Kappa Psi.

Expenses for 1997–98 State resident tuition: $1395 full-time. Nonresident tuition: $3900 full-time. Mandatory fees: $484 full-time. Full-time tuition and fees vary according to course level. College room and board: $2619. College room only: $848. Room and board charges vary according to board plan and housing facility. Special program-related fees: $28 per credit hour for applied music fee.

Financial Aid Program-specific awards for 1997: 65 partial tuition waivers for ensemble performers ($900–$1200), 8 Endowed Scholarships for upperclassmen ($200–$300).

Application Procedures Students admitted directly into the professional program freshman year. Deadline for freshmen and transfers: August 1. Required: high school transcript, college transcript(s) for transfer students, minimum 2.0 high school GPA, interview, audition, ACT test score only. Recommended: letter of recommendation. Auditions held 3 times on campus; recorded music is permissible as a substitute for live auditions when distance is prohibitive and

videotaped performances are permissible as a substitute for live auditions when distance is prohibitive.

Undergraduate Contact Dr. Walter Britt, Chairman, Department of Music, Southeastern Oklahoma State University, Box 4126, Durant, Oklahoma 74701-0609; 405-924-0121 ext. 2244, fax: 405-920-7475, E-mail address: wbritt@sosu.edu.

▼ SOUTHEAST MISSOURI STATE UNIVERSITY

Cape Girardeau, Missouri

State-supported, coed. Small town campus. Total enrollment: 8,231.

Degrees Bachelor of Music in the area of performance; Bachelor of Music Education in the areas of instrumental music education, vocal music education. Majors and concentrations: music, music education, piano/organ, stringed instruments, voice, wind and percussion instruments. Graduate degrees offered: Master of Music Education. Program accredited by NASM.

Enrollment Fall 1997: 125 total; 105 undergraduate, 20 graduate.

Music Student Profile 50% females, 50% males, 5% minorities, 5% international.

Music Faculty 21 total undergraduate and graduate (full-time and part-time). 95% of full-time faculty have terminal degrees. Graduate students do not teach undergraduate courses. Undergraduate student–faculty ratio: 9:1.

Student Life Student groups/activities include Collegiate Music Educators National Conference, Phi Mu Alpha Sinfonia, Sigma Alpha Iota.

Expenses for 1997–98 Application fee: $20. State resident tuition: $2799 full-time. Nonresident tuition: $5199 full-time. Mandatory fees: $201 full-time. College room and board: $6920. Room and board charges vary according to board plan and location. Special program-related fees: $50 per credit hour for applied music lesson fee, $10–$30 per semester for locker rental, $10 per instrument for instrument rental.

Financial Aid Program-specific awards for 1997: 4 Bea Limbaugh Scholarships for music students ($1200), 1 Mark Woods Allen Piano Scholarship for piano students ($480), 1 Charles Cox Scholarship for music students ($770), 1 Leroy Mason Scholarship for music students ($850), 1 Harold Lichtenegger Scholarship for music students ($1300), 1 O.L. Wilcox Scholarship for music students.

Application Procedures Students apply for admission into the professional program by sophomore, junior year. Deadline for freshmen and transfers: May 1. Required: high school transcript, college transcript(s) for transfer students, minimum 2.0 high school GPA, 2 letters of recommendation, interview, audition, SAT I or ACT test scores (minimum combined ACT score of 18), minimum 2.0 college GPA for transfer students. Auditions held continuously on campus and off campus in various cities throughout Missouri; recorded music is permissible as a substitute for live auditions when distance is prohibitive and videotaped performances are permissible as a substitute for live auditions when distance is prohibitive.

Undergraduate Contact Mr. Barry W. Bernhardt, Undergraduate Admissions, Department of Music, Southeast Missouri State University, 1 University Plaza, Cape Girardeau, Missouri 63701; 573-651-2335, fax: 573-651-2321.

Southeast Missouri State University *(continued)*

Graduate Contact Dr. Gary Miller, Graduate Admissions, Department of Music, Southeast Missouri State University, 1 University Plaza, Cape Girardeau, Missouri 63701; 573-651-2345, fax: 573-651-2321.

▼ SOUTHERN ADVENTIST UNIVERSITY

Collegedale, Tennessee

Independent-Seventh-day Adventist, coed. Small town campus. Total enrollment: 1,695.

Degrees Bachelor of Music Education in the areas of vocal music education, instrumental music education. Majors and concentrations: classical music, music education, piano/organ, stringed instruments, voice, wind and percussion instruments. Program accredited by NASM.

Enrollment Fall 1997: 48 total; 28 undergraduate, 20 non-professional degree.

Music Student Profile 57% females, 43% males, 20% minorities, 7% international.

Music Faculty 21 total (full-time and part-time). 33% of full-time faculty have terminal degrees. Graduate students do not teach undergraduate courses. Undergraduate student–faculty ratio: 4:1.

Expenses for 1997–98 Application fee: $20. Comprehensive fee: $13,364 includes full-time tuition ($9476), mandatory fees ($260), and college room and board ($3628). College room only: $1678. Full-time tuition and fees vary according to program. Room and board charges vary according to housing facility. Special program-related fees: $130 for lesson fee.

Financial Aid Program-specific awards for 1997: 28 Symphony Scholarships for string, wind, and percussion students ($1700), 15 band scholarships for wind and percussion students ($800), 19 Choral/Vocal Scholarships for vocal students ($420), 5 Keyboard Awards for organ/piano students ($500).

Application Procedures Students admitted directly into the professional program freshman year. Deadline for freshmen and transfers: continuous. Required: high school transcript, audition, SAT I or ACT test scores. Auditions held twice on campus; recorded music is permissible as a substitute for live auditions when distance is prohibitive and videotaped performances are permissible as a substitute for live auditions when distance is prohibitive.

Web Site http://www.southern.edu.

Undergraduate Contact Mr. Victor Czerkasij, Vice President for Admissions and College Relations, Southern Adventist University, PO Box 370, Collegedale, Tennessee 37315; 800-768-8437, fax: 423-238-3005.

▼ SOUTHERN ARKANSAS UNIVERSITY–MAGNOLIA

Magnolia, Arkansas

State-supported, coed. Small town campus. Total enrollment: 2,676.

Degrees Bachelor of Music Education. Program accredited by NASM.

Enrollment Fall 1997: 34 total; all undergraduate.

Music Student Profile 56% females, 44% males, 23% minorities, 3% international.

Music Faculty 12 total (full-time and part-time). 83% of full-time faculty have terminal degrees. Graduate students do not teach undergraduate courses.

Expenses for 1997–98 State resident tuition: $1848 full-time. Nonresident tuition: $2856 full-time. Mandatory fees: $48 full-time. College room and board: $2530. Room and board charges vary according to board plan. Special program-related fees: $40 per 2 semester hours for applied music fee.

Financial Aid Program-specific awards for 1997: 154 departmental scholarships for music majors/minors and participants in music activities ($196–$1848).

Application Procedures Students admitted directly into the professional program freshman year. Deadline for freshmen and transfers: August 15. Required: high school transcript, college transcript(s) for transfer students, interview, SAT I or ACT test scores (minimum combined ACT score of 19), audition for scholarship consideration. Recommended: minimum 2.0 high school GPA, audition. Auditions held by appointment on campus.

Web Site http://www.saumag.edu/music/index.htm.

Undergraduate Contact Dr. Kim Shirey, Chair, Music Department, Southern Arkansas University–Magnolia, Box 9358, Magnolia, Arkansas 71753-5000; 870-235-4251, fax: 870-235-5005, E-mail address: kfshirey@saumag.edu.

▼ SOUTHERN ILLINOIS UNIVERSITY AT CARBONDALE

Carbondale, Illinois

State-supported, coed. Small town campus. Total enrollment: 21,908.

Degrees Bachelor of Music in the areas of performance, piano pedagogy, music theory/composition, music education. Majors and concentrations: classical music, guitar, music education, opera, piano pedagogy, piano/organ, stringed instruments, voice, wind and percussion instruments. Graduate degrees offered: Master of Music in the areas of performance, piano pedagogy, music theory/composition, music history/literature, opera/music theater, music education. Program accredited by NASM.

Enrollment Fall 1997: 195 total; 140 undergraduate, 25 graduate, 30 non-professional degree.

Music Student Profile 45% females, 55% males, 5% minorities, 18% international.

Music Faculty 27 total undergraduate and graduate (full-time and part-time). 100% of full-time faculty have terminal degrees. Graduate students do not teach undergraduate courses. Undergraduate student–faculty ratio: 7:1.

Student Life Student groups/activities include Collegiate Music Educators National Conference, Phi Mu Alpha Sinfonia, Mu Phi Epsilon.

Expenses for 1997–98 State resident tuition: $2700 full-time. Nonresident tuition: $8100 full-time. Mandatory fees: $720 full-time. Full-time tuition and fees vary according to course load. College room and board: $3649. Room and board charges vary according to board plan and housing facility. Special program-related fees: $20 per semester for instrument rental.

Financial Aid Program-specific awards for 1997: 20–30 music scholarships for musically talented students ($300–$2000).

Application Procedures Students admitted directly into the professional program freshman year. Deadline for freshmen and transfers: continuous. Notification date for freshmen: August 15. Required: high school transcript, college transcript(s) for transfer students, audition, ACT test score only (minimum combined ACT score of 18). Auditions held 3 times and by appointment on campus; recorded music is permissible as a substitute for live auditions for out-of-state applicants and videotaped performances are permissible as a substitute for live auditions for international applicants and out-of-state applicants.

Web Site http://www.siu.edu/departments/cola/music001/.
Undergraduate Contact Dr. Daniel Mellado, Undergraduate Advisor, School of Music, Southern Illinois University at Carbondale, Mailcode 4302, Carbondale, Illinois 62901-4302; 618-453-5806, fax: 618-453-5808, E-mail address: dmellado@ siu.edu.
Graduate Contact Mr. Frank Stemper, Graduate Advisor, School of Music, Southern Illinois University at Carbondale, Mailcode 4302, Carbondale, Illinois 62901-4302; 618-536-8742, fax: 618-453-5808, E-mail address: fstemp@siu.edu.

▼ SOUTHERN ILLINOIS UNIVERSITY AT EDWARDSVILLE

Edwardsville, Illinois

State-supported, coed. Suburban campus. Total enrollment: 11,207. Music program established 1958.
Degrees Bachelor of Music in the areas of performance, music education, jazz performance, musical theater, theory/composition. Majors and concentrations: classical music, jazz, music, music education, music history and literature, music marketing, music theater, music theory and composition, performance. Graduate degrees offered: Master of Music in the areas of music education, performance. Program accredited by NASM.
Enrollment Fall 1997: 180 total; 120 undergraduate, 40 graduate, 20 non-professional degree.
Music Student Profile 55% females, 45% males, 16% minorities, 5% international.
Music Faculty 43 total undergraduate and graduate (full-time and part-time). 90% of full-time faculty have terminal degrees. Graduate students teach a few undergraduate courses. Undergraduate student–faculty ratio: 6:1.
Student Life Student groups/activities include Sigma Alpha Iota. Special housing available for music students.
Expenses for 1998–99 Application fee: $0. State resident tuition: $2081 full-time. Nonresident tuition: $6242 full-time. Mandatory fees: $584 full-time. College room and board: $4066. College room only: $2536. Room and board charges vary according to board plan and housing facility.
Financial Aid Program-specific awards for 1997: 20–40 Music Talent Awards for those demonstrating talent and academic achievement ($100–$1000), 6–12 Provost Scholarships for those demonstrating talent and academic achievement ($400–$900).
Application Procedures Students apply for admission into the professional program by sophomore year. Deadline for freshmen and transfers: August 1. Notification date for freshmen and transfers: August 19. Required: high school transcript, minimum 3.0 high school GPA, audition, SAT I or ACT test scores. Recommended: letter of recommendation. Auditions held 5 times and by appointment on campus;

recorded music is permissible as a substitute for live auditions when distance is prohibitive and videotaped performances are permissible as a substitute for live auditions when distance is prohibitive.
Web Site http://www.siue.edu/MUSIC/.
Undergraduate Contact Mr. Ronald D. Abraham, Chair, Music Department, Southern Illinois University at Edwardsville, Box 1771, Edwardsville, Illinois 62026-1771; 618-692-3900, fax: 618-692-5988.
Graduate Contact Dr. Allan Ho, Professor, Music Department, Southern Illinois University at Edwardsville, Box 1771, Edwardsville, Illinois 62026-1771; 618-692-3640, fax: 618-692-5988.

Meadows School of the Arts

▼ SOUTHERN METHODIST UNIVERSITY

Dallas, Texas

Independent, coed. Suburban campus. Total enrollment: 9,708. Music program established 1931.
Degrees Bachelor of Music in the areas of performance, music education, music theory, composition, piano pedagogy, music therapy. Majors and concentrations: bassoon, cello, clarinet, composition, double bass, flute, French horn, guitar, harp, harpsichord, music education, music theory, music therapy, oboe, organ, percussion, piano, piano pedagogy, saxophone, trombone, trumpet, tuba, viola, violin. Graduate degrees offered: Master of Music in the areas of performance, music education, music theory, composition, music history, sacred music, piano performance and pedagogy; Master of Music Therapy. Program accredited by NASM.
Enrollment Fall 1997: 306 total; 195 undergraduate, 84 graduate, 27 non-professional degree.
Music Student Profile 52% females, 48% males, 16% international.
Music Faculty 65 total undergraduate and graduate (full-time and part-time). 94% of full-time faculty have terminal degrees. Graduate students teach a few undergraduate courses. Undergraduate student–faculty ratio: 6:1.
Student Life Student groups/activities include Music Educators National Conference, National Association of Music Therapy. Special housing available for music students.
Expenses for 1997–98 Application fee: $40. Comprehensive fee: $23,244 includes full-time tuition ($14,896), mandatory fees ($1894), and college room and board ($6454). College room only: $3600. Room and board charges vary according to board plan and housing facility. Special program-related fees: $16 for practice room fee, $30 for recital recording fee, $18 for concert fee.
Financial Aid Program-specific awards for 1997: 160 Meadows Artistic Scholarships for talented program majors and minors ($2000–$10,000).
Application Procedures Students apply for admission into the professional program by freshman year. Deadline for freshmen and transfers: April 1. Notification date for freshmen: May 1; transfers: June 1. Required: essay, high school transcript, letter of recommendation, audition, SAT I or ACT test scores. Recommended: interview. Auditions held 24 times on campus and off campus in various locations; recorded music is permissible as a substitute for live auditions if a live audition is impossible and videotaped performances are permissible as a substitute for live auditions if a live audition is impossible.

Southern Methodist University (*continued*)

Web Site http://www.smu.edu/~music.
Contact Dr. Robert Stroker, Associate Dean for Student Affairs, Meadows School of the Arts, Southern Methodist University, PO Box 750356, Dallas, Texas 75275-0356; 214-768-3217, fax: 214-768-3272.

▼ SOUTHERN UNIVERSITY AND AGRICULTURAL AND MECHANICAL COLLEGE

Baton Rouge, Louisiana

State-supported, coed. Suburban campus. Total enrollment: 9,815.
Degrees Bachelor of Music in the area of performance. Majors and concentrations: instrumental music, jazz, music, music education, piano, voice, wind and percussion instruments. Cross-registration with Louisiana State University. Program accredited by NASM.
Enrollment Fall 1997: 112 total; 51 undergraduate, 61 non-professional degree.
Music Student Profile 24% females, 76% males, 99% minorities, 1% international.
Music Faculty 14 total (full-time and part-time). 21% of full-time faculty have terminal degrees. Graduate students do not teach undergraduate courses. Undergraduate student–faculty ratio: 9:1.
Student Life Student groups/activities include Music Educators National Conference, Phi Mu Alpha Sinfonia, Mu Phi Epsilon.
Expenses for 1997–98 Application fee: $5. State resident tuition: $2068 full-time. Nonresident tuition: $5852 full-time. College room and board: $3270. Room and board charges vary according to board plan and housing facility.
Financial Aid Program-specific awards for 1997: 12 Choir/Vocal Awards for choir singers ($2500), 1–8 Music (Jazz) Awards for jazz majors ($2500), 10–15 music awards for program majors ($100–$500), 6 Transfer Scholarships for transfer students ($1000).
Application Procedures Students admitted directly into the professional program freshman year. Deadline for freshmen and transfers: July 1. Notification date for freshmen and transfers: continuous. Required: high school transcript, audition, SAT I or ACT test scores, medical history. Auditions held twice and by appointment on campus; recorded music is permissible as a substitute for live auditions for out-of-state applicants and videotaped performances are permissible as a substitute for live auditions for out-of-state applicants.
Undergraduate Contact Mr. Wayne W. Brumfield, Director of Admissions, Southern University and Agricultural and Mechanical College, PO Box 9901, Southern University Station, Baton Rouge, Louisiana 70813; 504-771-2430.

▼ SOUTHWEST BAPTIST UNIVERSITY

Bolivar, Missouri

Independent-Southern Baptist, coed. Small town campus. Total enrollment: 3,593.
Degrees Bachelor of Music in the areas of church music, music education. Majors and concentrations: instrumental music education, sacred music, vocal music education. Program accredited by NASM.

Enrollment Fall 1997: 85 undergraduate.
Music Student Profile 60% females, 40% males, 4% minorities, 3% international.
Music Faculty 22 total undergraduate (full-time and part-time). 75% of full-time faculty have terminal degrees. Graduate students do not teach undergraduate courses. Undergraduate student–faculty ratio: 5:1.
Student Life Student groups/activities include Music Educators National Conference, Church Music Conference.
Expenses for 1997–98 Application fee: $25. Comprehensive fee: $10,927 includes full-time tuition ($8112), mandatory fees ($235), and college room and board ($2580). Room and board charges vary according to board plan and housing facility. Special program-related fees: $140 per credit hour for applied music fees, $13 per semester for practice room fee.
Financial Aid Program-specific awards for 1997: 110 Music Performance Scholarships for program majors ($500).
Application Procedures Students apply for admission into the professional program by sophomore year. Deadline for freshmen and transfers: continuous. Required: high school transcript, audition. Auditions held 3-4 times on campus and off campus in St. Louis, MO; Kansas City, MO; recorded music is permissible as a substitute for live auditions when distance is prohibitive or by request and videotaped performances are permissible as a substitute for live auditions when distance is prohibitive or by request.
Undergraduate Contact Mr. Ronn Ramey, Director of Admissions, Southwest Baptist University, 1600 University Avenue, Bolivar, Missouri 65613; 417-326-1810.

▼ SOUTHWESTERN COLLEGE

Winfield, Kansas

Independent-United Methodist, coed. Small town campus. Total enrollment: 826.
Degrees Bachelor of Music in the area of music education. Program accredited by NASM.
Enrollment Fall 1997: 25 undergraduate.
Music Student Profile 75% females, 25% males.
Music Faculty 10 total (full-time and part-time). 100% of full-time faculty have terminal degrees. Graduate students do not teach undergraduate courses. Undergraduate student–faculty ratio: 12:1.
Student Life Student groups/activities include Music Educators National Conference Student Chapter, Mu Phi Epsilon.
Expenses for 1997–98 Application fee: $15. Comprehensive fee: $13,100 includes full-time tuition ($9260) and college room and board ($3840). College room only: $1680. Full-time tuition varies according to location. Room and board charges vary according to board plan and housing facility. Special program-related fees: $100 per semester for private lesson fee.
Financial Aid Program-specific awards for 1997: 1–75 activity grants for music majors and minors, participants in music activities ($200–$2950).
Application Procedures Students admitted directly into the professional program freshman year. Deadline for freshmen and transfers: July 1. Required: high school transcript, college transcript(s) for transfer students, minimum 2.0 high school GPA, audition, ACT test score only. Recommended: minimum 3.0 high school GPA, letter of recommendation, interview. Auditions held at student's convenience on campus; recorded music is permissible as a substitute for live auditions for out-of-state applicants and videotaped performances are permissible as a substitute for live auditions for out-of-state applicants.

Undergraduate Contact Mr. Michael Wilder, Chair, Division of Performing Arts, Southwestern College, Darbeth Fine Arts Center, Winfield, Kansas 67156; 316-221-8272, fax: 316-221-8224, E-mail address: mwilder@jinx.sckans.edu.

▼ SOUTHWESTERN OKLAHOMA STATE UNIVERSITY

Weatherford, Oklahoma

State-supported, coed. Small town campus. Total enrollment: 4,478.

Degrees Bachelor of Music in the areas of sacred music, music therapy, music theory/composition; Bachelor of Music Education in the areas of instrumental music education, vocal/keyboard music education. Majors and concentrations: composition, music, music education, music theory, music therapy, performance, piano/organ, sacred music, stringed instruments, voice, wind and percussion instruments. Graduate degrees offered: Master of Music Education. Program accredited by NASM.

Enrollment Fall 1997: 164 undergraduate, 23 graduate.

Music Student Profile 67% females, 33% males, 5% minorities.

Music Faculty 21 total undergraduate and graduate (full-time and part-time). 64% of full-time faculty have terminal degrees. Graduate students teach a few undergraduate courses. Undergraduate student–faculty ratio: 10:1.

Student Life Student groups/activities include music fraternities and sororities, National Association of Music Therapy, Music Educators National Conference.

Expenses for 1997–98 Application fee: $15. State resident tuition: $1395 full-time. Nonresident tuition: $3878 full-time. Mandatory fees: $403 full-time. Full-time tuition and fees vary according to course level. College room and board: $2320. Room and board charges vary according to board plan. Special program-related fees: $30 per credit hour for applied lessons fee.

Financial Aid Program-specific awards for 1997: Ensemble Music Scholarships for ensemble performers, music scholarships for those passing audition evaluations.

Application Procedures Students admitted directly into the professional program freshman year. Deadline for freshmen and transfers: continuous. Required: high school transcript, college transcript(s) for transfer students, ACT test score only (minimum combined ACT score of 19), auditions for transfer students. Recommended: audition. Auditions held continuously by appointment on campus; recorded music is permissible as a substitute for live auditions when distance is prohibitive and videotaped performances are permissible as a substitute for live auditions when distance is prohibitive.

Undergraduate Contact Ms. Barbara Lane, Secretary, Department of Music, Southwestern Oklahoma State University, 100 Campus Drive, Weatherford, Oklahoma 73096; 405-774-3708, fax: 405-774-3795.

Graduate Contact Dr. Alan Spurgeon, Associate Professor, Department of Music, Southwestern Oklahoma State University, 100 Campus Drive, Weatherford, Oklahoma 73096; 405-774-3216, fax: 405-774-3795.

▼ SOUTHWESTERN UNIVERSITY

Georgetown, Texas

Independent-Methodist, coed. Suburban campus. Total enrollment: 1,215.

Degrees Bachelor of Music in the areas of performance, music education, music theory, music literature, sacred music. Majors and concentrations: guitar, organ, piano, stringed instruments, voice, wind and percussion instruments. Program accredited by NASM.

Enrollment Fall 1997: 45 total; all undergraduate.

Music Student Profile 60% females, 40% males, 10% minorities, 5% international.

Music Faculty 24 total (full-time and part-time). 87% of full-time faculty have terminal degrees. Graduate students do not teach undergraduate courses.

Student Life Student groups/activities include Pi Kappa Lambda, Delta Omicron, Texas Music Educators Association.

Expenses for 1997–98 Application fee: $40. Comprehensive fee: $19,270 includes full-time tuition ($14,000) and college room and board ($5270). College room only: $2470. Room and board charges vary according to board plan and housing facility. Special program-related fees: $150 for half-hour weekly private lessons, $300 for one hour weekly private lessons.

Financial Aid Program-specific awards for 1997: 18 music scholarships for talented program majors ($2000–$3000), 20 Performance Awards for non-music majors ($1000–$1500).

Application Procedures Students admitted directly into the professional program freshman year. Deadline for freshmen: February 15; transfers: continuous. Notification date for freshmen: May 1; transfers: continuous. Required: essay, high school transcript, college transcript(s) for transfer students, minimum 2.0 high school GPA, audition, SAT I or ACT test scores, minimum 3.0 college GPA for transfer students. Recommended: minimum 3.0 high school GPA, letter of recommendation, interview. Auditions held by appointment on campus; recorded music is permissible as a substitute for live auditions when distance is prohibitive and videotaped performances are permissible as a substitute for live auditions when distance is prohibitive.

Undergraduate Contact Dr. Kenneth Sheppard, Chair, Music Department, Southwestern University, Box 770, Georgetown, Texas 78627; 512-863-1358, fax: 512-863-1422.

▼ SOUTHWEST MISSOURI STATE UNIVERSITY

Springfield, Missouri

State-supported, coed. Suburban campus. Total enrollment: 16,468. Music program established 1907.

Degrees Bachelor of Music in the areas of performance, composition; Bachelor of Science in the area of vocal/instrumental education. Majors and concentrations: music, piano/organ, stringed instruments, voice, wind and percussion instruments. Graduate degrees offered: Master of Music in the areas of performance, theory/composition, conducting, piano pedagogy, music education. Program accredited by NASM.

Enrollment Fall 1997: 310 total; 270 undergraduate, 40 graduate.

Music Student Profile 41% females, 59% males, 5% minorities, 2% international.

Music Faculty 40 total undergraduate and graduate (full-time and part-time). 75% of full-time faculty have terminal degrees. Graduate students teach a few undergraduate courses. Undergraduate student–faculty ratio: 10:1.

Southwest Missouri State University (continued)

Student Life Student groups/activities include Phi Mu Alpha, Mu Phi Epsilon, Pi Kappa Lambda.

Expenses for 1998–99 Application fee: $15. State resident tuition: $2940 full-time. Nonresident tuition: $5880 full-time. Mandatory fees: $274 full-time. Full-time tuition and fees vary according to course load. College room and board: $3594. College room only: $2396. Room and board charges vary according to board plan and housing facility.

Financial Aid Program-specific awards for 1997: 50 Performance Awards for talented students ($2000), 100 Talent Awards for talented students ($100–$1000), 75 Band Grants for band members ($200–$1000).

Application Procedures Deadline for freshmen and transfers: August 1. Notification date for freshmen and transfers: continuous. Required: high school transcript, college transcript(s) for transfer students, minimum 2.0 high school GPA, audition, ACT test score only. Recommended: video. Auditions held by appointment on campus; recorded music is permissible as a substitute for live auditions when distance is prohibitive and videotaped performances are permissible as a substitute for live auditions when distance is prohibitive.

Web Site http://www.smsu.edu.

Undergraduate Contact Dr. John Prescott, Head, Department of Music, Southwest Missouri State University, 901 South National, Springfield, Missouri 65804; 417-836-5648, fax: 417-836-7665, E-mail address: jsp304f@vma.smsu.edu.

▼ SOUTHWEST TEXAS STATE UNIVERSITY

San Marcos, Texas

State-supported, coed. Small town campus. Total enrollment: 20,652.

Degrees Bachelor of Music in the areas of performance, sound recording technology, music education. Majors and concentrations: classical music, composition, guitar, jazz, music education, piano/organ, sound recording technology, stringed instruments, voice, wind and percussion instruments. Graduate degrees offered: Master of Music in the areas of music education, performance. Program accredited by NASM.

Enrollment Fall 1997: 400 undergraduate, 50 graduate.

Music Student Profile 50% females, 50% males, 40% minorities, 1% international.

Music Faculty 43 total undergraduate and graduate (full-time and part-time). 50% of full-time faculty have terminal degrees. Graduate students teach a few undergraduate courses. Undergraduate student–faculty ratio: 6:1.

Student Life Student groups/activities include Music Educators National Conference Student Chapter, American Choral Directors Association Student Chapter, professional music fraternities.

Expenses for 1997–98 Application fee: $25. State resident tuition: $816 full-time. Nonresident tuition: $5952 full-time. Mandatory fees: $1398 full-time. Full-time tuition and fees vary according to course load. College room and board: $3901. Room and board charges vary according to board plan and housing facility. Special program-related fees: $18 per credit hour for private lesson fee.

Financial Aid Program-specific awards for 1997: 5–10 Schneider Scholarships for Victoria, TX area students ($500–$1000).

Application Procedures Students admitted directly into the professional program freshman year. Deadline for freshmen

and transfers: July 1. Notification date for freshmen and transfers: July 15. Required: high school transcript, college transcript(s) for transfer students, audition, SAT I or ACT test scores (minimum combined SAT I score of 920, minimum combined ACT score of 20). Auditions held 5 times on campus; recorded music is permissible as a substitute for live auditions when distance is prohibitive or scheduling is difficult and videotaped performances are permissible as a substitute for live auditions if distance is prohibitive or scheduling is difficult.

Undergraduate Contact Ms. Kathy Hunt, Academic Advisor, Music Department, Southwest Texas State University, 601 University Drive, San Marcos, Texas 78666-4616; 512-245-7928, fax: 512-245-8181, E-mail address: mb10@swt.edu.

Graduate Contact Dr. Russell Riepe, Coordinator of Graduate Studies, Music Department, Southwest Texas State University, 601 University Drive, San Marcos, Texas 78666-4616; 512-245-2651, fax: 512-245-8181.

▼ STATE UNIVERSITY OF NEW YORK AT BINGHAMTON

Binghamton, New York

State-supported, coed. Suburban campus. Total enrollment: 12,156.

Degrees Bachelor of Music in the area of performance. Majors and concentrations: harpsichord, piano/organ, stringed instruments, voice, wind and percussion instruments. Graduate degrees offered: Master of Music in the areas of performance, composition, conducting. Program accredited by NASM.

Enrollment Fall 1997: 50 undergraduate, 30 graduate.

Music Faculty 33 total undergraduate and graduate (full-time and part-time). 50% of full-time faculty have terminal degrees. Graduate students do not teach undergraduate courses.

Expenses for 1997–98 Application fee: $30. State resident tuition: $3400 full-time. Nonresident tuition: $8300 full-time. Mandatory fees: $710 full-time. College room and board: $5114. College room only: $3070. Room and board charges vary according to board plan and housing facility. Special program-related fees: $10 per year for practice room fee.

Application Procedures Students apply for admission into the professional program by freshman year. Deadline for freshmen and transfers: January 15. Required: essay, high school transcript, college transcript(s) for transfer students, audition, SAT I or ACT test scores. Auditions held as needed on campus.

Web Site http://music.binghamton.edu/.

Undergraduate Contact Dr. Colleen Reardon, Director of Undergraduate Studies, Department of Music, State University of New York at Binghamton, PO Box 6000, Binghamton, New York 13902-6000; 607-777-2530, fax: 607-777-4425, E-mail address: reardon@binghamton.edu.

Graduate Contact Dr. Jonathan Biggers, Director of Graduate Studies, Department of Music, State University of New York at Binghamton, PO Box 6000, Binghamton, New York 13902-6000; 607-777-2595, fax: 607-777-4425, E-mail address: biggers@binghamton.edu.

▼ STATE UNIVERSITY OF NEW YORK AT BUFFALO

Buffalo, New York

State-supported, coed. Suburban campus. Total enrollment: 23,429. Music program established 1958.

Degrees Bachelor of Music in the areas of performance, music education. Majors and concentrations: classical guitar, harpsichord, music education, piano/organ, stringed instruments, voice, wind and percussion instruments. Graduate degrees offered: Master of Music in the areas of music education, music performance. Cross-registration with Buffalo Consortium. Program accredited by NASM.

Enrollment Fall 1997: 153 total; 54 undergraduate, 13 graduate, 86 non-professional degree.

Music Student Profile 45% females, 55% males, 2% minorities, 15% international.

Music Faculty 41 total undergraduate and graduate (full-time and part-time). 79% of full-time faculty have terminal degrees. Graduate students teach a few undergraduate courses. Undergraduate student–faculty ratio: 5:1.

Student Life Student groups/activities include Music Educators National Conference, New York State School Music Association Annual Conference.

Expenses for 1997–98 Application fee: $30. State resident tuition: $3400 full-time. Nonresident tuition: $8300 full-time. Mandatory fees: $940 full-time. College room and board: $5604. College room only: $3224. Room and board charges vary according to housing facility.

Financial Aid Program-specific awards for 1997: 14 departmental scholarships for program majors ($600–$1000), 4 Garahee Awards for program majors ($400–$500), 2 D. Bernard and Jill L. Simon Awards for program majors ($750), 2–3 Performing Arts Honors Awards for program majors ($2500), 4 Challengeships (Honors) for program majors ($2500), 4 Talentships (Honors) for program majors ($2500).

Application Procedures Students admitted directly into the professional program freshman year. Deadline for freshmen and transfers: continuous. Required: essay, high school transcript, college transcript(s) for transfer students, minimum 3.0 high school GPA, 2 letters of recommendation, audition, SAT I or ACT test scores (minimum combined SAT I score of 1130, minimum combined ACT score of 23), TOEFL score for international applicants. Auditions held 4 times on campus; recorded music is permissible as a substitute for live auditions if scheduling is difficult and videotaped performances are permissible as a substitute for live auditions if scheduling is difficult.

Web Site http://www.music.buffalo.edu/.

Contact Mr. Michael Burke, Director of Student Programs, Music Department, State University of New York at Buffalo, 226 Baird Hall, Buffalo, New York 14260; 716-645-2758, fax: 716-645-3824.

▼ STATE UNIVERSITY OF NEW YORK COLLEGE AT FREDONIA

Fredonia, New York

State-supported, coed. Small town campus. Total enrollment: 4,593.

Degrees Bachelor of Music in the areas of music education, performance, composition; Bachelor of Fine Arts in the area of music theater; Bachelor of Science in the areas of sound recording technology, music therapy. Majors and concentrations: composition, music education, music therapy, piano/organ, sound recording technology, stringed instruments, voice, wind and percussion instruments. Graduate degrees offered: Master of Music in the areas of music education, performance, composition. Program accredited by NASM, NAMT.

Enrollment Fall 1997: 475 total; 425 undergraduate, 40 graduate, 10 non-professional degree.

Music Student Profile 50% females, 50% males, 6% minorities, 5% international.

Music Faculty 50 total undergraduate and graduate (full-time and part-time). 90% of full-time faculty have terminal degrees. Graduate students do not teach undergraduate courses. Undergraduate student–faculty ratio: 10:1.

Student Life Student groups/activities include Music Educators National Conference Student Chapter, National Association of Music Therapy Student Chapter, professional music fraternities.

Expenses for 1997–98 Application fee: $30. State resident tuition: $3400 full-time. Nonresident tuition: $8300 full-time. Mandatory fees: $675 full-time. College room and board: $4650. College room only: $3000. Room and board charges vary according to board plan and housing facility. Special program-related fees: $90 per semester for comprehensive music fee (all majors).

Financial Aid Program-specific awards for 1997: 20–30 Hillman Foundation Awards for program majors ($500–$1000), 5–10 Directors Scholarships for program majors ($250–$750), 10–15 Piano Scholarships for program majors ($500–$750).

Application Procedures Students admitted directly into the professional program freshman year. Deadline for freshmen and transfers: continuous. Required: high school transcript, college transcript(s) for transfer students, 2 letters of recommendation, audition, SAT I or ACT test scores. Auditions held 6 times on campus and off campus in various locations in the Albany and Long Island areas; recorded music is permissible as a substitute for live auditions when distance is prohibitive and videotaped performances are permissible as a substitute for live auditions when distance is prohibitive.

Web Site http://www.fredonia.edu/som/.

Undergraduate Contact Mr. Barry Kilpatrick, Assistant Director (Admissions), School of Music, State University of New York College at Fredonia, Mason Hall, Fredonia, New York 14063; 716-673-3153, fax: 716-673-3154, E-mail address: kilpatrick@fredonia.edu.

Graduate Contact Mr. W. Stephen Mayo, Associate Director, School of Music, State University of New York College at Fredonia, Mason Hall, Fredonia, New York 14063; 716-673-3151, fax: 716-673-3154, E-mail address: mayo@fredonia.edu.

▼ STATE UNIVERSITY OF NEW YORK COLLEGE AT POTSDAM

See Crane School of Music

▼ STATE UNIVERSITY OF NEW YORK COLLEGE AT PURCHASE

See Purchase College, State University of New York

▼ STATE UNIVERSITY OF WEST GEORGIA

Carrollton, Georgia

State-supported, coed. Small town campus. Total enrollment: 8,422.

Degrees Bachelor of Music in the areas of performance, composition, music education, music. Majors and concentrations: jazz, music education, performance, piano pedagogy. Graduate degrees offered: Master of Music in the areas of music education, performance. Program accredited by NASM.

Enrollment Fall 1997: 125 total; 100 undergraduate, 20 graduate, 5 non-professional degree.

Music Student Profile 37% females, 63% males, 9% minorities, 1% international.

Music Faculty 19 total undergraduate and graduate (full-time and part-time). 70% of full-time faculty have terminal degrees. Graduate students do not teach undergraduate courses. Undergraduate student–faculty ratio: 10:1.

Student Life Student groups/activities include Music Educators National Conference Collegiate Chapter, Phi Mu Alpha Sinfonia, Sigma Alpha Iota.

Expenses for 1997–98 Application fee: $15. State resident tuition: $1680 full-time. Nonresident tuition: $4461 full-time. Mandatory fees: $408 full-time. College room and board: $3399. College room only: $1728. Room and board charges vary according to board plan. Special program-related fees: $25 per credit hour for applied music fee.

Financial Aid Program-specific awards for 1997: 34 Music Scholarships and Service Awards for music major and non-major ensemble members ($1000).

Application Procedures Students apply for admission into the professional program by freshman year. Deadline for freshmen and transfers: continuous. Notification date for freshmen and transfers: continuous. Required: high school transcript, college transcript(s) for transfer students, audition, SAT I or ACT test scores, minimum 2.5 high school GPA. Recommended: letter of recommendation, interview, portfolio. Auditions held 5 times on campus and off campus in Gainesville, GA; recorded music is permissible as a substitute for live auditions when distance is prohibitive and videotaped performances are permissible as a substitute for live auditions when distance is prohibitive. Portfolio reviews held 5 times on campus and off campus in Gainesville, GA.

Web Site http://www.westga.edu/~musicdpt.

Contact Dr. M. Scott McBride, Chair, Department of Music, State University of West Georgia, Carrollton, Georgia 30118-2210; 770-836-6516, fax: 770-836-4772, E-mail address: smcbride@westga.edu.

▼ STEPHEN F. AUSTIN STATE UNIVERSITY

Nacogdoches, Texas

State-supported, coed. Small town campus. Total enrollment: 12,041.

Degrees Bachelor of Music in the areas of performance, composition, music education. Majors and concentrations: music education, music theory and composition, orchestral instruments, piano/organ, voice, wind and percussion instruments. Graduate degrees offered: Master of Music in the areas of performance, conducting; Master of Arts in the area of music education. Program accredited by NASM.

Enrollment Fall 1997: 231 total; 214 undergraduate, 17 graduate.

Music Student Profile 49% females, 51% males, 19% minorities, 2% international.

Music Faculty 32 total undergraduate and graduate (full-time and part-time). 64% of full-time faculty have terminal degrees. Graduate students teach a few undergraduate courses. Undergraduate student–faculty ratio: 12:1.

Student Life Student groups/activities include Texas Music Educators Association, National Association of Teachers of Singing, Music Teachers National Association.

Expenses for 1997–98 Application fee: $0. One-time mandatory fee: $10. State resident tuition: $1020 full-time. Nonresident tuition: $7440 full-time. Mandatory fees: $1168 full-time. Full-time tuition and fees vary according to course load and reciprocity agreements. College room and board: $3682. Room and board charges vary according to board plan and housing facility. Special program-related fees: $20 per credit hour for applied music lesson fee, $15 for recital fee.

Financial Aid Program-specific awards for 1997: 12 Young Artists Scholarship Awards for incoming freshmen ($4200–$7500), 75 Music Activity Scholarships for program students ($600–$1200).

Application Procedures Students apply for admission into the professional program by freshman year. Deadline for freshmen and transfers: continuous. Notification date for freshmen and transfers: continuous. Required: high school transcript, audition, SAT I or ACT test scores (minimum combined SAT I score of 1010, minimum combined ACT score of 21). Auditions held as needed on campus; recorded music is permissible as a substitute for live auditions when distance is prohibitive and videotaped performances are permissible as a substitute for live auditions when distance is prohibitive.

Contact Dr. Ronald E. Anderson, Chair, Music Department, Stephen F. Austin State University, Box 13043, SFA Station, Nacogdoches, Texas 75962; 409-468-4602, fax: 409-468-5810, E-mail address: randerson@sfasu.edu.

▼ STETSON UNIVERSITY

DeLand, Florida

Independent, coed. Small town campus. Total enrollment: 2,857.

Degrees Bachelor of Music in the areas of performance, music theory and composition; Bachelor of Music Education in the areas of vocal music education, instrumental music education. Majors and concentrations: interdisciplinary studies, music, music education, music theory and composition, piano/organ, stringed instruments, voice, wind and percussion instruments. Program accredited by NASM.

Enrollment Fall 1997: 200 total; all undergraduate.

Music Student Profile 55% females, 45% males, 11% minorities, 3% international.

Music Faculty 43 total (full-time and part-time). 95% of full-time faculty have terminal degrees. Graduate students do not teach undergraduate courses. Undergraduate student–faculty ratio: 5:1.

Student Life Student groups/activities include Music Educators National Conference Student Chapter, Phi Mu Alpha, Sigma Alpha Iota.

Expenses for 1997–98 Application fee: $35. Comprehensive fee: $20,420 includes full-time tuition ($15,100), mandatory

fees ($665), and college room and board ($4655). College room only: $2835. Room and board charges vary according to gender and housing facility. Special program-related fees: $25 per course for practice room fee.

Financial Aid Program-specific awards for 1997: 255 Endowed Music Scholarships for program students ($4500).

Application Procedures Students admitted directly into the professional program freshman year. Deadline for freshmen: March 15; transfers: March 1. Notification date for freshmen: April 1; transfers: continuous. Required: essay, high school transcript, college transcript(s) for transfer students, audition, SAT I or ACT test scores. Recommended: minimum 3.0 high school GPA. Auditions held 4 times and scheduled as needed on campus and off campus in various locations; recorded music is permissible as a substitute for live auditions if a campus visit is impossible and videotaped performances are permissible as a substitute for live auditions if a campus visit is impossible.

Web Site http://www.stetson.edu/schools/music/.

Undergraduate Contact Ms. Crista Cueto, Admissions Counselor, School of Music, Stetson University, 421 North Woodland Boulevard, Unit 8399, DeLand, Florida 32720; 904-822-8975, fax: 904-822-8948.

▼ SUSQUEHANNA UNIVERSITY

Selinsgrove, Pennsylvania

Independent, coed. Small town campus. Total enrollment: 1,725. Music program established 1899.

Degrees Bachelor of Music in the areas of performance, music education, church music. Majors and concentrations: brass, guitar, piano/organ, stringed instruments, voice, wind and percussion instruments. Program accredited by NASM.

Enrollment Fall 1997: 106 total; 82 undergraduate, 24 non-professional degree.

Music Student Profile 63% females, 37% males, 2% minorities.

Music Faculty 27 total (full-time and part-time). 80% of full-time faculty have terminal degrees. Graduate students do not teach undergraduate courses.

Student Life Student groups/activities include Music Educators National Conference Student Chapter, Phi Mu Alpha Sinfonia, Sigma Alpha Iota. Special housing available for music students.

Expenses for 1997–98 Application fee: $30. Comprehensive fee: $23,580 includes full-time tuition ($18,060), mandatory fees ($290), and college room and board ($5230). College room only: $2770. Room and board charges vary according to board plan and housing facility. Special program-related fees: $25 per semester for organ practice fee, $15–$20 per semester for instrument rentals.

Financial Aid Program-specific awards for 1997: 2 Isaacs Scholarships for program majors ($5000), 10 music scholarships for program majors ($3000–$5000), 10 Performance Grants for program majors and non-majors ($1000–$1500).

Application Procedures Students admitted directly into the professional program freshman year. Deadline for freshmen and transfers: continuous. Required: essay, high school transcript, college transcript(s) for transfer students, 2 letters of recommendation, audition, SAT I or ACT test scores. Recommended: interview. Auditions held 5 times on campus; recorded music is permissible as a substitute for live auditions in special circumstances and videotaped performances are permissible as a substitute for live auditions in special circumstances.

Web Site http://www.susqu.edu/ac_depts/finearts/music/.

Undergraduate Contact Mr. Rick Ziegler, Director of Admissions, Susquehanna University, 514 University Avenue, Selinsgrove, Pennsylvania 17870; 717-372-4260, fax: 717-372-2722, E-mail address: ziegler@susqu.edu.

▼ THE SWINNEY CONSERVATORY OF MUSIC

See Central Methodist College

▼ SYBIL B. HARRINGTON COLLEGE OF FINE ARTS AND HUMANITIES

See West Texas A&M University

▼ SYRACUSE UNIVERSITY

Syracuse, New York

Independent, coed. Urban campus. Total enrollment: 14,557. Music program established 1877.

Degrees Bachelor of Music in the areas of music composition, music education, music industry, organ, percussion, piano, strings, voice, wind instruments; Bachelor of Arts in the area of music. Majors and concentrations: composition, music, music business, music education, performance, piano/organ, stringed instruments, voice, wind and percussion instruments. Graduate degrees offered: Master of Music in the areas of music composition, music education, organ, percussion, piano, strings, music theory, voice, wind instruments. Program accredited by NASM.

Enrollment Fall 1997: 207 total; 142 undergraduate, 19 graduate, 46 non-professional degree.

Music Student Profile 59% females, 41% males, 12% minorities, 3% international.

Music Faculty 55 total undergraduate and graduate (full-time and part-time). 92% of full-time faculty have terminal degrees. Graduate students teach a few undergraduate courses. Undergraduate student–faculty ratio: 9:1.

Student Life Student groups/activities include Sigma Alpha Iota, Music Educators National Conference, Pi Kappa Lambda.

Expenses for 1997–98 Application fee: $40. Comprehensive fee: $25,816 includes full-time tuition ($17,550), mandatory fees ($506), and college room and board ($7760). College room only: $4090. Room and board charges vary according to board plan and housing facility. Special program-related fees: $180–$360 per semester for private lessons, $15–$20 per course for practice room fee (piano), $36–$72 per course for practice room fee (organ).

Financial Aid Program-specific awards for 1997: 25 Special Music Awards for talented program majors, 1–40 Chancellor's Awards for those demonstrating academic achievement ($6000), 1–40 Dean's Awards for those demonstrating academic achievement ($4000).

Application Procedures Students admitted directly into the professional program freshman year. Deadline for freshmen: January 15; transfers: July 1. Notification date for freshmen: March 15; transfers: August 15. Required: essay, high school transcript, college transcript(s) for transfer students, minimum 2.0 high school GPA, 2 letters of recommendation, audition, SAT I or ACT test scores, high school counselor

Syracuse University (*continued*)

evaluation. Recommended: minimum 3.0 high school GPA, interview. Auditions held 10 times on campus and off campus in New York, NY; recorded music is permissible as a substitute for live auditions if a live audition is impossible and videotaped performances are permissible as a substitute for live auditions if a live audition is impossible.

Web Site http://vpa.syr.edu.

Undergraduate Contact Coordinator of Recruiting, College of Visual and Performing Arts, Syracuse University, 202P Crouse College, Syracuse, New York 13244-1010; 315-443-2769, fax: 315-443-1935, E-mail address: admissu@vpa.syr.edu.

Graduate Contact Graduate School, Syracuse University, Suite 303 Bowne Hall, Syracuse, New York 13244; 315-443-3028, fax: 315-443-3423, E-mail address: gradschl@suadmin.syr.edu.

More About the University

Program Facilities Crouse College houses acoustically rich Crouse Auditorium (750 seats); the 3,823-pipe Holtkamp organ; classrooms, practice rooms, and studios; an electronic music studio with equipment for sampling, 8-channel digital audio, FM and analog synthesis, and MIDI-based programming using Macintosh computers; Belfer Audio Archive (newly refurbished studio that offers study in sound archiving and digital multitrack and live acoustic recording); and the Music Education Resource Center.

Faculty, Resident Artists, and Alumni Included in the faculty are members of the Syracuse Symphony Orchestra, active recitalists and performers, published authors, and widely performed composers. Recent visiting artists have included the Kronos Quartet, the Peabody Trio, the Cassatt Quartet, the Atlantic Brass Quintet, Gunther Schuller, and the California EAR Unit. Alumni perform worldwide and are active in many areas of the music industry.

Student Performances Formal groups include chamber groups and small ensembles, Men's Glee Club, Women's Choir, Instrumental Jazz Ensemble, Opera Workshop, Orange Opus (new music ensemble that performs works by SU student composers), Oratorio Society, Pride of the Orange Marching Band (football pep band), Sour Sitrus Society (basketball pep band), SU Chimesmasters, Symphony Band, University Orchestra, University Singers, Weekly Convocation, Wind Ensemble, and Windjammer (vocal jazz).

Special Programs Guest artists perform and hold lectures and master classes on a regular basis, and internships–local or national–in many areas of the music industry, and merit scholarships for exceptionally qualified students are available. Performance honors program for nonperformance majors; students may study abroad in Europe and Asia through SU's Division of International Programs Abroad (DIPA); honors program available for students who desire a rigorous academic challenge.

▼

The School of Music encourages students to reach their musical and intellectual potential through preparation as performers, composers, arrangers, music educators, and music industry professionals. Students are a part of a vibrant creative environment led by faculty members who are absorbed in music making both on and off campus.

Although part of a large university, the School of Music enjoys an intimate atmosphere that allows each student to receive the individual attention and opportunity for regular performance that every serious young musician requires. In this inclusive programs with a classical basis, students are also

exposed to contemporary music of many genres. Students are immersed in music in many contexts: private lessons, ensemble rehearsals, recitals, guest artists, master classes, and performances. Qualified composition, music education, music industry, and AB music students may participate in a performance honors program that allows them to pursue a high level of proficiency on their instrument.

A wide array of ensembles provides ample variety for performance opportunities. All students in the School of Music are required to be involved in one of the School's ensembles every semester, although many participate in several groups. This experience helps students develop the important skill of functioning in group situations and complements the many hours every dedicated musician spends in solitary practice. A required weekly convocation provides a forum for music students and faculty members to convene as a community and features a lively mix of student, faculty, and guest performances. Academic electives, which provide a liberal arts component to the curriculum, can be selected from the broad range of courses offered at the University.

Students benefit from a faculty of active professionals who are members of the Syracuse Symphony Orchestra, composers whose works have been performed nationally and internationally, and recitalists who have won competitions worldwide and have performed with internationally known orchestras and ensembles. They are dedicated to challenging, inspiring, and encouraging students to explore all of their musical and intellectual potential.

The creative activities of the School of Music are an integral part of the College of Visual and Performing Arts, which also governs programs in art and design, drama, and speech communication. The College serves as the center of SU's cultural life, on a campus whose lively and diverse schedule of events could only be found at a large university.

The city of Syracuse itself offers a rich culture: it is home to the Syracuse Symphony Orchestra, the Syracuse Opera, the Society for New Music, and Syracuse Stage. Syracuse is also a regular stop for touring companies of Broadway's most popular musical comedies, experimental theater troupes, nationally known comedians, rock groups, and dance companies.

▼ TARLETON STATE UNIVERSITY

Stephenville, Texas

State-supported, coed. Small town campus. Music program established 1967.

Degrees Bachelor of Music in the area of music education; Bachelor of Arts in the area of music performance. Majors and concentrations: music education. Program accredited by NASM.

Enrollment Fall 1997: 60 total; all undergraduate.

Music Student Profile 55% females, 45% males, 12% minorities.

Music Faculty 10 total (full-time and part-time). 57% of full-time faculty have terminal degrees. Undergraduate student–faculty ratio: 8:1.

Student Life Student groups/activities include Texas Music Educators Association, National Association of Schools of Music, National Association of Teachers of Singing.

Expenses for 1997–98 Application fee: $20. State resident tuition: $1088 full-time. Nonresident tuition: $7872 full-time. Mandatory fees: $1376 full-time. Special program-related fees: $5–$20 per year for band equipment and uniform fees.

Financial Aid Program-specific awards for 1997: 3 Center Stage Scholarships for piano, vocal, instrumental students ($2000), 35 band scholarships for all students ($200–$1500), 28 music scholarships for instrumental/vocal majors ($400–$1500), 20 Hunewell Scholarships for instrumental majors ($150–$400), 1 Teat Scholarship for vocal majors ($200), 2–4 Piano Performance Scholarships for piano majors ($750–$1500), 3 Froh Scholarships for piano majors ($800–$1500), 1 Landress Scholarship for piano majors ($250–$500).

Application Procedures Students apply for admission into the professional program by freshman year. Deadline for freshmen and transfers: continuous. Required: high school transcript, college transcript(s) for transfer students, minimum 2.0 high school GPA, letter of recommendation, audition, SAT I or ACT test scores. Auditions held throughout the year on campus and off campus in various locations in Texas.

Undergraduate Contact Mr. Richard Denning, Head, Department of Fine Arts and Speech, Tarleton State University, Box T-0320, Stephenville, Texas 76402; 254-968-9245, fax: 254-968-9239, E-mail address: denning@tarleton.edu.

▼ TAYLOR UNIVERSITY

Upland, Indiana

Independent-interdenominational, coed. Rural campus. Total enrollment: 1,884. Music program established 1970.

Degrees Bachelor of Music in the areas of performance, composition; Bachelor of Music Education. Majors and concentrations: composition, music education, music management, music marketing, piano/organ, stringed instruments, theater arts/drama, voice, wind and percussion instruments. Program accredited by NASM.

Enrollment Fall 1997: 66 total; all undergraduate.

Music Student Profile 52% females, 48% males, 5% minorities, 5% international.

Music Faculty 28 total (full-time and part-time). 90% of full-time faculty have terminal degrees. Graduate students do not teach undergraduate courses.

Student Life Student groups/activities include Music Educators National Conference, National Association of Schools of Singing, Community Music Development.

Expenses for 1997–98 Application fee: $20. Comprehensive fee: $17,894 includes full-time tuition ($13,270), mandatory fees ($214), and college room and board ($4410). College room only: $2100. Room and board charges vary according to housing facility.

Financial Aid Program-specific awards for 1997: 3–5 Enrollment Awards for freshmen ($2000), 3–5 Music Merit Awards for freshmen ($500), 3–5 Applied Music Awards for freshmen ($250).

Application Procedures Students admitted directly into the professional program freshman year. Deadline for freshmen and transfers: January 15. Notification date for freshmen and transfers: continuous. Required: essay, high school transcript, college transcript(s) for transfer students, minimum 3.0 high school GPA, 3 letters of recommendation, interview, audition, SAT I or ACT test scores. Auditions held 4 times on campus; recorded music is permissible as a substitute for live auditions when distance is prohibitive and videotaped performances are permissible as a substitute for live auditions when distance is prohibitive.

Web Site http://www.tayloru.edu/~music/.

Undergraduate Contact Mr. Steve Mortland, Admissions Department, Taylor University, 236 West Reade Avenue, Upland, Indiana 46989; 317-998-5206.

▼ TEMPLE UNIVERSITY

See Esther Boyer College of Music at Temple University

▼ TENNESSEE TECHNOLOGICAL UNIVERSITY

Cookeville, Tennessee

State-supported, coed. Small town campus. Total enrollment: 8,263.

Degrees Bachelor of Music in the areas of performance, music education, music therapy. Program accredited by NASM.

Enrollment Fall 1997: 165 undergraduate.

Music Student Profile 62% females, 38% males, 5% minorities, 2% international.

Music Faculty 32 total (full-time and part-time). 75% of full-time faculty have terminal degrees. Graduate students do not teach undergraduate courses. Undergraduate student–faculty ratio: 7:1.

Student Life Student groups/activities include Phi Mu Alpha, Mu Phi Epsilon, Music Educators National Conference Student Chapter.

Expenses for 1997–98 Application fee: $15. State resident tuition: $0 full-time. Nonresident tuition: $4596 full-time. Mandatory fees: $2116 full-time. College room and board: $3180. College room only: $1700. Room and board charges vary according to board plan and housing facility. Special program-related fees: $55 per semester for recital and private lesson fees.

Financial Aid Program-specific awards for 1997: 8 departmental scholarships for students demonstrating need/talented students ($4000).

Application Procedures Students admitted directly into the professional program freshman year. Deadline for freshmen and transfers: continuous. Required: high school transcript, minimum 2.0 high school GPA, SAT I or ACT test scores. Recommended: audition. Auditions held twice on campus; recorded music is permissible as a substitute for live auditions when distance is prohibitive and videotaped performances are permissible as a substitute for live auditions when distance is prohibitive.

Undergraduate Contact Music Department, Tennessee Technological University, Box 5045, Cookeville, Tennessee 38505; 931-372-3161.

▼ TENNESSEE WESLEYAN COLLEGE

Athens, Tennessee

Independent-United Methodist, coed. Small town campus. Total enrollment: 756.

Degrees Bachelor of Music Education in the areas of teaching, church music. Majors and concentrations: music education.

Enrollment Fall 1997: 10 total; 3 undergraduate, 7 nonprofessional degree.

Music Student Profile 70% females, 30% males, 10% international.

Tennessee Wesleyan College (*continued*)

Music Faculty 4 total (full-time and part-time). 50% of full-time faculty have terminal degrees. Graduate students do not teach undergraduate courses. Undergraduate student–faculty ratio: 5:1.

Student Life Student groups/activities include Music Educators National Conference.

Estimated expenses for 1998–99 Application fee: $25. Comprehensive fee: $11,050 includes full-time tuition ($6950), mandatory fees ($100), and college room and board ($4000).

Application Procedures Students admitted directly into the professional program freshman year. Deadline for freshmen and transfers: continuous. Required: high school transcript, college transcript(s) for transfer students, minimum 2.0 high school GPA, letter of recommendation, SAT I or ACT test scores (minimum combined ACT score of 17). Recommended: audition. Auditions held by appointment on campus; recorded music is permissible as a substitute for live auditions when distance is prohibitive and videotaped performances are permissible as a substitute for live auditions when distance is prohibitive.

Undergraduate Contact Ms. Janice Ryberg, Chair, Music Department, Tennessee Wesleyan College, PO Box 40, Athens, Tennessee 37371; 423-745-7504, fax: 423-744-9968.

▼ Texas A&M University–Commerce

Commerce, Texas

State-supported, coed. Small town campus. Total enrollment: 7,693.

Degrees Bachelor of Music in the areas of performance, piano pedagogy. Majors and concentrations: brass, classical music, music, piano, voice, wind and percussion instruments. Graduate degrees offered: Master of Music in the areas of performance, music education; Master of Science in the area of music education. Program accredited by NASM.

Enrollment Fall 1997: 137 undergraduate, 25 graduate.

Music Student Profile 50% females, 50% males, 10% minorities, 2% international.

Music Faculty 25 total undergraduate and graduate (full-time and part-time). 30% of full-time faculty have terminal degrees. Graduate students do not teach undergraduate courses.

Student Life Student groups/activities include Phi Mu Alpha, professional fraternities and sororities, Gospel Choirs.

Expenses for 1997–98 Application fee: $0. State resident tuition: $1740 full-time. Nonresident tuition: $8160 full-time. Mandatory fees: $546 full-time. Full-time tuition and fees vary according to course load. College room and board: $3816. College room only: $1942. Room and board charges vary according to board plan and housing facility. Special program-related fees: $25 per semester for applied music fees.

Financial Aid Program-specific awards for 1997: 120 music scholarships for program students ($200–$1000).

Application Procedures Students admitted directly into the professional program freshman year. Deadline for freshmen and transfers: August 1. Required: high school transcript, college transcript(s) for transfer students, audition. Recommended: minimum 2.0 high school GPA, letter of recommendation, interview. Auditions held by appointment on campus; recorded music is permissible as a substitute for live

auditions if a campus visit is impossible, if unedited, and if of good quality and videotaped performances are permissible as a substitute for live auditions if a campus visit is impossible, if unedited, and if of good quality.

Undergraduate Contact Director of Admissions, Texas A&M University–Commerce, 2600 Neal Street, Commerce, Texas 75429; 903-886-5102.

Graduate Contact Dr. R. N. Singh, Dean of Graduate School, Texas A&M University–Commerce, Commerce, Texas 75429; 903-886-5163.

▼ Texas A&M University–Corpus Christi

Corpus Christi, Texas

State-supported, coed. Suburban campus. Total enrollment: 6,024. Music program established 1972.

Degrees Bachelor of Music in the areas of performance, music education. Majors and concentrations: classical guitar, keyboard, voice, wind and percussion instruments. Mandatory cross-registration with Del Mar College. Program accredited by NASM.

Enrollment Fall 1997: 63 total; 41 undergraduate, 22 non-professional degree.

Music Student Profile 46% females, 54% males, 48% minorities, 2% international.

Music Faculty 31 total (full-time and part-time). 33% of full-time faculty have terminal degrees. Graduate students do not teach undergraduate courses. Undergraduate student–faculty ratio: 8:1.

Expenses for 1997–98 Application fee: $10. State resident tuition: $816 full-time. Nonresident tuition: $5952 full-time. Mandatory fees: $1138 full-time. Special program-related fees: $40 per semester for applied music fee.

Financial Aid Program-specific awards for 1997: 30 Fine Arts Studio Scholarships for transfer students ($600).

Application Procedures Students apply for admission into the professional program by sophomore year. Deadline for freshmen and transfers: July 1. Notification date for freshmen and transfers: continuous. Required: high school transcript, college transcript(s) for transfer students, audition, SAT I or ACT test scores, theory assessment examination. Auditions held once on campus; recorded music is permissible as a substitute for live auditions when distance is prohibitive and videotaped performances are permissible as a substitute for live auditions when distance is prohibitive.

Undergraduate Contact Dr. Sam Logsdon, Music Program Coordinator, Department of Music, Texas A&M University–Corpus Christi, 6300 Ocean Drive, Corpus Christi, Texas 78412; 512-994-2761, fax: 512-994-6097, E-mail address: logsdons@falcon.tamucc.edu.

▼ Texas A&M University–Kingsville

Kingsville, Texas

State-supported, coed. Small town campus. Total enrollment: 6,050.

Degrees Bachelor of Music. Majors and concentrations: music education, performance. Graduate degrees offered: Master of Music in the area of music education. Program accredited by NASM.

Enrollment Fall 1997: 170 undergraduate, 15 graduate.

Music Student Profile 25% females, 75% males, 85% minorities.
Music Faculty 19 total undergraduate and graduate (full-time and part-time). 50% of full-time faculty have terminal degrees. Graduate students do not teach undergraduate courses. Undergraduate student–faculty ratio: 12:1.
Student Life Student groups/activities include Tau Beta Sigma, Kappa Kappa Psi.
Expenses for 1997–98 Application fee: $15. State resident tuition: $1054 full-time. Nonresident tuition: $7688 full-time. Mandatory fees: $1126 full-time. College room and board: $3484. College room only: $1784. Room and board charges vary according to board plan. Special program-related fees: $5 per course for lab fees, $18 per credit hour for applied music.
Financial Aid Program-specific awards for 1997: 75 departmental awards for music majors ($200–$400).
Application Procedures Students admitted directly into the professional program freshman year. Deadline for freshmen and transfers: continuous. Required: high school transcript, college transcript(s) for transfer students, audition, SAT I or ACT test scores (minimum combined SAT I score of 850, minimum combined ACT score of 21), completion of college preparatory courses, Texas Academic Skills Program test. Auditions held 3 times on campus; recorded music is permissible as a substitute for live auditions when distance is prohibitive and videotaped performances are permissible as a substitute for live auditions when distance is prohibitive.
Contact Department of Music, Texas A&M University–Kingsville, Box 174, Kingsville, Texas 78363; 512-593-2803, fax: 512-593-2816.

▼ TEXAS CHRISTIAN UNIVERSITY

Fort Worth, Texas

Independent, coed. Suburban campus. Total enrollment: 7,273. Music program established 1873.
Degrees Bachelor of Music in the areas of performance, piano pedagogy, music theory-composition, music history, church music; Bachelor of Music Education in the areas of vocal music education, instrumental music education. Majors and concentrations: guitar, music, music education, music theory and composition, musicology, piano/organ, sacred music, stringed instruments, voice, wind and percussion instruments. Graduate degrees offered: Master of Music in the areas of performance, pedagogy, musicology, music theory/composition/computer music; Master of Music Education. Program accredited by NASM.
Enrollment Fall 1997: 201 total; 150 undergraduate, 35 graduate, 16 non-professional degree.
Music Student Profile 60% females, 40% males, 10% minorities, 20% international.
Music Faculty 52 total undergraduate and graduate (full-time and part-time). 70% of full-time faculty have terminal degrees. Graduate students do not teach undergraduate courses. Undergraduate student–faculty ratio: 15:1.
Student Life Student groups/activities include professional music societies, American String Teachers Association, Music Educators Organization.
Expenses for 1997–98 Application fee: $30. One-time mandatory fee: $200. Comprehensive fee: $14,950 includes full-time tuition ($9900), mandatory fees ($1190), and college room and board ($3860). College room only: $2460. Room and board charges vary according to housing facility.

Financial Aid Program-specific awards for 1997: choral scholarships for vocalists ($800–$8500), orchestra scholarships for string players ($800–$8500), band scholarships for band instrumentalists ($800–$8500), Music Department Scholarships for program majors ($800–$8500).
Application Procedures Students apply for admission into the professional program by freshman year. Deadline for freshmen: February 15; transfers: August 1. Notification date for freshmen: March 15; transfers: August 15. Required: essay, high school transcript, college transcript(s) for transfer students, audition, SAT I or ACT test scores, portfolio for theory/composition majors. Recommended: minimum 3.0 high school GPA, 3 letters of recommendation, interview. Auditions held continuously by appointment on campus and off campus in various locations; recorded music is permissible as a substitute for live auditions if a campus visit is impossible. Portfolio reviews held by appointment on campus.
Web Site http://www.music.tcu.edu/music/.
Undergraduate Contact Dr. Kenneth R. Raessler, Chair, Department of Music, Texas Christian University, TCU Box 297500, Fort Worth, Texas 76129; 817-921-7602, fax: 817-921-7344, E-mail address: kraessler@gamma.is.tcu.edu.
Graduate Contact Dr. John Burton, Director of Graduate Studies, College of Fine Arts and Communication, Texas Christian University, TCU Box 298000, Fort Worth, Texas 76129; 817-921-7603, fax: 817-921-7703, E-mail address: jburton@tcu.edu.

▼ TEXAS SOUTHERN UNIVERSITY

Houston, Texas

State-supported, coed. Urban campus. Total enrollment: 7,282. Music program established 1947.
Degrees Bachelor of Arts in the area of fine arts. Majors and concentrations: composition, music, music history, performance. Graduate degrees offered: Master of Arts in the area of performance; Master of Education.
Enrollment Fall 1997: 67 total; 57 undergraduate, 10 graduate.
Music Student Profile 55% females, 45% males, 4% minorities, 5% international.
Music Faculty 13 total undergraduate and graduate (full-time and part-time). 40% of full-time faculty have terminal degrees. Graduate students do not teach undergraduate courses. Undergraduate student–faculty ratio: 7:1.
Student Life Student groups/activities include TSU Jazz Band, Concert Choir, Ocean of Soul Marching Band.
Expenses for 1997–98 Application fee: $25. State resident tuition: $1054 full-time. Nonresident tuition: $7688 full-time. Mandatory fees: $1010 full-time. Full-time tuition and fees vary according to course load. College room and board: $4000.
Financial Aid Program-specific awards for 1997: 2 Hines Vocal Awards for voice students ($1000), 3 Rollins/Stewart Awards for voice students ($1000), 16 Music Activities Awards for program students ($400–$800), 2 Lindquist Piano Awards for piano students ($400–$800), 35–40 Band Scholarship awards for band students ($400–$1000), 18 Jazz Band award for jazz band students ($400–$1000), 3 Merkle/Oliphint Voice Award for voice students ($400–$1000).
Application Procedures Students admitted directly into the professional program freshman year. Deadline for freshmen and transfers: June 31. Notification date for freshmen and transfers: August 20. Required: high school transcript,

Texas Southern University (*continued*)

college transcript(s) for transfer students, minimum 2.0 high school GPA, 2 letters of recommendation, audition, SAT I or ACT test scores. Auditions held by appointment on campus; recorded music is permissible as a substitute for live auditions when distance is prohibitive and videotaped performances are permissible as a substitute for live auditions when distance is prohibitive.

Contact Dr. Sarah Trotty, Chair, Department of Fine Arts, Texas Southern University, 3100 Cleburne Avenue, Houston, Texas 77004; 713-313-7337, fax: 713-313-1869.

▼ TEXAS TECH UNIVERSITY

Lubbock, Texas

State-supported, coed. Urban campus. Total enrollment: 25,022. Music program established 1923.

Degrees Bachelor of Music in the areas of performance, composition, music theory, music education. Majors and concentrations: music, music education, opera, piano/organ, stringed instruments, voice, wind and percussion instruments. Graduate degrees offered: Master of Music in the areas of performance, music history and literature, music theory; Master of Music Education. Doctor of Philosophy in the areas of performance, music theory, music history, music education, composition, music administration. Program accredited by NASM.

Enrollment Fall 1997: 1,346 total; 375 undergraduate, 71 graduate, 900 non-professional degree.

Music Student Profile 48% females, 52% males, 10% minorities, 2% international.

Music Faculty 78 total undergraduate and graduate (full-time and part-time). 95% of full-time faculty have terminal degrees. Graduate students teach a few undergraduate courses. Undergraduate student–faculty ratio: 7:1.

Student Life Student groups/activities include Texas Music Educators Conference Student Chapter, Music Educators National Conference Student Chapter, Texas Music Educators Association Student Chapter.

Expenses for 1997–98 Application fee: $25. State resident tuition: $1020 full-time. Nonresident tuition: $7440 full-time. Mandatory fees: $1587 full-time. Full-time tuition and fees vary according to course load. College room and board: $4290. Room and board charges vary according to board plan. Special program-related fees: $15 per semester hour for private music lessons, $15 per semester per instrument for instrument rental, $10 per semester for locker rental.

Financial Aid Program-specific awards for 1997: 230 Endowed Scholarships for program majors ($200–$8500).

Application Procedures Students admitted directly into the professional program freshman year. Deadline for freshmen and transfers: March 1. Required: high school transcript, college transcript(s) for transfer students, minimum 2.0 high school GPA, audition, SAT I or ACT test scores. Recommended: letter of recommendation. Auditions held 5 times and by request on campus; recorded music is permissible as a substitute for live auditions when distance is prohibitive and videotaped performances are permissible as a substitute for live auditions when distance is prohibitive.

Web Site http://www.ttu.edu.

Undergraduate Contact Dr. Robert Henry, Associate Director for Undergraduate Studies, School of Music, Texas Tech

University, Box 42033, Lubbock, Texas 79409-2033; 806-742-2270, fax: 806-742-2294, E-mail address: a5xrh@ttuvml.ttu.edu.

Graduate Contact Dr. Paul Cutter, Associate Director for Graduate Studies, School of Music, Texas Tech University, Box 42033, Lubbock, Texas 79409-2033; 806-742-2270, fax: 806-742-2294, E-mail address: mspfc@ttacs.ttu.edu.

▼ TEXAS WESLEYAN UNIVERSITY

Fort Worth, Texas

Independent-United Methodist, coed. Urban campus. Total enrollment: 3,136.

Degrees Bachelor of Music Education; Bachelor of Arts in the area of music. Majors and concentrations: piano, voice, wind and percussion instruments. Program accredited by NASM.

Enrollment Fall 1997: 90 total; 75 undergraduate, 15 non-professional degree.

Music Student Profile 50% females, 50% males, 35% minorities.

Music Faculty 13 total (full-time and part-time). 45% of full-time faculty have terminal degrees. Graduate students do not teach undergraduate courses.

Expenses for 1997–98 Application fee: $20. Comprehensive fee: $11,650 includes full-time tuition ($7550), mandatory fees ($400), and college room and board ($3700). Full-time tuition and fees vary according to course load and program. Room and board charges vary according to board plan. Special program-related fees: $240 per course for private instruction fee.

Financial Aid Program-specific awards for 1997: 25 departmental scholarships for talented music students ($1500).

Application Procedures Students admitted directly into the professional program freshman year. Deadline for freshmen and transfers: continuous. Required: high school transcript, college transcript(s) for transfer students, minimum 2.0 high school GPA, interview, audition, SAT I or ACT test scores. Auditions held twice on campus; recorded music is permissible as a substitute for live auditions when distance is prohibitive and videotaped performances are permissible as a substitute for live auditions when distance is prohibitive.

Undergraduate Contact Admissions Office, Texas Wesleyan University, 1201 Wesleyan, Fort Worth, Texas 76105; 817-531-4422.

▼ TOWSON UNIVERSITY

Towson, Maryland

State-supported, coed. Suburban campus. Total enrollment: 15,524. Music program established 1966.

Degrees Bachelor of Music in the areas of music performance, music composition, jazz studies, music literature; Bachelor of Science in the area of music education. Majors and concentrations: commercial music, composition, jazz, music education, music literature, performance. Graduate degrees offered: Master of Music in the areas of music performance, music composition, jazz studies; Master of Science in the area of music education. Program accredited by NASM.

Enrollment Fall 1997: 310 total; 250 undergraduate, 60 graduate.

Music Student Profile 59% females, 41% males, 20% minorities, 14% international.

Music Faculty 58 total undergraduate and graduate (full-time and part-time). 80% of full-time faculty have terminal degrees. Graduate students do not teach undergraduate courses. Undergraduate student–faculty ratio: 18:1.

Student Life Student groups/activities include Kappa Kappa Psi (band fraternity), Opera Club, American Choral Directors Association.

Expenses for 1997–98 Application fee: $30. State resident tuition: $3080 full-time. Nonresident tuition: $8158 full-time. Mandatory fees: $1040 full-time. College room and board: $5044. College room only: $2924. Special program-related fees: $85–$245 per credit for private lessons, $20 per year for practice room key rental, $75 per semester for instrument rental.

Financial Aid Program-specific awards for 1997: 10 Music Department Tuition Waiver Scholarships for Maryland resident orchestral instrumentalists ($3000), 3 Dean's Awards in the Fine Arts for program students ($2000), 20 Music Department Awards in the Fine Arts for program students ($1000), 5–10 Music Department Scholarships for program students, 1–2 double reed scholarships for bassoon/oboe players, 1 May Diekmann Scholarship for oboe majors, 1 Cello Scholarship for cello majors, 1 Livingston-Coulange Scholarship for pipe organ majors, 1 Stan Kenton Scholarship for jazz majors, 50 Marching Band Stipends for marching band participants, Marching Band Scholarships for marching band participants.

Application Procedures Students admitted directly into the professional program freshman year. Deadline for freshmen and transfers: continuous. Required: essay, high school transcript, college transcript(s) for transfer students, minimum 2.0 high school GPA, 2 letters of recommendation, audition, SAT I or ACT test scores (minimum combined SAT I score of 1100). Recommended: minimum 3.0 high school GPA, portfolio for composition majors. Auditions held 4 times on campus; videotaped performances are permissible as a substitute for live auditions on a case-by-case basis. Portfolio reviews held twice on campus.

Web Site http://www.towson.edu/music.

Undergraduate Contact Mary Ann Criss, Assistant to the Chair, Department of Music, Towson University, 8000 York Road, Towson , Maryland 21252; 410-830-2836, fax: 410-830-2841, E-mail address: mcriss@towson.edu.

Graduate Contact Graduate Coordinator, Department of Music, Towson University, 8000 York Road, Towson, Maryland 21252; 410-830-2821, fax: 410-830-2841.

▼ TRINITY UNIVERSITY

San Antonio, Texas

Independent, coed. Urban campus. Total enrollment: 2,560. Music program established 1975.

Degrees Bachelor of Music in the areas of performance, composition, music education. Majors and concentrations: choral music education, composition, guitar, harpsichord, instrumental music education, piano/organ, stringed instruments, voice, wind and percussion instruments. Program accredited by NASM.

Enrollment Fall 1997: 50 total; 10 undergraduate, 40 non-professional degree.

Music Student Profile 50% females, 50% males, 10% minorities, 3% international.

Music Faculty 28 total undergraduate (full-time and part-time). 92% of full-time faculty have terminal degrees. Graduate students do not teach undergraduate courses.

Student Life Student groups/activities include Opera Workshop/Musical Theater, Pep Band.

Estimated expenses for 1998–99 Application fee: $25. Comprehensive fee: $20,694 includes full-time tuition ($14,580), mandatory fees ($144), and college room and board ($5970). College room only: $3770. Room and board charges vary according to board plan. Special program-related fees: $200 per year for individual instruction.

Financial Aid Program-specific awards for 1997: 120 music awards for program students ($400–$2000).

Application Procedures Students apply for admission into the professional program by sophomore year. Deadline for freshmen and transfers: February 25. Notification date for freshmen and transfers: April 1. Required: essay, high school transcript, college transcript(s) for transfer students, minimum 2.0 high school GPA, letter of recommendation, SAT I or ACT test scores. Recommended: minimum 3.0 high school GPA, audition. Auditions held 6 times on campus and off campus in Dallas, TX; Houston, TX; recorded music is permissible as a substitute for live auditions if a campus visit is impossible and videotaped performances are permissible as a substitute for live auditions if a campus visit is impossible.

Web Site http://www.trinity.edu/departments/music/.

Undergraduate Contact Dr. Kenneth Greene, Chairman, Department of Music, Trinity University, 715 Stadium Drive, San Antonio, Texas 78212-7200; 210-736-8212, fax: 210-736-8170.

▼ TROY STATE UNIVERSITY

Troy, Alabama

State-supported, coed. Small town campus. Total enrollment: 6,468. Music program established 1965.

Degrees Bachelor of Music Education in the areas of instrumental music education, vocal/choral music education. Graduate degrees offered: Master of Science in the area of music education. Program accredited by NASM.

Enrollment Fall 1997: 118 total; 110 undergraduate, 8 graduate.

Music Student Profile 35% females, 65% males, 4% minorities.

Music Faculty 18 total undergraduate and graduate (full-time and part-time). 46% of full-time faculty have terminal degrees. Graduate students do not teach undergraduate courses. Undergraduate student–faculty ratio: 7:1.

Student Life Student groups/activities include Collegiate Music Educators National Conference, Phi Mu Alpha Sinfonia, Sigma Alpha Iota.

Expenses for 1997–98 Application fee: $20. State resident tuition: $2055 full-time. Nonresident tuition: $4110 full-time. Mandatory fees: $195 full-time. College room and board: $3480. College room only: $1680. Room and board charges vary according to board plan and housing facility. Special program-related fees: $40 per quarter for private lessons.

Financial Aid Program-specific awards for 1997: 80–100 band scholarships for instrumental majors ($300–$2000), 25–30 Choral Scholarships for singers or pianists ($150–$1000).

Application Procedures Students admitted directly into the professional program freshman year. Deadline for freshmen and transfers: continuous. Required: high school transcript, college transcript(s) for transfer students, minimum 2.0 high school GPA, audition, SAT I or ACT test scores (minimum combined SAT I score of 870, minimum combined ACT

Troy State University (continued)

score of 18), minimum 2.0 college GPA for transfer students. Recommended: interview. Auditions held by appointment on campus; recorded music is permissible as a substitute for live auditions if a campus visit is impossible and videotaped performances are permissible as a substitute for live auditions if a campus visit is impossible.

Undergraduate Contact Dr. William Denison, Director, School of Music, Troy State University, Smith Hall 101, University Avenue, Troy, Alabama 36082; 334-670-3322, fax: 334-670-3858.

Graduate Contact Mr. James Smith, Graduate Music Coordinator, School of Music, Troy State University, Long Hall 10, Troy, Alabama 36082; 334-670-3283, fax: 334-670-3858.

▼ TRUMAN STATE UNIVERSITY

Kirksville, Missouri

State-supported, coed. Small town campus. Total enrollment: 6,421.

Degrees Bachelor of Music in the area of performance. Majors and concentrations: piano, stringed instruments, voice, wind and percussion instruments. Graduate degrees offered: Master of Arts in the areas of performance, research, composition. Program accredited by NASM.

Enrollment Fall 1997: 127 total; 118 undergraduate, 9 graduate.

Music Student Profile 53% females, 47% males, 1% minorities, 1% international.

Music Faculty 25 total undergraduate and graduate (full-time and part-time). 89% of full-time faculty have terminal degrees. Graduate students teach a few undergraduate courses. Undergraduate student–faculty ratio: 9:1.

Student Life Student groups/activities include Phi Mu Alpha, Sigma Alpha Iota, Pi Kappa Lambda.

Expenses for 1997–98 Application fee: $0. State resident tuition: $3256 full-time. Nonresident tuition: $5736 full-time. Mandatory fees: $18 full-time. College room and board: $3992. Special program-related fees: $40–$80 for private lessons.

Financial Aid Program-specific awards for 1997: 10 Endowed Scholarships for program majors ($300–$1000), 100 Service Scholarships for program majors and non-majors ($300–$1500).

Application Procedures Students admitted directly into the professional program freshman year. Deadline for freshmen: November 15; transfers: May 1. Notification date for freshmen: December 5. Required: essay, high school transcript, college transcript(s) for transfer students, audition, SAT I or ACT test scores. Recommended: portfolio. Auditions held continuously on campus and off campus in Kansas City, MO; St. Louis, MO; Chicago, IL; Des Moines, IA; recorded music is permissible as a substitute for live auditions with approval from the department and videotaped performances are permissible as a substitute for live auditions with approval from the department. Portfolio reviews held twice on campus.

Web Site http://www.truman.edu.

Undergraduate Contact Mr. Robert L. Jones, Head, Division of Fine Arts, Truman State University, 100 East Normal, Baldwin Hall #118, Kirksville, Missouri 63501; 660-785-4417, fax: 660-785-7463, E-mail address: fa22@truman.edu.

Graduate Contact Dr. David Nichols, Professor of Music, Division of Fine Arts, Truman State University, 100 East Normal, Baldwin Hall #118, Kirksville, Missouri 63501; 660-785-4417, fax: 660-785-7463, E-mail address: dnichols@truman.edu.

▼ UNION COLLEGE

Barbourville, Kentucky

Independent-United Methodist, coed. Small town campus. Total enrollment: 1,016.

Degrees Bachelor of Music in the area of church music; Bachelor of Music Education in the areas of instrumental music education, vocal music education. Majors and concentrations: music, music education, sacred music, voice, wind and percussion instruments.

Enrollment Fall 1997: 20 undergraduate.

Music Student Profile 50% females, 50% males.

Music Faculty 8 total (full-time and part-time). 80% of full-time faculty have terminal degrees. Graduate students do not teach undergraduate courses. Undergraduate student–faculty ratio: 8:1.

Student Life Student groups/activities include Music Educators National Conference Student Chapter, American Guild of Organists, American Choral Directors Student Chapter.

Expenses for 1997–98 Application fee: $20. Comprehensive fee: $12,460 includes full-time tuition ($9340) and college room and board ($3120).

Financial Aid Program-specific awards for 1997: 10–20 departmental scholarships for voice/winds/keyboard majors ($2000).

Application Procedures Students admitted directly into the professional program freshman year. Deadline for freshmen and transfers: August 1. Notification date for freshmen and transfers: August 15. Required: high school transcript, college transcript(s) for transfer students, minimum 2.0 high school GPA, interview, audition, SAT I or ACT test scores. Recommended: letter of recommendation. Auditions held 3-4 times on campus; recorded music is permissible as a substitute for live auditions when distance is prohibitive and videotaped performances are permissible as a substitute for live auditions when distance is prohibitive.

Undergraduate Contact Dean of Admissions, Union College, 310 College Street, Barbourville, Kentucky 40906; 606-546-1220.

▼ UNION UNIVERSITY

Jackson, Tennessee

Independent-Southern Baptist, coed. Small town campus. Total enrollment: 1,953. Music program established 1920.

Degrees Bachelor of Music in the areas of voice, piano, organ, music education, sacred music, orchestral instruments, guitar, music theory and literature. Majors and concentrations: choral music education, instrumental music education, music theory and literature, performance, piano/organ, sacred music, voice. Cross-registration with Lambuth University, Freed-Hardeman University. Program accredited by NASM.

Enrollment Fall 1997: 87 total; all undergraduate.

Music Student Profile 60% females, 40% males, 3% minorities.

Music Faculty 17 total (full-time and part-time). 90% of full-time faculty have terminal degrees. Graduate students do not teach undergraduate courses. Undergraduate student–faculty ratio: 8:1.

Student Life Student groups/activities include Phi Mu Alpha Sinfonia, Sigma Alpha Iota, Pi Kappa Lambda (national music honor society).

Expenses for 1997–98 Application fee: $25. Comprehensive fee: $11,185 includes full-time tuition ($7990), mandatory fees ($190), and college room and board ($3005). Full-time tuition and fees vary according to class time, course load, location, and program. Room and board charges vary according to board plan and housing facility. Special program-related fees: $125–$225 per semester for private lessons, $50 per semester for class piano/voice fee.

Financial Aid Program-specific awards for 1997: 65 Talent Scholarships for program majors ($500–$2000), 20 Vocal Ensemble Scholarships for musically qualified students ($750–$1500), 30 Instrumental Ensemble Scholarships for musically qualified students ($200–$1000).

Application Procedures Students admitted directly into the professional program freshman year. Deadline for freshmen and transfers: continuous. Required: high school transcript, college transcript(s) for transfer students, interview, audition, SAT I or ACT test scores. Auditions held twice and individually by arrangement on campus; recorded music is permissible as a substitute for live auditions when distance is prohibitive and videotaped performances are permissible as a substitute for live auditions when distance is prohibitive.

Web Site http://www.uu.edu/dept/music/.

Undergraduate Contact Carroll Griffin, Director of Admissions, Union University, 1050 Union University Drive, Jackson, Tennessee 38305; 901-661-5000, fax: 901-661-5175, E-mail address: cgriffin@uu.edu.

▼ THE UNIVERSITY OF AKRON

Akron, Ohio

State-supported, coed. Urban campus. Total enrollment: 23,538.

Degrees Bachelor of Music in the areas of performance, music education, history/literature, theory/composition, jazz. Graduate degrees offered: Master of Music in the areas of performance, music education, history/literature, theory/composition, jazz, music technology. Program accredited by NASM.

Enrollment Fall 1997: 456 total; 368 undergraduate, 88 graduate.

Music Student Profile 55% females, 45% males, 7% minorities.

Music Faculty 74 total undergraduate and graduate (full-time and part-time). 100% of full-time faculty have terminal degrees. Graduate students do not teach undergraduate courses.

Student Life Student groups/activities include Phi Mu Alpha, Sigma Alpha Iota, Music Educators National Conference.

Expenses for 1997–98 Application fee: $25. State resident tuition: $3312 full-time. Nonresident tuition: $8772 full-time. Mandatory fees: $348 full-time. College room and board: $4490. College room only: $2820. Room and board charges vary according to board plan. Special program-related fees: $95–$190 per semester for applied music lesson fee.

Financial Aid Program-specific awards for 1997: 150 music scholarships for music majors and minors ($250–$2000).

Application Procedures Students apply for admission into the professional program by sophomore year. Deadline for freshmen: continuous. Required: high school transcript, college transcript(s) for transfer students, interview, audition, SAT I or ACT test scores, tests in rudimentary theory, ear training, and keyboard skills. Recommended: 3 letters of recommendation. Auditions held 5 times on campus; recorded music is permissible as a substitute for live auditions for out-of-state applicants and videotaped performances are permissible as a substitute for live auditions if a campus visit is impossible or for financial reasons.

Web Site http://www.uakron.edu.

Undergraduate Contact Office of Admissions, The University of Akron, Akron, Ohio 44325-2001; 800-655-4884.

Graduate Contact Graduate School, The University of Akron, 138 Fir Hill, Akron, Ohio 44325-2101; 330-972-7663.

▼ THE UNIVERSITY OF ALABAMA

Tuscaloosa, Alabama

State-supported, coed. Suburban campus. Total enrollment: 18,324. Music program established 1918.

Degrees Bachelor of Music in the areas of performance, music theory, composition, music therapy, arranging. Majors and concentrations: arranging, composition, jazz studies, music management, music theory, music therapy, piano/organ, stringed instruments, voice, wind and percussion instruments. Graduate degrees offered: Master of Music in the areas of performance, conducting, composition, arranging, theory, piano accompanying. Doctor of Musical Arts in the areas of performance, conducting, composition. Program accredited by NASM.

Enrollment Fall 1997: 265 total; 197 undergraduate, 52 graduate, 16 non-professional degree.

Music Student Profile 53% females, 47% males, 10% minorities, 12% international.

Music Faculty 44 total undergraduate and graduate (full-time and part-time). 100% of full-time faculty have terminal degrees. Graduate students teach a few undergraduate courses. Undergraduate student–faculty ratio: 6:1.

Expenses for 1997–98 Application fee: $25. State resident tuition: $2594 full-time. Nonresident tuition: $6808 full-time. Full-time tuition varies according to course load. College room and board: $3610. College room only: $2060. Room and board charges vary according to board plan and housing facility. Special program-related fees: $125 for applied music fee.

Financial Aid Program-specific awards for 1997: 30–40 music scholarships for program majors ($500–$5000).

Application Procedures Students admitted directly into the professional program freshman year. Deadline for freshmen and transfers: continuous. Required: high school transcript, college transcript(s) for transfer students, minimum 2.0 high school GPA, audition, SAT I or ACT test scores. Auditions held 4 times on campus; recorded music is permissible as a substitute for live auditions when distance is prohibitive or scheduling is difficult and videotaped performances are permissible as a substitute for live auditions when distance is prohibitive or scheduling is difficult.

Web Site http://www.music.ua.edu.

Undergraduate Contact Undergraduate Coordinator, School of Music, The University of Alabama, Box 870366, Tuscaloosa, Alabama 35487; 205-348-7110, fax: 205-348-1473, E-mail address: dfulford@music.ua.edu.

The University of Alabama *(continued)*

Graduate Contact Dr. Dennis Monk, Director of Graduate Studies, School of Music, The University of Alabama, Box 870366, Tuscaloosa, Alabama 35487; 205-348-7110, fax: 205-348-1473, E-mail address: dmonk@music.ua.edu.

▼ UNIVERSITY OF ALASKA ANCHORAGE

Anchorage, Alaska

State-supported, coed. Urban campus. Total enrollment: 14,765.

Degrees Bachelor of Music in the area of performance; Bachelor of Music Education in the areas of elementary music education, secondary music education. Majors and concentrations: classical music, music, piano/organ, stringed instruments, voice, wind and percussion instruments. Program accredited by NASM.

Enrollment Fall 1997: 453 total; 53 undergraduate, 400 non-professional degree.

Music Student Profile 65% females, 35% males, 10% minorities, 3% international.

Music Faculty 17 total (full-time and part-time). 50% of full-time faculty have terminal degrees. Graduate students do not teach undergraduate courses. Undergraduate student–faculty ratio: 3:1.

Student Life Student groups/activities include Music Educators National Conference Student Chapter.

Expenses for 1998–99 Application fee: $35. State resident tuition: $2168 full-time. Nonresident tuition: $6428 full-time. Mandatory fees: $298 full-time. Full-time tuition and fees vary according to class time, course level, and course load. College room and board: $6591. College room only: $3490. Room and board charges vary according to board plan and housing facility.

Financial Aid Program-specific awards for 1997: 1 music scholarship for incoming students ($2400).

Application Procedures Students admitted directly into the professional program freshman year. Deadline for freshmen and transfers: continuous. Required: high school transcript, college transcript(s) for transfer students. Recommended: minimum 2.0 high school GPA.

Web Site http://www.uaa.alaska.edu/music.

Undergraduate Contact Mr. Mike Turner, Counseling Coordinator, Advising and Counseling Department, University of Alaska Anchorage, 3211 Providence Drive, Anchorage, Alaska 99508; 907-786-4500, fax: 907-786-4519, E-mail address: afmtt@uaa.alaska.edu.

▼ UNIVERSITY OF ALASKA FAIRBANKS

Fairbanks, Alaska

State-supported, coed. Small town campus. Total enrollment: 7,686.

Degrees Bachelor of Music in the areas of performance, secondary music education, elementary music education. Majors and concentrations: classical music, jazz, music education, piano/organ, stringed instruments, voice, wind and percussion instruments. Program accredited by NASM.

Enrollment Fall 1997: 55 undergraduate.

Music Student Profile 50% females, 50% males, 1% minorities, 1% international.

Music Faculty 19 total (full-time and part-time). 90% of full-time faculty have terminal degrees. Graduate students teach a few undergraduate courses.

Expenses for 1997–98 Application fee: $35. State resident tuition: $2070 full-time. Nonresident tuition: $5478 full-time. Mandatory fees: $340 full-time. Full-time tuition and fees vary according to course level, course load, and reciprocity agreements. College room and board: $3690. College room only: $1800. Special program-related fees: $145 per semester for private lessons, $40 per semester for instrument rental fee, $5 per semester for locker rental.

Financial Aid Program-specific awards for 1997: 1–4 Friends of Music Awards for program majors ($500), 1–2 Glenmede Awards for string players ($500), 1–2 Fejes Music Scholarships for program majors ($500), 3–6 Fairbanks Symphony Scholarships for program majors ($500–$1000), 1 Anderson/DeRamus Scholarship for African-American program majors ($700).

Application Procedures Deadline for freshmen and transfers: August 1. Required: high school transcript, college transcript(s) for transfer students, 3 letters of recommendation, SAT I or ACT test scores. Recommended: audition. Auditions held once in the fall semester or by appointment on campus; recorded music is permissible as a substitute for live auditions with later audition on campus and videotaped performances are permissible as a substitute for live auditions with later audition on campus.

Web Site http://www.uaf.edu.

Undergraduate Contact Admissions and Records, University of Alaska Fairbanks, Signers' Hall, Suite 102, Fairbanks, Alaska 99775-0060; 907-474-7521.

▼ UNIVERSITY OF ALBERTA

Edmonton, AB, Canada

Province-supported, coed. Urban campus. Total enrollment: 28,613. Music program established 1947.

Degrees Bachelor of Music in the areas of school music, performance, music theory and composition, music history and literature; Bachelor of Music/Bachelor of Education in the area of music education. Majors and concentrations: classical music, composition, guitar, harp, music history and literature, music theory and composition, piano/organ, stringed instruments, voice, wind and percussion instruments. Graduate degrees offered: Master of Music in the areas of applied music, composition, choral conducting; Master of Arts in the areas of music, ethnomusicology, musicology, theory. Doctor of Music in the area of keyboard; Doctor of Philosophy in the areas of music, ethnomusicology, musicology, theory. Cross-registration with Grant MacEwan Community College. Program accredited by CUMS.

Enrollment Fall 1997: 379 total; 129 undergraduate, 50 graduate, 200 non-professional degree.

Music Student Profile 60% females, 40% males, 10% minorities, 4% international.

Music Faculty 45 total undergraduate and graduate (full-time and part-time). 100% of full-time faculty have terminal degrees. Graduate students teach a few undergraduate courses. Undergraduate student–faculty ratio: 9:1.

Expenses for 1997–98 Application fee: $60 Canadian dollars. Tuition, fee, and room and board charges are reported in Canadian dollars. Canadian resident tuition: $3056 full-time. Mandatory fees: $390 full-time. Full-time tuition and fees vary according to course load and program. College room and board: $3465. College room only: $1400. Room and board charges vary according to board plan, housing facility, and location. International student tuition: $6113 full-time. Special program-related fees: $10–$20 per year for lockers and keys.

Financial Aid Program-specific awards for 1997: 12 Beryl Barns Memorial Awards for academically and artistically talented students ($1000–$4000), 2 Richard Eaton Scholarship in Music and Voice for academically and artistically talented students ($1000–$2500), 1 Abigal Edith Condell Memorial Scholarship in Music for academically and artistically talented students ($1000), 1 Edmonton Musical Club Scholarship in Music for academically and artistically talented students ($1000), 1 Edmonton Opera Guild Award for academically and artistically talented students ($2000), 2 FM105 East Rock Prizes for academically and artistically talented students ($1000), 1 John Newman Memorial Scholarship for Performance of Contemporary Music for academically and artistically talented students ($750), 9 Peace River Pioneer Memorial Scholarship in Music for academically and artistically talented students ($750–$1500), 1 Mary Stinson Prize in Piano Accompaniment for academically and artistically talented students ($750), 1 Lloyd Thomas Award in Music for academically and artistically talented students ($1250).

Application Procedures Students admitted directly into the professional program freshman year. Deadline for freshmen and transfers: May 1. Notification date for freshmen and transfers: June 15. Required: high school transcript, college transcript(s) for transfer students, minimum 2.0 high school GPA, audition, music rudiments exam, aural skills exam. Recommended: minimum 3.0 high school GPA, interview. Auditions held once on campus; recorded music is permissible as a substitute for live auditions when distance is prohibitive and videotaped performances are permissible as a substitute for live auditions when distance is prohibitive.

Undergraduate Contact Ms. Donna Maskell, Executive Assistant, Department of Music, University of Alberta, FAB 3-82, Edmonton, AB T6G 2C9, Canada; 403-492-3263, fax: 403-492-9246.

Graduate Contact Dr. Marnie Giesbrecht, Graduate Coordinator, Department of Music, University of Alberta, FAB 3-82, Edmonton, AB T6G 2C9; 403-492-3263, fax: 403-492-9246.

▼ THE UNIVERSITY OF ARIZONA

Tucson, Arizona

State-supported, coed. Urban campus. Total enrollment: 33,737. Music program established 1893.

Degrees Bachelor of Music in the areas of performance, composition, jazz studies, music education. Majors and concentrations: choral music education, classical guitar, composition, instrumental music education, jazz, keyboard, stringed instruments, voice, wind and percussion instruments. Graduate degrees offered: Master of Music in the areas of composition, music education, musicology, conducting, performance, accompanying, theory. Doctor of Musical Arts in the areas of composition, conducting, performance, theory, music education. Cross-registration with Pima Community College. Program accredited by NASM.

Enrollment Fall 1997: 489 total; 322 undergraduate, 135 graduate, 32 non-professional degree.

Music Student Profile 50% females, 50% males, 25% minorities, 15% international.

Music Faculty 52 total undergraduate and graduate (full-time and part-time). 75% of full-time faculty have terminal degrees. Graduate students teach about a quarter undergraduate courses. Undergraduate student–faculty ratio: 7:1.

Expenses for 1997–98 Application fee: $40 for nonresidents. State resident tuition: $1988 full-time. Nonresident tuition: $8640 full-time. Mandatory fees: $70 full-time. College room and board: $4930. College room only: $2480. Room and board charges vary according to board plan and housing facility. Special program-related fees: $100 per semester for music lessons.

Financial Aid Program-specific awards for 1997: 167 tuition waivers for music majors ($2000–$9000).

Application Procedures Students admitted directly into the professional program freshman year. Deadline for freshmen: April 1; transfers: March 1. Required: high school transcript, college transcript(s) for transfer students, minimum 3.0 high school GPA, audition, portfolio, SAT I or ACT test scores (minimum combined SAT I score of 1040, minimum combined ACT score of 22). Recommended: interview. Auditions held several times on campus; recorded music is permissible as a substitute for live auditions if a live audition is impossible and videotaped performances are permissible as a substitute for live auditions if a live audition is impossible. Portfolio reviews held twice on campus.

Web Site http://www.arts.arizona.edu/music.

Contact Dr. Jeffrey Showell, Director of Academic Student Services, School of Music and Dance, The University of Arizona, PO Box 210004, Tucson, Arizona 85721; 520-621-1454, fax: 520-621-1351, E-mail address: showell@u.arizona.edu.

J. William Fulbright College of Arts and Sciences

▼ UNIVERSITY OF ARKANSAS

Fayetteville, Arkansas

State-supported, coed. Small town campus. Total enrollment: 14,322. Music program established 1952.

Degrees Bachelor of Music in the areas of performance, music education, composition, music history, music theory. Majors and concentrations: composition, guitar, harpsichord, music education, music history, music theory, piano/organ, stringed instruments, voice, wind and percussion instruments. Graduate degrees offered: Master of Music in the areas of performance, music education, composition, music history, music theory, accompanying, conducting. Program accredited by NASM.

Enrollment Fall 1997: 223 total; 190 undergraduate, 23 graduate, 10 non-professional degree.

Music Student Profile 60% females, 40% males, 10% minorities, 3% international.

Music Faculty 36 total undergraduate and graduate (full-time and part-time). 100% of full-time faculty have terminal degrees. Graduate students teach a few undergraduate courses. Undergraduate student–faculty ratio: 8:1.

Student Life Student groups/activities include drama department productions, North Arkansas Symphony Orchestra, North Arkansas Symphony Chorus.

Expenses for 1997–98 Application fee: $15. State resident tuition: $2470 full-time. Nonresident tuition: $6418 full-time. Mandatory fees: $191 full-time. Full-time tuition and fees vary according to program. College room and board: $3867.

University of Arkansas (continued)

Financial Aid Program-specific awards for 1997: 120 music scholarships for music major and non-major ensemble members ($1200–$2500), 220 band scholarships for music major and non-major ensemble members ($1200–$2500), 30 Inspirational Singers Awards for gospel choir members ($1200–$2500).

Application Procedures Students apply for admission into the professional program by junior year. Deadline for freshmen and transfers: May 1. Required: high school transcript, audition, SAT I or ACT test scores, minimum 2.75 high school GPA. Auditions held by appointment on campus; recorded music is permissible as a substitute for live auditions when distance is prohibitive and videotaped performances are permissible as a substitute for live auditions when distance is prohibitive.

Contact Dr. Stephen Gates, Chair, Department of Music, University of Arkansas, 201 Music Building, Fayetteville, Arkansas 72701; 501-575-4701, fax: 501-575-5409, E-mail address: sgates@comp.uark.edu.

▼ UNIVERSITY OF ARKANSAS AT MONTICELLO

Monticello, Arkansas

State-supported, coed. Small town campus.

Degrees Bachelor of Music Education in the areas of vocal music, keyboard, instrumental music. Majors and concentrations: music education, piano, voice, wind and percussion instruments. Cross-registration with University of Arkansas System. Program accredited by NASM.

Enrollment Fall 1997: 43 total; 38 undergraduate, 5 non-professional degree.

Music Student Profile 27% females, 73% males, 8% minorities.

Music Faculty 11 total (full-time and part-time). 50% of full-time faculty have terminal degrees. Graduate students do not teach undergraduate courses. Undergraduate student–faculty ratio: 8:1.

Student Life Student groups/activities include Music Educators National Conference Student Chapter, Kappa Kappa Psi.

Expenses for 1997–98 Application fee: $0. State resident tuition: $2040 full-time. Nonresident tuition: $4248 full-time. Full-time tuition varies according to reciprocity agreements. College room and board: $2510. Special program-related fees: $25–$40 per course for private lessons.

Financial Aid Program-specific awards for 1997: 60 Band Grants-in-Aid for band players ($375–$1500), 55 Choir Grants-in-Aid for choir singers ($375–$1500), 6 Keyboard Grants-in-Aid for keyboardists ($375–$1500), 4 departmental scholarships for program majors demonstrating talent and academic achievement ($600–$700).

Application Procedures Students admitted directly into the professional program freshman year. Deadline for freshmen and transfers: August 15. Required: high school transcript, college transcript(s) for transfer students, minimum 2.0 high school GPA, audition, ACT test score only. Auditions held 3 times on campus and off campus in various high schools.

Undergraduate Contact Ms. JoBeth Johnson, Director of Admissions, University of Arkansas at Monticello, PO Box 3600, Monticello, Arkansas 71656; 870-460-1026, fax: 870-460-1922.

▼ UNIVERSITY OF BRIDGEPORT

Bridgeport, Connecticut

Independent, coed. Urban campus. Total enrollment: 2,427.

Degrees Bachelor of Music in the areas of jazz studies, performance, music education.

Enrollment Fall 1997: 18 total; all undergraduate.

Music Student Profile 50% females, 50% males, 17% minorities, 56% international.

Music Faculty 20 total (full-time and part-time). 100% of full-time faculty have terminal degrees. Graduate students do not teach undergraduate courses.

Expenses for 1997–98 Application fee: $40. Comprehensive fee: $20,454 includes full-time tuition ($13,000), mandatory fees ($644), and college room and board ($6810). College room only: $3700. Full-time tuition and fees vary according to course load and program. Room and board charges vary according to board plan. Special program-related fees: $300–$600 per credit hour for private lessons.

Financial Aid Program-specific awards for 1997: 5–20 Music Department Scholarships for music majors ($3500–$19,310).

Application Procedures Students admitted directly into the professional program freshman year. Deadline for freshmen and transfers: continuous. Required: essay, high school transcript, college transcript(s) for transfer students, audition, SAT I or ACT test scores. Recommended: minimum 2.0 high school GPA, 3 letters of recommendation, interview. Auditions held as needed on campus; recorded music is permissible as a substitute for live auditions when distance is prohibitive and videotaped performances are permissible as a substitute for live auditions when distance is prohibitive.

Undergraduate Contact Dr. Suzanne Dale Wilcox, Dean of Admission and Financial Aid, Admissions Office, University of Bridgeport, 126 Park Avenue, Wahlstrom Library, Bridgeport, Connecticut 06601; 800-EXCEL-UB, fax: 203-576-4941, E-mail address: admit@cse.bridgeport.edu.

More About the University

The Music Program offers Bachelor of Music degrees in performance, music education, jazz studies, and music business. Facilities housed in the Bernhard Center include the 950-seat Mertens Theater, the 225-seat Littlefield Recital Hall, rehearsal halls, classrooms, individual practice rooms, a digital piano lab, a Macintosh MIDI lab, a music library, and a recording studio. Performing ensembles include sinfonietta, chorus, jazz ensemble, chamber music ensemble, and world music ensemble. The program features the annual Mertens Festival honoring leading contemporary composers, who visit the campus, supervise the performance of their music, and give seminars; past composers include Aaron Copland, Leonard Bernstein, Ned Rorem, Gerry Mulligan, and Stephen Sondheim. Performance-based, 4-year, full tuition and room and board scholarships are available for qualified students, as well as other partial scholarships and tuition assistance.

▼ UNIVERSITY OF BRITISH COLUMBIA

Vancouver, BC, Canada

Province-supported, coed. Urban campus. Total enrollment: 32,110. Music program established 1959.

Degrees Bachelor of Music in the areas of composition, general studies, elementary education stream, secondary education stream, guitar, music history and literature, music theory, opera, orchestral instruments, organ, piano, voice. Majors and concentrations: composition, guitar, music, music education, music history and literature, music theory, opera, orchestral instruments, piano/organ, voice. Graduate degrees offered: Master of Music in the areas of composition, piano, organ, voice, orchestral instruments, opera, guitar; Master of Arts in the areas of ethnomusicology, musicology, music theory. Doctor of Musical Arts in the areas of composition, piano, voice, orchestral instruments; Doctor of Philosophy in the areas of ethnomusicology, musicology, music theory.

Enrollment Fall 1997: 265 undergraduate, 85 graduate.

Music Student Profile 66% females, 34% males.

Music Faculty 83 total undergraduate and graduate (full-time and part-time). 70% of full-time faculty have terminal degrees. Graduate students teach a few undergraduate courses. Undergraduate student–faculty ratio: 3:1.

Expenses for 1997–98 Application fee: $72 Canadian dollars. Tuition, fee, and room and board charges are reported in Canadian dollars. Canadian resident tuition: $2333 full-time. Mandatory fees: $218 full-time. College room and board: $4516. College room only: $2600. Room and board charges vary according to board plan and housing facility. International student tuition: $13,830 full-time.

Financial Aid Program-specific awards for 1997: scholarships for program students ($100–$1800).

Application Procedures Students admitted directly into the professional program freshman year. Deadline for freshmen and transfers: April 15. Notification date for freshmen and transfers: June 1. Required: essay, high school transcript, college transcript(s) for transfer students, 2 letters of recommendation, audition, music theory examination, original music scores for composition applicants, minimum 2.5 high school GPA. Auditions held once on campus; recorded music is permissible as a substitute for live auditions when distance is prohibitive and videotaped performances are permissible as a substitute for live auditions when distance is prohibitive. Portfolio reviews held once on campus.

Web Site http://theory.music.ubc.ca/som/start.

Contact Ms. Isabel da Silva, Admissions Officer, School of Music, University of British Columbia, 6361 Memorial Road, Vancouver, BC V6T 1Z2, Canada; 604-822-2079, fax: 604-822-4884, E-mail address: isabelm@unixg.ubc.ca.

▼ THE UNIVERSITY OF CALGARY

Calgary, AB, Canada

Province-supported, coed. Urban campus. Total enrollment: 23,737. Music program established 1967.

Degrees Bachelor of Music in the areas of music education, performance, music theory, composition, music history. Majors and concentrations: brass, classical music, music education, music history, music theory and composition, piano/organ, stringed instruments, voice, wind and percussion instruments. Graduate degrees offered: Master of Music in the areas of performance, composition, pedagogy, conducting, school music. Doctor of Philosophy in the areas of music education, composition, musicology. Cross-registration with Mount Royal College. Program accredited by CUMS.

Enrollment Fall 1997: 230 total; 197 undergraduate, 33 graduate.

Music Student Profile 60% females, 40% males, 5% minorities, 10% international.

Music Faculty 44 total undergraduate and graduate (full-time and part-time). 90% of full-time faculty have terminal degrees. Graduate students teach a few undergraduate courses. Undergraduate student–faculty ratio: 12:1.

Student Life Student groups/activities include Wind Ensemble/Symphonic Band, Symphony Orchestra, choral ensembles.

Expenses for 1997–98 Application fee: $65 Canadian dollars. Tuition, fee, and room and board charges are reported in Canadian dollars. Canadian resident tuition: $3180 full-time. Mandatory fees: $186 full-time. Full-time tuition and fees vary according to course load. College room and board: $3153. College room only: $1228. Room and board charges vary according to board plan and housing facility. International student tuition: $6360 full-time. Special program-related fees: $100 per year for lab fee for recital.

Financial Aid Program-specific awards for 1997: 47 music awards for high academic and musical achievement ($150–$3000).

Application Procedures Students apply for admission into the professional program by freshman year. Deadline for freshmen and transfers: May 1. Notification date for freshmen and transfers: June 15. Required: high school transcript, college transcript(s) for transfer students, audition, Proof of Royal Conservatory of Music, grade III theory. Recommended: video. Auditions held once on campus; recorded music is permissible as a substitute for live auditions when distance is prohibitive and videotaped performances are permissible as a substitute for live auditions when distance is prohibitive.

Web Site http://www.ffa.ucalgary.ca/ffa/departments/music/.

Undergraduate Contact Ms. C. Te Kamp, Undergraduate Academic Advisor, Music Department, The University of Calgary, 2500 University Drive, NW, Calgary, AB T2N 1N4, Canada; 403-220-5383, fax: 403-284-0973, E-mail address: ctekampe@ucdasvm1.admin.ucalgary.ca.

Graduate Contact Dr. Kenneth De Long, Coordinator of Graduate Studies, Music Department, The University of Calgary, 2500 University Drive, NW, Calgary, AB T2N 1N4, Canada; 403-220-5381, E-mail address: delong@acs.ucalgary.ca.

▼ UNIVERSITY OF CALIFORNIA, IRVINE

Irvine, California

State-supported, coed. Suburban campus. Music program established 1965.

Degrees Bachelor of Music in the areas of voice, piano, wind and percussion instruments, stringed instruments; Bachelor of Arts in the area of music. Majors and concentrations: bassoon, clarinet, double bass, flute, French horn, guitar, harp, lute, oboe, percussion, piano, saxophone, trombone, trumpet, tuba, viola, violin, violoncello, voice. Graduate degrees offered: Master of Fine Arts in the area of music. Cross-registration with University of California System.

Enrollment Fall 1997: 170 total; 150 undergraduate, 20 graduate.

Music Student Profile 60% females, 40% males, 50% minorities, 20% international.

Music Faculty 38 total undergraduate and graduate (full-time and part-time). 100% of full-time faculty have terminal

University of California, Irvine (continued)

degrees. Graduate students do not teach undergraduate courses. Undergraduate student–faculty ratio: 6:1.

Student Life Special housing available for music students.

Financial Aid Program-specific awards for 1997: 4 Rawlins Scholarships for strings or piano majors ($4000), 3 Philharmonic Society of Orange County Scholarships for instrumental or voice majors ($2500), 1 Harry and Marjorie Slim Scholarship for instrumental or voice majors ($1000), 1 Mary Lyon Scholarship for instrumental or voice majors ($5000), 1 Tierney Scholarship for instrumental or voice majors ($4200), Artsbridge Scholarships for instrumental or voice majors ($2500), 10–12 music scholarships for instrumental or voice majors ($1000).

Application Procedures Students admitted directly into the professional program freshman year. Deadline for freshmen and transfers: November 30. Notification date for freshmen and transfers: continuous. Required: essay, high school transcript, college transcript(s) for transfer students, audition, SAT I or ACT test scores, minimum 3.0 college GPA for transfer students. Recommended: minimum 3.0 high school GPA. Auditions held once on campus; recorded music is permissible as a substitute for live auditions when distance is prohibitive and videotaped performances are permissible as a substitute for live auditions when distance is prohibitive.

Undergraduate Contact Ms. Amina El-Sadr, Admissions Counselor, Office of Admissions and Relations with Schools, University of California, Irvine, 206 Adminstration Building, Irvine, California 92697-1075; 714-824-4545, E-mail address: aelsadr@uci.edu.

Graduate Contact Ms. Sally Avila, Administrative Assistant, Department of Music, University of California, Irvine, 292 Music, Building 714, Irvine, California 92697-2775; 714-824-6615, fax: 714-824-4914, E-mail address: slavila@uci.edu.

▼ University of California, Santa Barbara

Santa Barbara, California

State-supported, coed. Suburban campus. Total enrollment: 18,940.

Degrees Bachelor of Music in the areas of composition, guitar, orchestral instruments, piano, piano accompanying, voice. Majors and concentrations: accompanying, brass, composition, guitar, orchestral instruments, stringed instruments, voice, wind and percussion instruments. Graduate degrees offered: Master of Music in the areas of piano accompanying, woodwinds and brass, conducting, keyboard, strings, voice. Doctor of Musical Arts in the areas of conducting, keyboard, strings, voice.

Enrollment Fall 1997: 120 undergraduate, 80 graduate.

Music Faculty 40 total undergraduate and graduate (full-time and part-time). 100% of full-time faculty have terminal degrees. Graduate students teach a few undergraduate courses. Undergraduate student–faculty ratio: 4:1.

Expenses for 1997–98 Application fee: $40. State resident tuition: $0 full-time. Nonresident tuition: $8989 full-time. Mandatory fees: $4098 full-time. College room and board: $6407. Room and board charges vary according to housing facility.

Financial Aid Program-specific awards for 1997: 10 Excellence in Entrance Awards for incoming freshmen ($300–$1500), 7 grants-in-aid for continuing program majors demonstrating need, musical and academic excellence ($300–$1500), 4 Quarterly Performance Awards for outstanding audition performers ($500), 1 Outstanding Early Music Award for early music program majors ($200), 1 Outstanding Service Award for program majors ($200).

Application Procedures Students admitted directly into the professional program freshman year. Deadline for freshmen and transfers: November 30. Notification date for freshmen: March 15; transfers: April 1. Required: essay, high school transcript, minimum 3.0 high school GPA, letter of recommendation, audition, SAT I or ACT test scores. Auditions held once and by appointment on campus; recorded music is permissible as a substitute for live auditions when distance is prohibitive and videotaped performances are permissible as a substitute for live auditions when distance is prohibitive.

Undergraduate Contact Ms. Donna Saar, Undergraduate Admissions, Department of Music, University of California, Santa Barbara, Santa Barbara, California 93106; 805-893-7748, fax: 805-893-7194, E-mail address: saar@humanitas.ucsb.edu.

Graduate Contact Ms. Robin Zierau-Cooper, Graduate Admissions, Department of Music, University of California, Santa Barbara, Santa Barbara, California 93106; 805-893-4603, fax: 805-893-7194, E-mail address: zierau@humanitas.ucsb.edu.

▼ University of Central Arkansas

Conway, Arkansas

State-supported, coed. Small town campus. Total enrollment: 8,938. Music program established 1908.

Degrees Bachelor of Music in the areas of performance, music education. Majors and concentrations: brass, music, music education, piano/organ, stringed instruments, voice, wind and percussion instruments. Graduate degrees offered: Master of Music in the areas of performance, music theory, music education, choral conducting, instrumental conducting. Program accredited by NASM.

Enrollment Fall 1997: 160 total; 130 undergraduate, 30 graduate.

Music Faculty 37 total undergraduate and graduate (full-time and part-time). 50% of full-time faculty have terminal degrees. Graduate students do not teach undergraduate courses. Undergraduate student–faculty ratio: 4:1.

Student Life Student groups/activities include Music Teachers National Association competitions, Arkansas Symphony Orchestra.

Expenses for 1997–98 State resident tuition: $2258 full-time. Nonresident tuition: $4478 full-time. Mandatory fees: $434 full-time. College room and board: $2920. Special program-related fees: $30–$40 per course for practice room fees.

Financial Aid Program-specific awards for 1997: 75 music scholarships for instrumental, orchestral, vocal, and keyboard students ($200–$1519).

Application Procedures Students admitted directly into the professional program freshman year. Deadline for freshmen and transfers: continuous. Required: minimum 2.0 high school GPA, audition, ACT test score only. Recommended: high school transcript, 3 letters of recommendation, interview. Auditions held 4 times and by appointment on campus; recorded music is permissible as a substitute for live auditions when distance is prohibitive, in special circumstances, or for international applicants and videotaped performances are permissible as a substitute for live auditions when distance is prohibitive, in special circumstances, or for international applicants.

Undergraduate Contact Mr. Gilbert Baker, Assistant Professor, Department of Music, University of Central Arkansas, UCA 201 Donaghey Avenue, Conway, Arkansas 72035-0001; 501-450-5754, fax: 501-450-5773, E-mail address: gilbertb@cc3.uca.edu.

Graduate Contact Dr. Anne Patterson, Interim Chair, Department of Music, University of Central Arkansas, UCA 201 Donaghey Avenue, Conway, Arkansas 72035-0001; 501-450-3163, fax: 501-450-5773, E-mail address: annep@cc1.uca.edu.

▼ UNIVERSITY OF CENTRAL FLORIDA

Orlando, Florida

State-supported, coed. Suburban campus. Total enrollment: 28,685.

Degrees Bachelor of Music in the area of performance; Bachelor of Music Education in the areas of instrumental music education, choral music education, elementary music education. Graduate degrees offered: Master of Music Education. Cross-registration with Seminole Community College, Valencia Community College. Program accredited by NASM.

Enrollment Fall 1997: 185 undergraduate, 17 graduate.

Music Student Profile 44% females, 56% males, 10% minorities, 1% international.

Music Faculty 30 total undergraduate and graduate (full-time and part-time). 80% of full-time faculty have terminal degrees. Graduate students do not teach undergraduate courses. Undergraduate student–faculty ratio: 11:1.

Student Life Student groups/activities include Phi Mu Alpha, Sigma Alpha Iota, Kappa Kappa Psi.

Expenses for 1997–98 Application fee: $20. State resident tuition: $1930 full-time. Nonresident tuition: $7846 full-time. Mandatory fees: $95 full-time. Full-time tuition and fees vary according to course load. College room and board: $4370. College room only: $2720. Room and board charges vary according to housing facility.

Financial Aid Program-specific awards for 1997: 20–30 Department Scholarships and Service Awards for those demonstrating talent and need ($600).

Application Procedures Deadline for freshmen and transfers: July 15. Notification date for freshmen and transfers: continuous. Required: high school transcript, minimum 2.0 high school GPA, audition, SAT I or ACT test scores. Auditions held 3 times on campus; recorded music is permissible as a substitute for live auditions when distance is prohibitive or scheduling is difficult and videotaped performances are permissible as a substitute for live auditions if distance is prohibitive or scheduling is difficult.

Contact Ms. Sue McKinnon, Director of Admission Services, University of Central Florida, PO Box 160111, Orlando, Florida 32816-0111; 407-823-3000, fax: 407-823-5625.

▼ UNIVERSITY OF CENTRAL OKLAHOMA

Edmond, Oklahoma

State-supported, coed. Suburban campus. Total enrollment: 13,928. Music program established 1890.

Degrees Bachelor of Music in the areas of instrumental music, piano, voice, music theater; Bachelor of Music Education in the areas of instrumental, vocal. Majors and concentrations: music education, music theater, piano/organ, stringed instruments, voice, wind and percussion instruments. Graduate degrees offered: Master of Music in the areas of music education, performance. Program accredited by NASM.

Enrollment Fall 1997: 203 undergraduate, 18 graduate.

Music Student Profile 50% females, 50% males, 10% minorities, 5% international.

Music Faculty 42 total undergraduate and graduate (full-time and part-time). 58% of full-time faculty have terminal degrees. Graduate students teach a few undergraduate courses. Undergraduate student–faculty ratio: 11:1.

Student Life Student groups/activities include Sigma Alpha Iota, Oklahoma Music Teachers Association, Music Educators National Conference.

Expenses for 1997–98 Application fee: $15. State resident tuition: $1380 full-time. Nonresident tuition: $3735 full-time. Mandatory fees: $426 full-time. Full-time tuition and fees vary according to course level, course load, and program. College room and board: $2481. Room and board charges vary according to board plan and housing facility. Special program-related fees: $40 per credit hour for private applied lessons, $18 per credit hour for semi-private lessons.

Financial Aid Program-specific awards for 1997: Parman Scholarships for music theater majors ($200).

Application Procedures Students apply for admission into the professional program by sophomore year. Deadline for freshmen and transfers: continuous. Required: high school transcript, college transcript(s) for transfer students, minimum 2.0 high school GPA, ACT test score only. Recommended: minimum 3.0 high school GPA, audition. Auditions held as needed on campus.

Undergraduate Contact Dr. Karen Carter, Chair, Department of Music, University of Central Oklahoma, 100 North University Drive, Edmond, Oklahoma 73034; 405-341-2980 ext. 5004, fax: 405-359-1147.

Graduate Contact Ms. Peggy Spence, Assistant Chair, Department of Music, University of Central Oklahoma, 100 North University Drive, Edmond, Oklahoma 73034; 405-341-2980 ext. 5754, fax: 405-359-1147, E-mail address: pspence@aix1.ucok.edu.

University of Cincinnati

▼ UNIVERSITY OF CINCINNATI COLLEGE CONSERVATORY OF MUSIC

Cincinnati, Ohio

State-supported, coed. Urban campus. Total enrollment: 28,161.

Degrees Bachelor of Music in the areas of performance, music education, keyboard, jazz, theory/history/composition, instrumental conducting. Majors and concentrations: classical guitar, classical music, composition, harpsichord, instrumental conducting, jazz, music, music education, music history, music theory, piano/organ, stringed instruments, voice, wind and percussion instruments. Graduate degrees offered: Master of Music in the areas of performance, music education, keyboard, theory/history/composition, conducting, accompanying. Doctor of Musical Arts in the areas of performance, keyboard, composition, conducting; Doctor of Music Education. Cross-registration with Greater Cincinnati Consortium of Colleges and Universities. Program accredited by NASM.

University of Cincinnati College Conservatory of Music
(continued)

Enrollment Fall 1997: 946 total; 323 undergraduate, 623 graduate.

Music Student Profile 51% females, 49% males, 7% minorities, 12% international.

Music Faculty 170 total undergraduate and graduate (full-time and part-time). 90% of full-time faculty have terminal degrees. Graduate students teach about a quarter undergraduate courses. Undergraduate student–faculty ratio: 7:1.

Student Life Student groups/activities include Student Artist Program, music fraternities and sororities.

Expenses for 1997–98 Application fee: $30. State resident tuition: $3879 full-time. Nonresident tuition: $10,986 full-time. Mandatory fees: $480 full-time. College room and board: $5643.

Financial Aid Program-specific awards for 1997: 76 Endowed Scholarships for program majors ($1600–$4500).

Application Procedures Students admitted directly into the professional program freshman year. Deadline for freshmen and transfers: February 15. Notification date for freshmen and transfers: continuous. Required: high school transcript, college transcript(s) for transfer students, letter of recommendation, interview, audition, SAT I or ACT test scores. Recommended: minimum 3.0 high school GPA. Auditions held 9 times on campus and off campus in Atlanta, GA; Chicago, IL; Interlochen, MI; Los Angeles, CA; New York, NY; San Francisco, CA; recorded music is permissible as a substitute for live auditions with approval from the department and videotaped performances are permissible as a substitute for live auditions with approval from the department.

Web Site http://www.uc.edu/www/ccm/.

Undergraduate Contact Mrs. Angela K. Vaubel, Admissions Officer, College-Conservatory of Music, University of Cincinnati, PO Box 210003, Cincinnati, Ohio 45221-0003; 513-556-5463, fax: 513-556-1028, E-mail address: angela.vaubel@uc.edu.

Graduate Contact Mr. Paul R. Hillner, Assistant Dean, College-Conservatory of Music, University of Cincinnati, PO Box 210003, Cincinnati, Ohio 45221-0003; 513-556-5462, fax: 513-556-1028, E-mail address: paul.hillner@uc.edu.

More About the University

Program Facilities The Corbett Center for the Performing Arts houses the newly renovated 736-seat Corbett Auditorium and the 400-seat Patricia Corbett Theatre. Renovation was recently completed this year on the 140-seat Watson Recital Hall, three dance studios, and four large rehearsal rooms. The Dieterle Vocal Arts Center, the 1995 addition to the CCM facility, is the home to the Voice, Opera, Choral, and Accompanying departments. It boasts 19 faculty studios, 3 private coaching rooms, the Italo Tajo Archive Room, 2 warm-up rooms, the 100-seat choral rehearsal room, and the choral library. The Center is also the location of the Nipper Rehearsal Studio, a large, grand opera–scale rehearsal space which has dressing rooms and technical support so that the space can double as a performance venue for workshops and concerts. The renovated Memorial Hall, which opened in 1996, includes teaching studios for piano, harpsichord, strings, and winds, plus practice rooms, chamber music rehearsal rooms, and the Electronic Music Studios. The Computer Music Studio contains Silicon Graphics and NeXTstep workstations equipped for digital sampling, editing, synthesis, signal processing, algorithmic composi-

Newly renovated Corbett Auditorium

tion, and interface programming. The Electronic Music Studio contains signal processing and MIDI hardware and software. Computer music research creating compositional software, performing live signal processing of acoustic instruments and sound/graphics collaborations is possible in five studios. Fiber connections between the studios and studio theater will facilitate live electronic music performances. The new Theater Production Wing adjacent to the Patricia Corbett Pavilion opened in 1996. The centerpiece of this highly praised facility is the scene shop where sets and props are constructed for CCM opera, musical theater, and drama productions. Also located in the wing are various design-oriented classrooms, labs, and faculty and staff offices. The lower level includes new facilities for the jazz department, including faculty studios, an ensemble rehearsal room, and practice rooms. The Gorno Memorial Music Library houses more than 110,000 volumes, including books, music scores, periodicals, and numerous special collections of rare books, music, and recordings. An extensive construction project to be completed in 1999 will result in a new studio theater, a new recital hall, expanded and renovated classroom and rehearsal facilities, and studios.

Faculty, Resident Artists, and Alumni CCM has more than 130 faculty members plus numerous adjuncts including Dorothy DeLay and Kurt Sassmannshaus (violin), Masao Kawasaki (viola), Yehuda Hanani (violincello), Al Laszlo (double bass), William Winstead (bassoon), Randy Gardner (horn), Mark

Ostoich (oboe), Brad Garner (flute), and James Tocco (piano and chamber music). Ensembles-In-Residence include the renowned Tokyo String Quartet, Amernet String Quartet, The Percussion Group/Cincinnati, and the Pridonoff Piano Duo. Alumni continue to hold key positions in the performing and media arts. Numbered among them are American and European opera stars Kathleen Battle, Barbara Daniels, Catherine Keen, David Malis, Stanford Olsen, and Mark Oswald; producers Earl Hamner ("The Waltons" and "Falconcrest") and Dan Guntzelman ("Growing Pains"); musical theater stars Faith Prince, Lee Roy Reams, Michele Pawk, Jason Graae, Jim Walton, and Vicki Lewis; prima ballerina Suzanne Farrell; jazz great Al Hirt; composers Albert Hague (*Plain and Fancy, Redhead, How the Grinch Stole Christmas*), Randy Edelman (*Last of the Mohicans, While You Were Sleeping*), and Stephen Flaherty (*Once on This Island, Ragtime*), and a host of international competition winners and instrumentalists who hold positions in the major orchestras, both in the United States and in Europe.

Student Performance Opportunities Nearly 1,000 performances a year take place at CCM by two large orchestras, three chamber orchestras, two wind ensembles, five choruses, more than forty chamber groups, dance productions and choreographers' workshops, jazz ensembles, early music ensembles, brass choir, and 24 mainstage and workshop productions in opera, musical theater, and drama.

▼

The University of Cincinnati College-Conservatory of Music (CCM) is the result of the merger of two distinguished schools of music–The Cincinnati Conservatory of Music, established in 1867, and The College of Music at Cincinnati, established in 1878. This merger in 1955, and subsequent union with the University of Cincinnati in 1962, brought together the professional training in the performing arts and media of a city long noted for its support of these areas.

Cited in the *New York Times* as "one of the nation's leading conservatories," CCM is among the nations most comprehensive conservatories–housing not only the standard disciplines of instrumental performance, voice, musicology, theory, and composition, but also music education, conducting, musical theater, drama, opera, theater design and production (makeup, lighting, scene design, stage management, costuming, sound design, and theater production), electronic media, jazz and studio music, dance, and a graduate program in arts administration, accompanying, and opera coaching.

Performing groups are continually recognized for their outstanding achievements. The jazz ensemble has regularly won the *Down Beat* magazine award for the best student ensemble; the National Opera Association has honored the CCM opera program with 16 first-place awards in the past nine years; and the wind department has been featured at major conventions and conferences in this country and in Japan and currently has twelve CDs on the market. Six additional outstanding CDs have been produced by the CCM Philharmonia orchestra, the Faculty Jazz Ensemble, and the Ensemble for Eighteenth Century Music. All have been recorded commercially. The CCM Philharmonia Orchestra was the only U.S. orchestra invited to perform at the One Hundred Days Festival that preceded Expo 98 in Lisbon, Portugal. The Orchestra received rave reviews for these March 1998 performances.

The CCM Dance Division–the first music school in the United States to offer courses in classical ballet–is the founding institution and affiliate of the Cincinnati Ballet. Both the Cincinnati Ballet Company and the Cincinnati Opera Association offer numerous performance opportunities to dance majors. The Dance Division also offers continual ballet performance experience, featuring works by Division faculty and guest choreographers. Other opportunities exist in productions by the opera and musical theater areas of CCM.

Theater training offers a unique opportunity for CCM students because of the combination of instruction in vocal coaching, dance, opera, musical theater, drama, theater design and production, and arts administration within one division. Students have the opportunity to share in a wide-ranging scope of classes, major productions, workshop productions, master classes, and internships, including mainstage and summer productions in the highly successful Hot Summer Nights series. This remarkable sharing of experiences among experts in all areas of theater and arts administration allows students exposure to a wealth of learning opportunities. In addition, the Division manages CCM's major theater and concert venues. Technical facilities currently include a state-of-the-art computerized lighting control mechanism for the theaters. The new technical support area, which opened in 1997, includes an 8,500 square foot scene shop, a 3,000 square foot costume shop plus wig, make-up, and prosthetics studios, a 1,500 square foot design/drafting studio, an 800 square foot light lab, and CAD drafting stations. The United States Institute of Technical Theater (USITT) has honored these programs with more than 30 awards in the past ten years.

In addition to the strengths of the College-Conservatory of Music, students have the resources of a major university at their disposal. The libraries of the University constitute a nationally recognized research center, with holdings that include 1.8 million bound volumes, 2.6 million microforms, and more than 19,500 serial subscriptions. They also offer access to an expanding number of libraries throughout the state via the OhioLINK online catalog.

Student support offices serve the entire University population and offer academic counseling and tutoring, resume and interview skills training, psychological and personal counseling, student health clinics, day-care centers; special programming for ethnic groups and women, and a host of activities such as special interest clubs, student government, and intramural sports.

The extensive physical facilities of the University provide residence halls for students; banking services; swimming, tennis, track, volleyball, basketball, racquetball/handball, and bowling; and six restaurants ranging from fast food to table service.

Cincinnati, "North America's most livable city" (*Places Rated Almanac*, 1993), is bordered on the south by the Ohio River and truly offers something for everyone. Nearby Mt. Adams and the adjoining Eden Park, a stylish urban area perched on top of a hill with spectacular views of the city and the Ohio River and the home of the playhouse in the Park, the Cincinnati Art Museum, and the Krohn Conservatory. Within walking distance is University Village, offering inexpensive restaurants and shops. And just beyond is the Ludlow Avenue of Clifton, with its boutiques, restaurants, and gaslit, tree-lined streets. At the heart of downtown, just a 5-minute bus ride, is Fountain Square–the place Cincinnatians go to celebrate, to demonstrate, to welcome hometown heroes, or to bring in the new year. Also downtown are numerous and diverse cultural opportunities–The Cincinnati Symphony Orchestra, the Pops, the Cincinnati Opera, the

University of Cincinnati College Conservatory of Music
(continued)

Cincinnati Ballet, Ensemble Theatre of Cincinnati, the Broadway Series, the Museum Center at Union Terminal, the Contemporary Art Center, the Playhouse in the Park, and more.

Both of CCM's founding schools, the Cincinnati Conservatory of Music and the College of Music of Cincinnati, were charter members of the National Association of Schools of Music (NASM), in which CCM continues to play a vital leadership role. All theater programs have received accreditation from the National Association of Schools of Theater (NAST), and the dance program holds accreditation from the National Association of Schools of Dance (NASD).

▼ University of Colorado at Boulder

Boulder, Colorado

State-supported, coed. Suburban campus. Total enrollment: 25,109. Music program established 1920.

Degrees Bachelor of Music in the areas of composition, history, all major instruments, voice; Bachelor of Music Education in the areas of instrumental music education, choral music education, general music. Majors and concentrations: brass, composition, music education, music history, opera, performance, piano/organ, sacred music, stringed instruments, voice, wind and percussion instruments. Graduate degrees offered: Master of Music in the areas of performance, composition, music technology, music literature, performance and pedagogy; Master of Music Education in the areas of choral conducting music education, instrumental conducting music education. Doctor of Musical Arts in the areas of performance, composition, instrumental conducting and literature, choral conducting and literature, performance and pedagogy; Doctor of Philosophy in the areas of music education, musicology. Cross-registration with University of Colorado System. Program accredited by NASM.

Enrollment Fall 1997: 718 total; 342 undergraduate, 241 graduate, 135 non-professional degree.

Music Student Profile 46% females, 54% males, 14% minorities, 8% international.

Music Faculty 56 total undergraduate and graduate (full-time and part-time). 75% of full-time faculty have terminal degrees. Graduate students teach a few undergraduate courses. Undergraduate student–faculty ratio: 6:1.

Student Life Student groups/activities include Sigma Alpha Iota, Phi Mu Alpha, Music Educators National Conference. Special housing available for music students.

Expenses for 1997–98 Application fee: $40. One-time mandatory fee: $35. State resident tuition: $2356 full-time. Nonresident tuition: $14,400 full-time. Mandatory fees: $583 full-time. Full-time tuition and fees vary according to program. College room and board: $4566. Room and board charges vary according to board plan, housing facility, and location.

Financial Aid Program-specific awards for 1997: 120 music scholarships for program majors ($1000).

Application Procedures Students admitted directly into the professional program freshman year. Deadline for freshmen and transfers: March 1. Notification date for freshmen and transfers: July 1. Required: essay, high school transcript, college transcript(s) for transfer students, minimum 2.0 high

school GPA, letter of recommendation, audition, SAT I or ACT test scores (minimum combined SAT I score of 1050, minimum combined ACT score of 23). Auditions held weekly in February and by appointment on campus; recorded music is permissible as a substitute for live auditions when distance is prohibitive and videotaped performances are permissible as a substitute for live auditions when distance is prohibitive.

Web Site http://www.colorado.edu/music.

Undergraduate Contact Dr. Tanya Gille, Associate Dean for Undergraduate Studies, College of Music, University of Colorado at Boulder, Campus Box 301, Boulder, Colorado 80309-0301; 303-492-6354, fax: 303-492-5619.

Graduate Contact Ms. Deborah Hayes, Associate Dean for Graduate Studies, College of Music, University of Colorado at Boulder, Campus Box 301, Boulder, Colorado 80309-0301; 303-492-2208, fax: 303-492-5619.

▼ University of Connecticut

Storrs, Connecticut

State-supported, coed. Rural campus. Total enrollment: 18,205.

Degrees Bachelor of Music in the areas of vocal performance, instrumental performance, music theory; Bachelor of Science in the area of music education; Bachelor of Arts in the area of music. Majors and concentrations: music education, music theory, piano/organ, stringed instruments, voice, wind and percussion instruments. Graduate degrees offered: Master of Music in the areas of performance, performance with conducting (instrumental, choral), music education; Master of Arts in the areas of music theory, musicology. Doctor of Musical Arts in the areas of performance, conducting; Doctor of Philosophy in the areas of music theory and history, music education. Program accredited by NASM.

Enrollment Fall 1997: 250 total; 164 undergraduate, 85 graduate, 1 non-professional degree.

Music Student Profile 60% females, 40% males, 3% minorities, 3% international.

Music Faculty 49 total undergraduate and graduate (full-time and part-time). 100% of full-time faculty have terminal degrees. Graduate students teach a few undergraduate courses. Undergraduate student–faculty ratio: 9:1.

Student Life Student groups/activities include Music Educators National Conference Student Chapter, American Choral Directors Association Student Chapter. Special housing available for music students.

Expenses for 1997–98 Application fee: $40. State resident tuition: $4158 full-time. Nonresident tuition: $12,676 full-time. Mandatory fees: $1084 full-time. College room and board: $5462. College room only: $2776. Room and board charges vary according to board plan and housing facility. Special program-related fees: $75–$145 per course for applied music fee.

Financial Aid Program-specific awards for 1997: 1–2 Victor Borge Awards for those demonstrating talent and academic achievement ($1000–$3000), 4–6 Dean's Scholarships for those demonstrating talent and academic achievement ($1500–$5000).

Application Procedures Students admitted directly into the professional program freshman year. Deadline for freshmen: April 1; transfers: May 1. Notification date for freshmen and transfers: July 1. Required: high school transcript, college transcript(s) for transfer students, 3 letters of recommenda-

tion, audition, SAT I test score only. Recommended: minimum 3.0 high school GPA. Auditions held 4 times on campus; recorded music is permissible as a substitute for live auditions when distance is prohibitive (beyond a 150-mile radius) and videotaped performances are permissible as a substitute for live auditions when distance is prohibitive (beyond a 150-mile radius).
Web Site http://www.sfa.uconn.edu/music.html.
Undergraduate Contact Prof. Peter Sacco, Director of Undergraduate Studies, Music Department, University of Connecticut, 876 Coventry Road, U-12, Storrs, Connecticut 06269-1012; 860-486-4793, fax: 860-486-3796, E-mail address: psacco@finearts.sfa.uconn.edu.
Graduate Contact Dr. Richard Bass, Director of Graduate Studies, Music Department, University of Connecticut, 876 Conventry Road,, U-12, Storrs, Connecticut 06269-1012; 860-486-3728, fax: 860-486-3796, E-mail address: rbass@finearts.sfa.uconn.edu.

▼ UNIVERSITY OF DAYTON

Dayton, Ohio

Independent-Roman Catholic, coed. Suburban campus. Total enrollment: 10,208.
Degrees Bachelor of Music in the areas of performance, composition, music therapy; Bachelor of Music Education. Majors and concentrations: composition, music education, music therapy, performance. Program accredited by NASM.
Enrollment Fall 1997: 110 undergraduate.
Music Student Profile 65% females, 35% males, 5% minorities.
Music Faculty 38 total (full-time and part-time). 75% of full-time faculty have terminal degrees. Graduate students do not teach undergraduate courses. Undergraduate student–faculty ratio: 15:1.
Student Life Student groups/activities include music fraternity and sorority, Ohio Student Music Educators Club, Music Therapy Club.
Expenses for 1998–99 Application fee: $30. Comprehensive fee: $19,340 includes full-time tuition ($14,170), mandatory fees ($500), and college room and board ($4670). College room only: $2480. Full-time tuition and fees vary according to program. Room and board charges vary according to board plan, housing facility, and student level. Special program-related fees: $110–$210 per semester for lesson fees, $40 per course for pedagogy classes.
Financial Aid Program-specific awards for 1997: 10–13 Music Talent Awards for program students ($3500), 12–18 Reichard Awards for program students ($500), 12–18 Band Grants for band members.
Application Procedures Students admitted directly into the professional program freshman year. Deadline for freshmen and transfers: continuous. Notification date for freshmen and transfers: continuous. Required: essay, high school transcript, 2 letters of recommendation, interview, audition, SAT I or ACT test scores, portfolio for composition and music theory applicants. Recommended: minimum 3.0 high school GPA. Auditions held 4 times and by appointment on campus; recorded music is permissible as a substitute for live auditions if a campus visit is impossible and videotaped performances are permissible as a substitute for live auditions if a campus visit is impossible. Portfolio reviews held once on campus.
Web Site http://www.udayton.edu/~music.

Undergraduate Contact Dr. Robert Jones, Coordinator, Music Admissions, Department of Music, University of Dayton, 300 College Park, Dayton, Ohio 45469-0290; 513-229-3936, fax: 513-229-3916, E-mail address: jonesr@yar.udayton.edu.

▼ UNIVERSITY OF DELAWARE

Newark, Delaware

State-related, coed. Small town campus. Total enrollment: 18,230. Music program established 1938.
Degrees Bachelor of Music in the areas of applied vocal and instrumental music, music theory and composition; Bachelor of Music Education in the areas of instrumental music education, choral music education. Majors and concentrations: classical music, music, music education, music theory and composition, piano, stringed instruments, voice, wind and percussion instruments. Graduate degrees offered: Master of Music in the areas of instrumental performance, music education, voice, strings, instrumental conducting. Program accredited by NASM.
Enrollment Fall 1997: 150 undergraduate, 15 graduate.
Music Student Profile 55% females, 45% males, 1% minorities, 1% international.
Music Faculty 37 total undergraduate and graduate (full-time and part-time). 80% of full-time faculty have terminal degrees. Graduate students do not teach undergraduate courses. Undergraduate student–faculty ratio: 3:1.
Student Life Student groups/activities include Sigma Alpha Iota, Phi Mu Alpha, Music Educators National Conference. Special housing available for music students.
Expenses for 1997–98 Application fee: $45. State resident tuition: $4120 full-time. Nonresident tuition: $11,750 full-time. Mandatory fees: $454 full-time. College room and board: $4770. College room only: $2590. Room and board charges vary according to housing facility.
Financial Aid Program-specific awards for 1997: 10 Jastak-Burgess Awards for those demonstrating musical achievement ($1000–$3000), 10–12 Arts and Humanities Awards for state residents demonstrating need/talent ($1500–$2000), 5 Quigley Awards for female state residents ($1000–$2500), 5 Music Department Awards for talented majors in needed instruments ($1000–$2500).
Application Procedures Students admitted directly into the professional program freshman year. Deadline for freshmen and transfers: March 1. Notification date for freshmen and transfers: April 15. Required: essay, high school transcript, college transcript(s) for transfer students, minimum 2.0 high school GPA, audition, SAT I or ACT test scores (minimum combined SAT I score of 1000), musicality test. Recommended: minimum 3.0 high school GPA, 2 letters of recommendation, interview. Auditions held 4 times on campus; recorded music is permissible as a substitute for live auditions when distance is prohibitive and videotaped performances are permissible as a substitute for live auditions when distance is prohibitive.
Web Site http://www.udel.edu/music.
Undergraduate Contact Mr. Frederic A. Siegel, Associate Provost for Enrollment Services, University of Delaware, 116 Hullihen Hall, Newark, Delaware 19716; 302-831-8125, fax: 302-831-6905.
Graduate Contact Dr. David Herman, Chair, Department of Music, University of Delaware, 209 Amy DuPont Music Building, Newark, Delaware 19716; 302-831-2577, fax: 302-831-3589, E-mail address: herman@udel.edu.

Lamont School of Music

▼ UNIVERSITY OF DENVER

Denver, Colorado

Independent, coed. Suburban campus. Total enrollment: 8,667.

Degrees Bachelor of Music in the areas of performance, jazz, piano/organ, wind, percussion, composition, commercial music. Majors and concentrations: accordion, arranging, classical music, commercial music, composition, jazz, music, music technology, piano/organ, stringed instruments, voice, wind and percussion instruments. Graduate degrees offered: Master of Music in the areas of performance, composition, conducting, piano pedagogy, Suzuki pedagogy; Master of Arts in the areas of music theory, music education, music history and literature. Program accredited by NASM.

Enrollment Fall 1997: 163 total; 125 undergraduate, 35 graduate, 3 non-professional degree.

Music Student Profile 50% females, 50% males, 10% minorities, 15% international.

Music Faculty 39 total undergraduate and graduate (full-time and part-time). 10% of full-time faculty have terminal degrees. Graduate students do not teach undergraduate courses. Undergraduate student–faculty ratio: 6:1.

Student Life Student groups/activities include professional music fraternities and sororities, various ensemble groups. Special housing available for music students.

Expenses for 1997–98 Application fee: $45. Comprehensive fee: $23,629 includes full-time tuition ($17,532), mandatory fees ($354), and college room and board ($5743). Full-time tuition and fees vary according to class time, course load, and program. Room and board charges vary according to board plan and housing facility.

Financial Aid Program-specific awards for 1997: 85 Music Activity Grants for program majors ($5000), 5 Endowed Awards for specific program majors ($6000), 2 Endowed Full Tuition Awards for program majors ($18,000).

Application Procedures Students admitted directly into the professional program freshman year. Deadline for freshmen and transfers: continuous. Required: essay, high school transcript, college transcript(s) for transfer students, 2 letters of recommendation, audition, SAT I or ACT test scores. Recommended: minimum 2.0 high school GPA, interview. Auditions held 4-6 times on campus and off campus in Chicago, IL and various cities; recorded music is permissible as a substitute for live auditions if a campus visit is impossible and videotaped performances are permissible as a substitute for live auditions if a campus visit is impossible.

Contact Mr. Malcolm Lynn Baker, Director of Admissions, Lamont School of Music, University of Denver, 7111 Montview Boulevard, Denver, Colorado 80220; 303-871-6973, fax: 303-871-3118, E-mail address: mbaker@du.edu.

▼ UNIVERSITY OF EVANSVILLE

Evansville, Indiana

Independent, coed. Suburban campus. Total enrollment: 3,023. Music program established 1933.

Degrees Bachelor of Music in the areas of performance, performance (Suzuki emphasis), music therapy, music education. Majors and concentrations: classical guitar, classical music, music, music education, music management, music therapy, piano/organ, stringed instruments, voice, wind and percussion instruments. Program accredited by NASM.

Enrollment Fall 1997: 100 total; all undergraduate.

Music Student Profile 60% females, 40% males, 5% minorities, 5% international.

Music Faculty 23 total (full-time and part-time). 100% of full-time faculty have terminal degrees. Graduate students do not teach undergraduate courses. Undergraduate student–faculty ratio: 8:1.

Student Life Student groups/activities include National Association of Music Therapy Student Chapter, Music Educators National Conference Student Chapter, Phi Mu Alpha/Sigma Alpha Iota.

Expenses for 1997–98 Application fee: $35. Comprehensive fee: $18,780 includes full-time tuition ($13,600), mandatory fees ($280), and college room and board ($4900). College room only: $2060. Room and board charges vary according to board plan and housing facility. Special program-related fees: $200 per credit hour for applied music fee.

Financial Aid Program-specific awards for 1997: academic scholarships for those demonstrating talent and academic achievement ($2000–$8000).

Application Procedures Students admitted directly into the professional program freshman year. Deadline for freshmen: May 1; transfers: June 1. Required: essay, high school transcript, college transcript(s) for transfer students, minimum 2.0 high school GPA, audition, SAT I or ACT test scores. Recommended: minimum 3.0 high school GPA, letter of recommendation. Auditions held 6 times on campus; recorded music is permissible as a substitute for live auditions when distance is prohibitive and videotaped performances are permissible as a substitute for live auditions when distance is prohibitive.

Web Site http://cedar.evansville.edu/~musicweb/index.html.

Undergraduate Contact Dr. Alan L. Solomon, Chair, Music Department, University of Evansville, 1800 Lincoln Avenue, Evansville, Indiana 47722; 812-479-2754, fax: 812-479-2101, E-mail address: as7@evansville.edu.

▼ UNIVERSITY OF FLORIDA

Gainesville, Florida

State-supported, coed. Suburban campus. Total enrollment: 41,713.

Degrees Bachelor of Music in the areas of performance, music history, music theory, composition, church music. Majors and concentrations: composition, music education, music history and literature, music liberal arts, music theory, piano/organ, sacred music, stringed instruments, voice, wind and percussion instruments. Graduate degrees offered: Master of Music in the areas of music education, performance, conducting, composition, music theory, music history and literature, sacred music, pedagogy. Program accredited by NASM.

Enrollment Fall 1997: 226 total; 160 undergraduate, 46 graduate, 20 non-professional degree.

Music Student Profile 53% females, 47% males, 10% minorities, 2% international.

Music Faculty 38 total undergraduate and graduate (full-time and part-time). 75% of full-time faculty have terminal degrees. Graduate students teach a few undergraduate courses. Undergraduate student–faculty ratio: 5:1.

Student Life Student groups/activities include Collegiate Music Educators National Conference, Sigma Alpha Iota, Phi Kappa Phi.

Expenses for 1997–98 Application fee: $20. State resident tuition: $1930 full-time. Nonresident tuition: $7570 full-time. College room and board: $4610. College room only: $2270. Room and board charges vary according to board plan and housing facility.

Financial Aid Program-specific awards for 1997: 100 Friends of Music Scholarships for program majors ($400–$1500), 40–55 band scholarships for band members ($400–$800).

Application Procedures Deadline for freshmen: February 1; transfers: June 1. Notification date for freshmen: May 1; transfers: July 31. Required: high school transcript, college transcript(s) for transfer students, minimum 2.0 high school GPA, letter of recommendation, interview, audition, SAT I or ACT test scores. Recommended: minimum 3.0 high school GPA. Auditions held 3-4 times on campus; recorded music is permissible as a substitute for live auditions for out-of-state applicants and videotaped performances are permissible as a substitute for live auditions for out-of-state applicants.

Web Site http://www.arts.ufl.edu/music.

Contact Dr. Linda Black, Director of Music Admissions, School of Music, University of Florida, 130 Music Building, PO Box 117900, Gainesville, Florida 32611-7900; 352-392-0223, fax: 352-392-0461, E-mail address: lin5353@nervm.nerdc.ufl.edu.

▼ UNIVERSITY OF GEORGIA

Athens, Georgia

State-supported, coed. Suburban campus. Total enrollment: 29,693. Music program established 1927.

Degrees Bachelor of Music in the areas of performance, composition, music therapy, music theory; Bachelor of Music Education. Majors and concentrations: composition, conducting, music, music education, music theory, music therapy, piano/organ, stringed instruments, voice, wind and percussion instruments. Graduate degrees offered: Master of Music in the areas of musicology, composition, music literature, performance; Master of Music Education in the areas of music education, music therapy. Doctor of Musical Arts in the areas of performance, composition, music education, choral conducting. Cross-registration with University System of Georgia. Program accredited by NASM, NAMT.

Enrollment Fall 1997: 495 total; 365 undergraduate, 130 graduate.

Music Student Profile 50% females, 50% males, 6% minorities, 8% international.

Music Faculty 55 total undergraduate and graduate (full-time and part-time). 98% of full-time faculty have terminal degrees. Graduate students teach a few undergraduate courses. Undergraduate student–faculty ratio: 10:1.

Student Life Student groups/activities include Music Educators National Conference, National Association of Music Therapy, Music Teachers National Association. Special housing available for music students.

Expenses for 1997–98 Application fee: $25. State resident tuition: $2838 full-time. Nonresident tuition: $8790 full-time. Full-time tuition varies according to program. College room and board: $4323. College room only: $2271. Room and board charges vary according to board plan and housing facility.

Financial Aid Program-specific awards for 1997: 90 music scholarships for performance majors ($2000–$2500).

Application Procedures Students admitted directly into the professional program freshman year. Deadline for freshmen: February 1; transfers: July 1. Notification date for freshmen and transfers: continuous. Required: high school transcript, college transcript(s) for transfer students, minimum 3.0 high school GPA, 3 letters of recommendation, interview, audition, SAT I or ACT test scores (minimum combined SAT I score of 1060), portfolio for composition applicants. Auditions held 4 times and by appointment on campus; recorded music is permissible as a substitute for live auditions when distance is prohibitive or scheduling is difficult and videotaped performances are permissible as a substitute for live auditions when distance is prohibitive or scheduling is difficult. Portfolio reviews held by appointment on campus.

Undergraduate Contact Dr. John Culvahouse, Coordinator of Undergraduate Studies, School of Music, University of Georgia, Music Building, Athens, Georgia 30602-3153; 706-542-2764, fax: 706-542-2773.

Graduate Contact Dr. Donald Lowe, Coordinator of Graduate Studies, School of Music, University of Georgia, Music Building, Athens, Georgia 30602-3153; 706-542-2743, fax: 706-542-2773.

The Hartt School

▼ UNIVERSITY OF HARTFORD

West Hartford, Connecticut

Independent, coed. Suburban campus. Total enrollment: 7,089. Music program established 1920.

Degrees Bachelor of Music in the areas of performance, jazz/African-American music, music management, composition, music history, music theory, music education, music production and technology; Bachelor of Arts in the area of performing arts management. Majors and concentrations: composition, instrumental music, jazz, music education, music history, music management, music theory, production/technology, voice. Graduate degrees offered: Master of Music in the areas of performance, opera, liturgical music, conducting, composition, music history, music theory, performance (Suzuki pedagogy), piano (accompanying or pedagogy emphasis); Master of Music Education in the areas of conducting (choral and instrumental) early childhood, performance, pedagogy, research, Kodály, technology. Doctor of Musical Arts in the areas of performance, composition, choral conducting, orchestral conducting, music education; Doctor of Philosophy in the area of music education. Cross-registration with Trinity College, Saint Joseph College, Hartford Seminary. Program accredited by NASM.

Enrollment Fall 1997: 510 total; 365 undergraduate, 125 graduate, 20 non-professional degree.

Music Student Profile 60% females, 40% males, 10% minorities, 18% international.

Music Faculty 120 total undergraduate and graduate (full-time and part-time). 70% of full-time faculty have terminal degrees. Graduate students teach a few undergraduate courses. Undergraduate student–faculty ratio: 8:1.

Student Life Student groups/activities include Music Educators National Conference, Pi Kappa Lambda, Epsilon Gamma Chapter, American Choral Directors Association. Special housing available for music students.

University of Hartford (continued)

Expenses for 1998–99 Application fee: $35. Comprehensive fee: $25,424 includes full-time tuition ($17,190), mandatory fees ($1034), and college room and board ($7200). College room only: $4440. Room and board charges vary according to board plan and housing facility.

Financial Aid Program-specific awards for 1997: 400 Performing Arts Scholarships for students passing audition evaluations ($7000).

Application Procedures Students admitted directly into the professional program freshman year. Deadline for freshmen and transfers: continuous. Required: high school transcript, college transcript(s) for transfer students, minimum 2.0 high school GPA, 3 letters of recommendation, interview, audition, SAT I or ACT test scores. Recommended: essay, minimum 3.0 high school GPA. Auditions held 3 times on campus; recorded music is permissible as a substitute for live auditions if a campus visit is impossible and videotaped performances are permissible as a substitute for live auditions when distance is prohibitive.

Undergraduate Contact Mr. James Jacobs, Director of Admissions, The Hartt School, University of Hartford, 200 Bloomfield Avenue, West Hartford, Connecticut 06117-1500; 860-768-4465, fax: 860-768-4441.

Graduate Contact Dr. Adrienne Maslin, Assistant Dean, The Hartt School, University of Hartford, 200 Bloomfield Avenue, West Hartford, Connecticut 06117-1500; 860-768-5389, fax: 860-768-4441, E-mail address: maslin@uhavax.hartford.edu.

▼ University of Hawaii at Manoa

Honolulu, Hawaii

State-supported, coed. Urban campus. Total enrollment: 17,356. Music program established 1947.

Degrees Bachelor of Music in the areas of composition, performance. Majors and concentrations: composition, ethnomusicology, guitar, music education, music theater, piano, stringed instruments, voice, wind and percussion instruments. Graduate degrees offered: Master of Music in the areas of composition, performance. Doctor of Philosophy in the area of music. Program accredited by NASM.

Enrollment Fall 1997: 190 total; 125 undergraduate, 55 graduate, 10 non-professional degree.

Music Student Profile 47% females, 53% males, 80% minorities, 18% international.

Music Faculty 53 total undergraduate and graduate (full-time and part-time). 100% of full-time faculty have terminal degrees. Graduate students teach a few undergraduate courses. Undergraduate student–faculty ratio: 7:1.

Student Life Student groups/activities include American Choral Directors Association Student Chapter, Circle of Fifths (departmental student organization), Music Educators National Conference Student Chapter.

Expenses for 1997–98 Application fee: $25 for nonresidents. State resident tuition: $2832 full-time. Nonresident tuition: $9312 full-time. Mandatory fees: $118 full-time. College room and board: $4740. College room only: $2660. Room and board charges vary according to board plan and housing facility.

Financial Aid Program-specific awards for 1997: 85 tuition waivers for band and orchestra members ($1400–$4260), 30 scholarships for program majors ($200–$9000).

Application Procedures Students apply for admission into the professional program by sophomore year. Deadline for freshmen and transfers: May 1. Required: high school transcript, college transcript(s) for transfer students, minimum 2.0 high school GPA, SAT I or ACT test scores, standing in top 40% of class for transfer students. Recommended: minimum 3.0 high school GPA, letter of recommendation, interview, audition, portfolio, video for out-of-state applicants. Auditions held once and by appointment on campus; recorded music is permissible as a substitute for live auditions for out-of-state applicants and videotaped performances are permissible as a substitute for live auditions for out-of-state applicants. Portfolio reviews held once and by appointment for composition applicants on campus.

Web Site http://www2.hawaii.edu/uhmmusic/.

Undergraduate Contact Mr. Dale Hall, Undergraduate Chairman, Music Department, University of Hawaii at Manoa, 2411 Dole Street, Honolulu, Hawaii 96822; 808-956-2129, fax: 808-956-9657, E-mail address: dhall@hawaii.edu.

Graduate Contact Mr. Byron K. Yasui, Graduate Chairman, Music Department, University of Hawaii at Manoa, 2411 Dole Street, Honolulu, Hawaii 96822; 808-956-2171, fax: 808-956-9657, E-mail address: byasui@hawaii.edu.

Moores School of Music

▼ University of Houston

Houston, Texas

State-supported, coed. Urban campus. Total enrollment: 31,602.

Degrees Bachelor of Music in the areas of applied music, music with teaching certificate, music theory, composition. Majors and concentrations: composition, music, music education, music theory, piano/organ, stringed instruments, voice, wind and percussion instruments. Graduate degrees offered: Master of Music in the areas of applied music, music theory, composition, music literature, music education, accompanying and chamber music, performance and pedagogy. Doctor of Musical Arts in the areas of performance, conducting, composition, music education. Program accredited by NASM.

Enrollment Fall 1997: 477 total; 218 undergraduate, 128 graduate, 131 non-professional degree.

Music Student Profile 49% females, 51% males, 23% minorities, 10% international.

Music Faculty 48 total undergraduate and graduate (full-time and part-time). 40% of full-time faculty have terminal degrees. Graduate students teach a few undergraduate courses. Undergraduate student–faculty ratio: 8:1.

Student Life Student groups/activities include Phi Mu Alpha Sinfonia, Sigma Alpha Iota.

Estimated expenses for 1998–99 Application fee: $30. State resident tuition: $864 full-time. Nonresident tuition: $5952 full-time. Mandatory fees: $1129 full-time. Full-time tuition and fees vary according to program. College room and board: $4405. College room only: $1960. Room and board charges vary according to board plan and housing facility. Special program-related fees: $25 per semester for piano use, $130 per semester for applied music courses, $4–$10 per semester for some music courses.

Financial Aid Program-specific awards for 1997: 350 music scholarships for program students ($1500), 100–125 Band Grants for program students ($200), 20–30 Delores Welder Mitchell Awards for outstanding scholars ($250).

Application Procedures Students admitted directly into the professional program freshman year. Deadline for freshmen and transfers: August 1. Required: high school transcript, college transcript(s) for transfer students, minimum 2.0 high school GPA, audition, SAT I or ACT test scores. Recommended: minimum 3.0 high school GPA, letter of recommendation, interview. Auditions held 4 times on campus; recorded music is permissible as a substitute for live auditions when distance is prohibitive or scheduling is difficult and videotaped performances are permissible as a substitute for live auditions when distance is prohibitive or scheduling is difficult.

Web Site http://www.uh.edu/music/.

Undergraduate Contact Ms. Jane Brewer, Academic Advisor, Moores School of Music, University of Houston, Houston, Texas 77204-4201; 713-743-3009, fax: 713-743-3166.

Graduate Contact Mr. David A. White, Graduate Advisor, Moores School of Music, University of Houston, Houston, Texas 77204-4201; 713-743-3009, fax: 713-743-3166.

More About the University

Program Facilities Performance spaces include the Moores Opera House (800 seats), Dudley Hall (300 seats), and Organ Hall (200 seats). Facilities also include an electronic music studio and a computer/synthesizer cluster. The Moores School of Music is housed in a new $24-million facility. The facility includes a recording studio, five large and six smaller chamber ensemble rehearsal rooms, and more than sixty practice rooms.

Faculty, Resident Artists, and Alumni Faculty are internationally recognized artists, members of the Houston Symphony, Houston Ballet Orchestra, and Houston Grand Opera Orchestra and have held principal positions in the orchestras of Houston, Pittsburgh, Indianapolis, Fort Worth, and Rochester and the New York Philharmonic. They also appear in chamber and solo recitals and as soloists with major orchestras and opera companies both in the United States and abroad. Alumni hold positions in leading orchestras and opera companies and pursue active solo careers. Music educators from the Moores School of Music are in great demand, receiving numerous honors and awards and directing some of the state's most successful music programs.

Student Performance/Exhibit Opportunities Performance opportunities include the University Orchestra, Chamber Orchestra, two wind ensembles, Concert Band, Marching Band, jazz ensembles, jazz combos, the Edythe Bates Old Opera Center, University Chorus, University Chorale, Chamber Singers, Women's Chorus, New Music Ensemble, Percussion Ensemble, Horn Ensemble, Trombone Ensemble, Trumpet Ensemble, and various chamber groups. There are numerous performance and teaching opportunities throughout the city for students.

Special Programs The Texas Music Festival, an intensive four-week summer orchestral and chamber music program attracts applicants from throughout the world; festival includes institutes in vocal chamber music, strings, piano, jazz, and junior high band; International Piano Festival presents 3 artists each year for recitals and master classes; A. I. Lack Music Master Series offers a number of master classes each year with internationally recognized performers.

Lionel Hampton School of Music

▼ UNIVERSITY OF IDAHO

Moscow, Idaho

State-supported, coed. Small town campus. Total enrollment: 11,027. Music program established 1893.

Degrees Bachelor of Music in the areas of performance, composition, business; Bachelor of Music Education in the areas of instrumental music education, choral music education, elementary music education. Majors and concentrations: composition, music and business, music education, piano/organ, stringed instruments, voice, wind and percussion instruments. Graduate degrees offered: Master of Music in the areas of performance, music education, pedagogy, accompanying, composition; Master of Arts in the area of music history. Cross-registration with Washington State University. Program accredited by NASM.

Enrollment Fall 1997: 226 total; 195 undergraduate, 13 graduate, 18 non-professional degree.

Music Student Profile 50% females, 50% males, 7% minorities, 2% international.

Music Faculty 28 total undergraduate and graduate (full-time and part-time). 90% of full-time faculty have terminal degrees. Graduate students teach a few undergraduate courses.

Student Life Student groups/activities include Sigma Alpha Iota (music honorary sorority), Pi Kappa Lambda (music honorary fraternity), Music Educators National Conference Student Chapter.

Expenses for 1997–98 Application fee: $30. State resident tuition: $0 full-time. Nonresident tuition: $5800 full-time. Mandatory fees: $1942 full-time. Full-time tuition and fees vary according to program and reciprocity agreements. College room and board: $3824. College room only: $1832. Room and board charges vary according to board plan and housing facility. Special program-related fees: $12–$20 for lab fee for equipment maintenance in specific courses.

Financial Aid Program-specific awards for 1997: 85 Music Merit Scholarships for those passing audition evaluations ($200–$2000), 12 out-of-state tuition waivers for out-of-state program majors ($6000).

Application Procedures Students admitted directly into the professional program freshman year. Deadline for freshmen and transfers: continuous. Required: high school transcript, college transcript(s) for transfer students, minimum 2.0 high school GPA, audition, SAT I or ACT test scores. Auditions held as needed on campus; recorded music is permissible as a substitute for live auditions by request and videotaped performances are permissible as a substitute for live auditions by request.

Web Site http://www.uidaho.edu/LS/music.

Undergraduate Contact Office of New Student Services, University of Idaho, Student Union Building, Moscow, Idaho 83844-4253; 208-885-6163.

Graduate Contact Mr. James Reid, Coordinator of Graduate Studies, Lionel Hampton School of Music, University of Idaho, Moscow, Idaho 83844-4015; 208-885-6231, fax: 208-885-7254, E-mail address: jreid@uidaho.edu.

▼ UNIVERSITY OF ILLINOIS AT URBANA–CHAMPAIGN

Champaign, Illinois

State-supported, coed. Small town campus. Total enrollment: 36,019.

Degrees Bachelor of Music in the areas of performance, composition/theory, music history; Bachelor of Music Education. Majors and concentrations: classical music, composition, jazz, music, music business, music history,

University of Illinois at Urbana–Champaign (continued)

music theory, piano/organ, sacred music, stringed instruments, voice, wind and percussion instruments. Graduate degrees offered: Master of Music in the areas of musicology, composition/theory, performance and literature, choral conducting, instrumental conducting, vocal accompanying and coaching, group piano pedagogy; Master of Music Education. Doctor of Musical Arts in the areas of composition, piano, organ, choral music, voice, violin, cello, wind instruments, percussion instruments. Program accredited by NASM.

Enrollment Fall 1997: 700 total; 420 undergraduate, 280 graduate.

Music Student Profile 52% females, 48% males, 11% minorities, 8% international.

Music Faculty 92 total undergraduate and graduate (full-time and part-time). 87% of full-time faculty have terminal degrees. Graduate students teach about a quarter undergraduate courses. Undergraduate student–faculty ratio: 5:1.

Student Life Student groups/activities include Music Educators National Conference, Sigma Alpha Iota, Phi Mu Alpha Sinfonia.

Expenses for 1997–98 Application fee: $40, $50 for international students. State resident tuition: $3308 full-time. Nonresident tuition: $9924 full-time. Mandatory fees: $812 full-time. Full-time tuition and fees vary according to program and student level. College room and board: $5078. College room only: $1958. Room and board charges vary according to board plan and housing facility. Special program-related fees: $200–$400 per year for additional music equipment and instructional support.

Financial Aid Program-specific awards for 1997: 16 Thomas J. Smith Scholarships for female students from Illinois ($3600), performance awards for program majors ($1000–$5000).

Application Procedures Students admitted directly into the professional program freshman year. Deadline for freshmen and transfers: continuous. Required: high school transcript, college transcript(s) for transfer students, 3 letters of recommendation, interview, audition, SAT I or ACT test scores (minimum combined ACT score of 20), standing in top 40% of graduating class, portfolio for composition/theory and music history applicants. Auditions held 7 times on campus; recorded music is permissible as a substitute for live auditions on a case-by-case basis. Portfolio reviews held 7 times on campus.

Web Site http://www.music.uiuc.edu/music/.

Undergraduate Contact Dr. Mark Sheridan-Rabideau, Coordinator of Undergraduate Admissions, School of Music, University of Illinois at Urbana–Champaign, 1114 West Nevada Street, Urbana, Illinois 61801; 217-244-0551, fax: 217-244-4585, E-mail address: mrabideau@uiuc.edu.

Graduate Contact Dr. Tom R. Ward, Coordinator, Graduate Studies in Music, School of Music, University of Illinois at Urbana–Champaign, 1114 West Nevada Street, Urbana, Illinois 61801; 217-333-1712, fax: 217-244-4585, E-mail address: t-ward2@uiuc.edu.

▼ THE UNIVERSITY OF IOWA

Iowa City, Iowa

State-supported, coed. Small town campus. Total enrollment: 28,409. Music program established 1856.

Degrees Bachelor of Music in the areas of performance, composition, music therapy. Majors and concentrations: composition, music education, music performance, music therapy, piano/organ, stringed instruments, voice, wind and percussion instruments. Graduate degrees offered: Master of Fine Arts in the area of performance; Master of Arts in the areas of performance, theory, composition, musicology, music education. Doctor of Musical Arts in the areas of performance, conducting; Doctor of Philosophy in the areas of composition, musicology, music education, theory, music literature. Program accredited by NASM.

Enrollment Fall 1997: 432 total; 227 undergraduate, 195 graduate, 10 non-professional degree.

Music Student Profile 4% minorities.

Music Faculty 56 total undergraduate and graduate (full-time and part-time). 99% of full-time faculty have terminal degrees. Graduate students teach about a quarter undergraduate courses. Undergraduate student–faculty ratio: 9:1.

Student Life Student groups/activities include Pi Kappa Lambda, Music Educators National Conference, Sigma Alpha Iota.

Expenses for 1997–98 Application fee: $20. State resident tuition: $2566 full-time. Nonresident tuition: $9422 full-time. Mandatory fees: $194 full-time. Full-time tuition and fees vary according to course load. College room and board: $4046. Room and board charges vary according to board plan. Special program-related fees: $70–$130 per credit hour for applied music fee.

Financial Aid Program-specific awards for 1997: 50 Music Activities Scholarships for composition and performance majors ($500–$2470).

Application Procedures Students admitted directly into the professional program freshman year. Deadline for freshmen and transfers: continuous. Required: high school transcript, college transcript(s) for transfer students, minimum 2.0 high school GPA, letter of recommendation, audition, SAT I or ACT test scores. Auditions held once in February and continuously by appointment on campus; recorded music is permissible as a substitute for live auditions if a campus visit is impossible and videotaped performances are permissible as a substitute for live auditions when distance is prohibitive.

Web Site http://www.uiowa.edu/~music/.

Undergraduate Contact Dr. Maurita Murphy Mead, Associate Director for Undergraduate Studies, School of Music, The University of Iowa, 1012 VMB, Iowa City, Iowa 52242; 319-335-1658, fax: 319-335-2637, E-mail address: music-admissions@uiowa.edu.

Graduate Contact Mr. Delbert Disselhorst, Associate Director for Graduate Studies, School of Music, The University of Iowa, 1011 VMB, Iowa City, Iowa 52242; 319-335-1603, fax: 319-335-2637, E-mail address: music-admissions@uiowa.edu.

▼ UNIVERSITY OF KANSAS

Lawrence, Kansas

State-supported, coed. Suburban campus. Total enrollment: 27,567. Music program established 1877.

Degrees Bachelor of Music in the areas of performance, music theory, history, composition, church music; Bachelor of Music Education in the areas of music education, music therapy; Bachelor of Fine Arts in the area of theater-voice. Majors and concentrations: composition, music, music education, music history, music theater, music therapy, piano/organ, sacred music, stringed instruments, voice, wind and percussion instruments. Graduate degrees offered: Master of Music in the areas of performance, musicology, music theory, composition, conducting, church music; Master of Music Education in the areas of music education, music therapy. Doctor of Musical Arts in the areas of performance, composition, conducting, church music; Doctor of Philosophy in the areas of music theory, musicology, music education. Program accredited by NASM.

Enrollment Fall 1997: 523 total; 361 undergraduate, 162 graduate.

Music Student Profile 50% females, 50% males, 5% minorities, 15% international.

Music Faculty 64 total undergraduate and graduate (full-time and part-time). 100% of full-time faculty have terminal degrees. Graduate students teach a few undergraduate courses.

Student Life Student groups/activities include Kappa Kappa Psi, Tau Beta Sigma, Music Educators National Conference Student Chapter.

Expenses for 1997–98 Application fee: $20. State resident tuition: $1965 full-time. Nonresident tuition: $8270 full-time. Mandatory fees: $420 full-time. Full-time tuition and fees vary according to course load. College room and board: $3736. Room and board charges vary according to board plan and housing facility.

Financial Aid Program-specific awards for 1997: 70–80 music scholarships for those demonstrating talent ($950).

Application Procedures Students admitted directly into the professional program freshman year. Deadline for freshmen and transfers: April 1. Required: high school transcript, college transcript(s) for transfer students, letter of recommendation, audition, SAT I or ACT test scores. Auditions held at various times on campus; recorded music is permissible as a substitute for live auditions when distance is prohibitive and videotaped performances are permissible as a substitute for live auditions when distance is prohibitive.

Undergraduate Contact Mr. Roger Stoner, Associate Chairman, Music and Dance Department, University of Kansas, 452 Murphy Hall, Lawrence, Kansas 66045; 913-864-3326, fax: 913-864-5387, E-mail address: rstoner@lark.cc.ukans.edu.

Graduate Contact Ms. Carole Ross, Associate Dean, School of Fine Arts, University of Kansas, 442 Murphy Hall, Lawrence, Kansas 66045; 913-864-3421, fax: 913-864-5387.

▼ UNIVERSITY OF KENTUCKY

Lexington, Kentucky

State-supported, coed. Urban campus. Total enrollment: 23,540. Music program established 1918.

Degrees Bachelor of Music in the areas of performance, music education. Majors and concentrations: music, music education, piano/organ, stringed instruments, voice, wind and percussion instruments. Graduate degrees offered: Master of Music in the areas of performance, music composition, music education; Master of Arts in the areas of musicology, music theory. Doctor of Musical Arts in the areas of performance, composition, conducting; Doctor of Philosophy in the areas of musicology, music theory, music education. Program accredited by NASM.

Enrollment Fall 1997: 386 total; 276 undergraduate, 90 graduate, 20 non-professional degree.

Music Student Profile 53% females, 47% males, 7% minorities, 2% international.

Music Faculty 44 total undergraduate and graduate (full-time and part-time). 53% of full-time faculty have terminal degrees. Graduate students teach about a quarter undergraduate courses. Undergraduate student–faculty ratio: 8:1.

Student Life Student groups/activities include Music Educators National Conference Student Chapter, Percussive Arts Society Student Chapter, music fraternities and sororities.

Expenses for 1997–98 Application fee: $20. State resident tuition: $2400 full-time. Nonresident tuition: $7200 full-time. Mandatory fees: $336 full-time. Full-time tuition and fees vary according to reciprocity agreements. College room and board: $3388. Room and board charges vary according to board plan and housing facility. Special program-related fees: $50 per semester for applied music fee.

Financial Aid Program-specific awards for 1997: 100 grants-in-aid for program majors/minors ($1500–$7500).

Application Procedures Students admitted directly into the professional program freshman year. Deadline for freshmen and transfers: August 1. Notification date for freshmen and transfers: August 23. Required: high school transcript, college transcript(s) for transfer students, minimum 2.0 high school GPA, audition, SAT I or ACT test scores. Recommended: letter of recommendation, interview. Auditions held 3 times on campus; recorded music is permissible as a substitute for live auditions if a campus visit is impossible and videotaped performances are permissible as a substitute for live auditions if a campus visit is impossible.

Web Site http://www.uky.edu/FineArts/Music.

Undergraduate Contact Director of Undergraduate Studies, School of Music, University of Kentucky, 105 Fine Arts Building, Lexington, Kentucky 40506-0022; 606-257-8181.

Graduate Contact Director of Graduate Studies, School of Music, University of Kentucky, 105 Fine Arts Building, Lexington, Kentucky 40506-0022; 606-257-8181, fax: 606-323-1050.

▼ UNIVERSITY OF LOUISVILLE

Louisville, Kentucky

State-supported, coed. Urban campus. Total enrollment: 20,283.

Degrees Bachelor of Music in the areas of performance, music history, music theory, composition, music education. Majors and concentrations: music education, music performance, piano/organ, stringed instruments, voice, wind and percussion instruments. Graduate degrees offered: Master of Music in the areas of performance, music history, music theory/composition; Master of Music Education in the areas of instrumental music education, vocal music education; Master of Arts in Teaching in the areas of instrumental music education, vocal music education. Cross-registration with Metroversity. Program accredited by NASM.

Enrollment Fall 1997: 370 total; 245 undergraduate, 80 graduate, 45 non-professional degree.

Music Student Profile 50% females, 50% males, 5% minorities, 2% international.

Music Faculty 49 total undergraduate and graduate (full-time and part-time). 70% of full-time faculty have terminal degrees. Graduate students teach a few undergraduate courses. Undergraduate student–faculty ratio: 9:1.

Student Life Student groups/activities include Music Educators National Conference Student Chapter, International Trumpet Guild, American Musicological Society.

University of Louisville *(continued)*

Expenses for 1997–98 Application fee: $25. State resident tuition: $2400 full-time. Nonresident tuition: $7200 full-time. Mandatory fees: $230 full-time. College room and board: $4982. College room only: $2338. Room and board charges vary according to board plan and housing facility.

Financial Aid Program-specific awards for 1997: 1 Sister Cities Award for program majors ($9000), 1 Presser Award for academically qualified applicants ($2100), 1 Babb Award for composition majors ($2000), 30 Performance Awards for music majors ($2500).

Application Procedures Students admitted directly into the professional program freshman year. Deadline for freshmen and transfers: continuous. Required: high school transcript, college transcript(s) for transfer students, 3 letters of recommendation, audition, SAT I or ACT test scores (minimum combined ACT score of 20), minimum 2.75 high school GPA. Recommended: interview. Auditions held 6 times on campus; recorded music is permissible as a substitute for live auditions when distance is prohibitive and videotaped performances are permissible as a substitute for live auditions when distance is prohibitive.

Undergraduate Contact Ms. Linda Smith, Admissions Coordinator, Admissions Office, University of Louisville, Louisville, Kentucky 40292; 502-852-1623, fax: 502-852-0520, E-mail address: lwsmit01@ulkyvm.louisville.edu.

Graduate Contact Dr. Jean Christensen, Director of Graduate Studies, School of Music, University of Louisville, Louisville, Kentucky 40292; 502-852-6907, fax: 502-852-0520, E-mail address: jmchri01@ulkyvm.louisville.edu.

▼ UNIVERSITY OF MAINE

Orono, Maine

State-supported, coed. Small town campus. Total enrollment: 8,917.

Degrees Bachelor of Music in the areas of classical vocal performance, classical instrumental performance, classical keyboard performance; Bachelor of Music Education in the areas of classical vocal performance, classical instrumental performance, classical keyboard performance. Majors and concentrations: classical music, music, music education, piano/organ, stringed instruments, voice, wind and percussion instruments. Graduate degrees offered: Master of Music in the areas of performance, music education, instrumental conducting, choral conducting; Master of Music Education in the areas of voice music education, instrumental music education, keyboard music education. Program accredited by NASM.

Enrollment Fall 1997: 92 undergraduate, 13 graduate.

Music Student Profile 1% international.

Music Faculty 22 total undergraduate and graduate (full-time and part-time). 43% of full-time faculty have terminal degrees. Graduate students teach a few undergraduate courses. Undergraduate student–faculty ratio: 4:1.

Expenses for 1997–98 Application fee: $25. State resident tuition: $3750 full-time. Nonresident tuition: $10,620 full-time. Mandatory fees: $594 full-time. Full-time tuition and fees vary according to course load and reciprocity agreements. College room and board: $4906. College room only: $2452. Room and board charges vary according to board

plan and housing facility. Special program-related fees: $30 for applied music lesson fee, $180 for applied music lesson fee (non-music majors).

Application Procedures Students admitted directly into the professional program freshman year. Deadline for freshmen: February 1; transfers: March 1. Notification date for transfers: continuous. Required: high school transcript, college transcript(s) for transfer students, letter of recommendation, audition, SAT I test score only. Recommended: essay. Auditions held continuously on campus; recorded music is permissible as a substitute for live auditions if of good quality and videotaped performances are permissible as a substitute for live auditions if of good quality.

Web Site http://www.ume.maine.edu/~spa/.

Undergraduate Contact Ms. Diane Roscetti, Director, Division of Music, University of Maine, 5788 Class of 1944 Hall, Orono, Maine 04469-5788; 207-581-4700, fax: 207-581-4701, E-mail address: roscetti@maine.maine.edu.

Graduate Contact Dr. Dennis Cox, Professor of Music, Division of Music, University of Maine, 5788 Class of 1944 Hall, Orono, Maine 04469-5788; 207-581-1245, fax: 207-581-4701, E-mail address: dkcox@maine.maine.edu.

▼ UNIVERSITY OF MARYLAND, COLLEGE PARK

College Park, Maryland

State-supported, coed. Suburban campus. Total enrollment: 32,711. Music program established 1964.

Degrees Bachelor of Music in the areas of theory, composition, music performance; Bachelor of Science in the area of music education; Bachelor of Arts in the area of performance. Majors and concentrations: choral music education, composition, instrumental music education, piano, stringed instruments, voice, wind and percussion instruments. Graduate degrees offered: Master of Music in the areas of performance, theory/composition, musicology, ethnomusicology, music education. Doctor of Musical Arts in the area of performance; Doctor of Philosophy in the areas of musicology, ethnomusicology, theory. Cross-registration with University of Maryland System. Program accredited by NASM.

Enrollment Fall 1997: 416 total; 178 undergraduate, 238 graduate.

Music Student Profile 53% females, 47% males, 10% minorities, 18% international.

Music Faculty 66 total undergraduate and graduate (full-time and part-time). 60% of full-time faculty have terminal degrees. Graduate students teach a few undergraduate courses. Undergraduate student–faculty ratio: 4:1.

Student Life Student groups/activities include Phi Mu Alpha, Sigma Alpha Iota, Pi Kappa Lambda.

Expenses for 1997–98 Application fee: $45, $65 for international students. State resident tuition: $3744 full-time. Nonresident tuition: $9873 full-time. Mandatory fees: $716 full-time. College room and board: $5667. College room only: $3218. Room and board charges vary according to board plan. Special program-related fees: $200 per semester for supplement to private music instruction.

Financial Aid Program-specific awards for 1997: 30 Creative and Performing Arts Scholarships for program majors ($2500–$5000), 35 Director's Scholarships for program majors ($1000–$6000).

Application Procedures Students admitted directly into the professional program freshman year. Deadline for freshmen and transfers: March 1. Notification date for freshmen and transfers: April 1. Required: essay, high school transcript, college transcript(s) for transfer students, minimum 3.0 high school GPA, letter of recommendation, audition, SAT I or ACT test scores (minimum combined SAT I score of 1140), portfolio for composition applicants. Recommended: interview, record of co-curricular activities. Auditions held 6 times on campus; recorded music is permissible as a substitute for live auditions when distance is prohibitive (beyond a 250-mile radius) and videotaped performances are permissible as a substitute for live auditions when distance is prohibitive (beyond a 250-mile radius). Portfolio reviews held as needed on campus.

Undergraduate Contact Ms. Kathleen Nicely, Assistant Director for Admissions, School of Music, University of Maryland, College Park, 2105 Tawes Fine Arts Building, College Park, Maryland 20742-9504; 301-405-1313, fax: 301-314-9504, E-mail address: knicely@deans.umd.edu.

Graduate Contact Mr. William Montgomery, Director of Graduate Studies, School of Music, University of Maryland, College Park, Tawes Fine Arts Building, College Park, Maryland 20742-9504; 301-405-5539, fax: 301-314-9504, E-mail address: wm26@umail.umd.edu.

▼ UNIVERSITY OF MASSACHUSETTS AMHERST

Amherst, Massachusetts

State-supported, coed. Small town campus. Total enrollment: 24,884.

Degrees Bachelor of Music in the areas of African-American music and jazz, music history, music education, performance, music theory/composition. Majors and concentrations: composition, jazz, music education, music history, music theory, piano/organ, stringed instruments, voice, wind and percussion instruments. Graduate degrees offered: Master of Music in the areas of piano accompanying, composition, music education, musicology, jazz composition and arranging, music theory, performance, choral conducting. Doctor of Philosophy in the areas of music theory, music education. Cross-registration with Amherst College, Hampshire College, Mount Holyoke College, Smith College. Program accredited by NASM.

Enrollment Fall 1997: 266 total; 189 undergraduate, 60 graduate, 17 non-professional degree.

Music Student Profile 43% females, 57% males, 6% minorities, 17% international.

Music Faculty 45 total undergraduate and graduate (full-time and part-time). 98% of full-time faculty have terminal degrees. Graduate students teach a few undergraduate courses. Undergraduate student–faculty ratio: 5:1.

Student Life Student groups/activities include Music Educators National Conference Student Chapter, Kappa Kappa Psi, Tau Beta Sigma.

Expenses for 1997–98 Application fee: $25, $40 for nonresidents. One-time mandatory fee: $143. State resident tuition: $2004 full-time. Nonresident tuition: $9017 full-time. Mandatory fees: $3568 full-time. Full-time tuition and fees vary according to reciprocity agreements. College room and board: $4520. Room and board charges vary according to board plan and student level.

Financial Aid Program-specific awards for 1997: 80 Chancellor's Talent Awards for program majors ($2725), 25 Alumni Scholarships for program majors ($330).

Application Procedures Students admitted directly into the professional program freshman year. Deadline for freshmen: February 15; transfers: April 1. Notification date for freshmen: May 1; transfers: June 15. Required: essay, high school transcript, college transcript(s) for transfer students, audition, SAT I test score only (minimum combined SAT I score of 1000). Auditions held 5 times and by request on campus; recorded music is permissible as a substitute for live auditions when distance is prohibitive and videotaped performances are permissible as a substitute for live auditions when distance is prohibitive.

Undergraduate Contact Auditions Coordinator, Department of Music and Dance, University of Massachusetts Amherst, 273 Fine Arts Center, Box 32520, Amherst, Massachusetts 01003-2520, 2520; 413-545-6048, fax: 413-545-2092.

Graduate Contact Ms. Miriam Whaples, Graduate Program Director, Department of Music and Dance, University of Massachusetts Amherst, 273 Fine Arts Center, Box 32520, Amherst, Massachusetts 01003-2520, 2520; 413-545-4313, fax: 413-545-2092.

▼ THE UNIVERSITY OF MEMPHIS

Memphis, Tennessee

State-supported, coed. Urban campus. Total enrollment: 19,851.

Degrees Bachelor of Music in the areas of performance, composition, music history, music education, sacred music, music business, recording technology, jazz/studio performance, jazz/studio composition and arranging. Majors and concentrations: composition, jazz, music business, music education, music history, performance, sacred music, sound recording technology. Graduate degrees offered: Master of Music in the areas of performance, sacred music, music history, Orff-Schulwerk, pedagogy, music education, jazz, studio music. Doctor of Musical Arts in the areas of composition, performance, sacred music, music education. Program accredited by NASM.

Enrollment Fall 1997: 525 total; 350 undergraduate, 165 graduate, 10 non-professional degree.

Music Student Profile 55% females, 45% males, 20% minorities, 5% international.

Music Faculty 63 total undergraduate and graduate (full-time and part-time). 80% of full-time faculty have terminal degrees. Graduate students teach a few undergraduate courses. Undergraduate student–faculty ratio: 10:1.

Student Life Student groups/activities include Music Educators National Conference Student Chapter, Phi Mu Alpha, American String Teachers Association Student Chapter.

Expenses for 1997–98 Application fee: $10. State resident tuition: $2344 full-time. Nonresident tuition: $6940 full-time. Mandatory fees: $68 full-time. College room and board: $3500. Special program-related fees: $90 per 1 hour lesson for applied lessons fee.

Financial Aid Program-specific awards available.

Application Procedures Students admitted directly into the professional program freshman year. Deadline for freshmen and transfers: August 1. Required: high school transcript, college transcript(s) for transfer students, audition, SAT I or ACT test scores (minimum combined SAT I score of 930, minimum combined ACT score of 20). Auditions held

The University of Memphis (continued)

continuously by appointment on campus; recorded music is permissible as a substitute for live auditions when distance is prohibitive and videotaped performances are permissible as a substitute for live auditions when distance is prohibitive.

Undergraduate Contact Dr. B. Glenn Chandler, Chair, Department of Music, The University of Memphis, 3775 Central Avenue, Memphis, Tennessee 38152; 901-678-3764, fax: 901-678-3096, E-mail address: bgchandler@cc.memphis.edu.

Graduate Contact Dr. John W. Baur, Associate Chair, Department of Music, The University of Memphis, 3775 Central Avenue, Memphis, Tennessee 38152; 901-678-3764, fax: 901-678-3096, E-mail address: jbaur@cc.memphis.edu.

▼ UNIVERSITY OF MIAMI

Coral Gables, Florida

Independent, coed. Suburban campus. Total enrollment: 13,651. Music program established 1926.

Degrees Bachelor of Music in the areas of composition, music education, music engineering technology, music business and entertainment industries, music therapy, musical theater, performance, studio music and jazz. Graduate degrees offered: Master of Music in the areas of accompanying/chamber music, conducting, electronic music, performance/pedagogy (jazz, keyboard), media writing/production, music education, theory/composition, music therapy, music business and entertainment industries, musicology, studio jazz writing; Master of Science in the area of music engineering. Doctor of Musical Arts in the areas of accompanying and chamber music, composition, jazz composition, conducting, keyboard performance and pedagogy, performance, jazz performance. Program accredited by NASM.

Enrollment Fall 1997: 699 total; 474 undergraduate, 225 graduate.

Music Student Profile 40% females, 60% males, 32% minorities, 13% international.

Music Faculty 114 total undergraduate and graduate (full-time and part-time). 80% of full-time faculty have terminal degrees. Graduate students teach a few undergraduate courses. Undergraduate student–faculty ratio: 7:1.

Student Life Student groups/activities include Phi Mu Alpha Sinfonia, Sigma Alpha Iota, Pi Kappa Lambda.

Expenses for 1997–98 Application fee: $40. Comprehensive fee: $26,864 includes full-time tuition ($19,140), mandatory fees ($372), and college room and board ($7352). College room only: $4194. Room and board charges vary according to board plan and housing facility.

Financial Aid Program-specific awards for 1997: 150 music scholarships for those demonstrating talent ($2000–$20,000), 75 academic scholarships for those demonstrating academic talent ($6700–$15,000), need-based grants, loans for those demonstrating need ($2000–$15,000).

Application Procedures Students admitted directly into the professional program freshman year. Deadline for freshmen and transfers: March 1. Notification date for freshmen and transfers: April 1. Required: essay, high school transcript, college transcript(s) for transfer students, letter of recommendation, audition, SAT I or ACT test scores. Recommended: minimum 3.0 high school GPA. Auditions held 4 times on campus and off campus in Atlanta, GA; Boston, MA; Charlotte, NC; Chicago, IL; Columbus, OH; Dallas, TX; Houston, TX; Interlochen, MI; Los Angeles, CA; New York,

NY; Philadelphia, PA; San Diego, CA; San Francisco, CA; Washington, DC; Hong Kong; Kuala Lumpur, Malaysia; Penang, Malaysia; Seoul, South Korea; Singapore; Taipei, Taiwan; Tokyo, Japan; recorded music is permissible as a substitute for live auditions when distance is prohibitive and videotaped performances are permissible as a substitute for live auditions for musical theater students.

Web Site http://www.music.miami.edu.

Undergraduate Contact Mr. Kenneth J. Moses, Director of Admission, School of Music, University of Miami, PO Box 248165, Coral Gables, Florida 33124; 305-284-2245, fax: 305-284-6475, E-mail address: kmoses@miami.edu.

Graduate Contact Dr. J. David Boyle, Associate Dean, School of Music, University of Miami, PO Box 248165, Coral Gables, Florida 33124; 305-284-2446, fax: 305-284-6475, E-mail address: dboyle@miami.edu.

More About the University

Facilities The music complex includes a 600-seat concert hall and 150-seat recital hall, 3 rehearsal halls, 2 state-of-the-art recording studios, 2 computer/MIDI keyboard labs, music library, instructional studios, practice rooms, and classrooms.

Faculty and Alumni There are more than 114 faculty members. Faculty members perform with the Florida Philharmonic, Florida Grand Opera, Miami City Ballet Orchestra, the Naples Philharmonic, and various jazz ensembles. Academic faculty members are widely published and recognized in their various fields. Alumni include Grammy winners Bruce Hornsby and Jon Secada; opera star Marvis Martin; assistant conductor of the Philadelphia Orchestra, Andre Raphel Smith; television star Dawnn Lewis; Keith Buterbaugh, Raoul in "Phantom of the Opera;" Gary Fry, arranger and producer of more than 1,800 commercials; Sam Pilafian, founder of the Empire Brass Quintet and Travelin' Light; and Matt Pierson, Senior Vice President/General Manager Jazz for Warner Brothers Records.

Performance The School of Music serves as a major cultural resource for the Greater Miami area, presenting more than 300 musical events annually. Complementing on-campus recitals and concerts by students and faculty are programs by guest artists, composers, conductors, and lecturers from virtually every corner of the world. Festival Miami, a monthlong international music festival held each fall, typically features performances by an array of faculty and guest artists, student ensembles, composers, and conductors, including many premiere performances of new compositions. Several of the School's more than 50 ensembles have performed in tours around the United States and the world.

▼

Each year, students from across the United States and more than two dozen countries pursue undergraduate and graduate study at the University of Miami School of Music. The School enjoys a reputation as a comprehensive and innovative music school, with more than 3 dozen degree, certificate, diploma, and international exchange program options available.

Since its founding in 1926 and accreditation in 1939 by the National Association of Schools of Music, the UM School of Music has become one of the largest schools of its kind in a private institution of higher learning in the United States. The School pioneered innovative programs in music industry, music engineering, and studio music and jazz. Since its inception, strong programs in composition/theory, performance, and music education have been a part of the curriculum. Flexible, well-rounded music instruction, designed to give graduates a professional edge, remains a hallmark of the School.

More than 58 full-time faculty members and 56 adjunct faculty members are active in the classroom and as dedicated music professionals. The diverse nature of the programs in the School of Music has attracted a faculty with a broad outlook in its approach to music education who imparts and encourages diversity in the music classroom.

Students choosing the UM School of Music are focused and serious about their studies and are eager for the academic and performance opportunities available to them at UM. The low ratio of students to faculty fosters close academic bonding. Every music student enjoys one-on-one studio instruction.

Many of the more than 4,000 students who have graduated from the UM School of Music have distinguished themselves professionally. Alumni provide a veritable "Who's Who" of both performance and related musical careers. UM graduates perform with major orchestras, operas, and jazz ensembles. Their compositions range from orchestral and operatic music to film and video scores. Some graduates are among the top solo performing artists in the country; others excel as arrangers, recording engineers, editors, therapists, teachers, publishers, distributors, and retailers.

The School of Music is situated on the University's Coral Gables campus, minutes away from the city of Miami, where students enjoy a delightful climate that lends itself to a myriad of activities. All the cultural advantages of a metropolitan center are available to UM music students. In addition to being the home of the Florida Philharmonic Orchestra, the New World Symphony, and the Florida Grand Opera, the Miami area is regularly included in concert tours of major symphonies, concert artists, jazz performers, and opera companies. Music students are able to participate in master classes given frequently by visiting artists performing in the greater Miami area.

▼ UNIVERSITY OF MICHIGAN

Ann Arbor, Michigan

State-supported, coed. Suburban campus. Total enrollment: 36,995. Music program established 1880.

Degrees Bachelor of Music in the areas of composition, music and technology, music education, music history, music theory, performance; Bachelor of Fine Arts in the areas of musical theater, performing arts technology, jazz and improvisational studies; Bachelor of Musical Arts in the areas of composition, jazz studies, music history, music theory, performance. Majors and concentrations: composition, jazz, music education, music history, music technology, music theater, music theory, piano/organ, stringed instruments, voice, wind and percussion instruments. Graduate degrees offered: Master of Music in the areas of arts administration, church music, composition, conducting, improvisation, music theory, piano pedagogy, performance, accompanying, chamber music, early keyboard instruments, music education. Doctor of Musical Arts in the areas of composition, conducting, performance. Program accredited by NASM.

Enrollment Fall 1997: 942 total; 644 undergraduate, 298 graduate.

Music Student Profile 52% females, 48% males, 15% minorities, 7% international.

Music Faculty 134 total undergraduate and graduate (full-time and part-time). 100% of full-time faculty have terminal degrees. Graduate students teach a few undergraduate courses. Undergraduate student–faculty ratio: 16:1.

Student Life Student groups/activities include Music Educators National Conference, Pi Kappa Lambda, Sigma Alpha Iota/Phi Mu Alpha.

Expenses for 1997–98 Application fee: $40. State resident tuition: $5694 full-time. Nonresident tuition: $18,260 full-time. Mandatory fees: $184 full-time. Full-time tuition and fees vary according to program and student level. College room and board: $5342. Room and board charges vary according to board plan and housing facility.

Financial Aid Program-specific awards for 1997: 120 Merit Awards for program students ($4962).

Application Procedures Students admitted directly into the professional program freshman year. Deadline for freshmen and transfers: continuous. Required: essay, high school transcript, college transcript(s) for transfer students, minimum 3.0 high school GPA, letter of recommendation, audition, SAT I or ACT test scores, portfolio for composition and performing arts technology students, interview for music education students. Auditions held 12 times on campus and off campus in New York, NY; Interlochen, MI; Los Angeles, CA; Seattle, WA; recorded music is permissible as a substitute for live auditions when distance is prohibitive and videotaped performances are permissible as a substitute for live auditions when distance is prohibitive. Portfolio reviews held continuously on campus.

Web Site http://www.music.umich.edu.

Contact Ms. Laura Strozeski, Senior Admissions Counselor, School of Music, University of Michigan, 1100 Baits Drive, Ann Arbor, Michigan 48109-2085; 734-764-0593, fax: 734-763-5097, E-mail address: music.admissions@umich.edu.

University of Michigan School of Music

More About the University

Program Facilities Performance venues: Hill Auditorium (4,200 seats), Power Center for the Performing Arts (1,400 seats), Rackham Auditorium (1,100 seats), Recital Hall, Lydia Mendelssohn Theatre, Trueblood Theatre, McIntosh Theatre, Blanche Anderson Moore Hall, Pease Studio Theatre (dance). Practice/study rooms: 135 practice rooms with pianos; ten organ practice rooms; special facilities for harp, harpsichord, carillon, and percussion; Rehearsal Hall for ensembles; listening room with ninety stations. The School has a professional-quality Electronic Music Studio, a Micro-

University of Michigan (continued)

computer and Synthesizer Laboratory, and one of the foremost music libraries in the country.

Faculty, Guest Artists, and Alumni Faculty members are performers currently active on the international stage; highly experienced musicians who are former members of major orchestras, opera houses, and dance and theater companies; prize-winning composers; and scholars and theorists who are renowned leaders in their disciplines. Guest artists to visit the school recently include Frederica von Stade, Marilyn Horne, Murray Perahia, Arleen Auger, Isaac Stern, Andre Watts, Ely Ameling, and the Cleveland Orchestra. Well-known alumni include Jessye Norman, Roberta Alexander, George Crumb, Ashley Putnam, Marian Mercer, Bob McGrath, and Michael Maguire.

Student Performance Opportunities Students and faculty members present more than 300 concerts, recitals, and staged performances each year. Student ensembles include the University Symphony, University Philharmonic, and University Chamber Orchestras, University Symphony and University Concert Bands, University Choir and Chamber Choir, Opera Production, Musical Theatre Production, Digital Music Ensemble, Jazz Orchestra, Men's and Women's Glee Clubs, Percussion Ensemble, Creative Arts Orchestra, Javanese Gamelan, Early Music Ensemble, Contemporary Directions Ensemble, and Composers' Forum. Concerts are frequently presented out of town and occasionally on international tours. Many solo and small-ensemble recitals augment these larger performances.

▼

The University of Michigan School of Music, founded in 1880, is one of the oldest and largest schools of music in the United States. *U.S. News & World Report* (March 14, 1994, and March 3, 1997) ranks it among the top four in both its rankings of conservatories and schools of music in this country. The School of Music has consistently received recognition in a variety of such evaluations. A special strength of the University of Michigan is that in addition to the University as a whole, many of its departments, schools, and colleges rank among the top ten in the nation. The School of Music, as a component of a major university, is advantageously positioned to offer its students a strong combination of breadth and depth of both an artistic and intellectual nature. Students in the School of Music benefit from the personal contact possible in a small unit of 900 students while at the same time taking advantage of the many opportunities and resources available at a major research university.

While conservatories address performance training, some university-based schools emphasize the academic aspects of musicianship, and many state universities provide music teacher training, the University of Michigan School of Music seeks to accomplish all three. Like a conservatory, the School offers studio instruction by some of the finest artist-pedagogues as well as plentiful performance opportunities. The Music Theory, Composition, Music History, and Musicology departments have historically been among the nation's best and continue to draw students who are also recruited by Ivy League schools. The School has long been regarded as an important center for the development of music education. For many decades it has been the overriding goal of the faculty at the School of Music to maintain distinction in all three separate but interrelated categories of music instruction.

An extensive array of degree programs enables each student to choose the curriculum that best meets individual interests and career goals. The Bachelor of Music degree offers intensive professional training in music, while the Bachelor of Fine Arts program provides professional training in dance, theater, or musical theater. The Bachelor of Musical Arts degree is designed for music students who want a greater emphasis on the liberal arts. It is also possible for undergraduate students to pursue dual-degree programs with other colleges within the University, such as the College of Engineering or the College of Literature, Science, and the Arts. Although many members of the Michigan faculty are highly active professionally, they all participate in the life of the School and are in every sense a resident faculty. Notable figures in today's musical world come to the School to present lecture-demonstrations, teach master classes, or meet informally with students to expand their contact with major performing artists. The School enjoys extraordinary facilities and the University and Ann Arbor both provide a rich extracurricular environment with an abundance of performance opportunities. Graduates of the School of Music have distinguished themselves in all areas of performance, composition, directing, choreography, scholarship, teaching, and arts administration.

▼ UNIVERSITY OF MICHIGAN–FLINT

Flint, Michigan

State-supported, coed. Urban campus. Total enrollment: 6,488. Music program established 1978.

Degrees Bachelor of Music Education. Program accredited by NASM.

Enrollment Fall 1997: 60 total; 45 undergraduate, 15 non-professional degree.

Music Student Profile 60% females, 40% males, 10% minorities, 10% international.

Music Faculty 20 total (full-time and part-time). 80% of full-time faculty have terminal degrees. Graduate students teach a few undergraduate courses.

Student Life Student groups/activities include Music Educators National Conference Student Chapter.

Expenses for 1997–98 State resident tuition: $3409 full-time. Nonresident tuition: $10,121 full-time. Mandatory fees: $150 full-time. Full-time tuition and fees vary according to program and student level.

Financial Aid Program-specific awards for 1997: 15–20 music awards and scholarships for instrumentalists ($400–$600), 3–4 friends of music scholarship for academically qualified students ($200–$800).

Application Procedures Students admitted directly into the professional program freshman year. Deadline for freshmen and transfers: continuous. Required: high school transcript, audition, SAT I or ACT test scores. Recommended: essay, minimum 3.0 high school GPA, letter of recommendation. Auditions held 4-5 times on campus.

Web Site http://www.flint.umich.edu/.

Undergraduate Contact Dr. Lois Alexander, Chairperson, Art and Music Department, University of Michigan–Flint, 126 CROB, Flint, Michigan 48502; 810-762-3377, fax: 810-762-3687, E-mail address: chumov@flint.umich.edu.

▼ UNIVERSITY OF MINNESOTA, DULUTH

Duluth, Minnesota

State-supported, coed. Suburban campus. Total enrollment: 9,653. Music program established 1942.

Degrees Bachelor of Music in the areas of piano pedagogy, jazz studies, performance, music education, theory-composition. Graduate degrees offered: Master of Music Education. Cross-registration with University of Wisconsin -Superior, College of St. Scholastica. Program accredited by NASM.

Enrollment Fall 1997: 335 total; 110 undergraduate, 25 graduate, 200 non-professional degree.

Music Student Profile 50% females, 50% males, 2% minorities.

Music Faculty 44 total undergraduate and graduate (full-time and part-time). 100% of full-time faculty have terminal degrees. Graduate students do not teach undergraduate courses. Undergraduate student–faculty ratio: 4:1.

Student Life Student groups/activities include Music Educators National Conference, American Choral Directors Association, International Association of Jazz Educators.

Expenses for 1997–98 Application fee: $25. State resident tuition: $3708 full-time. Nonresident tuition: $10,588 full-time. Mandatory fees: $608 full-time. Full-time tuition and fees vary according to course level, course load, reciprocity agreements, and student level. College room and board: $3912. Room and board charges vary according to board plan and housing facility. Special program-related fees: $50–$100 for lesson fees (music majors).

Financial Aid Program-specific awards for 1997: 1 Bernstein Jazz Scholarship for jazz players ($500), 1–3 Comella Scholarships for music education majors ($600), 1–3 Faricy Scholarships for trumpet players ($400), 1–3 Gauger Scholarships for keyboardists ($300), 3 Gendein Scholarships for state residents ($400), 2 Gershgol Scholarships for program majors ($800), 1–2 Oreck Scholarships for program majors ($500), 8 Gregg Johnson Scholarships for program majors ($400), 1 Opera Scholarship for voice performance majors ($300).

Application Procedures Students admitted directly into the professional program freshman year. Deadline for freshmen and transfers: continuous. Required: college transcript(s) for transfer students, interview, audition, SAT I or ACT test scores. Auditions held 3 times and by request on campus; recorded music is permissible as a substitute for live auditions when distance is prohibitive and videotaped performances are permissible as a substitute for live auditions when distance is prohibitive.

Undergraduate Contact Dr. Mark Whitlock, Chair, Scholarship Committee, Department of Music, University of Minnesota, Duluth, 231 H, 10 University Drive, Duluth, Minnesota 55812; 218-726-6124, fax: 218-726-8210, E-mail address: mwhitloc@d.umn.edu.

Graduate Contact Dr. Judith Kritzmire, Head, Department of Music, and Director of Graduate Studies, University of Minnesota, Duluth, 231 H, 10 University Drive, Duluth, Minnesota 55812; 218-726-8260, fax: 218-726-8210, E-mail address: jkritzmi@d.umn.edu.

▼ UNIVERSITY OF MINNESOTA, TWIN CITIES CAMPUS

Minneapolis, Minnesota

State-supported, coed. Urban campus. Total enrollment: 45,410. Music program established 1902.

Degrees Bachelor of Music in the areas of performance, music education, music therapy, jazz studies. Majors and concentrations: jazz, music education, music therapy, piano/organ, stringed instruments, voice, wind and percussion instruments. Graduate degrees offered: Master of Music in the areas of performance, piano pedagogy, choral conducting, orchestral conducting, wind/band conducting, accompanying/coaching. Doctor of Musical Arts in the areas of performance, orchestral conducting, accompanying/coaching. Program accredited by NASM.

Enrollment Fall 1997: 519 total; 290 undergraduate, 229 graduate.

Music Student Profile 60% females, 40% males, 10% minorities, 14% international.

Music Faculty 80 total undergraduate and graduate (full-time and part-time). 80% of full-time faculty have terminal degrees. Graduate students teach a few undergraduate courses.

Student Life Student groups/activities include Music Educators National Conference, Music Therapy Club, music fraternities and sororities.

Expenses for 1997–98 Application fee: $25. State resident tuition: $3976 full-time. Nonresident tuition: $11,378 full-time. Mandatory fees: $474 full-time. Full-time tuition and fees vary according to program, reciprocity agreements, and student level. College room and board: $4311. Room and board charges vary according to board plan, housing facility, and location. Special program-related fees: $60–$122 for applied music lessons, $22–$44 for practice rooms.

Financial Aid Program-specific awards for 1997: 75–100 School of Music Scholarships for exceptional talent ($500–$3500).

Application Procedures Students admitted directly into the professional program freshman year. Deadline for freshmen and transfers: continuous. Notification date for freshmen and transfers: continuous. Required: high school transcript, college transcript(s) for transfer students, audition, SAT I or ACT test scores, minimum 2.5 college GPA for transfer students. Recommended: 2 letters of recommendation. Auditions held 6 times on campus; recorded music is permissible as a substitute for live auditions when distance is prohibitive.

Web Site http://www.music.umn.edu.

Undergraduate Contact Mr. Rodney Loeffler, Assistant Director, School of Music, University of Minnesota, Twin Cities Campus, 2106 4th Street South, Minneapolis, Minnesota 55455; 612-624-4028, fax: 612-626-2200, E-mail address: loeff001@maroon.tc.umn.edu.

Graduate Contact Ms. Becky Drasin, Graduate Student Services, School of Music, University of Minnesota, Twin Cities Campus, 2106 4th Street South, Minneapolis, Minnesota 55455; 612-624-0071, fax: 612-626-2200, E-mail address: drasi001@tc.umn.edu.

▼ UNIVERSITY OF MISSISSIPPI

University, Mississippi

State-supported, coed. Small town campus. Total enrollment: 11,179.

Degrees Bachelor of Music in the areas of performance, music theory, instrumental music education, vocal music education. Majors and concentrations: classical music, music education, music theory, piano/organ, stringed instruments, voice, wind and percussion instruments. Graduate degrees offered: Master of Music in the areas of performance, music

University of Mississippi *(continued)*

theory, composition, instrumental music education, vocal music education, choral conducting. Doctor of Arts in the areas of music theory, music literature, performance pedagogy, music education. Program accredited by NASM.

Enrollment Fall 1997: 150 total; 110 undergraduate, 40 graduate.

Music Student Profile 40% females, 60% males, 3% minorities, 4% international.

Music Faculty 28 total undergraduate and graduate (full-time and part-time). 97% of full-time faculty have terminal degrees. Graduate students teach a few undergraduate courses. Undergraduate student–faculty ratio: 12:1.

Expenses for 1997–98 Application fee: $25 for nonresidents. State resident tuition: $1996 full-time. Nonresident tuition: $4816 full-time. Mandatory fees: $735 full-time. College room and board: $3186. College room only: $1786. Room and board charges vary according to board plan and housing facility.

Financial Aid Program-specific awards for 1997: 150 band scholarships for wind and percussion players ($1500), 25 Orchestra Scholarships for stringed instrument players ($500–$1500), 75 Chorus Scholarships for vocalists ($500–$1500), 15 Piano Scholarships for pianists ($1000–$2000), 4 Special Scholarships for music majors ($1000–$2000).

Application Procedures Students admitted directly into the professional program freshman year. Deadline for freshmen and transfers: continuous. Required: high school transcript, college transcript(s) for transfer students, minimum 2.0 high school GPA, interview, audition, SAT I or ACT test scores (minimum combined ACT score of 18). Recommended: 2 letters of recommendation. Auditions held by appointment on campus; recorded music is permissible as a substitute for live auditions with special permission and videotaped performances are permissible as a substitute for live auditions with special permission.

Contact Dr. Robert Riggs, Chairman, Music Department, University of Mississippi, 132 Meek Hall, University, Mississippi 38677; 601-232-7268, fax: 601-232-7830.

▼ UNIVERSITY OF MISSOURI–COLUMBIA

Columbia, Missouri

State-supported, coed. Small town campus. Total enrollment: 22,552.

Degrees Bachelor of Music in the areas of piano, strings, winds, percussion, voice, music theory, composition, music education, music history; Bachelor of Science in the area of music education. Majors and concentrations: composition, music education, music history, music theory, piano/organ, stringed instruments, voice, wind and percussion instruments. Graduate degrees offered: Master of Music in the areas of band conducting, choral conducting, orchestra conducting, piano, strings, winds, percussion, voice, music theory, composition, music education; Master of Arts in the area of music history; Master of Education in the area of music education. Doctor of Philosophy in the area of music education. Program accredited by NASM.

Enrollment Fall 1997: 221 total; 140 undergraduate, 48 graduate, 33 non-professional degree.

Music Student Profile 50% females, 50% males, 8% minorities, 5% international.

Music Faculty 37 total undergraduate and graduate (full-time and part-time). 45% of full-time faculty have terminal degrees. Graduate students teach a few undergraduate courses. Undergraduate student–faculty ratio: 5:1.

Student Life Special housing available for music students.

Expenses for 1997–98 Application fee: $25. State resident tuition: $3744 full-time. Nonresident tuition: $11,187 full-time. Mandatory fees: $536 full-time. College room and board: $4290. Room and board charges vary according to board plan and housing facility. Special program-related fees: $120 per semester for applied music fee.

Financial Aid Program-specific awards for 1997: 80 music scholarships for band, orchestra, chorus participants ($200–$2000).

Application Procedures Students admitted directly into the professional program freshman year. Deadline for freshmen and transfers: continuous. Notification date for freshmen and transfers: continuous. Required: high school transcript, minimum 2.0 high school GPA, audition, ACT test score only. Auditions held 9 times on campus and off campus in St. Louis, MO; Kansas City, MO; Springfield, MO; Poplar Bluff, MO; St. Joseph, MO; recorded music is permissible as a substitute for live auditions when distance is prohibitive and videotaped performances are permissible as a substitute for live auditions when distance is prohibitive.

Contact Mr. Dan L. Willett, Director of Graduate and Undergraduate Studies in Music, Department of Music, University of Missouri–Columbia, 138 Fine Arts, Columbia, Missouri 65211; 573-882-0933, E-mail address: musicdw@showme.missouri.edu.

▼ UNIVERSITY OF MISSOURI–KANSAS CITY

Kansas City, Missouri

State-supported, coed. Urban campus. Total enrollment: 10,445. Music program established 1907.

Degrees Bachelor of Music in the areas of composition, instrumental music, music theory, voice, piano pedagogy, music, applied music; Bachelor of Music Education in the areas of music education, music therapy. Majors and concentrations: accordion, composition, guitar, music education, music therapy, piano/organ, stringed instruments, voice, wind and percussion instruments. Graduate degrees offered: Master of Music in the areas of composition, applied music, music theory, voice, conducting; Master of Music Education in the area of music education. Doctor of Musical Arts in the areas of performance, composition, conducting. Program accredited by NASM.

Enrollment Fall 1997: 480 total; 235 undergraduate, 225 graduate, 20 non-professional degree.

Music Student Profile 50% females, 50% males, 10% minorities, 11% international.

Music Faculty 65 total undergraduate and graduate (full-time and part-time). 52% of full-time faculty have terminal degrees. Graduate students teach a few undergraduate courses. Undergraduate student–faculty ratio: 4:1.

Student Life Student groups/activities include Collegiate Music Educators National Conference, Music Therapy Association, American Choral Directors Association.

Expenses for 1997–98 Application fee: $25. State resident tuition: $4278 full-time. Nonresident tuition: $11,721 full-time. College room and board: $4270. Special program-related fees: $123 per semester for applied lesson fee.

Financial Aid Program-specific awards for 1997: music awards for program majors ($200–$5000).

Application Procedures Students admitted directly into the professional program freshman year. Deadline for freshmen and transfers: continuous. Required: high school transcript, audition, ACT score for state residents, SAT I or ACT score for out-of-state residents. Auditions held 6-8 times on campus; recorded music is permissible as a substitute for live auditions for provisional admission and videotaped performances are permissible as a substitute for live auditions for provisional acceptance.

Web Site http://cctr.umkc.edu/dept/conservatory/.

Contact Conservatory Admissions, University of Missouri–Kansas City, Conservatory of Music, 4949 Cherry, Kansas City, Missouri 64110-2229; 816-235-2900, fax: 816-235-5264, E-mail address: cadmissions@cctr.umkc.edu.

▼ UNIVERSITY OF MISSOURI–ST. LOUIS

St. Louis, Missouri

State-supported, coed. Suburban campus. Total enrollment: 15,576. Music program established 1965.

Degrees Bachelor of Music in the areas of music education, performance, music with elective studies in business. Majors and concentrations: music, music and business, music education, piano/organ, stringed instruments, voice, wind and percussion instruments. Graduate degrees offered: Master of Music Education. Program accredited by NASM.

Enrollment Fall 1997: 135 total; 100 undergraduate, 25 graduate, 10 non-professional degree.

Music Student Profile 55% females, 45% males, 8% minorities, 5% international.

Music Faculty 36 total undergraduate and graduate (full-time and part-time). 85% of full-time faculty have terminal degrees. Graduate students do not teach undergraduate courses.

Student Life Student groups/activities include Music Educators National Conference.

Expenses for 1997–98 State resident tuition: $3744 full-time. Nonresident tuition: $11,187 full-time. Mandatory fees: $652 full-time. College room and board: $4845. College room only: $3445. Special program-related fees: $125 per semester for applied music fee.

Financial Aid Program-specific awards for 1997: 35 Music Merit Scholarships for talented students ($1000), 4 UM/St. Louis Symphony Scholarships for minorities ($2000), 1–4 Opera Theatre of St. Louis Scholarships for vocalists ($2000), 7 Buder Foundation Scholarships for percussionists ($2000).

Application Procedures Students admitted directly into the professional program freshman year. Deadline for freshmen and transfers: continuous. Required: high school transcript, college transcript(s) for transfer students, minimum 2.0 high school GPA, audition, SAT I or ACT test scores. Recommended: interview. Auditions held 6 times on campus; recorded music is permissible as a substitute for live auditions when distance is prohibitive and videotaped performances are permissible as a substitute for live auditions when distance is prohibitive.

Web Site http://www.umsl.edu/.

Contact Dr. John Hylton, Chair, Department of Music, University of Missouri–St. Louis, 8001 Natural Bridge Road, St. Louis, Missouri 63121-4499; 314-516-5992, fax: 314-516-6593.

▼ THE UNIVERSITY OF MONTANA–MISSOULA

Missoula, Montana

State-supported, coed. Urban campus. Total enrollment: 12,124.

Degrees Bachelor of Music in the areas of performance, theory, composition, music technology; Bachelor of Music Education. Majors and concentrations: instrumental music, piano/organ, voice. Graduate degrees offered: Master of Music in the areas of performance, music history and literature, theory, technology/composition; Master of Music Education. Program accredited by NASM.

Enrollment Fall 1997: 205 total; 190 undergraduate, 15 graduate.

Music Student Profile 60% females, 40% males, 5% minorities, 5% international.

Music Faculty 25 total undergraduate and graduate (full-time and part-time). 90% of full-time faculty have terminal degrees. Graduate students do not teach undergraduate courses. Undergraduate student–faculty ratio: 15:1.

Student Life Student groups/activities include Collegiate Music Educators National Conference.

Expenses for 1997–98 Application fee: $30. State resident tuition: $2630 full-time. Nonresident tuition: $7192 full-time. Full-time tuition varies according to program and student level. College room and board: $3917. Room and board charges vary according to board plan and housing facility. Special program-related fees: $90 per semester for music fees.

Financial Aid Program-specific awards for 1997: 20 various awards for music majors ($300–$2500).

Application Procedures Students admitted directly into the professional program freshman year. Deadline for freshmen and transfers: July 1. Required: high school transcript, minimum 2.0 high school GPA, SAT I or ACT test scores, audition for voice majors. Recommended: interview. Auditions held by appointment on campus; recorded music is permissible as a substitute for live auditions when distance is prohibitive.

Contact Dr. Thomas H. Cook, Chair, Department of Music, The University of Montana–Missoula, Missoula, Montana 59812-1059; 406-243-6880, fax: 406-243-2441.

▼ UNIVERSITY OF MONTEVALLO

Montevallo, Alabama

State-supported, coed. Small town campus. Total enrollment: 3,125. Music program established 1924.

Degrees Bachelor of Music in the areas of performance, composition; Bachelor of Music Education in the areas of instrumental music education, choral music education. Majors and concentrations: classical music, composition, music, music education, piano/organ, voice, wind and percussion instruments. Graduate degrees offered: Master of Music in the areas of performance, music education. Cross-registration with Samford University, Birmingham-Southern University, University of Alabama at Birmingham, Miles College. Program accredited by NASM.

Enrollment Fall 1997: 127 total; 97 undergraduate, 23 graduate, 7 non-professional degree.

Music Student Profile 50% females, 50% males, 7% minorities.

University of Montevallo (continued)

Music Faculty 31 total undergraduate and graduate (full-time and part-time). 63% of full-time faculty have terminal degrees. Graduate students do not teach undergraduate courses. Undergraduate student–faculty ratio: 4:1.

Expenses for 1997–98 Application fee: $25. State resident tuition: $3040 full-time. Nonresident tuition: $6080 full-time. Mandatory fees: $140 full-time. College room and board: $3116. Room and board charges vary according to board plan and housing facility. Special program-related fees: $50 for applied music fees.

Financial Aid Program-specific awards for 1997: 35 College of Fine Arts Awards for talented students ($1500), 20 music awards for talented students ($750).

Application Procedures Students admitted directly into the professional program freshman year. Deadline for freshmen and transfers: July 29. Required: high school transcript, college transcript(s) for transfer students, minimum 2.0 high school GPA, interview, audition, SAT I or ACT test scores, music theory entrance test, piano placement examination. Recommended: 2 letters of recommendation. Auditions held twice in February and March and by appointment on campus.

Undergraduate Contact Dr. L. Frank McCoy, Chair, Department of Music, University of Montevallo, Station 6663, Montevallo, Alabama 35115; 205-665-6670, fax: 205-665-6676, E-mail address: mccoy@um.montevallo.edu.

Graduate Contact Dr. Robert Bean, Director, Graduate Studies in Music, Department of Music, University of Montevallo, Station 6670, Montevallo, Alabama 35115; 205-665-6673, fax: 205-665-6676, E-mail address: beanr@um.montevallo.edu.

▼ UNIVERSITY OF NEBRASKA AT KEARNEY

Kearney, Nebraska

State-supported, coed. Small town campus. Total enrollment: 7,133.

Degrees Bachelor of Fine Arts in the areas of classical music, music performance, music theater. Majors and concentrations: music, music business, music education, music theater, piano pedagogy, piano/organ, stringed instruments, voice, wind and percussion instruments. Graduate degrees offered: Master of Music Education. Cross-registration with members of the National Student Exchange Program, Nebraska Plains Alliance of Colleges. Program accredited by NASM.

Enrollment Fall 1997: 175 total; 152 undergraduate, 1 graduate, 22 non-professional degree.

Music Student Profile 60% females, 40% males, 2% minorities, 3% international.

Music Faculty 22 total undergraduate and graduate (full-time and part-time). 93% of full-time faculty have terminal degrees. Graduate students do not teach undergraduate courses. Undergraduate student–faculty ratio: 11:1.

Student Life Student groups/activities include Music Educators National Conference, Delta Omicron, Music Teachers National Association.

Expenses for 1997–98 Application fee: $25. One-time mandatory fee: $30. State resident tuition: $1906 full-time. Nonresident tuition: $3570 full-time. Mandatory fees: $363 full-time. Full-time tuition and fees vary according to course load. College room and board: $3034. College room only: $1450. Room and board charges vary according to board

plan, housing facility, and location. Special program-related fees: $20 per semester for practice room fee.

Financial Aid Program-specific awards for 1997: music awards for program majors ($300–$2500).

Application Procedures Students admitted directly into the professional program freshman year. Deadline for freshmen and transfers: continuous. Required: high school transcript, college transcript(s) for transfer students, minimum 2.0 high school GPA, audition, ACT test score only. Recommended: minimum 3.0 high school GPA, 2 letters of recommendation, interview, portfolio. Auditions held 4 times on campus; recorded music is permissible as a substitute for live auditions when distance is prohibitive and for international applicants and videotaped performances are permissible as a substitute for live auditions when distance is prohibitive and for international applicants. Portfolio reviews held twice on campus.

Undergraduate Contact Office of Admissions, University of Nebraska at Kearney, 905 West 25th Street, Kearney, Nebraska 68849; 308-865-8526.

Graduate Contact Ms. Linda Johnson, Coordinator of Graduate Admissions, Office of Graduate Studies and Research, University of Nebraska at Kearney, 905 West 25th Street, Founders Hall, Room 2131, Kearney, Nebraska 68849; 308-865-8838, fax: 308-865-8837.

▼ UNIVERSITY OF NEBRASKA AT OMAHA

Omaha, Nebraska

State-supported, coed. Urban campus. Total enrollment: 13,710.

Degrees Bachelor of Music in the areas of music education, music performance. Majors and concentrations: classical music, music, music education, piano/organ, stringed instruments, voice, wind and percussion instruments. Graduate degrees offered: Master of Music in the areas of music education, music performance. Cross-registration with University of Nebraska System. Program accredited by NASM.

Enrollment Fall 1997: 150 undergraduate, 45 graduate.

Music Student Profile 52% females, 48% males, 17% minorities, 6% international.

Music Faculty 39 total undergraduate and graduate (full-time and part-time). 95% of full-time faculty have terminal degrees. Graduate students teach a few undergraduate courses. Undergraduate student–faculty ratio: 9:1.

Student Life Student groups/activities include Music Educators National Conference, Nebraska State Bandmasters Association, professional sorority and fraternity.

Expenses for 1997–98 Application fee: $25. State resident tuition: $2145 full-time. Nonresident tuition: $5798 full-time. Mandatory fees: $211 full-time. Full-time tuition and fees vary according to course load and program. Special program-related fees: $15 for facilities fee.

Financial Aid Program-specific awards for 1997: 30–40 music scholarships for program majors ($200–$4200), 125–150 Ensemble Scholarships for program majors ($100–$800).

Application Procedures Students admitted directly into the professional program freshman year. Deadline for freshmen and transfers: continuous. Required: high school transcript, college transcript(s) for transfer students, audition. Auditions held 5 times on campus; recorded music is permissible as a substitute for live auditions when distance is prohibitive and videotaped performances are permissible as a substitute for live auditions when distance is prohibitive.

Undergraduate Contact Dr. James R. Saker, Chair, Music Department, University of Nebraska at Omaha, Strauss Performing Arts Center, Omaha, Nebraska 68182-0245; 402-554-2251, fax: 402-554-2252.

Graduate Contact Dr. W. Kenton Bales, Chair, Graduate Program Committee, Music Department, University of Nebraska at Omaha, Strauss Performing Arts Center, Omaha, Nebraska 68182-0245; 402-554-3359, fax: 402-554-2252, E-mail address: kbales@unomaha.edu.

▼ UNIVERSITY OF NEBRASKA–LINCOLN

Lincoln, Nebraska

State-supported, coed. Urban campus. Total enrollment: 22,827.

Degrees Bachelor of Music in the area of performance; Bachelor of Music Education. Graduate degrees offered: Master of Music in the areas of music theory, composition, performance, conducting, music education. Doctor of Musical Arts in the areas of performance, composition. Program accredited by NASM.

Enrollment Fall 1997: 220 undergraduate, 75 graduate.

Music Student Profile 51% females, 49% males, 8% minorities, 2% international.

Music Faculty 45 total undergraduate and graduate (full-time and part-time). 100% of full-time faculty have terminal degrees. Graduate students teach a few undergraduate courses. Undergraduate student–faculty ratio: 7:1.

Student Life Student groups/activities include Sigma Alpha Iota, Music Educators National Conference, Mu Phi Epsilon. Special housing available for music students.

Expenses for 1997–98 Application fee: $25. State resident tuition: $2355 full-time. Nonresident tuition: $6398 full-time. Mandatory fees: $474 full-time. Full-time tuition and fees vary according to course load. College room and board: $3700. College room only: $1638. Special program-related fees: $20 per semester for applied fees, $10 per instrument for instrument rental.

Financial Aid Program-specific awards for 1997: 125 Endowed Awards for music majors ($100–$6000).

Application Procedures Students admitted directly into the professional program freshman year. Deadline for freshmen and transfers: July 1. Required: high school transcript, college transcript(s) for transfer students, audition. Recommended: SAT I or ACT test scores. Auditions held 3 times on campus; recorded music is permissible as a substitute for live auditions for out-of-state applicants and videotaped performances are permissible as a substitute for live auditions for out-of-state applicants.

Undergraduate Contact Ms. Rosemary Petruconis, Administrative Assistant for Academic Affairs, School of Music, University of Nebraska–Lincoln, 120 Westbrook Music Building, Lincoln, Nebraska 68588-0100; 402-472-6845, fax: 402-472-8962, E-mail address: rgp@unlinfo.unl.edu.

Graduate Contact Ms. Colleen Nyhoff, Graduate Secretary, School of Music, University of Nebraska–Lincoln, 120 Westbrook Music Building, Lincoln, Nebraska 68588-0100; 402-472-2506, fax: 402-472-8962, E-mail address: cnyhoff@unlinfo.unl.edu.

▼ UNIVERSITY OF NEVADA, LAS VEGAS

Las Vegas, Nevada

State-supported, coed. Urban campus. Total enrollment: 19,249. Music program established 1968.

Degrees Bachelor of Music in the areas of jazz, applied music, composition, music education. Majors and concentrations: classical music, composition, jazz, music education, piano, stringed instruments, voice, wind and percussion instruments. Graduate degrees offered: Master of Music in the areas of performance, theory and composition, music education. Program accredited by NASM.

Enrollment Fall 1997: 290 total; 200 undergraduate, 55 graduate, 35 non-professional degree.

Music Student Profile 55% females, 45% males, 8% minorities, 2% international.

Music Faculty 49 total undergraduate and graduate (full-time and part-time). 50% of full-time faculty have terminal degrees. Graduate students teach a few undergraduate courses.

Student Life Student groups/activities include American Choral Directors Association, Music Educators National Conference.

Expenses for 1997–98 Application fee: $40. State resident tuition: $1596 full-time. Nonresident tuition: $8627 full-time. Mandatory fees: $46 full-time. Full-time tuition and fees vary according to course level, course load, and reciprocity agreements. College room and board: $5300. Room and board charges vary according to board plan. Special program-related fees: $150–$300 per semester for private lessons, $35 per semester for practice room fee.

Financial Aid Program-specific awards for 1997: 30 departmental scholarships for program majors ($500–$6000), 50 band scholarships for band members ($500–$6000), 30 Orchestra Scholarships for orchestra members ($500–$6000).

Application Procedures Students admitted directly into the professional program freshman year. Deadline for freshmen and transfers: July 15. Notification date for freshmen and transfers: September 1. Required: high school transcript, college transcript(s) for transfer students, audition, SAT I or ACT test scores, minimum 2.3 high school GPA. Recommended: interview. Auditions held once and as needed on campus and off campus in Reno, NV; recorded music is permissible as a substitute for live auditions for out-of-state applicants and videotaped performances are permissible as a substitute for live auditions for out-of-state applicants.

Web Site http://www.nscee.edu/unlv/Colleges/Fine_Arts/Music/.

Undergraduate Contact Dr. James Stivers, Associate Chair, Department of Music, University of Nevada, Las Vegas, 4505 South Maryland Parkway, Las Vegas, Nevada 89154-5025; 702-895-3736, fax: 702-895-4239, E-mail address: jstivers@cfpa.nevada.edu.

Graduate Contact Dr. Isabelle Emerson, Graduate Coordinator, Department of Music, University of Nevada, Las Vegas, 4505 South Maryland Parkway, Las Vegas, Nevada 89154-5025; 702-895-3114, fax: 702-895-4239, E-mail address: emerson@cfpa.nevada.edu.

▼ UNIVERSITY OF NEVADA, RENO

Reno, Nevada

State-supported, coed. Urban campus. Total enrollment: 12,442.

University of Nevada, Reno *(continued)*

Degrees Bachelor of Music in the areas of applied music, music education. Graduate degrees offered: Master of Music in the areas of applied music, music education; Master of Arts in the area of music. Program accredited by NASM.

Enrollment Fall 1997: 181 total; 101 undergraduate, 15 graduate, 65 non-professional degree.

Music Student Profile 50% females, 50% males, 3% minorities, 5% international.

Music Faculty 38 total undergraduate and graduate (full-time and part-time). 100% of full-time faculty have terminal degrees. Graduate students teach a few undergraduate courses. Undergraduate student–faculty ratio: 20:1.

Student Life Student groups/activities include Sigma Alpha Iota, Collegiate Music Educators National Conference, Phi Mu Alpha.

Expenses for 1997–98 Application fee: $40. State resident tuition: $1995 full-time. Nonresident tuition: $7430 full-time. Mandatory fees: $114 full-time. Full-time tuition and fees vary according to course load. College room and board: $5095. College room only: $2800. Room and board charges vary according to board plan and housing facility. Special program-related fees: $150 per credit hour for private applied lessons, $25 per course for instrument maintenance.

Financial Aid Program-specific awards for 1997: 144 Barringere Endowment Awards for program students ($800).

Application Procedures Students admitted directly into the professional program freshman year. Deadline for freshmen and transfers: March 1. Required: high school transcript, college transcript(s) for transfer students, SAT I or ACT test scores, minimum 2.5 high school GPA, audition for performance majors and for scholarship consideration. Auditions held twice on campus and off campus in Las Vegas, NV; recorded music is permissible as a substitute for live auditions when distance is prohibitive and videotaped performances are permissible as a substitute for live auditions when distance is prohibitive.

Contact Dr. Michael Cleveland, Chairman, Music Department (226), University of Nevada, Reno, Reno, Nevada 89557; 702-784-6145, fax: 702-784-6896.

▼ UNIVERSITY OF NEW HAMPSHIRE

Durham, New Hampshire

State-supported, coed. Small town campus. Total enrollment: 13,960. Music program established 1923.

Degrees Bachelor of Music in the areas of music education, organ, piano, strings, woodwind, brass, percussion, music theory/composition, voice. Majors and concentrations: music education, music theory and composition, piano/organ, stringed instruments, voice, wind and percussion instruments. Graduate degrees offered: Master of Science in the area of music education. Program accredited by NASM.

Enrollment Fall 1997: 145 total; 70 undergraduate, 15 graduate, 60 non-professional degree.

Music Student Profile 50% females, 50% males, 5% minorities, 3% international.

Music Faculty 38 total undergraduate and graduate (full-time and part-time). 100% of full-time faculty have terminal degrees. Graduate students do not teach undergraduate courses. Undergraduate student–faculty ratio: 7:1.

Student Life Student groups/activities include Music Educators National Conference, Music Teachers National Association.

Expenses for 1997–98 Application fee: $25. State resident tuition: $4600 full-time. Nonresident tuition: $13,460 full-time. Mandatory fees: $1289 full-time. College room and board: $4524. College room only: $2644. Room and board charges vary according to board plan. Special program-related fees: $105 per credit hour for applied music fee.

Financial Aid Program-specific awards for 1997: 50 University Music Scholarships for program students ($4600).

Application Procedures Students admitted directly into the professional program freshman year. Deadline for freshmen: February 1; transfers: March 1. Notification date for freshmen and transfers: May 1. Required: essay, high school transcript, college transcript(s) for transfer students, letter of recommendation, interview, audition, SAT I test score only. Recommended: portfolio for composition applicants. Auditions held 4 times and by appointment on campus; recorded music is permissible as a substitute for live auditions when distance is prohibitive and videotaped performances are permissible as a substitute for live auditions when distance is prohibitive. Portfolio reviews held continuously on campus.

Web Site http://www.unh.edu/music/index.html.

Undergraduate Contact Peggy Vagts, Chairperson, Music Department, University of New Hampshire, PCAC, Durham, New Hampshire 03824; 603-862-2404, fax: 603-862-3155, E-mail address: pav@hopper.unh.edu.

Graduate Contact Mr. Robert Stibler, Graduate Coordinator, Music Department, University of New Hampshire, PCAC, Durham, New Hampshire 03824; 603-862-2404, fax: 603-862-3155.

▼ UNIVERSITY OF NEW MEXICO

Albuquerque, New Mexico

State-supported, coed. Urban campus. Total enrollment: 23,956.

Degrees Bachelor of Music in the areas of performance, music theory; Bachelor of Music Education. Majors and concentrations: classical music, music, music education, opera, piano/organ, stringed instruments, voice, wind and percussion instruments. Graduate degrees offered: Master of Music in the areas of performance, music theory, conducting; Master of Music Education. Program accredited by NASM.

Enrollment Fall 1997: 290 total; 200 undergraduate, 70 graduate, 20 non-professional degree.

Music Student Profile 60% females, 40% males, 10% minorities, 5% international.

Music Faculty 42 total undergraduate and graduate (full-time and part-time). 40% of full-time faculty have terminal degrees. Graduate students teach a few undergraduate courses. Undergraduate student–faculty ratio: 10:1.

Student Life Student groups/activities include Music Educators National Conference, Collegiate Chorale, Jazz Festival.

Expenses for 1997–98 Application fee: $15. State resident tuition: $2165 full-time. Nonresident tuition: $8174 full-time. College room and board: $4119. Room and board charges vary according to board plan and housing facility. Special program-related fees: $10–$50 per course for lab and visiting artists and clinicians fees.

Financial Aid Program-specific awards for 1997: 20 Friends of Music Awards for freshmen ($1800), 7 Music Achievement Awards for program students ($2000), 7 Wind Symphony

Awards for program students ($2000), 6 Jones Scholarships for program students ($1500), 1 Orchestra Scholarship for program students ($1400), 2 Anderson Awards for program students ($1250), 13 University Bands Awards for program students ($1200), 30 individual scholarships for program students ($500–$1000).

Application Procedures Students admitted directly into the professional program freshman year. Deadline for freshmen and transfers: July 24. Notification date for freshmen and transfers: August 24. Required: essay, high school transcript, college transcript(s) for transfer students, minimum 2.0 high school GPA, 3 letters of recommendation, audition. Recommended: interview, video, portfolio for composition majors. Auditions held by request on campus; recorded music is permissible as a substitute for live auditions when distance is prohibitive and videotaped performances are permissible as a substitute for live auditions when distance is prohibitive. Portfolio reviews held by request on campus.

Undergraduate Contact Mr. Keith Lemmons, Undergraduate Advisor, Department of Music, University of New Mexico, Fine Arts Center, Room 1105, Albuquerque, New Mexico 87131-1411; 505-277-4905, fax: 505-277-0708.

Graduate Contact Mr. Karl Hinterbichler, Graduate Coordinator, Department of Music, University of New Mexico, Fine Arts Center, Albuquerque, New Mexico 87131-1411; 505-277-4331, fax: 505-277-0708.

▼ UNIVERSITY OF NORTH ALABAMA

Florence, Alabama

State-supported, coed. Urban campus. Total enrollment: 5,575.

Degrees Bachelor of Music in the area of performance; Bachelor of Music Education in the areas of instrumental music education, vocal/choral music education. Majors and concentrations: music education. Program accredited by NASM.

Enrollment Fall 1997: 154 undergraduate.

Music Student Profile 55% females, 45% males, 5% minorities, 1% international.

Music Faculty 21 total (full-time and part-time). 78% of full-time faculty have terminal degrees. Graduate students do not teach undergraduate courses.

Student Life Student groups/activities include Music Educators National Conference, Kappa Kappa Psi, Tau Beta Sigma.

Expenses for 1997–98 Application fee: $25. State resident tuition: $2064 full-time. Nonresident tuition: $4128 full-time. Mandatory fees: $120 full-time. College room and board: $3260. College room only: $1520. Special program-related fees: $60 per semester for applied music lesson fee.

Financial Aid Program-specific awards for 1997: 135 band scholarships for band members ($200–$800), 5 Choral Scholarships for accompanists ($400), 4 Choral Scholarships for section leaders ($500), 26 Choral Scholarships for chorus members ($250).

Application Procedures Students admitted directly into the professional program freshman year. Deadline for freshmen and transfers: August 5. Notification date for freshmen and transfers: continuous. Required: high school transcript, college transcript(s) for transfer students, minimum 2.0 high school GPA, audition. Auditions held as needed on campus and off campus in Panama City, FL; recorded music is permissible as a substitute for live auditions when distance is prohibitive and videotaped performances are permissible as a substitute for live auditions when distance is prohibitive.

Undergraduate Contact Dr. James Simpson, Chair, Department of Music, University of North Alabama, Box 5040, Florence, Alabama 35632-0001; 256-760-4361, fax: 256-765-4329, E-mail address: jsimpson@unanov.una.edu.

▼ THE UNIVERSITY OF NORTH CAROLINA AT CHAPEL HILL

Chapel Hill, North Carolina

State-supported, coed. Suburban campus. Total enrollment: 24,231.

Degrees Bachelor of Music in the areas of performance, composition. Majors and concentrations: composition, piano/organ, stringed instruments, voice, wind and percussion instruments. Graduate degrees offered: Master of Arts in Teaching in the area of music education. Cross-registration with Duke University.

Enrollment Fall 1997: 97 total; 85 undergraduate, 12 nonprofessional degree.

Music Faculty 50 total undergraduate and graduate (full-time and part-time). 100% of full-time faculty have terminal degrees. Graduate students teach a few undergraduate courses.

Student Life Student groups/activities include Phi Mu Alpha, Sigma Alpha Iota.

Expenses for 1997–98 Application fee: $55. State resident tuition: $1428 full-time. Nonresident tuition: $10,414 full-time. Mandatory fees: $796 full-time. Full-time tuition and fees vary according to program. College room and board: $4760. College room only: $2320. Room and board charges vary according to board plan, housing facility, and location. Special program-related fees: $290 per semester for private lessons, $25 per semester for practice room fees.

Financial Aid Program-specific awards for 1997: 2–3 Richard and Christopher Edward Adler Scholarships for program majors ($750–$1000), 2–6 D. W. Woodward Scholarships for viola players ($500–$1500), 1–2 J. M. Barham Scholarships for program majors ($500), 6–12 Sidney Dowd Scholarships for pianists ($500–$1500), 4 A. J. Fletcher Foundation Scholarships for program majors ($5000), 2–3 Janet and Newton Fischer Scholarships for vocalists ($1000), 1–2 Andy Griffith Fund Scholarships for program majors ($750–$1000), 2–6 Lemuel Sedberry Scholarships for program majors ($500–$750), 1–2 Paisley Scott Scholarships for program majors ($1000), 5–10 Vollmer Scholarships for program majors ($500–$1000).

Application Procedures Students admitted directly into the professional program freshman year. Deadline for freshmen: January 15; transfers: March 1. Notification date for freshmen and transfers: April 15. Required: high school transcript, college transcript(s) for transfer students, minimum 2.0 high school GPA, SAT I or ACT test scores (minimum combined SAT I score of 1150), minimum combined SAT score of 1300 for out-of-state applicants. Recommended: minimum 3.0 high school GPA, audition. Auditions held 3 times on campus; recorded music is permissible as a substitute for live auditions when distance is prohibitive and videotaped performances are permissible as a substitute for live auditions when distance is prohibitive.

Undergraduate Contact Mr. Michael Zenge, Professor, Music Department, The University of North Carolina at Chapel Hill, CB# 3320 Hill Hall, Chapel Hill, North Carolina 27599-3320; 919-962-1039, fax: 919-962-3376.

▼ UNIVERSITY OF NORTH CAROLINA AT CHARLOTTE

Charlotte, North Carolina

State-supported, coed. Urban campus. Total enrollment: 16,511. Music program established 1969.

Degrees Bachelor of Music in the areas of performance, music education. Majors and concentrations: classical music, music education, piano/organ, stringed instruments, voice, wind and percussion instruments. Cross-registration with Charlotte Area Educational Consortium.

Enrollment Fall 1997: 50 undergraduate.

Music Student Profile 50% females, 50% males, 5% international.

Music Faculty 24 total (full-time and part-time). 80% of full-time faculty have terminal degrees. Graduate students do not teach undergraduate courses. Undergraduate student–faculty ratio: 10:1.

Student Life Student groups/activities include Music Educators National Conference.

Expenses for 1997–98 Application fee: $35. State resident tuition: $900 full-time. Nonresident tuition: $8028 full-time. Mandatory fees: $877 full-time. Full-time tuition and fees vary according to course load. College room and board: $3446. Room and board charges vary according to board plan and housing facility. Special program-related fees: $45 for applied music courses.

Financial Aid Program-specific awards for 1997: 20 Music Department Scholarships for music majors ($750), 10 University merit awards for incoming freshmen ($1000), 1 Fleet-Green Jazz Scholarship for freshmen ($250).

Application Procedures Students admitted directly into the professional program freshman year. Deadline for freshmen and transfers: July 1. Required: high school transcript, college transcript(s) for transfer students, minimum 2.0 high school GPA, letter of recommendation, interview, audition, SAT I or ACT test scores, medical history. Auditions held 6 times on campus; recorded music is permissible as a substitute for live auditions when distance is prohibitive and videotaped performances are permissible as a substitute for live auditions when distance is prohibitive.

Web Site http://www.uncc.edu/colleges/arts_and_sciences/music/.

Undergraduate Contact Dr. Royce Lumpkin, Chair, Department of Music, University of North Carolina at Charlotte, Charlotte, North Carolina 28223; 704-547-2472, fax: 704-547-3795, E-mail address: rlumpkin@email.uncc.edu.

▼ UNIVERSITY OF NORTH CAROLINA AT GREENSBORO

Greensboro, North Carolina

State-supported, coed. Urban campus. Total enrollment: 12,308. Music program established 1892.

Degrees Bachelor of Music in the areas of performance, music education, composition. Majors and concentrations: classical music, composition, jazz, music education, music history, piano/organ, stringed instruments, voice, wind and percussion instruments. Graduate degrees offered: Master of Music in the areas of performance, music education, composition, music theory. Doctor of Musical Arts in the area of performance. Cross-registration with Bennett College,

Elon College, Greensboro College, Guilford College, High Point University, Guilford Technical Community College, North Carolina Agricultural and Technical State University. Program accredited by NASM.

Enrollment Fall 1997: 426 total; 271 undergraduate, 120 graduate, 35 non-professional degree.

Music Student Profile 60% females, 40% males, 11% minorities, 1% international.

Music Faculty 46 total undergraduate and graduate (full-time and part-time). 80% of full-time faculty have terminal degrees. Graduate students teach a few undergraduate courses. Undergraduate student–faculty ratio: 6:1.

Student Life Student groups/activities include Collegiate Music Educators National Conference, Phi Mu Alpha Sinfonia, Mu Phi Epsilon.

Expenses for 1997–98 Application fee: $35. State resident tuition: $1016 full-time. Nonresident tuition: $9304 full-time. Mandatory fees: $1015 full-time. College room and board: $3661. College room only: $2011.

Financial Aid Program-specific awards for 1997: 150–175 music scholarships for program students ($200–$4000).

Application Procedures Students admitted directly into the professional program freshman year. Deadline for freshmen and transfers: August 1. Required: high school transcript, college transcript(s) for transfer students, audition, SAT I or ACT test scores, minimum of 15 high school units. Auditions held 5 times and by appointment on campus; recorded music is permissible as a substitute for live auditions when distance is prohibitive, for provisional acceptance and videotaped performances are permissible as a substitute for live auditions when distance is prohibitive, for provisional acceptance.

Web Site http://www.uncg.edu/mus/.

Undergraduate Contact Dr. James Prodan, Associate Dean, School of Music, University of North Carolina at Greensboro, PO Box 26167, Greensboro, North Carolina 27402-6167; 336-334-5789, fax: 336-334-5497, E-mail address: j_prodan@uncg.edu.

Graduate Contact Dr. James Sherbon, Director of Graduate Studies, School of Music, University of North Carolina at Greensboro, PO Box 26167, Greensboro, North Carolina 27402-6167; 336-334-5794, fax: 336-334-5497, E-mail address: sherbonjw@hamlet.uncg.edu.

▼ UNIVERSITY OF NORTH CAROLINA AT PEMBROKE

Pembroke, North Carolina

State-supported, coed. Rural campus. Total enrollment: 3,034.

Degrees Bachelor of Music in the areas of music education, music business. Majors and concentrations: instrumental music education, keyboard, music education, vocal music education. Program accredited by NASM.

Enrollment Fall 1997: 31 total; 20 undergraduate, 11 non-professional degree.

Music Student Profile 42% females, 58% males, 45% minorities.

Music Faculty 15 total (full-time and part-time). 100% of full-time faculty have terminal degrees. Graduate students do not teach undergraduate courses.

Student Life Student groups/activities include Phi Mu Alpha, Sigma Alpha Iota, Music Educators National Conference.

Expenses for 1997–98 Application fee: $25. State resident tuition: $900 full-time. Nonresident tuition: $8028 full-time. Mandatory fees: $636 full-time. College room and board: $2910. Room and board charges vary according to board plan and housing facility.

Financial Aid Program-specific awards for 1997: 5–15 non-majors stipends for freshmen ensemble performers ($300), 10–20 majors scholarships for program majors ($600).

Application Procedures Students admitted directly into the professional program freshman year. Deadline for freshmen and transfers: continuous. Required: high school transcript, college transcript(s) for transfer students, 2 letters of recommendation, interview, audition, SAT I or ACT test scores. Auditions held twice and by arrangement on campus and off campus in various locations; recorded music is permissible as a substitute for live auditions for out-of-state applicants and videotaped performances are permissible as a substitute for live auditions for out-of-state applicants.

Web Site http://www.uncp.edu/music.

Undergraduate Contact Mr. George Walter, Chair, Department of Music, University of North Carolina at Pembroke, PO Box 1510, Pembroke, North Carolina 28372-1510; 910-521-6310, fax: 910-521-6649, E-mail address: gwalt@papa.uncp.edu.

▼ UNIVERSITY OF NORTH DAKOTA

Grand Forks, North Dakota

State-supported, coed. Small town campus. Total enrollment: 10,363. Music program established 1893.

Degrees Bachelor of Music in the areas of performance, music education. Majors and concentrations: music education, piano/organ, stringed instruments, voice, wind and percussion instruments. Graduate degrees offered: Master of Music in the areas of music education, composition, vocal performance, vocal pedagogy, keyboard performance, keyboard pedagogy, instrumental conducting, choral conducting. Program accredited by NASM.

Enrollment Fall 1997: 92 total; 43 undergraduate, 9 graduate, 40 non-professional degree.

Music Student Profile 50% females, 50% males, 2% minorities, 2% international.

Music Faculty 26 total undergraduate and graduate (full-time and part-time). 75% of full-time faculty have terminal degrees. Graduate students teach a few undergraduate courses. Undergraduate student–faculty ratio: 6:1.

Student Life Student groups/activities include Music Educators National Conference, American Choral Directors Association, professional sorority and fraternity.

Expenses for 1997–98 Application fee: $25. State resident tuition: $2677 full-time. Nonresident tuition: $6144 full-time. Mandatory fees: $441 full-time. Full-time tuition and fees vary according to program and reciprocity agreements. College room and board: $3117. College room only: $1216. Room and board charges vary according to board plan and housing facility. Special program-related fees: $50 for applied music fees.

Financial Aid Program-specific awards for 1997: 45 music scholarships for program majors/minors ($250–$1000).

Application Procedures Students admitted directly into the professional program freshman year. Deadline for freshmen and transfers: continuous. Required: high school transcript, college transcript(s) for transfer students, audition, ACT test score only. Auditions held 3 times on campus and off campus in various cities in North Dakota; recorded music is permissible as a substitute for live auditions when distance is prohibitive and videotaped performances are permissible as a substitute for live auditions when distance is prohibitive.

Web Site http://www.und.nodak.edu/dept/fac/m_home.html.

Contact Dr. E. John Miller, Chair, Music Department, University of North Dakota, Box 7125, Grand Forks, North Dakota 58202; 701-777-2644, fax: 701-777-3320, E-mail address: johmille@badlands.nodak.edu.

▼ UNIVERSITY OF NORTHERN COLORADO

Greeley, Colorado

State-supported, coed. Suburban campus. Total enrollment: 11,860. Music program established 1895.

Degrees Bachelor of Music in the areas of instrumental performance, piano, music theory and composition, voice performance; Bachelor of Music Education in the areas of instrumental music education, piano music education, general music education. Majors and concentrations: classical music, music, music education, music history, music theory and composition, piano/organ, stringed instruments, voice, wind and percussion instruments. Graduate degrees offered: Master of Music in the areas of choral conducting, instrumental performance, music history and literature, music theory and composition, wind/orchestral conducting; Master of Music Education. Doctor of Arts in the areas of music, chorale conducting, instrumental performance, music history and literature, music theory and composition, wind/orchestral conducting, music education; Doctor of Music Education. Program accredited by NASM.

Enrollment Fall 1997: 418 total; 358 undergraduate, 50 graduate, 10 non-professional degree.

Music Student Profile 58% females, 42% males, 8% minorities, 10% international.

Music Faculty 43 total undergraduate and graduate (full-time and part-time). 58% of full-time faculty have terminal degrees. Graduate students teach about a quarter undergraduate courses. Undergraduate student–faculty ratio: 9:1.

Student Life Student groups/activities include Kappa Kappa Psi, National Association of Jazz Educators, Collegiate Music Educators National Conference.

Expenses for 1997–98 Application fee: $30. State resident tuition: $1942 full-time. Nonresident tuition: $8710 full-time. Mandatory fees: $636 full-time. College room and board: $4420. College room only: $2160. Special program-related fees: $3 per semester for university technology fee, $20 per semester for music major fee, $10 per course for music technology fee, $10 per course for private lesson fee for non-majors.

Financial Aid Program-specific awards for 1997: 200 Music Talent Awards for program majors ($500), 24 academic scholarships for program majors ($1000).

Application Procedures Students apply for admission into the professional program by sophomore year. Deadline for freshmen and transfers: continuous. Required: high school transcript, interview, audition, SAT I or ACT test scores, minimum 2.8 high school GPA. Auditions held 5 times on campus; recorded music is permissible as a substitute for live auditions when distance is prohibitive and videotaped performances are permissible as a substitute for live auditions for conducting applicants.

Web Site http://arts.unco.edu.

University of Northern Colorado (*continued*)

Undergraduate Contact Dr. Shirley Howell, Director, School of Music, University of Northern Colorado, Frasier 108, Greeley, Colorado 80639; 970-351-2678, fax: 970-351-2679.

Graduate Contact Dr. Robert C. Ehle, Graduate Coordinator, School of Music, University of Northern Colorado, Frasier 108, Greeley, Colorado 80639; 970-351-2678, fax: 970-351-2679.

▼ UNIVERSITY OF NORTHERN IOWA

Cedar Falls, Iowa

State-supported, coed. Small town campus. Total enrollment: 13,503.

Degrees Bachelor of Music in the areas of performance, composition, music education. Majors and concentrations: composition, music education, piano/organ, stringed instruments, voice, wind and percussion instruments. Graduate degrees offered: Master of Music in the areas of music education, performance, music history, conducting, jazz pedagogy, composition, piano performance and pedagogy. Cross-registration with members of the National Student Exchange Program . Program accredited by NASM.

Enrollment Fall 1997: 280 total; 246 undergraduate, 34 graduate.

Music Student Profile 51% females, 49% males, 2% minorities, 6% international.

Music Faculty 43 total undergraduate and graduate (full-time and part-time). 56% of full-time faculty have terminal degrees. Graduate students teach a few undergraduate courses. Undergraduate student–faculty ratio: 6:1.

Student Life Student groups/activities include Music Educators National Conference, American Choral Directors Association.

Expenses for 1997–98 Application fee: $20. State resident tuition: $2566 full-time. Nonresident tuition: $6950 full-time. Mandatory fees: $186 full-time. College room and board: $3452. Special program-related fees: $90–$130 per semester for applied music fee, $15 per semester for instrument rental.

Financial Aid Program-specific awards for 1997: 120 School of Music Scholarship Awards for program majors ($200–$2500).

Application Procedures Students apply for admission into the professional program by freshman year. Deadline for freshmen and transfers: February 14. Required: high school transcript, college transcript(s) for transfer students, audition, SAT I or ACT test scores. Recommended: letter of recommendation, interview. Auditions held 3 times on campus; recorded music is permissible as a substitute for live auditions for out-of-state applicants and videotaped performances are permissible as a substitute for live auditions for out-of-state applicants.

Web Site http://www.uni.edu/music/web.

Undergraduate Contact Dr. Alan Schmitz, Associate Director of Undergraduate Studies, School of Music, University of Northern Iowa, Russell Hall Room 110, Cedar Falls, Iowa 50614-0246; 319-273-2024, fax: 319-273-7320, E-mail address: schmitz@uni.edu.

Graduate Contact Dr. Fred Rees, Associate Director of Graduate Studies, School of Music, University of Northern Iowa, Russell Hall Room 110, Cedar Falls, Iowa 50614-0246; 319-273-2024, fax: 319-273-7320, E-mail address: rees@uni.edu.

▼ UNIVERSITY OF NORTH FLORIDA

Jacksonville, Florida

State-supported, coed. Urban campus. Total enrollment: 11,389. Music program established 1972.

Degrees Bachelor of Music in the areas of jazz, classical music. Majors and concentrations: jazz. Cross-registration with Florida Community College at Jacksonville. Program accredited by NASM.

Enrollment Fall 1997: 145 total; all undergraduate.

Music Student Profile 50% females, 50% males, 8% minorities, 5% international.

Music Faculty 25 total (full-time and part-time). 90% of full-time faculty have terminal degrees. Graduate students do not teach undergraduate courses. Undergraduate student–faculty ratio: 10:1.

Student Life Student groups/activities include International Association of Jazz Educators Student Chapter.

Expenses for 1997–98 Application fee: $20. State resident tuition: $2006 full-time. Nonresident tuition: $7923 full-time. College room and board: $3492. College room only: $2342. Room and board charges vary according to board plan and housing facility.

Financial Aid Program-specific awards for 1997: 65 music scholarships for musically talented students ($1000).

Application Procedures Students admitted directly into the professional program freshman year. Deadline for freshmen and transfers: May 1. Notification date for freshmen and transfers: July 1. Required: high school transcript, college transcript(s) for transfer students, minimum 2.0 high school GPA, audition, SAT I or ACT test scores (minimum combined SAT I score of 1000, minimum combined ACT score of 17). Auditions held twice on campus; recorded music is permissible as a substitute for live auditions when distance is prohibitive and videotaped performances are permissible as a substitute for live auditions when distance is prohibitive.

Undergraduate Contact Dr. Gerson Yessin, Chair, Department of Music, University of North Florida, 4567 St. Johns Bluff Road South, Jacksonville, Florida 32224-2645; 904-620-2960, fax: 904-620-2568.

▼ UNIVERSITY OF NORTH TEXAS

Denton, Texas

State-supported, coed. Urban campus. Total enrollment: 25,013.

Degrees Bachelor of Music in the areas of composition, theory, music history and literature, performance, jazz studies, music education. Majors and concentrations: composition, jazz, music education, music history and literature, music theory, piano/organ, stringed instruments, voice, wind and percussion instruments. Graduate degrees offered: Master of Music in the areas of theory, composition, musicology, jazz studies, conducting, organ, piano, voice, performance, music education. Doctor of Musical Arts in the areas of performance, composition, conducting. Program accredited by NASM.

Enrollment Fall 1997: 1,000 undergraduate, 500 graduate.

Music Faculty 130 total undergraduate and graduate (full-time and part-time). 100% of full-time faculty have terminal degrees. Graduate students teach a few undergraduate courses. Undergraduate student–faculty ratio: 13:1.

Student Life Student groups/activities include Sigma Alpha Iota, Phi Mu Alpha Sinfonia, NT 40.

Expenses for 1997–98 Application fee: $25. State resident tuition: $1666 full-time. Nonresident tuition: $8300 full-time. Mandatory fees: $521 full-time. College room and board: $3842. Special program-related fees: $10–$40 per semester for practice room fee, $10 per semester for instrument rental, $30–$60 per semester for applied lesson fee.

Financial Aid Program-specific awards for 1997: music scholarships for out-of-state students ($200–$2000).

Application Procedures Students admitted directly into the professional program freshman year. Deadline for freshmen and transfers: June 15. Required: high school transcript, college transcript(s) for transfer students, 3 letters of recommendation, audition, SAT I or ACT test scores, taped audition for jazz applicants. Auditions held 3 times on campus and off campus in Chicago, IL; Interlochen, MI; New York, NY; recorded music is permissible as a substitute for live auditions if a live audition is impossible, for provisional acceptance and videotaped performances are permissible as a substitute for live auditions for provisional acceptance.

Web Site http://www.unt.edu.

Undergraduate Contact Ms. Judy Fisher, Undergraduate Advisor, College of Music, University of North Texas, PO Box 311367, Denton, Texas 76203-1367; 940-565-3734, fax: 940-565-2002, E-mail address: fisher@music.unt.edu.

Graduate Contact Ms. Sharon Gale, Administrative Assistant, Graduate Music Office, University of North Texas, PO Box 311367, Denton, Texas 76203-1367; 940-565-3721, fax: 940-565-2002, E-mail address: sgale@music.unt.edu.

▼ UNIVERSITY OF OKLAHOMA

Norman, Oklahoma

State-supported, coed. Suburban campus. Total enrollment: 25,975. Music program established 1898.

Degrees Bachelor of Music in the areas of performance, composition, piano pedagogy; Bachelor of Music Education in the areas of instrumental music education, vocal music education, combined vocal and instrumental music education; Bachelor of Fine Arts in the areas of music, musical theater; Bachelor of Musical Arts. Majors and concentrations: composition, music, music education, music theater, piano/organ, stringed instruments, voice, wind and percussion instruments. Graduate degrees offered: Master of Music in the areas of performance, composition, conducting, music theory, music history, piano pedagogy; Master of Music Education in the areas of instrumental music, vocal music, Kodály, conducting, piano pedagogy. Doctor of Musical Arts in the areas of performance, composition, conducting, piano pedagogy; Doctor of Philosophy in the area of music education. Program accredited by NASM.

Enrollment Fall 1997: 435 total; 295 undergraduate, 140 graduate.

Music Student Profile 52% females, 48% males, 12% minorities, 10% international.

Music Faculty 55 total undergraduate and graduate (full-time and part-time). 95% of full-time faculty have terminal degrees. Graduate students teach a few undergraduate courses. Undergraduate student–faculty ratio: 6:1.

Student Life Student groups/activities include music fraternities and sororities, Music Educators National Conference, Percussive Arts Society.

Expenses for 1997–98 Application fee: $25. State resident tuition: $1745 full-time. Nonresident tuition: $5785 full-time. Mandatory fees: $566 full-time. Full-time tuition and fees vary according to course level, course load, location, program, and reciprocity agreements. College room and board: $3800. College room only: $1884. Room and board charges vary according to board plan, housing facility, and student level. Special program-related fees: $40 for applied music fee, $5–$35 for special course fees.

Financial Aid Program-specific awards for 1997: 75–100 fee/tuition waivers for program majors ($1000–$3000), 20–40 scholarships for program students ($500–$3000).

Application Procedures Students admitted directly into the professional program freshman year. Deadline for freshmen and transfers: continuous. Required: high school transcript, college transcript(s) for transfer students, minimum 2.0 high school GPA, letter of recommendation, audition, SAT I or ACT test scores. Auditions held 3 times on campus; recorded music is permissible as a substitute for live auditions for out-of-state applicants and videotaped performances are permissible as a substitute for live auditions for out-of-state applicants.

Web Site http://www.ou.edu/finearts/.

Undergraduate Contact Undergraduate Admissions, School of Music, University of Oklahoma, 560 Parrington Oval, Norman, Oklahoma 73019; 405-325-2081, fax: 405-325-7574, E-mail address: oumusic@ou.edu.

Graduate Contact Graduate Admissions, School of Music, University of Oklahoma, 560 Parrington Oval, Norman, Oklahoma 73019; 405-325-2081, fax: 405-325-7574, E-mail address: oumusic@ou.edu.

More About the University

Faculty, Guest Artists, and Alumnae Seventeen members of the School of Music faculty perform with the Oklahoma City Philharmonic Orchestra and many perform regularly throughout Europe, Asia, and the Americas. The School of Music has been host to such guest artists as Elly Ameling, Richard Stoltzman, Vladimir Feltsman, Joshua Bell, John Browning, and Harvey Phillips. School of Music graduates enjoy a high placement record at secondary institutions; postsecondary institutions such as the state universities of Kansas, Mississippi, South Carolina, Florida, Oklahoma, Arkansas, and Nebraska; the Cincinnati Conservatory of Music; and institutions abroad. Students have also won positions with symphony orchestras in the United States and with opera companies in the U.S. and Europe. Faculty members and students are featured on CDs and tapes and in Early Music Television videos, while the University of Oklahoma Percussion Press regularly commissions new works for percussion for aspiring and established composers.

Facilities The $20-million Stanley B. Catlett Music Center will celebrate its completion in the fall of 1998. The Catlett Center will be the largest performing arts center in Oklahoma and, along with Holmberg Hall, will house one of the finest sets of electronic and MIDI equipment in the Southwest. The School of Music also houses the Journal of Music Theory Pedagogy—an internationally recognized journal devoted to the teaching of music theory.

▼ UNIVERSITY OF OREGON

Eugene, Oregon

State-supported, coed. Urban campus. Total enrollment: 17,530. Music program established 1886.

University of Oregon *(continued)*

Degrees Bachelor of Music in the areas of music composition, music education, music performance, music theory, jazz studies. Majors and concentrations: composition, jazz, music, music education, music theory, piano/organ, stringed instruments, voice, wind and percussion instruments. Graduate degrees offered: Master of Music in the areas of conducting, piano pedagogy, music composition, music performance, music education, jazz studies; Master of Arts in the areas of music history, music theory. Doctor of Musical Arts in the areas of music composition, music education, music performance; Doctor of Philosophy in the areas of music composition, music education, music history, music theory. Program accredited by NASM.

Enrollment Fall 1997: 461 total; 287 undergraduate, 174 graduate.

Music Student Profile 49% females, 51% males, 10% minorities, 9% international.

Music Faculty 59 total undergraduate and graduate (full-time and part-time). 79% of full-time faculty have terminal degrees. Graduate students teach a few undergraduate courses. Undergraduate student–faculty ratio: 15:1.

Student Life Student groups/activities include Oregon Bach Festival, Martin Luther King Celebration events, Children's Concert Series. Special housing available for music students.

Expenses for 1997–98 Application fee: $50. State resident tuition: $2694 full-time. Nonresident tuition: $11,145 full-time. Mandatory fees: $714 full-time. College room and board: $4646. Special program-related fees: $60–$80 per term for non-majors private lessons, $25 per term for music major fee, $10 per term for music education class instrument fee, $100 per term for group lessons, $10 per term for ensemble fee, $50 per term for synthesizer lab fee, $10 per term for organ, harpsichord, or percussion fee, $10 per term for locked grand piano practice room fee, $5–$50 per term for instrument rental, $5 per term for music locker rental, $50–$200 per term for accompanying fee, $85 per recital for recital and recording fee.

Financial Aid Program-specific awards for 1997: 1 Presser Scholarship for outstanding juniors and seniors ($2200), 1 Corbett Scholarship for Oregon students ($1200), 7 Stauffer Scholarships for male graduates of Oregon high schools ($1000), 3 Mu Phi Epsilon Patron Scholarships for program students ($1000), 1 Phi Beta Patrons (Saunders) Scholarship for pianists ($500), 2 Tuba Scholarships for tuba players ($375), 1 Moore Scholarship for vocalists ($800), 1 Maude Densmore Scholarship for continuing vocalists ($500), 4 Polastri Scholarships for voice majors ($1000), 67 Ruth Lorraine Close Scholarships for music majors ($1500).

Application Procedures Students admitted directly into the professional program freshman year. Deadline for freshmen: June 1; transfers: September 1. Notification date for freshmen and transfers: continuous. Required: high school transcript, college transcript(s) for transfer students, minimum 3.0 high school GPA, audition, SAT I or ACT test scores. Recommended: essay, 3 letters of recommendation. Auditions held 6 times and by appointment on campus and off campus in Portland, OR; recorded music is permissible as a substitute for live auditions when distance is prohibitive and videotaped performances are permissible as a substitute for live auditions when distance is prohibitive.

Web Site http://music1.uoregon.edu/.

Undergraduate Contact Ms. Marilyn Bradetich, Undergraduate Secretary, School of Music, University of Oregon, 1225 University of Oregon, Eugene, Oregon 97403-1225; 541-346-1164, fax: 541-346-0723, E-mail address: mbradeti@oregon. uoregon.edu.

Graduate Contact Ms. JillMichelle Cosart, Graduate Secretary, School of Music, University of Oregon, 1225 University of Oregon, Eugene, Oregon 97403-1225; 541-346-5664, fax: 541-346-0723, E-mail address: jmcosa@oregon.uoregon.edu.

▼ UNIVERSITY OF PORTLAND

Portland, Oregon

Independent-Roman Catholic, coed. Suburban campus. Total enrollment: 2,606.

Degrees Bachelor of Music Education. Graduate degrees offered: Master of Arts in the area of music. Cross-registration with Concordia University and other area universities. Program accredited by NASM.

Enrollment Fall 1997: 25 undergraduate, 10 graduate.

Music Student Profile 56% females, 44% males, 19% minorities.

Music Faculty 19 total undergraduate and graduate (full-time and part-time). 100% of full-time faculty have terminal degrees. Graduate students do not teach undergraduate courses. Undergraduate student–faculty ratio: 6:1.

Student Life Student groups/activities include Collegiate Music Educators National Conference, Music Club.

Expenses for 1997–98 Application fee: $40. Comprehensive fee: $20,230 includes full-time tuition ($15,420), mandatory fees ($100), and college room and board ($4710). Room and board charges vary according to board plan and housing facility. Special program-related fees: $30 per semester for electronic music lab fees.

Financial Aid Program-specific awards for 1997: 1–3 Dean's Scholarships for performers ($1750), 1–3 Vance Scholarships for music education majors ($1750), 10–20 Talent Grants for program majors and minors ($1250).

Application Procedures Students admitted directly into the professional program freshman year. Deadline for freshmen and transfers: continuous. Notification date for freshmen and transfers: continuous. Required: essay, high school transcript, college transcript(s) for transfer students, minimum 2.0 high school GPA, letter of recommendation, audition, SAT I or ACT test scores. Recommended: interview. Auditions held 4 times on campus; recorded music is permissible as a substitute for live auditions when distance is prohibitive or scheduling is difficult and videotaped performances are permissible as a substitute for live auditions if distance is prohibitive or scheduling is difficult.

Web Site http://www.uofport.edu.

Undergraduate Contact Office of Admissions, University of Portland, 5000 North Willamette Boulevard, Portland, Oregon 97203; 503-283-7147, fax: 503-283-7399, E-mail address: reilly@uofport.edu.

Graduate Contact Dr. Kenneth Kleszynski, Graduate Program Director/Music, Performing and Fine Arts Department, University of Portland, 5000 North Willamette Boulevard, Portland, Oregon 97203; 503-283-7294, fax: 503-283-7399, E-mail address: kkleszy@uofport.edu.

▼ UNIVERSITY OF PRINCE EDWARD ISLAND

Charlottetown, PE, Canada

Province-supported, coed. Small town campus. Total enrollment: 2,934.

Degrees Bachelor of Music in the areas of music education, general music. Majors and concentrations: classical music, music, music education, music history, music theory and composition, piano/organ, voice, wind and percussion instruments. Program accredited by CUMS.

Enrollment Fall 1997: 58 undergraduate.

Music Student Profile 57% females, 43% males.

Music Faculty 12 total (full-time and part-time). 100% of full-time faculty have terminal degrees. Graduate students do not teach undergraduate courses. Undergraduate student–faculty ratio: 8:1.

Student Life Student groups/activities include University of Prince Edward Island Music Society.

Expenses for 1997–98 Application fee: $35 Canadian dollars. Tuition, fee, and room and board charges are reported in Canadian dollars. Canadian resident tuition: $3150 full-time. Mandatory fees: $357 full-time. College room and board: $5040. College room only: $2352. International student tuition: $6550 full-time. Special program-related fees: $60 per year for instrument rental, locker, telephone.

Financial Aid Program-specific awards for 1997: 1 Tersteeg Music Scholarship for juniors ($250), 1 Bevan-MacRae Music Award for juniors ($250), 8 Music Alumni Scholarships for freshmen ($200–$750), 2 Music Society Scholarships for sophomores and seniors ($125), 2 Claude and Dr. Bernice Bell Awards for program students ($1000), 1 Elsie Cuthbertson Memorial Music Scholarship for program students ($250), 1 Frances Dindial Memorial Music Scholarship for freshmen ($600), 1 Eleanor Wheler Scholarship for entering students ($1000), 1 Carl Mathis Music Award for voice or horn majors ($250), 1 Reesor Music Award for organ majors ($300).

Application Procedures Students admitted directly into the professional program freshman year. Deadline for freshmen and transfers: August 15. Notification date for freshmen and transfers: August 25. Required: high school transcript, letter of recommendation, interview, audition, music theory test, ear test. Auditions held 5 times on campus; recorded music is permissible as a substitute for live auditions with later audition on campus and videotaped performances are permissible as a substitute for live auditions with later audition on campus.

Undergraduate Contact Ms. Gloria J. Jay, Audition Coordinator, Music Department, University of Prince Edward Island, 550 University Avenue, Charlottetown, PE C1A 4P3, Canada; 902-566-0507, fax: 902-566-0777, E-mail address: gjay@upei.ca.

▼ University of Puget Sound

Tacoma, Washington

Independent, coed. Suburban campus. Total enrollment: 3,011. Music program established 1892.

Degrees Bachelor of Music in the areas of performance, music education, with elective studies in business. Majors and concentrations: classical music, guitar, harp, harpsichord, music, music business, music education, piano/organ, stringed instruments, voice, wind and percussion instruments. Program accredited by NASM.

Enrollment Fall 1997: 590 total; 90 undergraduate, 500 non-professional degree.

Music Student Profile 48% females, 52% males, 12% minorities, 1% international.

Music Faculty 29 total (full-time and part-time). 90% of full-time faculty have terminal degrees. Graduate students do not teach undergraduate courses. Undergraduate student–faculty ratio: 12:1.

Student Life Student groups/activities include Music Educators National Conference, Phi Mu Alpha Sinfonia, Sigma Alpha Iota. Special housing available for music students.

Expenses for 1997–98 Application fee: $40. Comprehensive fee: $23,860 includes full-time tuition ($18,790), mandatory fees ($150), and college room and board ($4920). College room only: $2690. Special program-related fees: $75 per semester for applied music lessons.

Financial Aid Program-specific awards for 1997: 100 music scholarships for continuing students, 35 music scholarships for incoming students.

Application Procedures Students admitted directly into the professional program freshman year. Deadline for freshmen and transfers: February 1. Notification date for freshmen: June 1. Required: essay, high school transcript, college transcript(s) for transfer students, 3 letters of recommendation, interview, audition, SAT I or ACT test scores. Recommended: minimum 3.0 high school GPA. Auditions held once and by appointment on campus; recorded music is permissible as a substitute for live auditions when distance is prohibitive and videotaped performances are permissible as a substitute for live auditions when distance is prohibitive.

Undergraduate Contact Mr. Paul Gjording, Music Admission Coordinator, School of Music, University of Puget Sound, 1500 North Warner Street, Tacoma, Washington 98416; 206-756-3730, fax: 206-756-3500, E-mail address: pgjording@ups.edu.

▼ University of Redlands

Redlands, California

Independent, coed. Small town campus. Total enrollment: 1,490. Music program established 1907.

Degrees Bachelor of Music in the areas of performance, music education, composition, musical studies. Majors and concentrations: composition, music education, piano/organ, stringed instruments, voice, wind and percussion instruments. Graduate degrees offered: Master of Music in the areas of performance, music education, composition, woodwind doubling. Program accredited by NASM.

Enrollment Fall 1997: 158 total; 128 undergraduate, 28 graduate, 2 non-professional degree.

Music Student Profile 51% females, 49% males, 11% minorities, 18% international.

Music Faculty 27 total undergraduate and graduate (full-time and part-time). 100% of full-time faculty have terminal degrees. Graduate students do not teach undergraduate courses. Undergraduate student–faculty ratio: 7:1.

Student Life Student groups/activities include Sigma Alpha Iota, Phi Mu Alpha Sinfonia, Music Educators National Conference Student Chapter.

Expenses for 1997–98 Application fee: $40. Comprehensive fee: $25,641 includes full-time tuition ($18,300), mandatory fees ($245), and college room and board ($7096). College room only: $3954. Room and board charges vary according to board plan and housing facility.

Financial Aid Program-specific awards for 1997: 65 Music Merit Awards for incoming freshmen ($300–$4000), 10 Area Specific Awards for program students ($300–$4000), 4 Piano Awards ($2000), 2 Voice Awards ($1000).

University of Redlands (*continued*)

Application Procedures Students admitted directly into the professional program freshman year. Deadline for freshmen and transfers: May 1. Notification date for freshmen: September 1; transfers: August 1. Required: essay, high school transcript, college transcript(s) for transfer students, minimum 3.0 high school GPA, 2 letters of recommendation, interview, audition, SAT I or ACT test scores (minimum combined SAT I score of 1030, minimum combined ACT score of 25), portfolio for composition majors. Recommended: video for musical theater majors. Auditions held 4 times on campus; recorded music is permissible as a substitute for live auditions when distance is prohibitive (beyond a 200-mile radius) and videotaped performances are permissible as a substitute for live auditions when distance is prohibitive (beyond a 200-mile radius). Portfolio reviews held continuously for composition majors on campus.

Contact Ms. Pamela Stinson-Acha, Admissions Coordinator, School of Music, University of Redlands, 1200 East Colton Avenue, Box 3080, Redlands, California 92373; 909-335-4014, fax: 909-793-2029.

▼ University of Regina

Regina, SK, Canada

Province-supported, coed. Urban campus. Music program established 1968.

Degrees Bachelor of Music in the areas of performance, composition, music history; Bachelor of Music Education in the area of secondary music education. Majors and concentrations: classical music, composition, music education, music history, piano/organ, stringed instruments, voice, wind and percussion instruments. Graduate degrees offered: Master of Music in the areas of performance, composition, conducting, music theory; Master of Arts in the areas of musicology, music theory. Program accredited by CUMS.

Enrollment Fall 1997: 103 total; 95 undergraduate, 3 graduate, 5 non-professional degree.

Music Student Profile 63% females, 37% males, 1% minorities, 3% international.

Music Faculty 19 total undergraduate and graduate (full-time and part-time). 27% of full-time faculty have terminal degrees. Graduate students do not teach undergraduate courses. Undergraduate student–faculty ratio: 8:1.

Student Life Student groups/activities include Saskatchewan Music Educators Association, Music Students Association.

Expenses for 1997–98 Application fee: $25. Canadian resident tuition: $2813 full-time. Mandatory fees: $229 full-time. College room and board: $3680. International student tuition: $5625 full-time.

Financial Aid Program-specific awards for 1997: 2 Bachelor of Music Entrance Scholarships for Saskatchewan residents ($1300), 1 Entrance Scholarship for freshmen program majors ($750), 1 Laubach Scholarship for strings majors ($1000), 5 music scholarships for piano or voice majors ($250–$1000).

Application Procedures Students admitted directly into the professional program freshman year. Deadline for freshmen and transfers: July 31. Required: high school transcript, college transcript(s) for transfer students, minimum 2.0 high school GPA, interview, audition. Auditions held 5 times on campus; recorded music is permissible as a substitute for live auditions when distance is prohibitive and videotaped

performances are permissible as a substitute for live auditions when distance is prohibitive.

Web Site http://www.uregina.ca/~finearts/.

Undergraduate Contact Office of the Registrar, University of Regina, Regina, SK S4S 0A2, Canada; 306-585-4591, fax: 306-585-5203.

Graduate Contact Faculty of Graduate Studies and Research, University of Regina, Regina, SK S4S 0A2, Canada; 306-585-4161, fax: 306-585-4893.

▼ University of Rhode Island

Kingston, Rhode Island

State-supported, coed. Small town campus. Total enrollment: 13,437. Music program established 1933.

Degrees Bachelor of Music in the areas of music education, music composition, music performance; Bachelor of Arts in the areas of music, music history and literature. Majors and concentrations: composition, music, music education, music history and literature, performance. Graduate degrees offered: Master of Music in the areas of music education, performance. Program accredited by NASM, NCATE.

Enrollment Fall 1997: 140 total; 90 undergraduate, 25 graduate, 25 non-professional degree.

Music Student Profile 50% females, 50% males, 8% minorities, 5% international.

Music Faculty 90% of full-time faculty have terminal degrees. Graduate students do not teach undergraduate courses. Undergraduate student–faculty ratio: 8:1.

Student Life Student groups/activities include Music Educators National Conference Student Chapter, Kappa Kappa Psi, Tau Beta Sigma.

Expenses for 1997–98 Application fee: $30, $45 for nonresidents. State resident tuition: $3202 full-time. Nonresident tuition: $11,010 full-time. Mandatory fees: $1390 full-time. College room and board: $5764. College room only: $3338. Special program-related fees: $190 for applied music lesson fee.

Financial Aid Program-specific awards for 1997: 45 music scholarships for program majors/minors ($250–$4000), 4 Honors String Quartet Scholarships for top string players ($4577–$11,603), 25 University Centennial Scholarships for academically and musically talented students ($1000–$14,000).

Application Procedures Students admitted directly into the professional program freshman year. Deadline for freshmen and transfers: continuous. Notification date for freshmen and transfers: continuous. Required: high school transcript, college transcript(s) for transfer students, audition, SAT I or ACT test scores, minimum 2.5 college GPA for transfer students. Recommended: minimum 3.0 high school GPA, interview, video. Auditions held 7 times on campus; recorded music is permissible as a substitute for live auditions with approval from the department and videotaped performances are permissible as a substitute for live auditions with approval from the department.

Undergraduate Contact Mr. John Dempsey, Professor, Department of Music, University of Rhode Island, Fine Arts Center, Kingston, Rhode Island 02881; 401-874-2782, fax: 401-874-2772.

Graduate Contact Dr. Carolyn Livingston, Coordinator, Graduate Studies in Music, Department of Music, University of Rhode Island, Fine Arts Center, Kingston, Rhode Island 02881; 401-874-2763, fax: 401-874-2772.

▼ University of Richmond

University of Richmond, Virginia

Independent, coed. Suburban campus. Total enrollment: 4,425. Music program established 1954.

Degrees Bachelor of Music in the area of performance. Majors and concentrations: composition, music technology, performance, piano/organ, stringed instruments, voice, wind and percussion instruments. Program accredited by NASM.

Enrollment Fall 1997: 30 undergraduate.

Music Student Profile 60% females, 40% males.

Music Faculty 35 total (full-time and part-time). 100% of full-time faculty have terminal degrees. Graduate students do not teach undergraduate courses.

Expenses for 1998–99 Application fee: $40. Comprehensive fee: $22,738 includes full-time tuition ($18,595) and college room and board ($4143). College room only: $1923. Room and board charges vary according to board plan and housing facility.

Financial Aid Program-specific awards for 1997: 6–8 music scholarships for program majors ($2500–$15,000).

Application Procedures Students admitted directly into the professional program freshman year. Deadline for freshmen and transfers: February 1. Notification date for freshmen and transfers: April 1. Required: essay, high school transcript, college transcript(s) for transfer students, SAT I and SAT II (writing and math) or ACT. Recommended: minimum 3.0 high school GPA, 2 letters of recommendation, interview, video, audition, portfolio. Auditions held 3 times on campus; recorded music is permissible as a substitute for live auditions when distance is prohibitive and videotaped performances are permissible as a substitute for live auditions when distance is prohibitive. Portfolio reviews held twice on campus.

Web Site http://www.arts.richmond.edu/~music.

Undergraduate Contact Ms. Pam Spence, Dean of Admissions, University of Richmond, Sarah Brunet Hall, Richmond Way, Richmond, Virginia 23173; 804-289-8640.

▼ University of Rochester

See Eastman School of Music

▼ University of South Alabama

Mobile, Alabama

State-supported, coed. Suburban campus. Music program established 1963.

Degrees Bachelor of Music in the area of performance; Bachelor of Music Education in the areas of choral music education, instrumental music education. Majors and concentrations: classical music, music, music education, music technology, piano/organ, stringed instruments, voice, wind and percussion instruments. Graduate degrees offered: Master of Education in the area of music education. Program accredited by NASM, NCATE.

Enrollment Fall 1997: 94 total; 85 undergraduate, 6 graduate, 3 non-professional degree.

Music Student Profile 40% females, 60% males, 10% minorities, 1% international.

Music Faculty 32 total undergraduate and graduate (full-time and part-time). 91% of full-time faculty have terminal degrees. Graduate students do not teach undergraduate courses. Undergraduate student–faculty ratio: 7:1.

Student Life Student groups/activities include Music Educators National Conference, Sigma Alpha Iota, Phi Mu Alpha.

Expenses for 1997–98 Application fee: $25. State resident tuition: $2640 full-time. Nonresident tuition: $5280 full-time. Mandatory fees: $198 full-time. Special program-related fees: $40–$75 per quarter for private lessons.

Financial Aid Program-specific awards for 1997: 85 music scholarships for ensemble performers ($600–$1500), 1 Theodore Presser Award for senior program majors ($2250), 2 Chester Piano Scholarships for enrolled piano students ($300–$500).

Application Procedures Students admitted directly into the professional program freshman year. Deadline for freshmen and transfers: September 10. Required: high school transcript, college transcript(s) for transfer students, minimum 2.0 high school GPA, audition, SAT I or ACT test scores. Auditions held 3 times on campus; recorded music is permissible as a substitute for live auditions when distance is prohibitive and videotaped performances are permissible as a substitute for live auditions when distance is prohibitive.

Undergraduate Contact Dr. Andrew Harper, Chairman, Music Department, University of South Alabama, Laidlaw Performing Arts Center, Mobile, Alabama 36688; 334-460-6136, fax: 334-460-7328, E-mail address: aharper@jaguar1.usouthal.edu.

Graduate Contact Dr. Andrea Bohnet, Associate Professor of Music, Music Department, University of South Alabama, Laidlaw Performing Arts Center, Mobile, Alabama 36688; 334-460-6696, fax: 334-460-7328.

▼ University of South Carolina

Columbia, South Carolina

State-supported, coed. Urban campus. Total enrollment: 25,447. Music program established 1937.

Degrees Bachelor of Music in the areas of piano pedagogy, performance, music education, music theory/composition, jazz studies. Majors and concentrations: guitar, jazz, music education, music theory and composition, piano pedagogy, piano/organ, stringed instruments, voice, wind and percussion instruments. Graduate degrees offered: Master of Music in the areas of composition, performance, piano pedagogy, music history, music theory, conducting, jazz studies, opera theater; Master of Music Education. Doctor of Musical Arts in the areas of composition, performance, piano pedagogy, conducting; Doctor of Philosophy in the area of music education. Program accredited by NASM, NCATE.

Enrollment Fall 1997: 470 total; 310 undergraduate, 140 graduate, 20 non-professional degree.

Music Student Profile 44% females, 56% males, 16% minorities, 12% international.

Music Faculty 50 total undergraduate and graduate (full-time and part-time). 90% of full-time faculty have terminal degrees. Graduate students teach a few undergraduate courses. Undergraduate student–faculty ratio: 10:1.

Expenses for 1997–98 Application fee: $35. One-time mandatory fee: $25. State resident tuition: $3434 full-time. Nonresident tuition: $8840 full-time. Mandatory fees: $100 full-time. College room and board: $3830. Special program-related fees: $30 for recital fee.

University of South Carolina (continued)

Financial Aid Program-specific awards for 1997: 225 music scholarships for program majors ($100–$3500).

Application Procedures Students admitted directly into the professional program freshman year. Deadline for freshmen and transfers: August 15. Notification date for freshmen and transfers: continuous. Required: high school transcript, college transcript(s) for transfer students, minimum 2.0 high school GPA, audition, SAT I or ACT test scores (minimum combined SAT I score of 1100, minimum combined ACT score of 24). Auditions held 5 times on campus; recorded music is permissible as a substitute for live auditions when distance is prohibitive for provisional acceptance and videotaped performances are permissible as a substitute for live auditions when distance is prohibitive for provisional acceptance.

Web Site http://www.music.sc.edu/index.html.

Undergraduate Contact Ms. Jean Smith, Administrative Assistant, School of Music, University of South Carolina, Columbia, South Carolina 29208; 803-777-4335, fax: 803-777-6508, E-mail address: ugmusic@mozart.sc.edu.

Graduate Contact Ms. Dedra Stukes, Administrative Assistant, School of Music, University of South Carolina, Columbia, South Carolina 29208; 803-777-4106, fax: 803-777-6508, E-mail address: gradmusic@mozart.sc.edu.

▼ University of South Dakota

Vermillion, South Dakota

State-supported, coed. Small town campus. Total enrollment: 7,392. Music program established 1882.

Degrees Bachelor of Music in the areas of performance, music education. Majors and concentrations: music education, piano/organ, stringed instruments, voice. Graduate degrees offered: Master of Music in the areas of music education, performance, music literature, history of musical instruments. Cross-registration with South Dakota State University System . Program accredited by NASM.

Enrollment Fall 1997: 90 undergraduate, 30 graduate.

Music Student Profile 65% females, 35% males, 8% minorities, 6% international.

Music Faculty 17 total undergraduate and graduate (full-time). 80% of full-time faculty have terminal degrees. Graduate students teach a few undergraduate courses. Undergraduate student–faculty ratio: 10:1.

Student Life Student groups/activities include Music Educators National Conference.

Expenses for 1997–98 Application fee: $15. State resident tuition: $1728 full-time. Nonresident tuition: $5496 full-time. Mandatory fees: $1284 full-time. Full-time tuition and fees vary according to reciprocity agreements. College room and board: $2912. College room only: $1322. Room and board charges vary according to board plan.

Financial Aid Program-specific awards for 1997: 70 music scholarships for program majors ($300–$1500).

Application Procedures Students admitted directly into the professional program freshman year. Deadline for freshmen and transfers: continuous. Required: high school transcript, college transcript(s) for transfer students, audition, SAT I or ACT test scores. Auditions held twice on campus; recorded music is permissible as a substitute for live auditions when distance is prohibitive and videotaped performances are permissible as a substitute for live auditions by request.

Contact Dr. Lawrence Mitchell, Chair, Music Department, University of South Dakota, CFA 114a, 414 East Clark Street, Vermillion, South Dakota 57069; 605-677-5274, fax: 605-677-5988.

▼ University of Southern California

Los Angeles, California

Independent, coed. Urban campus. Total enrollment: 28,342. Music program established 1884.

Degrees Bachelor of Music in the areas of performance, composition, music education, jazz, music industry, composition with emphasis in film scoring. Majors and concentrations: classical guitar, composition, electronic music, film scoring, jazz, jazz guitar, music, music education, music industry, piano/organ, recording arts and sciences, stringed instruments, voice, wind and percussion instruments. Graduate degrees offered: Master of Music in the areas of choral music, church music, composition, jazz studies, music education, conducting, performance; Master of Music Education; Master of Arts in the areas of music history and literature, early music, performance. Doctor of Musical Arts in the areas of choral music, church music, composition, music education, performance. Program accredited by NASM.

Enrollment Fall 1997: 882 total; 438 undergraduate, 372 graduate, 72 non-professional degree.

Music Student Profile 48% females, 52% males, 12% minorities, 20% international.

Music Faculty 153 total undergraduate and graduate (full-time and part-time). 75% of full-time faculty have terminal degrees. Graduate students teach a few undergraduate courses. Undergraduate student–faculty ratio: 8:1.

Expenses for 1997–98 Application fee: $55. Comprehensive fee: $27,228 includes full-time tuition ($20,078), mandatory fees ($402), and college room and board ($6748). College room only: $3716. Room and board charges vary according to board plan and housing facility. Special program-related fees: $1040 per year for lessons for music majors.

Financial Aid Program-specific awards for 1997: music scholarships for talented students and those demonstrating need.

Application Procedures Students admitted directly into the professional program freshman year. Deadline for freshmen: February 1; transfers: March 1. Notification date for freshmen and transfers: April 1. Required: essay, high school transcript, college transcript(s) for transfer students, minimum 3.0 high school GPA, audition, SAT I or ACT test scores (minimum combined SAT I score of 1100), resume. Recommended: 3 letters of recommendation, interview. Auditions held 6 times and by appointment on campus and off campus in regional locations; recorded music is permissible as a substitute for live auditions if a campus visit is impossible (except vocalists) and videotaped performances are permissible as a substitute for live auditions if a campus visit is impossible (for vocalists only).

Web Site http://www.usc.edu.

Contact Mr. Christopher Sampson, Director of Admission and Financial Aid, School of Music, University of Southern California, Los Angeles, California 90089-0851; 213-740-8986, fax: 213-740-8995, E-mail address: uscmusic@usc.edu.

More About the University

The USC School of Music provides a comprehensive academic base in virtually all professional and scholarly branches of music, including instrumental and vocal performance, opera, composition, film scoring, music history and literature, jazz, musicology, theory, electronic music, pedagogy, conducting, choral and church music, early music, music education, music industry, and recording arts.

Alumni include Herb Alpert, Bruce Broughton, Jerry Goldsmith, Lionel Hampton, James Horner, Martin Katz, Marilyn Horne, Marni Nixon, Christopher Parkening, Nathaniel Rosen, Tom Scott, and Michael Tilson Thomas.

Faculty are solo, chamber, jazz, and motion picture/television recording artists active in the international and local professional music arenas. USC faculty are members of the Los Angeles Philharmonic, Los Angeles Chamber Orchestra, Music Center Opera, and many other distinguished institutions. USC routinely hosts a lengthy roster of touring artists. Former faculty members include Jascha Heifetz, Gregor Piatigorsky, William Primrose, Arnold Schoenberg, and Ingolf Dahl.

Facilities include the 1,573-seat Bovard Auditorium main concert hall, the 336-seat Hancock Auditorium for recitals, the 553-seat Bing Theatre for opera, and three other smaller performance venues. Three principal structures comprise the main School of Music complex: the Virginia Ramo Hall of Music, Booth Ferris Memorial Hall, and the Raubenheimer Music Faculty Memorial Building. These buildings house the school's primary rehearsal and teaching studios dedicated to percussion, organ, harp, individual instruction, electronic music, and recording arts. Practice rooms are located in the Performing Arts Annex. The Music Library is housed in the University's Doheny Memorial Library and includes 18,000 books and periodical volumes; 47,000 scores, historical sets and collected editions; 14,000 recordings; 100 videotapes and laser discs; and 1,400 microforms. Facilities also include extensive computer and multimedia workstations.

Performance Opportunities include the USC Symphony, Chamber Orchestra, Wind Ensemble and Symphonic Winds, SC Jazz Ensembles, Percussion Ensemble, Chamber Singers, Concert Choir, Opera, Early Music Ensemble, Contemporary Music Ensemble, and the Trojan Marching Band. A full range of piano, string, woodwind, brass, percussion, and guitar ensembles comprise chamber music opportunities.

▼ UNIVERSITY OF SOUTHERN MAINE

Portland, Maine

State-supported, coed. Suburban campus. Total enrollment: 10,236. Music program established 1957.

Degrees Bachelor of Music in the areas of music education, performance. Majors and concentrations: classical music, jazz, music education. Cross-registration with Greater Portland Alliance of Colleges and Universities. Program accredited by NASM.

Enrollment Fall 1997: 129 total; all undergraduate.

Music Student Profile 55% females, 45% males, 1% minorities, 1% international.

Music Faculty 41 total (full-time and part-time). 100% of full-time faculty have terminal degrees. Graduate students do not teach undergraduate courses. Undergraduate student–faculty ratio: 9:1.

Student Life Student groups/activities include Music Educators National Conference, American String Teachers Association, National Association of Teachers of Singing.

Expenses for 1997–98 Application fee: $25. One-time mandatory fee: $15. State resident tuition: $3450 full-time.

Nonresident tuition: $9540 full-time. Mandatory fees: $488 full-time. Full-time tuition and fees vary according to course load and reciprocity agreements. College room and board: $4646. College room only: $2406. Special program-related fees: $60 per year for applied music fees.

Financial Aid Program-specific awards for 1997: 10 Music Talent Scholarships for program majors ($600–$2400).

Application Procedures Students admitted directly into the professional program freshman year. Deadline for freshmen and transfers: September 6. Notification date for freshmen and transfers: September 6. Required: essay, high school transcript, college transcript(s) for transfer students, letter of recommendation, audition, SAT I or ACT test scores. Auditions held 5 times on campus; recorded music is permissible as a substitute for live auditions on a case-by-case basis and videotaped performances are permissible as a substitute for live auditions on a case-by-case basis.

Web Site http://www.usm.maine.edu/~mus.

Undergraduate Contact Dr. Ronald Cole, Chairman, Music Department, University of Southern Maine, 37 College Avenue, Gorham, Maine 04038-1032; 207-780-5265, fax: 207-780-5005, E-mail address: music@usm.maine.edu.

▼ UNIVERSITY OF SOUTHERN MISSISSIPPI

Hattiesburg, Mississippi

State-supported, coed. Suburban campus. Total enrollment: 14,599. Music program established 1938.

Degrees Bachelor of Music in the areas of performance, church music, music industry, jazz, music history and literature, composition; Bachelor of Music Education in the areas of instrumental music education, choral-vocal music education, choral-keyboard music education, choral-guitar music education. Majors and concentrations: composition, guitar, harpsichord, jazz, music education, music history and literature, music industry, piano/organ, sacred music, stringed instruments, voice, wind and percussion instruments. Graduate degrees offered: Master of Music in the areas of performance, church music, conducting, music history and literature, music theory/composition, woodwind performance/pedagogy; Master of Music Education. Doctor of Musical Arts in the areas of performance and pedagogy-applied music, performance and pedagogy-composition, performance and pedagogy-conducting. Program accredited by NASM, NCATE.

Enrollment Fall 1997: 397 total; 328 undergraduate, 69 graduate.

Music Student Profile 38% females, 62% males, 13% minorities, 5% international.

Music Faculty 44 total undergraduate and graduate (full-time and part-time). 56% of full-time faculty have terminal degrees. Graduate students teach a few undergraduate courses. Undergraduate student–faculty ratio: 9:1.

Student Life Student groups/activities include Phi Mu Alpha Sinfonia, Mu Phi Epsilon, Tau Beta Sigma.

Expenses for 1997–98 State resident tuition: $2590 full-time. Nonresident tuition: $5410 full-time. College room and board: $2565. Room and board charges vary according to board plan and housing facility. Special program-related fees: $15 per semester for instrument maintenance.

Financial Aid Program-specific awards for 1997: 450 Service Awards for program majors ($200–$2200), 30 Endowment Awards for program majors ($1200–$5000).

University of Southern Mississippi (continued)

Application Procedures Students admitted directly into the professional program freshman year. Deadline for freshmen and transfers: August 1. Notification date for freshmen and transfers: August 24. Required: high school transcript, college transcript(s) for transfer students, minimum 2.0 high school GPA, SAT I or ACT test scores, juried audition on major instrument at end of first year. Auditions held by appointment on campus; recorded music is permissible as a substitute for live auditions by request and videotaped performances are permissible as a substitute for live auditions by request.

Web Site http://www.arts.usm.edu/.

Contact Mrs. Tara Burcham, Academic Advisor, School of Music, University of Southern Mississippi, Box 5081, Hattiesburg, Mississippi 39406-5081; 601-266-5369, fax: 601-266-4127.

▼ University of South Florida

Tampa, Florida

State-supported, coed. Urban campus. Total enrollment: 34,036.

Degrees Bachelor of Music in the areas of jazz, performance, composition, piano pedagogy; Bachelor of Science in the area of music education; Bachelor of Arts in the area of music education. Graduate degrees offered: Master of Music in the areas of jazz, performance, composition, piano pedagogy, theory, conducting; Master of Arts in the area of music education. Doctor of Philosophy in the area of curriculum and instruction. Program accredited by NASM.

Enrollment Fall 1997: 249 total; 221 undergraduate, 28 graduate.

Music Student Profile 48% females, 52% males, 15% minorities, 2% international.

Music Faculty 39 total undergraduate and graduate (full-time and part-time). 96% of full-time faculty have terminal degrees. Graduate students teach a few undergraduate courses. Undergraduate student–faculty ratio: 10:1.

Student Life Student groups/activities include Collegiate Music Educators National Conference, professional music fraternities.

Expenses for 1997–98 Application fee: $20. State resident tuition: $2086 full-time. Nonresident tuition: $8003 full-time. Full-time tuition varies according to course level, course load, and location. College room and board: $4596. College room only: $2244. Room and board charges vary according to board plan, housing facility, and location. Special program-related fees: $10 per course for materials fees.

Financial Aid Program-specific awards for 1997: 50 music scholarships for music students ($400–$1600).

Application Procedures Students admitted directly into the professional program freshman year. Deadline for freshmen and transfers: continuous. Required: high school transcript, minimum 2.0 high school GPA, audition, SAT I or ACT test scores. Auditions held 3 times on campus; recorded music is permissible as a substitute for live auditions if a campus visit is impossible and videotaped performances are permissible as a substitute for live auditions if a campus visit is impossible.

Undergraduate Contact Dr. William Hayden, Undergraduate Advisor, School of Music, University of South Florida, 4204 East Fowler Avenue, Tampa, Florida 33620-7350; 813-974-1753, fax: 813-974-2091.

Graduate Contact Mr. Don Owen, Graduate Advisor, School of Music, University of South Florida, 4204 East Fowler Avenue, Tampa, Florida 33620-7350; 813-974-3976, fax: 813-974-2091.

▼ University of Southwestern Louisiana

Lafayette, Louisiana

State-supported, coed. Urban campus. Total enrollment: 17,020.

Degrees Bachelor of Music in the areas of performance, music theory/composition, music media, jazz studies, piano pedagogy; Bachelor of Music Education. Majors and concentrations: jazz, music education, music media, music theory and composition, performance, piano pedagogy. Graduate degrees offered: Master of Music in the areas of performance, conducting, music theory/composition. Program accredited by NASM.

Enrollment Fall 1997: 160 undergraduate, 15 graduate.

Music Faculty 22 total undergraduate and graduate (full-time and part-time). 60% of full-time faculty have terminal degrees. Graduate students teach a few undergraduate courses. Undergraduate student–faculty ratio: 6:1.

Student Life Student groups/activities include Music Educators National Conference, Sigma Alpha Iota, Phi Mu Alpha.

Expenses for 1997–98 Application fee: $5, $15 for international students. State resident tuition: $1947 full-time. Nonresident tuition: $6075 full-time. College room and board: $2592. Room and board charges vary according to board plan.

Financial Aid Program-specific awards for 1997: Marching Band Stipend for all students in marching band ($500), 100 Marching Band Housing Awards for all students in marching band.

Application Procedures Students admitted directly into the professional program freshman year. Deadline for freshmen and transfers: continuous. Required: high school transcript, college transcript(s) for transfer students, SAT I or ACT test scores, audition for scholarship consideration and for placement in wind ensemble. Auditions held in February and March on campus; recorded music is permissible as a substitute for live auditions when distance is prohibitive or scheduling is difficult and videotaped performances are permissible as a substitute for live auditions if distance is prohibitive or scheduling is difficult.

Web Site http://www.usl.edu.

Undergraduate Contact Dr. A. C. Himes, Director, School of Music, University of Southwestern Louisiana, Box 41207, Lafayette, Louisiana 70504-1207; 318-482-6016, fax: 318-482-5017.

Graduate Contact Dr. Andrea Loewy, Director of Graduate Studies, School of Music, University of Southwestern Louisiana, Box 41207, Lafayette, Louisiana 70504-1207; 318-482-5214, fax: 318-482-5017.

▼ The University of Tampa

Tampa, Florida

Independent, coed. Urban campus. Total enrollment: 2,896.

Degrees Bachelor of Music in the areas of music performance, music education. Program accredited by NASM.

Enrollment Fall 1997: 30 undergraduate.

Music Student Profile 50% females, 50% males.

Music Faculty 14 total (full-time and part-time). 100% of full-time faculty have terminal degrees. Graduate students do not teach undergraduate courses.

Student Life Student groups/activities include Cadenza (music service organization).

Expenses for 1997–98 Application fee: $25. Comprehensive fee: $19,432 includes full-time tuition ($13,890), mandatory fees ($762), and college room and board ($4780). College room only: $2280. Room and board charges vary according to board plan and housing facility.

Application Procedures Students admitted directly into the professional program freshman year. Deadline for freshmen and transfers: continuous. Notification date for freshmen and transfers: continuous. Required: essay, high school transcript, 2 letters of recommendation, audition, SAT I or ACT test scores, music theory placement test, evidence of constructive extracurricular activities. Auditions held twice and by appointment on campus; recorded music is permissible as a substitute for live auditions when distance is prohibitive and videotaped performances are permissible as a substitute for live auditions when distance is prohibitive.

Web Site http://www.utampa.edu.

Undergraduate Contact Ms. Barbara Strickler, Vice President for Enrollment Management, The University of Tampa, 401 West Kennedy Boulevard, Tampa, Florida 33606-1490; 813-253-6228.

▼ UNIVERSITY OF TENNESSEE AT CHATTANOOGA

Chattanooga, Tennessee

State-supported, coed. Urban campus. Total enrollment: 8,528.

Degrees Bachelor of Music in the areas of performance, sacred music, music theory/composition. Majors and concentrations: music theory and composition, piano/organ, sacred music, stringed instruments, voice, wind and percussion instruments. Graduate degrees offered: Master of Music in the areas of music education, performance. Program accredited by NASM.

Enrollment Fall 1997: 135 total; 43 undergraduate, 17 graduate, 75 non-professional degree.

Music Student Profile 54% females, 46% males, 8% minorities, 3% international.

Music Faculty 28 total undergraduate and graduate (full-time and part-time). 70% of full-time faculty have terminal degrees. Graduate students do not teach undergraduate courses.

Student Life Student groups/activities include Music Educators National Conference Student Chapter, Sigma Alpha Iota, Phi Mu Alpha Sinfonia.

Expenses for 1997–98 Application fee: $25. State resident tuition: $2200 full-time. Nonresident tuition: $6796 full-time. College room only: $1900. Special program-related fees: $30–$60 per semester for applied music fee.

Financial Aid Program-specific awards for 1997: performance grants for ensemble participants ($200–$1900).

Application Procedures Students admitted directly into the professional program freshman year. Deadline for freshmen and transfers: continuous. Required: high school transcript, college transcript(s) for transfer students, letter of recommendation, audition, SAT I or ACT test scores. Recommended:

essay. Auditions held 4 times on campus; recorded music is permissible as a substitute for live auditions when distance is prohibitive.

Undergraduate Contact Dr. Jocelyn Sanders, Head, Music Department, University of Tennessee at Chattanooga, 615 McCallie Avenue, Chattanooga, Tennessee 37403; 423-755-4601, fax: 423-755-4603.

Graduate Contact Dr. Monte Coulter, Coordinator, Graduate Programs in Music, Music Department, University of Tennessee at Chattanooga, 615 McCallie Avenue, Chattanooga, Tennessee 37403; 423-755-4601, fax: 423-755-4603.

▼ THE UNIVERSITY OF TENNESSEE AT MARTIN

Martin, Tennessee

State-supported, coed. Small town campus. Total enrollment: 5,997. Music program established 1970.

Degrees Bachelor of Music in the areas of music education, performance. Program accredited by NASM.

Enrollment Fall 1997: 86 undergraduate.

Music Student Profile 60% females, 40% males, 5% minorities, 2% international.

Music Faculty 16 total (full-time and part-time). 80% of full-time faculty have terminal degrees. Graduate students do not teach undergraduate courses. Undergraduate student–faculty ratio: 4:1.

Student Life Student groups/activities include Phi Mu Alpha Sinfonia, Sigma Alpha Iota, Music Educators National Conference.

Expenses for 1997–98 Application fee: $25. State resident tuition: $2240 full-time. Nonresident tuition: $6706 full-time. College room and board: $3104. College room only: $1600. Room and board charges vary according to board plan and housing facility. Special program-related fees: $180 per year for applied music fee.

Financial Aid Program-specific awards for 1997: 25 music scholarships ($600).

Application Procedures Students admitted directly into the professional program freshman year. Deadline for freshmen and transfers: continuous. Required: high school transcript, minimum 2.0 high school GPA, audition, SAT I or ACT test scores. Auditions held as needed on campus and off campus in various locations in Tennessee; recorded music is permissible as a substitute for live auditions if a campus visit is impossible and videotaped performances are permissible as a substitute for live auditions if a campus visit is impossible.

Web Site http://www.utm.edu/departments/finearts/music.htm.

Undergraduate Contact Dr. Earl Norwood, Director, Division of Fine and Performing Arts, The University of Tennessee at Martin, 102 Fine Arts Building, Martin, Tennessee 38238; 901-587-7400, fax: 901-587-7415, E-mail address: norwood@utm.edu.

▼ UNIVERSITY OF TENNESSEE, KNOXVILLE

Knoxville, Tennessee

State-supported, coed. Urban campus. Total enrollment: 25,397. Music program established 1947.

Degrees Bachelor of Music in the areas of music theory/composition, studio music and jazz, piano, organ, piano

University of Tennessee, Knoxville *(continued)*

pedagogy and literature, sacred music, strings, voice, woodwind, brass, and percussion instruments; Bachelor of Music Education in the areas of instrumental music, voice. Majors and concentrations: classical music, jazz, music, music education, music theory and composition, piano/organ, sacred music, stringed instruments, voice, wind and percussion instruments. Graduate degrees offered: Master of Music in the areas of accompanying, choral conducting, composition, instrumental conducting, jazz, music education, music theory, musicology, organ, piano, piano literature and pedagogy, strings, voice, winds and percussion instruments. Program accredited by NASM.

Enrollment Fall 1997: 235 total; 181 undergraduate, 54 graduate.

Music Student Profile 26% females, 74% males, 5% minorities, 12% international.

Music Faculty 55 total undergraduate and graduate (full-time and part-time). 90% of full-time faculty have terminal degrees. Graduate students teach a few undergraduate courses.

Student Life Student groups/activities include Sigma Alpha Iota, Phi Mu Alpha.

Expenses for 1997–98 Application fee: $25. State resident tuition: $2096 full-time. Nonresident tuition: $6778 full-time. Mandatory fees: $480 full-time. College room and board: $3802. College room only: $1890. Room and board charges vary according to board plan and housing facility. Special program-related fees: $60–$120 per semester for private lessons.

Financial Aid Program-specific awards for 1997: 30 music scholarships for high school seniors ($2000).

Application Procedures Students apply for admission into the professional program by freshman year. Deadline for freshmen and transfers: continuous. Required: high school transcript, college transcript(s) for transfer students, minimum 2.0 high school GPA, audition, SAT I or ACT test scores. Auditions held 3 times on campus; recorded music is permissible as a substitute for live auditions when distance is prohibitive and videotaped performances are permissible as a substitute for live auditions when distance is prohibitive.

Web Site http://orpheus.la.utk.edu.

Undergraduate Contact Ms. Dolly C. Davis, Advising Coordinator, Department of Music, University of Tennessee, Knoxville, Music Building, 1741 Volunteer Boulevard, Knoxville, Tennessee 37996-2600; 423-974-3241, fax: 423-974-1941, E-mail address: music@utk.edu.

Graduate Contact Mr. John Brock, Graduate Coordinator, Department of Music, University of Tennessee, Knoxville, 211 Music Building, 1741 Volunteer Boulevard, Knoxville, Tennessee 37996-2600; 423-974-3241, fax: 423-974-1941, E-mail address: music@utk.edu.

More About the University

Program Facilities Facilities include the main music building, consisting of an auditorium (seating approximately 550) that is adaptable for use as a recital hall, a concert hall, large ensemble performances, and small operatic productions. Additional rehearsal spaces are available for band, orchestra, and chorus. There are classroom facilities, two computer labs, and a laboratory for electronic music and piano instruction, in addition to the studios for keyboard and voice-applied instruction. There are six annexes in addition to the main music building that are devoted to woodwinds,

brass, strings, jazz, and multiuse. The Music Library is situated on the third floor in the main music building.

Faculty The faculty consists of performing artists, conductors and composers of international reputation, and active scholars.

Student Performance Opportunities Cooperative arrangements between the department and the Knoxville Symphony Orchestra provide opportunities for advanced students to gain valuable performance experience as orchestral players. Graduate students in voice often participate in the Knoxville Opera Studio Program, giving students more exposure on stage with professional singers while they pursue academic degrees. Students in the jazz program are actively involved in the local jazz scene in Knoxville and its environs. Many of them are recurrent performers at local clubs and restaurants.

▼ THE UNIVERSITY OF TEXAS AT ARLINGTON

Arlington, Texas

State-supported, coed. Suburban campus. Total enrollment: 19,286.

Degrees Bachelor of Music. Majors and concentrations: brass, jazz, music theory and composition, piano/organ, stringed instruments, voice, wind and percussion instruments. Program accredited by NASM.

Enrollment Fall 1997: 241 undergraduate.

Music Student Profile 40% females, 60% males, 16% minorities, 2% international.

Music Faculty 37 total (full-time and part-time). 48% of full-time faculty have terminal degrees. Graduate students do not teach undergraduate courses. Undergraduate student–faculty ratio: 7:1.

Student Life Student groups/activities include Texas Music Educators Association, Kappa Kappa Psi, Phi Mu Alpha.

Expenses for 1997–98 Application fee: $25. State resident tuition: $816 full-time. Nonresident tuition: $5952 full-time. Mandatory fees: $1272 full-time. Full-time tuition and fees vary according to course load. College room only: $1600. Room charges vary according to housing facility. Special program-related fees: $25 per semester for instrument rental fee.

Financial Aid Program-specific awards for 1997: 200 various scholarships for music majors ($400).

Application Procedures Students apply for admission into the professional program by junior year. Deadline for freshmen and transfers: August 4. Notification date for freshmen and transfers: continuous. Required: high school transcript, college transcript(s) for transfer students, SAT I or ACT test scores, audition for scholarship consideration. Auditions held once on campus.

Web Site http://www.uta.edu.

Undergraduate Contact Office of Admissions, The University of Texas at Arlington, Box 19111, Arlington, Texas 76019-0111; 817-272-2118, fax: 817-272-3435.

▼ THE UNIVERSITY OF TEXAS AT AUSTIN

Austin, Texas

State-supported, coed. Urban campus. Total enrollment: 48,857.

Degrees Bachelor of Music in the areas of performance, keyboard, voice, music studies, theory, composition, literature and pedagogy, musicology, ethnomusicology. Majors and concentrations: composition, harp, harpsichord, music education, music theory, orchestral instruments, organ, piano, voice. Graduate degrees offered: Master of Music in the areas of performance, keyboard, voice, music education, opera, conducting, literature and pedagogy, theory, composition, musicology, ethnomusicology. Doctor of Musical Arts in the areas of performance, composition, music education.

Enrollment Fall 1997: 759 total; 397 undergraduate, 358 graduate, 4 non-professional degree.

Music Faculty 87 total undergraduate and graduate (full-time and part-time).

Student Life Student groups/activities include professional fraternities and sororities.

Expenses for 1997–98 Application fee: $40. State resident tuition: $2040 full-time. Nonresident tuition: $8460 full-time. Mandatory fees: $826 full-time. Full-time tuition and fees vary according to course load and program. College room and board: $3901. College room only: $1950. Room and board charges vary according to board plan.

Application Procedures Students admitted directly into the professional program freshman year. Deadline for freshmen: February 1; transfers: March 1. Required: high school transcript, audition, SAT I or ACT test scores. Auditions held 5 times on campus; recorded music is permissible as a substitute for live auditions with permission of department.

Undergraduate Contact Ms. Martha Hilley, Associate Director, Undergraduate Studies, School of Music, The University of Texas at Austin, Austin, Texas 78712; 512-471-7764.

Graduate Contact Dr. Hunter C. Marsh, Director, School of Music, The University of Texas at Austin, Austin, Texas 78712; 512-471-1502.

▼ THE UNIVERSITY OF TEXAS AT EL PASO

El Paso, Texas

State-supported, coed. Urban campus. Total enrollment: 15,176.

Degrees Bachelor of Music in the areas of performance, theory/composition, music education. Majors and concentrations: music education, music theory, piano, stringed instruments, voice, wind and percussion instruments. Graduate degrees offered: Master of Music in the area of performance; Master of Music Education. Cross-registration with El Paso Community College. Program accredited by NASM.

Enrollment Fall 1997: 150 undergraduate, 20 graduate.

Music Student Profile 55% females, 45% males, 60% minorities.

Music Faculty 36 total undergraduate and graduate (full-time and part-time). 90% of full-time faculty have terminal degrees. Graduate students teach a few undergraduate courses.

Expenses for 1997–98 Application fee: $0. State resident tuition: $1020 full-time. Nonresident tuition: $7440 full-time. Mandatory fees: $1246 full-time. Full-time tuition and fees vary according to course load and reciprocity agreements. Special program-related fees: $50 for applied lessons.

Application Procedures Deadline for freshmen and transfers: continuous. Required: high school transcript, audition. Recommended: minimum 2.0 high school GPA. Auditions held continuously for instrumental and vocal applicants on campus; recorded music is permissible as a substitute for live auditions if a campus visit is impossible and videotaped performances are permissible as a substitute for live auditions if a campus visit is impossible.

Contact Dr. Ron Hufstader, Chair, Music Department, The University of Texas at El Paso, 500 West University Avenue, El Paso, Texas 79968-0552; 915-747-5606, fax: 915-747-5023.

▼ THE UNIVERSITY OF TEXAS AT SAN ANTONIO

San Antonio, Texas

State-supported, coed. Suburban campus. Total enrollment: 17,494. Music program established 1975.

Degrees Bachelor of Music in the areas of performance, composition, music marketing, music education. Majors and concentrations: classical music, composition, music education, music marketing, piano/organ, stringed instruments, voice, wind and percussion instruments. Graduate degrees offered: Master of Music in the areas of performance, music education, conducting. Program accredited by NASM.

Enrollment Fall 1997: 270 total; 240 undergraduate, 30 graduate.

Music Student Profile 50% females, 50% males, 49% minorities, 2% international.

Music Faculty 46 total undergraduate and graduate (full-time and part-time). 100% of full-time faculty have terminal degrees. Graduate students do not teach undergraduate courses. Undergraduate student–faculty ratio: 12:1.

Student Life Student groups/activities include Music Educators National Conference Student Chapter, Sigma Alpha Iota, Phi Mu Alpha Sinfonia.

Expenses for 1998–99 Application fee: $20. State resident tuition: $2010 full-time. Nonresident tuition: $8400 full-time. Mandatory fees: $734 full-time. Full-time tuition and fees vary according to course load. College room only: $3000. Room charges vary according to housing facility. Special program-related fees: $25–$75 per semester for music major fee, $50 per course for private lesson fee.

Financial Aid Program-specific awards for 1997: 75 Division of Music Scholarships for program majors ($400–$2000).

Application Procedures Students admitted directly into the professional program freshman year. Deadline for freshmen and transfers: July 1. Notification date for freshmen: August 1. Required: high school transcript, college transcript(s) for transfer students, SAT I or ACT test scores. Recommended: audition. Auditions held twice on campus; recorded music is permissible as a substitute for live auditions when distance is prohibitive and videotaped performances are permissible as a substitute for live auditions when distance is prohibitive.

Web Site http://music.utsa.edu.

Undergraduate Contact Dr. Diana Allan, Assistant Professor, Division of Music, The University of Texas at San Antonio, 6900 North Loop 1604 West, San Antonio, Texas 78249-1130; 210-458-4354, fax: 210-458-4381.

Graduate Contact Dr. David Heuser, Assistant Professor, Division of Music, The University of Texas at San Antonio, 6900 North Loop 1604 West, San Antonio, Texas 78249-1130; 210-458-4354, fax: 210-458-4381.

▼ THE UNIVERSITY OF TEXAS AT TYLER

Tyler, Texas

State-supported, coed. Urban campus. Total enrollment: 3,393.

Degrees Bachelor of Music in the areas of vocal music, instrumental music, keyboard, theory/composition. Majors and concentrations: instrumental music, music history, music theory and composition, piano, piano pedagogy, voice. Cross-registration with Tyler Junior College.

Enrollment Fall 1997: 37 undergraduate, 13 non-professional degree.

Music Student Profile 60% females, 40% males, 10% minorities, 10% international.

Music Faculty 17 total (full-time and part-time). 50% of full-time faculty have terminal degrees. Graduate students do not teach undergraduate courses. Undergraduate student–faculty ratio: 7:1.

Student Life Student groups/activities include Music Students Association.

Expenses for 1997–98 State resident tuition: $816 full-time. Nonresident tuition: $5952 full-time. Mandatory fees: $1268 full-time. Full-time tuition and fees vary according to course load. College room and board: $6029. Room and board charges vary according to board plan and housing facility. Special program-related fees: $30 per semester for Performing Arts Center fee.

Financial Aid Program-specific awards for 1997: 30 Performing Arts Scholarships for music majors ($700).

Application Procedures Students apply for admission into the professional program by freshman, sophomore, junior year. Deadline for freshmen and transfers: continuous. Required: high school transcript, college transcript(s) for transfer students, minimum 3.0 high school GPA, audition, 52 hours of college level course work and minimum 2.75 college GPA for transfer students. Recommended: 3 letters of recommendation. Auditions held twice on campus; recorded music is permissible as a substitute for live auditions when distance is prohibitive and videotaped performances are permissible as a substitute for live auditions when distance is prohibitive.

Undergraduate Contact Ms. Vicki Conway, Professor, Department of Music, The University of Texas at Tyler, 3900 Univeristy Boulevard, Tyler, Texas 75799; 903-566-7293, fax: 903-566-7287.

▼ UNIVERSITY OF THE ARTS

Philadelphia, Pennsylvania

Independent, coed. Urban campus. Total enrollment: 1,624. Music program established 1870.

Degrees Bachelor of Music in the areas of jazz performance, vocal performance, composition. Graduate degrees offered: Master of Music in the areas of jazz studies, performance; Master of Arts in Teaching in the area of music education. Program accredited by NASM.

Enrollment Fall 1997: 192 total; 177 undergraduate, 15 graduate.

Music Student Profile 15% females, 85% males, 10% minorities, 10% international.

Music Faculty 72 total undergraduate and graduate (full-time and part-time). 78% of full-time faculty have terminal degrees. Graduate students do not teach undergraduate courses. Undergraduate student–faculty ratio: 3:1.

Student Life Student groups/activities include Music Educators National Conference, National Academy of Recording Arts and Sciences, International Association of Jazz Educators. Special housing available for music students.

Expenses for 1997–98 Application fee: $40. Tuition: $14,570 full-time. Mandatory fees: $500 full-time. College room only: $4100.

Financial Aid Program-specific awards for 1997: 30 Merit Scholarships for incoming students ($500–$7900).

Application Procedures Students admitted directly into the professional program freshman year. Deadline for freshmen and transfers: continuous. Notification date for freshmen and transfers: September 1. Required: essay, high school transcript, college transcript(s) for transfer students, minimum 2.0 high school GPA, letter of recommendation, audition, SAT I or ACT test scores. Auditions held 8 times on campus; recorded music is permissible as a substitute for live auditions with approval from the department and videotaped performances are permissible as a substitute for live auditions with approval from the department.

Web Site http://www.uarts.edu.

Contact Ms. Barbara Elliott, Director of Admissions, University of the Arts, 320 South Broad Street, Philadelphia, Pennsylvania 19102; 800-616-ARTS.

▼ UNIVERSITY OF THE INCARNATE WORD

San Antonio, Texas

Independent-Roman Catholic, coed. Urban campus. Total enrollment: 3,312. Music program established 1932.

Degrees Bachelor of Music in the areas of classical music, composition, music, performance; Bachelor of Music Education; Bachelor of Music Therapy. Majors and concentrations: brass, composition, music, music business, music education, music therapy, piano/organ, stringed instruments, voice, wind and percussion instruments. Cross-registration with Our Lady of the Lake University of San Antonio, St. Mary's University of San Antonio, Alamo Community Colleges.

Enrollment Fall 1997: 51 total; 47 undergraduate, 4 non-professional degree.

Music Student Profile 60% females, 40% males, 60% minorities.

Music Faculty 23 total (full-time and part-time). 100% of full-time faculty have terminal degrees. Graduate students do not teach undergraduate courses. Undergraduate student–faculty ratio: 6:1.

Student Life Student groups/activities include American Association of Music Therapy.

Expenses for 1997–98 Application fee: $20. One-time mandatory fee: $100. Comprehensive fee: $15,467 includes full-time tuition ($10,600), mandatory fees ($240), and college room and board ($4627). College room only: $2580. Special program-related fees: $190 per semester for private lessons.

Financial Aid Program-specific awards for 1997: 1 Sarah Eliz Bell Endowed Scholarship for program majors ($1200), 1 Hortense Buchanan Award for program majors ($100), 1 Lamar Moreau Award for program majors ($100), 1 Sister Margaret Alacoque Colothan Endowed Scholarship for program majors ($700).

Application Procedures Students apply for admission into the professional program by freshman year. Deadline for freshmen and transfers: continuous. Required: high school transcript, college transcript(s) for transfer students, minimum 2.0 high school GPA, 3 letters of recommendation, interview, video, audition, SAT I or ACT test scores.

Auditions held 3 times on campus; recorded music is permissible as a substitute for live auditions with 3 letters of recommendation and videotaped performances are permissible as a substitute for live auditions with 3 letters of recommendation.

Undergraduate Contact Ms. D. E. Bussineau-King, Director, Music Department, University of the Incarnate Word, Box 67, 4301 Broadway, San Antonio, Texas 78209; 210-829-3858, fax: 210-829-3880, E-mail address: bussinea@universe.uiwtx.edu.

▼ UNIVERSITY OF THE PACIFIC
Stockton, California

Independent, coed. Suburban campus. Total enrollment: 5,585. Music program established 1878.

Degrees Bachelor of Music in the areas of performance, music education, music therapy, composition, music history; Bachelor of Arts in the area of music. Majors and concentrations: brass, composition, music education, music history, music management, music therapy, piano/organ, stringed instruments, voice, wind and percussion instruments. Graduate degrees offered: Master of Music in the area of music education; Master of Arts in the area of music therapy. Program accredited by NASM.

Enrollment Fall 1997: 192 total; 180 undergraduate, 12 graduate.

Music Student Profile 62% females, 38% males, 22% minorities, 8% international.

Music Faculty 42 total undergraduate and graduate (full-time and part-time). 65% of full-time faculty have terminal degrees. Graduate students do not teach undergraduate courses. Undergraduate student–faculty ratio: 7:1.

Student Life Student groups/activities include Music Educators National Conference Student Chapter, Music Therapy Association, professional music fraternities.

Expenses for 1998–99 Application fee: $50. One-time mandatory fee: $100. Comprehensive fee: $25,135 includes full-time tuition ($19,000), mandatory fees ($365), and college room and board ($5770). Full-time tuition and fees vary according to program. Room and board charges vary according to board plan and housing facility. Special program-related fees: $35–$100 per credit for applied music fee, $10–$15 per semester for practice room fee.

Financial Aid Program-specific awards for 1997: 118 music scholarships for those demonstrating talent and need ($3000–$15,000), 29 Conservatory Performance Scholarships for those demonstrating musical achievement ($1000–$9600).

Application Procedures Students admitted directly into the professional program freshman year. Deadline for freshmen and transfers: continuous. Required: essay, high school transcript, college transcript(s) for transfer students, letter of recommendation, audition, SAT I or ACT test scores. Recommended: minimum 3.0 high school GPA. Auditions held 9 times on campus and off campus in Los Angeles, CA; San Diego, CA; Portland, OR; recorded music is permissible as a substitute for live auditions if a campus visit is impossible and videotaped performances are permissible as a substitute for live auditions if a campus visit is impossible.

Undergraduate Contact Ms. Joanne Paine, Secretary of Student Services, Conservatory of Music, University of the Pacific, 3601 Pacific Avenue, Stockton, California 95211; 209-946-2418, fax: 209-946-2770, E-mail address: jpaine@uop.edu.

▼ UNIVERSITY OF TOLEDO
Toledo, Ohio

State-supported, coed. Suburban campus. Total enrollment: 20,307. Music program established 1948.

Degrees Bachelor of Music in the area of performance studies; Bachelor of Music Education. Majors and concentrations: music education, piano/organ, stringed instruments, voice, wind and percussion instruments. Graduate degrees offered: Master of Music in the area of performance studies; Master of Music Education. Cross-registration with Eastern Michigan University, Bowling Green State University. Program accredited by NASM.

Enrollment Fall 1997: 150 total; 100 undergraduate, 50 graduate.

Music Student Profile 52% females, 48% males, 10% minorities, 5% international.

Music Faculty 42 total undergraduate and graduate (full-time and part-time). 67% of full-time faculty have terminal degrees. Graduate students do not teach undergraduate courses. Undergraduate student–faculty ratio: 8:1.

Student Life Student groups/activities include Mu Phi Epsilon, Music Educators National Conference, Ohio Music Teachers Association.

Expenses for 1997–98 Application fee: $30. State resident tuition: $3171 full-time. Nonresident tuition: $8763 full-time. Mandatory fees: $781 full-time. College room and board: $4194. Room and board charges vary according to board plan and housing facility. Special program-related fees: $53–$83 per course for applied music fees, $23 per semester for ensemble and lab fees.

Financial Aid Program-specific awards for 1997: 20 Hassensall Awards for program majors ($100–$800), 7 Eckels Awards for upperclassmen ($200–$500), 2 Art Tatum Awards for African Americans ($200–$300), 8 Baer Awards for pianists ($150–$1200), 3 Key to the Sea Awards for brass/percussionists ($300–$600), Jacobson Awards for AGMA members, band scholarships for band members.

Application Procedures Students admitted directly into the professional program freshman year. Deadline for freshmen and transfers: continuous. Required: high school transcript, college transcript(s) for transfer students, minimum 2.0 high school GPA, audition, SAT I or ACT test scores. Auditions held 4 times and by appointment on campus; recorded music is permissible as a substitute for live auditions for international applicants and on a case-by-case basis and videotaped performances are permissible as a substitute for live auditions for international applicants.

Web Site http://www.utoledo.edu/college/arts-and-sciences/music/.

Undergraduate Contact Carolyn Olejownik, Recruiting Office, Department of Music, University of Toledo, 2801 West Bancroft, Toledo, Ohio 43606-3390; 419-530-2447, fax: 419-530-8483, E-mail address: rcofer@uoft02.utoledo.edu.

Graduate Contact Dr. Robert DeYarman, Chair, Department of Music, University of Toledo, 2801 West Bancroft, Toledo, Ohio 43606-3390; 419-530-4556, fax: 419-530-8483, E-mail address: rdeyarm@uoft02.utoledo.edu.

▼ UNIVERSITY OF TULSA
Tulsa, Oklahoma

Independent, coed. Urban campus. Total enrollment: 4,171.

University of Tulsa *(continued)*

Degrees Bachelor of Music in the areas of performance, composition; Bachelor of Music Education in the areas of instrumental music education, vocal music education. Majors and concentrations: composition, music education, piano, stringed instruments, voice, wind and percussion instruments. Program accredited by NASM.

Enrollment Fall 1997: 108 total; 69 undergraduate, 39 non-professional degree.

Music Student Profile 61% females, 39% males, 21% minorities, 3% international.

Music Faculty 30 total (full-time and part-time). 66% of full-time faculty have terminal degrees. Graduate students do not teach undergraduate courses.

Student Life Student groups/activities include Sigma Alpha Iota, Phi Mu Alpha Sinfonia, Music Educators National Conference.

Expenses for 1997–98 Application fee: $25. One-time mandatory fee: $200. Comprehensive fee: $17,340 includes full-time tuition ($12,850), mandatory fees ($80), and college room and board ($4410). College room only: $2260. Room and board charges vary according to board plan and housing facility.

Financial Aid Program-specific awards for 1997: 120 grants-in-aid for program students ($5400), 3 Kathleen C. Parriott Scholarships for music majors ($20,000), Roger P. Fenn Memorial Scholarship for string or wind music education majors ($750), 1 Presser Scholarship for senior music education majors ($2000), 1 Fourjay Scholarship in music for program majors ($2500), 1 Gretchen Ninan Gaither Memorial Scholarship for string majors ($1000), 1 Michael Houghton Memorial Scholarship for music education majors ($3000), 1 Albert and Florence Lukken Memorial Scholarship for voice or piano majors ($1250), 1 Maude B. Pape Memorial Scholarship for voice majors ($3500), 1 Sigma Alpha Iota Patroness Scholarship for outstanding Sigma Alpha Iota members ($2000).

Application Procedures Students admitted directly into the professional program freshman year. Deadline for freshmen and transfers: continuous. Required: essay, high school transcript, college transcript(s) for transfer students, minimum 2.0 high school GPA, letter of recommendation, interview, audition, SAT I or ACT test scores. Auditions held 5 times and by appointment on campus; recorded music is permissible as a substitute for live auditions when distance is prohibitive and videotaped performances are permissible as a substitute for live auditions when distance is prohibitive.

Undergraduate Contact Dr. Frank Ryan, Director, School of Music, University of Tulsa, 600 South College Avenue, Tulsa, Oklahoma 74104-3189; 918-631-2262, fax: 918-631-3589, E-mail address: frank-ryan@utulsa.edu.

▼ UNIVERSITY OF UTAH

Salt Lake City, Utah

State-supported, coed. Urban campus. Total enrollment: 25,883. Music program established 1908.

Degrees Bachelor of Music in the areas of performance, music education, theory, composition, piano pedagogy, history and literature; Bachelor of Music Education in the areas of instrumental music, choral music. Majors and concentrations: brass, classical music, composition, electronic music, harp, jazz, music education, music history and literature, music theory, piano, piano pedagogy, stringed instruments, voice, wind and percussion instruments. Graduate degrees offered: Master of Music in the areas of composition, history/literature, performance, music education, conducting, theory, musicology; Master of Music Education. Program accredited by NASM.

Enrollment Fall 1997: 322 undergraduate, 55 graduate.

Music Student Profile 53% females, 47% males, 2% minorities, 10% international.

Music Faculty 70 total undergraduate and graduate (full-time and part-time). 80% of full-time faculty have terminal degrees. Graduate students teach a few undergraduate courses. Undergraduate student–faculty ratio: 5:1.

Student Life Student groups/activities include Music Educators National Conference, world-wide competitions.

Expenses for 1997–98 Application fee: $30. State resident tuition: $2601 full-time. Nonresident tuition: $7,998 full-time. Full-time tuition varies according to course load. College room and board: $4620. College room only: $1708. Room and board charges vary according to board plan. Special program-related fees: $130–$300 per semester for private lessons, $90 per year for practice rooms.

Financial Aid Program-specific awards for 1997: 20–30 Tracy Piano Awards for pianists ($400–$5000), 20–30 Carmen Christensen Scholarships for program majors ($200–$5000), 4 departmental awards for program majors ($2000–$5000).

Application Procedures Students admitted directly into the professional program freshman year. Deadline for freshmen and transfers: July 1. Required: high school transcript, college transcript(s) for transfer students, minimum 3.0 high school GPA, audition, SAT I or ACT test scores. Recommended: essay, 3 letters of recommendation, interview, video, portfolio. Auditions held 3-4 times on campus; recorded music is permissible as a substitute for live auditions when distance is prohibitive and videotaped performances are permissible as a substitute for live auditions when distance is prohibitive. Portfolio reviews held as needed on campus.

Web Site http://www.music.utah.edu/.

Undergraduate Contact Dr. Mark Ely, Undergraduate Counselor, Music Department, University of Utah, 204 LCB, Salt Lake City, Utah 84112; 801-581-7163, fax: 801-581-5683.

Graduate Contact Dr. Edward Asmus, Director of Graduate Studies, Music Department, University of Utah, 204 LCB, Salt Lake City, Utah 84112; 801-585-7369, fax: 801-581-5683.

▼ UNIVERSITY OF VERMONT

Burlington, Vermont

State-supported, coed. Suburban campus. Total enrollment: 10,368.

Degrees Bachelor of Music in the areas of performance, music theory/composition; Bachelor of Science in the area of music education; Bachelor of Arts in the area of music. Majors and concentrations: classical guitar, classical music, harp, harpsichord, music history, music theory, performance, piano/organ, stringed instruments, voice, wind and percussion instruments. Program accredited by NCATE.

Enrollment Fall 1997: 80 total; 50 undergraduate, 30 non-professional degree.

Music Student Profile 50% females, 50% males, 5% minorities.

Music Faculty 33 total (full-time and part-time). 100% of full-time faculty have terminal degrees. Graduate students do not teach undergraduate courses. Undergraduate student–faculty ratio: 10:1.

Student Life Student groups/activities include Music Educators National Conference.

Expenses for 1997–98 Application fee: $45. State resident tuition: $7032 full-time. Nonresident tuition: $17,580 full-time. Mandatory fees: $518 full-time. Full-time tuition and fees vary according to course load. College room and board: $5272. Room and board charges vary according to board plan. Special program-related fees: $170 per credit hour for private music lessons.

Financial Aid Program-specific awards for 1997: 1 departmental awards for music major from New England, 30 Yandell Scholarships for music majors ($340).

Application Procedures Students apply for admission into the professional program by sophomore year. Deadline for freshmen: February 1; transfers: April 1. Required: essay, high school transcript, college transcript(s) for transfer students, SAT I or ACT test scores, completion of college preparatory courses. Recommended: minimum 3.0 high school GPA, 3 letters of recommendation, interview, video, audition. Auditions held by appointment on campus; recorded music is permissible as a substitute for live auditions when distance is prohibitive and videotaped performances are permissible as a substitute for live auditions when distance is prohibitive.

Undergraduate Contact Ms. Joanne Raymond, Administrative Assistant, Department of Music, University of Vermont, Redstone Campus, Burlington, Vermont 05405; 802-656-3040, fax: 802-656-0759, E-mail address: jraymond@zoo.uvm.edu.

▼ UNIVERSITY OF WASHINGTON

Seattle, Washington

State-supported, coed. Urban campus. Total enrollment: 35,367.

Degrees Bachelor of Music in the areas of performance, jazz studies, composition. Majors and concentrations: guitar, harp, jazz, music, music education, orchestral instruments, piano/organ, stringed instruments, voice. Graduate degrees offered: Master of Music in the areas of performance, composition, conducting. Doctor of Musical Arts in the areas of performance, composition, conducting. Program accredited by NASM.

Enrollment Fall 1997: 369 total; 169 undergraduate, 126 graduate, 74 non-professional degree.

Music Student Profile 46% females, 54% males, 14% minorities, 6% international.

Music Faculty 60 total undergraduate and graduate (full-time and part-time). 80% of full-time faculty have terminal degrees. Graduate students teach a few undergraduate courses. Undergraduate student–faculty ratio: 3:1.

Student Life Student groups/activities include Music Educators National Conference, Mu Phi Epsilon.

Expenses for 1997–98 Application fee: $35. State resident tuition: $3366 full-time. Nonresident tuition: $10,656 full-time. College room and board: $4671. College room only: $2556. Part-time tuition per term ranges from $226 to $1010 for state residents, $712 to $3197 for nonresidents. Special program-related fees: $100 per quarter for applied music lesson fee.

Application Procedures Students admitted directly into the professional program freshman year. Deadline for freshmen: February 1; transfers: April 15. Required: essay, high school transcript, college transcript(s) for transfer students, mini-

mum 3.0 high school GPA, audition, SAT I or ACT test scores. Auditions held 4 times on campus; recorded music is permissible as a substitute for live auditions for provisional acceptance and videotaped performances are permissible as a substitute for live auditions for provisional acceptance.

Web Site http://weber.u.washington.edu/~musicweb/.

Undergraduate Contact Ms. Beth Miquel Alipio, Undergraduate Advisor, School of Music, University of Washington, Box 352450, Seattle, Washington 98195-3450; 206-543-8273, fax: 206-685-9499.

Graduate Contact Ms. Elizabeth Westphal, Director, Counseling Services, School of Music, University of Washington, Box 353450, Seattle, Washington 98195-3450; 206-543-2726, fax: 206-685-9499, E-mail address: westphal@u.washington.edu.

▼ UNIVERSITY OF WISCONSIN–EAU CLAIRE

Eau Claire, Wisconsin

State-supported, coed. Urban campus. Total enrollment: 10,484. Music program established 1947.

Degrees Bachelor of Music in the areas of performance, theory, composition; Bachelor of Music Education in the areas of choral music education, instrumental music education; Bachelor of Music Therapy. Majors and concentrations: composition, harpsichord, music education, music theory, music therapy, piano/organ, stringed instruments, voice, wind and percussion instruments. Program accredited by NASM.

Enrollment Fall 1997: 280 total; all undergraduate.

Music Student Profile 60% females, 40% males, 5% minorities, 2% international.

Music Faculty 35 total (full-time and part-time). 60% of full-time faculty have terminal degrees. Graduate students do not teach undergraduate courses. Undergraduate student–faculty ratio: 10:1.

Expenses for 1997–98 Application fee: $28. State resident tuition: $2870 full-time. Nonresident tuition: $8812 full-time. Mandatory fees: $2 full-time. Full-time tuition and fees vary according to reciprocity agreements. College room and board: $2986. College room only: $1720.

Financial Aid Program-specific awards for 1997: 30 music scholarships for program majors ($500–$1000).

Application Procedures Students admitted directly into the professional program freshman year. Deadline for freshmen: January 1; transfers: continuous. Required: high school transcript, college transcript(s) for transfer students, minimum 2.0 high school GPA, 2 letters of recommendation, audition, ACT test score only (minimum combined ACT score of 23), standing in top half of graduating class. Recommended: minimum 3.0 high school GPA. Auditions held 3 times on campus; recorded music is permissible as a substitute for live auditions for international applicants and videotaped performances are permissible as a substitute for live auditions for international applicants.

Web Site http://www.uwec.edu/Academic/Mus-The.

Undergraduate Contact Mr. Timothy Lane, Admissions Coordinator, Department of Music and Theatre Arts, University of Wisconsin–Eau Claire, Room 156, Fine Arts Building, Eau Claire, Wisconsin 54702; 715-836-2284, E-mail address: lanet@uwec.edu.

▼ UNIVERSITY OF WISCONSIN–GREEN BAY

Green Bay, Wisconsin

State-supported, coed. Suburban campus. Total enrollment: 5,419.

Degrees Bachelor of Music in the areas of music education, performance. Majors and concentrations: bass, guitar, music education, piano/organ, voice, wind and percussion instruments. Program accredited by NASM.

Enrollment Fall 1997: 105 total; all undergraduate.

Music Student Profile 60% females, 40% males, 5% minorities.

Music Faculty 26 total (full-time and part-time). 45% of full-time faculty have terminal degrees. Graduate students do not teach undergraduate courses. Undergraduate student–faculty ratio: 11:1.

Student Life Student groups/activities include Music Educators National Conference Student Chapter, American Choral Directors Association College Chapter, Jazz Society.

Expenses for 1997–98 Application fee: $35. State resident tuition: $2312 full-time. Nonresident tuition: $8254 full-time. Mandatory fees: $426 full-time. Full-time tuition and fees vary according to reciprocity agreements. College room only: $1835. Room charges vary according to housing facility. Special program-related fees: $25 per semester for instrument rental fee.

Financial Aid Program-specific awards for 1997: 20–25 Music Talent Scholarships for freshmen music majors ($750), 9 Pep Band Awards for program majors and non-majors ($500), 7 Continuing Music Awards for upperclass program majors ($500).

Application Procedures Students admitted directly into the professional program freshman year. Deadline for freshmen: February 1; transfers: February 15. Required: high school transcript, college transcript(s) for transfer students, 2 letters of recommendation, interview, audition, ACT test score only (minimum combined ACT score of 20). Recommended: essay, minimum 3.0 high school GPA. Auditions held 4 times and by appointment on campus.

Undergraduate Contact Thomas Pfotenhauer, Chair of Music Scholarship and Recruitment Committee, Music Department, University of Wisconsin–Green Bay, 2420 Nicolet Drive, Green Bay, Wisconsin 54311-7001; 920-465-2440, fax: 920-465-2890, E-mail address: pfotenht@uwgb.edu.

▼ UNIVERSITY OF WISCONSIN–MADISON

Madison, Wisconsin

State-supported, coed. Urban campus. Total enrollment: 40,196. Music program established 1895.

Degrees Bachelor of Music in the areas of performance, music education. Majors and concentrations: composition, jazz, music, music education, piano/organ, stringed instruments, voice, wind and percussion instruments. Graduate degrees offered: Master of Music Education; Master of Musical Arts in the areas of brass instruments, choral conducting, composition, music education, ethnomusicology, musicology, instrumental conducting-orchestra, instrumental conducting-wind ensemble, opera, organ, percussion, piano, piano-accompanying, piano pedagogy/performance. Doctor of Musical Arts in the areas of brass instruments, choral conducting, composition, instrumental conducting-orchestra, instrumental conducting-wind ensemble, organ,

piano, stringed instruments, voice, woodwind instruments. Program accredited by NASM.

Enrollment Fall 1997: 290 undergraduate, 160 graduate.

Music Student Profile 50% females, 50% males, 10% minorities.

Music Faculty 54 total undergraduate and graduate (full-time and part-time). 90% of full-time faculty have terminal degrees. Graduate students teach a few undergraduate courses. Undergraduate student–faculty ratio: 20:1.

Student Life Student groups/activities include Sigma Alpha Iota, Music Educators National Conference Student Chapter, Music Teachers National Association Student Chapter.

Estimated expenses for 1998–99 Application fee: $35. State resident tuition: $3242 full-time. Nonresident tuition: $10,552 full-time. Full-time tuition varies according to reciprocity agreements. College room and board: $4880. Special program-related fees: $25 per semester for practice room, $30 per semester for recital recording, $40 per recital for non-required recital fee.

Financial Aid Program-specific awards for 1997: 15–20 Evelyn Steenbock Scholarships for program majors ($1000–$3000), 15 Elsa Sawyer Scholarships for those demonstrating need, talent and academic achievement ($1000–$3000), 10–15 Margaret Rupp Cooper Scholarships for state residents ($1000–$3000), 1–2 Gertrude Meyne Bates Scholarships for talented program majors.

Application Procedures Students apply for admission into the professional program by freshman, sophomore year. Deadline for freshmen: February 1; transfers: March 1. Notification date for freshmen: March 10; transfers: April 30. Required: high school transcript, minimum 3.0 high school GPA, 2 letters of recommendation, interview, audition. Auditions held 3 times on campus; recorded music is permissible as a substitute for live auditions when distance is prohibitive.

Undergraduate Contact Ms. Ellen Burmeister, Associate Director, School of Music, University of Wisconsin–Madison, 1621 Humanities, Madison, Wisconsin 53706; 608-263-5986, fax: 608-262-8876, E-mail address: coburmei@macc.wisc.edu.

Graduate Contact Dr. J. Chappell Stowe, Director of Graduate Studies, School of Music, University of Wisconsin–Madison, 4531 Humanities, Madison, Wisconsin 53706; 608-262-9295, fax: 608-262-8876, E-mail address: jcstow@facstaff.wisc.edu.

More About the University

Program Facilities Activities occur in three areas on campus, which is nestled on the shores of Lake Mendota in the state capitol. The Humanities Building, where most classrooms and faculty studios are located, houses three performance spaces: newly refurbished 770-seat Mills Concert Hall, 200-seat Morphy Recital Hall, and 175-seat Eastman Organ Recital Hall. The building contains the Wisconsin Center for Music Technology, a sophisticated computer laboratory that positions the School as a national leader in computer-based education. Music Hall, built in 1879 and renovated in 1985, and its 385-seat auditorium are the opera program's home. Mills Music Library serves the School's research mission with 42,000 monographs and serials, 120,000 recordings, and more than 1,000 microfilms.

Faculty, Resident Artists, and Alumni An international roster of 60 faculty artists and scholars strives to maintain a focus on individual student attention within the vast resources of the Madison campus. In 1939 the School gained distinction with the creation of the first musical artist-in-residence position at any American university. Today it has one of the nation's strongest chamber music programs, with three faculty resident ensembles: Pro Arte String Quartet, Wingra

Woodwind Quintet, and Wisconsin Brass Quintet. Master classes are taught by renowned musicians who visit Madison; recent guests include James Galway, Beaux Arts Trio, Max Roach, and Jeffrey Siegel. Living alumni number about 3,000, who perform and teach around the world.

Student Performances Three hundred annual performances include those by seven choral groups; three orchestras; six bands; ensembles in jazz, early music, percussion, African-American music, and Javanese gamelan; and fully staged opera productions.

▼ UNIVERSITY OF WISCONSIN–MILWAUKEE

Milwaukee, Wisconsin

State-supported, coed. Urban campus. Total enrollment: 21,525.

Degrees Bachelor of Fine Arts in the areas of music, performance, music history and literature, music theory/composition, music education/general, music education/instrumental, music education/choral. Majors and concentrations: brass, guitar, music education, music theory and composition, piano/organ, stringed instruments, voice, wind and percussion instruments. Graduate degrees offered: Master of Music in the areas of performance, music theory/composition, conducting, accompanying, music education, music history and literature. Mandatory cross-registration with Wisconsin Conservatory of Music. Program accredited by NASM.

Enrollment Fall 1997: 248 total; 193 undergraduate, 35 graduate, 20 non-professional degree.

Music Student Profile 55% females, 45% males, 1% minorities, 5% international.

Music Faculty 48 total undergraduate and graduate (full-time and part-time). 95% of full-time faculty have terminal degrees. Graduate students teach a few undergraduate courses. Undergraduate student–faculty ratio: 6:1.

Student Life Student groups/activities include Delta Omicron, Collegiate Music Educators National Conference.

Expenses for 1997–98 Application fee: $28. State resident tuition: $3327 full-time. Nonresident tuition: $10,790 full-time. Full-time tuition varies according to reciprocity agreements. College room only: $2457.

Financial Aid Program-specific awards for 1997: 50 music scholarships for program students ($200–$2000).

Application Procedures Students admitted directly into the professional program freshman year. Deadline for freshmen and transfers: continuous. Notification date for freshmen and transfers: continuous. Required: high school transcript, letter of recommendation, audition. Auditions held 4 times on campus; recorded music is permissible as a substitute for live auditions when distance is prohibitive and videotaped performances are permissible as a substitute for live auditions when distance is prohibitive.

Web Site http://www.uwm.edu/Dept/SFA/.

Undergraduate Contact Mr. Mitchell Brauner, Undergraduate Director, Fine Arts/Music Department, University of Wisconsin–Milwaukee, PO Box 413, Milwaukee, Wisconsin 53201; 414-229-6744, fax: 414-229-2776.

▼ UNIVERSITY OF WISCONSIN–OSHKOSH

Oshkosh, Wisconsin

State-supported, coed. Suburban campus. Total enrollment: 10,960.

Degrees Bachelor of Music in the areas of performance, music therapy, music merchandising; Bachelor of Music Education in the areas of general music, choral music, instrumental music. Majors and concentrations: brass, music education, music therapy, piano, retail music merchandising, sound recording technology, stringed instruments, voice, wind and percussion instruments. Program accredited by NASM.

Enrollment Fall 1997: 159 total; 156 undergraduate, 3 non-professional degree.

Music Student Profile 53% females, 47% males.

Music Faculty 33 total (full-time and part-time). 75% of full-time faculty have terminal degrees. Graduate students do not teach undergraduate courses. Undergraduate student–faculty ratio: 12:1.

Student Life Student groups/activities include Music Educators National Conference Student Chapter, National Association of Music Therapy Student Chapter, Oshkosh Recording Association.

Expenses for 1997–98 Application fee: $35. State resident tuition: $2607 full-time. Nonresident tuition: $8549 full-time. Mandatory fees: $2 full-time. Full-time tuition and fees vary according to reciprocity agreements. College room and board: $2658. College room only: $1628. Room and board charges vary according to board plan and housing facility.

Financial Aid Program-specific awards for 1997: 1 Willcockson Prize in the Arts for incoming freshmen ($300–$400), 10–12 music scholarships for music majors.

Application Procedures Students admitted directly into the professional program freshman year. Deadline for freshmen and transfers: continuous. Required: high school transcript, audition, ACT test score only. Auditions held 4 times on campus; recorded music is permissible as a substitute for live auditions when distance is prohibitive and videotaped performances are permissible as a substitute for live auditions when distance is prohibitive.

Undergraduate Contact Admissions Office, University of Wisconsin–Oshkosh, 800 Algoma Boulevard, Oshkosh, Wisconsin 54901; 920-424-0202.

▼ UNIVERSITY OF WISCONSIN–RIVER FALLS

River Falls, Wisconsin

State-supported, coed. Suburban campus. Total enrollment: 5,441.

Degrees Bachelor of Music Education in the areas of instrumental music, vocal music, piano/vocal music. Cross-registration with University of Wisconsin, University of Minnesota. Program accredited by NASM, NCATE.

Enrollment Fall 1997: 50 undergraduate.

Music Student Profile 50% females, 50% males, 5% minorities, 2% international.

Music Faculty 16 total (full-time and part-time). 33% of full-time faculty have terminal degrees. Graduate students do not teach undergraduate courses. Undergraduate student–faculty ratio: 8:1.

Student Life Student groups/activities include National Association of Schools of Music.

Estimated expenses for 1998–99 Application fee: $35. State resident tuition: $2750 full-time. Nonresident tuition: $8692 full-time. Full-time tuition varies according to reciprocity agreements. College room and board: $3036. College room only: $1640. Room and board charges vary according to

University of Wisconsin–River Falls (continued)

board plan. Part-time tuition and fees per term range from $153.75 to $1354.20 for state residents, $414.75 to $3730.20 for nonresidents.

Financial Aid Program-specific awards for 1997: 10 Music Performance Scholarships for incoming freshmen and program majors ($300).

Application Procedures Students admitted directly into the professional program freshman year. Deadline for freshmen and transfers: March 1. Required: high school transcript, college transcript(s) for transfer students, minimum 2.0 high school GPA, SAT I or ACT test scores. Recommended: minimum 3.0 high school GPA.

Web Site http://www.uwrf.edu/music/.

Undergraduate Contact Ms. Kris Tjornehoj, Recruitment Director, Music Department, University of Wisconsin–River Falls, 410 South Third Street, River Falls, Wisconsin 54022-5013; 715-425-3940, fax: 715-425-0657, E-mail address: music@uwrf.edu.

▼ UNIVERSITY OF WISCONSIN–STEVENS POINT

Stevens Point, Wisconsin

State-supported, coed. Small town campus. Total enrollment: 8,446.

Degrees Bachelor of Music in the areas of music education, jazz studies, performance, music literature. Graduate degrees offered: Master of Music Education in the areas of instrumental music education, choral music education, jazz pedagogy, studio pedagogy, Suzuki talent education. Program accredited by NASM.

Enrollment Fall 1997: 234 total; 186 undergraduate, 8 graduate, 40 non-professional degree.

Music Student Profile 60% females, 40% males, 3% minorities, 1% international.

Music Faculty 21 total undergraduate and graduate (full-time). 90% of full-time faculty have terminal degrees. Graduate students do not teach undergraduate courses. Undergraduate student–faculty ratio: 15:1.

Student Life Student groups/activities include Music Educators National Conference, American String Teachers Association.

Expenses for 1997–98 Application fee: $35. State resident tuition: $2790 full-time. Nonresident tuition: $8732 full-time. Full-time tuition varies according to course load and reciprocity agreements. College room and board: $3188. College room only: $1861. Room and board charges vary according to board plan.

Financial Aid Program-specific awards for 1997: music scholarships for those demonstrating talent, academic achievement, and need.

Application Procedures Students apply for admission into the professional program by sophomore year. Deadline for freshmen: January 15; transfers: February 15. Required: high school transcript, college transcript(s) for transfer students, audition, SAT I or ACT test scores. Auditions held 3 times and by appointment on campus; recorded music is permissible as a substitute for live auditions when distance is prohibitive and videotaped performances are permissible as a substitute for live auditions when distance is prohibitive.

Web Site http://www.uwsp.edu.

Undergraduate Contact Dr. Robert Kase, Chair, Music Department, University of Wisconsin–Stevens Point, Fine Arts Center, Stevens Point, Wisconsin 54481; 715-346-3107, fax: 715-346-2718, E-mail address: rkase@uwsp.edu.

Graduate Contact Dr. Patricia Holland, Coordinator of Graduate Studies, Music Department, University of Wisconsin–Stevens Point, Fine Arts Center, Stevens Point, Wisconsin 54481; 715-346-3119, fax: 715-346-2718, E-mail address: pholland@uwsp.edu.

▼ UNIVERSITY OF WISCONSIN–SUPERIOR

Superior, Wisconsin

State-supported, coed. Small town campus. Total enrollment: 2,574. Music program established 1939.

Degrees Bachelor of Music in the area of performance; Bachelor of Music Education in the areas of choral music, instrumental music, general music. Majors and concentrations: guitar, harpsichord, music education, piano/organ, stringed instruments, voice, wind and percussion instruments. Cross-registration with University of Minnesota-Duluth, College of St. Scholastica. Program accredited by NASM.

Enrollment Fall 1997: 51 undergraduate.

Music Student Profile 51% females, 49% males, 1% minorities, 1% international.

Music Faculty 19 total (full-time and part-time). 86% of full-time faculty have terminal degrees. Graduate students do not teach undergraduate courses. Undergraduate student–faculty ratio: 8:1.

Student Life Student groups/activities include Music Educators National Conference Student Chapter.

Expenses for 1997–98 Application fee: $35. State resident tuition: $2652 full-time. Nonresident tuition: $8600 full-time. Full-time tuition varies according to course load and reciprocity agreements. College room and board: $3200. College room only: $1600.

Financial Aid Program-specific awards for 1997: 1 NBC Keyboard Award for pianists and organists ($1000), 6 Foundation Awards for incoming freshmen ($500), 1 Rock Scholarship for junior and senior pianists ($1000).

Application Procedures Students admitted directly into the professional program freshman year. Deadline for freshmen and transfers: May 1. Notification date for freshmen and transfers: August 1. Required: high school transcript, college transcript(s) for transfer students, interview, audition, SAT I or ACT test scores, standing in top half of graduating class. Recommended: letter of recommendation. Auditions held 4 times on campus; recorded music is permissible as a substitute for live auditions when distance is prohibitive and videotaped performances are permissible as a substitute for live auditions when distance is prohibitive.

Web Site http://www.uwsuper.edu/acaddept/music.shtml.

Undergraduate Contact Mr. T. A. Bumgardner, Chairman, Department of Music, University of Wisconsin–Superior, 1800 Grand Avenue, Superior, Wisconsin 54880-2898; 715-394-8255, fax: 715-394-8454, E-mail address: abumgard@staff.uwsuper.edu.

▼ UNIVERSITY OF WISCONSIN–WHITEWATER

Whitewater, Wisconsin

State-supported, coed. Small town campus. Total enrollment: 10,563.

Degrees Bachelor of Music in the areas of music education, performance, music history, music theory. Majors and concentrations: music, music education, piano/organ, stringed instruments, voice, wind and percussion instruments. Graduate degrees offered: Master of Music Education. Program accredited by NASM.

Enrollment Fall 1997: 170 total; 159 undergraduate, 11 graduate.

Music Faculty 30 total undergraduate and graduate (full-time and part-time). 64% of full-time faculty have terminal degrees. Graduate students do not teach undergraduate courses. Undergraduate student–faculty ratio: 9:1.

Student Life Student groups/activities include Music Educators National Conference Student Chapter, International Association of Jazz Educators Student Chapter, music fraternities.

Expenses for 1997–98 Application fee: $35. State resident tuition: $2772 full-time. Nonresident tuition: $8714 full-time. Full-time tuition varies according to reciprocity agreements. College room and board: $2812. College room only: $1620.

Financial Aid Program-specific awards for 1997: 24 music scholarships for program majors ($400–$800).

Application Procedures Students admitted directly into the professional program freshman year. Deadline for freshmen and transfers: continuous. Notification date for freshmen and transfers: continuous. Required: high school transcript, letter of recommendation, audition, ACT test score only, standing in top half of graduating class. Auditions held 5 times on campus; recorded music is permissible as a substitute for live auditions if a campus visit is impossible and videotaped performances are permissible as a substitute for live auditions if a campus visit is impossible.

Undergraduate Contact Audition Coordinator, Department of Music, University of Wisconsin–Whitewater, 800 West Main Street, Whitewater, Wisconsin 53190; 414-472-1310, fax: 414-472-2808.

Graduate Contact Dr. Janet Barrett, Graduate Coordinator, Department of Music, University of Wisconsin–Whitewater, 800 West Main Street, Whitewater, Wisconsin 53190; 414-472-1310, fax: 414-472-2808, E-mail address: barrettj@uwwvax.uww.edu.

▼ UNIVERSITY OF WYOMING

Laramie, Wyoming

State-supported, coed. Small town campus. Total enrollment: 11,094.

Degrees Bachelor of Music in the area of music performance; Bachelor of Music Education. Graduate degrees offered: Master of Music in the areas of music performance, music history, music theory; Master of Music Education. Cross-registration with Wyoming community colleges. Program accredited by NASM.

Enrollment Fall 1997: 155 total; 130 undergraduate, 17 graduate, 8 non-professional degree.

Music Student Profile 65% females, 35% males, 5% minorities, 5% international.

Music Faculty 32 total undergraduate and graduate (full-time and part-time). 90% of full-time faculty have terminal degrees. Graduate students do not teach undergraduate courses. Undergraduate student–faculty ratio: 12:1.

Student Life Student groups/activities include Wyoming Music Educators Association, band fraternities.

Expenses for 1997–98 Application fee: $30. State resident tuition: $1944 full-time. Nonresident tuition: $7032 full-time. Mandatory fees: $386 full-time. College room and board: $4278. College room only: $1758. Room and board charges vary according to board plan. Special program-related fees: $5 per semester for practice room fees.

Financial Aid Program-specific awards for 1997: 20 Private Awards for music majors ($300–$500).

Application Procedures Students admitted directly into the professional program freshman year. Deadline for freshmen and transfers: August 28. Notification date for freshmen and transfers: continuous. Required: high school transcript, college transcript(s) for transfer students, minimum 2.0 high school GPA, 3 letters of recommendation, audition, SAT I or ACT test scores. Recommended: interview, portfolio. Auditions held twice and by appointment on campus; recorded music is permissible as a substitute for live auditions when distance is prohibitive and videotaped performances are permissible as a substitute for live auditions when distance is prohibitive. Portfolio reviews held once per semester and by appointment on campus.

Undergraduate Contact Office of Admissions, University of Wyoming, Knight Hall, PO Box 3435, Laramie, Wyoming 82071; 307-766-5160, fax: 307-766-4042.

Graduate Contact Dean, Graduate School, University of Wyoming, PO Box 3108, Laramie, Wyoming 82071-3108; 307-766-2287, fax: 307-766-4042.

▼ UTAH STATE UNIVERSITY

Logan, Utah

State-supported, coed. Urban campus. Total enrollment: 21,234.

Degrees Bachelor of Music in the areas of music education, performance, piano pedagogy; Bachelor of Science in the area of music therapy. Majors and concentrations: guitar, individualized major, music, music education, music therapy, piano pedagogy, piano/organ, stringed instruments, voice, wind and percussion instruments. Program accredited by NASM.

Enrollment Fall 1997: 270 total; all undergraduate.

Music Student Profile 70% females, 30% males, 3% minorities, 2% international.

Music Faculty 22 total (full-time and part-time). 70% of full-time faculty have terminal degrees. Graduate students teach a few undergraduate courses.

Student Life Student groups/activities include Music Therapy Student Association, Kappa Kappa Psi (band fraternity), Tau Beta Sigma (band sorority).

Expenses for 1997–98 Application fee: $35. State resident tuition: $1767 full-time. Nonresident tuition: $6207 full-time. Mandatory fees: $408 full-time. Full-time tuition and fees vary according to course load. College room and board: $3510. College room only: $1440. Room and board charges vary according to board plan and housing facility. Special program-related fees: $30 per quarter for piano/organ practice rooms, $5 per quarter for instrument locker rentals.

Application Procedures Students admitted directly into the professional program freshman year. Deadline for freshmen and transfers: July 1. Required: high school transcript, college transcript(s) for transfer students, interview, audition, ACT test score only, minimum 2.5 high school GPA. Recommended: minimum 3.0 high school GPA. Auditions held at various times on campus and off campus in Salt Lake

Utah State University *(continued)*

City, UT; Rexburg, ID; recorded music is permissible as a substitute for live auditions when distance is prohibitive and videotaped performances are permissible as a substitute for live auditions when distance is prohibitive.

Web Site http://www.usu.edu/~music/.

Undergraduate Contact Secretary, Student Services, Music Department, Utah State University, 4015 University Hill, Logan, Utah 84322-4015; 801-797-3015, fax: 801-797-1862, E-mail address: musicdep@cc.usu.edu.

▼ VALDOSTA STATE UNIVERSITY

Valdosta, Georgia

State-supported, coed. Small town campus. Total enrollment: 9,779.

Degrees Bachelor of Music in the areas of music performance, music education. Majors and concentrations: jazz, music education, piano/organ, stringed instruments, voice, wind and percussion instruments. Graduate degrees offered: Master of Music Education. Program accredited by NASM.

Enrollment Fall 1997: 195 total; 150 undergraduate, 30 graduate, 15 non-professional degree.

Music Student Profile 50% females, 50% males, 15% minorities, 1% international.

Music Faculty 29 total undergraduate and graduate (full-time and part-time). 90% of full-time faculty have terminal degrees. Graduate students do not teach undergraduate courses. Undergraduate student–faculty ratio: 5:1.

Student Life Student groups/activities include Music Educators National Conference, Tau Beta Sigma, Sigma Alpha Iota.

Expenses for 1997–98 Application fee: $10. State resident tuition: $1680 full-time. Nonresident tuition: $6141 full-time. Mandatory fees: $294 full-time. College room and board: $3465. College room only: $1665. Room and board charges vary according to board plan. Special program-related fees: $50 per quarter for applied music fee.

Financial Aid Program-specific awards for 1997: 2 Lucy Martin Stewart Scholarships for program students, 2 Elene Dorminey Scholarships for program students, 2 Robert F. Barr Scholarships for program students, 20 departmental awards for freshmen, 10 Valdosta Symphony Scholarships for program students.

Application Procedures Students admitted directly into the professional program freshman year. Deadline for freshmen and transfers: continuous. Required: high school transcript, college transcript(s) for transfer students, minimum 2.0 high school GPA, audition, SAT I test score only. Auditions held continuously on campus; recorded music is permissible as a substitute for live auditions when distance is prohibitive and videotaped performances are permissible as a substitute for live auditions when distance is prohibitive.

Web Site http://www.valdosta.edu/music/.

Undergraduate Contact Mr. Walter Peacock, Director, Admissions Office, Valdosta State University, 1500 North Patterson Street, Valdosta, Georgia 31698-0170; 800-618-1878.

Graduate Contact Dr. Robert Welch, Music Department, Valdosta State University, Valdosta, Georgia 31698-0115; 912-245-2151.

▼ VALPARAISO UNIVERSITY

Valparaiso, Indiana

Independent, coed. Small town campus. Total enrollment: 3,603. Music program established 1925.

Degrees Bachelor of Music in the areas of church music, performance, composition; Bachelor of Music Education in the area of combined vocal and instrumental music. Majors and concentrations: classical music, music, music education, piano/organ, sacred music, stringed instruments, voice, wind and percussion instruments. Graduate degrees offered: Master of Music in the areas of church music, music education. Program accredited by NASM.

Enrollment Fall 1997: 104 total; 100 undergraduate, 4 graduate.

Music Student Profile 56% females, 44% males, 7% minorities.

Music Faculty 32 total undergraduate and graduate (full-time and part-time). 88% of full-time faculty have terminal degrees. Graduate students do not teach undergraduate courses.

Student Life Student groups/activities include American Guild of Organists, Music Educators National Conference, Music Enterprises Student Association.

Expenses for 1997–98 Application fee: $30. Comprehensive fee: $18,990 includes full-time tuition ($14,560), mandatory fees ($500), and college room and board ($3930). College room only: $2450. Full-time tuition and fees vary according to program. Room and board charges vary according to board plan and housing facility. Special program-related fees: $200 for studio instruction fee.

Financial Aid Program-specific awards for 1997: 35–40 music scholarships for performers ($800–$1500).

Application Procedures Students admitted directly into the professional program freshman year. Deadline for freshmen and transfers: continuous. Notification date for freshmen and transfers: August 15. Required: high school transcript, college transcript(s) for transfer students, SAT I or ACT test scores, video or audition. Recommended: essay, letter of recommendation, interview. Auditions held twice on campus; recorded music is permissible as a substitute for live auditions by arrangement with department and videotaped performances are permissible as a substitute for live auditions when distance is prohibitive or if a campus visit is impossible.

Undergraduate Contact Dr. Linda C. Ferguson, Chair, Department of Music, Valparaiso University, Center for the Arts, Valparaiso, Indiana 46383-6493; 219-464-5454, fax: 219-464-5244, E-mail address: lferguson@exodus.valpo.edu.

Graduate Contact Dr. James Albers, Dean, Graduate Studies, Valparaiso University, Kretzmann Hall, Valparaiso, Indiana 46383; 219-464-5313, E-mail address: jalbers@exodus.valpo.edu.

Blair School of Music

▼ VANDERBILT UNIVERSITY

Nashville, Tennessee

Independent, coed. Urban campus. Total enrollment: 10,210. Music program established 1986.

Degrees Bachelor of Music in the areas of performance, musical arts, composition/music theory; Bachelor of Music/Master of Education in the area of musical arts/education. Majors and concentrations: classical guitar, piano/organ, stringed instruments, voice, wind and percussion instruments. Program accredited by NASM.

Enrollment Fall 1997: 154 undergraduate.

Music Student Profile 60% females, 40% males, 8% minorities.

Music Faculty 100 total (full-time and part-time). 84% of full-time faculty have terminal degrees. Graduate students do not teach undergraduate courses.

Student Life Student groups/activities include Pi Kappa Lambda, Voice Majors Association.

Expenses for 1997–98 Application fee: $50. Comprehensive fee: $28,908 includes full-time tuition ($20,900), mandatory fees ($578), and college room and board ($7430). College room only: $4780.

Financial Aid Program-specific awards for 1997: 1 Harold Sterling Vanderbilt Scholarship for program majors ($21,930), 1–50 Blair Dean's Honor Scholarships for program majors ($1000–$5000), Blair Help Loans for program majors ($500–$2400), 1 Frances Hampton Currey Music Scholarship for program majors ($21,930), 1 Laura Kemp Goad Honor Scholarship for program majors ($21,930), 1 Joel and Stella Hargrove Scholarship for program majors ($5000), 1 Rae S. Miller Piano Scholarship for piano majors ($5000), 1 Wilda and William Moennig Scholarship for program majors ($12,000), 1 Del Sawyer Trumpet Scholarship for trumpet majors ($21,930), 1 Wilma Ward Scholarship for voice majors ($21,930).

Application Procedures Students admitted directly into the professional program freshman year. Deadline for freshmen and transfers: continuous. Notification date for freshmen and transfers: April 1. Required: essay, high school transcript, college transcript(s) for transfer students, 2 letters of recommendation, audition, SAT I or ACT test scores, portfolio for composition/theory applicants. Recommended: minimum 3.0 high school GPA, video for voice majors. Auditions held 3 times on campus; recorded music is permissible as a substitute for live auditions for musical arts or performance majors (except in percussion) when distance is prohibitive and videotaped performances are permissible as a substitute for live auditions for percussion majors when distance is prohibitive. Portfolio reviews held by appointment on campus.

Undergraduate Contact Dr. Dwayne Sagen, Assistant Dean, Blair School of Music, Vanderbilt University, 2400 Blakemore Avenue, Nashville, Tennessee 37212-3499; 615-322-7679, fax: 615-343-0324, E-mail address: dwayne.p.sagen@vanderbilt.edu.

More About the School

The Blair School of Music offers superior musical training and a professional degree program at a comprehensive, top-ranked university, providing students with the opportunity to focus on their musical studies while maintaining a liberal arts base. Blair students take approximately 25 percent of their classes outside the School of Music, often selecting a second major or a minor in another field. While Vanderbilt University is home to more than 4,300 graduate students, there are no graduate students at Blair, so undergraduates are the sole focus of the faculty and have access to extensive performance opportunities.

Vanderbilt University is ideally located in Nashville, the capitol of Tennessee. The campus is located less than 2 miles from downtown Nashville and is a 333-acre, beautifully maintained national arboretum. Known as "Music City, USA" and "The Third Coast," Nashville is home to numerous publishers, production companies, record labels, and recording studios that rival those in New York City and Los Angeles.

Blair students have the rare opportunity to live and learn in one of America's preeminent music centers.

Students at Blair may receive performance instruction for credit in twenty-two areas, including all orchestral instruments, piano, organ, harpsichord, viola da gamba, recorder, guitar, fiddle, dulcimer, saxophone, and voice. Students may choose to major in performance, composition and theory, musical arts, or musical arts/teacher education track. Musical arts is the most flexible of the degree programs, reaching out to those with a commitment to the study of music in all its facets. The major provides equal preparation in three areas: performance, music theory, and music literature/history with optional concentrations in more specific areas. Musical arts majors have the opportunity to pursue careers in music as well as other areas of study, including medicine, law, and business.

The Blair School of Music is home to a world-class faculty. Though the faculty members perform as soloists and as members of touring ensembles, their commitment to teaching is paramount. The Blair resident string quartet, woodwind quintet, and brass quintet perform regularly on campus and throughout the country. Soloists such as Craig Nies, piano; John Johns, classical guitar; Kathryn Plummer, viola; Edger Meyer, double bass; Christian Teal, violin; Mark O'Connor, fiddle; Wilma Jensen, organ; Jonathan Retzlaff, voice; and William Wiggins, percussion, claim Blair as their home.

Blair hosts more than 200 concerts each year, including faculty and student recitals, as well as concerts and master classes by nationally and internationally renowned musicians such as Dorothy DeLay, violin; Ransom Wilson, flute; and Claude Frank, piano. The Blair concert series sponsors nearly twenty concerts each year, which has included John Browning, piano; Yo-Yo Ma, cello; Robert Craft, conducting; and Bela Fleck, banjo. Vanderbilt's Great Performances series brings to campus such performers as Wynton Marsalis, Stomp, the Academy of St. Martin in the Fields, and the King's Singers. Blair also hosts the BMI Composer in Residence Program.

The Blair School of Music at Vanderbilt University is noted for its flexibility, prestigious faculty, and outstanding facilities, but most of all for its commitment to students in their musical, academic, and personal development. Blair's goal is to graduate musicians thoroughly schooled in their art, broadly educated, and prepared for careers in music, related professions, or the finest graduate schools.

▼ VANDERCOOK COLLEGE OF MUSIC

Chicago, Illinois

Independent, coed. Urban campus. Music program established 1928.

Degrees Bachelor of Music Education in the areas of instrumental music education, choral music education. Graduate degrees offered: Master of Music Education in the areas of instrumental music education, choral music education. Cross-registration with Illinois Institute of Technology. Program accredited by NASM.

Enrollment Fall 1997: 938 total; 65 undergraduate, 123 graduate, 750 non-professional degree.

Music Student Profile 45% females, 55% males, 30% minorities, 2% international.

Music Faculty 25 total undergraduate and graduate (full-time and part-time). 60% of full-time faculty have terminal

VanderCook College of Music *(continued)*

degrees. Graduate students teach a few undergraduate courses. Undergraduate student–faculty ratio: 4:1.

Student Life Student groups/activities include Music Educators National Conference Student Chapter, International Association of Jazz Educators, Great Teachers Scholarship Fund Cabaret Benefit.

Expenses for 1997–98 Application fee: $25. Comprehensive fee: $15,350 includes full-time tuition ($10,000), mandatory fees ($350), and college room and board ($5000). Special program-related fees: $50 for techniques classes, $100 for computer lab use.

Financial Aid Program-specific awards for 1997: 30 scholarships for voice and instrument majors ($2500), 4 tuition assistance grants for program majors ($500), 15 VCM Work-Study Programs for program majors ($1000).

Application Procedures Students admitted directly into the professional program freshman year. Deadline for freshmen and transfers: continuous. Notification date for freshmen and transfers: continuous. Required: essay, high school transcript, college transcript(s) for transfer students, minimum 2.0 high school GPA, 3 letters of recommendation, interview, audition, SAT I or ACT test scores. Auditions held by appointment on campus; recorded music is permissible as a substitute for live auditions for out-of-state applicants or if a campus visit is impossible and videotaped performances are permissible as a substitute for live auditions for out-of-state applicants or if a campus visit is impossible.

Contact Mr. George Pierard, Director of Admissions, Admissions Office, VanderCook College of Music, 3140 South Federal Street, Chicago, Illinois 60616; 800-448-2655, fax: 312-225-5211.

▼ VIRGINIA COMMONWEALTH UNIVERSITY

Richmond, Virginia

State-supported, coed. Urban campus. Total enrollment: 22,702.

Degrees Bachelor of Music in the areas of music education, performance, composition, jazz studies. Majors and concentrations: guitar, jazz, music education, music history, music theory and composition, piano/organ, stringed instruments, voice, wind and percussion instruments. Graduate degrees offered: Master of Music in the areas of music education, performance, composition, conducting. Program accredited by NASM.

Enrollment Fall 1997: 370 total; 320 undergraduate, 35 graduate, 15 non-professional degree.

Music Student Profile 50% females, 50% males, 15% minorities, 2% international.

Music Faculty 59 total undergraduate and graduate (full-time and part-time). 56% of full-time faculty have terminal degrees. Graduate students do not teach undergraduate courses. Undergraduate student–faculty ratio: 10:1.

Student Life Student groups/activities include Music Educators National Conference Student Chapter, Pi Kappa Lambda.

Expenses for 1997–98 Application fee: $25. State resident tuition: $3125 full-time. Nonresident tuition: $11,382 full-time. Mandatory fees: $986 full-time. Full-time tuition and fees vary according to program. College room and board: $4540. College room only: $2715. Room and board charges vary according to board plan and housing facility. Special

program-related fees: $520 per 3 credits for private music lessons for majors, $300 per year for school of art fee.

Financial Aid Program-specific awards for 1997: 15 Merit Scholarships for program majors ($1500), 15 Applied Music Scholarships for program majors ($520), 5 Endowed Scholarships for program majors ($400–$700).

Application Procedures Students admitted directly into the professional program freshman year. Deadline for freshmen and transfers: continuous. Required: essay, high school transcript, college transcript(s) for transfer students, minimum 2.0 high school GPA, letter of recommendation, interview, audition, SAT I test score only. Auditions held 4 times and by appointment on campus; recorded music is permissible as a substitute for live auditions when distance is prohibitive and videotaped performances are permissible as a substitute for live auditions when distance is prohibitive.

Undergraduate Contact JoAnne Welling, Undergraduate Admissions Coordinator, Department of Music, Virginia Commonwealth University, 922 Park Avenue, PO Box 842004, Richmond, Virginia 23284-2004; 804-828-1166, fax: 804-828-6469, E-mail address: music@vcu.edu.

Graduate Contact Ms. Linda Johnston, Executive Secretary, Department of Music, Virginia Commonwealth University, 922 Park Avenue, PO Box 842004, Richmond, Virginia 23284-2004; 804-828-8008, fax: 804-828-6469, E-mail address: lsjohnst@vcu.edu.

▼ VIRGINIA INTERMONT COLLEGE

Bristol, Virginia

Independent, coed. Small town campus. Total enrollment: 848.

Degrees Bachelor of Fine Arts in the area of musical theater. Cross-registration with King College.

Enrollment Fall 1997: 1 undergraduate.

Music Faculty 1 total (full-time). 100% of full-time faculty have terminal degrees. Graduate students do not teach undergraduate courses.

Student Life Student groups/activities include Visiting Artists Workshop.

Expenses for 1997–98 Application fee: $15. Comprehensive fee: $15,350 includes full-time tuition ($10,650) and college room and board ($4700). Special program-related fees: $110 per course for private music lessons, $40 per semester for organ practice fees.

Financial Aid Program-specific awards for 1997: performance scholarships for program majors ($500–$1500).

Application Procedures Deadline for freshmen and transfers: continuous. Notification date for freshmen and transfers: continuous. Required: high school transcript, college transcript(s) for transfer students, minimum 2.0 high school GPA, SAT I or ACT test scores. Recommended: letter of recommendation, audition. Auditions held by appointment on campus.

Undergraduate Contact Ms. Robin Cozart, Director of Admissions, Virginia Intermont College, Box D-460, Bristol, Virginia 24201; 540-669-6101, fax: 540-466-7855, E-mail address: viadmit@vic.edu.

▼ VIRGINIA STATE UNIVERSITY

Petersburg, Virginia

State-supported, coed. Suburban campus. Total enrollment: 4,200. Music program established 1890.

Degrees Bachelor of Music in the area of performance; Bachelor of Music Education in the areas of choral music education, instrumental music education. Majors and concentrations: music education, piano/organ, stringed instruments, voice, wind and percussion instruments. Program accredited by NASM.

Enrollment Fall 1997: 61 undergraduate.

Music Student Profile 35% females, 65% males, 1% minorities.

Music Faculty 17 total (full-time and part-time). 70% of full-time faculty have terminal degrees. Graduate students do not teach undergraduate courses. Undergraduate student–faculty ratio: 9:1.

Student Life Student groups/activities include Music Educators National Conference, Kappa Kappa Psi (band fraternity), Tau Beta Sigma (band sorority).

Expenses for 1997–98 State resident tuition: $1951 full-time. Nonresident tuition: $6430 full-time. Mandatory fees: $1356 full-time. Full-time tuition and fees vary according to course level, course load, and program. College room and board: $4910. College room only: $2800. Room and board charges vary according to board plan and housing facility.

Financial Aid Program-specific awards for 1997: 4 Undine Smith Moore Awards for freshmen ($1000), 12 Aurelia Walford Awards for program majors ($500–$1000), 5 Provost Scholarships for freshmen and transfer students ($1500), 5 Performance Grants for incoming program majors ($3500), 50 Band and Choir Scholarships for band and choir students ($500–$2000).

Application Procedures Students admitted directly into the professional program freshman year. Deadline for freshmen and transfers: continuous. Required: high school transcript, college transcript(s) for transfer students, audition, SAT I or ACT test scores. Recommended: 2 letters of recommendation. Auditions held 3 times and by appointment on campus and off campus in Hartford, CT; New York, NY; Trenton, NJ; Raleigh, NC; Durham, NC; Pittsburgh, PA; Washington, DC; Atlanta, GA; various cities in Virginia; videotaped performances are permissible as a substitute for live auditions when distance is prohibitive.

Undergraduate Contact Dr. Mark Phillips, Chair, Department of Music, Virginia State University, PO Box 9007, Petersburg, Virginia 23806; 804-524-5311, fax: 804-524-6862.

▼ VITERBO COLLEGE

La Crosse, Wisconsin

Independent-Roman Catholic, coed. Urban campus. Total enrollment: 2,622. Music program established 1944.

Degrees Bachelor of Music in the area of applied music performance; Bachelor of Music Education. Majors and concentrations: applied music, music education. Program accredited by NASM.

Enrollment Fall 1997: 71 total; all undergraduate.

Music Student Profile 70% females, 30% males.

Music Faculty 12 total (full-time and part-time). 90% of full-time faculty have terminal degrees. Graduate students do not teach undergraduate courses.

Student Life Student groups/activities include Music Educators National Conference, Summer Theater, Viterbo Preparatory School of Arts.

Expenses for 1998–99 Application fee: $15. Comprehensive fee: $15,940 includes full-time tuition ($11,420), mandatory

fees ($270), and college room and board ($4250). College room only: $1860. Special program-related fees: $200 per credit for applied music fee.

Financial Aid Program-specific awards for 1997: 7 Fine Arts Scholarships for program majors ($1000).

Application Procedures Students apply for admission into the professional program by sophomore year. Deadline for freshmen and transfers: August 1. Required: high school transcript, college transcript(s) for transfer students, minimum 2.0 high school GPA, interview, audition, SAT I or ACT test scores. Recommended: minimum 3.0 high school GPA. Auditions held as needed on campus; recorded music is permissible as a substitute for live auditions when distance is prohibitive and videotaped performances are permissible as a substitute for live auditions when distance is prohibitive.

Undergraduate Contact Dr. Roland Nelson, Director of Admissions, Viterbo College, 815 South 9th Street, LaCrosse, Wisconsin 54601; 608-796-3012, fax: 608-796-3020.

▼ WALLA WALLA COLLEGE

College Place, Washington

Independent-Seventh-day Adventist, coed. Small town campus. Total enrollment: 1,653. Music program established 1892.

Degrees Bachelor of Music in the areas of performance, music education. Majors and concentrations: music education, piano/organ, stringed instruments, voice, wind instruments. Cross-registration with Whitman College . Program accredited by NASM.

Enrollment Fall 1997: 35 undergraduate.

Music Student Profile 57% females, 43% males, 11% minorities, 9% international.

Music Faculty 13 total (full-time and part-time). 67% of full-time faculty have terminal degrees. Graduate students do not teach undergraduate courses. Undergraduate student–faculty ratio: 5:1.

Student Life Student groups/activities include Music Club.

Expenses for 1997–98 Application fee: $30. Comprehensive fee: $16,073 includes full-time tuition ($12,570), mandatory fees ($123), and college room and board ($3380). College room only: $1836. Special program-related fees: $171–$207 per credit for music lesson fee (1/2 hour), $75 per quarter for music instrument rental.

Financial Aid Program-specific awards for 1997: 6 Music Lesson Scholarships for program students ($3000).

Application Procedures Students apply for admission into the professional program by freshman year. Deadline for freshmen and transfers: August 15. Required: high school transcript, college transcript(s) for transfer students, minimum 2.0 high school GPA, 3 letters of recommendation, audition, SAT I or ACT test scores. Auditions held once on campus; recorded music is permissible as a substitute for live auditions and videotaped performances are permissible as a substitute for live auditions when distance is prohibitive.

Undergraduate Contact Mr. Dan Shultz, Chair, Music Department, Walla Walla College, 204 South College Avenue, College Place, Washington 99324; 509-527-2562, fax: 509-527-2177, E-mail address: shulda@wwc.edu.

▼ WARTBURG COLLEGE

Waverly, Iowa

Independent-Lutheran, coed. Small town campus. Total enrollment: 1,528. Music program established 1952.

Degrees Bachelor of Music in the areas of voice, keyboard, instrumental music; Bachelor of Music Education in the areas of vocal music education, instrumental music education; Bachelor of Music Education/Music Therapy. Majors and concentrations: brass, guitar, piano/organ, stringed instruments, voice, wind and percussion instruments. Program accredited by NASM, NAMT.

Enrollment Fall 1997: 130 undergraduate.

Music Student Profile 65% females, 35% males, 2% minorities, 5% international.

Music Faculty 24 total (full-time and part-time). 82% of full-time faculty have terminal degrees. Graduate students do not teach undergraduate courses. Undergraduate student–faculty ratio: 12:1.

Student Life Student groups/activities include American Association of Music Therapy, Music Educators National Conference, Music Teachers National Association.

Expenses for 1997–98 Application fee: $20. Comprehensive fee: $17,620 includes full-time tuition ($13,470), mandatory fees ($140), and college room and board ($4010). College room only: $1860. Room and board charges vary according to board plan and housing facility. Special program-related fees: $190 per semester for applied lesson fee.

Financial Aid Program-specific awards for 1997: 60 Meistersinger Music Scholarships for talented students ($1500–$2500).

Application Procedures Students apply for admission into the professional program by freshman year. Deadline for freshmen and transfers: continuous. Notification date for freshmen and transfers: continuous. Required: high school transcript, college transcript(s) for transfer students, minimum 2.0 high school GPA, SAT I or ACT test scores. Recommended: minimum 3.0 high school GPA, interview, audition, portfolio. Auditions held 3 times and by appointment on campus; recorded music is permissible as a substitute for live auditions when distance is prohibitive (beyond a 250-mile radius) and videotaped performances are permissible as a substitute for live auditions when distance is prohibitive (beyond a 250-mile radius).

Undergraduate Contact Doug Bowman, Director of Admissions, Wartburg College, Whitehouse Business Center 201, Waverly, Iowa 50677-0903; 319-352-8264, fax: 319-352-8579.

▼ WASHBURN UNIVERSITY OF TOPEKA

Topeka, Kansas

City-supported, coed. Urban campus. Total enrollment: 6,281.

Degrees Bachelor of Music in the area of music performance; Bachelor of Music Education. Majors and concentrations: keyboard, music education, piano/organ, stringed instruments, voice, wind and percussion instruments. Program accredited by NASM.

Enrollment Fall 1997: 90 undergraduate.

Music Student Profile 52% females, 48% males, 10% minorities, 4% international.

Music Faculty 30 total (full-time and part-time). 80% of full-time faculty have terminal degrees. Graduate students do not teach undergraduate courses.

Expenses for 1997–98 State resident tuition: $3100 full-time. Nonresident tuition: $6758 full-time. Mandatory fees: $50 full-time. College room and board: $3300.

Financial Aid Program-specific awards for 1997: 25–30 music endowments for program majors ($1000–$2000).

Application Procedures Deadline for freshmen and transfers: August 6. Notification date for freshmen and transfers: August 15. Required: high school transcript, college transcript(s) for transfer students. Recommended: interview, audition, SAT I or ACT test scores. Auditions held 3 times on campus; recorded music is permissible as a substitute for live auditions when distance is prohibitive and videotaped performances are permissible as a substitute for live auditions when distance is prohibitive.

Undergraduate Contact Mr. Rodney Boyd, Associate Chair, Music Department, Washburn University of Topeka, 1700 Southwest College, Topeka, Kansas 66621; 785-231-1010 ext. 1520, fax: 785-357-4168, E-mail address: zzboyr@washburn.edu.

▼ WASHINGTON STATE UNIVERSITY

Pullman, Washington

State-supported, coed. Rural campus. Total enrollment: 20,243. Music program established 1904.

Degrees Bachelor of Music in the areas of voice, keyboard, instruments, composition; Bachelor of Music Education in the areas of choral music education, instrumental music education, general music education. Majors and concentrations: composition, music education, piano/organ, stringed instruments, voice, wind and percussion instruments. Graduate degrees offered: Master of Arts in the areas of performance, music education, composition. Cross-registration with University of Idaho. Program accredited by NASM.

Enrollment Fall 1997: 160 total.

Music Student Profile 50% females, 50% males, 5% minorities, 6% international.

Music Faculty 26 total undergraduate and graduate (full-time and part-time). 100% of full-time faculty have terminal degrees. Graduate students teach a few undergraduate courses. Undergraduate student–faculty ratio: 10:1.

Student Life Student groups/activities include Music Educators National Conference Student Chapter, American Choral Directors Association Student Chapter, Music Teachers National Association Student Chapter.

Expenses for 1997–98 Application fee: $35. State resident tuition: $2989 full-time. Nonresident tuition: $9871 full-time. Mandatory fees: $405 full-time. College room and board: $4426. Room and board charges vary according to board plan and housing facility. Special program-related fees: $10 per semester for instrument rental.

Financial Aid Program-specific awards for 1997: 35 Visual and Performing Arts Awards for program students ($500–$1200).

Application Procedures Students apply for admission into the professional program by sophomore year. Deadline for freshmen and transfers: May 1. Notification date for freshmen and transfers: August 22. Required: high school transcript, college transcript(s) for transfer students, minimum 2.0 high school GPA, audition, SAT I or ACT test scores. Auditions held by appointment on campus and off campus in various locations in the Washington area; recorded music is permissible as a substitute for live auditions if a campus visit is impossible.

Web Site http://www.wsu.edu/Music_and_Theatre/.

Undergraduate Contact Dr. Erich Lear, Director, School of Music and Theatre Arts, Washington State University, PO Box 645300, Pullman, Washington 99164-5300; 509-335-7757, fax: 509-335-4245.

Graduate Contact Dr. Khristopher von Baeyer, Coordinator of Graduate Programs in Music, School of Music and Theatre Arts, Washington State University, PO Box 645300, Pullman, Washington 99164-5300; 509-335-3973, fax: 509-335-4245.

▼ WAYLAND BAPTIST UNIVERSITY

Plainview, Texas

Independent-Baptist, coed. Small town campus. Total enrollment: 4,190. Music program established 1908.

Degrees Bachelor of Music in the areas of music education, church music. Majors and concentrations: music education, sacred music.

Enrollment Fall 1997: 165 total; 40 undergraduate, 125 non-professional degree.

Music Student Profile 60% females, 40% males, 15% minorities, 1% international.

Music Faculty 13 total undergraduate (full-time and part-time). 43% of full-time faculty have terminal degrees. Graduate students do not teach undergraduate courses. Undergraduate student–faculty ratio: 10:1.

Student Life Student groups/activities include Phi Mu Alpha, Sigma Alpha Iota, Music Educators National Conference.

Expenses for 1997–98 Application fee: $35. Comprehensive fee: $9784 includes full-time tuition ($6120), mandatory fees ($350), and college room and board ($3314). College room only: $1408. Room and board charges vary according to board plan and housing facility. Special program-related fees: $25 per semester for practice room fees, $50 per semester for private study fee.

Financial Aid Program-specific awards for 1997: 40 music scholarships for program majors ($500–$600).

Application Procedures Students admitted directly into the professional program freshman year. Deadline for freshmen and transfers: continuous. Required: high school transcript, college transcript(s) for transfer students, interview, audition, SAT I or ACT test scores (minimum combined SAT I score of 850, minimum combined ACT score of 18). Recommended: minimum 2.0 high school GPA. Auditions held 4 times on campus; recorded music is permissible as a substitute for live auditions when distance is prohibitive and videotaped performances are permissible as a substitute for live auditions when distance is prohibitive.

Undergraduate Contact Dr. Carl C. Moman, Chair, Music Division, Wayland Baptist University, 1900 West Seventh Street, Plainview, Texas 79072-6998; 806-296-4741, fax: 806-296-4718.

▼ WAYNE STATE UNIVERSITY

Detroit, Michigan

State-supported, coed. Urban campus. Total enrollment: 30,729. Music program established 1918.

Degrees Bachelor of Music in the areas of church music, composition, jazz studies, music education, music technology, music management, performance, music theory. Majors and concentrations: church music, composition, jazz, music, music education, music management, music technology, music theory, piano/organ, stringed instruments, voice, wind and percussion instruments. Graduate degrees offered: Master of Music in the areas of composition, choral conducting, music education, performance, music theory. Program accredited by NASM.

Enrollment Fall 1997: 287 total; 245 undergraduate, 42 graduate.

Music Student Profile 40% females, 60% males, 23% minorities, 3% international.

Music Faculty 87 total undergraduate and graduate (full-time and part-time). 100% of full-time faculty have terminal degrees. Graduate students teach a few undergraduate courses. Undergraduate student–faculty ratio: 12:1.

Student Life Student groups/activities include Delta Omicron, Phi Mu Alpha, Mu Phi Epsilon.

Expenses for 1997–98 Application fee: $20. State resident tuition: $3348 full-time. Nonresident tuition: $7471 full-time. Mandatory fees: $138 full-time. Full-time tuition and fees vary according to student level. College room only: $3875. Room charges vary according to housing facility. Special program-related fees: $79–$157 per semester for private lessons.

Financial Aid Program-specific awards for 1997: 70 Talent Scholarships for program majors ($1000), 270 Activity Awards for ensemble participants ($50–$1000), 60 awards for high academic and musical achievement ($150–$3750), 25–35 full scholarships for program majors ($2658–$3114).

Application Procedures Students admitted directly into the professional program freshman year. Deadline for freshmen and transfers: continuous. Required: high school transcript, college transcript(s) for transfer students, minimum 2.0 high school GPA, audition, SAT I or ACT test scores. Recommended: minimum 3.0 high school GPA. Auditions held twice and by appointment on campus; recorded music is permissible as a substitute for live auditions when distance is prohibitive and videotaped performances are permissible as a substitute for live auditions when distance is prohibitive.

Web Site http://www.comm.wayne.edu/music/.

Contact Mr. Dennis J. Tini, Chair, Department of Music, Wayne State University, 105 Schaver Music Building, Detroit, Michigan 48202; 313-577-1795, fax: 313-577-5420.

More About the University

Program Facilities Present facilities: Schaver Music Building, with administrative and faculty offices, rehearsal halls, classrooms, piano labs with twenty-seven Kawai and Korg MIDI keyboards, Macintosh-equipped listening lab/library, practice modules; the Community Arts Auditorium, with 550 seats, 50 rank organ; Music North Building, housing jazz, theory, composition, music technology programs, applied faculty studios, practice modules, up-to-date multitrack recording studio using Macintosh-based programs; the Music Annex, with offices and studios for vocal and choral faculty, rehearsal hall, practice rooms; and up to forty-five new pianos each year for student and faculty use.

Faculty, Resident Artists, and Alumni Honorary Adjunct Professors: Neemi Järvi, Music Director, Detroit Symphony Orchestra; David DiChiera, Director, Michigan Opera Theatre; Brazeal Dennard, Director/Founder, Brazeal Dennard Chorale.

Applied music faculty: twenty-six current or retired members of the Detroit Symphony Orchestra; some of Detroit's most respected and active music professionals in jazz, guitar, piano, and voice.

Distinguished alumni include: Metropolitan Opera stars George Shirley, Shirley Love; jazz guitarist Kenny Burrell; conductors Harry Begian, Robert Harris, Brazeal Dennard;

Wayne State University (*continued*)

saxophonist Donald Sinta; violinists Daniel Majeske, Isidor Saslav; organist Robert Bates; composer John Rea.

Student Performance Opportunities Department of Music: thirty-five regular ensemble performances annually; invitational performances with the Detroit Symphony and at festivals, corporate and government events; national and international ensemble tours; outreach performances for elementary through secondary students; extensive freelance opportunities in the Detroit metro area.

Special Programs Extensive outreach programs; internships with WSU, arts institutions, businesses.

▼ WEBSTER UNIVERSITY

St. Louis, Missouri

Independent, coed. Suburban campus. Total enrollment: 11,756. Music program established 1925.

Degrees Bachelor of Music in the areas of jazz, vocal performance, composition, piano performance, instrumental performance; Bachelor of Music Education in the areas of choral music education, instrumental music education. Majors and concentrations: classical music, composition, jazz, music, music education, piano/organ, voice, wind and percussion instruments. Graduate degrees offered: Master of Music in the areas of jazz, piano, vocal performance, composition, music education, church music, orchestral performance. Cross-registration with various colleges in St. Louis. Program accredited by NASM.

Enrollment Fall 1997: 118 total; 90 undergraduate, 18 graduate, 10 non-professional degree.

Music Student Profile 60% females, 40% males, 10% minorities, 5% international.

Music Faculty 37 total undergraduate and graduate (full-time and part-time). 90% of full-time faculty have terminal degrees. Graduate students do not teach undergraduate courses. Undergraduate student–faculty ratio: 10:1.

Student Life Student groups/activities include Sigma Alpha Iota.

Expenses for 1997–98 Application fee: $25. Comprehensive fee: $15,940 includes full-time tuition ($10,860), mandatory fees ($50), and college room and board ($5030). College room only: $3080. Room and board charges vary according to board plan and housing facility. Special program-related fees: $185–$370 per course for applied music fee.

Financial Aid Program-specific awards for 1997: 14 Buder Scholarships for incoming students ($740–$5000).

Application Procedures Students admitted directly into the professional program freshman year. Deadline for freshmen and transfers: continuous. Required: essay, high school transcript, college transcript(s) for transfer students, 2 letters of recommendation, audition, SAT I or ACT test scores. Auditions held 8 times on campus; recorded music is permissible as a substitute for live auditions when distance is prohibitive and videotaped performances are permissible as a substitute for live auditions when distance is prohibitive.

Web Site http://www.webster.edu.

Undergraduate Contact Ms. Bethany Wood, Auditions Coordinator, Office of Admissions, Webster University, 470 East Lockwood Avenue, St. Louis, Missouri 63119-3194; 314-968-7000, fax: 314-968-7115.

Graduate Contact Dr. Earl Henry, Director of Graduate Studies, Department of Music, Webster University, 470 East Lockwood Avenue, St. Louis, Missouri 63119-3194; 314-968-7032, fax: 314-963-6048.

▼ WEST CHESTER UNIVERSITY OF PENNSYLVANIA

West Chester, Pennsylvania

State-supported, coed. Small town campus. Total enrollment: 11,430.

Degrees Bachelor of Music in the areas of piano/organ, voice, wind and percussion instruments, stringed instruments, composition, theory; Bachelor of Science in the area of music education. Majors and concentrations: classical music, composition, music education, music theory, piano/organ, stringed instruments, voice, wind and percussion instruments. Graduate degrees offered: Master of Music in the areas of music education, performance, theory, composition, piano pedagogy. Cross-registration with Cheyney University of Pennsylvania. Program accredited by NASM.

Enrollment Fall 1997: 475 total; 400 undergraduate, 75 graduate.

Music Student Profile 50% females, 50% males, 5% minorities, 1% international.

Music Faculty 63 total undergraduate and graduate (full-time and part-time). 95% of full-time faculty have terminal degrees. Graduate students do not teach undergraduate courses. Undergraduate student–faculty ratio: 7:1.

Student Life Student groups/activities include Music Educators National Conference Student Chapter, Music Teachers National Association Student Chapter, professional music fraternities.

Expenses for 1997–98 Application fee: $25. State resident tuition: $3468 full-time. Nonresident tuition: $8824 full-time. Mandatory fees: $694 full-time. College room and board: $4376. College room only: $2776. Room and board charges vary according to board plan, housing facility, and location.

Financial Aid Program-specific awards for 1997: 30 Endowed Scholarships for music majors.

Application Procedures Students admitted directly into the professional program freshman year. Deadline for freshmen and transfers: April 1. Required: essay, high school transcript, college transcript(s) for transfer students, minimum 2.0 high school GPA, letter of recommendation, interview, audition, SAT I or ACT test scores (minimum combined SAT I score of 1000, minimum combined ACT score of 20). Recommended: minimum 3.0 high school GPA. Auditions held 10 times and by appointment on campus; recorded music is permissible as a substitute for live auditions when distance is prohibitive and videotaped performances are permissible as a substitute for live auditions when distance is prohibitive.

Undergraduate Contact Mr. Eugene Klein, Undergraduate Coordinator, School of Music, West Chester University of Pennsylvania, West Chester, Pennsylvania 19383; 610-436-2650, E-mail address: eklein@wcupa.edu.

Graduate Contact Dr. J. Bryan Burton, Interim Graduate Coordinator, School of Music, West Chester University of Pennsylvania, West Chester, Pennsylvania 19383; 610-436-2222, fax: 610-436-2873, E-mail address: jburton3@wcupa.edu.

▼ WESTERN CONNECTICUT STATE UNIVERSITY

Danbury, Connecticut

State-supported, coed. Urban campus. Music program established 1903.

Degrees Bachelor of Music; Bachelor of Science in the area of music education. Majors and concentrations: classical music, jazz. Graduate degrees offered: Master of Science in the area of awarded in music education.

Enrollment Fall 1997: 130 undergraduate, 25 graduate.

Music Student Profile 60% females, 40% males, 6% minorities.

Music Faculty 27 total undergraduate and graduate (full-time and part-time). 67% of full-time faculty have terminal degrees. Graduate students do not teach undergraduate courses. Undergraduate student–faculty ratio: 10:1.

Student Life Student groups/activities include Music Educators National Conference, International Association of Jazz Educators.

Expenses for 1997–98 State resident tuition: $2062 full-time. Nonresident tuition: $6674 full-time. College room and board: $4718. College room only: $2600. Special program-related fees: $150–$300 per semester for lessons for part-time students.

Financial Aid Program-specific awards for 1997: 1 Charles Murphy Percussion Scholarship for incoming freshmen percussionists ($750).

Application Procedures Students admitted directly into the professional program freshman year. Deadline for freshmen and transfers: continuous. Required: high school transcript, audition, SAT I or ACT test scores (minimum combined SAT I score of 900, minimum combined ACT score of 18), minimum 2.0 college GPA for transfer applicants. Recommended: letter of recommendation. Auditions held 4 times and by appointment on campus; recorded music is permissible as a substitute for live auditions when distance is prohibitive and videotaped performances are permissible as a substitute for live auditions when distance is prohibitive.

Undergraduate Contact Mrs. Roberta Watts, Secretary, Department of Music and Music Education, Western Connecticut State University, 181 White Street, Danbury, Connecticut 06810; 203-837-8350, fax: 203-837-8526, E-mail address: wattsr@wcsub.cstateu.edu.

Graduate Contact Dr. Kevin Isaacs, Professor, Department of Music and Music Education, Western Connecticut State University, 181 White Street, Danbury, Connecticut 06810; 203-837-8355, fax: 203-837-8526, E-mail address: wattsr@wcsub.cstateu.edu.

Potter College of Arts, Humanities, and Social Sciences

▼ WESTERN KENTUCKY UNIVERSITY

Bowling Green, Kentucky

State-supported, coed. Suburban campus. Total enrollment: 14,543.

Degrees Bachelor of Music in the areas of performance, music education (K-12). Majors and concentrations: guitar, piano, stringed instruments, voice, wind and percussion instruments. Program accredited by NASM.

Enrollment Fall 1997: 188 total; 148 undergraduate, 40 non-professional degree.

Music Student Profile 50% females, 50% males, 6% minorities.

Music Faculty 27 total (full-time and part-time). 76% of full-time faculty have terminal degrees. Graduate students do not teach undergraduate courses.

Student Life Student groups/activities include music fraternities and sororities, musical production sponsored by Theater Department.

Expenses for 1997–98 Application fee: $15. State resident tuition: $1800 full-time. Nonresident tuition: $5400 full-time. Mandatory fees: $340 full-time. College room and board: $2700. Special program-related fees: $50 per semester for applied lessons.

Financial Aid Program-specific awards for 1997: 30 Talent Grants for program majors ($900–$1800).

Application Procedures Students admitted directly into the professional program freshman year. Deadline for freshmen and transfers: August 1. Required: high school transcript, college transcript(s) for transfer students, minimum 2.0 high school GPA, audition, ACT test score only (minimum combined ACT score of 18). Recommended: minimum 3.0 high school GPA. Auditions held 3 times and by appointment on campus; recorded music is permissible as a substitute for live auditions for out-of-state applicants and videotaped performances are permissible as a substitute for live auditions for out-of-state applicants.

Web Site http://www.wku.edu/~kerstkt/music.html.

Undergraduate Contact Office of Admissions, Western Kentucky University, 1 Big Red Way, Bowling Green, Kentucky 42101; 502-745-5422.

▼ WESTERN MICHIGAN UNIVERSITY

Kalamazoo, Michigan

State-supported, coed. Urban campus. Total enrollment: 26,132. Music program established 1913.

Degrees Bachelor of Music in the areas of performance, music education, jazz studies, music therapy, music history, music composition. Majors and concentrations: classical music, composition, jazz, music, music education, music history, music therapy, piano/organ, stringed instruments, voice, wind and percussion instruments. Graduate degrees offered: Master of Music in the areas of performance, music education, composition, conducting, music therapy. Program accredited by NASM.

Enrollment Fall 1997: 483 total; 431 undergraduate, 52 graduate.

Music Student Profile 57% females, 43% males, 6% minorities, 3% international.

Music Faculty 53 total undergraduate and graduate (full-time and part-time). 88% of full-time faculty have terminal degrees. Graduate students teach a few undergraduate courses. Undergraduate student–faculty ratio: 13:1.

Student Life Student groups/activities include Collegiate Music Educators National Conference, Music Therapy Club, music fraternities.

Expenses for 1997–98 Application fee: $25. State resident tuition: $3061 full-time. Nonresident tuition: $7770 full-time. Mandatory fees: $594 full-time. Full-time tuition and fees vary according to course load and student level. College room and board: $4398. College room only: $1815. Room and board charges vary according to board plan. Special program-related fees: $60 per semester for music major fee, $7 per semester for applied music fee.

Western Michigan University (continued)

Financial Aid Program-specific awards for 1997: 80 School of Music Scholarships for program majors ($500–$7000).

Application Procedures Students admitted directly into the professional program freshman year. Deadline for freshmen and transfers: continuous. Required: high school transcript, college transcript(s) for transfer students, audition, ACT test score only. Recommended: minimum 3.0 high school GPA. Auditions held 3 times on campus; recorded music is permissible as a substitute for live auditions when distance is prohibitive and videotaped performances are permissible as a substitute for live auditions when distance is prohibitive.

Web Site http://www.wmich.edu/music.

Undergraduate Contact Ms. Margaret J. Hamilton, Assistant Director, School of Music, Western Michigan University, 1201 Oliver Street, Kalamazoo, Michigan 49008-3831; 616-387-4672, fax: 616-387-5809, E-mail address: margaret.hamilton@wmich.edu.

Graduate Contact Dr. David A. Sheldon, Coordinator of Graduate Studies, School of Music, Western Michigan University, 1201 Oliver Street, Kalamazoo, Michigan 49008-3831; 616-387-4672, fax: 616-387-5809, E-mail address: david.sheldon@wmich.edu.

▼ WESTERN WASHINGTON UNIVERSITY

Bellingham, Washington

State-supported, coed. Small town campus. Total enrollment: 11,476. Music program established 1947.

Degrees Bachelor of Music in the areas of performance, composition, music history and literature, jazz studies, music education. Majors and concentrations: composition, jazz, music education, music history and literature, performance. Graduate degrees offered: Master of Music in the areas of performance, composition, music history and literature, conducting, music education. Program accredited by NASM.

Enrollment Fall 1997: 540 total; 215 undergraduate, 25 graduate, 300 non-professional degree.

Music Student Profile 50% females, 50% males, 10% minorities, 4% international.

Music Faculty 33 total undergraduate and graduate (full-time and part-time). 50% of full-time faculty have terminal degrees. Graduate students teach a few undergraduate courses. Undergraduate student–faculty ratio: 15:1.

Student Life Student groups/activities include Music Educators National Conference Student Chapter.

Expenses for 1997–98 Application fee: $35. State resident tuition: $2772 full-time. Nonresident tuition: $9207 full-time. College room and board: $4635. Room and board charges vary according to board plan and housing facility. Special program-related fees: $15 for piano practice fee, $5 for accompanying fee, $20 for instrument rental.

Application Procedures Students admitted directly into the professional program freshman year. Deadline for freshmen: March 1; transfers: April 1. Notification date for freshmen and transfers: May 1. Required: high school transcript, college transcript(s) for transfer students, minimum 2.0 high school GPA, audition, SAT I or ACT test scores. Auditions held once and continuously by appointment on campus; recorded music is permissible as a substitute for live auditions when distance is prohibitive.

Undergraduate Contact Mr. David Wallace, Chairman, Music Department, Western Washington University, MS-9107, Bellingham, Washington 98225-9107; 360-650-3130, fax: 360-650-7538, E-mail address: dwallace@cc.wwu.edu.

Graduate Contact Mr. Edward Rutschman, Graduate Advisor, Music Department, Western Washington University, MS-9107, Bellingham, Washington 98225-9107; 360-650-3889, fax: 360-650-7538, E-mail address: rutsch@cc.wwu.edu.

Rider University

▼ WESTMINSTER CHOIR COLLEGE OF RIDER UNIVERSITY

Princeton, New Jersey

Independent, coed. Small town campus. Total enrollment: 437. Music program established 1926.

Degrees Bachelor of Music in the areas of sacred music, music education, piano pedagogy, theory and composition, organ performance, voice performance. Majors and concentrations: accompanying, music education, music theory and composition, organ, performance, piano, piano pedagogy, sacred music, voice. Graduate degrees offered: Master of Music in the areas of sacred music, music education, choral conducting, piano performance, piano pedagogy and performance, piano accompanying and coaching, composition, organ performance, voice pedagogy and performance. Cross-registration with Princeton University, Princeton Ballet School, Rider University. Program accredited by NASM, NCATE.

Enrollment Fall 1997: 437 total; 282 undergraduate, 112 graduate, 43 non-professional degree.

Music Student Profile 65% females, 35% males, 25% minorities, 19% international.

Music Faculty 72 total undergraduate and graduate (full-time and part-time). 80% of full-time faculty have terminal degrees. Graduate students do not teach undergraduate courses. Undergraduate student–faculty ratio: 7:1.

Student Life Student groups/activities include Music Educators National Conference, American Choral Directors Association, National Association of Teachers of Singing. Special housing available for music students.

Expenses for 1997–98 Application fee: $40, $50 for international students. Comprehensive fee: $22,040 includes full-time tuition ($15,120), mandatory fees ($310), and college room and board ($6610). Special program-related fees: $245 per semester for senior student teaching.

Financial Aid Program-specific awards for 1997: J. F. Williamson Awards for program students, Dean's Awards for program students ($6000), endowed scholarships for program students, Recognition Awards for program students ($3500).

Application Procedures Deadline for freshmen and transfers: continuous. Required: essay, high school transcript, college transcript(s) for transfer students, 2 letters of recommendation, audition, SAT I or ACT test scores, repertoire list. Recommended: minimum 3.0 high school GPA, interview. Auditions held 6 times on campus; recorded music is permissible as a substitute for live auditions when distance is prohibitive or in special circumstances and videotaped performances are permissible as a substitute for live auditions when distance is prohibitive or in special circumstances.

Web Site http://westminster.rider.edu.

Contact Ms. Heather J. Sano, Director of Admissions, Westminster Choir College of Rider University, 101 Walnut Lane, Princeton, New Jersey 08540-3899; 609-921-7144, fax: 609-921-2538.

More About the School

Program Facilities Performance halls include the fine Arts Theatre (550 seats), Bristol Chapel (350 seats), Williamson Hall (100 seats), Scheide Hall (100 seats), and the Playhouse/Opera Theatre (300 seats). Students play 120 pianos and twenty-one pipe organs. Talbott Library houses 55,000 scores and books, a state-of-the-art electronic music computer laboratory with fifteen Kurzweil synthesizers, sixteen Macintosh Power PCs running Finale and Performer, a multimedia center with CD-ROM and laser disc capabilities, computers customized for music theory and sight-singing programs, and 100 music fundamental programs.

Faculty and Alumni Faculty are all distinguished performers and scholars. Leonard Bernstein described Joseph Flummerfelt, principal Conductor and Artistic Director, as "the greatest choral conductor in the world." Joan Lippincott, organ professor and internationally known recitalist, was recently appointed University Organist at Princeton University. Recent Composers-in-Residence include Daniel Pinkham, Peter Schikele, and John Corigliano. Westminster's distinguished alumni include a senior who won the 1994 Metropolitan Opera National Competition; professors at Rice, Notre Dame, Manhattan School of Music, and the Cincinnati Conservatory; performers with the Metropolitan Opera, New York City Opera, and Chicago Lyric opera; and leading music ministers and teachers worldwide.

Student Performance Opportunities All Westminster students perform in professional concerts each year. The 200-student Westminster Symphonic Choir (all upperclass and graduate students) regularly performs and records with the New York Philharmonic and Philadelphia and New Jersey symphony orchestras. Moreover, students perform in Chapel Choir, Schola Cantorum, Westminster Singers, Westminster Jubilee Singers, Westminster Concert Bell Choir, and The Westminster Choir (Choir-in-Residence at the Spoleto Festival USA), which tours nationally.

Special Programs Westminster students can take classes at Westminster, Rider University, Princeton University, Princeton Theological Seminary, and the Princeton Ballet School. Rider and Westminster Career Development Offices provide specialized career services for musicians.

▼

Westminster Choir College, home of the famed Westminster Symphonic Choir, integrates music study with professional choral performances conducted in concert with major symphony orchestras. The Westminster Symphonic Choir performs regularly at Lincoln Center, Carnegie Hall, and the Philadelphia Academy of Music with the New York Philharmonic Orchestra, the Philadelphia Orchestra, and the New Jersey Symphony Orchestra. The Westminster Symphonic Choir has performed and recorded with such notable conductors as Toscanini, Bernstein, Leinsdorf, Mehta, Ozawa, and Muti.

Additional performance and touring opportunities include the Westminster Choir, freshman Chapel Choir, Schola Cantorum, Westminster Singers, Jubilee Singers, and Westminster Concert Bell Choir. Students who play orchestral instruments can participate in the Westminster Conservatory Community Orchestra and chamber ensembles.

Westminster students can also perform with orchestral musicians in Princeton, New Jersey.

Westminster's campus centers around elegant Williamson Hall in the original Georgian Quadrangle, providing an intimate setting for recitals and chamber ensembles. Stately Bristol Chapel, housing a 50-rank Aeolian-Skinner organ, a 16-rank Fisk organ, a 14-rank Noack organ, and a 9-foot Steinway grand piano, is a large recital facility for student, faculty, and guest performers. Nestled among the trees, the Playhouse/Opera Theatre offers a stage and two Steinway grand pianos. Beyond Bristol Chapel, Scheide Hall showcases a 44-rank Casavant organ.

Westminster offers practice rooms in each residence hall and has more than 120 pianos and twenty-one pipe organs, including practice organs by Flentrop, Holtkamp, Schantz, Moller, and Noack.

Talbott Library/Learning Center houses 55,000 books, periodicals, and microforms, plus 23,000 music scores and 160 periodical titles. The Performance Collection contains 6,000 titles in multiple copies for student study, class assignments, student teaching, and church choirs. A single-copy reference file of 45,000 individual octavos is the largest collection of its type in the United States. Voice students use a state-of-the-art voice laboratory, an invaluable resource for the scientific study of the vocal mechanism and singing. The Media Center contains more than 9,000 recordings and videos, with facilities for student playback. The Music Education Resource Collection contains 1,000 textbooks, recordings, filmstrips, charts, and resource materials, plus listening equipment and an electronic piano.

Princeton, 40 miles from New York and Philadelphia, is within easy reach by train or bus, offering students a wealth of educational, cultural, and recreational activities. Princeton University, a short walk from Westminster, offers lectures, art exhibits, recitals, and concerts. Westminster students may enroll in courses at Princeton University and use the university's athletic and recreational facilities. Near Westminster, the Tony Award–winning McCarter Theatre stages several major productions each year and hosts guest artists and performers.

Westminster Symphonic Choir and Westminster Choir performances scheduled for the 1997–98 school year included Beethoven's *Ninth Symphony* and Mahler's *Third Symphony* with the New Jersey Symphony Orchestra under the direction of Maestro Zdenek Macal; Bach's *Magnificat* and Orff's *Carmina Burana* with the Philadelphia Orchestra under Maestro Wolfgang Sawallisch; and Mendelssohn's *Elijah* with the New York Philharmonic under Maestro Kurt Masur.

▼ WESTMINSTER COLLEGE

New Wilmington, Pennsylvania

Independent, coed. Small town campus. Total enrollment: 1,571. Music program established 1947.

Degrees Bachelor of Music in the areas of performance, music education, church music, composition. Majors and concentrations: composition, music education, piano/organ, sacred music, voice. Program accredited by NASM.

Enrollment Fall 1997: 163 total; 70 undergraduate, 93 non-professional degree.

Music Student Profile 71% females, 29% males, 5% minorities, 1% international.

Westminster College (continued)

Music Faculty 27 total (full-time and part-time). 80% of full-time faculty have terminal degrees. Graduate students do not teach undergraduate courses. Undergraduate student–faculty ratio: 10:1.

Student Life Student groups/activities include Music Educators National Conference, Mu Phi Epsilon.

Expenses for 1998–99 Application fee: $20. Comprehensive fee: $19,745 includes full-time tuition ($14,745), mandatory fees ($685), and college room and board ($4315). College room only: $2260. Special program-related fees: $275 per semester for studio fee.

Financial Aid Program-specific awards for 1997: 30 music scholarships for program majors ($800–$2000).

Application Procedures Students admitted directly into the professional program freshman year. Deadline for freshmen and transfers: continuous. Required: essay, high school transcript, college transcript(s) for transfer students, minimum 3.0 high school GPA, 3 letters of recommendation, audition, SAT I or ACT test scores. Recommended: interview. Auditions held 10 times on campus and off campus in Pittsburgh, PA; Erie, PA; recorded music is permissible as a substitute for live auditions when distance is prohibitive and videotaped performances are permissible as a substitute for live auditions when distance is prohibitive.

Web Site http://westminster.edu/acad/musi/.

Undergraduate Contact Admissions, Westminster College, 319 South Market Street, New Wilmington, Pennsylvania 16172-0001; 412-946-7100, fax: 412-946-7171.

Sybil B. Harrington College of Fine Arts and Humanities

▼ WEST TEXAS A&M UNIVERSITY

Canyon, Texas

State-supported, coed. Small town campus. Total enrollment: 6,489.

Degrees Bachelor of Music in the areas of applied music, music therapy, music business, theory composition, music education. Majors and concentrations: music, piano/organ, stringed instruments, voice, wind and percussion instruments. Graduate degrees offered: Master of Music in the area of performance; Master of Arts in the area of music. Program accredited by NASM.

Enrollment Fall 1997: 225 undergraduate, 15 graduate.

Music Student Profile 50% females, 50% males, 10% minorities, 5% international.

Music Faculty 30 total undergraduate and graduate (full-time and part-time). 50% of full-time faculty have terminal degrees. Graduate students teach a few undergraduate courses. Undergraduate student–faculty ratio: 20:1.

Student Life Student groups/activities include National Association of Music Therapy Student Chapter, Kappa Kappa Psi, Mu Phi Epsilon.

Expenses for 1997–98 State resident tuition: $1296 full-time. Nonresident tuition: $6432 full-time. Mandatory fees: $448 full-time. Full-time tuition and fees vary according to course load. College room and board: $2969. College room only: $1308. Room and board charges vary according to board plan and housing facility. Special program-related fees: $60 for applied music fee.

Application Procedures Students admitted directly into the professional program freshman year. Deadline for freshmen and transfers: continuous. Required: high school transcript, college transcript(s) for transfer students, 3 letters of recommendation, audition, SAT I or ACT test scores. Auditions held 3 times on campus; recorded music is permissible as a substitute for live auditions if a campus visit is impossible and videotaped performances are permissible as a substitute for live auditions if a campus visit is impossible.

Contact Dr. Melvyn Raiman, Head, Department of Music and Dance, West Texas A&M University, WTAMU Box 60879, Canyon, Texas 79016; 806-651-2840, fax: 806-651-2958.

▼ WEST VIRGINIA UNIVERSITY

Morgantown, West Virginia

State-supported, coed. Small town campus. Total enrollment: 22,238. Music program established 1897.

Degrees Bachelor of Music in the areas of music theory, music history, composition, performance, music education. Majors and concentrations: classical music, composition, jazz, music, music education, music history, music performance, music theory, piano/organ, stringed instruments, voice, wind and percussion instruments. Graduate degrees offered: Master of Music in the areas of performance, composition, music history, music education. Doctor of Musical Arts in the areas of piano, voice, organ, percussion/world music, orchestral instruments. Program accredited by NASM.

Enrollment Fall 1997: 310 total; 249 undergraduate, 61 graduate.

Music Student Profile 49% females, 51% males, 4% minorities, 8% international.

Music Faculty 49 total undergraduate and graduate (full-time and part-time). 95% of full-time faculty have terminal degrees. Graduate students teach a few undergraduate courses. Undergraduate student–faculty ratio: 8:1.

Student Life Student groups/activities include Music Educators National Conference, Music Teachers National Association. Special housing available for music students.

Expenses for 1997–98 Application fee: $15, $35 for nonresidents. State resident tuition: $2336 full-time. Nonresident tuition: $7356 full-time. Full-time tuition varies according to location, program, and reciprocity agreements. College room and board: $4832. Room and board charges vary according to board plan, housing facility, and location. Special program-related fees: $15 per semester for practice room fee.

Financial Aid Program-specific awards for 1997: 1–2 Carolyn and Clifford Brown Music Alumni Scholarships for music majors ($1800), 1 Frank E. and Margaret S. Lorince Scholarship for music majors ($2000), 6 Music Faculty Recognition Scholarships for music majors ($8000), 2–3 Eleanor Tucker Donley Memorial Scholarships for music majors ($2000), 12 Ida Cope Tait Music Scholarships for music majors ($500–$1000), 2 Edith Roberts Williams Music Scholarships for music majors ($900), 3 Morgantown Music Club Scholarships for music majors ($2000), 14 Loyalty Permanent Endowment Awards for music majors ($500–$1000), 56 Performance Grants for music majors ($5357), 20 Performing Arts Scholarships for music majors ($1000).

Application Procedures Students admitted directly into the professional program freshman year. Deadline for freshmen and transfers: continuous. Notification date for freshmen and transfers: August 1. Required: high school transcript, college transcript(s) for transfer students, minimum 2.0 high

school GPA, audition, SAT I or ACT test scores. Recommended: letter of recommendation, interview. Auditions held 3 times and by appointment on campus; recorded music is permissible as a substitute for live auditions when distance is prohibitive and videotaped performances are permissible as a substitute for live auditions when distance is prohibitive.
Web Site http://www.wvu.edu/~music/index.htm.
Undergraduate Contact Dr. John Weigand, Director, Undergraduate Admissions, Music Department, West Virginia University, College of Creative Arts, PO Box 6111, Morgantown, West Virginia 26506-6111; 304-293-5511 ext. 3187, fax: 304-293-7491.
Graduate Contact Dr. Virginia Thompson, Director of Graduate Studies, Music Department, West Virginia University, College of Creative Arts, PO Box 6111, Morgantown, West Virginia 26506-6111; 304-293-5511 ext. 3165, fax: 304-293-7491, E-mail address: vthompso@wvu.edu.

▼ WEST VIRGINIA WESLEYAN COLLEGE

Buckhannon, West Virginia

Independent, coed. Small town campus. Total enrollment: 1,686.
Degrees Bachelor of Music; Bachelor of Music Education. Majors and concentrations: classical music, guitar, music, music education, piano, voice, wind and percussion instruments. Program accredited by NASM.
Enrollment Fall 1997: 60 undergraduate.
Music Student Profile 50% females, 50% males, 8% minorities, 4% international.
Music Faculty 14 total (full-time and part-time). 83% of full-time faculty have terminal degrees. Graduate students do not teach undergraduate courses.
Student Life Student groups/activities include Music Educators National Conference Student Chapter, Sigma Alpha Iota, Phi Mu Alpha Sinfonia.
Estimated expenses for 1998–99 Application fee: $25. One-time mandatory fee: $500. Comprehensive fee: $20,850 includes full-time tuition ($15,750), mandatory fees ($1000), and college room and board ($4100). College room only: $1855. Room and board charges vary according to housing facility. Special program-related fees: $150 per semester for applied music fees.
Financial Aid Program-specific awards for 1997: 25 music scholarships for incoming students ($1000–$6000), 25 Performing Arts Awards for incoming students ($1000–$6000).
Application Procedures Students apply for admission into the professional program by freshman year. Deadline for freshmen and transfers: continuous. Required: essay, high school transcript, college transcript(s) for transfer students, minimum 2.0 high school GPA, letter of recommendation, audition. Recommended: minimum 3.0 high school GPA, interview, video, SAT I or ACT test scores. Auditions held 6 times on campus and off campus in Washington, DC; recorded music is permissible as a substitute for live auditions if scheduling is difficult and videotaped performances are permissible as a substitute for live auditions if scheduling is difficult.
Undergraduate Contact Mr. Robert N. Skinner, Director of Admission, West Virginia Wesleyan College, 59 College Avenue, Buckhannon, West Virginia 26201; 800-722-9933, fax: 304-473-8108.

Wheaton Conservatory of Music

▼ WHEATON COLLEGE

Wheaton, Illinois

Independent-nondenominational, coed. Suburban campus. Total enrollment: 2,725. Music program established 1882.
Degrees Bachelor of Music in the areas of performance, composition, music history/literature, elective studies; Bachelor of Music Education. Majors and concentrations: composition, music education, music history and literature, piano/organ, stringed instruments, voice, wind and percussion instruments. Program accredited by NASM.
Enrollment Fall 1997: 200 total; all undergraduate.
Music Student Profile 52% females, 48% males, 6% minorities, 10% international.
Music Faculty 30 total (full-time and part-time). 75% of full-time faculty have terminal degrees. Graduate students do not teach undergraduate courses. Undergraduate student–faculty ratio: 9:1.
Student Life Student groups/activities include Music Educators National Conference, American Guild of Organists, National Association of Teachers of Singing.
Expenses for 1997–98 Application fee: $35. Comprehensive fee: $18,520 includes full-time tuition ($13,780) and college room and board ($4740). College room only: $2730. Special program-related fees: $16 per credit hour for music fee, $190 per semester for performance course, $45 per semester for second instrument lesson.
Financial Aid Program-specific awards for 1997: 3–4 Cording Awards for those demonstrating talent ($2000), 4 Presidential Honor Awards for those demonstrating talent ($1000), 4–5 Strickland Awards for those demonstrating need ($1000–$2000), 4–5 Special Achievement Awards for those demonstrating talent ($2000).
Application Procedures Students admitted directly into the professional program freshman year. Deadline for freshmen and transfers: March 1. Notification date for freshmen and transfers: April 1. Required: essay, high school transcript, college transcript(s) for transfer students, minimum 2.0 high school GPA, 4 letters of recommendation, interview, audition, SAT I or ACT test scores. Auditions held 6-8 times on campus; recorded music is permissible as a substitute for live auditions when distance is prohibitive and videotaped performances are permissible as a substitute for live auditions when distance is prohibitive.
Web Site http://wheaton.edu.
Undergraduate Contact Ms. Debbie Rodgers, Conservatory Admission Counselor, Wheaton Conservatory of Music, Wheaton College, Wheaton, Illinois 60187; 800-222-2419 ext. 3, fax: 630-752-5341, E-mail address: deborah.a.rodgers@wheaton.edu.

More About the Conservatory

Program Facilities Wheaton's main music facility is McAlister Hall, which houses most faculty offices and practice rooms. There are about seventy-five pianos on campus, including six concert grands. Performances take place in Edman Memorial Chapel, seating 2,350; in Pierce Chapel, seating 900; and in Barrows Auditorium, seating 500. There are five pipe organs, including a 65-rank, four-manual Schantz. The music library holds several thousand compact discs, tapes, and records, as well as an extensive collection of scores and music reference books. The Technomusic Studio is available with a

Wheaton College (*continued*)

Macintosh computer, sequencing and note-writing software, synthesizers, and digital recording capabilities.

Student Performance Opportunities There are nine performing ensembles directed by Conservatory faculty members. Vocal and choral ensembles include Chapel Choir, Concert Choir, Men's Glee Club, Music Theater Workshop, West Suburban Choral Union, and Women's Choral. Instrumental ensembles include Jazz Ensemble, Pep Band, Symphony Orchestra, and Wind Ensemble. In addition, chamber ensembles and soloists rehearse and perform regularly. Large ensembles join forces for the annual Christmas Festival and Festival of Faith, in addition to maintaining a busy schedule of concert events locally and throughout the United States.

▼ WICHITA STATE UNIVERSITY

Wichita, Kansas

State-supported, coed. Urban campus. Total enrollment: 14,061.

Degrees Bachelor of Music in the areas of performance, musicology-music theory/composition; Bachelor of Music Education in the areas of choral music education, instrumental music education, general music education, special music education. Majors and concentrations: classical music, conducting, jazz, music, music education, music theory and composition, opera, piano pedagogy, piano/organ, special music education, stringed instruments, voice, wind and percussion instruments. Graduate degrees offered: Master of Music in the areas of performance, musicology-music theory/composition, piano pedagogy, instrumental conducting, opera performance; Master of Music Education in the areas of choral music education, instrumental music education, general music education, special music education. Program accredited by NASM.

Enrollment Fall 1997: 375 undergraduate, 120 graduate.

Music Student Profile 52% females, 48% males, 10% minorities, 8% international.

Music Faculty 51 total undergraduate and graduate (full-time and part-time). 75% of full-time faculty have terminal degrees. Graduate students teach a few undergraduate courses.

Student Life Student groups/activities include Music Educators National Conference Student Chapter, Tau Beta Sigma/Kappa Kappa Psi, Music Teachers National Association Student Chapter. Special housing available for music students.

Expenses for 1997–98 Application fee: $20. State resident tuition: $1486 full-time. Nonresident tuition: $6414 full-time. Mandatory fees: $500 full-time. College room and board: $3760. Room and board charges vary according to board plan.

Financial Aid Program-specific awards for 1997: 300 scholarships for talented students ($500–$2000).

Application Procedures Students admitted directly into the professional program freshman year. Deadline for freshmen and transfers: continuous. Required: high school transcript, college transcript(s) for transfer students, minimum 2.0 high school GPA, audition for scholarship consideration. Recommended: minimum 3.0 high school GPA, letter of recommendation, interview, SAT I or ACT test scores. Auditions held twice and by appointment on campus; recorded music is permissible as a substitute for live auditions if a campus visit is impossible and videotaped performances are permissible as a substitute for live auditions if a campus visit is impossible.

Undergraduate Contact Dr. John William Thomson, Chair, School of Music, Wichita State University, Campus Box 53, Wichita, Kansas 67260-0053; 316-978-3500, fax: 316-978-3951, E-mail address: thomson@twsuvm.uc.twsu.edu.

▼ WILFRID LAURIER UNIVERSITY

Waterloo, ON, Canada

Province-supported, coed. Urban campus. Total enrollment: 7,857. Music program established 1975.

Degrees Bachelor of Music in the areas of comprehensive, church music, composition, music history, performance, music theory, music education; Bachelor of Music Therapy. Majors and concentrations: classical music, composition, music education, music history, music theory, music therapy, opera, piano/organ, sacred music, stringed instruments, voice, wind and percussion instruments. Cross-registration with University of Waterloo. Program accredited by CUMS.

Enrollment Fall 1997: 274 total; all undergraduate.

Music Student Profile 71% females, 29% males.

Music Faculty 74 total (full-time and part-time). 52% of full-time faculty have terminal degrees. Graduate students do not teach undergraduate courses. Undergraduate student–faculty ratio: 4:1.

Student Life Student groups/activities include Music Association, Music Therapy Association, Jazz Council.

Expenses for 1997–98 Application fee: $75 Canadian dollars. Tuition, fee, and room and board charges are reported in Canadian dollars. Canadian resident tuition: $3228 full-time. Mandatory fees: $260 full-time. College room and board: $5300. College room only: $3000. International student tuition: $7000 full-time. Special program-related fees: $30–$150 per term for accompanying fees.

Financial Aid Program-specific awards for 1997: 57 Faculty of Music Awards for program majors ($790).

Application Procedures Students admitted directly into the professional program freshman year. Deadline for freshmen and transfers: April 1. Notification date for freshmen and transfers: September 1. Required: high school transcript, minimum 3.0 high school GPA, letter of recommendation, interview, audition, music theory placement test. Auditions held once on campus; recorded music is permissible as a substitute for live auditions when distance is prohibitive and videotaped performances are permissible as a substitute for live auditions when distance is prohibitive.

Web Site http://www.wlu.ca.

Undergraduate Contact Ms. Robina Athavale, Admissions Officer (Music), Office of Admissions, Wilfrid Laurier University, 75 University Avenue West, Waterloo, ON N2L 3C5, Canada; 519-884-0710 ext. 6102, E-mail address: rathaval@mach2.wlu.ca.

▼ WILLAMETTE UNIVERSITY

Salem, Oregon

Independent-United Methodist, coed. Urban campus. Total enrollment: 2,502. Music program established 1842.

Degrees Bachelor of Music in the areas of music performance, music therapy, music education, composition. Majors and concentrations: brass, composition, guitar, harp, music,

music education, music therapy, piano/organ, stringed instruments, voice, wind and percussion instruments. Program accredited by NASM, NAMT.

Enrollment Fall 1997: 60 total; all undergraduate.

Music Student Profile 60% females, 40% males, 3% minorities, 12% international.

Music Faculty 34 total (full-time and part-time). 89% of full-time faculty have terminal degrees. Graduate students do not teach undergraduate courses. Undergraduate student–faculty ratio: 13:1.

Student Life Student groups/activities include Music Educators National Conference Student Chapter, Music Therapy Chapter, Mu Phi Epsilon.

Expenses for 1997–98 Application fee: $35. Comprehensive fee: $25,570 includes full-time tuition ($20,200), mandatory fees ($90), and college room and board ($5280). Special program-related fees: $200–$400 for applied music fee, $3 for locker rental fee.

Financial Aid Program-specific awards for 1997: 30 Music Scholarship Awards for talented performers ($1000–$2000), 20 Named Music Scholarships for talented performers ($500–$1000).

Application Procedures Students apply for admission into the professional program by freshman year. Deadline for freshmen and transfers: continuous. Notification date for freshmen and transfers: April 1. Required: essay, high school transcript, college transcript(s) for transfer students, 2 letters of recommendation, SAT I or ACT test scores. Recommended: minimum 3.0 high school GPA, interview, audition. Auditions held 3 times and through miscellaneous ad hoc auditions on campus; recorded music is permissible as a substitute for live auditions if a live audition is impossible and videotaped performances are permissible as a substitute for live auditions if a live audition is impossible.

Undergraduate Contact Mr. James Sumner, Dean of Admissions, Willamette University, 900 State Street, Salem, Oregon 97301; 503-370-6303, fax: 503-375-5363, E-mail address: jsumner@willamette.edu.

Winters School of Music

▼ WILLIAM CAREY COLLEGE

Hattiesburg, Mississippi

Independent-Southern Baptist, coed. Small town campus. Music program established 1966.

Degrees Bachelor of Music in the areas of music education, church music, performance, music therapy. Majors and concentrations: applied music, guitar, music education, music therapy, performance, piano/organ, sacred music, voice, wind and percussion instruments. Program accredited by NASM.

Enrollment Fall 1997: 80 undergraduate.

Music Student Profile 50% females, 50% males, 2% minorities.

Music Faculty 14 total (full-time and part-time). 75% of full-time faculty have terminal degrees. Graduate students do not teach undergraduate courses. Undergraduate student–faculty ratio: 8:1.

Student Life Student groups/activities include Delta Omicron, Phi Mu Alpha Sinfonia, Music Educators National Conference.

Expenses for 1997–98 Application fee: $10. Tuition: $6624 full-time. Special program-related fees: $300 per year for applied fee.

Financial Aid Program-specific awards for 1997: 75 departmental awards for program majors ($500–$5000).

Application Procedures Students admitted directly into the professional program freshman year. Deadline for freshmen and transfers: continuous. Required: high school transcript, college transcript(s) for transfer students, audition, SAT I or ACT test scores. Recommended: minimum 2.0 high school GPA. Auditions held continuously on campus and off campus in various regional cities; recorded music is permissible as a substitute for live auditions when distance is prohibitive and videotaped performances are permissible as a substitute for live auditions when distance is prohibitive.

Undergraduate Contact Dr. Milfred Valentine, Dean, Winters School of Music, William Carey College, 498 Tuscan Avenue, Hattiesburg, Mississippi 39401; 601-582-6175, fax: 601-582-6454.

▼ WILLIAM PATERSON UNIVERSITY OF NEW JERSEY

Wayne, New Jersey

State-supported, coed. Suburban campus. Total enrollment: 8,941.

Degrees Bachelor of Music in the areas of performance, jazz studies, music management, music education; Bachelor of Arts in the area of musical studies/audio recording. Majors and concentrations: classical music, jazz, music, music education, music management, piano/organ, stringed instruments, voice, wind and percussion instruments. Program accredited by NASM.

Enrollment Fall 1997: 275 total; all undergraduate.

Music Student Profile 35% females, 65% males, 8% minorities, 5% international.

Music Faculty 63 total undergraduate (full-time and part-time). 75% of full-time faculty have terminal degrees. Graduate students do not teach undergraduate courses. Undergraduate student–faculty ratio: 6:1.

Student Life Student groups/activities include Music Educators National Conference Student Chapter, Music Entertainment Industry Educators Student Association, National Association of Music Business Institutes.

Expenses for 1997–98 Application fee: $35. State resident tuition: $3786 full-time. Nonresident tuition: $6000 full-time. College room and board: $5100. College room only: $3200. Special program-related fees: $100 per course for applied music fees, $30 per semester for practice room fee, $30 per course for electronic music lab fee.

Financial Aid Program-specific awards for 1997: 10 departmental scholarships for talented music majors ($300).

Application Procedures Students admitted directly into the professional program freshman year. Deadline for freshmen and transfers: July 1. Required: essay, high school transcript, college transcript(s) for transfer students, audition, SAT I test score only (minimum combined SAT I score of 960). Recommended: minimum 3.0 high school GPA. Auditions held 5 times on campus; recorded music is permissible as a substitute for live auditions for jazz and classical music applicants.

Undergraduate Contact Dr. Joel Craig Davis, Director of Bands and Music Admissions, Music Department, William Paterson University of New Jersey, Shea Center for Performing Arts, Wayne, New Jersey 07470; 973-720-3466, fax: 973-720-2217.

▼ WINGATE UNIVERSITY

Wingate, North Carolina

Independent-Baptist, coed. Small town campus. Total enrollment: 1,230. Music program established 1977.

Degrees Bachelor of Music Education. Cross-registration with Charlotte Area Educational Consortium. Program accredited by NASM.

Enrollment Fall 1997: 34 total; all undergraduate.

Music Student Profile 52% females, 48% males, 10% minorities.

Music Faculty 13 total (full-time and part-time). 86% of full-time faculty have terminal degrees. Graduate students do not teach undergraduate courses. Undergraduate student–faculty ratio: 5:1.

Student Life Student groups/activities include Collegiate Music Educators National Conference.

Expenses for 1997–98 Application fee: $25. Comprehensive fee: $15,790 includes full-time tuition ($11,250), mandatory fees ($440), and college room and board ($4100). College room only: $2000. Special program-related fees: $80 per credit hour for applied music fee.

Financial Aid Program-specific awards for 1997: 24 music scholarships for program majors ($2000).

Application Procedures Students admitted directly into the professional program freshman year. Deadline for freshmen and transfers: continuous. Notification date for freshmen and transfers: August 15. Required: essay, high school transcript, college transcript(s) for transfer students, minimum 2.0 high school GPA, 2 letters of recommendation, interview, SAT I or ACT test scores. Recommended: minimum 3.0 high school GPA, audition. Auditions held 3 times on campus; recorded music is permissible as a substitute for live auditions when distance is prohibitive and videotaped performances are permissible as a substitute for live auditions when distance is prohibitive.

Undergraduate Contact Mr. Walt Crutchfield, Director of Admissions, Stegall Administration Building, Wingate University, Box 3059, Wingate, North Carolina 28174; 704-233-8201, fax: 704-233-8014, E-mail address: admit@wingate.edu.

▼ WINTERS SCHOOL OF MUSIC

See William Carey College

▼ WINTHROP UNIVERSITY

Rock Hill, South Carolina

State-supported, coed. Suburban campus. Total enrollment: 5,574. Music program established 1876.

Degrees Bachelor of Music in the area of performance; Bachelor of Music Education in the areas of choral music education, instrumental music education. Majors and concentrations: guitar, harpsichord, music education, piano/organ, stringed instruments, voice, wind and percussion instruments. Graduate degrees offered: Master of Music in the area of performance; Master of Music Education. Program accredited by NASM.

Enrollment Fall 1997: 160 total; 107 undergraduate, 11 graduate, 42 non-professional degree.

Music Student Profile 51% females, 49% males, 18% minorities, 2% international.

Music Faculty 31 total undergraduate and graduate (full-time and part-time). 75% of full-time faculty have terminal degrees. Graduate students do not teach undergraduate courses. Undergraduate student–faculty ratio: 7:1.

Student Life Student groups/activities include Delta Omicron, Phi Mu Alpha Sinfonia, Music Educators National Conference.

Expenses for 1997–98 Application fee: $35. State resident tuition: $3918 full-time. Nonresident tuition: $7046 full-time. Mandatory fees: $20 full-time. College room and board: $3764. College room only: $2260. Special program-related fees: $70–$100 per semester for applied music fees.

Financial Aid Program-specific awards for 1997: 50 music scholarships for above-average freshmen and continuing students with exceptional artistic ability ($600).

Application Procedures Students admitted directly into the professional program freshman year. Deadline for freshmen: May 1; transfers: June 1. Required: high school transcript, college transcript(s) for transfer students, letter of recommendation, audition, SAT I or ACT test scores. Recommended: essay. Auditions held 4 times on campus; recorded music is permissible as a substitute for live auditions when distance is prohibitive and videotaped performances are permissible as a substitute for live auditions when distance is prohibitive or scheduling is difficult.

Web Site http://www.winthrop.edu.

Undergraduate Contact Mr. Donald M. Rogers, Chair, Department of Music, Winthrop University, 129 Music Conservatory, Rock Hill, South Carolina 29733; 803-323-2255, fax: 803-323-2343, E-mail address: rogersd@winthrop.edu.

Graduate Contact Dr. Elda Franklin, Graduate Advisor in Music, Department of Music, Winthrop University, 129 Music Conservatory, Rock Hill, South Carolina 29733; 803-323-2224, fax: 803-323-2343, E-mail address: frankline@winthrop.edu.

▼ WITTENBERG UNIVERSITY

Springfield, Ohio

Independent, coed. Suburban campus. Total enrollment: 2,088. Music program established 1931.

Degrees Bachelor of Music in the areas of performance, church music; Bachelor of Music Education in the areas of choral music education, instrumental music education. Majors and concentrations: church music, music, music education, piano/organ, stringed instruments, voice, wind and percussion instruments. Cross-registration with Southwestern Consortium for Higher Education. Program accredited by NASM.

Enrollment Fall 1997: 40 total; 22 undergraduate, 18 non-professional degree.

Music Student Profile 58% females, 42% males, 3% minorities, 4% international.

Music Faculty 25 total (full-time and part-time). 63% of full-time faculty have terminal degrees. Graduate students do not teach undergraduate courses. Undergraduate student–faculty ratio: 14:1.

Student Life Student groups/activities include Ohio Collegiate Music Education Association.

Expenses for 1997–98 Application fee: $40. Comprehensive fee: $24,000 includes full-time tuition ($18,228), mandatory fees ($912), and college room and board ($4860). College room only: $2416. Room and board charges vary according to board plan and housing facility. Special program-related fees: $15 per semester for practice room rental.

Financial Aid Program-specific awards for 1997: 20 Music Alumni Scholarships for incoming students ($2500–$5000), 10 Alida Atwell Smith Scholarships for those demonstrating need and talent ($600–$3500), 10 Jan Bender Scholarships for those demonstrating need and talent ($600–$3500), 10 Pavlik Scholarships for those demonstrating need and talent ($600–$3500), 10 Sara Krieg Scholarship for those demonstrating need and talent ($600–$3500).

Application Procedures Students admitted directly into the professional program freshman year. Deadline for freshmen and transfers: continuous. Notification date for freshmen and transfers: August 1. Required: essay, high school transcript, college transcript(s) for transfer students, minimum 2.0 high school GPA, 2 letters of recommendation, SAT I or ACT test scores. Recommended: interview, audition. Auditions held 3 times and by appointment on campus; recorded music is permissible as a substitute for live auditions when distance is prohibitive and videotaped performances are permissible as a substitute for live auditions when distance is prohibitive.

Web Site http://www.wittenberg.edu/academics/music.

Undergraduate Contact Mr. Ken Benne, Dean of Admission, Wittenberg University, PO Box 720, Springfield, Ohio 45501-0720; 937-327-6314, fax: 937-327-6340, E-mail address: admission@wittenberg.edu.

▼ Wright State University

Dayton, Ohio

State-supported, coed. Suburban campus. Total enrollment: 15,343. Music program established 1966.

Degrees Bachelor of Music in the areas of performance, music history and literature, music education. Majors and concentrations: classical music, music, music education, piano/organ, stringed instruments, voice, wind and percussion instruments. Graduate degrees offered: Master of Music Education. Cross-registration with Southern Ohio Consortium of Higher Education. Program accredited by NASM.

Enrollment Fall 1997: 161 total; 138 undergraduate, 23 graduate.

Music Student Profile 55% females, 45% males, 6% minorities, 1% international.

Music Faculty 32 total undergraduate and graduate (full-time and part-time). 71% of full-time faculty have terminal degrees. Graduate students teach a few undergraduate courses. Undergraduate student–faculty ratio: 10:1.

Student Life Student groups/activities include Collegiate Music Educators National Conference, Phi Mu Alpha Sinfonia, Sigma Alpha Iota.

Expenses for 1997–98 Application fee: $30. State resident tuition: $3708 full-time. Nonresident tuition: $7416 full-time. College room and board: $4500. Room and board charges vary according to board plan and housing facility. Special program-related fees: $5 for practice room key rental, $50 for junior, senior recital fee, $120–$240 for applied music lesson fee, $15 for instrument rental fee.

Financial Aid Program-specific awards for 1997: 12–16 String Scholarships for string players ($1500–$3000), 50 music scholarships for program majors ($1500).

Application Procedures Students admitted directly into the professional program freshman year. Deadline for freshmen and transfers: continuous. Required: essay, high school

transcript, college transcript(s) for transfer students, minimum 2.0 high school GPA, 3 letters of recommendation, audition, SAT I or ACT test scores. Auditions held 7 times on campus; recorded music is permissible as a substitute for live auditions when distance is prohibitive and videotaped performances are permissible as a substitute for live auditions when distance is prohibitive.

Web Site http://www.wright.edu/.

Undergraduate Contact Ms. Kathie Barbour, Administrative Assistant, Music Department, Wright State University, Dayton, Ohio 45435; 937-775-2346, fax: 937-775-3786, E-mail address: cabarbou@wright.edu.

Graduate Contact Charles Larkowski, Director, Graduate Studies in Music, Music Department, Wright State University, Dayton, Ohio 45435; 937-775-2254, fax: 937-775-3786, E-mail address: clarkows@wright.edu.

▼ Xavier University of Louisiana

New Orleans, Louisiana

Independent-Roman Catholic, coed. Urban campus. Total enrollment: 3,506.

Degrees Bachelor of Music in the areas of performance, music education. Majors and concentrations: music education, piano/organ, stringed instruments, voice, wind and percussion instruments. Cross-registration with Loyola University-New Orleans. Program accredited by NASM.

Enrollment Fall 1997: 33 total; 16 undergraduate, 17 nonprofessional degree.

Music Student Profile 55% females, 45% males, 100% minorities, 1% international.

Music Faculty 14 total (full-time and part-time). 43% of full-time faculty have terminal degrees. Graduate students do not teach undergraduate courses. Undergraduate student–faculty ratio: 4:1.

Student Life Student groups/activities include Music Educators National Conference Student Chapter, Phi Mu Alpha Sinfonia.

Expenses for 1997–98 Application fee: $25. Comprehensive fee: $12,915 includes full-time tuition ($8100), mandatory fees ($115), and college room and board ($4700). Full-time tuition and fees vary according to program. Room and board charges vary according to housing facility. Special program-related fees: $150 per semester for applied music fee.

Financial Aid Program-specific awards for 1997: music talent scholarships for program majors ($2000–$3000).

Application Procedures Students admitted directly into the professional program freshman year. Deadline for freshmen and transfers: June 1. Required: high school transcript, letter of recommendation, audition, SAT I or ACT test scores. Auditions held twice and by appointment on campus; recorded music is permissible as a substitute for live auditions when distance is prohibitive and videotaped performances are permissible as a substitute for live auditions when distance is prohibitive.

Undergraduate Contact Mr. John E. Ware, Chairman, Department of Music, Xavier University of Louisiana, 7325 Palmetto Street, New Orleans, Louisiana 70125; 504-483-7597, fax: 504-482-2801.

▼ YORK UNIVERSITY

North York, ON, Canada

Province-supported, coed. Urban campus. Total enrollment: 37,900. Music program established 1969.

Degrees Bachelor of Fine Arts in the areas of music performance, composition. Majors and concentrations: classical performance, composition, electronic music, improvisation, jazz, world music.

Enrollment Fall 1997: 390 total; 330 undergraduate, 60 non-professional degree.

Music Student Profile 50% females, 50% males, 5% international.

Music Faculty 45 total (full-time and part-time). 100% of full-time faculty have terminal degrees. Graduate students teach a few undergraduate courses. Undergraduate student–faculty ratio: 7:1.

Student Life Student groups/activities include York Music Students Association, Creative Arts Students Association.

Expenses for 1997–98 Application fee: $60 Canadian dollars. Tuition, fee, and room and board charges are reported in Canadian dollars. Canadian resident tuition: $3750 full-time. Full-time tuition varies according to course load, degree level, and program. College room and board: $5000. Room and board charges vary according to board plan and housing facility. International student tuition: $10,800 full-time. Special program-related fees: $10–$40 per course for material fees.

Financial Aid Program-specific awards for 1997: 3 Talent Awards for applicants with outstanding auditions ($1000), 1 International Talent Award for international applicants with outstanding auditions ($2000), 1 Harry Rowe Bursary for demonstrated achievement or potential in artistic or scholarly work ($2000), 25 Fine Arts Bursary for academically qualified students demonstrating financial need ($250–$1500), Oscar Peterson Bursaries for outstanding jazz performers demonstrating need ($200–$700), 1 Alan Lessem Memorial Award for outstanding scholarly written work ($400), 1 Elaine Newton/Alan Wilder Achievement Bursary for students with a minimum B average demonstrating need ($1000), Oscar Peterson Scholarships for outstanding jazz performers ($1000–$1400), Ella Fitzgerald Award for Jazz Performances for applicants demonstrating artistic excellence ($500–$800), 1 Peggy Sampson Bursary for applicants demonstrating financial need ($300).

Application Procedures Students admitted directly into the professional program freshman year. Deadline for freshmen and transfers: March 1. Notification date for freshmen: June 30; transfers: July 15. Required: essay, high school transcript, college transcript(s) for transfer students, minimum 3.0 high school GPA, interview, audition, SAT I, ACT or Canadian equivalent. Recommended: 2 letters of recommendation. Auditions held once on campus; recorded music is permissible as a substitute for live auditions when distance is prohibitive and videotaped performances are permissible as a substitute for live auditions when distance is prohibitive.

Web Site http://www.yorku.ca/faculty/finearts/music/.

Undergraduate Contact Mr. Don Murdoch, Liaison Officer, Liaison and Advising, Faculty of Fine Arts, York University, 213 CFA, 4700 Keele Street, Toronto, ON M3J 1P3, Canada; 416-736-5135, fax: 416-736-5447, E-mail address: donm@yorku.ca.

More About the Department

Program Facilities Analogue and digital music studio; MIDI studio; acoustical lab and concert hall; jazz workshop studios; world music/percussion studio; ethnomusicology and jazz archives; computer-based research laboratory; Sound and Moving Image Library; piano/practice modules—pianos are replaced each year.

Faculty and Alumni York music faculty members are among Canada's leading music theorists, historians, composers, and performers and include Grammy Award–winning ethnomusicologist Rob Bowman, pianist Christina Petrowska, composer James Tenney, and South Indian master drummer Trichy Sankaran. Adjunct faculty members include First Nations recording artist Buffy Sainte-Marie and jazz icon Oscar Peterson. Many alumni have received national and international acclaim for their work.

Performance Opportunities Recitals, concerts, workshops, and master classes by faculty members, students, and guest artists are featured regularly in the program. Performance ensembles include jazz workshops and orchestra, guitar ensembles, contemporary improvisation groups, string ensembles and orchestra, wind symphony and brass ensembles, piano master classes, percussion ensembles, chamber and jazz choirs, and world music ensembles.

Special Programs Students benefit from being part of one of the largest faculties of fine arts in North America. Combined-degree programs are available with the Departments of Dance, Film & Video, Theatre, and Visual Arts and through an interdisciplinary program in fine arts cultural studies. Combined-degree programs are also available with the Faculties of Arts and Environmental Studies.

The Faculty of Education at York offers consecutive and concurrent teaching programs with the Faculty of Fine Arts, leading to teacher certification. Studies Abroad programs are available, as is support for students for whom English is their second language.

Dana School of Music

▼ YOUNGSTOWN STATE UNIVERSITY

Youngstown, Ohio

State-supported, coed. Urban campus. Total enrollment: 12,324. Music program established 1941.

Degrees Bachelor of Music in the areas of performance, music education, applied music, composition, accompanying, jazz studies. Majors and concentrations: accompanying, classical music, composition, jazz, music education, piano/organ, stringed instruments, voice, wind and percussion instruments. Graduate degrees offered: Master of Music in the areas of performance, music education, music theory and composition, music history and literature. Program accredited by NASM.

Enrollment Fall 1997: 307 total; 271 undergraduate, 36 graduate.

Music Student Profile 50% females, 50% males, 4% minorities, 1% international.

Music Faculty 37 total undergraduate and graduate (full-time and part-time). 60% of full-time faculty have terminal degrees. Graduate students teach a few undergraduate courses. Undergraduate student–faculty ratio: 8:1.

Expenses for 1997–98 Application fee: $25. State resident tuition: $2826 full-time. Nonresident tuition: $6609 full-time. Mandatory fees: $732 full-time. Full-time tuition and fees

vary according to course load and reciprocity agreements. College room and board: $4350. Room and board charges vary according to board plan and housing facility. Special program-related fees: $35 for applied music fee.

Financial Aid Program-specific awards for 1997: 70 Youngstown State University Foundation Music Awards for program students ($800), 4 University Grants-in-Aid for program students ($1800), 2 Monday Musical Awards for program students ($1000), 10 Showcase Awards for program students ($600).

Application Procedures Students admitted directly into the professional program freshman year. Deadline for freshmen and transfers: August 15. Required: high school transcript, college transcript(s) for transfer students, letter of recommen-

dation, audition, SAT I or ACT test scores. Recommended: minimum 2.0 high school GPA. Auditions held 4 times on campus; recorded music is permissible as a substitute for live auditions when distance is prohibitive and videotaped performances are permissible as a substitute for live auditions when distance is prohibitive.

Web Site http://www.cc.ysu.edu/dana-school-of-music.

Undergraduate Contact Bassam Deeb, Enrollment Management, Youngstown State University, 410 Wick Avenue, Youngstown, Ohio 44555; 216-742-3132, fax: 216-742-1998.

Graduate Contact Dr. Darla Funk, Coordinator of Graduate Studies/Music, Dana School of Music, Youngstown State University, Youngstown, Ohio 44555; 216-742-3636, fax: 216-742-2341.

THEATER PROGRAMS

If you're interested in acting, directing, costume design, lighting design, scenic design, technical direction, stage management, or theater management, you're in the right place. *Peterson's Professional Degree Programs in the Visual and Performing Arts* lists hundreds of degree-granting theater programs offered at universities and conservatories across the country. Faced with such a range of offerings, choosing a program isn't easy. You'll have to consider the program's features and your needs, talents, and career goals.

Your first decision will be the type of school you wish to attend. Conservatories devoted to the performing arts have a different feel than universities with a range of majors. If specialized and focused training is what you're looking for, conservatories may suit your needs more closely. If broader exposure to other subjects and students with other interests is important to you, then a university program will probably be a better fit.

Many universities offer students interested in theater a choice of either the Bachelor of Arts degree or the Bachelor of Fine Arts degree. The Bachelor of Arts (B.A.) track combines theater arts with a more traditional liberal arts range of course work. There is also a conservatory approach that's more focused on professional training. These programs, which lead to a Bachelor of Fine Arts (B.F.A.), offer specialties in acting, directing, design—the whole gamut of the theater. The courses are performance-oriented, and there are few outside liberal arts courses—perhaps fewer than a third.

REPORT FROM THE FIELD

Interview with stagehand Betsy Cutler

Betsy Cutler, a freelance stagehand in the Washington, D.C., area, received her degree in theater arts from Oberlin College. Cutler graduated with a concentration in acting and has been steadily employed for the past four years in theater, enjoying an incredible variety of working situations.

"It never in a million years occurred to me that I would be making my life in theater," says Cutler, who decided to "take a break" from her pursuit of an acting career after enduring a few grueling years of auditioning and rejection. She fell into her current occupation quite by accident, when she met some friends of a neighbor who worked as stagehands. When they learned of Cutler's extensive theater background, they were able to help her find employment in their field.

From sound and lighting design at the 9:30 Club, an alternative-music venue in the District, to frequent stints at the White House to parties at the home of the U.S. ambassador to Saudi Arabia, Cutler's work environment can hardly be called run-of-the-mill. In a physically demanding business where men far outnumber women, Cutler feels she has proven her worth. "I do what I'm hired to do and I do it extremely well," she says.

As to her future, Cutler admits she does not plan to remain a stagehand indefinitely. She's interested in returning to school at some future point, but for the present she is happy to have a career that is flexible and challenging.

"Had I not gotten that major or that education, there is no way I could be doing what I'm doing today. There's no way that one could have followed without the other," says Cutler.

"My advice to theater students would be to learn as much as you can about everything," Cutler says. "You never know where a window is going to open in this business, and you need to be prepared to do whatever you're asked to do."

WORDS OF WISDOM

How to Prepare a Successful Audition

- Relax—potential and natural talent are what the adjudicators are looking for. Many students are intimidated because they feel they should have some type of skill already inherent in their audition. Adjudicators aren't looking for perfection. What they are looking for are students whose natural talents can be developed.
- Overreaching won't win you points. Select pieces that suit your talent.
- Choose one upbeat number and one ballad—try to contrast them as much as possible.
- For singers: Work in as many tempo changes as you can to show a high degree of musicality.
- For actors: Prepare two monologues and, again, try to stick fairly closely to something within your castable range.

The Application Process

In a university program, students are usually required to complete an application, and the admission decision is made on criteria such as standardized test scores and academic record. Some schools also require a supplementary application geared toward theater. It usually includes questions related to theater and an essay on why you are pursuing this degree.

For the B.F.A. program, some schools require a university application and a supplementary application. The supplementary application is the starting point of the audition process.

Auditions

The standard audition is a 5-minute audition consisting of one classical and one contemporary piece, usually about 2 minutes each. For musical theater programs, you are required to prepare a song. Live auditions are usually held. There are so many individual requirements that it is best to contact the school to find out exactly what you need to produce. Schools usually require the students to come to them. Some schools or consortiums of schools hold regional or national auditions. Audition judges are typically faculty and staff members directly from the school of theater—not admissions officers. The panel normally includes from 2 to 4 judges; for a consortium audition, as many as 5 to 10 will judge auditions. Some auditions are very formal, very professional, and—unfortunately for the students—very intimidating. Others are very

HOW DO YOU KNOW A PROGRAM IS RIGHT FOR YOU?

Programs have their own personality and mission. You'll want to make sure that the one you choose meets your needs, talents, and professional goals. Here are some questions to ask to make the best match:

- Find out the program's methodology. For instance, if you know you want to study a particular acting technique, such as Strasberg or Meisner, make sure programs you're looking at focus on that type of training.
- How large is the school or university? How many people are in the program in which you're interested? What's the student-faculty ratio in your area of study?
- Does the school's location suit your needs and preferences?
- Does the program feature guest artists, artists-in-residence, or industry visitors so you can meet practicing professionals and learn the latest theories and techniques? How long do they stay on campus? Do they give lectures, teach classes, or offer workshops? Do they work with all students or with advanced students only?
- What opportunities are there to perform or practice? In the community? Does the program allow professional leave?
- Tour the facilities. Find out which ones are available to you to practice and perform. Is there adequate rehearsal space? Is the equipment state-of-the-art?
- Check out the faculty. Are instructors practicing in their field? The strongest faculty members are those who currently work in the field and bring their expertise into the classroom on a day-to-day basis.
- What are alumni of the program doing? Are they working in the field?
- Ask about career placement and counseling services. Does the program arrange internship opportunities? What kind of placement help does the program or school offer?

warm and informal. Some programs require call-backs, others don't. Some programs have an interview along with the audition; for some it's just the audition. Some are individual auditions, and others are "group auditions."

Auditions are the deciding factor for most programs. Some schools consider the audition as well as the academic component, and some base their admissions decisions primarily on auditions and do not place a great deal of emphasis on the academic component.

For more tips on the all-important audition, see the "Words of Wisdom" column within this article.

Once You Graduate

The competition for jobs in the performing arts is only increasing. Students should be keenly aware of this when they choose theater as their major and should take the opportunity as undergraduates to work in different areas within the theater. For example, if you're taking an acting track, focusing on stage management will enhance your job opportunities and make you more marketable. Some performance students who decide they don't want to perform go behind the scenes into production, casting, or directing. Some go on for a graduate degree to teach. Some go into an entirely different field. Most schools conduct a personal management class to give students a range of opportunities from which to choose.

Helping Graduates Get Jobs

Some schools stage a "showcase" at the end of the program where they invite industry people to see the students perform. Some schools open up their facilities for production companies to come in and actually hold auditions for film, television, and theater. Most schools do not have a traditional placement office that says, "We'll put your resume on file, and we'll get you a job." It is unrealistic to expect theater schools or programs to find jobs for their students, unless a school is associated with a professional theater company where it can place graduates.

Alumni can also provide good contacts. If your school's faculty members are working in the business, they may also be able to open doors for you. In fact, most networking is done through faculty members.

▼ Adelphi University

Garden City, New York

Independent, coed. Suburban campus. Total enrollment: 5,594.

Degrees Bachelor of Fine Arts in the area of theater. Majors and concentrations: technical theater, theater arts/drama.

Enrollment Fall 1997: 67 total; all undergraduate.

Theater Student Profile 60% females, 40% males, 18% minorities, 2% international.

Theater Faculty 13 total (full-time and part-time). 100% of full-time faculty have terminal degrees. Graduate students do not teach undergraduate courses. Undergraduate student–faculty ratio: 15:1.

Student Life Student groups/activities include INTERACT. Special housing available for theater students.

Expenses for 1997–98 Application fee: $35. Comprehensive fee: $21,320 includes full-time tuition ($14,000), mandatory fees ($720), and college room and board ($6600). College room only: $3700. Full-time tuition and fees vary according to program. Room and board charges vary according to board plan and housing facility.

Financial Aid Program-specific awards for 1997: 8–10 Barnes Scholarships for freshmen actors ($4000–$5000).

Application Procedures Students admitted directly into the professional program freshman year. Deadline for freshmen and transfers: continuous. Required: essay, high school transcript, college transcript(s) for transfer students, minimum 2.0 high school GPA, 2 letters of recommendation, audition, SAT I or ACT test scores (minimum combined SAT I score of 1000), portfolio for technical theater majors, interview or video. Auditions held 10 times on campus; videotaped performances are permissible as a substitute for live auditions when distance is prohibitive. Portfolio reviews held continuously on campus; the submission of slides may be substituted for portfolios.

Web Site http://www.adelphi.edu.

Undergraduate Contact Mr. Nicholas Petron, Chair, Department of Performing Arts, Adelphi University, Post Hall, Room 4, Garden City, New York 11530; 516-877-4930, fax: 516-877-4009, E-mail address: petron@adlibv.adelphi.edu.

More About the University

Adelphi University, the first liberal arts institution of higher education on Long Island, was chartered June 24, 1896, by the Board of Regents of the State of New York. The charter was one of the earliest granted by the Board of Regents to a coeducational college.

In keeping with its 100-year history, Adelphi University continues to make use of its rich resources to render significant service to Long Island, New York State, and the nation. The staging of cultural events in the University Center and the Olmsted Theatre, the strengthening of ties between the professional schools and the community, and, most essential to Adelphi's purpose, the education of a new generation of future leaders—all contribute to the University's mission to serve as a national center for liberal learning.

Today, Adelphi University reaffirms its commitment and dedication to providing excellence in education and to facing and surmounting the challenges of the twenty-first century with high standards and scholarship. In an era of increasing complexity in the nation's fundamental social fabric, society is changing and moving forward with momentum. In the face of the demands of rapid technological advances and worldwide social change, the University, with its faith in the rewards of individual merit, draws on a rich tradition of scholarly knowledge and human values to empower students for future leadership as learned and cultivated men and women.

The performing arts are concerned with supporting leadership in interpretive arts that gives living form to the performance of music, plays, and dance as well as to the production of original texts and dance pieces. The performing arts include acting, designing, directing, and producing choreography and dance theater. As a field of study, the performing arts involve the history and criticism of all forms of theater, dance, and playwriting.

The Department of Performing Arts offers programs leading to a B.F.A. degree in dance and theater arts, with specializations in acting and technical theater/design. The B.F.A. programs, designed to develop professional skills, craft, and attitudes, focus on professional training in the performing arts within a liberal learning context.

The proximity of New York City is a constant resource for observation and career opportunities for all performing arts programs.

▼ Albertus Magnus College

New Haven, Connecticut

Independent-Roman Catholic, coed. Suburban campus. Total enrollment: 1,549.

Degrees Bachelor of Fine Arts in the area of performance/theater. Cross-registration with University of New Haven, Southern Connecticut State University, Yale University.

Enrollment Fall 1997: 3 total; all undergraduate.

Theater Student Profile 72% females, 28% males, 20% minorities.

Theater Faculty 1 total (full-time and part-time). 100% of full-time faculty have terminal degrees. Graduate students do not teach undergraduate courses.

Student Life Student groups/activities include Non-Equity Professional Theatre/ACT 2 Theatre.

Expenses for 1997–98 Application fee: $35. Comprehensive fee: $24,898 includes full-time tuition ($16,864), mandatory fees ($398), and college room and board ($7636). Special program-related fees: $20–$100 per course for material fees for some studio classes.

Application Procedures Students apply for admission into the professional program by sophomore year. Deadline for freshmen and transfers: continuous. Required: high school transcript, college transcript(s) for transfer students, minimum 2.0 high school GPA, 2 letters of recommendation, SAT I or ACT test scores. Recommended: essay, interview.

Undergraduate Contact Mr. Richard Lolatte, Director of Admissions, Albertus Magnus College, 700 Prospect Street, New Haven, Connecticut 06511; 203-773-8501, fax: 203-785-8652.

▼ American Academy of Dramatic Arts

New York, New York

Independent, coed. Urban campus. Theater program established 1884.

Degrees Certificate in the area of advanced studies in actor training. Program accredited by NAST.

Enrollment Fall 1997: 186 undergraduate.

American Academy of Dramatic Arts *(continued)*

Theater Student Profile 58% females, 42% males, 15% minorities, 22% international.

Theater Faculty 23 total undergraduate (full-time and part-time). 70% of full-time faculty have terminal degrees. Graduate students do not teach undergraduate courses.

Expenses for 1998–99 Application fee: $50. Tuition: $9900 full-time. Mandatory fees: $200 full-time. Special program-related fees: $200 per year for library and classroom materials.

Financial Aid Program-specific awards for 1997: 1–2 Cleavon Little Scholarships for minority students ($500–$1500), 2–3 Spencer Tracy Scholarships for sophomores ($1000–$3000), 1–2 Philip Loeb Scholarships for sophomores demonstrating need ($750–$1500), 1–2 Greta Nissen Scholarships for female sophomores demonstrating need ($750–$2000), 1–2 Julie Harris Scholarships for sophomores ($500–$1500), 1–2 Hume Cronyn Scholarships for sophomores ($500–$1500), 1–6 Henrietta Alice Metcalf Memorial Scholarships for sophomores ($500–$3000), 1–2 Barbara Moore Jordan Scholarships for sophomores ($1000–$2000), 1–2 Kirk Douglas Scholarships for sophomores ($1500–$2500), 1–3 Suzanne Powers Scholarships for sophomores ($500–$1500).

Application Procedures Students admitted directly into the professional program freshman year. Deadline for freshmen and transfers: continuous. Required: high school transcript, college transcript(s) for transfer students, 2 letters of recommendation, interview, audition, health certificate. Recommended: essay, minimum 2.0 high school GPA, SAT I or ACT test scores. Auditions held weekly on campus and off campus in various cities in the U.S..

Web Site http://www.aada.org.

Undergraduate Contact Ms. Karen Higginbotham, Director of Admissions, American Academy of Dramatic Arts, 120 Madison Avenue, New York, New York 10016-7004; 800-463-8990, fax: 212-545-7934, E-mail address: admissions-ny@aada.org.

More About the Academy

Facilities AADA in New York is housed in a six-story landmark building located in midtown Manhattan. AADA/West is located on a small campus in the Los Angeles suburb of Pasadena. Each site includes classrooms, rehearsal halls, movement studios, student lounge, production and costume departments, library/learning center, video studio, and theaters.

Faculty and Alumni Academy faculty are seasoned professionals, well trained within their own disciplines, and exemplars of the commitment to excellence that the Academy hopes to instill in its students. The soundness of the Academy's training is reflected in the achievements of its alumni, a diverse body of distinguished professionals. (Performances by Academy alumni have been nominated for 70 Oscars, 50 Tonys, and 169 Emmys.)

Student Performances At each stage of development, the Academy student is tested in the disciplined arena of performance. In addition to classroom scene work, each student performs roles in four first-year performance projects and at least three second-year projects and full productions. The third-year Academy Company performs, on average, twelve fully mounted productions each year, including a showcase of scenes presented to casting directors and agents.

Special Programs Seminars offered in the second year provide the practical information actors need to initiate professional careers. A limited number of graduates are offered a third-year program of advanced performance training as members of the Academy Company. A career counselor works closely with Company members, advising them on matters of career management and serving as a liaison with the professional community. Students invited to the second or third years may apply to transfer from New York to California, or from California to New York. The Academy also offers a six-week summer conservatory for those wishing to begin to study acting, to refresh basic acting skills, or to test their interest and ability in an environment of professional training.

▼

An actor's talent, it's been said, begins in the soles of the feet and ends in a spirit than can vault beyond the stars. The American Academy of Dramatic Arts has been serving this talent for more than one hundred years.

The Academy's one purpose has remained constant from the start: "To provide a broad and practical education to those desiring to make acting their profession." The love of acting, as an art and as a profession, is the motivating spirit of the school. Every course and every activity is related to the disciplined development of actors. While the Academy is accredited as a college, it is different from traditional colleges for its focus on a single educational objective.

Founded in New York in 1884, the Academy was the first conservatory for actors in the English-speaking world. It has served as a model for many other acting schools and drama departments, both in America and abroad. This experience contributes to the effectiveness of the Academy's training, programs, and teaching methods that show a clear vision of the knowledge, skills, and discipline needed by today's professional actor.

The Academy's approach to training stresses self-awareness, self-discipline, and practical experience. The study of acting leads to many areas of knowledge, including knowledge of self. Academy training demands such self-discovery and emphasizes the development of the actor as an individual, unique in his or her artistic potential and experience of life.

Academy training aims to develop the well-rounded actor, giving equal attention to such "internal" aspects of technique as relaxation, concentration, emotional involvement, and imagination and to the "external" disciplines of speech, voice, and movement.

When the Academy began, motion pictures and television were still years away. To work as an actor in those days could only mean performing on stage. Today, it is likely that much of an actor's working life will be spent before a camera rather than in a theater. To prepare for this, Academy students— once they have mastered the basic discipline of truthful behavior in imaginary circumstances—learn adjustments needed for camera work.

With facilities in New York and California, the Academy offers accredited training in both of America's centers of professional activity. Whether a student chooses to attend the Academy in New York or California, the training program will be essentially the same, and it will be enriched by the professional and cultural advantages of New York City or southern California.

Academy students come from all parts of the United States, from Canada, and from other countries as well. About half of the entering students are recent high school graduates. Others transfer to the Academy from traditional colleges to study acting in a more concentrated, professional environment. Still others have worked in non-theatrical fields before deciding to commit to the study of acting. Whatever their age or background, once at the Academy, they are united by the shared commitment to acting and the challenge of working to become the best actors they can be.

▼ AMERICAN ACADEMY OF DRAMATIC ARTS/WEST

Pasadena, California

Independent, coed. Suburban campus. Theater program established 1974.

Degrees Certificate in the area of advanced studies in actor training. Program accredited by NAST.

Enrollment Fall 1997: 202 total; all undergraduate.

Theater Student Profile 57% females, 43% males, 14% minorities, 15% international.

Theater Faculty 47 total undergraduate (full-time and part-time). 75% of full-time faculty have terminal degrees. Graduate students do not teach undergraduate courses.

Expenses for 1997–98 Application fee: $50. Tuition: $9400 full-time. Mandatory fees: $200 full-time. Special program-related fees: $200 per year for library and classroom materials.

Financial Aid Program-specific awards for 1997: 1–2 Cleavon Little Scholarships for minority students ($500–$1500), 2–3 Spencer Tracy Scholarships for sophomores ($1000–$3000), 1–2 Philip Loeb Scholarships for sophomores demonstrating need ($750–$1500), 1–2 Greta Nissen Scholarships for female sophomores demonstrating need ($750–$2000), 1–3 Charles Jehlinger Scholarships for sophomores ($500–$1500), 1–2 Kirk Douglas Scholarships for sophomores ($500–$2000), 1–2 Hume Cronyn Scholarships for sophomores ($500–$1500), 1–2 Julie Harris Scholarships for sophomores ($500–$1500), 1–2 Neil Simon Scholarships for sophomores ($500–$1500).

Application Procedures Students admitted directly into the professional program freshman year. Deadline for freshmen and transfers: continuous. Required: high school transcript, college transcript(s) for transfer students, 2 letters of recommendation, interview, audition, health certificate. Recommended: essay, minimum 2.0 high school GPA, SAT I or ACT test scores. Auditions held weekly on campus and off campus in various cities in the U.S..

Web Site http://www.aada.org.

Undergraduate Contact Mr. James Wickline, Director of Admissions, American Academy of Dramatic Arts/West, 250-300 North Halstead Street, Pasadena, California 91107-3128; 800-222-2867, fax: 626-798-5047, E-mail address: admissions-ca@aada.org.

▼ ARIZONA STATE UNIVERSITY

Tempe, Arizona

State-supported, coed. Suburban campus. Total enrollment: 44,255. Theater program established 1963.

Degrees Bachelor of Fine Arts in the area of theater education; Bachelor of Arts in the area of theater. Majors and concentrations: acting, directing/stage management, theater design/technology, theater history. Graduate degrees offered: Master of Fine Arts in the areas of theater, acting,

theater for young audiences, scenography, playwriting. Doctor of Philosophy in the area of theater for young audiences. Cross-registration with Arizona State University West, Arizona State University East. Program accredited by NAST.

Enrollment Fall 1997: 325 total; 278 undergraduate, 47 graduate.

Theater Student Profile 60% females, 40% males, 12% minorities, 1% international.

Theater Faculty 33 total undergraduate and graduate (full-time and part-time). 60% of full-time faculty have terminal degrees. Graduate students teach about a quarter undergraduate courses. Undergraduate student–faculty ratio: 18:1.

Student Life Student groups/activities include Players Club, Arizona State University Repertory Theatre (ART). Special housing available for theater students.

Expenses for 1997–98 Application fee: $40 for nonresidents. State resident tuition: $1988 full-time. Nonresident tuition: $8640 full-time. Mandatory fees: $71 full-time. College room and board: $4500. College room only: $2700. Room and board charges vary according to board plan and housing facility. Special program-related fees: $5–$40 per course for supplies.

Financial Aid Program-specific awards for 1997: 10 Regents Out-of-State Tuition Awards for program students ($6400), 8 Regents In-State Tuition Awards for program students ($1950).

Application Procedures Students apply for admission into the professional program by sophomore year. Deadline for freshmen and transfers: continuous. Required: essay, high school transcript, college transcript(s) for transfer students, minimum 2.0 high school GPA, SAT I or ACT test scores. Recommended: minimum 3.0 high school GPA, letter of recommendation, interview, audition, portfolio. Auditions held twice on campus; videotaped performances are permissible as a substitute for live auditions by prior arrangement. Portfolio reviews held twice on campus; the submission of slides may be substituted for portfolios by prior arrangement.

Web Site http://www.asu.edu/cfa/theatre/.

Undergraduate Contact Ms. Marie Fay, Undergraduate Academic Advisor, Department of Theatre, Arizona State University, PO Box 872002, Tempe, Arizona 85287-2002; 602-965-9432, fax: 602-965-5351, E-mail address: idmlf@asuvm.inre.asu.edu.

Graduate Contact Ms. Luann Musser, Administrative Assistant, Department of Theatre, Arizona State University, PO Box 872002, Tempe, Arizona 85287-2002; 602-965-9547, fax: 602-965-5351, E-mail address: lmusser@asu.edu.

▼ ARKANSAS STATE UNIVERSITY

State University, Arkansas

State-supported, coed. Small town campus. Total enrollment: 10,012. Theater program established 1958.

Degrees Bachelor of Fine Arts in the areas of theater arts: performance, theater arts: production.

Enrollment Fall 1997: 35 undergraduate.

Theater Student Profile 53% females, 47% males, 9% minorities, 2% international.

Theater Faculty 5 total (full-time). 100% of full-time faculty have terminal degrees. Graduate students teach a few undergraduate courses. Undergraduate student–faculty ratio: 16:1.

Student Life Student groups/activities include Jonesboro Fine Arts Council, Imperial Theater, Paragould Fine Arts Council.

Arkansas State University (continued)

Expenses for 1997–98 Application fee: $15. State resident tuition: $2000 full-time. Nonresident tuition: $5090 full-time. Mandatory fees: $280 full-time. College room and board: $2840. Room and board charges vary according to board plan and housing facility.

Financial Aid Program-specific awards for 1997: 17 Theater Arts Scholarships for program majors ($250).

Application Procedures Students apply for admission into the professional program by freshman year. Deadline for freshmen and transfers: continuous. Required: high school transcript, SAT I or ACT test scores, minimum 2.3 high school GPA. Recommended: 2 letters of recommendation, interview and portfolio for production applicants, video and audition for performance applicants. Auditions held twice on campus; recorded music is permissible as a substitute for live auditions when distance is prohibitive and videotaped performances are permissible as a substitute for live auditions when distance is prohibitive. Portfolio reviews held once on campus; the submission of slides may be substituted for portfolios when distance is prohibitive.

Undergraduate Contact Mr. Bob W. Simpson, Director of Theater, Speech Communication and Theater Arts Department, Arkansas State University, PO Box 369, State University, Arkansas 72467; 870-972-3091, fax: 870-972-3932, E-mail address: bsimpson@aztec.astate.edu.

▼ AUBURN UNIVERSITY

Auburn University, Alabama

State-supported, coed. Small town campus. Total enrollment: 21,505.

Degrees Bachelor of Fine Arts in the areas of performance, technology/design, management. Majors and concentrations: design technology, performance. Program accredited by NAST.

Enrollment Fall 1997: 75 undergraduate.

Theater Student Profile 55% females, 45% males, 5% minorities.

Theater Faculty 10 total (full-time and part-time). 100% of full-time faculty have terminal degrees. Graduate students do not teach undergraduate courses. Undergraduate student–faculty ratio: 3:1.

Student Life Student groups/activities include Players Club, Alpha Psi Omega.

Expenses for 1997–98 Application fee: $25, $50 for international students. State resident tuition: $2610 full-time. Nonresident tuition: $7830 full-time. Full-time tuition varies according to program. College room only: $1905. Room charges vary according to housing facility. Part-time mandatory fees per term: $145 for state residents, $435 for nonresidents.

Financial Aid Program-specific awards for 1997: 15 Malone Fund Scholarships for program students ($400).

Application Procedures Students apply for admission into the professional program by sophomore year. Deadline for freshmen and transfers: April 1. Required: high school transcript, college transcript(s) for transfer students, minimum 2.0 high school GPA, letter of recommendation, SAT I or ACT test scores, audition for performance applicants, portfolio for design technology and theater management majors. Auditions held once on campus. Portfolio reviews held once on campus.

Undergraduate Contact Dr. Patricia D. McAdams, Head, Department of Theatre, Auburn University, 211 Telfair Peet Theatre, Auburn, Alabama 36849-5422; 334-844-4748, fax: 334-844-4743, E-mail address: mcadapd@mail.auburn.edu.

▼ AVILA COLLEGE

Kansas City, Missouri

Independent-Roman Catholic, coed. Suburban campus. Total enrollment: 1,246. Theater program established 1973.

Degrees Bachelor of Fine Arts in the area of theater; Bachelor of Arts in the area of theater. Majors and concentrations: acting, producing/directing, technical theater.

Enrollment Fall 1997: 42 total; 35 undergraduate, 7 nonprofessional degree.

Theater Student Profile 50% females, 50% males, 10% minorities, 10% international.

Theater Faculty 6 total (full-time and part-time). 100% of full-time faculty have terminal degrees. Graduate students do not teach undergraduate courses. Undergraduate student–faculty ratio: 12:1.

Student Life Student groups/activities include Alpha Psi Omega, American College Theatre Festival.

Expenses for 1997–98 Comprehensive fee: $15,260 includes full-time tuition ($10,700), mandatory fees ($160), and college room and board ($4400).

Financial Aid Program-specific awards for 1997: 30 performance grants for program majors and non-majors ($2000).

Application Procedures Students admitted directly into the professional program freshman year. Deadline for freshmen and transfers: continuous. Notification date for freshmen and transfers: July 31. Required: high school transcript, college transcript(s) for transfer students, 2 letters of recommendation, interview, audition, SAT I or ACT test scores (minimum combined ACT score of 20), minimum 2.5 high school GPA. Recommended: portfolio for technical theater majors. Auditions held by appointment on campus and off campus in various Kansas City high schools; videotaped performances are permissible as a substitute for live auditions when distance is prohibitive. Portfolio reviews held by appointment on campus; the submission of slides may be substituted for portfolios when distance is prohibitive.

Undergraduate Contact Mr. Todd Moore, Director, Admissions Department, Avila College, 11901 Wornall Road, Kansas City, Missouri 64145; 816-942-8400 ext. 3500, fax: 816-942-3362.

▼ BARRY UNIVERSITY

Miami Shores, Florida

Independent-Roman Catholic, coed. Suburban campus. Total enrollment: 6,899. Theater program established 1948.

Degrees Bachelor of Arts in the area of theater. Majors and concentrations: acting, technical theater.

Enrollment Fall 1997: 12 total; all undergraduate.

Theater Student Profile 48% females, 52% males, 84% minorities, 63% international.

Theater Faculty 3 total (full-time and part-time). 100% of full-time faculty have terminal degrees. Graduate students do not teach undergraduate courses. Undergraduate student–faculty ratio: 6:1.

Student Life Student groups/activities include Theater Club, Alpha Psi Omega.

Expenses for 1997–98 Application fee: $30. Comprehensive fee: $19,400 includes full-time tuition ($13,290), mandatory fees ($260), and college room and board ($5850). Full-time tuition and fees vary according to location. Room and board charges vary according to board plan.

Financial Aid Program-specific awards for 1997: 1 Minnaugh Scholarship for program majors ($2500), 2 Theater Arts League Awards for program majors ($500–$1500).

Application Procedures Students admitted directly into the professional program freshman year. Deadline for freshmen and transfers: continuous. Required: essay, high school transcript, college transcript(s) for transfer students, 3 letters of recommendation, interview, audition, SAT I or ACT test scores (minimum combined SAT I score of 1000), minimum 2.5 high school GPA. Auditions held once on campus; recorded music is permissible as a substitute for live auditions for musical theater applicants and videotaped performances are permissible as a substitute for live auditions.

Undergraduate Contact Ms. Derna M. Ford, Chair, Department of Fine Arts, Barry University, 11300 Northeast Second Avenue, Miami Shores, Florida 33161; 305-899-3422, fax: 305-899-2972, E-mail address: dford@buaxp1.barry.edu.

▼ BAYLOR UNIVERSITY

Waco, Texas

Independent-Baptist, coed. Urban campus. Total enrollment: 12,472.

Degrees Bachelor of Fine Arts in the areas of performance, design. Graduate degrees offered: Master of Fine Arts in the area of directing. Program accredited by NAST.

Enrollment Fall 1997: 35 undergraduate, 9 graduate.

Theater Student Profile 60% females, 40% males, 12% minorities.

Theater Faculty 9 total undergraduate and graduate (full-time and part-time). Graduate students teach a few undergraduate courses.

Student Life Student groups/activities include Student Theater Society.

Expenses for 1998–99 Application fee: $35. One-time mandatory fee: $50. Comprehensive fee: $14,832 includes full-time tuition ($9240), mandatory fees ($1026), and college room and board ($4566). College room only: $1958. Room and board charges vary according to board plan and housing facility. Special program-related fees: $25 per course for lab fee.

Financial Aid Program-specific awards for 1997: 8–10 theater scholarships for upperclass program students ($400–$1600).

Application Procedures Students admitted directly into the professional program freshman year. Deadline for freshmen and transfers: continuous. Required: high school transcript, SAT I or ACT test scores. Recommended: letter of recommendation, interview.

Undergraduate Contact Dr. Stan Denman, Director of Recruitment, Department of Theater Arts, Baylor University, BU Box 97262, Waco, Texas 76798; 254-710-1861, fax: 254-710-1765, E-mail address: bill_cook@baylor.edu.

Graduate Contact Dr. Steve Peters, Head of Graduate Program, Department of Theater Arts, Baylor University, BU Box 97262, Waco, Texas 76798; 254-710-1861, fax: 254-710-1765.

▼ BERNICE YOUNG JONES SCHOOL OF FINE ARTS

See Ouachita Baptist University

▼ BOSTON CONSERVATORY

Boston, Massachusetts

Independent, coed. Urban campus. Total enrollment: 501. Theater program established 1940.

Degrees Bachelor of Fine Arts in the area of musical theater. Graduate degrees offered: Master of Music in the area of musical theater. Cross-registration with ProArts Consortium. Program accredited by NASM.

Enrollment Fall 1997: 170 total; 150 undergraduate, 20 graduate.

Theater Student Profile 65% females, 35% males, 10% minorities, 5% international.

Theater Faculty 16 total undergraduate and graduate (full-time and part-time). 100% of full-time faculty have terminal degrees. Graduate students do not teach undergraduate courses. Undergraduate student–faculty ratio: 8:1.

Student Life Special housing available for theater students.

Expenses for 1997–98 Application fee: $60. Comprehensive fee: $23,075 includes full-time tuition ($15,300), mandatory fees ($625), and college room and board ($7150). Full-time tuition and fees vary according to course load, degree level, and program.

Financial Aid Program-specific awards for 1997: Conservatory Theater Scholarships for program majors ($5000–$9500).

Application Procedures Students admitted directly into the professional program freshman year. Deadline for freshmen and transfers: continuous. Notification date for freshmen and transfers: April 1. Required: essay, high school transcript, college transcript(s) for transfer students, 3 letters of recommendation, audition. Recommended: SAT I or ACT test scores. Auditions held 3 times and by appointment on campus and off campus in Chicago, IL; Seattle, WA; Houston, TX; Los Angeles, CA; Tampa/St. Petersburg, FL; Orlando, FL; Washington, DC; Las Vegas, NV; San Francisco, CA; videotaped performances are permissible as a substitute for live auditions if a campus visit is impossible.

Web Site http://www.bostonconservatory.edu.

Contact Mr. Richard Wallace, Director of Admissions, Boston Conservatory, 8 The Fenway, Boston, Massachusetts 02215; 617-536-6340 ext. 9148, fax: 617-536-3176, E-mail address: admissions@bostonconservatory.edu.

More About the Conservatory

Program Facilities Mainstage Proscenium Arch Theater (400 seats), Studio Theater (Black Box—75 seats), two recital halls (400 and 75 seats), five dance studios, costume shop, theater/technical shop, twenty-five practice rooms, computer lab (Apple), library of more than 60,000 volumes and scores and interlibrary loan availability with college network of Boston.

Faculty and Alumni Professional faculty members are active in all areas of acting, directing, voice, dance, and production. Alumni can be seen in major Broadway and Off-Broadway productions, national and international touring companies, television, and film.

Student Performance Opportunities Two mainstage musicals, one mainstage drama, Student Director Workshops (fifteen in

Boston Conservatory (*continued*)

1993–94), opera scenes, mainstage opera, dance theater concerts, regional theater productions, industrial films, acting/vocal gigs.

Special Programs Gig office providing performance opportunities throughout the greater Boston area, career seminar series, counseling and health services, international student ESL classes/orientation program, academic year ESL course work, and tutorial assistance.

▼

The Boston Conservatory, founded in 1867, is one of the oldest colleges offering training to serious students of the performing arts. The three divisions of the college—Music, Dance, and Theater—take full advantage of the wealth of cultural and academic offerings Boston has to offer. Guest artists, master classes, performance opportunities, and professional contacts and networking are provided to all students of the college. These experiences seek to ensure that each student receives a varied and professional level of education to augment the intensive study of the prescribed curriculum.

The Boston Conservatory was one of the first colleges to offer integrated training in theater encompassing acting, voice, and dance. Beginning as a full acting/drama program in the 1930s, the Theater Division now trains the "triple threat" actor/singer, offering a complete acting curriculum coupled with music and voice study and a full range of dance (ballet, modern, tap, jazz, and styles).

The Musical Theater Division faculty comprises experienced performers and teachers committed to bringing out the best each student has to offer. Potential is acknowledged and developed within a strong interactive theater curriculum. Frequent in-class performance with appropriate coaching and critique give guidance and constant evaluation of the student's work. The music and dance aspects of the program are presented both in-class and one-on-one to ensure individual attention for each student.

Performance opportunities are available throughout the year, from in-class and studio work to mainstage productions. All major productions have an open, professional casting policy in order for the most qualified person to get the role regardless of class standing. Technical and stagecraft experience is provided, and production assistance is required by all students during major runs.

In addition to these opportunities, the studio theater offers small-scale productions throughout the year, most often with a senior student directing project pieces.

Boston Conservatory alumni can be seen in major productions on Broadway, in Europe, and in National Touring companies. In addition, many alumni find acting work in television and film. As many musical theater students are very advanced in both classical voice and dance, additional performance experience may be gained in the opera and dance productions offered by the other two divisions of the college.

The Boston area provides varied outside work in theater and dance as well as industrials. Regional theater productions often cast students in both lead and ensemble parts.

Boston is a major center of higher education in America, with more than fifty major colleges and universities. The city provides a diverse student population and an endless array of courses, lectures, concerts, and social opportunities. The Conservatory is in the Pro-Arts Consortium with five area

colleges (Emerson College, Berklee College of Music, Museum School, Massachusetts College of Art, and Boston Architectural Center), which offers extensive cross-registration course possibilities to all students.

On-campus housing is provided to all interested students, offering brownstone-style living accommodations just a few steps from the main training and rehearsal buildings. For those students interested in off-campus housing, Boston offers a wide range of architectural styles and rent prices in neighborhoods throughout the city, which are all within easy access to the school by public transportation.

The Boston Conservatory strives to meet each student's needs, musically and personally, and provides a nurturing, safe environment in which to study, learn, and grow. The supportive atmosphere of the college extends to student life areas as well. More than a dozen special interest groups and organizations exist on campus, with new ones developing constantly as the student population grows and needs change. As part of the student services, a number of career seminars are given each year ranging from resume writing and audition anxiety to grant writing and tax laws for the performing artist. In addition, there is an active student government and a student-run newspaper.

▼ BOSTON UNIVERSITY

Boston, Massachusetts

Independent, coed. Urban campus. Total enrollment: 29,387.

Degrees Bachelor of Fine Arts in the areas of acting, design, stage management, independent theater study. Majors and concentrations: acting, costume design, costume production, lighting design, set design, sound design, stage management, technical production. Graduate degrees offered: Master of Fine Arts in the areas of directing, theater education, scene design, technical production, costume design, costume production, lighting design.

Enrollment Fall 1997: 230 total; 190 undergraduate, 40 graduate.

Theater Student Profile 60% females, 40% males, 5% minorities.

Theater Faculty 24 total undergraduate and graduate (full-time and part-time). 80% of full-time faculty have terminal degrees. Graduate students do not teach undergraduate courses.

Student Life Special housing available for theater students.

Expenses for 1998–99 Application fee: $50. Comprehensive fee: $31,018 includes full-time tuition ($22,830), mandatory fees ($318), and college room and board ($7870). College room only: $4830. Room and board charges vary according to board plan and housing facility.

Financial Aid Program-specific awards for 1997: grants/performance awards for program students.

Application Procedures Students admitted directly into the professional program freshman year. Deadline for freshmen: January 15; transfers: May 1. Notification date for freshmen: April 15. Required: essay, high school transcript, minimum 2.0 high school GPA, 2 letters of recommendation, SAT I or ACT test scores, audition for acting and independent theater study applicants, portfolio for design and stage management applicants. Recommended: minimum 3.0 high school GPA. Auditions held 20 times on campus and off campus in New York, NY; Chicago, IL; San Francisco, CA; Houston, TX; Miami, FL; Los Angeles, CA; Atlanta, GA; Seattle, WA. Portfolio reviews held 10 times on campus and off campus in

New York, NY; Chicago, IL; San Francisco, CA; Houston, TX; Miami, FL; Los Angeles, CA; Atlanta, GA; Seattle, WA; the submission of slides may be substituted for portfolios when distance is prohibitive.

Undergraduate Contact Ms. Eve B. Muson, Executive Assistant Director, Theatre Arts Department, Boston University, 855 Commonwealth Avenue, Room 470, Boston, Massachusetts 02215; 617-353-3390, fax: 617-353-4363.

More About the University

Program Facilities Performance spaces include the Boston University Theatre, an 850-seat proscenium house; Studio 210, a 100-seat black box space; and a 100-seat proscenium studio. The Theatre is equipped with a computerized lighting system, shops for scenery and costume construction, and an electronic sound studio. There are three movement studios and six additional rehearsal studios.

Faculty, Guest Artists, and Alumni Faculty members are not only master teachers but are also accomplished professionals who maintain vital careers in the theater. Distinguished faculty members include Peter Altman, Producing Director of the Huntington Theatre, and Jacques Cartier, founder of the Hartford Stage Company. Guest artists include director Caroline Eves, actors Claire Bloom and Campbell Scott, and designers Ralph Funicello and Desmond Heeley. Alumni include actors Olympia Dukakis, Alfre Woodard, Jason Alexander, and Julianne Moore and designer Wynn Thomas.

Student Performance Opportunities The Theatre Arts Division produces six fully mounted productions each year, as well as forty to sixty workshop productions directed by faculty members and graduate and undergraduate students. An annual festival of plays provides a showcase for work by undergraduate playwrights.

Special Programs The Huntington Theatre Company, one of Boston's leading professional companies, is in residence at the Boston University Theatre. A variety of assistantships and internships are available for students in the areas of design, production, directing, stage management, and theater management. Advanced acting majors have the opportunity to audition for understudy assignments and supporting roles in Huntington productions. Master classes are conducted for student by artists associated with the professional shows.

▼ BRADLEY UNIVERSITY

Peoria, Illinois

Independent, coed. Urban campus. Total enrollment: 5,861.

Degrees Bachelor of Science in the areas of performance, production, theater education; Bachelor of Arts in the areas of performance, production, theater education. Majors and concentrations: performance, production, theater education.

Enrollment Fall 1997: 47 total; all undergraduate.

Theater Student Profile 52% females, 48% males, 5% minorities.

Theater Faculty 7 total (full-time and part-time). 83% of full-time faculty have terminal degrees. Graduate students do not teach undergraduate courses. Undergraduate student–faculty ratio: 7:1.

Student Life Student groups/activities include Alpha Psi Omega, Cats Eye Theatre.

Expenses for 1997–98 Application fee: $35. Comprehensive fee: $17,380 includes full-time tuition ($12,610), mandatory fees ($80), and college room and board ($4690). College room only: $2840. Room and board charges vary according to board plan.

Financial Aid Program-specific awards for 1997: theater scholarships for theater majors ($1410).

Application Procedures Students admitted directly into the professional program freshman year. Deadline for freshmen and transfers: continuous. Required: high school transcript, college transcript(s) for transfer students, minimum 2.0 high school GPA, SAT I or ACT test scores, audition for scholarship consideration. Recommended: letter of recommendation. Auditions held on campus; recorded music is permissible as a substitute for live auditions when distance is prohibitive and videotaped performances are permissible as a substitute for live auditions when distance is prohibitive.

Web Site http://www.bradley.edu/cfa/theatre/.

Undergraduate Contact Ms. Nickie Roberson, Director of Admissions, Office of Undergraduate Admissions, Bradley University, Swords Hall, Peoria, Illinois 61625; 800-447-6460, fax: 309-677-2797, E-mail address: admissions@bradley.edu.

▼ BRENAU UNIVERSITY

Gainesville, Georgia

Independent, primarily women. Small town campus. Total enrollment: 2,366. Theater program established 1979.

Degrees Bachelor of Fine Arts in the areas of musical theater, arts management; Bachelor of Arts in the area of theater. Mandatory cross-registration with Gainesville College.

Enrollment Fall 1997: 30 total; all undergraduate.

Theater Student Profile 94% females, 6% males, 5% minorities, 1% international.

Theater Faculty 4 total (full-time and part-time). 100% of full-time faculty have terminal degrees. Graduate students do not teach undergraduate courses. Undergraduate student–faculty ratio: 10:1.

Student Life Student groups/activities include Gainesville Theatre Alliance, Alpha Psi Omega, Gainesville Children's Theatre.

Expenses for 1997–98 Application fee: $30. Comprehensive fee: $17,350 includes full-time tuition ($10,740) and college room and board ($6610).

Financial Aid Program-specific awards for 1997: 20 Talent Scholarships for program majors ($2000–$3500).

Application Procedures Students admitted directly into the professional program freshman year. Deadline for freshmen and transfers: continuous. Required: high school transcript, college transcript(s) for transfer students, minimum 2.0 high school GPA, audition, SAT I or ACT test scores (minimum combined SAT I score of 900, minimum combined ACT score of 19), health certificate. Recommended: minimum 3.0 high school GPA, portfolio for technical emphasis students. Auditions held 8 times and by appointment on campus; videotaped performances are permissible as a substitute for live auditions when distance is prohibitive. Portfolio reviews held upon request on campus; the submission of slides may be substituted for portfolios when distance is prohibitive.

Web Site http://www.brenau.edu.

Undergraduate Contact Dr. John D. Upchurch, Dean of Admissions, Brenau University, One Centennial Circle, Gainesville, Georgia 30501; 770-534-6264, fax: 770-534-6114.

▼ BRIGHAM YOUNG UNIVERSITY

Provo, Utah

Independent, coed. Suburban campus. Total enrollment: 32,161.

Brigham Young University (continued)

Degrees Bachelor of Fine Arts in the areas of music dance theater, acting. Graduate degrees offered: Master of Fine Arts in the area of theater design and technology. Program accredited by NAST.

Enrollment Fall 1997: 413 total; 394 undergraduate, 19 graduate.

Theater Faculty 26 total undergraduate and graduate (full-time and part-time). 85% of full-time faculty have terminal degrees. Graduate students teach a few undergraduate courses. Undergraduate student–faculty ratio: 15:1.

Expenses for 1997–98 Application fee: $25. Comprehensive fee: $6760 includes full-time tuition ($2630) and college room and board ($4130). Full-time tuition varies according to reciprocity agreements. Room and board charges vary according to board plan and housing facility.

Financial Aid Program-specific awards for 1997: 70 Performance Awards for program majors ($400).

Application Procedures Students apply for admission into the professional program by freshman year. Deadline for freshmen: February 15; transfers: March 15. Required: essay, high school transcript, college transcript(s) for transfer students, minimum 3.0 high school GPA, letter of recommendation, audition, SAT I or ACT test scores. Auditions held once on campus; recorded music is permissible as a substitute for live auditions if a campus visit is impossible and videotaped performances are permissible as a substitute for live auditions if a campus visit is impossible.

Undergraduate Contact Academic Advisement Center, Brigham Young University, D-444 HFAC, Provo, Utah 84602; 801-378-3777.

Graduate Contact Department of Graduate Studies, Brigham Young University, B-380 ASB, Provo, Utah 84602; 801-378-4091.

▼ BROOKLYN COLLEGE OF THE CITY UNIVERSITY OF NEW YORK

Brooklyn, New York

State and locally supported, coed. Urban campus. Total enrollment: 15,007. Theater program established 1973.

Degrees Bachelor of Fine Arts in the areas of acting, design and technical production. Majors and concentrations: acting, theater arts/drama, theater design and production. Graduate degrees offered: Master of Fine Arts in the areas of acting, design and technical production, directing, dramaturgy, performing arts management. Cross-registration with City University of New York System.

Enrollment Fall 1997: 187 total; 28 undergraduate, 79 graduate, 80 non-professional degree.

Theater Student Profile 60% females, 40% males, 25% minorities, 5% international.

Theater Faculty 28 total undergraduate and graduate (full-time and part-time). 100% of full-time faculty have terminal degrees. Graduate students teach a few undergraduate courses. Undergraduate student–faculty ratio: 2:1.

Student Life Student groups/activities include Undergraduate Theater Organization, Graduate Theater Organization.

Expenses for 1997–98 Application fee: $40. State resident tuition: $3200 full-time. Nonresident tuition: $6800 full-time. Mandatory fees: $213 full-time. Full-time tuition and fees vary according to class time and course load.

Financial Aid Program-specific awards for 1997: 1 Brooklyn College Foundation Performing Arts Scholarship for program majors ($2450), 1 Joseph Davidson Memorial Award for program majors ($800), 1 Theater Faculty Award for program majors ($300).

Application Procedures Students admitted directly into the professional program freshman year. Deadline for freshmen and transfers: June 30. Required: high school transcript, audition. Recommended: portfolio, SAT I or ACT test scores. Auditions held once on campus; recorded music is permissible as a substitute for live auditions for international applicants and videotaped performances are permissible as a substitute for live auditions for international applicants. Portfolio reviews held as needed on campus; the submission of slides may be substituted for portfolios for international applicants.

Undergraduate Contact Prof. Karen Barracuda, Undergraduate Deputy Chair, Theater Department, Brooklyn College of the City University of New York, 317 Whitehead Hall, 2900 Bedford Avenue, Brooklyn, New York 11210-2889; 718-951-3179, fax: 718-951-4606.

Graduate Contact Dr. Samuel L. Leiter, Graduate Deputy Chair, Theater Department, Brooklyn College of the City University of New York, 317 Whitehead Hall, 2900 Bedford Avenue, Brooklyn, New York 11210-2889; 718-951-5764, fax: 718-951-4606, E-mail address: sleiter@brooklyn.cuny.edu.

More About the College

Program Facilities Performance spaces include the Gershwin Theatre (550-seat, proscenium), the New Workshop Theatre (approximately 100-seat, black box), and Levinson Hall (160-seat, modern thrust). Classrooms include a directing studio, two acting studios, two movement studios, and fully equipped costume, carpentry, and design shops.

Faculty The 12 full-time faculty members of the department are all experienced professionals/scholars who are known for the personal attention given to each student and for supportive but realistic evaluation of student progress.

Student Performances The department produces ten shows a year—four mainstage and six black box productions—directed by faculty members and graduate directing majors, which provide the B.F.A. students plenty of hands-on experience in all phases of theatrical production. Casting for all departmental productions is by open call (undergraduate and graduate students), with a policy promoting multicultural and nontraditional casting. All B.F.A. acting majors are required to perform in a department production in their senior year. These are supplemented by Lunch-Time Theatre—informal presentation of monologues, class scenes, directing projects, etc.—and by scenes for directing classes. In addition, the College often collaborates with the Conservatory of Music on musicals, opera, and concert performances, and the departments of TV/Radio and Film often post calls for actors.

Special Programs The department maintains close ties with the Manhattan Theatre Club (a leading professional regional theater) and with New York City Technical College, which offers state-of-the-art computerized technology equipment. Independent study projects are encouraged, and some internships are available. Graduate students do internships at leading theater organizations in the New York area.

▼

A senior college of the City University of New York, Brooklyn College is located just 45 minutes from the Great White Way, enabling students to take advantage of the rich offerings of Broadway, Off-Broadway, and Off-Off Broadway. The department offers a performance-based program balanced by substantial humanistic studies. Its threefold purpose is to instill an appreciation and respect for the collaborative nature of theater by providing both intellectual and experiential opportunities in all areas of theater, to provide a solid liberal arts foundation on which to base a specialized degree, and to provide the skills and experiences needed to prepare for a career in theater.

Many alumni continue to work in the profession. Among the best-known actors trained at Brooklyn College are recent Academy Award nominee Michael Lerner; Herb Edelman, of numerous television series, including *Golden Girls*; Jimmy Smits, of *NYPD Blue*; film director Paul Mazursky (*Down and Out in Beverly Hills*); television director Joel Zwick (*Full House*); and Ken Garito of the Fox series *The Heights*.

While all faculty members are experienced professionals, special mention should be made of the following: Academy Award winner F. Murry Abraham, who provides acting majors with a bridge from the ivory tower to the professional world; Karen Barracuda, professional dancer and pioneer in ideokinetic acting techniques; Thomas Bullard, nationally known Obie-winning director and cofounder of the Manhattan Theatre Club; Rebecca Cunningham, costume designer and author of *The Magic Garment*; David Garfield, Broadway actor and author of *The Actors Studio*; Lynn M. Thomson, head of the M.F.A. dramaturgy program and professional dramaturgy (*Rent*); designer Richard Kearney; Tobie Stein, specialist on arts management and director of the department's M.F.A. program in performing arts management; Samuel L. Leiter, author/editor of thirteen books and editor of the *Asian Theatre Journal*; Margaret Linney, professional film, television, and stage actor and specialist in improvisation and arts education; Benito Ortolani, author of *The Japanese Theatre* and editor of the yearly *International Bibliography of Theatre*; John Scheffler, Obie-award winning scenic designer and member of the Scene Designer Union; and Michael Turque, Broadway stage manager.

In addition, visiting professors, adjuncts, and guest lecturers have included some of the most important figures of the theater world. The Sylvia Fine Kaye Chair in Musical Theatre has brought such distinguished guests as Betty Buckley, Betty Comden and Adolph Green, Joel Grey, Celeste Holm, and John Kander and Fred Ebb.

B.A. and B.F.A. students benefit from close association with M.A. and M.F.A. students from all over the world. They work together on productions, act in each others' classroom directing scenes, and are in daily contact with each other. Many professional opportunities have arisen from contacts made with former M.F.A. acting, directing, design, dramaturgy, performing arts, and management students.

Another feature that gives alumni an edge in the profession is their solid liberal arts education. B.F.A. students are subject to the same core studies requirements as the rest of the College. Brooklyn offers an unusually large history curriculum, with courses in Western and American as well as Asian, black, and musical theater.

While Brooklyn College does not offer campus housing, many students share apartments in nearby areas.

▼ CALIFORNIA INSTITUTE OF THE ARTS

Valencia, California

Independent, coed. Suburban campus. Total enrollment: 1,140. Theater program established 1961.

Degrees Bachelor of Fine Arts in the areas of acting, stage management, performing arts design and technology. Majors and concentrations: acting, costume design, directing, lighting design, set design, sound design, stage management, technical direction. Graduate degrees offered: Master of Fine Arts in the areas of acting, directing, stage management, performing arts design and technology, directing for theater, video and cinema. Program accredited by NAST.

Enrollment Fall 1997: 122 undergraduate, 77 graduate.

Theater Student Profile 44% females, 56% males, 23% minorities, 5% international.

Theater Faculty 43 total undergraduate and graduate (full-time and part-time). 80% of full-time faculty have terminal degrees. Graduate students do not teach undergraduate courses. Undergraduate student–faculty ratio: 7:1.

Student Life Student groups/activities include Community Arts Partnership (CAP). Special housing available for theater students.

Expenses for 1998–99 Application fee: $60. Tuition: $18,120 full-time. Mandatory fees: $65 full-time. College room only: $2800. Room charges vary according to housing facility.

Financial Aid Program-specific awards available.

Application Procedures Students admitted directly into the professional program freshman year. Deadline for freshmen and transfers: February 1. Required: essay, high school transcript, college transcript(s) for transfer students, audition, portfolio. Recommended: letter of recommendation, interview. Auditions held 15 times on campus and off campus in New York, NY; Chicago, IL; San Francisco, CA. Portfolio reviews held continuously for design majors on campus; the submission of slides may be substituted for portfolios by arrangement with the Office of Admissions.

Web Site http://www.calarts.edu.

Undergraduate Contact Mr. Kenneth Young, Director of Admissions, California Institute of the Arts, 24700 McBean Parkway, Valencia, California 91355; 805-253-7863, fax: 805-254-8352, E-mail address: kyoung@muse.calarts.edu.

More About the Institute

Program Facilities CalArts is a community of approximately 1,000 performing artists, visual artists, and writers located in the suburban hills north of Los Angeles. The college was incorporated in 1961 through the vision and generosity of Walt Disney. CalArts has been at its present 60-acre campus since 1971. On the campus are the main artistic/academic building, sound stages, rehearsal spaces, art studios, recreational facilities and two residence halls. At the undergraduate level in theater, CalArts offers B.F.A. degree programs in acting, scene design, lighting design, costume design, sound design, technical direction, and stage and production management. Admission is based on talent. Auditions for actors are conducted each winter in major cities in the United States. For design or management applicants, portfolios of recent work may be mailed in or brought to CalArts in person.

Faculty, Resident Artists, and Alumni Contact the admissions office for a free copy of the current admissions bulletin for complete and up-to-date biographies of all faculty members along with lists of alumni and visiting artists.

Special Programs The Community Arts Partnership links CalArts students and faculty members with high school and junior high school students in Watts, East Los Angeles, Pasadena, Santa Clarita, Hollywood, and Venice. The program enables CalArts students to teach, learn, and share their talents in community settings. Other special programs include exchanges with universities in other countries as well as

California Institute of the Arts (*continued*)

internships at companies and nonprofit organizations throughout southern California. Each spring the placement professionals in the Office of Student Affairs host a series of job fairs attended by companies well known in the world of entertainment and the arts.

▼ CARNEGIE MELLON UNIVERSITY

Pittsburgh, Pennsylvania

Independent, coed. Urban campus. Total enrollment: 7,912. Theater program established 1914.

Degrees Bachelor of Fine Arts in the area of drama. Majors and concentrations: design production, music theater, theater arts/drama. Graduate degrees offered: Master of Fine Arts in the area of drama. Cross-registration with University of Pittsburgh, Pittsburgh Filmmakers.

Enrollment Fall 1997: 289 total; 234 undergraduate, 55 graduate.

Theater Student Profile 40% females, 60% males, 8% minorities, 5% international.

Theater Faculty 42 total undergraduate and graduate (full-time and part-time). 95% of full-time faculty have terminal degrees. Graduate students do not teach undergraduate courses. Undergraduate student–faculty ratio: 6:1.

Student Life Student groups/activities include Scotch 'n Soda (student-run theater group). Special housing available for theater students.

Expenses for 1997–98 Application fee: $45. Comprehensive fee: $26,600 includes full-time tuition ($20,275), mandatory fees ($100), and college room and board ($6225). College room only: $3845. Room and board charges vary according to board plan. Special program-related fees: $20 per semester for class, script fees.

Application Procedures Students admitted directly into the professional program freshman year. Deadline for freshmen and transfers: January 1. Notification date for freshmen and transfers: April 1. Required: high school transcript, college transcript(s) for transfer students, minimum 2.0 high school GPA, 3 letters of recommendation, interview, audition, portfolio, SAT I or ACT test scores. Recommended: minimum 3.0 high school GPA. Auditions held once for acting, music theater, and directing applicants on campus and off campus in New York, NY; Chicago, IL; San Francisco, CA; Los Angeles, CA; Houston, TX; Miami, FL; Atlanta, GA. Portfolio reviews held once for design and production applicants on campus and off campus in New York, NY; Chicago, IL; San Francisco, CA; Los Angeles, CA; Houston, TX; Miami, FL; Atlanta, GA; the submission of slides may be substituted for portfolios if a campus visit is impossible.

Web Site http://www.cmu.edu.

Undergraduate Contact Office of Admissions, Carnegie Mellon University, Warner Hall 100, Pittsburgh, Pennsylvania 15213; 412-268-2082, fax: 412-261-0281.

Graduate Contact Ms. Denise Pullen, Admissions Coordinator, School of Drama, Carnegie Mellon University, College of Fine Arts 106, Pittsburgh, Pennsylvania 15213-3890; 412-268-2392, fax: 412-621-0281, E-mail address: dp2r@andrew.cmu.edu.

▼ CENTRAL CONNECTICUT STATE UNIVERSITY

New Britain, Connecticut

State-supported, coed. Suburban campus. Total enrollment: 11,625. Theater program established 1973.

Degrees Bachelor of Fine Arts in the areas of acting, dance, technical theater, general theater. Majors and concentrations: acting, dance, technical theater, theater arts/drama.

Enrollment Fall 1997: 55 total; all undergraduate.

Theater Student Profile 60% females, 40% males, 8% minorities, 2% international.

Theater Faculty 10 total (full-time and part-time). 100% of full-time faculty have terminal degrees. Graduate students do not teach undergraduate courses.

Student Life Student groups/activities include Theatre Unlimited (student producing organization), community outreach programs in children's theater and workshops.

Expenses for 1997–98 Application fee: $42. State resident tuition: $2062 full-time. Nonresident tuition: $6674 full-time. Mandatory fees: $1552 full-time. Full-time tuition and fees vary according to class time, course level, and reciprocity agreements. College room and board: $5300. College room only: $3000. Room and board charges vary according to board plan.

Financial Aid Program-specific awards for 1997: 1 Thad Torp Memorial Scholarship for juniors ($1000), 1 acting scholarship for sophomores ($1000).

Application Procedures Students admitted directly into the professional program freshman year. Deadline for freshmen: May 1; transfers: continuous. Required: high school transcript, college transcript(s) for transfer students, letter of recommendation, SAT I test score only, audition for acting majors. Recommended: minimum 2.0 high school GPA, interview, portfolio. Auditions held once on campus. Portfolio reviews held as needed on campus; the submission of slides may be substituted for portfolios for executed design projects.

Undergraduate Contact Office of Admissions, Central Connecticut State University, PO Box 4010, 1615 Stanley Street, New Britain, Connecticut 06050; 860-832-CCSU.

▼ CENTRAL MISSOURI STATE UNIVERSITY

Warrensburg, Missouri

State-supported, coed. Small town campus. Total enrollment: 10,320.

Degrees Bachelor of Fine Arts in the area of theater. Majors and concentrations: design technology, performance. Program accredited by NCATE.

Enrollment Fall 1997: 60 undergraduate.

Theater Student Profile 50% females, 50% males.

Theater Faculty 5 total (full-time and part-time). 100% of full-time faculty have terminal degrees. Graduate students teach a few undergraduate courses. Undergraduate student–faculty ratio: 11:1.

Student Life Student groups/activities include Theta Alpha Pi, University Players, American College Theatre Festival.

Expenses for 1997–98 Application fee: $25. State resident tuition: $2640 full-time. Nonresident tuition: $5280 full-time. College room and board: $4080. Room and board charges vary according to board plan and housing facility.

Financial Aid Program-specific awards for 1997: 5 Endowed Scholarships for program majors ($500–$600), 12–14 Theater Ambassador Scholarships for program majors ($500–$600).

Application Procedures Students admitted directly into the professional program freshman year. Deadline for freshmen and transfers: continuous. Required: high school transcript, SAT I or ACT test scores (minimum combined ACT score of 20), standing in top 66% of graduating class, completion of college preparatory courses. Recommended: letter of recommendation.

Undergraduate Contact Dr. Ed See, Chair, Theater Department, Central Missouri State University, Martin 113, Warrensburg, Missouri 64093; 660-543-4020, fax: 660-543-8006.

▼ CHAPMAN UNIVERSITY

Orange, California

Independent, coed. Suburban campus. Total enrollment: 3,806.

Degrees Bachelor of Fine Arts in the areas of theater performance, dance/theater, technical theater. Majors and concentrations: performance, technical theater.

Enrollment Fall 1997: 100 undergraduate.

Theater Student Profile 65% females, 35% males, 36% minorities, 4% international.

Theater Faculty 10 total (full-time and part-time). 75% of full-time faculty have terminal degrees. Graduate students do not teach undergraduate courses. Undergraduate student–faculty ratio: 10:1.

Student Life Student groups/activities include Shakespeare Orange County-Summer Professional Theaters, American Celebration, Performing Arts Society of Chapman.

Expenses for 1997–98 Application fee: $30. Comprehensive fee: $25,556 includes full-time tuition ($18,510), mandatory fees ($240), and college room and board ($6806). Room and board charges vary according to board plan and housing facility.

Financial Aid Program-specific awards for 1997: 20 Talent Awards for incoming students ($10,000).

Application Procedures Students admitted directly into the professional program freshman year. Deadline for freshmen and transfers: continuous. Required: high school transcript, college transcript(s) for transfer students, minimum 2.0 high school GPA, letter of recommendation, audition for performance majors. Recommended: essay, interview, video, portfolio for design/technical theater applicants. Auditions held twice on campus; videotaped performances are permissible as a substitute for live auditions with permission of the program director. Portfolio reviews held as needed on campus; the submission of slides may be substituted for portfolios with permission of the program director.

Web Site http://www.chapman.edu/comm/td/.

Undergraduate Contact Mr. Thomas Bradac, Chair, Theatre and Dance Department, Chapman University, 333 North Glassell Street, Orange, California 92666; 714-744-7016, fax: 714-744-7015.

▼ CLARION UNIVERSITY OF PENNSYLVANIA

Clarion, Pennsylvania

State-supported, coed. Rural campus. Total enrollment: 5,948.

Degrees Bachelor of Fine Arts in the areas of theater/acting, theater/technical direction and design, musical theater. Majors and concentrations: acting, music theater, theater design/technology.

Enrollment Fall 1997: 25 undergraduate.

Theater Student Profile 50% females, 50% males, 1% minorities.

Theater Faculty 4 total (full-time and part-time). 100% of full-time faculty have terminal degrees. Graduate students do not teach undergraduate courses. Undergraduate student–faculty ratio: 12:1.

Student Life Student groups/activities include Alpha Psi Omega, Zeta Phi Eta.

Expenses for 1997–98 Application fee: $25. State resident tuition: $3468 full-time. Nonresident tuition: $8824 full-time. Mandatory fees: $951 full-time. Full-time tuition and fees vary according to course load. College room and board: $3330. College room only: $1980.

Financial Aid Program-specific awards for 1997: 1 Cheri Aharrah Ried Scholarship for incoming freshmen program majors, 1 Mary Hardwick Scholarship for upperclass program majors.

Application Procedures Students apply for admission into the professional program by freshman year. Deadline for freshmen and transfers: continuous. Required: high school transcript, college transcript(s) for transfer students, SAT I or ACT test scores, portfolio for design/technical theater applicants, minimum 2.0 college GPA for transfer students, audition for acting and music theater applicants. Recommended: essay, 2 letters of recommendation, interview. Auditions held twice on campus; recorded music is permissible as a substitute for live auditions if a campus visit is impossible and videotaped performances are permissible as a substitute for live auditions if a campus visit is impossible. Portfolio reviews held twice on campus; the submission of slides may be substituted for portfolios on a case-by-case basis.

Undergraduate Contact Ms. Myrna Kuehn, Chair, Speech, Communication and Theatre Department, Clarion University of Pennsylvania, 165-B Marwick-Boyd, Clarion, Pennsylvania 16214; 814-226-2284, E-mail address: kuehn@mail.clarion.edu.

▼ COLLEGE OF SANTA FE

Santa Fe, New Mexico

Independent, coed. Suburban campus. Total enrollment: 1,417. Theater program established 1965.

Degrees Bachelor of Fine Arts in the areas of acting, design/theater technology, music theater. Majors and concentrations: acting, contemporary music, design, music theater, theater arts/drama, theater management.

Enrollment Fall 1997: 120 undergraduate.

Theater Student Profile 51% females, 49% males, 15% minorities.

Theater Faculty 15 total (full-time and part-time). 100% of full-time faculty have terminal degrees. Graduate students do not teach undergraduate courses. Undergraduate student–faculty ratio: 12:1.

Student Life Student groups/activities include Drama Club, Student Writers Association, Estranged Bedfellows (comedy troop).

Expenses for 1997–98 Application fee: $25. Comprehensive fee: $17,964 includes full-time tuition ($13,000), mandatory fees ($240), and college room and board ($4724). College

College of Santa Fe (continued)

room only: $2308. Room and board charges vary according to board plan and housing facility.

Financial Aid Program-specific awards for 1997: 12 departmental scholarships for freshmen ($1500), 15 Talent Scholarships for freshmen ($2000).

Application Procedures Students admitted directly into the professional program freshman year. Deadline for freshmen and transfers: March 1. Notification date for freshmen and transfers: July 1. Required: essay, high school transcript, college transcript(s) for transfer students, minimum 2.0 high school GPA, 2 letters of recommendation, interview, SAT I or ACT test scores (minimum combined SAT I score of 900, minimum combined ACT score of 20), portfolio for design/theater technology and theater management applicants, audition for acting and music theater applicants. Auditions held by appointment on campus and off campus in various cities in the U.S.; recorded music is permissible as a substitute for live auditions with approval from the department and videotaped performances are permissible as a substitute for live auditions with approval from the department. Portfolio reviews held by appointment on campus and off campus in various cities in the U.S.; the submission of slides may be substituted for portfolios (slides preferred).

Web Site http://www.csf.edu.

Undergraduate Contact Mr. John Weckesser, Chair, Performing Arts Department, College of Santa Fe, 1600 St. Michael's Drive, Santa Fe, New Mexico 87505; 505-473-6439, fax: 505-473-6016.

More About the College

Facilities The Greer Garson Theatre Center is home to the College of Santa Fe Performing Arts Department. It includes a 500-seat mainstage theater named after the Academy Award–winning actress as well as the Weckesser Studio Theatre, a 100-seat black box performance space. Practice rooms, a dance studio and classrooms, and scenery and costume shops round out the facility.

Faculty, Guest Artists, Lecturers, and Alumni The Performing Arts Department faculty is composed of 9 full-time members specializing in acting, directing, costume design, music, voice, playwriting, dance, and technical theater. CSF has welcomed such guest artists as actress Greer Garson, Theater Grottesco, actor Ben Kingsley, members of the Royal Shakespeare Company, and actress Maureen Stapleton. Guest lecturers at CSF have included director Paul Baker, actress Carol Burnett, playwright Howard Korder, actor Gregory Peck, and singer Harry Connick Jr. Guest directors include Elan Evans, Roger DeLaurien, and Ray Bukteniea. Alumni of the College of Santa Fe Performing Arts Department can be found in a wide variety of professional companies, regional theaters, and touring companies; on television; and in films. From New York's Carnegie Hall to *The Will Rogers Follies* on Broadway, CSF alumni have distinguished themselves in the field.

Special Programs Semester in London: To increase the depth of the artistic training experience available through the College of Santa Fe, a semester in London program exists. Acting majors will be eligible to study with leading actors, directors, and playwrights of the British stage one semester of the senior year. New York Arts Program: CSF students are also eligible to participate in the New York Arts Program, a semester-long internship in the performing, visual, and media arts. Students spend the semester working as apprentices with artists or art organizations, as well as

participating in seminars headed by professionals from various areas of the arts. Student Performances: Each theater season is packed with quality student productions ranging from dramas to musicals to comedies. CSF student performances continue to gain critical acclaim and recent mainstage productions have included *A Midsummer Night's Dream, Dancing at Lughnasa, Assassins, The Skin of Our Teeth, The Love of the Nightingale,* and *Once Upon a Mattress.*

▼ CONCORDIA UNIVERSITY

Montréal, PQ, Canada

Province-supported, coed. Urban campus. Total enrollment: 29,271. Theater program established 1975.

Degrees Bachelor of Fine Arts in the areas of theater, design for theater, drama for human development, theater performance, playwriting. Cross-registration with any university in Quebec.

Enrollment Fall 1997: 183 total; all undergraduate.

Theater Student Profile 4% international.

Theater Faculty 29 total (full-time and part-time). Graduate students teach a few undergraduate courses.

Student Life Student groups/activities include Concordia Association for Students in Theater.

Expenses for 1998–99 Application fee: $40 Canadian dollars. Tuition, fee, and room only charges are reported in Canadian dollars. Province resident tuition: $1668 full-time. Canadian resident tuition: $2868 full-time. Mandatory fees: $618 full-time. College room only: $2290. Room charges vary according to housing facility. International student tuition: $8268 full-time.

Application Procedures Students admitted directly into the professional program freshman year. Deadline for freshmen and transfers: March 1. Notification date for freshmen and transfers: July 15. Required: high school transcript, college transcript(s) for transfer students, interview, video, audition, portfolio. Auditions held monthly from April through August on campus; videotaped performances are permissible as a substitute for live auditions if a campus visit is impossible. Portfolio reviews held monthly from April through August on campus; the submission of slides may be substituted for portfolios for large works of art and three-dimensional pieces.

Web Site http://www-fofa.concordia.ca/theatre/.

Undergraduate Contact Ms. Jolanta Manowska, Communications Assistant, Office of the Registrar, Concordia University, 1455 de Maisonneuve Boulevard West, LB700, Montreal, PQ H3G 1M8, Canada; 514-848-2668, fax: 514-848-2837, E-mail address: admreg@alcor.concordia.ca.

▼ CORNISH COLLEGE OF THE ARTS

Seattle, Washington

Independent, coed. Urban campus. Total enrollment: 621. Theater program established 1914.

Degrees Bachelor of Fine Arts in the areas of acting, theater. Majors and concentrations: acting, performing arts, theater arts/drama.

Enrollment Fall 1997: 103 undergraduate.

Theater Student Profile 10% minorities.

Theater Faculty 18 total (full-time and part-time). 75% of full-time faculty have terminal degrees. Graduate students do not teach undergraduate courses. Undergraduate student–faculty ratio: 6:1.

Expenses for 1997–98 Application fee: $35. Tuition: $11,540 full-time. Mandatory fees: $118 full-time. Special program-related fees: $155 for photographs.

Financial Aid Program-specific awards for 1997: Presidential Scholarships for continuing students ($600–$4000), Nellie Scholarships for new students ($600–$4000), 1–6 Kreielsheimer Scholarships for new students from Washington, Oregon, or Alaska ($16,000), departmental scholarships for program students ($600–$4000).

Application Procedures Students admitted directly into the professional program freshman year. Deadline for freshmen and transfers: August 15. Required: essay, high school transcript, college transcript(s) for transfer students, minimum 2.0 high school GPA, interview, audition. Recommended: minimum 3.0 high school GPA, 2 letters of recommendation, SAT I or ACT test scores, current resume/head shot. Auditions held 12 times on campus and off campus in Los Angeles, CA; San Francisco, CA; videotaped performances are permissible as a substitute for live auditions when distance is prohibitive.

Web Site http://www.cornish.edu.

Undergraduate Contact Ms. Jane Buckman, Director of Admissions, Cornish College of the Arts, 710 East Roy Street, Seattle, Washington 98102; 800-726-ARTS, fax: 206-720-1011.

▼ CORNISH COLLEGE OF THE ARTS

Seattle, Washington

Independent, coed. Urban campus. Total enrollment: 621. Theater program established 1914.

Degrees Bachelor of Fine Arts in the area of performance production. Majors and concentrations: costume design, lighting design, set design, sound design, stage management, technical direction.

Enrollment Fall 1997: 24 total; all undergraduate.

Theater Student Profile 70% females, 30% males, 13% minorities, 10% international.

Theater Faculty 10 total (full-time and part-time). 75% of full-time faculty have terminal degrees. Graduate students do not teach undergraduate courses. Undergraduate student–faculty ratio: 3:1.

Student Life Student groups/activities include United States Institute for Theatre Technology.

Expenses for 1997–98 Application fee: $35. Tuition: $11,540 full-time. Mandatory fees: $118 full-time.

Financial Aid Program-specific awards for 1997: Presidential Scholarships for continuing students ($600–$4000), departmental scholarships for program students ($600–$4000), Nellie Scholarships for new students ($600–$4000), 1–6 Kreielsheimer Scholarships for new students from Washington, Oregon, or Alaska ($16,000).

Application Procedures Students admitted directly into the professional program freshman year. Deadline for freshmen and transfers: August 15. Required: essay, high school transcript, college transcript(s) for transfer students, minimum 2.0 high school GPA, interview. Recommended: 2 letters of recommendation, portfolio. Portfolio reviews held continuously on campus; the submission of slides may be substituted for portfolios when distance is prohibitive.

Web Site http://www.cornish.edu.

Undergraduate Contact Ms. Jane Buckman, Director of Admissions, Cornish College of the Arts, 710 East Roy Street, Seattle, Washington 98102; 800-726-ARTS, fax: 206-720-1011.

More About the College

Seattle's remarkable arts community features a wealth of professional theater and dance companies that provide exciting opportunities for the next generation of actors, designers, directors, playwrights, and technicians. Cornish College's philosophy encourages artists to use a wide range of techniques in connecting their work to the world around them.

The Theater Department's training philosophy is to provide a variety of approaches to any particular acting problem rather than requiring adherence to any one method. The department presents up to eighteen productions each year in three campus theaters and at several off-campus locations. Students may perform in one-acts as freshmen, create an original show as sophomores, and play in two to four productions during each of the junior and senior years, including an outdoor Shakespeare show and a guest-directed senior show. Students also have a chance to intern with many Equity theaters in Seattle.

The Performance Production Department offers studies in lighting, sound, set and costume design, technical direction, and stage management. Extensive hands-on experience and an intimate exploration of the aesthetics of performance comprise the core of the curriculum. Each year, students build, mount, and staff 125 productions for the Dance, Music, and Theater departments. A twelve-week internship with an arts organization is the final requirement of the B.F.A. degree.

Many Theater and Performance Production graduates have found work in Seattle, at organizations including the Seattle Repertory Theater, Intiman Theater, Empty Space Theater, Seattle Opera, and Seattle Children's Theater.

▼ CULVER-STOCKTON COLLEGE

Canton, Missouri

Independent, coed. Rural campus. Total enrollment: 994.

Degrees Bachelor of Fine Arts in the area of theater. Majors and concentrations: arts management, theater arts/drama, theater education.

Enrollment Fall 1997: 24 total; all undergraduate.

Theater Student Profile 60% females, 40% males, 8% minorities, 5% international.

Theater Faculty 4 total (full-time and part-time). 100% of full-time faculty have terminal degrees. Graduate students do not teach undergraduate courses.

Student Life Student groups/activities include Theta Alpha Phi.

Expenses for 1997–98 Comprehensive fee: $13,430 includes full-time tuition ($9200) and college room and board ($4230). College room only: $1930.

Financial Aid Program-specific awards for 1997: 14 theater awards for program majors ($2500), 20 Interest Awards for program minors ($1000).

Application Procedures Students admitted directly into the professional program freshman year. Deadline for freshmen and transfers: August 31. Required: high school transcript. Recommended: interview, video, audition, SAT I or ACT test scores, portfolio for technical theater applicants. Auditions held as needed on campus; recorded music is permissible as

Culver-Stockton College (continued)

a substitute for live auditions when distance is prohibitive and videotaped performances are permissible as a substitute for live auditions when distance is prohibitive. Portfolio reviews held as needed on campus; the submission of slides may be substituted for portfolios (slides preferred).

Web Site http://culver.edu.

Undergraduate Contact Director of Admissions, Culver-Stockton College, # 1 College Hill, Canton, Missouri 63435-1299; 217-231-6466, fax: 217-231-6611.

▼ DENISON UNIVERSITY

Granville, Ohio

Independent, coed. Small town campus. Total enrollment: 2,025. Theater program established 1960.

Degrees Bachelor of Fine Arts in the area of theater. Majors and concentrations: design/technical theater, performance.

Enrollment Fall 1997: 36 total; 17 undergraduate, 19 non-professional degree.

Theater Student Profile 60% females, 40% males.

Theater Faculty 5 total (full-time and part-time). 100% of full-time faculty have terminal degrees. Graduate students do not teach undergraduate courses. Undergraduate student–faculty ratio: 5:1.

Expenses for 1997–98 Application fee: $35. Comprehensive fee: $25,620 includes full-time tuition ($19,310), mandatory fees ($940), and college room and board ($5370). College room only: $2960.

Financial Aid Program-specific awards for 1997: departmental scholarships for program majors demonstrating need/talent ($250–$5000).

Application Procedures Deadline for freshmen: February 1; transfers: May 15. Notification date for freshmen: March 20; transfers: June 15. Required: essay, high school transcript, college transcript(s) for transfer students, minimum 2.0 high school GPA, 2 letters of recommendation, SAT I or ACT test scores (minimum combined SAT I score of 1040, minimum combined ACT score of 25), high school and college transcripts for transfer students, audition for performance applicants, portfolio for design/technical applicants. Recommended: interview. Auditions held by request on campus; videotaped performances are permissible as a substitute for live auditions if a campus visit is impossible. Portfolio reviews held by request on campus; the submission of slides may be substituted for portfolios if a campus visit is impossible.

Web Site http://www.denison.edu/theatre.

Undergraduate Contact Ms. Anne Marie McIntyre, Admissions Counselor, Office of Admissions, Denison University, Granville, Ohio 43023; 740-587-6276, fax: 740-587-6306, E-mail address: mcintyre@cc.denison.edu.

▼ DEPAUL UNIVERSITY

Chicago, Illinois

Independent-Roman Catholic, coed. Urban campus. Total enrollment: 17,804. Theater program established 1925.

Degrees Bachelor of Fine Arts in the areas of acting, scene design, lighting design, costume design, production management, theater technology, playwriting, theater management, dramaturgy/criticism, costume technology, general theater studies. Graduate degrees offered: Master of Fine Arts in the areas of acting, directing, scene design, lighting design, costume design.

Enrollment Fall 1997: 275 total; 230 undergraduate, 45 graduate.

Theater Student Profile 55% females, 45% males, 5% minorities, 1% international.

Theater Faculty 60 total undergraduate and graduate (full-time and part-time). 80% of full-time faculty have terminal degrees. Graduate students do not teach undergraduate courses.

Student Life Student groups/activities include new student mentors, The Theatre School Student Government.

Expenses for 1997–98 Application fee: $25. Comprehensive fee: $19,331 includes full-time tuition ($13,460), mandatory fees ($30), and college room and board ($5841). College room only: $4251. Full-time tuition and fees vary according to program. Room and board charges vary according to board plan and housing facility.

Financial Aid Program-specific awards for 1997: 5 Performance Scholarships for incoming actors ($5000), 10–20 Dean's Scholarships for incoming program majors (except acting) ($1000–$8000), 20–30 Merit Scholarships for upperclass program majors ($1500–$5000), 10–30 academic scholarships for freshmen ($1500–$8000).

Application Procedures Students admitted directly into the professional program freshman year. Deadline for freshmen and transfers: January 15. Notification date for freshmen and transfers: March 30. Required: high school transcript, college transcript(s) for transfer students, 3 letters of recommendation, interview, audition, portfolio, SAT I or ACT test scores, minimum 2.5 high school GPA, photo/resume. Recommended: essay. Auditions held 30-35 times on campus and off campus in Los Angeles, CA; San Francisco, CA; New York, NY; Seattle, WA: New Orleans, LA; Houston, TX; Washington, DC. Portfolio reviews held continuously on campus and off campus in Los Angeles, CA; San Francisco, CA; New York, NY; Seattle, WA; New Orleans, LA; Houston, TX; Washington, DC (off-campus only in February); the submission of slides may be substituted for portfolios if a campus visit is impossible or in special circumstances.

Web Site http://ttsweb.tht.depaul.edu.

Contact Ms. Melissa Meltzer, Director of Admissions, The Theatre School, DePaul University, 2135 North Kenmore Avenue, Chicago, Illinois 60614-4111; 773-325-7999, fax: 773-325-7920, E-mail address: mmeltzer@wppost.depaul.edu.

More About the University

The Theatre School, DePaul University, is a professional theater training conservatory located in Chicago. Founded as the Goodman School of Drama in 1925, The Theatre School's curricula prepare actors, designers, technicians, playwrights, dramaturges, theater managers, and other theater professionals for careers in theater and related fields. All applicants must audition or interview to be admitted.

Program Facilities Merle Reskin Theatre (formerly the Blackstone): 1,340 seats, proscenium, state-of-the-art technical equipment including fly space, trapped stage, computer and electronic lighting (240 dimmers), orchestra pit; The Theatre School Building and Annex: classrooms, rehearsal spaces, light lab, scene shop, costume shop, costume storage, script library, computer lab, makeup lab, design studios, faculty and staff offices, black box spaces; Victory Gardens Black Box Theatre: 60 seats, professional theater space.

Faculty, Resident Artists, and Alumni Distinguished faculty include Dr. Bella Itkin, master teacher and author, *Acting: Preparation,*

Practice, Performance (HarperCollins), and Nan Cibula-Jenkins, costume designer for Broadway, regional theater, and film. Recent resident artists and guest speakers include Joan Plowright, William Petersen, Ted Wass, and Gillian Anderson. Alumni include Gillian Anderson, Lois Nettleton, Concetta Tomei, Melinda Dillon, Lee Richardson, Jose Quintero, Carrie Snodgress, Harvey Korman, David Beron, Heidi Kling, Joe Mantegna, Kevin Anderson, Elizabeth Perkins, Linda Hunt, Karl Malden, Michael Rooker, Adrian Zmed, Scott Ellis, Kelly Coffield, Jacqueline Williams, Tom Amandes, the late Geraldine Page, Eugene Lee, and Theoni V. Aldredge.

Student Performance/Exhibit Opportunities More than thirty productions each year.

Special Programs Senior Showcases in Chicago and New York or Los Angeles; special program for students with learning disabilities; internships for design, technical, and theater studies majors.

▼ DRAKE UNIVERSITY

Des Moines, Iowa

Independent, coed. Suburban campus. Total enrollment: 5,184. Theater program established 1927.

Degrees Bachelor of Fine Arts in the area of theater; Bachelor of Arts/Bachelor of Fine Arts in the area of theater education. Majors and concentrations: acting, music theater, theater design/technology, theater education. Cross-registration with National Theatre Institute, Eugene O'Neill Centre.

Enrollment Fall 1997: 62 total; all undergraduate.

Theater Student Profile 65% females, 35% males, 6% minorities, 2% international.

Theater Faculty 7 total (full-time). 80% of full-time faculty have terminal degrees. Graduate students do not teach undergraduate courses. Undergraduate student–faculty ratio: 9:1.

Student Life Student groups/activities include United States Institute for Theatre Technology, American College Theatre Festival, Fiderlick Dramaturg.

Expenses for 1997–98 Application fee: $25. Comprehensive fee: $20,170 includes full-time tuition ($15,200) and college room and board ($4970). College room only: $2670. Full-time tuition varies according to student level. Room and board charges vary according to board plan.

Financial Aid Program-specific awards for 1997: 1 Fiderlick Award for junior program majors ($1000), 25 Fine Arts Awards for program majors ($1500–$3500).

Application Procedures Students admitted directly into the professional program freshman year. Deadline for freshmen and transfers: continuous. Required: essay, high school transcript, college transcript(s) for transfer students, minimum 2.0 high school GPA, SAT I or ACT test scores, portfolio for scholarship consideration, audition for scholarship consideration. Recommended: minimum 3.0 high school GPA, interview. Auditions held continuously through March 1 on campus; recorded music is permissible as a substitute for live auditions if a campus visit is impossible and videotaped performances are permissible as a substitute for live auditions if a campus visit is impossible. Portfolio reviews held continuously on campus; the submission of slides may be substituted for portfolios if a campus visit is impossible.

Web Site http://www.drake.edu/artsci/theatre/DrakeTheatre HomePage.html.

Undergraduate Contact Mr. Mike A. Barton, Chair, Department of Theatre Arts, Drake University, Harmon Fine Arts Center, Des Moines, Iowa 50311; 515-271-2867, fax: 515-271-2558, E-mail address: mike.barton@drake.edu.

▼ EAST CAROLINA UNIVERSITY

Greenville, North Carolina

State-supported, coed. Urban campus. Total enrollment: 18,271. Theater program established 1962.

Degrees Bachelor of Fine Arts in the areas of acting, musical theater, design, production. Majors and concentrations: acting, design production, music theater, theater arts/drama.

Enrollment Fall 1997: 200 total; all undergraduate.

Theater Student Profile 55% females, 45% males, 1% minorities.

Theater Faculty 21 total (full-time and part-time). 95% of full-time faculty have terminal degrees. Graduate students do not teach undergraduate courses. Undergraduate student–faculty ratio: 5:1.

Student Life Student groups/activities include East Carolina Playhouse, East Carolina Summer Theatre, studio theater workshops.

Expenses for 1997–98 Application fee: $35. State resident tuition: $916 full-time. Nonresident tuition: $8028 full-time. Mandatory fees: $932 full-time. College room and board: $3680. College room only: $1780. Room and board charges vary according to board plan and housing facility.

Financial Aid Program-specific awards available.

Application Procedures Students apply for admission into the professional program by sophomore year. Deadline for freshmen: March 15; transfers: April 15. Required: high school transcript, SAT I test score only. Recommended: minimum 2.0 high school GPA, 3 letters of recommendation.

Web Site http://www.theatre-dance.ecu.edu.

Undergraduate Contact Undergraduate Admissions, East Carolina University, Wichard Building, Greenville, North Carolina 27858; 252-328-6640.

▼ EASTERN KENTUCKY UNIVERSITY

Richmond, Kentucky

State-supported, coed. Small town campus. Total enrollment: 15,424.

Degrees Bachelor of Fine Arts in the area of performing arts.

Enrollment Fall 1997: 30 total; 7 undergraduate, 23 nonprofessional degree.

Theater Student Profile 60% females, 40% males, 10% minorities.

Theater Faculty 4 total (full-time). 75% of full-time faculty have terminal degrees. Graduate students do not teach undergraduate courses. Undergraduate student–faculty ratio: 8:1.

Student Life Student groups/activities include Alpha Psi Omega, Southeastern Theatre Conference.

Expenses for 1997–98 State resident tuition: $2060 full-time. Nonresident tuition: $5660 full-time. College room and board: $3240. College room only: $1316. Room and board charges vary according to board plan and housing facility.

Financial Aid Program-specific awards for 1997: 6 EKU Theater Scholarships for program majors ($100–$500).

Application Procedures Students admitted directly into the professional program freshman year. Deadline for freshmen and transfers: continuous. Required: high school transcript,

Eastern Kentucky University (continued)

college transcript(s) for transfer students, minimum 2.0 high school GPA, ACT test score only.

Undergraduate Contact Mr. James R. Moreton, Chair, Department of Theater, Eastern Kentucky University, Campbell 306, Richmond, Kentucky 40475; 606-622-1315, fax: 606-622-1020.

▼ EASTERN NEW MEXICO UNIVERSITY

Portales, New Mexico

State-supported, coed. Rural campus. Total enrollment: 3,495.

Degrees Bachelor of Fine Arts in the areas of theater performance, technical theater/design, university theater studies, dance. Majors and concentrations: dance, theater arts/drama, theater design/technology.

Enrollment Fall 1997: 50 undergraduate.

Theater Student Profile 55% females, 45% males, 9% minorities, 1% international.

Theater Faculty 5 total (full-time and part-time). 100% of full-time faculty have terminal degrees. Graduate students do not teach undergraduate courses. Undergraduate student–faculty ratio: 10:1.

Student Life Student groups/activities include Alpha Psi Omega.

Expenses for 1997–98 Application fee: $15. State resident tuition: $1170 full-time. Nonresident tuition: $5832 full-time. Mandatory fees: $546 full-time. College room and board: $2942. College room only: $1372.

Financial Aid Program-specific awards for 1997: 8 University Theater Scholarships for program majors ($800–$1500), 6 Talent Day Scholarships for program majors ($400), 20 Participation Grants for program majors ($200).

Application Procedures Students apply for admission into the professional program by sophomore year. Deadline for freshmen and transfers: continuous. Required: high school transcript, minimum 2.0 high school GPA, audition, SAT I or ACT test scores. Recommended: interview, portfolio. Auditions held twice in December and May on campus; recorded music is permissible as a substitute for live auditions when distance is prohibitive and videotaped performances are permissible as a substitute for live auditions when distance is prohibitive. Portfolio reviews held continuously on campus; the submission of slides may be substituted for portfolios for design/technical theater applicants.

Undergraduate Contact Chair, Theatre/Dance Department, Eastern New Mexico University, Station #37, Portales, New Mexico 88130; 505-562-2711, fax: 505-562-2961.

▼ EMERSON COLLEGE

Boston, Massachusetts

Independent, coed. Urban campus. Total enrollment: 3,885. Theater program established 1919.

Degrees Bachelor of Fine Arts in the area of performing arts. Majors and concentrations: acting, dance, music theater, stage management, theater design/technology, theater education, theater management, theater studies. Graduate degrees offered: Master of Arts in the area of theater education. Cross-registration with Boston Conservatory of Music, Massachusetts College of Art, Berklee College of Music, School of the Museum of Fine Arts, Boston Architectural Center.

Enrollment Fall 1997: 466 undergraduate, 39 graduate.

Theater Student Profile 61% females, 39% males, 9% minorities, 12% international.

Theater Faculty 39 total undergraduate and graduate (full-time and part-time). 90% of full-time faculty have terminal degrees. Graduate students do not teach undergraduate courses. Undergraduate student–faculty ratio: 17:1.

Expenses for 1997–98 Application fee: $45. Comprehensive fee: $26,076 includes full-time tuition ($17,376), mandatory fees ($450), and college room and board ($8250). College room only: $4890. Full-time tuition and fees vary according to course load and program. Room and board charges vary according to board plan.

Financial Aid Program-specific awards for 1997: 15 Emerson Stage Scholarships for performing arts freshmen ($3500), 35 Dean's Scholarships for performing arts freshmen ($4500), 50 Trustee Scholarships for honors program admission students ($8000), 50 Emerson Grants for those demonstrating financial need ($5000).

Application Procedures Students admitted directly into the professional program freshman year. Deadline for freshmen: February 1; transfers: March 1. Notification date for freshmen: April 1; transfers: May 1. Required: essay, high school transcript, college transcript(s) for transfer students, 2 letters of recommendation, audition, SAT I or ACT test scores. Recommended: minimum 3.0 high school GPA, interview, portfolio. Auditions held 10-14 times on campus and off campus in various locations; videotaped performances are permissible as a substitute for live auditions if a live audition is impossible. Portfolio reviews held 10-14 times on campus and off campus in various locations; the submission of slides may be substituted for portfolios for design applicants.

Undergraduate Contact Ms. Sara Ramirez, Director of Admission, Emerson College, 100 Beacon Street, Boston, Massachusetts 02116; 617-827-8600, fax: 617-824-8609, E-mail address: gdoyle@emerson.edu.

Graduate Contact Mr. Robert Colby, Head, Graduate Department, Department of Performing Arts, Emerson College, 100 Beacon Street, Boston, Massachusetts 02116; 617-824-8780, fax: 617-824-8799, E-mail address: rcolby@emerson.edu.

▼ EMPORIA STATE UNIVERSITY

Emporia, Kansas

State-supported, coed. Small town campus. Total enrollment: 5,320. Theater program established 1913.

Degrees Bachelor of Fine Arts in the area of dramatic art.

Enrollment Fall 1997: 75 undergraduate.

Theater Student Profile 50% females, 50% males, 5% minorities, 2% international.

Theater Faculty 7 total (full-time and part-time). 100% of full-time faculty have terminal degrees. Graduate students do not teach undergraduate courses. Undergraduate student–faculty ratio: 12:1.

Student Life Student groups/activities include Educational Theatre Company, Zoiks! - Improvisational Comedy Troupe.

Estimated expenses for 1998–99 Application fee: $20. State resident tuition: $1536 full-time. Nonresident tuition: $5900 full-time. Mandatory fees: $446 full-time. College room and board: $3560. College room only: $1720.

Financial Aid Program-specific awards for 1997: 1 Anderson Scholarship for outstanding theater students ($800), 1 Bruder Scholarship for outstanding theater students ($1800), 1 Wise Scholarship for outstanding theater students ($1000), 1 Pflam Scholarship for outstanding theater students ($1000), 1 Litchfield/Hume Scholarship for outstanding theater students ($600), 1 Karl Malden Scholarship for outstanding theater students ($1800), 1 Theatre Patrons Scholarship for outstanding theater students ($600), 1 Gilson Scholarship for future secondary teachers in theater ($600), 1 Halgedahl Scholarship for outstanding students in musical theater ($900), 4 Eubank Scholarships for outstanding theater students ($500).

Application Procedures Students admitted directly into the professional program freshman year. Deadline for freshmen and transfers: continuous. Required: high school transcript, college transcript(s) for transfer students. Recommended: interview, audition, portfolio, ACT test score only. Auditions held twice on campus; recorded music is permissible as a substitute for live auditions if a campus visit is impossible and videotaped performances are permissible as a substitute for live auditions if a campus visit is impossible. Portfolio reviews held on campus; the submission of slides may be substituted for portfolios if a campus visit is impossible.

Web Site http://www.emporia.edu/comta/commta.htm.

Undergraduate Contact Dr. Harry B. Parker, Director of Theater, Division of Communication and Theatre Arts, Emporia State University, 1200 Commercial,, Campus Box 4033, Emporia, Kansas 66801; 316-341-5256, fax: 316-341-6031, E-mail address: parkerha@esumail.emporia.edu.

Schmidt College of Arts and Letters

▼ FLORIDA ATLANTIC UNIVERSITY

Boca Raton, Florida

State-supported, coed. Suburban campus. Total enrollment: 18,823.

Degrees Bachelor of Fine Arts in the areas of acting/directing, design technical. Graduate degrees offered: Master of Fine Arts in the areas of acting/directing, design technical, arts management.

Enrollment Fall 1997: 103 total; 80 undergraduate, 23 graduate.

Theater Student Profile 57% females, 43% males, 8% minorities, 4% international.

Theater Faculty 15 total undergraduate and graduate (full-time and part-time). 90% of full-time faculty have terminal degrees. Graduate students teach a few undergraduate courses. Undergraduate student–faculty ratio: 11:1.

Student Life Student groups/activities include Coalition for the Advancement of Students in Theater.

Expenses for 1997–98 Application fee: $20. State resident tuition: $2022 full-time. Nonresident tuition: $7940 full-time. Full-time tuition varies according to course load. College room and board: $4680. College room only: $2360. Room and board charges vary according to board plan and housing facility. Special program-related fees: $50 per course for lab fee for technical theater.

Financial Aid Program-specific awards for 1997: 1 Esther Griswold Award for program majors ($500–$1000), 3 Harold Burris-Meyer Scholarship for technical students ($500).

Application Procedures Students apply for admission into the professional program by freshman year. Deadline for freshmen and transfers: continuous. Required: high school

transcript, minimum 2.0 high school GPA, 3 letters of recommendation, audition for acting/directing applicants, portfolio for design technical applicants. Auditions held 5 times on campus. Portfolio reviews held 10 times on campus and off campus in state thespian conference sites, Florida Theater Conference sites, University Resident Theater Association sites, Southeast Theater Conference sites; the submission of slides may be substituted for portfolios whenever needed.

Contact Mr. Jean Louis Baldet, Chair, Theatre Department, Florida Atlantic University, 777 Glades Road, Box 3091, Boca Raton, Florida 33431-6498; 561-297-3810, fax: 561-297-2180.

▼ FLORIDA INTERNATIONAL UNIVERSITY

Miami, Florida

State-supported, coed. Urban campus. Total enrollment: 30,012. Theater program established 1972.

Degrees Bachelor of Fine Arts in the area of theater. Majors and concentrations: acting, theater production. Program accredited by NAST.

Enrollment Fall 1997: 67 total; all undergraduate.

Theater Student Profile 60% females, 40% males, 65% minorities, 5% international.

Theater Faculty 8 total (full-time and part-time). 100% of full-time faculty have terminal degrees. Graduate students do not teach undergraduate courses. Undergraduate student–faculty ratio: 8:1.

Student Life Student groups/activities include Main Stage Players (student theater organization).

Expenses for 1997–98 Application fee: $20. State resident tuition: $1943 full-time. Nonresident tuition: $7859 full-time. Mandatory fees: $92 full-time. College room and board: $7378. College room only: $4448. Room and board charges vary according to board plan and housing facility.

Financial Aid Program-specific awards for 1997: 16 departmental scholarships for program majors ($500–$2000).

Application Procedures Students apply for admission into the professional program by sophomore year. Deadline for freshmen and transfers: August 1. Notification date for freshmen and transfers: August 15. Required: college transcript(s) for transfer students, minimum 2.0 high school GPA, audition, SAT I or ACT test scores (minimum combined SAT I score of 900). Recommended: 2 letters of recommendation, interview, portfolio. Auditions held 4 times on campus. Portfolio reviews held continuously on campus.

Undergraduate Contact Mr. Wayne Robinson, Director of Recruiting, Department of Theatre and Dance, Florida International University, University Park Campus, Miami, Florida 33199; 305-348-2895, fax: 305-348-1803, E-mail address: robinson@fiu.edu.

▼ FLORIDA STATE UNIVERSITY

Tallahassee, Florida

State-supported, coed. Suburban campus. Total enrollment: 30,401.

Degrees Bachelor of Fine Arts in the areas of acting, music theater, design technology. Majors and concentrations: theater arts/drama. Graduate degrees offered: Master of Fine Arts in the areas of acting, costume design, directing,

Florida State University *(continued)*

lighting design, scenic design, theater management, scenic technology. Program accredited by NAST.

Enrollment Fall 1997: 457 total; 63 undergraduate, 68 graduate, 326 non-professional degree.

Theater Student Profile 15% minorities, 1% international.

Theater Faculty 28 total undergraduate and graduate (full-time and part-time). 90% of full-time faculty have terminal degrees. Graduate students teach a few undergraduate courses. Undergraduate student–faculty ratio: 14:1.

Student Life Student groups/activities include Florida Theatre Conference, Southeastern Theatre Conference.

Expenses for 1997–98 Application fee: $20. State resident tuition: $1988 full-time. Nonresident tuition: $7905 full-time. College room and board: $4570. College room only: $2540. Room and board charges vary according to board plan and housing facility.

Financial Aid Program-specific awards for 1997: 2 Presidential Scholarships for program students ($1500), 5 Patron's Scholarships for program students ($1000), 1 Hoffman Chair Scholarship for program students ($1000), 3 Fallon Scholarships for program students ($500), 1–9 School of Theatre Scholarships for program students ($500–$1000).

Application Procedures Students admitted directly into the professional program freshman year. Deadline for freshmen: March 1; transfers: June 20. Notification date for freshmen: April 1; transfers: July 15. Required: high school transcript, letter of recommendation, SAT I or ACT test scores, interview for design technology applicants, audition for acting and music theater applicants. Recommended: portfolio for design technology applicants. Auditions held once on campus. Portfolio reviews held once on campus.

Contact Mr. Jim Bell, Student Affairs Director, School of Theatre, Florida State University, Fine Arts Building, Tallahassee, Florida 32306-2008; 850-644-5548, fax: 850-644-7246, E-mail address: jab9456@mailer.fsu.edu.

▼ THE HARTT SCHOOL

See University of Hartford

▼ HOFSTRA UNIVERSITY

Hempstead, New York

Independent, coed. Suburban campus. Total enrollment: 12,439. Theater program established 1956.

Degrees Bachelor of Fine Arts in the areas of performance, production. Majors and concentrations: acting, technical direction, theater arts/drama.

Enrollment Fall 1997: 96 undergraduate.

Theater Student Profile 65% females, 35% males, 2% minorities, 1% international.

Theater Faculty 12 total (full-time and part-time). 100% of full-time faculty have terminal degrees. Graduate students do not teach undergraduate courses. Undergraduate student–faculty ratio: 10:1.

Student Life Student groups/activities include Alpha Psi Omega, Spectrum Players, Masquerade Musical Theater Organization.

Expenses for 1997–98 Application fee: $40. Comprehensive fee: $20,274 includes full-time tuition ($12,790), mandatory fees ($754), and college room and board ($6730). College

room only: $4340. Room and board charges vary according to board plan and housing facility.

Financial Aid Program-specific awards for 1997: 8–10 Activity Grants for freshmen ($1000–$2500).

Application Procedures Students apply for admission into the professional program by sophomore year. Deadline for freshmen and transfers: continuous. Required: high school transcript, college transcript(s) for transfer students, minimum 3.0 high school GPA, SAT I or ACT test scores (minimum combined SAT I score of 1000), portfolio for technical direction applicants, audition for scholarship consideration. Recommended: essay, interview, video. Auditions held once in March on campus; videotaped performances are permissible as a substitute for live auditions when distance is prohibitive. Portfolio reviews held once in March on campus; the submission of slides may be substituted for portfolios when distance is prohibitive.

Web Site http://www.hofstra.edu.

Undergraduate Contact Admissions Counselor, Admissions Office, Hofstra University, Holland House, Hempstead, New York 11549-1000; 516-463-6700, fax: 516-463-5100, E-mail address: hofstra@hofstra.edu.

▼ HOWARD UNIVERSITY

Washington, District of Columbia

Independent, coed. Urban campus. Total enrollment: 10,438. Theater program established 1960.

Degrees Bachelor of Fine Arts in the areas of acting, musical theater, pre-directing, theater education, theater arts administration, theater technology. Majors and concentrations: acting, directing, music theater, theater arts administration, theater education, theater technology. Program accredited by NAST.

Enrollment Fall 1997: 139 total; all undergraduate.

Theater Student Profile 95% females, 5% males, 100% minorities.

Theater Faculty 13 total (full-time). Graduate students do not teach undergraduate courses.

Student Life Student groups/activities include Student Play Festival, Fine Arts Festival.

Expenses for 1997–98 Application fee: $45. Comprehensive fee: $13,147 includes full-time tuition ($8580), mandatory fees ($405), and college room and board ($4162).

Financial Aid Program-specific awards for 1997: Special Talent Awards for continuing students, Trustee Awards for continuing students.

Application Procedures Students admitted directly into the professional program freshman year. Deadline for freshmen and transfers: April 1. Required: high school transcript, college transcript(s) for transfer students, minimum 2.0 high school GPA, 2 letters of recommendation, audition, SAT I or ACT test scores (minimum combined SAT I score of 750), resume. Recommended: interview. Auditions held once on campus.

Undergraduate Contact Director, Office of Admissions, Howard University, 2400 6th Street, NW, Washington, District of Columbia 20059; 202-806-2700.

▼ IDAHO STATE UNIVERSITY

Pocatello, Idaho

State-supported, coed. Small town campus. Total enrollment: 11,886.

Degrees Bachelor of Fine Arts in the area of theater. Majors and concentrations: acting, costume design, theater arts/drama, theater design/technology. Graduate degrees offered: Master of Arts in the area of theater.

Enrollment Fall 1997: 34 total; 3 undergraduate, 4 graduate, 27 non-professional degree.

Theater Faculty 5 total undergraduate and graduate (full-time and part-time). 100% of full-time faculty have terminal degrees. Graduate students do not teach undergraduate courses.

Student Life Student groups/activities include Alpha Psi Omega, summer theater.

Expenses for 1997–98 Application fee: $20. State resident tuition: $0 full-time. Nonresident tuition: $5980 full-time. Mandatory fees: $1984 full-time. College room and board: $3580. College room only: $1520. Room and board charges vary according to board plan.

Financial Aid Program-specific awards for 1997: 15 Recognition Awards for program students, 15 Associated Students of ISU Awards for program students, 3–4 Service Awards for program students, 3 W. Jones Awards for program students.

Application Procedures Students admitted directly into the professional program freshman year. Deadline for freshmen and transfers: March 15. Notification date for freshmen and transfers: April 15. Required: high school transcript, college transcript(s) for transfer students, minimum 2.0 high school GPA, SAT I or ACT test scores. Recommended: 3 letters of recommendation for scholarship consideration.

Undergraduate Contact Dr. Sherri R. Dienstfrey, Professor, Department of Communication and Theatre, Idaho State University, Box 8115, Pocatello, Idaho 83209; 208-236-3561.

Graduate Contact Dr. Sherri R. Dienstfrey, Professor, Department of Communication and Theatre, Idaho State University, Box 8115, Pocatello, Idaho 83209; 208-236-3561.

▼ ILLINOIS WESLEYAN UNIVERSITY

Bloomington, Illinois

Independent, coed. Suburban campus. Total enrollment: 2,021. Theater program established 1948.

Degrees Bachelor of Fine Arts in the area of music theater; Bachelor of Arts/Bachelor of Fine Arts in the area of theater arts.

Enrollment Fall 1997: 114 total; all undergraduate.

Theater Student Profile 58% females, 42% males, 2% minorities.

Theater Faculty 14 total (full-time and part-time). 100% of full-time faculty have terminal degrees. Graduate students do not teach undergraduate courses. Undergraduate student–faculty ratio: 12:1.

Expenses for 1998–99 Comprehensive fee: $23,200 includes full-time tuition ($18,250), mandatory fees ($126), and college room and board ($4824). College room only: $2800.

Financial Aid Program-specific awards for 1997: talent awards for entering freshmen ($2500–$6000).

Application Procedures Students admitted directly into the professional program freshman year. Deadline for freshmen and transfers: continuous. Notification date for freshmen and transfers: May 1. Required: essay, high school transcript, college transcript(s) for transfer students, minimum 3.0 high school GPA, interview, SAT I or ACT test scores (minimum combined SAT I score of 1100, minimum combined ACT score of 24), audition for performance applicants, portfolio for design applicants. Recommended: 2 letters of recommendation. Auditions held weekly on campus; videotaped

performances are permissible as a substitute for live auditions if a campus visit is impossible. Portfolio reviews held weekly on campus; the submission of slides may be substituted for portfolios if a campus visit is impossible.

Web Site http://titan.iwu.edu/~theatre.

Undergraduate Contact Mr. Jared Brown, Director, School of Theatre Arts, Illinois Wesleyan University, Box 2900, Bloomington, Illinois 61702-2900; 309-556-3011, fax: 309-556-3411, E-mail address: jbrown@titan.iwu.edu.

▼ ITHACA COLLEGE

Ithaca, New York

Independent, coed. Small town campus. Total enrollment: 5,897. Theater program established 1927.

Degrees Bachelor of Fine Arts in the areas of acting, musical theater, theatrical production arts. Majors and concentrations: acting, music theater, theater design and production, theater production, theater technology. Cross-registration with Cornell University. Program accredited by NAST.

Enrollment Fall 1997: 242 total; 141 undergraduate, 101 non-professional degree.

Theater Student Profile 59% females, 41% males, 8% minorities, 2% international.

Theater Faculty 21 total (full-time and part-time). 88% of full-time faculty have terminal degrees. Graduate students do not teach undergraduate courses. Undergraduate student–faculty ratio: 14:1.

Student Life Student groups/activities include American College Theatre Festival, "IC Players" Drama Club.

Expenses for 1997–98 Application fee: $40. Comprehensive fee: $24,240 includes full-time tuition ($16,900) and college room and board ($7340). College room only: $3682.

Financial Aid Program-specific awards for 1997: Peter Bergstrom Scholarship for acting or musical theater majors ($200–$500), Katherine B. "Toby" Clarey Memorial Scholarships for acting or musical theater arts majors ($500–$1500), Richard M. Clark Memorial Scholarship for talented program majors ($1000–$2000), George Hoerner Memorial Scholarship for technical theater and scenic design majors ($200–$500), Theater Arts Alumni Memorial Scholarships for junior or senior theater arts majors ($200–$500), Jane Woods Werly Memorial Scholarships for sophomore, junior, or senior musical theater majors ($500–$2000), Ithaca Premier Talent Scholarships for theater arts majors ($10,000), Cissy Cheskis Scholarships for theater arts majors, Laura Hinkley Haver '23 Scholarships for theater arts majors.

Application Procedures Students admitted directly into the professional program freshman year. Deadline for freshmen: March 1; transfers: July 15. Notification date for freshmen: April 15; transfers: July 15. Required: essay, high school transcript, college transcript(s) for transfer students, letter of recommendation, SAT I or ACT test scores, audition for acting, drama, musical theater applicants, portfolio and interview for production arts applicants. Recommended: minimum 3.0 high school GPA. Auditions held 15-20 times for acting and musical theater applicants on campus and off campus in New York, NY; Houston, TX; Dallas, TX; Miami, FL; Sarasota, FL; Washington, DC; Chicago, IL; San Francisco, CA; Los Angeles, CA; Tampa, FL; Lakeland, FL; Seattle, WA; videotaped performances are permissible as a substitute for live auditions when distance is prohibitive. Portfolio reviews held 15-20 times and by appointment on campus and off campus in New York, NY; Houston, TX;

Ithaca College (continued)

Dallas, TX; Miami, FL; Sarasota, FL; Lakeland, FL; Tampa, FL; Washington, DC; Chicago, IL; San Francisco, CA; Los Angeles, CA; Seattle, WA; the submission of slides may be substituted for portfolios when distance is prohibitive.
Web Site http://www.ithaca.edu.
Undergraduate Contact Ms. Paula J. Mitchell, Director, Admission Department, Ithaca College, 100 Job Hall, Ithaca, New York 14850-7020; 607-274-3124, fax: 607-274-1900, E-mail address: admission@ithaca.edu.

More About the College

Program Facilities Performance facilities at Ithaca include a 525-seat proscenium theater, a 280-seat flexible theater, and a small studio theater, all featuring state-of-the-art equipment. Modern studios for acting, dance, and design combine with shops and workrooms for scenery, costumes, sound, electrics, and props to create a stimulating environment for artistic work. The School is a member of the National Association of Schools of Theatre.
Faculty, Resident Artists, and Alumni With 16 full-time theater faculty members and an extensive professional staff, the Department of Theatre Arts offers small classes and individualized instruction. Since there are no graduate students, many production opportunities in acting, directing, managing, technical direction, and design exist for the undergraduate student. Guest artists regularly visit campus, sharing their experience and insights and becoming valuable professional contacts for students. Ithaca alumni in the theater and entertainment world also actively provide career assistance.
Student Performance Opportunities The main-stage season includes five to seven productions; the studio season, two to four productions. Other opportunities include a student-directed season of six to eight productions.
Special Programs One of the most popular options for theater students is a semester at Ithaca College's London Center. Students spend their time studying and seeing plays—as many as twenty-five productions in a semester. Senior theater majors have an opportunity to participate in a field study for a week in New York City. Ithaca alumni discuss the theater and entertainment business, and qualified acting and musical theater majors present their annual showcase for agents and casting directors at an off-Broadway theater during this week.

▼

The Department of Theatre Arts offers a powerful combination of intensive classroom and performance experience that has made it one of the most effective and highly respected training programs in the nation. The goal is to prepare students for careers in the theater and entertainment business. It is a highly selective program, staffed by faculty members whose academic training and professional theater experience have prepared them for the focused, personalized instruction that is the key to successful theatrical training.

The Bachelor of Fine Arts programs in acting and musical theater are performance oriented, providing professional training and experience. The Bachelor of Fine Arts in theatrical production arts and the Bachelor of Science in theater arts management prepare students to enter the design, technical, and managerial aspects of the theater world. As with other programs at Ithaca College, the emphasis is on learning by doing. Students pursuing the

technology concentration in production, for example, will be involved in scenic carpentry, costume construction, drafting, electrics, sound, properties, stage management, and technical direction. The theatrical design concentration provides instruction in scenic design, costume design, lighting design, figure drawing, rendering, and art history, in addition to the technical areas. Students pursuing a Bachelor of Science in theater arts management have the opportunity to develop skills in marketing, advertising, publicity, fund-raising, grant writing, accounting, stage management, personnel management, booking, and tour organization. For students who elect the liberal arts–based drama degree, courses include directing, acting, theater history, stagecraft, dramatic literature, dance, and playwriting.

In addition to the annual senior showcase for New York City agents and casting directors, students and faculty members travel to New York City to see plays and participate in special theater events. Faculty members advise students about securing summer stock employment, graduate program admission, and work after graduation, taking extra time with individual students to prepare them for auditions or interviews. Design and technical students have an outstanding record of acceptance at some of the finest graduate programs.

Students direct all No Bucks Theatre productions; seniors may also direct studio theater productions. Student playwrights are encouraged to submit their plays for production.

Theater students may take advantage of courses outside their major within the School of Humanities and Sciences or at any of Ithaca College's four other schools: Business, Communications, Health Sciences and Human Performance, and Music. A comprehensive college, Ithaca offers some 1,900 courses and 100 different academic majors. Theater students may be particularly interested in exploring communications courses in areas such as audio production or film directing.

The city of Ithaca is one of the country's premier college towns, with nearly 25,000 students at Ithaca College and Cornell University. Surrounded by magnificent gorges, lakes, and countryside in the Finger Lakes region of New York State, Ithaca is a thriving cultural center. The community supports an impressive array of concerts, gallery shows, and movies as well as theater productions mounted by four local theater companies.

The combination of excellent undergraduate theater programs, a vibrant community, and a beautiful location make Ithaca College an exceptional choice for talented and motivated young artists who wish to make the theater and entertainment business their profession.

▼ JACKSONVILLE UNIVERSITY

Jacksonville, Florida

Independent, coed. Suburban campus. Total enrollment: 2,157. Theater program established 1957.
Degrees Bachelor of Fine Arts in the area of theater arts. Majors and concentrations: acting, theater design/technology.
Enrollment Fall 1997: 15 total; 13 undergraduate, 2 nonprofessional degree.
Theater Student Profile 65% females, 35% males, 7% minorities, 1% international.
Theater Faculty 4 total (full-time and part-time). 100% of full-time faculty have terminal degrees. Graduate students do not teach undergraduate courses.

Student Life Student groups/activities include Alpha Psi Omega.

Expenses for 1997–98 Application fee: $25. Comprehensive fee: $18,800 includes full-time tuition ($13,360), mandatory fees ($540), and college room and board ($4900). College room only: $2260. Room and board charges vary according to board plan. Special program-related fees: $15–$50 per course for materials.

Financial Aid Program-specific awards for 1997: 9 Theater Department Awards for program majors ($1000).

Application Procedures Students admitted directly into the professional program freshman year. Deadline for freshmen and transfers: continuous. Required: essay, high school transcript, college transcript(s) for transfer students, minimum 2.0 high school GPA, interview, SAT I or ACT test scores (minimum combined SAT I score of 820), portfolio for design/technical theater applicants, audition for acting applicants. Recommended: minimum 3.0 high school GPA, letter of recommendation. Auditions held 4 times and by appointment on campus and off campus in Southeastern Theatre Conference sites; videotaped performances are permissible as a substitute for live auditions if a campus visit is impossible. Portfolio reviews held 4 times and by appointment on campus and off campus in Southeastern Theatre Conference sites; the submission of slides may be substituted for portfolios if a campus visit is impossible.

Web Site http://www.ju.edu.

Undergraduate Contact Dr. Susan Hallenbeck, Director of Admissions, Jacksonville University, 2800 University Boulevard North, Jacksonville, Florida 32211; 904-745-7374, fax: 904-745-7375.

More About the University

Program Facilities Classes are held in the Swisher Auditorium and Phillips Fine Arts Building. Built in 1955, the auditorium offers acting and design classroom space, dressing rooms, and a fully equipped 550-seat auditorium with proscenium stage.

Faculty, Programs, and Alumni The faculty consists of 2 full-time and several adjunct members. Students broaden their skills in acting and design technology through a diverse curriculum that includes courses in acting and acting styles, playwriting, directing, scene design and construction, lighting design, costume history and design, theater history, and speech theater.

Student Performance Opportunities Performance and theater support opportunities are offered each semester, including two major productions directed by a faculty director and student-directed productions.

Special Programs The curriculum at JU is based on National Association of Schools of Theatre (NAST) guidelines. Independent study programs are offered for a one-on-one approach to a specific project or interest. Internships are also available within the Jacksonville community at many of the local community theaters. JU is accredited by the Commission on Colleges of the Southern Association of Colleges and Schools. Study-abroad programs are available.

▼ JOHNSON STATE COLLEGE

Johnson, Vermont

State-supported, coed. Rural campus. Total enrollment: 1,622. Theater program established 1982.

Degrees Bachelor of Fine Arts in the area of theater. Cross-registration with members of National Student Exchange Program, any school within the Vermont State College system.

Enrollment Fall 1997: 29 total; 10 undergraduate, 19 nonprofessional degree.

Theater Faculty 3 total (full-time and part-time). 100% of full-time faculty have terminal degrees. Graduate students do not teach undergraduate courses. Undergraduate student–faculty ratio: 15:1.

Student Life Student groups/activities include Children's Theatre, American College Theatre Festival, Campus Theatre Club.

Expenses for 1997–98 Application fee: $30. State resident tuition: $3780 full-time. Nonresident tuition: $8760 full-time. Mandatory fees: $861 full-time. Full-time tuition and fees vary according to reciprocity agreements. College room and board: $5086. College room only: $2928. Room and board charges vary according to board plan.

Financial Aid Program-specific awards for 1997: Arthur Dibden Talent Scholarships for program majors ($250–$500).

Application Procedures Students apply for admission into the professional program by sophomore year. Deadline for freshmen and transfers: continuous. Notification date for freshmen and transfers: continuous. Required: essay, high school transcript, college transcript(s) for transfer students, minimum 2.0 high school GPA, letter of recommendation, audition, SAT I or ACT test scores (minimum combined SAT I score of 980). Recommended: interview. Auditions held by appointment on campus; videotaped performances are permissible as a substitute for live auditions by prior arrangement.

Web Site http://www.jsc.vsc.edu.

Undergraduate Contact Mr. Jonathan Henry, Director of Admissions, Johnson State College, RR2 Box 75, Johnson, Vermont 05656; 800-635-2356, fax: 802-635-1230, E-mail address: jscapply@badger.jsc.vsc.edu.

▼ THE JUILLIARD SCHOOL

New York, New York

Independent, coed. Urban campus. Total enrollment: 782. Theater program established 1968.

Degrees Bachelor of Fine Arts in the area of theater.

Enrollment Fall 1997: 72 total; all undergraduate.

Theater Student Profile 37% females, 63% males, 32% minorities, 2% international.

Theater Faculty 29 total (full-time and part-time). 90% of full-time faculty have terminal degrees. Graduate students do not teach undergraduate courses. Undergraduate student–faculty ratio: 3:1.

Student Life Special housing available for theater students.

Expenses for 1997–98 Application fee: $85. Comprehensive fee: $21,500 includes full-time tuition ($14,400), mandatory fees ($600), and college room and board ($6500). Room and board charges vary according to housing facility.

Financial Aid Program-specific awards for 1997: drama scholarships for those demonstrating need.

Application Procedures Students admitted directly into the professional program freshman year. Deadline for freshmen: December 1. Notification date for freshmen: April 1. Required: essay, audition. Auditions held once on campus and off campus in Chicago, IL; San Francisco, CA.

Web Site http://www.juilliard.edu.

The Juilliard School (*continued*)

Undergraduate Contact Ms. Mary Gray, Director, Admissions Office, The Juilliard School, 60 Lincoln Center Plaza, New York, New York 10023-6590; 212-799-5000 ext. 223, fax: 212-724-0263.

▼ KENT STATE UNIVERSITY

Kent, Ohio

State-supported, coed. Small town campus. Total enrollment: 20,743. Theater program established 1983.

Degrees Bachelor of Fine Arts in the areas of theater, design/technology, musical theater. Majors and concentrations: acting, design technology, music theater. Graduate degrees offered: Master of Fine Arts in the area of theater.

Enrollment Fall 1997: 200 total; 70 undergraduate, 30 graduate, 100 non-professional degree.

Theater Student Profile 60% females, 40% males, 5% minorities, 5% international.

Theater Faculty 26 total undergraduate and graduate (full-time and part-time). 100% of full-time faculty have terminal degrees. Graduate students teach a few undergraduate courses. Undergraduate student–faculty ratio: 15:1.

Student Life Student groups/activities include Alpha Psi Omega, United States Institute for Theatre Technology, Kent Dance Association.

Expenses for 1997–98 Application fee: $30. State resident tuition: $4460 full-time. Nonresident tuition: $8920 full-time. Full-time tuition varies according to course load. College room and board: $4152. College room only: $2448.

Financial Aid Program-specific awards for 1997: 2–6 Creative Arts Awards for program majors ($1800–$2600).

Application Procedures Students admitted directly into the professional program freshman year. Deadline for freshmen and transfers: continuous. Required: high school transcript, college transcript(s) for transfer students, minimum 2.0 high school GPA, audition, portfolio, SAT I or ACT test scores, completion of college preparatory courses. Recommended: 3 letters of recommendation, interview. Auditions held twice on campus and off campus in Southeastern Theatre Conference sites, Ohio Theatre Alliance sites, United States Institute for Theatre Technology Conference sites. Portfolio reviews held twice on campus and off campus in Southeastern Theatre Conference sites, United States Institute for Theatre Technology Conference; the submission of slides may be substituted for portfolios when distance is prohibitive.

Web Site http://www.kent.edu/theatre/nav.htm.

Undergraduate Contact Dr. John R. Crawford, Chair, School of Theatre and Dance, Kent State University, P O Box 5190, Kent, Ohio 44242-0001; 330-672-2082, fax: 330-672-2889.

Graduate Contact Dr. Rosemarie K. Bank, Graduate Coordinator, School of Theatre and Dance, Kent State University, P O Box 5190, Kent, Ohio 44242; 330-672-2082, fax: 330-672-2889.

▼ LAKE ERIE COLLEGE

Painesville, Ohio

Independent, coed. Small town campus. Total enrollment: 701.

Degrees Bachelor of Fine Arts in the areas of theater, interdisciplinary studies; Bachelor of Arts in the area of theater. Majors and concentrations: acting, directing, interdisciplinary studies, lighting design, set design, theater history.

Enrollment Fall 1997: 2 undergraduate.

Theater Faculty 1 total (full-time and part-time). 100% of full-time faculty have terminal degrees. Graduate students do not teach undergraduate courses.

Student Life Student groups/activities include Alpha Psi Omega.

Expenses for 1997–98 Application fee: $20. Comprehensive fee: $18,690 includes full-time tuition ($12,950), mandatory fees ($800), and college room and board ($4940). College room only: $2540.

Financial Aid Program-specific awards for 1997: 1 Fine Arts Award for program majors ($500–$1000).

Application Procedures Deadline for freshmen: July 1; transfers: August 20. Required: essay, high school transcript, college transcript(s) for transfer students, minimum 2.0 high school GPA, 2 letters of recommendation, SAT I or ACT test scores, portfolio for design students, audition for scholarship consideration. Recommended: interview. Auditions held as needed on campus. Portfolio reviews held as needed on campus; the submission of slides may be substituted for portfolios.

Undergraduate Contact Mr. Paul Gothard, Director, Fine Arts Department, Lake Erie College, Box 354, 391 West Washington Street, Painesville, Ohio 44077; 440-639-7856.

▼ LONG ISLAND UNIVERSITY, C.W. POST CAMPUS

Brookville, New York

Independent, coed. Suburban campus. Total enrollment: 8,171.

Degrees Bachelor of Fine Arts in the areas of acting, film, production, dance. Majors and concentrations: dance, film, production, theater arts/drama. Graduate degrees offered: Master of Arts in the area of theater.

Enrollment Fall 1997: 90 total; 70 undergraduate, 10 graduate, 10 non-professional degree.

Theater Student Profile 55% females, 45% males, 30% minorities, 5% international.

Theater Faculty 11 total undergraduate and graduate (full-time and part-time). 100% of full-time faculty have terminal degrees. Graduate students do not teach undergraduate courses. Undergraduate student–faculty ratio: 7:1.

Student Life Student groups/activities include American College Dance Festival Association, Post Theatre Students Association, American College Theatre Festival.

Expenses for 1997–98 Application fee: $30. Comprehensive fee: $20,555 includes full-time tuition ($13,920), mandatory fees ($610), and college room and board ($6025). College room only: $3830. Room and board charges vary according to board plan. Special program-related fees: $30 per semester for dance accompanists, $35 per semester for production materials.

Financial Aid Program-specific awards for 1997: 10–12 Theatre Department Awards for program majors ($1000–$2000).

Application Procedures Students apply for admission into the professional program by freshman year. Deadline for freshmen and transfers: continuous. Notification date for

504

freshmen and transfers: continuous. Required: essay, high school transcript, college transcript(s) for transfer students, 2 letters of recommendation, interview, audition, SAT I or ACT test scores. Recommended: minimum 3.0 high school GPA. Auditions held by appointment on campus and off campus in Southeastern Theatre Conference sites, East Central Theater Conference sites, Theater Association of Pennsylvania sites, International Thespian Society sites; recorded music is permissible as a substitute for live auditions if a campus visit is impossible and videotaped performances are permissible as a substitute for live auditions if a campus visit is impossible.
Contact Dr. Cara Gargano, Chair, Department of Theatre, Film, and Dance, Long Island University, C.W. Post Campus, 720 Northern Boulevard, Brookville, New York 11548; 516-299-2353, fax: 516-299-3824.

▼ LONGWOOD COLLEGE

Farmville, Virginia

State-supported, coed. Small town campus. Total enrollment: 3,352. Theater program established 1966.
Degrees Bachelor of Fine Arts in the area of theater. Majors and concentrations: drama therapy, performance, technical theater. Cross-registration with Hampden-Sydney College. Program accredited by NAST.
Enrollment Fall 1997: 65 total; all undergraduate.
Theater Student Profile 56% females, 44% males, 2% minorities.
Theater Faculty 8 total (full-time and part-time). 100% of full-time faculty have terminal degrees. Graduate students do not teach undergraduate courses. Undergraduate student–faculty ratio: 10:1.
Student Life Student groups/activities include Alpha Psi Omega, Social Theatre/"Straight Talk", Longwood Players. Special housing available for theater students.
Expenses for 1997–98 Application fee: $25. State resident tuition: $2684 full-time. Nonresident tuition: $8156 full-time. Mandatory fees: $1732 full-time. College room and board: $4280. College room only: $2506. Room and board charges vary according to board plan. Special program-related fees: $25–$50 per course for lab fees, $100 per course for internship supervision.
Application Procedures Students admitted directly into the professional program freshman year. Deadline for freshmen and transfers: continuous. Notification date for freshmen and transfers: June 1. Required: essay, high school transcript, college transcript(s) for transfer students, SAT I or ACT test scores, minimum 2.5 high school GPA, portfolio and interview for technical theater applicants, audition for performance and drama therapy applicants. Recommended: minimum 3.0 high school GPA, interview. Auditions held 2-3 times in February and March on campus; videotaped performances are permissible as a substitute for live auditions when distance is prohibitive. Portfolio reviews held 2 to 3 times in February and March on campus.
Web Site http://web.lwc.edu/academic/LAS/Speech/spth.html.
Undergraduate Contact Dr. Gene Muto, Chair, Department of Speech and Theatre, Longwood College, 201 High Street, Farmville, Virginia 23909-1899; 804-395-2643, fax: 804-395-2680, E-mail address: theatre@longwood.lwc.edu.

▼ MARSHALL UNIVERSITY

Huntington, West Virginia

State-supported, coed. Urban campus. Total enrollment: 13,388.

Degrees Bachelor of Fine Arts in the area of theater. Majors and concentrations: acting and directing, theater design/technology.
Enrollment Fall 1997: 70 total; all undergraduate.
Theater Student Profile 60% females, 40% males, 4% minorities.
Theater Faculty 9 total (full-time and part-time). 100% of full-time faculty have terminal degrees. Graduate students do not teach undergraduate courses. Undergraduate student–faculty ratio: 15:1.
Student Life Student groups/activities include Alpha Psi Omega, West Virginia Theater Conference-Southeast Theater Conference, Theta Theta Omicron.
Expenses for 1997–98 Application fee: $10. State resident tuition: $1798 full-time. Nonresident tuition: $5680 full-time. Mandatory fees: $386 full-time. Full-time tuition and fees vary according to reciprocity agreements. College room and board: $4420. College room only: $2266. Room and board charges vary according to board plan and housing facility.
Financial Aid Program-specific awards for 1997: 5 tuition waivers for program majors ($2000–$6000), 21 theater scholarships for program majors ($500–$2000).
Application Procedures Students admitted directly into the professional program freshman year. Deadline for freshmen and transfers: continuous. Notification date for freshmen and transfers: continuous. Required: high school transcript, minimum 2.0 high school GPA, SAT I or ACT test scores, audition/portfolio for scholarship consideration. Recommended: interview. Auditions held once on campus; videotaped performances are permissible as a substitute for live auditions if a campus visit is impossible. Portfolio reviews held once on campus; the submission of slides may be substituted for portfolios if a campus visit is impossible.
Undergraduate Contact Dr. Jeffery Scott Elwell, Chair, Theatre Department, Marshall University, 400 Hal Greer Boulevard, Huntington, West Virginia 25755-2240; 304-696-6442, fax: 304-696-6582, E-mail address: elwell@marshal.edu.

▼ MARS HILL COLLEGE

Mars Hill, North Carolina

Independent-Baptist, coed. Small town campus. Total enrollment: 1,244. Theater program established 1980.
Degrees Bachelor of Fine Arts in the area of musical theater. Cross-registration with Warren Wilson College, University of North Carolina at Asheville. Program accredited by NAST.
Enrollment Fall 1997: 8 undergraduate.
Theater Student Profile 80% females, 20% males, 10% minorities.
Theater Faculty 7 total (full-time and part-time). 100% of full-time faculty have terminal degrees. Graduate students do not teach undergraduate courses.
Expenses for 1997–98 Application fee: $15. Comprehensive fee: $12,700 includes full-time tuition ($8350), mandatory fees ($550), and college room and board ($3800). College room only: $1700. Full-time tuition and fees vary according to course load. Room and board charges vary according to board plan and housing facility.
Application Procedures Students admitted directly into the professional program freshman year. Deadline for freshmen and transfers: continuous. Required: high school transcript, minimum 2.0 high school GPA, 2 letters of recommendation, interview, audition. Auditions held 4 times and by appointment on campus; recorded music is permissible as a substitute for live auditions when distance is prohibitive and

Mars Hill College *(continued)*

videotaped performances are permissible as a substitute for live auditions when distance is prohibitive.
Web Site http://www.mhc.edu.
Undergraduate Contact Ms. Peg Martin, Admissions Counselor, Admissions, Mars Hill College, Mars Hill, North Carolina 28754; 704-689-1201, fax: 704-689-1474, E-mail address: jfortney@mhc.edu.

▼ MARYMOUNT MANHATTAN COLLEGE

New York, New York

Independent, coed. Urban campus. Total enrollment: 2,140. Theater program established 1977.
Degrees Bachelor of Fine Arts in the area of acting. Cross-registration with Hunter College of the City University of New York.
Enrollment Fall 1997: 275 total; 125 undergraduate, 150 non-professional degree.
Theater Student Profile 53% females, 47% males, 20% minorities, 2% international.
Theater Faculty 52 total (full-time and part-time). 80% of full-time faculty have terminal degrees. Graduate students do not teach undergraduate courses.
Student Life Student groups/activities include Summer Theatre Festival.
Expenses for 1997–98 Application fee: $40. Tuition: $11,990 full-time. Mandatory fees: $300 full-time. College room only: $3182. Room charges vary according to housing facility. Special program-related fees: $15 per credit for studio/performance courses.
Financial Aid Program-specific awards for 1997: competitive merit scholarships for freshmen program majors ($500–$5000), Transfer Competitive Merit Scholarships for transfer program majors ($500–$5000).
Application Procedures Students admitted directly into the professional program freshman year. Deadline for freshmen and transfers: April 15. Notification date for freshmen and transfers: continuous. Required: high school transcript, college transcript(s) for transfer students, minimum 2.0 high school GPA, letter of recommendation, audition, SAT I or ACT test scores. Recommended: essay, minimum 3.0 high school GPA, interview. Auditions held 5 times on campus and off campus in Dallas, TX; videotaped performances are permissible as a substitute for live auditions when distance is prohibitive.
Undergraduate Contact Mr. Thomas Friebel, Admissions Office, Marymount Manhattan College, 221 East 71st Street, New York, New York 10021; 212-517-0555, fax: 212-517-0413.

Rutgers, The State University of New Jersey

▼ MASON GROSS SCHOOL OF THE ARTS

New Brunswick, New Jersey

State-supported, coed. Small town campus. Total university enrollment: 48,341. Total unit enrollment: 770. Theater program established 1976.
Degrees Bachelor of Fine Arts in the area of theater arts. Majors and concentrations: acting, design, production and management specialities. Graduate degrees offered: Master of Fine Arts in the area of theater arts. Program accredited by NAST.
Enrollment Fall 1997: 187 total; 107 undergraduate, 80 graduate.
Theater Student Profile 46% females, 54% males, 21% minorities, 2% international.
Theater Faculty 48 total undergraduate and graduate (full-time and part-time). 70% of full-time faculty have terminal degrees. Graduate students teach a few undergraduate courses.
Student Life Student groups/activities include The Shoestring Players (children's theater student-run company), The Cabaret Theater.
Expenses for 1997–98 Application fee: $50. State resident tuition: $4262 full-time. Nonresident tuition: $8676 full-time. Mandatory fees: $1104 full-time. Full-time tuition and fees vary according to location. College room and board: $5314. College room only: $3112. Room and board charges vary according to board plan and housing facility. Special program-related fees: $30–$100 per year for class supplies, models, transportation to museums, salon costumes, tickets.
Application Procedures Students admitted directly into the professional program freshman year. Deadline for freshmen: continuous; transfers: March 15. Required: high school transcript, college transcript(s) for transfer students, minimum 2.0 high school GPA, SAT I or ACT test scores, audition for acting majors, portfolio for design majors, interview for production and design majors. Recommended: essay, 2 letters of recommendation. Auditions held throughout spring term by appointment on campus and off campus in New York, NY; Evanston, IL; Long Beach, CA; videotaped performances are permissible as a substitute for live auditions when distance is prohibitive. Portfolio reviews held by appointment on campus; the submission of slides may be substituted for portfolios when distance is prohibitive.
Undergraduate Contact Assistant Vice President for University Undergraduate Admissions, Rutgers, The State University of New Jersey, Mason Gross School of the Arts, PO Box 2101, New Brunswick, New Jersey 08901-8527; 732-445-3770, fax: 732-445-0237.
Graduate Contact Mr. Donald J. Taylor, Director of Graduate and Professional Admissions, Admissions/Graduate, Rutgers, The State University of New Jersey, Mason Gross School of the Arts, Van Nest Hall, Room 204, New Brunswick, New Jersey 08901-8527; 732-932-7711, fax: 732-932-8231.

▼ MEADOWS SCHOOL OF THE ARTS

See Southern Methodist University

▼ MIAMI UNIVERSITY

Oxford, Ohio

State-related, coed. Small town campus. Total enrollment: 16,328. Theater program established 1905.
Degrees Bachelor of Fine Arts in the area of theater. Majors and concentrations: acting, theater design/technology. Graduate degrees offered: Master of Arts in the area of theater. Program accredited by NAST.
Enrollment Fall 1997: 82 total; 70 undergraduate, 9 graduate, 3 non-professional degree.
Theater Student Profile 60% females, 40% males, 4% minorities.

Theater Faculty 10 total undergraduate and graduate (full-time and part-time). 90% of full-time faculty have terminal degrees. Graduate students teach a few undergraduate courses. Undergraduate student–faculty ratio: 10:1.

Student Life Student groups/activities include Alpha Psi Omega.

Expenses for 1997–98 Application fee: $35. State resident tuition: $4482 full-time. Nonresident tuition: $10,582 full-time. Mandatory fees: $1030 full-time. Full-time tuition and fees vary according to course load. College room and board: $4810. Room and board charges vary according to board plan.

Financial Aid Program-specific awards for 1997: 5 departmental scholarships for program majors ($1000–$2000).

Application Procedures Students apply for admission into the professional program by freshman year. Deadline for freshmen: January 31; transfers: May 1. Notification date for freshmen: March 15; transfers: continuous. Required: high school transcript, college transcript(s) for transfer students, interview, audition, portfolio, SAT I or ACT test scores. Recommended: essay, letter of recommendation. Auditions held twice and by appointment on campus; videotaped performances are permissible as a substitute for live auditions if a campus visit is impossible. Portfolio reviews held twice and by appointment on campus; the submission of slides may be substituted for portfolios if a campus visit is impossible.

Undergraduate Contact Ms. Catherine Moore, Chair of Recruitment, Department of Theatre, Miami University, 131 Center for Performing Arts, Oxford, Ohio 45056; 513-529-3064, fax: 513-529-4048.

Graduate Contact Dr. Martin Bennison, Director of Graduate Studies, Theatre, Miami University, 131 Center for Performing Arts, Oxford, Ohio 45056; 513-529-3062, fax: 513-529-4048.

▼ MIDWESTERN STATE UNIVERSITY

Wichita Falls, Texas

State-supported, coed. Urban campus. Total enrollment: 5,770.

Degrees Bachelor of Fine Arts in the area of theater. Majors and concentrations: performance, technical theater.

Enrollment Fall 1997: 36 total; 30 undergraduate, 6 non-professional degree.

Theater Student Profile 65% females, 35% males, 4% minorities.

Theater Faculty 4 total (full-time and part-time). 100% of full-time faculty have terminal degrees. Graduate students do not teach undergraduate courses. Undergraduate student–faculty ratio: 6:1.

Student Life Student groups/activities include Alpha Psi Omega.

Expenses for 1997–98 State resident tuition: $1054 full-time. Nonresident tuition: $7688 full-time. Mandatory fees: $1037 full-time. Full-time tuition and fees vary according to course load. College room and board: $3633. Room and board charges vary according to board plan and housing facility.

Financial Aid Program-specific awards for 1997: 15–20 theater scholarships for program majors ($500–$2000).

Application Procedures Students admitted directly into the professional program freshman year. Deadline for freshmen and transfers: August 1. Required: high school transcript, college transcript(s) for transfer students, SAT I or ACT test scores, audition, interview, and/or portfolio for scholarship

consideration. Recommended: minimum 2.0 high school GPA, interview, audition, portfolio. Auditions held 5 times on campus and off campus in theater conference locations; videotaped performances are permissible as a substitute for live auditions when distance is prohibitive. Portfolio reviews held once on campus; the submission of slides may be substituted for portfolios whenever needed.

Undergraduate Contact Ms. Laura N. Wilson, Coordinator, Theatre Department, Midwestern State University, 3410 Taft Boulevard, Wichita Falls, Texas 76308; 940-397-4395.

▼ MILLIKIN UNIVERSITY

Decatur, Illinois

Independent, coed. Suburban campus. Total enrollment: 1,997.

Degrees Bachelor of Fine Arts in the areas of music theater, acting, technical theater, directing. Majors and concentrations: music theater, theater arts/drama.

Enrollment Fall 1997: 175 undergraduate.

Theater Student Profile 5% minorities, 1% international.

Theater Faculty 16 total (full-time and part-time). 100% of full-time faculty have terminal degrees. Graduate students do not teach undergraduate courses. Undergraduate student–faculty ratio: 16:1.

Student Life Student groups/activities include Alpha Psi Omega, Children's Theater, Illinois High School Association.

Expenses for 1997–98 Comprehensive fee: $19,208 includes full-time tuition ($13,988), mandatory fees ($150), and college room and board ($5070). College room only: $2638. Full-time tuition and fees vary according to course load. Room and board charges vary according to board plan and housing facility.

Financial Aid Program-specific awards for 1997: 135 Talent Awards for music theater, acting, directing majors ($1200–$2000), 20 Talent Awards for technology majors ($5500).

Application Procedures Deadline for freshmen and transfers: continuous. Required: high school transcript, letter of recommendation, video, audition, portfolio, SAT I or ACT test scores. Auditions held continuously on campus and off campus in Chicago, IL; Louisville, KY; recorded music is permissible as a substitute for live auditions when distance is prohibitive and videotaped performances are permissible as a substitute for live auditions when distance is prohibitive. Portfolio reviews held continuously for technology applicants on campus and off campus in Chicago, IL; Louisville, KY; the submission of slides may be substituted for portfolios.

Undergraduate Contact Mr. Barry Pearson, Chair, Theatre and Dance Department, Millikin University, 1184 West Main Street, Decatur, Illinois 62522; 217-424-6282, fax: 217-424-3993.

▼ MONTCLAIR STATE UNIVERSITY

Upper Montclair, New Jersey

State-supported, coed. Suburban campus. Total enrollment: 12,808.

Degrees Bachelor of Fine Arts in the areas of acting, production/design. Program accredited by NAST.

Enrollment Fall 1997: 130 total; 120 undergraduate, 10 graduate.

Theater Student Profile 60% females, 40% males, 8% minorities.

Montclair State University (continued)

Theater Faculty 17 total undergraduate (full-time and part-time). 80% of full-time faculty have terminal degrees. Graduate students do not teach undergraduate courses.

Student Life Student groups/activities include Departmental Productions-Mainstage, Studio, Experimental, Theta Alpha Phi, Theatre in the Raw.

Expenses for 1997–98 Application fee: $40. State resident tuition: $2912 full-time. Nonresident tuition: $4432 full-time. Mandatory fees: $782 full-time. College room and board: $5546. College room only: $3860.

Application Procedures Students admitted directly into the professional program freshman year. Deadline for freshmen: March 1; transfers: May 1. Notification date for freshmen and transfers: continuous. Required: high school transcript, college transcript(s) for transfer students, 2 letters of recommendation, interview, SAT I test score only, audition for acting applicants, portfolio for production/design applicants. Auditions held 4 times on campus. Portfolio reviews held continuously on campus.

Undergraduate Contact Dr. Suzanne Trauth, Chair, Theatre and Dance Department, Montclair State University, Normal Avenue, Upper Montclair, New Jersey 07043; 973-655-4217.

▼ Nebraska Wesleyan University

Lincoln, Nebraska

Independent-United Methodist, coed. Suburban campus. Total enrollment: 1,709.

Degrees Bachelor of Fine Arts in the area of theater. Majors and concentrations: acting, directing, technical theater. Cross-registration with University of Nebraska-Lincoln.

Enrollment Fall 1997: 22 total; 4 undergraduate, 18 nonprofessional degree.

Theater Student Profile 56% females, 44% males.

Theater Faculty 5 total undergraduate (full-time and part-time). 66% of full-time faculty have terminal degrees. Graduate students do not teach undergraduate courses. Undergraduate student–faculty ratio: 6:1.

Student Life Student groups/activities include Theta Alpha Phi (theater honorary society), American College Theatre Festival.

Expenses for 1997–98 Application fee: $20. One-time mandatory fee: $80. Comprehensive fee: $14,834 includes full-time tuition ($10,898), mandatory fees ($322), and college room and board ($3614). Room and board charges vary according to board plan.

Financial Aid Program-specific awards for 1997: 7–10 theater scholarships for program majors ($750).

Application Procedures Students admitted directly into the professional program freshman year. Deadline for freshmen and transfers: May 1. Notification date for freshmen and transfers: continuous. Required: high school transcript, minimum 3.0 high school GPA, SAT I or ACT test scores (minimum combined SAT I score of 920, minimum combined ACT score of 20), audition and two letters of recommendation for scholarship consideration. Auditions held by appointment on campus; videotaped performances are permissible as a substitute for live auditions when distance is prohibitive.

Undergraduate Contact Mr. David M. Clark, Director of Theatre, Communication and Theatre Arts Department, Nebraska Wesleyan University, 5000 St. Paul Avenue, Lincoln, Nebraska 68504; 402-465-2386, fax: 402-456-2179, E-mail address: dmc@nebrwesleyan.edu.

▼ New World School of the Arts

Miami, Florida

State-supported, coed. Urban campus. Total enrollment: 359. Theater program established 1987.

Degrees Bachelor of Fine Arts in the area of theater. Majors and concentrations: acting, music theater, playwriting, theater design and production. Mandatory cross-registration with University of Florida, Miami-Dade Community College. Program accredited by NAST.

Enrollment Fall 1997: 72 total; all undergraduate.

Theater Student Profile 60% females, 40% males, 48% minorities, 4% international.

Theater Faculty 21 total (full-time and part-time). 90% of full-time faculty have terminal degrees. Graduate students do not teach undergraduate courses. Undergraduate student–faculty ratio: 3:1.

Student Life Student groups/activities include Florida Theatre Association, State Thespians, Florida Association of Theater Education.

Estimated expenses for 1998–99 Application fee: $20. State resident tuition: $1478 full-time. Nonresident tuition: $5196 full-time. Full-time tuition varies according to course load and degree level.

Financial Aid Program-specific awards for 1997: 1 Robert Brenner Merit Scholarship for music theater majors ($1000), 1 Annett Foosaner Merit Scholarship for program majors ($1000), 2 Donald Khan Merit Scholarships for program majors ($1000), 1 Betty Ann Merit Scholarship for program majors ($1000), 1 Douglas Fairbanks/Southern Bell Merit Scholarship for program majors ($1000), 1 Tommy Tune Merit Scholarship for music theater majors ($500), 1 George Abbott Merit Scholarship for music theater majors ($500), 4 Nations Bank Merit Scholarships for program majors ($2000), 25 Miami-Dade Community College Merit Scholarships for program majors ($1500).

Application Procedures Students admitted directly into the professional program freshman year. Deadline for freshmen and transfers: continuous. Required: high school transcript, college transcript(s) for transfer students, audition. Recommended: essay, minimum 2.0 high school GPA, 2 letters of recommendation, interview, SAT I or ACT test scores. Auditions held continuously on campus and off campus in Southeastern Theatre Conference sites and Florida Theater Conference sites; videotaped performances are permissible as a substitute for live auditions for out-of-state applicants.

Web Site http://www.mdcc.edu/nwsa.

Undergraduate Contact Ms. Ileanna Gallagher, College Admissions Counselor, Student Services, New World School of the Arts, 300 North East 2nd Avenue, Miami, Florida 33132; 305-237-7007, fax: 305-237-3794.

More About the Conservatory

Program Facilities The Theater Division at New World School of the Arts is one of the most dynamic, comprehensive, and forward thinking conservatories in the country. Boldly drawing from a high standard of American and European techniques, New World emphasizes creativity, artistic rigor, and range versatility. The conservatory prepares highly competitive actors, music theater performers, playwrights,

and production majors for the real world, equipping them with the tools to be true innovators.

Special Programs The are several unique features about New World School including integrated curriculum with a professional edge; strong craft training as well as exploratory techniques; educational opportunities programs in England, Greece, Russia, and Australia; individualized training at competitive tuition costs; and an exciting environment for students to learn the art and craft of theater in synergy with a vibrant multicultural community.

Faculty, Resident Artists, and Alumni The conservatory has highly qualified faculty in all areas of training and internationally renowned visiting artists.

▼

Situated in the center of downtown Miami, New World School of the Arts draws unique energy from this vibrant multicultural setting. NWSA is surrounded by cultural and civic centers and public art produced by renowned artists. NWSA bridges the gap between the classroom and the performance world by affording each student opportunities to develop through immediate interaction with an accessible artistic community. Artists—aspiring and professional—form the creative environment of New World School of the Arts, a unique community celebrating individuality. The programs nurture the perspective of a new world, developing artists who express a multiplicity of ideas.

The dance division develops professional dancers qualified for high-caliber national or regional companies. Emphasis is placed upon building a strong technical base, learning a wide range of styles and techniques, and developing skills and craft through performance. Dance majors participate in a program of classical ballet, modern dance, jazz, and ethnic dance studies. The multicultural flavor of Miami is reflected in the strength of the classes offered in Spanish dance, Afro-Caribbean dance, and tap. Supporting these technical studies are courses in music, dance history, composition, anatomy, laban and dance production. Choreography and performance are integrated into the training process at all levels.

The music division guides students toward the highest professional standard. The pursuit of instrumental, composition, and vocal mastery is complemented by courses in theory, history, literature, and performance practice, so graduates are equipped with all the tools of the professional musician. The course of study caters to the individual through a unique blend of faculty members, interactive

performers and scholars, small classes, and abundant performance opportunities. The result is music making according to inspiration as opposed to according to a specific formula.

The theater division provides students with many opportunities to participate in main stage and studio productions, new play festivals, interdisciplinary collaborations, and student and class projects. Technique and execution are emphasized equally with research and experimentation. New World School nurtures actors, designers, writers, and directors who can compete in the existing professional world for career opportunities, as well as create new venues and jobs for themselves. Ultimately, we work for the preparation of a new kind of theater artist who understands and applies the multiplicity and richness of this ancestral art to the vibrant reality of today.

The visual art division degree programs provide a breadth of learning experiences which develop each student's personal vision and creative expression, technical skills in traditional and new media, and an understanding of the roles of art and design in society. Talented young artists draw on their unique personal visions to address issues emerging from the local and global communities and issues arising from the convergence of cyberspace and real space. In addition to painting, drawing, ceramics, and printmaking studios, students can be found in the community creating works of environmental and public art, working with top graphic designers and photographers on real-life projects, and creating electronic works of art and design in the School's cyberarts studio.

Tisch School of the Arts—Dramataic Writing Program

▼ NEW YORK UNIVERSITY

New York, New York

Independent, coed. Urban campus. Total enrollment: 36,684. Theater program established 1980.

Degrees Bachelor of Fine Arts in the area of dramatic writing. Graduate degrees offered: Master of Fine Arts in the area of dramatic writing.

Enrollment Fall 1997: 280 total; 200 undergraduate, 50 graduate, 30 non-professional degree.

Theater Student Profile 47% females, 53% males, 15% minorities, 5% international.

Theater Faculty 60 total undergraduate and graduate (full-time and part-time). 100% of full-time faculty have terminal degrees. Graduate students teach a few undergraduate courses. Undergraduate student–faculty ratio: 5:1.

Student Life Student groups/activities include Artists in the Community, Out Artists, United Artists of Color.

Expenses for 1997–98 Application fee: $45. Comprehensive fee: $29,900 includes full-time tuition ($21,730) and college room and board ($8170). Full-time tuition varies according to program. Room and board charges vary according to board plan and housing facility.

Financial Aid Program-specific awards available.

Application Procedures Students admitted directly into the professional program freshman year. Deadline for freshmen: January 15; transfers: April 1. Notification date for freshmen: April 1; transfers: May 15. Required: essay, high school transcript, college transcript(s) for transfer students, 2 letters of recommendation, portfolio, SAT I test score only.

New York University (*continued*)

Recommended: minimum 3.0 high school GPA. Portfolio reviews held continuously from November through May on campus.

Web Site http://www.nyu.edu/tisch.

Undergraduate Contact Mr. Elliot Dee, Director of Recruitment, Tisch School of the Arts, New York University, 721 Broadway, 8th Floor, New York, New York 10003-6807; 212-998-1902, fax: 212-995-4060, E-mail address: eddl@is6.nyu.edu.

Graduate Contact Mr. Dan Sandford, Director of Graduate Admissions, Tisch School of the Arts, New York University, 721 Broadway, 8th Floor, New York, New York 10003-6807; 212-998-1900, fax: 212-995-4060, E-mail address: dan.sandford@nyu.edu.

Tisch School of the Arts

▼ NEW YORK UNIVERSITY

New York, New York

Independent, coed. Urban campus. Total enrollment: 36,684. Theater program established 1965.

Degrees Bachelor of Fine Arts in the area of drama. Majors and concentrations: acting, directing, music theater, technical production, theater design and production. Graduate degrees offered: Master of Fine Arts in the area of acting.

Enrollment Fall 1997: 968 undergraduate.

Theater Faculty 188 total undergraduate and graduate (full-time and part-time). 100% of full-time faculty have terminal degrees. Graduate students do not teach undergraduate courses. Undergraduate student–faculty ratio: 5:1.

Student Life Student groups/activities include Artists in the Community, Out Artists, United Artists of Color.

Expenses for 1997–98 Application fee: $45. Comprehensive fee: $29,900 includes full-time tuition ($21,730) and college room and board ($8170). Full-time tuition varies according to program. Room and board charges vary according to board plan and housing facility.

Financial Aid Program-specific awards available.

Application Procedures Students admitted directly into the professional program freshman year. Deadline for freshmen: January 15; transfers: April 1. Notification date for freshmen: April 1; transfers: May 15. Required: essay, high school transcript, college transcript(s) for transfer students, 2 letters of recommendation, interview, audition, portfolio, SAT I or ACT test scores. Recommended: minimum 3.0 high school GPA. Auditions held continuously from October 15 through April 1 on campus and off campus in Chicago, IL; San Francisco, CA; Atlanta, GA; Los Angeles, CA; Houston, TX; videotaped performances are permissible as a substitute for live auditions with approval from the department. Portfolio reviews held continuously from October 15 through April 1 on campus and off campus in Chicago, IL; San Francisco, CA; Atlanta, GA; Los Angeles, CA; Houston, TX.

Web Site http://www.nyu.edu/tisch.

Undergraduate Contact Mr. Elliot Dee, Director of Recruitment, Tisch School of the Arts, New York University, 721 Broadway, 8th Floor, New York, New York 10003-6807; 212-998-1902, fax: 212-995-4060, E-mail address: eddl@is6.nyu.edu.

Graduate Contact Mr. Dan Sanford, Director of Graduate Admissions, Tisch School of the Arts, New York University, 721 Broadway, 8th Floor, New York, New York 10003-6807; 212-998-1900, fax: 212-995-4060, E-mail address: dan.sandford@nyu.edu.

▼ NIAGARA UNIVERSITY

Niagara University, New York

Independent, coed. Suburban campus. Total enrollment: 3,079. Theater program established 1981.

Degrees Bachelor of Fine Arts in the area of theater arts.

Enrollment Fall 1997: 70 undergraduate.

Theater Student Profile 60% females, 40% males, 4% minorities, 10% international.

Theater Faculty 12 total (full-time and part-time). 90% of full-time faculty have terminal degrees. Graduate students do not teach undergraduate courses. Undergraduate student–faculty ratio: 6:1.

Expenses for 1997–98 Application fee: $25. Comprehensive fee: $18,548 includes full-time tuition ($12,390), mandatory fees ($500), and college room and board ($5658). Room and board charges vary according to gender.

Financial Aid Program-specific awards for 1997: 8–10 departmental scholarships for program majors ($1000–$8000).

Application Procedures Students admitted directly into the professional program freshman year. Deadline for freshmen and transfers: continuous. Required: high school transcript, college transcript(s) for transfer students, interview, SAT I or ACT test scores, audition for scholarship consideration. Recommended: minimum 3.0 high school GPA, audition. Auditions held once on campus.

Undergraduate Contact Dr. Sharon O. Watkinson, Chair, Theater and Fine Arts Department, Niagara University, Niagara University, New York 14109; 716-286-8481, fax: 716-286-8495.

▼ NORTH CAROLINA AGRICULTURAL AND TECHNICAL STATE UNIVERSITY

Greensboro, North Carolina

State-supported, coed. Urban campus. Total enrollment: 7,468. Theater program established 1898.

Degrees Bachelor of Fine Arts in the areas of acting, directing, technology. Majors and concentrations: acting and directing, theater arts/drama, theater technology. Cross-registration with University of North Carolina System. Program accredited by NAST.

Enrollment Fall 1997: 60 total; 45 undergraduate, 15 non-professional degree.

Theater Student Profile 65% females, 35% males, 95% minorities, 5% international.

Theater Faculty 9 total (full-time and part-time). 100% of full-time faculty have terminal degrees. Graduate students do not teach undergraduate courses.

Student Life Student groups/activities include American College Theatre Festival, National Association of Dramatic and Speech Arts, Southeastern Theatre Conference.

Expenses for 1997–98 Application fee: $35. State resident tuition: $900 full-time. Nonresident tuition: $8028 full-time. Mandatory fees: $722 full-time. Full-time tuition and fees vary according to course load. College room and board: $3850. College room only: $2420. Room and board charges vary according to board plan.

Financial Aid Program-specific awards for 1997: 5 Chancellor's Awards for freshmen ($1000), 3 tuition remissions for upperclassmen ($1500).

Application Procedures Students apply for admission into the professional program by sophomore year. Deadline for freshmen and transfers: continuous. Required: high school transcript, college transcript(s) for transfer students, minimum 2.0 high school GPA, letter of recommendation, interview, audition, portfolio, SAT I or ACT test scores (minimum combined SAT I score of 830, minimum combined ACT score of 17), minimum combined SAT I score of 920 for out-of-state applicants, minimum composite ACT score of 21 for out-of-state applicants. Auditions held twice on campus; recorded music is permissible as a substitute for live auditions if pianist is not available. Portfolio reviews held twice on campus.

Undergraduate Contact Mr. Lucky Miller, Assistant Professor, Speech, Communication and Theatre Arts, North Carolina Agricultural and Technical State University, 1601 East Market Street, Greensboro, North Carolina 27411; 336-334-7221, fax: 336-334-7173.

▼ NORTH CAROLINA SCHOOL OF THE ARTS

Winston-Salem, North Carolina

State-supported, coed. Urban campus. Total enrollment: 773. Theater program established 1965.

Degrees Bachelor of Fine Arts in the areas of drama/acting, design and production, filmmaking. Majors and concentrations: acting, art direction, costume design, costume production, directing, film design, lighting design, makeup, scene painting, scenic design, stage management, technical direction. Graduate degrees offered: Master of Fine Arts in the area of design and production.

Enrollment Fall 1997: 294 total; 268 undergraduate, 26 graduate.

Theater Student Profile 40% females, 60% males, 11% minorities, 5% international.

Theater Faculty 32 total undergraduate and graduate (full-time and part-time). Graduate students do not teach undergraduate courses. Undergraduate student–faculty ratio: 9:1.

Student Life Special housing available for theater students.

Expenses for 1997–98 Application fee: $35. State resident tuition: $1401 full-time. Nonresident tuition: $9858 full-time. Mandatory fees: $1121 full-time. Full-time tuition and fees vary according to program. College room and board: $3970. College room only: $2060. Special program-related fees: $135 per year for educational and technology fee.

Financial Aid Program-specific awards for 1997: talent scholarships for artistically talented.

Application Procedures Students admitted directly into the professional program freshman year. Deadline for freshmen and transfers: March 1. Required: essay, college transcript(s) for transfer students, 2 letters of recommendation, interview, audition, SAT I or ACT test scores, portfolio for design and production applicants. Auditions held by request on campus and off campus in New York, NY; Seattle, WA; Houston, TX; Chicago, IL; Miami, Fl; San Francisco, CA; Los Angeles, CA. Portfolio reviews held 10 times on campus.

Web Site http://www.ncarts.edu.

Contact Ms. Carol J. Palm, Director of Admissions, North Carolina School of the Arts, 1533 South Main Street, Winston-Salem, North Carolina 27117-2189; 336-770-3291, fax: 336-770-3370, E-mail address: palmc@ncsavx.ncsart.edu.

▼ NORTH DAKOTA STATE UNIVERSITY

Fargo, North Dakota

State-supported, coed. Urban campus. Total enrollment: 9,408.

Degrees Bachelor of Fine Arts in the area of theater. Majors and concentrations: design/technical theater, performance. Graduate degrees offered: Master of Arts in the area of theater. Cross-registration with Moorhead State University, Concordia College (MN).

Enrollment Fall 1997: 24 total; 20 undergraduate, 4 graduate.

Theater Student Profile 60% females, 40% males.

Theater Faculty 5 total undergraduate and graduate (full-time and part-time). 80% of full-time faculty have terminal degrees. Graduate students teach a few undergraduate courses. Undergraduate student–faculty ratio: 3:1.

Expenses for 1997–98 Application fee: $25. One-time mandatory fee: $45. State resident tuition: $2236 full-time. Nonresident tuition: $5970 full-time. Mandatory fees: $330 full-time. Full-time tuition and fees vary according to course load, program, and reciprocity agreements. College room and board: $3135. College room only: $1163. Room and board charges vary according to board plan and housing facility. Special program-related fees: $25 per course for lab fee for makeup courses.

Financial Aid Program-specific awards for 1997: 1 Frederick Walsh Talent Grant for theater arts majors ($700), 3–5 Alfred G. Arnold Scholarships for theater arts majors ($700), 1 Jim and Sonja Ozbun Scholarship for the Fine Arts for upperclass theater arts majors ($700), 1 Arthur and Vera Johnson Scholarship for theater arts majors ($400).

Application Procedures Students apply for admission into the professional program by sophomore year. Deadline for freshmen and transfers: continuous. Required: high school transcript, college transcript(s) for transfer students, audition, portfolio, ACT test score only (minimum combined ACT score of 21), minimum 2.5 high school GPA, completion of college preparatory courses. Auditions held twice on campus. Portfolio reviews held twice on campus.

Undergraduate Contact Dr. Paul L Lifton, Coordinator, Division of Fine Arts, North Dakota State University, State University Station, Box 5691, Fargo, North Dakota 58105; 701-231-7785, fax: 701-231-2085, E-mail address: lifton@badlands.nodak.edu.

Graduate Contact Dr. Paul Lifton, Coordinator, Division of Fine Arts, North Dakota State University, State University Station, Box 5691, Fargo, North Dakota 58105; 701-231-7785, fax: 701-231-2085, E-mail address: lifton@badlands.nodak.edu.

▼ NORTHERN ILLINOIS UNIVERSITY

De Kalb, Illinois

State-supported, coed. Small town campus. Total enrollment: 22,082.

Degrees Bachelor of Fine Arts in the areas of acting, dance performance, design/technology, theater education. Graduate degrees offered: Master of Fine Arts in the areas of acting, directing, costume design, lighting design, scene design, technical production. Program accredited by NAST.

Enrollment Fall 1997: 161 total; 102 undergraduate, 38 graduate, 21 non-professional degree.

Theater Student Profile 40% females, 60% males, 12% minorities, 4% international.

Northern Illinois University *(continued)*

Theater Faculty 30 total undergraduate and graduate (full-time and part-time). 90% of full-time faculty have terminal degrees. Graduate students teach a few undergraduate courses. Undergraduate student–faculty ratio: 10:1.

Student Life Student groups/activities include American College Theatre Festival, American College Dance Festival, International Theatre Exchange Program.

Expenses for 1997–98 State resident tuition: $2952 full-time. Nonresident tuition: $8856 full-time. Mandatory fees: $885 full-time. Full-time tuition and fees vary according to course load. College room and board: $4000. Room and board charges vary according to housing facility. Special program-related fees: $25 per course for fees.

Financial Aid Program-specific awards for 1997: 10 Talented Student Scholarships for program majors ($1000–$6000), 1 Sidney Smith Award for outstanding incoming program majors ($1000–$6000), 3–5 Minority Student Scholarships for program majors ($1000–$6000).

Application Procedures Students apply for admission into the professional program by sophomore year. Deadline for freshmen and transfers: continuous. Notification date for freshmen and transfers: continuous. Required: high school transcript, college transcript(s) for transfer students, interview, audition, ACT test score only (minimum combined ACT score of 19). Recommended: portfolio. Auditions held 4 times on campus and off campus in Dallas, TX; Illinois High School Theatre Festival; Midwest Theatre Conference locations; recorded music is permissible as a substitute for live auditions when distance is prohibitive and videotaped performances are permissible as a substitute for live auditions when distance is prohibitive. Portfolio reviews held continuously on campus and off campus in Dallas, TX; Illinois High School Theatre Festival; the submission of slides may be substituted for portfolios when distance is prohibitive (beyond a 500-mile radius).

Undergraduate Contact JoAnne S. Fox, Undergraduate Advisor, School of Theatre Arts, Northern Illinois University, De Kalb, Illinois 60115; 815-753-8261, fax: 815-753-8415.

Graduate Contact Director of Graduate Studies, School of Theatre Arts, Northern Illinois University, De Kalb, Illinois 60115; 815-753-1335.

▼ NORTHERN KENTUCKY UNIVERSITY

Highland Heights, Kentucky

State-supported, coed. Suburban campus. Total enrollment: 11,763. Theater program established 1970.

Degrees Bachelor of Fine Arts in the areas of acting/directing, musical theater, design/technology, generalist/management, playwriting. Cross-registration with University of Cincinnati, Thomas More College, Xavier University.

Enrollment Fall 1997: 156 total; 150 undergraduate, 6 non-professional degree.

Theater Student Profile 45% females, 55% males, 5% minorities, 2% international.

Theater Faculty 18 total (full-time and part-time). 100% of full-time faculty have terminal degrees. Graduate students do not teach undergraduate courses. Undergraduate student–faculty ratio: 15:1.

Student Life Student groups/activities include Student Theater, Stage One-Student Service Organization, Tour Troupes. Special housing available for theater students.

Expenses for 1997–98 Application fee: $25. State resident tuition: $2120 full-time. Nonresident tuition: $5720 full-time. Full-time tuition varies according to course load. College room and board: $3439. College room only: $1769. Room and board charges vary according to board plan and housing facility. Special program-related fees: $20 per semester for technology fee.

Financial Aid Program-specific awards for 1997: 13 Theater Department Scholarships for program majors ($1500), 4 Corbett Scholarships for program majors ($2000).

Application Procedures Students apply for admission into the professional program by sophomore year. Deadline for freshmen and transfers: continuous. Required: high school transcript, college transcript(s) for transfer students, audition, ACT test score only, portfolio for design majors. Recommended: minimum 2.0 high school GPA, 3 letters of recommendation, interview. Auditions held twice on campus; videotaped performances are permissible as a substitute for live auditions if a campus visit is impossible and only for scholarship status, not BFA acceptance. Portfolio reviews held twice on campus.

Undergraduate Contact Office of Admissions, Administrative Centre, Northern Kentucky University, 4th Floor, Highland Heights, Kentucky 41099; 606-572-5220, fax: 606-572-5566.

▼ OHIO NORTHERN UNIVERSITY

Ada, Ohio

Independent-United Methodist, coed. Small town campus. Total enrollment: 2,927. Theater program established 1964.

Degrees Bachelor of Fine Arts in the area of musical theater. Majors and concentrations: music theater, theater arts/drama. Cross-registration with Queen Margaret College (United Kingdom).

Enrollment Fall 1997: 99 total; all undergraduate.

Theater Student Profile 65% females, 35% males, 3% minorities, 3% international.

Theater Faculty 9 total (full-time and part-time). 100% of full-time faculty have terminal degrees. Graduate students do not teach undergraduate courses. Undergraduate student–faculty ratio: 13:1.

Student Life Student groups/activities include Theta Alpha Phi, Touring Children's Company, Touring Broadway Revue.

Expenses for 1998–99 Application fee: $30. Comprehensive fee: $24,690 includes full-time tuition ($19,815) and college room and board ($4875). College room only: $2130. Full-time tuition varies according to program. Room and board charges vary according to board plan.

Financial Aid Program-specific awards for 1997: 10–12 Talent Awards for program majors ($2000–$6000).

Application Procedures Students admitted directly into the professional program freshman year. Deadline for freshmen and transfers: continuous. Notification date for freshmen and transfers: continuous. Required: high school transcript, minimum 2.0 high school GPA, interview, SAT I or ACT test scores. Recommended: essay, minimum 3.0 high school GPA, 2 letters of recommendation, video, audition, portfolio. Auditions held by appointment on campus; videotaped performances are permissible as a substitute for live auditions if a campus visit is impossible. Portfolio reviews held by appointment on campus.

Web Site http://www.onu.edu.

Undergraduate Contact Ms. Karen Condeni, Vice President and Dean of Admissions, Ohio Northern University, 525 South

Main Street, Ada, Ohio 45810; 419-772-2260, fax: 419-772-2313, E-mail address: admissions-ug@onu.edu.

▼ OHIO UNIVERSITY

Athens, Ohio

State-supported, coed. Small town campus. Total enrollment: 19,564. Theater program established 1890.

Degrees Bachelor of Fine Arts in the areas of performance, production, design and technology, theater arts/drama. Majors and concentrations: performance, theater arts/drama, theater design and production, theater technology. Graduate degrees offered: Master of Fine Arts in the areas of professional actor training, professional director training, professional playwriting, production, design and technology, general theater. Program accredited by NAST.

Enrollment Fall 1997: 250 total; 175 undergraduate, 75 graduate.

Theater Student Profile 63% females, 37% males, 10% minorities, 2% international.

Theater Faculty 17 total undergraduate and graduate (full-time and part-time). 88% of full-time faculty have terminal degrees. Graduate students teach a few undergraduate courses. Undergraduate student–faculty ratio: 12:1.

Student Life Student groups/activities include Ohio Valley Summer Theater, Monomoy Theatre.

Expenses for 1997–98 Application fee: $30. State resident tuition: $4275 full-time. Nonresident tuition: $8994 full-time. College room and board: $4698. College room only: $2310. Room and board charges vary according to board plan.

Financial Aid Program-specific awards for 1997: 15–25 Provost Talent Scholarships for incoming freshmen ($1500), 29 Dean's Scholarships for continuing students ($1000–$1500), 1 Third Century Scholarship for incoming freshmen ($3500), 1 President's Scholarship for incoming freshmen ($2500), 17 departmental scholarships for continuing students ($500–$1500).

Application Procedures Students apply for admission into the professional program by freshman year. Deadline for freshmen and transfers: continuous. Required: high school transcript, college transcript(s) for transfer students, minimum 3.0 high school GPA, SAT I or ACT test scores (minimum combined SAT I score of 990, minimum combined ACT score of 21), audition for scholarship consideration, portfolio for production design/technology applicants for scholarship consideration. Recommended: portfolio for production design/technology applicants. Auditions held twice in the winter on campus. Portfolio reviews held twice in the winter on campus.

Contact Ms. Vicki Hanson, Secretary, School of Theater, Ohio University, 307 Kantner Hall, Athens, Ohio 45701; 740-593-4818, fax: 740-593-4817, E-mail address: robbins@ouva.cats.ohiou.edu.

▼ OTTERBEIN COLLEGE

Westerville, Ohio

Independent-United Methodist, coed. Suburban campus. Total enrollment: 2,697.

Degrees Bachelor of Fine Arts in the areas of acting, design/technology, musical theater. Majors and concentrations: acting, design technology, music theater. Cross-

registration with members of the Higher Education Council of Columbus. Program accredited by NAST.

Enrollment Fall 1997: 128 total; all undergraduate.

Theater Student Profile 51% females, 49% males, 12% minorities.

Theater Faculty 30 total (full-time and part-time). 90% of full-time faculty have terminal degrees. Graduate students do not teach undergraduate courses.

Student Life Student groups/activities include Cap and Dagger (local theater honorary).

Expenses for 1997–98 Application fee: $20. Comprehensive fee: $19,747 includes full-time tuition ($14,997) and college room and board ($4750). College room only: $2100. Special program-related fees: $390 per quarter for private voice lessons (one hour weekly).

Financial Aid Program-specific awards for 1997: 20–35 Theater Talent Awards for program majors ($750–$4000), 400 Merit-based Scholarships for academically qualified students ($800–$8000), 100 Ammons-Thomas Awards for underrepresented students ($500–$5000).

Application Procedures Students admitted directly into the professional program freshman year. Deadline for freshmen and transfers: March 20. Notification date for freshmen and transfers: March 25. Required: high school transcript, college transcript(s) for transfer students, interview, audition, portfolio, SAT I or ACT test scores, 2 letters of recommendation for design/technology applicants. Recommended: minimum 2.5 high school GPA. Auditions held 7 times on campus; videotaped performances are permissible as a substitute for live auditions for out-of-state applicants with approval from the department. Portfolio reviews held at student's convenience on campus; the submission of slides may be substituted for portfolios for out-of-state applicants with the approval from the department.

Web Site http://www.otterbein.edu/dept/thr/index.html.

Undergraduate Contact Office of Admission, Otterbein College, One Otterbein College, Westerville, Ohio 43081-2006; 800-488-8144, fax: 614-823-1200, E-mail address: uotterb@otterbein.edu.

More About the College

Program Facilities Theater dance: 1,100-seat proscenium theater, 260-seat thrust theater, acting studio space, 5,000-square-foot scene shop, costume shop, design studio and electronic lighting system, 3-D CAD system, dance studio. Music: 275-seat recital hall, individual practice rooms, electronic music studio, computer lab, teaching and practice studios. Art: Dunlap Gallery, John Fisher Gallery, individual painting areas, ceramic and sculpture studio equipped with gas/electric kilns, pottery wheels and raku pit, Macintosh computer lab, photography darkroom, large drawing studio.

Student Performance/Exhibit Opportunities Theater/dance: six mainstage productions, nine to twelve senior workshop productions, dance concert and dance workshops, Summer Theater, directing projects. Music: four bands, Westerville Civic Symphony, percussion ensemble, small ensembles, three principal choirs, musical theater and jazz ensembles, Opera Theater, early music ensemble. Visual art: receptions and monthly exhibits for graduating seniors, interaction with visiting artists and exhibit installation opportunities.

Special Programs Theater/dance: professional guest artist program, ten-week internship program in Chicago, New York, Los Angeles, London, and regional theaters nationwide. Music: internships, opportunities to student teach abroad. Art: monthly lectures and exhibits by professional

Otterbein College (*continued*)

artists, opportunities to cross-register for course work at Columbus College of Art and Design, study-abroad programs.

Alumni Hundreds of alumni in various fields, including Dee Hoty, Tony Award nominee; David Weller, *ABC News* scenic designer, Robert Woods, Grammy Award winner and founder and president, Telarc, Inc.

▼

The arts at Otterbein College have been thriving since 1847. A solid liberal arts core of study, combined with practical career-training programs, provides students with a broad education in diverse areas of study as well as concentrated professional preparation in their chosen field.

The Department of Theater and Dance, styled as a conservatory atmosphere in a liberal arts setting, is committed to helping create artists that have both "depth and breadth." Professors strive to develop artists who have experience and knowledge not only in theater but also in other disciplines. This collage of experience gives artists the raw material to create great work as well as the tools with which to work. Students are prepared for the professional world, not only through the classroom but also through numerous audition and performance experiences. Design technology students are provided with intensive hands-on work on all productions. Utilizing guest artists, directors, and designers gives students the opportunity to work directly with professionals who are in "the business." The internship program offers students the opportunity to work with casting agents and regional theaters nationwide. NAST accredited.

The Department of Music is a member of the National Association of Schools of Music. Student performances are an academic requirement of the department as well as an integral medium of sharing by students, faculty, and guest artists. Excluding individual student recitals and cabarets, the department hosted more than fifty performances for the 1997–98 school year. Performances range from Opera Theater to faculty recitals to joint concerts with the Westerville Civic Symphony and Otterbein College Choirs. Voice and/or instrumental study is a vital part of each student's curriculum. Seven full-time and 25 adjunct faculty members work with students individually, building technique and exploring repertory.

The Department of Art faculty members are working artists who are regularly involved in all aspects of the profession. A series of foundation courses in design, drawing, and art history is integral for all students. From this conceptual, technical, and theoretical base, students then choose to concentrate in one of several art areas. Monthly exhibits and lectures coupled with an extensive College collection of African, Japanese, and Columbian art provide hands-on learning and enrich the classroom experience.

Columbus, Ohio's capital city, is becoming one of the most exciting cities in the Midwest. Points of interest span the continuum from the Columbus Museum of Art to City Center Mall, with its 160 shops and restaurants. The Columbus Symphony Orchestra, Ballet Met, Jazz Arts Group, Contemporary American Theater Company, and numerous community theaters provide a wide range of performances. Corporations such as Wendy's International and The Limited as well as historic German Village and the Short North round out this great city.

The College, which has always recognized and supported creativity as an important part of individual growth and development, believes that the arts, as an area of creative endeavor, are central to the human experience.

Bernice Young Jones School of Fine Arts

▼ OUACHITA BAPTIST UNIVERSITY

Arkadelphia, Arkansas

Independent-Baptist, coed. Small town campus. Total enrollment: 1,619. Theater program established 1996.

Degrees Bachelor of Arts in the area of musical theater (theater emphasis). Cross-registration with Henderson State University.

Enrollment Fall 1997: 40 total; all undergraduate.

Theater Student Profile 50% females, 50% males, 3% minorities, 10% international.

Theater Faculty 8 total (full-time and part-time). 67% of full-time faculty have terminal degrees. Graduate students do not teach undergraduate courses. Undergraduate student–faculty ratio: 5:1.

Student Life Student groups/activities include Broadway productions, Opera, Campus Spring Sings (Tiger Tunes).

Expenses for 1997–98 Application fee: $25. Comprehensive fee: $11,130 includes full-time tuition ($7970), mandatory fees ($120), and college room and board ($3040). College room only: $1390. Room and board charges vary according to board plan and housing facility.

Financial Aid Program-specific awards for 1997: performance grants for theater majors ($1000).

Application Procedures Students admitted directly into the professional program freshman year. Required: high school transcript, college transcript(s) for transfer students, audition, SAT I or ACT test scores (minimum combined SAT I score of 890, minimum combined ACT score of 20), Minimum 2.5 High School GPA (4.0 scale). Auditions held by appointment on campus; recorded music is permissible as a substitute for live auditions if a campus visit is impossible and videotaped performances are permissible as a substitute for live auditions if a campus visit is impossible.

Undergraduate Contact Randy Garner, Director, Admissions Department, Ouachita Baptist University, Box 3776, Arkadelphia, Arkansas 71998; 870-245-5110, fax: 870-245-5500.

▼ PACE UNIVERSITY

New York, New York

Independent, coed. Total enrollment: 13,317.

Degrees Bachelor of Fine Arts in the area of theater. Majors and concentrations: acting, directing, music theater, set design, technical theater.

Enrollment Fall 1997: 42 total; all undergraduate.

Theater Student Profile 74% females, 26% males, 30% minorities, 12% international.

Theater Faculty 9 total (full-time and part-time). 100% of full-time faculty have terminal degrees. Graduate students do not teach undergraduate courses.

Student Life Student groups/activities include Honors Program, Pace Players.

Expenses for 1997–98 Application fee: $35. Comprehensive fee: $19,920 includes full-time tuition ($13,470), mandatory

fees ($350), and college room and board ($6100). College room only: $4300. Room and board charges vary according to housing facility.

Application Procedures Students admitted directly into the professional program freshman year. Deadline for freshmen and transfers: continuous. Required: essay, high school transcript, college transcript(s) for transfer students, minimum 2.0 high school GPA, 2 letters of recommendation, interview, SAT I or ACT test scores, audition for performance majors, portfolio for design/technical theater majors. Recommended: video. Auditions held continuously on campus; videotaped performances are permissible as a substitute for live auditions. Portfolio reviews held continuously on campus.

Undergraduate Contact Undergraduate Admissions Department, Pace University, Pace Plaza, New York, New York 10038; 212-346-1323, fax: 212-346-1821.

▼ PENNSYLVANIA STATE UNIVERSITY UNIVERSITY PARK CAMPUS

University Park, Pennsylvania

State-related, coed. Small town campus. Total enrollment: 40,538. Theater program established 1935.

Degrees Bachelor of Fine Arts in the areas of production, music theater, stage management. Graduate degrees offered: Master of Fine Arts in the areas of acting, directing, costume, lighting, scene design, technical direction. Program accredited by NAST.

Enrollment Fall 1997: 187 total; 50 undergraduate, 37 graduate, 100 non-professional degree.

Theater Student Profile 63% females, 37% males, 9% minorities, 1% international.

Theater Faculty 26 total undergraduate and graduate (full-time and part-time). 98% of full-time faculty have terminal degrees. Graduate students teach a few undergraduate courses. Undergraduate student–faculty ratio: 8:1.

Student Life Student groups/activities include University Park Ensemble, Minority Theatre Workshop, Drama Duo. Special housing available for theater students.

Expenses for 1997–98 Application fee: $40. State resident tuition: $5632 full-time. Nonresident tuition: $12,206 full-time. Mandatory fees: $200 full-time. Full-time tuition and fees vary according to course level, course load, location, and program. College room and board: $4640. College room only: $2060. Room and board charges vary according to board plan.

Financial Aid Program-specific awards for 1997: 1 Mona Shibley Bird Scholarship for above-average students ($862), 2 Gallu Scholarships for freshmen ($820), 2 Lethbridge-Jackson Awards for outstanding achievement ($466), 25 Mabel Reed Knight Scholarships for those demonstrating financial need ($350–$1500), 2 Irene Richards Scholarships for sophomores demonstrating high academic achievement ($1609).

Application Procedures Deadline for freshmen and transfers: March 1. Notification date for freshmen and transfers: continuous. Required: essay, high school transcript, college transcript(s) for transfer students, minimum 2.0 high school GPA, 2 letters of recommendation, interview, audition, portfolio, SAT I or ACT test scores. Auditions held 7-8 times on campus and off campus in Chicago, IL; Irvine, CA; New York, NY; videotaped performances are permissible as a substitute for live auditions if distance is prohibitive or

scheduling is difficult. Portfolio reviews held 7-8 times on campus and off campus in Chicago, IL; Irvine, CA; New York, NY; the submission of slides may be substituted for portfolios only if accompanied by an interview.

Web Site http://www.psu.edu/dept/theatrearts/.

Undergraduate Contact Ms. Joane Stoneberg, Undergraduate Officer, School of Theatre Arts, Pennsylvania State University University Park Campus, 101B Arts Building, University Park, Pennsylvania 16802; 814-863-1451, fax: 814-865-7140, E-mail address: jrg3@psu.edu.

Graduate Contact Mr. Richard Nichols, Professor, School of Theatre Arts, Pennsylvania State University University Park Campus, 103 Arts Building, University Park, Pennsylvania 16802; 814-865-7586, fax: 814-865-7140, E-mail address: arn2@psu.edu.

▼ POINT PARK COLLEGE

Pittsburgh, Pennsylvania

Independent, coed. Urban campus. Total enrollment: 2,270.

Degrees Bachelor of Arts/Bachelor of Fine Arts in the areas of acting, musical theater, technical theater/design, arts management, stage management, children's theater. Majors and concentrations: arts management, music theater, stage management, theater arts/drama, theater design/technology. Cross-registration with Carnegie Mellon University, University of Pittsburgh, Chatham College, Robert Morris College, Duquesne University, Carlow College. Program accredited by NAST.

Enrollment Fall 1997: 210 total; all undergraduate.

Theater Student Profile 90% females, 10% males, 20% minorities, 10% international.

Theater Faculty 24 total (full-time and part-time). 80% of full-time faculty have terminal degrees. Graduate students do not teach undergraduate courses.

Student Life Student groups/activities include Theater Association of Pennsylvania, American College Theatre Foundation, University Resident Theater Association.

Expenses for 1997–98 Application fee: $20. Comprehensive fee: $16,580 includes full-time tuition ($11,050), mandatory fees ($356), and college room and board ($5174). College room only: $2550. Room and board charges vary according to board plan and housing facility. Special program-related fees: $325 per term for voice/piano private lessons, $20–$60 per term for music course fees, $35–$330 per term for performing arts instructional fee.

Financial Aid Program-specific awards for 1997: 35 Apprenticeships for those demonstrating academic achievement and talent ($500–$2000), 35 Talent Scholarships for those demonstrating academic achievement and talent ($500–$3500).

Application Procedures Deadline for freshmen and transfers: June 1. Required: high school transcript, college transcript(s) for transfer students, minimum 2.0 high school GPA, 2 letters of recommendation, interview, SAT I or ACT test scores, theater questionnaire and 2 photos, audition for acting and musical theater applicants, portfolio for technical theater, stage management and art management applicants. Auditions held 6 times on campus and off campus in Louisville, KY; state and international thespian conferences; recorded music is permissible as a substitute for live auditions if a live audition is impossible and videotaped performances are permissible as a substitute for live auditions by prior arrangement. Portfolio reviews held 6 times on campus and off campus in Louisville, KY and at state and international thespian conferences; the submission of slides may be substituted for portfolios whenever needed.

Undergraduate Contact Mr. Joseph McGoldrick, Assistant to the Chair, Department of Fine, Applied and Performing Arts, Point Park College, 201 Wood Street, Pittsburgh, Pennsylvania 15222-1984; 800-321-0129.

More About the Program

Program Facilities and Features Nine dance studios; a 3 theater complex at "The Playhouse" of Point Park College; performance opportunities for students in front of a subscription audience; on-site costume/set construction apprenticeships; 11 private singing and piano instructors; College Choir; art and design classes; more than 100 dance classes per week; ratio of 1 instructor to 14 students in acting classes; central to many educational, arts and entertainment activities; walking distance to boating, swimming, parks.

Alumni FAPA has more than 150 graduates performing in touring companies, on Broadway, in dance groups, in movies, on TV, and in other theaters, as well as many more teaching in schools, on faculties, choreographing, writing, directing, and stage managing across the world. Broadway and national touring productions of *Carousel, Cats, Joseph and the Amazing Technicolor Dreamcoat, Side Show, Tommy, Damn Yankees, The Rink, Kiss of the Spider Woman, Victor/Victoria, Les Miserables, Jekyll & Hyde, Ragtime,* and *Smokey Joe's Cafe* as well as movie and TV credits including *Pulp Fiction, NYPD Blue, Due South, The Guiding Light,* and *Leaving L.A.* are just a few of the vehicles showcasing FAPA graduates of theater and dance.

The Department of Fine, Applied and Performing Arts (FAPA) offers conservatory-oriented programs within a liberal arts context. Students receive intense training in their concentration as well as a thorough academic education. Because the faculty of FAPA believes that performing arts majors develop best in front of a live audience, the program offers many performing opportunities for students at The Playhouse.

Nationally renowned, The Playhouse of Point Park College (formerly The Pittsburgh Playhouse) is the performance facility for the Department of Fine, Applied and Performing Arts. Here students participate in live-theater/dance experiences before a subscription audience. Comprised of 3 working theaters, this 60-year-old facility is fully staffed by a production team of designers and artisans who train and supervise student apprentices in building, designing, lighting, and managing shows. The front-of-house staff, box office, and public relations personnel engage all students in the business aspect of running a theater. The season, which features student actors, dancers, designers, and stage managers, consists of 5 Playhouse, Jr., shows for children; 4 College Theatre Company dramas and musicals; and 2 Playhouse Theatre Company presentations for professional faculty, alumni, visiting artists, and selected undergraduates.

Dance students are featured in 3 Playhouse Dance Theatre productions, a student choreography showcase, and a Playhouse, Jr. Children's Dance Show as well as a public school outreach program in cooperation with the Gateway to Music organization.

The B.F.A. degree in Film and Video Production is offered in collaboration with Pittsburgh Filmmakers. Students take their academic courses at Point Park College and their film and video requirements at Pittsburgh Filmmakers'

newly built facility in the Oakland section of Pittsburgh. Both institutions work together to ensure that students receive a challenging educational experience.

The B.A. degree in Arts Management is designed for students who wish to pursue a career in arts management but who are not primarily interested in pursuing a professional performance career. The departmental requirements in business, finance, and management courses along with selected art courses provide a solid base from which entry-level employment in any one of a wide variety of arts management areas (marketing, development, financial management, performing company, etc.) is possible.

The B.F.A. degree in Arts Management is designed for students who wish to pursue a dual career in arts management and in performance. The curriculum includes the same foundation requirements as the B.A. program, but students choose one artistic focus: dance, theater, or music. A performance requirement focus is an expectation in the B.F.A. degree.

The innovative B.A. in Children's Theatre degree program provides opportunities for majors to plan, teach, and direct creative drama activities within the Children's School of the Education Department, Playhouse, Jr., or classes offered by the Community Conservatories of Dance, Music and Theatre (noncredit classes are also offered through FAPA). An Elementary Teaching Certificate for Pennsylvania is structured into this 4-year degree.

A Theater Communications degree prepares students to teach at the high school level in drama and English. A Secondary Teaching Certificate for Pennsylvania is part of this 4-year degree.

FAPA faculty are working professionals in acting, singing, dancing, writing, composing, painting, designing, choreography, and other specialties. Guest artists and master teachers in musical theater, voice and speech, and dance are regularly featured. Past guests include Chita Rivera, Michael Rupert, Jeff Shade, Rob Ashford, Sherry Zunker-Dow, Cicely Berry, Paul Gavert, Patricia Wilde, Albert Poland, Barbara Pontecorvo, Edward Villella, Maxine Sherman, Marshall Swiney, and Claire Bataille. The program also offers many workshops and collaborative efforts of an interdisciplinary nature with other college programs.

During the summer, FAPA offers an International Summer Dance program (open by audition) featuring renowned names in the world of dance. An exceptional theater program culminates in a play/musical presentation. The International Summer Dance program offers jazz, ballet, Alexander, and modern with famous names such as Laura Alonso, Roberto Munoz, Miguel Campaneria, Alexander Filipov, Michael Uthoff, and Whilheim Burman. The program culminates in a recital performance.

The community of Pittsburgh itself is an arts and education center with the Pittsburgh Symphony, Opera, Ballet, and Dance Council and the Pittsburgh Public Theaters supplemented by 8 other institutions of higher learning within a 15-minute drive. The whole city is truly the campus of the programs.

Prospective applicants must apply and be accepted by the college. An audition for and an interview with faculty is required for all prospective majors. Scholarships/Apprenticeships from $750 to $2500 are based on either talent or academics, or both. Presidential and Special academic full- and part-time awards are highly competitive.

Off-campus auditions are possible at Thespian and Dance conferences at San Juan, Puerto Rico, Chicago, New York,

Ohio, Philadelphia, Pennsylvania, and Louisville, Kentucky. Videotaped auditions acceptable under special circumstances.

For more information and audition guidelines, contact Joseph McGoldrick, Assistant to the Chair, Point Park College, 201 Wood Street, Pittsburgh, Pennsylvania 15222, or call 800-321-0129.

▼ POTTER COLLEGE OF ARTS, HUMANITIES, AND SOCIAL SCIENCES

See Western Kentucky University

▼ PURCHASE COLLEGE, STATE UNIVERSITY OF NEW YORK

Purchase, New York

State-supported, coed. Small town campus. Total enrollment: 3,297.

Degrees Bachelor of Fine Arts in the areas of acting, design technology, film. Graduate degrees offered: Master of Fine Arts in the areas of theater design, theater technology. Program accredited by CUPTP.

Enrollment Fall 1997: 233 total; 228 undergraduate, 5 graduate.

Theater Student Profile 40% females, 60% males, 15% minorities, 2% international.

Theater Faculty 40 total undergraduate and graduate (full-time and part-time). 100% of full-time faculty have terminal degrees. Graduate students do not teach undergraduate courses.

Expenses for 1997–98 Application fee: $30. State resident tuition: $3400 full-time. Nonresident tuition: $8300 full-time. Mandatory fees: $479 full-time. College room and board: $5264. College room only: $1930. Room and board charges vary according to board plan and housing facility.

Financial Aid Program-specific awards for 1997: 30–35 college scholarships for those demonstrating talent, academic achievement, and need ($500–$4500), 1–4 Empire Minority Awards for minority students from New York State ($1250), 7 Reed Scholarships for students with high academic and artistic achievement ($500).

Application Procedures Students admitted directly into the professional program freshman year. Deadline for freshmen and transfers: March 1. Notification date for freshmen and transfers: May 1. Required: high school transcript, essay for film applicants, audition for acting applicants, portfolio for design and technical theater applicants, minimun TOEFL score of 550 for international applicants. Recommended: letter of recommendation, picture and resume for acting applicants, interview for design, technical theater applicants. Auditions held at various times for acting students and in February and March for design tech students on campus and off campus in Seattle, WA; New York, NY; San Francisco, CA; Chicago, IL; Houston, TX; Miami, FL; Los Angeles, CA; Atlanta, GA; videotaped performances are permissible as a substitute for live auditions for international applicants or with approval from the department for domestic applicants. Portfolio reviews held at various times on campus and off campus in various locations; the submission of slides may be substituted for portfolios with some original work.

Undergraduate Contact Ms. Janicemarie Hamm, Admissions Counselor, Conservatory of Theatre Arts and Film, Purchase College, State University of New York, 735 Anderson Hill Road, Purchase, New York 10577-1400; 914-251-6300, fax: 914-251-6314.

Graduate Contact Mr. Michael Cesario, Coordinator, Theatre Design/Technology Program, Purchase College, State University of New York, 735 Anderson Hill Road, Purchase, New York 10577; 914-251-6851, fax: 914-251-6841.

More About the College

Professional training for a professional career in acting, design technology, and film is the dominant goal of the program. Young artists are selected for both the intensity of their interest in becoming professionals and their professional potential. The program offers focused and in-depth training in theater and film with a faculty that is itself working, creating, and succeeding in New York's professional world.

The community of students and professional faculty are constantly enriched by the creative bustle and aesthetic influence of New York City, just 30 minutes away. They work and strive together on the modern Purchase campus and Performing Arts Center located in Westchester County, a beautiful and elegant suburb of New York City.

Practical learning and practical experience is the daily life for the student artist at Purchase. State-of-the-art equipment, theaters, and work spaces for every aspect of training abound in this woods-surrounded center of contemporary art and learning.

All classes, rehearsals, productions, and filming are taught and supervised by men and women who are contributing participants in the professional artistic life of New York City, the United States, and the international arts communities. These artist-teachers have a common goal: to thoroughly train young artists so that the individual creativity of each student is preserved and augmented by the most strenuous and critical practice and performance standards possible.

In addition to this serious concentration in the arts, each student is offered one class a semester in liberal arts so that a grounding in our cultural heritage is part of his or her development. Life at Purchase consists of a rich social intermix of the performing and visual arts with the more traditional academic life of the Liberal Arts and Sciences.

The student's life after graduation is a powerfully active concern of the training program. Therefore, as the student gains proficiency, his or her work has gradually been presented to the professional community, and, by the time of graduation, when the work is formally introduced to that professional community using New York City presentations of actors; internships, portfolio reviews, and faculty personal contacts for designers; and completed student films (for filmmakers), Purchase students find that an extraordinary number of doors open for them: agents, producers, theaters, film companies, and television producers are available for the next creative and working step of the Purchase graduate.

The Conservatory of Theatre Arts and Film is now graduating some of the most exciting and successful young actors, designers, and filmmakers in America. It is not only the flagship program of the State University of New York but also among the finest and most prestigious of the conservatory programs offered in the disciplines of theater and film in the United States.

The Purchase College Conservatory of Theatre Arts and Film is a member of the Consortium of Undergraduate Professional Theatre Training Programs.

▼ ROOSEVELT UNIVERSITY
Chicago, Illinois

Independent, coed. Urban campus. Total enrollment: 6,605. Theater program established 1988.

Degrees Bachelor of Fine Arts in the areas of theater, musical theater. Majors and concentrations: music theater, performance. Graduate degrees offered: Master of Fine Arts in the areas of theater, musical theater, directing/dramaturgy.

Enrollment Fall 1997: 103 total; 65 undergraduate, 34 graduate, 4 non-professional degree.

Theater Student Profile 70% females, 30% males, 20% minorities, 10% international.

Theater Faculty 16 total undergraduate and graduate (full-time and part-time). 100% of full-time faculty have terminal degrees. Graduate students do not teach undergraduate courses. Undergraduate student–faculty ratio: 12:1.

Expenses for 1997–98 Application fee: $25. Comprehensive fee: $16,530 includes full-time tuition ($10,830), mandatory fees ($200), and college room and board ($5500).

Financial Aid Program-specific awards for 1997: 75 Theatre Award Scholarship ($1000–$7000), 60 Institutional Support Awards.

Application Procedures Students admitted directly into the professional program freshman year. Deadline for freshmen and transfers: continuous. Required: high school transcript, college transcript(s) for transfer students, minimum 2.0 high school GPA, 3 letters of recommendation, interview, audition, SAT I or ACT test scores, minimum 2.0 college GPA for transfer students. Recommended: essay, minimum 3.0 high school GPA. Auditions held continuously on campus and off campus in Lincoln, NE; Los Angeles, CA; Chicago, IL; New York, NY; Las Vegas, NV; San Francisco, CA; videotaped performances are permissible as a substitute for live auditions.

Web Site http://www.roosevelt.edu.

Contact Dr. Joel G. Fink, Director, Theatre Program, Roosevelt University, 430 South Michigan Avenue, Chicago, Illinois 60605; 312-341-3719, fax: 312-341-3814.

▼ RUTGERS, THE STATE UNIVERSITY OF NEW JERSEY
See Mason Gross School of the Arts

▼ SALEM STATE COLLEGE
Salem, Massachusetts

State-supported, coed. Small town campus. Theater program established 1984.

Degrees Bachelor of Fine Arts in the area of theater. Majors and concentrations: acting, costume design, lighting design, set design, technical theater.

Enrollment Fall 1997: 147 total; 81 undergraduate, 66 non-professional degree.

Theater Student Profile 75% females, 25% males, 2% minorities, 2% international.

Theater Faculty 19 total (full-time and part-time). 75% of full-time faculty have terminal degrees. Graduate students do not teach undergraduate courses. Undergraduate student–faculty ratio: 10:1.

Student Life Student groups/activities include Student Theater Ensemble, Salem State Summer Theater, Repertory Dance Theater.

Financial Aid Program-specific awards for 1997: 5–7 Presidential Arts Scholarships for program majors ($2500).

Application Procedures Students apply for admission into the professional program by freshman year. Deadline for freshmen and transfers: continuous. Required: high school transcript, college transcript(s) for transfer students, minimum 2.0 high school GPA, audition for acting majors, portfolio for design/technical theater majors. Recommended: essay, minimum 3.0 high school GPA, 2 letters of recommendation, interview, video. Auditions held twice on campus; recorded music is permissible as a substitute for live auditions if outside of the New England five state region and videotaped performances are permissible as a substitute for live auditions if out of the New England five state region. Portfolio reviews held twice on campus; the submission of slides may be substituted for portfolios if applicant is outside of the New England five state region.

Undergraduate Contact Mr. James Fallon, Chair, Department of Theatre and Speech Communication, Salem State College, Salem, Massachusetts 01970; 978-542-6290, fax: 978-542-6291.

▼ SCHMIDT COLLEGE OF ARTS AND LETTERS
See Florida Atlantic University

▼ SHENANDOAH UNIVERSITY
Winchester, Virginia

Independent-United Methodist, coed. Small town campus. Total enrollment: 1,927.

Degrees Bachelor of Fine Arts in the areas of music theater, theater for youth; Bachelor of Arts in the area of theater. Majors and concentrations: music theater, theater arts/drama, theater for youth.

Enrollment Fall 1997: 131 total; all undergraduate.

Theater Student Profile 58% females, 42% males, 5% minorities.

Theater Faculty 7 total (full-time and part-time). 67% of full-time faculty have terminal degrees. Graduate students do not teach undergraduate courses. Undergraduate student–faculty ratio: 19:1.

Student Life Student groups/activities include Alpha Psi Omega fraternity shows, Special Workshops, Children's Theater.

Expenses for 1997–98 Application fee: $30. Comprehensive fee: $19,450 includes full-time tuition ($14,400) and college room and board ($5050). Full-time tuition varies according to course load, degree level, and program. Room and board charges vary according to board plan.

Financial Aid Program-specific awards for 1997: 74 Talent Scholarships for program students ($250–$1600).

Application Procedures Students admitted directly into the professional program freshman year. Deadline for freshmen and transfers: continuous. Required: high school transcript, college transcript(s) for transfer students, minimum 2.0 high school GPA, interview, video, audition, SAT I or ACT test scores, portfolio for design majors. Recommended: letter of recommendation, portfolio. Auditions held 10 times on campus and off campus in various cities; recorded music is permissible as a substitute for live auditions if a campus visit is impossible and videotaped performances are permissible as a substitute for live auditions if a campus visit is impossible. Portfolio reviews held throughout the year on campus and off campus in various cities.

Undergraduate Contact Mr. Michael Carpenter, Director, Admissions Office, Shenandoah University, 1460 University Drive, Winchester, Virginia 22601-5195; 540-665-4581, fax: 540-665-4627, E-mail address: admit@su.edu.

▼ SIMON FRASER UNIVERSITY

Burnaby, BC, Canada

Province-supported, coed. Suburban campus. Total enrollment: 18,759. Theater program established 1992.

Degrees Bachelor of Fine Arts in the area of theater. Graduate degrees offered: Master of Fine Arts in the area of interdisciplinary studies.

Enrollment Fall 1997: 71 total.

Theater Faculty 3 total undergraduate and graduate (full-time). 75% of full-time faculty have terminal degrees. Graduate students teach a few undergraduate courses.

Student Life Student groups/activities include Black Box Theater Company.

Expenses for 1997–98 Application fee: $25 Canadian dollars. Tuition, fee, and room only charges are reported in Canadian dollars. Canadian resident tuition: $2310 full-time. Mandatory fees: $207 full-time. College room only: $2830. Room charges vary according to housing facility. International student tuition: $6930 full-time. Special program-related fees: $35 per course for materials fee.

Financial Aid Program-specific awards for 1997: 1 Murray Farr Award for program majors ($500), 5 Adaline May Clark Scholarships for program majors ($100–$500).

Application Procedures Students apply for admission into the professional program by sophomore year. Deadline for freshmen and transfers: May 1. Required: high school transcript, minimum 3.0 high school GPA, audition. Auditions held twice on campus.

Web Site http://www.sfu.ca/sca.

Undergraduate Contact Admissions Office, Simon Fraser University, 8888 University Drive, Burnaby, BC V5A 1S6; 604-291-3224, fax: 604-291-4969.

Graduate Contact Chair, MFA Program, School for the Contemporary Arts, Simon Fraser University, 8888 University Drive, Burnaby, BC V5A 1S6, Canada; 604-291-3492, fax: 604-291-5907, E-mail address: mfa_grad_office@sfu.ca.

Meadows School of the Arts

▼ SOUTHERN METHODIST UNIVERSITY

Dallas, Texas

Independent, coed. Suburban campus. Total enrollment: 9,708.

Degrees Bachelor of Fine Arts in the area of theater. Majors and concentrations: acting, theater studies. Graduate degrees offered: Master of Fine Arts in the areas of theater, acting, directing. Program accredited by NAST.

Enrollment Fall 1997: 138 total; 117 undergraduate, 21 graduate.

Theater Student Profile 49% females, 51% males, 16% minorities, 3% international.

Theater Faculty 23 total undergraduate and graduate (full-time and part-time). 89% of full-time faculty have terminal degrees. Graduate students teach a few undergraduate courses.

Student Life Special housing available for theater students.

Expenses for 1997–98 Application fee: $40. Comprehensive fee: $23,244 includes full-time tuition ($14,896), mandatory fees ($1894), and college room and board ($6454). College room only: $3600. Room and board charges vary according to board plan and housing facility.

Financial Aid Program-specific awards for 1997: 20 Meadows Artistic Scholarships for talented program majors ($1000–$5000).

Application Procedures Students admitted directly into the professional program freshman year. Deadline for freshmen and transfers: March 1. Required: essay, high school transcript, college transcript(s) for transfer students, letter of recommendation, audition, SAT I or ACT test scores. Recommended: interview. Auditions held 20 times on campus and off campus in various locations.

Web Site http://www.smu.edu/~meadows/.

Undergraduate Contact Cecil O'Neal, Professor of Theatre, Division of Theatre, Southern Methodist University, Meadows School of the Arts, PO Box 750356, Dallas, Texas 75275-0356; 214-768-2545, fax: 214-768-1136, E-mail address: coneal@mail.smu.edu.

Graduate Contact Division of Theatre, Southern Methodist University, Meadows School of the Arts, PO Box 750356, Dallas, Texas 75275-0356; 214-768-2558, fax: 214-768-1136.

▼ SOUTHERN OREGON UNIVERSITY

Ashland, Oregon

State-supported, coed. Small town campus. Total enrollment: 5,426.

Degrees Bachelor of Fine Arts in the area of theater arts. Majors and concentrations: theater arts/drama.

Enrollment Fall 1997: 133 undergraduate.

Theater Student Profile 53% females, 47% males, 8% minorities, 3% international.

Theater Faculty 9 total undergraduate (full-time and part-time). 100% of full-time faculty have terminal degrees. Graduate students do not teach undergraduate courses. Undergraduate student–faculty ratio: 20:1.

Expenses for 1997–98 Application fee: $50. State resident tuition: $3204 full-time. Nonresident tuition: $9153 full-time. Full-time tuition varies according to course load and reciprocity agreements. College room and board: $4380. Room and board charges vary according to board plan and housing facility.

Financial Aid Program-specific awards for 1997: 1 Angus Bowmer Award for acting, directing majors ($1000), 1 Harry Bartell Award for actors ($1500), 1 Leon Mulling Award for program majors ($1500), 10 departmental awards for program majors ($500).

Application Procedures Students apply for admission into the professional program by sophomore year. Deadline for freshmen and transfers: continuous. Required: high school transcript, college transcript(s) for transfer students, minimum 3.0 high school GPA, 3 letters of recommendation,

Southern Oregon University (continued)

interview, audition, portfolio, SAT I or ACT test scores. Auditions held twice on campus. Portfolio reviews held twice on campus; the submission of slides may be substituted for portfolios for applicants in technical areas.

Web Site http://www.sou.edu/thtr.

Undergraduate Contact Mr. Allen H. Blaszak, Director of Admissions, Southern Oregon University, 1250 Siskiyou Boulevard, Ashland, Oregon 97520; 541-552-6411, fax: 541-552-6329.

▼ SOUTHWESTERN UNIVERSITY

Georgetown, Texas

Independent-Methodist, coed. Suburban campus. Total enrollment: 1,215.

Degrees Bachelor of Fine Arts in the area of theater. Cross-registration with Ohio Wesleyan University.

Enrollment Fall 1997: 52 undergraduate.

Theater Student Profile 65% females, 35% males, 5% minorities.

Theater Faculty 6 total (full-time and part-time). 100% of full-time faculty have terminal degrees. Graduate students do not teach undergraduate courses. Undergraduate student–faculty ratio: 12:1.

Student Life Student groups/activities include Alpha Psi Omega, Mask and Wig Players.

Expenses for 1997–98 Application fee: $40. Comprehensive fee: $19,270 includes full-time tuition ($14,000) and college room and board ($5270). College room only: $2470. Room and board charges vary according to board plan and housing facility.

Financial Aid Program-specific awards for 1997: 15 departmental scholarships for program students ($1500).

Application Procedures Students apply for admission into the professional program by sophomore year. Deadline for freshmen and transfers: April 1. Required: essay, high school transcript, college transcript(s) for transfer students, minimum 3.0 high school GPA, letter of recommendation, interview, audition, SAT I or ACT test scores. Auditions held by appointment on campus; videotaped performances are permissible as a substitute for live auditions when distance is prohibitive.

Undergraduate Contact Dr. Richard J. Hossalla, Chair, Theater and Communications Department, Southwestern University, 1001 East University Avenue, Georgetown, Texas 78626; 512-863-1365, fax: 512-863-1422.

▼ SOUTHWEST MISSOURI STATE UNIVERSITY

Springfield, Missouri

State-supported, coed. Suburban campus. Total enrollment: 16,468.

Degrees Bachelor of Fine Arts in the area of theater. Program accredited by NAST.

Enrollment Fall 1997: 160 total; all undergraduate.

Theater Student Profile 60% females, 40% males, 5% minorities, 1% international.

Theater Faculty 13 total (full-time and part-time). 85% of full-time faculty have terminal degrees. Graduate students do not teach undergraduate courses. Undergraduate student–faculty ratio: 16:1.

Student Life Student groups/activities include In-School Players, Footnotes Entertainment Troupe, Bare Stage Peer Education Troupe.

Expenses for 1998–99 Application fee: $15. State resident tuition: $2940 full-time. Nonresident tuition: $5880 full-time. Mandatory fees: $274 full-time. Full-time tuition and fees vary according to course load. College room and board: $3594. College room only: $2396. Room and board charges vary according to board plan and housing facility.

Financial Aid Program-specific awards for 1997: 12 Theatre Activity Awards for program majors ($2000), 6 In-School Players Awards for program majors ($2000), 10 out-of-state waivers for program majors ($2000).

Application Procedures Students apply for admission into the professional program by sophomore year. Deadline for freshmen and transfers: August 1. Required: high school transcript, minimum 2.0 high school GPA, ACT test score only, standing in top 67% of graduating class.

Web Site http://www.smsu.edu¢ontrib he_dan.

Undergraduate Contact Dr. Robert H. Bradley, Head, Department of Theatre and Dance, Southwest Missouri State University, 901 South National, Springfield, Missouri 65804; 417-836-5268, fax: 417-836-6940, E-mail address: rhb072f@vma. smsu.edu.

▼ STATE UNIVERSITY OF NEW YORK AT NEW PALTZ

New Paltz, New York

State-supported, coed. Small town campus. Total enrollment: 7,641.

Degrees Bachelor of Fine Arts in the area of scenography. Program accredited by NAST.

Enrollment Fall 1997: 100 undergraduate.

Theater Faculty 14 total (full-time and part-time). 88% of full-time faculty have terminal degrees. Graduate students do not teach undergraduate courses.

Student Life Student groups/activities include New Paltz Players, Alpha Psi Omega.

Estimated expenses for 1998–99 Application fee: $30. State resident tuition: $3400 full-time. Nonresident tuition: $8300 full-time. Mandatory fees: $485 full-time. College room and board: $5020. College room only: $3000. Room and board charges vary according to board plan.

Financial Aid Program-specific awards for 1997: 10 Bruce Bennett Scholarships for program majors and non-majors ($500).

Application Procedures Students apply for admission into the professional program by freshman year. Deadline for freshmen and transfers: continuous. Notification date for freshmen and transfers: continuous. Required: high school transcript, audition, SAT I or ACT test scores (minimum combined SAT I score of 1100, minimum combined ACT score of 24). Recommended: interview. Auditions held twice in the spring and by appointment on campus; videotaped performances are permissible as a substitute for live auditions if a live audition is impossible.

Undergraduate Contact Ms. Beverly Brumm, Chair, Theatre Arts Department, State University of New York at New Paltz, 75

South Manheim Boulevard, New Paltz, New York 12561-2443; 914-257-3865, fax: 914-257-3882.

▼ STATE UNIVERSITY OF NEW YORK COLLEGE AT FREDONIA

Fredonia, New York

State-supported, coed. Small town campus. Total enrollment: 4,593. Theater program established 1970.

Degrees Bachelor of Fine Arts in the areas of acting, musical theater, production design. Program accredited by NAST.

Enrollment Fall 1997: 75 total; all undergraduate.

Theater Student Profile 65% females, 35% males, 5% minorities.

Theater Faculty 8 total (full-time and part-time). 100% of full-time faculty have terminal degrees. Graduate students do not teach undergraduate courses. Undergraduate student–faculty ratio: 12:1.

Student Life Student groups/activities include Performing Arts Company, Opera Theatre, Orchesis Dance.

Expenses for 1997–98 Application fee: $30. State resident tuition: $3400 full-time. Nonresident tuition: $8300 full-time. Mandatory fees: $675 full-time. College room and board: $4650. College room only: $3000. Room and board charges vary according to board plan and housing facility. Special program-related fees: $12 for visiting artist program.

Financial Aid Program-specific awards for 1997: 1 Jack Cogdill Scholarship for incoming freshmen ($1250).

Application Procedures Students admitted directly into the professional program freshman year. Deadline for freshmen and transfers: continuous. Required: high school transcript, college transcript(s) for transfer students, 2 letters of recommendation, interview, audition, SAT I or ACT test scores. Recommended: minimum 3.0 high school GPA, portfolio for production design applicants. Auditions held throughout the year by appointment on campus and off campus in Selden, NY; Troy, NY; recorded music is permissible as a substitute for live auditions if a live audition is impossible and videotaped performances are permissible as a substitute for live auditions if a live audition is impossible. Portfolio reviews held throughout the year by appointment on campus; the submission of slides may be substituted for portfolios if a campus visit is impossible.

Web Site http://www.fredonia.edu/department/theatre/index.htm.

Undergraduate Contact Dr. Robert Klassen, Chairperson, Department of Theatre Arts, State University of New York College at Fredonia, Rockefeller Arts Center, Fredonia, New York 14063; 716-673-3596, fax: 716-673-3621.

▼ STATE UNIVERSITY OF NEW YORK COLLEGE AT PURCHASE

See Purchase College, State University of New York

▼ STEPHEN F. AUSTIN STATE UNIVERSITY

Nacogdoches, Texas

State-supported, coed. Small town campus. Total enrollment: 12,041. Theater program established 1972.

Degrees Bachelor of Fine Arts in the area of theater. Majors and concentrations: performance, technical theater. Graduate degrees offered: Master of Arts in the area of theater. Cross-registration with Rose Bruford College (United Kingdom). Program accredited by NAST.

Enrollment Fall 1997: 110 total; 105 undergraduate, 5 graduate.

Theater Student Profile 65% females, 35% males, 2% minorities.

Theater Faculty 9 total undergraduate and graduate (full-time and part-time). 85% of full-time faculty have terminal degrees. Graduate students teach a few undergraduate courses. Undergraduate student–faculty ratio: 18:1.

Student Life Student groups/activities include Beta Phi Chapter of Alpha Psi Omega.

Expenses for 1997–98 Application fee: $0. One-time mandatory fee: $10. State resident tuition: $1020 full-time. Nonresident tuition: $7440 full-time. Mandatory fees: $1168 full-time. Full-time tuition and fees vary according to course load and reciprocity agreements. College room and board: $3682. Room and board charges vary according to board plan and housing facility. Special program-related fees: $7–$15 per course for supplies, $10 for theater admission.

Financial Aid Program-specific awards for 1997: 8–10 departmental scholarships for incoming students passing audition evaluations ($750–$1000), 1 Gray Scholarship for Nacogdoches County, TX residents ($500), 5–8 Stokes Foundation Scholarships for enrolled students ($600–$1000), 1 Cochran Scholarship for enrolled students ($700), 1 alumni scholarship for enrolled students ($500), 1 McGrath Scholarship for enrolled students ($700).

Application Procedures Students apply for admission into the professional program by sophomore year. Deadline for freshmen and transfers: continuous. Required: high school transcript, minimum 2.0 high school GPA, portfolio, SAT I or ACT test scores, evaluation interview at end of sophomore year. Recommended: audition for scholarship consideration. Auditions held 4 times on campus and off campus in conjunction with Texas Educational Theatre Association Convention and other regional festivals; videotaped performances are permissible as a substitute for live auditions when distance is prohibitive. Portfolio reviews held 4 times for design and technology applicants on campus and off campus in Texas Educational Theatre Association Convention; the submission of slides may be substituted for portfolios if a campus visit is impossible.

Undergraduate Contact Mr. Clarence W. Bahs, Chairman, Theatre Department, Stephen F. Austin State University, PO Box 9090 SFA Station, Nacogdoches, Texas 75962-9090; 409-468-4003, fax: 409-468-7601, E-mail address: cbahs@sfasu.edu.

Graduate Contact Dr. Alan Nielsen, Professor / Graduate Coordinator, Theatre Department, Stephen F. Austin State University, PO Box 9090 SFA Station, Nacogdoches, Texas 75962-9090; 409-468-4003, fax: 409-468-7601, E-mail address: anielsen@sfasu.edu.

▼ STEPHENS COLLEGE

Columbia, Missouri

Independent, women only. Urban campus. Total enrollment: 819. Theater program established 1833.

Degrees Bachelor of Fine Arts in the area of theater arts. Majors and concentrations: acting, design, directing, technical theater, theater arts/drama. Cross-registration with University of Missouri-Columbia.

Stephens College (continued)

Enrollment Fall 1997: 84 total.

Theater Student Profile 98% females, 2% males.

Theater Faculty 76 total (full-time and part-time). 80% of full-time faculty have terminal degrees. Graduate students do not teach undergraduate courses. Undergraduate student–faculty ratio: 11:1.

Student Life Student groups/activities include Warehouse Theatre, Velvetones-vocal group. Special housing available for theater students.

Expenses for 1997–98 Application fee: $25. Comprehensive fee: $20,530 includes full-time tuition ($14,830) and college room and board ($5700). College room only: $2990. Room and board charges vary according to board plan and housing facility.

Financial Aid Program-specific awards for 1997: 2 Musical Theater Awards for vocalists ($3000), 1 Annie Potts Award for actors ($3000), 1 Patricia Barry Award for actors ($1500), 1 Maude Adams Award for actors ($1000), Stephens Leadership Award ($1000–$3000).

Application Procedures Students admitted directly into the professional program freshman year. Deadline for freshmen and transfers: June 1. Notification date for freshmen: continuous; transfers: August 1. Required: essay, high school transcript, college transcript(s) for transfer students, minimum 2.0 high school GPA, 2 letters of recommendation, SAT I or ACT test scores, portfolio for design/technical applicants. Recommended: minimum 3.0 high school GPA, interview, video, audition. Auditions held at various times off campus in National Association of College Admission Counselor thespian festival locations; recorded music is permissible as a substitute for live auditions when distance is prohibitive and videotaped performances are permissible as a substitute for live auditions when distance is prohibitive. Portfolio reviews held as needed on campus and off campus in various locations.

Undergraduate Contact John F. Fluke, Dean of Enrollment Services, Office of Admissions, Stephens College, Box 2121, Columbia, Missouri 65215; 800-876-7207, fax: 573-876-7248.

▼ SYRACUSE UNIVERSITY

Syracuse, New York

Independent, coed. Urban campus. Total enrollment: 14,557. Theater program established 1921.

Degrees Bachelor of Fine Arts in the areas of drama, musical theater, design/technical theater; Bachelor of Science in the area of drama. Majors and concentrations: acting, design/technical theater, music theater, stage management, technical theater. Graduate degrees offered: Master of Fine Arts in the areas of drama, design theater. Program accredited by NAST.

Enrollment Fall 1997: 430 total; 200 undergraduate, 15 graduate, 215 non-professional degree.

Theater Student Profile 63% females, 37% males, 11% minorities, 1% international.

Theater Faculty 23 total undergraduate and graduate (full-time and part-time). 69% of full-time faculty have terminal degrees. Graduate students teach a few undergraduate courses. Undergraduate student–faculty ratio: 12:1.

Student Life Student groups/activities include Syracuse University Musical Stage, Danceworks, Black Box Players.

Expenses for 1997–98 Application fee: $40. Comprehensive fee: $25,816 includes full-time tuition ($17,550), mandatory fees ($506), and college room and board ($7760). College room only: $4090. Room and board charges vary according to board plan and housing facility. Special program-related fees: $180–$360 per credit hour for private music lessons, $10 per semester for piano maintenance.

Financial Aid Program-specific awards for 1997: 17 Chancellor's Awards for those demonstrating academic achievement ($6000), 40 Dean's Awards for those demonstrating academic achievement ($4000).

Application Procedures Students admitted directly into the professional program freshman year. Deadline for freshmen: January 15; transfers: July 1. Notification date for freshmen: March 15; transfers: August 15. Required: essay, high school transcript, college transcript(s) for transfer students, minimum 2.0 high school GPA, 2 letters of recommendation, SAT I or ACT test scores, audition for acting and musical theater applicants, high school counselor evaluation, portfolio for design/technical theater applicants. Recommended: minimum 3.0 high school GPA, interview. Auditions held 10 times on campus and off campus in New York, NY; Washington, DC; videotaped performances are permissible as a substitute for live auditions. Portfolio reviews held 7 times on campus; the submission of slides may be substituted for portfolios if original work is not available.

Web Site http://vpa.syr.edu.

Undergraduate Contact Coordinator of Recruiting, College of Visual and Performing Arts, Syracuse University, 202P Crouse College, Syracuse, New York 13244-1010; 315-443-2769, fax: 315-443-1935, E-mail address: admissu@vpa.syr.edu.

Graduate Contact Graduate School, Syracuse University, Suite 303 Bowne Hall, Syracuse, New York 13244; 315-443-3028, fax: 315-443-3423, E-mail address: gradschl@suadmin.syr.edu.

More About the University

Program Facilities Regent Theatre Complex: John D. Archbold Theatre (500 seats), Arthur Storch Theatre (200 seats), Black Box Theatre (60 seats), Sutton Pavilion (75-seat cabaret space); new studio and classroom building: dance studios, seminar rooms, design labs with a CAD lab, lecture rooms, performance/rehearsal studios, music practice rooms, and shower and locker rooms.

Faculty, Resident Artists, and Alumni Many faculty are members of the Actors' Equity Association; all are working artists as well as teachers. Several Syracuse Stage professionals, including the artistic director, teach in the drama program. Among the ranks of alumni are Tony award winners, New York City talent and casting agents, actors on Broadway and television and in movies, playwrights, screenplay and movie writers, and artistic and managing directors of theater companies.

Student Theater Opportunities Department of Drama productions, Syracuse Stage, Black Box Players student group, After Ours cabaret theater series.

Special Programs The Department of Drama's partnership with Syracuse Stage allows undergraduates to experience professional theater while in school. Study abroad in London is offered through SU's Division of International Programs Abroad (DIPA). Internships at Syracuse Stage, in New York City or Los Angeles, or through DIPA are available for credit or in a volunteer capacity. Each Wednesday, Drama Lab brings students together with visiting artists, alumni, agents, and union representatives, or to perform scenes from class. Qualified seniors travel to New York City in the spring for "Scene Night," a presentation of scenes and songs for New York agents and casting directors. All University activities are available to students in the Department of Drama. Honors program is available for students who desire a rigorous academic challenge.

▼

The Department of Drama at Syracuse University offers students the chance to study acting, musical theater, stage management, technical theater, or design/technical theater. Students nurture their creative abilities through a unique combination of active faculty members, diverse performance and staging opportunities, excellent facilities, and a liberal education. Students prepare for a professional career in theater beginning with the first semester; four years are spent in intensive work in the major in tandem with academic course work taken in other areas of the University.

The first year is a nonperformance year that allows young actors to focus on developing their basic acting and musical theater skills. From the second year on, drama students compete for roles in the thirty to forty productions produced each year by the Department of Drama, Syracuse Stage, the Black Box Players, and the After Ours cabaret series. Considered an extension of classroom work, mainstage drama department productions are reserved for drama majors only. In addition, drama majors may earn equity points by working in Syracuse Stage productions.

Design/technical theater majors at SU have a particular advantage: they can work as assistants to professional designers on Syracuse Stage productions and as assistants to faculty designers on mainstage Drama Department productions. They may also create their own designs in the Black Box and After Ours shows. Junior and senior design majors can create their own designs for the department mainstage shows. In addition, a unique partnership with the School of Art and Design provides opportunities for design/technical theater freshmen to develop their drawing and sketching skills.

The Regent Theatre Complex, shared by the Department of Drama and Syracuse Stage, houses four performance spaces that provide a broad range of possibilities.

The department's affiliation with Syracuse Stage, one of the country's outstanding Equity theater companies, opens the world of professional theater to students. Faculty members are not only outstanding teachers and mentors but also successful theater professionals. All performance and studio classes in acting, design, and musical theater are taught by full-time faculty members, including freshman courses.

Graduates of the Department of Drama are involved in every aspect of professional theater, from lead roles in Broadway plays and musicals and television dramas to casting directors and Actors' Equity Association staff members. Alumni return to campus each year for panel discussions, to bring their professional experiences to students.

Through the University's Division of International Programs Abroad (DIPA), students can study drama for a semester in London. Internships with one of London's Fringe theaters are also available for qualified students.

The activities of the Department of Drama are an integral part of the College of Visual and Performing Arts, which also governs programs in art and design, music, and speech communication. The College serves as the center of SU's cultural life, on a campus whose diverse schedule of events could only be found at a large university.

The city of Syracuse itself offers rich culture; it is a regular stop for touring companies of popular Broadway musicals and experimental theater troupes and is home to the Syracuse Symphony Orchestra, the Syracuse Opera, and the Society for New Music.

▼ TARLETON STATE UNIVERSITY

Stephenville, Texas

State-supported, coed. Small town campus. Theater program established 1984.

Degrees Bachelor of Fine Arts in the area of theater.

Enrollment Fall 1997: 32 total; all undergraduate.

Theater Student Profile 45% females, 55% males.

Theater Faculty 3 total (full-time and part-time). 100% of full-time faculty have terminal degrees. Undergraduate student–faculty ratio: 10:1.

Student Life Student groups/activities include United States Institute for Theatre Technology, Texas Educational Theatre Association, Southwest Theatre Association.

Expenses for 1997–98 Application fee: $20. State resident tuition: $1088 full-time. Nonresident tuition: $7872 full-time. Mandatory fees: $1376 full-time.

Financial Aid Program-specific awards for 1997: 4 Barry B. Thompson Scholarships for program students ($500–$1000), 1 Center Stage Scholarship for program students ($2000), 8–12 drama scholarships for program students ($600–$1000), 1 David C. Riggins Scholarship for program students ($1200), 1 Jerry Flemmons Scholarship for program students ($600), 1 Speech/Drama Scholarship for program students ($600).

Application Procedures Students admitted directly into the professional program freshman year. Deadline for freshmen and transfers: continuous. Notification date for freshmen and transfers: continuous. Required: high school transcript, college transcript(s) for transfer students, minimum 2.0 high school GPA, letter of recommendation, audition, SAT I or ACT test scores, portfolio for technical theater students. Auditions held throughout the year on campus and off campus in various locations in Texas. Portfolio reviews held throughout the year on campus; the submission of slides may be substituted for portfolios.

Undergraduate Contact Ms. Gail Mayfield, Director of Admissions, Tarleton State University, Box T-0030, Stephenville, Texas 76402; 254-968-9125, fax: 254-968-9951.

▼ TEXAS CHRISTIAN UNIVERSITY

Fort Worth, Texas

Independent, coed. Suburban campus. Total enrollment: 7,273.

Degrees Bachelor of Fine Arts in the areas of theater/ television, theater; Bachelor of Arts in the areas of scene design, lighting, theater. Majors and concentrations: design technology, performance. Program accredited by NAST.

Enrollment Fall 1997: 110 total; 80 undergraduate, 30 nonprofessional degree.

Theater Student Profile 66% females, 34% males, 16% minorities, 11% international.

Theater Faculty 8 total (full-time and part-time). 100% of full-time faculty have terminal degrees. Graduate students do not teach undergraduate courses. Undergraduate student–faculty ratio: 6:1.

Texas Christian University (continued)

Student Life Student groups/activities include Alpha Psi Omega, United States Institute for Theater Technology.

Expenses for 1997–98 Application fee: $30. One-time mandatory fee: $200. Comprehensive fee: $14,950 includes full-time tuition ($9900), mandatory fees ($1190), and college room and board ($3860). College room only: $2460. Room and board charges vary according to housing facility.

Financial Aid Program-specific awards for 1997: 14 Activity Grants for incoming students ($2000), 2 Nordan Grants for incoming students ($4000), 2 Stokes Grants for incoming students ($2000).

Application Procedures Students admitted directly into the professional program freshman year. Deadline for freshmen: February 15; transfers: August 1. Notification date for freshmen: May 1; transfers: August 1. Required: essay, high school transcript, college transcript(s) for transfer students, 2 letters of recommendation, SAT I or ACT test scores, minimum 2.0 college GPA for transfer students, audition for scholarship consideration. Recommended: minimum 3.0 high school GPA, interview. Auditions held once on campus; videotaped performances are permissible as a substitute for live auditions if distance is prohibitive or scheduling is difficult.

Undergraduate Contact Dr. Forrest Newlin, Chair, Theater Department, Texas Christian University, PO Box 297510, Fort Worth, Texas 76129; 817-921-7625, fax: 817-921-7344, E-mail address: f.newlin@tcu.edu.

▼ TEXAS SOUTHERN UNIVERSITY

Houston, Texas

State-supported, coed. Urban campus. Total enrollment: 7,282. Theater program established 1948.

Degrees Bachelor of Arts in the area of fine arts. Majors and concentrations: performance, technical theater.

Enrollment Fall 1997: 14 total; 11 undergraduate, 3 non-professional degree.

Theater Student Profile 59% females, 41% males.

Theater Faculty 2 total (full-time and part-time). Graduate students do not teach undergraduate courses. Undergraduate student–faculty ratio: 8:1.

Student Life Student groups/activities include University Players.

Expenses for 1997–98 Application fee: $25. State resident tuition: $1054 full-time. Nonresident tuition: $7688 full-time. Mandatory fees: $1010 full-time. Full-time tuition and fees vary according to course load. College room and board: $4000.

Financial Aid Program-specific awards for 1997: 4 Theater Activities Awards for program students ($200–$400).

Application Procedures Students admitted directly into the professional program freshman year. Deadline for freshmen and transfers: May 31. Required: high school transcript, college transcript(s) for transfer students, minimum 2.0 high school GPA, 2 letters of recommendation, audition, portfolio, SAT I or ACT test scores. Auditions held by appointment on campus; recorded music is permissible as a substitute for live auditions for out-of-state applicants and videotaped performances are permissible as a substitute for live auditions for out-of-state applicants. Portfolio reviews held continuously on campus; the submission of slides may be substituted for portfolios for out-of-state applicants.

Undergraduate Contact Dr. Sarah Trotty, Chair, Department of Fine Arts, Texas Southern University, 3100 Cleburne Avenue, Houston, Texas 77004; 713-313-7337, fax: 713-313-1869.

▼ TISCH SCHOOL OF THE ARTS

See New York University

▼ TULANE UNIVERSITY

New Orleans, Louisiana

Independent, coed. Urban campus. Total enrollment: 10,921. Theater program established 1937.

Degrees Bachelor of Fine Arts in the area of design/technical theater. Graduate degrees offered: Master of Fine Arts in the areas of design/technical theater, directing. Cross-registration with Loyola University-New Orleans.

Enrollment Fall 1997: 17 total; 3 undergraduate, 14 graduate.

Theater Faculty 15 total undergraduate and graduate (full-time and part-time). 100% of full-time faculty have terminal degrees. Graduate students teach a few undergraduate courses.

Student Life Student groups/activities include American College Theatre Festival.

Expenses for 1998–99 Application fee: $35. Comprehensive fee: $29,320 includes full-time tuition ($21,720), mandatory fees ($1000), and college room and board ($6600). College room only: $3650. Room and board charges vary according to board plan and housing facility. Special program-related fees: $15 per semester for design studio fee.

Application Procedures Students apply for admission into the professional program by freshman year. Deadline for freshmen: January 15; transfers: June 1. Notification date for freshmen: April 1; transfers: continuous. Required: essay, high school transcript, college transcript(s) for transfer students, SAT I or ACT test scores, minimum 3.0 college GPA for transfer students. Recommended: letter of recommendation, SAT II.

Web Site http://ps.theatre.tulane.edu/.

Contact Mr. Martin L. Sachs, Chair, Department of Theatre and Dance, Tulane University, New Orleans, Louisiana 70118; 504-862-8000 ext. 1744, fax: 504-865-6737, E-mail address: msachs@mailhost.tcs.tulane.edu.

▼ THE UNIVERSITY OF ARIZONA

Tucson, Arizona

State-supported, coed. Urban campus. Total enrollment: 33,737. Theater program established 1936.

Degrees Bachelor of Fine Arts in the areas of theater production, theater education, musical theater. Majors and concentrations: acting, design technology, music theater, theater education, theater production. Graduate degrees offered: Master of Fine Arts in the areas of acting/directing, theater production. Program accredited by NAST.

Enrollment Fall 1997: 311 total; 287 undergraduate, 24 graduate.

Theater Student Profile 60% females, 40% males, 14% minorities, 5% international.

Theater Faculty 22 total undergraduate and graduate (full-time and part-time). 100% of full-time faculty have terminal degrees. Graduate students teach about a quarter undergraduate courses. Undergraduate student–faculty ratio: 20:1.

Student Life Student groups/activities include Theta Alpha Phi.

Expenses for 1997–98 Application fee: $40 for nonresidents. State resident tuition: $1988 full-time. Nonresident tuition: $8640 full-time. Mandatory fees: $70 full-time. College room and board: $4930. College room only: $2480. Room and board charges vary according to board plan and housing facility. Special program-related fees: $10–$40 per semester for material fees for design/technology courses.

Financial Aid Program-specific awards for 1997: 1 Cajero Endowed Scholarship for Hispanic freshmen from Tucson High School ($300), 1 Livieratos Endowed Scholarship for freshmen from Tucson High School ($900), 1 Walzer Endowed Scholarship for junior, senior design technical student ($1000), 1 Talley Endowed Scholarship for outstanding juniors ($1425), 1 Voskuhler Endowed Scholarship for students demonstrating outstanding talent and need ($1400), 1 Landon Endowed Scholarship for students demonstrating outstanding talent and need ($1975).

Application Procedures Students apply for admission into the professional program by sophomore year. Deadline for freshmen and transfers: May 1. Notification date for freshmen and transfers: continuous. Required: high school transcript, college transcript(s) for transfer students, audition for music theater and acting applicants, minimum 3.0 high school GPA and minimum combined SAT I score of 930 or ACT score of 22; or standing in top half of graduating class for state applicants, minimum 3.0 high school GPA and minimum combined SAT I score of 1010 or ACT score of 24; or standing in the top 25% of graduating class for out-of-state applicants, interview for transfer applicants in theater education, portfolio for transfer students in design/technology. Recommended: 3 letters of recommendation. Auditions held once on campus and off campus in Irvine, CA; Evanston, IL; New York, NY; videotaped performances are permissible as a substitute for live auditions for out-of-state applicants. Portfolio reviews held once on campus and off campus in Irvine, CA; Evanston, IL; the submission of slides may be substituted for portfolios whenever needed.

Web Site http://www.arts.arizona.edu/theatre/index.html.

Undergraduate Contact Ms. Sandra Berthold, Undergraduate Secretary, Department of Theatre Arts, The University of Arizona, Box 210003, Tucson, Arizona 85721-0003; 520-621-7008, fax: 520-621-2412.

Graduate Contact Mrs. Justine Collins, Graduate Secretary, Department of Theatre Arts, The University of Arizona, Box 210003, Tucson, Arizona 85721-0003; 520-621-7008, fax: 520-621-2412.

▼ University of British Columbia

Vancouver, BC, Canada

Province-supported, coed. Urban campus. Total enrollment: 32,110. Theater program established 1962.

Degrees Bachelor of Fine Arts in the areas of theater, creative writing; Bachelor of Arts in the area of film production. Majors and concentrations: acting, creative writing, design, film, technical theater. Graduate degrees offered: Master of Fine Arts in the areas of theater, creative writing, film.

Enrollment Fall 1997: 212 total; 80 undergraduate, 72 graduate, 60 non-professional degree.

Theater Student Profile 60% females, 40% males, 4% international.

Theater Faculty 36 total undergraduate and graduate (full-time and part-time). 90% of full-time faculty have terminal degrees. Graduate students teach a few undergraduate courses. Undergraduate student–faculty ratio: 8:1.

Student Life Student groups/activities include Theatre at UBC, Brave New Play Rites.

Expenses for 1997–98 Application fee: $72 Canadian dollars. Tuition, fee, and room and board charges are reported in Canadian dollars. Canadian resident tuition: $2333 full-time. Mandatory fees: $218 full-time. College room and board: $4516. College room only: $2600. Room and board charges vary according to board plan and housing facility. International student tuition: $13,830 full-time.

Application Procedures Students apply for admission into the professional program by sophomore year. Deadline for freshmen and transfers: March 31. Required: high school transcript, college transcript(s) for transfer students, minimum 2.75 high school GPA, audition for acting majors, portfolio for design/technical theater and creative writing majors, video for film majors. Auditions held once on campus and off campus in Edmonton, AB; Toronto, ON. Portfolio reviews held once on campus; the submission of slides may be substituted for portfolios.

Web Site http://www.arts.ubc.ca/theatre/theatre.html.

Contact Head, Department of Theatre, Film, and Creative Writing, University of British Columbia, 6354 Crescent Road, Vancouver, BC V6T 1Z2; 604-822-3880, fax: 604-822-5985.

▼ University of California, Santa Barbara

Santa Barbara, California

State-supported, coed. Suburban campus. Total enrollment: 18,940. Theater program established 1970.

Degrees Bachelor of Fine Arts in the area of acting.

Enrollment Fall 1997: 153 total; 53 undergraduate, 100 non-professional degree.

Theater Faculty 18 total (full-time and part-time). 90% of full-time faculty have terminal degrees. Graduate students teach a few undergraduate courses. Undergraduate student–faculty ratio: 6:1.

Student Life Student groups/activities include American College Theatre Festival, Intercampus Arts Festival.

Expenses for 1997–98 Application fee: $40. State resident tuition: $0 full-time. Nonresident tuition: $8989 full-time. Mandatory fees: $4098 full-time. College room and board: $6407. Room and board charges vary according to housing facility.

Financial Aid Program-specific awards for 1997: 4–5 Drama and Dance Affiliate Scholarships for seniors ($200–$400), 1 Stanley Glen Scholarship for program majors ($800), 1–2 Theodore Hatten Scholarships for program majors ($1000).

Application Procedures Students apply for admission into the professional program by sophomore year. Deadline for freshmen and transfers: November 30. Notification date for freshmen: March 15; transfers: April 1. Required: essay, high school transcript, college transcript(s) for transfer students, minimum 3.0 high school GPA, audition. Auditions held twice on campus.

Undergraduate Contact Ms. Marilyn Romine, Undergraduate Advisor, Department of Dramatic Art and Dance, University

University of California, Santa Barbara (*continued*)

of California, Santa Barbara, Snidecor 2645, Santa Barbara, California 93106; 805-893-3241, fax: 805-893-3242, E-mail address: romine@humanitas.ucsb.edu.

▼ UNIVERSITY OF CENTRAL FLORIDA

Orlando, Florida

State-supported, coed. Suburban campus. Total enrollment: 28,685.

Degrees Bachelor of Fine Arts in the areas of theater performance, technical theater/design, stage management. Majors and concentrations: theater arts/drama.

Enrollment Fall 1997: 412 total; 112 undergraduate, 300 non-professional degree.

Theater Student Profile 55% females, 45% males, 10% minorities.

Theater Faculty 18 total (full-time and part-time). 100% of full-time faculty have terminal degrees. Graduate students do not teach undergraduate courses.

Student Life Student groups/activities include Alpha Psi Omega, Florida Theatre Association.

Expenses for 1997–98 Application fee: $20. State resident tuition: $1930 full-time. Nonresident tuition: $7846 full-time. Mandatory fees: $95 full-time. Full-time tuition and fees vary according to course load. College room and board: $4370. College room only: $2720. Room and board charges vary according to housing facility.

Financial Aid Program-specific awards for 1997: 20 Talent Grants for program majors ($500).

Application Procedures Deadline for freshmen and transfers: August 1. Notification date for freshmen and transfers: August 15. Required: high school transcript, minimum 3.0 high school GPA, 3 letters of recommendation, interview, audition, portfolio, SAT I or ACT test scores. Auditions held 6 times on campus; videotaped performances are permissible as a substitute for live auditions when distance is prohibitive. Portfolio reviews held 6 times on campus; the submission of slides may be substituted for portfolios when distance is prohibitive.

Undergraduate Contact Office of Admissions, University of Central Florida, PO Box 160111, Orlando, Florida 32816; 407-823-3180.

University of Cincinnati

▼ UNIVERSITY OF CINCINNATI COLLEGE CONSERVATORY OF MUSIC

Cincinnati, Ohio

State-supported, coed. Urban campus. Total enrollment: 28,161.

Degrees Bachelor of Fine Arts in the areas of musical theater, dramatic performance, theater design and production. Graduate degrees offered: Master of Fine Arts in the areas of theater performance, directing, theater design and production, musical theater. Cross-registration with Greater Cincinnati Consortium of Colleges and Universities. Program accredited by NAST, NASM, NASD.

Enrollment Fall 1997: 184 total; 147 undergraduate, 37 graduate.

Theater Student Profile 51% females, 49% males, 11% minorities, 12% international.

Theater Faculty 18 total undergraduate and graduate (full-time and part-time). 95% of full-time faculty have terminal degrees. Graduate students teach a few undergraduate courses. Undergraduate student–faculty ratio: 7:1.

Expenses for 1997–98 Application fee: $30. State resident tuition: $3879 full-time. Nonresident tuition: $10,986 full-time. Mandatory fees: $480 full-time. College room and board: $5643.

Financial Aid Program-specific awards for 1997: 12–50 Honors Awards for program majors ($800–$3200).

Application Procedures Students admitted directly into the professional program freshman year. Deadline for freshmen and transfers: February 1. Notification date for freshmen and transfers: continuous. Required: high school transcript, college transcript(s) for transfer students, letter of recommendation, audition, SAT I or ACT test scores, portfolio, interview, essay, and 3 letters of recommendation for theater design and production applicants. Recommended: minimum 3.0 high school GPA. Auditions held 8 times on campus and off campus in New York, NY; Chicago, IL; Los Angeles, CA; San Francisco, CA; Southeastern Theatre Conference sites. Portfolio reviews held 8 times for theater design and production applicants on campus and off campus in New York, NY; Chicago, IL; Los Angeles, CA; San Francisco, CA; Southeastern Theatre Conference sites; the submission of slides may be substituted for portfolios with approval from the department.

Web Site http://www.uc.edu/www/ccm/CCMOMDA.html.

Undergraduate Contact Mrs. Angela K. Vaubel, Admissions Officer, College-Conservatory of Music, University of Cincinnati, PO Box 210003, Cincinnati, Ohio 45221-0003; 513-556-5463, fax: 513-556-1028, E-mail address: angela.vaubel@uc.edu.

Graduate Contact Mr. Paul R. Hillner, Assistant Dean, College-Conservatory of Music, University of Cincinnati, PO Box 210003, Cincinnati, Ohio 45221-0003; 513-556-5462, fax: 513-556-1028, E-mail address: paul.hillner@uc.edu.

▼ UNIVERSITY OF COLORADO AT BOULDER

Boulder, Colorado

State-supported, coed. Suburban campus. Total enrollment: 25,109.

Degrees Bachelor of Fine Arts in the area of theater. Majors and concentrations: acting, design/technical theater. Graduate degrees offered: Doctor of Philosophy in the area of theater.

Enrollment Fall 1997: 215 total; 38 undergraduate, 26 graduate, 151 non-professional degree.

Theater Student Profile 62% females, 38% males, 7% minorities, 1% international.

Theater Faculty 15 total undergraduate and graduate (full-time and part-time). 100% of full-time faculty have terminal degrees. Graduate students teach a few undergraduate courses.

Student Life Student groups/activities include On Stage, Colorado Shakespeare Festival.

Expenses for 1997–98 Application fee: $40. One-time mandatory fee: $35. State resident tuition: $2356 full-time. Nonresident tuition: $14,400 full-time. Mandatory fees: $583 full-time. Full-time tuition and fees vary according to program. College room and board: $4566. Room and board charges vary according to board plan, housing facility, and location.

Financial Aid Program-specific awards for 1997: 14 Technical Assistant Awards for program students ($4400), 5 University Theatre Awards for production majors ($550), 2 University Theatre Awards for incoming freshmen ($1250), 1 David A. Busse Scholarship for upperclass design majors ($450), 1 Dorothy and Anthony Riddle Scholarship for acting majors ($450), 1 Mabel Gaiser Borgmann Scholarship for female drama students ($450), 1 Bonnie Potts Memorial Scholarship for senior theater majors ($100).

Application Procedures Students apply for admission into the professional program by sophomore year. Deadline for freshmen: February 15; transfers: April 1. Required: essay, high school transcript, college transcript(s) for transfer students, 3 letters of recommendation, interview, audition, portfolio, SAT I or ACT test scores. Recommended: minimum 3.0 high school GPA. Auditions held once on campus. Portfolio reviews held twice on campus.

Web Site http://www.colorado.edu/TheatreDance/.

Undergraduate Contact Sean Kelley, Undergraduate Advisor, Department of Theatre and Dance, University of Colorado at Boulder, CB 261, Boulder, Colorado 80309-0261; 303-492-2785, fax: 303-492-7722, E-mail address: sean.kelley@colorado.edu.

Graduate Contact Ms. Marcia Richardson, Graduate Studies Assistant, Department of Theatre and Dance, University of Colorado at Boulder, CB 261, Boulder, Colorado 80309-0261; 303-492-7356, fax: 303-492-7722, E-mail address: marcia. richardson@colorado.edu.

More About the University

The Department of Theatre and Dance at the University of Colorado, Boulder, is part of the College of Arts and Sciences. The department's theater curriculum, especially the BFA degree program, is designed for students with serious career goals in the areas of acting, designing, directing, and technical theatre. The BA degree program is open to all interested students; for the BFA program, applicants must audition in the fall of their sophomore year.

Program Facilities The department is housed in the recently renovated University Theatre consisting of classrooms, studios, costume shops, offices, a 450-seat main stage proscenium theatre, a 150-seat black box flexible theater, and a 150-seat theater for dance.

Faculty, Resident Artists, Alumni Distinguished faculty members include Dr. James Symons, author of *Meyerhold's Theatre and the Grotesque*, and Richard Devin, lighting designer for numerous professional theatre productions and Producing Artistic Director of the Colorado Shakespeare Festival. Recent guest artists include lighting designer Jim Moody, performance artist Holly Hughes, and Russian playwright Alexander Galin. Alumni include performers in Off-Broadway's *Blue Man Group*, and the Broadway revival of *Cabaret*. Alumni also include Christopher Duncan from television's *Jamie Foxx Show* and Tony Award winning Broadway and television actress Patricia Elliott.

Student Performance Opportunities The department usually presents nine major productions during the year. There are also student-directed productions presented during the year and sponsored by the student organization, On Stage.

Special Programs The Colorado Shakespeare Festival is produced by the department and plays to more than 40,000 people each summer. As paid apprentice actors and crew members, advanced undergraduates comprise approximately 30 percent of the 175-member company.

▼ UNIVERSITY OF CONNECTICUT

Storrs, Connecticut

State-supported, coed. Rural campus. Total enrollment: 18,205. Theater program established 1960.

Degrees Bachelor of Fine Arts in the areas of acting, design/technical theater, puppetry. Graduate degrees offered: Master of Fine Arts in the areas of acting, design, puppetry, technical direction; Master of Arts in the area of production-puppetry. Program accredited by NAST.

Enrollment Fall 1997: 180 total; 115 undergraduate, 43 graduate, 22 non-professional degree.

Theater Student Profile 51% females, 49% males.

Theater Faculty 24 total undergraduate and graduate (full-time and part-time). 85% of full-time faculty have terminal degrees. Graduate students teach a few undergraduate courses. Undergraduate student–faculty ratio: 5:1.

Student Life Student groups/activities include Connecticut Repertory Theatre.

Expenses for 1997–98 Application fee: $40. State resident tuition: $4158 full-time. Nonresident tuition: $12,676 full-time. Mandatory fees: $1084 full-time. College room and board: $5462. College room only: $2776. Room and board charges vary according to board plan and housing facility.

Financial Aid Program-specific awards for 1997: 18 University Drama Scholarships for incoming students ($1000).

Application Procedures Students admitted directly into the professional program freshman year. Deadline for freshmen: April 1; transfers: May 1. Notification date for freshmen and transfers: continuous. Required: essay, high school transcript, college transcript(s) for transfer students, audition, SAT I or ACT test scores. Recommended: 2 letters of recommendation, portfolio for design/technical theater applicants. Auditions held by appointment for acting and puppetry majors on campus. Portfolio reviews held by appointment on campus; the submission of slides may be substituted for portfolios if a campus visit is impossible.

Web Site http://www.sfa.uconn.edu.

Undergraduate Contact Stephanie Stoops, Admissions Assistant, Department of Dramatic Arts, University of Connecticut, U-127, 802 Bolton Road, Storrs, Connecticut 06269-1127; 860-486-4025, fax: 860-486-3110.

Graduate Contact Stephanie Stoops, Graduate Admissions Assistant, Department of Dramatic Arts, University of Connecticut, U-127, 802 Bolton Road, Storrs, Connecticut 06269-1127; 860-486-4025, fax: 860-486-3110.

▼ UNIVERSITY OF EVANSVILLE

Evansville, Indiana

Independent, coed. Suburban campus. Total enrollment: 3,023.

Degrees Bachelor of Arts/Bachelor of Fine Arts in the areas of performance, design and technology. Majors and concentrations: design, performance, theater management, theater technology. Cross-registration with Harlaxton College (England). Program accredited by NASM.

Enrollment Fall 1997: 113 undergraduate.

Theater Student Profile 65% females, 35% males, 7% minorities, 2% international.

University of Evansville (continued)

Theater Faculty 11 total (full-time and part-time). 100% of full-time faculty have terminal degrees. Graduate students do not teach undergraduate courses. Undergraduate student–faculty ratio: 7:1.

Student Life Student groups/activities include United States Institute for Theatre Technology.

Expenses for 1997–98 Application fee: $35. Comprehensive fee: $18,780 includes full-time tuition ($13,600), mandatory fees ($280), and college room and board ($4900). College room only: $2060. Room and board charges vary according to board plan and housing facility.

Financial Aid Program-specific awards for 1997: 28 Academic/Department Scholarships for program students ($2000–$6000).

Application Procedures Students admitted directly into the professional program freshman year. Deadline for freshmen: March 1; transfers: June 1. Notification date for freshmen: May 1; transfers: continuous. Required: high school transcript, minimum 2.0 high school GPA, SAT I or ACT test scores (minimum combined SAT I score of 1000, minimum combined ACT score of 20), audition for performance applicants, portfolio for design/technology applicants. Recommended: minimum 3.0 high school GPA, letter of recommendation. Auditions held 17 times on campus and off campus in Denver, CO; Indianapolis, IN; New York, NY; Chicago, IL; Los Angeles, CA; San Francisco, CA; Las Vegas, NV; Louisville, KY; Atlanta, GA; videotaped performances are permissible as a substitute for live auditions if a campus visit is impossible, with permission. Portfolio reviews held 17 times on campus and off campus in Denver, CO; Indianapolis, IN; New York, NY; Chicago, IL; Los Angeles, CA; San Francisco, CA; Las Vegas, NV; Louisville, KY; Atlanta, GA.

Web Site http://www.evansville.edu/~thtrweb.

Undergraduate Contact Mr. John David Lutz, Director, Department of Theatre, University of Evansville, 1800 Lincoln Avenue, Evansville, Indiana 47722; 812-479-2744, fax: 812-471-6995.

▼ University of Florida

Gainesville, Florida

State-supported, coed. Suburban campus. Total enrollment: 41,713. Theater program established 1975.

Degrees Bachelor of Fine Arts in the areas of theater performance, theater production. Graduate degrees offered: Master of Fine Arts in the area of theater. Cross-registration with Florida State University System. Program accredited by NAST.

Enrollment Fall 1997: 123 total; 101 undergraduate, 22 graduate.

Theater Student Profile 70% females, 30% males, 20% minorities, 1% international.

Theater Faculty 25 total undergraduate and graduate (full-time and part-time). 100% of full-time faculty have terminal degrees. Graduate students teach a few undergraduate courses. Undergraduate student–faculty ratio: 7:1.

Student Life Student groups/activities include Alpha Psi Omega, Florida Players, Floridance.

Expenses for 1997–98 Application fee: $20. State resident tuition: $1930 full-time. Nonresident tuition: $7570 full-time.

College room and board: $4610. College room only: $2270. Room and board charges vary according to board plan and housing facility.

Financial Aid Program-specific awards for 1997: 10 theater scholarships for program majors ($500–$1000).

Application Procedures Students admitted directly into the professional program freshman year. Deadline for freshmen: February 1; transfers: July 15. Notification date for freshmen and transfers: continuous. Required: high school transcript, college transcript(s) for transfer students, minimum 3.0 high school GPA, audition, portfolio, SAT I or ACT test scores. Recommended: essay. Auditions held twice and by appointment on campus and off campus in various sites of National Theater Associations throughout the U.S.; videotaped performances are permissible as a substitute for live auditions with approval from the department. Portfolio reviews held twice on campus; the submission of slides may be substituted for portfolios with approval from the department.

Web Site http://www.arts.ufl.edu.

Undergraduate Contact Dr. Louise Rothman, Undergraduate Coordinator, Department of Theatre and Dance, University of Florida, McCarty C, 4th Floor, PO Box 115900, Gainesville, Florida 32611-5900; 352-392-2038 ext. 202, fax: 352-392-5114, E-mail address: lrothman@ufl.edu.

Graduate Contact Dr. David Shelton, Graduate Coordinator, Department of Theatre and Dance, University of Florida, McCarty C, 4th Floor, PO Box 115900, Gainesville, Florida 32611-5900; 352-392-2038 ext. 206, fax: 352-392-5114, E-mail address: dlshel@nervm.nerdc.ufl.edu.

The Hartt School

▼ University of Hartford

West Hartford, Connecticut

Independent, coed. Suburban campus. Total enrollment: 7,089. Theater program established 1996.

Degrees Bachelor of Fine Arts in the areas of theater arts, music theater. Cross-registration with Trinity College, Saint Joseph College, Hartford Seminary.

Enrollment Fall 1997: 105 total; all undergraduate.

Theater Student Profile 60% females, 40% males, 1% minorities, 1% international.

Theater Faculty 12 total (full-time and part-time). 100% of full-time faculty have terminal degrees. Graduate students do not teach undergraduate courses.

Student Life Special housing available for theater students.

Expenses for 1998–99 Application fee: $35. Comprehensive fee: $25,424 includes full-time tuition ($17,190), mandatory fees ($1034), and college room and board ($7200). College room only: $4440. Room and board charges vary according to board plan and housing facility.

Financial Aid Program-specific awards for 1997: 25 Performing Arts Scholarships for students passing audition evaluations ($7000).

Application Procedures Students admitted directly into the professional program freshman year. Deadline for freshmen and transfers: continuous. Required: high school transcript, college transcript(s) for transfer students, minimum 2.0 high school GPA, 3 letters of recommendation, interview, audition, SAT I or ACT test scores. Recommended: essay, minimum 3.0 high school GPA. Auditions held 6 times on campus and off campus in Hartford, CT; Boston, MA; New York, NY; Chicago, IL; Miami, FL; San Francisco, CA;

videotaped performances are permissible as a substitute for live auditions when distance is prohibitive.

Undergraduate Contact Mr. James Jacobs, Director of Admissions, The Hartt School, University of Hartford, 200 Bloomfield Avenue, West Hartford, Connecticut 06117-1500; 860-768-4465, fax: 860-768-4441.

▼ University of Houston

Houston, Texas

State-supported, coed. Urban campus. Total enrollment: 31,602. Theater program established 1970.

Degrees Bachelor of Arts in the area of theater. Majors and concentrations: acting, dance, design, directing. Graduate degrees offered: Master of Fine Arts in the area of theater; Master of Arts in the area of theater.

Enrollment Fall 1997: 283 total; 175 undergraduate, 106 graduate, 2 non-professional degree.

Theater Student Profile 68% females, 32% males, 29% minorities, 1% international.

Theater Faculty 13 total undergraduate and graduate (full-time and part-time). 46% of full-time faculty have terminal degrees. Graduate students teach a few undergraduate courses. Undergraduate student–faculty ratio: 16:1.

Estimated expenses for 1998–99 Application fee: $30. State resident tuition: $864 full-time. Nonresident tuition: $5952 full-time. Mandatory fees: $1129 full-time. Full-time tuition and fees vary according to program. College room and board: $4405. College room only: $1960. Room and board charges vary according to board plan and housing facility. Special program-related fees: $20–$50 per course for equipment maintenance and supplies fee.

Financial Aid Program-specific awards for 1997: 5 Theatre Scholarships for all theater students ($750), 1 Trey Wilson for all theater students ($1000), 1 Robert Bullard for all theater students ($500), 1 Cecil Pickett for all theater students ($1000), 1 Joseph Michael Adamo for all theater students ($500).

Application Procedures Students admitted directly into the professional program freshman year. Deadline for freshmen and transfers: July 1. Required: high school transcript, college transcript(s) for transfer students, SAT I or ACT test scores.

Web Site http://bentley.uh.edu/theatre/theatre.home.html.

Undergraduate Contact Admission Office, University of Houston, 4800 Calhoun, Houston, Texas 77204; 713-743-1010.

Graduate Contact Dr. Sidney Berger, Director, School of Theatre, University of Houston, 4800 Calhoun, Houston, Texas 77204-5071; 713-743-2930, fax: 713-749-1420, E-mail address: sberger@uh.edu.

▼ University of Illinois at Urbana–Champaign

Champaign, Illinois

State-supported, coed. Small town campus. Total enrollment: 36,019. Theater program established 1969.

Degrees Bachelor of Fine Arts in the areas of acting, design, technology and management, performance studies. Majors and concentrations: acting, costume design, design technology, lighting design, performance studies, set design, stage management, theater technology. Graduate degrees offered: Master of Fine Arts in the areas of acting, design, technology and management. Doctor of Philosophy in the area of theater history and criticism. Cross-registration with Parkland College. Program accredited by NAST.

Enrollment Fall 1997: 206 total; 140 undergraduate, 66 graduate.

Theater Student Profile 45% females, 9% minorities, 6% international.

Theater Faculty 31 total undergraduate and graduate (full-time and part-time). 100% of full-time faculty have terminal degrees. Graduate students teach a few undergraduate courses. Undergraduate student–faculty ratio: 3:1.

Student Life Student groups/activities include American College Theatre Festival.

Expenses for 1997–98 Application fee: $40, $50 for international students. State resident tuition: $3308 full-time. Nonresident tuition: $9924 full-time. Mandatory fees: $812 full-time. Full-time tuition and fees vary according to program and student level. College room and board: $5078. College room only: $1958. Room and board charges vary according to board plan and housing facility. Special program-related fees: $5–$15 per semester for CAD lab fee.

Financial Aid Program-specific awards for 1997: 50 Talented Undergraduate Student Tuition Waivers for program students ($500–$1000), 3 Bernard Gold Awards for program students ($1000).

Application Procedures Students apply for admission into the professional program by sophomore year. Deadline for freshmen and transfers: continuous. Notification date for freshmen and transfers: April 15. Required: high school transcript, college transcript(s) for transfer students, SAT I or ACT test scores, interview for performance studies applicants, audition for acting applicants, portfolio for design/technology applicants. Recommended: essay, letter of recommendation. Auditions held 6 times on campus and off campus in Chicago, IL; videotaped performances are permissible as a substitute for live auditions if a campus visit is impossible. Portfolio reviews held 6 times on campus; the submission of slides may be substituted for portfolios for international applicants.

Web Site http://www.theatre.uiuc.edu/theatre/theat.html.

Undergraduate Contact Office of Admissions and Records, University of Illinois at Urbana–Champaign, 901 West Illinois Street, 506 South Wright, Urbana, Illinois 61801; 217-333-0302.

Graduate Contact Department of Theatre, University of Illinois at Urbana–Champaign, 4-122 Krannert Center for the Performing Arts, 500 South Goodwin Avenue, Urbana, Illinois 61801; 217-333-2371, fax: 217-244-1861.

▼ University of Kansas

Lawrence, Kansas

State-supported, coed. Suburban campus. Total enrollment: 27,567.

Degrees Bachelor of Fine Arts in the area of theater scenography. Graduate degrees offered: Master of Fine Arts in the area of theater scenography. Program accredited by NAST.

Enrollment Fall 1997: 12 undergraduate, 6 graduate.

Theater Student Profile 50% females, 50% males, 10% minorities, 20% international.

Theater Faculty 4 total undergraduate and graduate (full-time and part-time). 100% of full-time faculty have terminal

University of Kansas (continued)

degrees. Graduate students teach a few undergraduate courses. Undergraduate student–faculty ratio: 4:1.

Student Life Student groups/activities include American College Theatre Festival, United States Institute for Theatre Technology.

Expenses for 1997–98 Application fee: $20. State resident tuition: $1965 full-time. Nonresident tuition: $8270 full-time. Mandatory fees: $420 full-time. Full-time tuition and fees vary according to course load. College room and board: $3736. Room and board charges vary according to board plan and housing facility.

Application Procedures Students admitted directly into the professional program freshman year. Deadline for freshmen: February 1; transfers: June 1. Required: high school transcript, college transcript(s) for transfer students, portfolio, SAT I or ACT test scores, minimum 2.0 high school GPA for out-of-state applicants. Recommended: interview. Portfolio reviews held continuously until February 1 on campus and off campus in American College Theatre Festivals, United States Institute for Theatre Technology sites; the submission of slides may be substituted for portfolios whenever needed.

Contact Ms. Delores Ringer, Coordinator of Design Program, Department of Theatre and Film, University of Kansas, 356 Murphy Hall, Lawrence, Kansas 66045; 785-864-3381, fax: 785-864-5251.

▼ UNIVERSITY OF KENTUCKY

Lexington, Kentucky

State-supported, coed. Urban campus. Total enrollment: 23,540. Theater program established 1928.

Degrees Bachelor of Fine Arts in the areas of acting, design and technology. Cross-registration with University of Kentucky Community College System . Program accredited by NAST.

Enrollment Fall 1997: 105 total; all undergraduate.

Theater Student Profile 46% females, 54% males, 10% minorities, 1% international.

Theater Faculty 14 total (full-time and part-time). 91% of full-time faculty have terminal degrees. Graduate students do not teach undergraduate courses. Undergraduate student–faculty ratio: 10:1.

Student Life Student groups/activities include United States Institute for Theatre Technology, American College Theatre Festival, Southeastern Theatre Conference.

Expenses for 1997–98 Application fee: $20. State resident tuition: $2400 full-time. Nonresident tuition: $7200 full-time. Mandatory fees: $336 full-time. Full-time tuition and fees vary according to reciprocity agreements. College room and board: $3388. Room and board charges vary according to board plan and housing facility. Special program-related fees: $15–$75 per semester for materials fee for design courses.

Financial Aid Program-specific awards for 1997: 10–15 Wallace Briggs Freshman Scholarships for entering freshmen ($1000), 1 John and Ruth Koch Scholarship for entering freshmen acting majors ($1000), 2 Wallace and Olive Briggs Scholarships for entering freshmen ($4000), 5 UK Theatre Sophomore Scholarships for freshmen theater majors ($1000), 4 Lolo Robinson Scholarships for sophomore, junior, and senior theater majors ($500), 2 Raymond A. Smith Scholarships for junior and senior theater majors ($500).

Application Procedures Students admitted directly into the professional program freshman year. Deadline for freshmen and transfers: continuous. Required: high school transcript, college transcript(s) for transfer students, minimum 3.0 high school GPA, 2 letters of recommendation, SAT I or ACT test scores (minimum combined SAT I score of 950, minimum combined ACT score of 22), audition for acting applicants, portfolio for design applicants. Auditions held twice on campus and off campus in Louisville, KY; videotaped performances are permissible as a substitute for live auditions with permission of the chair. Portfolio reviews held once on campus; the submission of slides may be substituted for portfolios with permission of the program director.

Web Site http://www.uky.edu/FineArts/Theatre.

Undergraduate Contact Mr. A. J. Pinkney, Director of Undergraduate Studies, Department of Theatre, University of Kentucky, 114 Fine Arts Building, Lexington, Kentucky 40506; 606-257-3297, fax: 606-257-3042.

▼ THE UNIVERSITY OF MEMPHIS

Memphis, Tennessee

State-supported, coed. Urban campus. Total enrollment: 19,851. Theater program established 1950.

Degrees Bachelor of Fine Arts in the area of theater. Majors and concentrations: dance, design/technical theater, performance. Graduate degrees offered: Master of Fine Arts in the area of theater. Program accredited by NAST.

Enrollment Fall 1997: 128 total; 97 undergraduate, 22 graduate, 9 non-professional degree.

Theater Student Profile 61% females, 39% males, 18% minorities, 1% international.

Theater Faculty 23 total undergraduate and graduate (full-time and part-time). 75% of full-time faculty have terminal degrees. Graduate students teach a few undergraduate courses. Undergraduate student–faculty ratio: 7:1.

Student Life Student groups/activities include Fred Mertz Student Activity Group, University Dance Company, Memphis Moving Line.

Expenses for 1997–98 Application fee: $10. State resident tuition: $2344 full-time. Nonresident tuition: $6940 full-time. Mandatory fees: $68 full-time. College room and board: $3500.

Financial Aid Program-specific awards for 1997: 3 University Talent Scholarships for program majors ($4821), 4–9 Department Talent Scholarships for program majors ($100–$400).

Application Procedures Students apply for admission into the professional program by freshman, sophomore year. Deadline for freshmen and transfers: August 1. Required: high school transcript, college transcript(s) for transfer students, audition, SAT I or ACT test scores (minimum combined SAT I score of 930, minimum combined ACT score of 20), 3.0 GPA for auto-admission. Auditions held twice on campus. Portfolio reviews held twice on campus; the submission of slides may be substituted for portfolios for technical and design students.

Undergraduate Contact Ms. Joanna Helming, BFA Performance Coordinator, Department of Theatre and Dance, The University of Memphis, Campus Box 526524, Memphis, Tennessee 38152-6524; 901-678-2523, fax: 901-678-4331, E-mail address: theatrelib@memphis.edu.

Graduate Contact Ms. Gloria Baxter, Coordinator of Graduate Studies, Department of Theatre and Dance, The University of Memphis, Campus Box 526524, Memphis, Tennessee 38152-6524; 901-678-2523, fax: 901-678-4331, E-mail address: theatrelib@memphis.edu.

▼ UNIVERSITY OF MIAMI

Coral Gables, Florida

Independent, coed. Suburban campus. Total enrollment: 13,651. Theater program established 1936.

Degrees Bachelor of Fine Arts in the area of theater arts. Majors and concentrations: design production, music theater, performance, stage management, theater management.

Enrollment Fall 1997: 85 undergraduate.

Theater Student Profile 60% females, 40% males, 17% minorities.

Theater Faculty 17 total (full-time and part-time). 100% of full-time faculty have terminal degrees. Graduate students do not teach undergraduate courses. Undergraduate student–faculty ratio: 6:1.

Student Life Student groups/activities include Jerry Herman Ring Theatre.

Expenses for 1997–98 Application fee: $40. Comprehensive fee: $26,864 includes full-time tuition ($19,140), mandatory fees ($372), and college room and board ($7352). College room only: $4194. Room and board charges vary according to board plan and housing facility.

Financial Aid Program-specific awards for 1997: 12 department scholarships for program majors demonstrating need/talent ($1000–$3000).

Application Procedures Students admitted directly into the professional program freshman year. Deadline for freshmen and transfers: March 1. Notification date for freshmen and transfers: April 1. Required: essay, high school transcript, letter of recommendation, interview, audition, SAT I or ACT test scores. Recommended: minimum 3.0 high school GPA, portfolio. Auditions held by appointment on campus and off campus in New York, NY; Washington, DC; Chicago, IL; Louisville, KY; Southeastern Theatre Conference sites; International Thespian Conference sites; videotaped performances are permissible as a substitute for live auditions if a campus visit is impossible. Portfolio reviews held by appointment on campus and off campus in New York, NY; Chicago, IL; Louisville, KY; Southeastern Theatre Conference sites; International Thespian Conference sites; the submission of slides may be substituted for portfolios for design, production, management applicants.

Web Site http://www.miami.edu/tha/.

Undergraduate Contact Mr. Kent Lantaff, Associate Chairman, Theatre Arts Department, University of Miami, PO Box 248273, Coral Gables, Florida 33124; 305-284-6439, fax: 305-284-5702, E-mail address: klantaff@miami.edu.

More About the University

Programs Bachelor of Fine Arts Conservatory offers intensive training in a professional environment. Bachelor of Arts program offers a more liberal arts approach. Both programs offer specializations in performance, musical theater, stage or theater management, and design or technical theater. Admission to the University required for both degrees; admission to the Conservatory requires additional application and audition or portfolio review. Courses include acting, musical theater, dance, voice and speech, movement and stage combat as well as theater history, technical theater, design, directing, and management.

Program Facilities The Jerry Herman Ring Theatre is a flexible theater that can be configured into a 300-seat proscenium, 450-seat arena, 350-seat thrust, or any other combination. Equipment includes state-of-the-art sound and lighting, dressing and green rooms and scenic and costume shops. Classroom facilities feature classrooms, dance studio, lighting and design lab with CAD stations, and 45-seat studio theater.

Faculty, Guest Artists, and Alumni Full-time faculty members are chosen not only for their excellent teaching skills but also for professional expertise. Each year, guest directors and designers work with students on selected mainstage productions. Graduates include: Jerry Herman (*Hello Dolly!, Mame*), Ray Liotta (*Field of Dreams, Unlawful Entry*), Ernie Sabella (Broadway actor), Susan Elrod and Sherry Cohen (Broadway managers), and Riccardo Hernandez (Broadway designer).

Student Performances Recent productions have included *Hair, The Colored Museum, SubUrbia, Anything Goes, Reckless, A Piece of My Heart,* and *Into the Woods.* Both B.F.A. and B.A. students are eligible to audition. Students are actively encouraged to audition for summer stock opportunities.

▼ UNIVERSITY OF MICHIGAN

Ann Arbor, Michigan

State-supported, coed. Suburban campus. Total enrollment: 36,995. Theater program established 1915.

Degrees Bachelor of Fine Arts in the areas of performance, design and production, directing. Majors and concentrations: acting, directing, theater arts/drama. Graduate degrees offered: Master of Fine Arts in the areas of design, directing, playwriting. Doctor of Philosophy in the area of theater practice. Cross-registration with Welsh College of Music and Drama (Wales), Middlesex University (England). Program accredited by NASM.

Enrollment Fall 1997: 119 total; 98 undergraduate, 6 graduate, 15 non-professional degree.

Theater Student Profile 60% females, 40% males, 10% minorities, 2% international.

Theater Faculty 34 total undergraduate and graduate (full-time and part-time). 78% of full-time faculty have terminal degrees. Graduate students teach a few undergraduate courses. Undergraduate student–faculty ratio: 5:1.

Student Life Student groups/activities include Basement Arts, Musket Theatre Productions, Soph Show.

Expenses for 1997–98 Application fee: $40. State resident tuition: $5694 full-time. Nonresident tuition: $18,260 full-time. Mandatory fees: $184 full-time. Full-time tuition and fees vary according to program and student level. College room and board: $5342. Room and board charges vary according to board plan and housing facility.

Financial Aid Program-specific awards for 1997: 16 Merit Awards for continuing students ($800–$3000), 20 scholarships for continuing students ($500–$4000).

Application Procedures Students admitted directly into the professional program freshman year. Deadline for freshmen and transfers: continuous. Required: essay, high school transcript, college transcript(s) for transfer students, minimum 3.0 high school GPA, letter of recommendation, interview, SAT I or ACT test scores, portfolio for design, production and directing applicants, audition for acting applicants. Recommended: production photos for design and production applicants. Auditions held 9 times on campus and off campus in Chicago, IL; Las Vegas, NV; New York, NY; Los Angeles, CA. Portfolio reviews held 11 times

University of Michigan (continued)

and by appointment on campus and off campus in Chicago, IL; Las Vegas, NV; Los Angeles, CA, and at Southeastern Theatre Conference and United States Institute for Theater Technology Conference sites; the submission of slides may be substituted for portfolios when distance is prohibitive.

Web Site http://www.theatre.music.umich.edu.

Undergraduate Contact Ms. Laura Strozeski, Senior Admissions Counselor, School of Music, Department of Theatre and Drama, University of Michigan, 1100 Baits Drive, Ann Arbor, Michigan 48109-2085; 734-764-0593, fax: 734-763-5097, E-mail address: music.admissions@umich.edu.

Graduate Contact Department of Theatre and Drama, University of Michigan, 2550 Frieze Building, Ann Arbor, Michigan 48109-1285; 734-764-5350, fax: 734-747-2297, E-mail address: theatre.info@umich.edu.

More About the University

Program Facilities Performance spaces: Power Center (1,400 seats), with a thrust stage of flexible size and shape; Lydia Mendelssohn Theatre (650 seats), a lovely, intimate theater built in 1928; Trueblood Theatre (open-space seating for 175), with flexibility of thrust, three-quarter, and arena staging; and Arena Theatre (100 seats), a black-box space suitable for workshops, studios, and student-produced works. Spacious design studios are fully equipped and include a Macintosh workstation with a variety of state-of-the-art design software.

Faculty, Guest Artists, and Alumni Performance and design faculty members are all theater professionals with experience on the Broadway, London, and regional stage. Michigan is dedicated to maintaining ties with the professional theater community; actors, designers, and directors frequently visit campus to teach master classes and direct or design productions. Recent guests have included artistic director Libby Appel, actress Christine Lahti (alumna), actress and director Michele Shay, actor James Earl Jones (alumnus), producer Hal Cooper (alumnus), actor Jeff Daniels, director Lloyd Richards, and designers Susan Benson and Dawn Chiang.

Performance Opportunities The department mounts five mainstage productions each year. Recent productions include works by Shakespeare, Molière, Euripides, Shaw, Shepard, Wilder, and Pinter. The School of Music produces operas, dance concerts, and musical theater, and resident student groups also mount full productions. Local theater groups, from the nontraditional to the Civic Theatre, are all in need of a constant supply of performers, designers, and technicians. The department also has professional ties with The Purple Rose Theatre, founded by actor Jeff Daniels.

▼ UNIVERSITY OF MICHIGAN–FLINT

Flint, Michigan

State-supported, coed. Urban campus. Total enrollment: 6,488.

Degrees Bachelor of Fine Arts in the area of performance.

Enrollment Fall 1997: 52 total; 2 undergraduate, 50 non-professional degree.

Theater Student Profile 50% females, 50% males, 8% minorities.

Theater Faculty 11 total (full-time and part-time). 100% of full-time faculty have terminal degrees. Graduate students do not teach undergraduate courses. Undergraduate student–faculty ratio: 9:1.

Student Life Student groups/activities include Chicago Showcase.

Expenses for 1997–98 State resident tuition: $3409 full-time. Nonresident tuition: $10,121 full-time. Mandatory fees: $150 full-time. Full-time tuition and fees vary according to program and student level.

Financial Aid Program-specific awards for 1997: Carl and Sarah Morgan Trust Awards for theater majors ($1000–$3300), 1 Jeffrey F. Garfield Scholarship for theater majors ($1000–$3300), departmental awards for theater majors ($1000–$3300).

Application Procedures Students apply for admission into the professional program by sophomore year. Deadline for freshmen and transfers: continuous. Required: high school transcript, college transcript(s) for transfer students, interview, audition, SAT I or ACT test scores, minimum 2.7 high school GPA in academic courses in grades 10-12. Recommended: letter of recommendation. Auditions held once in January on campus.

Undergraduate Contact Ms. Carolyn Gillespie, Chair, Department of Theater, University of Michigan–Flint, 303 East Kearsley Street, Flint, Michigan 48502-2186; 810-762-3230, fax: 810-762-3687, E-mail address: cmgil@flint.umich.edu.

▼ UNIVERSITY OF MINNESOTA, DULUTH

Duluth, Minnesota

State-supported, coed. Suburban campus. Total enrollment: 9,653.

Degrees Bachelor of Fine Arts in the area of theater. Majors and concentrations: acting, costume design, design/technical theater, lighting design, music theater, scenic design. Cross-registration with University of Minnesota-Twin Cities, University of Minnesota-Morris, College of St. Scholastica, University of Wisconsin-Superior.

Enrollment Fall 1997: 92 undergraduate.

Theater Student Profile 60% females, 40% males, 1% minorities.

Theater Faculty 11 total (full-time and part-time). 100% of full-time faculty have terminal degrees. Graduate students do not teach undergraduate courses. Undergraduate student–faculty ratio: 10:1.

Student Life Student groups/activities include American College Theatre Festival, United States Institute for Theatre Technology, American College Dance Festival.

Expenses for 1997–98 Application fee: $25. State resident tuition: $3708 full-time. Nonresident tuition: $10,588 full-time. Mandatory fees: $608 full-time. Full-time tuition and fees vary according to course level, course load, reciprocity agreements, and student level. College room and board: $3912. Room and board charges vary according to board plan and housing facility. Special program-related fees: $10 per course for consumable materials, $25 per course for specialized needs (pianist).

Financial Aid Program-specific awards for 1997: 6 Marshall Center Awards for program majors ($600–$1200), 1 Earl Jensen Award for technical/design majors ($600), 1 Ann Upgren Award for program majors ($600), 2 Gersghol Awards for program majors ($900), 1 Erin Wright Memorial Award for program majors ($500), 1 Teazla Award for program majors ($500).

Application Procedures Students apply for admission into the professional program by freshman year. Deadline for freshmen and transfers: continuous. Required: high school transcript, college transcript(s) for transfer students, ACT

test score only (minimum combined ACT score of 19). Recommended: letter of recommendation, interview.
Web Site http://www.d.umn.edu/theatre/.
Undergraduate Contact Ms. Patricia Dennis, Chair, Department of Theatre, University of Minnesota, Duluth, 141 MPAC, 10 University Drive, Duluth, Minnesota 55812; 218-726-8778, fax: 218-726-6798, E-mail address: pdennis@d.umn.edu.

▼ THE UNIVERSITY OF MONTANA–MISSOULA

Missoula, Montana

State-supported, coed. Urban campus. Total enrollment: 12,124.
Degrees Bachelor of Fine Arts in the areas of acting, design/technical theater. Graduate degrees offered: Master of Fine Arts in the areas of directing, acting, design/technical theater. Program accredited by NAST.
Enrollment Fall 1997: 189 total; 140 undergraduate, 19 graduate, 30 non-professional degree.
Theater Student Profile 65% females, 35% males, 1% minorities, 1% international.
Theater Faculty 17 total undergraduate and graduate (full-time and part-time). 100% of full-time faculty have terminal degrees. Graduate students teach a few undergraduate courses. Undergraduate student–faculty ratio: 16:1.
Student Life Student groups/activities include Montana Repertory Theatre, The Young Rep.
Expenses for 1997–98 Application fee: $30. State resident tuition: $2630 full-time. Nonresident tuition: $7192 full-time. Full-time tuition varies according to program and student level. College room and board: $3917. Room and board charges vary according to board plan and housing facility. Special program-related fees: $20–$60 per course for materials, accompanist fees.
Financial Aid Program-specific awards for 1997: 2 Wallace Scholarships for incoming freshmen ($500), 1 Gordon Scholarship for state resident acting students ($350), 6 Dean Scholarships for upperclassmen ($600), 1 Carol Scholarship for those demonstrating need ($500).
Application Procedures Students admitted directly into the professional program freshman year. Deadline for freshmen and transfers: March 15. Notification date for freshmen and transfers: continuous. Required: high school transcript, minimum 2.0 high school GPA, SAT I or ACT test scores, audition for acting majors, portfolio for design/technical theater applicants at end of freshman year. Auditions held once on campus. Portfolio reviews held twice on campus; the submission of slides may be substituted for portfolios whenever necessary.
Contact Co-Chairs, Drama/Dance Department, The University of Montana–Missoula, Missoula, Montana 59812-1058; 406-243-4481, fax: 406-243-5726.

▼ UNIVERSITY OF MONTEVALLO

Montevallo, Alabama

State-supported, coed. Small town campus. Total enrollment: 3,125. Theater program established 1923.
Degrees Bachelor of Fine Arts in the area of theater. Majors and concentrations: acting, directing, music theater, technical theater. Cross-registration with Birmingham Area Consortium for Higher Education (BACHE): Samford University, Birmingham Southern College, Miles College, University of Alabama, Birmingham.
Enrollment Fall 1997: 51 total; 35 undergraduate, 16 non-professional degree.
Theater Student Profile 65% females, 35% males, 5% minorities.
Theater Faculty 5 total (full-time and part-time). 100% of full-time faculty have terminal degrees. Graduate students do not teach undergraduate courses. Undergraduate student–faculty ratio: 10:1.
Student Life Student groups/activities include Children's Theatre Series.
Expenses for 1997–98 Application fee: $25. State resident tuition: $3040 full-time. Nonresident tuition: $6080 full-time. Mandatory fees: $140 full-time. College room and board: $3116. Room and board charges vary according to board plan and housing facility. Special program-related fees: $35 per semester for computer lab and printer use (unlimited).
Financial Aid Program-specific awards for 1997: 5–10 Dean of Fine Arts Awards for talented students ($2000), 15 Endowed Awards for talented students ($1000), 4 Presidents Scholarships for talented students ($3600).
Application Procedures Students apply for admission into the professional program by sophomore year. Deadline for freshmen and transfers: August 15. Notification date for freshmen and transfers: continuous. Required: high school transcript, minimum 2.0 high school GPA, audition for scholarship consideration, portfolio for technical theater scholarship consideration. Recommended: letter of recommendation, interview for directing and technical theater applicants, audition for acting and music theater applicants. Auditions held twice on campus. Portfolio reviews held twice on campus; the submission of slides may be substituted for portfolios as part of interview.
Web Site http://www.montevallo.edu/thea/.
Undergraduate Contact Director of Theatre, Communication Arts Department, University of Montevallo, Station 6210, Montevallo, Alabama 35115; 205-665-6210, fax: 205-665-6211, E-mail address: theatre@um.montevallo.edu.

▼ UNIVERSITY OF NEBRASKA–LINCOLN

Lincoln, Nebraska

State-supported, coed. Urban campus. Total enrollment: 22,827. Theater program established 1900.
Degrees Bachelor of Fine Arts in the areas of technical theater, theater arts. Graduate degrees offered: Master of Fine Arts in the areas of acting, design. Program accredited by NAST.
Enrollment Fall 1997: 100 total; 12 undergraduate, 18 graduate, 70 non-professional degree.
Theater Student Profile 60% females, 40% males, 1% minorities, 1% international.
Theater Faculty 14 total undergraduate and graduate (full-time and part-time). 100% of full-time faculty have terminal degrees. Graduate students teach a few undergraduate courses. Undergraduate student–faculty ratio: 7:1.
Student Life Student groups/activities include American College Theatre Festival, National Association of Schools of Theatre/University Resident Theatre Association.
Expenses for 1997–98 Application fee: $25. State resident tuition: $2355 full-time. Nonresident tuition: $6398 full-time. Mandatory fees: $474 full-time. Full-time tuition and fees

University of Nebraska–Lincoln *(continued)*

vary according to course load. College room and board: $3700. College room only: $1638.

Financial Aid Program-specific awards for 1997: 4 Hal Floyd Scholarships for freshmen ($500), 1–2 Williams-H. Alice Howell Awards for upperclass program majors ($750–$1500), 1 Dame Judith Anderson Award for sophomores ($100), 1 Eunice Vivian Peterson Memorial Scholarship for upperclass program majors ($400–$550), 4 Joseph R. Moore Fund Awards for freshmen ($200), 1–2 Helen Hayes MacArthur scholarships for upperclass program majors ($500–$1000).

Application Procedures Students admitted directly into the professional program freshman year. Deadline for freshmen and transfers: continuous. Required: high school transcript, college transcript(s) for transfer students, minimum 3.0 high school GPA, SAT I or ACT test scores, audition for scholarship consideration. Recommended: 3 letters of recommendation, interview, portfolio for design/technical theater applicants. Auditions held twice on campus. Portfolio reviews held twice on campus.

Undergraduate Contact Ms. Shirley Carr Mason, Associate Professor, Department of Theatre Arts and Dance, University of Nebraska–Lincoln, PO Box 880201, 215 Temple Building, Lincoln, Nebraska 68588-0201; 402-472-1603, fax: 402-472-9055, E-mail address: smason@unlinfo.unl.edu.

Graduate Contact Dr. Patricia Behrendt, Associate Professor, Department of Theatre Arts and Dance, University of Nebraska–Lincoln, PO Box 880201, 215 Temple Building, Lincoln, Nebraska 68588-0201; 402-472-1617, fax: 402-472-9055, E-mail address: pbehrendt@unlinfo.unl.edu.

▼ UNIVERSITY OF NEVADA, RENO

Reno, Nevada

State-supported, coed. Urban campus. Total enrollment: 12,442. Theater program established 1988.

Degrees Bachelor of Fine Arts in the areas of performance, design/technology.

Enrollment Fall 1997: 40 total; 5 undergraduate, 35 non-professional degree.

Theater Student Profile 50% females, 50% males.

Theater Faculty 8 total (full-time and part-time). 100% of full-time faculty have terminal degrees. Graduate students do not teach undergraduate courses. Undergraduate student–faculty ratio: 2:1.

Expenses for 1997–98 Application fee: $40. State resident tuition: $1995 full-time. Nonresident tuition: $7430 full-time. Mandatory fees: $114 full-time. Full-time tuition and fees vary according to course load. College room and board: $5095. College room only: $2800. Room and board charges vary according to board plan and housing facility.

Application Procedures Students apply for admission into the professional program by junior year. Deadline for freshmen and transfers: continuous. Notification date for freshmen and transfers: continuous. Required: high school transcript, college transcript(s) for transfer students, SAT I or ACT test scores, minimum 2.5 high school GPA, minimum 2.0 college GPA for transfer students.

Undergraduate Contact Dr. Bob Dillard, Director, Department of Theatre, University of Nevada, Reno, Reno, Nevada 89557; 702-784-6123.

▼ UNIVERSITY OF NORTH CAROLINA AT GREENSBORO

Greensboro, North Carolina

State-supported, coed. Urban campus. Total enrollment: 12,308. Theater program established 1953.

Degrees Bachelor of Fine Arts in the areas of acting, design and technical theater, theater education. Majors and concentrations: theater arts/drama, theater education. Graduate degrees offered: Master of Fine Arts in the areas of acting, design, directing, film/video production, theater for youth. Program accredited by NAST.

Enrollment Fall 1997: 226 total; 166 undergraduate, 60 graduate.

Theater Student Profile 59% females, 41% males, 5% minorities.

Theater Faculty 24 total undergraduate and graduate (full-time and part-time). 100% of full-time faculty have terminal degrees. Graduate students teach a few undergraduate courses. Undergraduate student–faculty ratio: 15:1.

Student Life Student groups/activities include Alpha Psi Omega, North Carolina Theatre for Young People, North Carolina Theatre Conference.

Expenses for 1997–98 Application fee: $35. State resident tuition: $1016 full-time. Nonresident tuition: $9304 full-time. Mandatory fees: $1015 full-time. College room and board: $3661. College room only: $2011.

Financial Aid Program-specific awards for 1997: 1 W. Raymond Taylor Scholarship for drama majors ($500).

Application Procedures Students apply for admission into the professional program by sophomore year. Deadline for freshmen and transfers: August 1. Notification date for freshmen and transfers: continuous. Required: high school transcript, minimum 2.0 high school GPA, SAT I test score only, portfolio review for design students, audition for acting students. Recommended: 3 letters of recommendation. Auditions held twice on campus; videotaped performances are permissible as a substitute for live auditions if a campus visit is impossible. Portfolio reviews held twice on campus; the submission of slides may be substituted for portfolios when distance is prohibitive.

Web Site http://www.uncg.edu.

Contact Dr. Robert C. Hansen, Head, Broadcasting/Cinema and Theatre Department, University of North Carolina at Greensboro, 201 Taylor, Greensboro, North Carolina 27412; 336-334-5576, fax: 336-334-5039.

▼ UNIVERSITY OF NORTH DAKOTA

Grand Forks, North Dakota

State-supported, coed. Small town campus. Total enrollment: 10,363.

Degrees Bachelor of Fine Arts in the areas of performance, design/technology. Majors and concentrations: design technology, performance, theater arts/drama. Program accredited by NAST.

Enrollment Fall 1997: 40 total; 25 undergraduate, 15 non-professional degree.

Theater Student Profile 60% females, 40% males, 5% minorities, 2% international.

Theater Faculty 10 total (full-time and part-time). 100% of full-time faculty have terminal degrees. Graduate students teach a few undergraduate courses. Undergraduate student–faculty ratio: 5:1.

Expenses for 1997–98 Application fee: $25. State resident tuition: $2677 full-time. Nonresident tuition: $6144 full-time. Mandatory fees: $441 full-time. Full-time tuition and fees vary according to program and reciprocity agreements. College room and board: $3117. College room only: $1216. Room and board charges vary according to board plan and housing facility. Special program-related fees: $15 per semester for makeup class fees.

Financial Aid Program-specific awards for 1997: 2–3 Donors awards for program majors ($1200), 10–15 departmental awards for program majors ($600).

Application Procedures Students admitted directly into the professional program freshman year. Deadline for freshmen and transfers: continuous. Required: high school transcript, minimum 2.0 high school GPA. Recommended: 2 letters of recommendation, interview, video, audition for performance applicants, portfolio for design/technology applicants. Auditions held once on campus; videotaped performances are permissible as a substitute for live auditions when distance is prohibitive. Portfolio reviews held once on campus.

Undergraduate Contact Kathleen McLennan, Chair, Theatre Arts Department, University of North Dakota, Box 8136, Grand Forks, North Dakota 58202; 701-777-3446, fax: 701-777-3522.

▼ UNIVERSITY OF OKLAHOMA

Norman, Oklahoma

State-supported, coed. Suburban campus. Total enrollment: 25,975. Theater program established 1923.

Degrees Bachelor of Fine Arts in the area of drama. Majors and concentrations: design technology, music theater, performance. Graduate degrees offered: Master of Fine Arts in the area of drama; Master of Arts in the area of drama.

Enrollment Fall 1997: 150 total; 125 undergraduate, 25 graduate.

Theater Student Profile 55% females, 45% males, 10% minorities, 3% international.

Theater Faculty 18 total undergraduate and graduate (full-time and part-time). 100% of full-time faculty have terminal degrees. Graduate students teach a few undergraduate courses. Undergraduate student–faculty ratio: 12:1.

Student Life Student groups/activities include Drama and Dance Association.

Expenses for 1997–98 Application fee: $25. State resident tuition: $1745 full-time. Nonresident tuition: $5785 full-time. Mandatory fees: $566 full-time. Full-time tuition and fees vary according to course level, course load, location, program, and reciprocity agreements. College room and board: $3800. College room only: $1884. Room and board charges vary according to board plan, housing facility, and student level. Special program-related fees: $5–$95 per course for lab fees.

Financial Aid Program-specific awards for 1997: 55 departmental scholarships for program majors ($500–$1500), 10 assistantships for program majors ($3300).

Application Procedures Students apply for admission into the professional program by sophomore year. Deadline for freshmen and transfers: July 1. Required: high school transcript, college transcript(s) for transfer students, interview, audition, portfolio, SAT I or ACT test scores (minimum combined SAT I score of 1070, minimum combined ACT score of 23), minimum 2.5 high school GPA. Recommended: essay, minimum 3.0 high school GPA, 3 letters of recommendation. Auditions held 3 times and as needed on campus and off campus in University Resident Theatre Association locations, Texas Educational Theatre Association locations, and various other theater association sites; videotaped performances are permissible as a substitute for live auditions with permission of the director. Portfolio reviews held 3 times and as needed on campus and off campus in University Resident Theatre Association locations, Texas Educational Theatre Association locations, and various other theater association sites; the submission of slides may be substituted for portfolios (slides preferred).

Undergraduate Contact Mr. Steven W. Wallace, Director, School of Drama, University of Oklahoma, 563 Elm Avenue, #209, Norman, Oklahoma 73019-0310; 405-325-4021, fax: 405-325-0400, E-mail address: swallace@ou.edu.

Graduate Contact Dr. Kae Koger, Graduate Liaison, School of Drama, University of Oklahoma, 563 Elm Avenue, #209, Norman, Oklahoma 73019-0310; 405-325-5328, fax: 405-325-0400, E-mail address: alicia-kaekoger-1@ou.edu.

More About the University

Program Facilities The School of Drama utilizes three outstanding performance facilities: Rupel J. Jones Theatre, a highly flexible 650-seat hall; Weitzenhoffer Theatre, an intimate and state-of-the-art 200-seat space; and Lab Theatre at Old Science Hall, a student-run 90-seat theater. Classrooms, rehearsal space, and the Rupel J. Jones and Weitzenhoffer Theatres are housed in the Fine Arts Center, conveniently located on the northwest quadrant of the main campus.

Faculty, Resident Artists, and Alumni The School of Drama has more than fourteen excellent faculty members and has vital contacts on both the east and west coasts. Tony Award-winning producer Max Weitzenhoffer is an adjunct faculty member and producing director of the Musical Theatre Program. Students are often used to develop Broadway-bound materials. Guest artists, including John Cullum, Ming Cho Lee, Jane Alexander, Tom Sawyer, Stewart Lane, and Mark Medoff, often visit the campus to conduct workshops and master classes for students.

Student Performance/Design Opportunities The School of Drama produces ten to twelve mainstage productions and eight Lab Theatre productions each year. In addition, OU SummerStage, a professional summer stock company, produces three to four productions each summer. This high number of performance and design opportunities provide ample experience for our students. The School of Drama is very active in the Kennedy Center/American College Theatre Festival. This venture allows students an opportunity to evaluate their work on a regional level and make vital contacts for future job prospects.

▼ UNIVERSITY OF RHODE ISLAND

Kingston, Rhode Island

State-supported, coed. Small town campus. Total enrollment: 13,437. Theater program established 1966.

Degrees Bachelor of Fine Arts in the areas of acting, directing, design and technology, theater management. Cross-registration with Rhode Island College.

Enrollment Fall 1997: 87 total; all undergraduate.

Theater Student Profile 53% females, 47% males, 1% minorities.

University of Rhode Island (*continued*)

Theater Faculty 13 total (full-time and part-time). 80% of full-time faculty have terminal degrees. Graduate students do not teach undergraduate courses.

Student Life Student groups/activities include Afternoon Theatre Productions, Staged Reading Series, 10 Minute Play Festival.

Expenses for 1997–98 Application fee: $30, $45 for nonresidents. State resident tuition: $3202 full-time. Nonresident tuition: $11,010 full-time. Mandatory fees: $1390 full-time. College room and board: $5764. College room only: $3338. Special program-related fees: $5–$50 per course for lab/materials fees.

Financial Aid Program-specific awards for 1997: 4 Theatre Department Merit Awards for theater majors ($500), 1–2 Thomas Pezzullo Scholarships for theater majors ($900).

Application Procedures Students admitted directly into the professional program freshman year. Deadline for freshmen: March 1; transfers: May 1. Notification date for freshmen: May 1. Required: essay, high school transcript, college transcript(s) for transfer students, SAT I or ACT test scores (minimum combined SAT I score of 900, minimum combined ACT score of 18), minimum 2.5 high school GPA. Recommended: interview.

Undergraduate Contact Joy Emery, Acting Chair, Department of Theatre, University of Rhode Island, 105 Upper College Road, Suite 3, Kingston, Rhode Island 02881; 401-874-2713, fax: 401-874-5618, E-mail address: jemery@uriacc.uri.edu.

▼ University of South Alabama

Mobile, Alabama

State-supported, coed. Suburban campus.

Degrees Bachelor of Fine Arts in the area of theater arts/drama.

Enrollment Fall 1997: 25 total; all undergraduate.

Theater Student Profile 51% females, 49% males, 10% minorities, 1% international.

Theater Faculty 5 total (full-time and part-time). 50% of full-time faculty have terminal degrees. Graduate students do not teach undergraduate courses.

Expenses for 1997–98 Application fee: $25. State resident tuition: $2640 full-time. Nonresident tuition: $5280 full-time. Mandatory fees: $198 full-time.

Financial Aid Program-specific awards for 1997: 6 Assistantship Awards for drama majors ($625).

Application Procedures Students admitted directly into the professional program freshman year. Deadline for freshmen and transfers: continuous. Required: essay, college transcript(s) for transfer students, SAT I or ACT test scores (minimum combined SAT I score of 800, minimum combined ACT score of 20). Recommended: high school transcript.

Web Site http://usouthal.edu/drama.

Undergraduate Contact Dr. R. Eugene Jackson, Chairman, Dramatic Arts Department, University of South Alabama, 1052 PAC, USA, Mobile, Alabama 36688-0002; 334-460-6305, fax: 334-461-1511.

▼ University of South Dakota

Vermillion, South Dakota

State-supported, coed. Small town campus. Total enrollment: 7,392. Theater program established 1935.

Degrees Bachelor of Fine Arts in the areas of acting, theater, design and theater technology. Majors and concentrations: acting, costume design, lighting design, set design, sound design, technical direction, theater arts/drama. Graduate degrees offered: Master of Fine Arts in the areas of directing, design and theater technology. Program accredited by NAST.

Enrollment Fall 1997: 69 total; 37 undergraduate, 7 graduate, 25 non-professional degree.

Theater Student Profile 48% females, 52% males, 4% minorities, 4% international.

Theater Faculty 9 total undergraduate and graduate (full-time). 100% of full-time faculty have terminal degrees. Graduate students teach a few undergraduate courses. Undergraduate student–faculty ratio: 6:1.

Student Life Student groups/activities include Strollers, Coyote Capers, Ye Olde Comedy Troupe.

Expenses for 1997–98 Application fee: $15. State resident tuition: $1728 full-time. Nonresident tuition: $5496 full-time. Mandatory fees: $1284 full-time. Full-time tuition and fees vary according to reciprocity agreements. College room and board: $2912. College room only: $1322. Room and board charges vary according to board plan.

Financial Aid Program-specific awards for 1997: 1–10 Freshman Talent Scholarships for entering freshmen theater majors ($300–$1000), 10–12 Endowed Scholarships for sophomore, junior, and senior theater majors ($200–$750).

Application Procedures Deadline for freshmen and transfers: continuous. Required: high school transcript, college transcript(s) for transfer students, interview, SAT I or ACT test scores, standing in top 60% of graduating class or minimum ACT score of 18 or minimum 2.6 high school GPA, portfolio for design/technology applicants, audition for acting applicants. Auditions held during February and March by appointment on campus and off campus in Lincoln, NE; Denver, CO; videotaped performances are permissible as a substitute for live auditions when distance is prohibitive. Portfolio reviews held during February and March by appointment on campus and off campus in Lincoln, NE; Denver, CO; the submission of slides may be substituted for portfolios when distance is prohibitive.

Web Site http://www.usd.edu/cfa/Theatre/theatre.html.

Undergraduate Contact Department of Theatre, University of South Dakota, CFA 184A, 414 East Clark Street, Vermillion, South Dakota 57069-2390; 605-677-5418, fax: 605-677-5988, E-mail address: cfa@usd.edu.

Graduate Contact Dr. Ronald L. Moyer, Director of Graduate Studies, Department of Theatre, University of South Dakota, CFA 184B, 414 East Clark Street, Vermillion, South Dakota 57069-2390; 605-677-5735, fax: 605-677-5988, E-mail address: rmoyer@usd.edu.

▼ University of Southern California

Los Angeles, California

Independent, coed. Urban campus. Total enrollment: 28,342. Theater program established 1990.

Degrees Bachelor of Fine Arts in the areas of acting, stage management, technical direction, design. Majors and concentrations: acting, design, stage management, technical direction. Graduate degrees offered: Master of Fine Arts in the areas of acting, playwriting, design, directing.

Enrollment Fall 1997: 351 total; 330 undergraduate, 21 graduate.

Theater Student Profile 57% females, 43% males, 12% minorities, 2% international.

Theater Faculty 41 total undergraduate and graduate (full-time and part-time). 100% of full-time faculty have terminal degrees. Graduate students teach a few undergraduate courses.

Student Life Student groups/activities include community-based theater lab, Theatre for Youth, Theater Representative Council.

Expenses for 1997–98 Application fee: $55. Comprehensive fee: $27,228 includes full-time tuition ($20,078), mandatory fees ($402), and college room and board ($6748). College room only: $3716. Room and board charges vary according to board plan and housing facility.

Financial Aid Program-specific awards for 1997: 1–2 Trustee Scholarships for program majors demonstrating talent and academic achievement ($16,500), 10–11 Dean's Scholarships for program majors demonstrating talent and academic achievement ($6000), 2 Jack Nicholson Awards for performers demonstrating talent and academic achievement ($8000), 2 Stanley Musgrove Awards for those demonstrating talent and academic achievement ($2500), 2 John Blankenship/William C. White Awards for those demonstrating talent and academic achievement ($2000), 1 James Pendleton Award for program majors demonstrating talent and academic achievement ($2500), 2–3 Presidential Scholarships for program majors demonstrating talent and academic achievement ($8000).

Application Procedures Students admitted directly into the professional program freshman year. Deadline for freshmen and transfers: January 2. Notification date for freshmen and transfers: continuous. Required: essay, high school transcript, college transcript(s) for transfer students, minimum 2.0 high school GPA, 2 letters of recommendation, interview, SAT I or ACT test scores, audition for acting applicant, portfolio for stage management, technical and design applicants. Recommended: minimum 3.0 high school GPA. Auditions held 9 times on campus and off campus in Chicago, IL; New York, NY; San Francisco, CA; Dallas, TX; videotaped performances are permissible as a substitute for live auditions for international students and U.S. students from a great distance. Portfolio reviews held 9 times on campus and off campus in Chicago, IL; New York, NY; San Francisco, CA; Dallas, TX; the submission of slides may be substituted for portfolios if a campus visit is impossible.

Web Site http://www.usc.edu/dept/theatre/DramaNet/.

Contact Ms. Lori Ray Fisher, Director, Academic Services, University of Southern California, Los Angeles, California 90089-0791; 213-740-1286, fax: 213-740-8888, E-mail address: dramaapp@mizar.usc.edu.

More About the University

Program of Study The B.A. combines a theater and liberal arts education. This program is designed for students many a passion for theater and a desire to explore one of the many other major/minor combinations at USC. The B.F.A. in acting is a rigorous four-year professional training program comprising an integrated four-year sequence of training in acting, voice, and body movement. The B.F.A. production program incorporates study in scenic, lighting, and costume design; management; technical direction; stage; and theater management.

Program Facilities Bing Theatre, a modern proscenium 589-seat house; Massman Theatre, an intimate studio that seats 60; and a newly constructed theater, a second studio with flexible seating for 75 people.

Faculty/Visiting Artists Faculty members are award-winners in their fields and maintain active professional lives in theater, film, and television while teaching. The School invites leading international artists to interact with students as directors, lecturers, and teachers of specialized workshops.

Program Supplements The Theatre Council, an elected body of students, represents their peers in meetings with the School's administration and faculty. The Casting Office maintains students' résumés and headshots on file for use by student filmmakers and outside agencies. Students are encouraged to seek professional experience through internship opportunities. Overseas study programs are available. The School of Cinema and Television also offers theater students a unique opportunity to gain experience in these media.

▼ UNIVERSITY OF SOUTHERN MISSISSIPPI

Hattiesburg, Mississippi

State-supported, coed. Suburban campus. Total enrollment: 14,599. Theater program established 1956.

Degrees Bachelor of Fine Arts in the areas of acting, design and technical theater. Majors and concentrations: acting, design/technical theater, theater arts/drama. Graduate degrees offered: Master of Fine Arts in the areas of performance (acting and directing), design and technical theater. Program accredited by NAST.

Enrollment Fall 1997: 82 undergraduate, 21 graduate.

Theater Student Profile 50% females, 50% males, 10% minorities, 3% international.

Theater Faculty 7 total undergraduate and graduate (full-time). 72% of full-time faculty have terminal degrees. Graduate students teach about a quarter undergraduate courses. Undergraduate student–faculty ratio: 9:1.

Student Life Student groups/activities include Southern Arena Theater.

Expenses for 1997–98 State resident tuition: $2590 full-time. Nonresident tuition: $5410 full-time. College room and board: $2565. Room and board charges vary according to board plan and housing facility.

Financial Aid Program-specific awards for 1997: 15–20 Service Awards for talented students with high test scores ($500).

Application Procedures Students admitted directly into the professional program freshman year. Deadline for freshmen and transfers: August 15. Required: high school transcript, college transcript(s) for transfer students, minimum 2.0 high school GPA, SAT I or ACT test scores. Recommended: 2 letters of recommendation.

Contact Mr. George Crook, Chair, Department of Theater and Dance, University of Southern Mississippi, Box 5052, Hattiesburg, Mississippi 39406-5052; 601-266-4994.

▼ UNIVERSITY OF SOUTHWESTERN LOUISIANA

Lafayette, Louisiana

State-supported, coed. Urban campus. Total enrollment: 17,020. Theater program established 1994.

Degrees Bachelor of Fine Arts in the area of performing arts. Majors and concentrations: dance, theater arts/drama.

Enrollment Fall 1997: 50 total; all undergraduate.

Theater Student Profile 40% females, 60% males, 8% minorities, 2% international.

University of Southwestern Louisiana *(continued)*

Theater Faculty 7 total (full-time and part-time). 100% of full-time faculty have terminal degrees. Graduate students do not teach undergraduate courses. Undergraduate student–faculty ratio: 10:1.

Expenses for 1997–98 Application fee: $5, $15 for international students. State resident tuition: $1947 full-time. Nonresident tuition: $6075 full-time. College room and board: $2592. Room and board charges vary according to board plan.

Financial Aid Program-specific awards for 1997: 4 departmental scholarships for program majors ($500–$1500).

Application Procedures Students admitted directly into the professional program freshman year. Deadline for freshmen and transfers: continuous. Required: high school transcript, college transcript(s) for transfer students, minimum 2.0 high school GPA, SAT I or ACT test scores, minimum 2.75 high school GPA and audition for scholarship consideration. Auditions held once in the Spring or by appointment on campus; videotaped performances are permissible as a substitute for live auditions for provisional scholarship consideration.

Web Site http://www.usl.edu.

Undergraduate Contact Dr. Stephen Taft, Chairman, Performing Arts Department, University of Southwestern Louisiana, Box 43850, Lafayette, Louisiana 70504; 318-482-6357, fax: 318-482-5089.

▼ THE UNIVERSITY OF TENNESSEE AT MARTIN

Martin, Tennessee

State-supported, coed. Small town campus. Total enrollment: 5,997. Theater program established 1989.

Degrees Bachelor of Fine Arts in the area of fine and performing arts. Majors and concentrations: theater arts/drama.

Enrollment Fall 1997: 17 undergraduate.

Theater Student Profile 60% females, 40% males, 5% minorities, 2% international.

Theater Faculty 2 total (full-time). 100% of full-time faculty have terminal degrees. Graduate students do not teach undergraduate courses. Undergraduate student–faculty ratio: 9:1.

Student Life Student groups/activities include Vanguard Theatre.

Expenses for 1997–98 Application fee: $25. State resident tuition: $2240 full-time. Nonresident tuition: $6706 full-time. College room and board: $3104. College room only: $1600. Room and board charges vary according to board plan and housing facility.

Financial Aid Program-specific awards for 1997: 1 Endowment for the Arts Scholarship for theater majors ($750).

Application Procedures Students admitted directly into the professional program freshman year. Deadline for freshmen and transfers: continuous. Required: high school transcript, minimum 2.0 high school GPA, audition, SAT I or ACT test scores. Auditions held once on campus; videotaped performances are permissible as a substitute for live auditions when distance is prohibitive.

Web Site http://www.utm.edu/departments/finearts/dfpa.htm.

Undergraduate Contact Dr. Earl Norwood, Director, Division of Fine and Performing Arts, The University of Tennessee at Martin, 102 Fine Arts Building, Martin, Tennessee 38238; 901-587-7400, fax: 901-587-7415, E-mail address: norwood@utm.edu.

▼ THE UNIVERSITY OF TEXAS AT AUSTIN

Austin, Texas

State-supported, coed. Urban campus. Total enrollment: 48,857. Theater program established 1938.

Degrees Bachelor of Fine Arts in the area of theater studies. Graduate degrees offered: Master of Fine Arts in the areas of acting, creative drama, directing, playwriting, theater technology, design. Doctor of Philosophy in the area of theater. Program accredited by NAST.

Enrollment Fall 1997: 530 total; 100 undergraduate, 90 graduate, 340 non-professional degree.

Theater Student Profile 55% females, 45% males, 18% minorities, 1% international.

Theater Faculty 43 total undergraduate and graduate (full-time and part-time). 99% of full-time faculty have terminal degrees. Graduate students teach a few undergraduate courses. Undergraduate student–faculty ratio: 12:1.

Student Life Student groups/activities include Drama Education Organization, Student Advisory Council, Fine Arts Advisory Council.

Expenses for 1997–98 Application fee: $40. State resident tuition: $2040 full-time. Nonresident tuition: $8460 full-time. Mandatory fees: $826 full-time. Full-time tuition and fees vary according to course load and program. College room and board: $3901. College room only: $1950. Room and board charges vary according to board plan. Special program-related fees: $48 per course for production and performance fee.

Financial Aid Program-specific awards for 1997: 1 Barton-Berry Scholarship for theater students ($2000), 2 Crain Scholarships for theater students ($2000), 2 Denney Scholarships for theater students ($2000), 1 Hanna CES in Drama Scholarship for theater students ($8600), 2 Hexter Scholarships for theater students ($5000), 1 Hingle Scholarship for theater students ($2000).

Application Procedures Students admitted directly into the professional program freshman year. Deadline for freshmen and transfers: February 1. Notification date for freshmen and transfers: April 1. Required: essay, high school transcript, college transcript(s) for transfer students, SAT I or ACT test scores, resume for transfer students.

Web Site http://www.utexas.edu/cofa/theatre/.

Undergraduate Contact Mr. Stephen Gerald, Undergraduate Program Coordinator, Department of Theatre and Dance, The University of Texas at Austin, WIN 1.120, Austin, Texas 78712; 512-471-5793, fax: 512-471-0824.

Graduate Contact Dr. David Nancarrow, Graduate Advisor, Department of Theatre and Dance, The University of Texas at Austin, WIN 2.160, Austin, Texas 78712; 512-471-5793, fax: 512-471-0824.

▼ UNIVERSITY OF THE ARTS

Philadelphia, Pennsylvania

Independent, coed. Urban campus. Total enrollment: 1,624. Theater program established 1983.

Degrees Bachelor of Fine Arts in the area of theater arts and writing for media and performance. Majors and concentrations: acting, music theater.

Enrollment Fall 1997: 164 total; all undergraduate.

Theater Student Profile 55% females, 45% males, 18% minorities, 1% international.

Theater Faculty 38 total (full-time and part-time). 60% of full-time faculty have terminal degrees. Graduate students do not teach undergraduate courses. Undergraduate student–faculty ratio: 8:1.

Student Life Student groups/activities include Students for Environmental Education, Student Government. Special housing available for theater students.

Expenses for 1997–98 Application fee: $40. Tuition: $14,570 full-time. Mandatory fees: $500 full-time. College room only: $4100.

Financial Aid Program-specific awards for 1997: 30 Merit Scholarships for incoming students ($500–$5000).

Application Procedures Students admitted directly into the professional program freshman year. Deadline for freshmen and transfers: continuous. Required: essay, high school transcript, college transcript(s) for transfer students, minimum 2.0 high school GPA, letter of recommendation, audition, SAT I or ACT test scores, resume and photograph. Recommended: minimum 3.0 high school GPA, interview. Auditions held 8 times on campus and off campus in various thespian festival locations; videotaped performances are permissible as a substitute for live auditions when distance is prohibitive.

Undergraduate Contact Ms. Barbara Elliott, Director of Admissions, University of the Arts, 320 South Broad Street, Philadelphia, Pennsylvania 19102; 800-616-ARTS, fax: 215-875-5458.

▼ UNIVERSITY OF TOLEDO

Toledo, Ohio

State-supported, coed. Suburban campus. Total enrollment: 20,307.

Degrees Bachelor of Fine Arts in the area of theater. Majors and concentrations: acting, directing. Cross-registration with Bowling Green State University.

Enrollment Fall 1997: 60 total; 10 undergraduate, 50 non-professional degree.

Theater Student Profile 65% females, 35% males, 10% minorities.

Theater Faculty 5 total (full-time and part-time). 100% of full-time faculty have terminal degrees. Graduate students do not teach undergraduate courses. Undergraduate student–faculty ratio: 15:1.

Expenses for 1997–98 Application fee: $30. State resident tuition: $3171 full-time. Nonresident tuition: $8763 full-time. Mandatory fees: $781 full-time. College room and board: $4194. Room and board charges vary according to board plan and housing facility.

Financial Aid Program-specific awards for 1997: 1 Wolfe Award for graduates of Ohio high schools ($1500).

Application Procedures Students apply for admission into the professional program by sophomore year. Deadline for freshmen and transfers: continuous. Required: college transcript(s) for transfer students, audition. Recommended: SAT I or ACT test scores. Auditions held once on campus.

Web Site http://www.utoledo.edu/colleges/arts-and-sciences/theatre.

Undergraduate Contact Mr. James Hill, Chair, Department of Theatre, Film and Dance, University of Toledo, Toledo , Ohio 43606-3390; 419-530-2202, fax: 419-530-8439.

▼ UNIVERSITY OF UTAH

Salt Lake City, Utah

State-supported, coed. Urban campus. Total enrollment: 25,883. Theater program established 1947.

Degrees Bachelor of Fine Arts in the areas of actor training, teaching, design, stage management. Majors and concentrations: acting, design, film and video production, stage management, theater arts/drama, theater education. Graduate degrees offered: Master of Fine Arts in the areas of directing, film.

Enrollment Fall 1997: 266 total; 241 undergraduate, 25 graduate.

Theater Student Profile 45% females, 55% males, 5% minorities, 5% international.

Theater Faculty 36 total undergraduate and graduate (full-time and part-time). 100% of full-time faculty have terminal degrees. Graduate students do not teach undergraduate courses. Undergraduate student–faculty ratio: 12:1.

Student Life Student groups/activities include Kingsbury Hall Young Persons Drama Season, National Student Film and Video Festival.

Expenses for 1997–98 Application fee: $30. State resident tuition: $2601 full-time. Nonresident tuition: $7,998 full-time. Full-time tuition varies according to course load. College room and board: $4620. College room only: $1708. Room and board charges vary according to board plan.

Financial Aid Program-specific awards for 1997: 3 Special Departmental Scholarships for resident incoming freshmen ($2000), 2 Continuing Student Scholarships for continuing students ($2000).

Application Procedures Students admitted directly into the professional program freshman year. Deadline for freshmen and transfers: March 1. Required: high school transcript, college transcript(s) for transfer students, minimum 2.0 high school GPA, letter of recommendation, audition, portfolio, SAT I or ACT test scores. Recommended: essay, minimum 3.0 high school GPA, interview, video. Auditions held twice on campus; videotaped performances are permissible as a substitute for live auditions for out-of-state applicants. Portfolio reviews held twice on campus; the submission of slides may be substituted for portfolios for design applicants.

Web Site http://www.theatre.utah.edu/.

Undergraduate Contact Undergraduate Advisor, Theatre and Film Department, University of Utah, 206 Performing Arts Building, Salt Lake City, Utah 84112; 801-581-6448, fax: 801-585-6154.

Graduate Contact Dr. Thomas B. Sobchack, Director of Graduate Studies, Theatre and Film Department, University of Utah, 206 Performing Arts Building, Salt Lake City, Utah 84112; 801-581-5761.

▼ UNIVERSITY OF WISCONSIN–MILWAUKEE

Milwaukee, Wisconsin

State-supported, coed. Urban campus. Total enrollment: 21,525. Theater program established 1978.

University of Wisconsin–Milwaukee *(continued)*

Degrees Bachelor of Fine Arts in the area of theater. Majors and concentrations: acting, costume production, stage management, technical production. Graduate degrees offered: Master of Fine Arts in the area of performing arts.
Enrollment Fall 1997: 66 total; 36 undergraduate, 30 graduate.
Theater Student Profile 55% females, 45% males, 5% minorities, 6% international.
Theater Faculty 17 total undergraduate and graduate (full-time and part-time). 64% of full-time faculty have terminal degrees. Graduate students do not teach undergraduate courses. Undergraduate student–faculty ratio: 1:1.
Student Life Student groups/activities include Professional Theatre Training Program Student Support.
Expenses for 1997–98 Application fee: $28. State resident tuition: $3327 full-time. Nonresident tuition: $10,790 full-time. Full-time tuition varies according to reciprocity agreements. College room only: $2457.
Financial Aid Program-specific awards for 1997: 10–15 Professional Theatre Training Program Scholarships for program students ($1000–$3000).
Application Procedures Students admitted directly into the professional program freshman year. Deadline for freshmen and transfers: March 1. Notification date for freshmen and transfers: April 1. Required: high school transcript, college transcript(s) for transfer students, minimum 2.0 high school GPA, 2 letters of recommendation, interview, audition, SAT I or ACT test scores. Recommended: portfolio. Auditions held once every other year on campus and off campus in Chicago, IL; New York, NY; San Francisco, CA. Portfolio reviews held once every other year on campus and off campus in various locations.
Web Site http://www.uwm.edu/Dept/SFA/.
Undergraduate Contact Department of Recruitment and Outreach, University of Wisconsin–Milwaukee, PO Box 749, Milwaukee, Wisconsin 53201; 414-229-2222, fax: 414-229-6940, E-mail address: uwmtours@cgd.uwm.edu.
Graduate Contact The Graduate School, University of Wisconsin–Milwaukee, PO Box 340, Milwaukee, Wisconsin 53201; 414-229-4982, fax: 414-229-6967, E-mail address: gradschool@csd.uwm.edu.

▼ University of Wisconsin–Stevens Point

Stevens Point, Wisconsin

State-supported, coed. Small town campus. Total enrollment: 8,446. Theater program established 1985.
Degrees Bachelor of Fine Arts in the areas of acting, design/technology, musical theater. Majors and concentrations: acting, design technology, music theater. Program accredited by NAST.
Enrollment Fall 1997: 45 undergraduate.
Theater Student Profile 50% females, 50% males, 1% minorities.
Theater Faculty 9 total (full-time and part-time). 100% of full-time faculty have terminal degrees. Graduate students do not teach undergraduate courses. Undergraduate student–faculty ratio: 10:1.
Expenses for 1997–98 Application fee: $35. State resident tuition: $2790 full-time. Nonresident tuition: $8732 full-time. Full-time tuition varies according to course load and

reciprocity agreements. College room and board: $3188. College room only: $1861. Room and board charges vary according to board plan.
Financial Aid Program-specific awards for 1997: 6 theater scholarships for incoming students ($500–$800).
Application Procedures Deadline for freshmen and transfers: March 1. Required: high school transcript, 3 letters of recommendation, audition, portfolio, standing in top half of graduating class or minimum ACT score of 23. Auditions held 3 times on campus. Portfolio reviews held once on campus.
Undergraduate Contact Dr. Arthur B. Hopper, Chair, Department of Theatre and Dance, University of Wisconsin–Stevens Point, COFAC, Stevens Point, Wisconsin 54481; 715-346-4429, fax: 715-346-2718.

▼ University of Wisconsin–Superior

Superior, Wisconsin

State-supported, coed. Small town campus. Total enrollment: 2,574.
Degrees Bachelor of Fine Arts in the area of theater. Majors and concentrations: acting, directing, lighting design, scenic design, sound design, technical theater, theater management. Cross-registration with University of Minnesota-Duluth.
Enrollment Fall 1997: 30 total; 10 undergraduate, 20 non-professional degree.
Theater Faculty 9 total (full-time and part-time). 100% of full-time faculty have terminal degrees. Graduate students do not teach undergraduate courses. Undergraduate student–faculty ratio: 12:1.
Student Life Student groups/activities include student-directed shows, drama honorary organization.
Expenses for 1997–98 Application fee: $35. State resident tuition: $2652 full-time. Nonresident tuition: $8600 full-time. Full-time tuition varies according to course load and reciprocity agreements. College room and board: $3200. College room only: $1600.
Financial Aid Program-specific awards for 1997: 5 departmental scholarships for program students ($100–$500).
Application Procedures Students admitted directly into the professional program freshman year. Deadline for freshmen and transfers: continuous. Notification date for freshmen and transfers: continuous. Required: high school transcript, college transcript(s) for transfer students, minimum 2.0 high school GPA, SAT I or ACT test scores.
Web Site http://staff.uwsuper.edu/commarts/.
Undergraduate Contact Mr. Jon Wojciechowski, Director, Admissions Office, University of Wisconsin–Superior, 1800 Grand Avenue, Superior, Wisconsin 54880-2898; 715-394-8396, E-mail address: jwojciec@staff.uwsuper.edu.

▼ University of Wyoming

Laramie, Wyoming

State-supported, coed. Small town campus. Total enrollment: 11,094.
Degrees Bachelor of Fine Arts in the areas of theater, performance, design, theater/English. Majors and concentrations: acting, costume design, lighting design, set design, technical direction, theater/English.

Enrollment Fall 1997: 60 total; 30 undergraduate, 30 non-professional degree.

Theater Student Profile 17% minorities.

Theater Faculty 11 total (full-time and part-time). 90% of full-time faculty have terminal degrees. Graduate students do not teach undergraduate courses. Undergraduate student–faculty ratio: 10:1.

Student Life Student groups/activities include Associated Students.

Expenses for 1997–98 Application fee: $30. State resident tuition: $1944 full-time. Nonresident tuition: $7032 full-time. Mandatory fees: $386 full-time. College room and board: $4278. College room only: $1758. Room and board charges vary according to board plan.

Financial Aid Program-specific awards for 1997: 21 departmental awards for program majors ($2144).

Application Procedures Students admitted directly into the professional program freshman year. Deadline for freshmen and transfers: August 31. Required: high school transcript, college transcript(s) for transfer students, minimum 3.0 high school GPA, SAT I or ACT test scores, audition for scholarship consideration, minimum 2.75 high school GPA for Wyoming residents. Recommended: letter of recommendation, interview, portfolio. Auditions held twice on campus and off campus in Rocky Mountain Theatre Association Festival locations; videotaped performances are permissible as a substitute for live auditions if a campus visit is impossible. Portfolio reviews held twice on campus and off campus in Rocky Mountain Theatre Association Festival locations; the submission of slides may be substituted for portfolios if a campus visit is impossible.

Undergraduate Contact Dr. Rebecca Hilliker, Head, Department of Theatre and Dance, University of Wyoming, Box 3951 University Station, Laramie, Wyoming 82071-3951; 307-766-2198, fax: 307-766-2197, E-mail address: hilliker@uwyo.edu.

▼ UTAH STATE UNIVERSITY

Logan, Utah

State-supported, coed. Urban campus. Total enrollment: 21,234. Theater program established 1967.

Degrees Bachelor of Fine Arts in the area of theater arts. Graduate degrees offered: Master of Fine Arts in the area of theater arts.

Enrollment Fall 1997: 79 total; 65 undergraduate, 10 graduate, 4 non-professional degree.

Theater Student Profile 60% females, 40% males, 3% minorities, 3% international.

Theater Faculty 11 total undergraduate and graduate (full-time and part-time). 100% of full-time faculty have terminal degrees. Graduate students teach a few undergraduate courses.

Expenses for 1997–98 Application fee: $35. State resident tuition: $1767 full-time. Nonresident tuition: $6207 full-time. Mandatory fees: $408 full-time. Full-time tuition and fees vary according to course load. College room and board: $3510. College room only: $1440. Room and board charges vary according to board plan and housing facility.

Financial Aid Program-specific awards for 1997: 75 Talent Awards for program students ($570).

Application Procedures Students apply for admission into the professional program by freshman year. Deadline for freshmen and transfers: July 15. Notification date for freshmen and transfers: August 1. Required: high school

transcript, college transcript(s) for transfer students, minimum 2.0 high school GPA, ACT test score only, audition/portfolio for scholarship consideration. Auditions held 5 times on campus and off campus in Rocky Mountain Theatre Association locations, American College Theatre Association locations; recorded music is permissible as a substitute for live auditions if a campus visit is impossible and videotaped performances are permissible as a substitute for live auditions if a campus visit is impossible. Portfolio reviews held 5 times on campus and off campus in Rocky Mountain Theatre Association locations, American College Theatre Association locations; the submission of slides may be substituted for portfolios if a campus visit is impossible.

Web Site http://www.usu.edu/~theatre/index.html.

Undergraduate Contact Dr. Colin Johnson, Department Head, Department of Theatre Arts, Utah State University, 4025 Old Main Hill, Logan, Utah 84322-4025; 801-797-3046, fax: 801-797-0086, E-mail address: colinj@wpo.hass.usu.edu.

Graduate Contact Ms. Nancy Hills, Graduate Program Coordinator, Department of Theatre Arts, Utah State University, 4025 Old Main Hill, Logan, Utah 84322-4025; 801-797-3049, fax: 801-797-0086, E-mail address: nhills@wpo.hass.usu.edu.

▼ VALDOSTA STATE UNIVERSITY

Valdosta, Georgia

State-supported, coed. Small town campus. Total enrollment: 9,779. Theater program established 1964.

Degrees Bachelor of Fine Arts in the area of theater arts.

Enrollment Fall 1997: 80 total; all undergraduate.

Theater Student Profile 60% females, 40% males, 10% minorities, 5% international.

Theater Faculty 9 total (full-time and part-time). 100% of full-time faculty have terminal degrees. Graduate students do not teach undergraduate courses.

Student Life Student groups/activities include College Theater, Georgia Theatre Conference, Southeastern Theatre Conference.

Expenses for 1997–98 Application fee: $10. State resident tuition: $1680 full-time. Nonresident tuition: $6141 full-time. Mandatory fees: $294 full-time. College room and board: $3465. College room only: $1665. Room and board charges vary according to board plan.

Financial Aid Program-specific awards for 1997: 20 theater scholarships for program students ($600–$1500).

Application Procedures Students admitted directly into the professional program freshman year. Deadline for freshmen and transfers: continuous. Required: high school transcript, audition/portfolio for scholarship consideration. Recommended: minimum 2.0 high school GPA, interview. Auditions held twice on campus and off campus in Atlanta, GA; recorded music is permissible as a substitute for live auditions when distance is prohibitive and videotaped performances are permissible as a substitute for live auditions when distance is prohibitive. Portfolio reviews held twice on campus and off campus in Atlanta, GA; the submission of slides may be substituted for portfolios when distance is prohibitive.

Undergraduate Contact Mr. Walter Peacock, Director, Admissions Office, Valdosta State University, 1500 North Patterson Street, Valdosta, Georgia 31698; 800-618-1878.

▼ VIRGINIA COMMONWEALTH UNIVERSITY

Richmond, Virginia

State-supported, coed. Urban campus. Total enrollment: 22,702. Theater program established 1940.

Degrees Bachelor of Fine Arts in the areas of theater, theater education. Majors and concentrations: costume design, costume management, costume production, design, performance, scenic design, stage management, theater education, theater history. Graduate degrees offered: Master of Fine Arts in the area of theater.

Enrollment Fall 1997: 255 total; 205 undergraduate, 50 graduate.

Theater Student Profile 60% females, 40% males.

Theater Faculty 33 total undergraduate and graduate (full-time and part-time). 90% of full-time faculty have terminal degrees. Graduate students teach a few undergraduate courses. Undergraduate student–faculty ratio: 20:1.

Student Life Student groups/activities include League of Resident Theaters.

Expenses for 1997–98 Application fee: $25. State resident tuition: $3125 full-time. Nonresident tuition: $11,382 full-time. Mandatory fees: $986 full-time. Full-time tuition and fees vary according to program. College room and board: $4540. College room only: $2715. Room and board charges vary according to board plan and housing facility. Special program-related fees: $150 per semester for materials for design students.

Application Procedures Students admitted directly into the professional program freshman year. Deadline for freshmen and transfers: continuous. Notification date for freshmen and transfers: continuous. Required: essay, high school transcript, college transcript(s) for transfer students, minimum 2.0 high school GPA, letter of recommendation, interview, SAT I test score only, portfolio for design applicants, audition for theater studies, performance, and theater education applicants. Auditions held 6 times on campus and off campus in Southeastern Theatre Conference sites; Virginia Theater Association sites; videotaped performances are permissible as a substitute for live auditions when distance is prohibitive. Portfolio reviews held by appointment on campus and off campus in Chicago, IL; New York, NY; Virginia Theater Association sites; the submission of slides may be substituted for portfolios with some original work.

Undergraduate Contact Ms. Patricia Archer, Admissions Auditions Coordinator, Theatre Department, Virginia Commonwealth University, Box 842524, Richmond, Virginia 23284-2524; 804-828-1514, fax: 804-828-6741.

Graduate Contact Dr. James W. Parker, Director of Graduate Studies, Theatre Department, Virginia Commonwealth University, Box 842524, Richmond, Virginia 23284-2524; 804-828-1514, fax: 804-828-6741.

▼ VIRGINIA INTERMONT COLLEGE

Bristol, Virginia

Independent, coed. Small town campus. Total enrollment: 848.

Degrees Bachelor of Fine Arts in the area of performing arts (theater and musical theater). Majors and concentrations: music theater, theater arts/drama. Cross-registration with King College.

Enrollment Fall 1997: 10 undergraduate.

Theater Faculty 3 total (full-time and part-time). 100% of full-time faculty have terminal degrees. Graduate students do not teach undergraduate courses. Undergraduate student–faculty ratio: 6:1.

Student Life Student groups/activities include Southeastern Theatre Conference, American College Theatre Festival, WETS Live Radio Theater.

Expenses for 1997–98 Application fee: $15. Comprehensive fee: $15,350 includes full-time tuition ($10,650) and college room and board ($4700).

Financial Aid Program-specific awards for 1997: performance scholarships for program majors ($500–$1500), 15 departmental scholarships for program majors ($1200).

Application Procedures Deadline for freshmen and transfers: continuous. Notification date for freshmen and transfers: continuous. Required: high school transcript, college transcript(s) for transfer students, minimum 2.0 high school GPA, SAT I or ACT test scores, audition for scholarship consideration. Recommended: letter of recommendation, audition. Auditions held by request on campus.

Undergraduate Contact Ms. Robin Cozart, Director of Admissions, Virginia Intermont College, Box D-460, Bristol, Virginia 24201; 540-669-6101, fax: 540-466-7855.

▼ WAYNE STATE UNIVERSITY

Detroit, Michigan

State-supported, coed. Urban campus. Total enrollment: 30,729.

Degrees Bachelor of Fine Arts in the area of theater. Graduate degrees offered: Master of Fine Arts in the areas of acting, lighting, costuming, management, scenography, stage management. Doctor of Arts in the areas of theater history, criticism. Program accredited by NAST.

Enrollment Fall 1997: 280 total; 198 undergraduate, 82 graduate.

Theater Student Profile 42% females, 58% males, 10% minorities, 1% international.

Theater Faculty 17 total undergraduate and graduate (full-time and part-time). 100% of full-time faculty have terminal degrees. Graduate students teach a few undergraduate courses. Undergraduate student–faculty ratio: 16:1.

Expenses for 1997–98 Application fee: $20. State resident tuition: $3348 full-time. Nonresident tuition: $7471 full-time. Mandatory fees: $138 full-time. Full-time tuition and fees vary according to student level. College room only: $3875. Room charges vary according to housing facility.

Financial Aid Program-specific awards for 1997: 10 Freshman Incentive Awards for incoming freshmen ($1500).

Application Procedures Students admitted directly into the professional program freshman year. Deadline for freshmen and transfers: August 1. Notification date for freshmen and transfers: continuous. Required: college transcript(s) for transfer students, minimum 2.0 high school GPA. Recommended: minimum 3.0 high school GPA.

Undergraduate Contact Undergraduate Admissions, Wayne State University, 3 East, Joy Student Services Building, Detroit, Michigan 48202; 313-577-3577, fax: 313-577-7536.

Graduate Contact Mr. James Thomas, Chair, Theatre Department, Wayne State University, 4841 Cass, Suite 3225, Detroit, Michigan 48202; 313-577-3511, fax: 313-577-0935, E-mail address: aa4732@wayne.edu.

▼ WEBSTER UNIVERSITY

St. Louis, Missouri

Independent, coed. Suburban campus. Total enrollment: 11,756. Theater program established 1967.

Degrees Bachelor of Fine Arts in the areas of theater, musical theater. Majors and concentrations: costume design, lighting design, music theater, performance, scene painting, set design, sound design, stage management, technical production. Cross-registration with various colleges in St. Louis.

Enrollment Fall 1997: 140 total; all undergraduate.

Theater Student Profile 50% females, 50% males, 10% minorities, 1% international.

Theater Faculty 32 total (full-time and part-time). 100% of full-time faculty have terminal degrees. Graduate students do not teach undergraduate courses. Undergraduate student–faculty ratio: 12:1.

Student Life Student groups/activities include United States Institute for Theatre Technology.

Expenses for 1997–98 Application fee: $25. Comprehensive fee: $15,940 includes full-time tuition ($10,860), mandatory fees ($50), and college room and board ($5030). College room only: $3080. Room and board charges vary according to board plan and housing facility. Special program-related fees: $300 per year for technical theater materials.

Application Procedures Students admitted directly into the professional program freshman year. Deadline for freshmen and transfers: continuous. Required: essay, high school transcript, college transcript(s) for transfer students, minimum 2.0 high school GPA, 2 letters of recommendation, audition, portfolio, SAT I or ACT test scores. Recommended: minimum 3.0 high school GPA. Auditions held 8 times on campus and off campus in New York, NY; San Francisco, CA; Los Angeles, CA; Dallas, TX; Houston, TX; Atlanta, GA; Las Vegas, NV; Cincinnati, OH. Portfolio reviews held 8 times on campus and off campus in New York, NY; San Francisco, CA; Los Angeles, CA; Dallas, TX; Houston, TX; Atlanta, GA; Cincinnati, OH; Las Vegas, NV; the submission of slides may be substituted for portfolios when distance is prohibitive.

Web Site http://www.webster.edu.

Undergraduate Contact Ms. Bethany Wood, Auditions Coordinator, Office of Admissions, Webster University, 470 East Lockwood Avenue, St. Louis, Missouri 63119-3194; 314-968-7000, fax: 314-968-7115.

More About the University

The Conservatory of Theatre Arts is a four-year, sequential professional training program located within a strong liberal arts teaching university. The Conservatory is among the few undergraduate programs in the country that utilize on-campus performing organizations: The Repertory Theatre of Saint Louis and the Opera Theatre of Saint Louis. They present their seasons in Webster's Loretto-Hilton Center for the Performing Arts, which is also the home for the Conservatory's six-play season of student-performed and -designed productions.

Students are selected through a national audition/interview process for their academic strengths and perceived professional potential. It is important that potential participants in the program exhibit a positive interest in combining study in the liberal arts with the discipline that a significant professional program demands.

The graduating class presents an annual showcase in New York. Webster hosts the annual Mid-West Theatre Auditions that presents opportunities for employment in the summer and year-round professional theaters. A regularly updated list of alumni activities is available upon request.

The Conservatory's goal is to present to its students the best possible opportunities to be challenged and to excel in all of the disciplines of theater. Because the program demands hard work in an intense situation, students tend to be goal-oriented.

The Department of Music provides outstanding music training in both the classical and jazz studies areas that utilize the St. Louis region's outstanding musicians as regular contributing members of the faculty. The department enjoys significant relationships with The Opera Theatre of Saint Louis and the Saint Louis Symphony Orchestra. Both are nationally recognized. The department strives to provide performance opportunities for students at the highest attainable levels. The Jazz Studies Program uses the recognized cadre of jazz artists as its faculty and as leaders of the various groups in this combo-based process of development.

In 1998–99, the department will present more than 100 recitals, performances, and concerts that represent the work of students, faculty, and visiting artists. Performing organizations on campus include the Webster University Symphony, the Webster University Big Band, three choral ensembles, Voices St. Louis, the Webster Wind Ensemble, and the Opera Studio. Students have opportunities to work with their studio faculty in these opportunities and are constantly challenged to reach the highest musical standards.

The primary focus of the Department of Music is on undergraduate experiences. While a significant part of a strong liberal arts teaching university, the College of Fine Arts is the leader in training of undergraduates for the St. Louis region. There are 100 undergraduates and twenty majors that comprise those studying in a variety of musical fields. Excellence is expected and excellence is the tradition. Students find music education at Webster to be a challenging and exciting experience.

▼ WESTERN CAROLINA UNIVERSITY

Cullowhee, North Carolina

State-supported, coed. Rural campus. Theater program established 1975.

Degrees Bachelor of Fine Arts in the area of theater arts.

Enrollment Fall 1997: 24 total; all undergraduate.

Theater Student Profile 60% females, 40% males.

Theater Faculty 5 total (full-time and part-time). 100% of full-time faculty have terminal degrees. Graduate students do not teach undergraduate courses.

Student Life Student groups/activities include Alpha Psi Omega, University Players.

Financial Aid Program-specific awards for 1997: 8 Fine and Performing Arts Awards for those demonstrating talent and academic achievement ($500).

Application Procedures Students apply for admission into the professional program by sophomore year. Deadline for freshmen and transfers: continuous. Required: essay, high school transcript, college transcript(s) for transfer students, 3 letters of recommendation, interview, audition, SAT I or ACT test scores. Auditions held 3-4 times on campus; videotaped performances are permissible as a substitute for live auditions with prior approval.

Undergraduate Contact Dr. Lawrence J. Hill, Professor, Department of Communication/Theatre Arts, Western Carolina

Western Carolina University *(continued)*

University, 123 Stillwell, Cullowhee, North Carolina 28723; 704-227-7491, fax: 704-227-7647, E-mail address: hill@wcuvax1.wcu.edu.

Potter College of Arts, Humanities, and Social Sciences

▼ WESTERN KENTUCKY UNIVERSITY

Bowling Green, Kentucky

State-supported, coed. Suburban campus. Total enrollment: 14,543. Theater program established 1987.

Degrees Bachelor of Fine Arts in the area of theater. Majors and concentrations: acting, technical theater.

Enrollment Fall 1997: 13 undergraduate.

Theater Student Profile 64% females, 36% males, 8% international.

Theater Faculty 6 total (full-time and part-time). 100% of full-time faculty have terminal degrees. Graduate students do not teach undergraduate courses.

Student Life Student groups/activities include Alpha Psi Omega.

Expenses for 1997–98 Application fee: $15. State resident tuition: $1800 full-time. Nonresident tuition: $5400 full-time. Mandatory fees: $340 full-time. College room and board: $2700.

Financial Aid Program-specific awards for 1997: 10 Governor's School of the Arts Award for students who complete Governor's School of the Arts ($1130–$3050).

Application Procedures Students apply for admission into the professional program by sophomore year. Deadline for freshmen and transfers: June 1. Required: high school transcript, minimum 2.0 high school GPA.

Web Site http://www.wku.edu/Dept/Academic/AHSS/Theatre/.

Undergraduate Contact Office of Admissions, Western Kentucky University, 101 Cravens Center, One Big Red Way, Bowling Green, Kentucky 42101-3576; 502-745-5422.

▼ WESTERN MICHIGAN UNIVERSITY

Kalamazoo, Michigan

State-supported, coed. Urban campus. Total enrollment: 26,132. Theater program established 1976.

Degrees Bachelor of Fine Arts in the area of music theater performance. Majors and concentrations: arts management, design technology, music theater, performance, theater education, theater studies. Cross-registration with Kalamazoo Valley Community College, Kalamazoo College. Program accredited by NAST.

Enrollment Fall 1997: 220 total; all undergraduate.

Theater Student Profile 55% females, 45% males, 9% minorities, 2% international.

Theater Faculty 15 total (full-time and part-time). 100% of full-time faculty have terminal degrees. Graduate students do not teach undergraduate courses. Undergraduate student–faculty ratio: 13:1.

Student Life Student groups/activities include Association for Theater in Higher Learning, National Association of Schools of Theater, American Alliance for Theatre and Education. Special housing available for theater students.

Expenses for 1997–98 Application fee: $25. State resident tuition: $3061 full-time. Nonresident tuition: $7770 full-time. Mandatory fees: $594 full-time. Full-time tuition and fees vary according to course load and student level. College room and board: $4398. College room only: $1815. Room and board charges vary according to board plan. Special program-related fees: $20 per credit hour for practicum lab fee, $20 per course for stagecraft fee.

Financial Aid Program-specific awards for 1997: 6 Minority Theater Scholarships for minority program majors ($500–$8000), 6 Music Theater Scholarships for music theater majors ($500–$8000), 6 theater scholarships for theater majors ($500–$8000).

Application Procedures Students admitted directly into the professional program freshman year. Deadline for freshmen and transfers: March 1. Notification date for freshmen and transfers: April 1. Required: high school transcript, college transcript(s) for transfer students, minimum 3.0 high school GPA, letter of recommendation, interview, audition, portfolio, SAT I or ACT test scores (minimum combined ACT score of 20), resume. Recommended: essay. Auditions held 3 times on campus; videotaped performances are permissible as a substitute for live auditions when the video is of adequate quality. Portfolio reviews held 3 times on campus.

Web Site http://www.wmich.edu/theatre/.

Undergraduate Contact Dr. D. Terry Williams, Chairman, Department of Theatre, Western Michigan University, Kalamazoo, Michigan 49008; 616-387-3224, fax: 616-387-3222, E-mail address: williamst@wmich.edu.

▼ WEST VIRGINIA UNIVERSITY

Morgantown, West Virginia

State-supported, coed. Small town campus. Total enrollment: 22,238. Theater program established 1970.

Degrees Bachelor of Fine Arts in the area of theater. Graduate degrees offered: Master of Fine Arts in the area of theater. Program accredited by NAST.

Enrollment Fall 1997: 150 total; 134 undergraduate, 16 graduate.

Theater Student Profile 60% females, 40% males, 5% minorities, 2% international.

Theater Faculty 16 total undergraduate and graduate (full-time and part-time). 97% of full-time faculty have terminal degrees. Graduate students teach a few undergraduate courses. Undergraduate student–faculty ratio: 12:1.

Student Life Student groups/activities include Puppetry Touring Program. Special housing available for theater students.

Expenses for 1997–98 Application fee: $15, $35 for nonresidents. State resident tuition: $2336 full-time. Nonresident tuition: $7356 full-time. Full-time tuition varies according to location, program, and reciprocity agreements. College room and board: $4832. Room and board charges vary according to board plan, housing facility, and location.

Financial Aid Program-specific awards for 1997: 16 Performance Grants for incoming freshmen ($1750–$4800), 1 Tanner Scholarship for state residents ($500–$2000), 1–2 Boyd Scholarships for program majors ($500–$1000), 1–4 Tate-Ensley Scholarships for program students ($500–$2000), 1 Selby Scholarship for program juniors ($750).

Application Procedures Students admitted directly into the professional program freshman year. Deadline for freshmen and transfers: continuous. Notification date for freshmen and transfers: continuous. Required: high school transcript, college transcript(s) for transfer students, minimum 2.0 high school GPA, 2 letters of recommendation, interview, audition, portfolio, SAT I or ACT test scores. Auditions held 4 times and by appointment on campus and off campus in University Resident Theatre Association regional auditions, Southeastern Theatre Conference auditions; videotaped performances are permissible as a substitute for live auditions when distance is prohibitive (beyond a 500-mile radius). Portfolio reviews held 4 times and by appointment on campus and off campus in University Resident Theatre Association regional reviews, Southeastern Theatre Conference reviews; the submission of slides may be substituted for portfolios when distance is prohibitive.

Web Site http://www.edu/~theatre/.

Undergraduate Contact Registrar, Admissions and Records, West Virginia University, PO Box 6009, Morgantown, West Virginia 26506-6009; 304-293-2124 ext. 3510.

Graduate Contact Division of Theatre and Dance, West Virginia University, PO Box 6111, Morgantown, West Virginia 26506-6111; 304-293-2020, fax: 304-293-3550.

▼ WICHITA STATE UNIVERSITY

Wichita, Kansas

State-supported, coed. Urban campus. Total enrollment: 14,061.

Degrees Bachelor of Fine Arts in the area of performing arts/theater. Majors and concentrations: design/technical theater, music theater, performance.

Enrollment Fall 1997: 62 undergraduate, 383 non-professional degree.

Theater Student Profile 51% females, 8% minorities, 12% international.

Theater Faculty 10 total (full-time and part-time). 90% of full-time faculty have terminal degrees. Graduate students teach a few undergraduate courses. Undergraduate student–faculty ratio: 7:1.

Student Life Student groups/activities include American College Theatre Festival, Alpha Psi Omega, Theatre in Public Schools Project. Special housing available for theater students.

Expenses for 1997–98 Application fee: $20. State resident tuition: $1486 full-time. Nonresident tuition: $6414 full-time. Mandatory fees: $500 full-time. College room and board: $3760. Room and board charges vary according to board plan.

Financial Aid Program-specific awards for 1997: 34 Miller Theatre Scholarships for incoming students ($650–$1500).

Application Procedures Students admitted directly into the professional program freshman year. Deadline for freshmen and transfers: continuous. Required: high school transcript, college transcript(s) for transfer students, minimum 2.0 high school GPA, SAT I or ACT test scores. Recommended: interview, audition, portfolio. Auditions held 3 times and by arrangement on campus; videotaped performances are permissible as a substitute for live auditions for international applicants and U.S. students from great distances. Portfolio reviews held 3 times and by arrangement on campus; the submission of slides may be substituted for portfolios.

Undergraduate Contact Ms. Christine Schneikart-Luebbe, Director of Admissions, Wichita State University, 1845 Fairmount, Wichita, Kansas 67260-0124; 316-978-3085.

▼ WILLIAM CAREY COLLEGE

Hattiesburg, Mississippi

Independent-Southern Baptist, coed. Small town campus.

Degrees Bachelor of Fine Arts in the area of theater. Majors and concentrations: music theater, theater arts/drama.

Enrollment Fall 1997: 24 undergraduate.

Theater Student Profile 50% females, 50% males, 4% minorities.

Theater Faculty 5 total (full-time and part-time). 67% of full-time faculty have terminal degrees. Graduate students do not teach undergraduate courses. Undergraduate student–faculty ratio: 6:1.

Student Life Student groups/activities include Alpha Psi Omega, Serampore Players.

Expenses for 1997–98 Application fee: $10. Tuition: $6624 full-time.

Financial Aid Program-specific awards for 1997: 3 Named Scholarships for enrolled program students ($500–$5000), 15 Theater Talent Awards for program majors ($500–$5000).

Application Procedures Students admitted directly into the professional program freshman year. Deadline for freshmen and transfers: August 1. Notification date for freshmen and transfers: August 1. Required: high school transcript, college transcript(s) for transfer students, minimum 2.0 high school GPA, letter of recommendation, SAT I or ACT test scores. Recommended: interview, video, audition, portfolio. Auditions held at various times on campus; videotaped performances are permissible as a substitute for live auditions when distance is prohibitive. Portfolio reviews held at various times on campus; the submission of slides may be substituted for portfolios whenever needed.

Undergraduate Contact Mr. O. L. Quave, Chair, Department of Theatre and Communication, William Carey College, 498 Tuscan Avenue, Hattiesburg, Mississippi 39401-5499; 601-582-6218, fax: 601-582-6454, E-mail address: thecom@umcarey.edu.

▼ WRIGHT STATE UNIVERSITY

Dayton, Ohio

State-supported, coed. Suburban campus. Total enrollment: 15,343.

Degrees Bachelor of Fine Arts in the areas of acting/musical theatre, theatre design/technology, stage management. Majors and concentrations: music theater, stage management, theater arts/drama, theater design/technology.

Enrollment Fall 1997: 175 undergraduate.

Theater Student Profile 50% females, 50% males, 5% minorities, 5% international.

Theater Faculty 21 total undergraduate (full-time and part-time). 75% of full-time faculty have terminal degrees. Graduate students do not teach undergraduate courses.

Expenses for 1997–98 Application fee: $30. State resident tuition: $3708 full-time. Nonresident tuition: $7416 full-time. College room and board: $4500. Room and board charges vary according to board plan and housing facility. Special program-related fees: $125–$250 per quarter for private voice lessons.

Financial Aid Program-specific awards for 1997: Theatre Arts Talent Awards for incoming program students ($500–$4000), Milton Augsburger and Francisco Estevez Scholarships for

Wright State University *(continued)*

incoming program students ($500–$4000), Faculty Academic Scholarships for out-of-state incoming program students ($3708).

Application Procedures Students admitted directly into the professional program freshman year. Deadline for freshmen and transfers: March 13. Required: high school transcript, college transcript(s) for transfer students, interview, SAT I or ACT test scores, photograph, video if unavailable to audition in person, audition for acting and musical theatre applicants. Auditions held 6-8 times on campus and off campus in Louisville, KY; Lincoln, NE.

Web Site http://www.wright.edu/.

Undergraduate Contact Ms. Victoria Oleen, Administrative Coordinator, Department of Theatre Arts, Wright State University, 3640 Colonel Glenn Highway, T148 CAC, Dayton, Ohio 45435; 937-775-3072, fax: 937-775-3787, E-mail address: voleen@desire.wright.edu.

Wright State University

More About the University

Program Facilities The Department of Theatre Arts is housed in a newly constructed, state-of-the-art facility that includes acting studios, a ninety-five-seat directing lab, design labs, dance studios, a movement studio, a lighting lab, and motion picture production facilities. Mainstage theater productions are held in the Festival Playhouse, a 376-seat proscenium theater. Studio productions are in a 100-seat black box theater. The department has access to a comprehensive collection of playscripts, musical theater scores and soundtracks, and a videotape library.

Faculty, Resident Artists, and Alumni Chair W. Stuart McDowell is the founder and former artistic director of the Riverside Shakespeare Company in New York City and stage director of numerous professional productions in New York and across the country. Music theater faculty members include Broadway actor and choreographer Joe Deer, Broadway dancer and choreographer Suzanne Walker (*Coco, Barishnykov on Broadway*), and Rocco Dal Vera, noted voice teacher and coauthor of *Voice: On Stage and Off*. Other faculty members have worked professionally at the Stratford Festival of Canada, the Alabama Shakespeare Festival, the Milwaukee Repertory Theatre, the Cincinnati Playhouse in the Park, the Dayton Ballet, the Dayton Contemporary Dance Company, and the Human Race Theatre Company. Motion picture professors have been nominated for the Academy Award, and student-directed films have received recognition at leading film festivals internationally.

Student Performance Opportunities Students may work on six mainstage and three studio productions as actors, designers, dancers, or technicians. Students are also offered directing, design, choreography, acting, and dance opportunities in student productions in the directing lab and studio theater. Motion picture production majors are required to complete two fully realized films prior to graduation. Performance opportunities are also offered with the Human Race Theatre Company, Dayton's professional Equity theater, and the Dayton Ballet and the Dayton Contemporary Dance Company.

▼

The Department of Theatre Arts' production of *1913: The Great Dayton Flood*, coauthored by W. Stuart McDowell, chair, and student Tim Nevits, was selected to be presented at the National American College Theatre Festival XXIX at the Kennedy Center in Washington, D.C., in 1997, winning a record number of ACTF awards. This is the second time the department has been honored with this prestigious award.

For the second time in three years, the design/technology students won first place in competition at the National United Scenic Institute of Theatre Technology Conference in 1997.

The B.F.A. in acting is essentially a classically oriented program that includes various styles and periods, including Greek, Shakespearean, Restoration, modern, contemporary, and acting in film and television and basic musical theater instruction. All acting majors are required to study one year of fundamentals of modern dance, followed by jazz/theater dance or ballet as electives. The acting faculty endorses the concept that all actors must be trained to sing. Students who study singing learn the rudiments of breathing, vocal support, and placement. Singing is required during all four years of the training program. Upper-division students are also trained to become certified stage combatants.

The B.F.A. in acting with musical theater emphasis includes the same initial acting classes as the acting program, with additional courses in music theory, keyboard skills, classical speech, and dialect and speech production, and private singing lessons. Dance classes include ballet, jazz, tap, and modern. Acting courses include film and television and musical theater performance. Performance opportunities for musical theater actors include revues and a small musical that may tour. Recent musical productions include *Show Boat*, *The Secret Garden*, and *Chicago*.

The B.F.A. program in design/technology prepares students for careers as designers, technicians, and stage managers in the professional theater. Students approach their studies from three viewpoints: general theater knowledge, with classes in acting, dramatic literature, theater history, and theory; artistic design skills, with classes in design, drawing, theater graphics, deco and costume history, and style and concept; and theater technology, with classes in technical theory, application, and craft.

▼ YORK UNIVERSITY

North York, ON, Canada

Province-supported, coed. Urban campus. Total enrollment: 37,900. Theater program established 1969.

Degrees Bachelor of Fine Arts in the areas of acting, production, directing. Graduate degrees offered: Master of Fine Arts in the areas of acting, playwriting, directing.

Enrollment Fall 1997: 378 total; 320 undergraduate, 18 graduate, 40 non-professional degree.

Theater Student Profile 60% females, 40% males, 5% international.

Theater Faculty 43 total undergraduate and graduate (full-time and part-time). 80% of full-time faculty have terminal degrees. Graduate students teach a few undergraduate courses. Undergraduate student–faculty ratio: 8:1.

Student Life Student groups/activities include Theatre Students Association, Creative Arts Students Association.

Expenses for 1997–98 Application fee: $60 Canadian dollars. Tuition, fee, and room and board charges are reported in Canadian dollars. Canadian resident tuition: $3750 full-time. Full-time tuition varies according to course load, degree level, and program. College room and board: $5000. Room and board charges vary according to board plan and housing facility. International student tuition: $10,800 full-time. Special program-related fees: $10–$40 per course for materials and supplies.

Financial Aid Program-specific awards for 1997: 3 Talent Awards for applicants with outstanding auditions ($1000), 1 International Talent Award for international applicants with outstanding auditions ($2000), 1 Harry Rowe Bursary for demonstrated achievement or potential in artistic or scholarly work ($2000), 25 Fine Arts Bursary for academically qualified students demonstrating financial need ($250–$1500), 1 Cheryl Rosen Bursary for upperclassmen demonstrating need ($175), 1 Elaine Newton/Alan Wilder Achievement Bursary for applicants with a minimum B average demonstrating need ($1000).

Application Procedures Students admitted directly into the professional program freshman year. Deadline for freshmen and transfers: March 1. Notification date for freshmen: June 30; transfers: July 15. Required: essay, high school transcript, college transcript(s) for transfer students, minimum 3.0 high school GPA, 2 letters of recommendation, interview, SAT I, ACT or Canadian equivalent, portfolio for theatre production applicants, audition for acting applicants. Auditions held once on campus; videotaped performances are permissible as a substitute for live auditions. Portfolio reviews held by appointment on campus; the submission of slides may be substituted for portfolios when distance is prohibitive.

Web Site http://www.yorku.ca/faculty/finearts/theatre/.

Undergraduate Contact Mr. Don Murdoch, Liaison Officer, Liaison and Advising, Faculty of Fine Arts, York University, 213 CFA, 4700 Keele Street, Toronto, ON M3J 1P3, Canada; 416-736-5135, fax: 416-736-5447, E-mail address: donm@yorku.ca.

Graduate Contact Ron Singer, Graduate Director, Department of Theatre, York University, 318 CFT, 4700 Keele Street, Toronto, ON M3J 1P3, Canada; 416-736-5172, fax: 416-736-5785, E-mail address: rsinger@yorku.ca.

More About the Department

Program Facilities The largest theater and film teaching complex in Canada includes three acting/rehearsal studios, a lighting lab, a carpentry shop, drafting and design studios, a wardrobe shop and dressing rooms, an extensive costume collection, the Joseph G. Green Studio Theatre, and Burton Auditorium (600 seats, thrust stage).

Faculty, Staff, and Alumni York Theatre faculty are among Canada's leading theater scholars, playwrights, dramaturges, designers, actors, directors, and educators. The department also employs a substantial technical staff to assist with productions, supervise crew work, and ensure the safe operation of all studio facilities. Alumni include Los Angeles–based casting director Risa Bramon-Garcia (*Twister, Natural Born Killers, Speed*), comic actor Scott Thompson (*Kids in the Hall, The Larry Sanders Show*), and award-winning designer Charlotte Dean.

Performance Opportunities Theatre at York mounts an ambitious season each year, with full productions at both the undergraduate and graduate levels. The department's annual weeklong festival, PlayGround, showcases the work of student directors and playwrights. Theater students also have the unique opportunity to participate in projects produced by students in the Department of Film & Video.

Special Programs Students benefit from being part of one of the largest faculties of fine arts in North America. Combined-degree programs are available with the Departments of Dance, Film & Video, Music, and Visual Arts and through an interdisciplinary program in fine arts cultural studies. Combined-degree programs are also available with the Faculties of Arts, Education, and Environmental Studies.

GALLERY OF SUMMER PROGRAMS

M aybe you're looking for help in building a portfolio. Or you'd like to get another audition or two under your belt before applying to a conservatory. Or maybe you'd just like to get a feel for campus living before choosing a particular school. Whatever your interest—visual arts, dance, music, theater, writing, or some combination of the above—the Gallery of Summer Programs can turn your next summer break into the learning experience of a lifetime. Program directors provided Peterson's with the following descriptions. To find out how to contact them for more information, turn to page 550. You can find out more about these and other great summer programs by visiting us on the Web at http://www.petersons.com (look for summer programs). Happy hunting!

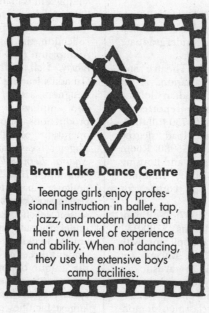

Brant Lake Dance Centre

Teenage girls enjoy professional instruction in ballet, tap, jazz, and modern dance at their own level of experience and ability. When not dancing, they use the extensive boys' camp facilities.

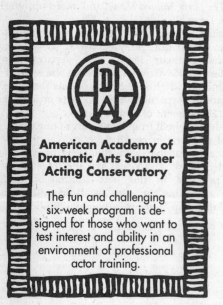

American Academy of Dramatic Arts Summer Acting Conservatory

The fun and challenging six-week program is designed for those who want to test interest and ability in an environment of professional actor training.

California State Summer School for the Arts

A preprofessional program in the visual and performing arts, creative writing, animation, and film for talented high school artists. Students can hone acquired skills and explore new techniques and ideas.

A Full Scholarship Summer at Interlochen

The Emerson Electric Co. Scholars Program offers talented high school musicians 8 weeks of intensive study and performance opportunities at Interlochen Arts Camp.

MARYLAND INSTITUTE
COLLEGE OF ART

Maryland Institute, College of Art

Students expand their art experiences and strengthen their skills with other high school sophomores and juniors who are serious about art making. The four-week Pre-College Summer Program offers courses in computer imaging, illustration, interior design, drawing, painting, sculpture, bookmaking, photography, and more.

Northwestern University National High School Music Institute

Through seminars, course work, lessons, ensemble, and solo performance, NHSMI students "walk in music majors' shoes." Chamber music, close work with Northwestern's renowned artists and faculty members, and visits to Chicago's cultural institutions featured.

CONTACT INFORMATION FOR THE GALLERY OF SUMMER PROGRAMS

 f you are interested in finding out more about a program in the Gallery of Summer Programs, call or write to the person listed below who is affiliated with that program.

Karen Higginbotham, Director of Admissions
American Academy of Dramatic Arts
120 Madison Avenue
New York, New York 10016
212-686-9244
800-463-8990 (toll-free)

Karen Meltzer
Brant Lake's Dance Centre
19 East 80th Street
New York, New York 10028
212-734-6216
Fax: 212-288-0937
E-mail: brantlakec@aol.com

Joseph Alameida, Director
California State Summer School for the Arts
4825 J Street, Suite 120
Sacramento, California 95819
916-227-9320
Fax: 916-227-9455
E-mail: sabrina@csssa.org

Anne Brasie, Marketing Director
Interlochen Center for the Arts
P.O. Box 199
Interlochen, MI 49643-0199
616-276-7603
Fax: 616-276-6321

Theresa Lynch-Bedoya, Dean of Admissions
Maryland Institute, College of Art
1300 Mount Royal Avenue
Baltimore, MD 21217-4192
410-225-2294
Fax: 410-225-2337

Heather Landes, Coordinator of Graduate
Admissions and Financial Aid
Northwestern University School of Music
711 Elgin Road
Evanston, IL 60208-1200
847-467-3367
Fax: 847-467-1317

Majors Index

▲

Art Majors

Advertising design
Atlanta College of Art **A54**
Kutztown University of Pennsylvania **A102**
Minneapolis College of Art and Design **A118**
School of Visual Arts **A154**
Syracuse University **A164**
University of Delaware **A176**
University of Mary Hardin-Baylor **A182**
The University of Texas–Pan American **A200**
Washington University in St. Louis **A209**

Advertising design and communication
Art Center College of Design **A51**

Advertising graphic design
Cazenovia College **A67**

Animation
Art Institute of Boston **A52**
Center for Creative Studies—College of Art and Design **A68**
Eastern New Mexico University **A84**
Edinboro University of Pennsylvania **A85**
The Illinois Institute of Art **A92**
Minneapolis College of Art and Design **A118**
Mississippi State University **A119**
Parsons School of Design, New School for Social Research **A135**
Radford University **A141**
School of the Museum of Fine Arts **A153**
School of Visual Arts **A154**
University of Central Florida **A174**
University of Illinois at Chicago **A179**
University of Oregon **A194**
University of the Arts **A200**

Apparel design
The Art Institutes International at Portland **A54**

Applied art
Culver-Stockton College **A80**
Eastern New Mexico University **A84**
Memphis College of Art **A114**
Millikin University **A117**

Northern Illinois University **A127**
Parsons School of Design, New School for Social Research **A135**
School of Visual Arts **A154**
University of the Arts **A200**

Applied design
University of Wisconsin–Oshkosh **A204**

Applied photography
Northern Kentucky University **A127**
University of Delaware **A176**

Architectural design
Massachusetts College of Art **A114**
University of Massachusetts Amherst **A182**

Architectural history
Savannah College of Art and Design **A150**

Architectural illustration
Lawrence Technological University **A104**

Architecture
California College of Arts and Crafts **A62**
Savannah College of Art and Design **A150**

Art and technology
School of the Art Institute of Chicago **A151**
Seton Hill College **A156**

Art direction
Center for Creative Studies—College of Art and Design **A68**
Pratt Institute **A138**
Texas A&M University–Commerce **A165**

Art education
Adrian College **A42**
Alfred University **A44**
Appalachian State University **A49**
Arizona State University **A49**
Arkansas State University **A50**
Austin Peay State University **A56**
Baylor University **A57**
Beaver College **A58**
Belmont University **A59**
Bradley University **A60**

Brigham Young University **A61**
California State University, Long Beach **A65**
Capital University **A66**
Cardinal Stritch University **A66**
Central Michigan University **A69**
Central Missouri State University **A69**
College of New Rochelle **A72**
Columbia College **A75**
Converse College **A76**
Daemen College **A80**
Drake University **A82**
East Carolina University **A83**
East Tennessee State University **A84**
Edinboro University of Pennsylvania **A85**
Emmanuel College **A85**
Emporia State University **A85**
Fort Hays State University **A88**
Indiana University–Purdue University Indianapolis **A95**
Jacksonville University **A98**
Kansas State University **A99**
Kent State University **A101**
La Sierra University **A103**
Lindenwood University **A104**
Long Island University, C.W. Post Campus **A105**
Longwood College **A106**
Massachusetts College of Art **A114**
Metropolitan State College of Denver **A115**
Miami University **A115**
Michigan State University **A116**
Millikin University **A117**
Mississippi University for Women **A120**
Montserrat College of Art **A120**
Moore College of Art and Design **A122**
New York Institute of Technology **A125**
Ohio University **A129**
Old Dominion University **A130**
Pittsburg State University **A138**
Pratt Institute **A138**
Rhode Island College **A141**
Saint Mary's College **A148**
School of the Art Institute of Chicago **A151**
School of the Museum of Fine Arts **A153**
School of Visual Arts **A154**
Seton Hill College **A156**
Shorter College **A156**
Southern Illinois University at Carbondale **A158**

Millikin University **A117**
Mississippi University for Women **A120**
Montserrat College of Art **A120**
Mount Allison University **A123**
New Jersey City University **A124**
Northern Illinois University **A127**
Nova Scotia College of Art and Design **A127**
Oregon State University **A132**
Otis College of Art and Design **A132**
Pacific Lutheran University **A133**
Paier College of Art, Inc. **A135**
Parsons School of Design, New School for Social Research **A135**
Pittsburg State University **A138**
Purchase College, State University of New York **A140**
Radford University **A141**
Saint Mary's College **A148**
Salisbury State University **A148**
San Francisco Art Institute **A149**
San Jose State University **A150**
School of the Museum of Fine Arts **A153**
School of Visual Arts **A154**
Seton Hill College **A156**
Shepherd College **A156**
Sonoma State University **A158**
Southern Illinois University at Edwardsville **A158**
Sul Ross State University **A164**
Texas A&M University–Commerce **A165**
Texas Woman's University **A167**
The University of Alabama **A170**
The University of Alabama at Birmingham **A170**
University of Alaska Anchorage **A171**
University of Arkansas **A172**
University of British Columbia **A173**
University of Colorado at Boulder **A174**
University of Colorado at Denver **A175**
University of Connecticut **A175**
University of Dayton **A175**
University of Delaware **A176**
The University of Iowa **A180**
University of Louisville **A181**
University of Mary Hardin-Baylor **A182**
The University of Memphis **A184**
University of Michigan **A185**
University of Missouri–St. Louis **A188**
The University of Montana–Missoula **A188**
University of Nebraska–Lincoln **A189**
University of New Mexico **A190**
University of North Carolina at Charlotte **A191**
University of North Texas **A193**
University of Notre Dame **A193**
University of Southern California **A196**

The University of Texas at Arlington **A198**
University of the Arts **A200**
University of West Florida **A202**
University of Wisconsin–Madison **A203**
University of Wisconsin–Whitewater **A205**
Virginia Intermont College **A207**
Washington State University **A208**
West Chester University of Pennsylvania **A210**
Western Illinois University **A211**
Western Michigan University **A212**
West Virginia University **A213**
Xavier University **A214**

Arts administration
American University **A48**
Appalachian State University **A49**
Lindenwood University **A104**
Millikin University **A117**

Arts management
Adrian College **A42**
Seton Hill College **A156**

Book arts
Oregon College of Art and Craft **A131**
Purchase College, State University of New York **A140**
Western Carolina University **A211**

CAD/CAM
Temple University **A168**

Cartooning
Minneapolis College of Art and Design **A118**
Savannah College of Art and Design **A150**
School of Visual Arts **A154**

Ceramic art and design
Abilene Christian University **A41**
Alberta College of Art and Design **A43**
Appalachian State University **A49**
Ball State University **A56**
Baylor University **A57**
Beaver College **A58**
California College of Arts and Crafts **A62**
California State University, Chico **A65**
California State University, Fullerton **A65**
Center for Creative Studies—College of Art and Design **A68**
East Carolina University **A83**
Eastern New Mexico University **A84**
East Tennessee State University **A84**
Emporia State University **A85**
Fort Hays State University **A88**

Georgia Southwestern State University **A89**
Georgia State University **A90**
Grand Valley State University **A90**
Howard University **A92**
Illinois Wesleyan University **A93**
Indiana State University **A93**
Indiana University Bloomington **A94**
Indiana University–Purdue University Fort Wayne **A95**
Indiana University–Purdue University Indianapolis **A95**
James Madison University **A98**
Kansas City Art Institute **A99**
Kansas State University **A99**
Kent State University **A101**
Lakehead University **A103**
Lehman College of the City University of New York **A104**
Lindenwood University **A104**
Louisiana Tech University **A107**
Maine College of Art **A108**
Maryland Institute, College of Art **A110**
Marywood University **A113**
Massachusetts College of Art **A114**
Memphis College of Art **A114**
Miami University **A115**
Middle Tennessee State University **A116**
Millikin University **A117**
Mississippi State University **A119**
Mississippi University for Women **A120**
New Jersey City University **A124**
New Mexico Highlands University **A124**
New Mexico State University **A125**
Northern Illinois University **A127**
Northern Kentucky University **A127**
Ohio University **A129**
Ohio Wesleyan University **A129**
Oregon State University **A132**
Pacific Lutheran University **A133**
Parsons School of Design, New School for Social Research **A135**
Pennsylvania State University University Park Campus **A137**
Pittsburg State University **A138**
Pratt Institute **A138**
Saint Mary's College **A148**
San Francisco Art Institute **A149**
School of the Art Institute of Chicago **A151**
School of the Museum of Fine Arts **A153**
Southern Illinois University at Carbondale **A158**
Southern Illinois University at Edwardsville **A158**
State University of New York at New Paltz **A161**
Sul Ross State University **A164**
Temple University **A168**
Texas A&M University–Commerce **A165**

Texas Woman's University **A167**
Truman State University **A168**
The University of Akron **A170**
The University of Alabama **A170**
University of Alaska Anchorage **A171**
The University of Arizona **A171**
University of Arkansas **A172**
University of Central Florida **A174**
University of Colorado at Boulder **A174**
University of Denver **A176**
University of Louisville **A181**
University of Manitoba **A181**
The University of Memphis **A184**
University of Miami **A184**
University of Minnesota, Twin Cities Campus **A187**
University of Mississippi **A187**
University of Montevallo **A188**
University of Nebraska–Lincoln **A189**
University of Nevada, Las Vegas **A189**
University of North Carolina at Charlotte **A191**
University of North Carolina at Greensboro **A191**
University of North Dakota **A192**
University of North Texas **A193**
University of Notre Dame **A193**
University of Oklahoma **A193**
University of Southern California **A196**
The University of Texas at Arlington **A198**
The University of Texas at Austin **A198**
The University of Texas–Pan American **A200**
University of the Arts **A200**
University of Utah **A202**
University of Wisconsin–Milwaukee **A203**
University of Wisconsin–Oshkosh **A204**
Utah State University **A205**
Wayne State University **A209**
Webster University **A210**
Western Carolina University **A211**
Western Illinois University **A211**
Western Michigan University **A212**
West Virginia University **A213**
Wichita State University **A213**
Xavier University **A214**

Ceramics

Alfred University **A44**
Arizona State University **A49**
Arkansas State University **A50**
Auburn University **A55**
Austin Peay State University **A56**
Barry University **A57**
Bellevue University **A59**
Brenau University **A61**
Brigham Young University **A61**
California State University, Long Beach **A65**
Central Michigan University **A69**

Clarion University of Pennsylvania **A69**
Clarke College **A70**
Cleveland Institute of Art **A70**
Columbia College **A75**
Concordia University **A76**
Dominican College of San Rafael **A82**
Edinboro University of Pennsylvania **A85**
Florida Atlantic University **A87**
Florida International University **A88**
Georgia Southern University **A89**
Guilford College **A90**
Illinois State University **A93**
Indiana University of Pennsylvania **A94**
Jacksonville State University **A97**
Johnson State College **A99**
Kutztown University of Pennsylvania **A102**
Lake Erie College **A103**
Long Island University, C.W. Post Campus **A105**
Louisiana State University and Agricultural and Mechanical College **A107**
Maharishi University of Management **A108**
Mankato State University **A110**
Metropolitan State College of Denver **A115**
Michigan State University **A116**
Murray State University **A124**
Nova Scotia College of Art and Design **A127**
Oklahoma State University **A130**
Oregon College of Art and Craft **A131**
Otis College of Art and Design **A132**
Radford University **A141**
Rhode Island College **A141**
Rochester Institute of Technology **A146**
Rutgers, The State University of New Jersey, Mason Gross School of the Arts **A113**
St. Cloud State University **A147**
Shorter College **A156**
Siena Heights University **A157**
Slippery Rock University of Pennsylvania **A157**
Southern Oregon University **A159**
Southwest Missouri State University **A160**
Southwest Texas State University **A160**
State University of New York College at Fredonia **A161**
State University of West Georgia **A162**
Syracuse University **A164**
Texas Southern University **A167**
Texas Tech University **A167**
University of Cincinnati **A174**
University of Delaware **A176**

University of Florida **A177**
University of Georgia **A178**
University of Hartford **A178**
University of Hawaii at Manoa **A179**
The University of Iowa **A180**
University of Massachusetts Amherst **A182**
University of Massachusetts Dartmouth **A182**
University of Michigan **A185**
University of Missouri–Columbia **A187**
The University of Montana–Missoula **A188**
University of New Hampshire **A189**
University of North Alabama **A190**
University of North Carolina at Asheville **A190**
University of Northern Iowa **A192**
University of Oregon **A194**
University of Regina **A195**
University of South Alabama **A195**
University of South Carolina **A195**
University of Southern Maine **A196**
University of Tennessee, Knoxville **A198**
The University of Texas at San Antonio **A199**
The University of Texas at Tyler **A199**
University of Washington **A202**
University of Wisconsin–Stevens Point **A204**
University of Wisconsin–Superior **A205**
Washington State University **A208**
Washington University in St. Louis **A209**
West Chester University of Pennsylvania **A210**
Western Kentucky University **A211**
West Texas A&M University **A212**
Winthrop University **A214**

Clay and metal
Old Dominion University **A130**

Combined media
Cornell University **A78**

Commercial art
Alberta College of Art and Design **A43**
Baylor University **A57**
Center for Creative Studies—College of Art and Design **A68**
Central Missouri State University **A69**
East Tennessee State University **A84**
Emporia State University **A85**
Fort Hays State University **A88**
Georgia Southwestern State University **A89**
Illinois Wesleyan University **A93**
Indiana University–Purdue University Fort Wayne **A95**

Art Institute of Southern California
A53
Atlanta College of Art **A54**
Auburn University **A55**
Austin Peay State University **A56**
Brigham Young University **A61**
California College of Arts and Crafts
A62
California State University, Fullerton
A65
California State University, Long
Beach **A65**
Cazenovia College **A67**
Center for Creative Studies—College
of Art and Design **A68**
Central Missouri State University **A69**
Cleveland Institute of Art **A70**
College of Visual Arts **A73**
Columbia College **A75**
Columbus College of Art and Design
A75
Cornish College of the Arts **A80**
Daemen College **A80**
East Carolina University **A83**
Fort Hays State University **A88**
Grand Valley State University **A90**
Kansas City Art Institute **A99**
Kansas State University **A99**
Kent State University **A101**
Kutztown University of Pennsylvania
A102
Louisiana Tech University **A107**
Maryland Institute, College of Art
A110
Marywood University **A113**
Massachusetts College of Art **A114**
Memphis College of Art **A114**
Minneapolis College of Art and Design
A118
Montserrat College of Art **A120**
Moore College of Art and Design
A122
New Jersey City University **A124**
Northern Illinois University **A127**
Oklahoma State University **A130**
Otis College of Art and Design **A132**
Paier College of Art, Inc. **A135**
Parsons School of Design, New School
for Social Research **A135**
Pratt Institute **A138**
Rivier College **A145**
Rochester Institute of Technology
A146
Rocky Mountain College of Art &
Design **A147**
San Jose State University **A150**
Savannah College of Art and Design
A150
School of the Museum of Fine Arts
A153
School of Visual Arts **A154**
Southwest Missouri State University
A160
State University of New York at Buffalo
A160

State University of New York College
at Fredonia **A161**
Syracuse University **A164**
Temple University **A168**
Texas A&M University–Commerce
A165
University of Alaska Anchorage **A171**
University of Connecticut **A175**
University of Dayton **A175**
University of Delaware **A176**
University of Hartford **A178**
University of Massachusetts Dartmouth
A182
University of Miami **A184**
University of Nebraska–Lincoln **A189**
University of North Carolina at
Charlotte **A191**
University of the Arts **A200**
University of Utah **A202**
Utah State University **A205**
Virginia Commonwealth University
A206
Washington University in St. Louis
A209

Image design

East Carolina University **A83**

Individualized major

Atlanta College of Art **A54**
Maine College of Art **A108**
University of Connecticut **A175**

Industrial design

Academy of Art College **A41**
Art Center College of Design **A51**
Brigham Young University **A61**
California College of Arts and Crafts
A62
Cleveland Institute of Art **A70**
Columbus College of Art and Design
A75
Massachusetts College of Art **A114**
Pratt Institute **A138**
Rochester Institute of Technology
A146
San Jose State University **A150**
Savannah College of Art and Design
A150
Southern Illinois University at
Carbondale **A158**
Syracuse University **A164**
University of Illinois at Chicago **A179**
University of Michigan **A185**
University of Notre Dame **A193**
University of the Arts **A200**
University of Washington **A202**
University of Wisconsin–Stout **A204**
Wayne State University **A209**

Intaglio

Illinois State University **A93**
The University of Texas at Austin
A198

Interactive mutli-media

Minneapolis College of Art and Design
A118

Interdisciplinary studies

Alberta College of Art and Design
A43
Cardinal Stritch University **A66**
Concordia University **A76**
Lake Erie College **A103**
University of Washington **A202**

Interior architecture

California College of Arts and Crafts
A62
Lawrence Technological University
A104
Longwood College **A106**
School of the Art Institute of Chicago
A151

Interior design

Adrian College **A42**
American InterContinental
University **A46**
American InterContinental
University **A47**
The Art Institutes International at
Portland **A54**
Atlanta College of Art **A54**
Beaver College **A58**
Brigham Young University **A61**
California State University, Chico
A65
Center for Creative Studies—College
of Art and Design **A68**
Central Missouri State University **A69**
Cleveland Institute of Art **A70**
Columbus College of Art and Design
A75
Converse College **A76**
Cornish College of the Arts **A80**
Culver-Stockton College **A80**
Drake University **A82**
Fort Hays State University **A88**
Georgia State University **A90**
Harding University **A91**
The Illinois Institute of Art **A92**
Iowa State University of Science and
Technology **A96**
James Madison University **A98**
Maryland Institute, College of Art
A110
Marylhurst University **A112**
Marywood University **A113**
Mississippi University for Women
A120
Moore College of Art and Design
A122
Northern Illinois University **A127**
O'More College of Design **A130**
Paier College of Art, Inc. **A135**
Parsons School of Design, New School
for Social Research **A135**
Pratt Institute **A138**

Siena Heights University **A157**
Slippery Rock University of
    Pennsylvania **A157**
University of Oklahoma **A193**
University of Washington **A202**

Multimedia

College of Santa Fe **A72**
Johnson State College **A99**
Mississippi State University **A119**
University of the Arts **A200**
University of Wisconsin–Stout **A204**

Multimedia communications

The Illinois Institute of Art **A92**

Museum studies

University of North Carolina at
    Charlotte **A191**

New genre

Otis College of Art and Design **A132**
Radford University **A141**
San Francisco Art Institute **A149**
The University of Arizona **A171**
University of Southern California
    A196

New media

York University **A215**

Painting

Arizona State University **A49**
Art Institute of Boston **A52**
Austin Peay State University **A56**
Ball State University **A56**
Barry University **A57**
Brigham Young University **A61**
Clarion University of Pennsylvania
    A69
Clarke College **A70**
Cleveland Institute of Art **A70**
The College of Saint Rose **A72**
College of Visual Arts **A73**
Colorado State University **A74**
The Corcoran School of Art **A77**
Daemen College **A80**
Dominican College of San Rafael
    A82
Drake University **A82**
Edinboro University of Pennsylvania
    A85
Florida International University **A88**
Georgia Southern University **A89**
Illinois Wesleyan University **A93**
Indiana University of Pennsylvania
    A94
Johnson State College **A99**
Kansas State University **A99**
Lakehead University **A103**
Longwood College **A106**
Maine College of Art **A108**
Mankato State University **A110**
Marshall University **A110**

Minneapolis College of Art and Design
    A118
Old Dominion University **A130**
Radford University **A141**
Rhode Island College **A141**
St. Cloud State University **A147**
Savannah College of Art and Design
    A150
Siena Heights University **A157**
Slippery Rock University of
    Pennsylvania **A157**
Southwest Missouri State University
    A160
State University of New York College
    at Fredonia **A161**
Truman State University **A168**
University of Massachusetts Amherst
    A182
University of
    Missouri–Columbia **A187**
University of Missouri–St. Louis **A188**
University of Nebraska–Lincoln **A189**
University of North Carolina at
    Asheville **A190**
University of Northern Iowa **A192**
University of Southern Maine **A196**
The University of Texas at San
    Antonio **A199**
The University of Texas at Tyler
    A199
University of Washington **A202**
University of
    Wisconsin–Oshkosh **A204**
University of Wisconsin–Stevens
    Point **A204**
University of
    Wisconsin–Superior **A205**
Washington University in St. Louis
    A209
Western Kentucky University **A211**
Wright State University **A214**
York University **A215**

Painting/drawing

Abilene Christian University **A41**
Academy of Art College **A41**
Alberta College of Art and Design
    A43
Alfred University **A44**
American University **A48**
Appalachian State University **A49**
Arkansas State University **A50**
Art Academy of Cincinnati **A50**
Art Center College of Design **A51**
Art Institute of Boston **A52**
Atlanta College of Art **A54**
Auburn University **A55**
Baylor University **A57**
Beaver College **A58**
Bellevue University **A59**
Brenau University **A61**
Brooklyn College of the City University
    of New York **A62**
Caldwell College **A62**
California College of Arts and Crafts
    A62

California Institute of the Arts **A64**
California State University, Chico
    A65
California State University, Fullerton
    A65
California State University, Long
    Beach **A65**
Cardinal Stritch University **A66**
Center for Creative Studies—College
    of Art and Design **A68**
Central Michigan University **A69**
College of Santa Fe **A72**
Columbia College **A75**
Concordia University **A76**
Cornell University **A78**
Cornish College of the Arts **A80**
Drake University **A82**
East Carolina University **A83**
Eastern New Mexico University **A84**
East Tennessee State University **A84**
Emmanuel College **A85**
Emporia State University **A85**
Florida Atlantic University **A87**
Fort Hays State University **A88**
Georgia Southwestern State University
    A89
Georgia State University **A90**
Grand Valley State University **A90**
Guilford College **A90**
Howard University **A92**
Illinois State University **A93**
Indiana State University **A93**
Indiana University Bloomington **A94**
Indiana University–Purdue University
    Fort Wayne **A95**
Indiana University–Purdue University
    Indianapolis **A95**
Indiana University South Bend **A95**
Iowa State University of Science and
    Technology **A96**
Jacksonville State University **A97**
James Madison University **A98**
Kansas City Art Institute **A99**
Kent State University **A101**
Kutztown University of Pennsylvania
    A102
Lehman College of the City University
    of New York **A104**
Lindenwood University **A104**
Louisiana State University and
    Agricultural and Mechanical
    College **A107**
Louisiana Tech University **A107**
Maharishi University of Management
    A108
Maryland Institute, College of Art
    A110
Marylhurst University **A112**
Marywood University **A113**
Massachusetts College of Art **A114**
Memphis College of Art **A114**
Metropolitan State College of Denver
    A115
Miami University **A115**
Michigan State University **A116**

Papermaking

Performance

Performance art

Photography

Rutgers, The State University of New Jersey, Mason Gross School of the Arts **A113**

St. Cloud State University **A147**

Saint Mary's College **A148**

San Francisco Art Institute **A149**

School of the Art Institute of Chicago **A151**

School of the Museum of Fine Arts **A153**

School of Visual Arts **A154**

Shepherd College **A156**

Siena Heights University **A157**

Slippery Rock University of Pennsylvania **A157**

Sonoma State University **A158**

Southern Illinois University at Carbondale **A158**

Southern Illinois University at Edwardsville **A158**

Southern Oregon University **A159**

Southwest Missouri State University **A160**

Southwest Texas State University **A160**

State University of New York at Buffalo **A160**

State University of New York at New Paltz **A161**

State University of West Georgia **A162**

Sul Ross State University **A164**

Syracuse University **A164**

Temple University **A168**

Texas A&M University–Commerce **A165**

Texas Christian University **A166**

Texas Southern University **A167**

Texas Tech University **A167**

Truman State University **A168**

The University of Akron **A170**

The University of Alabama **A170**

University of Alaska Anchorage **A171**

The University of Arizona **A171**

University of Arkansas **A172**

University of British Columbia **A173**

The University of Calgary **A173**

University of Central Florida **A174**

University of Cincinnati **A174**

University of Colorado at Boulder **A174**

University of Connecticut **A175**

University of Delaware **A176**

University of Denver **A176**

University of Florida **A177**

University of Georgia **A178**

University of Hartford **A178**

University of Hawaii at Manoa **A179**

University of Illinois at Chicago **A179**

The University of Iowa **A180**

University of Louisville **A181**

University of Manitoba **A181**

University of Massachusetts Amherst **A182**

University of Massachusetts Dartmouth **A182**

The University of Memphis **A184**

University of Miami **A184**

University of Michigan **A185**

University of Minnesota, Twin Cities Campus **A187**

University of Mississippi **A187**

University of Missouri–Columbia **A187**

University of Missouri–St. Louis **A188**

The University of Montana–Missoula **A188**

University of Montevallo **A188**

University of Nebraska–Lincoln **A189**

University of Nevada, Las Vegas **A189**

University of New Hampshire **A189**

University of North Alabama **A190**

University of North Carolina at Asheville **A190**

University of North Carolina at Charlotte **A191**

University of North Dakota **A192**

University of Northern Iowa **A192**

University of North Texas **A193**

University of Notre Dame **A193**

University of Oklahoma **A193**

University of Oregon **A194**

University of Regina **A195**

University of South Alabama **A195**

University of South Carolina **A195**

University of Southern California **A196**

University of Southern Maine **A196**

University of Tennessee, Knoxville **A198**

The University of Texas at Arlington **A198**

The University of Texas at Austin **A198**

The University of Texas at San Antonio **A199**

The University of Texas at Tyler **A199**

The University of Texas–Pan American **A200**

University of the Arts **A200**

University of Utah **A202**

University of Washington **A202**

University of Wisconsin–Milwaukee **A203**

University of Wisconsin–Oshkosh **A204**

University of Wisconsin–Stevens Point **A204**

University of Wisconsin–Superior **A205**

Utah State University **A205**

Virginia Commonwealth University **A206**

Washington State University **A208**

Washington University in St. Louis **A209**

Wayne State University **A209**

Webster University **A210**

Western Carolina University **A211**

Western Illinois University **A211**

Western Kentucky University **A211**

Western Michigan University **A212**

West Texas A&M University **A212**

West Virginia University **A213**

Wichita State University **A213**

Winthrop University **A214**

Wright State University **A214**

Xavier University **A214**

York University **A215**

Product design

Art Center College of Design **A51**

Center for Creative Studies—College of Art and Design **A68**

Retail management

The Art Institutes International at Portland **A54**

Scientific illustration

Beaver College **A58**

University of Georgia **A178**

University of Michigan **A185**

Screenwriting

The University of Texas at Arlington **A198**

Sculpture

Abilene Christian University **A41**

Academy of Art College **A41**

Alberta College of Art and Design **A43**

Alfred University **A44**

American University **A48**

Appalachian State University **A49**

Arizona State University **A49**

Arkansas State University **A50**

Art Academy of Cincinnati **A50**

Art Institute of Boston **A52**

Atlanta College of Art **A54**

Auburn University **A55**

Austin Peay State University **A56**

Ball State University **A56**

Baylor University **A57**

Bellevue University **A59**

Brenau University **A61**

Brigham Young University **A61**

Brooklyn College of the City University of New York **A62**

Caldwell College **A62**

California College of Arts and Crafts **A62**

California Institute of the Arts **A64**

California State University, Chico **A65**

California State University, Fullerton **A65**

California State University, Long Beach **A65**

Center for Creative Studies—College of Art and Design **A68**

Central Michigan University **A69**

Clarion University of Pennsylvania **A69**

Clarke College **A70**

Dance Majors

Ballet

Barat College **D221**
Butler University **D223**
Cornish College of the Arts **D226**
East Carolina University **D227**
The Juilliard School **D229**
North Carolina School of the Arts **D232**
Purchase College, State University of New York **D235**
Radford University **D236**
Southern Methodist University **D238**
The University of Arizona **D240**
University of Cincinnati **D241**
The University of Iowa **D244**
University of Nebraska–Lincoln **D246**
University of Oklahoma **D247**
The University of Texas at Austin **D248**
University of the Arts **D249**
University of Utah **D249**
University of Wyoming **D250**
Western Kentucky University **D251**
West Texas A&M University **D252**
York University **D253**

Ballet pedagogy

University of Hartford **D242**
University of Utah **D249**

Children's dance

University of Hartford **D242**

Choreography

George Mason University **D228**
Temple University **D239**
The University of Iowa **D244**

Choreography and performance

Arizona State University **D221**
Cornish College of the Arts **D226**
Lake Erie College **D230**
University of California, Santa Barbara **D241**
University of Florida **D242**
University of Illinois at Urbana–Champaign **D243**
University of Michigan **D244**
The University of Montana–Missoula **D246**
University of Southern Mississippi **D247**
The University of Texas at Austin **D248**

Composition

Purchase College, State University of New York **D235**

York University **D253**

Contemporary dance

North Carolina School of the Arts **D232**

Dance

Butler University **D223**
East Carolina University **D227**
Lake Erie College **D230**
Sam Houston State University **D237**
Shenandoah University **D237**
Temple University **D239**
University of Florida **D242**
University of North Carolina at Greensboro **D246**
University of Southwestern Louisiana **D248**
The University of Tennessee at Martin **D248**
The University of Texas at Austin **D248**
West Texas A&M University **D252**

Dance education

Arizona State University **D221**
Brenau University **D222**
The Ohio State University **D233**
Shenandoah University **D237**
The University of Montana–Missoula **D246**
University of North Carolina at Greensboro **D246**
University of the Arts **D249**

Dance in medicine

University of Florida **D242**

Dance performance

Chapman University **D225**

Dance theater

Chapman University **D225**

Ethnic dance

University of Utah **D249**

Interdisciplinary studies

Lake Erie College **D230**

Jazz dance

East Carolina University **D227**
Southern Methodist University **D238**
The University of Arizona **D240**
University of the Arts **D249**
University of Wyoming **D250**
Western Kentucky University **D251**
West Texas A&M University **D252**

Modern dance

Barat College **D221**
Cornish College of the Arts **D226**
East Carolina University **D227**
The Juilliard School **D229**
Purchase College, State University of New York **D235**
Radford University **D236**
Rutgers, The State University of New Jersey, Mason Gross School of the Arts **D231**
Southern Methodist University **D238**
The University of Arizona **D240**
University of Colorado at Boulder **D242**
The University of Iowa **D244**
University of Michigan **D244**
University of Nebraska–Lincoln **D246**
University of Oklahoma **D247**
The University of Texas at Austin **D248**
University of the Arts **D249**
University of Wisconsin–Milwaukee **D250**
University of Wyoming **D250**
Virginia Commonwealth University **D250**
Wichita State University **D252**
York University **D253**

Music theater

Western Kentucky University **D251**
Wichita State University **D252**

Pedagogy

Brenau University **D222**

Performance

Brenau University **D222**
George Mason University **D228**
New World School of the Arts **D231**
The Ohio State University **D233**
Temple University **D239**
University of Hartford **D242**
University of Utah **D249**

Production

Purchase College, State University of New York **D235**

Tap dance

Western Kentucky University **D251**
West Texas A&M University **D252**

Theater arts/drama

University of Florida **D242**
University of Southwestern Louisiana **D248**

Music Majors

Accompanying
Arizona State University **M262**
Florida Atlantic University **M311**
James Madison University **M330**
The Juilliard School **M331**
Oberlin College **M371**
University of California, Santa Barbara **M416**
Westminster Choir College of Rider University **M470**
Youngstown State University **M478**

Accordion
University of Denver **M422**
University of Missouri–Kansas City **M434**

Applied music
Seton Hall University **M390**
Viterbo College **M465**
William Carey College **M475**

Arranging
American Conservatory of Music **M260**
The University of Alabama **M411**
University of Denver **M422**

Arts management
Shenandoah University **M391**

Audio recording technology
Cleveland Institute of Music **M289**
Five Towns College **M310**

Band
Auburn University **M264**
Slippery Rock University of Pennsylvania **M394**
Southeastern Louisiana University **M394**

Bass
Musicians Institute **M359**
St. Francis Xavier University **M385**
University of Wisconsin–Green Bay **M458**

Bass trombone
The Harid Conservatory **M319**

Bassoon
The Harid Conservatory **M319**
The Juilliard School **M331**
Southern Methodist University **M397**
Temple University **M308**
University of California, Irvine **M415**

Brass
Alcorn State University **M259**
Baldwin-Wallace College **M265**
Berry College **M270**

Boston Conservatory **M272**
Boston University **M273**
Brewton-Parker College **M275**
Brigham Young University **M275**
Cincinnati Bible College and Seminary **M287**
Dalhousie University **M300**
The George Washington University **M315**
Georgia College and State University **M315**
Houghton College **M321**
Longwood College **M340**
North Park University **M368**
Oberlin College **M371**
Queens College of the City University of New York **M382**
St. Francis Xavier University **M385**
Susquehanna University **M403**
Texas A&M University–Commerce **M406**
The University of Calgary **M415**
University of California, Santa Barbara **M416**
University of Central Arkansas **M416**
University of Colorado at Boulder **M420**
The University of Texas at Arlington **M452**
University of the Incarnate Word **M454**
University of the Pacific **M455**
University of Utah **M456**
University of Wisconsin–Milwaukee **M459**
University of Wisconsin–Oshkosh **M459**
Wartburg College **M466**
Willamette University **M474**

Cello
The Harid Conservatory **M319**
Southern Methodist University **M397**
Temple University **M308**

Choral music
Auburn University **M264**
Lawrence University **M336**

Choral music education
Alabama State University **M258**
Calvin College **M280**
Christopher Newport University **M287**
Georgia College and State University **M315**
Northern Arizona University **M366**
Silver Lake College **M392**
Trinity University **M409**
Union University **M410**
The University of Arizona **M413**
University of Maryland, College Park **M428**

Church music
Belmont University **M268**
Birmingham-Southern College **M271**

Cedarville College **M284**
Cornerstone College **M296**
Dalhousie University **M300**
Drake University **M302**
Furman University **M313**
Hardin-Simmons University **M318**
Oakland City University **M370**
Palm Beach Atlantic College **M377**
Samford University **M387**
Shorter College **M392**
Wayne State University **M467**
Wittenberg University **M476**

Clarinet
The Harid Conservatory **M319**
The Juilliard School **M331**
Southern Methodist University **M397**
Temple University **M308**
University of California, Irvine **M415**

Classical guitar
Baldwin-Wallace College **M265**
Dalhousie University **M300**
The George Washington University **M315**
Illinois State University **M323**
Keene State College **M332**
Kennesaw State University **M332**
Lawrence University **M336**
Mars Hill College **M347**
St. Olaf College **M386**
San Francisco Conservatory of Music **M388**
Simpson College **M393**
State University of New York at Buffalo **M401**
Temple University **M308**
Texas A&M University–Corpus Christi **M406**
The University of Arizona **M413**
University of Cincinnati **M417**
University of Evansville **M422**
University of Southern California **M448**
University of Vermont **M456**
Vanderbilt University **M462**

Classical music
Appalachian State University **M261**
Baylor University **M267**
Birmingham-Southern College **M271**
Boise State University **M271**
Brooklyn College of the City University of New York **M276**
California Institute of the Arts **M277**
California State University, Long Beach **M278**
Carleton University **M282**
Central Methodist College **M284**
Central Washington University **M286**
City College of the City University of New York **M288**
Cleveland Institute of Music **M289**
Coe College **M290**
The College of New Jersey **M291**

Classical performance

Commercial music

Composition

English horn

The Juilliard School **M331**

Ethnomusicology

Carleton University **M282**
University of Hawaii at Manoa **M424**

Euphonium

Temple University **M308**

Eurythmics

Cleveland Institute of Music **M289**

Film scoring

Berklee College of Music **M268**
University of Southern California
  M448

Flute

The Harid Conservatory **M319**
The Juilliard School **M331**
Southern Methodist University **M397**
Temple University **M308**
University of California, Irvine **M415**

French horn

The Harid Conservatory **M319**
Southern Methodist University **M397**
University of California, Irvine **M415**

Guitar

Alcorn State University **M259**
American Conservatory of Music
  M260
Aquinas College **M262**
Atlantic Union College **M264**
Barry University **M267**
Birmingham-Southern College **M271**
Boston Conservatory **M272**
California State University, Northridge
  M279
California State University, Sacramento
  M279
Central Washington University **M286**
Coe College **M290**
Duquesne University **M302**
Eastern Michigan University **M304**
Georgia College and State University
  M315
Indiana University South Bend **M326**
Ithaca College **M327**
Johns Hopkins University **M331**
The Juilliard School **M331**
Mannes College of Music, New School
  for Social Research **M344**
Millikin University **M353**
Musicians Institute **M359**
North Carolina School of the Arts
  M364
Northern Kentucky University **M367**
Oakland City University **M370**
Philadelphia College of Bible **M378**
Queens College **M381**
Southern Illinois University at
  Carbondale **M396**

Southern Methodist University **M397**
Southwestern University **M399**
Southwest Texas State University
  M400
Susquehanna University **M403**
Texas Christian University **M407**
Trinity University **M409**
University of Alberta **M412**
University of Arkansas **M413**
University of British Columbia **M414**
University of California, Irvine **M415**
University of California, Santa Barbara
  M416
University of Hawaii at Manoa **M424**
University of Missouri–Kansas
  City **M434**
University of Puget Sound **M445**
University of Rochester **M305**
University of South Carolina **M447**
University of Southern Mississippi
  M449
University of Washington **M457**
University of Wisconsin–Green
  Bay **M458**
University of
  Wisconsin–Milwaukee **M459**
University of
  Wisconsin–Superior **M460**
Utah State University **M461**
Virginia Commonwealth University
  M464
Wartburg College **M466**
Western Kentucky University **M469**
West Virginia Wesleyan College
  M473
Willamette University **M474**
William Carey College **M475**
Winthrop University **M476**

Harp

College of Notre Dame **M291**
Holy Names College **M320**
The Juilliard School **M331**
Lawrence University **M336**
Louisiana State University and
  Agricultural and Mechanical
  College **M340**
North Carolina School of the Arts
  M364
Northern Kentucky University **M367**
Queens College **M381**
Southern Methodist University **M397**
State University of New York College
  at Potsdam **M298**
Temple University **M308**
University of Alberta **M412**
University of California, Irvine **M415**
University of Puget Sound **M445**
The University of Texas at Austin
  M452
University of Utah **M456**
University of Vermont **M456**
University of Washington **M457**
Willamette University **M474**

Harpsichord

Acadia University **M258**
American Conservatory of Music
  M260
Coe College **M290**
Dalhousie University **M300**
The Juilliard School **M331**
Lawrence University **M336**
Roosevelt University **M383**
Southern Methodist University **M397**
State University of New York at
  Binghamton **M400**
State University of New York at Buffalo
  M401
Trinity University **M409**
University of Arkansas **M413**
University of Cincinnati **M417**
University of Puget Sound **M445**
University of Rochester **M305**
University of Southern Mississippi
  M449
The University of Texas at Austin
  M452
University of Vermont **M456**
University of Wisconsin–Eau
  Claire **M457**
University of
  Wisconsin–Superior **M460**
Winthrop University **M476**

Historical performance

Oberlin College **M371**

Horn

The Juilliard School **M331**
Temple University **M308**

Improvisation

New England Conservatory of Music
  M360
York University **M478**

Individualized major

Utah State University **M461**

Instrumental conducting

University of Cincinnati **M417**

Instrumental music

Carnegie Mellon University **M282**
Cornish College of the Arts **M297**
Cumberland College **M299**
Eastern Kentucky University **M304**
Fisk University **M309**
Lake Erie College **M334**
Lander University **M335**
Lawrence University **M336**
Lincoln University **M339**
Louisiana Tech University **M341**
Millikin University **M353**
Moravian College **M356**
New York University **M361**
Northern Arizona University **M366**
Northern State University **M367**
San Francisco State University **M390**

Southern University and Agricultural and Mechanical College **M398**
University of Hartford **M423**
The University of Montana–Missoula **M435**
The University of Texas at Tyler **M454**

Instrumental music education

Alabama State University **M258**
Calvin College **M280**
Christopher Newport University **M287**
Georgia College and State University **M315**
Mississippi State University **M354**
Northern Arizona University **M366**
Silver Lake College **M392**
Southwest Baptist University **M398**
Trinity University **M409**
Union University **M410**
The University of Arizona **M413**
University of Maryland, College Park **M428**
University of North Carolina at Pembroke **M440**

Instrumental performance

San Francisco State University **M390**

Interdisciplinary studies

Indiana University–Purdue University Fort Wayne **M326**
Lake Erie College **M334**
Stetson University **M402**

Jazz

American Conservatory of Music **M260**
Arizona State University **M262**
Boise State University **M271**
Bowling Green State University **M273**
California Institute of the Arts **M277**
California State University, Long Beach **M278**
California State University, Los Angeles **M279**
California State University, Northridge **M279**
Capital University **M281**
Carleton University **M282**
Central Missouri State University **M285**
Central Washington University **M286**
City College of the City University of New York **M288**
Colorado Christian University **M293**
Cornish College of the Arts **M297**
Dalhousie University **M300**
Duquesne University **M302**
Eastern Illinois University **M303**
Florida Atlantic University **M311**
Florida International University **M311**

Florida State University **M312**
Hope College **M321**
Hunter College of the City University of New York **M322**
Ithaca College **M327**
Jackson State University **M329**
Lawrence University **M336**
Loyola University New Orleans **M341**
Manhattan School of Music **M342**
McNeese State University **M349**
Millikin University **M353**
Moravian College **M356**
Morehead State University **M357**
Murray State University **M359**
New England Conservatory of Music **M360**
New School Jazz and Contemporary Music **M345**
New York University **M361**
North Carolina Central University **M364**
Northern Illinois University **M366**
Oberlin College **M371**
The Ohio State University **M372**
Purchase College, State University of New York **M380**
Roosevelt University **M383**
Rowan University **M384**
Rutgers, The State University of New Jersey, Mason Gross School of the Arts **M349**
St. Cloud State University **M385**
St. Francis Xavier University **M385**
San Diego State University **M388**
Shenandoah University **M391**
Southern Illinois University at Edwardsville **M397**
Southern University and Agricultural and Mechanical College **M398**
Southwest Texas State University **M400**
State University of New York College at Potsdam **M298**
State University of West Georgia **M402**
Towson University **M408**
University of Alaska Fairbanks **M412**
The University of Arizona **M413**
University of Cincinnati **M417**
University of Denver **M422**
University of Hartford **M423**
University of Illinois at Urbana–Champaign **M425**
University of Massachusetts Amherst **M429**
The University of Memphis **M429**
University of Michigan **M431**
University of Minnesota, Twin Cities Campus **M433**
University of Nevada, Las Vegas **M437**
University of North Carolina at Greensboro **M440**
University of North Florida **M442**
University of North Texas **M442**
University of Oregon **M443**

University of Rochester **M305**
University of South Carolina **M447**
University of Southern California **M448**
University of Southern Maine **M449**
University of Southern Mississippi **M449**
University of Southwestern Louisiana **M450**
University of Tennessee, Knoxville **M451**
The University of Texas at Arlington **M452**
University of Utah **M456**
University of Washington **M457**
University of Wisconsin–Madison **M458**
Valdosta State University **M462**
Virginia Commonwealth University **M464**
Wayne State University **M467**
Webster University **M468**
Western Connecticut State University **M469**
Western Michigan University **M469**
Western Washington University **M470**
West Virginia University **M472**
Wichita State University **M474**
William Paterson University of New Jersey **M475**
York University **M478**
Youngstown State University **M478**

Jazz bass

Temple University **M308**

Jazz composition

Berklee College of Music **M268**

Jazz drums

Temple University **M308**

Jazz guitar

Kennesaw State University **M332**
St. Francis Xavier University **M385**
Temple University **M308**
University of Southern California **M448**

Jazz piano

Temple University **M308**

Jazz saxophone

Temple University **M308**

Jazz studies

Northwestern University **M369**
Portland State University **M379**
The University of Alabama **M411**

Jazz trombone

Temple University **M308**

University of Puget Sound **M445**
University of Rhode Island **M446**
University of South Alabama **M447**
University of Southern California **M448**
University of Tennessee, Knoxville **M451**
University of the Incarnate Word **M454**
University of Washington **M457**
University of Wisconsin–Madison **M458**
University of Wisconsin–Whitewater **M460**
Utah State University **M461**
Valparaiso University **M462**
Wayne State University **M467**
Webster University **M468**
Western Michigan University **M469**
West Texas A&M University **M472**
West Virginia University **M472**
West Virginia Wesleyan College **M473**
Wichita State University **M474**
Willamette University **M474**
William Paterson University of New Jersey **M475**
Wittenberg University **M476**
Wright State University **M477**

Music and business

Berry College **M270**
Boise State University **M271**
DePauw University **M301**
Drake University **M302**
Otterbein College **M376**
State University of New York College at Potsdam **M298**
University of Idaho **M425**
University of Missouri–St. Louis **M435**

Music business

Acadia University **M258**
Berklee College of Music **M268**
Central Washington University **M286**
Eastern New Mexico University **M305**
Five Towns College **M310**
Indiana State University **M325**
James Madison University **M330**
Mansfield University of Pennsylvania **M346**
New Mexico State University **M361**
New York University **M361**
Radford University **M382**
Roosevelt University **M383**
Syracuse University **M403**
University of Illinois at Urbana–Champaign **M425**
The University of Memphis **M429**
University of Nebraska at Kearney **M436**
University of Puget Sound **M445**
University of the Incarnate Word **M454**

Music education

Acadia University **M258**
Alcorn State University **M259**
Anderson College **M260**
Andrews University **M260**
Angelo State University **M261**
Appalachian State University **M261**
Aquinas College **M262**
Arizona State University **M262**
Arkansas State University **M263**
Ashland University **M263**
Atlantic Union College **M264**
Augsburg College **M264**
Augusta State University **M265**
Baker University **M265**
Baldwin-Wallace College **M265**
Ball State University **M266**
Baylor University **M267**
Belmont University **M268**
Berklee College of Music **M268**
Berry College **M270**
Bethel College **M270**
Biola University **M270**
Boise State University **M271**
Boston Conservatory **M272**
Boston University **M273**
Bowling Green State University **M273**
Bradley University **M274**
Brenau University **M274**
Brewton-Parker College **M275**
Brigham Young University **M275**
Brooklyn College of the City University of New York **M276**
Bucknell University **M276**
Butler University **M277**
California State University, Fullerton **M278**
California State University, Long Beach **M278**
California State University, Los Angeles **M279**
Calvary Bible College and Theological Seminary **M280**
Cameron University **M280**
Campbellsville University **M281**
Capital University **M281**
Carson-Newman College **M282**
Cedarville College **M284**
Centenary College of Louisiana **M284**
Central Methodist College **M284**
Central Michigan University **M285**
Central Missouri State University **M285**
Central Washington University **M286**
Chapman University **M286**
Cleveland State University **M290**
Coe College **M290**
The College of New Jersey **M291**
The College of Wooster **M292**
Colorado State University **M293**
Columbia College **M294**
Columbus State University **M294**
Concordia College **M295**

Converse College **M296**
Cornerstone College **M296**
Crown College **M298**
Culver-Stockton College **M299**
Dalhousie University **M300**
Dallas Baptist University **M300**
DePauw University **M301**
Duquesne University **M302**
East Carolina University **M303**
East Central University **M303**
Eastern Illinois University **M303**
Eastern Michigan University **M304**
Eastern New Mexico University **M305**
East Tennessee State University **M307**
Emporia State University **M308**
Evangel College **M309**
Five Towns College **M310**
Florida Atlantic University **M311**
Florida Southern College **M312**
Florida State University **M312**
Fort Hays State University **M313**
Furman University **M313**
Georgetown College **M314**
Gordon College **M316**
Grand Valley State University **M317**
Hardin-Simmons University **M318**
Hastings College **M319**
Heidelberg College **M319**
Henderson State University **M320**
Hope College **M321**
Houghton College **M321**
Howard Payne University **M321**
Huntington College **M323**
Idaho State University **M323**
Illinois State University **M323**
Illinois Wesleyan University **M324**
Indiana State University **M325**
Indiana University–Purdue University Fort Wayne **M326**
Indiana University South Bend **M326**
Iowa State University of Science and Technology **M327**
Ithaca College **M327**
Jackson State University **M329**
Jacksonville State University **M329**
Jacksonville University **M329**
James Madison University **M330**
Johns Hopkins University **M331**
Kansas State University **M332**
Keene State College **M332**
Kennesaw State University **M332**
Kent State University **M333**
Kentucky State University **M333**
Kentucky Wesleyan College **M334**
Lamar University **M335**
Lander University **M335**
Lawrence University **M336**
Liberty University **M338**
Lincoln University **M339**
Longwood College **M340**
Louisiana College **M340**
Loyola University New Orleans **M341**
Manhattanville College **M343**
Mankato State University **M343**

Augsburg College **M264**
Baldwin-Wallace College **M265**
Berklee College of Music **M268**
Chapman University **M286**
The College of Wooster **M292**
Colorado State University **M293**
Duquesne University **M302**
East Carolina University **M303**
Eastern Michigan University **M304**
Florida State University **M312**
Illinois State University **M323**
Indiana University–Purdue University
  Fort Wayne **M326**
Loyola University New Orleans **M341**
Mansfield University of Pennsylvania
  M346
Michigan State University **M351**
Montclair State University **M355**
Ohio University **M373**
Queens College **M381**
Radford University **M382**
Sam Houston State University **M387**
Shenandoah University **M391**
Southern Methodist University **M397**
Southwestern Oklahoma State
  University **M399**
State University of New York College
  at Fredonia **M401**
The University of Alabama **M411**
University of Dayton **M421**
University of Evansville **M422**
University of Georgia **M423**
The University of Iowa **M426**
University of Kansas **M426**
University of Minnesota, Twin Cities
  Campus **M433**
University of Missouri–Kansas
  City **M434**
University of the Incarnate Word
  M454
University of the Pacific **M455**
University of Wisconsin–Eau
  Claire **M457**
University of
  Wisconsin–Oshkosh **M459**
Utah State University **M461**
Western Michigan University **M469**
Wilfrid Laurier University **M474**
Willamette University **M474**
William Carey College **M475**

Musical instrument technology
Appalachian State University **M261**

Musicology
Oberlin College **M371**
Texas Christian University **M407**

New genre
Cornish College of the Arts **M297**

New media
California Institute of the Arts **M277**

Oboe
The Harid Conservatory **M319**
The Juilliard School **M331**
Southern Methodist University **M397**
Temple University **M308**
University of California, Irvine **M415**

Opera
Baylor University **M267**
Birmingham-Southern College **M271**
Boise State University **M271**
Boston Conservatory **M272**
Brooklyn College of the City University
  of New York **M276**
California State University, Long
  Beach **M278**
Dalhousie University **M300**
Indiana University South Bend **M326**
Murray State University **M359**
Northwestern University **M369**
Purchase College, State University of
  New York **M380**
Sam Houston State University **M387**
Southern Illinois University at
  Carbondale **M396**
State University of New York College
  at Potsdam **M298**
Texas Tech University **M408**
University of British Columbia **M414**
University of Colorado at Boulder
  M420
University of New Mexico **M438**
Wichita State University **M474**
Wilfrid Laurier University **M474**

Orchestral instruments
California State University, Northridge
  M279
New York University **M361**
Slippery Rock University of
  Pennsylvania **M394**
Stephen F. Austin State University
  M402
University of British Columbia **M414**
University of California, Santa Barbara
  M416
The University of Texas at Austin
  M452
University of Washington **M457**

Organ
American Conservatory of Music
  M260
Aquinas College **M262**
Fisk University **M309**
The Juilliard School **M331**
San Francisco State University **M390**
Shorter College **M392**
Southern Methodist University **M397**
Southwestern University **M399**
The University of Texas at Austin
  M452
Westminster Choir College of Rider
  University **M470**

Pedagogy
Shenandoah University **M391**

Percussion
Boston University **M273**
The Harid Conservatory **M319**
The Juilliard School **M331**
Musicians Institute **M359**
Southern Methodist University **M397**
Temple University **M308**
University of California, Irvine **M415**

Performance
Berklee College of Music **M268**
Brooklyn College of the City University
  of New York **M276**
California State University, Northridge
  M279
Cameron University **M280**
Capital University **M281**
City College of the City University of
  New York **M288**
College of Santa Fe **M292**
Five Towns College **M310**
Florida International University
  M311
Furman University **M313**
Ithaca College **M327**
Lawrence University **M336**
Mannes College of Music, New School
  for Social Research **M344**
Marygrove College **M347**
Marylhurst University **M348**
Montclair State University **M355**
Moorhead State University **M356**
Moravian College **M356**
Mount St. Mary's College **M358**
New England Conservatory of Music
  M360
New York University **M361**
North Carolina School of the Arts
  M364
Pacific Lutheran University **M377**
Palm Beach Atlantic College **M377**
Radford University **M382**
Rowan University **M384**
Southern Illinois University at
  Edwardsville **M397**
Southwestern Oklahoma State
  University **M399**
State University of West Georgia
  M402
Syracuse University **M403**
Texas A&M
  University–Kingsville **M406**
Texas Southern University **M407**
Towson University **M408**
Union University **M410**
University of Colorado at Boulder
  M420
University of Dayton **M421**
The University of Memphis **M429**
University of Rhode Island **M446**
University of Richmond **M447**

University of Southwestern Louisiana
M450
University of Vermont M456
Western Washington University
M470
Westminster Choir College of Rider
University M470
William Carey College M475

Piano

Abilene Christian University M258
American Conservatory of Music
M260
Aquinas College M262
Barry University M267
Brenau University M274
California Institute of the Arts M277
California State University, Long
Beach M278
Cameron University M280
Cumberland College M299
DePaul University M301
Eastern Washington University M305
Fisk University M309
Florida Atlantic University M311
Fort Hays State University M313
The Harid Conservatory M319
Idaho State University M323
Indiana State University M325
The Juilliard School M331
Kennesaw State University M332
Lamar University M335
Lee University M337
Lock Haven University of Pennsylvania
M339
Louisiana College M340
Louisiana State University and
Agricultural and Mechanical
College M340
Mansfield University of Pennsylvania
M346
Michigan State University M351
Mount St. Mary's College M358
Northern Kentucky University M367
North Park University M368
Oakland University M371
The Ohio State University M372
Oral Roberts University M376
St. Francis Xavier University M385
San Francisco State University M390
Shorter College M392
Slippery Rock University of
Pennsylvania M394
Southern Methodist University M397
Southern University and Agricultural
and Mechanical College M398
Southwestern University M399
Temple University M308
Texas A&M University–Commerce
M406
Texas Wesleyan University M408
Truman State University M410
University of Arkansas at Monticello
M414
University of California, Irvine M415
University of Delaware M421

University of Hawaii at Manoa M424
University of Maryland, College Park
M428
University of Nevada, Las Vegas
M437
The University of Texas at Austin
M452
The University of Texas at El Paso
M453
The University of Texas at Tyler
M454
University of Tulsa M455
University of Utah M456
University of
Wisconsin–Oshkosh M459
Western Kentucky University M469
Westminster Choir College of Rider
University M470
West Virginia Wesleyan College
M473

Piano pedagogy

Belmont University M268
Bowling Green State University
M273
Butler University M277
Central Missouri State University
M285
Colorado State University M293
Columbus State University M294
Converse College M296
Drake University M302
East Carolina University M303
Hastings College M319
Louisiana State University and
Agricultural and Mechanical
College M340
Marygrove College M347
McNeese State University M349
Meredith College M350
Michigan State University M351
Northeast Louisiana University M366
Northern Kentucky University M367
Pittsburg State University M379
Roosevelt University M383
Shorter College M392
Southern Illinois University at
Carbondale M396
Southern Methodist University M397
State University of New York College
at Potsdam M298
State University of West Georgia
M402
University of Nebraska at Kearney
M436
University of South Carolina M447
University of Southwestern Louisiana
M450
The University of Texas at Tyler
M454
University of Utah M456
Utah State University M461
Westminster Choir College of Rider
University M470
Wichita State University M474

Piano/organ

Acadia University M258
Alcorn State University M259
Andrews University M260
Angelo State University M261
Anna Maria College M261
Appalachian State University M261
Arizona State University M262
Arkansas State University M263
Ashland University M263
Atlantic Union College M264
Augusta State University M265
Baker University M265
Baldwin-Wallace College M265
Ball State University M266
Baylor University M267
Berry College M270
Bethel College M270
Biola University M270
Birmingham-Southern College M271
Boise State University M271
Boston Conservatory M272
Boston University M273
Bowling Green State University
M273
Brewton-Parker College M275
Brigham Young University M275
Bucknell University M276
Butler University M277
California State University, Fullerton
M278
California State University, Los
Angeles M279
California State University, Northridge
M279
California State University, Sacramento
M279
Campbellsville University M281
Carleton University M282
Carnegie Mellon University M282
Carson-Newman College M282
Cedarville College M284
Centenary College of Louisiana
M284
Central Methodist College M284
Central Michigan University M285
Central Missouri State University
M285
Central Washington University M286
Chapman University M286
Christopher Newport University
M287
Cincinnati Bible College and Seminary
M287
Cleveland Institute of Music M289
Cleveland State University M290
Coe College M290
The College of New Jersey M291
College of Notre Dame M291
The College of Wooster M292
Colorado Christian University M293
Colorado State University M293
Columbia College M294
Columbus State University M294
Concordia College M295

Converse College **M296**
Cornerstone College **M296**
Covenant College **M297**
Crown College **M298**
Culver-Stockton College **M299**
The Curtis Institute of Music **M299**
Dalhousie University **M300**
Dallas Baptist University **M300**
Delta State University **M301**
DePauw University **M301**
Drake University **M302**
Duquesne University **M302**
East Carolina University **M303**
East Central University **M303**
Eastern Illinois University **M303**
Eastern Michigan University **M304**
Eastern New Mexico University **M305**
East Tennessee State University **M307**
Emporia State University **M308**
Evangel College **M309**
Florida Southern College **M312**
Florida State University **M312**
Furman University **M313**
Georgetown College **M314**
The George Washington University **M315**
Georgia College and State University **M315**
Gordon College **M316**
Grace College **M317**
Grand Valley State University **M317**
Hardin-Simmons University **M318**
Hastings College **M319**
Heidelberg College **M319**
Henderson State University **M320**
Holy Names College **M320**
Hope College **M321**
Houghton College **M321**
Howard Payne University **M321**
Hunter College of the City University of New York **M322**
Illinois State University **M323**
Illinois Wesleyan University **M324**
Indiana University–Purdue University Fort Wayne **M326**
Indiana University South Bend **M326**
Iowa State University of Science and Technology **M327**
Ithaca College **M327**
Jackson State University **M329**
Jacksonville University **M329**
James Madison University **M330**
Johns Hopkins University **M331**
Kansas State University **M332**
Keene State College **M332**
Kent State University **M333**
Kentucky Wesleyan College **M334**
Lawrence University **M336**
Lenoir-Rhyne College **M338**
Longwood College **M340**
Loyola University New Orleans **M341**
Manhattan School of Music **M342**
Mankato State University **M343**

Mannes College of Music, New School for Social Research **M344**
Marshall University **M346**
Mars Hill College **M347**
Maryville College **M348**
McNeese State University **M349**
Mercer University **M350**
Meredith College **M350**
Methodist College **M350**
Miami University **M351**
Middle Tennessee State University **M352**
Midwestern State University **M353**
Millikin University **M353**
Mississippi College **M353**
Montana State University–Bozeman **M355**
Montclair State University **M355**
Morehead State University **M357**
Morningside College **M357**
Mount Union College **M358**
Murray State University **M359**
Newberry College **M360**
New England Conservatory of Music **M360**
New Mexico State University **M361**
New York University **M361**
Norfolk State University **M363**
North Carolina Central University **M364**
North Carolina School of the Arts **M364**
Northeast Louisiana University **M366**
Northern Illinois University **M366**
Northern State University **M367**
Northwestern Oklahoma State University **M368**
Northwestern State University of Louisiana **M369**
Northwestern University **M369**
Nyack College **M370**
Oakland City University **M370**
Oberlin College **M371**
Ohio University **M373**
Ohio Wesleyan University **M373**
Oklahoma Baptist University **M374**
Oklahoma City University **M374**
Oklahoma State University **M375**
Old Dominion University **M375**
Otterbein College **M376**
Ouachita Baptist University **M376**
Pacific Union College **M377**
Pennsylvania State University University Park Campus **M378**
Philadelphia College of Bible **M378**
Pittsburg State University **M379**
Portland State University **M379**
Prairie View A&M University **M380**
Purchase College, State University of New York **M380**
Queens College **M381**
Queens College of the City University of New York **M382**
Rice University **M383**
Roosevelt University **M383**
St. Cloud State University **M385**

St. Norbert College **M386**
St. Olaf College **M386**
Saint Xavier University **M386**
Samford University **M387**
Sam Houston State University **M387**
San Diego State University **M388**
San Francisco Conservatory of Music **M388**
Shenandoah University **M391**
Simpson College **M393**
Southeastern Louisiana University **M394**
Southeast Missouri State University **M395**
Southern Adventist University **M396**
Southern Illinois University at Carbondale **M396**
Southwestern Oklahoma State University **M399**
Southwest Missouri State University **M399**
Southwest Texas State University **M400**
State University of New York at Binghamton **M400**
State University of New York at Buffalo **M401**
State University of New York College at Fredonia **M401**
State University of New York College at Potsdam **M298**
Stephen F. Austin State University **M402**
Stetson University **M402**
Susquehanna University **M403**
Syracuse University **M403**
Taylor University **M405**
Texas Christian University **M407**
Texas Tech University **M408**
Trinity University **M409**
Union University **M410**
The University of Alabama **M411**
University of Alaska Anchorage **M412**
University of Alaska Fairbanks **M412**
University of Alberta **M412**
University of Arkansas **M413**
University of British Columbia **M414**
The University of Calgary **M415**
University of Central Arkansas **M416**
University of Central Oklahoma **M417**
University of Cincinnati **M417**
University of Colorado at Boulder **M420**
University of Connecticut **M420**
University of Denver **M422**
University of Evansville **M422**
University of Florida **M422**
University of Georgia **M423**
University of Houston **M424**
University of Idaho **M425**
University of Illinois at Urbana–Champaign **M425**
The University of Iowa **M426**
University of Kansas **M426**

Saxophone

North Carolina School of the Arts **M364**
Southern Methodist University **M397**
Temple University **M308**
University of California, Irvine **M415**

Sociology of music

Carleton University **M282**

Songwriting

Berklee College of Music **M268**

Sound recording technology

Brigham Young University **M275**
Colorado Christian University **M293**
Duquesne University **M302**
Southwest Texas State University **M400**
State University of New York College at Fredonia **M401**
The University of Memphis **M429**
University of Wisconsin–Oshkosh **M459**

Special music education

State University of New York College at Potsdam **M298**
Wichita State University **M474**

String pedagogy

Colorado State University **M293**

Stringed instruments

Abilene Christian University **M258**
Acadia University **M258**
American Conservatory of Music **M260**
Andrews University **M260**
Appalachian State University **M261**
Arizona State University **M262**
Arkansas State University **M263**
Ashland University **M263**
Atlantic Union College **M264**
Augusta State University **M265**
Baldwin-Wallace College **M265**
Ball State University **M266**
Baylor University **M267**
Bethel College **M270**
Biola University **M270**
Birmingham-Southern College **M271**
Boise State University **M271**
Boston Conservatory **M272**
Boston University **M273**
Bowling Green State University **M273**
Brigham Young University **M275**
Brooklyn College of the City University of New York **M276**
Bucknell University **M276**
Butler University **M277**
California Institute of the Arts **M277**
California State University, Fullerton **M278**

California State University, Long Beach **M278**
California State University, Los Angeles **M279**
California State University, Sacramento **M279**
Cameron University **M280**
Campbellsville University **M281**
Carleton University **M282**
Cedarville College **M284**
Centenary College of Louisiana **M284**
Central Michigan University **M285**
Central Missouri State University **M285**
Central Washington University **M286**
Chapman University **M286**
Christopher Newport University **M287**
Clayton College & State University **M288**
Cleveland Institute of Music **M289**
Cleveland State University **M290**
Coe College **M290**
The College of New Jersey **M291**
College of Notre Dame **M291**
The College of Wooster **M292**
Colorado Christian University **M293**
Colorado State University **M293**
Columbia College **M294**
Columbus State University **M294**
Concordia College **M295**
Converse College **M296**
Covenant College **M297**
The Curtis Institute of Music **M299**
Dalhousie University **M300**
DePaul University **M301**
DePauw University **M301**
Drake University **M302**
Duquesne University **M302**
East Carolina University **M303**
Eastern Illinois University **M303**
Eastern Michigan University **M304**
Eastern New Mexico University **M305**
Eastern Washington University **M305**
East Tennessee State University **M307**
Emporia State University **M308**
Evangel College **M309**
Fisk University **M309**
Florida Atlantic University **M311**
Florida Southern College **M312**
Florida State University **M312**
Fort Hays State University **M313**
Furman University **M313**
The George Washington University **M315**
Gordon College **M316**
Grace College **M317**
Grand Valley State University **M317**
Hardin-Simmons University **M318**
Hastings College **M319**
Heidelberg College **M319**
Holy Names College **M320**
Hope College **M321**

Houghton College **M321**
Hunter College of the City University of New York **M322**
Idaho State University **M323**
Illinois State University **M323**
Illinois Wesleyan University **M324**
Indiana State University **M325**
Indiana University–Purdue University Fort Wayne **M326**
Indiana University South Bend **M326**
Iowa State University of Science and Technology **M327**
Ithaca College **M327**
Jackson State University **M329**
Jacksonville University **M329**
James Madison University **M330**
Johns Hopkins University **M331**
Kansas State University **M332**
Keene State College **M332**
Kennesaw State University **M332**
Kent State University **M333**
Lamar University **M335**
Lawrence University **M336**
Lock Haven University of Pennsylvania **M339**
Longwood College **M340**
Louisiana State University and Agricultural and Mechanical College **M340**
Loyola University New Orleans **M341**
Manhattan School of Music **M342**
Mankato State University **M343**
Mannes College of Music, New School for Social Research **M344**
Mansfield University of Pennsylvania **M346**
Marshall University **M346**
McNeese State University **M349**
Mercer University **M350**
Meredith College **M350**
Methodist College **M350**
Miami University **M351**
Michigan State University **M351**
Middle Tennessee State University **M352**
Millikin University **M353**
Mississippi College **M353**
Montana State University–Bozeman **M355**
Montclair State University **M355**
Morehead State University **M357**
Morningside College **M357**
Mount Union College **M358**
Murray State University **M359**
New England Conservatory of Music **M360**
New Mexico State University **M361**
New York University **M361**
Norfolk State University **M363**
North Carolina Central University **M364**
North Carolina School of the Arts **M364**
Northeast Louisiana University **M366**
Northern Illinois University **M366**
Northern Kentucky University **M367**

Winthrop University **M476**
Wittenberg University **M476**
Wright State University **M477**
Xavier University of Louisiana **M477**
Youngstown State University **M478**

Studio composition
Purchase College, State University of
    New York **M380**

Theater arts/drama
Taylor University **M405**

Trombone
The Harid Conservatory **M319**
The Juilliard School **M331**
Southern Methodist University **M397**
Temple University **M308**
University of California, Irvine **M415**

Trumpet
The Harid Conservatory **M319**
The Juilliard School **M331**
Southern Methodist University **M397**
Temple University **M308**
University of California, Irvine **M415**

Tuba
The Harid Conservatory **M319**
The Juilliard School **M331**
Southern Methodist University **M397**
Temple University **M308**
University of California, Irvine **M415**

Video music
Five Towns College **M310**

Viola
The Harid Conservatory **M319**
The Juilliard School **M331**
Southern Methodist University **M397**
Temple University **M308**
University of California, Irvine **M415**

Violin
The Harid Conservatory **M319**
The Juilliard School **M331**
Southern Methodist University **M397**
Temple University **M308**
University of California, Irvine **M415**

Violoncello
The Juilliard School **M331**
University of California, Irvine **M415**

Vocal music
Cumberland College **M299**

Vocal music education
Mississippi State University **M354**
Southwest Baptist University **M398**
University of North Carolina at
    Pembroke **M440**

Vocal pedagogy
Roosevelt University **M383**

Voice
Abilene Christian University **M258**
Acadia University **M258**
Alcorn State University **M259**
American Conservatory of Music
    M260
Andrews University **M260**
Angelo State University **M261**
Anna Maria College **M261**
Appalachian State University **M261**
Aquinas College **M262**
Arizona State University **M262**
Arkansas State University **M263**
Ashland University **M263**
Atlantic Union College **M264**
Augusta State University **M265**
Baker University **M265**
Baldwin-Wallace College **M265**
Ball State University **M266**
Barry University **M267**
Baylor University **M267**
Berry College **M270**
Bethel College **M270**
Biola University **M270**
Birmingham-Southern College **M271**
Boise State University **M271**
Boston Conservatory **M272**
Boston University **M273**
Bowling Green State University
    M273
Brenau University **M274**
Brewton-Parker College **M275**
Brigham Young University **M275**
Brooklyn College of the City University
    of New York **M276**
Bucknell University **M276**
Butler University **M277**
California Institute of the Arts **M277**
California State University, Fullerton
    M278
California State University, Long
    Beach **M278**
California State University, Los
    Angeles **M279**
California State University, Northridge
    M279
California State University, Sacramento
    M279
Cameron University **M280**
Campbellsville University **M281**
Carleton University **M282**
Carnegie Mellon University **M282**
Carson-Newman College **M282**
Cedarville College **M284**
Centenary College of Louisiana
    M284
Central Methodist College **M284**
Central Michigan University **M285**
Central Missouri State University
    M285
Central Washington University **M286**
Chapman University **M286**

Christopher Newport University
    M287
Cincinnati Bible College and Seminary
    M287
Clayton College & State University
    M288
Cleveland Institute of Music **M289**
Cleveland State University **M290**
Coe College **M290**
The College of New Jersey **M291**
College of Notre Dame **M291**
The College of Wooster **M292**
Colorado Christian University **M293**
Colorado State University **M293**
Columbia College **M294**
Columbus State University **M294**
Concordia College **M295**
Converse College **M296**
Cornerstone College **M296**
Cornish College of the Arts **M297**
Covenant College **M297**
Crown College **M298**
Culver-Stockton College **M299**
The Curtis Institute of Music **M299**
Dalhousie University **M300**
Dallas Baptist University **M300**
Delta State University **M301**
DePaul University **M301**
DePauw University **M301**
Drake University **M302**
Duquesne University **M302**
East Carolina University **M303**
East Central University **M303**
Eastern Illinois University **M303**
Eastern Kentucky University **M304**
Eastern Michigan University **M304**
Eastern New Mexico University
    M305
Eastern Washington University **M305**
East Tennessee State University
    M307
Emporia State University **M308**
Evangel College **M309**
Fisk University **M309**
Florida Atlantic University **M311**
Florida Southern College **M312**
Florida State University **M312**
Fort Hays State University **M313**
Furman University **M313**
Georgetown College **M314**
The George Washington University
    M315
Georgia College and State University
    M315
Gordon College **M316**
Grace College **M317**
Grand Valley State University **M317**
Hardin-Simmons University **M318**
Hastings College **M319**
Heidelberg College **M319**
Henderson State University **M320**
Holy Names College **M320**
Hope College **M321**
Houghton College **M321**
Howard Payne University **M321**

University of Connecticut **M420**
University of Delaware **M421**
University of Denver **M422**
University of Evansville **M422**
University of Florida **M422**
University of Georgia **M423**
University of Hartford **M423**
University of Hawaii at Manoa **M424**
University of Houston **M424**
University of Idaho **M425**
University of Illinois at Urbana–
Champaign **M425**
The University of Iowa **M426**
University of Kansas **M426**
University of Kentucky **M427**
University of Louisville **M427**
University of Maine **M428**
University of Maryland, College Park
M428
University of Massachusetts Amherst
M429
University of Michigan **M431**
University of Minnesota, Twin Cities
Campus **M433**
University of Mississippi **M433**
University of
Missouri–Columbia **M434**
University of Missouri–Kansas
City **M434**
University of Missouri–St. Louis **M435**
The University of Montana–Missoula
M435
University of Montevallo **M435**
University of Nebraska at Kearney
M436
University of Nebraska at Omaha
M436
University of Nevada, Las Vegas
M437
University of New Hampshire **M438**
University of New Mexico **M438**
The University of North Carolina at
Chapel Hill **M439**
University of North Carolina at
Charlotte **M440**
University of North Carolina at
Greensboro **M440**
University of North Dakota **M441**
University of Northern Colorado
M441
University of Northern Iowa **M442**
University of North Texas **M442**
University of Oklahoma **M443**
University of Oregon **M443**
University of Prince Edward Island
M444
University of Puget Sound **M445**
University of Redlands **M445**
University of Regina **M446**
University of Richmond **M447**
University of Rochester **M305**
University of South Alabama **M447**
University of South Carolina **M447**
University of South Dakota **M448**
University of Southern California
M448

University of Southern Mississippi
M449
University of Tennessee at
Chattanooga **M451**
University of Tennessee, Knoxville
M451
The University of Texas at Arlington
M452
The University of Texas at Austin
M452
The University of Texas at El Paso
M453
The University of Texas at San
Antonio **M453**
The University of Texas at Tyler
M454
University of the Incarnate Word
M454
University of the Pacific **M455**
University of Toledo **M455**
University of Tulsa **M455**
University of Utah **M456**
University of Vermont **M456**
University of Washington **M457**
University of Wisconsin–Eau
Claire **M457**
University of Wisconsin–Green
Bay **M458**
University of
Wisconsin–Madison **M458**
University of
Wisconsin–Milwaukee **M459**
University of
Wisconsin–Oshkosh **M459**
University of
Wisconsin–Superior **M460**
University of
Wisconsin–Whitewater **M460**
Utah State University **M461**
Valdosta State University **M462**
Valparaiso University **M462**
Vanderbilt University **M462**
Virginia Commonwealth University
M464
Virginia State University **M464**
Walla Walla College **M465**
Wartburg College **M466**
Washburn University of Topeka
M466
Washington State University **M466**
Wayne State University **M467**
Webster University **M468**
West Chester University of
Pennsylvania **M468**
Western Kentucky University **M469**
Western Michigan University **M469**
Westminster Choir College of Rider
University **M470**
Westminster College **M471**
West Texas A&M University **M472**
West Virginia University **M472**
West Virginia Wesleyan College
M473
Wheaton College **M473**
Wichita State University **M474**
Wilfrid Laurier University **M474**

Willamette University **M474**
William Carey College **M475**
William Paterson University of New
Jersey **M475**
Winthrop University **M476**
Wittenberg University **M476**
Wright State University **M477**
Xavier University of Louisiana **M477**
Youngstown State University **M478**

Wind and percussion instruments

Abilene Christian University **M258**
Acadia University **M258**
Alcorn State University **M259**
American Conservatory of Music
M260
Andrews University **M260**
Angelo State University **M261**
Appalachian State University **M261**
Arizona State University **M262**
Arkansas State University **M263**
Ashland University **M263**
Atlantic Union College **M264**
Augusta State University **M265**
Baker University **M265**
Baldwin-Wallace College **M265**
Ball State University **M266**
Baylor University **M267**
Berry College **M270**
Bethel College **M270**
Biola University **M270**
Birmingham-Southern College **M271**
Boise State University **M271**
Boston Conservatory **M272**
Bowling Green State University
M273
Brewton-Parker College **M275**
Brigham Young University **M275**
Brooklyn College of the City University
of New York **M276**
Butler University **M277**
California Institute of the Arts **M277**
California State University, Fullerton
M278
California State University, Long
Beach **M278**
California State University, Los
Angeles **M279**
California State University, Northridge
M279
California State University, Sacramento
M279
Cameron University **M280**
Campbellsville University **M281**
Carleton University **M282**
Cedarville College **M284**
Centenary College of Louisiana
M284
Central Michigan University **M285**
Central Missouri State University
M285
Central Washington University **M286**
Chapman University **M286**
Christopher Newport University
M287

Wind instruments

World music

World music instruments

Theater Majors

Acting

Arizona State University **T485**
Avila College **T486**
Barry University **T486**
Boston University **T488**
Brooklyn College of the City University of New York **T490**
California Institute of the Arts **T491**
Central Connecticut State University **T492**
Clarion University of Pennsylvania **T493**
College of Santa Fe **T493**
Cornish College of the Arts **T495**
Drake University **T497**
East Carolina University **T497**
Emerson College **T498**
Florida International University **T499**
Hofstra University **T500**
Howard University **T500**
Idaho State University **T500**
Ithaca College **T501**
Jacksonville University **T502**
Kent State University **T504**
Lake Erie College **T504**
Miami University **T506**
Nebraska Wesleyan University **T508**
New World School of the Arts **T508**
New York University **T509**
North Carolina School of the Arts **T511**
Otterbein College **T513**
Pace University **T514**
Rutgers, The State University of New Jersey, Mason Gross School of the Arts **T506**
Salem State College **T518**
Southern Methodist University **T519**
Stephens College **T521**
Syracuse University **T522**
The University of Arizona **T524**
University of British Columbia **T525**
University of Colorado at Boulder **T526**
University of Houston **T529**
University of Illinois at Urbana–Champaign **T529**
University of Michigan **T531**
University of Minnesota, Duluth **T532**
University of Montevallo **T533**
University of South Dakota **T536**
University of Southern California **T536**
University of Southern Mississippi **T537**
University of the Arts **T538**
University of Toledo **T539**
University of Utah **T539**
University of Wisconsin–Milwaukee **T539**
University of Wisconsin–Stevens Point **T540**
University of Wisconsin–Superior **T540**
University of Wyoming **T540**
Western Kentucky University **T544**

Acting and directing

Marshall University **T505**
North Carolina Agricultural and Technical State University **T510**

Art direction

North Carolina School of the Arts **T511**

Arts management

Culver-Stockton College **T495**
Point Park College **T515**
Western Michigan University **T544**

Contemporary music

College of Santa Fe **T493**

Costume design

Boston University **T488**
California Institute of the Arts **T491**
Cornish College of the Arts **T495**
Idaho State University **T500**
North Carolina School of the Arts **T511**
Salem State College **T518**
University of Illinois at Urbana–Champaign **T529**
University of Minnesota, Duluth **T532**
University of South Dakota **T536**
University of Wyoming **T540**
Virginia Commonwealth University **T542**
Webster University **T543**

Costume management

Virginia Commonwealth University **T542**

Costume production

Boston University **T488**
North Carolina School of the Arts **T511**
University of Wisconsin–Milwaukee **T539**
Virginia Commonwealth University **T542**

Creative writing

University of British Columbia **T525**

Dance

Central Connecticut State University **T492**
Eastern New Mexico University **T498**
Emerson College **T498**
Long Island University, C.W. Post Campus **T504**

University of Houston **T529**
The University of Memphis **T530**
University of Southwestern Louisiana **T537**

Design

College of Santa Fe **T493**
Rutgers, The State University of New Jersey, Mason Gross School of the Arts **T506**
Stephens College **T521**
University of British Columbia **T525**
University of Evansville **T527**
University of Houston **T529**
University of Southern California **T536**
University of Utah **T539**
Virginia Commonwealth University **T542**

Design production

Carnegie Mellon University **T492**
East Carolina University **T497**
University of Miami **T531**

Design technology

Auburn University **T486**
Central Missouri State University **T492**
Kent State University **T504**
Otterbein College **T513**
Texas Christian University **T523**
The University of Arizona **T524**
University of Illinois at Urbana–Champaign **T529**
University of North Dakota **T534**
University of Oklahoma **T535**
University of Wisconsin–Stevens Point **T540**
Western Michigan University **T544**

Design/technical theater

Denison University **T496**
North Dakota State University **T511**
Syracuse University **T522**
University of Colorado at Boulder **T526**
The University of Memphis **T530**
University of Minnesota, Duluth **T532**
University of Southern Mississippi **T537**
Wichita State University **T545**

Directing

California Institute of the Arts **T491**
Howard University **T500**
Lake Erie College **T504**
Nebraska Wesleyan University **T508**
New York University **T509**
North Carolina School of the Arts **T511**
Pace University **T514**
Stephens College **T521**
University of Houston **T529**

Technical direction
California Institute of the Arts **T491**
Cornish College of the Arts **T495**
Hofstra University **T500**
North Carolina School of the Arts **T511**
University of South Dakota **T536**
University of Southern California **T536**
University of Wyoming **T540**

Technical production
Boston University **T488**
New York University **T509**
University of Wisconsin–Milwaukee **T539**
Webster University **T543**

Technical theater
Adelphi University **T483**
Avila College **T486**
Barry University **T486**
Central Connecticut State University **T492**
Chapman University **T493**
Longwood College **T505**
Midwestern State University **T507**
Nebraska Wesleyan University **T508**
Pace University **T514**
Salem State College **T518**
Stephen F. Austin State University **T521**
Stephens College **T521**
Syracuse University **T522**
Texas Southern University **T524**
University of British Columbia **T525**
University of Montevallo **T533**
University of Wisconsin–Superior **T540**
Western Kentucky University **T544**

Theater arts administration
Howard University **T500**

Theater arts/drama
Adelphi University **T483**
Brooklyn College of the City University of New York **T490**
Carnegie Mellon University **T492**
Central Connecticut State University **T492**
College of Santa Fe **T493**
Cornish College of the Arts **T495**
Culver-Stockton College **T495**

East Carolina University **T497**
Eastern New Mexico University **T498**
Florida State University **T499**
Hofstra University **T500**
Idaho State University **T500**
Long Island University, C.W. Post Campus **T504**
Millikin University **T507**
North Carolina Agricultural and Technical State University **T510**
Ohio Northern University **T512**
Ohio University **T513**
Point Park College **T515**
Shenandoah University **T518**
Southern Oregon University **T519**
Stephens College **T521**
University of Central Florida **T526**
University of Michigan **T531**
University of North Carolina at Greensboro **T534**
University of North Dakota **T534**
University of South Dakota **T536**
University of Southern Mississippi **T537**
University of Southwestern Louisiana **T537**
The University of Tennessee at Martin **T538**
University of Utah **T539**
Virginia Intermont College **T542**
William Carey College **T545**
Wright State University **T545**

Theater design and production
Brooklyn College of the City University of New York **T490**
Ithaca College **T501**
New World School of the Arts **T508**
New York University **T509**
Ohio University **T513**

Theater design/technology
Arizona State University **T485**
Clarion University of Pennsylvania **T493**
Drake University **T497**
Eastern New Mexico University **T498**
Emerson College **T498**
Idaho State University **T500**
Jacksonville University **T502**
Marshall University **T505**
Miami University **T506**
Point Park College **T515**
Wright State University **T545**

Theater education
Bradley University **T489**
Culver-Stockton College **T495**
Drake University **T497**
Emerson College **T498**
Howard University **T500**
The University of Arizona **T524**
University of North Carolina at Greensboro **T534**
University of Utah **T539**
Virginia Commonwealth University **T542**
Western Michigan University **T544**

Theater for youth
Shenandoah University **T518**

Theater history
Arizona State University **T485**
Lake Erie College **T504**
Virginia Commonwealth University **T542**

Theater management
College of Santa Fe **T493**
Emerson College **T498**
University of Evansville **T527**
University of Miami **T531**
University of Wisconsin–Superior **T540**

Theater production
Florida International University **T499**
Ithaca College **T501**
The University of Arizona **T524**

Theater studies
Emerson College **T498**
Southern Methodist University **T519**
Western Michigan University **T544**

Theater technology
Howard University **T500**
Ithaca College **T501**
North Carolina Agricultural and Technical State University **T510**
Ohio University **T513**
University of Evansville **T527**
University of Illinois at Urbana–Champaign **T529**

Theater/English
University of Wyoming **T540**

SCHOOL INDEX

▲

A

Aaron Copland School of Music—See Queens College of the City University of New York

Abilene Christian University, Abilene, TX **A41, M258**

Academy of Art College, San Francisco, CA **A41**

Acadia University, Wolfville, NS, Canada **M258**

Adelphi University, Garden City, NY **T483**

Adrian College, Adrian, MI **A42**

Alabama State University, Montgomery, AL **M258**

Alberta College of Art and Design, Calgary, AB, Canada **A43**

Albertus Magnus College, New Haven, CT **A43, T483**

Albion College, Albion, MI **A44**

Al Collins Graphic Design School, Tempe, AZ **A44**

Alcorn State University, Lorman, MS **M259**

Alfred University, Alfred, NY **A44**

Allen R. Hite Art Institute—See University of Louisville

Alma College, Alma, MI **M259**

Alverno College, Milwaukee, WI **M259**

American Academy of Art, Chicago, IL **A45**

American Academy of Dramatic Arts, New York, NY **T483**

American Academy of Dramatic Arts/West, Pasadena, CA **T485**

American Conservatory of Music, Chicago, IL **M260**

American InterContinental University, Los Angeles, CA **A46**

American InterContinental University, Atlanta, GA **A47**

American University, Washington, DC **A48**

Anderson College, Anderson, SC **M260**

Andrews University, Berrien Springs, MI **A48, M260**

Angelo State University, San Angelo, TX **M261**

Anna Maria College, Paxton, MA **A49, M261**

Appalachian State University, Boone, NC **A49, M261**

Aquinas College, Grand Rapids, MI **A49, M262**

Arizona State University, Tempe, AZ **A49, D221, M262, T485**

Arkansas State University, State University, AR **A50, M263, T485**

Armstrong Atlantic State University, Savannah, GA **M263**

Art Academy of Cincinnati, Cincinnati, OH **A50**

Art Center College of Design, Pasadena, CA **A51**

Art Institute of Boston, Boston, MA **A52**

Art Institute of Southern California, Laguna Beach, CA **A53**

The Art Institutes International at Portland, Portland, OR **A54**

Ashland University, Ashland, OH **M263**

Atlanta College of Art, Atlanta, GA **A54**

Atlantic Union College, South Lancaster, MA **M264**

Auburn University, Auburn University, AL **A55, M264, T486**

Augsburg College, Minneapolis, MN **M264**

Augusta State University, Augusta, GA **A56, M265**

Austin Peay State University, Clarksville, TN **A56**

Avila College, Kansas City, MO **T486**

B

Baker University, Baldwin City, KS **M265**

Baldwin-Wallace College, Berea, OH **M265**

Ball State University, Muncie, IN **A56, M266**

Barat College, Lake Forest, IL **D221**

Barry University, Miami Shores, FL **A57, M267, T486**

Barton College, Wilson, NC **A57**

Baylor University, Waco, TX **A57, M267, T487**

Beaver College, Glenside, PA **A58**

Bellevue University, Bellevue, NE **A59**

Belmont University, Nashville, TN **A59, M268**

Benjamin T. Rome School of Music—See The Catholic University of America

Berklee College of Music, Boston, MA **M268**

Bernice Young Jones School of Fine Arts—See Ouachita Baptist University

Berry College, Mount Berry, GA **M270**

Bethel College, St. Paul, MN **M270**

Biola University, La Mirada, CA **M270**

Birmingham-Southern College, Birmingham, AL **M271**

Blair School of Music—See Vanderbilt University

Boise State University, Boise, ID **M271**

Boston Architectural Center, Boston, MA **A59**

Boston Conservatory, Boston, MA **D221, M272, T487**

Boston University, Boston, MA **A60, M273, T488**

Bowling Green State University, Bowling Green, OH **A60, M273**

Bradley University, Peoria, IL **A60, M274, T489**

Brenau University, Gainesville, GA **A61, D222, M274, T489**

Brewton-Parker College, Mt. Vernon, GA **M275**

Brigham Young University, Provo, UT **A61, M275, T489**

Brock University, St. Catharines, ON, Canada **M275**

Brooklyn College of the City University of New York, Brooklyn, NY **A62, M276, T490**

Bucknell University, Lewisburg, PA **M276**

Butler University, Indianapolis, IN **D223, M277**

C

Caldwell College, Caldwell, NJ **A62**

California College of Arts and Crafts, San Francisco, CA **A62**

California Institute of the Arts, Valencia, CA **A64, D224, M277, T491**

California State University, Chico, Chico, CA **A65**

California State University, Fullerton, Fullerton, CA **A65, M278**

California State University, Long Beach, Long Beach, CA **A65, D225, M278**

California State University, Los Angeles, Los Angeles, CA **M279**

California State University, Northridge, Northridge, CA **M279**

California State University, Sacramento, Sacramento, CA **M279**

NOTES

GETTING ██████ GE ISN'T AS HARD A ████ AS LON ████ NK PETERSON'S!

Get on line at petersons.com for a jump start on your college search.

- Search our college database
- Get financial aid tips
- Browse our bookstore

And when you're ready to apply, you're ready for ApplyToCollege.com!

ApplyToCollege.com is our **free** online college application service that lets you apply to *more colleges than anyone else on the Internet!*

Why ApplyToCollege.com?
- Fill out one application for over 1,000 colleges!
- Talk with admissions deans!
- Keep track of your applications!
- IT'S FREE!

Peterson's is on your side with everything you need to get ready for college. And it's all just a mouse click away!

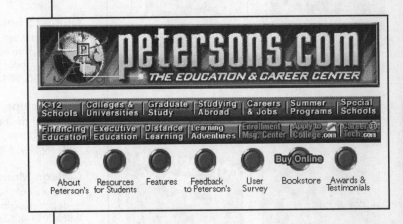

P ETERSON'S
Princeton, New Jersey
www.petersons.com

1-800-338-3282

Wait! There's more!➔